Becoming George
The Life of Mrs W. B. Yeats

all life is a return to its beginnings—there is no new thought or feeling
(the Instructors)

'Think more intimately'
'What do you mean by intimately'
'Do not see the flower without the petal
The stream without its stones
The child without its smile
The house without its windows'
(the control Ecanentu and Willy)

BECOMING GEORGE

THE LIFE OF MRS W. B. YEATS

ANN SADDLEMYER

OXFORD

UNIVERSITY PRESS

OXFORD
UNIVERSITY PRESS

Great Clarendon Street, Oxford OX2 6DP

Oxford University Press is a department of the University of Oxford.
It furthers the University's objective of excellence in research, scholarship,
and education by publishing worldwide in

Oxford New York

Auckland Bangkok Buenos Aires Cape Town Chennai
Dar es Salaam Delhi Hong Kong Istanbul Karachi Kolkata
Kuala Lumpur Madrid Melbourne Mexico City Mumbai Nairobi
São Paulo Shanghai Singapore Taipei Tokyo Toronto

and an associated company in Berlin

Oxford is a registered trade mark of Oxford University Press
in the UK and in certain other countries

Published in the United States
by Oxford University Press Inc., New York

British Library Cataloguing in Publication Data

Data available

Library of Congress Cataloging in Publication Data
Saddlemyer, Ann.
Becoming George : the life of Mrs. W. B. Yeats / Ann Saddlemyer.
p. cm.
1. Yeats, Georgie, d. 1968. 2. Yeats, W. B. (William Butler), 1865-1939—Marriage. 3.
Authors' spouses—Ireland—Biography. 4. Married people—Ireland—Biography. 5.
Spiritualists—Ireland—Biography. 6. Occultists—Ireland—Biography. I. Title.

PR5906 .S28 2002 821'.8—dc21 [B] 2002019040

ISBN 0-19-811232-7

1 3 5 7 9 10 8 6 4 2

Typeset in 11/13 pt Bulmer MT
by Graphicraft Limited, Hong Kong
Printed in Great Britain
on acid-free paper by
T.J. International Ltd,
Padstow, Cornwall

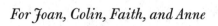

For Joan, Colin, Faith, and Anne

Acknowledgements

The late Anne Yeats, Michael and Gráinne Yeats, and their family, have supported this project from the beginning, while at the same time allowing me complete freedom. I hope I will be forgiven when my versions of events vary from theirs. Other family members who have offered help and friendship are Charles Lane-Poole Burston, Grace Spurway Jaffe, the late Sister Brigid Younghughes, the late Frances Fielden, Nancy Threlfall, and Joy C. Gordon. Anthony Reyntiens kindly gave access to the Woodmass family papers he inherited from his mother, and Kim Woodmass Ridley helped to identify these and other photographs. Omar Shakespear Pound assisted in every way possible from his own collection of memories and treasures.

A list of all those who have over the years patiently answered my queries and volunteered information is impossible, and I hope they will accept this general note of gratitude. It would however be ungracious of me not to mention the following, beginning with George Mills Harper and William M. Murphy, both of whom gave access to their vast store of materials and memorabilia, and have been steadfast in their support. Roy Foster, biographer of W. B. Yeats, has been generous and helpful, and John Kelly, General Editor of the ongoing *Collected Letters of W. B. Yeats*, gave me access to materials in his possession when I embarked on this project. A. N. Jeffares and the late Richard Ellmann were a source of encouragement and information, as were the late Virginia Moore and Birgit Bramsbäck. Memories of George were freely and generously shared also by Diane and Hazard Adams, John Byars, David Clark, Saros Cowasjee, Alan Denson, the late H. Lovat Dickson, Sister de Lourdes Fahy, Daphne Fullwood, Bridget Ganly, the late Evelyn O'Donovan Garbary, Donna Gerstenberger, Michael Gill, Oliver D. Gogarty, David H. Greene, Elaine Hall, the late Patrick Hall, the late Rupert Hart-Davis, Marjorie Hobson, Daniel Hoffman, the late Hugh Hunt, Richard Kain, John V. Kelleher, Hugh Kenner, John Keohane, Louis LeBrocquy, Delia McAllel, Alf MacLochlainn, Tanya Moiseiwitsch, John Montague, John O'Meara, Michael J. O'Neill, Roger Parisious, Donald Pearce, Kathleen Raine, Michael G. Reade, B. L. Reid, Michael Reyntiens, Harriet O'Donovan Sheehy, Elizabeth Curran Solterer, Jon Stallworthy, Melanie LeBrocquy Stewart, the late Hanna Taylor, and Donald Torchiana. I recall conversations with Jo and Liam Miller with affection.

Stone Cottage was hospitably opened to me by Rosemary and Tim Hammond and William Hearst, The Prelude (now End House) by Victor and Judith Benjamin, the Yeatses' flat in Rapallo by Matilde Frisenden, Ashdown Forest Hotel by Allan Pratt, and Garsington Manor by Mrs L. Ingram; Pauline and Andrew Rankine sought out Georgie's birthplace, and Malcolm Payne discovered the house where Willy proposed.

Eric Binnie, Rochford Brady, Jim Brennan, Graham Buckley, Cosimo Cordella, Kathy Chung, Andrew Cunningham, Nicholas Daly, Sarah Gibson-Bray, Rachel Grahame, Selina Guinness, Rob Hanks, Ann Hutchison, Janet Hutchison, R. Bruce Kirkley, Matthew Lamberti, Joan Lawrence, Margaret Montgomery, and Paul Murray all provided assistance with my research; Valerie Eliot, Warwick Gould, Richard Lancelyn Green, Dr Roger Lancelyn Green, the late Rupert Hart-Davis, Harriet O'Donovan Sheehy and Melanie Stewart generously offered letters in their possession, and Diana Poteat Hobby, Susan Dailey, and Gary Phillips sent me their theses; R. G. S. Bidwell provided his grandfather's unpublished memoirs. William Gaddes spent many hours discussing automatic writing; R. A. Gilbert advised on the Order of the Golden Dawn; John Harwood generously provided materials from his research on Olivia Shakespear; Nicola Gordon Bowe, Nick Bowlin, and Keith Parsons provided much-needed photography; Elizabeth Heine advised me on astrological matters and Gwladys Downes guided me through French legal documents. Hilary Thomas spent many hours following leads in public archives tracking down George's ancestors and making exciting discoveries; this book and George's family trees would have been much poorer without her enthusiastic assistance. The staff of the William Butler Yeats Microfilmed Manuscripts Collection, Special Collections Department, Library, State University of New York at Stony Brook, in particular Kristen J. Nyitray and Ann Becker, have been exceptionally patient and helpful.

Other librarians, friends, and scholars who have come to my aid include Bruce Arnold, Conrad Balliet, John Barrett, Alan Batten, Janet Bavelas, Karl Beckson, William Benzie, Joan Bigwood, Larry Bongie, George Bornstein, Michael Bott, Patricia Boylan, Mrs Curtis Bradford, Janice Westley Braun, Diana Burnham, the late Flann Campbell, Nancy Cardozo, Bernadette Chambers, Wayne Chapman, Stella Chappell, the late Julia Ching, Dardis Clarke, Lester Connor, Eleanor Cook, Karen S. Cook, Ellen Cooper, Lori N. Curtis, M. Roe d'Albert, the late Adele Dalsimer, Ann and George Dannatt, Iris Dargon, Alfred Daveigas, C. S. L. Davies, Mairead Delaney, Mary Diaz, Ann de Klerk, Josie Dixon, Yvonne Dixon, Kildare Dobbs, Karen Drickamer, Dennis Duffy, Pam Duncan, Mairead Dunleavy, Marjorie Esson, Stephen Enniss, Judith Etherton, Brian Fanning, T. Finlayson, Christine Finn, Richard Finneran, the late Mary FitzGerald, Peter Fitzpatrick, Corrina Flanagan, Brendan Flynn, Barbara Frieling, C. J. E. Fryer, D. G. Gamble, Brigid O'Brien Ganly, J. G. Gasteaud, Milton McC Gatch, J. Gent, Isaac Gewirtz, Stanley Gilliam, David Griffin, Lillie Hall, M. Hamilton, John Handford, Melissa Hardie, Maurice Harmon, Margaret Mills Harper, Joseph Hassett, Ann Hearle, Charmian

Hearne, Victoria Hesford, Cathy Henderson, Bernard Hickey, Sue Hodson, D. H. Hoeniger, Brooke Holdack, Ken Hogue, A. J. Hutchison, Michael Hutchison, Joan Hyland, Robin Jeffrey, Toni O'Brien Johnson, Irene Johnston, Margaret Jonas, John Keohane, K. A. Jowett, Alex Kidson, Declan Kiely, Margaret J. Kimball, V. J. D. Kirwan, Noel Kissane, Elizabeth Knowles, David V. Koch, Morine Krissdottir, Lorna Knight, Sabine Lacaze, Richard Landon, Catríona Lawlor, Dan H. Laurence, M. M. Lees, M. M. Liberman, A. Walton Litz, Laura D. Logie, Janis and Richard Londraville, James Longenbach, James McGarry, Mari McKay, Wallace McLeod, Jay Macpherson, Johannes Maczewski, Phillip Marcus, John Sayre Martin, Alexandra Mason, R. Russell Maylone, J. C. C. Mays, Bernard Meehan, L. Rebecca Johnson Melvin, Laura Micham, Val Milgate, the late Peggy Miller, Laura V. Monti, Maureen Murphy, Timothy D. Murray, Dónal Ó Luanaigh, Felicity O'Mahony, Stuart Ó Seanóir, Sean O'Tuama, Nancy Oliver, Harold Orel, the late Margaret Ormsby, Stephen Parks, Stephen L. Parrish, Melinda Parsons, Ronald Patkus, Jamie Peele, Michael Peters, Mary Peterson, James Pethica, Gary Phillips, Rodney Phillips, Lis Pihl, Lionel Pilkington, Clare Porac, Ann Porter, Anne Posega, Mrs W. Poynton, Eric Pumroy, P. R. Quarrie, Jennifer M. Rampton, Michael G. Reade, Darryl Rehr, the late Laura Rièse, Roy Robertson, Wendell Robinson, Ruth R. Rogers, Joseph Ronsley, Betsy Rosasco, Lynn Roundtree, Carol Rudisell, Stephen Rupp, R. K. Rycroft, Edward Safarian, George Sandelescu, Susan Schreibman, Ronald and Keith Schuchard, Rosa Shand, Linda Shaughnessy, Ruth Sherry, Elizabeth K. Shoemaker, Gordon Shrimpton, C. Anderson Silber, Evelyn Silber, Kate Slattery, Peter L. Smith, Martha Mann Southgate, Karin Strand, Bruce Stewart, Leon Surette, Hiroshi Suzuki, Richard Taylor, Saundra Taylor, Carroll F. Terrell, Thierry Terrier, French Embassy in Ireland, Gillian Thomas, M. Wynn Thomas, Mary Thompson, Donal Tinney, Steven Tomlinson, Deirdre Toomey, Demetres Tryphonopolus, David Vaisey, Janet Wallace, Elizabeth Webby, Tara Wenger, Alan Wesencraft, Nancy Weyant, Anna MacBride White, Faith White, James White, R. N. White, Shane White, the late Terence de Vere White, Patricia Willis, Richard Winter, the late Georgie Wynne, Judith Zilczer, Elaine Z. Zinkham, Sheldon Zitner.

   Staff and officers of the following institutions courteously dealt with my needs: Anthroposophical Society of Great Britain, BBC Sound Archives, Bodleian Library, Boston Public Library, British Museum Central Archives, British Red Cross Society Archives, Bryn Mawr College, Cheltenham Ladies' College, Convent of Sisters of Mercy, Clewer, Eton College Library, Heatherley School of Fine Art, Irish Architectural Archives, Irish Department of Foreign Affairs, Mills College, National Archives of Canada, National Archives of Ireland, National Library of Ireland, Princess Grace Irish Library, Monaco, Queen's Gate School, Red Cross Society, Society for Psychical Research, Rudolf Steiner Centre Library, St Hugh's College, Oxford, St James' School, West Malvern, University

College Dublin, Wheaton College, Library & Museum of United Grand Lodge of England Freemasons.

A grant from the Social Sciences and Humanities Research Council of Canada greatly assisted me in the early stages of my research; travel grants from the University of Toronto and Victoria University allowed me to pursue it; the library resources of the University of Victoria, British Columbia—in particular the Inter Library Loan, Special Collections, Microfilm, and Photographic Departments— helped me to the finish line.

Permission to quote has been granted by Marcia Geraldine Anderson and Hodder and Stoughton Limited for letters of Edmund Dulac and reproduction of his drawings; The Earl of Chichester for the unpublished letter from Lady Elizabeth Beazley (née Pelham); Lucy and Maud Ellmann for letters and inter- view notes of Richard Ellmann; Oliver D. Gogarty and Colin Smythe on behalf of the estate of Oliver St John Gogarty; Colin Smythe on behalf of Anne Gregory de Winton and the estate of the late Catherine Kennedy for writings of Lady Gregory; R. J. Gluckstein on behalf of the estates of Gluck and Edith Shackleton Heald; Andrew Schuller for the unpublished letter by E. F. Jourdain; Palgrave Publishers Ltd. for letters in the Macmillan files by H. Lovat Dickson, Harold Macmillan, and Thomas Mark; Margaret Farrington and Elizabeth Ryan for letters of Thomas MacGreevy; Jean Faulks for letters and notes by Ethel Mannin; Adrian Mitchell for his poetry; Society of Authors as the Literary Representative of the Estate of John Masefield; Omar Shakespear Pound for letters and painting of Dorothy Shakespear Pound; unpublished letters of Ezra Pound to WBY and George Yeats, Copyright 2002 by Mary de Rachewiltz and Omar S. Pound; Poetry and prose by Ezra Pound used by permission of New Directions Publishing Corporation; unpublished letter from H.D. to Vera Hone, copyright 2002 by Perdita Schaffner, used by permission of New Directions Publishing Corporation; Trustees of the Abbey Theatre for the letters of Lennox and Dorothy Robinson; Society of Authors on behalf of the Bernard Shaw Estate; Leonie Sturge-Moore, Charmian O'Neill and the University of London Library for the letters of Thomas Sturge Moore and Marie Moore; Brigid O'Brien Ganly for letters of Dermod and Mabel O'Brien; Letters of Frank O'Connor to George Yeats and Evelyn O'Donovan reprinted by permission of PFD on behalf of The Estate of Frank O'Connor; David Higham Associates on behalf of Ethel Smyth estate; Christina Bridg- water for letters of Iseult Gonne Stuart; Brian Read on behalf of Arthur Symons estate; the Trustees of the late Dorothy Wellesley, Duchess of Wellington Will Trust for letters of Dorothy Wellesley; Paul Mellon Centre for Studies in British Art and the Yale Center for British Art for permission to make use of material first published on pages 152–3 of my article, 'Spirits in Space: Theatricality and the Occult in Tissot's Life and Art', *Seductive Surfaces: The Art of Tissot*, ed. Katharine Lochnan (Yale University Press, 1999); A. P. Watt for permission to quote from the files of A. P. Watt Ltd., on behalf of Michael Holroyd for John S. Collis, and on behalf of Michael Yeats and the estate of Anne Butler Yeats for unpublished correspondence of the Yeats family and selections from the poetry and prose of W. B. Yeats. Access to and permission to quote from materials in their possession as indicated in the relevant notes has been granted by the Berg Collections of English and American Literature, The New York Public Library, Astor, Lenox and Tilden Foundations; Frank O'Connor papers, Ethel Mannin papers and Yeats Collection, Burns Library, Boston College; Mariam Coffin Canaday Library, Bryn Mawr College; Yeats Collection, Burns Library, Boston College; W. B. Yeats Collection, University of Delaware Library, Newark, Delaware; Special Collections, Robert W. Woodruff Library, Emory University; W. B. Yeats Collection, University of Delaware Library; Houghton Library, Harvard University; The Huntington Library, San Marino, California; Lilly Library, Indiana University, Bloomington, IN; The Council of Trustees of the National Library of Ireland; Kenneth Spencer Research Library, University of Kansas Libraries; University of London Library; John Quinn Memorial Collection, Manuscripts and Archives Division, The New York Public Library, Astor Lenox and Tilden Foundations; Sligo County Library; Special Collections, Morris Library, Southern Illinois University at Carbondale; Department of Special Collections, Stanford University Libraries; William Butler Yeats Microfilmed Manuscripts Collection, Special Collections Department, Library, State University of New York at Stony Brook; Harry Ransom Humanities Research Center, The University of Texas at Austin; Thomas Fisher Rare Book Library, University of Toronto; The Board of Trinity College Dublin; Richard Ellmann Papers, Special Collections, McFarlin Library, The University of Tulsa; The Babette Deutsch Papers, Washington University Libraries, Department of Special Collections; Wellesley College Library, Special Collections; Marion E. Wade Center, The Yale Collection of American Literature, and the James M. and Mariel-Louise Osborn Collection, Beinecke Rare Book and Manuscript Library, Yale University. Every effort has been made to establish contact with the other holders of original copyrights.

I owe special thanks to Kevin Nowlan for offering wise counsel and a home in Dublin, to Christopher Murray who smoothed many a path in Ireland and elsewhere, and to Colin Smythe, as always generous with his time and extensive knowledge. I am grateful to Jackie Pritchard for her care in copy-editing, to Paul Cleal and Sue Tipping for their work on design, and to Frances Whistler who gallantly and cheerfully shepherded this book through the press. My greatest debt, as always, is to Joan Coldwell for advice, support, and encouragement.

Ann Saddlemyer
Deep Cove
Vancouver Island

Contents

Mrs W.B.

List of Illustrations

In-Text Illustrations

Introduction

> Thank you for leaving me out. I am quite sure that 'wives' are a part of
> literary gossip, just as I hate reading a poet's work for the first time if I know
> anything about him (or her), or about the circumstance from which a poem
> arose.[1]

This book—which she would not have approved of—tells the story of George
Yeats. Other figures walk across, then disappear offstage; often we hear their voices
from the wings, muffled by memory and personal perspective. But my main
task, to hear hers, has controlled and directed this narrative. The telling has not
been easy, for, unlike her husband who refined his at every opportunity, George
frequently and cunningly subverted her own voice, leaving only questionable
echoes to track. She destroyed papers and writings she thought unnecessary to
the story of others, doled out personal information only to a chosen few when she
felt it was safe to do so, and frequently offered varying versions of what she was
prepared to tell.

Promised for more than a dozen years and heralded before then, this telling
has been delayed by personal and academic lives. I apologize to all those friends
and colleagues who have lived through it with me, and especially to Anne,
Michael, and Gráinne Yeats, who initiated a project none of us knew would hover
for so long, and who have been generous in their patience and encouragement
throughout. They have also been generous with their memories, and I ask their
pardon for sometimes telling a different version.

We all have our secret lives, disclosed little by little and part by part to our
intimate friends and family; no one sees the whole, nor is that even possible.
George Yeats concealed her secret lives more successfully than most: she had few
women friends (five or six at most) and only two male confidants, both of whom
at various times distanced themselves. There was Willy, of course. But even from
her husband, her closest friend, she concealed much, and there will forever
be debate as to whether the bond that first linked them was her hoax, a joint
self-deception, or daimonic intervention.

No wonder then, that it has taken over a decade to discover the barest bones of
her story. As much as possible, I have tried to tell it in her words, helped by the
public documents, letters, and diaries that are available. Even there, amongst the
institutional archives biographers must depend upon, George Yeats managed to
conceal her tracks. For only after her death did her children discover where their

mother was born, and that they had (possibly) been celebrating her birthday on the wrong day. Perhaps her natural reserve was so strong she could not bear any public scrutiny; perhaps she was even more adept than her husband at creating a private mask. I too am caught in her net: the papers held by the family were the ones considered worth preservation by her; those letters between husband and wife that exist are what she chose to keep. Only the 'magic books' and automatic scripts seem to be intact—or are they? The first few weeks of the automatic writing are absent, and there are lacunae throughout.

A third complexity of voices belongs to her family and friends, whose chorus I have tried faithfully to take note of without distortion. By marrying Willy in her mid-twenties she found herself in the centre of all the Yeatses—but she remained indomitably herself throughout. In telling this story I have been helped by that chorus, but WBY and his circle remain peripheral to the central figure, entering only as she encountered them or they somehow affected her life. And finally this narrator herself appears, and here I play a double role: as a minor member of the large cast of 'seekers' who were so generously assisted by 'Mrs W. B.', and, much later, as the recipient of the many memories dredged up by her family, friends, and those scholars still living who gained entrance to Palmerston Road.

These three sets of voices, then, the personal, the institutional, and the recollected, form the basis for what follows. It can never be the complete story of a remarkably clever, creative, witty, energetic, and wily woman, but it is a beginning. I never thought this adventure would be mine—for one thing, I'd have taken notes—but for me the search for this remarkable woman has been rewarding and illuminating. It has also, increasingly, been a labour of love.

A NOTE ON NAMING

Throughout, a distinction is made between the young Georgie Hyde Lees and George Yeats, the role she gradually grew into. After her husband's death, she tended to appear in public only as Mrs W. B. Yeats or, as Dublin knew her, 'Mrs W. B.' Similarly, WBY the public figure and Yeats the poet are identified separately from George's husband Willy. In later years George herself, when speaking of her husband, alternated among the three names.

A NOTE ON SOURCES

I have used George's own wording and spelling wherever possible. I am indebted to the entire world of Yeats scholarship, and have been assisted with generosity and grace by them and a host of friends and colleagues; any errors are mine alone. Where not indicated otherwise, most notes come from unpublished material when it was still in the possession of Michael and Anne Yeats; later copies when they come from the University of Stony Brook or Boston College are identified as such. I am particularly grateful to W. M. Murphy for use of his transcriptions of letters from Lily to Ruth Lane-Poole and John Butler Yeats to Rosa Butt; when I have depended upon these I have identified them as WMM. Other transcriptions came from George Mills Harper and are identified as such. John Kelly kindly allowed me to read through the relevant period of his collection of Yeats letters; again, when I have depended upon these transcriptions they are identified.

The multitudinous notes are for the Yeats scholars, who quite naturally will expect them.

GEORGIE HYDE LEES' MATERNAL ANCESTRY

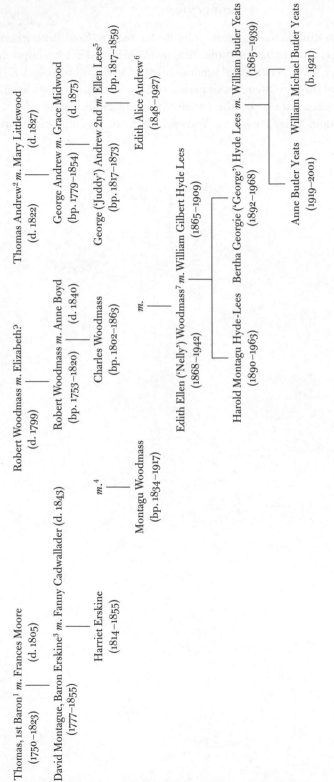

ERSKINE

Thomas, 1st Baron[1] m. Frances Moore
(1750–1823)   (d. 1805)

David Montague, Baron Erskine[3] m. Fanny Cadwallader (d. 1843)
(1777–1855)

Harriet Erskine
(1814–1855)

m.[4]

WOODMASS

Robert Woodmass m. Elizabeth?
(d. 1799)

Robert Woodmass m. Anne Boyd
(bp. 1753–1820)   (d. 1840)

Charles Woodmass
(bp. 1802–1863)

Montagu Woodmass
(bp. 1834–1917)

m.

Edith Ellen ('Nelly') Woodmass[7] m. William Gilbert Hyde Lees
(1868–1942)   (1865–1909)

Harold Montagu Hyde-Lees   Bertha Georgie ('George') Hyde Lees m. William Butler Yeats
(1890–1963)   (1892–1968)   (1865–1939)

Anne Butler Yeats   William Michael Butler Yeats
(1919–2001)   (b. 1921)

ANDREW

Thomas Andrew[2] m. Mary Littlewood
(d. 1822)   (d. 1827)

George Andrew m. Grace Midwood
(bp. 1779–1854)   (d. 1875)

George ('Juddy') Andrew 2nd m. Ellen Lees[5]
(bp. 1817–1873)   (bp. 1817–1859)

Edith Alice Andrew[6]
(1848–1927)

bp. = baptized

1. 1st Baron Erskine of Restormel Castle, Lord High Chancellor of England, third son of Henry David, 10th Earl of Buchan and Agnes Steuart.

2. Like Georgie's maternal ancestors, the Andrew family all came from near Manchester.

3. The eldest son of Thomas 1st Baron Erskine; by this marriage he had six sons and six other daughters; his second wife was Anne Bond, his third wife Anna Durham, née Cunninghame Graham.

4. Harriet and Charles were married first in Munich in 1833 and again in Warwick in 1834.

5. Ellen Lees was a younger sister of William Gilbert Hyde's grandmother, Anne Lees.

6. Her only brother died in infancy; she had four sisters, Grace (m. Revd Kenrick Prescot), Agnes (m. William Edward Hollwey Steeds and resided in Ireland), Ellen (m. first, Walter Raleigh Gilbert Hamley and second, George Frederick Munn), and Alice Maude (m. Robert Maddison Warwick).

7. Her sister Gertrude Elizabeth married Revd Richmond William Spurway and had two daughters (Gertrude Annie, m. her great-uncle Robert Maddison Warwick, and Grace Mary m. William Jaffe), and one son (William Langdon); other four brothers, and Montagu George Erskine married, and by his first wife Katharine Angel Hobson had three daughters.

GEORGIE HYDE LEES' PATERNAL ANCESTRY

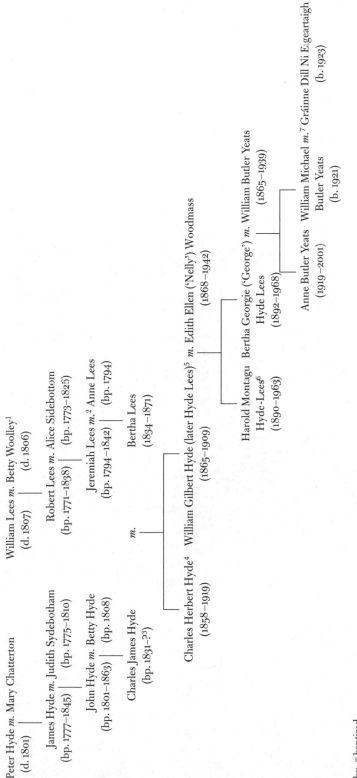

bp. = baptized

[1] Peter and Mary Hyde, William and Betty Lees all came from Mottram in Longdendale, now part of Greater Manchester.

[2] Had seven other daughters and one son, Harold, who married Ellen Preston and named as heir his sister Bertha's son William Gilbert Hyde.

[3] No death certificate has been found.

[4] Married Ellen Doyle; died in workhouse.

[5] Upon inheriting his Uncle Harold Lees' estate, took the name of Hyde Lees.

[6] Married Ada Gwynne Younghughes; they had no children.

[7] Have four children, Caitríona Dill (b. 1951), Siobhán Máire (b. 1953), Síle Áine (b. 1955), and Pádraig Butler (b. 1959).

Prelude: Ballylee

The tower is for the medium alone—not for you—it is a symbol of the human
arm & the human heart—arm and human heart
(the control Thomas)

> Tower renew renew
> alone in it
> yes [*space*] *through your wife*
> (the control Thomas)

The image of conditional memory is your rose—the tower your spiritual
memory
(the control Thomas)

Do not forget that the Tower is still your symbol | in all lives
(the control Ameritus)[1]

The journey to Ballylee began in Dublin at the Broadstone Station, near the
King's Inns. But the train ride to Gort had always been indirect, after three hours
requiring a change at Athenry onto the Limerick lines. Passing many ruined
towers on its way through Craughwell, Castle Taylor on the right, jogging south
at Ardrahan, the train skirts the village of Labane and Edward Martyn's home at
Tillyra Castle on the left, edges by Kiltartan Castle and Ballinamantan House on
the other side, with the leafy entrance to Coole just beyond, and eventually halts
at Gort, separated from the market square by Gort River. Here the rail journey
ends. At the river, George's Street leaves the village forge behind and becomes
Bridge Street, flanked by Glynn's Hotel and the town shops, then, once through
the square, branches off towards Coole and Galway.

The old road, despite its leisurely ups and downs and around, is the most
direct to Ballylee, following Gort River out of town as far as Rinneen, then north-
east to Ballyaneen, passing the neighbouring farms of the Fahys, Brennans, and
Hynes. Further to the right, flowing from the hill range Slieve Aughty, is a stream
(called here the Turra, Streamstown, or Cloon River, depending on its location).

Where river and road meet, as the land dips downwards, Ballylee Castle stands surrounded by water, for yet another stream breaks off from the river (here named after the castle), and rejoins it some fifty yards lower down. Beyond the tower, at the curve of the river, is Martin Linnane's old mill, and about a mile further on, the river disappears into a field, runs underground through the honeycombed limestone, eventually contributing its share to the turlough or seasonal lake named after the Coole demesne. In early summer the countryside is white with the mayflower, the hawthorn in blossom all along the river banks.

In the spring of 1918 when George first saw Ballylee, a right of way had been built through the castle yard, separating the tower and the dilapidated cottage at its foot from a grove of ash trees on the river bank. Soon the cottage would be habitable again, with flowers along the roadside, and a second, larger, white-washed cottage, parallel to the first, built to create an inner cloister leading into her treasured walled garden where she would plant apple trees and roses. Then, across the right of way beside the duck shed, a garage was built, awaiting the Ford car that never materialized.

High in the south-east wall of the tower, facing Coole demesne, is a carved stone head. Willy's poem, intended to enhance the new entrance on the other side, would never be carved in his lifetime:

> I, the poet William Yeats,
> With old mill boards and sea-green slates,
> And smithy work from the Gort forge,
> Restored this tower for my wife George;
> And may these characters remain
> When all is ruin once again.[2]

No matter, it was not long before George possessed Ballylee, proclaimed by both script and poetry, created with her hands and eyes. Year by year, floor by floor, the four single rooms of the castle were shaped in her vision: dining room, study above, bedroom above that, though the 'stranger's room', originally conceived as a study, was never furnished. Connected to the cottages by an open-timbered entrance porch, guarded by a 'great castle door with its 14th or 15th century arched top',[3] the castle took five years to complete. They would not sleep in the great bed, it and the chairs made from felled elms rescued from the neighbours and cut into planks by the old miller, until 1922, and then only on the first floor which doubled as Willy's study. The iron fittings over the hearth, like the hinges, were wrought at the forge in Gort. The hundred-year-old timbers for ceilings and floors, and slates and stones, were from long abandoned Kininclea Mill, just north of Gort to the west of the railway, belonging to old Lord Gough of Lough Cutra Castle. Despite the great fireplaces on the lower two floors, the four-foot thick limestone slate walls did sweat; but the rooms were brightened by deep blue cotton or white bainín curtains and the bedroom had a fine panelled ceiling. Inside the walls, starting anew at a corner on each floor, the ancient winding stairway—seventy silent stone steps in all—climbed to a cemented roof, terraced with waist-high walls where one could sit on a deckchair, hidden from sight.[4]

While the tower, with its broken crown, stood against the cloud-wrapped sky, below all was rooted in time and locality. Even the stone for the cottage was from their own garden. Once while George was digging, 'suddenly out of the air came a voice thanking her, an old owner of the garden, she was told later, long since reborn, yet still in the garden'.[5] Eventually a specially designed sturdy gate kept out merely mortal uninvited guests, including the children, who were never allowed into the walled garden unattended. Their play area was in the enclosed courtyard outside the new three-bedroomed cottage where they slept near faithful Nana Reade, within easy access of the kitchen in the rebuilt cottage next door.

All remained simple. There was no electricity; candles and lanterns cast shadows against the whitewashed walls. The new cottage had the only indoor water closet; the kitchen a good range with copper boiler for hot water. Water for general purposes was drawn from the river in a large galvanized iron water carrier on wheels; the nearest well for drinking water was half a mile away. Milk was fetched from Fahys' farm (avoiding the cowpats) and chickens from local farmers; and there were twice-weekly visits to the shops of Paddy Lally, Gerard Keane, and Bartley Finnegan in Gort, when for this purpose a horse and side-car were borrowed from Coole or hired. The rest of the week George or a servant travelled four and a half miles to Gort by bicycle. (Once the Troubles were over, Matt O'Connor's Garage could provide a motor car to bring visitors or supplies from the village.) To visit Lady Gregory Willy regularly walked across the fields near Kiltartan Cross and through the woods of Coole.

Willy had insisted on bright red for the castle window frames and shutters; though George preferred blue (like the cottage windows), they later compromised on green. Now, during the summer of 1923, upstairs in the first-floor room destined for the dining room but serving temporarily as their bedroom, with its deep blue cotton curtains against freshly whitewashed walls, George painted the ceiling in brilliant, powerful, colours. Red, blue, and gold, rich colours symbolizing Fire and Air, Passion and Power, Construction and Reception, Truth and Spirit—and the Moon and Sun.[6]

Ballylee, August 1923. shhhhstp! shhhhstp! shhhhstp! The methodical strokes of her brush follow her thoughts as George transforms the old mill beams above her.

shhhhstp! shhhhstp! If only the rain would stop, no use bicycling into Gort in this weather. Only one and a half feet above the flood and no sign of Willy coming. Even the jackdaws in the chimneys are restive, and still no sighting of young moorhens. How profligate nature can be!—the gale tears down the winding staircase of the tower turning her hair inside out like one's umbrella in a storm.[7] No wonder over at Clonsilla great-aunt Agnes strengthened her favourite egg-flip with so much whiskey. At least she could tell **that** *story to Nelly; and perhaps distract her from the news of Willy's rapprochement with grandmother Woodmass. Mother and grandmother so alike, in the philosophical system both typical 19s, yet such bitter enemies. Living so close to each other, but never meeting (although both had ways of keeping informed!). What could have caused the rift? Perhaps it came unbidden, like her own strong feeling against Nelly before Anne was born. Strange how, afterwards, when Nelly visited at Oxford, Anne howled whenever she came near.[8] If only she knew more about her own family, now that she had children of her own. If only there was a family circle outside the elderly Yeatses. She could remember young, handsome uncles in their uniforms. What had she missed by not knowing her own grandparents? WHY WHY WHY is it that we all have to deceive our parents? Is it because they began our lives by deceiving us?[9]*

shhhhstp! Willy has asked for a list of the books on philosophy she has read. Where to begin? James (William, so much a better writer than Henry), Hegel, Croce, Descartes, Wundt, Bergson . . . Agrippa, Aventinus, Molinos, Börne, Kircher, Zetzner's Theatrum Chemicum *(British Library resources!) . . . and always Pico and the divine Hermes—a struggle those, in Italian; though not as much as the Latin of old Khunrath. Thank goodness she picked up languages easily, for WBY certainly did not! Ptolemy, foremost of all astrologers. Plotinus and Iamblichus of course; a coup to have introduced Willy to Taylor, and to Hölderlin. Who first told her of Blavatsky, Swedenborg? Probably George Mead. Though Ezra was always a useful source for arcana.*

Blue might be an expansive colour for the staircase. A pity Willy insisted on changing it for the windows and shutters; even Lady Gregory agrees the brilliant red he had insisted upon was too harsh—so like the stairs at Woburn Buildings, sealing-wax red against black walls! Surely the Order's five elemental colours elsewhere are enough? Perhaps he will consent to a compromise green next time round, one of her favourite colours. They must have decided on the brilliant colours for this room when they changed the name to 'Thoor Ballylee'; there is still some stationery headed 'Ballylee Castle'.

Would Willy be able to rescue the Order properties? History now for them, who no longer needed the burnished secrets of the Stella Matutina, but they must be saved. It would be appropriate to store them in this upper room, next to the gilded chest which holds their own magical scripts.

shhhhstp

Her brush continues to move across the great beams above, creating a galaxy of blue, black, and gold. Strong colours for their bedroom and Willy's study, colours redolent of William Blake, even more of the North Kensington temple where nine years ago Willy led her through those first intricate steps into the Outer Order of the Stella Matutina. He so impressive in his Imperator robes and incantatory manner, so knowledgeable of the mysteries of the Order of the Golden Dawn, so transfigured from the mischievous, gossiping, excitable, vulnerable creature who sat on Olivia's hearthrug or at her mother's tea table; she, the earnest student of astrology and the occult, so achingly private. Half-mockingly, Ezra and Dorothy called him 'The Eagle'; secretly, she dreamed of assisting this tall, darkly attractive magician and his wondrous crafts. Little did she know it would yield such mysteries, including their own 'Black Eagle'[10]—one more aspect of her life her mother must never find out.

shhhhstp! shhhhstp! Naming was sacred; it bore responsibilities.

Brother Harold always signs his name with a hyphen; she prefers her father's style. She must stop Willy and Ezra from calling Anne that ridiculous 'Wattles'.[11] Ezra was one of the first to call her 'George'. Does she still dream as Georgie? An intolerable name. But names do stick—like 'Dobbs', which must have come from a round man, a character in one of their children's books perhaps. As Harold would be her 'Hokel', she would forever be 'Dobbs' to him, even to Eva Ducat and Jelly d'Aranyi. Willy always refuses to call her that, though he sometimes addresses her so in letters. 'George' is so much more a serviceable name; and at least saves her from those gratuitous extensions 'Georgina' or even—god help us!—'Georgiana'! Of course, to Dorothy she will always be 'Coz'□.

George was not the only name she chose: to members of the Order of the Golden Dawn she was 'Nemo Sciat', Let Nobody Know. 'Nemo' scrambled becomes 'Omen'; rescramble it, add a 'D', and we have 'Demon', short for 'Demon est Deus Inversus', Willy's motto.

Her brush moves smoothly, expertly avoiding the cornices and moulded edges. The ceiling is almost finished, though more gold paint will have to be ordered from Dublin.[12] Canaries are nesting, and the tower will soon be completed and Willy can return to his poetry—the most important of their partnerships. She and Willy both lost so much by changes of place in childhood; now Anne and Michael will have a special place to remember always, a place to come home to, to bring their friends.[13] Perhaps now, also, there will be an opportunity for that long-promised trip to Italy. Those journeys with Olivia and Dorothy had been important in so many ways. Strange that she was never really homesick for England, but Italy . . . everything nice has always been in Italy.[14]

GEORGIE

Part I
Progressions 1892–1918

1

ANCESTRY

On the morning of 18 December 1889 the entire village of Compstall, Cheshire, in the ancient Township and Manor of Werneth, was in celebratory mood. Flags and banners flew from the church tower, the stables, the mill, the Athenaeum, reading room, brass band pavilion, hotel, taverns, and all the houses; streamers criss-crossed the churchyard gateway and main streets; three triumphal arches—each with intricately designed mottoes—spanned the roads from stables, schools, and manor house; and bunting flourished everywhere. For that afternoon a marriage was to take place in the Church of St Paul between Edith Ellen ('Nelly'), the eldest daughter of Montagu Woodmass, manufacturer, and Captain William Gilbert Hyde Lees, gentleman. Despite heavy morning showers the church was packed to its capacity of 750 well before 2 p.m., when the bridegroom and his friends took their places to greet the bride.

No less than three clergymen officiated, the attendants including Nelly's only sister Ghita, two of her five brothers as sailor-suited pages, Mary Bradshawe-Isherwood from nearby Marple Hill, and, of great interest to the village chroniclers, the Hon. Greta, daughter of the fifth Baron Erskine. After the ceremony, the village brass band assembled to greet the wedding party as their carriages were escorted by cheering villagers up the long drive to Compstall Hall and a lavish dinner. Nelly and Gilbert left on the 4.27 train from Marple for their honeymoon in the south, but the celebrations continued. By special dispensation work at the mill and printworks had stopped at noon, and bonfires and fireworks were at the ready on each hillside. The villagers, the vast majority of whom were employees of the bride's father, deserved this holiday: all through the previous week special committees, teachers, and scholars had laboured over decorations; speeches had been delivered with becoming solemnity, and platforms erected for individual presentations to the handsome couple.

No one would have guessed that this, the marriage of Georgie Hyde Lees's parents, was to be the last great wedding of the Woodmasses of Compstall Hall. Two years later Nelly's only sister Ghita would elope with the penurious Revd William Spurway, and be rapidly disinherited; all five brothers chose military or naval careers and four would die young and unmarried—Harry (consumption),

John (pneumonia), Robert (in an 'asylum for gentlemen of unsound mind'), and Kenny at Ypres. Only George Montagu, the eldest, would survive, shell-shocked and passionate by turn, outliving all his siblings and two wives to inherit the family fortune. There were distant cousins in Turkey, America, Australia, and India, but the direct Woodmass line soon burned itself out.

On this December day, however, the family was out in full force. Nelly's father Montagu[1] traced his family to east Yorkshire, already independently wealthy in the eighteenth century, possibly from whaling; there were tales of a seafaring tradition. Through connections with Lloyd's of London that fortune had increased, and his grandfather rose to the gentry with a fashionable residence in London's Montagu Square. The Woodmasses continued to marry well; a great-aunt, Mrs Thomas Bradshaw, had enjoyed 'grace and favour apartments' at Hampton Court Palace.[2] Montagu himself was great-grandson to Baron Lord Erskine of Restormel Castle, son of the tenth Earl of Buchan, briefly Lord High Chancellor of England, friend of Johnson, Burns, Sheridan, Fox, and—until he rashly pleaded on behalf of Queen Caroline—George IV. In his prime 'an incomparable advocate and orator' who once defended Thomas Paine, the Baron lived up to his family motto 'Trial by Jury'. Sir Walter Scott dismissed him as 'moody and maddish' in old age, but Lord Byron considered him 'the most brilliant person imaginable, quick, vivacious, and sparkling, he spoke so well that I never felt tired of listening to him, even when he abandoned himself to the subject of which all his dear friends expressed themselves so much fatigued—self'.[3] Montagu's grandmother came from equally rebellious stock, being the daughter of General John Cadwallader of Philadelphia, who was a companion of George Washington and one of the leaders of the American Revolution. That Erskine connection remained the Woodmass family's social measure, offering further connections with the Cunningham Grahames, the Mordaunts, the Yeats-Browns; all these names would appear prominently on Woodmass legal and clerical documents for several generations. At Montagu's own wedding, his stepmother Charlotte Cunningham Grahame and her sister the Dowager Lady Anna Erskine were witnesses, while the Dowager's second husband the Archdeacon of Coventry officiated.[4]

Georgie's grandfather Montagu met Edith Alice Andrew while travelling the Midland Circuit of Compstall as a young barrister of the Inner Temple. Although he had attended Eton and, like his titled ancestor, Trinity College, Cambridge, his interests did not tend towards politics. In 1863 his father committed suicide, and as eldest son of an eldest son of an eldest son he came into considerable property. The same year he was elected to the Alpine Club and was a member of the first team to ascend the Dent d'Hérens.[5] After his marriage in 1867 he quickly forsook the bar and turned to the more profitable business of cotton manufacturing and printing. By 1869 he had purchased from his wife's uncle a half share in his father-in-law's business; four years later he inherited the other half ownership of George Andrew and Company.

'The earth is the Lord's and the fullness thereof, But Compstall and all within is Juddy Andrew's.'[6] Justice of the Peace and Deputy Lieutenant of the county, cotton manufacturer, calico printer, collier, and merchant, Edith Alice's father George Andrew the Second believed in property; a quarrel over purchasing yet another mill had alienated his brother and partner, making Montagu's entry into the firm possible. As 'Lord of the Manor of Werneth' George (familiar to all as 'Juddy') Andrew ruled the village of Compstall and his 2,000 employees with Victorian strictness: girls were expected to curtsy and boys remove their hats as the carriage from the big house passed by—if not, their parents were summoned to the mill office for a stern warning; each evening at precisely 10 o'clock a blunderbuss, fired from the mill roof, signalled curfew. After the death of his wife in childbirth, Juddy appears to have been equally demanding at home, later extending control from beyond the grave: a codicil to his will decreed that his daughter Ellen be disinherited if she should marry a certain doctor of the Royal Horse Artillery (wisely, she did not). With no son surviving, he made 'handsome provision' in his will (approximately £150,000) for his son-in-law; in 1873 Montagu therefore became sole owner of Compstall on condition that he provide a generous £10,000 each to his wife and his four sisters-in-law.

George Andrew's only son had died in infancy. However, all five of his daughters survived and married: Agnes and Captain Hollwey Steeds had settled in Ireland as early as 1878; Alice Maude died young and her husband Robert Maddison Warwick would re-enter family history two generations later by marrying his own great-niece; the wilful Ellen survived her second husband, American landscape and still life painter George Frederick Munn; Grace married the Revd Kenrick Prescot. While Montagu looked after the family's legal and financial concerns, the vicar consecrated them: baptisms, funerals, and marriages.

Family gossip suggests that the Andrew women were an eccentric bunch. Nelly Munn, obese in her later years, sensibly insisted on travelling with her own bathtub. Another covered a footstool with the hide of her favourite horse, on which only the chosen few were invited to sit; this may have been Agnes Steeds, still alive in 1924, who barricaded herself in with wood and iron, relived her riding days by jumping over the footstools in her drawing room, and entertained her great-niece Georgie with an egg-flip made from a full glass of whiskey.[7] Montagu's wife Edith Alice, strikingly beautiful, was noted for the number of her lovers; of the seven Woodmass children only Nelly the eldest, Georgie's mother, was known for certain to be legitimate. 'If I had known then about birth control what I know now, I would never have had any children,' she once said to her second daughter (who did not look at all like her sister Nelly). 'The Royal Family does not love their children. There is no reason why I should love mine.'[8] Given the impressive list of godfathers (all wealthy, some titled) for each of those children, it is tempting to wonder whether paternity stood next to godliness.

Exactly five feet tall, Edith Alice was as hard as her father Juddy must have been. Villagers recall that when Montagu and his wife took over the family business their manner changed perceptibly from working industrialists to squire and lady, who presided graciously and generously over social events but left the mill and machinery to competent managers and foremen. By 1870 Montagu was granted his own arms and crest, unlike his ostentatious ancestor modestly selecting the motto 'Pro Deo et Patria'. While his wife entertained her many admirers Montagu, despite his responsibilities as Justice of the Peace for Chester, spent most of his time at the Keg, a hunting lodge built by his father-in-law; he was clearly 'more happy with a dog and a gun than with a bobbin of weft'. Improvements to the property tended to lie in stocking the land with game and widening the river to create a fish pond, rather than with the needs of the factory.[9]

But times had also changed in the industry. In 1899 George Andrew and Company joined the newly formed Calico Printers' Association which took over mills, mines, water supplies, houses, and public buildings; two years later the uneconomic printing section was completely closed, the machinery sold, and most of the buildings demolished. By 1902 the Woodmasses forsook Compstall altogether and settled in a fine house in Kensington, number 7 Southwell Gardens, where portraits of the revered Lord High Chancellor (one by Romney and two by Gainsborough) reigned over the dining room.[10] As iron-willed as she was beautiful, more interested in music than family, Edith Alice Woodmass was terrifying to those children and grandchildren, trembling on the doorstep, whom she did receive; the rebellious Ghita seems to have regained entrance and a small allowance only after it was clear her impecunious clergyman husband could not support their three children. Montagu lived in private quarters at the top of the house, descending formally dressed every evening at 7 p.m. for dinner, which he ate in absolute silence before adjourning to his rooms or his club. There is no record of either returning to Compstall. At his death in 1917, Montagu was loyally described by the local paper in Cheshire as 'a great sportsman, a generous landlord, and a typical English gentleman of the Old School'. Edith Alice determinedly outlived her husband by ten years; his will left everything to her.

The strain of unconventionality continued. Georgie's mother Nelly inherited Edith Alice's appearance, love of the arts, and temperament; like her she was easily bored, infinitely preferred the company of men to women, and encouraged courtiers. Although 'by centuries of tradition an "English Christian lady" ', she pronounced 'the game of flirtation' her favourite pastime, which she claimed she had learned in her youth in Ireland (perhaps while visiting Aunt Agnes Steeds).[11] That may be why her younger sister Ghita was sent instead to finishing school in

Dresden. It is no surprise that mother and daughter became sworn enemies. Not long after her marriage to Gilbert, Nelly seems to have spoken too frequently and publicly about her mother's affairs; whereupon 'that snake in the grass' was banished and disinherited, a decree that was only partially rescinded a few months before the formidable Mrs Woodmass's death in 1927. Hardly a deathbed repentance—that was not in her nature—although she did admit to Ghita's daughter Grace that she wished she had been 'a better grandmother'.[12] She also seems to have been sufficiently conscientious to preserve photographs and memorabilia, left to her son George.[13] Regrets only went so far, however. Some provision was made for Nelly's children, but there is no sign of the 'diamond suite necklace, earrings and locket' Edith Alice inherited from her father on condition that they pass to her eldest daughter—Nelly—and that daughter's eldest daughter—Georgie—in turn. Similarities between mother and daughter extended to choice of marriage partner, for not many years after their rousing send-off, Nelly and Gilbert seemed to spend most of their time apart.

On her father's side also Georgie's ancestors were northerners. William Gilbert Hyde Lees owed his fortune to his maternal uncle Harold Lees. Even by the time of his marriage, details of Gilbert's paternal line—the Hydes—had vanished into obscurity along with all traces of his father. Like the Andrew family, his father Charles James Hyde was descended from eighteenth-century cotton manufacturers but with less social pretension; all staunch Nonconformists, the Hydes prospered in propinquity, building through marriage with neighbouring Chattertons, Sidebottoms, and other Hydes a thriving trade based in Dukinfield and environs. By marriage with Bertha Lees of Kelsall House in Staleybridge, Charles James, eldest son of a prosperous master spinner and manufacturer, continued that tradition. Nelly and Gilbert were, in fact, distantly related, for Nelly's grandmother Ellen Lees (wife of the strict Juddy Andrew) was sister to Gilbert's grandmother Anne Lees (wife of yet another Lees). The busy Revd Prescot officiated at both unions. And in the same church eight years before Gilbert's marriage, his uncle and benefactor Harold Lees had stood godfather (along with the Hon. W. W. Vivian) to Nelly's youngest brother, the unhappy Robert.

Among the wedding gifts on display at Compstall Hall that December day in 1889 was a Worcester tea service from a Miss Ann Lees, but despite close family and business connections, the Hyde family was not represented. (The name Ann would not, however, be forgotten.) Gilbert's mother, who had suffered from a weak heart for a number of years, died at 36 when her younger son was not yet 6. Her husband identified himself on the marriage certificate as an 'American commissions merchant', and the Hydes had begun married life as gentry living in The Larches in Eccles. But by the time of Bertha's death Charles James Hyde is included in the 1871 census as 'retired merchant' residing in a much smaller house; this process would be repeated until the last record we have of him ten years later is as a lodger in a clothier's home in Manchester. No death certificate has ever been traced, but when Gilbert's brother Charles Herbert married in 1885, their father was described as deceased. Older than Gilbert by seven years, Charles Herbert Hyde seems to have left home as a young man in some disfavour: an 'engineer' on his marriage certificate, he had been reduced to 'maintenance work labourer' when he died in the Barrow workhouse in 1919.

Although the surname Hyde Lees began with her father, Georgie's ancestors the Hydes and Lees, wealthy cotton manufacturers, had previously intermarried in the eighteenth century. By the early nineteenth century they had added a more distinguished branch to their tree when through the Dumville Lees they married with the Luxmoores of Okehampton, Devon; in later years this was the only branch of her husband's relations that Nelly acknowledged. Gilbert, however, was the more direct product of Jeremiah Lees, cotton spinner, and Anne, eldest child of Robert Lees, cotton manufacturer, both, like the Hydes, of Dukinfield. Their only son Harold, 10 when his father died, was somewhat unfairly dismissed by Nelly as 'a rather commonplace country squire' who 'increased his fortune by a speculation in the days of early rail-roads'.[14] Wealthy enough to purchase Pickhill Hall, a freehold estate of close to 200 acres in the Dee Valley of north Wales, Harold Lees's life as country squire and Justice of the Peace ended suddenly in 1887, following a hunting accident. Childless, in his will Harold appointed his sister Bertha's son Gilbert his heir on condition he take the name Lees, specifically excluding Gilbert's brother and another of his own sisters from inheritance. That will did, however, make generous provision for Harold's young wife Ellen: the interest from £100,000 should she remain widowed, and, should neither she nor Gilbert wish to live in Pickhill Hall, an equal share of the sale proceeds; a codicil increased his wife's share of the estate from £25,000 to £50,000 should she remarry. Ellen Lees did remarry—twice—became Mayor of Worthing, and lived on till 1925, thereby delaying and reducing (for she was known for her philanthropy) great expectations for the next two generations, notably Georgie's.[15]

Charming, witty, musically inclined, but notably unambitious, Georgie's father Gilbert had been brought up by his uncle Harold to appreciate the good life. Like his father-in-law he attended Eton, although before any of the Woodmass sons; on 19 October 1885 aged 19 he was admitted to Wadham College, Oxford, then a small college of only about seventy students. The one distinction of Gilbert's university career seems to have been his role as no. 3 on the winning team for the 'Oxford Fours' 1886 boat race. One of the few items stipulated in his will was that the cabinet made out of the winning boat be preserved by his son; the cabinet has, unfortunately, since disappeared, but a pewter tankard with its triumphant inscription celebrating the victory remains with the family. His name does not appear on the College honours list and there is no indication that he actually took a degree. What little else we know of those Oxford years is dependent upon the unpublished memoirs of Edward John Bidwell, Bishop of Ontario, with whom Gilbert shared lodgings in 'Hell' (St Helen's) Passage in their fourth year and whose clergy family he stayed with more than once at Worthing.[16] Since Bidwell was one of the founders of the Wadham Association Football Club, it was presumably athletic rather than intellectual or theological interests that led to their friendship; he noted in his memoirs with some disapproval that agnosticism was fashionable at the time. The description probably extended to Gilbert, who would later earn his pious brother-in-law's disapproval by singing outrageous verses to the tunes of traditional hymns.

While still at Oxford Gilbert became a volunteer in the Manchester Regiment, 4th Battalion (a recent amalgamation of the 63rd and 96th regiments of foot nicknamed 'The Bloodsuckers'); by 27 June 1885 he was Lieutenant Hyde Lees. That the militia headquarters was at Ashton under Lyne suggests that he kept some connection with his home region; the uniform was also attractive, scarlet with white facings. On 12 June 1887 he was made up to captain and on 21 October of that year came into his inheritance. By then also he seems to have taken lodgings in London: the *North Cheshire Herald* report of his marriage to Nelly (which does not mention Oxford) gives his address as 22 Emperor's Gate, London, but on the marriage certificate the bridegroom's address is 6 Charles Street, in the clubland of St James's, London.

By November 1890 when their son Harold Montagu was born, Gilbert and Nelly Hyde Lees were living at 40 Montpelier Road, Brighton. A move the following year to Hampshire may have been because Gilbert enjoyed the companionship of fellow officers, for The Grove, Branksome Wood, Fleet, was within an easy ride of Aldershot. Now with the more prosaic address of 60 Church Road, not far off Fleet High Street, The Grove still stands—a two-storey building large enough for a household which included nurse, cook, two housemaids, and a parlourmaid.[17] And here, in December 1892, their daughter was born. Change of name would come later, from the stolid Bertha Georgie (names acknowledging the source of family fortunes) to the more euphoniously ambiguous George. It seems that Gilbert and Nelly's only daughter later not only chose the name by which she would be known for most of her adult life, but also determined her date of arrival. For although birth certificate and passport clearly state 17 October, she and her family always celebrated her birthday on the 16th;[18] in later years her horoscope would be even more specific, stipulating the time of birth as 8.25 a.m.[19] Since the informant indicated on the birth certificate is her mother, this may have been a later astrological rectification, for long before she married Georgie was a firm believer in the power of heavenly bodies. It may also of course have been purely a clerical error, as Nelly did not report the birth until 17 November.

From this time on records of Gilbert's military career are sparse: he was promoted to major on 2 March 1894, but disappears from the Army Lists after 1896,
thereby escaping his regiment's (and his brothers-in-law's) experiences at
Ladysmith. *Walford's Directory* continued to give The Grove as his address until
1899, although it also lists membership in two London clubs, the Wellington and
the Junior United Service (noted for their military relics and big-game trophies).
Records of the young Georgie are also sparse: later references suggest that
something may have happened to her and her mother on 29 November 1896,
and to Nelly on 27 December 1897, but there are no further records until the end
of the century.[20] According to the electoral registers from 1899 to 1901, the Hyde
Lees family had settled in London with an address at 17D de Vere Gardens,
Kensington. Although by this time alienated from her mother, for the next two
decades Nelly Hyde Lees would never live more than a mile from her parents'
home at 7 Southwell Gardens. When she *was* in London, that is.

2

CHILDHOOD

We know nothing of Georgie's seven years at Fleet; presumably in time a governess replaced the nurse. But by 1898 Harold was 8, and required preparation —whether through private tutoring or at a preparatory school is unknown— if he was to follow his father, grandfather, and uncles to Eton. Although Georgie doubtless continued to receive schooling at home, the move to 17D de Vere Gardens in 1898 precipitated both children into an intoxicatingly new world. Still a suburb at the turn of the century, Kensington for many represented the summit of the good life: well served by two great shopping areas, the Royal Albert Hall, several fine museums with another under construction, and within a short cab ride of the gentlemen's clubs of St James's, the West End theatres, and the Queen's Hall (site of the popular 'Proms' since 1895), it was bounded on the north by Kensington Palace and its gardens and by Hyde Park, while to the east lay Belgravia and Westminster. Harrod's (with London's first escalator) had expanded on Brompton Road, and north in Westbourne Grove stood Whitely's, self-styled 'universal purveyor', first of the many great department stores that would appear within the decade. De Vere Gardens, overlooked by the Albert Memorial, a few hundred yards south of Kensington Palace and almost directly across from Palace Gate and the great parkland, offered green spaces which compensated somewhat for the smut and smog of the world's largest city. The terraced houses were large enough to be divided into roomy flats such as 17D, which could accommodate not only the children but the essential household staff. Except for brief intervals in Westminster and Chelsea, Kensington would remain Georgie's London address until 1911.

It was a world of sharp class distinctions and even greater economic extremes. Wages were low, but unemployment was high—one reason servants were so plentiful and still prepared to work long hours and sleep in basements or attics of grand houses, following their employers from place to place. In the back streets drab crowded tenement houses were lit by gas or candles and hot water was rare; in the parks and under the bridges the homeless huddled, and beggars were a familiar sight. From their privileged viewpoint, Georgie and Harold observed elegant ladies and gentlemen ride in Rotten Row or sweep by in open carriages, while along Kensington Road proud, beautifully groomed horses drew the gleaming leather and burnished brasses of the 'four-in-hands'. Infantry from Hyde Park barracks, smart in scarlet tunics and pillbox caps, marched briskly past on their way to the Boer War. Occasionally in nearby squares straw might be laid down to protect the sick from the jarring sound of wheels on cobblestones, but the air was full of the sounds of the city: barrel-organs, brass bands, street cries, muffin-bells, calls from the newsboys and cart vendors, and the bells of horse-drawn traffic (omnibuses, trams, draywagons, carts, cabs, private carriages). The bicycle was by now a familiar sight, with teams of boy cyclists dressed in khaki uniform and red sash bearing the words 'Bovril war cables' sent out from hour to hour to various London shops, announcing special war news. But although the speed limit on highways rose in 1896 from four to fourteen miles per hour, locomotives were still a surprise in London, while the motor bus did not arrive until 1906. London's first electric railway, the Central Line, began operating in 1900, the same year electric trams were introduced; the first underground tube stations did not open until 1910, the year the Victoria and Albert Museum was finally completed.

For those who could afford it, travel above ground was simpler and more suitable: within a four-mile radius of Charing Cross a hansom cab cost a shilling for the first two miles and sixpence for each extra mile, while a package outside the cab raised the charge another twopence. It cost sixpence to keep a four-wheeler (the hackney carriage or 'growler') waiting fifteen minutes, and eightpence for a two-wheeler. The South African War pushed income tax higher, but goods were still comparatively inexpensive: most newspapers cost a halfpenny, cigarettes a penny for five, a glass of beer twopence, the best tea could be had for one shilling and sixpence a pound and coffee a shilling a pound; really good cigars were fifteen shillings a hundred, while a dozen bottles of fine champagne cost forty-eight shillings. The newly invented phonograph could be purchased for as little as two guineas, a Brownie camera from five shillings. It was possible to furnish a fair-sized house completely and adequately for £100. Velveteen sold for two shillings a yard and gentlemen could purchase six good white shirts for thirty shillings (post free). It cost a penny to send a letter, a halfpenny for a postcard; in central London there were up to twelve postal deliveries daily.[1]

For children fresh from the country, even the local shops with their overhead cash-railway system, whistling from assistant to cashier and back, were an adventure, while a visit to Harrod's meant exploring the vast Meat Hall (designed in the finest Arts and Crafts style) or the glories of the pastry counters. Accompanied by their governess, they took walks in Hyde Park, on Sunday dressed in their finest hats and gloves. On August Bank Holidays all twenty-four air balloons of the Spencer brothers would be in use throughout London; while at the Crystal Palace if one were lucky one might see balloon ascents and parachute descents by the brothers themselves. At night over the rooftops it was still possible to see the Great Wheel of Earl's Court Exhibition grounds, and just around the corner the annual sheepshearing took place in the palace gardens. Madame Tussaud's waxworks had opened in 1884 and Astley's circus was still operating, but surely one of the greatest attractions was the zoo in Regent's Park where one could feed the sea lions, visit the monkey house, or queue for an elephant ride. Georgie continued to visit the zoo for the rest of her life. At Christmas there were pantos at the Theatre Royal with the incomparable Dan Leno, while films of up to thirteen minutes chronicled the dear Queen's final years and Lord Roberts's triumphant return from South Africa; by 1912 there would be more than five hundred cinemas in London and its suburbs.

By now too every borough had a public library; and then there were the bookshops, Hatchard's of Piccadilly and Bumpus Brothers next to Marshall and Snelgrove on Oxford Street, both frequented by Nelly, soon by Georgie herself. Art galleries, public and private, were all within a short distance of the privileged.[2]

Not long after their arrival in London, the Hyde Leeses, restless even for the landless upper middle classes, began a decade on the move. On 1 November 1900, a passport was issued to W. G. H. Lees; such travel documents were then a matter of courtesy and convenience, not necessity. We have no idea when they departed for the Continent; this may have been for a short jaunt to Paris to visit the Exposition. The sudden death of Queen Victoria in January 1901 might well have delayed their plans for a lengthier stay abroad; they were probably still in London in February when Nelly purchased W. B. Yeats's *The Wind among the Reeds* (and copied on the endpapers the lines 'But I being poor, have only my dreams; I have spread my dreams under your feet. Tread softly because you tread on my dreams'). Or, out of concern for Nelly's four brothers, they may have waited until the most destructive period of the South African War had ceased (reeling from Kitchener's 'scorched earth policy', the Boers unsuccessfully sued for peace in March). Though it is likely that Paris was one of the cities they first visited, we do not pick up the trail again until November 1901, when the *Florence Gazette* notes that Mr and Mrs Hyde Lees were residing at the Villa Bonaini, La Pietra, in the hills above Florence. By late March 1902 they had moved to the Hotel Minerva on the piazza Santa Maria Novella. One friend who lived in Florence (also known to Lady Gregory) was Helen Lawless, wife of a military man, who was to follow Georgie's life 'with love & interest', see her as a married woman, and console her in her widowhood.[3] Apparently they returned to London later that year, for an entry in the 1902 Death Duty Registers for Gilbert's uncle Harold Lees gives Edith Ellen's address as 38 Montpelier Street, Kensington.[4] A copy of Yeats's 1901 edition of *Poems* is inscribed 'Nelly Hyde Lees July 1902'.[5]

No sooner had they returned from the Continent than Georgie was sent away to school (where she carefully entered her name, new address, and the date in her Bible). Although it was not unusual for children to be sent from home at an early age, Nelly may have had more pressing reasons, if Gilbert was already showing signs of alcoholism. Under the control of the Anglican order of Sisters of Mercy, St Stephen's High School on Arthur Road, Clewer, Somerset, catered for local girls, but also had a small boarding house for about fifty children.[6] With 225 boys, 179 girls, and 336 infants under their care, Master Joseph W. Steadman and Mistresses Elizabeth and Mary Fenemore would have had little time for individual supervision. But Nelly herself had grown up with ten boys (brothers and cousins all younger than herself),[7] and no maternal care, and clearly had definite ideas about both children's education.

Georgie was already monitoring her reading by indicating the year, often the month and day, of each new purchase. It may have been while at Clewer that she received Mrs Gatty's *Parables from Nature* as a school prize, with the expectation that she would find them both 'amusing and instructive'.[8] But she had by then developed her own taste and was not averse to declaring it. Nelly preserved this letter of 1901 from the author and illustrator Laurence Housman:

Dear Georgie When I got your letter I consulted my magic crystal, asking where in the world lived a child so considerate, who would trouble to tell me my stories pleased her, but didn't want to trouble me to write back to her. 'What is her name?' I asked, 'Where does she live? And how old is she? Also is she a he or a she?' And the crystal answered 'She is a she, and she lives in a flat, not far from the house Robert Browning lived at; it's rude to name ages, don't ask it me please, but the name of her mother is Mrs. Hyde-Lees.'

Having got that information out of my crystal, I write to thank you for loving the one end of me you have got hold of. Here at a distance the other end of me puts your letter in lavender; and years hence may come across you and find you have quite left off caring for fairy-tales. But until that day comes I shall go on writing them and shall still hope to please you.

Your grateful fairy-tale maker
LAURENCE HOUSMAN.[9]

Housman was well known for his originality as book designer and illustrator, most notably of Christina Rossetti's *Goblin Market and Other Poems*. By this time he had turned to writing his own tales of 'weird fantasy' and 'mystic glamour',[10] three collections of which had been published: *A Farm in Fairyland* (1894), *The House of Joy* (1895), and *The Field of Clover* (1898). Strongly individual in approach, his work was refreshingly unique in a period in which much of children's literature was intended, like Mrs Gatty's, to amuse and instruct. 'The true end and object of a fairy tale is the expression of the joy of living. There begins and ends the morality of the fairy tale; its value consists in its optimism,' he declared. It must be pure in the sense of being 'wholly unconcerned with any question of morals', and 'wholly unconscious of its simplicity'.[11] Again and again moonlight carries a special magic (in 'The Horse with a Hump' the golden queen is joined by the silvery king[12]), an entrance to the 'what if' world of wonders multiplied within wonders, the smooth translation from natural to supernatural and back again. His stories of transformation and dreams, full of giants and witches and magicians, emphasized a will to believe and achieve, where the grotesque and the beautiful walked together, and the unique and strange were embraced and encouraged. Clearly Georgie learned such lessons early.

But Housman's illustrations were not popular with all; he tells in his autobiography of a friend overhearing a discussion between two children, 'one objecting to them, and the other saying that she must try to like them because now they were "the thing"'.[13] It is tempting to think the young critics might have been Harold, already a budding art collector, and his younger sister Georgie. Later Housman would collaborate with other artists, most notably Edmund Dulac, who in 1907 provided the drawings for his *Stories from the Arabian Nights*. Born in 1865 and thus the same age as Georgie's father, Housman became friendly with her brother and mother also. But soon he was actively supporting the suffragettes and pacifism, activities Nelly found distasteful; by the time of her marriage to Harry Tucker in 1911, the relationship seems to have become more distant. And there is no record of further contact, especially after Housman's co-founding with Edward Carpenter of the British Society for the Study of Sex Psychology in 1914. They had 'each become different people'.[14]

Meanwhile, the Hyde Leeses moved again. From 1902 to 1904 they are registered at 4 Carlisle Mansions, Westminster; Somerset Maugham was their neighbour at number 27. An increased demand for middle-class housing and lack of building space meant that in the decade before the construction slump of 1906, dozens of such large mansion blocks (all with lifts) were built in the fashionable parts of the city. These were luxury flats, spacious and rich in architectural detail, with imposing entrances and central staircases, large enough for entertaining and for a considerable staff. Somewhat more modest 'mansion houses' frequently nestled at the end of streets of terraced houses. Private gardens were a rarity, but with the public gardens and parks of Kensington, the area around which the Hyde Leeses gravitated, this was hardly a drawback. By now Gilbert's life may have begun to disintegrate, for his aunt Ellen, holder of the family treasury, refers to him in her will in 1925 as 'late of' Carlisle Mansions.

The next few years are murky. We do not know how long Georgie stayed at school at Clewer, or when in 1905 Nelly moved with the peripatetic Gilbert to nearby 26 Yeomans Row, a house recently vacated by the artist Charles Stacey Knight. Harold seems to have oscillated between the Victorian puritanism of his aunt and uncle in the Edworth rectory (perhaps as a paying guest—cousin Grace was shocked when on one occasion both Georgie and Harold complained of the food) and the decadence of travels with his father; he later claimed he had learned everything there was to know about evil from visits to Paris with Gilbert before he was 14.[15] However, when Nelly and her children joined the Spurways at Edworth, they went alone. Given to anti-clerical pranks, Gilbert was not welcome at the rectory, the Revd Spurway declaring more than once, 'I will not have that man in my house.' Grace Spurway, who would have much preferred the company of Georgie to the dissolute Harold, remembered her aunt and beloved cousin spending much time travelling in Europe;[16] dates provided by Nelly in George's horoscope books include 'Florence 1899 Feb 1906'. Georgie's mastery of foreign languages and familiarity with foreign travel support this; she always spoke longingly of the days in Italy when she was 'very happy as a child'.[17] Italy, especially Florence, would long be her promised land.

It is difficult to determine just when Georgie's parents parted permanently; there is no trace even of a formal separation,[18] and social courtesies were maintained. In November 1906, for example, 'Mr and Mrs Hyde Lees' sent a wreath to the funeral of cousin George Dumville Lees. During that winter of 1906–7 Nelly was living at 22 Priory Mansions, Drayton Gardens, with both her children (and presumably Gilbert when he was in London). A letter about this time to Laurence Housman suggests that her situation would soon change: 'I haven't been able to make any engagements here for some months, except with intimate friends, so you will guess that I have not been living a quite normal life; I hope however to be freer very soon.'[19] Nelly's 'intimate friends' by then included the novelist Olivia Shakespear's family and circle; her friendship with Housman, who was much more comfortable with his homosexuality than was his brother Alfred, would be unlikely to cause much speculation—a lesson Georgie would later heed to her own advantage. Unless there had been a marriage settlement Nelly, alienated from her own family, was probably dependent on the reckless Gilbert's generosity. In any case, socially conscious Nelly would hardly risk the public opprobrium attached to divorce. However, some time between 1907 and 1908, Georgie's parents appear to have formally separated at last. By 1907 Nelly had settled into Kensington Palace Mansions, up the road in de Vere Gardens from her first home in London as a young married woman, and there she remained for the next four years. Gilbert meanwhile stayed nearby in Drayton Gardens, moving from number 22 to number 16 Priory Mansions.

In 1907, while Harold was in his last year at Eton, Georgie, now 15, enrolled in St James's School for Girls in West Malvern. Run by the four Baird sisters, the school had an established reputation, but Nelly would probably have heard of it from her Kensington neighbours. Olivia Shakespear had sent her daughter to St James's when it was still in Crowborough, and Dorothy had happily moved with the school to Malvern. There, the gardens established by the late Lady de

Walden, whose home it had been, were justly famous. The curriculum, too, was known for the originality with which traditional subjects (English literature, Latin, German, French) were presented, and an openness to new approaches to the arts such as the Dalcroze method of expressing music by movement. Here, under the beneficent tutoring of the twin headmistresses Alice and Katrine Baird, reading was encouraged and composition enlighteningly taught with wit and imagination.[20] Perhaps urged by her teachers, from 1907 on Georgie added to her collection, from Christmas and birthday 'tips', the entire eighteen volumes of Thomas Hardy's Wessex novels. However, Georgie was not happy at school.[21] She must have chafed under the customary lessons in sewing, cookery, dancing, and deportment—and suffered even more from the intrusive sound of bells ordering the day; always independent and valuing her solitude, one morning she was discovered in the headmistresses' garden alone and without permission before the getting-up bell.[22] Whatever the reason, she left St James's after five terms; when she returned with Dorothy Shakespear for a visit four years later and wandered (this time with permission) down the avenues of golden cypress and weeping wych elms, through the Japanese magnolias and gardens of heather, double narcissus, gentians, and michaelmas daisies, she was startled to discover that her memory of swans on the ponds was imaginary. The incident would have repercussions in years to come.[23]

Their father's departure brought Georgie (called 'Dobbs' from infancy) and Harold ('Hokel', her nickname for him) more closely together, and some semblance of normality was restored at Kensington Palace Mansions. Was it now they were joined by 'Binks' the dog? Naughty Binks has gone down in family legend—during the annual ceremonial visit to the Bishop (a remote relative) he broke loose and killed one of the deer in the park; another time he disgraced himself by consuming an entire hambone and as punishment was locked in overnight without his water bowl; until, that is, the children sneaked down to give him a drink.[24] Starting in July 1908, while her brother prepared for Oxford, Georgie each day journeyed to 133 Queens Gate, where at Miss Amabel Douglas's school for girls there were more classes in French and German, elocution, piano, and singing, as well as ballet and ballroom dancing, flower arranging and dressmaking. Art and music history were supplemented by regular visits to the theatre, opera, and art galleries.[25] Crossing Gloucester Road, she passed directly by 7 Southwell Gardens—would she have recognized as her grandmother the elegant old woman being handed into a cab on her way to an afternoon concert?

Not until after her marriage was Georgie invited to Southwell Gardens; by then her grandfather was dead.[26] Although she never met him, there seems to have been some contact, if not a rapprochement, with Montagu Woodmass through Herbert Vincent Reade, a younger fellow member of the Alpine Club who became her close friend. Great-nephew of the novelist, playwright, and theatre manager

Charles Reade and nephew of the explorer Winwood Reade (whose ambitious and controversial 'universal history' *The Martyrdom of Man* went through more than two dozen editions), Reade was a graduate of Corpus Christi College, Oxford, but spent his entire working life in the civil service, gradually ascending the various levels of the Board of Customs and Excise. His heart however was in climbing, and he seems to have harboured some ambition to be a travel writer himself. By the time the Woodmasses had settled in London he was a regular contributor to the *Alpine Journal*, writing graceful reports lavishly interspersed with quotations from nineteenth-century poets and sly comments on his Alpine companions. Shy and reserved (except with close friends and at the Club's annual general meetings), he and his wife Georgina had a flat in Queen's Gate close to Georgie's school, and later at Palace Gardens Terrace; but they spent as much time as possible at the extensive Ipsden Estate, in the Chilterns near Oxford, inherited from Herbert's father. 'Ba', as Mrs Reade was known to her friends and family, like her husband came from a clerical background, the only daughter of the Revd Edmond Thomas Butler, rector of Trotten, Sussex; her love of Ireland and all things Irish suggests she may have been related to the Irish Butlers and hence perhaps a distant relative of the Yeatses.[27] Georgie was clearly fond of 'dear little 'Erb', who seems to have taken a special interest in her education, judging by the books still in her library: Plato's *Republic* was his Christmas gift in 1913, and later, volumes of Shelley and George Moore among others, with accompanying letters both arch and courtly. Until Reade's death in 1929, she often sought refuge from London at Ipsden House ('part 13th century and part Queen Anne'), like the adjoining village comparatively unchanged for centuries.[28]

Sometime late in 1908 Gilbert became a patient at Highshot House, East Twickenham, a private nursing home for alcoholics.[29] His final address was in Pimlico where, on 18 November 1909, he died; the death certificate describes symptoms consistent with syphilis. Like his father before him, and his brother later, he seems to have died among strangers; even his executor and residuary legatee Arthur Tolfrey Christie was apparently a casual acquaintance, a quondam soldier who soon returned home to Australia an aimless wandering pensioner, dying intestate.[30] Gilbert left his most valued possession, the cabinet made from the boat in which he rowed for Oxford, to Harold. Although it is not specifically mentioned in his brief will,[31] Georgie throughout her life cherished the writing desk her father had carried with him on his peripatetic journey.

But to live with an alcoholic, especially one's handsome, witty father, takes its toll. It is now generally acknowledged that susceptibility to alcoholism and alcohol abuse is genetically transferred;[32] George would later confide to John Butler Yeats that her father, grandfather, and great-grandfather were all alcoholics,[33] and it is reasonable to assume that explains the disappearance of Gilbert's father from public records. While still a child Georgie seems to have exhibited the personality traits that psychologists observe in some children of alcoholic parents, who compensate by becoming 'overly controlled supercopers' or 'care-takers', 'high achievers' who 'discount [themselves] by putting others first'.[34] She was remembered as being solitary at school, and remarkably mature and 'alarmingly intuitive' for her age.[35] Although she always had a keen sense of humour,[36] very early on an outward gaiety masked her innate seriousness. The shock of her father's sudden and unexpected death would remain with her for many years.[37] Was it now that she began to have nightmares and walk in her sleep? The high colouring Georgie (like her brother) had all her life might also have been a symptom of the facial flushing or rosacea noted as an inherited factor.[38]

Well before Gilbert's death Nelly had become part of the only society that mattered, 'the one thing that makes the world tolerable', the Arts[39] (which she always thought of with a capital A), and had begun the social round of afternoon teas and soirées where talented musicians performed and poets read. She was an intimate member of the circle surrounding Olivia Shakespear in Brunswick Gardens, a retinue which included Olivia's former lover W. B. Yeats and three younger poets vying for the affections of her daughter Dorothy—the Australians Frederick Manning and James Griffyth Fairfax, and the American Ezra Pound. As Georgie matured she dutifully accompanied her vivacious mother, observing the scene with those intense, wide eyes. Jelly d'Aranyi, Hungarian violinist and grand-niece of the virtuoso performer and teacher Joseph Joachim, became a devoted lifelong friend to both mother and daughter; Walter Rummel, the handsome young German-American pianist recently arrived from Paris, performed works by his friend Debussy especially for Nelly.[40] Yeats nicknamed her 'the Gad Fly'.[41] Gentle, philosophical Harry Tucker, Olivia's beloved brother, fell in love with her. Nelly and 'H.T.T.', as he habitually signed himself, were sufficiently friendly by 1906 for him to present her or her daughter with a copy of Max Beerbohm's recently published *The Happy Hypocrite*.[42]

Olivia Shakespear was in Florence at the same time as the Hyde Leeses in March 1902, where their paths may well have crossed;[43] but it is likely they knew each other as early as 1900 through the ubiquitous Erskine connections. In 1899 Beatrice Caroline Strong (whose mother was one of Kenny Woodmass's godparents) married Robert Steuart Erskine, a distant cousin of Georgie's grandfather Montagu. In 1901 she was editor of the *Kensington*, a new magazine 'of art, literature, and the drama', which included articles on stage costume by Ellen Terry's daughter Edith Craig and on music by composer Martin Shaw, illustrations by Gordon Craig, Pamela Colman Smith, and Beatrice herself, and poetry by Alix Egerton and W. B. Yeats, all of whom frequented the same artistic circles in London. The review section was dominated in its first months by Olivia Shakespear, who proved a harsh if discerning critic.[44] 'Intended to be good in matter, small in price and catholic in taste', the first issue was sold out in three days, but like most such worthy endeavours the *Kensington* seems to have disappeared after only seven issues. It did however launch Mrs Steuart Erskine on a career as novelist, dramatist, translator, prolific travel writer, biographer, and editor of letters with a special interest in women and the arts. Even more significant to Nelly and her mother, she published the memoirs of both the Earl of Sandwich and Sir David Erskine. Beatrice Erskine remained on good terms with all the Woodmasses, doubtless serving at times as a useful conduit of information between mother and daughter; later, through her exploration of the occult, she was to become an even closer associate of Georgie.

None of the Andrew family seems to have returned to Compstall.[45] But more careful than Edith Woodmass had been of reputation, Nelly ensured respectability by inviting Ghita Spurway to join her for seaside holidays, though the two sisters apparently rarely met in London; there was, Nelly admitted later, 'the usual dissatisfaction born of love where is no liking'.[46] Two of their brothers were now dead—Harry, whose promising career in the Merchant Navy was cut short by consumption in 1898, and John, who after the war returned to South Africa as a commercial traveller and died of pneumonia in a Cape Town hotel in 1907. It was clear that Robert would never recover from his wartime experiences, and George, who had recently married Kitty Hobson, would soon depart for Canada. Of all the tall, handsome brothers Grace Spurway recalled as having visited the rectory at Edworth, only Kenny remained in uniform. Having distinguished himself during the South African War as an Imperial Yeoman in the famous Rough Riders (who were required to pass special riding tests), he accepted a commission as lieutenant in the 2nd East Yorkshire Regiment. The two sisters had in fact very little in common apart from their devotion to music— Ghita was a fine pianist and cellist—dread of their mother, and concern for their children. Georgie was clearly fond of Ghita's younger daughter Grace, whom she nicknamed 'sandy cat' and alternately teased and advised; recognizing her unprepared cousin's distress over the sudden onset of menstruation, she was able to offer comfort and explanation. Older by five years and infinitely wiser, Georgie remained Grace's ideal for the rest of her life.

Although sometimes Grace's young brother William accompanied them, the seaside holidays rarely included Georgie's brother Harold or the Spurways' elder daughter Annie. For by this time it was obvious that Annie was emotionally and mentally unstable, suffering from the dementia praecox that would, as with her uncle Robert and, later, her uncle George's eldest daughter, eventually lead to permanent confinement. Harold, too, as a young child had such severe tantrums that the doctor had to be called in to calm him. Harold was always physically awkward and heavily built; Grace remembered that once while the children were picking daisies, he had fallen in a ditch and his 'Uncle Rich' had to seek help to pull him out. His father's lifestyle served as no model for moderation, and, as he approached puberty, he found it even more difficult to control his emotions; his cousin recalls escaping rape only by the timely arrival of her father. Years later Harold would blame his early transgressions on the influence of his father combined with 'the seamier side' of Eton. Georgie, ever loyal to her beloved brother and adored father, made excuses to Grace, explaining that 'some people take a very long time to grow up'.[47]

Like most of her circle, Nelly was interested in occult matters; she read cards[48] and believed in psychic powers. Olivia Shakespear considered herself a firm agnostic inclining towards Buddhism, believed in reincarnation, psychometrized objects,[49] was familiar with Tattwa and Tarot cards, and was often consulted by Yeats while in semi-trance. As early as 1906 Harold too was discovered to have clairvoyant faculties; holding a letter in his hand he could accurately describe the personality and whereabouts of the writer, eventually with practice in such detail that Nelly felt as if she was eavesdropping and discouraged the budding psychic. One of his subjects was Laurence Housman, to whom she sent her notes of the reading, saying, 'I will not let him do it again without getting the consent of the writer of any letter. . . . I do hope you will not be annoyed. . . . We haven't told any one except Mrs Shakespear about it as he is shy. He has improved with practice. . . . but I really feel very uncomfortable about it.'[50] Now the shock of attending his dying father had a profound long-range effect on Harold, which might well also have led to the poltergeist activities the family suffered during a summer holiday in 1910. Instead of going to Devon or Cornwall, Nelly had arranged to spend that entire summer at Hinxworth, in the hamlet next to the Spurways of Edworth. The experiment was not a success; the Hyde Leeses and their guests, including Harry Tucker and his niece Dorothy Shakespear, were subjected to disturbing nightly noises and ghostly hair pulling. Years later when Grace jokingly suggested to Harold that he might have been the cause of the disturbance, 'he turned as white as the proverbial sheet'. But Georgie, whom the family always credited with second sight,[51] insisted that the bachelor incumbent Revd Atkins, who had let them his rectory for the summer months while he went elsewhere, was the evil perpetrator of the ghostly visits. Despite Revd Spurway's disdain of the superstitious town-dwellers, everyone departed for London early except for the unfortunate Harold, who once more remained with his aunt and uncle before going up to Oxford. Before she left, Georgie herself created a memorable impact by arguing fiercely with 'Uncle Rich', perhaps because he refused to acknowledge ghosts in the neighbourhood. 'You're talking through your hat,' she announced on one occasion, leaving the room to return with a large paper bag which she proceeded to put over the Revd Spurway's head. To the surprise of his shocked children, her uncle quietly accepted the rebuke. Many years later, visitors to the Hinxworth rectory and residents of the nearby manor house reported stories of hauntings in both places.[52]

Once a widow, Nelly was no longer that social misfit, the abandoned but not-quite-divorced wife, and although Georgie's share of her father's estate was not munificent (Harold received twice as much as she did) her children ceased to be a drain on a 'very small' private income. In fact, Nelly would on later occasions have her daughter co-sign her overdrafts.[53] Despite the limitations of her income, Nelly, like her own mother and aunts, believed in travelling in comfort— never second class and always in good hotels, a practice her daughter was to continue. There may have been another trip to Nelly's 'beloved Florence'[54] when Georgie left finishing school, for George recalled sharing a compartment with the ebullient Jelly d'Aranyi, who undressed in full sight of the platform as the train passed by, explaining unperturbedly to her shocked companion, 'they will not see me again'.[55]

The Hyde Leeses seem to have met Jelly d'Aranyi, who was a few months younger than Georgie, soon after the three d'Aranyi sisters (Jelly, Adila, and Hortense) first visited England in 1909 where they gave concerts at various private houses; from March 1910 till June 1911 they performed both publicly and privately, and again lived in London during the winter of 1913–14. When war came they and their mother lived as 'enemy aliens' in Beaufort Gardens, Chelsea, performing frequently at Lady Ottoline Morrell's 'Thursdays', and in 1915 both of Jelly's sisters married. Her own career took off: Vaughan Williams, Ravel, and Bartok dedicated compositions to her; from 1917 on she toured for many years with Myra Hess; she became close friends with Margot Asquith, Aldous Huxley, and Baron Erik Palmstierna, Sweden's Minister in London (later a friend of the W. B. Yeatses). The latter would describe occult experiments with Jelly and Adila in the 1930s which led to the first performances of Schumann's suppressed 'D Minor Concerto'.[56] Jelly adored Nelly, dashing off affectionate messages while on tour and visiting her frequently. To Nelly, she confirmed the belief that 'nothing matters, nothing really counts, for us, except the Arts, in the Arts alone can we find our salvation'.[57] She remained one of the few women Georgie accepted into intimate friendship; all loved her openness, wit, and charm.[58]

Eva Ducat was another lifelong friend of Nelly and her daughter. 'Born with a passion for music, not as a performer but as a listener,' she had studied piano with Mimie and her father William Shakespeare, friends of Brahms and Clara Schumann. Eva's book *Another Way of Music*, in which she urges 'the ideals, manner of work, and standards of the Classical School', draws on Schopenhauer, Nietzsche, and Bernard Shaw as well as musicians past and present to argue her belief in the active function of the listener. 'A good listener by reinforcing the feeling of the player, fills a more important place than people imagine. His function is first to receive, then to respond in his turn. . . . His ear must be open to shades and delicacies, and his mind and heart empty, ready to receive the impression given him,'[59] advice which would have profound significance for the young

Georgie. They attended concerts together, and Georgie's record collection included, in addition to the customary samples of Chaliapin and Caruso, recordings by Jelly and a considerable number of Schubert arias by soprano Elena Gerhardt.[60] Eva may have influenced the younger woman in other ways, too, for as soon as she came of age she had left a comfortable home (and, while her disapproving father remained alive, an assured income) in order to pursue her studies in her own way. She probably sponsored Georgie's membership in the Three Arts Club for women, founded by the actress and activist Lena Ashwell, for she was a member from its early years.[61] In the 1930s and 1940s she would publish a number of children's books. Also a friend of Olivia Shakespear, she later acted for a time as Yeats's musical agent (on one occasion causing the poet some embarrassment).[62] Eva's connections with Olivia's circle extended further still, for she and Nelly were both friends of Helen Lawless, née Bayly, whom Lady Gregory had taken Yeats to visit in her home in Florence.[63]

Jelly, Eva, Nelly, and Olivia all belonged to the circle entertained by the wealthy American Eva Fowler, who opened her London home and Daisy Meadow, her cottage in Kent, to devotees of the arts and the occult. Tea at Mrs Fowler's might include readings by the young poets Ezra Pound, Frederick Manning, James Griffyth Fairfax, and their friends; recitals by Jelly and Rummel, an early collaborator with Pound and known as much for his psychic tendencies as his appeal to women; experiments with the ouija board and table-rapping; discussions of automatic writing.[64] There were intense debates on Egyptian mythology with the erratically erudite actress-producer Florence Farr, who had written and performed two esoteric plays with Olivia and had been a power in the occult society the Order of the Golden Dawn; Olivia believed that she herself had an Egyptian incarnation.[65] In this receptive atmosphere poetry, music, and occultism grew ever more closely together. Meanwhile, in October 1910, Georgie reached 18, the traditional 'coming out' age for young ladies. Although not in either an economic or social circle to be presented at Court, she was duly photographed in evening dress of prescribed style ('bodice cut in a round decolletage, showing the shoulders, and with short sleeves').[66] Standing tall and serious, challenging the camera with those unforgettable dark hazel eyes —everyone remembers their penetrating intensity—she was already a person to be reckoned with.

On 1 February 1911, a decent fourteen months after Gilbert's death, Edith Ellen Hyde Lees and Harry Tucker were married in the Register Office, St George, Hanover Square, London. The witnesses were Harry's sister Olivia Shakespear and her daughter Dorothy. The Tuckers took up residence very close to their friend Eva Fowler, at 16 Montpelier Square, a pleasant house on the corner which, when they were not in the country, was their address for the next eight years. Bachelor son of a major general in the Indian Army, Harry had lived with his widowed mother until her death in 1900, and probably first met Nelly at the Shakespears' home in Brunswick Square. They were in many ways well suited; both fervently nationalist, Nelly later histrionically claimed that, fearing England would not enter the war in 1914, they went so far as to arrange to live in France 'as the only way, bar suicide, to bear the shame'.[67] (Fortunately for them, the move became unnecessary.) Thanks to a number of inheritances and shrewd investments, Harry was able to indulge in his love of golf and art, which he started collecting at the age of 13; by the mid-1930s his collection of Japanese prints, works by Augustus John, Henri Gaudier-Brzeska, Wyndham Lewis, Charles Conder, and other contemporary painters was professionally valued at more than £2,000. Fiercely opinionated yet outwardly polished and gentle,[68] Harry's violent nature, Nelly recognized, kept her 'in the divine state of uncertainty and alarm I need'.[69] ('My mother loves to make a whirlpool and especially if she can suck me in to it', George once confided to a friend.[70]) Eventually that violence would break through and engulf her husband, leaving Nelly in her last years again uncertain, unhappy, and lonely.

But in 1911 all was serene. Georgie joined her mother and new stepfather at Montpelier Square. Harold, though not quite 21 already independently wealthy (throughout his life he kept a shrewd eye on the stock market), was now up at Wadham College, taking, failing, and taking again Oxford's preliminary Devotional exams (or 'Divvers'). Still shattered by the experience of watching his father die (he was responsible for identifying the body), he began deliberately a conversion of personality, conscientiously making himself over into 'what the world calls a good man', as his young sister-in-law would later describe him.[71] As he matured he also grew more handsome, with 'high-coloured, florid good looks' (probably also a legacy from his father), filling out (with an early tendency to over-weight) the large six foot four frame that had burdened him as a clumsy young-ster. Unfortunately he also became dull and humourless in the progress towards improvement ('The dismal Hyde descends for tea,' once lamented Pound),[72] rigidly disapproving in his outlook, rabidly anti-Semitic,[73] and parsimonious in all things but his developing art collection, an interest no doubt encouraged by Harry Tucker. Georgie, always loyal, continued to have some influence on her brother until his marriage, although their cousin Grace felt that not even his mother cared much for Harold, especially once he became a clergyman.[74] It is possible, although there is now no record, that he had also inherited part of his considerable fortune from a Woodmass relation; the Spurway family always resented his wealth, feeling it should have been distributed more evenly. Perhaps because of this (as well as lingering guilt), Harold was prevailed upon to pay his cousin Grace's school fees and, while she was at Oxford, to provide an allowance supplementing her scholarship, which he abruptly reduced by three-quarters when—a rebel like her aunt and mother—she declared her agnosticism.

Georgie meanwhile, now 18 and determined not to spend her afternoons tagging along after her mother, asserted *her* independence by becoming an art student. A university education never seems to have been contemplated. This may have been a reflection of Nelly Tucker's conventional attitude towards women and her own personal leaning towards the arts, but Georgie was sufficiently independent and financially able to embark on an academic career had she wished. Certainly her desultory schooling had not prepared her for university life, nor despite her eagerness to learn did her interests turn her in that direction; throughout her life she found academics slightly suspect, and with very few exceptions ranked them well below the creative artist.[75] Whatever the reasons, in the very month Nelly embarked on her new life as Mrs Tucker, Georgie enrolled in the Heatherley School of Art. Conveniently situated at 75 Newman Street off Oxford Street and tracing its origins through a series of distinguished principals as far back as 1845, the Heatherley was an independent school with emphasis on the French atelier system, an extensive collection of costumes, armour, and casts, and, most importantly, life classes (though ladies and gentlemen attended on different days). Its pedigree was impeccable, boasting such former students as Burne-Jones, D. G. Rossetti, Millais, Walter Crane, du Maurier, Samuel Butler, Walter Sickert, Lewis Carroll, Ernest Shepard, Kate Greenaway, and John Butler Yeats. Another reason for her choice of school may have been that she was left-handed and so saw things from the opposite direction, which might have made learning more difficult at the conservative Slade. No doubt encouraged by her art-loving husband, Nelly could hardly object to Georgie's avocation, especially as the new principal's wife, Gertrude (Mrs Henry) Massey, was herself well known as a miniaturist and watercolour painter admired by royalty.[76] In any case, her daughter now had money of her own, although her inheritance seems unlikely to have provided more than £300 or £400 a year.[77] Still, that put her firmly in the leisure class, allowing her to travel, buy books, and pursue her own interests.

Georgie studied at Heatherley's from February 1911 until January 1912. Between terms, she seems to have attended other studios at Newlyn, Rye, Southwold, Ilfracombe, Lynton, Margate, Aldeburgh, Brighton, wherever Nelly chose seaside retreats, and eventually, often accompanied by Dorothy, without her mother. Her cousin Grace recalled one memorable holiday which she, her mother, and her young brother William spent with Nelly in Cornwall (thereby escaping a long hot summer of workers' strikes in London[78]). Grace remembered that Nelly used to take her and William out in a boat when the black flag was up (signifying danger from squalls), and scoffed at their fear when the boat keeled, saying death by drowning would not be too bad. Georgie was rarely with them; she and Dorothy were painting in the studio of a well-known artist. This was most likely Stanhope Forbes, who in 1899 with his wife Elizabeth had established a 'School of Painting' in three wooden huts in 'the Meadows' area of Newlyn, on the slope of a hill above Mount's Bay, near Penzance: beginners started in the cast-room; the more experienced drew or painted from the living model in the head-room (or outside in the open), while students of the nude worked in the life-room. Emphasizing study of the human figure and offering a solid grounding in drawing and painting, the School attracted not only such dedicated young artists as Gladys Hynes (later to illustrate Pound's *Cantos*) but a great many transitory students. 'Crits' were conducted in public by Forbes on Saturday mornings in the head-room. Everybody was encouraged to participate in the social activities, musical gatherings, play readings, and outings to the cinema in canopied wagonettes (called 'jingles'), where they mingled freely with other members of the 'plein air' Newlyn School, such as Laura and Harold Knight, Charles and Ruth Simpson, Dod and Ernest Proctor, and Alethea Garstin (who had also studied at Heatherley's).[79] The high-spirited students (and their teachers) were considered a godless group by the locals, many of whom, notwithstanding, served as modestly dressed models. However, one student later recalled that sketching in the open on a Sunday was unsafe: 'some of the students who did so were pelted by the righteous; one or two of the more daring had their pictures and easels thrown into the harbour.'[80] Years later George entertained her own artist daughter with tales of hearing the Salvation Army singing under the window of her lodgings, wondering whether 'The bells of hell . . .' rang for her.

Georgie had always painted; Grace remembers her complaining at Hinxworth that 'everything was too green to paint'. (A particular shade of dark green was clearly significant, becoming her trademark in clothing and jewellery.) Later, she would take a keen interest in Abbey Theatre productions, occasionally lend a hand painting sets for the Dublin Drama League, create designs for Cuala embroideries, and supervise the printing for the press; she cared deeply about the designs of their plates and her husband's books; and her supervision of the restoration and furnishing of Ballylee drew upon all her skills of draughtsmanship and eye for colour. But whatever work of her own George thought worth preserving has since disappeared. One day her daughter Anne noticed a portfolio that had always been in the study was no longer there. A deliberate suppression? As with her phonograph collection, we can glean only a slight indication of her interests among the scattered photos of cathedral interiors, sculptures, and a very few paintings; even these may be of a later date, collected for Willy's benefit. But to be an art student in the pre-war years provided legitimate reason to escape from the domestic circle into museums, galleries, lectures, and unchaperoned into the country. Until she married she was never without a sketchbook and paints. More important still, she finally had a treasured companion with whom to share her interests.

Despite the six years' difference in their ages, given the closeness of the Shakespear and Tucker families it was inevitable that Dorothy Shakespear and

Georgie Hyde Lees should become friends. More remarkable is the similar pattern their lives would later follow, each devoting her life, considerable artistic talents, and inheritance to nurturing a husband whose poetry was paramount. Each with the capability of absenting—but in no way diminishing—herself in the process. Each knowing how, in their friend Eva Ducat's sense, to listen. Neither would embrace painting as a profession, preferring the comfortable seclusion of amateur status: George appears to have destroyed her portfolio; although contributing illustrations to some of her husband's publications, Dorothy pointedly rejected invitations to exhibit her work.[81] They were alike, too, in being self-possessed daughters of strong-willed mothers, eventually choosing life partners against considerable maternal opposition. As well-bred Englishwomen of the professional middle classes, no matter—perhaps in spite of—their own romantic interludes, Nelly and Olivia were protective of their daughters, hoping for more fulfilling, financially secure marriages than they themselves had experienced. Her son-in-law would later characterize Nelly as good-hearted but 'always on the watch for the wolf with "privy paw" '.[82] Neither mother succeeded in her ambitions: Dorothy finally wore down parental opposition and married—at 27— Ezra Pound, her parents' allowance supporting them both; while Georgie— at 25—joined her income to the even lesser one of W. B. Yeats. Although Olivia seems to have tolerated her histrionic, artistically inclined, occasionally 'tiresome' sister-in-law Nelly mainly for Harry's sake, in February 1911 the Shakespear and Tucker households (nicknamed by Dorothy 'the Bunks' after her childhood name for her uncle, or 'the Montpels' after their street address) became even more closely interlocked. Olivia was always kind and generous, observing and encouraging Georgie's intellectual interests and including her in holidays both in England and Italy. Acknowledging that her own daughter was 'fundamentally selfish and self-absorbed',[83] perhaps an exaggeration in an attempt to dissuade Ezra Pound's determined courtship, Olivia may have welcomed the younger woman's openness, wit, and sensitivity. But with Dorothy, her beloved 'Coz', Georgie, self-styled 'the step-pest', could be herself at last.

FRIENDS

'Georgie's face *is* square: but she is very handsome, I think, as well. She is awfully intelligent, & I believe admires yr. poems—what more can be said? Alarmingly intuitive at 18.'[1] Dorothy's description to Ezra of her 'Coz' is confirmed by a 1910 studio photograph treasured by Grace.[2] Georgie is dressed fashionably with an elegant hat partially hiding her luxuriant waving hair, dark strong eyebrows, the nose a little too large for customary 'good looks', the chin and mouth determined with just the possibility of a smile, as Grace says, 'a mature face for a child'. The right cheek is in shadow, perhaps to hide a disfiguring mole which had not yet been removed, or its scar.[3] But it is the eyes that catch and hold, in a penetrating gaze that looks into one's very soul. So striking were those eyes that, although they were definitely hazel in colour, even her observant sisters-in-law thought them 'rather remarkable eyes of green-blue';[4] they are later variously remembered as 'really beautiful', 'piercing', 'sparkling', 'bright and darting', 'twinkling', 'glinting', 'scrutinizing', 'glittering', even 'terrifying'. Painter Louis LeBrocquy had only seen one other pair with the same intensity—on Pablo Picasso.[5] The black and white photographs of this period do not reveal the glossy auburn hair or her high colouring (too high, some thought).[6] Nor do they show the 'animated sceptical' face that so charmed her family and friends; 'she has gaiety and is I am sure intuitive.'[7] Later she would be thought of as short, no more than five foot three; but her 1956 passport measures her at five foot six; at the time these portraits were taken, she was an inch taller still. Sturdy in build, she had a firm, quick step but thick ankles that later made her wish for the return of the long skirts that disappeared with the onset of war.[8] She took great care of her appearance, brushing the lovely thick hair a hundred strokes each night and wearing vividly coloured dresses and earrings of 'Irish green'.

Georgie and Dorothy shared much more than a love of clothes—which they designed themselves (and, in Georgie's case, carefully tended[9])—and keen appreciation of hairstyles and elegant hats. Only a few postcards of that period survive from Georgie, but Dorothy's letters to Ezra Pound from 1910 to 1914 record many of their joint activities. Enjoined by custom to the social pattern embraced by their mothers, in London they took tea with Olivia's and Nelly's friends, listened to discourse on literature and the occult, were entertained by private concerts featuring 'dear Walter' Rummel[10] and impulsive, affectionate Jelly d'Aranyi, attended the same soirées at Eva Fowler's, who in 1912 had moved with her pet lemur from Knightsbridge to Mayfair. In the country Georgie and her mother visited relatives, sought the fresh air of the coast or the Norfolk Broads, and, with increasing frequency, they and Harry were joined by Olivia and Dorothy in furnished apartments or small hotels in Southwold (1911), Margate, Ilfracombe, Lynton (1912), Coleman's Hatch (1913), Aldeburgh, and Brighton (1914).

Dorothy was not as adventurous as her companion, reporting from Ilfracombe:

Georgie has gone off this morning to paint alone: it is a queer uncanny place down, down, at the bottom of Cliffs and I simply daren't go there to paint—Its chiefly because it makes me horribly giddy—but slightly because its so cold & alarming. We had awful adventures the other day: we scrambled round at low tide among such gorgeous places which are certainly 10ft. & more, under water at High [Tide]. It scares me all the time—but G. seems calm & leads the way.[11]

Despite a happy camaraderie, although sympathetically aware, both were naturally reticent about personal matters, but the friendship was close and empathetic, and would last. 'G is very depressed with life I fancy—But we paint a lot & take as little notice as possible of the Family—which I am not sure they don't think nasty tempered of us. Nelly said yesterday à propos some frivolous remark, that she would "believe anything of the Young" (that's us).'[12] 'It is a pleasant place. G. and I sketched in a wood inland this morning. We have a pianola—G. plays it beautifully & we have Brahms & Schumann (Oh dear Walter!) in the evenings . . . Thank goodness there isn't much need here for mental efforts—I paint & eat & hold desultory conversations with G. They think I am cross, or dull or queer—accordingly—but if I can do the rocks I don't care!'[13] Despite her fear of the cliffs, Dorothy painted watercolours of Ilfracombe and Rapparce Cove which she thought worthy of preserving.[14]

Sometimes Georgie went with Dorothy, without their mothers, to the home of Shakespear cousins in Canterbury. Gradually, once she had come of age, they were allowed to go off sketching by themselves; during one trip in Devon they were welcomed as bearers of news as they moved from cottage to cottage.[15] In May 1912 they were at the Broomhill Hotel, in West Malvern, where they visited their former teachers of St James's School and received permission to wander through the grounds. 'It is very pleasant to be away from one's family and "on the loose".'[16] Later Dorothy joined Georgie in Margate, where her 'step-pest' seems to have been attending art classes; together they practised their Italian and explored 'the Grotto', an eighteenth-century folly with a network of serpentine underground passages in a chalk hill nearby, speculating about possible Masonic or occult significance.[17] In turn, Dorothy introduced her to other friends: 'Hilda

[Strutt, an Australian schoolmate at St James's] and her Frank are coming down to the hotel for Whitsuntide—I wonder how she and Georgie will get on.' After Hilda's marriage they visited her at St Catharine's Court, Bath. Another of her schoolmates, Nancy Maude, married the poet Joseph Campbell, and both these women would remain part of Georgie's life also.[18]

Although never formally enrolled in an art school, Dorothy also took her painting seriously. Her uncle collected prints and etchings, and watercolour drawing, especially landscapes, had been 'a traditional family hobby' for both her father and grandfather.[19] But her own work at this time tended towards the visionary, dreamscapes and romantic drawing from architecture. Yet both she and Georgie were interested in contemporary movements and eventually Dorothy became a disciple of modernism. Gallery-going was a regular occupation for both young women and their mothers.

Accompanied by Olivia, and to their annoyance joined by Shakespear cousins[20] at different stages of the journey, the two friends twice went to the Continent on sketching holidays. They spent six weeks in Italy in 1913, the month of April at Tivoli twenty miles across the plain from Rome in the Villa S. Antonio, 'a lovely old house', 'the nicest place in the world'. Housekeeping in Italian offered 'queer adventures'; Cecilia, the parlourmaid, their prime adviser, sent them an announcement of her wedding six months later.[21] Although the weather made outdoor sketching difficult, they were excited by discoveries of Roman remains and mosaics in the neighbourhood. The first two weeks of May were spent in the Hotel Flora on the via Veneto after a weekend at Subiaco in a convent of French nuns to see frescos in two mountain monasteries. The following year, on a last trip before Dorothy's marriage, they returned to Rome for the month of March, where they were joined at the end of their stay by James Fairfax, too late to press his suit for Dorothy's hand.[22] Georgie's careful totting up of generous tips for the staff at the Hotel Élysée survives in the back flyleaf of one of her books.[23] They spent a night in Paris on the way back.

The 1913 and 1914 visits enhanced Georgie's love of Italy, and throughout her life she longed especially for Florence. 'I am never really homesick for England but Italy . . . everything nice has always been in Italy,' she confided years later to a friend.[24] Equally enamoured of things ancient and Italian, both young women took their sketching and their Baedekers seriously: despite transportation strikes in Rome they managed to see Hadrian's villa a number of times ('[Georgie] likes it all I fancy very much') and visit Mithraic temples at Ostia and Tivoli.[25] Dorothy thought the Baths of Caracalla sinister but Georgie, excited by the 'magnificent, almost perfect mosaics', sent postcards to both her mother and brother,[26] and romantically recalled that Shelley had written *Prometheus Unbound* among its ruins.[27] Dorothy preserved a green piece she saw 'dug up from under about 4 ft. of soil . . . hadn't seen the light for nearly 2000 years';[28] Georgie, fascinated by the 'queer (mystical?) shape' of one excavation, 'played at making triangles fit into it all the afternoon, instead of sleeping: then she had bad indigestion'.[29] But they also frequented the zoo, where Georgie, who loved cats of all kinds, persuaded the leopard keeper to allow her into the cages to play with the cubs.

Naturally they toured the art galleries. It is likely that Georgie had gone with Dorothy to the Futurist exhibition in London in 1912, also the accompanying aggressive, inflammatory lectures (in Italian) at Bechstein Hall on the celebration of industrialized life by Futurist founder Filippo Marinetti. They may even have heard him read his first manifesto at the Lyceum Club in 1910, for Georgie seems at one time to have been a member. Marinetti returned to London in November 1913 to give 'Futurist evenings' at the Poet's Club, Poetry Bookshop, and the Doré Galleries; on one of these occasions he noisily disrupted Yeats's Monday 'At Home'.[30] At this stage Marinetti was fêted by artists like Wyndham Lewis and Christopher Nevinson, who would later distance their own furious attack on the status quo, Vorticism, from Futurism.[31] (When Marinetti returned in 1914 they in turn heckled his lecture.[32]) Doubtless affected by the interest in Marinetti in London, Georgie and Dorothy visited the Galleria Futurista in Rome in 1913 where two 'enlightening' paintings by Gino Severini—who had a one-man exhibition in London that year—especially intrigued them, and they responded in language learned from Rabindranath Tagore's lectures: 'One was centripetal force and the other c.fugal. The former, yellows and white, outside, and blues & greens inside. Centrifugal was a [sketch] of yellow & white in centre & blues & greens solidly surrounding it . . . we decided my receptive yellow outside— her ferment inside, being calmed by the ring of blue & green!' The works seem to anticipate Severini's gradual move towards Cubist structure and theories of mathematical proportions. In the same exhibition Dorothy also admired the technique of Giacomo Balla (as Lewis would also), but felt 'one would go mad quickly with them in a room'.[33] Balla's series of charcoal drawings, enticingly called *Vortice*, had been completed that winter.[34]

Shopping ('G has bought a very fine green enamel chain') culminated in prowls of old bookshops. It is not surprising that books were on the agenda, for Georgie was a voracious reader, more systematic than Dorothy. Nelly was careless with her books, leaving even the proscribed lying about;[35] by the time her daughter was 12 she had covertly read all that George Moore had published. Before she was 16 Georgie was reading Balzac. Grace Spurway never forgot her cousin's instructions on learning a language, later applied also to Anne and Michael's education:

What impressed me most at that time was my cousin's ability to speak and read French—not the silly little classroom French with which I struggled at Saint George's school, but grown-up novels by an author called Balzac. And I remember that she told me to learn French by taking a novel and reading it, not looking up every word I didn't know, but trying to guess words by understanding their context. . . . I was less successful with Georgie's system of memorizing, which, in all truth, I never understood. At school we were required to memorize long poems, to be recited in class. The only way I knew was to say the words over and over again until I knew them by heart. 'That's not the right way', my cousin said, but she failed to explain what the 'right way' was. I think she first absorbed the meaning of the passage and then worked her way, so to speak, into the outer crust of the words.[36]

Thomas Hardy was read cover to cover. In October 1910 she purchased Swinburne's *Song of Italy* and *Poems and Ballads*; the following month *The Lyrical Poems of William Blake*.[37] That autumn she also began a two-year study of Dante while learning Italian, buying the Temple edition translations one by one as she progressed: The *Paradiso* was 'first read at Rye' in November 1910 and annotated with quotations from da Vinci in Italian and Börne in German; she moved on to the *Purgatorio* and *Inferno* in January 1911, the *Vita Nuova* following in December 1911. She completed her collection with the *Convivio* (though she did not date her copy) and received the other prose works[38] for Christmas in 1912.

It is perhaps no accident that Georgie embarked on her study of Dante shortly after the publication of Ezra Pound's *The Spirit of Romance*, the final chapters of which the author read out in the Shakespears' drawing room in February 1910.[39] Published in June 1910 but based on his London Polytechnic lectures which Dorothy and Olivia had attended the previous winter, Ezra used the Temple edition of Dante as his preferred text.[40] Pound met Olivia, 'undoubtedly the most charming woman in London', in January 1909 shortly after his arrival in England, and Dorothy several weeks later, by which time he had become a regular visitor at Brunswick Gardens.[41] Georgie knew Ezra well enough by July 1909 for Harry Tucker to confide his worries about the relationship with his beloved niece Dorothy; she later recalled, 'HTT who was very bald said to me in July—about Ezra—"a good brain needs no bush!"'.[42] Soon Ezra became Georgie's friend also, and to a certain extent her mentor as well as Dorothy's, providing advice on topics ranging from philology to philosophy and modern art. She seems to have agreed with his comment in *The Spirit of Romance*, 'I am always filled with a sort of angry wonder that any one professing to care for poetry can remain in ignorance of the tongue in which the poem is written. It shows a dulness, a stolidity, which is incomprehensible to any one who knows the *Commedia*.'[43] By then she was conversant in French, German, Italian, and, using her own methods, was well on with Spanish, appealing to Ezra for advice on what to read 'beside Lopez & Calderon. She has tried some modern verse, but seems to have pitched upon rubbish.'[44] But much as Georgie admired Ezra, she was not always prepared to accept Dorothy's belief in his omniscience. Pound had devoted a chapter to Lope de Vega in *The Spirit of Romance*; her copy of *Exultations*, a Christmas gift in

1909, compares Ezra's translation of 'A Song of the Virgin Mother' with Lope's original and includes in a much more mature hand on a separate sheet—probably in response to his poem entitled 'Guido Invites You Thus'—her Italian transcription of Dante's 'Guido, vorrei che tu e La po ed io . . .'.[45] Ezra gave Georgie a copy of his translation of *Sonnets and Ballate of Guido Cavalcanti* on its publication in June 1912; while in Rome the following year she purchased an Italian edition of Cavalcanti and compared her own translation with Ezra's.[46]

Also at his urging Georgie subscribed to the Chicago-based *Poetry* when Pound became the magazine's foreign correspondent in September 1912. A year later he sent her the prospectus for Wyndham Lewis and Kate Lechmere's short-lived Rebel Art Centre at 38 Great Ormond Street, a movement which had a strong influence on Dorothy's artwork.[47] Ezra's invention of 'Vortex' for the name of the new revolutionary movement which was to link all the arts was celebrated in the two issues of another magazine, *Blast*, the 'review of the great English Vortex'.[48] As Lewis later explained the theory of 'Vorticism', 'You think at once of a whirlpool, at the heart of the whirlpool is a great silent place where all the energy is concentrated, and there at the point of concentration is the Vorticist.'[49] Wyndham Lewis would continue to be a strong influence on Dorothy; she contributed drawings to the second (and final) issue of *Blast* in 1915, and further announced her allegiance with striking cover designs for a reissue of Ezra's *Ripostes* and his *Catholic Anthology*.[50] The concept, if not the actual terminology, would surface later in Georgie's automatic writing. It was doubtless with Ezra's and Dorothy's encouragement that she became sufficiently impressed by this aspect of modernism to purchase in 1917 a drawing by Lewis (for £12) and the same year a small alabaster sculpture carved in 1914 by Gaudier-Brzeska. The sculpture, described as a 'letter-weight', had originally belonged to T. E. Hulme, like Gaudier-Brzeska killed in the war, and was later stolen.[51] Geometric design with its cubes, cones, circles, and triangles would continue to fascinate her, the Vorticist combination of 'dissonance and asymmetry' less so.[52] In 1913 Ezra also tried to persuade her brother Harold to visit Gaudier-Brzeska's studio. He encouraged her to attend other lectures, and when Douglas Ainslie lectured on Benedetto Croce and Hegel, he took her along.[53] It is possible that she also occasionally attended Hulme's Thursday philosophical discussions with Dorothy and Ezra; she would have appreciated Hulme's devotion to the French philosopher Henri Bergson more than Dorothy did.[54]

Georgie, as Dorothy had said, admired Ezra's poems. She continued to read the *Cantos*, buying each volume as it appeared, although in later years she would regret Ezra's 'always preferring the lesser man to the greater (I am thinking of Ezra's passion for Cavalcanti as against Dante. Both have their place but sociology shouldn't come into it).'[55] Even more than his genius, she appreciated his sense of fun and irrepressibility which was as vibrant as his uncontrollable head of hair. 'He was just like his hair,' she was to recall many years later: 'If you put your hand on Gabriel D'Annunzio's hair—he had a great shock of silver hair—and pressed down, it would stay flat. But if you pressed down on Ezra's hair—poof!—it would spring right up again!'[56] Sometimes he startled even her: 'I upset [Georgie] by whispering confidentially that the toothbrush had arrived & so on,' reported Dorothy. 'She thinks your flippancy terrible—She is used to mine.'[57] And he too loved cats. Perhaps seeing her as a useful chaperone, Olivia also encouraged the friendship; although she once confessed that she 'never understood anything he said', she routinely presented Georgie with copies of Ezra's publications.[58] Although very soon a salacious couplet about Pound's promiscuity went the London rounds ('Ezra Pound and Augustus John / Bless the bed that I lie on'[59]), the relationship between Georgie and Ezra remained one of 'just good friends'; besides, in his eyes she was Shakespear property, and therefore sacrosanct.

Pound had come to England to meet W. B. Yeats, and achieved his goal when Olivia and Dorothy took him in early May 1909 to one of the poet's regular Monday 'At Homes'. J. M. Synge, co-Director of the Abbey Theatre with Yeats and Lady Gregory, had recently died, and it could well be that this bouncy, out-rageous, American poet-playboy provided a missing flint.[60] Yeats quickly grew to appreciate the 'headlong ragged creature' who was 'always hurting people's feel-ings, but he has I think some genius and great good will . . . Hercules cannot help seeming a little more than life size in our European Garden of the Hesperides,' he once explained. 'His voice is too loud, his stride too resounding.'[61] Pound in turn encouraged Yeats's new experiments with plays and poetry: Yeats wrote, 'He is full of the Middle Ages & helps me to get back to the definite & the concrete away from modern abstractions,'[62] and (perhaps unwisely) told the young opinionated critic himself how much he valued his comments. Within a very short time, to the alarm of some of the older habitués, Pound was a fixture at Yeats's Woburn Buildings 'Mondays' as well as at Brunswick Gardens.[63] Yeats contemplated, but resisted, accompanying him to Italy;[64] despite Olivia's misgivings, she and Dorothy did join him in Sirmione and Venice in the spring of 1910 before Pound made a brief return to the United States.[65] By then certainly Dorothy had deter-mined she would share her life with Ezra and no other; Georgie was clearly in her friend's confidence—always loyal and discreet, whether she was ever entrusted with forbidden correspondence during Ezra's winter exile in America, we will never know.[66]

Perhaps introduced by Olivia, Georgie's mother Nelly had known Yeats for many years and treasured his poetry although apparently their friendship was never close. By 1910 the relationship between Yeats and Olivia Shakespear seems to have been stronger than ever, although Yeats was simultaneously having what George herself later dismissed as 'a purely amorous affair' with Mabel Dickinson, begun in April 1908.[67] Did Georgie and Dorothy ever discuss the nature of this friendship between their elders? George thought Olivia and Willy had become lovers again as early as 1903, and further evidence points to increased intimacy in 1910, but if so, it was a comfortable unexplosive arrangement in which Willy was a familiar presence at Brunswick Gardens.[68] In any case, Georgie was always most precise about the date of her own first official meeting with 'The Eagle' or 'Dante' (names given to Yeats by Dorothy and Ezra with mischievous respect): 'I did not meet WBY until May 1911 but knew EP quite well from 1910.' Given their relatively small London circle, there may well have been sightings in April 1909 and October 1910 (both identified later as significant moments in her life) and February 1911.[69] Certainly Georgie could not have avoided observing this tall dark figure at the theatre and perhaps even at lectures for several years. However, she repeatedly stated that they met in 1911. She recalled the occasion of their introduction in vivid detail: 'one morning when her mother thought she was at art school, she went to the British Museum, where she saw Yeats rush past her like a meteor; and that very afternoon, taking tea with her mother at Olivia Shakespear's, was formally introduced.'[70] Still, with Nelly's frequent attendance in Olivia's drawing room, and Georgie's closeness to Dorothy, it is surprising the introduction did not come sooner. By early December 1911, after a three weeks' stay with the Shakespears in Brunswick Gardens, Georgie's presence was sufficiently acknowledged for her to be invited with Dorothy and Ezra for an evening in Yeats's flat in Woburn Buildings.[71] She was not yet 19; he was 46, three years older than her mother, the same age as her beloved late father. Despite her early-won maturity, Yeats would always consider George and Ezra a younger, slightly foreign, generation.[72]

Whatever the status of Olivia and Willy's relationship, after Nelly's marriage to Harry Tucker, both mothers and daughters were often joined on their frequent country visits by the poet, whose companionship was also appreciated by Harry. (Olivia's husband Hope Shakespear rarely took leave from his solicitor's office except for his own extended—and private—painting holiday each September.) Yeats reported confidentially to Lady Gregory in February 1912, 'I am at Margate staying with a Mr and Mrs Tucker (she was a Mrs Hyde Lees who I have known vaguely for years). I got rather out of sorts, digestion wrong & so on & wanted to do nothing for a day or two. . . . This is a dismal place & it rains all day [but] it is very quiet & a good change & I am with pleasant people & out of the Dublin atmosphere.'[73] Georgie, having just completed her studies at Heatherley's, may not have been present during Yeats's visit to Margate, for she and Dorothy attended a lecture in London on 20 February.[74] But when in October he again visited the Tuckers, Nelly, Harry, and Georgie were sharing an apartment with Olivia and Dorothy in Lynton, north Devon.[75] In March 1913 the Tuckers (and probably Georgie) were back in Devon at a much superior hotel, where Yeats joined them for a week. 'My address will be Valley of Rocks Hotel, Lynton, North Devon.' On those visits he gave as good as he got—tales of Tagore and other writers, excitement over his research into the occult, revising his 'ghost theory' in connection with various séances; the year they met, Yeats had once again become interested in Swedenborg, George remembered.[76] And always a batch of new plays and poems to read and be read to. But he also showed his vulnerable side, suffering frequently from digestive problems and rheumatism, and clearly delighted to be out of the city.

By then, too, the annual Irish invasions of London had become staple summer fare; Georgie had been attending the Abbey Theatre performances with her mother since at least 1909 when she saw a play by Lord Dunsany.[77] This may have been when she first had Yeats pointed out to her; whenever it was, the recollection was vivid.[78] In June 1912, when the Irish Players began their season at the Royal Court, Dorothy saw *Patriots*, a new play by Lennox Robinson, who (perhaps along with WBY) on 22 June attended a party at the Shakespears at which Rummel performed. Georgie and the Tuckers were in attendance, for 'someone took Mrs Fagan [wife of the actor and theatre impresario] for Harry's new wife'; Nelly would have reason to remember that encounter with Fagan some years later. Also in June, Dorothy reported that Walter and Hilda Strutt joined them 'to see a Synge: & we go alone to "Countess Cathleen":[Gordon] Craig production.'[79] Coincidentally at the Walker Art Gallery Jack Yeats was showing his 'Pictures of Life in the West of Ireland' during the first two weeks of July, an exhibition which so charmed Georgie that for Christmas 1912 Harry Tucker presented her with *Life in the West of Ireland Drawn and Painted by Jack B. Yeats*. Jack's paintings and the Abbey both returned in succeeding summers; Lady Gregory's son Robert exhibited works at the Baillie Gallery in the spring of 1912 and had his own show at the Chenil Gallery in April 1914. Nor could Irish politics be ignored: in April 1912 Asquith introduced the third Home Rule Bill, which finally passed its third reading in the House of Commons the following January, only to be held up for another year by the House of Lords. During the same months the suffragette movement had also escalated, with organized window smashing campaigns throughout London's West End and Knightsbridge.[80] Georgie's interests, however, were increasingly turning towards other worlds.

4
STUDIES

Yeats's enthusiastic engagement with the occult struck a strong, receptive chord in Georgie. Her father had died on 18 November 1909; the anniversary brooded over her life for many years, as did his birthday, 21 December.[1] Grief may well have led her to Cesare Lombroso's recently translated apologia, *After Death—what? Spiritistic Phenomena and their Interpretation*, which she had read in 1909.[2] However, with her usual diligence she pursued the study of spiritualism far beyond the French psychiatrist's somewhat naive and heavy-handed discussion of conversion to belief in the reality of thought transference and finally, through experiments with the medium Eusapia Paladino, phantasmic activity and reincarnation. (Ironically, Lombroso, who held the chair of criminal anthropology at the University of Turin, began his career as a sceptical scientist concentrating on the study of cretins and criminals in an attempt to establish a theory of degeneracy; by examining their brain structure, he concluded that women also are natural criminals.) While reading the *Paradiso*, she had made a note of R. M. Bucke's *Cosmic Consciousness*, 'a study in the evolution of the human mind', with its examples of individuals through history who had experienced Illumination.[3] In 1911 Harry Tucker gave her a copy of *Pragmatism* by the distinguished psychologist and president of the American Society for Psychical Research, William James. In it James questioned the 'pretence of finality in truth' and asserted that 'the true is the name of whatever proves itself to be good in the way of belief '. That the 'true' theory was one that 'will carry us prosperously from any one part of our experience, to any other part, linking things satisfactorily, working securely, simplifying, saving labor' became her prevailing philosophy. She might already have discovered his sympathetic treatment of mysticism in *The Varieties of Religious Experience*—hypothetical like a belief in the existence of God, an uncertainty about which he withholds judgement, but not an illusion. James's book went through innumerable editions after its publication in 1902; particularly impressed by Bucke's own experience of a mystical state of consciousness, the psychologist quotes him extensively. James's famous essay 'The Will to Believe' (1897) had insisted that 'we must will to act and act on our beliefs'; his 'Confidences of a "Psychical Researcher" ' (1909) acknowledged a belief in 'the presence, in the midst of all the humbug, of really supernormal knowledge'.[4] Throughout Georgie's life, William James would remain a model of clear thought and fine writing, and a better writer than his brother.[5] It may have been now that she first delved into Descartes, for she possessed a copy of his *Discourse on Method and Metaphysical Meditations*.[6] From there it was a short step to the German psychologist Wilhelm Wundt's *Principles of Physiological Psychology* with his emphasis on introspection in investigating the immediate experiences of consciousness and his concept of the 'folk soul'.[7] All of this the young Georgie read and inwardly digested.

In the summer of 1911 Pound had contemplated a book 'about philosophy from Richard St. Victor to Pico della Mirandola'.[8] But another influence was even more prevalent. Early in 1912 Ezra gave a lecture on 'Psychology and Troubadours' to the Quest Society, founded three years earlier by G. R. S. Mead 'to promote investigation and comparative study of religion, philosophy, and science, on the basis of experience' and 'to encourage the expression of the ideal in beautiful forms'.[9] Mead had served as private secretary to Madame Blavatsky, founder of the Theosophical Society, from 1889 until her death in 1891, had worked with her on the second edition of *The Secret Doctrine*, and been general secretary of the Society; he resigned (with approximately 700 other members) in protest against the scandals surrounding Blavatsky's colleague C. W. Leadbeater, and this dissident group became the nucleus of the 'Questors' the following year. On 1 February 1912, Yeats nervously lectured to 'hundreds' of 'Questors', developing his new theories on the physical form taken by ghosts or 'spirit bodies'.[10] That same month, perhaps encouraged by Ezra's and Yeats's lectures to the Society, Georgie and Dorothy began to attend Mead's Tuesday lectures at the Kensington Town Hall; Dorothy was 'deeply interested in Mead—so, I think, was G.'[11] They also probably attended at least one of Ezra's lectures on medieval poetry on 14, 19, and 21 March 1912 at 34 Queen Anne's Gate (Lord and Lady Glenconner's private gallery); however, Dorothy at least chose to attend Marinetti's lecture on the 19th instead. That spring a copy of Mead's *The World Mystery* (which 'intensely excited' Dorothy) was in their luggage at West Malvern, and *Fragments of a Faith Forgotten*, subtitled 'a Contribution to the Study of the Origins of Christianity', went with the two young women to Ilfracombe eight months later, in October 1912.[12] Intrigued by Mead's elaboration of Gnosticism (a system of secret knowledge, of religious and magical beliefs drawn from Egypt, Greece, the Hebrews, and the first Christians, emphasizing a theory of cosmic cycles or 'aeons' and affirming the significance of the 'feminine principle'[13]), the following year they attended his lectures again, from October to December 1913. Mead's quarterly journal the *Quest* became a preferred symposium for discussion of the possibility of a meeting ground between science (especially empirical psychology) and mysticism, and William James's optimistic caution was reflected in many of the debates Georgie would have read there.[14] Not surprisingly, Laura and George Mead—also friends of Eva Fowler—soon became part of Olivia's circle: 'The Meads here at tea yesterday; they both have so much, and such pleasant, personality.'[15] Whether influenced by Ezra or Olivia or both, Yeats, who had dismissed Mead in 1889 as having 'the intellect of a good-sized whelk', changed his mind; Ezra recalled that Mead used to turn up 'about twice a month' to the Monday 'At Homes' at Woburn Buildings.[16] The first surviving letter from Georgie to her husband would mention a visit of the Meads to her in Oxford.[17]

Soon Georgie's library showed the effect of this learned medieval scholar and syncretist, whose books and lectures on Gnosticism, mysticism, and early religion led her to range through explorations of hermeticism, the Kabbalah, alchemy, astrology, ritual magic, and even Quietism. She polished up her medieval Latin with a copy of Henricus Khunrath's *Amphitheatreum Sapientiae Aeternae Solius Verae, Christiano-Kabalisticum, Divino-magicum.* (1609), probably discovered in Rome in the spring of 1913 and later with copious notes compared to a copy in the British Museum. Fortunately the notebook of her studies survives. In July 1913 she purchased Mead's edition of *Select Works of Plotinus*, translated from the Greek by Thomas Taylor; typically, the following year she found a copy of Taylor's original 1817 edition with Porphyry's 'Life of Plotinus', and heavily marked both copies, with emphasis on the soul and its virtues ('the endeavour is not to be without sin, but to be a God'). She also possessed Taylor's translation of *Iamblichus on the Mysteries of the Egyptians, Chaldeans, and Assyrians*; the Syrian philosopher had been a student of Porphyry who had himself been a student of Plotinus. Later she would proudly claim to have introduced WBY to Taylor.[18] George's study of Plotinus continued for many years; the first volume of Stephen MacKenna's magisterial edition—*The Ethical Treatises* (1917)— bears her bookplate. Doubtless she also knew Ezra's poem 'Plotinus'.[19] Noting her interest, and perhaps hoping to steer her back to a less militantly pagan Platonism, the ever-vigilant Herbert Reade of Ipsden presented her with a copy of *The Republic* for Christmas.

Then in August 1913 Georgie discovered *The Spiritual Guide which Disentangles the Soul* by the founder of Quietism, the Spanish priest and mystic Miguel de Molinos, and marked it with quotations from Solomon, da Vinci, and Manes, founder of Manichaeism. Perhaps it was now that she also added Carl du Prel's *The Philosophy of Mysticism*.[20] One annotation on the back flyleaf of *The Spiritual Guide* seems to have had special significance: 'And will you harken to the Hebrew Rabbins? "Your young men shall see visions, and your old men shall dream dreams." ' Without acknowledging its origin, she repeated this quotation from the Old Testament Book of Joel[21] on the inside back cover of her copy of Yeats's *The Celtic Twilight*, purchased two months later, in October 1913.

That same month her dream of that other, younger, visionary Pound was duly reported by Dorothy:

Georgie had an amusing dream about you two nights ago. You were hanging to the top of a very straight pine tree-all-stem-&-a-burst-of-branches-at-the-top-kind, and you had not climbed it—but got there 'by translation' as she says. You seemed very happy—but hanged—(which latter I feel is due to her own throat trouble). You had on a yellow tie— (a few other clothes too) and your hair was standing bolt upright, and was very long. She won't tell me more—more there was, I feel sure.

Ezra replied on 11 October, 'If [Georgie] has any more such dreams we shall end as a ménage à trois. . . . she takes me for a corn-god.'[22] Freudian interpretations notwithstanding, the image was more likely drawn from the Tarot card of the Hanged Man than Frazer's *The Golden Bough*.

When Georgie returned from Italy in May 1913 after her first trip with Dorothy, she had immediately embarked on an exhaustive series of lecture attendances, most notably those by the Bengali poet and Nobel laureate Rabindranath Tagore who was visiting England. Praised by Yeats and Pound, inevitably he was entertained in the Shakespear and Fowler drawing rooms and given a private musical performance by Rummel.[23] Either at tea discussing Tagore's poetry and philosophy or Yeats's own latest researches into automatic writing ('performed through the agency of subconscious intelligence'[24]), clearly something made a profound impact on Georgie which elicited a response from Yeats; 'a Sunday 1:30pm' in May 1913 would later be considered significant for both of them, in Georgie's case 'new knowledge' which created a 'shock to belief'.[25] Her copy of Tagore's prose translations, *Gitanjali* (*Song Offerings*), with an introduction by Yeats, is dated that month. From 19 May to 16 June 1913 she and Dorothy attended Tagore's Monday lectures on Indian philosophy at Caxton Hall;[26] he also lectured to the Quest Society early in June. In his lectures, which were later published, Tagore took issue with Greek and Western civilizations. Although he is silent on the subject of yogic philosophy, his discussion of reality as 'a reconciliation of pairs of opposing forces', 'the positive and the negative, the centripetal force and the centrifugal, attraction and repulsion', was evocative: 'when at last we find a relation between these two, and thereby see them as one in essence, we feel that we have come to the truth.'[27] Another message Georgie would remember (and which she and Dorothy would apply to Severini's paintings in Rome the following spring). Breaking precedent, the Irish Players included Tagore's play *The Post Office* in their summer programme at the Court Theatre. When his *The King of the Dark Chamber* was published the following year, Georgie immediately bought a copy, perhaps by now less influenced by Ezra than by Yeats, who was already talking of a journey to India. Tagore clearly made such an impact that he would appear as a 'perfected man' in her own occult adventures six years later.[28]

At the same time, Georgie continued to study contemporary European literature: on the back free endpaper of her volume of Tagore's *Gitanjali*, she duly noted that University College was offering a series in June on 'L'esprit romantique de la littérature française de 1800 à 1900',[29] and at Bedford College on 26 May 1913, 'Influence of Poe on Baudelaire'. She also followed Irish literature with interest. In November Dorothy was urging Ezra to read James Stephens's recently published *Here Are Ladies*; several weeks later Yeats presented the Royal Society of Literature Polignac prize, worth £100, to Stephens for *The Crock of Gold*, which Georgie bought six months later.[30] Then on the afternoons of 18 and 19 December 1913, as trial runs for his American tour, WBY lectured at Mrs Fowler's in Gilbert Street. Shortly after its reissue Georgie added his *Plays for an Irish Theatre* to her library.[31]

That dream of Ezra as Hanged Man at the top of a pine tree took place at The Prelude, a pleasant three-storey house near Coleman's Hatch, East Sussex, which the Tuckers had taken in the summer of 1913 for an extended stay. Its owner, Mrs W. F. Adeney, a writer herself, married to a doctor, and mother of a painter and textile designer, had enlarged the house the previous year in what would now be considered an 'arts and crafts' style, but since she would not move permanently from Hampstead for another few years, the furnished house (presumably with local household staff) was available to let.[32] On the very edge of Ashdown Forest, familiar now as the haunt of A. A. Milne's Pooh and his friends, one looked from an open porch across lush gardens down to Five Hundred Acre Wood in the east; to the west a short path led from the rose garden down across the dry bed of a stream into the very woods themselves which, Georgie assured Dorothy, were haunted. And well they might be; the area has long been known for its spiritistic associations, ley lines,[33] and as host to numerous occult groups. Covering 6,500 acres of woods, gorse, and heather, this had originally been a royal hunting ground, preserved by tenacious 'Commoners' since the thirteenth century; more heath than woodland, from the high ground you can see four counties. At one time more than two thousand animals grazed within the enormous deer park; was it here that Georgie first saw a fox dancing to mesmerize hares?[34] The Prelude was the last of four dwellings at the end of a winding lane less than a mile and a half through heathland from the village of Coleman's Hatch, which took its name from the old coalmen's gate onto the forest and boasted a post office, a chapel, and the Hatch Inn. Carts still delivered bread, milk, and meat on regular rounds. It took only an hour and a half by train from Victoria station in London to reach the larger village of Forest Row, where a trap met those travellers who were not prepared for the three-mile walk to the house.

In August Yeats joined the Tuckers and Georgie at The Prelude for ten days and wrote enthusiastically, 'I propose to take rooms for Ezra and myself in a Farm House near this. We are on the edge of Ashdown Forest and have on the other side of the House a great Heath. It is a most perfect and most lonely place.'[35] A week later he sent a postcard to Pound, showing a photograph of Stone Cottage, some 200 yards closer to the village.[36] Daisy Meadow, Eva Fowler's cottage in Brasted, Kent, which had been Yeats's original choice, was closer to London. 'Give my love to them all at "The Prelude",' Eva wrote on 22 August, '—and I hope they'll manage one day to get over here.'[37] The area was a familiar one: Dorothy had attended school in the district, and all knew the Fowlers' country home, 'a charming little cottage looking out over a wooded valley'.[38] Olivia and Dorothy, just back from Dorset, arrived at the end of August for a month's stay with the Tuckers and Georgie at The Prelude, and Yeats took Olivia to see Stone Cottage before he departed for London and Ireland.[39] To Ezra, Dorothy described what would become the two poets' winter retreat for three seasons: 'It is a pretty place—common, heather, & woods—Georgie says the latter are haunted. . . . —they are gloomy—& were v. wet after heavy rain. . . . Your cottage is next door nearly to us. Its plain grey stone & right on the moor. There is a queer lake in the forest—with wonderful-coloured trees reflecting in it—It is a weird place—and possibly faerie.'[40] Georgie meanwhile had developed tonsilitis, and although she and Dorothy made several sketching and mushroom-hunting forays, she finally became so ill that medical attention was required; Dorothy accompanied her to London to have her tonsils removed and returned with her on 7 October to keep her company for a further week.

Recuperation was encouraged by the presence of two kittens ('Henry André James' and 'Brahms') and occasional additional visitors including Hilda Strutt, now married to Frank Deverell, who collaborated in practical jokes on the patient. As always there were books to explore: Dorothy had discovered a translation of the Koran ('mighty dull') and Pater's Plato ('terrible stodge'); everyone, she reported, was reading plays by Paul Claudel, doubtless influenced by Willy. Georgie was studying the second-century Christian commentaries of Origen, whose speculations about the pre-existence of souls, world cycles, the doctrine of correspondences, belief in free will, and allegorical interpretation of the scriptures strongly influenced later biblical scholars.[41]

However, more immediately intriguing was the evidence Yeats had brought with him concerning a mysterious medium who 'puts her fist through Religion and her toes through Philosophy'.[42] Yeats first met Elizabeth ('Bessie') Radcliffe during the winter of 1911–12, most likely through Eva Fowler who, though not a sensitive herself, was deeply committed to spiritualist studies and had for some time been experimenting with Bessie's psychic skills.[43] Bessie's mother, who lived nearby in Kensington Square, seems to have sought Eva's advice about the automatic writing that was taking over more than one daughter,[44] and Eva and Bessie soon became lifelong friends.[45] It was not long before Yeats was drawn in: 'I think perhaps we have to help one another on—though I marvel at the odd conjunction of the three of us,' Eva would later write to him.[46] Throughout that first summer and autumn, the three experimented with automatic and slate writing, frequently at Daisy Meadow in Kent, and finally in May 1913 Yeats was allowed to take away the entire script for study and investigation.

I have had a most wonderful psychic experience—I think one that is entirely conclusive. You remember that girl I told you of whose automatic script I hoped to get. After much difficulty I have seen it all. It was all put into my hands last week at Mrs Fowlers & the girl herself was there. She is a very gentle, well-bred charming & not very clever girl of 27, but seems four or five years younger. She knows a little French & Italian. I find in the script eleven languages. A great deal of Greek & Latin, long passages in Welsh & even a little Chinese or Japanese. The Greek & Latin are most constant—long conversations sometimes about practical things & in one case in answer to mental questions. . . . On Thursday we went out for a walk and left the pad of clean paper in a cupboard & when we came back there was writing—made as if with a slate pencil—indented—just legible—on the pad. It was made by what is called direct writing in the absence of the medium. . . . I have now the proof, the overwhelming conviction I have been waiting for.[47]

Two days later he reported his success at the British Museum:

Perfectly correct Hebrew, perfectly correct Greek, perfectly correct Latin, perfectly correct Welsh, perfectly correct Chinese, and apparently correct ancient Egyptian (B.C.600). . . . The contents of the inscription were as remarkable as the form. They were evidently carefully arranged so as to make impossible every scientific theory which accounts for things of the kind by the emergence of submerged memories, memories that is of things perceived by the unconscious, though not necessarily by the conscious mind . . . ; it is probably the most sensational page in psychical research. . . . Unfortunately the controls themselves forbid publication. I can use it for my own conviction—that is all, but it is what I have been waiting for.[48]

Bessie Radcliffe was not quite the naive and 'comparatively ignorant girl' represented by Yeats: the daughter of the Chief Commissioner of the Metropolitan Police, she came from a long line of eminent clergy and barristers (Yeats observed that her messages came from 'always very ardent Christians'). At this time a close friend of the historian A. L. Smith, master of Balliol, and his son-in-law Harold Hartley, then science don at Balliol, she would eventually marry Ronald Barnes, who had been at Oxford with her brother, when he was Under-Secretary of State for Air. After her marriage she continued to be in touch with Yeats but by then the automatic writing seems to have been channelled into more acceptable forms, and as Baroness Gorell she later published a number of children's books and essays.[49] However, at the time Eva involved Yeats and Olivia—always an interested observer—supernatural phenomena were familiar to Bessie (and to her younger sister, who dealt with her experiences with less equanimity[50]); although she and her family shunned publicity, she was anxious like Yeats to prove the authenticity of the spirit messages, especially to her Oxford friends.

Coming from an 'intelligent but not imaginative, and decidedly conventional' family, she was described by a family friend as of 'unassailable integrity, . . . attractive, well-educated . . . of rather downright speech . . . candid, uncomplicated and matter-of-fact'.[51] She and Georgie may well have already encountered each other, at the very least known each other by sight, for as well as becoming Eva Fowler's accomplice, Bessie too took tea with Olivia Shakespear, saw the Abbey Theatre perform, and Yeats had even suggested that she consult Tagore for assistance with meditation.[52] Like Georgie, Bessie attended at least one of WBY's lectures at the Fowler residence on the afternoons of 18 and 19 December 1913, for she saw him at Brunswick Square on the 18th, a spirit standing behind his chair.[53] By then Eva, Bessie, and WBY were meeting regularly at Gilbert Street each Tuesday afternoon for sessions with the intriguing script. In late July when Georgie and her mother were holidaying on the Broads of Norfolk (where, she wrote to Dorothy, 'they have had to have the cocks shut up 'cos they crow so early in the morning'[54]), they were only a few miles from Yeats, who was careering about the country following up hints from Bessie's controls. They may have met on 28 July, the date of one of Georgie's horoscopes.[55] By mid-August 1913, when Yeats arrived at The Prelude bearing yet more automatic script and corresponding daily with either Eva or Bessie—quotations in Greek with their translations are written on 'Prelude' stationery—Georgie was ready to offer assistance in seeking out identifications which would provide the aspiring magus with the proofs he longed for.

Messages had been received from Anna Luise Karsch (or Karschin), a minor nature poet known as the 'deutsche Sappho' (although this spirit at first evidently found even three observers too many and demanded privacy). Much discussion ensued concerning quotations from Goethe, whom Karsch evidently knew. As soon as Georgie had recovered from her throat operation and since she had at last reached the age of admittance, she applied for a reading ticket to the British Museum, indicating her desire to read 'all available literature on the religious history of the 1st 3 centuries AD', clearly the influence of Mead's work. Her letter of recommendation came from a Montpelier Square neighbour, the novelist Richard Pryce.[56] On 18 November she presented herself promptly at 9 a.m. for what would be the first of many sojourns under the library's imposing dome in Great Russell Street.[57] But her first foray had nothing to do with early religious history and much to do with her knowledge of German, for she immediately submitted a report to Stone Cottage:

Concerning Anna Luise Karschin There is no evidence in any biography, biographical sketch or other source of Karschin's having belonged to any mysticall [sic] society. She seems to have had no inner mysticall life, but to have been religious & a good church-woman. Schlichtegroll says of her that she was very reserved, & that no one knew much of her life, save the externals.

Three letters from Goethe to K., none of particular interest. He is writing to her in 1775-6-7 & visits her in 1778 on which occasion she writes him a poem. (she was then 56, G:29) Till she goes to Berlin in 1761 K. had but little education & few books. There is no mention of Goethe's having met her *before* 1778 & her correspondance [*sic*] & acquaintance with him is not mentioned in any written matter concerning her life.

If details of G's letters or other matters are of any use to you, or you want anything else looked up, send me a post card.[58]

That she formally signed her name 'G. Hyde Lees' in full suggests that she and Yeats were not yet on the familiar terms she enjoyed with Ezra and Dorothy, despite the fact that their common interests were creating ever more opportunities to meet.[59] By late September Eva Fowler had gained more information about Karsch's life from her niece in Germany; an unsigned typed extract identifying lines from Goethe's *Faust* part II quoted in the automatic script may also have been typed out by Georgie while she was in London.[60] Certainly that year no one could escape Yeats's obsession; as he explained somewhat defensively to his father: 'I know all the rationalist theories, fraud, unconscious fraud, unconscious action of the mind, forgotten memories, and so on and have after long analysis shown that none can account for this case. . . . I am now elaborating a curious theory of spirit action which may I believe make philosophic study of mediums possible. I am really absorbed in this for the moment.'[61]

Nelly Tucker also contributed to the ongoing research: a copy in her hand of Henri Bergson's presidential address to the Society for Psychical Research (published in January 1914) exists in an old French workbook of Harold's, doubtless the result of that exciting summer at The Prelude.[62] It is quite likely therefore that Georgie, and certainly Olivia, read the manuscript of Yeats's 'Preliminary Examination' of Bessie's script which he began in October 1913 and revised the following June but never published. In it he quotes from Bergson's lecture and tentatively puts forward a number of conclusions about spirit communication ('a sort of double mediumship, a spirit medium and a human medium'), describing the methods used by both interlocutor and responder. Although couched in terms used by the Society, of which he was by now an associate member, Yeats's interpretation of 'secondary or tertiary personalities' that 'once formed may act independently of the medium' differed considerably from that of Frederic Myers, one of the founders and early presidents of the Society for Psychical Research, whose 1885 article on double consciousness in automatic writing suggested the possibility of complex telepathic communication.[63] (The terms 'telepathy', 'supernormal', and 'veridical' were all coined by Myers, who argued that most supernormal phenomena were caused not by spirits of the dead but by the continuing 'subliminal self'.[64])

Within a year Georgie would become the fourth enquirer into the spirit scripts. Later, perhaps because of the overriding importance of her own experience, she would deny the significance of Bessie's automatic writing, suggesting that the influence on Yeats was not that great. She insisted that 'E. R. was better educated than he said; she knew German. He was very excited with her for about a year, referred to her later on[ly] occasionally.'[65] But by the summer of 1913 Georgie was thoroughly committed to her own studies of the supernormal, and the concept of automatic writing would have been long familiar to her. In her reading, she had already encountered the long history of occultism, the study of things hidden or mysterious, an acknowledgement of the secret forces of nature beyond the range of ordinary knowledge; the practices of alchemy, astrology, geomancy, witchcraft, and magic were common property. Nor was it possible to ignore the growing interest in spiritualism (of which the Society for Psychical Research was a by-product), when in addition to the rejection of philosophical materialism many grieving over the loss of loved ones in the Crimean, South African, and First World Wars sought reassurance that life continues beyond bodily death. Closer to home, Ezra had read Swedenborg as early as 1904;[66] Georgie noted that Yeats returned to the Swedish mystic (who had influenced Blake) about the time she first met him,[67] and Swedenborg is referred to in his notes on Elizabeth Radcliffe. Shortly after his own marriage Pound wrote pompously to Yeats, who was then writing his essay 'Swedenborg: Mediums and the Desolate Places', 'I don't want to be stuffy about Swedenborg's originality but I have just come on a line in the 11th book of the Odyssey . . . "The departing soul hovers about as a dream". It might not make a bad chapter heading or motto.'[68]

    Second sight, clairvoyance and clairaudience, telepathy or what is now referred to as extrasensory perception, had long been acknowledged as gifts possessed by the select and strange few. But the phenomenon that swept North America and Europe in the late nineteenth and early twentieth centuries claimed to be a science, a philosophy, and a religion all in one. Spiritualists believe in the continuity of personality after death, and that spirits of the departed communicate through a living person who is sensitive to these forces. Their belief was also democratic, for everyone has the potential to be a medium; however, spirits will be naturally attracted to those individuals whose qualities resemble their own (which tended toward class distinctions among groups exploring spiritism).[69] Eventually most spirits progress to a higher plane and lose contact altogether with the earthbound, although they can continue to watch over and even influence the living through 'controls', spirits on a less advanced level—an intermediary realm familiar to those who, like Yeats and Georgie, had read their Swedenborg and the Cambridge Platonist Henry More.[70]

    It is commonly accepted that spiritualism received its impetus in strange rappings heard by the American Fox family in 1848; once decoded, the messages spelled out showed an impressive knowledge of a murder, and much less remarkable information about the neighbours. Although the Fox sisters later admitted the strange knocking was the result of talented joint-snapping, 'table-rapping' spread like wildfire as séances bred further mediums who in turn developed greater powers: such improvements as automatic writing, direct writing, slate writing (where two slates are fastened together awaiting spirit writing—an experience that occurred once during the Radcliffe sittings), spirit music, voice through trance, direct voice, speaking in tongues, apports (unaided movement of objects), tele-portation, levitation, materialization. New professions arose to accommodate the phenomena: spirit photography, astral projection, and spirit healing. Within four years spiritualism had gained ground in England and a new generation of mediums emerged, many of them remaining within the privacy of the family circle, but also professionals who travelled a fairly extensive circuit and were fre-quently subjected to tests devised by scientists and other sceptics. Table-turning and tilting reached epidemic proportions not only in England (most notably in the north); it is reported that in France those in the know enquired not after one's health, but one's table manners ('Thank you, mine turns beautifully—how goes yours?'[71]). Fraud was frequently detected, especially among nubile young mediums from whose darkened cabinets emerged charming, often mischievous and pro-vocative controls, but the movement advanced.[72] Home circles were common, especially among the lower and middle classes; clientele for professional séances included members of the aristocracy and royalty as well as a considerable num-ber of professionals, artists, and writers. Balzac's *Seraphita*, beloved of Yeats and early devoured by Pound, was a recognized textbook of occult practices. Abraham Lincoln, Elizabeth Barrett Browning, Harriet Beecher Stowe, Bulwer Lytton, Dion Boucicault, John Ruskin, the entire Rossetti circle, all frequented the tables. Victor Hugo in exile in Jersey was greatly impressed by table-turning; perhaps not unexpectedly, the messages he received were of a high literary calibre, including a challenge by Shakespeare to a literary competition, and again not surprisingly the spirit of Hugo himself briefly took control of a medium seven years after his death. Victorien Sardou, whose 'well-made plays' made him one of the most popular dramatists in France and England, was himself a medium, his most memorable achievement automatic drawings of dwellings on the planet Jupiter. On a no less serious level, Charles Dickens celebrated a revival of mesmerism (briefly endorsed by prominent physicians) and Walt Whitman consulted a phrenologist's chart of his 'bumps'.

Spiritualism in England and North America preferred to ally itself with Christianity despite warnings of devil possession. Although disagreeing with the resurrection of the body (while usually accepting the doctrine of transubstantia-tion), many believed in a world beyond which is in most ways a copy of life on earth, conducted in a much more rarefied atmosphere—translating the Hermetic 'as above, so below' in frequently banal terms. In France, although spiritualism had its adherents, spiritism, which denied certain basic Christian tenets, gradually became the ascendant belief. Under the leadership of the French educator Allan Kardec (Hippolyte Rivail) who had previously been interested in mesmerism and phrenology, the doctrine of reincarnation and a belief in the astral body were added to the spiritualists' belief in physical phenomena. Basing his teachings on spirit messages received through clairvoyants, Kardec tended to play down aspects such as materialization in favour of more direct contact through automatic writing, during which the subject holding pen or pencil is not necessarily conscious. A series of works published by Kardec in the 1850s and 1860s became the standard textbooks of spiritism, which is still an acknowledged practice in South America, especially Brazil, where it is the basis for, among other procedures, psychic surgery. Today, the crude methods of phrenology have been replaced by sophisticated techniques of measuring the chemistry and energy of the multiple circuits in the brain; but neuroscientists, although they have traced the systems related to the senses, still do not understand the role of consciousness, understanding, or personality, nor can they identify their whereabouts. Mesmerism has given way to hypnotism, now an established and respectable practical treatment technique by psychiatrists, dentists, clinical psychologists, and other therapists. Medical practitioners in the nineteenth century began to use it for producing psychological anaesthesia before chemical anaesthetics were generally available; then Freud and many of his contemporaries turned to hypnosis for personality analysis and for revealing repressed memories. Not all people will respond to such therapy, which makes use of trance states and automatic writing and drawing; nor is it fully understood why there is such a variability in susceptibility, which does not appear to be a matter of strength or weakness of will. But persons with a natural (or cultural) susceptibility to hypnotic suggestions may even induce the state by themselves in a matter of seconds; as we shall see later, Georgie seems to have developed this skill.[73]

It was the continental form of spiritism represented by Kardec that Georgie inclined to; despite the initiatory impulse of her father's death, she always distrusted Spiritualism as a religion.[74] Dorothy remained firmly against all forms of spiritism, and like many of Yeats's other friends was becoming bored with his enthusiasm for spooks.[75] But Georgie, still grieving for her father and intent on her researches into the supernatural, was soon attending séances both with Yeats and independently.[76] Her first experience may have been with a famous 'direct voice' medium who visited England at least five times. In 1911 Mrs Etta Wriedt of Detroit had been invited to attend meetings at 'Julia's Bureau', which operated out of Cambridge House in Wimbledon, the country home of journalist and confirmed spiritualist W. T. Stead. Named after the American Julia Ames, his 'friend in spirit-life', the Bureau, which included an extensive library, was established and funded by Stead as an office where grieving men and women could register their names and be put in touch with mediums incognito. In addition, every

Wednesday a religious service was held at Cambridge House, followed by a séance with a medium. Those who attended 'Julia's Circle' came regularly, sitting in the large upper room furnished for the purpose with a cabinet, a semicircle of chairs, and tables on which were placed vases of fresh flowers brought by the sitters to enhance 'the power' or, as it was sometimes called, the 'light'.[77]

In 1911, at Stead's invitation, Mrs Etta Wriedt arrived to conduct these séances, staying for two and a half months through July and August. Her sittings were so successful that she was invited to return the following summer; in April 1912 Stead sailed for America to accompany her, and was one of the casualties on the *Titanic*. (This did not prevent him from reappearing frequently both to 'Julia's Circle' and, daily, to his daughter.[78]) Vice-Admiral W. Usborne Moore then guaranteed Mrs Wriedt's visit in Stead's place, and she arrived at the beginning of May, providing both public and private sittings until early July. As a frequent visitor to the 'Julia Circles' Yeats would have heard of Etta Wriedt's séances in 1911; we are certain of his attendance at some of the sittings in 1912 when 'Leo Africanus' presented himself on 9 and 12 May, 5, 8, 28 June, and again on 12 May and 23 June 1913.

It appears probable that Georgie joined the circle as early as 1912. Mediums were accustomed to 'tests' by which seekers attempt to satisfy themselves of the authenticity of the spirit voices presenting themselves. But Wriedt finally ejected Yeats in August 1913 'because she says "nothing ever satisfies me" '.[79] Much to Willy's annoyance when he found out, Georgie was allowed to continue; she delighted in relating that Yeats was expelled for two years: 'He was too critical. He was furious when he heard that I was allowed to go to the séances.'[80] 'Two years' was something of an exaggeration, for Yeats records séances with Mrs Wriedt in America on 19 February 1914 and back at Cambridge House on 6 June 1914 (when Leo discussed both Anna Luise Karsch and Bessie Radcliffe's waning powers); in 1915 Yeats and Lady Gregory consulted her concerning Hugh Lane's will. George's memory however implies that she was at least sometimes present at the same sessions as Yeats, and was bound to have heard of his encounters with the spirit calling himself 'Leo Africanus' who encouraged Yeats to try his own hand at automatic writing, with limited if any success. Olivia Shakespear was also on familiar terms with Leo; on 31 October 1915 while she and Yeats were conducting experiments with Tattwa cards, the spirit held a long conversation with her.[81]

The American medium was a woman of independence, some might even say unpredictability; 'she alters her plans twenty times in a week', complained Admiral Moore. But as a psychic Etta Wriedt was considered sincere, honest, and tireless. Séances might take place in full daylight, in the red light of two shaded electric lamps, or in absolute darkness (though lights could be turned on at any time). She refused to use a cabinet although Stead had furnished 'Julia's room' with one on which an earlier generation of materializing mediums had depended; she never went into a trance or lost consciousness, talking normally throughout to both mundane and ultramundane visitors. Her only props aside from the flowers brought by sitters were two aluminium trumpets made in three lengths of thirteen inches each to magnify the voices of the spirit communicators, and even then Admiral Moore's trumpets were frequently used instead. These trumpets were apparently not always necessary (though helpful to tentative spirits visiting for the first time) and sitters were convinced that as many as three voices might speak at once while Mrs Wriedt conversed in her own voice. Sitters heard messages in at least thirteen languages ranging from Arabic and Croatian to Hindustani and Welsh, although the medium claimed she understood only English. Nothing as vulgar as ectoplasm was produced although occasionally flashes or discs of light were seen; but usually only Mrs Wriedt could read the names, inverted and fleeting, that appeared in the air. Sessions often began with a gentle sprinkling of water over the sitters, which the medium explained 'was the way her control had of showing he was present and that it was a kind of baptism'.[82] Sitters reported that they were touched ('never groped') by ghostly hands and swore the flowers were dropped in their laps or strewn about the room; unless firmly grasped the trumpets never seemed to remain still, often at the end of the sitting dropping to the floor from the ceiling. At what was probably the regular Wednesday evening 'Julia Circle', early in June 1912, Yeats was presented with violets, which he asked Olivia to 'psychometrize' for him; puzzled by the impression of 'illusion', 'grey mists', and 'unreality', she identified 'some fundamental insincerity'. He later thought they had come from Maud Gonne, whose voice he was convinced he had heard at the sitting.[83]

Much depended upon the co-operative energy of the sitters. 'I am preying [sic] for an uneventful day tomorrow,' Yeats wrote to Lady Gregory. 'Tomorrow night I get the seance from Mrs Wriedt, the American medium, which I have been trying to get for weeks. It is my best chance about Hugh's will & if I lose vitality during the day nothing whatever will happen. I have already had one absolute blank through going tired. No one knows why this is, but every one finds it so.'[84] Meetings always began with music, either from a mechanical box which played softly at private sittings or, in the public circles, a recitation of the Lord's Prayer followed by the singing of a hymn or doxology; 'Lead Kindly Light' was particularly favoured. Ezra, who once accompanied Georgie to Cambridge House, was the only person present who knew all the verses, which 'he sang out loud and clear'.[85]

During Etta Wriedt's absence in the winter of 1915 Georgie frequented other mediums, giving her name as 'Miss Hyde' (to her and the mediums' great amusement Willy used to go as 'Mr Smith'). She went once to a Mrs Handcock, wife of a London barrister; Yeats also went to her at 1 Egerton Mansions, considering her 'not much good as a mere clairvoyant . . . best as a trance medium'.[86] More important, Georgie had a 'great many' sittings with Mrs Gladys Osborne Leonard, who later became famous as the medium in *Raymond*, Oliver Lodge's account of the search for communication with his dead soldier-son, first published in 1916.[87] Gladys Leonard, a quiet, reserved woman with a forthright manner, was ten years older than Georgie; a sometime actress married to an actor, she had discovered her gift while playing at table-tipping with fellow actors while waiting for their cues.[88] Georgie seems to have been one of her early sitters, for at that time she 'only charged 5/- She said to me of Lodge—before the book came out—"Sir Oliver Lodge is having sittings with me. He accepts too much on faith. I don't think he is critical enough". . . . She *used* to be remarkable. . . [and] she *was* excellent.'[89] Later Leonard was the co-operative subject of thousands of hours of study by the Society for Psychical Research, none of whom ever doubted her honesty, despite their misgivings.[90]

Leonard offered trance séances with her child control 'Feda', who claimed to be her Hindu ancestor and to her own annoyance was occasionally 'dispossessed' by other eager communicators. Although far less frequently than with Wriedt, voices would be heard apparently from an empty space some distance in front of her; she also held, while remaining conscious, sittings with the ouija board and table-tiltings. Lodge, who experienced all these forms with Gladys Leonard and considered her 'a very straight forward and honest medium, but not a particularly strong one', was especially impressed by the 'cross correspondences' he received —messages purporting to come from the late Frederic Myers through several mediums at about the same time—and the results of the 'proxy sittings' and 'book tests' he and his colleagues devised.[91] Six years later, writing to a grieving Ottoline Morrell (whose young lover had recently died in her arms), Georgie admitted that after a while she gave up going to mediums for two reasons—

partly because I found the meagre communications one got, so poor a substitute for the real & *tangible* thing that one longed for—and also that it exhausted vitality and absorbed all my thought almost to a mania. The excitement never fails. Even a bad medium was exciting—something always *might* happen. But the one real & permanent thing I did get was that the terrible remorse one sometimes feels after a person has died—that feeling— if I had only done or said something I did *not* do or say—all that vanished. And that at least is something achieved.[92]

By the time Georgie started attending such sessions she had lost not only her father, but two of her uncles, and would soon lose two more. Much later still Leonard would publish a book about her experiences in which she recommended 'conscious or semi-trance' over 'full trance' in mediumship and automatic writing—perhaps because she did not really care for her childlike control 'Feda' (the feeling was apparently mutual).[93] Clearly this method was also the one which would be preferred by George herself.

Etta Wriedt returned to England at least once more, in 1919. However, by then Georgie had no need of such external phenomena, and had even managed to banish Leo Africanus.[94] The pain of her father's death had eased and attendance at séances, having lost its urgency, became just one of the projects in her joint research with Willy. But for many years after their marriage they continued to visit mediums, and she retained an interest in the subject throughout her life. She never gave up her belief in ghosts of some form, once startling her daughter by objecting that 'ghosts weren't white';[95] and in the 1950s she was intrigued by Kathleen Raine's experiences in a haunted cottage on Achill.[96] But she was also cautious: 'Your account of the Mrs Crandon séance is very interesting,' she commented on one of Yeats's visits in New York; 'especially interesting in the mechanical control of the tongue by the instrument during the "direct voice" '.[97] She admitted that 'Yeats was very credulous at most séances, incredulous only at a few. He believed in phenomena.'[98] But then, even mediums' 'controls' were occasionally known to reprimand him severely for leaping to conclusions.

In 1913, while Georgie was still exploring Italian bookshops and studying Plotinus, and Willy was pursuing automatic messages at Daisy Meadow, another charismatic lecturer visited London. Rudolf Steiner arrived at the beginning of May; he gave two lectures for members of a group which had been established within the Theosophical Society for the sole purpose of studying his writings, and held other meetings and a great number of private interviews before departing a week later. As leader of the German section of the Theosophical Society, Steiner had attended congresses in London in 1902, 1903, and 1905; but this was the first visit since his banishment by Annie Besant (who had by then taken over from Madame Blavatsky and disapproved of Steiner's independent views) and the legitimization of his own Anthroposophical Society. By the time of his visit, the English group of breakaway theosophists who had turned to him for leadership (by now there were two Lodges, the 'Zarathrustra' and the 'Myrdhin') numbered 200.[99] Believing that through an enhanced consciousness man could once again perceive spiritual worlds, Steiner encouraged and developed his system of 'spiritual science' through exercises of the intellect and acknowledgement of the spirit's previous incarnations and, through a complex process of visualization, 'astral travel'.[100] Steiner's major work, *Occult Science: An Outline*, did not appear until 1913, but Clifford Bax's translation from the German of his *Initiation and its Results: A Sequel to 'The Way of Initiation'*, had been published by the Theosophical Society in 1909.[101] Although she read Madame Blavatsky's works,[102] Georgie never joined the Theosophical Society; however, some time after Steiner's London visit she did become a member of the Anthroposophical Society, which offered lectures four times a week on Steiner's work (much of it not yet in translation).[103] Although William James discusses the work of the German physicist and philosopher Gustav Fechner, this may have been when she first encountered Fechner's *On Life after Death*, a system that bears considerable resemblance to Steiner's.[104] There was another connection, too, for in the company of one of its members, Steiner apparently attended at least one meeting of yet another independent occult society which also included many former theosophists (Yeats among them), the Order of the Golden Dawn.[105]

Georgie was never a member of the Society for Psychical Research despite her growing interest in the occult; she may however have attended some of the Society's meetings, which were open to both 'Associates and friends'.[106] However, given Mead's and Steiner's earlier involvement with the Theosophical Society, her own developing friendship with Yeats, and her independent studies of ancient and medieval esoteric doctrines, it was inevitable that February 1914 should see Georgie buying *The Kabbalah Unveiled* by the erstwhile leader of the Golden Dawn, S. L. MacGregor Mathers. (A reference on the flyleaf to Austin Freeman's *The Silent Witness*, featuring the forensic detective Dr Thorndyke, shows her equally early love of mystery novels.) Mathers's *Kabbalah Unveiled* was a translation of three books of the *Zohar* or 'Book of Splendour', a thirteenth-century commentary on the Pentateuch which draws on the earlier *Sepher Yetzirah* or 'Book of Formation'. Both the *Sepher Yetzirah* and the *Zohar* deal with the doctrine of the sephiroth or spheres, a hierarchical series of intelligences which emanate from God and are expressed in the Three Pillars of the Tree of Life; both envisage four different worlds ranging from that of God to the dwelling of evil spirits: the world of emanations or the heavenly man, the Briatic world of pure nature or creation, the Yetziratic world of formation, and the world of action or matter. Emphasis is on immanence rather than transcendence, engagement with the world through the 'cosmic dance' where every part of the universe is in constant interaction with every other part. Accompanying Mathers's text are the equally important tables and diagrams ascribing a sacred name, planet, sign of the zodiac, numerical value (especially combinations of one, three, four, and ten), colour, and other qualities to each of the twenty-two letters of the Hebrew alphabet, showing parallels and correspondences with the parts of the human body—all intricately relating the microcosm of man to the macrocosm of the world.

This purchase by Georgie was speedily followed by an Italian version of the works ascribed to Hermes Trismegistos, bought while she was in Rome with Dorothy later that month.[107] Composed by Alexandrian scholars in the first two centuries AD and dealing with alchemy, astrology, and magic, and fusing Eastern, Platonic, Stoic, and neo-Pythagorean philosophies, the *corpus hermeticum* was written in the form of Platonic dialogues, emphasizing the maxim traditionally attributed to the 'Tabula Smaragdina' or Emerald Tablet—'as above, so below'. Again Georgie's volume is heavily annotated, including a list of other texts to be examined; many of these were mentioned in Mathers's introduction: Raymon Llull (or 'Raymond Lully') the mystic, Simon Magus 'the Sorcerer', the 'Tabula

Smaragdina' itself, and Khunrath (which on her list is triumphantly marked 'found'). Inserted on hotel stationery are her notes on the Daityos in the Indian pantheon, personal magnetism, and astrology.[108] Clearly her stated application to the British Museum was no mere excuse; she was indeed 'desirous of reading all available literature on the religious history of the 1st 3 centuries AD'. Interest in Hebrew, Greek, and Roman history led to further additions to her library, including studies by Franz Cumont and John Estens, and the sixteenth-century Bavarian Chronicles by Aventinus.[109]

Alongside Chapman's Homer, another significant purchase was an Italian edition of the works of Pico della Mirandola, whose syncretic humanism would engross her for at least the next decade. She immediately set about comparing Pico's commentary to the Kabbalah; her notebook transcribes his '31 conclusions concerning his own opinion of the manner of understanding the Hymns of Orpheus concerning Magic, that is the secret of divine and natural things'.[110] Perhaps this was when she also began to read Hölderlin's lyrics, with their prophecy of 'the return of the gods' of ancient Greece, which she later introduced to Yeats.[111] Immediately on her return from Italy she also found a copy of *Sepher Yetzirah: The Book of Formation, with the Fifty Gates of Intelligence and the Thirty-Two Paths of Wisdom*, the earliest known Jewish text on magic and cosmology, translated by Dr Wynn Westcott, another of the founders of the Order of the Golden Dawn. Complementing Mathers's *Kabbalah*, her copy of the *Sepher Yetzirah* includes cross-references to Pico's *Heptapolus*, a seven-point exposition of Genesis.[112] At the same time she was studying philosophers both medieval and modern, including *De Occulta Philosophia* by the sixteenth-century German astrologer and magician Cornelius Agrippa (recommended by Mathers who betrayed considerable familiarity with Agrippa's system of numerical and alphabetical tables for summoning spirits), and the works of Hegel and Benedetto Croce (on whom Pound had brought her to hear Douglas Ainslie lecture).[113] Small wonder that, after attending a church service with her then devout cousin while Grace was attending Miss Sparkes's finishing school in Eastbourne, she should explosively declare that she 'doesn't believe in a word of it'. But then, neither did Nelly, who claimed, 'I have no use for "God" in the Person Singular; Gods = yes, as many as you like, all delightful and archeological: all classic and romantic. Art made the Gods.'[114]

Other events were gradually separating the 'step-pest' from her dearest friend. In February 1914 Olivia finally relented and asked Hope Shakespear to sanction Dorothy and Ezra's engagement, even without the wished-for £500 a year. 'I told Georgie all about it yesterday afternoon,' Dorothy wrote to Pound: 'but she is secret as the grave abt. it until I say she may know. She was pleased, I think. I am sure she was—She didn't say much—I particularly don't want her to feel 'deserted' by my marrying—I know how it is when one's girl-friends marry—Of course it can't be helped in a way—but you can help, if you like her—which I believe you do?'[115] By the end of that month, while Georgie and Dorothy returned to Rome (their last trip on the Continent together until 1924), news of the 'bombshell' (Eva Fowler's word) spread through their circle; Georgie's mountaineer friend Herbert Reade recommended that the newly-weds furnish their rooms at 5 Holland Place Chambers with a canvas bath such as that used by hikers.[116] Word reached Yeats in Pittsburgh, where he wrote to Ezra on 8 March, perhaps with some chagrin at his own continuing single state: 'I congratulate you very heartily. You will have a beautiful & clever wife & that is what few men get. I doubt not too that you will do better work from getting the great business of life settled. I hope to be back for your marriage but will not know for certain for a few days.'[117]

On Saturday, 18 April, two days before the wedding, Olivia and Hope Shakespear hosted a reception for friends and relatives at Brunswick Gardens from 3.30 to 6.30; at Hope's insistence, the ceremony itself took place in a church. Dorothy's father and 'Uncle Bunk' (Henry Tucker) signed as witnesses; Nelly, Georgie, and Yeats were among the 'half-a-dozen observers'.[118] Later Yeats reported, 'Ezra Pound was married yesterday & the day before I had to listen to Mrs Fowler & her sister denouncing him for a whole morning (I was waiting in hope of automatic writing). One or other had asked him to dinner soon after he came from America & he had not been able to eat anything owing to his having "eaten the table-ornaments before the dinner began." '[119] Flushed with the success of his American tour, Yeats's wedding gift was a cheque, which was put towards the purchase of a clavichord from Arnold Dolmetsch, the musician and musicologist who had created Florence Farr's psaltery. Georgie's gift is not recorded, nor does the marriage appear to have been noticed in the newspapers, except in Philadelphia, home of the Pounds Senior.

Three days after the wedding Yeats lectured to the London Spiritualist Alliance at the Salon of the Royal Society of British Artists on 'Ghosts and Dreams', in which he discussed, among others, Cesare Lombroso and F. W. H. Myers, and described his séances with Etta Wriedt. Open to 'Members, Associates and friends', the audience may have included Georgie, but in any case, the lecture was later summarized in the Alliance's magazine *Light* and there was nothing new in it for her by now.[120] Meanwhile Ezra and Dorothy were honeymooning at Stone Cottage, where they were cared for by the Misses Welfare; Eva Fowler's offer of servantless Daisy Meadow was rejected, because the bride refused to cook. Wilfrid Scawen Blunt, who lived nearby, entertained them with champagne, a return perhaps for the poets' tribute Ezra had organized for his seventy-fifth birthday the year before.[121] After the couple returned to London Georgie was a regular visitor in their angular-shaped rooms (across the hall from Ezra's former fiancée H.D.—whose horoscope Georgie cast—and her new husband Richard Aldington), and would remain so until the Pounds moved to Paris six and a half years later. In May Olivia gave Georgie a copy of Ezra's anthology *Des Imagistes* (published by Poetry Bookshop in February); the same month she received a prospectus to the Rebel Art Centre, newly established by Wyndham Lewis as a counter to the Omega Workshops of Bloomsbury, and its blatantly propagandist magazine *Blast*, which Ezra was busily proof-reading in the country.[122] Yeats went off to Paris until the end of the month, visiting a series of materializing mediums, enthusiastic at this 'chance of a lifetime',[123] and, accompanied by Maud Gonne and the SPR investigator Everard Feilding, on the search for a 'miraculous' bleeding oleograph of the image of Christ; all investigations were failures. Meanwhile in London Georgie added the 1830 edition of Walter Scott's *Letters on Demonology and Witchcraft* to her library. She also possessed a copy of Aleister Crowley's *Mortadello* (1912) (which she later twice gave away, first to the Dublin Drama League library and then in 1945 to Oliver Edwards).[124] Another purchase was James Stephens's *The Crock of Gold* which, significantly, she signed 'George Hyde Lees'. This was the first indication of her departure from 'Georgie'; such gestures towards self-construction would become more frequent over the next four years.

The spring of 1914 saw the opening of an exhibition of paintings by Robert Gregory (with William Orpen and Augustus John) at the Chenil Gallery. When Lady Gregory arrived in preparation for the annual Abbey Theatre season at the Royal Court, Willy was in attendance with Georgie and her mother (and perhaps Olivia), who were duly introduced. The meeting made no impact on the chatelaine of Coole, who would on an occasion so important to her only son's career have been too interested in more influential people to notice one other young woman in the party. But George always bitterly remembered that, the next time they met, Lady Gregory 'cut her dead'. To give Yeats's long-time friend her due, this probably took place at the theatre, when once again the playwright would have had other matters on her mind, this time her own career. Nelly however recalled with pleasure being taken by Lady Gregory to Marlborough House, 'a never forgotten treat'.[125]

5
THE GOLDEN DAWN

Georgie's occult readings inevitably led to the study of astrology, which she seems to have taken up with typical earnestness and enthusiasm. Horoscopes cast by her exist from 1913, but astrology, reinforced by her study of the *Zohar* and *Sepher Yetzirah*, was an essential aspect of her reading for several years earlier. If the motions of the heavens could be predicted well in advance, surely here was another key to both the past and the future, an explanation of personality and world events. Like many before her, she studied the art by casting natal (or 'birth') horoscopes not only of her friends and family, but of those individuals who had —and were having—a profound effect on world events.[1] As usual she collected works on the subject, both ancient and modern. Dorothy reported from Rome in 1914, 'G. & I have been for an old-book-shop prowl: She found one work on astrology—for 10c. It is in Latin, & has nice looking diagrams.'[2] In October 1910 Yeats had cast a horoscope for Dorothy,[3] who regularly visited her favourite palmist Sara; but Georgie's research into astrology went far beyond casual attempts at prediction, for she took seriously the doctrine of correspondences as understood by medieval philosophy. 'What is below is like that which is above, and what is above is like to that which is below, to accomplish the miracles of one thing. And as all things were produced by the one word of the Being, so all things were produced from this one thing by adaptation. Its father is the Sun, its mother is the Moon.'[4]

'As above, so below': the order of the universe (the macrocosm) is reflected in the order in man (the microcosm); history repeats itself like the cycles in the natural world where every thing vibrates against everything else and opposites frequently alternate; by understanding the cosmic order, we can begin to understand ourselves. This is the basis of both astrology and alchemy, from Ptolemy onwards. In 1921, in reply to a query about 'Lunar Symbolism', the Yeatses would recommend Ptolemy's *Tetrabiblos* from which 'all our astrology is derived'.[5] Birth-patterns did not predetermine fate, for there always remained the exercise of free will, but knowledge of certain celestial influences and possible trends could help one avoid mistakes. And such knowledge led one even closer to an understanding of things beyond our senses. Madame Blavatsky herself had insisted, 'In astrology and psychology one has to step beyond the visible world of matter, and enter into the domain of transcendent spirit.'[6]

And so the casting of natal horoscopes became a regular practice for Georgie, as did mundane astrology which studies the relationship between certain moments such as eclipses or floods and historical events such as those leading up to the First World War. In fact, by calculating 'primaries' (the motion of the horoscope during the first day of birth) and 'secondaries' (the motion during subsequent days) one could correlate not only forward in time but back, as Georgie did to satisfy the vexed question of her birthdate (16 or 17 October) and determine her birth time (she finally settled on 8.25 a.m.).[7] Although well aware that 'the stars impel rather than compel,'[8] from as early as 1914 she celebrated her birthday by casting 'secondary progressions' for the coming year. The use of an ephemeris (giving the positions of Sun, Moon, and planets for every day of that particular year) is needed to calculate secondary progressions, but not for primary directions; both however require considerable skill for accurate calculations.[9] A British Museum library call slip, dated by her 19 February 1914, requests Thomas Oxley's *A Supplement, or Only True Key to the Use and Construction of the Celestial Planispheres, for Working Nativities, etc.* (1833); thanks to Harry Tucker's 1909 Christmas gift (a book in German about Dürer's engravings), she would have known of the first pair of planispheres, drawn by Albrecht Dürer in 1515.[10] The artist apparently remained an interest; on her birthday in 1925 Lennox Robinson presented her with a copy of *The Little Passion of Albert Dürer* (1894), which included plates with Latin poems on facing pages. She also practised interrogatory astrology, casting horaries that focus on questions of the moment: 'to decide for the asking of a certain letter, or no'; a lost brooch; seeking a missing letter ('will be found in stagnant place probably dustbin'[11]). And catarchic or electional astrology, to determine the appropriate time for a journey, an operation, a wedding. Horaries took her into the art of divination. They required much tact and skill, especially if the querent (person asking the question) was also the astrologer making the analysis: the wording must be precise, the chart fit the situation, place, and significant moment (otherwise the chart was not 'radical', or fit to be judged), and circumstances carefully considered to avoid self-deception.

One of the earliest detailed analyses of birth charts surviving among Georgie's papers is actually double, for Dorothy and Ezra Pound. Probably cast just before their marriage, either in Rome or after the two friends returned to London, the exercise not only suggests that the months of April and May 1914 are distinctly favourable to a union, but analyses the strengths of their relationship. The immense detail involved and time consumed in geometric and trigonometric calculations in order to synthesize all the planetary details ('transits', 'progressions', 'directions') marks this truly a labour of love. Impressed, Ezra paid a visit to one of Yeats's professional astrologers to have further mathematical horoscopes done for himself and Dorothy.[12] But it also shows how much Georgie had already learned about the movements of the heavens. By 1915, or even earlier, she was such a practised astrologer that Yeats was making use of 'Miss Hyde Lees rectifications' when exploring the 'lunar secondaries in my own horoscope'; one of her horoscopes lists his progressed Moon positions from month to month, starting with June 1914. Needless to say, the information she required concerning precise dates and events in order to correlate them with his charts led to an intimate knowledge not only of Yeats's present circumstances and preoccupations, but also those of his past. Their close collaboration on astrology, particularly lunar aspects which deal with instinctive and emotional responses, clearly began very early; to be successful, it demanded precision, honesty, and openness.

Without evidence of her artwork beyond rough sketches, it is difficult to know whether astrology and its accompanying geometrical work replaced or accompanied her own commitment to artistic creation; we will never know, for example, whether she like Dorothy was influenced by the Vorticists beyond an interest in their use of geometrical form. There exist among her papers many astrological maps, including several workbooks which show her rapid progress in casting horoscopes for herself and her family and of specific events.[13] These demonstrate her conviction as well as her skill: the character of her generous old friend Herbert Reade is closely examined in one careful horoscope, concluding that he is 'sceptical, critical of all religions yet interested, an unbeliever in accepted dogma, unorthodox . . . inclined towards the occult, but intellectually irreligious'. With the exception of the last phrase, she might have been describing herself. Astrology remained a subject of deep interest throughout her life, and as late as 1946 she offered to cast one visitor's natal horoscope.[14] More important, later charts re-examined events which in hindsight she and her husband saw as significant to the story of their lives and relationship: horoscopes for 1913 isolate as memorable 'a Sunday 1.30 p.m.' in May, 24 June,[15] 28 July, 2.30 p.m. on 29 July. The date 29 June 1913 seems especially important, for it is compared with a 'horary to decide for the asking of a certain letter, or no' of 12 June 1914.[16]

These dates allow us to track the most momentous decision in Georgie's life so far. Yeats's influence might have led her to Rudolf Steiner's Anthroposophical Society, in which he was interested although never a member himself.[17] Certainly he was responsible for her induction, at 3.15 p.m. on 24 July 1914, into the Hermetic Order of the Golden Dawn, the occult society he had joined twenty-four years earlier. It is likely that they first discussed the matter one Sunday afternoon in May and again on 29 June the previous year; either she approached him, or, aware of her interest, he suggested it. But whereas the Anthroposophical Society does not appear to have had an age limit, from its beginning in 1888 the Golden Dawn had insisted that all candidates for initiation be 'over 21 years of age'. Admission of Neophytes took place in the regular January, July, and

December meetings, and at the equinox ceremonies in March and September. Although Georgie was eligible by mid-October 1913, clearly she waited for the appropriate moment to request Yeats's sponsorship. When he was in London that winter, he was preoccupied with chasing down the details of Bessie Radcliffe's automatic script and had little time even for Lady Gregory or the Abbey Theatre. While he was based at Stone Cottage with Ezra Pound from mid-November, Georgie spent part of the winter at Margate. He returned to London in mid-January and left almost immediately for Dublin and his American tour, while Georgie went to Italy with Dorothy and Olivia. Meanwhile however she was steadily preparing herself for initiation: attending Anthroposophical meetings,[18] comparing Mathers's Kabbalah with Pico's, working through the *Sepher Yetzirah* with its Fifty Gates of Intelligence and the Thirty-Two Paths of Wisdom, poring over Cornelius Agrippa and Khunrath, practising her astrology. And then there was Dorothy and Ezra's wedding.

Finally, at 11.50 a.m. on 19 June 1914 she presented herself at 47 Bassett Road, North Kensington, home of Dr R. W. Felkin, Chief of the Stella Matutina branch of the Order of the Golden Dawn. Two days later Georgie signed the Preliminary Pledge to join the Order's Amoun Temple:

I the undersigned do hereby solemnly pledge myself:
  (1) That I am above the age of 21 years.
  (2) That I join this Order of my own free will and accord.
  (3) To keep secret this Order, its Name, its Members, and its Proceedings, from every person outside its pale; and even from Initiates unless in actual possession of the Pass-Word for the time being. I further promise to keep secret any information relative to this Order which may become known to me before my admission; and I also pledge myself to divulge nothing whatsoever to the outside World concerning this Order in case either of my Resignation, Demission, or Expulsion therefrom.
  (4) I undertake to prosecute with zeal the study of the Occult Sciences.
  (5) If accepted as a Candidate, I undertake to persevere through the Ceremony of my Admission.

Her formal application was addressed to the Cancellarius (treasurer and supervisor of examinations and instructor in healing), Revd Father Fitzgerald, and Sub-Cancellarius Sybil Childers; a sister to the Irish revolutionary Erskine Childers, Miss Childers ('Rosa in Cruce') remained a friend long after the Amoun Temple had disbanded.[19]

Her personal motto, by which she would be called in all Order transactions, was of great importance, expressing 'the candidate's highest occult aims or aspirations'; Georgie selected 'Nemo Sciat' ('Let Nobody Know').[20] The two words rarely appear together in classical Latin, and only twice in the Vulgate—although there the exhortation 'let no man know' resonates with implications for Georgie's later automatic script.[21] In casual address and correspondence within the Order, the name was frequently abbreviated to 'Nemo', suggesting less portentous associations such as Winsor McCay's character strip 'Little Nemo' (1906) and Captain Nemo's Nautilus submarine in Jules Verne's *2000 Leagues under the Sea* (1870), Trinculo's reference in *The Tempest* to the early English broadsheets depicting 'Nobody' as a head placed above a vast pair of trunk hose—or perhaps even Alice's famous exchange in *Through the Looking Glass*. More serious antecedents were 'Nobody', the name by which Odysseus tricks Polyphemus; and in her forays in the British Museum Georgie may also have encountered Radulphus' thirteenth-century 'Sermo Neminis', consisting of a collection of biblical, patristic, and liturgical references to Nemo, thereby introducing a new heresy, Neminianism.[22] But 'Let Nobody Know' with its multiple references and interpretation—invocation, instruction, warning—was also a solid indicator of her passion for illumination as well as the reserve and innate timidity she managed to hide by impressive organizational skills and a ready wit. Not for her the bravado of Yeats's final choice for motto, the Neoplatonic 'Demon est Deus Inversus' ('The Devil is the converse of God'); as a chapter heading in Blavatsky's *The Secret Doctrine* this was a familiar saying; it is also employed by Eliphas Lévi in his translation of Pico's 'Kabalistic Conclusions'.[23]

At 3.15 p.m. on 24 July, Georgie's formal admission took place—a suitable date according to her horary, which indicated exactness and boxed conjunctions (all extremely favourable and powerful); she was number 471 on the roll. It appears from Georgie's horoscopes that this and succeeding ceremonies took place a few doors away from the Felkins, at 56 Bassett Road, the address of Christina Mary Stoddart ('Il faut chercher'), later Chief of the Amoun Temple and later still the cause of its downfall.[24] Like all the Order's rituals, the ceremony was designed to impress upon the candidate the solemnity of the occasion. Dressed in a black tunic fastened by a cord passed three times round her waist and wearing red shoes, she was blindfolded; after completion of the ritual the cord was replaced by a black sash crossing from the left shoulder to her right side. What must surely have been the most dramatic moment occurred when, kneeling with her right hand in the centre of the Holy Symbol (a triangle), she swore 'to persevere in the labours of the Divine Science' or be expelled and overwhelmed with misfortunes which 'journey as upon the winds, . . . strike where no man strikes . . . slay where no sword slays'. At these words the Hiereus 'suddenly lays the blade of his Sword upon the Candidate's neck, and withdraws it again' as the Pledge continues 'and as I bow my neck under the sword of the Hiereus so do I commit myself into the hands of [the Divine Guardians of this Order] for vengeance or reward'. Seated on the Throne of the West before the door of the Temple ('The Gate of the Declarers of Judgment'), Hiereus, expounder of the mysteries and Master of Darkness, splendid in his black robe with its white cross on the left breast and the symbol of his office (white equilateral triangle on black ground) suspended from a scarlet collar matching the hilt of his Sword of Strength and Severity, was 'Demon est Deus Inversus'. This was the year Yeats was appointed Imperator, one of the chief officers of the Temple, his mantle 'the Flame Scarlet Robe of Fire and Severity'.

The Hierophant, Master of the Hall, then explained the secret modes of recognition, the 'Step' and the 'Grip', and released the password—which was changed for security reasons at each festival of the equinox—and the 'Grand Word' ('Har-par-krat', a variation on the Egyptian name of the God of Silence). Once initiated and wearing the badge of her grade, the Neophyte was immediately instructed in the practice of a simple 'Pentagram Ritual with the Cabbalistic Cross', so that she might 'form some idea of how to attract and come into communication with spiritual and invisible forces'.[25] (This first sash was provided by the Cancellarius; succeeding ones could be purchased or made and embroidered by the candidate.) Georgie remained faithful to her vow of secrecy throughout her life; nor did she ever disparage the Order, although she may well have agreed with Yeats's later conclusions: 'I am confident from internal evidence that the rituals, as I knew them, were in substance ancient though never so in language unless some ancient text was incorporated. There was a little that I thought obvious and melodramatic, and it was precisely in this little I am told that they resembled Masonic rituals, but much that I thought beautiful and profound.'[26]

Surely no initiate was better prepared than 'Nemo Sciat'. The manuals, 'knowledge lectures' for each grade, and 'flying rolls' (occasional 'side lectures') of the Order drew heavily upon the very texts Georgie had already added to her library, whether by chance or following Yeats's veiled suggestions. The titles of the officers were taken from the Eleusinian Mysteries she had been introduced to by Mead; alchemy was by now old hat to her. The Tree of Life, 'an objective diagram of the principles working through the Universe', was essential to all other studies in the Order. Both a picture of Creation and a 'comprehensive view of man', it is the central image of the Kabbalah which she had learned from reading Mathers and others: the ten emanations of the sephiroth on the Tree connect the Divine Crown (Malkuth) and this Kingdom (Kether) in two directions, 'the long straight path up through the centre' and the 'winding paths of nature or instinct' symbolized by the jagged flash of lightning downwards through the intermediate sephiroth.[27] The angelic orders of Aquinas are modelled on the Kabbalistic work of Dionysius the Aeropagite and that of Aristotle, all of whom she had also studied by this time. One wonders what her instructors in astrology (Miss K. Moffat and Miss Midgeley) made of their new pupil, already with more knowledge than the rudimentary skills the Order required.

The Outer Order of the Stella Matutina, to which she had now been admitted, consisted of five grades modelled on the first five ascending spheres of the sephiroth (identified with 'various spiritual principles existing in the universe'[28]) from 'the Land of Night' towards 'the Light of the Spirit', each requiring an examination, with admission into the next grade occurring at specified times throughout the year. For the next few years Georgie's life would be regulated by lessons, study, and regular meetings. Assemblies appear to have been held the second Monday of every month except during equinox months; a formal apology was required for missing the equinox ceremonies which 'should be celebrated within at least 48 hours . . . of the actual solar entry' in March and September, at which time the password for the next six months was announced.[29] Examinations, which were strictly monitored, took place in between the regular assemblies:

The Chief Adept in charge desires that each Adept will procure a small M. S. S. Book and enter for himself the Titles and Sub-Divisions of all the Examinations. with this phrase written out for each Examination. 'I the undersigned to this day certify that I have duly examined Quicumque Vault and am satisfied with attainments which have been shown.' This Book must then be produced at each Examination and also on admission to the Grade of Theoricus.[30]

Armed with her prior knowledge, there remained for Georgie before examination as Neophyte (0=0) only to learn the characters and values of the twenty-two letters of the Hebrew alphabet, which she scrupulously copied in the workbook every frater and soror was also required to keep.[31] The 'History for Neophytes 1888' (a somewhat specious account of the Order's origins[32]) was the first document issued. Two months after her initiation, on 27 August, she took notes on 'the angelical hierarchies'; a horoscope for 21 September 1914 at 5.45 p.m. may have marked her attendance at the September equinox festival[33] and advancement to Zelator (1=10, '1 as seen from the earth, 10 as seen from heaven'[34]). A month later, on 23 October, she signed out a copy of 'The Address of the Pillars', one of the early 'Subjects of Study'. Again she encountered much with which she was already familiar—the three pillars, the arrangement of the ten sephiroth, and the Serpent on the Tree of Life with the 'Divine Names' attributed in both Hebrew and English ('This is especially important.'). There was further work in alchemy and astrology: according to the *Sepher Yetzirah*, which she had studied with reference to Pico, each letter of the Hebrew alphabet was linked with a planet, a sign of the zodiac, and assigned a numerical number; in various combinations these in turn were arranged with the different trinities such as the alchemical air, water, and fire. What might have been new—though requiring for accurate divination the same skills of the astrologer—was the introduction to the Tarot, the symbolism of which would later find its way even into her bookplate, as did the Order's symbol for the soul, the Unicorn.[35] Although the well-known Rider pack designed by Pamela Colman Smith was by then in circulation, it had been commissioned by A. E. Waite of the rival mystical Independent and

Rectified Rite; Georgie's own Tarot cards were of French origin. Very early also she received training in the practice of meditation, the first stage towards gaining occult knowledge through one's own inner powers of concentration, and a step towards mastering self-hypnosis.

Horoscopes for 1914, 2 November and 18 December, suggest examinations and advancement to Theoricus (2=9), either before or after she went to Brighton with the Tuckers. While at the seaside they were joined by Yeats and Olivia for a week, but the situation was hardly conducive to extensive discussions of secret rites.[36] She worked hard at her studies, reading far beyond the lectures and flying rolls put at her disposal by the Cancellarius. There must have been some piquancy—as well as confirmation of the equality insisted upon for women in the Order—in studying *The Way of Wisdom* by 'Sapientia Sapienti Dono Data', Olivia's old friend and co-author and the Order's former Chief Adept Florence Farr Emery, now in Ceylon; Georgie had seen her once or twice, probably at the Shakespears.[37]

She returned to her work on Pico, and in the British Museum found other commentaries on the Kabbalah, some of which she had already identified before her admission: five volumes of the *Zohar*, the seventeenth-century *Theatrum Chemicum* by Lazarus Zetzner, Georg von Welling's eighteenth-century *Opus Mago-Kabbalisticum*, a commentary on the apocryphal Book of Enoch, and much more, all of which she scrupulously commented on and quoted in her study books. The sections on reincarnation and the transmigration of souls seem to have been considered especially significant.

Also preserved among Georgie's papers are the ceremony for 3=8, notes on the 'angelical hierarchies', and 'Formula for personal spiritual development' (with diagrams of cones or gyres); she probably received her sash for Practicus at the 24 May 1915 meeting (10.25 p.m.).[38] The next grade, Philosophus, had no specific 'Subjects of Study' designated, although Georgie's notebook for 4=7 includes 'Lecture on the Shemhamphoresch' (and the seventy-two names of God, the fifth knowledge lecture) and 'The Aura of the Earth', a lecture by Dr Felkin dated August 1915. This commentary on the fourth of the six or seven layers of the earth's aura had a profound impact, for here is where 'earth-bound spirits who have sufficiently advanced to become teachers' reside, and from where they draw 'vitality and sustenance from the thoughts and aspirations of their adherents on earth'. Such spiritual beings are constantly on the lookout for any likely and willing candidate 'who by training has gained occult knowledge'. The lecture ends with a stern reminder to do with the use of the Tattwa cards (done at first only under the supervision of a senior member): 'Avoid the tendency to get *individual* teaching through them. Keep to the definite things of each plane.'[39] Two months later she passed examinations on polygons and polygrams, ranging from the triangle, square, and pentangle to the enneagram, dodekagon, and combinations within talismans;[40] a horary for 13 November coincides with the next Order meeting. With the examinations as Philosophus, the candidate had completed all the rituals of the Outer Order of the Stella Matutina, and was allowed to have in her possession the grade rituals and flying rolls.

If invited, one could then pursue studies further in practical magic, eventually becoming a member of the Second or Inner Order, the RR et AC (Rosae Rubeae et Aureae Crucis), 'our link with the invisible Degrees'.[41] This was a serious step, not to be taken lightly:

Your instructions in the several Grades of the 'G.D. in the Outer' have been intellectual exercises in the symbolism of medieval and ancient occult science. . . . But it is not only an intellectual study of these pages which is needed; it is hoped that you have, to some extent, clothed the dry bones with life and force and have been able to spiritualize and idealize the names and forms and symbols laid before you; for it is especially to the psychic and then to the spiritual places of thought and formation that you will be in future led. . . . For this new development of yourself, two requirements are essential; a *Clean Life*, and an *Indomitable Will*. . . . In the Second Order, we are still very human but not only human—we are *attempting* to be ultra-human, i. e. divine. If you enter there, you must be in thought and practice like an Angel, one who has passed beyond contract worship. . . . The occult burden is not light, it is not easy to bear, be warned in time, for the higher you rise—the more terrible the fall—if you should fall.[42]

No wonder Georgie, when she reached 5=6 in 1916, was 'upset' during the ceremony.[43] But her studies continued to circle back to that 'practical mystic'[44] Plotinus, from whom she had first learned that 'the endeavour is not to be without sin, but to be a God'.

First, however, she had to cross the bridge or portal between the orders. Nine months must elapse before the 'Lords and Ladies of the Portal' were allowed to move to Zelator Adeptus Minor, the first stage of 5=6. Practical instruction was given in ritual or Enochian magic (a language received by the Elizabethan John Dee and his skryer Edward Kelley from the angels appearing in their crystal),[45] and 'Enochian chess', devised by MacGregor Mathers. Entry into the Inner Order required that she present herself carrying a Lotus wand of her own making, decorated with the twelve colours of the zodiac plus black and white, which she must then consecrate on her own. (The white end was for invocation, the black end for banishing.[46]) The ritual of Self-Transformation evoked the goddess Isis; the ritual of Contemplation demanded that she ponder upon masks of Osiris ('the Redeemer'), lion, eagle, and ox and, standing outside herself and beholding her own mask, attempt to observe her personality as others see it.[47] Now theory was fortified by practice: the production of visions through skrying (using a symbol as a mirror, with or without the aid of implements), meditation on symbols designed to lead to astral travel, invocations, the creation of talismans. Much time was devoted to the making and consecration of instruments involved in the rituals, all of which were designed, like the methods of divination taught in the Outer Order, to stimulate further 'the faculties of clairvoyance, imagination, and intuition'.[48]

Exclusive to the Inner Order and central to its ceremonies was the seven-sided Vault of the Adepti, containing a circular altar and the Pastos which represented the tomb of the allegorical Christian Rosencreutz; the walls, floor, and ceiling were painted with astrological, alchemical symbols and Hebrew letters.[49] According to Yeats's recorded impression, the candidate for 6=5 lay down blindfolded in the Pastos, while the ritual continued through the ringing of thirty-six bells.[50] 'After being symbolically buried, triumphantly he rises from the tomb of Osiris in a glorious resurrection through the descent of the white Light of the Spirit.'[51] Thereafter, once purified, the Adept could enter the Vault, either singly or with others, to participate in magical work. It was even permissible to lie down in the Pastos and meditate.

By now the Adept was expected to be familiar with all aspects of the syncretist doctrine of the Golden Dawn. There exists among the papers preserved by Georgie, in her hand and others, an intricately detailed diagram illustrating the 'Minutum Mundum' or 'Hodos Chameleonis', drawing together in the Tree of Life and its three columns the four colour scales relating to the four elements and Tarot symbols, Hebrew letters, Kabbalistic and sephirothic names, various combinations of the cross, pentagram, and circle, branches of the Tree of Knowledge of Good and Evil, the zigzag descent of the lightning flash, the serpentine movement upwards through the middle column, the parts of the human body, the angelic hierarchy, and quotations from the New Testament narrating the various stages in the life of Christ. This knowledge was expected of the candidate who had passed through the portal. 'D.E.D.I.' had warned his fellow Adepts over a decade earlier, 'The link that unites us to that Supreme Life. . . is a double link. It is not merely an ascent, that has for symbols the climbing of the Serpent through the Tree of life and of the Adepti through the Degrees that we know of, but a descent that is symbolised by the Lightning Flash among the sacred leaves.' The message would reappear in Georgie's automatic script.[52]

It is tempting to think that 'Demon', in addition to being her sponsor, may have been the Adept in charge of training the newly admitted 'Nemo'; given the strict insistence upon secrecy, this might explain Yeats's later evasive explanation to Nelly Tucker that in November 1915 he and her daughter shared 'only a mutual interest in astrology'.[53] Clearly by now they had considerably more mutual interests. Yeats, whose initiation had taken place on 7 March 1890, was promoted on 10 January 1912 to the second stage of the first grade of the Inner Order, Theoricus Adeptus Minor (5=6); he reached 6=5 (Adeptus Major) on 16 October 1914 (with a newly devised ritual by Dr Felkin) and may have advanced as far as 7=4 (Adeptus Exemptus) by 1916.[54] Georgie Hyde Lees reached Zelator Adeptus

Minor (5=6 first stage) in May 1916. According to General Orders compiled by
the Chief Dr Felkin in 1914, five years must elapse between 5=6 and 6=5, requiring eight more examinations and five stages, although she told Richard Ellmann
that she had reached 6=5.[55] Unless the situation altered after the Felkins left
England for New Zealand in 1916, 'Nemo Sciat' could not have reached Theoricus
AM until 1921. But it had taken her less than three years to accomplish what
had taken Willy Yeats twenty-two. When they withdrew from the Golden Dawn,
there was only one degree between them.

Both Orders were governed by three ruling chiefs; officers in the Outer Order
were appointed for six months, each member installed in office as he or she
became eligible. The office of Hierophant was reserved for those fratres and
sorores who had reached Zelator Adeptus Minor; but even a Neophyte could
hold the office of Sentinel. Once reaching the Inner Order, however, 'Members
find for themselves whether their line is in taking Office, Astral watching, or in
serving the group in some other capacity.' They might even leave the group and
work alone. One special duty of Inner members required attendance—unless there
was 'a reasonable excuse for absence'—at the annual ceremony on the summer
solstice (the Day of Corpus Christi) to reconsecrate the Vault; in addition 'certain
kinds of outside work or service may be considered as Order Work'.[56] Georgie
seems to have remained active within the Order, serving as an examiner until at
least 1920 and teaching the use of Tattwa symbols, 'the earliest experiments in
clairvoyance', closely integrated with the study of the first and second layers of
the earth's aura.[57] For this, members were expected to make their own set of cards
of five coloured forms symbolizing the four elements—yellow square or cube for
earth, sky-blue disc or circle for air, red equilateral triangle for fire, silver crescent
for water—and a black oval or egg for the ether or spirit. Beginning with simple
'mirror-like vision' (a double experience for left-handed Georgie), meditation
in time produced a series of images leading one through the chosen element as
through a door; with practice one symbol could be superimposed on another,
offering further trance truths and clairvoyant experiences.[58] Additional symbols
employed for meditation and active visions were the pentagram (five-pointed
star), the seal of Solomon (six-pointed star), and the Tarot cards themselves.

Symbols were powerful, could 'act in their own right and with little consideration for our intentions, however excellent', Yeats had warned his fellow magicians
many years previously.[59] Georgie would have been familiar with his special
lecture on 'The Power of Symbols', taken down at great speed by an anonymous
scribe. The names of Freud and Jung are evoked in passing; although Yeats took
issue with Frederic Myers's terminology for subliminal ('that mysterious part
which influences us without our consciousness') and superliminal consciousness ('occupied with the daily details of life'), preferring the terms '*impersonal* &
personal consciousness':

I understand impersonal consciousness to be that condition when in profound sleep the ordinary observation of dreams & physical twilight passes away & we get into another state of intense psychical *life* when we see scenes of beauty & persons so vividly that the individual is simply a 'seeing' eye & a 'hearing' ear & all his thinking powers are vividly alert & as it were *more* alive than ever before. . . . occultism is the power of getting into our daily lives this 'impersonal consciousness' this intense spiritual individuality, which is not personal. . . . The aim of occultism is to acquire this power of impersonal being. . . . All nature is a ritual of symbols & when we analyse it we find something powerful & mysterious in these symbols. . . . There is symbolism of the arts just as much as a symbolism of magic. The symbolism of nature is too vague to be used consciously therefore temples and orders have created and used symbolism from it. . . .

With this narrowed ritual which we create we find symbol is answered by the starting out from the depths of our own mind of symbols & powers we have never known with our ordinary mind. . . . We may be forced into another concept altogether—that this is not memory but entrance into a world that is timeless—that ideas of past present & future are mere forms of perception & that the events of the past are still taking place. The final result of evocation & meditation is to enter into such relations that you could share in the multiform life of this world. There you enter into the presence of a great mystery & receive a curious sense of great things doing around you for which you are occasionally used. The mere repetition of symbols is nothing in itself. To fix yourself on groups of symbols by which you put yourself into new relations is not successful unless you have a sense of being more alive than ever before.[60]

Neither Yeats nor Georgie would have guessed the 'great mystery' that would arise 'from the depths' of their own minds in just a few more years.

Before then Georgie in her turn would sponsor other candidates. On 8 August 1915 her grandmother's friend and Nelly's cousin by marriage, Beatrice Caroline Erskine, was admitted as number 482 on the roll, her motto 'Carpe Diem'. Mrs Erskine reached 4=7 by May 1916, at the same ceremony in which Harold Montagu Hyde-Lees was admitted as 'Amore Sitis Uniti' (number 503 on the roll). Doubtless coached by his sister, Harold's advancement was extraordinarily quick: he was admitted to 4=7 by 8 December and the portal on 30 July 1917, entering the Second Order (number 245) on 1 May 1918.[61]

But no ceremony, secret sign, or invocation could ward off the threat hovering over the external world in 1914, however much Georgie and her colleagues fixed their gaze on celestial matters. Just fifteen weeks after Dorothy and Ezra's marriage, Germany invaded Belgium; obliged by treaty, the next day Britain joined her allies Russia and France by declaring war on Germany and, a week later, on Austria-Hungary. Although Germany had long been prepared to fight a land war (and Britain long considered an enemy to progress), no one could foresee the toll this long drawn-out deadlock would take—an estimated eight and a half million soldiers dead as a result of wounds or disease, perhaps as many more maimed for life, countless civilian casualties—and the catapulting of the entire world into a state of mechanized murderous tension. At first few took the situation seriously, although Prime Minister Asquith persuaded the Irish leaders to accept postponement of Home Rule, and many eager young men, including Lady Gregory's only son Robert, rushed to enlist with public school fervour. Ezra watched as first Richard Aldington, then Wyndham Lewis and Gaudier-Brzeska (whose hieratic head of Pound graced the pages of the second and final number of *Blast*) donned uniforms; as an American he remained aloof. Instead, punctuated by weekly dinner gatherings he and Violet Hunt arranged in Soho, Ezra wrote his essay on Vorticism, borrowing liberally from G. R. S. Mead.[62] Yeats meanwhile continued to write *his* essay on 'Swedenborg, Mediums and the Desolate Places' and to pursue Elizabeth Radcliffe's controls for advice on his complex personal life, but postponed his journey to India. By October the d'Aranyi sisters and their mother were settled in London, soon to embark on a series of benefit concerts in Lady Ottoline Morrell's drawing room.

Georgie's life at first was affected only by seeing her uncles once more in uniform and listening to the speculations of the aged soldiers who gathered around Olivia's tea table.[63] It was still difficult to believe activities in England could be disrupted. This may have been the summer Nelly invited Grace and her brother to holiday in Southwold; in August Ezra's parents had arrived from Philadelphia to meet their new daughter-in-law; in September, after Homer Pound had returned to his work, Georgie joined the Shakespears, Dorothy, Ezra, and his mother in Aldeburgh,[64] coming back to London in time for the solstice meeting of the Golden Dawn. Harold, down from Oxford, started work at Oxford House, a Settlement House in the East End of London, the first step on his path towards clerical orders; according to his cousin Grace, his anti-Semitism was becoming increasingly obvious in the lives he chose (or did not choose) to improve.[65] Then in September John Redmond created disenchantment within the Irish Parliamentary Party by pledging the National Volunteers to support the war. 'London is strange', wrote May Morris from Hammersmith,'—quiet in the day, dark at night: at Charing Cross a great search-light sweeps over the dark city after dark, and a little while back in the day one might watch the great Admiralty air-ships in the flawless mid-day sky.'[66] By the end of 1914 Egypt had been declared a British protectorate and some British troops were massed for the attack on the Dardanelles, but still people were reluctant to acknowledge that the war would not soon be over.[67]

Ezra and Dorothy both by inclination and American citizenship were unhappy bystanders; when the barracks installed across from Kensington Church Street caused constant anti-aircraft noise, they were doubtless relieved to accompany Yeats to Stone Cottage from January to March 1915. Unaware that as 'registered aliens' they should not have been in a restricted area, they were visited by the police early in February. Seeking the necessary routine for his writing, Yeats reported to Lady Gregory, 'I am working well here at Coleman's Hatch, I go up to London for my Monday evenings. . . . Ezra and his wife are very pleasant companions. One likes having young people about one—they fit with one's way.'[68] However, he did not approve of Dorothy's chosen painting style. He described his companions in more detail to the ailing Mabel Beardsley:

[Dorothy] looks as if her face was made out of Dresden china. I look at her in perpetual wonder. It is so hard to believe she is real; yet she spends all her daylight hours drawing the most monstrous cubist pictures. I am sure her real test would be to paint with very little brushes, & draw neat outlines with a pencil she took half the morning making sharp enough. She is merely playing up to the revolutionary energy of her husband. . . . I feel quite sure that Ezra & his wife who are obviously devoted must have fallen in love out of sheer surprise & bewilderment they are so unlike each other.[69]

Later Ezra would claim that Lady Gregory used to motor down to Stone Cottage with prospective brides, including Elizabeth Asquith, for the older poet. Aside from the occasional inquisitive visit this is highly unlikely given her responsibilities at Coole and the reputed candidate's involved personal life in London.[70]

The Pounds never mentioned any visit by Georgie during the two winters they were with Yeats at Coleman's Hatch. Nor within the Pound circle is there any hint of other close male friendships Georgie may have enjoyed, at least of her own age. There were pleasant forays to the Reades' country home at Ipsden where she could enjoy the country walks and a rich library. In London there was always art and music—performances both private and public by Walter Rummel on his frequent visits from Paris, recitals by the d'Aranyi sisters at the Aeolian Hall or the Classical Concert Society, exhibitions and tea at the Three Arts Club and elsewhere with Eva Ducat, lectures at the Lyceum Club, meetings with Dorothy and Ezra on their regular journeys back to Kensington.[71] She was a cheerful, witty companion, always ready for the next adventure.

She was also becoming increasingly interested in those scripts by Bessie Radcliffe that so absorbed WBY and Eva Fowler. In addition to the languages and personal identifications intriguing to Yeats, there were numerous symbols—crosses, candles, flames, hands, hearts; crescents, orbs, sun, moon, star, squares, and triangles; antique vases, flowers, vessels of incense; arrows, boats, helmets, pennants, bridges, and gates; serpents, wings, books, eyes open and shut; and, most frequently, birds. Though crudely drawn, the images were often arranged in patterns as complex as the secret diagrams of the Golden Dawn. On 4 March 1915 Eva Fowler wrote concerning the statement 'There will be four', which occurred a number of times in Bessie's automatic writing. 'Dearest G. . . . Your letter *hasn't* come. Bring your symbols etc up with you and we will try to compare notes. With love E. Written in awful haste just off to work.'[72] Their meeting may well have been related to a further unspecified significant moment (for Georgie or Yeats or both) which occurred that same month. Was Georgie to be the fourth investigator, or something more personal still? Bessie's scripts were beginning to reveal more about Willy than he realized.

Eva's 'work' had doubtless to do with the war, which more and more civilians were required to support. Zeppelin attacks on England began in January 1915; there would be many more that year. The German raids were scheduled to arrive over the target area at night in the dark of the moon, and very soon a system of blackouts darkened both countryside and cities, making movement about the streets treacherous and adventurous.[73] But it was not until March and the Battle of Neuve-Chapelle, first of the siege warfare battles, that the strange sight of dirigibles floating silently overhead caused more than a frisson of excitement. In April, the Germans introduced chemical warfare; 'For me', Vera Brittain wrote in her diary, 'I think the days are over of sheltered physical comfort and unruffled peace of mind. I don't think they will ever come again.'[74]

Three days later, on 25 April, Georgie's maternal uncle Kenny Woodmass died in action at Ypres; he was 38. Two weeks passed and a German U-boat sank the *Lusitania*, a loss of 1,195 passengers and crew, including Lady Gregory's nephew and Yeats's friend Hugh Lane. By now long convoys of casualties began their progress through the London streets. 'London . . . looks distinctly more abnormal now—more soldiers, more bandages and limps, and more nurses— quite a sensational sense of strain. Raw recruits led by band still make one cry and everywhere the rather undignified, bullying posters—very, very dark at night,' noted Cynthia Asquith. Maud Gonne wrote to Yeats from Paris, where she and her daughter Iseult (always referred to publicly as her 'niece', later her 'cousin'[75]) were nursing, 'It seems quite natural now to have a Zeppelin or an airship overhead & to watch for the falling bombs as one would watch a display of fireworks & to listen to shrapnel rattling on the roofs of the houses like hail stones, & to open the windows & get a better view.'[76] Italy joined the Allies by signing the Treaty of London in April and formally entering the war in May. Later that month London experienced its first Zeppelin raid; the giant airship hovered above for more than ten minutes, releasing more than 150 bombs and incendiaries; forty-two were killed or wounded. By mid-October 1915 there had been twenty-two raids, mainly against London and its suburbs, not only causing many casualties but starting large fires. St Paul's barely escaped; the theatrical district was decimated. The Zeppelins still brought out excited onlookers, as enthusiastically described by one court reporter: 'The giant airship was played upon by two searchlights and in their radiance she looked a thing of silvery beauty sailing serenely through the cool night, indifferent to the big gun roaring at her from the Green Park, whose shells seemed to burst in the manner of sparkling fireworks just below her, more like a welcome than a threat.'[77] May Morris's description of the raid might have been taken over wholesale by Bernard Shaw for *Heartbreak House*:

It came on a still night of the most majestic starlight I've ever seen, after a lovely sunset with delicate crescent moon. Across the water opposite, a huge booming (of the biggest gun round the city) travelled up the great path of light that was searching the N. E. sky, and there, among the stars were little sparks and moving stars—the anti-air-craft aeroplane guns . . . worrying the big monster. I was not in the least alarmed, it was all too strange, but spent the night in a state of intense excitement—waiting (foolishly enough) for *more*.[78]

Dictating to Miss Jacobs in her office across from the British Museum, Yeats rushed out to join the crowd. The next day he added a footnote in his letter to Lady Gregory: 'The Zeppelin was much nearer than I thought the other night. It smashed a house or two in Greys [*sic*] Inn & in Kings Way & in Chancery Lane. A friends housekeeper has written to him from somewhere in that neighbourhood "Providence has preserved us but we are very shook up." '[79] Then all was quiet over London until the end of January.[80]

The devastating failure of the joint offensive at Champagne and Loos (where the British retaliated with their own use of chlorine) led to further horrific convoys of wounded men to the London hospitals. 'September 25th remains with July 1st and March 21st, one of the three dates on which the "In Memoriam" notices in *The Times* fill the whole of one column and run on into the next,' observed Brittain.[81] Yeats wrote to New York lawyer John Quinn that to him the war 'is merely the most expensive outbreak of insolence and stupidity the world has ever seen, and I give it as little of my thoughts as I can'.[82] But he sympathized with his friend Augusta Gregory's 'daily terror overshadowing everything' while her son was fighting, and with her he visited mediums in an effort to contact Hugh Lane.[83] Bessie Radcliffe's duties as a nurse interfered with their regular sessions, and besides, many of the messages she now received were, she reported, 'just snatches from a few people who died fighting—nothing interesting'.[84] Dorothy's father Hope Shakespear volunteered his skills as a craftsman, making wooden limbs for returning amputees; he would receive a Red Cross award for his work. Meanwhile Yeats contemplated the purchase of Ballylee Castle, the Norman keep which had been part of the original Coole estate, 'though if I remain unmarried I would find it useless (I am too blind for the country alone & too fond of company)'.[85]

Georgie continued to haunt antiquarian bookstores, in June 1915 discovering a reprint of the sixteenth-century anthology compiled by Silvestro Meuccio, *Abbas Joachim Magnus Propheta*, a collection of works attributed to Joachim de Fiore. And she diligently practised her astrology, adding to her library further volumes by 'Sepharial' (Walter Gorn Old) and consulting the works in French of Jean Baptiste Morin de Villefranche in the British Museum.[86] At Yeats's request, she devoted much time to calculating his 'primaries' and providing rectifications to his own calculations; drawing up a progressed horoscope for himself at the age of 50, he glumly noted, 'probably as I grow older [Venus] does less mischief'.[87] But Georgie's remarkable ability to compartmentalize her interests that would be so valuable in future years could not blot out the horrors of war. In mid-October 1915 she turned 23, the minimum age accepted for nurses in an army hospital under the War Office, and by November she had reported for duty as part-time member of the Voluntary Aid Detachment Programme, London/50 detachment, Kensington Division. However, her first assignment by Commandant Lady Florence Norman was not in Kensington but to Endsleigh Palace Hospital for Officers at 25 Gordon Street, just yards away from Yeats's home in Woburn Buildings. Formerly a hotel, the Endsleigh Palace was but one of some 4,500 buildings which were offered for use as temporary hospitals; many were private mansions, and the Red Cross Society was responsible for equipping and staffing those deemed suitable. VAD members were also carefully scrutinized, for members of the nursing units were considered to have the same status as male commissioned officers, chosen as they were primarily from the middle and upper classes.[88] Young Jiddu Krishnamurti, already selected by Annie Besant as theosophy's next 'World Teacher', helped scrub out the Endsleigh Palace in preparation, but was not allowed to nurse because of his colour.[89]

Alongside obligatory courses in first aid and home nursing which were taught at the Kensington Training Centre—and for those destined to nurse in the hospitals, a month-long course in the local infirmary—Georgie studied hygiene and cookery; Miss Phoenix Norton 'gave practical cooking classes and lectures, and two demonstrations on War Rationing and Daily Application'.[90] George never forgot her indignation when, being taught to make Neaves food for invalids, one of her classmates ate all the lumps before submitting her sample for approval. Her first appointment was as pantry orderly, where she helped with the serving of meals, clearing, and washing up. Every VAD remembers scrubbing oilskin tables, washing lockers, 'a long blur of mops, taps, brooms, and plates'. She then became a nursing assistant, working on the wards. The hours were long—twelve-hour shifts with three hours' break—and the semi-trained Volunteers were frequently looked upon as a threat to the trained nurses' struggle for registration. Dressed in her street uniform of dark blue crêpe de chine veil and the orthodox cloak, Georgie could feel useful.[91] In the Red Cross archives, her address is given as Tavistock Square, possibly a temporary nurses' hostel, but more likely the address recorded after her marriage. During her first few days as a VAD a bomb smashed buildings in Gray's Inn Square, uncomfortably nearby.[92]

The Golden Dawn was stimulated to greater efforts, even the contemplation of 'The Second Coming'. In November Dr Felkin announced that he had been told by members of the 'Third' Order that

C. R. C. [Father Christian Rosenkreuz] himself expects to manifest again on the material plane before very long. I do not know whether he will return as an infant, or whether as sometimes happens he may assume a suitable body which has already reached maturity. . . . Now it will be possible to define a little more clearly the different Grades . . . Kether

10=1 Rosenkreuz (Sixth Order); Chokmah and Bina, 9=2 members on the Material Plane, but secluded (Fifth Order); Daath 8=3. Members who may be contacted actively (Fourth Order); Chesed, 7=4 Your own highest Members and Geburah, 6=5 Next highest Members (Third Order); Tipareth 5=6 (Second Order 0=0 to Portal inclusive (First Order).

Satisfied with his reorganization (which borrowed directly from the Kabbalist *sephiroth*), Felkin then departed for New Zealand.[93]

Work in Georgie's Golden Dawn notebook is interrupted by a page of nourishing beef tea recipes, lists of metallic poisons, acids, and alkalis, and a diagram depicting the structure of the heart. On the opposite page is a horary for 13 November 1915; although later George and Willy had difficulty recalling the specific date—17, 22, or 'a Sunday 2.15 p.m.', probably Sunday 21 November— both agreed that the occasion was profoundly significant.[94] It is likely that, as their meetings both public and private became more frequent, Yeats now first began to consider her as candidate for the 'woman That gives up all her mind', as he had expressed his longing the previous year in the poem 'On Woman'. Nelly was certainly alert to that possibility, fearing as early as November 1915 that he meant to propose to her daughter. Her suspicions would be confirmed by his admission to Lady Gregory in September 1917, 'We had our talk alone two years ago.'[95] His sister Lily also noticed that he was thinking more about marriage; to her he was just as evasive in his reply, 'No I have not found anybody on a staircase. It may be symbolic—I have been doing psychic work it might refer to—but that is all too vague. One never knows what goes on in the dream life.'[96] I have discovered no hint of any other romance for Georgie, who may have been captivated by Yeats as early as 1911, when she was only 18. Yeats on the other hand was a very experienced lover, as Nelly astutely realized, and by now Georgie herself was familiar with much of his private life. Sometime after mid-November 1915, on a visit to her cousin Grace who was attending Cheltenham Ladies College, she confided that she was 'engaged to marry the well-known poet, William Butler Yeats'—and made her promise not to tell Nelly.[97] Hers would be a long, one-sided commitment.

At the end of December 1915 the Pounds once more joined Yeats at Stone Cottage; they were there until 6 March, while the German raids increased in intensity and Britain introduced conscription. Yeats refused a knighthood and spoke more and more of buying property at Ballylee. Georgie quite enjoyed her shifts as cook at Endsleigh Hospital, but the experience may have encouraged her attendance at séances—where she regularly encountered grieving relatives seeking solace. Even non-believers snatched at the hope of a message; Vera Brittain described one of her last discussions with her fiancé, 'We could not honestly admit that we thought we should survive, though we would have given anything in the world to believe in a life to come, but he promised me that if he died in

France he would try to come back and tell me that the grave was not the end of our love.'⁹⁸ Georgie attended séances with Etta Wriedt, and as 'Miss Hyde' visited Mrs Handcock, whom she thought 'exceedingly good'. Clearly more important for her were the sittings with Gladys Osborne Leonard, not yet popular or well known. By then Georgie's youngest uncle Robert Woodmass had died in an asylum for 'gentlemen of unsound mind' (most likely aggravated by his experiences in the South African War) and only Nelly's eldest brother George (retired after a distinguished military career but still a member of the Reserve), survived.

Eager for experiences, 'something always *might* happen', she sent the following record, in an envelope with her signature over the seal, to Stone Cottage:

January 21.1916.
Mrs Leonard & G Hyde Lees. Table sitting.
— — — — — —
Several too personal things— — — — — —
—I. 'But I am not going to India on Government work'—
Table. 'Not *you*.'
I. 'Who is going?'
T. 'George'
I. 'What George?'
T. 'Uncle'.
I. 'My uncle'
T. '*Yes*.'
. . .
I. 'What government work?'
T. 'Soldier'
I. 'When will he go?'
T. 'March'
I. 'Will he be there long'
T. 'No'
I. 'How soon will he come back?'
T. 'No'
I. 'Is he going to live there?'
T. 'No'
I. 'Then is he going to die there?'
T. 'Yes' (very slow & hard)
I. 'In connection with the war?'
T. 'No'
I. 'Will Kitty go?'
T. 'No.'
I. 'When shall we hear that he is going?'
T. 'February.'
I. 'What date?'
T. No answer.

I. 'Early in February'
T. 'No'
I. 'Middle?'
T. 'Yes'
I. 'Are you sure?'
T. 'Yes' (again very slow, slower)
I. 'Will he die through an accident?
T. 'No'
                                                    (Then on to something else.)[99]

Unfortunately, there is no record of the Pounds'—or Yeats's—reaction. Captain Woodmass moved not to India but Canada, and lived on to divorce his wife Kitty, and to remarry.

In February 1916 Georgie was seconded to London/30 detachment at 27 Berkeley Square, Westminster Division, to work as a nursing assistant under Commandant Mrs Salisbury Jones, who had turned her home over to the Red Cross. The hospital, which opened on 1 March 1916, was again for officers only but much smaller than the Endsleigh Palace, with twenty-two beds tended by two trained nurses (who were put up next door), and twelve whole-time and nine part-time VAD members. Here Georgie's work increased, washing floors, making beds, helping with dressings, emptying bedpans, and generally caring for the patients; there were many cases of trench feet and the deathly chill that followed shell-shock.[100] Once she gained experience, she was responsible for carrying out treatments on her own, and while on night duty was expected to take charge of the ward. Cynthia Asquith describes what Georgie too must have endured: 'A ghastly afternoon of blanket baths. . . . Some of the men had to be washed in bed, others given the wherewithal and left, and others had to go to the bathroom; some had to be rubbed with methylated spirit in one place, some in two, and some not at all; and some had to be given clean top sheet and clothes, some clothes not sheets, . . . Strange how quickly I have grown reconciled to the word "pus".'[101] The Red Cross reported approvingly of 'the discipline which prevailed; in very few cases was advantage taken of the comparative freedom from restriction'. Brittain, while admiring the 'first-rate physical type' of many of the patients, and coming to terms with day-by-day contact with male anatomy, records the shock of the 'butcher's-shop appearance of the uncovered wounds'. Especially after the Battle of the Somme, when the British Army suffered 57,470 casualties on 1 July 1916 alone, the wounded included 'men without faces, without eyes, without limbs, men almost disembowelled, men with hideous truncated stumps of bodies'.[102]

Working part-time in a small hospital which recorded only one death among 496 admissions, Georgie was spared much of the horror, but was never comfortable with her nursing duties. Once on the wards her watch stopped and all the wounded men laughed, telling her that was a sign of fear. Years later, when her daughter was practising for her first aid badge in the Girl Guides, 'she shied away and said "Oh no, it brought back the war memories and she couldn't bear it." ' By now she was sleepwalking frequently and had to be tied to the bed.[103] Determined to maintain some normalcy, she continued her studies of early religious history, spending long hours in the British Museum, and—encouraged perhaps by her experience at séances—purchased the popular *Apotheosis and After Life* by Mrs Arthur Strong (Eugenie Sellers), a friend of Thomas Sturge Moore.[104]

Much as he tried, Yeats could not escape wartime activities either. The first performance of his Noh-style play *At the Hawk's Well* was in Lady Cunard's drawing room at 20 Cavendish Square on the afternoon of 2 April 1916; Olivia and Eva Fowler had attended the dress rehearsal the previous Friday. In the audience at Emerald Cunard's was Miss Stoddart ('Il faut chercher') of the Golden Dawn, and probably Dorothy, for Ezra was very much involved backstage. The society pages do not include Georgie and her mother among those present either then or two days later at Lady Islington's, 8 Chesterfield Gardens, when the play was again performed for the Social Institutes' Union for Women and Girls in the presence of Queen Alexandra (and T. S. Eliot, brought by Ezra). But they were not really 'in society' and their presence (or absence) would not have been noted; it would be surprising if neither Olivia nor Georgie attended if 'Il faut chercher' had. The masks and dresses were designed by Edmund Dulac, who played the role of the Chief Musician and seems also to have been stage director. Yeats was already contemplating another dance play on the subject of Cuchulain, *The Only Jealousy of Emer*, but was having difficulty determining the roles of the characters.[105] Nine days later he was one of the ten poets reading in aid of the Star and Garter Fund, organized by Elizabeth Asquith. 'Yeats recited four poems preciously, but really rather beautifully. Wonderful to be able to do it, no paralysing sense of humour there.'[106] Touched by Iseult's paleness when she arrived in London from nursing alongside her mother in France, Yeats agreed to return with her to Maud Gonne's country home in Normandy. Looking 'very distinguished and . . . full of self-possession', Iseult accompanied him to lunch with Bernard Shaw and to William Rothenstein's exhibition of portraits at the Leicester Gallery. Proud of the 'little stir' her beauty was making, he reported to Lady Gregory, 'She seems to have suddenly grown up, & has thrown off all her old anarchic ideas about life. She explained to me yesterday that because of her birth she must never be bohemian in any way'; no matter that she was conventionally introduced as Maud's cousin, her illegitimacy was well recognized.[107] On 22 May he invited her to dine at Woburn Buildings to meet the Pounds. It is impossible to believe that by now Georgie had not met, or at least heard of, the beauteous Iseult.

Georgie continued to advance in the Amoun Temple, which with the Felkins' departure was now in the care of Dr William Hammond, librarian at Freemasons'

Hall, and Christina Stoddart. Yeats was struck at how unusually emotional Georgie was when taking the 5=6 obligation as Zelator Adeptus Minor in May 1916.[108] She was now his colleague in the Second Order, swearing to 'keep secret all things connected with this order & its secret knowledge from the whole world, equally from him who is a member of the first order of the Golden Dawn as from an uninitiated person, & that I will maintain the veil of strict secrecy between the First and Second orders'. Gaining admission to 'the Vault of the Mystic Mountain', she was now herself qualified to serve as Hiereus, although there is no record that she actually did.[109] Eight further examinations were required:

A—Preliminary written and Viva Voce and Practical—covering the Obligation, Minutum Mundum Diagram, use of Tarot cards, Rose Cross and Sigils, Ritual of Pentagram and Ritual of Hexagram.; B—Elemental (on the magical implements); C—Psychic (judging visions from Tattwa cards); D—Divination (astrology, geomancy and Tarot); E—Magic (talismans, flashing tablets, ascending planes, vibratory mode, etc); F—Elemental Enochian Tablet (especially 'the 16 Servient Squares of each Lesser Angle, as to angel, Sphynx and God'); G—Symbolical ('Symbols and Formulae from the Neophyte Ritual'); and finally, H—Consecration or Evocation.[110]

There was more than one reason for Georgie's agitation during the ceremony that May. The Easter Monday uprising had turned all eyes towards Ireland once again, and among the small band proclaiming an Irish Republic was John MacBride. On 5 May he was executed and his estranged wife Maud Gonne was now free. Yeats consulted various mediums as to whether he should marry Maud, though with her visit to London Iseult was rapidly becoming another possible candidate for 'the torch's splendour'.[111] Georgie, twenty-two months older than Iseult, might already have divined that further threat; in any case, a retrospective horoscope would identify July 1916 as one of her 'moments of greatest disquiet'. Her chief weapon in capturing Yeats's interest, in addition to partnership in the Order, was her skill as astrologer. It can be no coincidence that the following letter to the editor appeared in the July 1916 issue of the *Occult Review*, 'A monthly magazine devoted to the investigation of supernormal phenomena and the study of psychological problems':

Probably among the readers of the OCCULT REVIEW there are some who could supply the information for which I am seeking and for which I should be most grateful. Would you be so kind as to include this letter among the correspondence of your next issue?

I want the hour, and for preference the *exact time*, of birth of the following persons:—

Theobald Wolfe Tone, Daniel O'Connell, Lord Frederick Cavendish, Charles Stewart Parnell, Burke, Lord Edward Fitzgerald, Isaac Butt, William Pitt, Robert Emmet, Henry Grattan, O'Leary, Cavour, Garibaldi, Cardinal Antonelli, Von Moltke, Metternich, John Henry Newman, Rousseau, Pope Leo XIII, Pope Pius IX, J. H.[*sic*] Pearse, Connolly Jim Larkin, Napoleon III.

If any one is good enough to communicate any information as to these dates, would they very kindly mention on what authority their statements are founded. The times are required for certain calculations in Mundane Astrology connected with the events preceding the War, and a misquoted time makes all conclusions hopelessly incorrect.[112]

By design, or editorial carelessness, the letter was signed 'George Hyde Lees'. Either way, like the occasional signature in her library, it signified an important change to come.

Georgie may have got the original idea for this ambitious project from *A Thousand and One Notable Nativities: 'The Astrologer's "Who's Who"'* by Alan Leo (William Frederick Allen), a volume recommended by the Golden Dawn; her copy is heavily underlined and annotated, the correspondences between England and Ireland noted. She may also have been influenced by Steiner's concept of great 'individualities' directing history; her papers include a series of astrological horoscopes for philosophers, royalties, politicians, soldiers, scientists, as well as for the Union of England and Ireland in 1801. It would appear, given the inconsistency (and occasional error) in naming, especially the Irish notables included in her letter, that she enlisted Willy's help in compiling her list. She bought further astrological textbooks.[113]

Busily preparing for his journey to France with Iseult, Yeats was meanwhile reassuring Lady Gregory that Ireland and the Abbey Theatre were not being overlooked. He recommended Ezra as manager, for 'the army cannot touch him & . . . he showed over "At the Hawk's Well" real theatrical capacity'. Reluctantly Pound agreed to go to Dublin for four months if he was required, but, given his own frenzied schedule, was doubtless relieved that an Irishman was found instead. The same letter to Lady Gregory expressed Yeats's ambivalence towards any marriage:

I very nearly wrote to make a compact with you as a refuge from some moment of weakness in myself. Then as my mind grew more settled that did not seem necessary. The compact would have been that for the sake of the movement I should not marry unless Maud Gonne gave up all politics including amnesty . . . I think this resolution of mine may make marriage impossible & yet I see no other way. I would gladly see her work at charity such as her movement for feeding the children or any movement that combined different political parties. I do not see much likelihood of any other marriage for only a violent shock & a claim such as this could persuade me to give so much pain deliberately. As I grow older impulse declines.

Maud rejected him; it would be bad for their work, and anyway, she claimed she was 'too old' for him. He then became 'very much taken up' with Iseult. He felt 'very unsure of everything'.[114] Georgie had every reason to be emotional that hot sultry summer.

The devastating losses from the Battle of the Somme—57,470 casualties in
the British army on 1 July alone—resulted in further long convoys of wounded
soldiers in a 'prevailing odour of wounds and stinking streets'. The vibration of
the guns could be felt as far as London.[115] On 3 August Roger Casement joined
the lengthening list of Irish executions. Still Yeats remained in France, now
openly courting Iseult, 'established not as husband not as father'. Eva Fowler
gardened all day in Kent, entertained Jelly d'Aranyi (who would soon begin her
musical partnership with Myra Hess), and worried over Bessie's script each
evening; whether from the raids, casualties, or a more personal cause, Olivia was
also in the country, ill from an undentified shock.[116] Later that month London
experienced its first raid by a 'superzeppelin', and on 2 September an attack
by thirteen German airships. When the scorched skeleton of a German ship,
downed by one lonely fighter pilot, fell to the north of London in a field behind a
pub, 'all London went mad. For hours after the downfall of SL-11, people sang
and danced in the streets. Sirens that had previously been sounded only to
announce air raids let loose as their operators discarded all caution and openly
flaunted regulations. Locomotive whistles squealed in the cool night air; auto
Klaxons along the city streets were earsplitting; ships' foghorns along the docks
blared ceaselessly; church bells rang.'[117] By then back in Woburn Buildings,
Yeats caught a violent cold rushing out to see the raid at 2.15 a.m.[118]

By mid-November 1916, with heavy rains, the four-month Battle of the Somme
ended, and Georgie's nursing duties finally eased. When Yeats returned from
a theatre trip to Dublin, he brought with him sketches of Ballylee; his dream of
owning a castle was becoming a reality. But more and more he acknowledged that
the castle needed a wife. Word was going the rounds of Dublin that he was to
marry Iseult; his sister Lily's matter-of-fact response was, 'I don't think Willy
would be such a fool. Isolde is 30 years his junior—as well as other drawbacks.'[119]
The major drawback—his long vain public courtship of her mother—was obvious
to everybody but Willy. A horary cast by Georgie for 22 November at 7.15 p.m.
bears the tantalizing partially legible phrase 'Tower [?burn]ing'; could it refer
to more than the Tree of Life or a Tarot card?[120] She continued her sittings
with Mrs Leonard. In December Yeats also returned to astrology, casting his and
Iseult's horoscopes, most of which seemed to be 'bad'. His friend Horton, however, predicted 'some regeneration in September' the following year.[121]

The year 1917 opened with family matters: Georgie's cousin George Barbara
Woodmass, uncle George's third daughter, was born; precisely a month later,
on 2 February, her grandfather Montagu Woodmass died. It is unlikely that
Nelly or her children were present at her father's funeral or had attended, just
two weeks earlier, the memorial service and unveiling of tablets to her brothers
Kenny, John, and Robert at St Paul's Church, Compstall. It was probably about
now that Georgie did some research on her ancestors—the Erskines, Hydes, and

Lees—in the British Museum. Yeats, newly elected to the Savile Club, spent most
of that spring worrying about the purchase of Ballylee—he settled for £35—and
planning renovations. Margaret Gregory, an artist like her husband Robert, was
advising, but Yeats confided to Lady Gregory that all 'will depend on my wife if
I marry'. George always believed that Lady Gregory was in favour of Iseult as
a likely pliant wife—or as the most obvious candidate (although her refusal to
invite Iseult to Coole in July 1916 certainly does not suggest approval[122]); Olivia
began to urge Georgie's case, possibly the reason for Willy's 'slight difference'
with her in March.[123] That same month Yeats confided in his old friend and
sometime lover Florence Farr Emery, 'I am 51 myself and do not like it at all and
keep thinking of all the follies I have committed not to have somebody to talk
to after nightfall and to bring me gossip of the neighbours. Especially now that
I am going to own a castle and a whole acre of land.'[124] Hedging all bets as usual,
he also arranged to take over the two rooms of the floor below him in Woburn
Buildings. He was spending sleepless nights, worrying himself ill over the plans
for Ballylee.

    Then once again his and Georgie's lives converged—at the end of February
they met in St James's Street and together they went on to a séance; later she
would confide that she heard a 'voice telling of which way to turn'.[125] Was she
hoping to make contact with her recently deceased grandfather Woodmass? Less
than a month later, 'feeling a little unkind at [her] long neglect of him', Nelly
Tucker invited Yeats to call. Although its significance would only be seen in hindsight two years later, a horary drawn up by Yeats for 18 March at 9 p.m. (and
placed just around the corner from the Tuckers' home in Montpelier Square)
is annotated the next day and again on 5 September, suggesting a number of
consultations: Venus conjunct Mars was favourable and 'promises completion',
but 'Neptune promises deception'; 'Suggest man and woman in full sympathy
but deception pulls them apart'; 'Square may mean difficult and slow'. How right
the stars were. However, on 20 March 1917 (the Order's equinox festival may have
been celebrated now or the day before) for the second time Yeats introduced to
Georgie the possibility of marriage.[126] Yet within two days he was still asking controls whether he was to marry Maud or Iseult. Still burning no bridges, ten days
later he wrote to Lady Gregory, 'I wonder if I could get a photograph made from
Robert's drawing of Ballylee—it might make a postcard & at any rate interest
Iseult.'[127] A special meeting with Bessie Radcliffe and her mother at which he
silently asked whether he should marry Maud Gonne produced a surprising
answer: 'after some scribbles "Rabshakeh" which means "cup bearer". . . . The
writing came slowly as if from "far off".'[128] He noted that Rabshakeh was closest
to the king. By mid-May he was at Coole, finishing the 'elaborate philosophical
essay' which became *Per Amica Silentia Lunae* ('Through the friendly silences
of the moon') and making equally detailed plans for the rebuilding of his castle

and the cottage at its foot. Fearing that for want of routine he might break down like his brother Jack (who was undergoing a serious depression), he told Olivia he hoped to be out of town for most of the summer; there was no mention of Georgie, or of his plans to go to France.[129] But when he returned to London he was triumphantly carrying 'the symbols of possession' for Ballylee.

Earlier this year the Germans had declared unrestricted submarine warfare. England was now suffering from a shortage of both food and coal; bread was rationed by February 1917. 'Food encroaches more and more as a topic for table talk,' Cynthia Asquith noted in her diary;[130] rationing of meats, cheese, tea, jam, syrup, sugar would not cease until May 1919. June saw some of the worst raids London had yet experienced; a daylight air raid on the 13th brought 'the sinister group of giant mosquitoes sweeping in close formation over London . . . shrapnel raining down like a thunder-shower.'[131] Five days later after yet another attack Willy telegraphed his sisters that he was all right; 'I wish he was safe in Galway,' Lily wrote to her father, safe in New York.[132] But he reluctantly participated in the second Poets' Reading on 21 June, described by one observer as 'the stage poet—a pale hand checking a lock trained into rebellion—a cathedral voice and a few editing remarks before delivering a poem'. This year's event was not as well attended as the previous one; the war had gone on too long and people were feeling numb or hopeless.[133] By now 'formations of twin-engined Gothas and four-engine Giants were being launched on a succession of raids over the heart of London, not only at night but also in daring strikes during daylight'. The fashionable Irish artist John Lavery painted his wife Hazel observing the Zeppelins from his studio window; Edgware Road was reported to be in ruins.[134] Yeats returned to Coole, from where he wrote to Olivia of Florence Emery's death in Ceylon adding, 'I am glad to be out of London where I was disconsolate & mostly tired. I have got to the last state of a man where only work is of interest.'[135] He was also very nervous of the raids, and resented urchins shouting 'Kitchener wants you!' as he walked to his club.[136] As if determined to maintain some kind of normalcy, Georgie bought more books on astrology and a drawing by Wyndham Lewis. On 17 August Ezra reported to the artist, then on the battlefield, 'The female who bought your £12 picture, told me last night she would send on the cheque, she is already two weeks late, but her bank account is solid if not extensive, so it will in due time come. I don't imagine you have much use [for] it where you are.'[137]

Always generous to her young cousin, that summer she promised Grace a book allowance for Oxford to supplement the funds provided by Harold; Grace was always mystified that the money never came and Georgie never explained. But other events had interfered, for she suffered an accident where the tips of her fingers were damaged by acid.[138] This probably occurred while she was at the hospital; Brittain describes the danger of 'young untried women . . . continually in contact with septic wounds and sputum cups and bed-pans'.[139] She was also exhausted, and this combination led to her withdrawing from active duties with the Red Cross in August.[140] By September she was staying with her mother in a rented house near Tunbridge Wells before beginning work 'of a very interesting nature' at the Foreign Office in October;[141] although no further details are known of this possible appointment, doubtless Georgie's skill in modern languages would be considered useful, for by now she spoke Italian, German, French, and Spanish. Like her sister Ghita, who disapproved of Grace scrubbing floors at a local hospital during vacation, Nelly would consider the Foreign Office a far more appropriate—and safer—place for her daughter.

Early in August Yeats left for Maud Gonne's house in Colleville, planning to stay on in September to deliver some lectures in France and Italy; he would, he explained to the patient Lady Gregory, not consider the situation with Iseult final ('she has not the impulse') until the Gonnes left for England and, they hoped, Ireland. Life in Normandy was pleasant, Maud Gonne 'no longer bitter', and he was working well and reading Blake; Walter Rummel was writing the music for his Noh play *The Dreaming of the Bones*.[142] But by early September his life was once again in turmoil: Iseult had been ambivalent about his proposal since the previous summer, confiding in her cousin that her first rejection 'didn't seem to affect him much, he lost no appetite through this; so I came to the conviction that he had merely done it to follow a code of politeness which he has made for himself.' Later, she would recall challenging him, 'You wouldn't say you loved me, would you?'; he could not say yes.[143] He wrote to Lady Gregory on 8 September reporting that, his Paris lectures having been postponed, he was accompanying the Gonnes back to England:

I am really getting ready a mass of work to start in Dublin and London if I can make some settlement in my life. I am just now too restless. Iseult has always been something like a daughter to me and so I am less upset than I might have been—I am chiefly unhappy about her general prospects. Just at the moment she is in one of her alarming moods— deep melancholy and apathy, the result of having left the country—and is always accusing herself of sins—sins of omission not of commission. She has a horoscope that makes me dread melancholia. Only in the country is she amused and free of this mood for long. Maud Gonne on the other hand is in a joyous and self forgetting condition of political hate the like of which I have not yet encountered. As soon as I reach London I shall be in the midst of another crisis of my affairs . . . so you must not expect to get much good of me for a while.[144]

Georgie was once more back in the picture, and by mid-September, before reaching London, he had written to Mrs Tucker asking if he might call, evidently indicating his intentions.

But whether Iseult was entirely out was another matter. It is not clear when or whether he delivered the ultimatum on the boat as reported by Jeffares, that 'she must make up her mind one way or the other, that he found the whole business an immense strain, and that if she would not marry him he had a friend who would be very suitable, a girl strikingly beautiful in a barbaric manner'.[145] More likely, after a sleepless, worrying night, on 18 September he had a further consultation with the Gonnes, who had been served with a notice under the Defence of the Realm Act (DORA) forbidding their landing in Ireland. 'Poor Iseult was very depressed on the journey and at Havre went off by herself and cried. Because she was so ashamed "at being so selfish" "in not wanting me to marry and so break her friendship with me". I need hardly say she had said nothing to me of "not wanting". Meanwhile she has not faltered in her refusal of me but as you can imagine life is a good deal at white heat.'[146] He and Iseult met again at Lyons Corner House, where Yeats 'became very decisive'. Years later Iseult confessed to Ellmann that she had toyed with the idea of 'keep[ing] Yeats about as her mother had done', but by now it was too late. Though worried that Maud would 'do something wild' in order to get to Ireland, and more and more convinced that he must look after Iseult, he also now felt more committed to Georgie. 'Mrs Tucker has asked me down to where she and her daughter are. I am however in rather a whirlpool. . . . I would be glad of a letter of counsel,' he begged Lady Gregory. 'I wrote to Mrs Tucker from France thinking that Iseult was going to Dublin and that I would not see her for months.'[147] The next day another visit to Chelsea, where Maud had taken a flat for six months in the King's Road, seems to have unsettled him further, and he postponed his journey to east Sussex. Still equivocal, he reported to Coole on 19 September,

I wrote you a very disturbed letter yesterday. Since writing I have decided to be what some Indian calls 'true of voice'. I am going to Mrs Tucker's in the country on Saturday or Monday at latest and I will ask her daughter to marry me. Perhaps she is tired of the idea. I shall however make it clear that I will still be friend and guardian to Iseult. Last night Maud Gonne returned to that strange conviction of hers that Iseult is my child because when Iseult was born she was full of my ideas. Perhaps at that time Maud Gonne was in love with me. I have seen Iseult to-day and am doing as she wishes. All last night the darkness was full of writing, now on stone, now on paper, now on parchment, but I could not read it. Were spirits trying to communicate? I prayed a great deal and believe I am doing right.[148]

Spirits were indeed trying to communicate. On 17 September Bessie's sister Margaret Radcliffe had sent a message from her dead grandfather:

'First of all, will you tell "Mr WBY" to let the Evening Star rule,' I think that was the message. Later I got some more (which might I think be intended for you) 'Continue in thy course, for the risings be propitious, Mars be thy guide, he being dispossessed by Saturn. Go and good attend thee, oh thou of golden tongue'. This was signed 'The Protector' and was most indistinct, the word I have just given as 'dispossessed' might as well be 'dissuaded'. It ended with a little drawing [a bird with open wings like a herald].[149]

Did he recall Horton's warning of the previous October? 'You seem to have taken up a certain course which experience only will convince you of its unwisdom,' his old friend had written. 'The time . . . is rapidly drawing near when you are to learn by bitter experience. . . . your House has to be put in order. This will be done in a way peculiarly fitted to your personal idiosyncracies [*sic*] & individual state. Some day you will attain to the Grail; today you are pursuing its shadow leading into black pools & quagmires.'[150] Possibly, for in his letter he echoed another old comrade, Florence Emery, who had written him in 1914 from Ceylon,

I am rounding off my life trying to become 'true of voice' as the old Egyptians used to call it. I am told it is necessary to do this if one is to attain anything in the way of adeptship & yet not in the way I used to understand it. . . . if you once decide that something must be done & say so you must carry it through even if it costs you your life & the lives of everyone you value most. That seems to be the Superhuman Morality. Another part of it is 'The great must always give'. [151]

The 'whirlpool' state continued. On 20 September after he had written to Nelly Tucker settling his visit, he attempted to tidy his affairs by inviting Horton and Ezra Pound to meet the Gonnes; he seems to have contemplated the older artist as a possible suitor for Iseult, ironically, as it would turn out. He saw Iseult again the next day; it was the date of the autumn equinox festival, but mundane matters were temporarily in the ascendancy. Lady Gregory's 'letter of counsel' finally arrived on the 22nd, to which he immediately responded:

Since I wrote you I have had talks with both Iseult & Maud Gonne. I had done exactly what you suggest. I have explained that I might be occupied with the political difficulty for some time. Iseult said to me yesterday 'Even if I loved you wildly (and I do not love) I would not marry you because it would distress Moura [the children's name for Maud] so deeply'. I acted as I did when I wrote to Mrs Tucker from Paris because I wished to start my new life so seemingly heart free that my wife would not be jealous of Iseult & would make no difficulty in the kind of guardianship I have taken up. Strange to say I think that guardian ship possible & Maud Gonne insists upon it. The strange conviction that Iseult is my child has grown upon her. I have not I think been in love with Iseult—I have been nearly mad with pity & it is difficult to distinguish between the two emotions perhaps. I want to get rid now of all ambiguity & to make my relationship definite & final. I go to Mrs Tuckers on Monday, & now that Iseult knows that I will not allow anything to break our friendship (I had for a time thought it my duty to break it) she seems to be content, though a little indignant, as Maud is also, with what they think my prosaic marriage plans. Both wish me to settle things so decisively that Mrs Tucker will not think there is any-thing to dread from either. Both on these grounds disapproved of my letter putting things off. I am doing little things for them both. I think I can persuade Maud to study design at the Central London art school, instead of taking up some wild political plan. All this will seem strangely cold & calculating. But I have only come to it—in my way—after sleepless nights & prayer. About 3 mornings ago I awakened calm & decided & had a last interview with Iseult & wrote the deciding letter. I need hardly say that all this has left me but little time to think or plan of my own future, but I believe all will go well. Perhaps Iseult's account is true—she gave it to Maud—'he is tired of romance & the normal & ordinary is now to him the romantic'. I certainly feel very tired & have a great longing for order, for routine and shall be content if I find a friendly serviceable woman. I merely know— we had our talk alone two years ago—that I think [this] girl both friendly, serviceable & very able. After all I want quiet more than any other thing & with me quiet & habit create great affection.[152]

Finally, on 24 September Yeats appeared at Rosewood, Beeches Road, in Crowborough, a semi-detached Victorian-style villa where Georgie was recuperating under her mother's watchful care. The area was familiar, for it was not far from Coleman's Hatch and Dorothy had attended school here; one of their neighbours was Conan Doyle who, as private in the local Volunteer Forces he had founded, drilled regularly through the streets of Crowborough.[153] Since the two leading performers in this extraordinary drama duly cast horoscopes of the event ('critical moments' for both of them), it is possible to give precise times for what followed. The worried suitor seems to have asked permission of Nelly, who then discussed the matter with her daughter on 25 September. At 10 a.m. on Wednesday, 26 September, Yeats formally proposed to Georgie, who remembered his describing himself as 'a Sinbad who after many misadventures had at last found port'; given her personal knowledge of his astrological aspects and what was common (and public) currency, he could hardly deny previous attachments.[154] Within twenty minutes, she accepted. Yeats annotated his horary 'good result must have come from moon trined with sun in Jupiter a "triple trine"'—trines were extremely favourable—and, later, 'Moon in major aspect to *all* Planets'—a busy, interesting time, full of stress but moving fast. At noon the next day he sent a telegram asking if he could come to Coole 'Monday or Tuesday'.

Communication for the following two days was obviously not all the usual lovers' talk, though they discussed Georgie's wish to go to Italy and plans for Ballylee; Willy seems to have expressed in more detail (and doubtless with considerable emotion) his commitment of responsibility for the hapless Iseult. He was probably also correcting the proofs of *Per Amica Silentia Lunae*, which were awaiting him when he returned from France.[155] This 'elaborate bit of writing'[156] contained a prologue and epilogue addressed in easy, familiar terms to 'Maurice' (Iseult). Even more tellingly, the framework and the second essay 'Anima Mundi', with its concluding lines 'we may love unhappily', are all dated May 1917, not long after he had again raised the prospect of marriage with Georgie. Long aware—who could not be?—of his relationship with Maud Gonne, she was clearly prepared to face the spectre of lost love. However, Iseult was another matter. Sufficiently disturbed by this indication of intimacy with another young woman, she seems to have confided in her mother.

On Sunday, 30 September, without (she hoped) her daughter's knowledge, Nelly wrote to Lady Gregory:

Georgie has sent you her photograph and Mr Yeats tells me he has written to you to say they are engaged.

I now find that this engagement is based on a series of misconceptions so incredible that only the context can prove them to be misconceptions, on my part and my daughter's. I was very much afraid that Mr Yeats meant to propose to my daughter in Nov. 15. I did not consider him free to do so then. But it was only a mutual interest in astrology which they shared, which is, so Mr Yeats tells me 'a very flirtatious business'! The war and its interests helped to keep us apart for some time, but unluckily, last March, having no idea that Mr Yeats's life was in any way changed, and feeling a little unkind at my long neglect of him I asked him to come & see me, never supposing that there could be any question of his marrying my daughter.

Other, and most annoying misconceptions arose, a mutual friend interested him in my daughter, the idea occurred to him that as he wanted to marry, she might do. Fortunately she has no idea of all this unpleasant background, she thinks he has wanted her since the time of the astrological experiments, and when he proposed to come & see us here, I told her he was now free. But it has dawned upon her that there is something amiss, after a long talk with Mr Yeats yesterday I have decided that the best thing to do is to write to you, and I have told him to confide in you frankly and without any idea of consideration for me or my daughter's possible feelings. She is under the glamour of a great man 30 years older than herself & with a talent for love-making. But she has a strong and vivid character and I can honestly assure you that nothing could be worse for her than to be married in this manner, so there will be no harm done and a rather unpleasant episode can be closed. She has told no one of the affair, and only a few intimate friends of Mr Yeats (who we do not know) are aware of the matter. Mr Yeats has the kindest heart and I feel that only you can convince him of the entire undesirability of this engagement. Georgie is only 24 and is to have work at the F. O. in October of a very interesting nature, I am not selfishly trying to keep her from marrying, but the present idea seems to me impracticable. . . .
P. S. I feel sure you will understand that my knowledge of the deep affection and reverence that Mr Yeats has for you is my justification in writing to you. If Georgie had an inkling of the real state of affairs she would never consent to see him again, if she realised it after her marriage to him she would leave him at once.

My letter to you is his release if he wishes it.[157]

Whether Yeats was the unwilling courier is not known, but Nelly's letter offering release must have arrived at Coole about the same time he did. Meanwhile, undeterred, Georgie returned to London with her fiancé on 1 October and the same day took out the ten-shilling application for a licence to marry. Dorothy, who accompanied her friend to the Harrow Road Registry Office in Paddington, recalled that Georgie was 'uncharacteristically nervous'.[158] Small wonder. Since fifteen days' previous residence was required by one of the parties, she took an apartment in 21 Kildare Gardens, a pleasant, quiet square off Westbourne Grove, about 500 yards north of the Shakespears' old home on Moscow Road; Harry Tucker had lived at 5 Kildare Gardens before his marriage. That evening there was another air raid, 'much more desultory' than the preceding ones, 'going on intermittently for about three hours—there were long intervals of complete silence'.[159] Either then or the next day Yeats introduced Georgie to Iseult and Maud; that accomplished, he took the night boat for Dublin. Nelly and her husband meanwhile moved on to Bexhill, still in search of country quiet. She had done her best; but Georgie was after all of age and, with her 'strong and vivid character', determined to take control of her own life. Nelly had once confided to her niece Grace that 'she really didn't know anyone Georgie *could* marry'.[160] The mother–daughter pattern Edith Ellen had endured with Edith Alice was beginning to repeat itself.

Four years earlier Maud Gonne had warned Willy, 'you are thinking dangerously much about a wife, think how she would disarrange your things! Matrimony I think requires great space either a castle & vast rooms or a cottage where one only enters to sleep & all the wide world outside.' He had replied, lamenting his loneliness after nightfall: 'A mistress cannot give one a home & a home I shall never have.'[161] Now that he was on the verge of both wife and castle, a gracious letter from Maud followed him to Coole:

I think your betrothed charming & I am sure we will be great friends. I am so glad of this, it would have been dreadful if you had chosen someone who would have broken our friendship, I feel Georgie will not, I think she will enter into it & add to it. I find her graceful & beautiful, & in her bright picturesque dresses, she will give life & added beauty to the grey walls of Ballylee.

I think she has an intense spiritual life of her own & on this side you must be careful not to disappoint her.

I am glad we are going to see her again on Friday. Iseult likes her very much, and Iseult is difficult & does not take to many people—Yes I think you have chosen well—I am so glad, for I want you to be very happy—[162]

What arrangements were made for which Friday is not recorded, nor is Georgie's reaction to the Gonnes, but we know from others that Maud was not always so generous in her remarks about her former suitor's 'prosaic marriage'. 'I wish you had heard Maude [*sic*] laugh at Yeats' marriage', Arthur Symons wrote to John Quinn, '—a good woman of 25—rich of course—who has to look after him; who might either become his slave or run away from him after a certain length of time.'[163] Both Maud and Iseult thought her somewhat strange, certainly different.[164] Yeats duly reported Maud's praise to Georgie, but far more important was Lady Gregory's influence in allaying Nelly's fears—though not before she had briskly interrogated Willy, reproving him for marrying Georgie in the clothes he bought to court Iseult in.[165] Her reassuring letter from Coole does not survive, but it was clearly satisfactory, judging by Nelly's reply of 9 October, written the day Yeats returned to London: 'Many thanks for your kind letter in answer to mine which seems to have been unnecessary. As long as Georgie has no idea of what I told you I think all will be well now. I am much reassured by your opinion of Mr Yeats's feelings.' Tactfully, his old friend and sponsor had written a welcoming letter to Georgie as well:

My dear Georgie—(if I may call you so)—I thank you very much for sending me your photograph I hope I may soon see you yourself, before the winter floods rise around Ballylee. I hope and believe you will have a very happy life, and I know you can make Willie very happy—very sincerely yours A Gregory.[166]

It is highly unlikely that Georgie was unaware, as others naively thought, of what had transpired. Her anxious suitor's letters were clearly forced as he tried to envision a life which would finally and irrevocably include her. In them astrological forecasts (especially worry about Neptune's dark influence), the Abbey Theatre, Lady Gregory's influence, Maud's opinions, the restoration of Ballylee, plans for travel, his longing for stability and order, her help with his work, her home-making, his helplessness in practical matters—all outlined the blueprint of the next twenty-one years:

3 October Stephen's Green Club Dublin My beloved: I forgot that wretched sugar card after all. I have now filled it up. Will you be very kind & ask a policeman what is the food office for the neighbourhood of St Pancras & post it. Probably it is enough to write 'St Pancras' on the blank space & put it into the nearest pillar box to where you live. I cannot it seems post it here. I am sorry to give you this trouble & yet glad too It makes me think of the time when I shall find you, when my work is over, sitting at the gass [*sic*] fire or dealing firmly with Mrs Old [his housekeeper at Woburn Buildings]. As the train passed through Wales I noticed a little house at the roadside & thought of Stone Cottage & myself walking home from the post to find you at the tea table. . . . Yours with love W. B. Yeats

4 October Coole My beloved: I arrived an hour ago. The masons are at work at Ballylee. Lady Gregory thinks that we should get married as soon as possible & that I should bring you here before the weather grows very cold & gloomy that we may make our Ballylee plans together while the castle looks well. She does not want us however till we are married—that one candle being I think the danger, or at least what the neighbours might say about the possible number of our candles. I was at the theatre last night, & I know that today or tomorrow Lady Gregory will show me a list of proposed plays with several of mine. I shall cross mine off the list, for this winter at least I will have no rehearsals to distract us. We shall be together in the country, here I hope & in Stone Cottage & then we shall be alone in France & Italy. You found me amid crowd but you will lead me to lonely places. Let us begin at once our life of study, of common interests & hopes. Lady Gregory is very pleased at the thought of our marriage, & thinks it the best thing that could have befallen me. I grow more fond of you every time we meet, but never quite escape my dread of that old intreaguer Neptune. I shall have no ease of mind till he has been finally put to rout. Lady Gregory is writing to your mother & I think her letter will compell [*sic*] him to take his trident out of our flesh. You will soon see me

again—what day I cannot say till I have had another talk with Lady Gregory & learn what necessary business there is, if there is any. There are generally a few plays which I have to be read—and then I long to receive from you one or two letters. Remember you have never yet written to me. I think I must go downstairs as I am to row the children across the lake. I kiss your hands. Yours affectionately W. B. Yeats

(Lady Gregory's version was less romantic; although originally it was intended that Georgie join Willy at Coole, the castle 'looked so dreary on what was a day of wind and rain that they decided to postpone her visit till after the marriage'.[167])

5 October My beloved: My thoughts are always with you—at first you were but a plan & a dream & then you became a real woman, & then all in a moment that real woman became very dear. And now I watch every post for your first letter. I keep wondering how you will begin it, what you will say. I cannot yet say upon what date I shall return to you. I have to read eight plays & that seems to be all there is to do—that and to decide on the theatre programme. This afternoon I drive to Ballylee to give some directions to the workmen. Lady Gregory comes with me. I have slipped into my old routines, writing from 11 to 2 & then again after five. Last night my first night here was difficult for dark comes early, & after a very little writing I must sit with my hands before me grudging the passing hours to empty talk with a couple of not interesting visitors. O my dear child if you can add your eyes to mine we will do together fine & stirring things. Endless hours will be saved from sheer non-being. I kiss the tops of your fingers where they are marked by the acid. Yrs affecly WBY

6 October My beloved: no letter yet from you. I keep wondering how you will begin the letter which seems full of mystery. A letter has come from Maud Gonne praising you. . . . She is sure that you & I will be very happy. I have noticed that though she judges badly when she uses her intellect she judges subtly & truly when as now she uses her intuition & sympathy.

    I went to Ballylee yesterday to see the men at work on the cottage— . . . & thought it was a pity you would see it in no better weather. It looks so different in spring with the island full of daffodils—but then spring may find us in Italy. They think they may get the roof on the castle some time in November. I have tried to start an essay (the one for Per Amica Silentia Lunae) & could not and then a poem and could not. I am therefore but reading plays. Ah dear you are in my blood & I must get back to you. Perhaps tomorrow will bring a letter from your mother settling all. Tomorrow at any rate I will decide what day we are to meet again—Tuesday perhaps. I shall be almost at peace when I see you though only the day when we begin to live together always shall give me full peace. Yours with love WBY

(It is possible that the projected new essay may have been an attempt to assuage her feelings about the ones already written to Iseult.)

7 October My beloved: I am sad that there is no letter and perhaps I shall not get one at all for I go to Dublin tomorrow. I have asked the architect to wire if he can see me. If he can I shall not cross to England until Tuesday. If he cannot I shall go straight through & if you could hear the wind howling in the chimney you would know how great is my longing to

see you. I shall have a damnable crossing. This separation has made you dearer to me—& strangely disquieting Years ago knowing that I had [Mars] in my [VIIth house] I feared your strong magnetism. I know now that the strong magnetism is not a thing to dread but a foundation for lasting love. Did you notice that [Venus] conjoins [Mars] and trines Saturn & Venus [is] in mutual reception with [Jupiter]?

When I hear this howling wind I no longer wish you to come to Ireland. I think we will go straight to Stone Cottage & then when I have roofed and cleared this castle you can come & see it & add what you will & add nothing at all if it does not please you. When we come from Italy, if we return at all before the end of the war, it will be surrounded by green boughs & wild flowers. O my dearest I kiss your hands full of gratitude & affection—do not draw them away while my lips are still hungry. Am I not Sinbad thrown upon the rocks & weary of the seas? I will live for my work & your happiness & when we are dead our names shall be remembered—perhaps we shall become a part of the strange legendary life of this country. My work shall become yours and yours mine & do not think that because your body and your strong bones fill me with desire that I do not seek also the secret things of the soul. That magnetic [Mars] will not make me the less the student of your soul. Yours always WBY

P. S. Probably—for Scott the architect will probably forget to send the wire I have asked for—I shall be in London when this reaches you. Unless I wire from Dublin I shall go to see you at the first possible moment—before noon certainly.[168]

Perhaps wisely, Georgie never replied to his letters, though his astrological readings would have been appealing: the Venus Mars conjunction with Venus and Jupiter, in signs which are each ruled by the other, harked back to horoscopes cast for 18 and 20 March, when marriage had been discussed earlier that year (and Moon was in opposition to Neptune). Woman's Mars to man's Moon suggests a less passive role for her in the seventh house of partnership; while the fortunate trine of Venus with Saturn was a reminder of the grand trines they shared in their natal horoscopes; she would recall with pleasure that Willy always said Mars in his Seventh House was her 'strong Saturnian influence'.[169] Astrologically, their union promised much good fortune.[170] Surely deceitful Neptune would not hold sway forever. Perhaps also Georgie held the same wistful view Yeats expressed before she was born about his courtship of Maud Gonne, that in time need and their shared occultism would become love.[171]

On the afternoon of 10 October Yeats sent a telegram to Coole baldly stating, 'October 20 matter still private Yeats'. The same day Georgie finally put pen to paper. Stiff with shyness, her letter was not franked until the afternoon of the 11th, suggesting that she delayed posting until Willy had read it:

Dear Lady Gregory I must write to thank you for your note. It is a great thing to me that Willy's friends, & you above all others, should be happy at the thought of his marriage; and I am grateful to you that you should have had the kind thought of writing so reassuringly to me.

I hope that before many months pass I will meet you. Ever sincerely yours Georgie.

Nelly's approval finally gained, the wedding date itself was reached after careful consideration of the stars. Elizabeth Heine has pointed out the grand trines in air they both had in their natal horoscopes, 'signifying good fortune in things of the mind'; these were matched by the major transiting planets on their wedding day, 'a kind of doubling and tripling of fortunate angles', while transiting Saturn added stability to the union. If Saturn represented the groom and Venus the bride, 'of the two feminine planets, transiting Venus—a loving young woman —was in Sagittarius, trine Yeats's Mars-Saturn-progressed Sun combination in Leo, and the Moon, goddess of marriage and all things female, was also in Sagittarius, approaching Yeats's fortunate Jupiter, itself in trine to George's Jupiter in Aries'.[172]

But whether due to Neptune's influence or his own continuing 'whirlpool', as soon as the day was fixed Yeats again 'fell into wild misery', convinced that he would forever love Iseult and had written 'that letter to Mrs Tucker to end by a kind of suicide an emotional strain that had become unendurable—my sheer bodily strength was worn out'. Probably there was a little truth in both; but he then reasoned himself out of despair by thinking that 'a long vain courtship' could only bring unhappiness to him, while an acceptance 'out of mere kindness and gratitude' would make Iseult unhappy. Whether she was fully aware of his moods or simply shy—doubtless both—Georgie refused to go with him to see Iseult on Friday, 12 October, insisting that they should be alone. This was a wise move, for Iseult, 'so noble and sweet', persuaded him that 'neither of us could think of anything now but Georgie's happiness'. By the morning of the 13th, 'more content', he confided to Lady Gregory that

the storm has shifted and I think the marriage a great promise of happiness and tranquil work. . . . 'not easily did we three come to this'. I know I have not been selfish or had any vulgar motive. I am longing for all to be over that a new life of work and common interest may give Georgie and myself one mind and drive away after a time these wild gusts of feeling. I believe that in spite of all I shall make her happy and that in seeking to do so I shall make myself happy. She has great nobility of feeling, and I have always believed that the chief happiness and favour of my life has been the nobility of three or four woman friends.

But he cautiously added, 'When you write you need not speak of this letter. I send it you that I may keep nothing back.'[173]

Only then did he tell his father and sisters of his wedding plans, writing to John Butler Yeats on Monday, 15 October:

My betrothed is a Miss Hyde Lees, comely and joyous and aged but 24. She is a great student of my subjects and has enough money to put us above anxiety and not too much money. Her means are a little more than my earnings and will increase later, but our two incomes together will keep us in comfort. I have known her for some years, and a very dear friend of mine has long wanted to bring this match about. Then when I found the girls mother wished it, I thought I might marry so young a girl and yet not do her wrong. I will send you her photograph as soon as I can get one. She is of good family, speaks French and Italian and reads German and Spanish and was an art student for a time.

His income for the year ending April 1917 was £429 3s. 5d.; they contributed approximately the same amount to the union, but Georgie would wait for almost ten years before receiving anything further from her father's estate. However, gossip in Dublin and elsewhere insisted on believing that when they married, Yeats was penniless and his wife very wealthy.[174]

That week Willy dutifully paid court, entertaining Georgie at Woburn Buildings and introducing her to other friends. She recalled his proudly cooking chops in a paper bag (a method he had demonstrated to Synge and Masefield many years before); she did not have the nerve to tell him they tasted only of brown paper.[175] They were shyly coming to terms with their new situation, and each other: 'My beloved: I was so sorry not to have seen you today. I wanted to tell you that I did not mean to chaff you last night about Macchiavelli. I got up all that discussion about books in youth to get you to explain your liking. But you were too modest—you had not our gay self-assertion. You are only confident I think in the service of others. Tomorrow at 3 Yours always.'[176]

His assessment marked the difference he would always recognize in her; she lacked 'our gay self-assertion', but he was astute enough in isolating the origin of her self-confidence. He probably did not even know that the 16th marked another rite of passage—her twenty-fifth birthday. On Friday, 19 October—a fine, starlit night—at a few minutes past ten, air-raid alarms signalled a 'silent raid' that struck at strategic points in London, including Piccadilly Circus. Yeats later claimed that he spent the night at the Gonnes; other evidence suggests he spent at least part of it at Kildare Gardens, when their union was consummated.[177]

At 11.20 the next morning the marriage ceremony took place at the Harrow Road Registry Office in Paddington; the witnesses were Nelly Tucker and Ezra Pound.[178] The setting reinforced the businesslike arrangements of the contract that had been reflected in their astrological calculations, for 'there is nothing attractive in a Register Office marriage: it is the bare civil contract and nothing more'. Leonard Woolf describes his own marriage two years earlier, also on a Saturday, at St Pancras Register Office 'in a room which, in those days, looked down into a cemetery. In the ceremony before a Registrar one makes no promise "to love and to cherish, till death do us part, according to God's holy ordinance." '[179] Fourteen years later the experience still rankled, and George would graphically try to dissuade Lennox and Dolly Robinson from the same fate:

nasty frowzy places where you cant get married before ten-thirty a.m. even though
they open at 10 a.m., but the officials spend at least half an hour taking off their greatcoats
and hats and recovering from train or bus journeys and undigested breakfasts (very
vulgar . . .) . . . Also, in Church one's relations may weep quietly in or in front pews
which is quite OKE in the best 1830 tradition, whereas in registry offices the formality
may lead to outbursts. . . . speaking Dolly with full experience of registry offices, and a
very great prejudice in favour of the church, I have, as you see, very strong feelings on
the subject![180]

On the way from the wedding Yeats felt it necessary to instruct Ezra (who *had*,
surprisingly, been respectably married in a church) to word his telegram to Coole
Park so that it would not be talked about throughout the countryside for generations.[181] Pound may also have been responsible for the curt announcement
that appeared on the first page of the *Irish Times* on 23 October: 'Yeats and
Hyde-Lees—Oct 20, 1917. In London, W. B. Yeats, to Georgie, only daughter of
the late W. G. Hyde-Lees, of Pick Hill Hall, Wrexham, and of Mrs Henry Tucker,
of 16 Montpelier Square, London.' His sister Lily reported to their father that
Rose, their aged servant, 'does not like at all the way Willy put in the announcement of his wedding. "He did not say who's son he was, or nothing." '[182] Word
rapidly got round London and beyond; Ezra nonchalantly reported to Wyndham
Lewis at the front, 'Yeats was married on Saturday. To the purchaser of your
£12 drawing at that. I don't know that that was your intention when you composed it.'[183] Grandmother Woodmass, doubtless hearing the news through
Nelly's sister or their joint Erskine connections, telegraphed a blunt query, 'Is
Yeats a Catholic?' Apparently satisfied, she lapsed once again into silence.[184] The
day after the wedding Lily Yeats wrote to their friend and patron the lawyer John
Quinn in New York,

We are very pleased & excited over Willy's marriage. His mother in law sent a photograph of Willy's wife yesterday. She is charming dark—regular features, & strongly
marked eyebrows—it is one of those faint sketchy photographs, very little to get hold of at
all. I am sure Papa is pleased I suppose Willy wrote—reporters were here & at the Abbey
on Saturday looking for news—but we all kept the secret till after the wedding. I told
Susan [Mitchell] by telephone asking her to tell A. E. [George Russell]. She got me to
repeat it—& then said—'the telephone has burst.'[185]

Meanwhile, 'the great business of life settled',[186] the couple retired to Woburn
Buildings where a fresh outbreak of the bridegroom's nervous stomach disorders delayed their honeymoon departure. No matter what the stars promised,
it was not an auspicious beginning. They had planned to go immediately to
Stone Cottage, but the Welfares could not take them in until 7 November. Meanwhile, anxious to be in that enchanted neighbourhood, they had booked into
the Ashdown Forest Hotel nearby in Forest Row.[187] They also contemplated

spending a few weeks in Ireland, where Georgie could at last enter Ballylee. Georgie immediately made herself useful not just as nurse but as amanuensis. On Monday the 22nd, still in London, Yeats dictated a letter to his good friend and collaborator Edmund Dulac arranging a visit 'next Saturday if you have not filled up the day . . . I would have written before but life has been a little hurried as you can imagine and I have had two days' illness.'[188] Later that day they finally reached the hotel, taking room number 6 on the third floor; reached by private stairs directly above the entrance, today there are suggestions that section is haunted.[189] But Willy was still morose and unwell, not helped by unsettled weather and the continuing procession of khaki-clad soldiers marching from the picturesque 'timber-town' artillery camp near Greenhall down the Eastbourne Road to the Forest Row station.[190] A well-meant letter from Iseult arrived, assuring him that Georgie would only increase their friendship and wishing them both great happiness and mutual understanding; perceptively, she likened his bride to a sphinx.[191] This only increased his misery, and, feeling that he 'had betrayed three people' in his haste to marry, he fired off yet another missive to Iseult. Georgie watched helplessly as she saw Willy 'drifting away from her'.[192]

On 24 October, both wretched, they questioned the heavens, casting horaries within minutes of each other. Yeats timed his 5.45 p.m.; a phrase he later struck out in his commentary reads 'letter to I G':

Sympathy strong so that is in accord with querient though some trouble in that accord but all events of Vth house [love affairs] & 11 [hopes] caught in the most evil construction [Saturn rules delays, Neptune dissolution and lack of clarity, Uranus accidents and sudden happenings], aspects with which Moon [women] is mixed up. Signification to querient not seriously injured by this in the mind and character—personal relations good. Events bad as can be Oct 1917.

Georgie's horary was more discreet; timed 6.40 p.m., while making use of the same list of aspects or planetary positions as his, she employed a language her husband did not know: 'Per dimandera [domandare] perche noi siamo infelice' ('to ask why we are unhappy'). Unusually for her, though not surprising considering her frantic state, she made a few errors in her calculations as well as in her Italian. But the message both consultations provided was clear: the oppositions at Moon and Uranus to Mars and Saturn and Neptune, and of Jupiter and Venus across the partnership axis, all signify tension.[193] Later Yeats would acknowledge George's 'moment of greatest disquiet' as 'caused by me': some time between 4 and 5 p.m. he told her of his letter to Iseult, perhaps in his self-abnegation even showed Iseult's reply.[194] He turned also to poetry, beginning 'The Lover Speaks', with its use of astrological quadrants. Given his carelessness in leaving papers around, she probably read that too, either then or when the first draft was completed the following day:

1

A strange thing surely that my heart when love had come unsought
upon that Norman upland or in that poplar shade,
Should find no burden but itself & yet should be worn out;
It could not bear that burden & therefore it went mad.

2

The south wind brought it longing, & the East brought in despair,
The west wind made it pityful, & the North wind afraid;
It feared to give its love a hurt with all that tempest there;
It feared the hurt that she could give & therefore it went mad.

3

I can exchange opinion with any neighbouring mind
I have as healthy flesh & blood as any rhymer's had
But oh my heart could bear no more when the upland caught the wind;
I ran, I ran from my love's side because my heart went mad.[195]

What followed has been described several times by George herself. The very process of casting and analysing a horary chart may well have clarified the situation, as it frequently did. Fully aware of the reason for his unhappiness, first she contemplated leaving him. But then, reluctant to surrender what had been for so many years her destination, she considered arousing his interest through their joint fascination with the occult. She decided to 'make an attempt to fake automatic writing' and then confess to her deception once her distracted husband was calmer.[196] Announcing that she felt 'she had lived through this before' and was impelled to write, while talking to him all the while (a favoured device among automatists so that the hand may remain independent of the conscious will), she put pencil to paper. As Yeats recalled them, the words that came were 'with the bird all is well at heart. Your action was right for both but in London you mistook its meaning.'[197] Years later George remembered her reassurance as 'What you have done is right for both the cat and the hare.' Probably neither memory is completely accurate, but neither is totally wrong. In the Kabbalah, the pathway by way of the middle pillar which connects Malkuth (the Kingdom or Queen) and Tiphareth (Beauty, the Sun or King) passes through Yesod (the Foundation, the sexual centre, Moon), and later they would identify themselves in these spheres; in the animal kingdom Yesod corresponds to both hare and cat. Not surprisingly, the images of bird, 'speckled cat', and 'tame hare' would reappear in Georgie's script and Willy's poems; eventually their menagerie at Ballylee would include all three as pets.[198] Whatever the wording, the message was taken as she hoped, and interpreted as a statement reassuring her new husband about Iseult and herself.[199] A second sentence followed: 'after Georgie had written that sentence I asked mentally "when shall I have peace of mind" and her hand wrote "you will never regret nor repine" and I think certainly that I never shall again.'[200] But the writing did not stop; 'to her utter amazement, her hand acted as if "seized by a superior power". The loosely held pencil scribbled out fragments of sentences on a subject of which she was ignorant.'[201]

Within days Willy, still hoping and believing that 'George knew nothing', was to describe this 'miraculous intervention' to Lady Gregory:

I had begun to believe just before my marriage that I had acted, not as I thought more for Iseult's sake than for my own, but because my mind was unhinged by strain. The strange thing was that within half an hour after writing of this message my rheumatic pains & my neuralgia & my fatigue had gone & I was very happy. From being more miserable than I ever remember being since Maud Gonne's marriage I became extremely happy. That sense of happiness has lasted ever since.[202]

The word 'fake' would continue to haunt George, even though it was the phrase she herself employed in speaking with Virginia Moore and Ellmann. She had always been aware of Willy's 'remarkable sense of how an event would look to posterity';[203] after his death she assumed that responsibility as well. Over forty years later she objected to its use in the first draft of A. Norman Jeffares's introduction to *Selected Poems*: 'I dislike your use of the word "Fake" in Introduction. I told you this before & you had a happier phrasing in your book. However, I cannot ask you to alter this. The word "Fake" will go down to posterity.' Jeffares returned to his original phrasing, adopting Yeats's own words: 'A few days after their marriage, Mrs Yeats for the first time in her life attempted automatic writing.'[204] But the damage was done, not only by later biographers, but by Yeats himself when, against her will, in 1937 he published his version of the 'incredible experience':

On the afternoon of October 24th 1917, four days after my marriage, my wife surprised me by attempting automatic writing. What came in disjointed sentences, in almost illegible writing, was so exciting, sometimes so profound, that I persuaded her to give an hour or two day after day to the unknown writer, and after some half-dozen such hours offered to spend what remained of life explaining and piecing together those scattered sentences. 'No', was the answer, 'we have come to give you metaphors for poetry.'[205]

An earlier draft revealingly includes, then struck out, the lines 'and after some vague sentences it was as though her hand were grasped by another hand.'[206]

Iseult's reply sympathizing in her quondam lover's distress arrived from Chelsea on 26 October. In it she described how on receiving his first letter (which she had burned as requested) she had entered a little Protestant church to ask God why Willy was unhappy and what part she herself had played in this. 'Why should I who love you so much be happy when you are not?' Begging him to try to be happy if only as a kindness to her, she recommended that he renounce for a while the life of emotion; it was both too late, and too early, to look into himself for answers. 'An abruptly new condition is bound to have a little of the fearfulness of a birth. . . . all I know is that I share your sadness and will share your joy when you will tell me "All is well." ' And she sent Georgie her love.[207]

By then all was indeed well. The following day, Saturday, 27 October, Yeats wrote 'The Heart Replies', echoing lines from a poem by Tagore which Georgie knew, and five years earlier Iseult had translated:[208]

[1]
The Heart behind its rib laughed out, 'You have called me mad' it said
'Because I made you turn away & run from that young child;
How could she mate with fifty years that was so wildly bred?
Let the cage bird & the cage bird mate & the wild bird mate in the wild'

2
'You but imagine lies all day O murderer' I replied
'And all those lies have but one end poor wretches to betray;
I did not find in any cage the woman at my side
O it would break her should she learn my thoughts are far away

3
'Speak all your mind' my heart sang out 'speak all your mind who cares
Now that your tongue cannot persuade that child till she mistake
Her gratitude for love himself & wed your fifty years
O let her choose a young man now & all for his wild sake.[209]

Above, there was 'a very precise emphasis on Mercury and Uranus, planets astrologers associate with communication and heightened mental activity; Uranus adds qualities of the unexpected, the unusual, the extraordinary.'[210] Below, Georgie had played her trump card; instead of renouncing 'the life of emotion' as Iseult had advised, they embraced it.

6
FOREST ROW

Late in August 1924 George wrote from Ballylee to London, 'My dearest Willy . . .
You ought to finish the book on October 24—then it will be exactly seven years
since we started it.' 'The book' was, of course, *A Vision*, based upon the teachings
of the 'Instructors' who spoke through George's automatic script and trances,
codified and elaborated from their discussions and library research, and finally
published privately in 1925.[1] Clearly they had both agreed on Wednesday, 24
October, as the day the automatic script began; the date of the two preserved
horoscopes may have been the deciding factor.[2] Not surprisingly, however, critics
have since raised some doubts about the accuracy of this timing: George later
variously dated 'The Lover Speaks' 24 October and 25/26 October, but corrected
the date of 'His Heart Replies' from the 30th to the 27th. The automatic script
itself ambiguously identifies George's 'moment of greatest disquiet' as 'October
24th—5 1917 | 4 to 5', 'caused by two people . . . you & I[seult] G[onne]—IG
through your letter'; however the first '5' may, as is the nature of the script, be the
hour clarified in the next line, '4 to 5'. But a letter to Lady Gregory postmarked
29 October speaks of 'the miraculous intervention' having occurred 'two days
ago'; primarily on the basis of this letter, George Harper and others believe the
writing began as late as 27 October.[3]

Whether the automatic writing began on the 24th, 25th, or 27th, and I think the
evidence points towards the 24th, little did either realize in 1917 what forces Willy's
new wife in her highly emotional state had unleashed, or what long-term impact
this would have on their lives and his creativity. As far as we know, although
familiar with the practice, Georgie had never before attempted to write automatically (so she assured Ellmann and Moore); it must have taken time to adjust
to yet another new role. We have only their memories of that first session, and
the first few days were either too hesitant and chaotic or too personal—probably
both—to be preserved. Even the control admitted, 'I communicated with her by
chance.' Whatever the reason, despite her husband's excitement, it appears that
it was not until after a fortnight of experimenting that they began to look upon
Georgie's script as an ongoing record of revelation which should be properly
annotated and preserved; even later, questions were not always filed away with

the answers. No questions seem to have been recorded until 8 November and then haphazardly until a few days later, by which time a pattern began to emerge. Gradually, as the two partners established a routine for the dialogue they were calling forth, the 'disjointed sentences, in almost illegible writing' became easier to decipher, the answers to their carefully composed questions more germane, until a system evolved which would satisfy at last Willy's need to comprehend the macrocosm in relation to the microcosm, this world and the other, 'all thought, all history and the difference between man and man'.[4] Despite the fact that it was, as she admitted later, 'a very disconcerting way to spend a honeymoon', Georgie's impulse had been effective.[5]

The scripts that have so far been discovered, and transcribed by George Harper and his team of editors, plunge us *in medias res*. However, from these and other sources it is possible to piece together something of those first heightened weeks in Georgie's 'haunted woods'.[6] Still in an intense state of excitement, Yeats sent a telegram to the Dulacs on the morning of the 25th and followed it later that day with a letter: 'We can go to you whenever it is convenient, for we have our rooms here till the fifth, but Stone Cottage is by an old arrangement to be ready for us. So you see one day will suit us as well as another. Our life has no date. I am writing verses. My wife is casting horoscopes. . . . We are both looking forward very much to our visit to you and your wife.'[7] The work of 'writing verses' and 'casting horoscopes' hinted at, but did not reveal, what was happening in the enchanted forest. Despite the control's famous answer, 'we have come to give you metaphors for poetry', Yeats seemed determined to devote himself to the mysterious script.[8] If that is so, they made remarkable progress; a letter on the 27th to Allan Wade suggests that he had already committed himself wholeheartedly to the new venture: 'I am married as I daresay someone has told you. I am keeping away from London for the present. I will let you know as soon as I come back & will ask you to come round one evening. I am not sure if we shall go on with the Mondays as we shall be going abroad soon.'[9]

By the next day it is clear from a letter to Bessie Radcliffe that enough of the script was making sense for him to seek possible cross-correspondences: 'my wife is a friend of Mrs Fowler and of other friends of yours & she is a close student of all my subjects. I wish you would tell me exactly what intimation came to you on Oct 4, I have a strong reason, not curiosity for asking this.'[10] Too busy nursing, Bessie did not reply; after a fortnight he sent a second request, adding, 'a great deal has happened both lucky & the reverse . . . My wife is a great student of my subject & I think we shall [have] a cheerful & busy life.'[11] This finally elicited the reassurance sought by the two sensitives:

I couldn't write before—the hospital work was so hard I had not time to think & hardly any time to breathe. About Oct 4th I saw you on the stairs as I was rushing down with a tray & stopped to speak but you vanished away rather rudely. Every night after that till I heard from Mrs Fowler about your marriage I caught sudden & short glimpses of you. The only writing during that time which might have been meant for anyone was a repetition of what we had before 'And they departed with the rewards of divination in their hands'. . . . I look forward to meeting your wife when you come back to London.[12]

Either he (and Eva Fowler) neglected to tell her whom he had married, or, surprisingly, Bessie and Georgie had never met; however, the spirit message sent through Bessie must have been especially encouraging.

Willy was far less reticent in his report to Coole which began, 'The last two days Georgie and I have been very happy. Yesterday we walked to a distant inn on the edge of the Forest & had tea.' Relying as always on his friend and collaborator, he added, 'The misery produced two poems which I will send you presently to hide away for me—they are among the best I have done.' The poems were finally sent to Ireland for safe keeping on his first trip to London in early November, 'for they can hardly be published for years, if ever. I got some peace of mind by writing them & they are quite sincere. The last verse was my mood very often in Colleville & Paris though not always—it was I think the mood I acted on.'[13]

Despite their shared pleasure in the countryside, a greater part of each day was spent on the new experiments, two long daily sessions at least, in which Georgie drew upon all her inner resources to fulfil her fascinated husband's needs.[14] On one occasion, clearly in response to Yeats's impatient questioning, the control sternly commented, 'she has no definite message and is trying to get one before she writes'. Later Georgie would remember to state the time as well as place and date for each script, but the early sessions appear to have taken place in the afternoon and again later in the day. By 1919 there were even some morning sessions, although 'Thomas' did not really like coming to them before 9 p.m.[15] It is clear that from the beginning this was a collaboration, drawing on their joint experiences as students of the Golden Dawn (especially the Kabbalah), astrology, Georgie's extensive reading, and the productions of Bessie Radcliffe and other mediums. Although Georgie's frequent attendance at séances offered her some direction, and Yeats was known for his adroitness at formulating questions, this was new and different.[16] Despite Willy's eagerness, the control insisted on Georgie's power: 'you must use her for question.' Later his own role was pithily distinguished, and so, in the process, was Georgie's: 'you cannot be both a psychic and an artist.'[17] The role of Sibyl, successful though it was, would force much of her creativity, like her voice, underground; in the eyes of the world she dwindled into the efficient organizer Yeats described to Lady Gregory: 'My wife is a perfect wife, kind, wise, and unselfish. . . . She has made my life serene and full of order.'[18] But to Ellmann she admitted that she had not liked the gruelling experience of automatist and offered further excuses for complying: '—great strain—but at first she thought it would keep his mind off the mediums, who had become almost an obsession with him—he had lost many of the habitués of his Woburn Bldgs Mondays because he insisted on talking about occult experiments—none of which went much further than the ones before.'[19] Some of this was probably seen more clearly in retrospect. There were other reasons for not enjoying the role of Sibyl. From the beginning she was prone to nightmares, which would plague her for many years; as early as 7 November the control recommends that Willy 'make a mantra over a small object give it to her to wear in sleep without saying what it is use[d] on'.[20] Although by now her damaged fingertips had obviously healed, she was still suffering from somnambulism and would continue to do so, especially after their psychic endeavours; frequently on coming out of a trance she would burst into tears.[21]

From professional mediums of the time such as Hester Travers Smith, we can gain some sense of the physical demands involved in automatic writing:

A pencil is held generally between the first and third fingers of the hand of the medium; it touches the paper, and as a rule, after some preliminary flourishes and twirls, the pencil begins to write coherent words and messages. These messages vary according to the communicator, and the handwriting changes as different personalities appear. . . . the script is generally difficult to decipher, as . . . the pencil cannot be lifted as in ordinary handwriting, and the MS. is full of scrawls and hard to read.[22]

Georgie and her controls forbade any onlookers: the circle of two must remain inviolate. But with no other sitters to share the preparation and subsequent tension, the sessions were even more exhausting. Travers Smith, who preferred the ouija board herself, objected to automatic writing in part because 'for some unknown reason, [it] leads in certain cases to continual pain in the arm, an irresistible desire to write, nervous upset, and consequent physical prostration'. The Communicators, concerned that Georgie would become exhausted, regularly warned that the power depended upon her physical strength. Recognizing the toll it took on his bride, although too committed to moderate his demands, Willy was evasive in his letters to Lady Gregory: 'I find that George is still very fateagued [*sic*] with her hospital work and I have to watch that she does not overtire herself. At ordinary times she has been full of work and energy.'[23] In years to come she would suffer considerably from rheumatism and arthritis, which may well have originated in the many intense sessions from October 1917 to March 1920 and beyond.[24] But it is evident from the script itself that she was as committed to the experiment as he was, no matter what toll it took.

The Society for Psychical Research tended to call the producers of automatic writing 'automatists'; perhaps in an effort to differentiate herself from spiritualists (or to disengage herself from so much responsibility), George would eventually prefer the term 'Interpreter' to 'Medium'.[25] Georgie knew many spiritualists who dabbled in automatic writing; like sessions at the table and ouija board, it was an acceptable social activity. Walter Rummel, himself deeply engrossed in psychical matters, performed 'his new Debussys' for friends in the home of the American writer and magazine editor Elsa Barker (also a member of the Golden Dawn), who would herself produce three volumes of 'spiritualistic messages'.[26] Yet especially at the beginning the Yeatses' sittings bore some of the trademarks of the professional medium, and even of some trance speaking. The first recorded sessions reflect the results, if not the methods, of Etta Wriedt and Gladys Leonard: the control complained, 'I am trying to get through to you but too many others round.' These 'others' included an eighteenth-century shopkeeper named Bolton, an unknown 'Isabella', and a malignant and dishonest 'Leo'. Isabella and Bolton never returned, but Leo, 'one of several' of that name, would continue to interfere on occasion, perhaps drawing on his familiarity with Willy's own early attempt at automatic writing, of which Georgie surely knew.[27] Later—again attempting to distance their experiments from that of others—her guides would openly disapprove of 'the lying tales told through writing mediums' as 'subliminal romancing of the medium from a partial spirit communication'.[28] On those first days variations of the 'book test' also appeared, appropriately making use of a French edition of the astrologer-poet Lully (Raymon Llull), with the acknowledgement that 'she once looked it up in catalogue'; clearly the spirits were aware of Georgie's researches in the British Museum library.[29]

Like Bessie Radcliffe's scripts, Georgie's were interspersed with drawings and considerable mirror, upside down, and backwards writing (these much easier for someone left-handed as she was). Neither of them would have appreciated Frederic Myers's comment that 'reversed script' or 'mirror-writing' 'is not very rare with left-handed children and imbeciles, and has been observed in association with aphasia'.[30] At first, sentence fragments and broken phrases were common, although once the dialogue form was established, Willy usually asking the questions and Georgie's hand always providing the answers, the lines of communication became clearer and the discussions more complex and germane to their own studies. Most professional sittings devoted considerable time to matters of health and personal habits; with George and Willy too we find interspersed among the philosophical discourses advice to him on drinking more water, discreet eating habits, taking long walks, keeping more regular hours and to her, not surprisingly, the need for more rest ('fatigue is the safeguard against excess'). At least some of this advice Willy took seriously, for he writes to Lady Gregory from Stone Cottage, 'I must go out now for my daily walk. I go alone for my work's sake.'[31] In a circle of strangers, such advice would have been far less frank than in the Yeatses' case where the most intimate aspects of their marriage were discussed, especially their sexual habits. The most respected mediums preferred however to deal with questions of significance to all of humanity rather than being restricted to providing proof of life after death; this is reflected in Yeats's subtitle for *A Vision*, 'an explanation of life'.[32] Again, as with most mediums, there was a clearly defined hierarchical structure to the voices of their discarnate teachers: Georgie's control not only dictated the length of sitting but what would be addressed; nearly always masculine, he frequently was accompanied by a helper or 'lesser guide', many of whose names suggested the feminine. Sometimes questions were left unanswered; it was traditional for controls to acknowledge their need and use of the medium yet to retain the right not to respond, and when they did reply to claim superior understanding in particular areas of knowledge. At the first recorded session, 'Thomas of Dorlowicz', who would be their major control for the next eighteen months, insisted, 'I am here for a purpose & must go when that is done | I am here for her only.' A few days later he repeated, 'I was sent to the medium for various reasons of which I have fulfilled one . . . I was sent as part of my duties.' But he also warned, 'I cant say what is not in my province.'[33]

But despite these predominantly masculine higher 'intelligences', George was definitely more than the provider of a physical body or 'borrowed brain mechanism'.[34] Never merely an instrument taking dictation, like Wriedt and Leonard she was always mentally engaged at some level of consciousness, though she fluctuated from alertness to accommodation.[35] Nor, after the first shock of 'possession', did she disavow responsibility for her writing, she and the controls persistently making it clear that the active presence of both herself and her husband was necessary to the project; together they provided the necessary 'double force'.[36] Later when 'new methods' were devised and the control spoke through her sleep, this required some ingenuity, but again the procedure is reminiscent of Mrs Leonard, whose control 'Feda' claimed that she required the medium's husband to be present to facilitate the power.

Unlike the controls of many mediums, Georgie's while oddly named are not particularly exotic; there are no guttural North American savages, ancient Chinese philosophers, lisping children, or Hindu maidens. When new methods of trance speaking were introduced much later, they generally came through George's recognizable voice. (In a wry acknowledgement of the esoterica of the period, the Eastern flavour would turn up later in Willy's fictional Arabic framework to *A Vision* and related poetry, especially the Solomon and Sheba poems and 'The Gift of Harun Al-Raschid'.) Instead, the major names tended to bear strong, if playful, echoes from her studies, inviting the reader to puzzle out word games. Thomas of Dorlowicz, for example, suggests Dr Ochorowicz the psychical researcher as well as an East European place name.[37] Thomas, who would return when certain discussions were necessary, was followed by Dionertes (Thomas Aquinas wrote a commentary on the dialectical writings of the mystic theologian Dionysius the Areopagite, while astronomer Dionysius Exiguus was considered the inventor of the Christian calendar); Aymor (god of love or Aymon, the hero of an Old French *chanson de geste* well known to Pound); Arnaud—also known as

AR (troubadour Arnaut Daniel was beloved of both Dante and Ezra Pound). AR seems to have been especially keen on astrological interpretations of history. Other controls, who departed after one or more sessions, were similarly reminiscent of literary or philosophical subjects—Zoretti (nineteenth-century Italian dialect poet Pieri Zorut—or 'little foxes'?), Terhemly (anagram for hermet[ical]ly), Erontius (Elgar's oratorio *The Dream of Gerontius*), Eurectha (Thomas's name in a 'new state', 'means the builder';[38] several sections of the Erechtheum, temple of Athena, went to London with Lord Elgin), Eliorus (nineteenth-century French magus 'Eliphas Lévi' or fourth-century historian Heliodorus), El Bahir (the twelfth-century *Sepher ha-bahir* or Book of Brightness, which introduced to Kabbalistic criticism the notion of the transmigration of souls), and a deceiver called Ontelos (ontology, the study of being, Aristotle's 'first philosophy'). The sole female control Epilamia (epithalamium, nuptial love song) made only two visits in 1920; Ecanentu (untenac[ious]?) appeared briefly in July 1919 to emphasize the solar, lunar, and beatific visions and advise Willy to 'think more intimately'; Frazzlepat, a highly refined spirit, might well have been a pet name for one of their cats, as well as Georgie's recurring dream of being a kitten herself. Later, when 'sleeps' replaced the automatic writing in 1920, other messengers would surface briefly, such as the crusty Carmichael whom Willy with Lily's help traced to a former Dublin clergyman of that disposition.[39] A passage in 'Hodos Chameliontos' refers to 'personifying spirits that we had best call but Gates and Gate-keepers, because through their dramatic power they bring our souls to crisis', suggesting a more generic term for certain guides or controls ('the Gates') they consulted in April 1921 and as late as August 1923.[40]

George's controls—or Instructors and Communicators as the Yeatses preferred to call them—claimed to be spirits, some of whom had been great persons, while those referred to as guides had a limited purpose, to 'affect action directly . . . to bring the living into a condition to receive spiritual or emotional influence'.[41] Their individual daimons (variously described as a 'distinct spirit', 'the ghostly self or soul', 'another mind or another part of our mind', and always of the opposite sex) appear to be different again. These were first discussed in *Per Amica Silentia Lunae*:

The good, unlearned books say that He who keeps the distant stars within His fold comes without intermediary, but Plutarch's precepts and the experience of old women in Soho, ministering their witchcraft to servant girls at a shilling a piece, will have it that a strange living man may win for Daemon an illustrious dead man; but now I add another thought: the Daemon comes not as like to like but seeking its own opposite, for man and Daemon feed the hunger in one another's hearts. Because the ghost is simple, the man heterogeneous and confused, they are but knit together when the man has found a mask whose lineaments permit the expression of all the man most lacks, and it may be dreads, and of that only.

Educated through his wife, Yeats would later annotate these lines, 'I could not distinguish at the time between the permanent Daemon and the impermanent, who may be "an illustrious dead man", though I knew the distinction was there.'[42] In the script George and Willy's (and later their children's) daimons only worked with positive qualities or emotions, acting on events from their habitation in the 'thirteenth cone', 'a phaseless sphere' from whence they transferred images to the mind of the communicant; by 1920 Tagore—whose lectures had impressed the young Georgie, and whom they met again that year—was identified as one of the perfected spirits who became a daimon.[43] Daimons, George and Willy were told, especially made use of what they called the sixth sense, the sexual, to 'collect imagery'. The Moorish traveller and geographer Leo Africanus, who first came to Yeats on 3 May 1909, was one of the 'impermanent' daimons, which may be why later Frustrators adopted the name Leo; on the other hand the permanent daimon resembled the daimon of Socrates, on whom Plutarch had discoursed and about which both Yeatses had read.[44] The word daimon also echoes Yeats's final Golden Dawn motto, 'Demon est Deus Inversus'. Ameritus, pointedly introduced as 'Speaking for Interpreter's Daimon', may indicate a relationship with Thomas Americus, third Baron Erskine, brother of George's great-grandmother. A distinction was made by Thomas: 'he [Ameritus] speaks through her voice—I through hand.'[45] Later, while sleeping, George would associate Ameritus with Willy.[46]

Thomas of Odessa, who made a brief appearance in those early days and then retreated, resurfaced a decade later through the automatic writing of George's close friend Dolly Travers Smith, herself the accomplished daughter of a medium. Either then or earlier he was identified by WBY on a scrap of paper as 'Thomas of Odessa really from Durlowicz (south Russia) trader—great boats black sea'. In the summer of 1928 George had urged Dolly to 'do automatic writing' to keep her ailing husband occupied. As Willy reported the return to Olivia, 'Thomas of Odessa was the first spirit who came to George and myself ten years ago. He stayed so short a time that I had almost forgotten his existence.' Fretting that he would not be able through ill health to finish *A Vision*, he was 'cheered . . . greatly' by this message from the other world—as he had been in the past.[47]

The Instructors—apart from the occasional Frustrator—were sophisticated and intelligent, with an impressive English vocabulary and an extensive knowledge of literature and philosophy. On the other hand Georgie's four guides, Leaf, Fish, Apple, and Rose, were, like the familiars of Marlowe and Goethe, related to the natural world. Notably reminiscent of Willy's early poetry, a few may also have borrowed names from contemporaries—RoseMary La Roche Shakespear, Hope Shakespear's youngest sister, married Herbert Leaf; Dr Walter Leaf was a member of the Council of the Society for Psychical Research who examined the renowned American medium admired by William James, Mrs Leonore Piper;[48]

Horace Leaf was a well-known medium;[49] Mrs Charlotte Herbine's control, who
had strongly advised Willy to marry in 1913, drew strength from a table heaped
with apples, roses, and heather.[50] The guides, especially Apple, were particularly
solicitous of Georgie's physical and emotional welfare (and later of her baby
daughter). That their names were reminiscent of her experience would not
surprise either of them. Yeats, in *Per Amica Silentia Lunae* admitted what most
aspirants already knew:

If you suspend the critical faculty, . . . either as the result of training, or, if you have
the gift, by passing into a slight trance, images pass rapidly before you . . . But the
images pass before you linked by certain associations, and indeed in the first instance
you have called them up by their association with traditional forms and sounds. You
have discovered how, if you can but suspend will and intellect, to bring up from the
'subconscious' anything you already possess a fragment of.[51]

There were other striking differences from the usual séance. After the tentative
beginning, there was no groping for words, although in the haste of writing some
misspellings did occur. With one notable exception (Anne Hyde, of whom more
later; Hugh Lane seems to have momentarily made himself known by accident),
no attempts were made to call up family members, friends, or other recognizable
voices from the dead; nor were the controls as personalized as Leonard's childish
'Feda', or that medium's consultations with the deceased investigators Frederic
Myers and Edmund Gurney. If a parallel can be found, it was with Leonore Piper
(admired by William James) and her 'Imperator' group, who insisted on excluding
'inferior' intelligences, 'earthbound' spirits, and who, while the medium passed
smoothly in and out of trance, seemed able to divine the most secret thoughts of
sitters.[52] Although Georgie did not employ Mrs Piper's use of psychometry, like
the 'Imperators' her disembodied Instructors came for one purpose only; when
their portion was done, they were replaced. Nor were Georgie and Willy allowed
to stray far from their appointed task; for the Instructors preferred to restrict discussion as much as possible to assisting with Willy's Cuchulain cycle, by which
means Maud and Iseult were put in their place, and formulating a theory of the
whole, so complex that only part would be employed in *A Vision*. Towards the
end of his life Yeats would admit, '(The *Vision* is my "public philosophy"). My
"private philosophy" is the material dealing with individual mind which came to
me with that on which the mainly historical *Vision* is based. I have not published
it because I only half understand it.'[53]

The purpose of the visitations gradually became clear: a philosophical system
was to be revealed that explained the 'psychology of the individual', 'the mathematical law of history', 'the adventure of the soul after death', and 'the interaction
between the living and the dead'.[54] Yeats later recalled that the first discussion
with Thomas began with a theme from *Per Amica Silentia Lunae*, the proofs of

which he brought with him to Crowborough and the title of which was drawn from the writings of the Platonic philosopher Henry More, an author familiar to Georgie:

I had made a distinction between the perfection that is from a man's combat with himself and that which is from a combat with circumstance, and upon this simple distinction he built up an elaborate classification of men according to their more or less complete expression of one type or the other. He supported his classification by a series of geometrical symbols and put these symbols in an order that answered the question in my essay as to whether some prophet could not prick upon the calendar the birth of a Napoleon or a Christ. A system of symbolism, strange to my wife and to myself, certainly awaited expression, and when I asked how long that would take I was told years.[55]

The script also drew upon his essay for certain terminology, such as the title of one section, 'Anima Mundi'—'the soul of the world', which he would later define as a world memory 'independent of embodied individual memories, though they constantly enrich it with their images and their thoughts'.[56] And it would reflect the imagery and dialogue structure of the prefatory poem 'Ego Dominus Tuus' ('I am thy master', a line taken from Dante):

> Hic.   Why should you leave the lamp
> Burning alone beside an open book,
> And trace these characters upon the sands?
> A style is found by sedentary toil
> And by the imitation of great masters.
> Ille.   Because I seek an image, not a book.
> Those men that in their writings are most wise
> Own nothing but their blind, stupefied hearts.
> I call to the mysterious one who yet
> Shall walk the wet sand by the edge of the stream
> And look most like me, being indeed my double,
> And prove of all imaginable things
> The most unlike, being my anti-self . . .

In his card file under 'Symbols', recalling some cross-correspondences that had come to him three years earlier, Yeats later noted, 'System said to develope [*sic*] from a spirit script showed me in 1913 & 14. An image in that script used. (This refers to script of Mrs Lytelton, & a scrap of paper by Houghton [Horton] concerning chariot with black & white horses). This told in almost earliest script of 1917.'[57] During the second sitting of 5 November, the script insisted 'one white one black both winged both necessary to you | One you have the other found—the one you have by seeking it | you find by seeking it in the one you have.' If Georgie had not already known of the earlier messages from Lady Edith Lyttelton (who began experimenting with automatic writing through

Yeats's influence) and the artist-mystic Horton, they were bound to be analysed now. But that session closed with Thomas of Dorlowicz cautioning, 'do not lay yourself too open to belief'. This was, as the first Communicator had warned, going to take time. The codification of history, psychology, personality, and spiritism would demand at least 450 sessions in the first three years of their marriage alone.[58]

The Golden Dawn officially disapproved of 'passive mediumship' and automatic writing was forbidden, as explicitly stated in the 1902 by-laws: 'Members are forbidden to permit themselves to be mesmerized, hypnotized, or to lose the control of their thoughts, words, or actions.' Theosophists also disapproved of séances and attempts to make contact with the dead, not because they denied the existence of spirits, but because they believed that the astral plane was inhabited by unsavoury 'spooks, elementaries and elementals'.[59] But the examples of Madame Blavatsky, Moina Mathers, and Mrs Felkin—all of whom received instructions through automatic writing—were common knowledge to members of the Golden Dawn; and William Stainton Moses, one of the founders of the SPR who claimed to have been occasionally visited by Plotinus himself, so intrigued the Yeatses that Georgie cast his horoscope and 220 typed pages of his script were preserved in their library.[60] But there were other examples closer to home: Florence Farr Emery had joined Yeats in 'skrying' adventures; Olivia, while not claiming to be a medium, appears to have been a satisfactory enough seer to engage in Tattwa and psychometric sessions with him; even without seeing his early 'vision notebooks' Georgie would have been aware of his extensive occult adventures with Maud Gonne, culminating in their 'spiritual marriage'.[61] All of these collaborations encouraged but at the same time challenged her to higher achievements. An element of rivalry may also explain her later dismissal of the importance of Bessie Radcliffe's automatic writing, and her dislike of Lennox Robinson's and Tom MacGreevy's friend Hester Travers Smith. *Her* experience was different, unique, special.

It is generally accepted that automatic writing is produced without control of the conscious self who may be at some level of trance or hypnosis. In the early 1950s George would discreetly describe the process as 'writing after suspending the will. To others it would not appear different from normal writing. A planchette would not necessarily be used, though some of Yeats' friends did try it. However, it aimed at evoking the "subconscious", through which, it was believed, revelation was possible.'[62] She might well have been providing a gloss on Yeats's own lecture on symbols to the Order many years earlier: 'The final result of evocation & meditation is to enter into such relations that you could share in the multiform life of this world. There you enter into the presence of a great mystery & receive a curious sense of great things doing around you for which you are occasionally used.'[63]

Despite these illustrious examples, the script itself provides very few hints as to the methods they employed to assist pencil and paper. Later she told John Montague that they eschewed any mechanical means, such as ouija board, planchette, crystal, or the many other devices or 'autoscopes', as William Barrett called them.[64] In the main, this was so, although at one time after she had been unpacking several objects, Ameritus requested that Willy make a crystal from them and charge it astrologically: 'to go on your chain I say a crystal for my own use | yes [*space*] a crystal for me to see in.'[65] Both had long been familiar with the practice of Yoga, through readings of Tagore and Blavatsky as well as the Tattwa doctrines Georgie taught within the Order; their instructors occasionally referred to breath control (the Tattwa Vayu or Air) as preparation for sessions; and talismans were recommended for specific purposes.[66] However, even Tarot cards were eventually banished, Thomas insisting on 21 January 1919, 'I will *not* have this dabbling in cards or anything else of the sort— | It upsets the links [*space*] I wont come tonight | Quite wrong connections | Occult worse than psychical research.'[67]

After their trip to the United States in 1920, the Japanese sword with which Yeats was presented—itself to become famously symbolic, more potent and infinitely more beautiful than the sword of Hiereus which Willy wielded when admitting Georgie into the Order—was incorporated in some of their rituals, usually to ward off evil.[68] However they drew primarily on shared experience, especially their Golden Dawn training in meditation and invocation: Thomas recognized the Order's diagram of a rose on the cross as 'one of the few formulae which is true symbol', and instructed them both to 'do daily some religious exercise—whatever you will—& once the evocation of the higher self ', another Golden Dawn practice.[69] Later, when communications came through George's induced 'sleeps', Willy employed hypnosis, with which, despite the Order by-laws, he was notably skilful. Atmosphere was invoked through incense, candles, flowers ('personal relation'), scent ('increase instinct'), and ritual, especially 'prayer & ceremony' lest they let slip the necessary intensity. Most of all, by their own sense of communion.[70] There were occasional mishaps: 'Whenever I received a certain signal . . . I would get pencil and paper ready. After they had entranced my wife suddenly when sitting in a chair, I suggested that she must always be lying down before they put her to sleep.'[71] Signals included whistles (until the servants complained of 'ghost whistles'[72]); 'sweet smells' (violets were especially comforting[73]); the ringing of a bell heard only by George; bursts of music; occasionally actual speech heard by either or both. George later saw apparitions; other 'still stranger phenomena . . . seemed so incredible' that Yeats preferred to remain silent about them.

Thoughtful professional mediums were always aware of the problem of 'colouring', when the medium becomes interested, and fragments of her own opinions and associations may intrude.[74] Two years earlier, in his report on the clairvoyant search for Hugh Lane's will, Yeats had admitted,

The greatest difficulty in judging communications through mediums or clairvoyants is to separate the communication that one seeks from what is merely dramatic. Only the most literal-minded spiritualist thinks there is no dramatic element and one school of investigators think that all except the underlying thought itself, is dramatic . . . It was possible that we should look upon communications from the dead as the communication of thoughts which take a dramatic form upon entering our minds, or if you will a dream form. Only in the communications which I have received through Miss X. [Radcliffe] have I found reason to believe that the communicators are exactly what they say they are.[75]

Now Yeats had perfect confidence in his control, although the Instructors— distinguishing between the unconscious (invisible means) and subconscious (human memory)—also warned that 'The subconsciousness should be emptied absolutely'; 'that is what the medium wants badly—then the anti[thetical] is free & *may* have the power of prophecy'.[76] Unlike professional mediums, however, George was not expected to deal with a full range of questions; Thomas would reiterate, 'nothing will be accurate with this medium but the philosophy.'[77] Both discussed the questions beforehand and the answers after; doubtless they drew upon Willy's past for details as much as from their shared reading. Very soon they learned to write out their questions, entering them in a separate notebook and carefully indicating who was responsible for which question; on 10 November 1917, George seems to have asked a series of them, effectively participating in a dialogue with herself—was Willy out of the room? Later, clearly less entranced, she would record both question and answer in the same book, indicating with their initials who was responsible for the questions.

After remaining silent throughout his brief epistolary courtship, Georgie was now writing to Willy every day, creating a shared language out of the symbols, rituals, theories, and concepts of eight years of intensive study. Using primarily this alphabet and geometry of imagery, she soon outgrew the familiar structure of the séance room and began to chart a territory of her own, gaining confidence in her powers as the philosophical system began to take shape before their eyes. More visual than verbal, in this rapid shorthand there was no need for polished presentation or stylistic precision (which might have invited literary criticism); images and concepts piled one on the other, creating a vast palimpsest over which each day, after the sessions, the artist-medium and the poet-philosopher would together pick and probe, marshalling their findings into a format for further exploration. The messages can be roughly divided into three categories: domestic instructions—at the beginning or end of the sessions before Georgie fell into or emerged from a deeper trance; attempts to unravel and dissect the 'knots' of

Willy's past emotional life, which included lengthy discussions about Iseult's 'complexes' (they had both read their Freud); and, gradually taking precedence, the exploration and building of the 'system' itself, only a part of which would be taken over by Willy in *A Vision*.

The early automatic writing devoted considerable time to the relationship between the spiritual and the material world, inner and outer nature, process and concept. The psychological polarities of the 'primary' or daily self and the 'antithetical' self, the 'point of vortex'—which would soon become the 'funnel', then the 'gyre' (Willy did not like the word 'spiral'[78])—all so essential to the entire philosophy, are present from the beginning. Not just words but drawings, tables, and diagrams appeared on page after page, providing the basis for the 'more than mathematical' structure Yeats would incorporate in *A Vision*.[79] Did she remember her early studies of Dante, with the Temple edition's detailed diagrams of round towers and double gyres tracing the poet's spiralling journey from death to birth, purgatory to heaven? Dante was a major figure in the early discussions especially.[80] Examples of various psychological phases were drawn from their reading and close acquaintances; while the evolving system was 'to a degree' their 'original thought', the symbolism of the system, Thomas admitted, was rooted in both mythology and astrology.[81]

At the beginning, however, it was necessary to sort out some personal matters. It is clear from the first surviving script of 5 November that the roles of Maud and Iseult had already been discussed and would have to be understood before progress could be made not merely on the system but with Willy's creativity. Fascination with his own obsessions took up many sittings before sense was made of twenty years of barren passion for Maud Gonne, his ambivalent feelings towards Iseult, and, increasingly important as the full significance of George's relationship with the Communicators became clear, the happy chance in choice of wife. As sessions continued, confident in George's sympathetic understanding, Willy more and more openly questioned the Instructors on intimate details of his own past emotional adventures. Fictional results can be seen in the dance play with which he was then struggling, *The Only Jealousy of Emer*, in which in addition to development of the character of Cuchulain he attempts to order the three women in his life. 'I have just begun a new Cuchulain play on the Noh model—I think it very dramatic & strange. It is the "only jealousy of Emer" story & much that I have felt lately seems coming in to it,' he wrote to Lady Gregory on 3 November.[82] An elaborate outline evolved with George as Emer (Race, then Love, Fire, Emotion), Iseult as Eithne (Passion, Water, Desire), and Maud as Fand (Love, Air, Intellect). The script was at first silent, then coy, concerning which woman Cuchulain (WBY, Earth, Instinct), should love; Willy was assured the play was 'a true dream' only after he had answered correctly (appropriately, George) a few weeks later.[83]

The entire Cuchulain cycle would soon be used as examples also of the rapidly developing concepts of historical cycles, 'funnels', the twenty-eight phases identifying individual psychological states, and masks.[84] 'You must seek *truth* | we can only suggest by help', Thomas advised. 'But where your mind can help us is by criticism & proof.' Of the forms of truth, Willy at phase 17 represented artistic genius; George at phase 18 represented a form of innocence, the 'war between philosophy and art'.[85] In fact George's talent for collaboration is evident in the extent to which through the script she provided imagery, scenarios, and even the style of some of her husband's poems and plays.[86] If their exploration proved nothing else, her generosity of spirit was obvious from the beginning, for on a daily basis she had to make room for the other women in her husband's life—Mabel Dickinson and lighter loves were readily dismissed; surprisingly, Maud was easily disposed of, rapidly becoming the icon of his later poetry; Iseult, Olivia, and Lady Gregory were more problematical, and would remain forces to be dealt with throughout their married life. Jealousy of Olivia seems to have been difficult to eradicate despite her obvious encouragement of the marriage, and the script took pains to distinguish Willy's previous collaboration with Lady Gregory, a '24' in the range of personalities ('Imbalanced—you created she transferred—not real colaboration [*sic*]').[87] Even so, Willy remained aware that his wife was still persecuted by 'the thought that she had come between old friends by an accident'.[88] Much depended upon George's strength of will and willingness to face the brutal facts of her own place in his life story; 'Fish' openly reminded Willy of the medium's courage and 'Sacrifice of all & self for an idea or perhaps an ideal'.[89] Despite the revelations of the script, it would be many months before theirs became, in Yeats's words, the 'natural, deep, satisfying love' which 'must precede the Beatific Vision'.[90]

That 'sixth sense', the sexual, became increasingly important as the Yeatses explored and developed the concept of a balanced relationship between creativity and sexuality, leading to that secular Holy Grail, Unity of Being. This, as the script prescribed, required 'Complete harmony between physical body intellect & spiritual desire—all may be imperfect but if harmony is perfect it is unity', adding cryptically that the physical was necessary for 'Sensuous desire emotional desire spiritual desire'. Month after month the same message reappeared: 'What reveals the new' 'Equal balance—that is also why equal balance in sexual intercourse is not tiring—but it must be in both' 'equal instinct & emotion'.[91] Years before John Butler Yeats had written of his eldest son, 'If only the fates would send him a very affectionate wife who would insist on being visibly and audibly loved—insist on it with tears and anger—she would be like Aaron's rod striking the rock in the desert.'[92] George's automatic writing had become that rod.

Due acknowledgement to the marriage bed as 'symbol of the solved antinomy' would be made in *A Vision*, but emphasis on their physical union was repeatedly stressed within the script. On the 28 May 1919, for example, there was a lengthy discussion which concluded with Willy's question 'At what moment of sexual act does energy attain its greatest purity' and the script's reply 'The moment just after entering'.[93] Although the Instructors at times had to encourage regularity and discuss the pattern of intercourse, it appears that Georgie and Willy were from the beginning sexually compatible; a question of September 1919, 'How are we to dream', provoked the answer, 'mental questions & answers *seen* as on marriage night | dreams lying close | dreams *in*voked by prayer | dreams *e*voked by [?vision]'. The script's acknowledgement of the relationship between creative genius and sexual intercourse is also reminiscent of Pound's theories, and in later years would provide encouragement for Willy's Steinach operation and its amatory effects. But long after their initial passion had evaporated, Yeats's passage on transfiguration through sexual union as emphasized in the Hindu Tantric philosophy reflects the intensity and intention of those early years:

There are married people who, though they do not forbid the passage of the seed, practise, nor necessarily at the moment of union, a meditation, wherein the man seeks the divine Self as present in his wife, the wife the divine Self as present in the man. There may be trance, and the presence of one with another though a great distance separates. If one alone meditates, the other knows; one may call for, and receive through the other, divine protection.[94]

The index book in which George and Willy entered phrases drawn from early material emphasizes the 'Wisdom of Two' where, as in their case, 'sex & emotions must be alike (in harmony) mind & soul unlike in tendency & nature'.[95] Their Instructors insisted that 'visual desire' was used by them 'to collect imagery', 'to get in touch with the pam [personal Anima Mundi] & the am [Anima Mundi]'; there would be 'satisfaction only if *both* people are being used by us', for 'when one only is used then we give only fragments'; 'to attain B. V. [the 'Beatific Vision'] 2 people were necessary—both actives.' '[A]ll depends on the writer . . . because we cant use you alone—must have you & medium *equally*.'[96] After the birth of their daughter, there was a further forcible reminder of the need for their union: 'This system is *not* preexistent—it is developed and created by us & by you two or you three now from a preexisting psychology—all the bones are *in* the world—we only select & our selection is subordinate to *you both*—therefore *we* are dependent on you & you influence our ability to develop & create by every small detail of your joint life'; 'we can force true thought into a philosophic system . . . *we never draw analogies*.'[97] From the start, this was to be a crowded marriage, but both parties were encouraged to accept responsibility.

Intercourse as a metaphor for the alchemical union leading to the conception of the Philosopher's Stone is often depicted as 'an embrace of Sun and Moon, in the guise of a King and Queen'.[98] The beggar's vision of 'golden king and silver lady' in Yeats's poem 'Under the Round Tower', 'prancing round and prancing up | Until they pranced upon the top', is an obvious use of terms from alchemy and astrology to celebrate both sexual and psychic revelations. Almost a domestic tease, for 'prancing' was one of George's favourite words for joyful adventuring, the implications of the wild cosmic dance are serious enough:

> That golden king and that wild lady
> Sang till stars began to fade,
> Hands gripped in hands, toes close together,
> Hair spread on the wind they made;
> That lady and that golden king
> Could like a brace of blackbirds sing.

Yeats frequently used 'the old symbol' of the 'gold sun' and 'silver moon' on going to sleep in order to evoke dreams. But the orbital dance of sun and moon was also symbolic of the polarity of male and female and day and night, hence yet another reminder of the oppositions emphasized in George's script.[99] As she once implied to John Montague, the backbone to the script and later the system as discussed in *A Vision* was geometrical; what Yeats would describe as its 'arbitrary, harsh, difficult symbolism' in which he could 'survey all art and letters under the glare of [his] mathematical lightning'.[100] Some of the system's terminology was reminiscent of Vorticism, especially Gaudier-Brzeska's triumphant announcement, 'we have crystallized the sphere into the circle . . . will and consciousness are our vortex.'[101] But a more immediate derivation was their extensive practice as astrologers.[102] Willy hinted as much in his letter to Dulac of 25 October when he said that his wife was 'casting horoscopes'; a month later he would proudly comment to Lady Gregory, 'She is working now at a big Latin edition of Pico della Mirandola and finds there much profound astrology.'[103] (The script for 20 November 1917 includes a question by 'GY', 'Is vulcan in Pico energy?' to which Thomas replies 'vulcan=energy? Yes.') Shortly after their marriage one of Yeats's favourite astrologers, the curmudgeonly 'Kymry' (Hamilton Minchin), who had provided horoscopes for his earlier loves and in 1910 predicted that Dorothy's marriage would take place in 1914, worked out Georgie's progressions from 1909 as far forward as 1960; one of the signposts given was the sudden death of her father (which he estimated as '*very near 8am*'), identified in the script as her first 'moment of crisis'.[104] In Oxford a few months later, as the script progressed, Willy confided to Dulac, 'We are very busy, and for a part of every morning at work in the Bodleian and in the evening the system reveals itself, growing always more subtle and more profound. We can do wonderful things now with a horoscope if only we had the time to use our knowledge.'[105]

As the script gained complexity while George and the Instructors attempted to answer Willy's questions, and as the system itself expanded, more and more frequently the solutions turned on astrological shorthand. Consequently the symbols of 'Sun in Moon' reflected not only their physical union, but as the first script clearly stated, 'sanity of feeling & thinking'. When at Capri in February 1925 Yeats put the final touches to *A Vision*, his final statement recapitulated a belief in the mystic's ideal with the same formula: 'when the two halves of man can define each its own unity in the other as in a mirror, Sun in Moon, Moon in Sun, and so escape out of the Wheel.'[106] Similarly, the instruction to 'melt Saturn in Venus', while sexually explicit, also referred to their individual ruling planets: a proper balance of forces required invocation by Willy of Sun; while he considered himself an Aquarian ruled by Saturn; George's ruler was Venus, planet of love and beauty. As we shall see, the importance of Saturn and Venus was so great that the two symbols were inscribed on the inner side of a ring designed for them by Dulac. Later, when Ameritus was asked, 'Why did you put so much importance to [Saturn Venus] just after we were married, so that I have it now in my ring', he curtly replied, 'her [Venus] parallel [Sun]—your [Saturn] on her [Sun] | 2nd CM [critical moment]'. Years later George would hint to Ellmann of this significance, telling him that Willy's horoscope showed Mars in the Seventh House, which he always claimed was her 'strong Saturnian influence'.[107]

Very early the script implied that Georgie's power came from the threefold 'source of human energy', identical with the three forms of magic ('material astral spiritual') common to early geomancy.[108] In addition to the astrological and alchemical symbolism of this prevailing imagery there is, of course, the ritualism of the Golden Dawn, whose first five grades took the candidate from the 'Land of Night' towards the 'Light of the Spirit'; the contrast was repeated in the candidate's Lotus wand, one end black, the other white. Willy as Hiereus had worn a black robe with a white cross on the left breast and the symbol of his office was a white equilateral triangle on black ground. The spring and autumn equinoxes, marking the intersection of the sun's annual path across the equator, were significant dates in the Order's calendar. Mead, Georgie's old mentor, had dealt much with the doctrines of reincarnation and transmigration of souls, and of 'the life-swirl or vortex . . . the finger of fire, as it were, or light-spark, shot forth by the light-aeons, in their positive phases'.[109] And Felkin's lecture 'The Aura of the Earth', which Georgie had studied just two years previously, described the fourth layer where 'earth-bound spirits', now teachers, draw vitality from likely candidates still living.[110] The cosmic dance of the *Zohar*, with its emphasis on engagement with the world, immanence rather than transcendence, insisted that everything in the universe is connected to everything else, every part in constant inter-action and interplay with every other part, the direct link between sexual and spiritual union, and—a point increasingly emphasized by the script—the uniting of the male and female within one's self. But perhaps the greatest visual influence was the Kabbalah, with its tetrads, triads, and cones, the four worlds or levels of energy, the three triads of the Tree of Life, down which knowledge descends like 'the Lightning Flash among the sacred leaves'. Zigzagging in the order of creation from Kether to the active right pillar to the passive left through the middle pillar where it achieves equilibrium, the lightning flash is grounded at last in Malkuth.[111] The Neophyte's Oath warned that the lightning flash could destroy as well as illuminate: 'the awful penalty of voluntarily submitting myself to a deadly and hostile Current of Will set in motion by the Chiefs of the Order by which I should fall slain or paralysed without visible weapon, as if blasted by the Lightning Flash.'[112] The zigzag of the lightning flash would recur in the script, identifying the various points of 'affinities of souls' until George and Willy reached their partnership: he, predictably, moved from 16 (Maud) through 14 (Iseult) to 18 (George); she from 8 (her father) through 25 (an unidentified person who seems to have caused a 'personal spiritual experience'—Tagore?) to 17 (Willy). Interestingly Ezra, who shares 12 with the hero Cuchulain, occurs in Willy's flash but does not appear in hers.[113]

Even the various moments of crisis—one of the most original contributions in the system—can be plotted along the Tree of Life, moving through time from one sephiroth to the next. And by placing the zodiac on the sacred Tree, with some assistance from the Tattwa and Tarot cards, Georgie and Willy could identify the space each inhabited in this incarnation. For her, it was Yesod or Foundation, the ninth sephiroth on the middle column, corresponding in the human body to the genitals and sex, in alchemy to water, in astrology to the Moon, in mythology to Hecate the lunar goddess of enchantments (Willy would teasingly call her 'a witch'), in psychology to the subconscious, represented by the four 9s of the Tarot, the cat and hare of the animal world. 'As Yesod is connected to both our personal and collective past, the psychological and direct healing work we do in this sphere helps release us from the ties that bind us, including those from our past-life emotional identifications.'[114] According to Demon's notebook for Zelator Adeptus Minor, Yesod 'is the special seat of the Automatic Consciousness'.[115] Directly above on the middle column, at the sixth sephiroth, is Tiphareth or beauty and harmony, the Sun, king, or bridegroom. Here on the axis of human conscious-ness stands Willy, corresponding to the heart or solar plexus, in psychology to the essential self or 'I', in mythology to Apollo, the four 6s of the Tarot, the lion and spider of the animal world; the banner of Hiereus bore the red cross of Tiphareth within a white triangle on a black field, 'the symbol of twilight . . . the equation of the light and the darkness'.[116] 'When we become more centred in ourselves, we become more in control of our own destiny, and our own ability to stay in touch with the unfolding of the soul's individual purposes'; 'thoroughly grounding any inspirational spiritual contacts that may be made . . . we need a firm base.'[117] All nine spheres or sephira are circled or bound by the tenth sephiroth at the base of the Tree, Malkuth or Shekinah, the female presence, bride or queen, sometimes

known as the Holy Spirit, equivalent in Tantra to Shakti, who enters the particip-
ants at the moment of orgasm. It was the vision of Shekinah Willy had beheld
in 1914 when entering the Vault for the 6=5 ceremony of Adeptus Major.[118]

This is far too cursory a generalization to account for the intricacies of more
than 4,000 pages of script, 'sleeps', and 'meditations' over a period of five years;
after July 1922, when the script ceased, there were sporadic 'dream visions'
until the second edition of *A Vision* was published in 1937. But we can safely
acknowledge what critics (and there will be many more as the published script is
studied and digested separately from the *Vision* books[119]) have always known: the
'Wisdom of Two' was constructed by Georgie on a foundation of shared knowledge and experience of which Willy's previous writing and study played no small
a part. In practice, it would appear that they depended on hypnosis, in the beginning self-induced by Georgie; later, in the 'sleeps' and 'visions' which followed
the automatic writing, more of a joint effort. Although not accessible to all,
self-hypnosis is possible for some, especially those trained as they both were in
meditation and methods of achieving inner powers of concentration; it seems
likely that Georgie had the ability to put herself under very quickly. Once in this
state, a willing subject becomes subject to 'trance logic' which, among other
qualities, is characterized by 'the ability to tolerate logical inconsistencies that
would be disturbing to the individual in the wake state'.[120] Reality and imagination,
conscious knowledge and unconscious reactions flow smoothly back and forth.
This could explain why at times George seems to be consciously controlling the
answers, other times apparently not; it also explains why the advice on personal
matters tended to occur at the beginning and end of the sessions, when George's
own concerns and daily thoughts would be uppermost. Again, the frequent use of
mirror or backwards writing when the subject was likely to be one distressing to
George could either suggest an element of deception or, more likely, an unwilling-
ness to acknowledge responsibility for what is being said—as psychologists have
recognized by deliberately encouraging recalcitrant patients to practise automatic
writing. Though it would be foolhardy to ignore the strength of her will power,
we will never know how aware she was during the process. More than likely the
levels fluctuated, for psychiatrists and clinical psychologists acknowledge that
the element of 'dissociation' shifts considerably during hypnosis: the subject may
realize what is happening but be powerless to intervene, may even be capable of
expressing her reactions, and, if not completely 'under', of dramatizing. Much
depends upon the relationship between the entranced and the entrancer, and the
eagerness to fulfil expectations. Modern psychologists confirm that, writing automatically when in a deep trance, a hypnotized individual 'literally does not know
what his right (or left) hand is doing. The suggestion is given . . . that without his
awareness and even while he is concentrating on other matters, his hand will guide
his pen in writing a message from the unconscious.'[121] In persons sufficiently

susceptible, these skills can be learned and polished; urged on by Willy, Georgie had plenty of opportunity to practise. She had, after all, initiated them.

But even if this process of automatic writing explains George's insistence that after her first few sentences she was no longer 'faking', what of the script that emerged in her altered state, or states, of consciousness?[122] For even more astonishing, apart from her extraordinary critical and codifying skills, is her ability for total recall and, beyond that, her creativity in making use of what surfaced. Where did it come from?

Neuropsychologists would confidently answer from Georgie herself, more specifically the result of electro-chemical activity in both the language and motor centres of her brain. No one can explain how the content is selected, any more than why some are naturally good hypnotic subjects and others not. But thanks to studies made during brain surgery and brain scans, although we are only at the beginning of understanding the full interaction between brain and mind, we now know much more about how the brain works, and the relationship between its function and human consciousness.[123] Dr Wilder Penfield, one of the first neuro-surgeons to carry out brain surgery while the patient was awake and able to describe what occurred, found that electro-stimulation of various parts of the cortex produced certain involuntary or automatic movement. When stimulating certain parts of the verbal-memory centres, 'the patient re-lived an early child-hood episode or emotion, experienced what had reappeared in dreams, saw herself at certain times in the past in original surroundings, heard voices, recalled previous experiences and recognized them as authentic'. Penfield was intrigued to discover that in this 'flash-back' or 'double consciousness', the patient while re-experiencing an event complete with details from the past was at the same time aware of the present as well; they were not 'memories' as we understand them, but an apparent actual reliving of certain moments. Further research suggests that the hippocampus plays a role in the formation or preservation of this record of the past or its recall, by controlling the record of the stream of consciousness which is then somehow stored in the temporal lobe.[124] Penfield concluded that

there is a neuronal record of the stream of consciousness that seems to preserve all those things of which a man was aware, even the unimportant experiences, in a continuous succession from minute to minute to minute. This record of the stream of former con-sciousness can be activated, occasionally, by electrical stimulation of the interpretive cortex of a conscious man. Under normal conditions the recording mechanism must be called upon subconsciously when a man judges that present experience is familiar or strange, or when he compares the present with past similar experience. But a man can voluntarily recall the detail of comparatively few past experiences.[125]

Although some psychologists question the suggestion that *everything* is remembered, it is possible that somewhere within the inner depths of the brain a continuous film records what we have observed, heard, or felt, buried until an abnormal occurrence causes it to be re-enacted. This might partly account for some of the sensations experienced by sitters at séances when they 'recognize' voices of deceased loved ones—and for the storehouse of images Georgie was able to draw on, even perhaps for the 'power' that grasped and directed her hand. Certainly on 24 October 1917 she underwent an emotional shock equivalent only to the sudden death of her father eight years previously; the dark night of the soul endured in the Ashdown Forest Hotel galvanized all her resources and threw up what she did not know she knew. As another automatist once put it, 'When emotion is roused . . . it strengthens desire and stimulates the imagination, which enables the higher mind or subliminal to function smoothly as a channel for authentic messages.'[126]

Such research can explain the surfacing, if not the selection, of ideas that were stored electro-chemically in the neural tissues of George's cerebral cortex, and even the shared memories of husband and wife. Her own creative resources and training in image-making, both graphic and literary, could account for the multiple characters who served as guides and instructors in sorting out and expanding on those original memories; the dialogue form was remarkably consistent. One might even go further and attempt to explain the Instructors as examples of a *healthy* schizotypal trait in her nature; recent studies suggest that heredity plays some part in schizophrenia, a condition suffered by at least one of Georgie's uncles and two of her cousins.[127] Sympathy and increased intimacy could also help explain how attuned wife and husband became not only as the script progressed, but in their many shared dreams, visions, and even co-creations. But these speculations provide only partial answers.

It is tempting to enlist one of the more recent categories of psychological disorder to explain the appearance in the script of so many controls or Instructors. But the criteria set out for Multiple Personality Disorder and Dissociative Identity Disorder imply that there is no 'executive control' when alternate personalities take over. This appears to be an unnecessary minefield, where, unlike the clinical understanding of hypnosis and automatic writing, psychiatrists and psychologists are in considerable disagreement.[128] In contrast, George seems always to have been at some level or another aware and in control, stage-managing the transition to Instructors and back with Willy's help (and curiosity) and her own skills in autohypnosis. In any case, the process of automatic writing itself requires a certain degree of concentration and control.

What did they themselves believe? 'Overwhelmed by miracle as all men must be when in the midst of it',[129] Yeats was by nature and inclination receptive to the conviction that in the trance state such revelations could occur. He had, after all, decided that 'the ER case' had finally proved spirit identity. What Elizabeth Radcliffe's scripts and his many sittings with other mediums had *not* offered was 'speculative power, or at any rate not equal to the mind's action at its best . . . only in speculation, wit, the highest choice of the mind that they fail'.[130] There was no question of the scripts provided by George lacking such qualities. Nor was there any doubt that these powers were doubled by the 'Wisdom of Two'. Yeats's note to his poem 'An Image from a Past Life', which is based on a shared dream he and George experienced at Ballylee, offers one explanation: 'No mind's contents are necessarily shut off from another and in moments of excitement images pass from one mind to the other with extraordinary ease, perhaps most easily from that portion of the mind which for the time being is outside consciousness. . . . The second mind sees what the first has already seen—that is all.'[131]

The concept of thought transference or mental telepathy had been a major concern of the Society for Psychical Research ever since its founding.[132] Four of its presidents in particular had written specifically of the relationship between the brain and memory, moving on to consider the possibility of supranormal powers. As early as 1889 Frederic Myers in his discussion of the secondary (or multiple) personality had associated Socrates' daimon with 'a wiser self' that could 'use the products of unconscious thought'. A few years later he wrote of the Subliminal Consciousness (preferring that and 'supraliminal' to sub- and superconscious), 'Each of us is in reality an abiding psychical entity far more extensive than he knows—an individuality which can never express itself completely through any corporeal manifestation. The Self manifests through the organism; but there is always some part of the Self unmanifested; and always, as it seems, some power of organic expression in abeyance or in reserve.'[133] It was Myers who first suggested the name telepathy (and related its activities to the right side of the brain), explaining automatic writing as 'the operation, first of unconscious cerebral action of the already recognized kind, but much more complex and definite than is commonly supposed to be discernible in waking persons; and secondly, of telepathic action—of the transference, that is to say, of thoughts or ideas from the conscious or unconscious mind of one person to the conscious or unconscious mind of another person, from whence they emerge in the shape of automatically written words or sentences.' And, in language which seems to predict Penfield's findings, 'It may be that the unconscious self moves more readily than the conscious along these old-established and stale mnemonic tracts, that we constantly retrace our early memories without knowing it, and that when some recollection seems to have *left* us it has only passed into a storehouse from which we can no longer summon it at will.'[134]

Psychologist William James, whose writing George so admired, while not going as far as his British counterpart in asserting the survival of the individual personality, accepted long before Jung's belief in inherited symbols and a world soul Bucke's concept of a 'cosmic consciousness' (about which Georgie had also read), and eventually became convinced of the reality of supernormal powers. He concluded his lectures on *Varieties of Religious Experience*, 'The whole drift of my education goes to persuade me that the world of our present consciousness is only one out of many worlds of consciousness that exist, and that those other worlds must contain experiences which have a meaning for our life also; and that although in the main their experiences and those of this world keep discrete, yet the two become continuous at certain points, and higher energies filter in.'[135]

Philosopher Henri Bergson, whose 1913 presidential lecture had been copied out by Nelly Tucker for either Willy or Georgie, suggested, 'may there not be, around our normal perception, a fringe of perceptions mainly unconscious, but always ready to enter into the consciousness and actually introducing itself into it in exceptional instances or with predisposed subjects. . . . If consciousness is proved to have an even partial independence of relation to the body we have no reason for admitting the extinction of consciousness after death.'[136] And physicist Sir William Barrett, with whom George and Willy both attended séances, became convinced 'that whilst many super-normal psychical phenomena may ultimately be proved to be due to abnormal conditions of the brain, yet there will be found to remain well attested facts which will compel science to admit the existence of a soul; and also of a spiritual world, peopled with discarnate intelligent beings, some of whom can occasionally, but more or less imperfectly, get into communication with us.'[137]

Although George rejected what she referred to as 'the old psychical research theory of the "subconscious" ', she did believe that memory was a large part of all psychic phenomena; but she also insisted that discarnate beings appeared at séances.[138] Neither she nor Willy appears to have doubted this link between telepathy and belief in an external consciousness. Their ghostly Instructors informed them that the process of automatic writing bore in fact some resemblance to telepathy in that both were mechanical; unlike the Anima Mundi which drew upon dream images, 'The automatic faculty is a machinery & not a reservoir. . . . It selects from memory in conscious waking states.'[139] An element of dramatization may be necessary, and the conscious mind could play on the form the messages took:

in a recent sleap [*sic*] communicator said that all communications such as ours were begun by the transference of an image later from another mind. The image is selected by the daimon from telepathic impacts & one is chosen not necessarily a recent one. . . . The image or bundle of images was symbolic of the state of mind at start of communication in the mind for whom the communication was sent. In this case my mind. They cannot use an image formed by that mind because a mind cannot see its own states objectively. They develop their communication from the image. The mind from which the image comes is not conscious of the transference where the communication is as in present case of a subjective nature. It is because of the relation between image & state that the system is within human life. The system of Swedenborg was not so begun & is out side human life.[140]

Later, Willy dictated to George Dionertes' simple explanation during a 'sleep': 'She finds the words, we send the wave & she as it were catches it in a box.' Clearly familiar with at least some contemporary methods of communication, Dionertes elsewhere described his own role as 'a kind of telephone between us & a central group of spirits'.[141]

Thus, they and their Instructors continued to insist that *their* experience was different—distinguishing it from séances they had attended, articles they had read, examples they had heard of. On the other hand they believed that dreams were messages from the spiritual state; like astrology, dreaming might provide what could not be explained by telepathy. When a letter arrived from John Quinn after George dreamt of the same subject, Willy triumphantly announced: 'This dream proves (like much else) that people explain by telepathy what telepathy has nothing to do with. No telepathy could have told George that your letter was about to arrive.'[142] By the time he wrote the second version of *A Vision*, Yeats had come to the conclusion that his and George's knowledge, combined with help and encouragement from their personal daimons, may in fact have invented the entire system:

one said in the first month of communication, 'We are often but created forms', and another, that spirits do not tell a man what is true but create such conditions, such a crisis of fate, that the man is compelled to listen to his Daimon. And again and again they have insisted that the whole system is the creation of my wife's Daimon and of mine, and that it is as startling to them as to us. . . . The blessed spirits must be sought within the self which is common to all. Much that has happened, much that has been said, suggests that the communicators are the personalities of a dream shared by my wife, by myself, occasionally by others—they have . . . spoken through others without change of knowledge or loss of power—a dream that can take objective form in sounds, in hallucinations, in scents, in flashes of light, in movements of external objects.[143]

But like George he never entirely gave up his belief in discarnate spirits, explaining one day to a startled Lady Gregory, 'I believe there are emanations that communicate with me, giving knowledge now, but sometimes sent by the beings that exist somewhere outside us, to seek knowledge. In séances they give foolish answers because of want of knowledge; they are sent as questioners.'[144] He was somewhat less open, understandably, in print, but in 1928, having told the true story—against her wishes—of George's automatic script, he went as far as he could: 'Some will ask if I believe all that this book contains, and I will not know how to answer. Does the word belief, used as they will use it, belong to our age, can I think of the world as there and I standing here to judge it. I will never think any thoughts but these, or some modification or extension of these; when I write prose or verse they must be somewhere present though not it may be in the words; they must affect my judgment of friends and of events.'[145]

Few who later came to know George Yeats personally would doubt her honesty. As Virginia Moore has argued, 'Mrs Yeats says that what happened was a complete surprise; and certainly an impulse to fake an hour's automatic writing is very different from a decision to sustain years of deception. I myself found her forthright and transparently honest.'[146] Most of the scholars who have left reports would agree with Moore (herself a philosopher) that George was one of the most intelligent persons they had ever met and remarkably sensitive to others—in fact, an extraordinarily perceptive woman.[147] There are many valid reasons why she did not want her share in the making of *A Vision* to become widely known, although it was impossible for her to prevent Willy from dropping hints. Nor, while her mother was alive, was she keen to have their activities broadcast. Besides, if Willy were to invite onlookers or publicize her mediumship a request by the Society for Psychic Research would inevitably follow. She disapproved intensely of the nineteenth-century antics provoked in the name of spiritualism. To be subjected to the same kind of scrutiny would have been embarrassing and demeaning. George was after all a product of her time, with a strong sense of Victorian dignity; to open herself to possible mockery would have been intolerable. But she also disapproved of the framework of myth round which Willy wove the system in the first edition of *A Vision*; that too was demeaning to their close joint work.[148] It is clear that at least during the first five years of marriage George believed that there were supernormal powers which certain gifted persons could tap. Certainly she never gave up her belief in ghosts, poltergeists, or other indications of supernatural forces at work in the universe, although in her later years it would lead her in other more conventional directions, even to a flirtation with Roman Catholicism.

As the long process of analysis and structuring continued, the tone of the script becomes more confident, her ability to plumb the depths more striking. She would never have considered herself a mystic, and shunned the popular image of the medium (further reasons she never wanted her role stated in print). Yet her contribution to their system seems to have fallen somewhere between these two poles. Summoning memories and energies she did not know she had, day after day fresh material came from her pen. Where did it come from? Certainly much of the initial structure of the developing philosophy reflected her own reading and thoughts; but no matter the extent of the willingness to suspend disbelief, it is clear from the script and the ensuing dreams and 'sleeps' that in digging deep she was throwing up more than scattered recollections and snatched imagery. As we have seen, even neuropsychologists confess that nobody knows what goes on in the cortex, how information is stored and retrieved. In 1929 Jean Cocteau, speaking of his new book, told Tom MacGreevy that 'it wasnt he wrote it all that something queer happened'; MacGreevy assured him that 'W. B. could probably explain all about those things.' So, of course could William Blake, whose authors

'were in eternity'.[149] Present-day automatists speak of their experience in much
the same terms as George had—'It just happened to me, there was no forcing,
I sense it, then write as fast as I can.'[150]

Although I am reluctant to claim what is commonly thought of as mystical
powers for George Yeats, it would appear that, in her entranced state, something
did indeed 'grasp her hand'. That something was akin to the ecstatic state in which,
as Northrop Frye describes it, 'the real self, whatever reality is and whatever the
self is in this context, enters a different order of things from that of the now dispossessed ego' and 'all the doors of perception in the psyche, the doors of dream
and fantasy as well as of waking consciousness, are thrown open'.[151] So slender
is the thread between this and the normal state that anything might disrupt concentration, which would explain in part the script's frequent annoyance with Willy's
insistent questioning and persistence in pursuing one line of thought. While
still in the Ashdown Forest Hotel the control insisted, 'when you are doubting we
begin to doubt too', and later, 'I don't like you misdoubting script as it upset the
communication. Much better not ask for facts No No but never for veryfication
[*sic*].'[152] Analysis could only come later when on reflection a theory was elaborated,
or a Frustrator identified. Frequently the Instructors would hesitate, ask for a
postponement, even delay for several days before they dealt with specific questions
('I must think a coherent answer'[153]). From the beginning, the script warned
that when George's powers weakened, as they often did from tiredness or other
physical causes, they could not continue. 'The automatic script will only continue
for a time because it will be too bad for her,' and 'she will lose it for a while perhaps
a few months'.[154] This tenuousness provides a further explanation for Georgie's
refusal to have any observers; if she became self-conscious the miracle might
not happen. Their experience was special, personal; the bond which had been
created was not yet strong enough to allow for any doubts. It is a sign of the great
trust they shared that the experiment continued as long as it did. Her husband
recognized this, and clearly had Georgie in mind when he remarked to William
Barrett concerning a séance all three had recently attended:

I think that one should deal with a control on the working hypothesis that it is genuine.
This does not mean that I feel any certainty on the point, but even if it is a secondary
personality that should be the right treatment. The control believes that it is present for
a purpose & is tortured by the feeling that it cannot carry out this purpose because we
doubt its existence. As all experiments increase that torture by seeming a part of our
doubt, they should be given up so far as that control is concerned, until it has regained
tranquility. In fact the control should be treated as a doctor would treat a nervous
patient.[155]

By 1952 George was prepared to admit to Virginia Moore that while in the
beginning they did believe that the messages were 'spirit-sent, and therefore

proof of communion between the living and dead', they later saw them 'as a dramatized "apprehension of the truth". . . . from their own higher selves'.[156] Five years later, when Thomas Parkinson boldly asked her 'exactly what she and Yeats thought when the automatic writing began and was followed by dictation, what were those voices? She sat silent for a moment and then said, "We thought they were expressing our best thought".'[157] Probably she would have agreed with the conclusion of the philosopher she most admired. I think she would have sympathized entirely with William James's admission that he himself was a 'piecemeal' supernaturalist who believed 'that in communion with the Ideal new force comes into the world, and new departures are made here below'.[158] But she continued to 'draw an opaque curtain' across the making of the script and, understandably, the personal and intimate details intermingled with the philosophical. It is clear that in the 1940s she read through the scripts herself to answer Ellmann's questions. She did go so far as to tell Virginia Moore, whom she trusted even more than she did Ellmann, that she 'might leave some notes'. If so, they have not yet been discovered.[159]

As her letters to Willy and her friends illustrate, there was a strong streak of common sense in George, and an insistence upon facing facts. The pragmatism that had caused her to initiate the script in the first place, and would later enable her to accept her ageing poet-husband's amorous forays elsewhere, was a strong trait in her nature. Although the notebooks transcribed by George Harper and his indefatigable team provide some evidence of the Yeatses' discussions, it is difficult to know how much of the rigidity implied in the diagrams of *A Vision* comes from George, who dictated them through the script and later drew them for publication. Peter Allt, whom George knew well, has wisely pointed out that the Instructors proposed

a working hypothesis merely, and not a gospel; not a creed by which he must live but a cosmic symbol by which he might organize his thought; not a school for his will but an instrument for his invention . . . But . . . by no means a religion in the scope and type of its teaching. It was essentially an hypothesis, like a scientific theory . . . not imposed as a dogma: therefore acceptance of it could always remain hypothetical, partial, conditional . . . it set his imagination free, but established no law for his will . . . religious belief unrestrained by the trammels of any religious faith.[160]

Yeats himself claimed that the doctrine of the gyres was not fatalistic 'because the mathematical figure is an expression of the mind's desire and the more rapid the development of the figure the greater the freedom of the soul'.[161] George would have agreed; as the days, months, and years went on, she and the Instructors insisted that the system was there to serve his writing, not the other way round, that the ecstatic state of the poet was paramount.[162] Later she would insist to Ellmann that free will was represented by the true and false masks and escape into the thirteenth cone, even suggesting that the twelve cones could be interpreted as the twelve disciples, the thirteenth Christ, thereby having it more than both ways.[163] In any case, her personal choices were influenced by what she had to do to help the marriage and 'perfection of the work', and in this way she differed most obviously from his previous muse: Maud had grown disillusioned with the Golden Dawn and replaced it with the Castle of Heroes which she fervently believed in but would not commit herself to; Georgie provided revelation itself. Hers was not to be merely a spiritual, but a mystical marriage. Willy exulted in one of his almost daily letters to Coole,

A very profound, very exciting mystical philosophy—which seems the fulfilment of many dreams and prophecies—is coming in strange ways to George and myself. It began of a sudden when things were at their worst with me, and just when it started came this curious message from Bessie Radcliffe 'They departed with the rewards of divination in their hands'. It is coming into my work a great deal and makes me feel that for the first time I understand human life. . . . I live with a strange sense of revelation and never know what the day will bring. You will be astonished at the change in my work, at its intricate passion.[164]

Whether you choose to call the extraordinary phenomenon that occurred in Ashdown Forest subconscious direction, cross-dreaming, extrasensory perception, subliminal consciousness, split subjectivity, telepathy, clairvoyance, channelling, psychic transcription, 'faculty X', 'Mind Energy',[165] or plain hocus-pocus, the results are obvious. Clearly there were strong psychological advantages and equally strong emotional benefits to the role Georgie consciously chose to play in selecting automatic writing as her creative medium: as they worked out the system of what would become *A Vision*, George's place in Willy's affections was assured and their marriage forged with a confidence and trust in each other's frank responses which would last until death. More than that 'friendly, serviceable & very able' domestic partner he had hoped for, she was immediately established as the voice of truth, and for the rest of their lives together would continue to serve as unquestioned extension of his senses.[166] If poetry was the essence of his creative genius, then the automatic writing, whether consciously initiated or not, became the essence of hers. In helping provide those metaphors for poetry, might not the poet in turn have become her form of creation?

> Where got I that truth?
> Out of a medium's mouth,
> Out of nothing it came,
> Out of the forest loam,
> Out of dark night where lay
> The crowns of Nineveh.[167]

7

LONDON, OXFORD, AND DUBLIN

There were other bridges to build on the more mundane sphere. Willy's first letter to his sister Lily as a married man was dictated to Georgie:

I have just reminded her that we have never written you any thanks for your letter of Oct: 16 and for the presents you speak of in it. We thank you very much both for the promise of the Fire screen and the pearl ring. I think the best thing to do will be for you to keep both for the present, for we shall be in Ireland before long to have a look at Ballylee. . . . Mrs. Tucker has sent on a letter of yours in which you ask if she is tall or short. She says she is short, but that is a question of definition. We are keeping Woburn Buildings for the present, and expect to be there in December; and after that probably in Ireland; and after that in France where I am to deliver some lectures.[1]

Plans would change, as they frequently did throughout their married life, but ever since the news of his marriage—which arrived after the event—John Butler Yeats and his daughters Lily and Lolly had been excitedly relaying bits and pieces of information back and forth across the ocean. 'I would that my new daughter-in-law were 34 rather than 24', the patriarch-in-exile complained to his younger daughter Lolly. 'Willie won't need a heavy hand, but his abstract and self concentrated mind has produced a kind of *personal isolation*. Therefore his wife must do a little guiding and forewarning. He would surrender to her instantly, and be greatly improved in himself and in his poetry.'[2]

Relieved on hearing Georgie was five foot seven (her brother Harold towered over Willy at six foot four), he exulted to the family's patron John Quinn in appropriately astrological terms: 'Willie has always had luck—he is *well constellated*. . . . I am to receive a photo—which I wait anxiously. . . . I think tall women are easier to get on with and live with than little women. They have more sentiment and gentleness, and because they are more conspicuous are more watchful of themselves. The little women are constantly out of sight so that you don't know what they are up to.'[3]

Georgie and her mother wrote dutifully to Willy's sisters, even Harold introduced himself ('I am your brother-in-law') with the excuse of ordering books from the Cuala Press, which Lolly had founded and for which Willy served as editor.

All correspondence was in turn forwarded to New York, provoking further response. Never had words been pored over so assiduously outside the schoolroom. 'The letters you enclose are written without any appearance of literary culture or style, yet Willie says the young lady is very cultivated. They were very British, with a sort of robust frankness.' 'I am still wondering and guessing about Willie's marriage. It took me completely by surprise. The two letters Lollie copied for me don't shed any light—they were so businesslike. They may be horrid people and philistine and utterly without sympathy, and Willie's wife for all we know may be quite under their influence so that Willie may miss the old freedom. Still money and position are good things in themselves.'[4] One can only wonder what Georgie thought when the old artist sent his son a perceptive pen portrait of his new daughter-in-law, drawn from such limited information:

I am indeed delighted to hear of your marriage, and since I got the news have thought of nothing else. Please give your wife, my new daughter-in-law, my love. . . . I think it will help you in your poetical development. . . . But there is something from which to draw an inference. She is full of guile, but good guile, like mother nature's or Penelope's. There is also fire in the flint. Beware. Someday there may come a flash and you will see angles where you thought were only curves, yet so momentarily that you will think you have dreamed and rub your eyes and resolve to be more cautious in future. . . . About your wife let me add another conjecture. She is not critical. She loves to give and receive praise and likes it in full measure, her mind synthetic, not at all analytic. She is like the other 'George' who was 'such a good comrade', as Flaubert and Tourgenieff and Balzac described her. The suffragettes would scold her, and she would laugh at them.[5]

The comparison with George Sand may well have been flattering if inaccurate, but when he finally wrote to Georgie directly, already aware of her husband's financial commitments to keeping JBY in bed and board, she doubtless took his words with a pinch of salt. 'I bragged a little about the family,' he told Lolly, 'but I think delicately, so as not to set her back up. Indeed I could not brag except delicately. I told her my father's family were to me the most loveable, just because they never got on or expected or wanted to *get on*, yet always paid their debts.'[6] But Willy was not averse to some (less discreet) bragging himself:

I enclose her photograph. She permits me to say that it flatters her good looks at the expense of her character. She is not so black and white, but has red brown hair and a high colour which she sets off by much Irish green in her clothes and earrings, etc. You are right in saying that towns are bad for me and my wife is ready to seem to dislike them too. I hope to see very little of them henceforth. We are going after Christmas to Ireland, where Dr Gogarty has lent us a Connemara house, a great 17th century place which once belonged to the Blakes. We shall take a couple of servants and have a friend to stay with us.[7]

Of this offer of Gogarty's recently purchased Renvyle House, JBY wryly noted, 'the "two servants" was an artistic touch, and lets me see that they are in a sort of atmosphere not common hitherto in Willie's rather bare and lonely life'.[8] However, the censor returned Georgie's photograph. Not until they finally met in New York two years later would he be able to trace her likeness, or discover that he and his new daughter-in-law had both attended the same art school in London.

Willy then wrote, through his wife, to John Quinn in much the same vein, once again emphasizing the newly-weds' affinities. 'We have known each other for some years, and she is a deep student in all my subjects, and is at present deep in the Latin edition of the astrological works of Pico della Mirandola. She consents for my sake to pretend to a hatred of town life & we shall live in many country places, Ireland or England, or after the war is over Italy and France. I daresay you will see us in America too.'[9] Pound also gave his opinion of the match to Quinn, with typical nonchalance and somewhat less candour: 'I dare say it is not so bad as it might be. The girl is 25, not bad looking, sensible, will perhaps dust a few cobwebs out of his belfry. At any rate, she wont be a flaming nuissance [sic] to him or his friends. She is the step-daughter of an uncle of my wife's, so it is not an incursion.' He then added, 'The Gonne family seem pleased with her, also Lady G.'[10]

Meanwhile, Lady Gregory herself wrote to Willy of her relief at his safe harbour: 'It is really an ease to my mind your going into good hands. I had often felt remorseful at having been able to do so little for you now, with the increasing claims here, looking after this place for Robert, and teaching and playing with the children, and trying to keep the wheels working. . . . And there is only half of me here while Robert is in danger.'[11] Though she had not yet met Georgie, her report to New York was equally encouraging, unconsciously echoing the wishes he had expressed that distracted previous September:

you want to know about Willie's marriage. Well, I am satisfied it will be a happy one—& that he has found a good companion & helpmate. He had come to have a passionate, almost romantic, longing for a hearth & home of his own—& as in gaining this he has also gained a young & charming & well endowed wife, she is naturally the centre, the shrine in that romantic setting. . . . Woburn Buildings will be their London house for the present.[12]

Nelly Tucker sent Georgie's photograph to Ireland, but it was not sufficiently detailed for the eager in-laws; Lily had shrewdly guessed that her brother's description of his bride as 'comely' 'may mean not good-looking'.[13] But a few months later she was able to report a much more revealing picture to her father after a visit from Maud Gonne:

She told me more about Georgie in five minutes than all others or all letters. The photograph she says, is hardly even like. She is not nearly so dark as it shows her. Her eyebrows are very marked, her eyes blue, her colour high, rather too high. She dresses well in rather vivid colours which suit her. She is most unselfish, never appears to assert herself at all, but from her face Maud thinks she could assert herself. She thinks her life has not been altogether happy, because of her Mother, who is 'charming' but very neurotic. Her tastes are serious so she will find life with Willy pleasant—smooth anchorage. Willy does not like his only brother-in-law, but Maud thinks he has no good reason for it.[14]

Years later Iseult Gonne—doubtless influenced by her mother's lifelong theatrical costume of black—still recalled their disapproval of George's 'strangeness' and 'high colours, somewhat too high'.[15] Yet Iseult was quickly wound into a more intimate—yet safer—relationship by Georgie herself.

On 3 November, a week after completing his confessional poems, Willy went up to London for the day and sent them to Coole for safe keeping. Ostensibly to visit the dentist, his primary motive was to see Iseult, whose position at the School of Oriental Languages had been secured by him. Concerned about the young woman's lack of self-confidence, he took her to the Tuckers—a visit engineered by Georgie and her mother. His letter to Lady Gregory is as revealing for its naivety as its delight in his good fortune: 'Mrs Tucker suggested this she wishes to show her some kindness. I think she will be a better adviser than Madame Gonne. Georgie has I believe no idea of what has happened but I think Mrs Tucker has divined something of it. Georgie is a good friend and an always pleasant companion & seems to me entirely unselfish as good a wife as a man could have—indeed a very perfect character.'[16] As Lily described her brother's state of mind to Quinn, 'He is in the mood in which a child could play with him.'[17]

But there were more serious players to deal with, closer to home. Willy was especially anxious to introduce his wife to his friends, and so as soon as they had gained access to Stone Cottage on 8 November, plans were made to visit London. On Tuesday, 13 November, Georgie for the first time took her place as hostess at Woburn Buildings when Willy invited the visionary artist W. T. Horton around to 'meet my wife'. Yeats seems to have openly discussed their experiments, for, distressed by what he was told, the next morning Horton (whose own experiments with the planchette had ceased with the death of his companion Audrey Locke) sent, along with a jar with 'sweet smelling herbs' as a wedding gift, a lengthy warning:

I have given up all spiritistic things & all things automatic or unconscious for I have found them all unreliable, foolish or dangerous. Nothing new or great is obtained by unconscious means & at the best come nowhere near anything that has been done consciously by the great or good in the world. Automatism etc. lead to obsession, depletion, hallucination, utter lack of self reliance & self control, weakness & moral disintegration. It robs the Creative Artist of all.

This was not the first time Horton had attempted to rouse Yeats against 'these lower things . . . & ascend to the heights'; a note three years previously had, Willy was convinced, introduced the imagery revealed in the earliest scripts and repeated in Edith Lyttelton's automatic messages: 'The fight is still raging round you while you are trying to increase the speed & usefulness of your chariot by means of a dark horse you have paired with the winged white one which for so long has served you so faithfully & well.' Undeterred, and all too familiar with his long-time friend and adversary's 'profound and lonely temperament', Yeats continued to woo him whenever they were in London; doubtless he hoped for further revelations concerning Horton's white horse of reason and creativity, the dark horse of belief and spiritism, and their relationship to Georgie's automatic writing.[18] Desperate to find her a safe harbour, Willy also had a fleeting, bizarre hope that Iseult might find some consolation in a relationship with his visionary friend.[19] George's script seems to have had the last word: after his death Horton apologizes by sending a message through Thomas that 'he believes now much that he denied before', and asks that a chair be left for him on Monday.[20]

Willy was still concerned about Iseult's welfare. George's spirits instructed him to make a box charged with symbols to help her over her attacks of depression; it is clear from the script that he was also to encourage her to remove 'complexes' by talking about the incident—the sexual attack by her stepfather—that caused her to feel worthless.[21] It may also have been on this occasion that, doubtless in company with the Pounds, they paid a surprise visit to Richard Aldington and his wife Hilda Doolittle (the poet H.D.). Their reaction echoed that of most of Yeats's London friends:

It seemed to me that marriage with its realities and responsibilities would interfere hopelessly with Yeats's habits of dawdling meditation and dim moods. You may imagine my surprise then when I came back to England on leave from the front in 1917, and next morning Mr and Mrs W. B. Yeats were announced as callers. Mrs Yeats turned out to be Georgie Hyde-Lees, a distant relative of Mrs Ezra Pound. Miss Hyde-Lees was versed in occult learning, and I knew she had done research for Yeats in the British Museum Library, but I never dreamed they would marry. The idea of there being a Mrs Yeats and she not an inhabitant of the land of faery but a girl I had known slightly for some time seemed fantastic.[22]

But their most important visit was to Edmund and Elsa Dulac, who had taken refuge from air raids in Cranleigh, Surrey, with Elsa's mother and other artist friends. In a letter now lost, the irrepressible Willy had obviously already hinted of their special studies, for he promised to 'bring all our magic formulae and whatever sympathy nature has given us. You will find us reasonably cheerful.'[23] During those five days from 15 to 20 November, apparently with Georgie's permission, the secret of the automatic writing was revealed. It is likely that Georgie had already met Dulac, perhaps at one of Yeats's Monday evenings or, through Ezra, during the preparations for the April 1916 production of *At the Hawk's Well*, for which he had been Chief Musician and designer. Yeats never forgot Dulac's mask for Cuchulain, a 'noble, half-Greek, half-Asiatic face, [which] will appear perhaps like an image seen in reverie by some Orphic worshipper'.[24] Georgie would also have heard of his involvement with WBY and Denison Ross in the investigation of the 'Metallic Homunculus' or 'psychic machine' at St Leonards earlier that year.[25] Despite Madame Dulac's nervous illness (which would eventually lead to permanent invalidism and separation), the two couples became fast friends, sharing common interests from the occult to the aesthetic. Like the early Yeats, Dulac had strong connections with Pre-Raphaelitism and Orientalism as reflected in the peacock gowns, mysterious caves and palaces, ghostly fingered trees, brilliant blues, lustrous greens, and smoky oranges of his famous illustrations to *Stories from the Arabian Nights* in her old friend Laurence Housman's version. At the Leicester Galleries in June 1920, Edmund exhibited a portrait of Georgie strongly reminiscent of 'Pirouze the fairest and most honourably born' in that 1907 edition that had catapulted him to fame as a major illustrator; he later presented it to George and Willy.[26]

Yeats and Dulac had first met about 1912 or 1913 when they often saw each other in Pound's rooms or Charles Ricketts's studio.[27] A man of astounding versatility and zest (he died at 71 after a strenuous evening of flamenco dancing), for more than a quarter of a century he would serve as Willy's closest male confidant. French by birth though by now a confirmed Anglophile, he understood Arabic and Chinese, was an authority on carpets and furniture which he also designed, illustrated books (including three of Yeats's, a *Broadside*, and the unicorn logo that appeared on three of the Cuala Press books), composed and directed the music to some of Yeats's later poems (and rewrote the music for *At the Hawk's Well*), wrote parodies and poetry, was a successful designer of the ballet, posters, stamps, bank notes, tapestries, and drew caricatures as well as portraits.[28] Georgie had doubtless seen, at the spring exhibition of the 'International' in 1915, his cartoon of Yeats leaning on a harp while attached marionette-like to the Irish theatre.[29]

On that first visit to Cranleigh in November 1917 Dulac, also a keen astrologer and believer in arcana, was enlisted as designer-collaborator to the system. His guests brought astrological books by Waite and Flambert, which they forgot to pack on their departure.[30] First came Willy's ring, probably commissioned by Georgie as a special gift for her husband. On 2 December she wrote to Dulac from Stone Cottage, 'Willy and I both want to thank you so much for the design for the ring which we think really a beautiful thing, and it would be impossible to imagine a design we should like better. It is perfect just as it is. Really one cannot thank you enough.' At his friend's request, Willy forwarded 'the formula' for Dulac's design, symbols for Sun in Moon/Venus/Saturn/Moon in Sun, adding, 'If you like you could put [sign for Sun] on one side and [sign for Moon] on the other of the Eagle design but if you do to exorcise ill luck, scratch a butterfly on the inside with this formula or instead of it.'[31] Dissatisfied with his first design, and taking his hint from the formula, Dulac made another 'more Keltic in feeling'.[32] The symbolism of the finished project was dictated by the automatic script, and remarkably perceptive concerning their relationship and personalities:

Symbols
Eagle. Butterfly
were George & I chosen for each other
'one needs material protection one emotional protection—the eagle & the butterfly'
'In her seen distrust of self'
'Butterfly her & another thing'

Two days after they returned from Surrey Willy sought further confirmation of the ring's power:

'Is butterfly symbolic of cleared subconsciousness'
'No Butterfly symbol of innocence of emotion Eagle complexity & unbalanced emotion anger overcoming wisdom—Butterfly wisdom overcoming anger—the clearing of subconscious destroys anger' . . .
'destroying anger does not imply the begetting of wisdom' . . .
'Butterfly symbol not anything to do with subconscious—Relates absolutely to the formula'

   That formula was astrological, 'Butterflie & eagle | Two forms of Saturn'. Inside the ring were incised their signs, Venus and Saturn: 'her [Venus] parallel [Sun]—your [Saturn] on her [Sun]', love lightening wisdom's seriousness, wisdom in turn steadying beauty.[33] On 14 January Thomas described the butterfly as the 'wisdom of love'.[34] Willy informed Dulac, 'I shall have an explanation for the ring ready always, for I have written a poem to explain it.' By February 1918 Yeats had written the lines sung by the beggar in 'Tom O'Roughley' which he would favour when inscribing his books: 'And wisdom is a butterfly | And not a gloomy bird of prey.' The emblem remained significant, as did Georgie's role. Evidently for Yeats hawk and eagle were synonymous. In response to a vision described by William Force Stead in 1934, he explained, 'The Butterfly is the main symbol in my ring—the ring I always wear. The other symbol is the Hawk. The Hawk is the straight road of logic, the Butterfly the crooked road of intuition—the Hawk pounces, the Butterfly flutters. . . . I suggest that your candle is knowledge, conscious effort, thought; & the butterfly the wisdom out of the unconscious that follows.'[35] Once made, Willy removed the ring only when instructed to give it to George while putting her into a hypnotic sleep.[36] One of her last gestures at his death was to remove it from his left hand. It would have pleased George that, unknowingly, here too she was wooing her husband away from his former muse. When Maud learned of his play *At the Hawk's Well*, she had claimed the hawk symbol for herself: 'I did not feel at all surprised when you told me about the Hawk influence—I always knew it in a vague way that you & I are both connected with a hawk. It has been my symbol which I designated in certain occult work—& I think it has been in several of the visions we have had together though when I tried to find it in some of our old records I could only find it in one.'[37] But the fluttering butterfly—the spiritual 'which drives & inspires the soul' (and which the script also associated with the tower)—had won.[38]

Willy duly kept Dulac informed of their progress. 'Our familiar continues to bring us wisdom,' he wrote in November.[39] Indeed, immediately on their return to Stone Cottage the Instructors turned their attention to his plays, relating them to various states of his life. To his question 'is there symbolism not apparent to me in my Cuchulain plays', Thomas replied, 'There is a symbolism of the growth of the soul—If you take certain symbols & use them on the medium['s] prevision you may get information I can not give you.'[40] Georgie was gaining more than magical authority; soon the structure and characterization of *The Only Jealousy of Emer*, the new Cuchulain play with which Yeats had been struggling for some time, would take their place in the discussions. They were also reading plays sent them by Lady Gregory, to whom he happily reported that his wife was 'full of service and friendly speech—I think my work will prosper as it never has in the past. The country life gives me concentration and is giving me health.'[41]

Then on Sunday, 2 December, yet another of Willy's old friends, the artist-poet Thomas Sturge Moore, paid them a visit. Although he too had been a regular for many years at the Monday 'At Homes' in Woburn Buildings, it was only now, as Mrs W. B. Yeats, that Georgie was noticed (although like Maud Gonne and even Lolly he attributed the wrong colour to her eyes): 'I spent the week end before last at Yeats's Stone Cottage in Ashdown Forest. A lovely country with mouse-coloured woods, bear-coloured heaths. Mrs W. B. seems very nice with a big boned face and blue eyes and reddish complexion, in a bright green jumper with up to date embroidery on it. She is only 25, and they seem very happy.'[42] To another friend he added, 'she is very nice and they seem perfectly happy . . . I do not suppose they will be much in London in future.'[43]

Sturge Moore and Yeats had been friends since 1900, first as rival poets, later as collaborators in various experimental theatre projects and enthusiasts of chanting, and finally as philosophical disputants. A poet, playwright, and artist, he was responsible for the stage setting for *The Hour-Glass*, based on a sketch by Robert Gregory, which Georgie had by now seen. Candid and exacting as a critic, he steadfastly refused to be overwhelmed by his more eloquent friend on subjects ranging from verse-speaking to editing. But it was as a designer and wood engraver (he had studied at the Lambeth School with Housman, Ricketts, and Shannon and later worked at the Vale Press) that his sensitivity to Yeats's imagery was most apparent. Over the years he would make designs for ten of his friend's books and perform various commissions for the Cuala Industries.

Fig. 1. George's bookplate, designed by T. Sturge Moore, completed by November 1918.

Georgie would have appreciated Moore's gentleness, even more the wit that
ranged from impish to acerbic.[44] Either on that visit or shortly after she established
her own relationship with the artist, commissioning him to design a bookplate
for her to accompany the one he had already designed for Willy. Completed by
November the following year, it featured a unicorn leaping from a broken tower
which has been struck by lightning, with a hawk in the lower right-hand corner.
Like Willy's ring, the symbolism married their past studies with current preoccupations. The unicorn, Yeats once informed his sister concerning the early
play *The Unicorn from the Stars*, was 'a private symbol belonging to my mystical
order & nobody knows what it comes from. It is the soul'; it was also George's
daimon.[45] The tower, which by the middle of January 1918 had become 'medium's

symbol not yours',[46] was illuminated by the lightning flash as it made its zigzag movement down the Tree of Life from Kether to Malkuth. In the corner, anchoring all, was the hawk. Despite the script's repetitive insistence that 'The information is not to be betrayed as to *source*,' Sturge Moore, too, was clearly included among those confidants who learned of the revelations; he had after all been a participant in earlier planchette experiments with Horton and Audrey Locke.[47] Later Willy would find himself in the somewhat embarrassing position of having to withdraw a request for frontispiece to *A Vision* in favour of Dulac's portrait of Giraldus; but so enchanted were they by Moore's bookplate for George, 'a masterpiece', that even before their daughter could read they asked for one for Anne. By then, however, Willy's memory had altered the unicorn to 'that admirable faun or stag springing from the broken tower'.[48]

By the time they went up to London on 10 December for their second stay in Woburn Buildings, she was George. 'We have abolished Georgie—she is now George,' Willy told Lady Gregory on 25 November, and five days later while dictating a letter to his father, 'I call her George to avoid Georgie which she has been called hitherto in spite of her protests.'[49] It would take some time before the old habit died and for legal purposes she would continue to sign her name Bertha Georgie, but the change reflected the purposefulness with which she embraced her new career. Not surprisingly, Ezra had been the first to acknowledge and embrace this conscious decision to rename herself; perhaps even more than WBY, he appreciated the need to remake oneself.

George's influence over the metaphorical environment extended to the physical when they set up house together; this was, after all, a natural extension of the pre-occupations of their Instructors. By the time of their marriage Willy had taken over five rooms (for £50 a year), all of Woburn Buildings but the ground floor with its 'queer old paved court'.[50] Although bathing was still somewhat primitive —'the bath water was dumped out a window in the stair landing that opened onto a roof; it flowed across the roof, into the gutter, and down the drain pipe'—it was luxurious compared with the chill of Stone Cottage where, 'after washing the upper half you put on all the clothes you could find before starting on the lower'.[51] Now it was his young wife's genius for decoration that charmed Willy. 'I wish you could see Woburn Buildings now,' he wrote to his old friend at Coole, 'nothing changed in plan but little touches here and there, and my own bedroom (the old bathroom) with furniture of unpainted unpolished wood such as for years I have wished for. Then there is a dinner service of great purple plates for meat and various earthenware bowls for other purposes.'[52] As a young man he had delighted in sitting around William Morris's 'unpolished and unpainted trestle table of new wood' but had also been disappointed that Morris, 'an ageing man', was 'content at last to gather beautiful things rather than to arrange a beautiful house'.[53] With his talented wife, herself schooled in the Pre-Raphaelites, that would not happen to him.

George especially disliked the black walls, chairs, and picture frames Willy had favoured.[54] But imbued with the sense of history with which she was already rescuing Willy's discarded manuscripts, she preserved a sample of the wallpaper with Indian design that they found on the walls when redecorating.[55] And she added her twenty-one engravings of the Book of Job to his collection of Blake's seven illustrations to Dante's *Inferno*. As she would be always, the new housewife was tactful and considerate of household servants, her own and others. 'All is very clean yet Mrs. Old is not unhappy,' Willy continued his letter to Coole. 'She comes in the evening for better pay and someone else does the rough work in the mornings.' Presumably George also waged battle with the long-time resident bedbugs that had plagued others as well as Willy, though stoutly denied by the ageing housekeeper he had inherited from Arthur Symons, and whose husband held the lease.[56]

Nowhere was George's tact more striking than the way she came to terms with Iseult, by embracing Willy's commitment to serve as quasi-guardian to a woman just twenty-two months her junior. By the middle of November she and Willy had invited Maud and her children to join them for Christmas near the Dulacs in Surrey. But Maud refused to fall in with their plans. 'We have found it impossible to get Madame Gonne, Iseult, and the boy to come away. They have a servant who speaks no English and a whole Zoological Gardens.' George suggested an alternative: Iseult would join them in Ashdown Forest for Christmas week, then later they would go to the Dulacs at Cranleigh, taking 'a lodging near for Madame Gonne if she can come for a couple of days. . . She is longing to have a talk with you over the Persian miniatures, etc.'[57] From Woburn Buildings Willy rhapsodized to Lady Gregory on his young wife's perfections:

George has formed the kind idea of our taking Iseult to Stone Cottage for Xmas that she may be a few days in the country. She and Iseult are becoming great friends—Iseult stayed here last night as she seemed too tired to go home and they have spent the morning talking dress. And now I find that George is giving Iseult a dress as a Xmas present. They made friends first for my sake but now it is for each other's, and as both according to the new fashion for young girls are full of serious studies (both work at Sanskrit) it should ripen. My wife is a perfect wife, kind, wise, and unselfish. I think you were such another young girl once. She has made my life serene and full of order.

Then, whether embroidery or not, came a further brilliant touch. 'George is reading your *Gods and Fighting men* and is about half way through. She prefers it to the Eddas which she had been reading just before.'[58] Georgie was clearly leaving no stone unturned in preparation for the meeting with her husband's oldest friend and confidante.

Evidently while in London they also planned to meet with members of the Golden Dawn, for just before Thomas departed, having 'finished what I came for this time', Willy was once again warned that 'The information is not to be betrayed as to *source*—all else may be done.' Their Instructor then relented sufficiently to allow some of the philosophy to be revealed: 'Your order can—no others—your order will think it secret—you can say it is a sequence & your original thought— that is to a degree true—You are very quick too quick sometimes.'[59] Thomas returned briefly a few nights later to tell Willy not to work while in London, 'or read late at night'. Assuring them that Iseult 'is all right—take her about while you are both in London & get her affairs fixed', he continued in George's mirror writing, 'you need not have any of the old fear about her and need not doubt that you should have done otherwise—she will assert herself'.[60]

On 17 December, the day after Iseult's overnight visit, the Abbey playwright Lennox Robinson joined the newly-weds for dinner. What would become one of the most important of George's friendships began somewhat hesitantly; Lennox thought her 'nice . . . but too young for him; and a learned person—just starting on Sanscrit!'[61] (But in time, encouraged by George, he himself would marry a much younger woman.) Then came a brief trip to Brighton for a courtesy call on Nelly and Harry Tucker; the situation had changed considerably since Willy had visited them at these same lodgings three years earlier, when he was accompanied by Olivia.

During their idyllic weeks at Stone Cottage, while developing the relationship of cones and gyres to the soul's judgement after death and pursuing the concept of 'dreaming back', they had managed to escape some of the most severe raids over London, which had caused the authorities to decree blackouts even earlier, by 5.30 p.m.[62] On 7 December the United States officially entered the war; a week later Lenin's Bolshevik regime signed an armistice with the Central Powers (Germany, Austria-Hungary, and Turkey). The air raids increased in intensity, and Willy, who at first had, like other Londoners, enjoyed the drama, now admitted, 'Air-raids are fond of my neighbourhood and I have had quite a number, and I cannot say that they grow on one in any way. We had a couple of hours of racket on Wednesday with intervals of whizzing shrapnel, and occasional explosions in the near neighbourhood. I liked my first raid but dislike them extremely now.'[63] He was, in fact (as George later told Ellmann), becoming very frightened, so much so that they fled to Sussex in advance of a dinner arranged by his fellow researcher William Barrett and his wife:

I hope you will forgive my wife and myself for not staying in town for your dinner party. We had finished the work that brought us to London, and were lingering on without aim, and the air raid hurried us away. The risk is no doubt small, but neither of us can do any work with that racket going on, and they are very fond of our neighbourhood, and much of our work is done in the evenings. Or to put it in plain words without any further excuses we are panic-stricken refugees. And everything must be forgiven to refugees.[64]

Their 'work' had included—in addition to the arrangements with Iseult and Maud, who was furiously trying to arrange permits for Ireland—a number of séances to do with the will and unsigned codicil of Gregory's nephew Hugh Lane, and research at the British Museum in connection with their own studies. This experience with other mediums led to Willy's attempt to question his Instructors about Bessie Radcliffe's automatic writing; the script was prompt and dismissive: 'Nothing to do with Bessie—only relates to you.'[65] But the spirit of Hugh Lane hung around, making an abortive attempt to speak about a third codicil and 'an ikon I gave Aunt Augusta'.[66] A few weeks later when Willy attempted to contact Lane again, the guide Leaf was scornful, evidently referring to the messages reportedly received by Lennox Robinson and Hester Travers Smith on the day Lane was drowned: 'I will try—I know from your mind but those two will never help him—I think he is much better now—I will do what I can for him. . . . he hates those people who write for him—wants sympathy & to be instructed.'[67] Thomas then returned to emphasize his disapproval of this departure from their main purpose:

the newly dead seem to be able to communicate but I think myself it is through spirits at number one [phase] *except when it is through a medium in trance which is wrong* . . . All mediumship which aims at obtaining contact with newly dead is wrong because it disturbs & obsesses the spirit. This is very important But if the spirit wishes to contact with some special individual *he can always do it some* way or another without going to a medium—they hate mediums they *dont know*[68]

Evidently George's communicants were brooking no competition, and she clearly agreed. Willy made no further effort to use his wife to call on the dead.[69]

So precipitous had been their departure from London that they discovered Stone Cottage already let. A temporary resting place was found in Ashdown Cottage on Chapel Lane in Forest Row, not far from the hotel where their married life had begun. A charming five-bedroom house built in 1904, with servant's quarters on the third storey and apple trees in the garden, this was considerably more comfortable than Stone Cottage, and more hospitable to visitors. Some half a century later, it would be visited by the Dalai Lama.[70] Here on 20 December George and Willy settled down to their private explorations and caught up on correspondence. 'My marriage has been very fortunate for me & in the order & quiet it has brought I feel my work taking on a new integrity,' he wrote to Charles Ricketts in response to a note reproaching him for not announcing his change of status; and to Horton, an assurance that he was 'no longer anxious' about Iseult now that she was working at the School of Oriental Languages.[71] Though still close enough to enjoy the snow-covered woods and heath, they could not entirely escape from the war, as soldiers marched from the artillery camp to Forest Row. But Iseult arrived in time to enjoy the carollers in the village square on Christmas Eve, accompanied by the village brass band, and watch their Boxing Day progress past the Hatch Inn. The band's motley uniform of peaked cap in blue and white stripes and ex-police jackets was still innocent of the black-and-tan horrors to come in Ireland.

Willy may not have been quite as sanguine as he claimed, for immediately after Iseult's departure they made the postponed visit to the Dulacs, where he came down with a severe flu-like cold. And so instead of making their way to Ireland and Lady Gregory, by 2 January they were in Oxford, where after a few nights at the Mitre Hotel George found 'charming old rooms' at 45 Broad Street, across from Christopher Wren's semicircular Sheldonian Theatre. The green-shuttered house 'with a rickety staircase, and low ceilings', later destroyed to make way for the New Bodleian Library,[72] had its idiosyncrasies as did their landlady, who placed a notice on the lavatory door reading 'beware of the dog' to prevent tampering with the gas meter. George recalled to Oliver Edwards that once, finding the bathroom door unlocked, she entered to encounter the broad naked back of young Beverley Nichols. Nichols in turn remembered that 'It was a time when the servant problem was at its height, and occasionally, if the house was more than usually under-staffed, all the undergraduates and other occupants of rooms, including Yeats himself, used to gather to eat a communal luncheon.'[73] 'The Broad', short and wide enough to accommodate the horse fairs that were once held there, was still patrolled at night by university proctors in mortar board, gown, and white tie, ensuring that gowns were in evidence, and only second- and third-year men could keep a car. (In 1914, only 4,000 of the 54,000 residents of Oxford were undergraduates.) A stationer's and post office were just next door, and a typing service and physician and dental surgeon conveniently nearby. Blackwell's Bookshop, not yet enlarged, was just down the Broad next to the White Horse public house.[74]

Lady Gregory, who had received a telegram on their arrival in Oxford putting off their visit until 'this day six months', tartly observed, 'I think Oxford must have looked warmer & more settled than the vision of Ballylee with its feet in the floods & raids for arms going on.'[75] But she was clearly nervous about how her friend's young English bride would take to the country and a dilapidated Norman tower, and had already suggested that Ballylee would be less daunting once spring had come. Having dissuaded Yeats from inviting Georgie over before they were married, now she continued to temporize: she would only be able to offer hospitality for a week if they did come in January to examine Ballylee, but on the other hand it was now snowing and 'I would not like you to come till the harshness of March is over—say Thursday in Easter week. The children will be coming back then and the house will not look so cheerless. I should not like your wife to see it as it is now.'[76] Oliver St John Gogarty, who had described his house in Galway as '18 miles from a railway—forty rooms, only three or four furnished—the gardener and his wife in charge', had also encouraged them to delay their journey, warning of food and petrol shortages; although these were not as severe as the rationing affecting all parts of Britain, where butter and ham were now scarce.[77] Although neither correspondent mentioned it, there were the increased activities of the Irish Volunteers to contend with, now estimated to number close to 100,000 and more opposed than ever to British rule.[78]

Life was not only comfortable but convenient in Oxford. Woburn Buildings had been let but, wartime restrictions permitting, they were within an hour and a half's journey to London, a return rail ticket costing only ten shillings and sixpence; it was possible to travel down in the morning, returning by the fast 4.40 from Paddington. Quinn had written congratulating him, especially pleased that both Lady Gregory and Maud approved of his choice ('All that I have heard about her has been pleasant'). Willy replied with uxorious pride, 'My wife never knows which to be most surprised at, the hats or the minds of the dons wives, and is convinced that if we live here every winter, which is possible, she will be driven to great extravagance out of the desire for contrast.'[79] He was writing poetry, including another 1916 poem ('Sixteen Dead Men'), preparing for publication his play *The Dreaming of the Bones*, also based on the Easter Rising, finally finishing his Noh play *The Only Jealousy of Emer*, and contemplating new ones. All projects were fed through the automatic script; in fact the scenario for a fifth Noh play, never named or completed, was later described by George as 'a summary of the events of 1918'.[80]

Meanwhile, by typing his work and rescuing old manuscripts, reading Abbey Theatre submissions aloud in the evenings, listening to Willy's testiness about the fight for the Hugh Lane pictures, following the troubling news of raids, baton charges, ominous disturbances throughout the country, and the looming threat of conscription there, George was finding Ireland, and its politics, more of a reality. Anxious to involve her in all of his activities, Yeats consulted the Instructors as to whether his artist-wife might become the Abbey Theatre's much-needed stage designer: 'I think of asking medium to help with plays etc.' But the moving finger quickly responded,

'Not good—not enough constructive ability'
'Do you mean she cannot design costumes Etc?'
'not well done' . . .
'She cant do anything till this is done—no good trying plenty of activity but we use it all'.[81]

In turn, the script kept reminding him of what his own work must be: 'your genius is not for teaching nor preaching' (possibly a warning against too many lecture commitments), and 'Artistic Genius & moral Genius are the two works of man and in these he has to develop his own powers,' advice which would, like most of Thomas's wisdom, later work its way into poetry.[82]

By early January Willy was planning a discussion of the system 'in a series of dialogues about a supposed medieval book the *Speculorum Angelorum et Hominum* of Giraldus, and a sect of Arabs called the Judwalis (diagrammatists)'.[83] Despite Georgie's misgivings, at the end of a lengthy section the evening of 12 January Giraldus appears in the script as an example of the primary self; he would surface again two years later as an abstraction, concerning messages of a 'supernormal origin received through a person we will call Gyraldus'.[84] And as the system developed, the hoax became more elaborate, as he explained to Dulac: 'Every evening the Speculum of Gyraldus becomes more imposing. I am more and more astonished at the profundity of that learned author and at the neglect into which he has fallen, a neglect only comparable to that which has covered with the moss of oblivion the even more profound work of Kusta ibm Luka of Bagdad, whose honour remains alone in the obscure sect of the Judwalis.'[85] His friend responded with a sketch of Giraldus Cambrensis, expressing mock concern at the anachronism, for 'he could not have his portrait at the beginning of a book printed in the early fifteenth century unless it be a faulty one.'[86] Four years later they finally settled on the sly self-important philosopher, surrounded by the symbols and images of his trade and bearing a strong resemblance to WBY, whose portrait appeared as frontispiece to *A Vision*. Ever inventive, Dulac achieved the effect of antique Gothic woodcuts on vellum by dipping the paper in tea before working on it. Meanwhile, he promised to design a bedcover for the embroidery section of the Cuala Industries, run by Lily Yeats, but it is not known whether she ever received the drawing of 'centaurs male & female, with trees' (unless it too contributed to the poem 'On a Picture of a Black Centaur by Edmund Dulac').[87]

Apart from those, like Nichols and L. A. G. Strong, who were too young for military service, this was an Oxford empty of its customary overwhelmingly male students. Somerville, the women's college, had been commandeered by the War Office for conversion into a military hospital, its students taking over the St Mary Hall quadrangle of Oriel.[88] One of those women students was Grace Spurway, George's young cousin, who was at St Hugh's until the spring of 1920 and with whom she enjoyed morning coffee discussions upstairs in the popular Cadena Café, around the corner in Cornmarket Street.[89] Unaware of the olfactory signals emphasized by the automatic script, Grace was indignant when George suggested there was 'a bad smell around her'. They never talked about art, but a lot about books. Willy's health was, Grace recalled, always a regular topic of conversation but not his poetry or his friends—apart from her cousin's indignation at George Moore's memoirs. Nor was Nelly mentioned; clearly Grace was not amongst her adored cousin's confidantes. Harold Hyde-Lees, who was subsidizing Grace's Oxford expenses, must have paid the occasional visit, for it was through his young cousin that he met his future wife, a fellow student at St Hilda's.

George and Willy met few people on this first stay. Yeats's friend John Masefield, who had recently moved to Boars Hill nearby, was on a lecture tour of the United States; an evening was spent with Gilbert Murray to discuss Willy's plan to make Oxford a centre for his Noh plays; they met with Robert Bridges. Sir Walter Raleigh, Oxford's first Professor of English Literature (whose edition of William Blake Georgie still prized but who now 'seemed very old & shaky'), signed their applications for reader's tickets; at one time interested in geomancy, he was now committed to his official history of the air force.[90] On 19 January, the very day after *Per Amica Silentia Lunae* was published, Iseult joined them for the weekend and, concerned about her talk of London companions, in a few days Willy had written 'To a Young Beauty'. Other invitations followed—to Eva Ducat, Horton, Bessie Radcliffe, H.D.

However, so charmed were they by their surroundings that within a week of their arrival they had decided to make Oxford a more permanent base and started searching for a house to rent. While George was in London arranging for an extension of the Woburn Buildings lease, Willy broke the news to Augusta Gregory: 'It looks as if we shall take a house here & furnish it with the Montpelier Square furniture (house now let unfurnished) for the present that we may keep on Woburn Buildings too till I know what my new plays require, or till Ballylee is ready. We have Woburn Buildings for a year at any rate. I spend a good deal of time in the Bodleian.'[91] George was now writing more freely to her sisters-in-law:

We have been meeting this afternoon Mr and Mrs Ball. We had tea with them at St. John's College. They have a house to let which we are going to look at.

Willy has bought himself a fawn-coloured corduroy jacket which he wears to work in and is most becoming. He strides about in a dark blue French Student's Cloak. I think Oxford is the only place in England where it could be worn, and look romantic and not odd! Life is very pleasant here. We go to the Bodleian in the morning, walk in the afternoon, and in the evening work or read and write letters—and now we are beginning to know a few people, so the charm grows.

Thanking her sister-in-law for the 'charming' patterns she had sent, she placed another order to Cuala. Noting that Georgie's arithmetic was no better than her own—'she sent too much before—now 10/- too little'—Lily sent the letter on to her father with approval.[92] For the rest of his life in consultation with his wife Willy would favour light browns, blues, and greys; there was no further need for him to persevere in the black costume Symons had encouraged as being both elegant and inexpensive. But it would be over a year before they settled into a house in Oxford.

Early in February 1918 their new-found serenity was shattered by the news that Lady Gregory's son had been killed in action, and from then on plans were being formulated—and reformulated—towards the delayed journey to Ireland.

But Gregory, still dealing with her own grief as well as her daughter-in-law's, did not want them until Easter. Maud Gonne was, as usual, ahead of them. She, Iseult, her young son Seán, and their devoted servant Josephine had been temporarily living in Woburn Buildings while campaigning for the authorities to lift their ban on her travel to Ireland. By late January, anarchic as ever, she had escaped with Seán to Dublin, jubilant at evading the British authorities in the disguise of a poor old Irishwoman;[93] this time Dublin Castle decided to ignore her presence, and by the end of March she had purchased a house at 73 St Stephen's Green. Iseult, meanwhile, still doing secretarial work at the School for Oriental Studies, would also soon leave Woburn Buildings for a flat in Chelsea. Yeats wrote to Iseult with the newly acquired confidence the automatic script bestowed,

my sister writes that she has told Moura [Maud] of a fine old house where Emmet once lived 'as it seems a suitable place for Shawn, who is being bred up and trained for martyrdom. He is being brought to all the meetings.' I am getting the encyclicals of Leo XIII and Pius X for Moura, and suggesting to her Catholic economics. Help me to keep her enthusiasms, for that will keep her sane. . . . I hope in the next month to convict her of several damnable heresies.[94]

George no longer needed to worry about her husband's obsession with Maud Gonne.

She was beginning however to tire of the stress of daily sessions on the script; the Instructors threatened not to come for two weeks, but then relented. Willy was reproved for allowing his mind to stray while George drew diagrams for them; then either he or George was not sufficiently 'passive'. It was possible that they would meet 'certain mystic associates' of 'the orderly and philosophic' kind. There was clairvoyant work to be done, but it must be 'natural & unconscious'; 'you are in too great a hurry—be content with a little very little—if you say much the intellectual bias will be against you.' The mysterious 'high medium' did not appear, and may well have been a product of wishful thinking on George's part.[95] The first stage of their work was ending; the second brought new guides. Again, they were counselled against revealing their source; the script was not to be spoken of. But shortly after Iseult's visit, Willy could not resist. 'We have learned new & wonderful things,' he wrote to her. 'I have just finished a new Cuchulain poem full of this new philosophy. I wish I could tell you of what has come but it is all so vast & one part depends upon another. Our last teaching has been on the relation between the passionate body (astral body) and celestial body after death.'[96]

By now the script was drawing on their knowledge of astrology, the Tree of Life, and perhaps even Chaucer to establish the twenty-eight lunar phases representing the cycle of personality or 'the psychology of the individual', and there was much deliberation in placing historical figures, family, friends, and acquaintances in their appropriate categories.[97] Later Thomas would explain that the Instructors must obtain their symbolism through the living and therefore, in choosing for symbol the phases of the Moon, they were drawing 'from intellectual experience in this life'; George and Willy 'had both read of them'.[98] With the coveted 'Unity of Being' only possible in phases 16, 17, and 18, George (like Dulac and Goethe) was decreed to be an 18 (whose characteristics were 'emotional', 'wisdom of the heart' always desiring 'the unchanging'[99]) verging on 19; Nelly and Mrs Woodmass were now regularly referred to as typical 19s ('assertive'), while George acknowledged her father's alcoholism in phase 8 ('obscure wastrels who seem powerless to free themselves from some sensual temptation').[100] Willy (like Dante and Shelley) was a 17 ('Daimonic man'). Iseult and Maud were placed on either side of 'entire beauty' (15), Maud 'positive' (in company with Blake and Rabelais) at 16, and Iseult (with Keats) 'obsessed' at 14. This habit of speaking of themselves and others at one or two removes encouraged a process Yeats would develop more and more, later writing in great glee to Lady Gregory, 'I am working hard and have just finished a denunciation of Carlyle, whom I have placed at one of my lunar crescents—it is a great satisfaction at last to bless and curse as I please.'[101] George noticed that as a result of their work on the phases of personality, her husband began to take more interest in people.[102] This was not immediately apparent to others, however. Lady Gregory sympathized with Quinn's complaint that both Willy and his father tended to 'tag' him as 'a man of great energy' and downplay his intellectual strengths: 'Poor old Yeats, he does "tag" one, and so does W. B. Y. And having tied on the tag, they try to justify it. I have often told W. B. Y. this.'[103]

Research in the Bodleian was by contrast almost a relaxation, and day by day George, more regularly than Willy who had to save his eyes, crossed the cobblestones and climbed the steep narrow stair to the Duke Humfrey Library. Under the superb painted ceiling, they found comfortable seats in the bay next to the window, and from there ordered up titles ranging from seventeenth-century ephemerides and almanacks, eighteenth-century peerages, to twentieth-century histories and primers on astronomy.[104] Simultaneously exploring the relationship of the communicators' statements to the historical world, they were intent on verification; the script was also starting to wander into prognostication, requiring consultation with, among other relevant volumes, Walter Gorn Old's 1914 astrological survey of the Great War. That very day, 23 February, there occurred the startling appearance of a persistent spirit who interfered with both Old and their study of colour symbolism (especially important to Willy who believed that only dreams in colour could be considered true),[105] provoking George's seventh 'moment of crisis'. The spirit, who announced herself to be Anne Hyde, Duchess of Ormonde, was finally discovered to be the Countess of Ossory, a historical figure who had died in childbirth.

The Countess had in fact attempted to make contact much earlier, while they were still at Ashdown Cottage, on the eve of Iseult's arrival. On 23 December 1917, she slipped sideways into the script with the mysterious comment 'Choice had to be made from Anne but she may have chosen for warni[ng]'. Since no questions for this session were recorded—or preserved—we do not know whether the invitation came from them or their spirit advisers, or whether Anne Hyde had previously surfaced during that first week of Georgie's automatic writing in the Ashdown Forest Hotel. Other disjointed remarks on 23 December 1917, some in mirror writing, also appear to refer to Anne as well as to the early days of their experiment: 'That was to enable us to make medium forget old script Script one is dark', '1681 I think', 'The *message* came through You were *incarnated* during 16th phase before your birth.' A further response may have been to a question from Willy about the script's authenticity: 'I don't think she invented it—better not talk of it—it creates a centre of undesirable kind if in thought of many people.'[106] However, the mysterious Anne was then silent for a further two months.

Now she firmly took over the script. Willy removed—but did not destroy as recommended—many of the pages in which her messages appeared, but his card file provides a later summary of what then transpired.[107] On 4 March 1918 Anne announced in George's mirror writing that they were to have a child—but only if Willy wished it. This 'would only give her happiness in being your child she does not want a child for its own sake' but for 'family tradition name etc'. 'She will on the whole be equally happy during your life whether you want a child or no It will always be you she will love in the child.' 'The decision on your part must be honest and unbiased wrong because *that* would destroy the link between you . . . you must not wait till you are growing old. . . . If you make a false decision in self-sacrifice you are not true.' He was to make his decision without telling George, not too hastily, but definitely within three months: 'youll go on meandering for 10 years if I dont fix a time.' The following day Aymor reluctantly admitted that he had 'permitted' Anne's arrival 'but I cannot accept responsibility'. He added further particulars—Willy would probably not be able to decide until they had reached 'the third stage' of their relationship. And he promised to respond to further questions. 'Anything you like except backwards | not through medium don't say through medium.'

On the day of Anne's first revelation, George ordered Alan Leo's *Astrology for All* at the Bodleian; it must have been at this time that she carefully worked out all the family horoscopes—including Anne Hyde's. The next few weeks were devoted to tracing Anne's history and that of her Ormonde ancestry. Willy looked up Burke's peerage in the Oxford Union and 'found that in 1682 July 15 Anne Hyde daughter of Laurence Hyde (afterwards Lord Rochester) married James, afterwards Duke of Ormonde. She was however never Duchess of Ormonde, but only Countess of Ossory. I found nothing further in the peerage except that she

died in January 1685 & that she left one daughter who lived for a few years.'
George meanwhile called up from the Bodleian further works on Edward Hyde,
first Earl of Clarendon, including his autobiography (two volumes, 1857), the
correspondence and diaries of Hyde and his brother Laurence, Earl of Rochester
(two volumes, 1828), and Thomas Henry Lister's *Life and Administration of
Edward, First Earl of Clarendon* (three volumes, 1837–8). The following day they
both worked through the six volumes of Thomas Carte's *History of the Life of
James, Duke of Ormonde*, where they were intrigued to discover that Anne 'had
indeed died in childbirth & had forseen her death in a prophetic dream'.[108]

Was George also rehabilitating her father's family history, the Hydes, as well as
Willy's? For a time her automatic writing ceased to concentrate on the system in
general and more on their own place on the 'Great Wheel'; there was now even
more urgency to reach Ireland. There was also more reason for secrecy. On the
day of Anne's return, the script had begun with yet again a severe warning to
Willy, emphasized by the solemn presence of all six Communicators:

we are not pleased because you talk too freely of spirits & of initiation—you may *yes* not
speak of any personal thing we give—you may speak of the actual system but ye may not
tell of any personal thought image or information we give nor of the forms & processes
we give for your own contemplation nor of such demand & restrictions as we make nor of
the life we demand that you should live—only speak of those actual machineries of the
philosophy that may be in the book
Yes [*space*] but do not imply that it is through your own initiation or psychic power
Imply *intervention* if need be
Yes [*space*] dream—*yes* [*space*] but not *guidance of spirits in your life*
That is always wrong—because you speak to unbelievers you destroy our help. . . .
The only value is in the whole—you may say a good deal is of supernormal & the rest
invention & deduction—I do not *wish* the spirit source revealed
Never mention *any* personal message—these (*no*) are the most important of all our
communications—(no)
All those things are personal but essentially those that appertain to any nature of
initiation
You can say what you will but no *personal*[109]

This was followed by a drawing of a large sailing vessel on a body of water; a
butterfly on the sail and a second butterfly (Iseult?) trailing the ship. As George
was fully aware, the warning would continue to be necessary; she would soon
dub her husband 'William Tell'.

The next day Anne Hyde's intentions were made clearer (although still in
mirror writing). They were startled to learn that Anne's 'mission' was 'to reincarnate
—and the dead child that never lived—a boy—reincarnate . . . both'. The message was again directed specifically at Willy: 'Ann wishes her boy to reincarnate
because she cannot leave him till he— | she will not want you to reincarnate

herself only her boy because she looks on you as on her husband and on medium as on herself.' She 'would like' to be reincarnated herself 'but that would have to depend on mediums willingness—she wants the boy to incarnate first'. Then, with a certain amount of backtracking, 'under certain circumstances it might first be the latter | The circumstances might bring the latter instead of former though she is most anxious for former.'[110] Additional, more mundane pressure was also brought to bear, perhaps the result of Willy's poem 'Pardon, old fathers . . .' or his family's concern over the family line: 'She came to medium for a purpose & your sisters minds helped her in that by thinking of the same thought . . . of continuation of human life.'[111] Then George laid down her pencil and started packing for Ireland and Ballylee.

They left Oxford on Wednesday, 6 March, even earlier than planned, and in some confusion. Iseult was still occupying Woburn Buildings, and the Tuckers had let their house in Montpelier Square unfurnished. Whether through Nelly or other friends, they were promised the loan of a flat 'for a few days' at 38 Montpelier Street, just yards away from Georgie's old home,[112] and set about inviting friends to simple meals—the Dulacs (who were up from the country), Horton (with the promise of Iseult's presence).[113] However, instead of seeing anyone, on the evening of Friday, 8 March, the Yeatses abruptly took the train from Liverpool Street Station, changed at Chester, and at 10 p.m. sailed from Nelson Dock on the British and Irish Steam Packet.

Saloon passengers were allowed to stay on board the next day until 8 a.m., at which time the Yeatses took a cab to the Royal Hibernian Hotel in Dawson Street. Like her mother and aunts, Georgie was accustomed to travelling first class, but this was still a new experience for Willy; it may well have been the first time her husband had stayed at the Hibernian, advertised as 'The Most Fashionable First-Class Hotel in Dublin, with an electric elevator, and orchestra daily'. In later years the hotel would become George's favourite place for tea. A. Norman Jeffares has described the town Georgie would have smelled and heard on that first morning:

In the twenties there was still the sound of ironshod drays, still the clop of hoofs, still the hoarse hooting of ships downriver and of Guinness barges as they lowered their funnels under the city's bridges in a cloud of steam. Cabs, outside cars, high-swung delivery vans and bicycles moved easily through streets not yet filled with the pervasive convergence of private cars, which, even into the thirties, could be easily parked. There were no official bus stops, the few buses responding—somewhat at the whim of individualistic drivers —to requests to stop from passengers within or would-be passengers without. The newsboys cried 'Harolomail'; the shawlies chanted 'Fine vi'lets, fine vi'lets, a peddy a budch of vi'lets'.

There was also the sound of talk. There was time to chat when friends or acquaintances happened on each other in the street.[114]

In 1925 the speed limit on most roads was still ten miles an hour, less in the towns; Page Dickinson recalls a tram being stopped just so the hailer could light a match on the side of the car.[115]

Threat of further air raids may have determined their early flight, for by departing from England on a 'remarkably bright and clear' night, George and Willy had just missed an especially frightening raid over north London, which killed twenty, injured forty-five, and destroyed considerable property. They arrived in Dublin to the usual soft Irish morning mist; a proclamation by Major-General W. Fry, Competent Military Authority for Ireland, prohibiting the holding of any meeting or procession within the Dublin Metropolital Police Area between 6 and 27 March; rigid censorship over all printed and written matter in County Clare (neighbouring Coole and Ballylee); the news that certain Sinn Féin prisoners in Mountjoy and Dundalk jails were on hunger strike demanding the promised special person treatment for 'political' offenders convicted under the Defence of the Realm Act; the threat of a Dublin Tramway strike; and word that the Sinn Féin Food Controller had been charged with conspiracy to seize pigs and other animals to prevent their export. *The Irish Times*, doubtless the paper delivered at the Royal Hibernian with breakfast, advertised the titles of Sunday sermons, insurance for 'passengers to London and England . . . owing to a war and for Marine peril', the opening of Slyne and Company's new premises for 'Fascinating Underwear', Charlie Chaplin's *The Vagabond* at Kingstown Pavilion, and D. W. Griffith's 'half million pound film' *Intolerance* at the Gaiety; while the Irish Paper Mills in Clondalkin urged everyone to save paper. On the international front that day, war news continued to be grave—especially troubling for Georgie whose brother was being sent to France; Moscow became the new Russian capital and Trotsky resigned as Commissioner of Foreign Affairs. Perhaps the most telling single detail of the political mood was the announcement that, while a film of the public funeral in Wexford of John Redmond, leader of the Irish Parliamentary Party, would be shown in all six Dublin cinemas, the Cork Guardians rejected a motion for adjournment out of respect; later in the month the Bishop of Limerick would refuse to allow a requiem mass on the somewhat transparent excuse—given the rejection of conscription by all clergy a few weeks later—that there should be no 'politics in the church'. The same issue reported a baton charge on a farm in Boyle, County Roscommon, and that a mass meeting of Dublin tram workers was to be held at midnight to discuss whether to go on strike. This was reality with a vengeance, but perhaps that morning Georgie took some comfort in the literary pages, where an anonymous reviewer rejected the new book *The Question*, in which the author (Edward Clodd) dismissed spiritualism, instead urging 'the singular nature and importance of those phenomena which engage the attention of the Psychical Research Society. These well deserve careful, scientific study.'

George put away her pencil and special notebook for a week. Not that there was much time for meditation or contemplation: Dublin was a busy, talkative town, and there were many people Willy wanted her to meet. Gossip had been rife ever since the announcement of his marriage. 'It is all very sudden and suggests she is furniture for the castle,' was one comment; while Willy's old friend George Russell, who had probably heard more than he should have from Maud Gonne, wrote to Quinn, 'I gather she will write for him, read for him . . . communicate with the dead or living for him, and will make the ideal poet's wife.'[116]

The young English bride's initiation into Irish hospitality began, appropriately enough, at Lily and Lolly Yeats's home Gurteen Dhas in Dundrum, just outside the centre of Dublin, where the day after their arrival his sisters had called in brother Jack and his wife Cottie, and—perhaps for protection against or for George—critic-biographer Joseph Hone and his wife Vera. In her customary breathless style Lolly described the evening for their father in New York,

on Saturday Willie and his wife came to Dublin—they telegraphed from Chester to say they were crossing and would come out to us on Sunday evening, asking us to get Jack and Cottie. . . . Lily . . . went into town leaving a note at the Hibernian Hotel for Willie saying to come out as early as they could—then on she went and arranged with Jack and Cottie to come after supper—they could not come *to* supper as the Gogartys were going *there* in the afternoon—all worked out beautifully. . . . at six o'clock Willie and George walked up the path—Maria opened the door for them (Rose was out—being a person of routine) before we could and Willie asked for Rose and said 'This is my wife, Maria'— Maria was awfully pleased and said 'hasn't she nice manners' George shook hands with her and was evidently very nice altogether.

We like George *greatly* already—she looks older than her years. I think it is the marked features—a very large nose—her hair is reddish brown—very waving and curling and worn low over her ears—she has a good deal of colour and very nice eyes—really beautiful eyes—blue—a charming expression—you feel that she has plenty of personality but that her disposition is so amiable that she does not often assert herself—not from inertness but because she is happiest in agreement with the people around her—this is the impression she gave us—she has gaiety and is I am sure intuitive—she would fit in anywhere—*Cottie* at first was a little self-conscious but George was so nice Cottie was soon quite at ease—and not afraid the new sister in law would try to supplant her with all of us. I think *Cottie* just felt nervous and fussed up; but all this evaporated in a few moments and we were all at ease. Willie and Jack and Cottie and George walked off to the Dartry tram together at 11 o'clock to get the last tram.[117]

Lily would forward her reaction a few days later: 'George is better looking every time you see her. Now I think her very good looking.'[118] Father Yeats wrote with relief to Lady Gregory, 'My daughters have seen their new sister-in-law, and are enthusiastic about her.'[119] He was also pleased at last to receive some description of his young daughter-in-law.

Lolly's narrative continues with a description of George's introduction to the Abbey players in the Green Room (apparently, at the Yeats sisters' urging, repainted for the occasion without Lady Gregory's permission[120]):

the Company had tea ready—the first they have had in the Green Room for years—so it was all very pleasant—after the play Lily and I walked back to their Hotel with them and today they go down to Glendalough—a lot of letters have come for them we have sent them on to the Royal Hotel Glendalough—they were to buy fishing rods to take with them—in about a fortnight they are to go to Coole. Yesterday Willie took George to see Uncle Isaac and Aunt Gracie and Aunt Jenny and the Gordons & Jack and Cottie went there too. First glance George is not *at all* like her photograph—not so handsome— stranger looking—but soon you see that line for line the photograph is exactly her— but gives another impression—she has more character and personality altogether than the photograph but is less handsome—although Miss Bushell of the Abbey Theatre who shows the people to their seats in the stalls—said 'she is *far* handsomer than the photograph & she has a *beautiful expression*'.

Lily noticed that 'When the lights went down George used to sit forward and look round me at him [Willy], smile to herself and sit back again.'[121]

Lolly once distinguished her siblings by the way they talked about themselves. 'I tell people too much—& Jack too little—& Willie tells almost all his own affairs but generally with great apparent secrecy—& then one finds he has told ever so many other people the same thing (as a secret) & Lily makes a witty story of it all.'[122] That evening as they all gathered in the small dining room of Gurteen Dhas, George in turn sized up her new family. Both Lily and Lolly were attractive and graceful—W. G. Fay used to instruct the Abbey actors to glide across the room the way Miss Lily Yeats walked. They believed in 'keeping up appearances' despite their poverty; they dressed elegantly and were conscious of 'good form'. (The villagers distinguished the two sisters by the colours they wore: Lily was 'the Blue Miss Yeats', while her younger sister Lolly was 'the Purple Miss Yeats'.[123]) Both were clairvoyant and had 'previsions' which were frequently shown to be accurate. Both had lively minds, strong wills, and even stronger opinions. Each was a fine artist in her chosen profession. George would soon discover how incompatible they were, however, doomed to be unevenly harnessed by financial need throughout their lives. The sisters could not have been more different, physically and temperamentally. Lily needed routine, Lolly thrived on gaiety and adventure (George would later say she saw life as a series of one-act plays). Lolly was direct and forthright—too much so most of the time, for she could be extremely tactless; Lily more reserved, passive, and devious, anything for peace in the family. A natural historian, Lily was always treated by her brothers as 'a book of reference'; but Lolly, a stimulating teacher, was the most formally educated of the four Yeats children. 'I want people, Lily can get on without,' Lolly once wrote to her father. Even now there were signs of physical distress in Lily—she moved slowly and breathed loudly; Lolly was energetically active, outgoing, and at her best in company, especially, Lily once commented, in a new hat. Lolly looked like Jack, but had the unyielding attitude and hasty temper of Willy. Now, however, the two sisters sparkled with excitement and pleasure; perhaps influenced by her husband, George was especially attracted to Lily, his favourite sister.

It was harder to assess her new artist brother-in-law and his wife. Their father had once confessed that 'with all his faults' Willy was 'more lovable than Jack', whom he found 'a little cold and a little self complacent'. Even Jack's jokes were serious.[124] Always courteous and elegantly dressed, he was obviously loved by his sisters, who appreciated his wife Cottie for her self-effacing devotion. Like Willy, Jack had married an Englishwoman of independent means who was also an artist —George would come to appreciate her portrait painting especially.[125] Cottie too was a smart dresser, fond of hats and jewellery; a slim brunette, she was five years older than her husband but hid the age difference well. Although inclined to gossip, she jealously protected Jack and his need for privacy. And although Jack's career always came first, she continued to paint, contributing designs for both Lily's embroidery and Lolly's press. It was a close-knit family group, but unlike the two sisters, neither Jack nor Cottie recorded their responses to Willy's young wife. They would always keep a polite but pleasant distance, which George and Willy reciprocated.

'Willy *has* got such a lot of relations,' George would later ruefully exclaim. On this first visit she was also taken to meet an even older generation of Yeatses. Uncle Isaac, Aunt Grace, and Aunt Jane, all unmarried, lived together at 52 Morehampton Road; their widowed sister Fanny Gordon (who, at least three inches shorter, was once heard referring to 'Willy's dear little wife'[126]) lived nearby at number 26 with her daughters Violet and Eileen. One of the few remotely close to George's age and different from her conservative and conventional family, Violet would become a trusted friend.[127]

The putative ancestor Anne Hyde had also followed them to Dublin. On 11 March, although Aymor and Apple were both present, it was she who controlled George's pencil. Willy was informed in mirror writing that she did not 'wish medium to know and if you say name familiar she will know at once Anne Hyde is writing'. However she could always be called up, 'If you ask personally for me—you said you wanted me to come.'[128] There is no further reference to Anne in the scripts until 18 July, when, although she was not allowed to come herself, Thomas pronounced that Anne was 'content'. Later when re-examining his notes Willy commented, 'conception had taken place on May 24 or 25 & this question & answer may have referred to it'. On that day she also suggested that something more might be found about her in 'British manuscripts probably' letters to a 'fair haired woman not a good friend' who seems to have expected too much. The session ended in confusion with some lines in 'imitation Arabic' by

Thomas Hyde and comments about Anne and her son's previous incarnations. One answer stood out clearly; to the question 'Why did you choose us not people of great station for your sons parents' the reply was abrupt, 'No freedom'.[129]

Meanwhile, however, after a few days of Dublin, the couple took a train for Rathdrum, where Glendalough's Royal Hotel motor rescued them from family and the gossip of Dublin. There—and over the Easter weekend at the much more modest Glenmalure Hotel, in the glen so reminiscent of Synge's plays—they returned to their studies of the automatic script and the poetry that strangely arose from it. Although questions were not always recorded the answers were straightforward, as the incorporeal guides further explained their methods: 'we gather up your memories when we come . . . if we wish we see all . . . we remember most easily by emotions . . . They come by a link they have with you a telepathic link.' Again there was reassurance, though no new information, 'about London' (presumably Iseult) where 'all will be well'.[130] By now the Instructors were beginning to express concern for Georgie's health, fearing that she would be too fatigued by 'new visits etc'. But when at Glendalough Yeats wrote the happy poem 'Under the Round Tower', while the script was much concerned with spirals, cones, and what would become known as gyres. Although it rained occasionally, this was the hottest Easter on record, reaching 108 degrees Fahrenheit in the sun.

More than Georgie's pencil and Willy's notebook was taken to Glendalough, though strangely their companion is not mentioned in any of the family correspondence. 'We have begun domestic life in earnest', Willy reported to Dulac,

for we have bought a cat; a small cat; very regular in his habits; tho' his digestion is liable to be upset after a journey. He is our absorbing interest. We judge by the thickness of his waist whether he had made a good breakfast. [At] our hotel where we were staying they shut him into the larder and 'in the morning there he was sleeping grandly on an old sack as if it were a silk cushion'. He had eaten the chops and for 24 hours after would look at neither milk nor meat or do anything but sleep.[131]

The kitten seems to have come from Cuala; at any rate, he was very much a part of their luggage from the day they arrived in Dublin.[132] Many years later a Sandycove acquaintance recalled having first met George at Glenmalure with 'a darling kitten in a basket'.[133]

He also became part of a psychological tug-of-war between Willy and Lady Gregory, for on Sunday, 9 March, the day of the family party, Yeats wrote to his formidable old friend, 'May we bring a kitten to Coole or should I leave it with my sisters.' To which she firmly replied, 'I hope to see you in Easter week—but I am afraid the kitten must be left behind.' Only a few days later, however, obviously torn between the desire to appear hospitable to Willy's bride and her wish to protect the considerable treasures of Coole, Gregory had somewhat relented:

I dont think you can settle any plans till you have both seen Ballylee, & have decided what you will go on with there. We can talk it all over when you come. I am seeing about the cat—Raftery could probably consent to it—tho' the scarcity of milk seems even greater this year . . . I thought of Mike John, & John Diviney—but they have dogs in the house.

By the next day she had found a solution: the kitten could share the room of 'a nice Connemara boy who sleeps over the coach house. I cannot have it in the house but you could see it in the [?stable] . . . or take it into the garden.'

Willy gracefully replied, 'We accept with gratitude your arrangement about the Cat. We were disturbed by the thought at leaving the engaging beast in Dublin. His record of good conduct is still impeccable except that at this moment he is escaped into the kitchen.'[134] A mollifying postscript reports that he has finished a pastoral poem on Robert ('Shepherd and Goatherd') which 'My wife thinks . . . good'. Needless to say, the incident of the kitten and the chops was not mentioned. It was inevitable that they should name their cat Pangur, after the well-known medieval poem 'The Monk and his Cat':

> I and Pangur Ban, my cat,
> 'Tis a like task we are at;
> Hunting mice is his delight,
> Hunting words I sit all night.
>
> Better far than praise of men
> 'Tis to sit with book and pen;
> Pangur bears me no ill will,
> He too plies his simple skill.[135]

Easter once over, there was one more brief stopover in Dublin, this time at the Gresham Hotel on Sackville Street, to introduce Georgie to more friends (James Stephens, Douglas Hyde), pay another visit to the Abbey Theatre, and attend brother Jack's one-man show where George bought a 'small but very good drawing'. Such were the disrupted postal conditions in the country, when it was later sent on to Coole 'it contained a number of other letters sealed up in it; like the sponge which certain doctors are supposed to leave in a patient after an operation'.[136] Their chance encounter with his old friend Katharine Tynan Hinkson provided Father Yeats with yet another impression of 'Willy's new bride': 'She is a delightful creature, pretty, charming, and beautifully dressed. I think it is great happiness for him. They stayed a night at Maple's Hotel when they passed through in April. . . . I was very much taken with the pretty creature. I should long to be friends with her.'[137]

Finally, on 6 April they took the train to Gort and were transported down the long two-mile tree-arched driveway to Coole. Georgie was received graciously by Lady Gregory; but her mischievous husband crept down to the stables every night after their hostess had retired, to rescue the kitten and bring him up to their bedroom. In time the tale of the kitten became a set piece recounted by George to visitors. According to Frank O'Connor's version, Pangur was sneaked into Coole without permission, 'But as the outside car drove up the avenue of Coole the married, mature, famous man grew panic-stricken at the thought of the old lady's forbidding countenance. He bade the jarvey drive him first to the stables. There Pangur was deposited until, everyone having gone to bed, Yeats crept out in his slippers and brought him up to the bedroom.' By the time Ellmann had heard the story it illustrated Willy's 'fine sense of humour': 'Sometimes this took the form of prankishness, as when he allowed his wife, on their first visit together to Coole, to bring their cat along. . . . Yeats had to wait until their hostess was asleep to bring the cat in, and to take it out early in the morning before she woke up. Mrs Yeats asked why he had not forewarned her, and he replied, "I wanted to see what she'd say." '[138] Whatever version one accepted, Pangur became one of Willy's first strokes of independence from Coole. And with him came Mrs W. B. Yeats. She was Georgie no more, and Ballylee within reach at last.

GEORGE

PART II

CONJUNCTIONS 1919–1921

It seems strange to me that I have no feeling of fear over the future, but this very lack of anxiety increases my belief that there is no need for fear, for if I do not fear for you when you are my whole world surely my instinct is right?   (George to Willy)[1]

After this little time away, after this necessary service, I shall return to you more completely yours than ever before.   (Willy to George)[2]

The more you keep this medium emotionally and intellectually happy the more will script be possible now—at first it was better when she was emotionally unhappy but now the passivity is as small the opposite
                                                                    (the control Thomas)[3]

Her happiness will always depend on you only but the child would only give her happiness in being your child she does not want a child for its own sake
                                                                      (the Instructors)[4]

8

COOLE

While they moved from Ashdown Forest to London and then to Oxford, Ballylee was never far from their minds. Even before their marriage, masons were at work restoring the cottage at its foot.[5] It had been more than twenty years since Yeats, charmed by the old castle when he first visited the old miller nearby, returned again and again to solicit tales of the healer Biddy Early and Mary Hynes, 'the flower of Ballylee':

I have been lately to a little group of houses, not many enough to be called a village, in the barony of Kiltartan in County Galway, whose name, Ballylee, is known through all the west of Ireland. There is the old square castle, Ballylee, inhabited by a farmer and his wife, and a cottage where their daughter and their son-in-law live, and a little mill with an old miller, and old ash trees throwing green shadows upon a little river and great stepping-stones. I went there two or three times last year to talk to the miller about Biddy Early, a wise woman that lived in Clare some years ago, and about her saying 'There is a cure for all evils between the two mill-wheels of Ballylee.'[6]

In 1912, Georgie purchased her copy of *The Celtic Twilight* in which this essay appeared and wrote inside the cover, 'your young men shall see visions; your old men shall dream dreams'. This particular dream would take a long time to build.

A stone later dug from the property was dated 1657; the tower, then called Islandmore Castle, was listed in the *Book of Connaught* in 1585 as property of the de Burgo (or Burke) family; by the nineteenth century it was owned by James Colgan of Kilcolgan Castle and leased to his nephew Patrick Spellman, the retired master of the Loughrea Workhouse. When Yeats first visited Ballylee in 1896, walking south from Edward Martyn's home in Tillyra, Colgan's nephew and his wife still lived there; after her death in 1902 Ballylee Castle and the adjoining cottage they had built for their family reverted to the Gregory estate.[7] As Yeats approached north-eastward from Coole, it became part of his visionary landscape. Lady Gregory encouraged his interest in the old castle; in 1914, hearing that neighbours had cut down the elm trees, she reported, 'I drove to Ballylee, alas only one elm tree left! However it looked well all the same.' By 1916, when the property was turned over to the Congested Districts Board for redistribution, she was active on his behalf.[8] The sitting tenant was soon encouraged to abandon plans to turn it into a quarry and migrate elsewhere. Nobody else wanted that portion of Lot 31, with its broken tower and ruined outbuildings on a barren acre (plus two rods and twenty-five perches 'or thereabouts') by the edge of a flooding stream—essentially an island created by the stream briefly separating from Ballylee (or Turra) River and then joining it again. Yeats had to agree to a further division, 'a public right of way over the bridge to the entrance of the Castle and roadway through the Castle yard . . . for the use of persons needing same for horses, carts, and passengers'. But he saved the stepping stones. The 'symbols of possession' were handed over on 16 May 1917 although there was still some delay in the Board's arrangement with the Gregorys; keen to have him as a neighbour and concerned about the prevailing damp of the castle, Lady Gregory then suggested he consider buying instead the dower house opposite the road into Coole. But Willy was set on Ballylee:

Ballymantane would not please me at all. If I did not get Ballylee I would probably have built a thatched cottage on a site I chose long ago in Sligo. I only want a couple of sitting rooms from castle & it will not be too damp I think. Martyn says the castle wall 'sweats' at times & the board of works architect said if serious one could amend with laths & plaster a little out from wall. . . . I am really only anxious about the flood. I must have somewhere to keep my books safe. . . . Surely as I am to sleep in cottage there is nothing to be alarmed about in Castle. You certainly cannot wash your face from the castle walls in summer. All those heavy old walls 'sweat' a little.[9]

Besides, photographs had already been exhibited to his interested friends. The agreement was finally signed, sealed, and delivered on 30 June 1917, and he had his castle.[10]

As Lady Gregory told his father, from the beginning the medieval tower, within walking distance across the fields from Coole, was for Yeats inextricably tied to the idea of marriage. In 1915, when the prospect of acquiring Ballylee from the Congested Districts Board was first mooted, and several months before he and George first reached an understanding, he reluctantly wrote to Lady Gregory from Stone Cottage that he could not bid on it, for 'If I remained unmarried I would find it useless'.[11] But by 1916, the situation had changed, with Yeats determined on the married state—if not the precise bride—and the purchase of Ballylee was confirmed. At first, he did not conceive of actually living in the tower itself: on the advice of his architect, he thought of having 'the necessities' in the cottage and devoting the castle to 'a couple of great rooms'.[12] 'He wavers between beginning by putting a roof on the castle—or rebuilding the Cottage, in which he could encamp & oversee repairs being done,' Lady Gregory reported, including in her letter to JBY a fine pen and ink drawing of the tower. 'When he left, the cottage was in the ascendant. It is really a lovely & romantic place—but far from being habitable—There are trout in the little river—you can fish from the window but I don't know if anyone has ever caught anything from it.'[13]

Within weeks of marriage, plans changed once again—even before she visited Ireland George had taken possession of arrangements for the restoration of Ballylee (and it appears paid for most of it). Very soon the dream replaced even Italy as her ideal goal, and within days of the 'miraculous intervention', Willy was asking Lady Gregory, 'Is Raftery at work on Ballylee? If he is I will write to Gogarty and ask him to stir up [his architect] Scott.' Gregory in turn reported to his father, 'I look forward to having her as a neighbour at Ballylee. He wanted to bring her to see it at once—but he came over just before the marriage & the roofless castle & the ragged-roofed cottage looked bleak in the autumn floods & he put off till next summer. But now again he is anxious to show it, & straw was hurriedly bought yesterday in Gort market for the thatching'.[14] By late November Georgie was in regular correspondence with the local builder, Michael Rafferty of Glenbrack, Gort (whom Yeats and Gregory both persisted in calling Raftery, after the eighteenth-century Gaelic poet who had sung of Mary Hynes).[15] Nor did their search for a more permanent residence in Oxford deter them. 'Meanwhile there are various things Raferty can do at Ballylee (George is in correspondence with him) & when we go to see the daffodils may be in flower.' 'Raftery gets on slowly but fairly steadily with his work at Ballylee, & has just written that the rats are eating the thatch. Scott has asked for dimensions of fire-places so evidently will send designs and the Castle has been cleared out. It looks as if this spring may see the roof on but I dont want my wife to spend more money till she has seen the place.'[16] By George's reckoning, in addition to the original purchase price of £35, it had already cost them £150.[17] It would cost them considerably more. And there were still details of the purchase to attend to—arrangements concerning the bit of land on the other side of the road, and the building of a wall.[18]

Unrealistically worried that Rafferty would finish the cottage without them ('we are circumstantial here'), his old friend once again suggested that, instead of accepting Gogarty's offer of Renvyle where they would be 'thrust between bogs and ocean', they take Ballinamantan 'at an easy rent so as to be near Ballylee & able to superintend the work. Furniture for Ballylee could then be used at the dower house and easily carted over once the castle was habitable.'[19] From Oxford, Willy instructed his sister Lily to enquire about hiring furniture from Dublin 'for three bedrooms and two sitting rooms and kitchen. We shall bring our own plate and linen but shall want to have carpets and bedroom crockery. It would be for about six months.'[20] But again Lady Gregory had other suggestions: it might be better to bring furniture from Limerick, with its direct railway line to Gort.[21] In the event, fearing it would be too expensive to hire, George seems to have decided even before they left Oxford to purchase the minimum until they could have furniture made for the castle.[22] Despite the occasional disclaimer, 'No need to decide about this until Ballylee has been seen by its new mistress,' clearly Gregory was having difficulty withdrawing from her role as primary adviser. Even though she confided to John Quinn (who promptly informed JBY) that 'Yeats had for some years been longing for a home and fixity', it would be some time before she could recognize in George what JBY assumed intuitively: 'Probably she is sensible and practical as well as clever and will for the future decide everything for Willie.'[23] But she was somewhat uneasy about how her relationship with Georgie would evolve; in acknowledging a copy of *Per Amica Silentia Lunae* with its reference to a 'close friend' whose 'only fault is a habit of harsh judgment with those who have not her sympathy', she added:

I have at last realised you are a married man by the arrival of the Macmillan book so beautifully packed & 'with the Author's compliments' instead of the home tied parcel & scribbled autograph—I liked the untidy parcel better—but I don't mean that I like the married man less! . . . Are you not a little hard on me? Poor 'George' will think I am a Gorgon—I hope she wont, like Lady Anne Blunt, spend her time in 'looking for facts with which to bolster up her husband's arguments'![24]

For anyone aware of Gregory's early love affair with Wilfrid Scawen Blunt, this last comparison is telling.[25] Perhaps even more distressing was her realization that she would no longer be at the centre of his creativity; 'It is quite a strange sensation', she later wrote when reading his poems as they appeared in papers and journals, '—a little sad too, seeing for the first time in print a poem of yours, & not in your own writing.'[26]

Despite her excitement at being within reach of Ballylee, George must also have had mixed feelings about this first visit to Coole; she remembered, if her hostess did not, being snubbed at their previous encounter. There had also been varying excuses for delaying their arrival. Willy's version had been that 'She does not want us however till we are married—that one candle being I think the danger, or at least what the neighbours might say about the possible number of our candles.'[27] But Gregory's first note of welcome had betrayed some doubt as to the young English bride's perception of what might well still prove to be Willy's folly: 'I hope I may soon see you yourself, before the winter floods rise around Ballylee.'[28] Faced with the coming of winter, even Willy's courtship letters had showed some concern about her reaction to his dream castle: 'Lady Gregory thinks that we should get married as soon as possible & that I should bring you here before the weather grows very cold & gloomy that we may make our Ballylee plans together while the castle looks well.' 'It looks so different in spring with the island full of daffodils.'[29] Now spring had finally arrived, and the next morning they walked the three miles across the fields to Ballylee.

We can only guess at George's reaction on that first day. No building site is ever inviting, and Rafferty, despite his probity and avowed determination to fulfil the various contracts to the best of his ability, was a victim not only of the weather and the occasional undependable worker, but of the architect's delays. He was also working for Margaret Gregory on Ballinamantan, in preparation for the Yeatses' arrival. Acknowledging Georgie's cheque in February, he had promised shutters and windows for the cottage, but could do nothing to the castle until he received the architect's plans for the ceiling and fireplaces. By now however the castle had been cleaned and the old material removed, the thatching on the original cottage roof completed, and work was proceeding on a second cottage parallel with the first and extending from the original castle porch. Charging £3 a week for his own labour, Rafferty punctiliously reported on his expenditures each week, his letters offering more insight as to country life in the west of Ireland than even Jack Yeats's paintings. For the next six years, despite shortages of material, the political situation, other responsibilities, and the occasional misjudgement, he and George were to work harmoniously together. His regular reports do not betray Willy's description of 'a morbid man who cries when anything goes wrong', nor his excuse to Dulac that 'my wife would not leave Ballylee where the builder does something wrong the moment our heads are turned'.[30]

The architect was another matter. Willy had already received considerable advice from his English friends: Dulac had offered to decorate the rooms for nothing, but there was no place to accommodate him during the process;[31] Ricketts, who also lived in a castle (though there the similarity with Ballylee ends), was always free with advice. Margaret Gregory had been consulted on the original layout of cottage and roadway. But even before negotiations were completed, Willy had turned to William Alphonsus Scott, himself the son of a well-known architect. Professor of Architecture at the National University and the acknowledged expert of the Arts and Crafts movement as it flourished in Ireland, his efforts to rescue the Hiberno-Romanesque design once earned him the sobriquet 'architect by appointment to the Celtic Revival'.[32] Edward Martyn had commissioned Scott to remodel the tower house in which he lived at Tillyra, the nearby Catholic church at Laban, and the parochial hall (which was later burned down by the Black and Tans). But Scott's most important contributions to the Celtic Revival were St Enda's, the small stone parish church in Spiddal designed for Lord Killanin, and much of the interior fittings for the Cathedral of St Brendan at Loughrea. Well known for his ecclesiastical work, he had been equally successful with commissions for private homes—a house for the Countess of Desart in Kilkenny, an extension of Lord Killanin's Spiddal House (burned down in 1923), a renovation on Lough Gill for the Gore-Booth family. This was someone about whom Willy could feel confident, providing he could be found in a receptive condition. Edward Martyn once complained to Lady Gregory, 'Scott never does anything—but then there's nobody else!'[33] Equally important, Scott was familiar with the local craftsmen and keen to use materials at hand; he sent George off to the blacksmith at Liscannor village on the Clare coast for wrought-iron hinges, and while she was at it to look at 'the flag-slate roof on the barn near the Priests House', made from the light blue-green flags of the Liscannor quarries.[34] He advised Rafferty on cutting the sedge ('and save as one would hay'), negotiated the price (£25) for the materials—'great beams and three-inch planks and old paving stones'—from Lord Gough's disused mill and recommended using the mill wheel as hearthstone, and designed window sashes and frames, doors, fireplaces, and chairs (modelled on old Galway furniture), two beds for the castle, hanging cupboards for the cottages, and George's garden gate. Rafferty had the shutter hinges made at the Gort forge, and employed two carpenters to work with him, one of whom, John Hallanan, he reported, 'was doing real well'; Patrick Connolly, a craftsman joiner from Gort, made the furniture. Meanwhile, advised by Scott, George bought more furniture in Dublin, and was writing 'constant letters to shops, etc.' Willy was proud to report that 'by staying here we have succeeded in getting open timbers cut with an adze to support our hall roof instead of machine sawn timbers'.[35]

In March 1918 Lily informed an equally intrigued John Quinn, 'Ballylee Castle is being repaired, the Cottage beside it is thatched and ready—if the architect was more often sober things would be quicker.'[36] Willy reported to Maud, 'We hope to be in Ballylee in a month and there I dream of making a house that may encourage people to avoid ugly manufactured things—an ideal poor man's house. Except a very few things imported as models we should get all made in Galway or Limerick. I am told that our neighbours are pleased that we are not getting "grand things but old Irish furniture." '[37] When 'rumoured to be sober' and 'taken while in the mood', Scott, he admitted, 'has done beautiful work for us and is perhaps the finest imagination working at architecture but he is very difficult'.[38] Again, Willy turned over to George the responsibility for basic decisions, apparently content to have her decide on roof, shed, and archway, and oversee the many details involved in reconstruction. Throughout the summer of 1918 and into the next winter while his clients were in Ireland, Scott was attentive; then silence seems to have fallen. In 1921 he died of pneumonia, having caught a chill at Archbishop Walsh's funeral. Designs, still extant, for a magnificent wrought-iron floor candelabrum, great oak hall table, and other furnishings were never executed. Nor was the inscription which was to go on a stone tablet on the front of the castle. Already revised once, the poem was longer than its published version:

I the poet William Yeats
With common sedge and sea-green slates
And smithy work from the Gort forge
Restored this tower for my wife George
And on my heirs I lay a curse
If they should alter for the worse
From fashion or an empty mind
What Raftery built and Scott designed

In the template, Scott spelled the builder's name correctly. But rats ate the sedge he had so carefully instructed be preserved and, as Michael Yeats recalls, the cottages required further roofing to prevent 'creatures' from falling from the thatch onto their beds in the cottage. Later still they discovered that the sea-green slates, purchased at some expense, were rejected by the contractor; the tower roof was concreted instead.[39] Willy's lines underwent several further versions; when they were finally published, the castle was still a gift for 'my wife George', but their children were released from responsibility for its inevitable ruin and decay. Encouraged by George, he was beginning to see the tower not as an adjunct but a complement to the work done in Coole by Lady Gregory: 'I am making a setting for my old age, a place to influence lawless youth, with its severity & antiquity. If I had had this tower of mine when Joyce began to write I dare say I might have been of use to him, have got him to meet those who might have helped him'.[40]

Attention was not lacking from friends and neighbours. In an effort to ensure historical accuracy, George and Willy consulted local antiquarians concerning traditional fireplaces and mantels.[41] Their nearest neighbour Edward Martyn, now badly crippled by rheumatism, called by in his motor at least once a week and often invited them to Tillyra; there luncheon was drawn out until at least 7 p.m., or their host feared he had 'bored' them. Obviously relaxed with George, he once complained to her that both Willy and Lady Gregory used to tell stories of how Martyn, unlike his cousin George Moore, hated women; 'with her special emphasis and her particular twinkle of the eyes, Mrs Yeats said "Don't believe it. It is not true".' Like Willy and Lady Gregory, George enjoyed a good story: 'Martyn's mother tried to get her son married, and once to a girl who ruined her chances badly. She went up to some picture of some French painter, and said, "I do love those Beardsleys". That was the end for ever.'[42]

Lord Gough of Lough Cultra Castle, who had 'made light of the damp' and willingly sold the contents of his disused mill, had also alerted others to the distinguished new occupants of Ballylee. A letter survives in which he advises a descendant of the original Burkes: 'I think the Gort R. D. C should bid him welcome, and assure him that we are not such barbarians here as to be indifferent to the advent of the leading poet of Ireland to dwell amongst us.'[43] George later regaled Lily with tales of their eccentric neighbour, 'so loyal that his mind has become a little confused and he is said to turn to the east when "God save the King" is played'; but they lamented Lord Gough's death the following year, for he was always interested in Ballylee.[44]

Later that summer Willy took to Ricketts the plans they had received from their 'talented but drunken architect'. 'I went to Ricketts and showed him the designs,' he reported to his wife. 'He says we should risk the wicker hoods and that at the worst they would smoulder but will he thinks be safe. He thought the bed too like a bed for "King Lear's wife" but liked the big fireplace. Said he "had not seen it before". He suggests our using a millstone as flagging for the castle floor. He retouched the candlestick design and to demonstrate a point gave me a beautiful brass candlestick.'[45] A month later, responding to the rather puzzling advice to add soot, presumably to the whitewash, Ricketts replied, 'The pinch of soot may be an old Morris receipt it is the first I have heard of it. We always put a pinch of black and a pinch of ochre yellow they prevent the white looking blue. The quantities are very small, like salt in soups.'[46] Ever generous, he and his partner Charles Shannon would later present them with a 'rather charming' stained-glass window by Burne-Jones depicting St Cecilia; it eventually found an appropriate place not in Ballylee but at Rathfarnham, in the window from Willy's study into the greenhouse.[47] But the reference to William Morris was apt, for George was sensitive to her husband's ambition for the three traditions —unspoiled simplicity, uniqueness, and fantasy—he had admired in Morris's work. Now he sat at his own 'unpolished and unpainted trestle table of new wood', his wife arranging 'a beautiful house'. Once they were settled in the little cottage he rhapsodized to Ezra, 'As George moves about she would shock your modern mind by composing into 14th century pictures against the little windows with their orange curtains, and the rough whitewashed walls.'[48] As always, his gratitude came out in poetry:

> God grant a blessing on this tower and cottage
> And on my heirs, if all remain unspoiled,
> No table or chair or stool not simple enough
> For shepherd lads in Galilee; and grant
> That I myself for portions of the year
> May handle nothing and set eyes on nothing
> But what the great and passionate have used
> Throughout so many varying centuries[49]

But they were not in Ballylee yet. And the atmosphere was becoming unpleasant at Coole. The Gregorys' unassuming plain oblong Georgian house of local stone with its square porch and slate roof could not have been more different from

Georgie's comfortable retreat when visiting the Reades at Ipsden. Vines threatened the yellowish-white outer walls of the house, and one of the first tasks spring visitors were given was to sow wallflowers in the holes and crevices in the walls around the garden, an annual job which George for one found particularly boring.[50] Despite the magnificent library and artwork within, the Seven Woods and autograph tree without, perhaps also on that first visit she felt the way John Masefield did when he confided to Cottie Yeats: 'Coole *has* a bad aura. While I was there I had a continual feeling of something malignant and uncanny surrounding the house every night.'[51] It may, of course, have been the rats, for which Coole was notorious. When Willy returned to Dublin to lecture on William Blake at the Abbey, George eagerly joined him for the weekend of 13 April. While entertaining her sister-in-law, she provided the latest instalment in the Pangur saga, duly relayed to New York: 'George said "the Gregorys dont like pets unless they are useful"—she tried to get Lady Gregory to pat the cat—it lived in the stables at Coole.' But she was pleased that 'George is in love with Galway County.'[52]

Conditions at Coole deteriorated. Lady Gregory's daughter-in-law Margaret had been helpful to Willy on his first plans for the cottage, perhaps relieved that he would at last be out of Coole. Now, still grief-stricken over Robert's death, she could no longer hide her obvious dislike and resentment of the role Yeats unquestioningly took in the household. On 17 April, two days after George and Willy returned from Dublin, the façade of cordiality cracked with unexpected results:

In April we went to Coole. Margaret Gregory received us both rather rudely. One night . . . she began at dinner to contradict as usual every thing I said & instead of avoiding reply as I had done hitherto I turned on her. I had come down to dinner in the highest of spirits with this wicked intention & at the end of dinner went up stairs in the highest spirits. George told me I had behaved badly but had so much sympathy with me, that we omited [*sic*] our usual precaution against conception . . . the spirit approved & treated my quarrel at dinner as a [Sun sign] against [Saturn] symbolism. He seemed indifferent to the ethics of the matter. From then on we expected the conception of a child. We had not waited as long as the spirit had advised thanks to Margaret Gregory.[53]

With 'sympathy complete' at last, 17 April marked the 'third stage' of their relationship, which the spirit had said was necessary for completion of the 'birth of third Daimon', a process which had begun with their marriage. This and succeeding events were marked as usual by horoscopes, one for 17 April '9.40 p.m. old time', another for 25 April '10–12 p.m. Old Time', and more explicit horaries by George for 29 April 1918 at 7.10 p.m. enquiring 'é consevato o no?', for 24 May 1918 at 9.30 p.m. 'probable date Anne's conception', and for 1 June at 10.30 p.m. 'Anne's conception improbable date'. According to the script these events were progressive; the night of Willy's quarrel with Margaret also marked the conception of the fourth daimon. By 24 September the automatic writing was suggesting that the child—regularly referred to as the 'heir or son'—would be connected with an avatar.[54]

Even before leaving Oxford, Willy had contemplated a period of houselessness. Lady Gregory's letter of welcome, written just weeks after news of her son's death, had been unusually precise: 'As to your plans, I think you may like to arrange definitely to come, say for a fortnight at or after Easter, & look about. I don't say, come for an indefinite time—because even if you make a payment for food, it may be difficult to get it—supplies seem to be getting short. But we'll see when you come what will be best.' Almost as an afterthought, she had added, 'of course I look forward very much to seeing you—& Margaret said she wd. like it.'[55] Willy had reassured her; they could 'if need be fill up a little time at small hotels by some inland water. I noticed the hotels were good along the Shannon. As we are both students we can entertain ourselves & each other.'[56] Now, three days after his encounter with Margaret, he and George fled from Coole, before they left reporting on their progress to Dulac,

We are here and gone tomorrow. We drift about from place to place and with a country on the verge of God knows what disturbances heaven knows when we shall get into our own house, although a month's steady work would make it ready. . . . We fish, and we catch nothing. And tomorrow we go to Galway where our luck may be better. What will happen to us there we do not know, for it is reported that all the young men are buying hatchets and crowbars with the intention of using them on the Railway lines and telegraph poles. We have chosen Galway Town because at the worst we can walk back here, 16 miles, and Lady Gregory can kill a sheep and cook it on the lawn.[57]

Unlike the idyllic Easter sojourn in Wicklow, however, they could no longer ignore the political unrest so evident around them. Despite his jaunty tone to Dulac, these were troubling times: the day after they had reached Coole, Sinn Féin leaders were rounded up on the strength of a mythical 'German plot'; their arrival in Galway coincided with a general strike protesting conscription. 'We cant remain here any longer,' Yeats wrote to Lady Gregory from their Galway lodgings (c/o Mrs Little, The Crescent), 'there is too much danger of being drawn into politics, or of seeming to shirk the business.' A month later he cancelled a planned lecture on war poetry in Dublin, explaining, 'I cannot imagine a more dangerous condition of things, the old historical passion is at its greatest intensity. I hear of an old cabinet maker saying two years ago "There will be more wild work. The young men are mad jealous of their leaders for being shot." '[58] Even Ballylee was part of the political saga; he had been told that 'the local Sinn Feiners . . . used to meet in it before we took possession.'[59]

Margaret Gregory was also keen to see them settled outside Coole (even if only as far as the gate), urging Rafferty to whitewash the bedrooms of Ballinamantan.

Lady Gregory loaned them bedsteads and armchairs to eke out the furnishings George had already purchased. 'We shall go to Ballynamantan on Thursday [2 May]. If there are only a couple of mattresses & bedding we can spend the night there,' Willy wrote from Galway. 'George is writing to Nora Dooly to know what is there & if the place is quite uninhabitable we shall go to Oughterard for a couple of days.'[60] Once again George had made her own decisions; Norah Dooley, daughter of Mike John, Lady Gregory's gamekeeper, although described as unable to boil an egg, would be malleable, whereas her sister-in-law Kate, suggested by Lady Gregory, might not.

The very day they moved into the dower house, the eagle and butterfly ring arrived from Dulac. 'George made me promise the other day when she expected to be away for a day that if the parcel arrived in her absence I was not to open it,' Willy had written to his friend. 'So you see with what ceremony we treat it. Neither must open it without the other.' Now, on their 'first escape from lodgings and hotels', they rejoiced in the 'very beautiful and mysterious looking object'—a 'good omen' indeed.[61] During their wanderings they had managed only one session with the Instructors; although rife with unintelligible answers interspersed amongst the discussion of phases of personality, one passage again linked their unborn child to the mysterious Anne Hyde:

myhrrh is medium
frankincense is you—one rising
one to preserve—one to create
one to initiate—one to renew
one to be born—one to be reborne [*sic*][62]

Ballinamantan at last provided the stability and peace they sought for work on the system, and Thomas gave them a timetable—'Work five mornings a week— idle one morning—potter over paper one morning | afternoon & evening go out as much as possible & sleep.' He promised to come '2 nights a week for system & two evenings when you codify to help now', adding, 'You must codify from the very beginning of system & then medium can sort out each division & make a summary of each.'[63] They were getting closer to understanding their responsibilities. The dower house was also closer to Ballylee, and George immediately started planning her garden of roses, wallflowers, and vegetables and sowing a narrow bed of sunflowers in front of the cottage. Across the road they planted trees; seventy years later one of the dead elms would become the cover of 'The Great Book of Ireland'.[64]

George enjoyed fishing from the castle windows. More than thirty years later she recalled her pleasure in the sport: when she had informed Willy that 'I dont like country occupations at all but I do like fishing,' they went to Lyden's in Galway where she was bought 'the most beautiful little fishing rod, the most enchanting little rod and flies and all the appurtenances'. She horrified her husband by preferring fishing with worms from a boat, unaware that experienced fishermen cast with the mayfly.[65] But her success was broadcast to Lily and beyond: 'We had a fine dish of trout from our own river the other day—grey trout and some salmon trout.'[66] Impressed by this knowledge of country ways, JBY sent a sketch from New York with the heading, 'Mrs W. B. Yeats catches the biggest fish ever known,' adding 'I am so glad George is a fisherman—we were all great fishers.'[67] Once they had actually moved in it became a daily sport, to Willy's delight also: 'My wife is now fishing for trout under one of the windows & says through the window that she has had several bites. It is in flood & she is fishing with a worm. At lunch we shall have a dish of trout caught under the same window. Last night she was fishing out of another window but caught nothing though she had some good tugs on the line.'[68]

Though they promised themselves each week would be the last on the Coole estate, by July they were becoming reconciled to the slow though steady progress on the castle. George had brought her typewriter to Ireland, and Willy was catching up on his correspondence as well as his lecture preparations.[69] Meanwhile they were expanding their menagerie; Pangur was joined by another angora cat from Cuala named Thomas, two big brown hares, one small brown hare, and two small black hares. The hares sat up and washed their faces with their paws; Pangur proved to be sturdy and independent (and frequently dirty), but Thomas, like his master, had digestive problems, exacerbated by the mainly liquid diet Norah kept him on while George and Willy were away.[70] In time canaries were added to the bestiary, and the first of a series of dogs. But despite her fishing skills still an urban romantic, George anxiously asked Willy whether he thought somebody might give them some crows to nest in the big tree by the tower—an unnecessary concern as it soon turned out.[71] Later Willy in turn badgered his wife until she gave in and—to the glee of the children—agreed to two Aylesbury ducks.

George was also growing familiar with country ways. In addition to con- sultations with the blacksmith and carpenters, there were the twice-weekly shopping visits to Gort in a horse-drawn side-car borrowed from Coole. Willy usually stayed outside while George visited the grocer. When horse and cart were not available, she bicycled. With a population of about 1,000, Gort, especially its post office on Saturday market day, yielded many opportunities for getting and spreading the news. There were also visitors off the road, more often at the castle with its door onto the right of way. The miller nearby was a man who believed in being prepared: he had a boat ready for the floods, and was rumoured even to have cut the boards for his own coffin. Across the bridge, left at the crossroads and right down the boreen, lived fey old Mrs Cusack, who brushed her teeth outside so the ogre up the chimney would not catch her with her mouth open. Later she berated George for planting sunflowers by the roadside—lizards might leap out from them into the children's mouths, the only known cure to make them thirsty and hold them upside down over the river until the lizards jumped out for a drink.[72] A strong element of Mrs Cusack entered into the persona of 'Crazy Jane' about whom, as 'Cracked Mary', George had a number of stories:

she was a bit touched in the head. But it was a head full of amusing, often obscene stories about things she'd see on her rambles. I used to seek her out and get her to tell them to me. Then I'd go home and tell W. B. . . . . He loved them. He asked me to get as many as I could for him. And so I saw a good deal of Cracked Mary at that time. . . . One day she told me—and leaned confidentially over a roadside bench on which she'd put down her basket: 'I was comin' down the lane up beyont, and was just passin' a large bush that grows by the side of the road, when I see appearin' from beneath the bush two pairs of feet, the one pair above the other. And the top pair was diggin' with its toes into the dirt, just like that'—and George here extended her hands, palms down, as cracked Mary had done, and worked her fingers as if digging them into the roadside dirt, and laughed delightedly, her eyes a-twinkle.[73]

They were not as solitary as it would seem that summer. There were regular visits to Coole, by Willy more often than George. The O'Neills spent a day with them, reporting later to Lily that 'George "is the nicest person he ever met or expects to meet in this existence or any other" and so she is, she is that comfortable and pleasant thing a good woman with good brains—and no axe of her own to grind. After all this is the right mixture to make a good wife and the best of mothers.'[74] The four would become fast friends; Joseph, 'a big kindly man', had left academia to become Secretary of the Department of Education, and his wife Mary, a poet, later had many long discussions over *A Vision*.[75] The young poet Austin Clarke had lunch at Ballinamantan with WBY alone who, rushing off to the 4 p.m. train, promised, 'You must come and see me again, when I am in my castle!'[76]

On 27 June at 2 p.m. the script brought Thomas, Aymor, Rose, Arnaud, and later Fish in solemn conclave; Willy was instructed to 'begin writing—not question'.[77] By the middle of July Ezra received poems born of the system for publication in *The Little Review*, for which he was serving as foreign editor. And Willy, apparently with George's permission (the script had specifically suggested the system be put 'into story romance image'[78]), was well into the Robartes–Aherne dialogues that would elaborate their new philosophy and in a revised form frame the first edition of *A Vision*. Asking the irascible young American to 'read my symbol with patience', for 'After all ones art is not the chief end of life but an accident in ones search for reality or rather perhaps ones method of search,' he reported his progress to Pound:

I am now at the 30th page of my prose dialogue, expounding this symbol & there will be 3 dialogues of some 40 pages each, full of my sort of violence & passion. The mere mathematic discord and concord between different phases needs many pages—17 is in one mathematical relation with 3 other phases—13–3–27 & in another mathematical relation with 12 and 24 so you see I am precise enough . . . I survey all art and letters under the glare of my mathematical lightning.[79]

As previously promised, he sent Ezra 'The Double Vision of Michael Robartes' and, far more revealing, 'The Phases of the Moon', describing them as 'two philosophic poems, both of which I think good (George says are very good). They are nothing like as abstract as the Paradiso; an attempt to get subjective hardness.'[80] Like his pastoral elegy in memory of Robert Gregory, 'Shepherd and Goatherd', 'The Phases of the Moon' draws directly on the questions and answers recorded in the automatic script during these months, with some acknowledgement to both Swedenborg and William Blake's 'The Mental Traveller'. Pound, who with Dorothy had been indoctrinated into the workings of the system, soon decided Willy had gone 'queer in his head about "moon"'.[81]

Then in late July the Yeatses finally paid the long-promised visit to the Gogartys in Connemara. Yeats's witty doctor friend had recently purchased Renvyle, an old house surrounded by trout lakes and less than a hundred yards from the sea, and was turning a portion of the 'sixty rooms or more' into a hotel. The house boasted superb views of fir trees, water, and mountains, and an old library with first editions of More's *Utopia* and Chaucer's lessons on the astrolabe to his son. It also housed a ghost, which, although the visitors sensed its presence, would not be exorcized until they returned the following year.[82] Apparently they did not attempt any automatic writing while at Renvyle, and although much was doubtless hinted at, little was said of their own ghostly encounters on this first meeting. But no matter how much he mocked, Gogarty had a healthy respect for his friend's occult skills: 'I have never looked lightly upon Yeats's tampering with the spirit world—not since the time he entered a room in my house in Ely Place, Dublin, stood in the doorway and said, "There is a presence here, I smell incense." Yeats had had no way of knowing that my wife and I had just been talking about a friend—a priest—lately dead. Yeats used to say that to talk about a dead person is to bring their ghost about you.'[83] It was probably in this company that Willy tried to protect his young wife from their host's more salacious stories and limericks by sending her out of the room—until George roundly challenged him.[84]

Other responsibilities also invaded their retreat. Almost as soon as they had left England in March Ezra wrote to them, concerned about financial arrangements for 'Maurice', as they continued to call Iseult in all correspondence. Despite Willy's careful arrangements with his friend Sir Denison Ross, the Arabic scholar and director of the School of Oriental Studies, it appeared that regulations prevented Iseult from working part-time as an assistant librarian.

'The present arrangement certainly does not leave her sufficient leisure to write, or even prepare for writing,' Ezra fretted. But he could not commit more than £5 a month, his entire salary from *The Little Review*, as payment to Iseult for three days' work each week; would Willy provide the further £3 necessary for a living wage? Moreover she had no typewriter; if George's had gone with her, perhaps Eliot's might be available. More serious still was her official role. His own poems 'are too Ithyphallic for any secretary of her years to be officially in my possession. . . . She might, of course, be doing typing for both of us.'[85] The question of Iseult's position continued to plague the two men, although this apparently did not prevent Ezra from seducing her. That spring two publications by Iseult appeared in the *English Review*, a poem and a prose vision, and, planted by Ezra, the July issue of *The Little Review* published her brief essay on an epic by the Bengali poet Saptam Edoyarder Svargabohan—slim fruits at last of Yeats's encouragement.[86] As her mother had frequently said, Iseult did not have the staying power required to be a writer; she did not have the self-confidence either. 'Though she has written some charming & some subtle & profound things to please herself finds great difficulty in working on a set theme,' Willy admitted.[87] Thomas tried to reassure him; the script for 14 May began with an obvious reference to his earlier poem about Iseult and George:

The bird was in no cage do not shut the door
Let it find its own seed & worms as it will & where it will
No be careful
. . . do not obliterate the marks of its feet on the soft ground . . .
Do not be afraid the script will cease—it will not until its time & all is through[88]

By the end of March Maud had moved into her house at 73 St Stephen's Green, but on 17 May, just three days after the script's optimism, she was arrested and sent with other Sinn Féin sympathizers back to England under the threat of a 'German plot' which had apparently been concocted to silence anti-conscription. Despite efforts from Willy and all her friends, she would remain in Holloway Jail throughout the summer. Iseult, still working at the College of Oriental Studies, was in Woburn Buildings with their French servant and at the mercy of Mrs Old's onslaught on the housekeeping budget. Although suffering from a reduced income herself, George sent money to Iseult and they made plans for a summer visit to London. 'Thank Georgie for her sweet letter to me,' Maurice replied in a letter to Willy; all were in 'a great state of excited politics'. There was also the question of Seán MacBride, Maud's son, who had left AE's charge in Dublin and was with Iseult in the Woburn flat, supposedly being tutored by Ezra. Another possibility was to offer the Oxford house they had now rented to the Gonnes (and Maud if they could get her out of prison), thereby keeping the entire family out of the country. But Willy knew his old friend too well, she 'will refuse to leave London where she can see MPs & the like'. Keeping a shrewd eye on the situation, Lily informed her father, 'Willy and George offered to take Maud's son—but AE is waiting to hear what plans his mother has for him, at present he is at AE's. A rest far from men is what the boy wants I think.'[89] Seán, now just 15, joined them at Ballinamantan towards the end of June.

Meanwhile George, signing her name with the square □ by which the Pounds identified her, called on Ezra:

I want you to do 2 things for me. I am worried about Maurice. I wrote some time ago telling her we were coming to England in either July or August; & I asked her, if she had made no other arrangement, to spend her holiday with us in the country. I told her we would choose whichever month was convenient for her. I have had no answer. Several of our letters, especially those to Shawn & MG, have been lately stopped, presumably by Censor. This letter may therefore not have reached Maurice. I must know soon, as we will have to write about lodgings, passports & the divil of the rest of it, & there is only about a month now before July. I would also like to know if she has made other arrangements; in that case we shall not come at all. We were only coming for her holiday *see end as she must be able to get away for a time. It will be damnably expensive & we are both feeling this war on our incomes rather seriously just now. Find out if you can when you see her, & suggest she makes up her mind as soon as she can.

Then, now MG is in gaol I do not know how Maurice's financial affairs will prosper. MG may or may *not* have made arrangements about her allowance & Josephine's board & lodging allowance. Also Shawn may be going over to England & also have no money!

I have sent Maurice £5 for emergencies but she will not like going on borrowing with no prospect of paying back; or accepting money. I therefore enclose a cheque to you for £5 & you can apply it in case of need—as payment for work or some other quibble your ingenious mind can invent. The stoppage of payments from MG will probably only be temporary but it might be very serious for a short time. We have not been able to find out yet what money Shawn has. He may have gone to England yesterday; Russell wrote he was bent on doing so. If not, he will probably come to us—Anyhow you must look after his & M's finance if he goes to England & see they get enough to eat etc. Maurice certainly cannot feed him & Josephine herself on £2 a week.

I have urged WBY to make her take the plunge of leaving the School at end of June. She ought to be able to make £3 a month beyond what you give her, and in any case we'd have to be responsible if she didnt so she wouldnt starve & it would be much better for her in every way. I believe he has written her about it.

NONE of this is to be spread outside the flat, especially of our possible coming to England.
*You will *not* of course tell Maurice we are only coming for her holiday, or of the question of raising means.[90]

Suffering from a 'raging toothache', she went to Dublin and made enquiries of Maud's friend Barry Delaney, who so adored Seán that at his birth she had sent a telegram to the Pope announcing 'the King of Ireland had been born'.[91]

Reassured, George then wrote once again to Ezra, heading it 'PRIVATE' in large letters. Her self-confident tone puts paid to any suggestion that she held the literary world, Lady Gregory, or her poet-husband in awe or that by now she suffered any delusions as to the roles she must play in their life together:

I gather from Delaney that they have at present enough cash—
In view of my great knowledge of reviews etc as gold mines—needless to say my information dates from WBY. Anyhow M. will have to be got work from some other source than the L.R. with its social reputation—No dynamite or gelignite will alter that—As a matter of fact Shorter[92] is in a sentimental condition over Ireland & might get Maurice a job on the Bookman or some other godforsaken bilge. Turpitude can easily be produced in WB's brain & hashed up by M. Anyway it wont do for you to have M on whole time with your appearance etc etc etc. So something nominal must be got.
WB has *stacks* of stuff eating its head off for want of printing In fact he is going to take two weeks holiday to recover from overwork! I left him reluctantly turning it over in view to sending you some stuff.
WB spent many hours over a french dictionary reading the French no. [of] L.R. [*Little Review*]—As I remarked, no dynamite will reconcile WB to let us try Eliot Lewis & Co—whether Maurice will consent to any machine work I doubt. But then I am not cautious. Anyway a little review writing will be good for WB as he wont write prose at the moment & is doing too much of t'other for his own good—tho' the stuff is good enough.
I also left him writing to Quinn to extol the LR its purity & literal excellence. His unnatural honesty over *known* facts is difficult to assuage.
WB will be unpersuadable over the whole time job. He will be less so if he does not imagine you are paying from your own pocket for the workhouse fare of distressed beauty. But his view of LR is of course final. Even if she doesnt get some machine work it wont matter. If we dont come over we'll be about £30 to the good & something can be wangled. WB has an exaggerated view of M's suspicious nature. In other words I dont imagine she'll have the faintest ideas if she gets 10/- more than normal in a note. (You can do it out of the £5 & write me when its all gone.) I imagine she'll have to give a month's notice at the school?
However meanwhile I will on returning home
1. See WB writes a sufficient letter to Quinn
2. Get him to write urging M again to L.R.
I dislike forcing people to do things especially as he trots up to Coole—Lady G & I cant *both* be right! And she's as cautious as any priest. LR no place for a young gal etc! G[93]

When she returned to Ballinamantan, Willy informed Ezra—as if they were his own idea—of all the plans for Iseult, Quinn, *The Little Review*, and his own work that his wife had already hatched.

While she was away Willy was desolate. 'I miss you beyond words & have carefully watered your seeds on the windowsill as the only form of attention I can show you & am now going to the garden to water the rest. They do not require watering but I am doing it to satisfy my feelings so they must endure it.'

Your two letters dated Monday & Tuesday came this morning. Both very good letters—vivid and wise. The worst of it is that your account of the acting of 'A Little Bit of Youth' makes it the more desirable that I should stay for a while in Dublin while your absence from me now makes it seem quite impossible. I cannot bear the thought of being away from you again. I say to myself every day that is one day less of parting, she will be home in so many days. I have done nothing but tidy the table & read my books & discuss with Lady Gregory the new stanza that is to commend Robert's courage in the hunting field. . . .

I have opened the big parcel of books which has come addressed for you. One book [Spinoza] will give me all I want for Thomas. On looking over Mrs Fowlers copy of that old script I have found the form ▷◁ surely the two cones.

I think of spending the afternoon perch fishing. I feel always that I am just filling up an empty space in life waiting your return.[94]

George seems to have accomplished a great deal on this quick visit to Dublin. Armed with a letter of introduction from Willy ('She is a Latin scholar and has some knowledge of the kind of thought in the MSS') she examined Larminie's translation of Johannes Scotus Erigena in the National Library, reported unfavourably on Fred O'Donovan's production of Christian Callister's one-act comedy *A Little Bit of Youth* at the Abbey ('an amusing play we cast at Glendalough'), ordered furniture for Ballylee, and with considerable self-satisfaction entertained her sisters-in-law with reports of Willy's attentiveness. Both daughters promptly reported all to New York:

[Lily] She is really good looking and as happy as possible—her clothes becoming and with personality—we dined one night at the Hotel with her. You know how long it takes to get a letter from Willy, she got a long one every day—he was carefully watering all her seedlings. They have taken an old house in Oxford 5 [*sic*] Broad St—and will move all their possessions from Woburn Buildings there in the Autumn— . . . Willy has been writing very hard and is now going to break off for a fortnight.

[Lolly] Lily had tea with her in town one day—& I the next day—& I went with her to see about some furniture they want to get made in Dublin for the Castle—we ordered some things beds & chairs etc to be made of unpolished mahogany—a fine big chair for Willie good simple lines but comfortable—I think George enjoys the *thrill* she gets when she gives her name in shops—'Mrs W. B. Yeats' It was a shop near the pro-cathedral— . . . They were most anxious to do all George wanted—& are to send designs & estimates at once down to Galway. On Friday night Lily & I dined with her at the Hibernian Hotel—& went on afterwards to the Abbey plays—& we went up to the Green Room & saw the company between the acts—everyone likes her—*now* she seems to be a very handsome glowing girl—I think she must have been tired out (she had a bad cold) when we saw her first—for now you would say *at once* she is very charming & pretty—her colouring very good & glowing—she is *evidently* very happy—& the clothes she is wearing now are most becoming—So I take back all I said about her way of dressing—she is very well dressed—wears lots of brilliant colour most becoming to her—very expensive clothes—& distinctive in style—fashionable & artistic at the same time—the things we saw her in first were eccentric but we did not think them pretty—*perhaps* she *thought* they would be what we *would* like so put them on—she went back to Galway on the 7.30 a.m. train on Sunday taking the Cuala kitten with her[95]

Lolly took photographs, which were also forwarded to their father, provoking Lily to even further encomium: 'Lolly has sent you some snapshots she did of Georgie when she was here, lately—the light wasn't very good, but still it will give you an idea of her—she is delightfully sane, just think of all the pests of women that are going about who suffer from nerves and think it soul—and so does some unlucky man till he marries them—Willy is in luck.'[96]

George returned to glorious weather, work progressing slowly on the cottage and tower ground floor, and a relieved husband who for once agreed with both his sisters. They immediately set about making arrangements for the journey to London, asking the ever-willing Dulac to find them a cottage with 'local assistance' for a few weeks, with room for Iseult and Seán and possibly a servant. 'We *must* have three bedrooms and if possible four (of course, the servant, if we took a cottage, would have to be provided for).'[97]

Circumstances altered their plans once again. George was apparently not yet prepared for such a long encounter with Iseult, or still felt her relationship with Willy too fragile. She also began to suspect that she was pregnant, another reason for being unusually emotional. Some incident obviously upset her, for on 16 June Thomas advised in mirror writing, 'private—you had better prevent the medium going away now—she will not get accustomed to conditions from the mind | will only become more depressed . . . constant renewal of . . . problems deductions . . . it accentuates the feeling of *alienation* . . . not loneliness quite happy here now but events such as this morning make the situation lose reality by seeming to have no right of intimacy only that of law.'[98] Thomas then proceeded with discussion of the cycles and their relation to the birth of an avatar. They postponed their visit to London, and George went instead to the coast of Clare for several days in mid-July, doubtless with Scott's designs for James Nestor, the blacksmith at Liscannor, and an introduction to the knowledgeable local priest, Father O'Fahey. A card from Willy to the Aberdeen Arms Hotel, Lahinch, kept her informed of the slow progress on the castle: 'MacDonough has returned design to "G. Yeats Esq." and says he has no seasoned ash or oak. We may have to use red larch or the like and perhaps paint door. We cannot move in without a front door. . . . No news here except an obscure message from Rafferty about sedge—"Steward had not time to go with him"—he is to come in today.'[99] While she was away he too made plans for their expected child, suggesting to Lily that she ask Sturge Moore to use his 'infinite fold' design for 'a cover for a child's cot (you need not say it is for our use)'.[100] They would make their own announcements in time.

Iseult had by now moved to a flat in Beaufort Mansions, Chelsea, which she shared with Iris Barry, the penurious mistress of Wyndham Lewis (by whom she would have two children) and later to become a respected film critic for the *Spectator*. There are differing accounts of what seems to have become very rapidly a deteriorating arrangement. According to later biographers of Barry, 'For Iris it was a largely sandwich existence. She shared a room for a time with another, better-off girl, but got turned out, involuntarily involved in personal feuds and complications she never fathomed.'[101] But according to Willy, perhaps revealing more of his own fears than Iseult's, and based on a report from Seán, rescue was essential. So in early August George and Willy rushed over to London, staying in the de Vere Hotel while they installed Iseult, Josephine, cat, birds, and furniture once again in Woburn Buildings. As usual, Gregory received the fullest account of this extraordinary comedy, which also indicates how far Willy had travelled on his emotional road:

I cannot yet return though we had shifted Iseult two days after our arrival. She was going into the country for two or three days & with the understanding that she was to seem to know nothing about it we kidnapped her maid, her cat & birds & all her furniture & transferred them to Woburn buildings. The young woman turned up too late (warned it seems by Aleck Sheppeler of our arrival—Chelsea clings together). She is a scandalous person & seems to have kept Iseult in submission with tears & temper. Iseult was of great practical use to her, especially as she had frequently omitted to pay her half of the rent or for the meals she eat whenever she quarrelled with Lewis her lover. The trouble is that Iseult after gratitude for delivery has seen her again & is full of remorse for having got rid of her. Maud Gonne has brought Iseult up in such a strange world that she is not shocked at what other girls are shocked at. As long as she herself lives & thinks rightly she thinks nothing else matters. I am playing the stern uncle sent by her mother to carry off a foolish niece. The neice [*sic*] says that she must obey. It is an absurd comedy but I think there will be no talk as both Lewis & the young woman have been warned that if anything reaches Ross (head of school where young woman works) & he questions me I will tell all.

Of course nothing to anybody least of all to Aleck Sheppeler who can hardly be expected to sympathize with ones dislike for Comus & his rout (John & his troup to translate it). . . . Iseult is afraid of this young woman, of Ezra, of me, of everybody, & thats the very devil. It was George who got the furniture van & seized the furniture glad to exercise her hatred of Chelsea.[102]

After Willy's return to Ballinamantan, the still-incarcerated Maud received an edited and reassuring, if somewhat defensive, version of the *coup d'état*. 'Iseult had feared to [be] unkind but was grateful to be rid of Barry by the act of others. She can stay at Woburn Buildings until March next without rent to pay as we are moving to Oxford.' But Seán's education also concerned them; during the summer he was being tutored by the Gort schoolteacher. 'He went to Martyn while I was away. I have made many enquiries about Irish school. I think Clongowes would be best. . . . I am very much struck by Seán. He is the most remarkable boy I have met—self possessed and very just, seeing all round a question and full of tact.'[103]

Both Yeatses seem to have enjoyed the London adventure, although Willy returned to Seán and the animals a week ahead of George. In addition to meeting with friends (Herbert Reade presented her with a copy of Shelley), she had news to break to her mother which was not entirely welcome—the expected conception had at last taken place. After Anne was born Willy confided to Lady Gregory, 'in the months before her birth George had a strong feeling against her mother, who on her side regretted Annes arrival'.[104] Nelly was not yet ready to give up her own bit of youth by becoming a grandmother. It was also an opportunity to see Harold, who had been called up, but, because of some weakness of the ligatures at the back of his knees, was exempt from active service; by early October, he would be in France, working in a Church Army Hut.[105] She may even have had time to join him at the August meeting of the Golden Dawn, for on 1 May he had crossed the portal and entered the Inner Order. Certainly she met with various members of the Stella Matutina, and it was probably now that she asked 'Il faut chercher' the 'innocent question' that precipitated a final schism among the members, which in a few years' time would threaten to engulf them also. Even more solicitous of his wife, Willy instructed her either to take the 6.40 evening train from Euston where she could board the boat when she arrived, or the early morning train, sleeping at the Euston Hotel in spite of the noise. Either way, 'you have to be on platform at least 40 minutes before the train starts to get a good seat'. 'No dining car so bring food.'[106]

He also immediately began mending fences with Iseult. Having introduced her to Charles Ricketts and Eva Ducat as safer acquaintances, he wrote as soon as he reached Dublin:

We must not let the old 'link' be broken. For so many years you were to me like a very dear daughter, and cannot you be that again. Nothing ended can break this link—never up to this broken in my thoughts—but the unhappiness of another. Every year of life has shown me that there is nothing in life worth having but intensity and that there can not be intensity without a certain harmlessness and sweetness in the common things of life. . . . Your Mask is at 28 . . . The ego is folding up into itself and scales as an escape the absorption in God. By this Mask and by the creative genius (from 16) which is a kind of emotional intuition (I will write more of this and less vaguely when I have sought the help of Thomas) the ego escapes from 'the enforced love of the world' the personality of Fate from 2 (where Natural life the vehement life of the race begins). Tell me if you can understand this.

When I come to London next, we will have some long talks and we will see each other at Oxford when you will come and stay with us. Later on you will come to Ballylee. Meanwhile my dear child be friends with George and with her friends too if you can.

George has become happy only very lately but in a little while she will have become used to happiness and then I shall dread no more that thought that used to persecute her—the thought that she had come between old friends by an accident. Write to me more often and send me your work.[107]

Iseult was not impressed. 'Those revelations from your spirits are certainly very curious and interesting but . . . May I speak frankly? I can hardly attach much spiritual value to them.'[108] It seems that by then, and even after her return to Ireland, she and Ezra were lovers, though, concerned about her mother's health, she refused his invitation to travel with him to the Italian lakes.[109] Seán stayed with George and Willy until early September; although it would be some time before they or Maud found out, later that autumn, lying about his age, he joined the IRA. On 1 September, the day before Seán left Ballinamantan, something untoward occurred, which remains mysterious. When Willy asked the Instructors 'Was there serious danger,' the reply was 'Much upset'; he was doubtless disappointed when the control would not acknowledge any correspondence 'between what happened to us & happened in your world'.[110]

Meanwhile, something had to be done about the feline Thomas; they turned to Gogarty for medical advice:

We have a sick angora cat; each time we have been away it has been left with a servant, and each time it has been ill when we came back, and this time for over three weeks. Is there a vet who takes in cats in Dublin? This beast was probably fed on milk diet exclusively with the result, from being the most exemplary cat, it has gone to pieces morally. Now I am not consulting you professionally, but you can perhaps tell us if there is in Dublin a vet for domestic animals. We go into Ballylee on Thursday and exchange the bare boards of this house for perishable floor covers. Would you mind sending me a wire with the address if you know one, that we may send the cat off in its basket before Thursday.[111]

Gogarty seems to have found care for Thomas in Galway, for the following month Gregory reported that 'the vet couldn't hear from you—& the cat had to be taken on a visit by some lady who has a gt many other cats & is pressured for room'.[112]

By the middle of the month, while their furnishings and the remaining animals were being transferred from Ballinamantan, Willy took George on a visit to Pollexfen and Middleton country. They spent several days at Rosses Point, much loved by the Yeats family since childhood, where George, now in her fourth month of pregnancy, required rest. They then moved on to Sligo and a further round of Yeats relatives, dining with Arthur Jackson who, through marriage with Willy's Aunt Alice, had taken over the Pollexfen firm. Anxious to show off all his childhood haunts, Willy hired a rowing boat and set off around Lough Gill, but no matter which direction they took, he never could identify Innisfree. The incident was to become another set piece in George's repertory.[113]

By 21 September they had moved into the 'picturesque old cottage which opens into the castle', just in time for the autumn equinox. Now they had their own secret space and the Communicators were becoming more demanding in their request for incense and flowers, and sometimes a bowl of water for meditation. Although the printed stationery proudly bore the address 'Ballylee Castle', Willy was providing mixed signals: 'We shall have a wonder house, a house full of history & yet quite without pretence—a farmers house in dreamland.' 'We shall live on the road like a country man, our white walled cottage with its border of flowers like any country cottage and then the gaunt castle.'[114] George had ordered curtains for the cottage from Cuala, 'wonderful brilliant colours, orange & deep blue' of 'strange canvas like stuff like hand-woven things'.[115] Whether their ailing cat Thomas returned in time to enjoy the castle is unclear, although Pangur and a companion appear in the images Willy conjured up to that other cat-lover, Pound: 'We have moved in. Little of house is yet habitable but we have kitchen and servants room, and our bedroom, and a sitting room with a most romantic old cottage fireplace, with a great hood [picture of fireplace, hearth, and hood] and a great flat hearth that makes our two cats purr whenever they think of it.'[116]

Still worried about Iseult and protective towards his pregnant wife, Yeats wrote 'Two Songs of a Fool' during the first week they were in the cottage:

> A speckled cat & a tame hare
> Eat at my hearth stone
> And sleap there
> And both look up to me alone
> Their wardour & their defence
> As I look up to providence.
>
> I start up in my bed & I think
> Someday I may forget
> Their food & drink
> Or the house door left unshut
> The hare may run till its found
> The horns sweet note & the tooth of the hound. . . .
>
> I slept on my three legged stool by the fire
> The speckled cat slept on my knee
> we never thought to enquire
> Where the brown hare might be
> And whether the door were shut. . . .[117]

Did he by now suspect that the 'brown hare' might be with a hound named Ezra?

Other poetry that summer, although still drawing upon the vocabulary of their philosophical system, must have pleased George better. The poems in which he draws upon the legendary Solomon and Queen of Sheba and images and figures from *The Arabian Nights* openly celebrate their collaboration, especially the responsibility of lovers to offer each other corresponding images. Truly epithalamic poems, they give away far more than they ostensibly conceal, slyly acknowledging her contribution as both sibyl and philosophical partner. The way George's nightly narrative held Willy captive cannot but remind one of Scheherazade, the enthralling story-teller of *The Arabian Nights*—the Oriental style was popular not only in the theatre but in architecture and decoration; traces of Bewley's 'Egyptian' decor can still be seen in that well-known coffee bar and restaurant in Grafton Street. The wisdom of Solomon was familiar not only from the Old Testament, but through *The Key of Solomon the King* ('Clavicula Salomonis'), translated and edited by MacGregor Mathers and, with its detailed instructions for ceremonial magic, standard reading for the Order of the Golden Dawn.[118] Yeats had for many years been intrigued by the person of Sheba, and as early as 1909 had confided to his diary, 'It seems to me that true love is a discipline, and it needs so much wisdom that the love of Solomon and Sheba must have lasted, for all the silence of the Scriptures. Each divines the secret self of the other, and refusing to believe in the mere daily self, creates a mirror where the lover or the beloved sees an image to copy in daily life; for love also creates the Mask.'[119]

In May 1914, when he and Georgie were attending séances together, he had written 'On Woman', with its longing reference to the legendary lovers:

> Though pedantry denies
> Its plain the bible means
> That Solomon grew wise
> While Talking with his queens
> Yet never could, although
> They say he counted grass
> Count all the praises due
> When Sheba was his lass . . .[120]

'Solomon to Sheba' (dated 8 April 1918), a dialogue between two people equally matched in both wit and passion and written with all the gaiety and frankness of marital affection, acknowledges his good fortune:

> . . . Sang Solomon to Sheba
> And kissed her Arab eyes
> There ['s] not a man or woman
> Born under the skies
> Dare match in learning with us two
> And all day long we have found
> There s not a thing but love can make
> The world a narrow pound.[121]

Written the same year, 'Solomon and the Witch' even more explicitly states the relationship between the sexual act and creative or philosophical energy. Denser and more complex in its imagery, drawing heavily not only on legend and primal mythology, it also expresses the system's recently developed distinctions between Chance and Choice, time present and the timeless world of infinity, and the cycles between. Significantly, in this poem it is Sheba who initiates the conversation, and it is she, not Solomon, who urges another attempt at bringing Chance and Choice together under the blessed moon. The poem is, in fact, as much or even more about Sheba's power as Solomon's, and its first stanza accurately reflects the circumstances of George's sleeping trance voice (in which she sometimes made animal cries) and the equal contribution made by both to the knowledge that later evolved into the 'System' behind *A Vision* ('a strange tongue | Not his, not mine'). The poem was originally entitled 'Chance and Choice'; the script for 26 January 1919 speaks of 'The [*space*] joyous [*space*] luck [*space*] through choice [*space*] The gregarious luck through chance'.[122]

Sheba's 'dusky' beauty has more than a little of Georgie Yeats's high colouring, and the legend of the African queen was now even more relevant. Depicted in the Koran as a pagan and sun worshipper, in both Arabic and Jewish legends she is a riddle-maker who tests Solomon's wisdom. 'The Queen said, "Seven depart. Nine enter. Two pour. One drinks." To which Solomon replied, "Seven days represents the period of a woman's menstruation; nine months the period of her pregnancy; two pouring is a reference to her breasts; and one drinking, a reference to her baby."' Astrologically too there were points of comparison. In the ancient Abyssinian book *Kebra-Nagasht* this marvellous creature is named Makeda ('woman of fire'), an Ethiopian princess whom Solomon tricks into marriage and whose son was the first of the royal line of Ethiopian kings. Although hardly needed, here was another reminder of George Russell's vision of twenty years previously, predicting the appearance of 'a new Avatar . . . one of the kingly Avatars, who is at once ruler of men and magic sage'. 'The gods have returned to Erin and have centred themselves in the sacred mountains and blow the fires through the country.'[123] AE's dream would duly turn up in Willy's questions to Thomas that September, after they had visited the western home of his forebears in the shadow of Ben Bulben.[124]

At least one more quatrain probably belongs to this period, reflecting more directly the Yeatses' domestic situation:

> Queen of Sheba's busy packing
> King Solomon is mute   .
> For a busy woman
> Is a savage brute.[125]

The lines were more prophetic than either, happily contemplating a long sojourn in the tower, could have imagined. Sheba eventually faded into the background, but George/Scheherazade continued to encourage her husband to make poetry out of personal experience. In fact, to her, the only poetry worth anything was rooted in the personal. Whether she was comfortable with the revelatory poems that followed, especially 'The Gift of Harun Al-Rashid', is another matter.

Meanwhile relations with Coole improved, with regular invitations to tea and dinner; these included young Seán (although he then blotted his copy-book by forgetting to return one of Robert's books[126]). Now that his young wife could serve as amanuensis and typist, Willy need not call upon Lady Gregory's services to the extent he had; although he continued to confide in her, their relationship altered slightly, became in some ways more equal. In addition to the care of Willy, the two women were to discover how much they had in common: both were gardeners, accomplished linguists (as well as Irish, Lady Gregory too was knowledgeable in French, Italian, and German, while George also knew Spanish). No mean painter herself, Gregory was like George a reader, fond of quoting the classics. They were shrewd judges of character, and generous in the service of others; although good listeners, neither suffered fools or deceivers gladly. 'You may be sure she means what she says,' Willy once wrote of his wife; the same could be said of Augusta Gregory. And despite their warmth and sympathy, both were reluctant to display personal emotions. Neither was born to aristocracy or exceptional wealth, yet both had a certain hauteur about them, a confidence born of an awareness of position and economic status. And both were conscientious in their responsibilities as householders, earning respect and devotion from their employees. Until her grandchildren went off to school, Coole was their home and Gregory was accustomed to juggling the care of her 'chicks' alongside many other responsibilities; she would later appreciate George's concern when, torn between loyalties, she had to leave her children in the care of others in order to dash off more than once to her husband's sickbed. Although Lady Gregory never seems to have put in writing her feelings about the Yeatses' occult activities, she herself was sensitive to folk and fairy belief, and had attended at least one séance with Yeats in their efforts to find Hugh Lane's will.

Most important, both women acknowledged their belief in the poet and were prepared to put his needs foremost; in turn, they realized his need of them. It had been many years since Yeats, 'dazed' at the news that his friend had been seriously ill, had written, 'You have been more to me than father or mother or friend, a second self. The only person in the world to whom I could tell every thought.' She in turn had once told him, 'You gave me faith in myself (following on faith in you).'[127] The same process had strengthened George. Recognizing their common loyalties, the two worked out a convenient *modus vivendi*. When the floods overtook Ballylee, Coole could always be counted on as a refuge; and later the Yeats children would always be welcome visitors. When the Black and Tans were perpetrating horror in Galway, Lady Gregory risked much by writing to the English papers; but she also took time to keep an eye on Ballylee and report to

George in Oxford, pregnant with her second child and distressed by the fate of the tower. As age and ill health overtook Lady Gregory, George in turn was a willing and efficient messenger. The countrywoman was of great assistance over Ballylee: Gregory knew the tradespeople, sources of supply, and could advise on local niceties. For all of this, George was grateful, although she remained sturdily independent: when, for example the decorum of entertaining the clergy was tactfully pointed out—the rector came to lunch, the curate to tea, and the bishop to dinner—George continued to invite the curate, being the most intelligent and interesting, to dine.[128]

The two neighbours were also clever enough to be wary of each other, as JBY was to note when he had finally met his daughter-in-law: 'I could see that she was always on the watch with Lady Gregory, too intelligent not to see her great merit, but yet alive to the necessities of self-defence.' To his brother Isaac he commented, 'George is the only woman I have met who is not scared of Lady Gregory. I fancy Lady Gregory is extra-civil with her—naturally.'[129] Early in their collaboration, Gregory had 'turned [Yeats's] dream' into *Cathleen ni Houlihan* and other plays; she had provided the substance for some of his articles on folklore. George could offer even more, for now through her automatic writing and subsequent research she was providing the dream itself. In so doing the centre of creativity moved from Coole to Ballylee, and beyond. It is significant, however, that both women waived first rights to authorship (although occasionally Gregory let it be known she begrudged the dwindling acknowledgement of her share in *Cathleen ni Houlihan*).[130] And Coole was always a presence: from Ballylee one could hear the workmen's bell at 8.00 a.m., noon, 1 p.m., and 6 p.m.; on very clear evenings one might also hear the angelus ringing at sunset from Gort.[131]

In late September George and Willy were in Dublin when the Abbey Theatre opened the season with its first play about the 1916 Rising (Maurice Dalton's *Sable and Gold*)—especially interesting for George, since that summer Willy had been revising *The Dreaming of the Bones*, *his* play based on the Rising. Anxious to return to workmen and 'the beasts' at Ballylee, George stayed only a few days, thereby avoiding the scheduled debate between Chesterton and the labour leader Thomas Johnson on 'Private Property' (Bernard Shaw, en route to Coole, was an interested member of the audience present), and an evening at Dundrum, where the sisters-in-law entertained thirty-four people to meet Frances and Gilbert Chesterton.

Once again George and Willy changed course. Delighted with the house they had finally discovered in Oxford, George had already confirmed the rental of 4 Broad Street (conveniently on a six-month renewable lease). To fortify Ballylee against thieves while they were in England, they had urgently extracted from Scott a design for the castle door.[132] Now they would not be returning to

Oxford that winter after all; their first child was to be born in Ireland. George was fortunate enough to delay the Oxford rental for another year. The decision to stay in Ireland was as always sudden, for it had only been a few weeks earlier that Willy had promised Iseult the use of Woburn Buildings 'until March next without rent to pay as we are moving to Oxford'.[133] Dining with George at the Hibernian Hotel, Lily was delighted at the news: 'Jack is the only Yeats born out of Ireland for 200 years so it would have been a pity if this record had been broken'. George, she reported, 'is very happy over the future, she has to go quietly and be careful and is going nowhere—people tire her . . . She says she "will be perfectly mad if he hasnt dark hair" she said this right in the midst of talk with me about the new play at the Abbey—she looks very pretty and it would take a very observant person to guess her secret.'[134] Preparations included a commission to Sturge Moore for a design for a quilt of 'a rich colour and unshiny surface', a subtle announcement of their news to England; word to Dulac would soon follow.[135]

House-hunting had yielded strange fruits, for they settled on Maud's house across from St Stephen's Green, apparently arranging a rental through the obliging Barry Delaney. Although 'freshly but inadequately furnished', George and Lily decided that it could be made comfortable. Entrusted by George to interview servants, Lily had already engaged a cook, formerly with the Purser family and still referred to by the aged but indomitable painter Sarah as 'my Eliza'; Willy, staying on for theatre business, would finalize the arrangements. On 2 October he informed Maud,

George & I have taken your Dublin house at £2.10.0 a week . . . for four months. Should you be released and allowed to live in Ireland we will move out which strangers would not. George was not well enough to go to England and to manage a move to Oxford. She is now at Ballylee Castle, which has all charm I hoped for.

I hear from Iseult at times and I know she is writing beautiful things . . . My own sorrow at not getting to Oxford is that I can do little for her from so far off. I think she is learning a great deal and growing more confident. It is often the best thing that can happen to a timid sensitive nature to be forced to rely upon itself for a while.[136]

Little did he know what troubles that promise to Maud would cause. Meanwhile, assisted by his sister, he bought 'for £7.11.0 one chest of drawers (not bad) two small tables (one mahogany & quite decent) two washstands'. Lily loaned them a kitchen armchair, and 'I can get a padded basket chair for 24/-'. His sister would also arrange for the delivery of wood and turf. 'With luck', he reported with husbandly satisfaction, 'house should be clean & habitable on Oct 9.'[137]

Number 73, now demolished, was at the other end of the street from the Hotel Russell on the south side of St Stephen's Green; next door was a private school and a little further on two hostels for women students. The historian Alice

Stopford Green lived at number 90, while in between from 78 to 81 stood the palatial town house of the brewer Edward Guinness, now Lord Iveagh, whose wife Lady Ardilaun had turned adjoining houses into handsome winter quarters 'with sumptuous marble halls and enough bedrooms to accommodate large house parties'. Later that winter Yeats was invited to recite his poems to Ardilaun's guests; 'he spoke of the moon but did not stay for tea'.[138]

George seems by now to have overcome her reluctance to write to her poet-husband, but unfortunately none of her early letters have been preserved. That she wrote regularly and in glowing detail of the life they were forging can be deduced from Willy's replies—'your description of our household has relieved my mind, & I am grateful to the crows & the sea gulls'; even at this early stage she was kept busy packing up forgotten belongings such as a shaving brush and necessary bits of clothing. But she would never match the almost daily detailed reports he sent to her throughout their married life. On 8 October George herself reluctantly left Ballylee, her final act to leave generous gratuities for Mike John Dooley, Lady Gregory's gamekeeper and general factotum, and his daughter Norah.[139] She brought with her all the beasts, including three baby hares 'as tame as pet cats—sleek shining coats and twitching ears'; Maud never forgave the devastation of her garden, and without the cats Rafferty was plagued by mice at Ballylee.[140] Wise Thomas too when called upon was at first reluctant to pursue their studies in this 'strange & alien place'. He called upon his namesake—who had rejoined the other animals—for additional force, but he still had trouble sorting out the mathematical arrangement of cycles. Things were not well with George; Thomas advised her not to go out in the morning 'unless to sit in the garden'. And now that Willy was back in town, he was talking too much to his cronies: 'it draws whirlpool round you—you have little resistance,' the script warned. 'Do not talk psychics too much—you draw in strangers I do not like.' Lamenting that 'there is no force no good', he offered by now familiar advice: 'you must begin regular days—work without interruption in morning—always walk at least $1/2$ hour afternoon . . . I feel no precision in your mind—it is no good forcing script . . . You must not upset things again talking about your psychic experiences personal.' By the end of the month Willy was instructed, in mirror writing, to 'make a protective symbol round medium now—a sheltering symbol'.[141] A few days later Thomas accepted 'a few questions', again warning in mirror writing 'but build the tower & gild the sun the moon is cold and worried and nervous and needs plenty of sun and quiet—nervous'.

Thomas was briefly replaced by Erontius, who was not nearly as aware of the cat, but had trouble getting 'a grip when you have thought of nothing else all day . . . like a stale flower'. The force was definitely winding down; Thomas fretted about irrelevancies and Willy needed to 'do some regular work'. More-over, George required extra attention at this stage of her pregnancy: 'the more you keep this medium emotionally and intellectually happy the more will script be possible now—at first it was better when she was emotionally unhappy but now the passivity is as small the opposite'. By 11 November—Armistice Day, when Willy talked freely of the twenty-eight phases at AE's Hermetic Society[142]— Thomas admitted that his communication 'is more & more influenced by her will therefore become less automatic . . . the form is less the automatic though the bones are still automatic—when the passivity grows less the bones may not be able to get through'.[143] 'Church incense and charcoal' were required; Frustrators were abroad. Then on 17 November the script ceased entirely.

The war had ended none too soon. On 10 October, the very evening Yeats was chairing the inaugural meeting of the Dublin Drama League, the mailboat *Leinster* was torpedoed a few miles out of Kingstown, with between 400 and 500 lost. Writing to urge Maud's release now that conscription was no longer a threat, Willy realized that they might have to give up the house before the baby was born.[144] George's progressed horoscope, cast as usual on her birthday, depicted Mars as the ruling planet for the year, with an interesting great collection of planets just rising with Uranus on the ascendant in the twelfth house, involved with hidden things. Weekly reports from Rafferty were also mixed: floods had reached the hall and castle floor and were only one and a half inches below the cottage, and the yard was three feet below water. But with the thatching complete all was watertight inside, the shutters were finally on, the castle windows made, corner cupboards and outer doors were being hung, and he was staying overnight to plaster the back cottage. By the middle of November the chimneys were built and the fireplaces almost finished, the eaves installed, and he was beginning to turn his attention to the castle itself. Conscientious to the last detail, before leaving off work for Christmas he bought two mousetraps.[145] Rafferty regularly ended his report with enquiries after George's health; he was worried about the heavy rains she had experienced before leaving Ballylee.

It was not a good time to be in the city, for in October the so-called Spanish Influenza Epidemic, the worst in human history, had reached Dublin, with 250 deaths recorded by 2 November. The last pandemic had occurred in 1889–90, but this virus altered structure so swiftly that scientists could not keep up with the rapid worldwide transmission of the new strain; nor could they identify its cause, although later it was thought there may have been a connection with dormant swine flu. All they knew was that the virus was transmitted from person to person through airborne respiratory secretions, and once gaining hold selectively attacked and destroyed the cells lining the upper respiratory tract, bronchial tubes, and trachea. Occurring in three waves, the first onslaught of this strange new flu was comparatively mild and seems to have originated on an army base in Kansas, early in March 1918. When American troops arrived in western Europe in April the virus travelled with them; by July it had spread to Poland, but within a month a more severe strain had emerged; if pneumonia developed, death usually followed within a few days. With winter, usually the most receptive time for such illnesses, the third lethal wave occurred, and the virus had not run its course until the spring of 1919. Striking nearly every inhabited part of the world, it was responsible for the deaths of an estimated 30 million people (a greater toll than in four years of war), with close to half the deaths among those aged from 15 to 40, usually considered the strongest and healthiest. Although the virus itself might be completely wiped out by the body's immune system within a few days, the effects continued with sudden chills, fatigue, muscular pains and headaches, and a rapidly rising temperature. The greatest danger occurred from the immune system's own response, flooding the lungs with white blood cells and fluids; then there was the danger of cyanosis from a lack of oxygen and death from asphyxiation as the lungs filled with fluid. Survivors suffered from lingering feelings of weakness and debility, and possible susceptibility to bronchial infections.[146]

Willy's attack of influenza the previous year, followed by a slight case in the autumn (he spent their first wedding anniversary in bed with a temperature), seems to have given him immunity.[147] But on 18 November, the anniversary of her father's death, George herself succumbed. At first her husband thought this was the result of Quinn's notification of his father's pneumonia (which had arrived, as had news of her father's death, by wire), and the hasty arrangements made for Lily to go to New York if necessary. Not yet aware of the seriousness of George's condition, he wrote to his sister, 'She said tonight "I want Lilly" but made me promise not to send for you as she says she may be quite well in the morning. If she is not I will send you a wire. She has had too much to do lately.'[148] George's obstetrician Bethel Solomons called in a specialist,[149] and pneumonia was diagnosed, which then developed into the dreaded influenza. As both a day and a night nurse were necessary, Willy moved to the Stephen's Green Club to make room. It was not long before he feared that George was dying; desperate, he went looking for Lily, calling her out of a committee meeting. On the 26 November he wrote to Lady Gregory, 'Poor George is very ill. She has pneumonia—not thank God septic pneumonia—but the ordinary kind but that is serious enough to a woman in her condition. . . . I am very anxious. . . . She is very weak but sweet & patient through it all, trying to think of everybodys comfort.' But it was another three days before he could hope she might at last be out of danger: 'the inflammation of the lung is being "absorbed" & she can sleep without a drug. She sleeps constantly now or half sleeps & is of course very week [sic]. The doctor thinks she will be able to leave her bed in a week & that in a couple of weeks more my sister can take her away into the country. She longs for my sister Lilly & they are to go alone.'[150] His old friend's letter of consolation would have done nothing to ease his concerns, for she reported that influenza was so bad in the country that Gort was crowded 'with hearses and funerals'.[151]

It was not until later that George knew what took place in the hallway of their rented house as she lay gasping for breath upstairs. Maud, too, had been ill, and after much agitation from her family, Willy, and other friends including John Quinn in New York, and medical reports that she was suffering from a recurrence of pulmonary tuberculosis, the Home Office relented sufficiently to allow her to be moved to a nursing home 'for a week'. By the end of that week she was back, not in Holloway, but in Woburn Buildings. She wrote to Willy immediately, joyful at being with her family but insisting that 'My home in Dublin is best place for all of us, with Josephine to cook for us. Please try & arrange that.'[152] On 15 November, in response to a number of cables from a worried Quinn, Pound sent the latest bulletin to New York, adding, 'I hope no one will be ass enough to let her get to Ireland. . . . It is a great pity, with all her charm, that the mind twists everything that goes into it, on this particular subject [politics]. (Just like Yeats on his ghosts.)'[153] But Maud continued to agitate for permission to return to Ireland. Iseult described her to Willy as 'not really bitter, but very tired and needs a lot of looking after . . . if they drag her away now, it would really be a bad shock to her nerves.'[154] A week later Arthur Symons visited Woburn Buildings, where Iseult confided that all four of them were leaving for Ireland on Saturday, 23 November, 'with no passports—but taking every risk of being discovered. I rarely saw such fear in a girl's eyes as in hers; she hated to have to go and yet had to.'[155] The next morning, disguised as an emaciated Red Cross nurse (perhaps in the very uniform Georgie had cast off on her marriage), Maud slipped through the immigration line and arrived at the door of 73 St Stephen's Green, demanding shelter.

Maud had observed to the Yeats sisters that George, while 'most unselfish, never appears to assert herself at all, but from her face Maud thinks she could assert herself'. But George was helpless; now it was Willy's turn to assert. Fearing disruption from the police raids that inevitably followed in Maud's wake, he refused the party entry; fortunately during the row the doctor appeared 'and declared that Maud's continued presence might endanger George's life'. Still she refused to leave. Aware at last of his priorities, Willy 'had a scene with her and turned her out'.[156] From the country, where she was staying near Glenmalure with Ella Young, Maud sent her former lover 'venomous letters', denouncing him for ejecting her from her own house and accusing him of unpatriotic cowardice. Later she would complain that, although married to a rich wife, he took advantage of her in prison by offering such a low rent, and she never forgot that George's pet hares ate all the greenery in her garden. He retaliated by saying she had a 'pure and disinterested love of mischief', privately describing her as suffering from 'neurasthenia'. Cumann na mBan (Irishwomen's Council) joined in the chorus, charging Yeats with conspiring with the Chief Secretary to shut up Maud in an English sanatorium that he 'might keep possession of her house'; to which Willy countered, 'It would be much simpler to call it possession by the devil & then one could believe that it might be over after a Mass or two'. Iseult described them both as 'equally to blame and both in need of keepers'.[157] By 29 November Lily wrote a relieved but loyal letter to Quinn. Her father was recovering in New York, and the situation at home was 'much better':

George had some natural sleep & was better, & the doctors thought the worst was over. Willy and I went out with a doctor's permit for cream for her—and fish, Willy was less anxious, & had disposed of the patriots for the present. Maud is reported to have gone to the country. I can't imagine her in the country, no limelight, no audience, no one but her very difficult family—but it shows that for the present she has abandoned the 'arrested on her death bed' tableau, or perhaps only postponed it.[158]

Finally on 10 December the doctors declared George well enough to be moved by cab to furnished rooms just down the street in number 96; Maud returned from the country and turned her attention to the intolerable conditions her former cellmates (Kathleen Clarke and Constance Markievicz) were still suffering in Holloway; and Willy went off to speak about the phases of the Moon to a gathering in Mrs Gogarty's drawing room.[159] News of the quarrel went far beyond the borders of Ireland. Wounded by what he felt was Maud's apparent ingratitude for his own efforts on her behalf, John Quinn wrote to Yeats in sympathy, 'I know that it must have been a strain upon you to have any differences with her. But at the same time you had to protect your wife and your wife's health.'[160] Eventually peace was restored and Willy was once more seen at Maud's Tuesday 'At Homes' in number 73, but things were never quite the same again between them. George and Willy continued however to keep a concerned eye on the younger generation. 'The patriot has graciously forgiven Willy,' Lily reported in early January, '& the boy has consented to go to school, on condition that he can leave at the end of a month if he doesn't like it. Isolde says he feels as if a statesman was asked to go to school . . . Willy was rather tired out, but quite cheerful.'[161] Maud was also buoyed up by the results of the 14 December election, when Sinn Féin won seventy-three seats against the Irish Parliamentary Party's six, a strong response to Lloyd George's announcement the previous month that Home Rule would be withheld 'until the condition of Ireland makes it possible'.[162]

The day after their move out of Maud's house, work on the script began again. But Thomas was clearly aware of what had been going on, and shut down for another few days. 'Your business to get normal shut out & isolate yourselves | Shut out rows—shut out the irrelevant . . . medium must go very slowly or bad bad,' he warned, adding with emphasis '*Tower to protect*'. But he liked the new place they were in.[163] George was too weak to go to Lily in Dundrum; instead on 16 December she and Willy went to Enniskerry, where Thomas recommended a banishing ritual and solar invocations to prevent nightmares. Willy apparently suggested turning to other mediums (probably Hester Travers Smith) to save George's strength, but this was brusquely shot down: 'no mediums no if voluntary not through you Script must be mentioned to no one & no one must be told you are sworn to secrecy.' George must rest each half-hour before an equal time on the script, but even so (in mirror writing) she was 'not strong enough to write every day'. Thomas himself was distressed by noise.[164] They returned to Dublin for Christmas, but did not join in any of the traditional family festivities; George was still in a highly nervous condition and Willy was not much better. The next day Thomas had once more to remind him, torn between his anxiety to pursue the psychology of the phases and concern for his wife's health, 'it all depends on the writer writers *nerves* . . . because we cant use you alone—must have you & medium *equally*'. He recommended a permanently lighted flame in oil as a good night light, a candle lit from it would call him 'at unusual hours'; 'it creates a physical link one world to next—candle your world oil flame mine.'[165]

But still things got muddled, and Apple joined forces with Thomas. The candle, however, seems to have worked, for on 7 January 1919, in a script headed by George 'Personal Only', an example is given them of a 'dream each'. The session that day opened with a drawing of Mount Cashel (the setting for 'The Double Vision of Michael Robartes'), and their Instructor's charge to go 'back in thought', far earlier than their own castle in the west: 'You are empty—drained dry—the true moment for vision . . . you are drained dry from looking into the future & exhausted by the present . . . *so go to the past*—a historical & spiritual past—the church the Castle on the hill.'

The vision which George and Willy invoked led to a 'corresponding dream' similar to those encouraged by their Order training. Thomas promised more, however:

I gave you dream each—now I give you two more in one—at Castle

> Hand & eye
> waterfall & stag
> Hand—eye
> waterfall
> touch—desire to grasp
> eye—desire to see
> possessive hand—desiring eye

Again, an explanation was forthcoming for such phenomena: 'in nervous states you are more closely linked psychically—the nightmare of one runs along this link—creates a shock to the other & then reacts on the dreamer that form gave the dream I gave medium dream automatic.' Almost two years later, through dream speech, the interaction between them would be described as 'the way in which we share dreams & visions . . . this sharing came through telepathy & everything.'

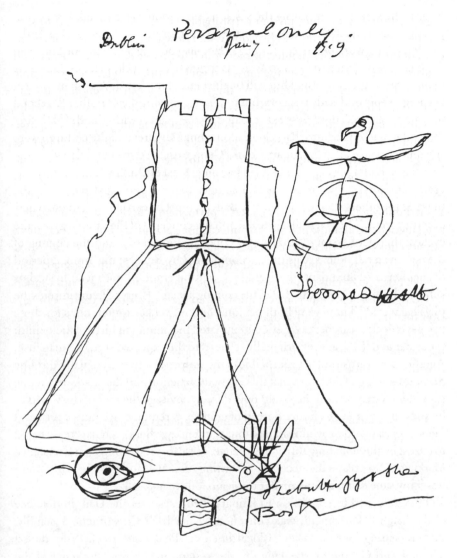

Fig. 2. George's Automatic Script for 7 January 1919 with a drawing of Mount Cashel, providing scenarios for two of Willy's poems.

The scenarios provided on 7 January led to Willy's poem 'Towards Break of Day' (originally entitled 'The Double Dream'). 'Another Song of a Fool' was written in conjunction with it. Literally as well as symbolically, 'George's ghosts' were providing metaphors for poetry.[166]

It seems obvious from the questions recorded that Willy was reading the answers as they were being written. Thomas was also encouraging them to discuss the script either during the session ('now 10 minutes & talk') or as preparation for the next. Sometimes he ordered them to stop and read back over the previous day's work before continuing. Place also became more important; even Thomas was ordering them to go away. 'George is nearly well, so far as the effects of pneumonia are concerned but will be the better for a few days with no housekeeping', Willy told Lady Gregory, but now *he* was having 'heart bother & general nervous weakness', doubtless exacerbated by the quarrel with Maud.[167] His first thought was to invite himself to Coole alone, but Margaret and the children were still there, so instead on 9 January he and George escaped the hateful town to the Lucan Spa Hotel, a 'very solar place' a few miles west of Dublin. There Willy was again reminded, 'The woman is still solitary better—You must remain in the tower & the others all outside.' Clearly Ballylee must be carried with them, wherever they went. They were also working on the concepts of the double gyres, the cyclical theory of history ('each single cone is 2000 years'), and the coming of the new avatar. Thomas, this time accompanied by Rose, spoke from 'a period of shepherds & abundant physical life & natural emotion not metaphysical or subtle. The opposite state to that of the coming avatar.' 'Unity of being implies the physical world.' There were both personal and universal connotations for these two psychical researchers as they contemplated the imminent birth of their child; the avatar and 'J.B.', as they originally referred to the expected son, began to fuse. Another poem arose out of the crucible of the script as Willy started work on 'The Second Coming'. Confident that this era of destruction and distrust was but one turn of the Great Wheel, he could now dare to envisage the end of the world as he knew it, a vision of a future devoid of culture, ceremony, sweetness, pity, and innocence, a world drowning in passionate intensity where even nature is stirred to unrest by the slouching threat of violence. He also wrote a poem on Constance Markievicz 'to escape the necessity of writing one on Maud Gonne'. But Maud was 'now sane & amiable again & I think anxious to make up'.[168]

They returned to Dublin on 10 January; two days later the Dáil, in defiance of the English Parliament, was convened by the Irish Constituent Assembly, thereby setting loose a series of local horrors. That same week Willy defied Thomas and George by speaking on 'the system' to a private audience at the United Arts Club,[169] where he claims to have converted James Stephens, and then on 26 January participated in a long-postponed discussion on 'Psychical Phenomena in Belfast and Elsewhere' at the Abbey Theatre. This was too much for Thomas who crossly informed them, 'Occult worse than psychical research', and 'be careful not let those physical psychics get into my area'. The 'physical psychic' was Dr Wm. J. Crawford from Belfast, who described experiments where a young girl had caused a table to levitate; Yeats on his part quoted from Frederic Myers, and showed slides borrowed from Mead of materializations. 'The time had come, above all, in this country to cease treating this whole subject with derision,' he was reported to have stated. 'An age of belief was passing, and an age of unbelief was coming.'[170] 2 February saw him on the stage again, this time in a debate with Prof. John Howley of University College, Galway, on 'Psychical Research from the Catholic Point of View'. Lady Gregory, who came up from Coole for the occasion, took some credit for his success: 'Yeats spoke very finely, saying that only the belief in the immortality of the soul could lead to that perfecting of the soul of the whole being, that perfect faith that brings us nearer to God. And he used my suggestion that the Research should be left to men of Science and of balanced mind just as medical research is, and not rushed into by unhappy people, unbalanced by grief, as one would not leave to the suffering patient to experiment in drugs.'[171] Given the direct influence of the script and the sources Willy quoted in his two discussions, it is difficult to imagine that George could disagree with the substance, no matter how much she may have agreed with Thomas that all these activities made him 'so scattered'.

When George was not sharing dreams with Willy or having nightmares, she was once more walking in her sleep. One night, 'awakened by the cold, she found herself sitting on a chair with all the baby clothes on her knees'.[172] The script for 30 January ended with an outburst:

I don't like you
You neglect me
You don't give me physical symbols to use[173]

Although the words came through Thomas who recommended a lighted candle, incense, and the banishing ritual, George was clearly getting tired of Willy's enthusiasm for lecturing and a consequent lessening of their physical relationship.

They were also, however, worried about finances, for, as Willy confessed to Ezra in a letter dictated to George, 'our feudal ambitions have left us both impecunious'. They were anxious to rent Woburn Buildings until the lease was up in June, and H.D. (Hilda Aldington), now separated from her husband, and 'a friend', were potential tenants. Again they turned to Pound for advice:

Have you any idea what rent we should ask them. We pay 20/- a week & if they want to use my study as a bedroom we would have to take the basement at 5/- a week for storage. Now the neighbourhood is bad, 'offices' poor, but the rooms are large & the literary associations distinguished; & however shabby the rooms may look by daylight, they put on glory by the light of candles . . . The matter is urgent, & we do not want to be lost through our ignorance. . . . So please inform us immediately, or if there must be delay let it only be so long that you may consult the wisest woman of your acquaintance. . . . George recollects that you may have a charwoman & that she might be set to clean down W. B. (If she has any spare time) before the new tenants moved in.[174]

Hilda changed her mind, but by mid-February the rooms had been rented at thirty shillings a week to Douglas Goldring, recently married to the daughter of Ellen Duncan, founder of the United Arts Club and first curator of the Municipal Gallery of Modern Art. Obviously the Gonnes had left in some disarray, for Willy returned the first week's rent money to Betty and Douglas Goldring, 'as there is so much missing', and asked Mrs Old to find them a 'kettle, coffee machine, and pan' which he would pay for. The newly-weds, inexperienced at housekeeping and 'desperately poor', were not comfortable:

It was a strange, ghost-haunted flat, heavy with Celtic twilight and magical influences. The hall, from the bottom of the stairs to the front door, was so thickly charged with unseen presences that Betty, who was to some extent psychic, used to send me on ahead to open the door for her, so that she could run straight out. I remember one morning when I descended to the study to write a letter and found the desk covered all over with chalk marks shaped like a hen's claws. I rubbed then out hastily and was careful to say nothing about them.

Two of their visitors, Franklin Dyall and Mary Merrall, who had hired the Abbey Theatre during the summer of 1918 as independent producers, were however so charmed that they took over the lease when George and Willy gave it up.[175]

Although she had apparently remained out of sight while Willy was lecturing on the system, George was not entirely a recluse. On 10 January Willy finally felt well enough to attend rehearsals of his play *On Baile's Strand*, which was being revived for the spring season under the direction of Fred O'Donovan, one of the Abbey's most accomplished actors and now the theatre manager. George, always a keen theatregoer, seems to have taken an active interest, with not always happy results according to an entry in Augusta Gregory's *Journal* for 31 January 1919:

Harris [theatre accountant] had written urging me to come up, there was something wrong, O'Donovan had talked of 'interference' and Millington [business manager] had written in the same way that there was a 'strain'. I . . . saw Donovan. His grievance is that Mrs Yeats looks on and criticises and, 'not understanding the difficulties or business', makes suggestions and criticism to Yeats who carries them on. However, I told him we mustn't grumble at anything. It is such a great matter getting a verse play on again.[176]

Fred O'Donovan had been dissatisfied for some time with his position at the Abbey, and by March had resigned to form his own company; the indefatigable diarist and theatregoer Joseph Holloway recorded that as early as November there had been complaints to Yeats concerning his English wife's interference.[177]

Apart from her habitual theatregoing, there were other reasons for George's interest. Willy and Lennox Robinson had recently established the Dublin Drama League to present plays outside the theatre mandate; she would later become actively involved in the project. More immediately, the script was encouraging Willy to proceed with a play—contemplated the year before—which would become *Calvary*. In fact, through George Thomas was serving as a metaphysical dramaturge, offering suggestions that Willy incorporated. On 26 January, while Willy was immersed in preparations for his public lectures, George 'felt' Thomas's presence and the session began with the words 'I like the idea of your play—*put it much later* | Why not | Starting at the end of his life'. Two weeks later, during what was clearly intended to be his farewell appearance during this 'abnormal' time, Thomas returned to the subject:

Now I want to give you instructions for the next two months—I cant write much so I want a medium of getting in touch with you—I do not want you to write on system [*space*] I would like you to write something *through which* I can give you ideas . . .
Christ Judas lazarus—2 maries Pilate—John Paul & Peter . . .
I want natural heroic life & you will hover round the abstract the intellectual the concrete—that is why I say write the Christ—you cant be abstract there
I would much prefer play
I am afraid of a mechanical turn to natural life in the Cuchulain unless you are living it[178]

After this message Lazarus first made his appearance in the play; Willy however exercised his creative judgement by not including Peter. Then, apart from a hasty summary from Rose on 16 February in response to an earlier question, George's pencil again fell silent.

But work on the system continued, and that month she purchased William Inge's two-volume *The Philosophy of Plotinus* (signing the first volume 'George Yeats February 1919', the second 'Georgie'); the first volume in particular was read with care and annotated with reference to their own terminology. It may have been now that yet another 'Yeats story' was circulated in Dublin, told to the Dunsanys by Padraic and Mary Colum:

Yeats: My wife can read Plotinus in the original Latin
Gogarty: Arabic Yeats
Yeats: Er, Arabic[179]

Plotinus may have been a welcome antidote while she rested at Dundrum, for on 11 February Lily wrote to her father, 'George is here and going to stay for a few days, she is well and has her breakfast in bed and is looked after by Rose and Maria all day, they take great care of her—and because of her presence, we are being waited on by Maria as only the great are waited on in plays in expensive theatres.'[180] The unaccustomed luxury may have been the reason for her temporary return to 'Georgie'. Willy meanwhile was looking after the animals at number 96:

I enclose a note from Rafferty. You had better wire about roof of shed. We can talk over arch though I shall be content if you decide that too.

I am just recovering from violent cold. I spent Tuesday either half asleep in bedroom or in sitting room quarrelling with Pangur who was in a damnable mood. He howled at the door, & he filled the room with a smell of singed hair by putting his tail in the candle & then nearly pulled the electric lamp down by getting his tale [*sic*] lassoed in by the cord of his toy—further more he eat a whole herring without gratitude.[181]

We do not have George's reply, but on the reverse she cast a horoscope for the period 23 February to 10 March 1919.

The weather was unpleasant and there were many strikes on in Dublin, including one by the road cleaners. The Yeatses left Stephen's Green on Saturday, 22 February, Willy back to his club while George moved to the Hibernian Hotel to await developments in greater comfort. The unrepentant Pangur seems to have been packed off to Ranelagh, an arrangement doubtless made by resourceful Lily.[182] On the 25th a further report was sent to New York:

Willy will I think have news to cable to you this week. George was not at all well all yesterday and has gone into the Nursing Home today. I saw her last night, very uncomfortable rather ill and a little frightened. She was not to go into the home till March 1st but Willy and I were firm and said 'no' but at once—she said we were bullies and wanted to get rid of her—we agreed and said we did so that we could sleep easy. We will be glad when the news comes and all is well and your grand-child snug in his cradle. She is too anxious to save Willy anxiety and forgets herself. When I left last night she said 'remember you are to come in the moment you get Willys message'. The home is in Upper Fitzwilliam St.[183]

The next morning George gave birth to a daughter.

9

ANNE

Anne Butler Yeats was born at 10 a.m. (or two minutes earlier) in A. Smyth's private nursing home, 40 Upper Fitzwilliam Street, Dublin, on Wednesday, 26 February 1919. In attendance was Beatrice Marsh, chief maternity nurse to Bethel Solomons, one of Dublin's leading obstetricians (later to become master of the Rotunda Hospital) who lived conveniently nearby at 42 Fitzwilliam Square. Advanced in his views and also, incidentally, interested in psychic matters, young Dr Solomons was responsible for the change from two-hour to four-hour feeding for the new-born; however, mothers were still expected to remain in the nursing home for a month, the baby in a crib next to the bed.[1] Later Lily would recall 'the barricades of silence you put up between you and your husband on one side of you and Nurse Marsh on the other side of you'.[2] But after remaining stoical through all her labour pains, George burst into tears at the news she had given birth to a daughter.

George immediately cast her child's horoscope, announcing that she 'will be good looking & lucky, but not have any great talent'.[3] Later more accurate forecasts were provided by Cyril Fagan, the president of the Irish Astrological Society, and Miss Mary Lane, a friend of Lily in Cork. A Gemini with her sun in Pisces, Anne would have an 'essentially harmonious inner nature, trustful, straight, honest & conscientious'. The Moon in the ninth house 'favours philosophy, also mysticism, will be sure to probe into hidden mysteries, but will investigate with her head, prophetic, inspirational and intuitive; "variety" "joy" the two keynotes of the character, important to help her to learn to concentrate.' Her ruling planet Mercury suggests 'an active, flexible, witty brain, will be a success in society, strong artistic sense, certain feeling for order and method and fitness of things, mediumistic'. She would take pleasure in travel and could succeed as a teacher. Willy was proud of his daughter's horoscope: 'the stars only affect passionate people. My daughter's horoscope shows a very passionate life.'[4] But what would interest her parents most was that Anne was born 'at a moment when Mars and Venus were just past conjunction'. Fifteen years later in his short poem 'Conjunctions' Yeats would identify this moment with the passing of the objective historical cycle of Christianity or democracy, associated with the conjunction of war and love, making way for its antithesis, the subjective.

The sword's a cross; thereon He died:
On breast of Mars the goddess sighed.[5]

Ameritus, George's daimon, in turn added his commentary—a spirit provided Anne at the moment of birth with the subjective sequences 'Sweetness & beauty of mind', while the objective sequence suffered at birth was the 'thought and the gayety [sic] of the Fool and of God'.[6] He seems to have been watching Willy at work, for this reflects the 'Anne poem' already begun by late March.[7] 'A Prayer for my Daughter' is also a hymn of thanksgiving to the woman whose 'glad kindness', magnanimity, and wisdom had made his present contentment possible. The Instructors insisted that the personality does not find its phase on the Great Wheel until the age of 7; as George and Willy studied the development of the soul each night in the script, so they were to observe the making of a soul in their daughter.[8]

Family lore has it that the doctor thought she said 'Damn' on hearing her child was a girl; as late as 1937 her father endorsed the legend when he presented the young Abbey stage designer with a copy of the theatre's 25th anniversary programme, signing it 'Anne, or Damn from W. B. Yeats'. But George always insisted the word was 'Anne'; if a boy he would have been named James Butler ('J.B.' in the script) after Anne Hyde's husband, the second Duke of Ormonde. 'Anne', Willy insisted, was a name which ' "cannot be clipped", and has the advantage of not being too poetical'. Perhaps unknowingly he was correct in claiming that 'It is a family name on both sides',[9] for there were at least two Ann Hyde ancestors in George's family dating back to the eighteenth and nineteenth centuries, and Willy's great-grandfather the Revd John Yeats of Drumcliffe had a sister named Anne. It would not be until 1925 that the Yeatses' legendary connection with the Butlers of Ormonde was finally disproved, and by 1928 George had refused to have it mentioned in 'the family book' kept by Lily in case it would embarrass their children (although Willy persevered in his search for at least another few years).[10] But for now, with the birth of their daughter, Anne Hyde's situation in the discarnate world and her influence in this one were paramount.

It was Anne Hyde's insistence, reflecting George's natural desire for the persistence of the family name, that had led them to expect a boy; the previous year she had several times used the word 'wain', explaining 'wain *old word* wain means heir or son'.[11] On 24 September 1918, encouraged by Willy's leading questions, the script had gone even further by suggesting that their child 'would be in some way connected with an "avatar" '. With the images 'The child the avatar the mountain the work', the word was again linked to the vision experienced by AE twenty years previously, 'of a child seen rising up above Ben Bulben'. But with the arrival of a daughter rather than a son, the Instructors had some explaining to do.

On 20 March 1919, in the first script after their child's birth, Thomas was somewhat defensive:

. . . one spirit cannot call another—only through special permission | I knew it was not Annes son—it could never be—I did not say so—I said John or a son
Anne . . .
She could choose for her son not for herself—she *was not deceived* [*space*] She had the choice & chose well . . .
She chose so that they might be born together—otherwise she might have been delayed
Yes [*space*] if she had chosen *you* she would have had to want & also her son was not for you by nature although by birth
As I said a son . . .
Anne could never have so fierce a horary
It evokes but *cannot create*
Physically we cannot create nor cause you to create—*we cannot influence sex*—your system is all we think of—only that matters
It would be folly to command—such a son could not be *willed*—to will sterilises choice & chance . . .
. . . I say nothing matters but system because I do not want others than the one I evoke
. . . We gave you Anne—is not that horary remarkable enough?????

He also made it clear that a second child was necessary for the completion of the system: 'not pure symbol *but* only one *choice* more | child is chosen *but* remember we have not complete control & *only* one more—more would destroy system | *too domestic* | luck exactly *but* the March horary held good . . . if one then no more.'[12]

Unexpectedly, a letter from John Quinn agreed with the spirits' advice. 'I hope you are not disappointed that the child is not a boy. If I were married and the first child were a girl, I should not know whether to be disappointed or not. But I should have another child, hoping that the second one would be a boy. Two children have a much better time than one. One child is likely to be lonely and the mother of one child is likely to be over-anxious about it.'[13] As far as Thomas was concerned, however, the second child should not arrive too soon: 'Must begin soon though no nervous strain One the beginning but the other *must* be the *end* . . . we must have at least 16 months *work*.' Evidently there was still much to do on both planes.

The date of this session was also auspicious, for it was exactly two years earlier, on 18 and 20 March 1917, that first Willy and then Georgie had cast horoscopes concerning the possibility of marriage. Not surprisingly, therefore, before closing the session of 20 March 1919 Thomas again referred to horoscopes both recent and past, linking George and Willy's union (the first horary, Moon conjunct Saturn) with Anne's birth (the first nativity, Mars conjunct Venus) and predicting the nature of a second child in the conjunction of Sun and Uranus: 'First came [Moon] & [Saturn]—then [Mars] [Venus] [Sun] [Uranus] *study the third* . . . It is a symbol for you both as well as two nativities & a horary—find it in the horary & compare with sun.'[14] The next day he returned once more to the subject, introducing a concept which would occupy them for some time, and again send them back to their astrological workbooks. This was the 'impregnating' or, as they were later called, 'initiatory' and 'critical moments', occasions on which the symbol dominates and thereby alters the course of an individual's life. At these points in one's life, the spirits invoke symbols 'that a third [occasion] may be invoked'. That third was already predicted in the horary of 18 March 1917, drawn up by Willy after he had been visiting the Tuckers in London; in it, Venus conjunct Mars was favourable and 'promises completion', and on the strength of that reading he had once again suggested marriage to Georgie.[15] As Thomas had intimated the previous day, Anne, whose conception had marked a 'sympathy complete' giving rise to the third stage of their relationship, was born under that very conjunction; hence his reference to a 'remarkable' horary. Nelly's impulsive invitation to Willy that day in March 1917 had indeed produced lasting results. Impressed by these correspondences, Willy remarked to their control, 'In many cases you must control a life for years.' Chance and choice were beginning to take on new meaning. But Thomas also insisted that there were not just one but two events evoked by that memorable evening two years previously: 'The individual represented by that horary', that is, their daughter Anne, and 'The end or systematisation of the philosophy'. Astrologically, however, Jupiter was 'outside both', 'a reference to "J.B."'—another prediction which would turn out to be accurate, for two years later their son was born at the conjunction of Jupiter with Saturn.[16] Despite the fact that their first child was a girl, the system and the promised avatar were still linked, with George the vessel for both. Significantly it is at this stage of their experiment, on the first dated script after Anne's birth while discussing those earlier critical moments, that George was given a different name. No longer 'the medium', she was henceforth to be referred to as 'Interpreter'.[17]

George's month in the nursing home gave her some much-needed rest while she grew to know her baby girl. 'George goes on well & the child too,' Willy reported. 'Lilly says the child is the most healthy looking child of its years she has seen. It certainly sleeps much & cries little.'[18] Staying at the Stephen's Green Club, he spent every afternoon from 4.30 until 7 with his wife and daughter. 'My brother is delighted with her—& already speaks about her as if she was months instead of days old,' Lolly observed. All considered her 'a very pretty baby' who 'promises to be absolutely healthy & strong'.[19] Lyrical in delight, Lily described the new mother (and her own role) for the absent grandfather:

I spent some time yesterday with George and the Baby—they are both well—George now able to lean up on her elbow and look about her—she is very happy and told me how the night before Baby had stirred in her cradle as if she was going to cry and how she George had just put out her hand through the bars of the cradle and Baby had closed her hand on her fingers and went off to sleep again. The Baby is really very pretty with black hair and dark eyes—her head a good shape—her temper very amiable. George loves all the things she sees in her that are like Willy. I am to spend Sunday afternoon there, to let the Nurse out. I am 'considered capable' of looking after the Baby—the Baby is the very best thing that has happened for as long as I can remember. George likes the Nurse and the Nursing Home and she is going to have the Nurse with her for three weeks after she leaves the Home.[20]

Even childless Jack was moved to write to a friend, 'Willy is very pleased to have a daughter,'[21] while words of praise travelled throughout New York city: 'My daughter's letters are full of the granddaughter & her loveliness,' wrote JBY to one of his American friends. 'Never was such a baby. Lilly says she herself must have been mother of many children, she so loves this baby & all babies —& Lollie writes that as it lies in its crib breathing peacefully, it makes her think of a little fish in a pool of sunny water. As soon as it was born Willie did its horoscope (which is very good). He said "it is a nice little child." . . . He is very busy writing verse. His wife is praised by every one.'[22] Just weeks after his daughter's birth, Willy began 'A Prayer for my Daughter'. But a rival poet got his lines in before him, publishing 'The Sidhe Come to Stephen's Green: Ode of Welcome for A Poet's Child' in the *Freeman's Journal* on the Saturday after Anne's birth. The final lines read:

> As they camp in the lilies and wait there unseen,
> Dark fairies, thin fairies, big fairies and all
> For the love of a child who shall hold them in thrall,
> And her father, who first with the word of his pen,
> Made them free of the thresholds and firesides of men

Proud Aunt Lolly sent out cuttings ('It is not every baby that gets poems written at its birth'); there is no record of George's or Willy's reaction.[23]

On 19 March, now truly a family, they were reunited in Dundrum, where Dundrum Lodge, a furnished house in Sydenham Road, had been rented for six weeks, with 'garden, apple trees & singing birds—a green oasis of peace in a turbulent country'.[24] They had originally thought of staying in Howth, but influenza had not yet run its course and many workers in the city were on strike; it seemed wiser to be within reach of help, especially Lily's. On the 21st George cast a horary of the 'vernal Equinox'; the date may be one reason Thomas insisted that the entire house be fumigated, and was quite cross when they procrastinated.[25] He was also disturbed by Willy's behaviour, for too much energy was being devoted to theatre business and especially the winter's lecture series: the next day, 30 March, he was to be joined on the stage by Lennox Robinson in a discussion of 'The Abbey Theatre, Past and Future'.[26] 'For every public speech or lecture you give after tomorrow during the next 6 months I shall stop script one month,' Thomas warned. Willy was also speaking too freely about the philosophy, and had recently given a talk on the subject at the United Arts Club. 'For every occasion you talk system in private conversation one month . . . You must begin writing.'[27] Two weeks later, the script opened in upside down writing with exasperation: 'What did you pray for—not faith of course—nor for your two daimons—oh no | Why should I tell you—you don't help me—why should I bother about you—you arent in the least sorry so don't tell . . .' This was followed a few minutes later by the abrupt rejoinder 'do please think'. George struck out the even sharper retort, 'don't worry that word [daimon] to death'.[28] It is well that George and her Instructors did not know that news of their experiments had reached further than England. The Australian writer Louis Esson informed Padraic Colum, 'A friend of mine, Vance Palmer, who has since returned to Australia, paid a visit to Dublin just before he left. . . . He heard that W. B. Yeats had retired to a castle in the South of Ireland to finish an abstruse metaphysical or mathematical work, showing by figures and diagrams the stages of consciousness various modern writers had preached.'[29]

Clearly, discussion of the system was beginning to become a time-consuming obsession. But it was also therapeutic. George's active role as 'Interpreter' was now acknowledged and the union of their daimons 'phisically complete', leading to 'positive correspondence instead of negative', 'the will to live—self preservation, assertion of self'.[30] Sufficiently at ease with each other and the system that was revealing itself, painful subjects could once again be examined. Thomas's explication of critical moments and the lightning flash pattern which connected them led to a much more dispassionate discussion of Yeats's relationship with Maud, Olivia, and even Mabel Dickinson. However, Thomas felt no compunction about counselling Willy to leave the past alone and concentrate on the future, including 'house planning'. 'Your future at present will be system but if future & past are too separate system suffers . . . interpreter among others'.[31] Interestingly, with the change from 'Medium' to 'Interpreter', George's clairvoyant powers were also openly acknowledged; her self-confidence now pervaded the script's sessions.[32] This allowed George to express her own emotional history, including the relationship with her parents and stepfather; various lists of 'impregnating moments' included the date of her father's death and her mother's remarriage as well as her previous experiences with Willy.[33] Ongoing elaboration of the concept of 'victimage' (purgation for another either living or dead) provided an honest appraisal of 'Mediums rejected state' on the day she began the automatic writing, for 'The victim is the one who suffers that he or another may harden subjectively.' According to the script her decision not to leave Willy when 'told of the letter' to Iseult was a combination of 'pity & reason', the knife of reason hardening away self-pity. Willy was learning to examine himself through George's eyes: 'Did she become knife for pity because she had pitied or a knife in deception because once deceived', to which the answer was simply, 'exactly'.[34] The role of pity would again dominate the script three months later, this time with the spotlight turned on George.

Willy's sisters were daily visitors to Sydenham Road. 'The baby is the most happy small thing, never cries, lying in her cradle and smiles at the world,' Lolly enthused to John Quinn. Secretly Lily was relieved that Anne was 'pale so it seems will not have her mother's colour'.[35] 'I get good news from home,' JBY reported, 'The grand child is so interesting that it makes all my people forget everything else. I better understand the worship of the Virgin Mary & her infant.'[36] On 8 April the two spinsters gave a party for their only niece's parents, inviting fifty guests including AE, James Stephens, Susan Mitchell, Ernest Boyd, and other artists. 'The 50 people represented the most diverse political opinions, —from extreme Protestant Unionist to Sinn Fein—& everyone who was at it seemed to enjoy themselves immensely.'[37] Susan Mitchell, a close friend of the family with whom she had lived in London some twenty years earlier, had been privileged with an earlier glimpse of old JBY's granddaughter: 'she is a nice small woman, with rather a strong face for so young an infant. It will be most interesting to watch her, Lily is perfectly happy over her—I never saw anything like it, I believe it was for Lily's happiness she was born, and I hope she will be a treasure.' Known for her own wit, Susan was quick to recognize George's sense of humour: 'Mrs Willie is very nice, & a very amusing person to talk to. She is a vigorous handsome creature and the baby ought to grow up well.'[38]

As Lolly remarked, Lily became 'a second mother to Anne'.[39] She had already adopted in all but name their young cousin Ruth Pollexfen when her parents' marriage dissolved. Ruth had lived with the Yeats family until her marriage in 1911, had been a member of Lily's embroidery team, and, although eventually living in Australia, was Lily's closest confidante. So devoted in fact was Lily that when Ruth's first daughter Charlotte was born, she experienced a vision in which Ruth was close beside her; the vision coincided precisely with the beginning of Ruth's labour pains. In her weekly letters to Ruth Lily was even more open and confiding than she was to 'Papa' in New York. And with the birth of Anne, never was a child's progress recorded so intimately and broadcast so widely: ' "the little Creature" is waxing big she grows at the rate of 9 oz a week, she is weighed every Wednesday morning, every Wednesday morning at 10 a.m. she has a birthday— she is so content and lies sometimes for over an hour wide awake in her cradle just thinking—Willy looks at her shyly—but is writing a poem on her. George knows every little inch of her and says—one ear is Willys and the other Jack.'

Lily was also delighted with signs of her brother's domestic felicity; George was clearly everything that was needed in the Yeats circle. 'The other morning I came on George and Willy finishing breakfast, Willy got up saying his tea was cold, so George ran at him and shook him saying he was doing the neglected husband, as the night before he had said, he would write his own letters if she wanted to go to Baby—he assured her he wasnt feeling neglected and had no second meaning at all in what he said.'[40] In turn Willy informed Ezra, 'George & her child are well & I think happy.'[41] He was fitting comfortably into the role of *paterfamilias*: 'I find that having a child seems to prolong ones own life,' he admitted to Quinn, 'One thinks of oneself as perhaps living to 1970 or even with luck to the year 2000 (That would be Anne's 91st year). It makes ones family seem venerable too now that ones grandfathers are all great grandfathers.'[42] No matter that his mathematics was questionable; she would enter the next century in her early eighties.

Anne was becoming everything that could be desired in a child. 'She is the best tempered baby I ever came across—lies placidly wide awake in her cradle looking as if her mind was full of pleasant dreams,' Lolly thought.[43] The controls would have applauded, for very early on, when discussing Iseult's unhappy emotional state, they had emphasized that 'a conception in sorrow gives sorrow to the child'.[44] (This was probably a recognition of Maud's determination to have another child when her first little son died, and Iseult's conception in his burial vault.) Certainly Anne was a contented baby, had been even in the womb when George was able to keep her quiet 'by suggestion'. This would become especially important for her father, for as George noted, while Willy was working, 'he had to be in absolute isolation in a room wherever he was writing.'[45] Yeats was even disturbed by silent activities, such as George's embroidering.

George had been preoccupied with the colour yellow before Anne's birth, which later in the script is identified with space and 'all that is natural'.[46] She may have been recalling the colour table in Willy's edition of William Blake, in which, as with their own system, all the colours are given both good and bad aspects: 'A warm golden light, which is highest of things in one aspect, is, when considered as the falling beam descending towards the nadir, the not very obscure symbol for this theft, which is none other than the theft of Prometheus.' 'Yellow Physical—Warm light Mind. When the yellow is of a ruddy or golden colour it is symbolic of the love.'[47]

Anne's christening on 27 April was a family affair at St Mary's in Donnybrook, where Willy had been christened. The ceremony was officiated by black-haired Canon Wilson; looking 'far more like a Priest than a Parson', the Revd David Wilson would eventually become the Dean of St Patrick's Cathedral. Lily and Cottie stood as godmothers, while Harold Hyde-Lees, now studying at Wells Theological College, was godfather *in absentia*. Lily's department at Cuala had made a special cloak of gold and white brocade with little roses embroidered on it; over it Anne wore the robe her father had worn at his christening fifty-four years earlier, preserved by Lily the family archivist. Then everyone went to Aunt Fanny Gordon's in Morehampton Road for tea 'so that all the Great Aunts can see Anne Butler'. Products of an earlier time, doubtless they all shared Lily's concern that, as Anne later remembered it, if the children were not christened 'the Catholics would get them'. And if they did not entirely agree with Lily, both George and Willy seemed determined that their daughter should have every form of social and spiritual endorsement. For the one absent member Lolly conjured up an image of George, 'so pretty . . . with Ann in her arms—so motherly and anxious she should not cry—the two heads came close together as she bent over her cooing softly to her'.[48] Lolly's christening gift arrived later in Ballylee—a hand-painted wooden cradle.[49]

But it was necessary to find a permanent nurse, especially since George was planning to leave Anne with Willy's eager sisters while they made a journey to England. There was the move from Woburn Buildings to Oxford to arrange, and Willy was anxious to attend rehearsals of the Stage Society's production of *The Player Queen* in London. Then, too, Ballylee required a visit. The first nurse George tried, 'a nice easy going South of Ireland woman', proved 'too timid' with the tiny baby and so departed after a week. On 30 April instead of their going to Galway as planned, George moved into Gurteen Dhas and Willy, thrown back on his own resources, found a bed elsewhere.

'If your afternoon solitude becomes less sweet wire or phone to me but as I think, after having had so little of it, you will continue to find it sweet I shall not come unless I hear,' he wrote from his club. 'I have taken the fur-coat to Mitchell, got my ticket, phoned to many people & generally done my duty.' 'Did I leave my pen with you?'[50] They resorted to meeting at the local 'DBC' in order to have some privacy before he took the boat train ahead of her.[51] Meanwhile, determined to keep an eye on the castle and plant her garden during a spell of hot summer weather, George arranged to spend a week there herself even without a nurse. She assured the concerned aunts that as soon as she reached Galway 'her progress with Anne would be like a Royal procession—she wouldnt have to look after anything'. Lolly made a point of telling her father the travel was first class 'because of Anne'; Willy had even asked about hiring a motor from Athenry to avoid changing trains.[52]

George was making her wishes known concerning child-rearing. Inevitably, she sought out the best advice she could, depending especially on a book by Dr Truby King, the New Zealand children's specialist.[53] George was also determined that Anne should not be spoiled 'by rocking her when she cried, or by taking her out of her cradle and coaxing her to sleep'. Nor was she to be overwhelmed with praise: 'Its mother says her baby has become big and plain, & this makes Lilly indignant,' JBY was told.[54] This suited George, who despite her warmth and humour never lost her English reserve when it came to expressing her emotions directly, either physically or verbally. Thinking ahead to when her daughter could talk (and perhaps showing her own preference for Lily), she decided to call her sister-in-law 'Elizabeth' rather than the diminutive 'Lolly'.[55] On the return from County Galway on 19 May, Dr Solomons sent yet another nurse—who again proved unsatisfactory. Eventually George, rejecting her sister-in-law's preference for someone older and more experienced, chose a young woman whom she could train herself. 'Nana', as the children called their greatly loved Florence Reade, stayed with them for ten years and then with her employer's sponsorship formally trained at the Rotunda Hospital.

George arrived at the castle on 13 May, where to the intense interest of the neighbourhood work was apparently still going on; Lady Gregory reported a case of assault in Galway—'W. Fahy accusing W. Brennan of having pelted him with stones & mortar from the top of Ballylee castle.'[56] Before leaving Ballylee George was joined there on the 15th by Iseult who, 'looking very pale & needs to be much in the open air', had been invited to spend three weeks in the country during their absence. Perhaps recalling earlier days when Gregory had refused to invite Iseult to Coole, Willy made a point of informing his old friend that 'It was George's idea to offer Ballylee to Iseult.' 'You might show her the woods as she is going into the country to wander about alone. Town life which she hates has brought on a rather serious old complaint. If she can find her way over the fields I am sure she will spend much time in the woods. . . . She will probably take her lunch with her & spend all day out.'[57]

With Ballylee inhabited and the question of a 'most satisfactory nurse' settled, George sailed for London, where Willy had been staying with the Tuckers. Nelly had already accompanied him on an inspection of Woburn Buildings in preparation for her arrival and its final dismantling, and he conscientiously reported (two or three times) their findings: 'all kinds of damage and dirt but nothing that will not be put reasonably right before you come. A strange banjo in the study which suggests a lodger of Mrs Old, & also a strange & very common hearth rug beside the bed in my bed room. I have asked Mrs Old to clean up & will ask Mrs Robinson (Ezra's char) to finish up after. This was your mothers idea.'[58] They were in England together for three weeks, from 21 May to mid-June. Probably neither George nor her mother ever knew that eight days after she arrived in London Charles Herbert Hyde, her father's elder brother, had died in a workhouse in Barrow-in-Furness, Cumberland.[59] While she was away Lily, ecstatic at seeing the baby 'ever so often a day instead of once', sent a daily postcard report and 'at George's expense' spent her free Saturdays touring the family with her prize.[60] The lease for Woburn Buildings expired on 25 June, and George energetically set about arranging the move by van to Oxford, which was planned for 11 June. In addition to Willy's furnishings in Woburn Square, they were taking her possessions from the house in Montpelier Square, which the Tuckers had let unfurnished while deciding their own future plans. In particular, there was her father's bureau which she had treasured since his death; it would figure later in the script.

George stayed long enough in London to attend the opening night of *The Player Queen* on 25 May and then went ahead to Oxford, where Willy joined her at the Boars Hill Hotel after a second performance of his play two days later. They arranged for the winter lease of 4 Broad Street, just down the road from the rooms they had happily shared as students of the system the previous year. Although it was bound to be a wrench for Willy to leave Woburn Buildings after so many years and memories, George may well have felt it a release for the same reasons. At any rate, during their few nights in Oxford the script became highly personal, discussing the relationship between the sexual act and energy at its 'greatest purity'. For the rest of his life Willy, and perhaps George also, would continue to believe that 'pure energy [is] confined to creative genius & to sex intercourse'.[61] This may be the only point on which both would later agree with Ezra Pound.

There was other business to attend to when they returned to London at the end of the month. George, who was still involved in conducting examinations for the Order, seems to have been drawn even further into Golden Dawn affairs. Although they did not realize it at the time, 'Nemo Sciat' was partly responsible for a crisis that had erupted. In an effort to understand what was happening, apparently George had asked about 'Sapiens Dominabitur Astris', the mysterious Anna Sprengel of Nuremberg whose name was allegedly on the 'discovered' cipher manuscript on which the Golden Dawn was based. When Anna Sprengel conveniently 'died', Dr Felkin claimed to have made his own contact with the Third Order, through the discarnate Arab adept Ara Ben Shemesh, who communicated new rituals to the Felkins by means of automatic writing and put him in touch with other astral figures, notably 'the hidden masters of a Sun Order'. The ensuing confusion among members, and George's innocent question, prompted Christina Mary Stoddart ('Il faut chercher'), who had prepared Georgie for her initiation and was now one of the chiefs of the Amoun Temple, to search for facts. Determined to be 'quite sure of our foundations' and to eliminate 'All that is not purely Order teaching', Miss Stoddart embarked on three years of investigation.[62]

The strain was evident as early as April that year when Stoddart had a vision at a Tenebrae service in the Anglican Church, followed by 'the most extraordinary astral persecution, unexpected attacks, forces, overpowering scents and projections of astral light, etc.'[63] Felkin being in New Zealand and in any case unsympathetic, she turned to 'Nemo' and 'Demon' for help. Back in Woburn Buildings George and Willy consulted their own discarnate teachers: 'What is the cause of the obsession [*sic*] Miss S spoke of', to which Thomas (in his new state as Eurectha, 'the builder') responded, 'to break up & reinstate—cause is lack of lunar activity—too much sun'. Obviously Thomas did not approve of the new astral entities who had taken over the Stella Matutina. The evil influence, he reported, originated in 'five people—2 dead three living'—that is, the Felkins' new Arabic familiar Ara Ben Shemesh, the recently deceased MacGregor Mathers, and Dr and Mrs Felkin and their daughter Ethel (who was now representing her father as head of the Order). Expulsion 'for the good of the order' was necessary. George, referred to only as 'the woman here', was not to learn their names lest she recognize the identities of the five evil influences.

The reason for Thomas/Eurectha's insistence upon secrecy then became clear: the Interpreter and 'Miss S' were to 'abolish & burn all rosy cross rituals' and exorcize and reconsecrate the cross 'with hands *wet*'; they were then to 'see Arab' and, each with a bowl of clear water, 'throw it at obsessing force'. Willy was 'not to appear at all'. Three days later Eurectha forbade any further script 'till after medium has been to Arab etc.'[64] He did, however, allow them to be present 'at consecration of vault' (presumably part of the cleansing ritual as they banished Ara Ben Shemesh). But they must practise their own rituals more regularly: incense, flowers, and other 'scent signels [*sic*]' 'to bring you back to an intensity you are letting slip'. Miss Stoddart and the Golden Dawn were clearly considered too much of a distraction for Willy: 'Do not too much pass into spiritual life— keep in emotional life in your phase & not beyond it | I do not want you to communicate with her too much—the medium is quite safe but not you.' Decreeing there was to be no further script until they returned to Ireland, he relented sufficiently to admit that the balance between Willy's spiritual and emotional life was satisfactory.[65]

While they were in London something occurred to cause a further 'critical moment' for George, and again it was not pleasant. This one seems to have arisen from a phrase quoted from one of Willy's letters, whether the one to Iseult which had served as catalyst on 24 October 1917 or another is not clear. Analysed a few months later in the tower, this second critical moment 'in case of woman' was described as 'always a revealing of her own pride—the complete departure of vanity—the realisation of isolation of identity—of pride of identity', which also suggests that George's second critical moment casts back to 24 October 1917. 'Real pity', their Instructor continued, 'has pride of self—it says go and I am still I . . . It says go if that were better for you—do if it is better for you to do [*space*] Think as you will [*space*] I am always I—pity is real pity is the unity of self with another self . . . if the I is not in unity with itself the other would be able to hurt it or change it & it would lose its identity or else it could not be approached through *fear* of hurting or changing.'

In the first critical moment 'she wishes chance to be free . . . hers must be the choice—clear reasoning choice—in 2nd hers the chance . . . she is waiting for the decision'.[66] Thanks to Ameritus, her personal guide, George was coming to terms with her own history and the 'painful process' they had both undergone to reach the present unity.[67]

They did not restrict their visits to colleagues in the Order. The Pounds were in Europe for the summer, but there were other friends to see, including Olivia and the Tuckers. When Dulac first learned of George's pregnancy, consumed with curiosity as to how Willy would behave as a father, he had written a letter of congratulation: 'The result ought to be remarkable: I hope you will manage to have him or her born in the Castle, it would be a good start, the planets' impressions on his microscopic sphere would be purer.'[68] But in addition to Anne there were other subjects to discuss with the Dulacs—Ballylee Castle and the disturbed state of the Irish countryside; Willy's play *Calvary* and his search for 'a new Noh play plot';[69] their work on the system. Coached by George, Willy tried hard not to mention Dulac's designs for the play *Cyrano de Bergerac*, which he had disliked.[70] Perhaps they brought with them the sketch of the legendary 'Giraldus' that Dulac had sent the previous year; it would not resurface until 1923 when a part of the philosophy was about to be published as *A Vision*.

While at the Dulacs on 10 June George had smelt incense, which the Instructors informed them represented, among other symbols, the voyage myth.[71] Certainly some time during their visit to London they began to talk seriously of a lecture tour in the United States and Canada. This was doubtless precipitated not only by the income tax forms George was preparing, but by a meticulous account Quinn had sent Willy of the monies ($759) which had been advanced by him to John Butler Yeats over the past three years. No matter how optimistic the old painter was, he could never earn enough to pay his bills. Earlier in 1919 Willy had already sent cheques of £40 and £35, but there was still some £90 outstanding, a debt to his old friend which was embarrassing and needed to be cleared before they met. Throughout their lives both George and Willy were painfully scrupulous about such matters—and about their family responsibilities. Just before they took the boat train to Ireland on 14 June Willy sent a cable to John Quinn, 'Have sent two hundred thirty four pounds to pay father's debt. Writing about manuscripts.'[72] A long-standing private agreement with Quinn had arranged for the sale of manuscripts in compensation for payment of his father's expenses, but 1918 had been 'a lean year' for Willy, and George—who had taken financial responsibility for the construction and furnishing of Ballylee, and probably the move to Oxford—had been forced to sell £100 of investments to pay for her illness and confinement. Faced with his debt to Quinn, Willy informed his father that he had sold out most of his Sligo legacy 'at rather a loss'.[73] No matter how careful he had always been with money, he and his wife were, he later admitted, neophytes at housekeeping and domestic finances. Financial concerns and plans for the American trip would loom large in the months to come.

They stayed in Dublin just long enough for the anxious mother to see her daughter, but then, still leaving Anne in the safe care of her nurse and aunt Lily, went directly on to Ballylee to assess Rafferty's progress, check how the garden

was doing, and prepare for the summer occupation. Again, a neighbouring family provided domestic help: Norah Dooley having married, they were joined by
Mary Anne Molloy of a farming family living on the main road to Gort just down
from the Coole demesne;[74] she would prove so satisfactory that she later went
with them to Oxford, while her parents could always be counted on to keep an
eye on Ballylee. George and Willy's two weeks in the west also offered an opportunity for serious uninterrupted work on the philosophy. There had been some
indication in London that George was getting tired of the daily questioning, for
at Woburn Buildings Thomas had suggested, 'Not sure medium isnt right & it
might be better to stop for 3 months'; when Willy asked permission to write prose
rather than poetry he had replied, 'write anything except system'. There would
be 'no synthesis for some time'.[75] (George may have had other plans for the
summer in Ballylee.) However, Thomas did not object to a lecture on the system
to their old friend Mead's Quest Society that autumn, or to the journey to
America 'next spring'.[76] By 18 June George's automatic writing had taken on a
more normal appearance—she stopped running words together, added more
regular punctuation and capitalization, and whereas a few months earlier she was
already occasionally recording both questions and answers, now the questions
were enclosed in parentheses.[77] Whether some of these changes were made later
during their analysis of the scripts, or whether this was a deliberate effort on
her part to emphasize her own contribution, is impossible to determine. If
not completely conscious, George was certainly allowing her personality and
opinions to intrude more and more openly. It is probably no coincidence that
the next day Ameritus, identified so closely with her daimon, took over the script.

'The Case of Anne Hyde' continued to obsess them; Thomas had even
suggested they try finding her letters in the British Museum before they left
London.[78] Now the Earl of Rochester, Anne's father, entered the script and also
a request from 'a personality' identifying himself with Anne's tutor: 'We would
like you to write what you know of Annes history—it would help some of us.'
The narrative should include 'all we have told you', but they were to seek a burial
place in Kilkenny, and look for Anne's diary and other Hyde papers. He then
provided a drawing of three birds, refusing to offer any explanation.[79] For his part
Ameritus had 'wonderful things to tell you', but warned against self-deception,
especially in 'writing about personal script'; this may have referred to a message
Willy had sent to Coole with Mary Anne that morning.[80] He also reminded them
—as if either needed it—that 'proofs are no certainty to a philosophical mind
—never convince any subjective person by objective experience'; scientific
methods would never be satisfactory when it came to doctrines of belief.[81] Then
Apple and Rose, George's personal caretaker guides, joined Ameritus, apparently
in connection with the bird imagery that had haunted the script from the beginning and with which the messages from Anne Hyde now intermingled.

Willy had recalled George's first words of automatic writing as 'with the bird all is well at heart. Your action was right for both but in London you mistook its meaning.'[82] Whether his memory was accurate or not, from then on the three birds that kept turning up in messages and drawings were usually understood to refer to the three women who dominated Willy's imagination: Maud, Iseult, and George. Throughout December 1917 the script had kept providing this bird imagery, including the day Anne Hyde's name first appears. On 23 December the Instructors explained that '3 birds only symbols to medium', who continued to open many sessions with a diagram which, although the setting would vary, always included the birds. A week later Iseult was identified with 'bird & shell' ('one symbol only not two'), a reference to the opening song of his play *The Only Jealousy of Emer*:

> A woman's beauty is like a white
> Frail bird, like a white sea-bird alone
> At daybreak after stormy night
> Between two furrows upon the ploughed land:
> A sudden storm, and it was thrown
> Between dark furrows upon the ploughed land. . . .
> A strange, unserviceable thing,
> A fragile, exquisite, pale shell,
> That the vast troubled waters bring
> To the loud sands before day has broken.[83]

Finally in mid-January 1918 the following exchange took place with Thomas:

What is the significance of birds?
Different forms of intellect when connected *with water*—with air *emotion* . . .
Are birds of the air live.
Love . . .
A butterfly different from a bird in wisdom is it not?
No   wisdom of love . . .
. . . birds of sea—intellectual intellect
    birds of air—intellectual love . . .
all flying things without sting & not birds—forms of wisdom

Maud was identified as the 'speckled bird', a reminder of Willy's unfinished novel of the 1890s.[84]

They had also consulted others about the persistent bird imagery, including Horton and Bessie Radcliffe. Just two months before he died Horton had written to congratulate them on their expected child, adding, 'Remind your wife of my interpretation of the *birds* when I saw her last.'[85] Unfortunately there does not seem to be a record of what he had said. Birds, once as many as twenty-three, had made frequent appearances in Elizabeth Radcliffe's automatic writing throughout 1913. But the ones that most interested George and Willy were the so-called 'Salisbury birds' that came to Bessie in connection with a brief message from Bishop Moberly of Salisbury. As recorded in medieval archives and more recently in *Dulce Domum*, the history of the Moberly family, two 'great white birds' were said to herald the death of the Bishop of Salisbury. The author Anne Moberly, who claimed to have seen them herself on the occasion of her father's death, was the first principal of St Hugh's College in Oxford. She was also known to be the pseudonymous 'E. Morison', co-author with 'Frances Lamont' (Eleanor Jourdain) of *An Adventure*, a description of an unexpected psychic experience on a visit to Versailles when the two women encountered the ghosts of Marie Antoinette and others. The book, first published in 1911, was widely read; an enlarged edition appeared in 1913 and both George and Willy seem to have owned copies.[86] In addition the *Occult Review*, which they both regularly read, had carried a description in 1912 of a similar experience at Versailles in which Margaret and Robert Gregory had been transported back to an earlier period; Willy's assistance had been requested by the journal editor in initiating a correspondence between Miss Moberly and Margaret Gregory.[87]

The coincidence between Bessie's birds and the Versailles adventure intrigued George as it had Willy. As early as March 1918 they made the acquaintance of both Anne Moberly and the scholar Eleanor Jourdain, who by then had succeeded her co-author as principal of St Hugh's. Although firmly denying any suggestion that the late Bishop might have attempted communication with Bessie, they did show the Yeatses yet more manuscript material: 'We are much exercised at present to know whether to publish the book you saw or not. There seem so many reasons, both private and public, for and against it. Have you a view and would you let us know it? Of course The Salisbury Birds could not be part of it.'[88] Meanwhile Bessie was considering publication of her own experiences with the spirit world,[89] but insisted that she had never read *Dulce Domum* and that she had read *An Adventure* only after the Bishop and his birds had reached her. However, she sent the relevant drawings Willy requested, innocently enquiring, 'Has your wife had any interesting writing?'[90] Evidently Bessie's birds did nothing to assist their research, but George was determined to pursue the question with Eleanor Jourdain when they got back to Oxford.

Birds returned to the script after the birth of Anne who is, appropriately, linked with the drawing of a feather; 'feathers grow & grow till they make birds.'[91] Eventually one of George's personal guides, associated with a lake and, through drawings, Ballylee, shifted her allegiance to baby Anne ('Rose belongs to feather').[92] However, Thomas insisted that the Interpreter is not always one of the birds in Willy's horoscope; there would, after all, have to be room for Olivia in his 'Lightning Flash'.[93] Some birds were not as welcome; in March 1919 Thomas indignantly announced—twice—'no more peackcocks [*sic*]'; as usual, however, there was no explanation of this new addition to the supernatural aviary.[94] Maud is now not only speckled, but 'the bird with yellow beak' and likely to become a nuisance; the session ended in upside down writing, 'home truths Too many feathers pulled out of your tail . . . yellow beak tail feathers very dragled [sic].'[95] Evidently Thomas and Rose were not without a sense of humour at times. But the birds persisted as a message to Willy to 'look into the likenesses'. There was also a reminder of the hawk and butterfly on the ring representing their own union; 'eagle is Saturn'. And by then there is no doubt of the relationship of 'feather' to the Countess of Ossory:

Could Anne write now, there being such a very little of her in the cradle
No . . .
Does the soul of Anne, so little being in the cradle, remember her past life
For three days—not after[96]

There seems to have been an attempt to shift this imagery from the personal to the philosophical plane, for by mid-May 1918 the diagram had expanded to include four birds, identified as the four faculties being developed as part of the structure of the system.[97] In July during a discussion of the Yeatses' relationship with the third and fourth daimons, the number of birds grew to five: 'notice *all* Birds that you may study all . . . there you have five people all 3rd & yet all so dissimilar [*space*] I do not in these "five" include feather.' This fifth bird was 'The Black Bird you have not yet quite discovered.' As George and Willy, encouraged by Anne Hyde, looked forward to their second child, 'Black Bird' would soon become 'Black Eagle', their son and heir. Perhaps that is why this particular session had begun in such a playful mood: 'The interpreter had better do a course of metaphysics & algebra or botany | She is making things very difficult . . . you cant warm a frog . . .'[98]

Another interesting discovery was made while they were alone at Ballylee in June 1919. Rafferty had found a drain-like excavation while digging in George's garden; Ameritus when consulted drew a chapel underneath the new road. It is, he informed them, 'Later than Castle', but they were to 'go on digging' in order to 'free . . . the spirits of the place'.[99] There was no further discussion of this romantic concept. However, again following Ameritus' instructions, they made plans to travel to Kilkenny to inspect Anne Hyde's burial place. They stopped in Dublin to see their daughter, who was now growing so fast she was too big for her long robes. George had made Lily promise that 'no matter what her age or what her size—no one was to short coat her till she was here to do it herself'.[100] The young mother was already feeling the pressure of divided loyalties. Ameritus took the occasion to remind Willy (in mirror writing) that 'script depends on the love of medium for you—all intensity comes from that.'[101] But two days of exploration in Kilkenny yielded little, even though a new guide, Briennach or Brienan, arrived briefly to assist. George's automatic writing provided two different floor plans of the cathedral and recommended a search of the church register, Lady Kildare's letters, Rochester's diary, and archaeological journals; but when he returned Ameritus confessed to having 'so great difficulty without Anne [Hyde]' to advise him.[102] They then returned to Dublin and the baby Anne.

When George went back to Ballylee on 7 July this time she triumphantly carried her daughter with her. Willy meanwhile stayed on in Dublin, for the nurse was using his room while Rafferty plastered the ceilings in an effort to reduce the risk of insects falling from the thatch.[103] Enough of the tower itself was completed that they could make use of the ground floor as Willy's writing space and a dining room; now with two servants, it was getting a little crowded in the two adjoining cottages. Aware of the dangers once Willy was at loose in Dublin, Ameritus had already warned him 'not to be drawn into anything'; there was 'possible trouble in Ireland . . . you may be tempted to join in political schemes if there is trouble & you must not.' Ireland had been in political ferment since Sinn Féin had won a sweeping majority in the December election, although many of those elected were still in jail. But de Valera, Sinn Féin's leader, had escaped from prison in February and was on his way to America to secure recognition for the outlawed Dáil Eireann; under Michael Collins's direction there were frequent skirmishes between the IRA and the constabulary as representatives of the British government —even the Gort post office had been robbed more than once. The 'Bird with white & black head & wings' (an obvious reference to Maud whom he would see in Dublin) was 'dangerous':

. . . some are brewing rebellion—useless. . . .
Danger it being National holiday
Nothing must be said *unless* she speaks of it—then simply say you are destroying the souls of hundreds of young men
That method is most wicked in this country—wholesale slaughter because a few are cruel
The leader should never incite   That is always done through *hate & deception*
It is being planned   I am not sure of her
more than half are against it

Besides, Willy had work to do on the script, which he must not speak of; 'be silent when you cannot deceive.'[104]

Lonely in the Stephen's Green Club, Willy sent daily bulletins to Ballylee:

I went on Monday morning to College Library to find it closed for two weeks. I am now trying to get in as a special favour. As I had not you to take care of me I talked much, read in bed & smoked much—result two days headache. Fit for nothing else I spent yester-day evening wandering about Chapel-Izod looking for the ruins of the great house of the Ormonds—a tower was still left in 1830—but there is not a trace. I have looked through all the histories of Dublin & of Christ Church but found nothing except that we should have gone into the crypt. One gets into the crypt for I think 1/-. There is no use my going as it is clearly job for Ameritus. . . . I think the mills are on the site of the Ormonds house.

'I suppose you are fishing for trout & that you have set all your plants,' he wrote wistfully the next day. George meanwhile lunched at Coole; he dined with the O'Neills and finally managed to gain entrance to the library, but as there was 'no ephemeris there of any kind', it was a frustrating time all round.[105] By 14 July he had rejoined his wife and daughter at Ballylee, bringing with him on the one o'clock train an exciting invitation to spend two years at the Keio Gejuken University in Tokyo as a lecturer on English literature. At least it would give 'time perhaps to finish the system away from all distractions'; but much depended upon 'what Ameritus thinks'.[106]

He had already written a lengthy letter to John Quinn concerning both his personal and the political situations, informing him of the invitation to Japan:

We are reeling back into the middle ages, without growing more picturesque. George has gone back to Ballylee where she is, I hope, catching trout, and I follow in a few days . . . It looks as if I may have a spirited old age. It would be pleasant to go away until the tumult of war had died down, and perhaps Home Rule established, and even the price of coal settled on. . . . I think my chief difficulty in accepting will be my tower, which needs another year's work under our own eyes before it is a fitting monument and symbol, and my garden, which will need several years if it is to be green and shady during my lifetime. Ballylee is a good house for a child to grow up in—a place full of history and romance, with plenty to do every day.[107]

By the 16th they were strongly inclined to Japan—at least George was. Willy informed Ezra of their plans, at the same time painting an idyllic picture of life at Ballylee:

I am writing in what will be the castle garden and a young otter has just glided through a still place in the moss. Wattles and George are beside me, George sewing an orange curtain and Wattles crowing softly. Both are I think happy. You may not see much of us for some time. I have been invited to lecture on English literature to the University of Tokio for two years and am hesitating. Probably we shall accept. George, Wattles and I— George wants & I—I in sheer joy of escaping from my country for two years, during which it may not be at its best . . . I have not yet dared to tell Lady Gregory who will think I am deserting all my duties but must walk over tomorrow and tell her. I shall come back to find Ballylee finished so far as structure goes and all trees planted. It is beautiful now but untidy here and there, and a man is at this moment painting the windows a brilliant blue.[108]

Later that day, he described the scene—and drew a sketch of the hallway—for his father:

I have been driven in by rain from the river bank where I have been writing & catching a distant glimpse of a young otter fishing, I suppose for trout. . . . We saw just his brown head & a long ripple on the water. Anne & George were there too, George sewing & Anne lying wide awake in her seventeenth century cradle. I am writing in the great ground floor room of the castle—pleasantest room I have yet seen, a great wide window opening on the river & a round arched door leading to the thatched hall . . . I am writing at a great trestle table which George keeps covered with wild flowers.[109]

Never had he been so contented.

George soon put a stop to the nickname 'Wattles', doubtless the result of photographs of the new baby being shown around London, and she had also won the battle over the colour of the windows. But Ezra was unsure about Japan, for which he blamed George, and Quinn and JBY were even more strongly against the idea. Throughout the winter letters would arrive from New York, advising them against the project. 'The Japan part is all right—but the word lecture *dismays* me,' his father wrote, 'Can you stand it? Remember that you inherited a certain constitution and that means that tho' you have high vitality it ebbs very quickly—so dont play any tricks with yourself . . . *Remember you must take care of your own health* and resist others who would give you bad advice—they knowing nothing of your nervous system. You cant expect your wife to take care of you—she is too young to be cautious and wise and knowing and she because of her quite other sex is all for activity and adventure—whereas you are a man of thought who loves the quiet.'[110] However by 9 August, still with Ballylee in mind, Willy had accepted the offer 'subject to reasonable terms etc'. He replied persuasively to Quinn, 'The work on this old tower will be finished before my return. As I write I can see the river, where two water hens have just passed, through the big window & when the cat purrs it sounds very loud because of the echo in the stone vaulting.'[111] Lily was delighted at the thought of once more taking care of Baby until she and Nurse Reade were to join her parents for the long journey across the Pacific.[112]

Every few days Willy walked over to Coole to consult Lady Gregory on such affairs as the theatre and the ongoing battle to bring Hugh Lane's pictures to Ireland. While she was with her family in the Burren, he and George decided to take a fishing holiday themselves. And so on 25 July they were on the road again, but only as far as Galway, where they stayed overnight before choosing which direction to take into Connemara.[113] Based in Oughterard on the shores of Lough Corrib, they fished during the day, while each evening Ameritus elaborated on the complex concept of 'victimage'. Evidently Willy was still pursuing proof, for the session of 28 July began with Ameritus' complaint, 'Oh Lord forgive the hard of belief.' Occasionally the questions again strayed into their intimate relationship, for a few days later Ameritus was called upon to counsel on the frequency and method of sexual intercourse, apparently in answer to

Willy's concern about his own stamina: 'Sexual health unaccustomed for some time to twice—therefore gradually try twice as always once will increase fatigue —But you must accustom yourself to gradually declining power & rest assured your power will always be amply sufficient.' Reassuring him that it was 'psychically all right last night', he advised that it would be 'better [to] have no script those nights'.[114]

Although their fishing seems to have been less satisfactory than their personal relationship, George looked back on the holiday with pleasure and a certain amount of wry wit:

We started off one day after lunch after Yeats's morning work and we got our boat. . . . a marvellous clear cloudless day, still water showing only your own reflection. Hopeless to catch a fish of any sort. Yeats insisted on rowing to the island to fish with the fly. Rowed in silence for about 10 minutes with that extraordinary short-armed action he always used as if backing against very strong waves. Then 'George. I row, you scull'. Rowed for another 15 minutes to island in silence. WBY emptied boat sat down in the only spot of shade available, and talked, surrounded by thousands of insects.

For the entire afternoon he talked, telling her the whole life story of Florence Farr Emery, of his involvement in magic, his interest in Horton. 'Then a little breeze got up, fishing began to be possible. WBY sat up suddenly, sat up on his haunches and, unaware that this was well past May, said "George, which among all these insects is the mayfly?" '[115]

On their last evening in Oughterard both Willy and Ameritus were getting tired and cranky. The session began with their Instructor snapping, '*Please attend & dont fidget* . . . get a new topic—as symbol of a new interest.' It ended with an even more heated exchange: 'You say exasperating—I am told you are to get script only in the degree that you become ready . . . You claim you will do as we tell you but you do nothing to make your lives more easy for us.' And he commanded them to consider 'What is lacking in your form of prayer'. However, the next day back at home in Ballylee, Ameritus relented, explaining that a Frustrator had interfered with their work, and perhaps even caused a temporary illness.[116]

While fishing they had evidently continued to develop the astrological relationships between the Hydes and Yeatses. Perhaps Willy's account of his earlier life had included a description of his Uncle George Pollexfen, fellow member of the Golden Dawn and practising astrologer, for on their return to Ballylee the scripts include a number of family horoscopes, a progressed horoscope for George, and an addition to their symbolical aviary—the 'Pol-ex-fen', an 'outlandish name meaning a solitary bird from a marsh'. 'The Pen' (George) married to 'the Pol' (Willy) seems to have been bent on a little mischief after her holiday.[117]

The following week a deceiver named Ontelos succeeded in ousting Ameritus, leading them a merry but interesting chase through their supposed past lives, including George's husbands and her relationship with her mother in previous incarnations, and Willy's affair with Anne Hyde. Unfortunately Willy's taste for his previous history was whetted; two weeks later he returned to the old subject, 'What life gave me my craze for MG. when did I meet her.' Although occasionally obliging, Ameritus warned 'All personal is DANGEROUS,' and brusquely dismissed Willy's question about the 'relation between parentage & truth & beauty' with 'I cant see this leads anywhere except to platitudes'.[118]

The weather continued to be very hot, and an invitation from the Gogartys was accepted with pleasure, especially at the thought of Renvyle's trout lake. Perhaps at Willy's suggestion Iseult had been included in the invitation, but when they once more turned towards Connemara, they went alone, this time travelling through Joyce Country, past the rugged grandeur of the Twelve Pins towards the Atlantic ocean. Renvyle Castle had originally been in the possession of the Joyces, then the O'Flahertys, and finally the Blakes. It was known to be haunted; according to Gogarty 'Some of the indoor walls were six feet thick, and where they were pierced, the doors were double. Sometimes the doors would open and shut by themselves . . . a window of an upstairs room, the only room at the house with a northern aspect, was heavily guarded. . . . No servants would sleep in that room. There was a "presence" there which could be felt, they said.'[119] George, always a believer in ghosts, saw a young man who promised to appear to her in the haunted room while the rest of the party waited below. Gogarty described George's reappearance, carrying a lighted candle; extinguishing it, she nodded curtly to Willy, 'Yes. It is just as you said.' Willy then explained to the assembled company, 'My wife saw a pale-faced, red-haired boy of about fourteen years of age standing in the middle of the north room. She was by the fireside when he first took shape. . . . He resents the presence of strangers in the home of his ancestors. He is Athelstone Blake. He is to be placated with incense and flowers.'[120] Back in Ballylee on 22 August, Ameritus was quizzed about their experience. Yes, he had wished them to go to Gogarty's, but not to exorcise the 14-year-old Blake; rather it had to do with the 'J.B. disaster'. He too demanded incense, from the 'hinged chest'. Evidently the conception of an heir was very much on their minds; they were advised to 'Keep quite apart for 3 days—no touch at all.'[121] Perhaps an early miscarriage had taken place?

In their search for documentation on Anne, Willy had turned to Miss Jacobs, the trusted typist in Great Russell Street who had worked for him for many years. The data on Anne Hyde's birth which she gleaned from an ephemeris in the British Museum excited them both, and they immediately sought signs in common for Anne Ossory and Anne Butler Yeats. 'I am very much obliged to you,' Willy wrote to Miss Jacobs on stationery stamped 'Ballylee Castle':

You have helped me in the most important piece of psychic research I have ever done. A year before my daughter was born a certain spirit told me through a friend, who is a writing medium, that this spirit had belonged to my wife's family in the 17th century and was seeking rebirth. We had never heard of her but found after some research that she existed and that various facts told us about her were correct. When our daughter was born the most marked feature in her horoscope was a strongly placed conjunction of Mars, & Mercury and Herschel. I then had another sitting with the spirit & told him that I did not consider that mere telling me of a certain obscure person of the past, & the claim that this person has now returned, was proof. I said the horoscopes must show continuity of character. The spirit said if you can find the birth date you will find the conjunction of Mars. Venus. After research in the Record Office Dublin my wife found the birth date. You have sent me the stats for her birthdate in the extract from the Ephemeris of Andrea Orgoli & they contain not only the conjunction of Mars & Venus (within 7 degrees is an astrological conjunction) but of them with [symbol for Mercury]. There are other resemblances Herschel (which is not in ephemeris) but easy to calculate is also in conjunction

The importance of the case is that no juggling ingenuity of the subliminal could, before our daughters birth, have picked a person of a past century whose horoscope resembled that of an unborn child.

If you have my letter please keep it & keep this letter. If you have destroyed my letter please make a record of the date when the research was made. Some day I may publish it all though not for some years. The sceptics will of course say I invented the automatic script after my child's birth & picked the 17th century date myself but evidence of research though not conclusive carries some weight. I am also asking one or two people to whom I spoke about the spirit before the childs birth to state so in writing. I do not tell you at present the name of the 17th century person, as I think if the name is known it may interfere with my research by creating thoughts which will confuse the controls. I am looking for a diary and some letters the control has spoken of.[122]

As always, he and George were concerned about what future critics would say.

Throughout August and September 1919 the script pursued Anne Hyde and their own previous incarnations. Willy's suggestion that he might have been a member of the Digby family may have been the result of rereading George's copy of *The Closet of Sir Kenelm Digby, Knight, Opened*, a book he had previously mentioned in his writings with 'Leo Africanus'.[123] George was still suffering from nightmares; Ameritus opened one session with 'I gave you that nightmare last night to show you how similar shocks affect secondly.' One cure for nightmares was to change the bird's feathers to black, a 'black swan'—once again a reminder of J.B. 'the heir', whose conception he warned was not to take place under Saturn or Neptune.[124] Even more revealing is the exchange two days later when Ameritus answered Willy's question, 'Have I met my wife of that life again,' with 'Yes . . . She whom you had to defend from tendency to drink.'[125] Evidently George's research into her own ancestry was giving rise to some serious fears about inherited tendencies, reflected also in a description of Nelly's previous incarnations and the necessity of purgation in her marriage with the luckless Gilbert Hyde Lees: 'In 19 [Nelly] a dreaming back to victimage but a victimage to expiate a wrong *done to her in past life*—a tyranny done to her—she has a drunken husband to expiate wrong done to tyrant—victimage for ghostly self done for present life as clearing up of gnots [knots].' In this life 'she has to care for a blundering man that she may expiate ignorance', an unflattering description of Nelly's second husband Harry Tucker.

George was clearly uncomfortable about this probing: 'medium . . . dislikes this case to go into on personal grounds as much as one or two others but if you cant grasp it without personal then you must have it.' However, a further session that evening brought little but a number of diagrams of birds and cats and the complaint, 'The robin does not sing. He is not on his tree.' The next day Ameritus relented sufficiently to pursue a discussion of 'critical moments' in relation to their union: to Willy's question, 'Have only 2 children of such a marriage correspondential significance' the answer was firmly 'Only 2'.[126] Still concerned about parallels between herself and her parents, George's script later loyally insisted that the Hyde Lees marriage had been 'happy for a time'; but there is an implication that for George there might still be some residual uncertainty about the permanence of her own happiness in marriage.[127]

Other related admissions surfaced in upside down and mirror writing:

[Q] Who was my wife jealous of in 1700 incarnation
[A] The woman who is now [upside down writing] Olivia Shakespere . . .
[Q] Did that jealousy create a knot
[A] Yes . . . necessitated expiation in life
[Q] That expiation now complete
[A] nearly 4 years ago . . .
[Q] What caused the jealousy
[A] [mirror writing] he wrote a poem to her[128]

'Nearly 4 years ago' harks back to November 1915, when Willy first raised the topic of marriage to George, a suggestion encouraged by Olivia and feared by Nelly. Whether Olivia had also had a discussion with Georgie we will never know, but by then apparently there was no hint of a continued liaison between Yeats and the woman he wrote of as 'Diana Vernon'.

Meanwhile Ameritus continued in his efforts to divert Willy from this persistent inquisitiveness about past lives: 'No no more Script you *must* write poetry . . . I have also given you material for a Noh play.'[129] A few weeks later Ameritus and Thomas both appeared 'To show we do not always come to blame & scold—for aprobation [*sic*] of you also to herald your new rhymes.'[130] They were not averse to advising on medical matters, either: 'Water morning & evening—Milk at night —no *root* vegetables—grape nuts or porridge & cream every breakfast—You eat too fast Coffee breakfast—Coco supper.'[131]

The summer was not entirely devoted to admiring Anne in her cradle by the river (which Willy could look down upon from his window in the tower[132]), watching the water hens and otters gliding by, contemplation (and conception) of the heir 'J.B.', fishing, and work on the script. They were often invited to Coole when Lady Gregory was in residence; after attending a dinner there with Edward Martyn and Joseph Vendryes, the editor of the *Revue celtique*, George returned to Anne while Willy stayed overnight to help Lady Gregory with her biography of Hugh Lane.[133] Willy was also encouraging his father 'to write at length on the time when he was an art student at Heatherley's and knew Butler, Nettleship, and the two Ellises', a project that George would find of special interest and, given her own experience at Heatherley's, might even have suggested.[134] They were getting to know other neighbours; one woman, a nearby farmer, asked for advice concerning some silver coins she had inherited.[135]

Immediately after the autumn equinox they left Ballylee; but in Dublin George insisted on keeping the baby with her while Nurse had a brief holiday with her family. 'Lolly and I are to dine at the Hotel with them, and we are promised a sight of Anne Butler's eel trick in her bath, quite a new trick learnt since she left us,' Lily wrote to Quinn. However, the delighted aunt was once more given the opportunity to babysit while George and Willy dined out. 'Baby is a splendid child—so sturdy & friendly & good-tempered. Willy says the people about Ballylee come to see the wonderful Baby, who sleeps out of doors and who never cries.'[136] Her New York bachelor friend must have been getting a little tired of these bulletins.

George, Anne, and the nurse sailed for England on 24 September. But Willy remained in Dublin suffering from a sore throat, his plan to join them in a few days thwarted first by the onset of tonsilitis, and then by a British transport strike.[137] Once again George was torn between two loyalties, concern for her husband's health and care for her child, a pattern that would become increasingly prevalent during their married life. In London, alone in her mother's milieu for the first time since Willy's proposal exactly two years ago, she cast a horoscope to mark the event.[138] With the small, happy baby beside her, it was a moment to reflect on the radical changes that had occurred since that 'critical moment' in her life— marriage, the automatic writing, childbirth, and, encircling all, Ballylee. Shortly before they had left Galway, Ameritus had opened the script with the following message:

Do not forget that the Tower is still your symbol | In all lives
[Q] Why do you say that especially tonight.
[A] Because you are soon leaving it[139]

Whatever else might happen, for George Ballylee had become the symbol of permanence. But not even their ghostly Instructors could foretell how long it would be before she returned to that blessed place.

10

Oxford and New York

London was already suffering from a shortage of supplies because of the railway strike, and so beyond seeing a few friends—the Pounds had only just returned from their summer in France—George moved on to Oxford. She was there by early October 1919, alone with Anne and her nurse while cleaning up after the tenants and arranging the furnishings they had moved from London. Apart from the magical tower, this would be the first house of their married life, and she was determined to create an environment that would not only be comfortable and aesthetically pleasing, but permanent. It was also the first time they were surrounded by their own belongings: books, paintings, new curtains, all had to be ready for Willy's arrival on 12 October. Willy meanwhile, should the strike continue, dreamed romantically of getting passage on a tramp steamer and then walking to join her; though he admitted that not having a map he had no idea 'where the sea runs nearest to Broad St Oxford'. He worried that George would tire herself, and find it hard to get milk for Anne.[1]

By the time Willy had made his more prosaic way to Oxford the servants had also arrived from Ireland. Norah Dooley, who had so longed to be with them in England,[2] had been replaced by Mary Anne Molloy, whose father James, a local farmer, looked after George's garden, and Mary Anne was joined in Oxford by her equally attractive sister Delia. The soft voices and gentle accents of the two sisters—one demure, one merry—seemed foreign in the new world they had entered. They in turn were sometimes bewildered: one day a prospective tenant knocked at the door and asked if the 'ouse was taken'; the puzzled Miss Molloy had to ask George what an 'ouse was.[3]

Number 4 Broad Street was a delightful seventeenth-century house opposite Balliol College, with 'queer narrow windows' overhanging Broad Street that reminded Lolly of Florence, and floors, stairs, and dark oak panels brightened by George with many cushions and curtains—orange in the sitting room, cherry red in the landing and hall windows, plum-coloured in the dining room against whitewashed walls, deep blue Morris hangings in the guest bedroom. 'There are odd steps up and down—down into Willys big study,' Lily later reported to her father; 'the floors are so uneven from age that I go up stage to bed and down stage to my cupboard.'[4] George painted the panelled oak walls of Anne's large nursery, and added a dull gold to the black bookcases Willy had brought from Woburn Buildings. John Butler Yeats's self-portrait in watercolour took pride of place over the fireplace, while Mancini's oil of his son hung by the window; the staircase up to the dimly lit drawing room on the first floor was lined with Blake's etchings—George's twenty-one of the Book of Job and Willy's seven of Dante's *Inferno*. As little Anne began to take notice of her surroundings, she would pat Job's beard when she was being carried up to bed. She also recalled being told they had so many paintings that a Rossetti was placed in the lavatory—it hung there until shy young visitors returning to the sitting room invariably spoke of the artist and provoked George and Willy to unseemly giggles.

Harold Hyde-Lees had presented them with an entire set of bedroom furniture in modern oak, but all else was designed to seem timeless. A Burmese gong summoned them to meals, where they dined off unpatterned, dark red china set on a long refectory table covered only by a narrow strip of brilliant Chinese embroidery. Having no silver and rejecting silver-plate, they ate with old Dublin forks of two or three prongs and horn spoons (pronounced by Lolly 'as flat as the blade of an oar'[5]), and served drinks in oddly shaped curved glasses.[6] George sought out old furnishings, diligently consulting catalogues and auction sales to achieve the effect admired by Lily: 'There is nothing new but Baby all looks old and long established and settled.'[7] It was a house with grace and learning, one such as Willy had long dreamed of.

It was also a house to which he could proudly invite guests, and they immediately set about arranging Wednesday as their 'At Home' day. They were getting to know more people: Robert Bridges entertained them, and Sir Walter Raleigh eased their way into the university; George's brother Harold maintained a close connection with Wadham College, which he and their father had both attended. But most important to George was the blossoming friendship with Lady Ottoline Morrell, who would become a regular caller and with whom they could both talk frankly about books and people.[8] Ottoline had been a familiar figure in the London arts world, and George may well have attended some of the wartime concerts given by Jelly d'Aranyi and her sisters in the Morrells' London house.[9] Also during the war though on a very limited income Ottoline and Philip Morrell had opened their home to like-minded pacifists, and Garsington had become a gathering place for artists, writers, and other brave swimmers against the social tide; a typical weekend might include appearances by Virginia and Leonard Woolf, Bertrand Russell, Frieda and D. H. Lawrence, Lytton Strachey, Aldous Huxley, Mr and Mrs T. S. Eliot, Mark Gertler, Siegfried Sassoon, and soon George and W. B. Yeats.

Lady Ottoline was aristocratic in appearance yet democratic and artistic in her interests, strikingly original in her tastes and passions, beautiful in a strangely grotesque way. The house was the same—built in the time of James I but decorated with a range of paintings, packed full of books, full of eighteenth-century furniture and smelling of incense, a jewel box with a shabbiness that enhanced rather than detracted from the overall effect of ancient romance. On Sunday afternoons the brightest and most stimulating of undergraduates would walk the six miles from Oxford—or take the winding bus ride to Cowley Village—to join the party. In summer they sat in the loggia or wandered on the terraces leading down to a swimming pool surrounded by yews, Italian statues, and an ilex tree; never out of hearing were conversational murmurs, peacocks' screams, and the yapping of pugs and Pekinese. In winter they played chess with their handsome host or sat by the fire in the Venetian-red drawing room listening to the talk and poetry readings. Among them were a very young David Cecil (who was too nervous to accept Willy's invitation to meet with 'old friends and a few witches'), L. A. G. Strong (who did, and never forgot George's 'glittering eyes', perhaps the reason so many had difficulty remembering their colour), and Christine Trew (who would later, as Lady Longford, become a respected fixture in Dublin theatrical circles).[10] Ottoline Morrell's distinctive appearance and fervent approach to life were, to one awed undergraduate, 'Elizabethan', but most agreed that she tended to orchestrate the conversation rather than lead it. Witty and intense, she was also a sympathetic listener, which George especially appreciated, while one cynical young observer noted that Willy 'liked to enunciate at their full value the words "the Lady Ottoline Morrell." '[11]

The Yeatses seem to have made their first visit to the Jacobean manor in mid-December 1919 according to George's punctilious note of thanks (as she always called it, her 'roofer'): 'You gave us a most delightful & refreshing time with you & we are both full of thanks to you for it. We returned full of envy for your beautiful house. . . . We shall hope to see you some Wednesday before we go.'[12] Their stay had clearly delighted Ottoline as well; 'such a relief to me after these dry English . . . we talked by the hour and I enjoyed him enormously,' she wrote of Yeats in her diary after they left. Having just given up her London house, it was important to her too to have such stimulating companionship. From then on she was a regular visitor to the Broad, driving herself there with abandon in phaeton and pair or bicycling through the streets of Oxford, scarves and shawls billowing behind.[13] Her bright red shoes with their incredibly high heels elicited from Anne her first complete sentence, 'Who is that?'[14]

Following Ottoline's example, they too made their house a welcoming gathering place for precocious undergraduates. Willy spoke at college meetings, and even accepted the position of president of the newly established Irish Society.[15] A list of 'Oxford Students & Societies 1919-1921' was preserved by George. Neither of them having attended university, they obviously enjoyed participating vicariously in student life. Once Willy rescued a girl undergraduate who had unwittingly taken a book away from the Bodleian: 'Overcome with horror, she rushed to the fountain-head of wisdom, and presented herself sobbing to the astonished poet. He gave her his complete attention, and, satisfied on the facts, sent for Mrs Yeats, who comforted the girl with tea and aspirin. Yeats then took the book back to the Bodleian and handed it to a stupefied official with a long and flamboyant explanation.'[16] The students were also good copy for the ongoing game of classifying personalities—'a 17 [or other category], I think' was a common remark after some oblivious guest had gone down the stairs. Strong recalled that they altered his particular phase once they discovered he wrote poetry.[17] Although she remembered sewing a white dress for little Anne, Grace Spurway was rarely invited to Broad Street; she felt that Willy did not care for her outspokenness, and so she and her cousin continued to meet at the Cadena Café.

However, the principal of Grace's college, Eleanor Jourdain, shared many interests with the Yeatses. A member of a distinguished family and a Dante scholar, she may have been the catalyst behind Ameritus' advice, shortly after Willy arrived from Ireland, that George read aloud the whole of Dante's *Il Convito* (*The Banquet*), 'only a little every day'; as George was aware from her intensive early studies, Dante's analysis of the four levels of meaning provided an interesting parallel to their own philosophical patterning.[18] Miss Jourdain also seemed more prepared to discuss her early Versailles 'Adventure' and was soon drawn in to George's continuing quest for the meaning of the bird images in the script and their possible connection with the Clarendon family. Towards the end of December Jourdain wrote to George from St Hugh's College that she had received 'what purported to be a message for you the other night. It was . . . "three winged *birds*, hence the woman." ' Recalling that St Peter's in the East, a church of Queen's College, had as its arms three winged birds, she volunteered to search the register for possible entries.[19] Perhaps because of this, she was sympathetic to Grace's friend Gwynne Younghughes, who had organized a table-turning circle in the college; sent for by the principal, who informed the startled student that she was aware of what was happening as her aura had changed dangerously, Gwynne gave up the table-turning. But her sisters think that, influenced by George and Willy, Gwynne may also have attended some séances.[20]

There were other reasons for Gwynne Younghughes's entry into the Yeats circle. A sensitive young poet, she had captured the attention of George's brother Harold when he visited Grace. Soon they were engaged, although the marriage was delayed until Gwynne completed her degree—to Harold's relief, although she came close, she did not get the first everybody expected of her—and he was ordained. A possible attraction in addition to his wealth and good looks was that Harold was still an active member of the Stella Matutina; while to him Gwynne, a penurious clergyman's daughter, was 'the first truly good person he had ever met'. Giving up both the idea of a teaching career and poetry, she was a loyal, devoted wife until her death just days after Nelly Tucker's. Although unlike her new sister-in-law without any financial or clothes sense, she was adored by her husband. She did have the Younghughes temper, however, and her own sisters always assumed that was how she managed her husband; once in a rage with Harold she threatened to break a valuable vase—and did.[21] Willy considered as a wedding gift the Stratford Shakespeare, which 'might mitigate certain theological asperities', but Harold's bigotry would simply increase with age.[22]

Willy meanwhile was having his own family worries. Pressured by Quinn, who was tiring of responsibility for the elderly artist, he urged his father to return to Ireland. He and George paid off all JBY's debts—which was probably a mistake, for it encouraged further guilt-free delay—and guaranteed a first-class passage home. They may also have felt that an American tour would be more pleasant if it was not encumbered by a father's interests and a friend's disapproval. But still the old man refused to leave New York. Meanwhile, counselled by Ameritus, plans for Japan were quietly shelved; happily settled in Oxford, George at least was having second thoughts.[23] But the idea of a visit to India was left open, surfacing in Willy more than a decade later.

Despite their increased social life, work continued on the system. On the evening before they left Ballylee Ameritus' last recorded words on the four faculties, employed by the soul as it rounds the Great Wheel of incarnations, had been 'There is so much more to be got on this.'[24] Now, once the Broad Street house had been ceremoniously cleansed ('never write in a strange house without first using incense'), he returned with further instructions: they were to go back to Ireland after the American tour; the invitation to Japan 'was produced by us to break lack of lure'. Evidently not only George understood Willy's need for continual intellectual stimulation. They were also to get in touch with members of the Order, after first protecting the medium from an erratic Miss Stoddart by water. Furthermore, as the script had so often belaboured without too much success, there was to be no more talk of the past; they were to preserve 'The silence of the grave'.[25]

Influenced by her belief in astrology, George was always conscious of anniversary dates, regularly observing her father's birth and death;[26] as usual she cast a progressed horoscope for 16 October. The script went even further, by a series of diagrams using both her birthdates (the 16th and 17th) as reminders of their union. Evidently, after the move to Oxford and several weeks of silence, Ameritus was having difficulty finding the right language ('I dont know what you call the thing [space] I cant get at it by words') and resorted to demands for 'a crystal for me to see in', perhaps made out of a birthday gift recently sent to George. He was also disturbed by Willy's demand for 'veryfication' about their past lives: 'I dont like you misdoubting script as it upset the communication Much better not ask for facts.' The entire week was 'muddled'; 'water images' were required. It seems that they were all missing Ballylee.[27] Finally on 23 October he brought in rein-forcements to 'continue the script for a while'. El Bahir demanded precision, there was too much vagueness in Willy's thought and questions: 'meandering over your dreams—*make a complete* statement & not 15 dozen questions . . . either abandon forever or finish forever . . . No speech about it—if you wish script at same time as search you take confidence away.' He in his turn felt the need for support, suggesting that it was time to call again on Anne Hyde.[28] El Bahir was not much pleasanter the following day, 24 October, although he did acknowledge its significance by suggesting they compare today's horoscope with that of two years ago, when George first attempted automatic writing.

In the weeks that followed, while they pursued the significance of thought transference and continued their analysis of the twenty-eight phases of the Great Wheel (now expanded to include historical events as well as phases of personal-ity), George also required additional support. For the first time she fell back on an old séance device, the book test. Instructions to find the 'fourth volume on the right' led Willy to the first volume of Frazer's *The Golden Bough*, where on page 25 there was a note on the 'hair of Berenice'. Impressed, George later wrote a note: 'On looking up page 25 of Vol 1 Magic art we find many pages of offering of hair to God or Godess [*sic*]—pages *cut* but book 2nd hand—WBY no memory of having read & I no memory of ever having opened or seen book.' Ameritus then recalled the '*Two horsed chariot*' of 'the *original* system', Horton's black horse.[29] The script seemed to be circling in.

Work also continued at the Bodleian, where George went almost daily to check seventeenth-century ephemerides, almanacks, predictions, and prognostications by Crooke, Llull, and others. Instructed by Ameritus to 'look up Rochester papers', she once again studied the papers and biographies of Henry and Edward Hyde and the entire Clarendon family, casting her net as far as Joachim's proph-ecies, Burke's history of extinct peerages, and the records of the Oxford Ladies' Archaeological and Brass-rubbing Society. It was probably a relief when they went to London for a few days at the end of October to arrange for their passports, meet with Lady Gregory, and dine with friends at the popular Mont Blanc Restaurant in Gerrard Street, conveniently close to George's club.[30]

Anne, in the charge of a competent nurse, was flourishing. George wrote regular bulletins to Lily: 'our Baby is splendid and sits up alone and tries to stand, she weighs 17 lbs 12 oz and puts on 8 oz a week.'[31] Now, a week after their return from London, Nelly paid a visit to see her grandchild and probably take a look at Gwynne Younghughes. George and Willy were amused that she had 'comprom-ised with the grandmother so far as to permit herself grey hair instead of the snow white it was a week ago'.[32] (She continued until old age to use as an addi-tional hairpiece a lock of the original auburn colour.) George was dismayed at the thought of her mother's arrival to the extent that Ameritus instructed Willy to make 'tower *symbol* over her'.[33] Nelly Tucker's visit was not a success. 'I will not write with unbelievers in the house atmosphere,' Ameritus grumpily stated after her arrival, and again insisted on protective symbols over 'Venus' and Anne.[34] Willy watched with interest this renewed contest between mother and daughter, so reminiscent of Nelly's battle of wills with her own mother. 'Ann is well and growing in mirth,' he told Gregory. 'She does not get on with her grandmother & howled when ever she came near. She never behaved to anybody else in this way. It is curious because in the months before her birth George had a strong feeling against her mother, who on her side regretted Annes arrival. It is rather tragic now & when Mrs Tucker went away she said "some grandmothers would cry." She had been very nice & brought toys.[35] Another visitor (unidentified) was even less welcome, perhaps because he reminded George of her father's unsavoury past: 'I strongly object to that Lees man—don't go near him again,' Ameritus sternly commanded before one question and answer session began.[36]

They were also trying their hand at matchmaking. As early as December 1917 a mysterious 'Isabella—of the Rose' had promised in mirror writing that there would soon be 'a marriage ring' on Iseult's hand, but so far nothing of the sort had materialized.[37] But Lennox Robinson had fallen in love with her, and Willy wrote to Iseult advising her to reconsider her rejection. Lily and Lolly were soon involved, inviting both Lennox and Iseult out to supper at Gurteen Dhas, but Lily remained doubtful: 'I can't tell from her anything of her thoughts, she is charming—has very little self confidence, is indolent and something of a charming humbug—enormously tall and rather gaunt—like Maud says little but looks much—she hates politics and her mother's political friends—so cant be very happy—her position is too uncomfortable.'[38]

With all these activities and company, their own relationship was becoming less ardent, so much so that throughout November Ameritus complained of lack of 'creative force'. There followed another open discussion concerning their sexual activity, with Willy slightly on the defensive:

[Willy] There were about 3 months before Anne was coming when [Sun] in [Moon] was impossible & yet there was script
[Ameritus] Depends on subject—in the present complex script it would be impossible because the sex element is a part of the matter—There was no sex element in last Nov Dec Jan Feb Script . . . Mediumship in this case arises because of certain sexual emotions—When those lack there is no mediumship . . . both the desire of the medium and her desire for your desire should be satisfied . . . there cannot be intellectual desire (not intellectual interests) without sexual & emotional satisfaction—therefore without intellectual desire there is no force or truth especially truth because truth is intensity

Ameritus insisted that in their case the obligation for regular intercourse is 'largely horoscopic'. Willy finally got the point: 'it cannot be complete for one &

not for the other because neither can be deceived about the other.'[39] Incense and the Tarot were recommended; they were also encouraged to take regular breaks during the script sessions for discussion, reading over, and analysing before proceeding. This not only gave George as 'Interpreter' a rest (Ameritus had to remind Willy again she was no longer 'medium'), but allowed them to orchestrate the questions.[40] Diagrams in the script continued to invoke images of the tower, while Willy covered pages of notes on the phases of the Moon and their relationship to personality and the history of both the soul and the world. An article on his new form of 'drawing room' drama speaks of 'those moments of revelation which are as a flash of lightning'.[41]

He was also openly referring to their psychic experiences in his poetry. 'An Image from a Past Life', written just before they left Ballylee, has its origin in their belief in reincarnation and one of George's vivid and revealing nightmares: a lover from a previous life hovers, taking possession of the man's mind without his being conscious of it, thereby shattering the woman's recently won peace and confidence. When 'He' offers fumbling attempts at reassurance, 'She' is not comforted. The poem also draws directly upon George's script where three classes of dream images are described: those coming directly from spiritual memory, those from one's personal Anima Mundi, and those between sleeping and waking which come from personal memory. The imagery describing 'the hovering thing' 'loosen[ing] out a tress | Among the starry eddies of her hair | Upon the paleness of a finger' seems more reminiscent of Olivia Shakespear than of Maud Gonne.

Only a few months later Willy wrote another confessional poem, 'Under Saturn', this time drawing on his own dreams as well as their astrological knowledge. Asking forgiveness for his gloomy mood, the speaker once again attempts to reassure the woman in the poem that he does not pine for the lost love of his youth, but rather for kin and country, lamenting his vain vow as a child 'Never to leave that valley his fathers called their home':

> Do not because this day I have grown saturnine
> Imagine that lost love, inseparable from my thought
> Because I have no other youth, can make me pine;
> For how should I forget the wisdom that you brought,
> The comfort that you made? . . .

Although happy in their Oxford nest, the thoughts of both were turning over and over again towards Ireland.

Their studies focused on the revelations of George's script, but commitment had not been withdrawn from the Stella Matutina. Miss Stoddart was continuing to call on them for advice for her research into the origin of the Order of the Golden Dawn, and George was also still very much involved in administering examinations. Her cousin by marriage Beatrice Erskine was preparing to enter the Inner Order and needed to pass the 5=6 tests. More significantly, Stoddart was lobbying to have Yeats appointed the new Chief of the Stella Matutina; there is no indication of how 'Demon' and 'Nemo' reacted to this proposal, but in any event Dr Felkin, fearing Willy's propensity to gossip, rejected the idea. Sometime while at Oxford 'Georgie Yeats' was being urged to apply to the 'Golden Rule No.1 Lodge of Antient Masonry', sponsored by the Grand Matron Marion L. Halsey, who was also a member of the Stella Matutina. Since George's unsigned application remains in their Golden Dawn papers, apparently the matter was not pursued.[42]

Plans for the trip to America were now settled, and George arranged for the rental of their house—at £4 10s. a week—to an Oxford professor, who, they felt, 'would know how to care for it'. 'I hear we shall always be able to let it,' Willy assured Lady Gregory. As always they were torn between the desire for new adventure and enjoyment of their present comfort: 'We are sad leaving this house, which is now such a house as I love—all harmonious and serene, nothing looking expensive or too cheap but a dignified natural house for intellectual people.'[43] And it was a wrench for George to part from her baby girl once again. However, by 30 December Anne and the servants were on their way to Ireland where the aunts eagerly awaited their charge, and George and Willy spent the week next door in the Cranston Hotel while they prepared the house for its new tenant.[44] In a gesture of confidence that they would return, they bought each other the complete works of William Morris in twenty-four volumes. Willy's Christmas gift to George was a bracelet, symbol of 'Daimonic concordance between two people'; Dionertes suggested he also 'do a marriage invocation over one of the interpreters rings'. And once again their commanding spirit insisted that 'You must always now *refuse* any script which refers to your past present or future relations.'[45] George's supportive guide Apple joined them during their last few days in Oxford. On the last day of 1919 Willy wrote to John Quinn how 'very excited' his wife was 'at the thought of America & many people, having been practically alone with me since our marriage, every evening in my study helping me at my work'. He added, 'I think Japan has faded. My own work has grown more engrossing and Europe less unendurable.'[46] One adventure at a time was enough.

Their actual date of departure was still uncertain, for the American steamship line was plagued by strikes. While waiting in London George cast a horary 'for sailing of Carmania, *say* 6 p.m. January 13 1920 Liverpool', which promised to be full of incident:

Should be a good journey on the whole. Weather inclined to warm drizzle with intervals of sunshine. There may be a violent storm beginning about one p.m. on Wednesday 14th, which will be at its height when moon reaches Scorpio 18 degrees that is to say about 5 a.m. Thursday morning when the moon will also be parallel Uranus & Jupiter. Some one on the boat may have an accident, break an arm or a rib on January 20th when there will be another storm & many people will fall down owing to movement of boat.

Interestingly, she signed her forecast 'GHL'; perhaps the prospect of the new world and yet another of Willy's relatives was making her more insecure than she acknowledged.[47] However, although the journey on the SS *Carmania* was, as predicted, pleasant, what incidents there were might be described as more socially disturbing than physically harmful. George had an amusing time with a group of nice young men on deck, and then when they all came down to dinner wearing clerical collars was mortified by what she might have said. Especially clothes conscious at this time in her life, she had purchased a new dress in her favourite colour, but after all the Americans on board commented on her 'cleverness' in choosing an Irish green, she could never wear it again.[48] Their arrival in New York on Saturday, 24 January 1920, was greeted by the flashing bulbs of newspaper reporters, yet another reminder of her public role as wife of the famous Irish poet.

It was inevitable that they should stay at the Algonquin Hotel, already famous as the haven of artists and writers. As soon as they were settled in George telephoned her father-in-law, who in turn called John Quinn; JBY may also have been nervous at this first meeting with his son's wife. Quinn immediately drove to the Algonquin and escorted the Yeatses to the four-storey brownstone lodging house at 317 West 29th Street where John Butler Yeats awaited them, smartly turned out in a suit (provided as usual by Quinn) but, to his patron's consternation, wearing 'some sort of dancing slippers'. The old artist eyed his daughter-in-law warily; after only a moment's hesitation, George stepped forward and kissed him. Quinn then tactfully left the three Yeatses together.[49] It would be some time before George and JBY were entirely comfortable with each other; after worrying only half-humorously that 'probably she thinks me a sort of hobgoblin with great teeth & that I devour daughters-in-law', he was today faced with the reality.[50] 'Willie with a wife will be as great a surprise as Willie with an income,' he had once predicted.[51] Now his lucky son had both (though he would always assume they had more money than they did).

The next day Quinn invited all three to dinner and the afternoon at his apartment, crammed with paintings, books, and manuscripts, on fashionable Central Park West. JBY wore the new coat purchased for him by Quinn for the occasion. The talk ranged widely, and George made an immediate impact; both men at once forwarded their impressions to Lily. Later Quinn, enjoying his self-appointed role as stage manager, described the scene to Ezra Pound: 'Yeats seemed to be devoted to her, and she seems to be interested in and devoted to Yeats. And the old man beamed upon both of them and was evidently pleased and delighted with the wife.'[52] When Quinn discovered her passion for music he advised her on the operas she might attend, recommending the Metropolitan's 'beautifully staged' production of *Oberon* rather than the Chicago Company's *Rip van Winkle*, and he generously offered to arrange for tickets the following Friday.

He was also relieved that the plans for Japan were off, having earlier predicted that the poet 'would be a fish out of water' and within two months would have committed 'murder or bigamy or suicide'.[53]

Meanwhile the artist father-in-law was perceptively observing George, who pleased him 'very much'. On their first meeting he realized 'She looked at me so searchingly that I said to myself that I was under observation. But no, she was really wanting to find out what I thought of her.' After pleading for descriptions, photographs, and even portraits for more than two years, he was delighted to find her 'pretty & distinguished looking—& very merry', 'good looking & but for a drawn look in her mouth would be very good looking'. And he was finally reconciled to the age difference: 'They look very well. The disparity of years is not apparent to the superficial eye.' He was also impressed by her knowledge of four languages; nor did it hurt that his new daughter-in-law 'is descended from several Earls—So that our family descent from King Bryan Boroo (see Peerage) seems quite small.'[54] A week later he confided to his brother Isaac, 'I like her, I think, very much, but am cautious, as *I think she is with me*. We have not yet tested each other, although we are both of us quite frank. But *liking needs time*.'[55] It was not long before they had taken each other's measure, and approved.

That first week was a crowded one. The next day, 29 January, Willy was the guest of honour at the annual dinner of the Poetry Society of America. While her husband was lionized George watched and listened to the guests, later annotating her programme, the sharpest observations restricted to the women. Of all the women she met, she later decided that only the charming and beautiful poet and journalist Jeanne Robert Foster, seated at Table Twenty-One with JBY, could hold her own as an interesting, sensitive conversationalist.[56] It was as a writer for the *American Review of Reviews* that Mrs Foster had first heard of the elderly artist, whose conversation 'was the best to be heard this side of Dublin'.[57] They soon became friends and she and George would meet frequently in the company of John Quinn, to whom JBY had introduced her with lasting results. A former student of William James and ardent follower of Hindu teachings, a friend of poets and artists, like the younger George Jeanne Robert Foster had a reputation for putting the needs of others ahead of her own, and although an outspoken feminist and socialist in her political essays, she too was content to serve. George did not realize that she was also a poet, but would not have cared for the sentimentality revealed in her writing. Nor did she know that they also shared a belief in reincarnation.[58]

Laurence Housman was also at the head table that evening, but sadly George was not seated near the man whom she had so admired as a child.[59] Instead she suffered through the evening next to Robert Haven Schauffler, whom she pronounced 'an awful bore'; later his novelist wife Margaret Widdemer —'a dreadful woman'—thought her husband 'got on all right with Mrs Yeats. It seems that she did fluent automatic writing . . . Robert could do it too.' Widdemer sat beside Willy, who silenced her within seconds by announcing gloomily, 'I never talk when I have to speak at a dinner.'[60] George reserved her wittiest appraisal for another guest, copying out Max Beerbohm's lines, 'I love to think of Lady Speyer, Climbing ever higher and higher.'[61] Then and later she would dismiss most of the women she met in New York as boring social climbers, tartly observing of her father-in-law's patron the wealthy Julia Ford, when they later attended one of her 'At Homes' in Rye, that her hostess's breath smelt of whiskey. Delighted at this indication of 'the salt of malice', he wrote to Lily, 'In these prohibition days there are men who would kiss any woman for the sake of that smell, though George thinks that Mrs Ford even with that addition would not tempt anyone.' No doubt with a certain secret satisfaction she declared she was becoming 'sick of her own name', as the magic words 'Mrs William Butler Yeats' were uttered in Mrs Ford's 'shrill strident voice'.[62]

To George's surprise John Quinn did not attend the Poetry Society dinner, although the busy lawyer was already devoting a great deal of the week to the man he considered his best friend and his new wife, to whom he had taken an immediate liking. They again spent the following evening with him, rounding out the week at the opera. Willy then departed for the first leg of his lecture tour to Toronto, Montreal, and Vassar, returning to New York by 12 February. George accompanied him to Yale, where she was presented with a reprint by the Elizabethan Club,[63] and then on to Washington. All she remembered of their one night in Washington was that she was 'politely asked not to *smoke* in the public rooms'.[64] It was probably on one of these occasions that a woman leaned across the dinner table and said, 'You are Georgie Hyde Lees aren't you? I was at school with you,' at which George, whose childhood memories were not the happiest, panicked and claimed she had never been to school.[65] A happier moment occurred either here or in Chicago when Vachel Lindsay recited from his poem on the Congo and all the black serving staff stopped and took up a rhythmic hand-clapping until he finished.[66] There were other visiting poets on tour—although the gentle John Drinkwater's readings were popular, his wife had blotted her copybook, complaining to George, 'How do you manage with the nuisance of American hospitality so lavishly thrust upon you. I find *rudeness* the only method by which to meet it.'[67] George would find the second Mrs Drinkwater much more pleasant when they met in Dublin many years later.[68]

New York in the early 1920s was vibrant, energetic, and prosperous. George especially liked the tall skyscrapers reaching above Manhattan. But while Willy was away George saw very little of the city itself, remaining snugly at the Algonquin or trudging the eighteen blocks through the snow almost daily to visit her new father at the lodging house and its restaurant run by the dour French Petitpas sisters. Passing through the open kitchen to reach the small dining room on the lower floor, she would dine with Father and his circle, who gathered there as much for the talk as the food. When she did go out, it was usually in his company to a society hostess's luncheon party or 'At Home', where she reacted as unfavourably as she had to Mrs Ford. She was happiest talking with JBY's friends over the Petitpas' table on West 29th Street. Soon however she was sitting for a portrait, a situation allowing the old artist to draw conclusions as well as likeness. He enjoyed sketching George; as usual, feeling he had not captured her charm, he was not satisfied with the result although the sitter was pleased.[69] 'She has an aquiline nose, rosy cheeks, the sanguine temperament, hopeful and eager to please, loving,' but at first he had thought that 'There are no vast depths in her, but endless kindness and sympathy and . . . a lot of practical talent.'[70] In retrospect he would fondly believe her 'scanty words' betrayed 'an acuteness so profound there that it is genius'.[71] She was, he decided, 'shrewd and sympathetic and just'.[72] Her practical skills and 'business instinct' impressed him first, as he watched her manage the train schedules and telephone (neither he nor Willy could), organize her husband's life smoothly and efficiently, even look up quotations and make notes for his lectures so that the poet 'has only to lecture and make himself agreeable in conversation'. He noted approvingly that George watched her husband's diet carefully; when he returned from a lecture a glass of fresh milk was ready for him. Under George's careful supervision Willy now weighed fourteen stone, but was 'very nervous' in the streets.[73] As JBY grew to know George better he decided that she was 'very likable, gay and affectionate and very friendly, and very popular with every one. . . . she likes to be kind to people, even though she is laughing at them and bored by them. And she is easily *bored.*' Lily would later complain of the same fault in her sister-in-law, but their father acknowledged that Willy too could become easily bored, 'because he hates to be asked to be interested in small matters which don't appeal to his imagination'. George, evidently, was not to be allowed the same latitude. However, he readily believed Lolly's earlier comment that 'you don't find out how nice she is till she has lived in the house with you'.[74]

To her the old artist was 'a man of overpowering personality',[75] and she found herself speaking more openly than usual about her family, her interests, and her aspirations. She confessed that although not quite 'cottoning' to Lady Gregory, she appreciated her good qualities. And she regretted that Cottie did not go on with portrait painting.[76] They probably also compared notes about their experience at Heatherley's; certainly it provided a bond beyond family ties. Did she suspect that all was then shared with his correspondents? As they grew to know each other better, they confided in each other. He admitted that he had only loved two women in his life—his wife Susan Pollexfen and Rosa Butt, with whom he still affectionately corresponded (Lily later told George she believed the second attachment had remained platonic).[77] She in turn confessed her loneliness for baby Anne, and how torn she was between returning to her daughter and leaving Willy to fend for himself. 'George seems always thinking of Ballylee or of Anne,' Willy had admitted to Gregory. 'One night I heard her saying something in her sleep—it was hush a by baby in the tree top. A week ago I thought she would go home—Anne had not been gaining weight and then came a letter to say Anne had gained so many ounces.'[78] Impressed by her loyalty, his father was amused by how well she handled her husband: 'She can always conquer him by pretending not to sympathize with what he is telling her. She has merely to remain silent while he talks, she says. He will change the subject and do everything to get her to reply to him and be interested. After this has gone on for a while she ends it by bursting out laughing. I think they are well mated.' When she confessed the Hyde family dreaded secret, that 'her father, grandfather, and greatgrandfather all died of drink', he decided that she had enough self-control not to fall into the same trap.

Perhaps most of all JBY appreciated her frankness and directness, and, as he watched her converse at dinner in the Petipas' French restaurant, was proud to be seen with such a good-looking and well-dressed daughter-in-law. 'She is very popular, and has democratic manners, though in herself I fancy a good deal of an aristocrat,' he noted shrewdly.[79] But, suspecting that 'in her heart she despises all the Americans, but she never shows it', he regretted that she had met only the social climbers and not his own closest associates. On the one occasion when he did attempt a private meeting with two intimate friends, Professor Frans Bellinger and his novelist wife (who had been responsible for collecting and seeing through the press a volume of JBY's essays), Willy collapsed just as they were sitting down to tea—he was allergic to the clam broth he had eaten at lunch. The disaster was multiplied by their taxi getting stuck in the snow as they attempted to get back to a doctor at the hotel, but after spending the next day in bed Willy had recovered and both, his father was relieved to find, were 'merry as birds'.[80]

This was their last weekend in New York before embarking on the extensive part of the tour, and the indefatigable Quinn had managed to cram in one more appointment, a dinner interview with the two newly appointed editors of the *Dial*. George phoned to cancel and after the dinner—where Quinn persuaded the editors to appoint Pound their European representative—he appeared at the hotel to find Willy stretched out on the bed wearing a long, cassock-like light blue nightgown open at the front. 'His wife should have propped pillows up behind him,' Quinn thought, but the patient seemed not to mind his uncomfortable position. He also noticed that during the hours he was there George smoked three or four cigarettes to Quinn's three cigars. Either now or the next day, when the discussion continued, Quinn brought with him as note-taker Jeanne Foster, experienced as editor and reporter. Aware of his audience, Willy at one stage exclaimed during the lengthy meeting, 'You ought to marry the youngest girl of your acquaintance and come to Oxford and take a house and live there.' George may have been flattered, but one wonders about Foster's reaction.

On Monday evening, 23 February, Quinn accompanied them to the railway station as they departed for their journey westward, noting with some disapproval that they were travelling in a stateroom: 'Nobody but presidents travel in staterooms these days. . . . After you leave Chicago I think you would be quite comfortable in a berth, your wife taking the upper.'[81] Evidently the aristocratic nature her father-in-law had noted for once had taken over from George's practical streak. The tour, arranged by the J. B. Pond Lyceum Bureau, took them on a circuitous route to Oberlin, then Chicago (where George again stayed behind at the Auditorium Hotel while Willy took a side trip to Pittsburgh), through Utah, Oregon, and down the coast of California, then eastward again through Texas, Missouri, and Louisiana, northward to Ohio and eventually on 30 April back to New York, then on to Boston and Wellesley. The journey was eventful in more ways than one: by the time they reached Santa Barbara they learned that the Pond Agency was close to bankruptcy.[82] To Quinn's chagrin, Pond had persuaded them to take a young man as courier as far as Portland, an additional expense that his friend calculated cost them between $800 and $1,000. From Pittsburgh Willy had written optimistically, if naively, to Coole: 'We are travelling in much comfort as one of Ponds men wanted to get to Oregon, where we go in middle of March as his mother was sick so we are paying his expenses & he is booking our railway seats & looking after our hotel bills etc. In spite of all the expense & the high rate of living (this room costs 6 dollars a night) I hope to bring home more money than ever before.'[83]

Chicago was exciting and bustling: in the train compartment even before they arrived both noticed the scent of violets that 'seemed to flow from Georges head & shoulders'—connected with the tower symbol, this was always a comforting signal.[84] They managed to slip in a visit to a clairvoyant between Willy's scheduled lectures, and then on 3 March were entertained at a banquet organized by the founder of *Poetry* magazine, Harriet Monroe (who had thoughtfully greeted them at their hotel with a half-pint flask of prohibited liquid). Willy was openly disapproving of prohibition, announcing in an interview, 'but prohibition's hell, isn't it?', and elaborating on his view of the phenomenon: 'Prohibition, I believe, is the direct outcome of woman suffrage. After women become more accustomed to political freedom they will seek less reform. They will become constructive. I understand they are even going to bar cigarets in this country.'[85] It would be interesting to know whether George agreed with her husband's conservative views about women, but this may have been where they locked a bottle of their own in the hotel cabinet, then lost the key and had to appeal to the negro attendant for assistance.[86] They lunched with Mary and Padraic Colum and St John Ervine, who was also on a lecture tour; a guest later recalled George as 'an energetic, auburn-haired, efficient-looking little woman . . . an adequate balance of practicality in a marriage where there was so much ethereality'.[87] He might have changed his tune had he followed George one day when, passing a bookshop, she 'heard a voice say "fourth shelf from window third from floor, seventh book". . . . went in & bought the book so pointed out. It was Freud, "Totemism" [*Totem and Taboo*] which answered a question she had been bothered over—her three birds.'[88]

Leaving Chicago on 10 March, they stopped in Utah, where the Mormon 'doctrine of continuous inspiration' intrigued them; they too had experienced miraculous intervention.[89] On 19 March they finally relieved themselves of the extra expenses of Pond's courier. Later Willy confided to Lady Gregory the full extent of the young man's perfidy: 'Pond, who has made many mistakes is in difficulties so I am as far as possible drawing all money myself. I hope to return with about £500 & should have had rather more but for a very expensive young man sent round with us by Pond—this private—who has kept no accounts & could not even recollect what money he collected & was always abusing Pond & warning us against him.'[90] By then, Quinn was authorized to collect all Willy's fees; in Texas alone these amounted to $944.[91]

The evening they arrived in Portland Willy lectured in the Masonic Temple to the Drama League on 'The Theatre of the People'; a young Japanese student was in the audience. So impressed was Junzo Sato that he paid a ceremonial visit to the Yeatses the following day. As he himself later recalled the incident, their discussion 'so exceeded my expectations that I decided to reciprocate the poet's friendliness and understanding by presenting him with something which I treasured very highly.' He returned the next day with one of the three swords he treasured most. Forged 600 years earlier by Bishu Motoshige, Motoshige the Second, of Osafune in the province of Bizon, it was wrapped in an embroidered silken cloth 'made from one of the garments worn in feudal times by ladies of the Daimyos'.[92] Instead of journeying to Japan, Japan had come to them; that the presentation of such a treasure took place at the spring equinox could only intensify the experience. Embarrassed by this munificent gesture, after consultation with George Willy finally accepted the sword on condition that he will it back to Sato's family.[93] (In the event, it remained with Michael Yeats.) After refusing to perform, except for two unsatisfactory attempts since they left England, Dionertes resurfaced that evening, delighted with the conversation and even more by the sword. 'You have got to begin to write soon | life should be a ritual', he pronounced, and, in upside down writing, suggested December 1920 as the ideal time for conception of the new avatar. His astrological prediction was not far off; their son would be born in August 1921. A few days later while supervising the Tarot method, their communicator explained, 'We wanted an eastern symbolically incarnation . . . the Sword is the daimon.'[94]

Although Dionertes continued to expound on matters as various as the avatar, politics, and how sounds and sensations are recorded 'in a strata between your world & ours',[95] he announced on 29 March, in Pasadena, that he did not 'really want script here—I prefer to use other methods—sleeps—I have given you three opportunities lately and you have not taken any of them.'[96] George was to speak while asleep, Willy then taking notes; apart from a few sporadic attempts over the years by Dionertes and others to communicate, this effectively brought an end to the automatic writing.

Dream-speaking had been suggested before as a means less tiring for George than automatic writing. As early as 9 November 1918 Thomas had warned them that 'this method of communication will not go on very long'; in January 1919 he announced that 'You are to develop a new method', but after several weeks they had still not had any success:

I will come late tonight & *talk not write* | in dark | I will make myself heard—heard—go on | I am going to try a new method—talking—an experiment less tiring for medium as no nervous force wasted—last night I tried but needs two consciousnesses dovetaled [*sic*] into each other . . . two distinct individual consciousnesses—this is as well as script to be used for the more difficult parts . . . Whichever first sees or hears me calls the other or sees or hears Rose | Bed is easier because the body is relaxed & all the senses are free[97]

By December 1919 they had been employing the 'trance' or 'mesmeric' method more frequently, but 'only at certain *lunar* periods', to call up visions which 'make a link between the conscious & the subconscious that the subconscious should not be repressed'. The method involved Willy putting George into a deep sleep, suggesting a dream of the sea or a still lake ('like using a fire tatwa after a water one') and that her 'will is to become active in 30 minutes'. 'When she speaks you will know the sleep has changed' and it was time for questioning. Although Willy was an experienced hypnotist, finding the correct depth was difficult; visualization—a method frequently employed by the Golden Dawn—was also necessary. And he was warned that he 'must never use hypnotism without our permission as if you use it without you entangle your personalities but with our permission we give the force & you merely the symbol'.[98] George (having obviously re-examined the notebooks) later informed Ellmann that exposition in sleep ended in 1920. Willy wrote in early April 1920 that 'All communication by external means—sleaps [*sic*]—whistles—voices—renounced, as too exausting [*sic*] for George. . . . Philosophy is now coming in a new way. I am getting it in sleep & when half awake, & George has correspondential dreams or visions.'[99] However, this decision was premature, for 'philosophical sleeps' continued on a fairly regular basis during their tour—they became adept in such communications on train journeys[100]—and for the next two years, then tapering off; but George occasionally fell into a trance, apparently self-induced, as late as 1933.[101]

Later Yeats would describe his impression of the voice—or voices—he heard while George was in trance:

My teachers did not seem to speak out of her sleep but as if from above it, as though it were a tide upon which they floated. A chance word spoken before she fell asleep would some-times start a dream that broke in upon the communications, as if from below, to trouble or overwhelm, as when she dreamed she was a cat lapping milk or a cat curled up asleep and therefore dumb. The cat returned night after night, and once when I tried to drive it away by making the sound one makes when playing at being a dog to amuse a child, she awoke trembling, and the shock was so violent that I never dared repeat it.[102]

Evidently, just as the Yeatses' real cats had disturbed their Communicators during earlier sessions of the automatic script, now the tables were turned. Sometimes also they were alerted by whistles, pipe notes, or other sounds. There is no suggestion that they considered these communications the same as the 'direct voice' messages familiar to the séance room of Etta Wriedt and other mediums; it is probable that George was in a genuine state of trance as she had been for most of the automatic script sessions. However, by now they were accus-tomed, both singly and together, to slipping easily from alert discussion into meditations on the system; the entries in their notebooks, in either hand, record alternately what they remember of dreams, visions, dream-speaking, and occa-sionally automatic writing. Sometimes these communications are elaborations of the system, other times corrections or refinements of previous discussions or of Willy's writing, for he was now committed to an account of this new description of reality he and George had developed from her script. Finally, in July 1922, all such methods would cease on a regular basis, mediumship was discouraged, and they sought further elucidation by such 'positive means' as research and discussion.[103] By then the outline of their philosophy had been typed and—with George's reluctant permission—Willy was well embarked on what would become A Vision. However, their spirits did not ever entirely desert them, and in addition they both continued to visit other mediums.

But in the spring of 1920, as their train swung through the south and west, they invoked colours and other means to induce 'sleep talk'. Once in Pasadena George 'sees herself dead', surrounded by many other 'sleapers' who had not yet achieved the state of spirits, shades, or ghosts. The lengthy discussion which pro-ceeded from this, the first of a series, would find its way not only into A Vision, but into Yeats's poetry and drama.[104] But it also led back to the case of Anne Hyde and another book test. In New Orleans other more personal experiences disturbed George's calm: 'Before waking second time she thought noises of shunting trains were bombs.'[105] Whether because of the frequent dream sessions or relief that the tour was nearing an end, both seem to have made an impression in New Orleans. When Lennox Robinson lectured there eight years later, he wrote to George,

'I have met charming people here whose one question is "when is Mr Yeats coming back?" I have to say "Probably never" and they say "Tell him we shall never forget his beautiful reading". And they are quite genuine people. And they remember you—but you puzzled them, you were so different—so I burst out and say "Can you imagine *two* W. B. Ys going around?" and they admit they can't, and I tell them you're just as queer (or queerer) in your way as he is in his.'[106] When they returned to New York so did Dionertes, to warn Willy against 'abstractions & hatred'; he was to 'avoid reading abstract qualities into George . . . because they would destroy her spontaneity. Because system was abstract & deliberate our lives must be happy spontaneous full of impulse.'[107]

To anyone who met her, there was no question that, apart from missing her daughter, George was happy. As JBY once wrote after receiving a particularly entertaining letter from her, 'Balzac says that happiness is a woman's poetry— when happy she is poetry.'[108] The tour had been a financial success and £100 had already been sent back so that work might begin on the coloured slates for the Ballylee roof.[109] In addition George had seen her husband acknowledged as the leading poet of the age. Together in the west they had enjoyed interesting company and new scenery. Willy sent a postcard to Lady Gregory from 'this lovely place', the Hotel Maryland in Pasadena: 'We are in a bungalow connected with the hotel—the hotel is not one building but a beautiful village. We walk to our meals through the garden in the post-card—birds all a little different from our birds . . . a sort of sparrow . . . sing & chirp continually & in the evening the grasshoppers make a great noise.'[110] Now on their return to New York there was time to relax before sailing for home. Willy finished reading all of Jane Austen, while George saw more of New York; at least its architecture delighted her.[111]

They were also faced with Quinn's insistence that they persuade Father Yeats to return to Ireland. He meanwhile, fretting because 'No 2 Daughter in law' was not, like the rest of his family, a letter-writer (two telegrams had been sent by George but not the epistles he attempted to elicit),[112] tried to persuade them to stay until summer; it had been a cold, late spring in the east. But after five days in Quinn's apartment, they were off again, this time to Boston and then Wellesley College for the weekend. George's 'roofer' to the principal was a model of courtesy, but it reflected her longing for home:

We have to thank *you* for the very delightful three days we spent at Wellesley. They were a great rest and we brought away a memory which will always be a pleasure to look back upon. My husband is sending, under separate cover, the book which contains the cat and hare poems. It seemed to him the only thing of his you had not already in your collection, and so was the only book he could think of. And I, alas, have nothing to offer in gratitude and thanks, but as a writer's printed work is the thing it gives him most pleasure to send as an offering, so I send a snapshot of my daughter who is as much my most precious thing, as a writer's work is to him! She is holding a fish which I sent her from Chicago! We are always at 4 Broad St. Oxford from October 1 to May 1 and so if you are ever there during those months I hope you will give us the great pleasure of a visit.[113]

It may have been at Wellesley that they heard someone announce with proud but disconcerting arithmetic, '50 per cent of our girls get married and 60 per cent have babies'.[114]

They returned to a few days at the Algonquin Hotel, then went for the remaining two weeks to Quinn's luxurious Central Park apartment. Distressed that they had not spent their entire time with him, their friend industriously set about organizing their lives. Willy was suffering from rheumatism, so was carried off to a specialist and for X-rays, which revealed nothing more serious than tonsilitis.[115] One night Quinn himself had a sore throat; George calmly took charge, prescribing remedies to his Japanese valet and countermanding her host's orders for the usual early morning call. All held their breath at her temerity, 'for Quinn is a terrible bully in his own apartment'.[116] But Quinn liked George, was impressed by her practical nursing experience, and was doubtless heartened by Ezra's comment that 'Mrs. Y. approves of you, but of very little else save the architecture'.[117] Aware of Ezra and George's friendship, he presented her with a copy of Pound's *Instigations*, just published under his auspices, 'To Mrs W. B. Yeats with the kind regards of John Quinn 58 Central Park West New York May 5, 1920'.[118] Later Pound would write of Willy's American tour, '*I* shall reap the full profit in G's account of the migration.'[119] He would bear no grudge that an invitation from his mother in Philadelphia had to be rejected.[120]

George thought John Quinn the most 'groomed' man she had ever met; he even once persuaded Willy to join him when he had his weekly manicure.[121] 'For once Quinn liked a friend's wife,' JBY exulted. 'He mostly hates them. He told me that she is always "*calm*", which she is, because she has a sense of fact. When he or Willie get excited or vehement about anything, she waits till she knows the facts, and that was like a little douche of cold water which cooled the situation.'[122] 'They are very pleasant people with each other and everybody else,' he noted. And he himself enjoyed the attention: 'Last night I was sitting all alone—every other table with its guests, but mine empty—and as the dinner had proceeded somewhat I was resigned to seeing nobody to exchange a word with, when in entered Willie and George, and we had a real talk. No mysteries this time. It was a domestic and friendly and personal atmosphere, and not a thin air in which a fellow can hardly breathe. At 9 o'clock they rose and departed and I could not keep them.' He was lonely without them, but memories of his time with George, and her pleasure at his portrait of her, sustained him. George, not unaware of the values of tipping, may also have been responsible for the change he observed in the attitude of the Petitpases, who became 'smiling and friendly'.[123] She always referred to JBY's portrait of her as the 'Roman matron'.[124]

It was while in Quinn's apartment that Yeats came in close contact with one of his friend's most enduring enthusiasms, works of the Romanian pioneer of abstract sculpture Constantin Brancusi, but he did not like them. George later described how he went through their rooms 'turning all the Brancusis over, or face down, on sofas and cushions'. 'All those ovoids—those smooth, curved surfaces, and rounded figures, with their egg-shaped heads—seemed to put him off. He called them "featureless".' She insisted to Donald Pearce that WBY's reference to Brancusi in *A Vision* ('stylistic arrangements of experience comparable to the cubes in the drawing of Wyndham Lewis and to the ovoids in the sculpture of Brancusi') 'is made with a certain amount of humor, you see— which you earnest Americans never seem to catch!'[125]

Quinn played his own trick on the pair. One day when George and Willy arrived, Jeanne Foster was about to leave. Doubtless for propriety's sake as well as mischief, Quinn pushed her into a closet adjoining the Yeatses' rooms. Within hearing but not sight, she heard what she later described as 'a lively discussion' concerning a second child. She thought George insistent, Willy reluctant. So impressed was she by this unintentional eavesdropping, she related the story a number of times to biographers and—many years later—to 'the heir' himself, Michael Yeats and his eldest daughter.[126] It would not be surprising if she had inadvertently stumbled on one of their astrological sessions, or even a script or trance sitting; there were 'sleeps' on 14 and 15 May, and two scripts are dated 16 and 17 May. Certainly by then for both Willy and George the decision was not *whether*, but *when*, to have their second child.

Hospitable as ever and obviously reluctant to say goodbye, Quinn entertained lavishly. There were small dinner parties—at one his former mistress Dorothy Coates was also a guest; since she had been the mischievous cause of a previous rift between Quinn and Yeats (by claiming that Willy had attempted to seduce her), George was less than cordial.[127] Miss Coates's replacement, Jeanne Foster, was in favour with all of them. At one large dinner party another guest was the American sculptor Gutzon Borglum, now known for his giant heads of Lincoln and the presidential façade of Mount Rushmore; he made a stir by denouncing Americans for not having suffered enough during the war.[128] Willy was filmed for posterity, his first experience of talking pictures, and Quinn took him off to hear de Valera.[129] On 26 May, after a dinner in the apartment, he and Quinn jointly signed a presentation copy of *Responsibilities and Other Poems* to the French performer Yvette Gilbert; no doubt on that occasion George wisely stayed behind in Central Park West.[130]

But one wish of Quinn's was destined to remain unfulfilled. John Butler Yeats would not agree to return to Ireland, pleading the necessity to complete Quinn's commission of a self-portrait. In vain, much embarrassed by the heavy responsibility on a busy lawyer's shoulders, George and Willy tried to persuade the frail, elderly man to book his passage. They promised a studio in Dublin, and George volunteered to meet him at Liverpool and bring him first to Oxford to meet his grandchild.[131] Still he refused, explaining defensively to Rosa Butt that if he went home he 'would have to bid farewell to painting and be just an old man in his second childhood. He and she said they only wanted me to do what I liked to do, but said he would get me a studio in Dundrum if I liked. But for my illness I have not cost them very much, earning money myself.'[132] This incurable optimism was further encouraged by Willy unwisely guaranteeing his expenses; he refused to accept the fact that his eldest son and his wife were not now rich.[133] Later in exasperation Willy would equally defensively blame his father's dithering on 'infirmity of will', 'which has prevented him from finishing his pictures and ruined his career. He even hates the sign of will in others. It used to cause quarrels between me and him, for the qualities which I thought necessary to success in art or in life seemed to him "egotism" or "selfishness" or brutality. I had to escape this family drifting.'[134]

But George knew, as soon as she met him, that her father-in-law would never return. In New York JBY had freedom, an appreciative audience, and the space to dream. In Dublin, the reality of his failure would have always been before him. As she explained later, 'he was free in New York to give his clothes away, eat when he chose, sleep when he chose, come and go as he liked'.[135] She was not the only one who had noticed; Mary Colum had been a frequent visitor to the Petitpas boarding house:

In Dublin . . . J. B.'s wardrobe was supervised by his daughters so that he always presented a handsome, well-groomed appearance. Here in New York he felt freer to wear anything that was handy, and his occasionally ravelled collars and shirt cuffs, and his much darned woolen gloves mended anew every winter by Mlle. Petitpas would have shocked his daughters and his carefully garbed poet son. Here J. B. also felt freer to choose his friends, and much as he loved and admired his family he seemed pleased to be at a distance from all domestic bonds.[136]

JBY did, however, allow them to take the manuscript of his *Early Memories*. And although admitting to George that 'The sight of you and Willy has generated a longing to return to Ireland—I part from you with much reluctance,' part with them he did.[137] From then until his death less than two years later, a constant bombardment of letters would continue to keep the dream alive.

Drawing upon the Texas lecture fees, Quinn had arranged for their passage on the White Star Line's SS *Megantic* (room 80 on the 'Shelter Deck'), due to sail from Montreal on 22 May; their first-class passage cost $515.[138] George cast a horary for their journey: 'As far as *we* are concerned, with Mars on my Sun & Mercury Saturn on my Moon Venus I should say I am bound to be very seasick Moon Venus being in Scorpio & Pisces Neptune which affects digestion. WBY

Fig. 3. John Butler Yeats's last recollection of George and Willy in New York, included in a letter to his family of 24 May 1920.

will probably have one bad day (Thursday) & will be very inclined to active forms of Saturn—forbodings & nightmare. We shall probably survive the evening of Friday 23rd but this may be the landing of passengers or food at Halifax.'[139] The ship was delayed for a week; hoping to escape the American tax of 8 per cent on their earnings, they crossed the border into Canada at 4.30 in the morning of 28 May. They seem to have been successful in this ruse, but in their haste to depart forgot to return a key to the apartment, and to pack one of George's bracelets.[140] In Montreal that evening they celebrated their arrival at the Windsor Hotel with both automatic script and a 'sleap'.

Once on board and turned towards home, they concentrated on the system with a series of sessions. On the 30th, Dionertes dictated a summary of the details of the departing spirits that had been accumulating in George's visions. 'I need a ritual of burial. If there is no ritual I am longer in the grave for the thoughts of those on whom I am dependent are not focussed upon me. The ritual is a discipline of thought, and intensifies thought. The flowers set on my grave are the only light I see. It is through these flowers that I am first able to enter into the thoughts of the living to discover my own identity—until I have found that I may not leave my body.'[141] She would have cause to honour these directions in another country almost two decades later.

Everyone sent assessments of the visit. Willy's final report to Coole was triumphant: 'I shall have made enough to do nearly all structural work at Ballylee—roof, floor etc. I have had however to do more work for every £100 than before for hotel & railway rates are enormous. . . . I am not tired thanks to George & shall come back eager for work.'[142] The journey to America had accomplished more than the money for Ballylee—JBY had met his daughter-in-law and was happy in Willy's stability. As important, friendship with Quinn was confirmed. After they had left he sent on a number of letters and the bracelet his housemaid Marie had found in George's bed:

It was a genuine pleasure to have you and your wife at my apartment during those few days. I hope some time in the next one or two years that I may see both of you at Ballylee. I feel the attraction of the place for you and I was glad to know that your wife shared your liking for it. I enclose with this three letters that have come in my care, one for you and Mrs Yeats, one for her from abroad, and one for you. . . . When you wrote me about your marriage, I wrote to you telling you that I was certain it would be a happy marriage because you were a lucky man. That was before I met your wife. Then I felt sure it would be happy, but that was based upon my belief in your good fortune, in your good luck. Now, I know that your good luck came true. . . . The number of new real friends seems to grow fewer each year. But it is a real satisfaction to me to feel that your wife and I have become good friends.[143]

George too was pleased, her report to Dundrum as usual relayed back to New York: 'She wanted you to like her and she wanted John Quinn to like her. You liked her at once and John Quinn liked her in the end in spite of her being his friend's wife.'[144]

But most of all, she was glad to be home.

11
MICHAEL

Even before they left New York George and Willy were planning the return to Ballylee. But stories of cattle-driving and land seizures were disturbing, controlled though they were in many areas by the courts set up by the nationalist Dáil as an alternative to the British government's judiciary.[1] From Quinn's apartment Willy wrote anxiously to Lady Gregory,

In the disturbed state of Ireland will it be right to bring Anne to Ballylee? Has there been much cattle driving? & if so is it enough to endanger the supply of milk? The papers here give a very alarming account & at Ballylee we are dependent on Fahy's cows & Fahy has enemies. . . . If Ballylee is unwise for Anne we will give our tenants at Oxford notice—we can resume possession on July 1. George and I would go to Ballylee for a short time to see how the work has gone leaving Anne in Dublin & then fetch Anne to Oxford. We shall be sorry.[2]

The reply was encouraging: there was no milk shortage nor cattle-driving in the district, and their arrival with American news was eagerly awaited.[3]

While Willy stayed on in London to consult his publishers, George went immediately to Dublin; she had been away from her daughter for twenty-four weeks. According to Lily, the reunion was tentative: 'George arrived in Dublin last night at the Hibernian Hotel and I handed back her daughter to her, she was very shy, smiled but would not go to her—held tight to my collar but went on smiling, she never sends anyone away with a sore heart. George thought her greatly grown and very well. . . . I am half ashamed of myself I miss Baby so much.' Scrupulous as always in dealing with Willy's sisters, George entertained them to lunch singly, then took Lily with her when visiting the older generation at Morehampton Road. Then Lily delivered 'very careful accounts of the change left of George's money'. The sisters—and presumably the elder Yeatses—agreed that George 'gets better looking, she is far better looking than she was when she was married'.[4]

In London they had gone first to the Gwalia Hotel just around the corner from Woburn Buildings, but while George was away Willy was staying with the Tuckers at 27 Royal Crescent. They had celebrated their return with the purchase of a set of pewter dinner plates for Oxford and a green parrot, the first of their 'caged birds'. Willy wrote to her almost immediately that the parrot 'has just given its first screech for joy . . . His cage hangs by a cord on the balcony outside the drawing room and he looks more gay than hitherto.'[5] Worrying, however, was George's news of delay over Ballylee. Mr Binns, the builder responsible for installing the new slates on the tower roof, although authorized to spend up to £400 had not yet begun work and did not reply to their urgent messages. There were more serious concerns. The Molloy sisters, who went over to make the cottages ready for habitation, received threatening letters because some time the previous winter they had gone to mass in a cart drawn by a mule owned by their neighbour Fahy, whose cows provided milk for Ballylee and 'whose land someone else wants'. Lily advised her brother to appeal to the courts established by the outlawed Dáil; she may have been slightly ironic, for Maud was one of the appointed justices. As it turned out, the threatening anonymous letter had come from the Sinn Féin Club;[6] when they finally saw the letter, Willy noticed that 'there was an ungrammatical postscript, which may mean a threat to my wife also'.[7] To complicate matters further, the railwaymen, refusing to transport British troops or supplies for military and police, were poised to go on strike. George reluctantly decided that she would have to return to London. 'Baby's chance of "life in some dear perpetual place" seems unlikely to come true,' Lily noted with more truth than she realized.[8]

While George in Dublin calculated the progression of his stars, Willy celebrated his birthday by writing a duty letter for his mother-in-law. Nelly Tucker had taken to playwriting, adapting George Meredith's comedy of social class *Evan Harrington*. The subject is interesting, for Evan comes from a family of tailors; was Nelly influenced by her own family background, which had risen from trade to landowning? Willy managed to write an adroit letter of introduction to the Irish playwright and manager James B. Fagan without actually recommending the play itself, beyond suggesting that it had a part 'that might suit Mrs Patrick Campbell', who was then performing in Shaw's *Pygmalion*. Fully aware that his Dublin theatre was prohibited by patent from producing non-Irish plays, he continued, 'I know little of the London stage and nothing of the general merit of the plays sent to London managers probably in great abundance. However if this play were sent to me for the Abbey Theatre I would accept & think its author had a future.'[9]

George returned with Anne from Dublin the next day, and they moved into the Pounds' 'very small and unclean little flat' at 5 Holland Place Chambers, vacant while Dorothy and Ezra were in Italy. Pronouncing the space unsatisfactory for her baby girl (and in any case too small), while the nurse went on holiday George arranged for Anne to be cared for in 'a horribly expensive house where all the babies are guaranteed born in wedlock'. From there George took her into

Kensington Gardens every day—when not struggling with the chaos of the flat.[10] The gesture did not go unnoticed in Ireland; rumour immediately reached Lady Gregory that they had put their child in an orphanage. Perhaps remembering that she herself had left her two-month-old son behind when Sir William took her first to the Continent and then on an extended trip to Egypt, Gregory held her peace.[11] With this additional stress, George again began to suffer from nightmares, which continued for some time. These had begun while she was in Ireland, associated in her mind with Willy in London—Ameritus had warned them he would suffer from psychic interference should they be apart for as much as a week.[12] Concerned about his wife's health and forgoing his customary round of visits, to distract her Willy took her to see Philip Moeller's *Madame Sand* at the Duke of York Theatre—'bad enough to be amusing, and is pleasant to look at'.[13] To 'break the nightmares' their Instructors counselled a week with neither script nor 'sleeps'; concerning Willy's understanding of the system, 'all is sufficiently correct and there is no need to rewrite the whole'. However, instruction in George's sleep continued intermittently with Ameritus cross when George really *was* in a natural state of sleep and beyond his call.[14]

Willy was anxious to introduce George to more of his London friends, describing her to one as 'a scholar in several languages but young and nothing of a pedant'.[15] They dined with the Dulacs, and may also have seen Miss Stoddart, who was still campaigning to install Willy as Ruling Chief of the Order. However rumour had reached Australia that 'he or his wife have been talking too freely in America about the Order and its present troubles', and so Felkin awarded the dubious honour instead to Dr William Hammond, in charge of the Freemasons' Library, who was not any happier about his limited authority.[16] In any case, the Order had been temporarily suspended and there were no equinox ceremonies this year. A more welcome surprise was their meeting with Rabindranath Tagore, back in England with his son and daughter-in-law, with whom they spent a pleasant evening nearby at William Rothenstein's studio. At Willy's request Tagore sang some *Gitanjali* songs and Jelly d'Aranyi played 'piece after piece, as she declared she had never played before'. Unable to see them again before leaving England, Tagore sent George a piece of old Indian silk 'as homage'.[17]

By the end of June no trains were running to Galway and they reluctantly postponed the return to Ballylee until September; even that was uncertain, for there was still no response from Binns or Rafferty. Again news came indirectly, this time from Anne's nurse, who had heard from Delia and Mary Anne Molloy that 'the workmen who were to have begun work at Ballylee two weeks ago, cannot begin for another month'.[18] Furthermore, Scott's foreman was unhappy about the condition, number, and colour of the expensive slates (purchased on the advice of the architect Edwin Lutyens and approved by Scott). 'I am spending almost the whole of my American money on Ballylee straight off; but it will mean an efficient home where we can have a guest,' Willy had written to Lady Gregory. But he and the builder were both overly optimistic: the slates were finally declared unsuitable for Galway's high winds, and the 'stranger's room' was never completed. Anxious as always to be of service, Lady Gregory collared Rafferty, who confirmed the state of affairs.[19] They moved to Oxford on 12 July; the Molloy sisters, whose mother was looking after Pangur, again joined them from Gort.

Despite disappointment over Ballylee, they were delighted to reclaim their Oxford house. 'It is a great joy to be in this house again after so many journeys,' Willy wrote to Coole, '& it looks very solemn & dignified to our eyes wearied by many irrelevant things. . . . It is not "arty" to use the new word; there is no undue mark of present taste; all looks I think as if it had some history behind it & yet there is unity. I have many little pictures by my father, & by various members of the family, you have never seen; & all our furniture, or nearly all, is old & so suited to the 17th century house.'[20] Willy concentrated on writing about the script while George settled in; 'through lack of momentum' there were few successful 'sleeps' for several weeks. Instead they shared vivid dreams of a beautiful young man; the heir, 'J.B.', was much on their minds.[21] Lily was invited to visit, her fare paid; she had not been in England since 1916. Lolly, who saw her off on the Saturday mailboat, was shocked to see the pier 'festooned with rusty barbed wire' and guarded by so many young armed soldiers.[22] Anne meanwhile had come down with chickenpox, probably contracted in the 'horribly expensive home' in London.

But Willy would have no time that summer to luxuriate in his familial Oxford surroundings. Even before Lily arrived on 29 July, he was summoned back to Ireland, this time by Maud who had recently written to tell him the story of Iseult's marriage. Against her mother's wishes, on 6 April Iseult had married 18-year-old Francis ('Harry') Stuart. Doubtless Willy had been kept informed of the events, for Lady Gregory had been told of the engagement by Iseult herself in early January; then on the evening of their wedding, as the couple were on their way to London, they encountered Lennox Robinson, the rejected suitor, who had also told the Yeatses.[23] Now, however, the news was anything but promising: both Iseult and Maud had written to Willy of 'horrible family trouble' between the Stuarts. Replying to Willy's letters and telegram, Maud thanked them for 'George's idea . . . both kind & wise' of asking the pair to Oxford in order to try and influence Francis: 'He admires you greatly. . . . for Iseult it would mean peace to be with you & George.'[24] But despite Willy's advice that Iseult leave her husband unless 'some satisfactory arrangement' could be made about money, it became clear that she would do no such thing. George and Willy decided that he must go there himself; telling everyone that he was returning to consult Lady Gregory on Abbey business, he set off just minutes after his sister arrived in Oxford.[25]

Iseult had taken refuge in Maud's cottage in Glenmalure and there Yeats was horrified by what he heard from them and other witnesses: she had been deprived of food, money, and sleep and 'several times knocked down by her husband'; worse still in this desperate state, she was pregnant. As the story unfolded, details of the situation were relayed daily to Oxford and Coole Park. Willy's first plan was to install Iseult in a nursing home for a few days under the care of their friend the obstetrician Bethel Solomons, and while she was there her husband would be delivered an ultimatum to sign a financial agreement or lose his wife. Events of the past few years had been so intense for both Iseult and Willy that, surprisingly, she considered him unbiased because he had never met Stuart. Confident therefore that Iseult would listen to him far more readily than to her mother, Willy then appealed to Lady Gregory to offer safe harbour. But Coole was full of guests and children, and privacy would have been impossible; to give Gregory her due, this was not simply an excuse, for she had herself tried to contact Iseult earlier that spring without success. Eventually a refuge for Iseult and her mother was found elsewhere, but in the meantime, Willy turned to George (who had seen Stuart once while in Dublin)—would she invite the young man, for whom Iseult claimed 'charm & certain gifts of poetical phantasy', to Oxford, where he might have some influence? To Lady Gregory he spoke of Iseult's insistence on excusing Stuart, adding 'thus spake Griselda'. Grimly he recalled his own lines written during the happy summer of 1918, 'Alas "the horn's sweet note and the tooth of the hound." '[26] Having made what arrangements he could, now there was nothing to do but wait; he was anxious to get home to Oxford, to a settled routine, and, most of all, to his wife.

George's first reaction was to cast a horary—'e infelice per amore d'ella, e come se finire questa dolore?'—which was accurate enough:

one side of the affair, i.e. 'X' does not wish to separate but yet is willing to play with the idea and will in all probability lead the ambassador to believe that she is in agreement with him. There seems deception and entanglements of all kinds Mars in seventh house probably represents young man who appears to have control of situation . . . delusion and false idealism. The person in question will make no definite decision but probably will return to husband

Her letter to Willy (the first to survive) once again displays the mixture of sensibility and pragmatism that would carry them through the various crises in their emotional life together: 'No settlement can be very satisfactory that is made *after* marriage & you should be very careful to go to the best possible lawyer about it. I hope negociations [*sic*] will fall through & that she will not return to him. It will be far better. Sadism in so young a man is incurable. Is she in great despair about the child? My thought is so much more for you than for her, because the spectator suffers more poignantly than the victim.' As to her own 'goodness' in letting him go to Iseult's assistance—'that was really nothing but the forseeing that you would have found it difficult to forgive me had I dissuaded you.

If you cannot do much, at least you can do something.' However, she was finding Lily's 'chatter' and desire for small talk 'maddening', especially since there were a number of visitors '& I do not know whether having to adjust one's thought to their needs is more a distraction or a worry'. The Meads were staying overnight and there were so many things she wished to discuss with them; in addition to details from the script, doubtless she would have wanted to hear about her old mentor's most recent publication, which was on astral projection and out-of-body experiences.[27]

The next day she warned Willy to keep his visit to Dr Solomons a secret, for Lily was becoming increasingly curious about his absence. Iseult's horoscope suggested that, if not 'a false alarm', the child would not live—yet another accurate prediction. But her letter also brought sad news of her own miscarriage, 'another six weeks mishap', which she carefully concealed from Lily. Apparently Willy had heard the cry of a banshee; the heir's arrival was to be once more delayed.

Willy was writing to her every day, Lily noted. His next crossed with George's, and was 'so great a relief' that it caused her, unaware, to weep 'as sometimes after the Dionertian sleep'. She was longing 'for a mind that has "bite" . . . I am too dependent on you—I am lost when you are away.' But she also recognized his dependency on her: 'Remember to take your ticket to Paddington & label your box Paddington, as otherwise it goes via Crewe & gets lost on the way.' Willy's letter had acknowledged, perhaps for the first time to her, although regularly affirmed by the script and broadcast by him to all and sundry, how well mated he and George were: 'I give you my word of honour that to my own surprise I have suffered little. I have had bad hours, but they are nothing compared to the even serenity that rather shocks me. The truth is that so much has happened since that time in Normandy that though I admire Iseults subtle thought I have no contact with her mind.'[28]

The next day brought further confirmation. 'After this little time away, after this necessary service, I shall return to you more completely yours than ever before. Is it not enough to say that through this week of painful discoveries, but for a few hours, mainly at the start, I have been tranquil, even happy, even gay. That strange first morning, when Robinson smelt the violets, seemed to make me see all objectively.'[29] 'The caged bird' could feel secure at last. Years later, when Oliver Edwards had the temerity to ask her whether she minded being so described, she merely laughed.[30]

George's reply was bound to turn his mind towards less mundane matters:

Some strange things have happened here. Lily feels a hand every night either pressing against her pillow or even stroking her head & one night the hand pulled her hair over her face! Then nurse came to me last night (Saturday) & said she had found a bill dated 1865 to a Miss Bonham 'in the press'. That is, in the lower part of my father's bureau. It was lying on top of Anne's clothes! I investigated this morning & found about a dozen more, dates 1855 to '83. All stuffed in a small space between the desk (which pulls out like a drawer) & the boards, a space of at the most 1¹/₄ inches in height & about 3 feet in length. It is *inconceivable* how they got there & how, if there since those dates they were not found before. I have used that bureau ever since 1908 & my father had used it to my certain knowledge for 18 years before that & probably longer. I remember him using it ever since *I can* remember. An apport? *And why?* . . . the letters *cannot* have slipped out of the desk part or got in to the crevasse [*sic*] in any normal way. I had great difficulty in getting them out as only one finger would go in.

At the time of discovery both Nurse and Lily had smelt incense near the nursery door, close by the bureau. More intriguing still, the crest on the Bonham stationery was 'either a unicorn's or a stag's head rising out of a stumpy tower & a long tail with *arrow* and issuing out of the door of the tower!' As if these details were not enough to turn them back to their psychic explorations, George—who since receiving Willy's letter had slept peacefully with 'the strangest feeling of liberation & of all calamity passed'—heard a voice saying, 'Let the 3rd element begin its operation, for now Jupiter has no antagonists.' Once again, their emblems and desires—tower, unicorn, arrow, and heir—were circling in. George rejected Willy's plea to go over at once to Dublin to be examined by Dr Solomons; she wanted him home—and if he did go to Coole, could he not bring Pangur, still with the Molloy family?[31]

But Willy did not go west. At George's suggestion they met in London on 12 August, where through one of her 'sleaps' they consulted Dionertes about Willy's adventures in Dublin, the crested stationery found in George's bureau, and the sentence she had overheard. Francis Stuart was deemed to belong to phase 14 (the same as Iseult), but was not homicidal. Again many of the references were astrological: the tower represented Mars, the stag Venus, the conjunctions that had led to so many of George's 'initiatory moments' to do with WBY. 'Jupiter is 3rd element. First was Neptune, second Saturn. It would begin with conception of a child.' Dionertes preferred 13 August (if not tired) for conception, or later when the moon was full; clearly Jupiter was still an essential aspect of the heir's daimon—as it turned out he was born the following August. Once again, Willy was warned not to speak of their 'method of communication'. A few days later Tagore was elevated to the rare status of a fourth daimon personality, 'free from frustration . . . self moving'. [32] It would be some time before 'the Bonham papers' were discussed; evidently, according to their Instructors, Miss Bonham 'was in need of help', but they showed no further interest, recommending that the problem be turned over to Bessie Radcliffe. Nor, apparently, did the Yeatses pursue the matter further; they may have decided that the letters, no matter how they were discovered, were secreted in the desk long before it came into the possession of Gilbert Hyde Lees.[33]

The 'sleeps' continued, again intermittently. George smelt incense and returned briefly to automatic writing, producing a drawing of a tower, flying birds, flowering trees, a mask, and a unicorn's horn—the tower, obviously evoking Ballylee, was circled by water and had flowers at its base. They were still making plans for their return to the castle; Willy asked Lady Gregory how much they should pay James Molloy for taking care of George's garden at Ballylee. Surprisingly, she 'had not an idea'.[34] They bought two canaries to keep the parrot company, and Olivia sent a nest.

Lily finally left on 21 August; 'like a migrating bird that has found rest for a moment on some island of the blest', she had reported every detail of her visit to New York, and doubtless also to Dundrum.[35] Number 4 Broad Street was 'a delightful old house—full of mellow colour and light'. She even took pleasure in the snatches of Catholic hymns she heard Delia and Mary Anne singing; they sounded 'pretty and foreign' in the dark, rainy English evenings. Lily loved having her breakfast and the newspaper brought on a tray each morning; 'I am like the heroine of a penny novel with nothing to do but rest and see other people busy—but I do go out and knit pretty coats for Baby and write a few letters.'[36] Her greatest joy was of course Anne, 'splendid, a real character, & very big';[37] now staggering about with feet wide apart; she was just beginning to talk and take notice of the activities outside her nursery window. Her brother took Lily on visits to Robert Bridges and other old friends, while George, pleading Nurse's day off, stayed home with the baby. Lily had dismissed the Meads as 'a pair of cranks'; when Lady Ottoline Morrell appeared, her bright red shoes eliciting from Anne her surprised question ('Who is that?'), Lily was determined not to be too impressed by either visitor or niece, deciding that Anne 'may have meant it as something quite different'.[38]

They were, Willy wrote to Gregory, 'beginning to make friends here as well as to see something of various people passing through. Lady Ottoline often comes and we go to her next week.'[39] George and Ottoline compared notes on their reading: Ottoline gave her Eliot's volume of essays, *The Sacred Wood*;[40] George confessed she was 'a little disappointed in the Tchekov letters. Too much abstraction & too little passion.'[41] She always took care to make her own letters entertaining. By now sufficiently relaxed with Ottoline Morrell to gossip about other celebrities in the neighbourhood, she ended one letter with 'Mrs Masefield has just departed & has left us such bad headaches!' Both stylishly minded, neither woman would have appreciated Constance Masefield's 'extraordinary shapeless garments and strange hats, which made her look quite uncouth', any more than they could accept her dry, humourless manner.[42] To Quinn Willy described the discomfiture created on one occasion over Constance's daughter Judith, who was 'not allowed to know us because we might talk astrology, or magic, or say something unclassifiably wicked. She was sent out when we were expected to tea and by a stroke of providential irony landed in the society of Lady

Ottoline Morrell, who is still more disapproved, being suspected of being always unclassifiably wicked.'[43] On this second visit to Garsington, the weekend of 4 September, they discussed astrology—George later cast the horoscopes of both Ottoline and her daughter Julian—and Willy, still searching about for a house of refuge for Iseult, confided enough of her story to prompt an invitation to Garsington. Ottoline had also enjoyed their company and, interested to know the results of George's astrological calculations, promised to visit them 'very soon'.[44] She would become a regular visitor, not only to their Sunday 'At Homes' but dropping by when she drove in to Oxford. An entranced undergraduate vividly recalled one such occasion:

A little phaeton with two beautifully groomed horses was drawn up . . . with a man in a great fur coat and a 'high-low' hat at the reins. A groom in a blue tailed coat with britches and a cockaded top hat stood holding the horses. A door opened and two remarkable figures came out. . . . Lady Ottoline Morrell, . . . a tall wraithlike creature fantastically costumed in clothes suggesting some bygone period of aristocratic grandeur, the other was William Butler Yeats in dim coloured tweeds and a large knotted black silk tie, hatless, his long greying hair blown by the wind. Lady Ottoline paused, took the poet's arm and descended the curved steps to the pavement. Yeats, bowing low, kissed her hand and helped her into the seat beside the driver, her husband Philip Morrell.[45]

Buoyed by the stimulation of Garsington and life in Oxford with George, Willy wrote gaily to Quinn suggesting he rent Ottoline Morrell's house for six months for £100 (with servants and gardener): 'I would not have dared on my own responsibility to make *you* so masterly a suggestion but my wife is the source of the mischief & she is a witch & sees into the future which makes me confident that if you dont do it, you will have missed your true destiny.' George, to whom he was dictating, added in parentheses, 'Dont you believe this! George Yeats.'[46]

Even Dionertes grew more relaxed. One night he requested silence that he might listen to the cry of an owl, and later enjoyed the striking of the clocks at midnight. 'When the last strike was finished he said "Sounds like that are sometimes a great pleasure to us".'[47] But George's dreams were not always so pleasant—readily suggestible, her mouth filled with feathers at the mention of Maud (the 'speckled bird'); another time, Titania-like, she dreamed Willy had the ears of a donkey; frequently she herself was a cat. Even the spirits were animalistic: 'In sleep Dionertes said they took cat form by day owl form by night, when acting in connection with daimon. Always animal or bird for daimon.'[48] Towards the end of September there was an intriguing intervention, apparently introduced by Dionertes; 'the Lunar group' made an appearance, shortly followed by 'the Solar group'. The Lunar group, also called 'the Poseidon group', came for three nights and, although they discussed some aspects of the philosophy, were primarily concerned about the birth of a child. Poseidon, brother of Zeus and

Hades and father of Pegasus, was a reminder also of that 'intriguer Neptune' who had caused problems with their union. (George may have also been recalling Leonore Piper's 'Imperator group' which so impressed William James.) When 'the Solar group' spoke through Dionertes they recommended meditation (with the customary colour symbolism) 'for 5 minutes between 2 & 3 p.m. on the subject of "the Heir" & to do this lying on our backs. We were to attend to the secondary images that arose from the first idea.' George saw a tiger on a desert island (Mars in Saturn), Willy an elephant (Saturn in Mars). George later told him that she had that very morning purchased 'a little Indian tiger & elephant'. The two 'groups' never returned; evidently Dionertes had no further need of them, although the terms 'coven' (later changed to 'Dragon') and 'unicorn' were introduced to distinguish between a 'group' and the 'group mind'.[49]

By then Dionertes had departed and was replaced by Alastor—who was accompanied occasionally by Apple when George required assistance on personal matters (such as the loss of an earring), and the crusty Carmichael. Quite a different character, Carmichael was curious about their modern bath and disapproved of their new cat, Harry, who insisted upon washing himself as he lay between them ('Washing, washing, more washing & swallowing all the dirt').[50] Whether Harry was named after George's stepfather gentle Harry Tucker, we will probably never know. For months George continued to dream that she was a cat, and this sometimes led to difficulties when Willy attempted to break the spell by pretending to be a dog. In early October 'the Heir' was identified as 'Black Eagle', reminiscent of the nickname Dorothy and Ezra had given Willy so many years before. His mission was 'to change the quality of the idea of time in men's minds'; the system was attempting to do the same thing. However, now when George spoke in her sleep it was 'in her own character, hearing Alastors words spoken to her'.[51] Perhaps some of the power was running out that autumn; George's energies were concentrating more and more on the future.

There was still no word from Iseult. Willy had sent a long letter relating her situation to their astrological studies, using the vocabulary of the system:

There are 'Initiatory moments' of great importance to a life, perhaps decid[ing] its whole future. I was told some time ago that we were going through one & I knew it to be one of a type that begins with Venus and Saturn in conjunction and ends with Venus & Neptune in conjunction. I have looked up your dates. When you accepted Francis, Venus & Saturn were in conjunction & when you decided to go to the Nursing Home Venus & Neptune were in conjunction. This should mean that the worst is over and as the object of all such moments is to compel a too subjective nature into objective action & in the case of your phase into action implying practical expedience & prudence. . . . it gives you some guidance also. To you it may mean the start of a new & stronger life. Take this too as certain, no fool, no person without a possible future of spiritual importance has ever had an 'initiatory moment'.[52]

At last he received a response. Alone and back in her flat in Dublin, Iseult reported that the situation with Francis, who was with his mother in the north, was still not settled; but she refused to entertain the idea of a financial settlement. If her husband did not join her in Dublin within the next five days, she would go to her aunt in London for a few weeks and seek work for the sake of her child, due in March. As for visiting Lady Ottoline, that was out of the question; nobody but Willy and George was to know of her affairs. Loyal, heart-broken Lennox was doing everything he could to help place her writing; people in Dublin who tried to sympathize drove her 'wild' and caused her to snub them. But what Willy had written of the initiatory moments was 'a great stimulus'. As always, she sent her love to George.[53]

George was meanwhile also casting horoscopes for Willy. Should he go to Dublin where Gogarty would remove his tonsils, or follow Quinn's advice and have the operation done in London? Willy went to consult a Harley Street surgeon, could not find the address, and returned to Oxford. Finally, after first advising delay, George's stars ('Venus, with all her ribbons floating, poised upon the mid-heaven!') recommended Gogarty.[54] There were other worries about making the journey across the Irish Sea—a coal strike in England might prevent them from returning to Anne, left in the care of Nurse and the control Apple. (Anne now had 'eleven teeth and can say eleven words', Lily was informed.[55]) Willy's needs finally prevailed and they arrived in Dublin on 9 October. Almost immediately he was required at Glenmalure where Maud was once more in distress: young Seán was being drawn into the Republican maelstrom and had been arrested for driving without a military permit. George meanwhile visited her sisters-in-law in Dundrum, leading them to believe that Willy was at Sir Horace Plunkett's; at least the two houses were in the same direction.[56] On 13 October, in the Elpis Nursing Home (where Synge had died a decade earlier), Dr Gogarty removed Willy's tonsils; it was not a simple operation, for the patient haemorrhaged. 'No one could say that he had *sluggish* blood,' Gogarty commented many years later.[57] Although the condition may have been exacerbated by the patient having allowed himself 'a little brandy', as Willy aged so did his tendency to bleed easily. But that morning Gogarty was clearly concerned about his patient, visiting him at least six times and arranging for private nurses both day and night. George, accompanied by Lily, stayed on at Elpis until late in the evening when the danger was finally declared over.

Lily took the opportunity to hand over to them some of Willy's manuscripts; she had been saving them for years in 'an old oak chest', mindful that they did not disappear into 'the archives at Coole'. But she was somewhat brusquely informed that they were a disappointing cache, 'all early versions of Countess Cathleen, Mosada, etc etc, in some cases several versions, but in no case the final version— so merely interesting but not valuable. George says they ought to make Willy kind to young poets,—, some of it is so bad.'[58] It would not be long before George would learn to value such manuscripts as part of her husband's 'history'.[59] But with more immediate pressing financial needs, she may have hoped them suitable to send to Quinn. Or perhaps, so excited were they by their new philosophy, Willy's earlier work no longer interested him. Just before leaving Oxford, he had written to Ezra, 'I have just finished a long poem, 100 lines, & I think it good, at least as good as "The Prayer for my Daughter" & much the same sort of thing. It describes Horton & Mrs Emery & Macgregor.'[60] 'All Souls' Night' would take its place as an epilogue to *A Vision*. Written somewhat in advance of the festival which honoured the souls of Purgatory (2 November), the poem also celebrated their work together and the excitement George's philosophical script had brought. Although George was still against public revelation, both were by now convinced that there was 'a marvellous thing to say':

> Such thought—such thought have I that hold it tight
> Till meditation master all its parts. . . .
> Such thought, that in it bound
> I need no other thing,
> Wound in mind's wandering
> As mummies in the mummy-cloth are wound.[61]

On their arrival in Dublin they had dined with Lennox Robinson, who was to become one of George's closest friends; doubtless during the evening the discussion touched on Iseult's problems as well as theatre business. It may have been Lennox who introduced George to Dermott MacManus whom she met this year; a Mayo man greatly interested in magic and Hinduism, he would later be Willy's confidant and Tantric teacher, but now as a Trinity College student he was one more entry for George into Dublin's intellectual life.[62] After the operation by Gogarty, performed 'with his usual exuberant gaiety', they had intended to spend a few days with Lady Gregory 'to see after Ballylee which certainly needs some attention'. Binns was clearly unsatisfactory, and they had decided a caretaker was necessary to keep the rats under control.[63] However, with the threat of a railway strike and despite Willy's weakened state, instead they made a hasty retreat to get back to 'Feathers' (Anne). He left the nursing home on 17 October, and after a final visit to Maud (who again expressed gratitude for the trouble they had taken over Iseult's affairs[64]) boarded the steamer the next night. Concerned to save her husband's strength, George arranged that their journey back to Oxford took three days, with overnight stops at both Holyhead and Chester.

Unable to concentrate on work, Willy found convalescence boring. He asked Quinn for a likeness to join the other portraits in his study and confessed, 'when I am dressing in the morning I look out of the window at Anne strapped into her perambulator in the garden. I watch her twisting about trying to get into the bottom of the perambulator, with her heels up, and I say to myself, "Which is the greater bore, convalescence or infancy?" "[65] With family matters uppermost and the prospect of Ballylee as a permanent home receding, they were also considering what their future should be. 'We find that this beautiful house is to be pulled down in ten years and think of moving as soon as we can get another old house. We want Anne, before she begins to remember, to be settled in a house where she can live till maturity if not always. We both feel we have lost so much by changes of place in our childhood. We want to buy our house that our children may have it after us.'[66] However, all these additional expenditures were worrying, and he wrote to Quinn again, offering to send some manuscripts for sale and as payment for his father's accounts. 'We have reduced our expenses here to the minimum but the expense of living is very high & is still rising. All my money & George's goes to mere living expenses.'[67] Publication of his poetry in the *Dial*—before it was issued by the Cuala Press in *Michael Robartes and the Dancer*—did little to ease the ongoing financial worry, although it gained him accolades from his father ('magnificent—there is no other word for them—cut deep in marble and destined to last for ever').[68] Having worked through much of his premarital turmoil with their ghostly Instructors, he resumed writing his memoirs, for sale to the *Dial*.

There were few 'sleeps' until late November, when once again there was 'cat trouble'; but Willy doggedly persevered with their philosophical problems throughout the winter as he struggled to put all this information into some sort of order. There were also visitors who interfered with their extramundane communicators. Dorothy and Ezra, back from Italy and planning their permanent move to France, came for at least a week. Although friendly, the spirits again found Ezra's presence disruptive ('The communicator likes him but says communication impossible while he is in the house'); perhaps because he had dismissed Willy's essay 'If I Were Four-and-Twenty' as 'the worst rubbish he has ever written'.[69] Dorothy, 'looking like a little Dresden china shepherdess', stayed on after Ezra departed.[70] The following week, after she had left, Sturge Moore arrived, during which time they also entertained the Masefields. 'It is a great pleasure to see my friend really comfortable and cared for at last and no longer as one used to feel in circumstances quite unworthy of him,' Moore wrote in his letter of thanks to George. 'You have created a home which it will be nice to picture to oneself at odd moments.' But he forgot to collect the wools and silk samples sent by Lily for the long-promised cot cover—still not designed.[71]

George then invited the Dulacs to join them in Oxford after Christmas, but that visit was postponed until early January while they traced 'a mysterious, atrocious, smell' in Willy's bedroom; as George had insisted all along, it turned out to be nothing more arcane than a leaking gas stove.[72] That winter the Australian playwright Louis Esson also stayed for a night, and was entertained by 'good stories' at lunch and dinner; afterwards Willy took him into the study where he admired the family portraits on the walls and the two four-and-a-half-foot brass candlesticks flanking a blue lectern on which the Kelmscott Chaucer lay open with a gold marker.[73] Perhaps the most important object in the room, however, was the 'gilded Moorish wedding-chest' where Yeats had kept his 'barbarous words' [of invocation] and now the automatic script.[74] Like Sturge Moore, Esson heard much on the theme of 'unity of personality'.[75] Thanks to George, Willy was beginning—as he described it in the essay so ignominiously rejected by Ezra—to 'hammer his thoughts into unity', providing 'a form of philosophy' for his 'love of literature' and 'belief in nationality'.[76] (George and Willy were by now preparing to turn their attention to the phases or 'cones' of history.) Willy's 'ordered life of routine (now having lasted for many months for the first time in my life)' had, he remarked in his regular letters to Coole, made him 'exceedingly tidy. I cannot bare [sic] a paper knife crooked on my table.'[77]

They had also begun to hold Monday 'At Homes' for undergraduates only —thereby freeing Sunday for other visitors. Unlike the later gatherings in Dublin which tended to be for men only, here George was very much in evidence. 'Mrs Yeats was very often the catalyst, saying little, but filling the room with an aura of humorous perception without which Yeats could not have achieved what he did,' marked one perceptive observer.[78] Invariably there was discussion of phases and related matters, giving rise to Robert Graves's later barbed witticism: 'Undergraduate: Have you written any poems recently, sir? Yeats: No, my wife has been feeling poorly and disinclined.'[79]

In mid-December Nelly Tucker paid a visit, and fortunately this time her granddaughter was more receptive. The relieved father reported that 'Anne is well—always gay & friendly, noticing everybody & everything.'[80] On 4 January Harold, now ordained, married Gwynne Younghughes in her father's parish church in Caldicot, Wales. His sister does not seem to have gone to the wedding. But despite domestic happiness in Oxford, news was not all that satisfactory from New York. Although repeatedly urged to do so by all (except Jack), John Butler Yeats refused to come home. He preferred to converse by post, although worried about how to write to George in response to her entertaining but infrequent letters. Willy negotiated an agreement to publish his father's two Cuala books, both editions from his letters, with George making the arrangement 'in a shape like "Samuel Butler's Note Books" ', but the project never materialized. Perhaps George's reluctance to deal with correspondence was one of the reasons; however, she was not well enough that winter to tackle her father-in-law on any terms.[81]

Finally Willy, hounded by Quinn, wrote a series of missives, each one more exasperated than the last: 'Lilly & Lolly want you home, I want you home & what should be decisive John Quinn wants you home.' Another winter in New York might kill him; a studio would be his in Dublin, as well as the conviviality of the University Club; neither he nor George could afford to keep him in New York. To all these arguments the old artist serenely replied, 'I like the accounts that come floating to me about your life—I would like to see it before my eyes. People used to say to me—Don't you want to see your grandchild and I would reply that I want to see my son with his daughter all of which I think is natural. I also want to see it with its mother but about you and that new relative I am all curiosity.' Willy played his last card—if father would not go to Dublin, then son would have to make another lecture tour; meanwhile he would 'pay present expenses with some manuscripts'. But the only response was a series of letters cautioning him against another tour, especially without George even though her presence 'would lessen the profit'. Not even the financial crash in America that winter, which greatly affected Quinn, would move him.[82] George had been right all along—that hard-won liberty would be compromised by a return to Ireland. At 82, he remained obstinately convinced that his own fortune was just around the corner.

Then there was the situation in Ireland, where the clashes between Republicans and the British forces, supplemented by the hated motley-uniformed 'Black and Tans', had escalated into outright warfare. Before going to Ireland, the Yeatses had received a surprise visit from Herbert Asquith, former Prime Minister and still leader of the Liberals; they spent 'some time talking of Ireland', and a few days later Asquith wrote a letter to *The Times* urging that Ireland be given the status of an autonomous Dominion.[83] But war fever continued to mount and retaliatory raids became so brutal that Lady Gregory published a series of reports anonymously signed 'an Irish Landlord', describing 'the Black and Tan Terror' in her own neighbourhood—bleak records of threats and drunkenness, looting and robbery, assault and rape, torture and murder. The first was published on 16 October, just days before the Republican Terence MacSwiney, Mayor of Cork, died of a hunger strike; a report of the funeral ended with lines from Yeats and Lady Gregory's *Cathleen ni Houlihan*.[84] Her last account appeared on 1 January 1921, a week after the Government of Ireland Act set up a six-county parliament and administration in the north, ignoring any provision for the south.[85] Augusta Gregory's journals for these months are a litany of such stories. There were atrocities on both sides, for the police were also under siege. Reprisals became more savage and the boycotting, firings, and intimidation increased. The attack and counter-attack in Dublin of 'Bloody Sunday', 21 November, marked the nadir of violence.[86]

One image in particular haunted Yeats and his wife, safely in Oxford watching their little daughter at play. Ellen Quinn, who lived near the crossroads of Kiltartan, was killed with a child in her arms by the random shooting of troops in a passing lorry; she was pregnant. Enraged by this and other atrocities, Yeats wrote a fourth poem in memory of Robert Gregory entitled simply 'Reprisals', which he sent to Lady Gregory and to *The Times*. 'I have not asked your leave,' he wrote in his accompanying letter, 'as I think one must make what appeal one can now & at once. I think the poem is good & good for its purpose. . . . I am glad to be out of Ireland & by the ordinary mistakes of life not from any "flight".' This last comment was not designed to comfort a besieged landowner. Moreover, the poem itself deeply pained Gregory; she did not think it good or honest—after all, although never accusing him directly, she and her family were in the eye of the storm while he was comfortably in Oxford, and she could not bear 'the dragging of R[obert] from his grave to make . . . a not very sincere poem'. She also pointed out that 'it is already rather late—poor Mrs Quinn's case has been used & overused—and so has the "cheated dead" "motif" '.[87] Chastened, Willy immediately withdrew the poem from *The Times*, but her criticism—both direct and implied—stung: 'I think the poem good and wrote it, after the subject had been six weeks in my head, less because it would be a good poem than because I thought it might touch some one individual mind of a man in power.'[88] Lennox Robinson in 1926 would incorporate the horror of young Mrs Quinn's murder by the Black and Tans in his play *The Big House*; Yeats's 'Reprisals' remained unpublished until 1948.[89] His old friend's bitterness emerged in a comment to John Quinn in New York: 'His wife has money, though perhaps not so much as he was led to believe, and they live in extreme comfort and ease.'[90]

A quarrel with Lolly, which prompted him to threaten resigning as editor of her Cuala Press, provided occasion for more direct criticism from Gregory: 'when so much is being torn down one likes to keep any work going, & without you it will fizzle out & lose its good name'.[91] Marriage was combining with politics to separate the two colleagues.[92] But Yeats's determination to speak out publicly was strengthened by the exchange; from now on his and George's feelings about living outside Ireland became less ambiguous. Within months they were talking about moving permanently to Ireland, and on 17 February Willy's seven-minute speech denouncing British policy in Ireland during an Oxford Union debate made headlines.[93] He wrote to Coole with satisfaction, 'My speech at "The Union" the other night seems to have moved the audience a good deal. We carried our anti-government resolution by a large majority. I see much of the students & lecture to small groups a good deal.'[94]

Reports about Ballylee were distressing George more and more. On 21 December Lady Gregory had written, 'Your Oxford life sounds very peaceful— All chaos here still . . . The Black & Tans visited Ballylee opened the door with a key & went in & there were rumours they were going to settle there "as it has greater facilities than Drumhasna for hanging their prisoners from the bridge" but I haven't heard of their being actually in it. I don't suppose they could do it much harm.' Alarmed, Willy responded immediately. 'The castle contains £72 worth of slates & garden tyles [*sic*] & also quantities of timber & bedding & furniture. George talks of going over to find out, which I am most anxious she should not do as I don't think the journey wise for her at present—we have both been ill. . . . There must be £300 worth of our property in Ballylee apart from the new floor & roof & the building.'[95] Further details were provided by the Molloy sisters. 'George went into the kitchen to find one of our servants reading out a letter to the other, very pale & supporting her tottering body by resting on the table. "Is not this dreadful about Ballylee?" she said and read out an account from her father of how every window was broken & the mirror of glass "trodden into the linoleum" on the kitchen floor. Further all doors had been burst open & all locks stolen.'[96] Yeats, to Gregory's wry amusement, wrote enquiring as to the name of the commandant at Gort so they might send a formal complaint and demand compensation. George went to London to consult her solicitors, dropping in to Holland Chambers to say goodbye to Dorothy and Ezra on the eve of their departure for Paris. 'George just in to say that the Blackantans have tanned Ballylee,' Ezra reported laconically to Quinn.[97]

This news of Ballylee could not have come at a worse time for George, for she was at last pregnant. But despite their triumph at the promise of the heir's arrival ('we were told that there had been success & also that it was a boy as they had desired'[98]), she was having a much more difficult time with this pregnancy. She is 'constantly ill & very restless', he confided to Gregory: 'I am sometimes a little anxious. I dare not take her to Ireland till things are quiet there. I know not what shock she might get and yet she is always thinking about Ballylee. The nervous system of a psychic is terribly subject to certain kinds of strain.'[99] Since George could not have Ballylee, they talked once more of Italy. Besides, if they let the Oxford house, they might save money; but Willy was feeling beleaguered by concern for his wife, responsibility to the Abbey which required some fund-raising lectures, and the incessant drain of his father's financial needs (£4 a week for his hotel alone).

All our plans for the year depend on letting this house for half the year & living economically in the country during the summer. We propose to go to Italy, to get a small villa near Florence probably & stay away for a long time. We must go fairly soon for George is expecting another child, which can be born in Italy. (She has not even told her mother this so I suppose does not want it talked of—it certainly makes Ireland impossible). We can live cheaply in Italy, getting our servants temporary situations here. . . .

I am very anxious to get George away as soon as possible, as long as she is here she will be restless & upset about Ballylee, to which she is devoted, thinking she should go over and so on. It will be better for her child if she is surrounded with pleasant things and she has a great friend in Florence (before marriage Hellen Bailey whom you brought me to see and now the wife of a General whose name I forget). . . . I think the only desire George has ever expressed to me has been this desire to go to Italy, where she was very happy as a child, and it was growing on her even before the last news. Please do not speak of it for the present for we have not told the servants. I write it now that we may come to some understanding about the Abbey . . . I want to get George away.

Although he would never have said this to his wife, even Ballylee in its present state could be sacrificed: 'If they would only burn Ballylee I might go next winter & light a fire of my own out there & when I come back roof it with copper & panel it with oak'. But with all these expenses and his father's care he needed 'peace & routine' to finish the memoirs.[100]

His plea for advice must have seemed like old times to Augusta Gregory, especially as he wrote again the next day:

We wish to go for at least six months for we count on living cheaply during the summers and no place is as cheap as Italy just now (80 and odd lira to the £—so that you can board in Florence for £1 a week). Even if we stay away a year you must not think we are deserting Ireland. It is probably that on our return we shall decide to live altogether in Ireland and we think of Cork for our autumns and winter. If I were a richer man I might be tempted to put one leg of the compass fully in Florence and leave the other in Ballylee but as it is I must keep the legs close together.

Somewhat mollified, she assured him that, despite the Abbey's parlous state (curfews had meant great losses the previous quarter), his offer to return to lecture was unnecessary. 'Ireland is too much out of fashion for the moment to fix a time . . . so go ahead.'[101]

It was a relief when word finally came from Coole that Ballylee had not been ransacked after all. First there was cautious encouragement—the Black and Tans do not seem to have returned to Ballylee, perhaps because it was flooded at the time of their inspection—or too much publicity was attending their activities. Rafferty then reported that, according to young John Molloy, who regularly visited the castle to light fires, cupboards had been broken into but nothing taken.[102] Recovering some of his equanimity at last, Willy commented that 'Ballylee wreckage seems a fine example of "Spreading the News" ' (Gregory's most popular Kiltartan comedy):

On receipt of your news George questioned the nurse, who merely looked as if she knew all & said 'maybe those that did the damage got afraid & mended it all again'. The girls father was supposed to have seen all with his own eyes. The only thing I can think of is that Binns man went to the castle & put the timber in, & that the neighbours spread the news & that old Molloy met it on the way to Ballylee & ran home & has not been seen since. I fortunately refrained from writing to the Times. I wonder if B & Ts were ever near the place at all.[103]

Before the welcome news about Ballylee, George had consulted the stars as to their future plans: a horary the evening of 9 January posed the question, 'Journey to Italy for 7 months. Good or bad?' The Dulacs, who were present and also interested in astrology, were invited to join them in Florence, but decided against it.[104] However, the stars did not apparently alert them to another potential family catastrophe. By mid-January, shortly after her son's wedding, Nelly Tucker became seriously ill; histrionic as always, she refused institutional treatment, for that would 'merely prolong things', and went to Torquay instead. The preliminary diagnosis of consumption proved to be false, but plans for Italy had once again to be abandoned.

Before news of Nelly's mysterious illness George had already decided that she would prefer Ballylee even to Florence, and they had resolved to accept a friend's offer to take the Molloy sisters as servants for six months. As with her first pregnancy, George was restless; Willy hoped that going elsewhere would produce the same peaceful effect this time. 'She will not be content or well till she breathes some new air, here it is dull & wet. She is very happy & satisfied so far as the future is concerned & of course hopes for a son.'[105] With George still in a nervous state of anxiety, shortly after 19 January they went on a fortnight's journey to Wells and Glastonbury, then moved on to Stone Cottage for a few days.[106] For some years they had been intrigued by the experiences of Frederick Bligh Bond, director of excavations, who through a series of sittings with a medium had ascertained the foundations of a lost chapel at Glastonbury. Their journey was accompanied by scents, whistles, and, while in Ashdown Forest, 'a very serious frustration'. In Wells Cathedral George identified a 'sweet Odour' emanating from Willy's pockets first as roses, then 'like May flower'; by the time they reached Glastonbury, accepting a suggestion made by their Instructor during a 'sleep', Willy had decided the scent was that of the Glastonbury thorn. The 'sleeps' sometimes caused confusion; in his introduction to *A Vision* he would claim this was George's attribution. The Frustrator who joined them at Stone Cottage threatened to kill 'the fourth daimon', a reference to the heir or 'Black Eagle'.[107] Perhaps in an effort to allay George's fears, Willy suspected 'this may not be more than dramatic machinery'. He decided to 'stop all sleaps for the present'; their notebook records nothing further until early April when all external means were renounced as too exhausting for his pregnant wife. But the sweet odours continued to follow Willy about, and husband and wife experienced a number of interesting double and converse dreams.[108] There were also examples of 'bilocation': George saw Willy sitting at his desk when he was 'walking in the street a mile off'.[109]

George was anxious to meet F. P. Sturm, a medical doctor, poet, skilled astrologer, and amateur philosopher, who had been advising WBY on magical matters for many years. Both admired his volume of essays, *Umbrae Silentes*, and George had taken a personal interest in his poetry which they would later include in *The Oxford Book of Modern Verse*: 'My wife thinks that you would strengthen your work by being more personal, but perhaps if you did you might lose your dreams.' Willy had divulged as early as 1918 the 'Startling and I think profound thoughts which have come to me from a supernormal source'; now he was anxious to consult his learned friend about the system. When Sturm arrived on 12 February

George was in London, and while on the train back had premonitions warning against Sturm being told too much. Apparently the current Communicators ('the Pulons' and Carmichael) did not like him, feeling, with George, that he was 'too mediumistic' and 'had brought frustration'.

Unaware of the confusion he had caused, after he left the learned doctor sent 'Kindest regards to your wife, to yourself, and to charming Anne who kissed the chair and ate sugar as if it were a ritual of innocence'.[110] Obviously George, in her heightened emotional state, was not prepared to share her visionary powers even with a proven believer. She may have been right, for Sturm, 'on the track of a cosmic law' and contemplating a book on the fourteenth-century alchemist and occultist Nicholas Flamel, continued to worry the problems of gyres and the phases of the Moon, attempting to apply both rational and astrological logic to their geometry. Willy advised him to read his poems 'The Phases of the Moon' and 'The Double Vision of Michael Robartes', 'for all is there'. 'The first part of "The Double Vision" describes spirits at phase 1 and the last part is spirits at phase 15. There are also in the same book my poems on "The Hunchback" and "The Fool", the 26th and 28th phases.' Doubtless urged by George, he warned Sturm not to speak 'of what is still in MSS. I do not yet fully understand the geometry and what I wrote only a few months ago I now know to be superficial.'[111] When *A Vision* was finally published, Sturm's barrage of corrections and comments continued, although personally he thought 'your philosophy smells of the fagot. Some dead and damned Chaldean mathematikoi have got hold of your wife and are trying to revive a dead system.'[112] Undeterred, Yeats continued to consult his 'very learned doctor in the north'.[113] We do not know how George reacted, but clearly she remained jealous of making her spiritual property known to the world.

By the time they had returned to Oxford from Stone Cottage George was determined to explore the possibility of moving to Cork, despite the fires deliberately set in that city the previous November (celebrated by the Black and Tans with a bit of burned cork in their caps[114]). Although he would prefer to stay out of Ireland until the system was finished, 'It is her idea to leave this for Cork on our return,' Yeats wrote to Gregory:

I had suggested it half seriously—partly because she wants to be near Ballylee to look after it and partly because she hopes to get a house on the edge of Cork city, a town house, and yet with a garden and thinks we can economise enough by the move to have a motor which she would carry on to Ballylee and back. . . . I had proposed Oxford as a place to live in because I thought it unfair to George to live wholly in Ireland. I now find she would have preferred Ireland from the start.[115]

Lily later confirmed the misunderstanding: 'George says that she only went there [Oxford] to please W. B., and W. B. says that he only went there because he thought that it would please George.'[116]

Later Willy would facetiously claim that George had 'finally revolted against dons' wives, their hats being their principal offence'.[117] In fact both of them were beginning to tire of Oxford society, and with the drying up of the automatic writing they no longer required frequent access to the Bodleian. Also, Willy too was becoming somewhat restless; although insisting that he would always be 'somewhat solitary' because of his 'strange work', the thought of creating a new theatre movement for his Noh plays appealed. 'Willy and George are splendid for plans,' Lily wrote to her father. 'They find the people of Oxford too dull, and the house will be pulled down a year or so to widen the street—the old saying says that "Dublin was—Belfast is and Cork will be" —so they must feel this in their bones.'[118] JBY immediately advised George to take a house in the hills, if there were any.[119]

Early in February Lennox Robinson, a Corkman himself, joined them overnight so that George could consult him about houses. By early March their enthusiasm was waning, and plans for Cork gradually began to recede; they had 'almost decided to move to Cork', Willy informed Quinn, 'that being within motoring distance of Ballylee and very far from Oxford education. There are too many people here who can read and write, especially among the Dons' wives.'[120] Once again financial matters carried them forward—by late February they had let the Oxford house at £5 10s. a week for six months from 4 April; they would be able to recoup their rent and taxes while living more cheaply in the country. It took George some time to find a place for them to live, which had to be within walking distance of a Roman Catholic church for the maids. Eventually with just days to spare, they found a two-storeyed roadside cottage with a garden in Shillingford, a hamlet about fifteen miles from Oxford, and at a rent their depleted funds could spare. Willy confided his money worries to Lily: 'George and I a few months ago decided to move into a smaller house but I have done rather well this year so it may not be necessary but I am not sure. We are inexperienced in housekeeping and cannot yet calculate ahead. Of course a new child incurs expense.' JBY was also a constant yet unpredictable drain on their resources; if only he were settled in Dundrum, it would be easier to calculate expenses. Willy sent most of his remaining Sligo inheritance to Quinn and again wrote insisting his father return, though he feared 'his inability to recognize curfew'.[121] In the midst of all this uncertainty, he was trying to finish a section of his memoirs and write enough poetry for a volume for Macmillan; letters were left unopened on George's mantelpiece so that he would not be tempted 'till the day's work was finished'.[122]

But Willy's greatest concern was George, still restless and uncharacteristically shrinking from his touch, longing for Ballylee 'as if it were a human being'.[123] He dreaded Ireland for both of them, fearing another relapse if further bad news reached her; but perhaps 'she would be in better health there with even an occasional murder in the district than in this place or any other spot'. Gregory urged

Willy to come over for a week to see 'what is going on, & report to George'. Irish trains seemed to be running again.[124] By the time they had moved to the country Anne had come down with whooping cough, which to Willy 'seems a long business'—but his daughter recovered surprisingly easily, though still coughing 'when crossed—she has discovered what a fine weapon a good whoop is'.[125] George took turns with the nurse on night duty, which did not improve her nerves. Willy noticed that despite the bad news from Ireland, his wife talked 'constantly of the trees and of her garden and of the river'. Again he consulted Coole: would it be wise to take George to Ballylee? 'She is however pining for Ballylee with that curious intensity about things & places that seems a symptom of her state.' They also consulted the stars, but Gregory's advice carried the day; the incendiary climate around Gort was not a suitable place for him to take his nervy, pregnant wife.[126] They remained uncomfortably in Shillingford, buying 'firing & food in small amounts at a time from trades mens carts that go their rounds daily'; their coal supply lasted a month and they hoped for an early summer.[127]

Willy spent two weeks in London in May, joining Lady Gregory for a series of lectures to support the Abbey Theatre. He visited St Paul's Church in Knightsbridge, 'to see if his [the vicar's] brand of Anglican faith would suit Anne', and attempted to mediate among the warring factions of the Stella Matutina. But he longed to return to George and their cottage, despite its discomfort. 'Dont be surprised if I just wire "get me a room at New Inn" and turn up soon after my wire.' He was 'lonely, bored, tired, becolded in the head, toothachy, out of temper, Saturnian, noise-destructed, excemaish [*sic*], bathless, theatre-hating, woman-hating, but otherwise well and cheerful'.[128] Another journey later that month was to give a reading at the Training College for Women in Lincoln, where Grace Spurway, newly graduated from Oxford, was teaching. Returning home, he wrote to Quinn, 'I am working more steadily than I have worked for years, thanks to marriage & the country life marriage has made possible.' His friend's response was to congratulate him again on a successful marriage, adding, 'You must miss Ireland very much. I cannot say that I see Ballylee except as a thing to write about. It is not a place to live in.'[129]

Quinn was more perceptive than he realized. Work had still not resumed on the tower, their architect had recently died, and Rafferty could get no satisfactory answer out of Binns. George then considered going to Ireland herself; but that very week, while Lady Gregory was in London, her daughter-in-law Margaret was the only survivor in an ambush of British soldiers and their wives, while returning from a harmless tennis party.[130] 'I suppose one day we will look back calmly on this awful time,' Lolly wrote to her father, 'the papers *every morning* full of accounts of murders and shootings of men under arrest (really murder)—executions etc. and no-one knows what may happen next? Of course Willie and

George and Anne cannot go to Galway—that is certain now—things are very bad there—Margaret Gregory was the only survivor of a motor party that was ambushed—you will see about it in the papers—so like Margaret Gregory to go about with *military* and things as they are.'[131]

Minchins' Cottage in Shillingford, flea-racked and uncomfortably small, was becoming increasingly unbearable, and so once again George looked for a house to rent until their own in Oxford would again be available. She found Cuttlebrook House in the picturesque town of Thame, just twelve miles away. Belonging to 'three old maids and their old mother, now in Switzerland', number 42 High Street was large, old, and pleasantly situated; beyond the church on the other side of the seventeenth-century main street they could see the old schoolhouse where the seventeenth-century radical Parliamentarian John Hampden had lived and died. The house amused them, with its Victorian furnishings and decorations, including 'all sorts of obsolete sporting guns'. But it had a lovely garden, where Anne was happily engrossed in her playpen.[132] Anne was already showing her independence in other ways. 'She is very gay and pretty,' her father wrote, 'She calls me Villy (Willy) and when I remonstrate merely changes it to papa Villy. There could not be a child more vivacious or alert. She is put at the far end of the garden so that the maids may not play with her and talk with her till she is too excited to eat or sleep.'[133] To Olivia he enlarged on the attractions of domestic life:

Our canaries are now feeding four strapping but very ugly chicks—their third attempt—and I had hoped that young canaries would be as engaging as kittens. Meanwhile Anne is as energetic as possible. The other day she asked me to put on her shoes (which she had pulled off). I got on one but could not get on the second. Then I found that she had screwed up her toes to prevent me. It was sheer coquetry and she has never been known to ask a woman to put her shoes on. In fact she cannot bear shoes.[134]

He confessed to another friend, 'Marriage and its consequent quiet has made me a man of habit and anchored me as never before.'[135] The experience of fatherhood would enter his discussion of the system:

When I watch my child, who is not yet three years old, I can see so many signs of knowledge from beyond her own mind; why else should she be so excited when a little boy passes outside the window, and take so little interest in a girl; why should she put a cloak about her, and look over her shoulder to see it trailing upon the stairs, as she will some day trail a dress; and why, above all, as she lay against her mother's side, and felt the unborn child moving within, did she murmur, 'Baby, baby'?[136]

But he was in trouble with his own father, who had complained to Lily and Lolly of the description of their family life in the recently published instalment of his memoirs. Once again he turned to Gregory for help: 'He says, it seems, that as a "back-ground" I have invented for myself "sisters & parents, rather a dreadful lot" & "vulgar family" etc.' Lolly's objections were not treated seriously, but would Augusta Gregory please assess his treatment of his father? 'In writing of someone not of my family I could judge for myself, but when writing of one's family one has no objectivity.' Family matters were weighing heavily on George as well. 'Here are the true comedies of family life,' he added. 'When JBY found that I was going to pay his expenses he decided to put aside "money making" and "acquire skill" (he is 86) & spent all his time on his own portrait many years ago "a palmist" had so advised him. George's mother, having persuaded George to guarantee a large over draft—has showered gifts upon us out of the overdraft which, as she has never lived within her income, George will sooner or later have to pay.'[137]

George was also worried about her cousin Grace, who was spending the summer in France and from there wrote a letter criticizing her parents and strict upbringing. Describing an innocent adventure with Bill Jaffe, an American student who was to become her husband, her diatribe was apparently less than coherent; her older cousin replied with a long letter warning her against 'white marriages', for 'nothing can be more disastrous than a platonic relationship'. Since such an arrangement had never entered Grace's head, she always considered this her cousin's 'one big error of judgment'.[138] George may have been thinking of Dorothy Pound's situation, for tales of Ezra's infidelity were by now widespread.

In early July 1921 the long road to an Anglo-Irish treaty began with a tentative truce. Heartened, the Yeatses again turned their thoughts to Ballylee. Binns was dismissed and the design for the tower roof sent to Rafferty (who as early as 1918 had foreseen the necessity of a cement waterproofing[139]). Once again, there were worrying reports that the doors had been entered, but Rafferty's inspection yielded no serious damage. However, Lady Gregory's letter was less comforting —barricades were still up on the roads, and young men in Galway were drilling every night.[140] Then they learned from Iseult that her baby girl, just four months old, had died of meningitis. Willy described her long letter: 'very touching & heart broken—full of intimate little details such as the closing of the child's fingers about her fingers when it was ill. . . . George said some months ago that it would not live . . . Perhaps it is well that a race of tragic women should die out.'[141] The thought came from his philosophy, but the event was ominous to George. Only days later they heard that Eva Fowler had died suddenly at the age of 50, yet another break with the London life they had once shared.

As her confinement drew closer, George invited Lily to visit for a few days, instructing Willy 'to see to it that she does not even remain in the same house when the event comes'. Enveloped in a big cloak, she took Anne with her to meet Lily at the station. The little niece was pronounced more enchanting than ever. 'Such a lovely Anne—her hair is bright gold dark in the shadows—her eyes bright gray. She is so vivid like a brilliant firefly or a dragon fly. She darts about—talks little laughs and is really beautiful all friendliness very well behaved and lives under strict rule—George is fairly well . . . She dresses Anne very prettily in gay colours—Willy is working very hard, but is uneasy I see about George.' Even before Lily departed the maternity nurse, Beatrice Marsh who had been present at Anne's birth, had arrived—'very nice a lady and moves a young baby about as if it was a soap bubble'.[142] George was distressed, tired, and suffering from the heat. She saw apparitions, including 'a great black bird'—heralding 'Black Eagle' or some more dangerous portent?[143] Concerned also about her daughter's reaction, she asked Willy to be present when Anne was first shown the new baby, so that he could tell her just how she looked.[144] In a horary cast in early February George had begun to contemplate the possibility of giving birth to a second daughter—'Stuarta' after the Erskine line—rather than to 'Black Eagle'.[145] But Willy worried that 'If the child is Stuarta and not William Michael, it will be a blow to George made all the worse because Mrs Tucker says that all the Stuartas in her family have been "corkers"; and the probable horoscope does rather suggest a "corker".'[146]

Michael was born in Cuttlebrook House at 6.15 a.m. on Monday, 22 August; a Leo with Virgo rising; Jupiter was conjunct Saturn as the Communicators had predicted over two years earlier. (Although given no explanation, Willy was instructed to make the Saturn evocation while George was awake, and the Jupiter while she slept.) In 'Conjunctions' (1934), with a couplet matching the one about Anne, Yeats would celebrate this particular phenomenon as representative of the objective dispensation:

> If Jupiter and Saturn meet,
> What a crop of mummy wheat![147]

Their son, however, was not to be named after 'J.B.' or even, as George had earlier led his aunts to expect, 'John'[148] after his grandfather. The horoscope Willy drew up first read 'William Michael', then 'Michael Butler'. Willy had never liked his first name, considering it 'a soft, wishy washy moist day sort of name'.[149] But the birth certificate reads 'William Michael Butler Yeats', probably at George's insistence, for William was also her father's first name. In later years her son would never use it, even on school reports.

Congratulations flowed in immediately at the birth of a son (despite the *Star*'s announcement that George had given birth to a girl[150]). 'You hankered for a son yourself—tho' you were prepared to put up with a daughter', wrote Lady Gregory. 'He will be an immense interest to you & you must both feel very proud of bringing an heir into the family.'[151] But within two days of his birth, George thought her little son was dying; his bowels were haemorrhaging—a rare natal disease. Refusing to have Willy told, she and the doctor arranged for a bacteriologist, in the guise of a chemist's assistant, to come from Oxford; George's blood type found satisfactory, little William Michael was injected with serum mixed with his mother's blood and survived. Willy meanwhile, oblivious to the danger and the servants' tears, passed to and fro with congratulatory telegrams. Not surprisingly, George saw more apparitions; Willy then smelt burnt feathers and, fearing the attack of Frustrators, felt 'the mediaeval helpless horror at witchcraft'. Later he was told by Carmichael that 'They can compell [sic] a spirit to reveal its nature by always causing a particular odour. It is our warning.'[152]

By the beginning of September mother and child were well enough to sit in the garden, from where George sent a word-picture to Lily. 'He has "a marked straight nose, short upper lip well curved, small face, large head, smooth brown hair, black eyelashes, very determined expression". Very obstinate says Willy. Anne is delighted with him and Willy plays with her every day to keep her from feeling neglected.'[153] Very soon Michael was putting on weight and appeared 'very healthy', but a further 'slight operation' was necessary and his parents would not be satisfied until he had been examined by Bethel Solomons in Dublin. Still wary of Frustrators, as an additional precaution Willy composed 'A Prayer for my Son', with the first lines that would torment Michael as a schoolboy:

> Bid a strong ghost stand at the head
> That my Michael may sleep sound,
> Nor cry, nor turn in the bed
> Til his morning meal come round;
> And may departing twilight keep
> All dread afar till morning's back,
> That his mother may not lack
> Her fill of sleep.
>
> Bid the ghost have sword in fist:
> Some there are, for I avow
> Such devilish things exist,
> Who have planned his murder, for they know
> Of some most haughty deed or thought
> That waits upon his future days,
> And would through hatred of the bays
> Bring that to nought. . . .[154]

He did not register William Michael's birth until 12 September, the day before they set off for Dublin, again accompanied by Nurse Marsh. While waiting for the boat train in the Euston Hotel, Willy dashed off another poem drawn from the system, 'The Wheel'.[155]

Carefully avoiding the question of a name, Lily wrote to her father, 'Your grandson is here—a beautiful child—he is a fine strong child and has the dearest little dark head just the same shape as Willys a fine fair skin, dark deep set eyes

—a big nose and a grave expression—George knows every hair of his head.'[156] In 1911 while in London Lily had had a vision in which she saw 'a tall young man, about 38 or 40, like Willy in some way, but different. He had gray or light blue eyes, was lively and a success in some way. I knew that he was in and out of the Embassies that are all about that part of London. Then in another flash I saw him looking at my portrait which hung on a panelled wall. He was talking about it to someone and laughing.' Would Michael be in politics? Now she told Willy, who thought that 'the boys horoscope is quite compatible with a diplomatic career'.[157] (Michael did indeed become a statesman, and his aunt's portrait hangs in a panelled room.) His parents were not the only family members concerned about the baby boy. Three months after Michael's birth Lily received a message from their cousin Ruth Lane-Poole, living in Australia. 'Ruth writes that her little Charlotte was so pleased to hear of Michael & said "now we have a boy in the family"—but she doesn't like his name—Michael. She told Ruth to write and ask you not to call him that, because "it is such a delicate name—he will be very ill if they call him that" she said. Wasn't it strange?'[158]

However Dr Solomons pronounced Michael 'very fine in every way', and he continued to gain weight at the rate of nine ounces a week. With that worry behind them, George and Willy spent several weeks in the Hibernian Hotel. Lady Gregory was also in town; after a quiet dinner with Willy alone she recorded in her diary, 'We sat late talking pleasantly enough, it seemed like old times. But he has been very much cut off from Ireland, and if he "can't stand England" talks of South Italy.'[159] Again George made sure to include Willy's sisters; together they went to the Abbey, and were entertained to Sunday dinner at Gurteen Dhas where Susan Mitchell was the other guest. As always, Lolly took advantage of the occasion to use her camera.[160] Any strain over Willy's memoirs seems to have evaporated with the excitement of the heir's arrival; Lily and Lolly did not have the heart to tell them that their father refused to come back.[161] Touched by what he heard of George's bravery, the old painter wrote a conciliatory letter:

I have just heard from Lily of your great anxiety when your little son was so ill—and that you went through the crisis without letting Willie know—how grateful to you he must be!—grateful all his life—and how clever of you!—Lily sends me a delightful account of your son—a long nose and short upper lip and this will suggest that he is mild and gentle. Hitherto Lily has only liked girl babies. . . . probably she will now enlarge her heart and include baby boys . . . Your account of people is always interesting because shrewd and sympathetic and just—[162]

On his way back to Oxford, Willy once again initiated a series of arguments to bring his father home, stressing the expenses incurred by his son's birth and illness and, even more strongly, Quinn's objections to his staying in New York. 'I can keep you comfortably in Dublin but the expense of New York is too much for my resources,' he warned. His father's only response was to ask George if he was in her 'bad books that you don't write' and that he was 'hustling to make a living', having written 'two articles which will flutter the dovecotes of the critics to whom Quinn attaches his faith'. A month later Willy wrote much more bluntly: 'I consider your present position undignified because it forces upon Quinn a responsibility which he greatly objects to. He resents your delays most intensely.'[163] Quinn was invited to be godfather to their son, Willy assuring him that 'It is George's idea. She is very set on your taking the post.' 'I should love to have a boy and a girl, and wish I had a boy and a girl, or a boy, at any rate,' the confirmed bachelor replied. Later, despite his distrust of Ballylee, Quinn asked George for photographs of castle and children, 'particularly if she gets a good one of my godson'.[164]

They were delighted to be back in their 'old beautiful house' in Oxford, retrieved at the beginning of October. But all was still not well. 'George is wholly taken up with William Michael who gets various little ailments and seems more delicate than Anne was,' Willy wrote worriedly to Coole. There was need for yet another operation, this time for a triple rupture 'and some other complication all arising from that attack when he was two days old, or so it seems'.[165] The further complication was a hydrocele, a collection of clear fluid in the testes. The operation, performed by Tyrell Grey in London, took place on 30 October. Willy, who accompanied his wife to London, took her to the ballet as a distraction before returning to Oxford and Anne ('gay and well and has taken to occasional joyous yells in the manner of the parrot'). Picking up her mother's desires, Anne announced that 'Baby has gone to Ballylee'. Dublin was not informed until a week after the operation.[166]

Again George protected her husband: since telegrams could not be sent on Sunday, she told him the surgery would take place the next day. 'Michael stood the operation very well,' she reported: 'Under chloroform for 1 hour 25 minutes. Both ruptures and the hydrocele done. The ruptures were *large*. He has slept a good deal today & not been as uncomfortable as I feared. Both doctors were in this evening & say he is in fine condition . . . *Unless* I wire to the contrary I shall arrive at Oxford by the 4.45 (arriving at *5 to 6 p.m.*) on Tuesday evening for the night & can pack you for Scotland & return on Wed.'[167] Assured that his son would be all right, Willy then went on a financially essential lecture tour, but from Glasgow he anxiously awaited George's regular bulletins: 'I know he is out of danger but I hope to hear that he begins to get back his colour.'[168]

George was staying with the Tuckers at 27 Royal Crescent, and Nelly also wrote to Willy:

I am so very sorry about the new trouble Michael looks so well & strong we hope he will outgrow these weaknesses. Why He wanted children to have these vagaries is a mystery. I suppose it is Nature's method of warning us away from civilization! However, in spite of broken nights and anxiety Georgie looks very well, and so radiantly happy. . . . Tonight we are going to hear Jelly d'Aranyi play at Mr Fowlers & (I hope) George too.

I found an old Peerage at Okehampton & copied out my Erskine genealogy. I see my great uncle John Cadwallader Erskine married in 1829 *John Martyn of Tyrone*. I am trying to collect the *Lees* genealogy. I found a lot of data at Okehampton which is owned by George Dumville Lees wife who [was a] Luxmoore There are in her house some good portraits of old Lees—about 1830—one (her great-grandfather Lees) exactly like Georgie! The Lees appear to have followed strange gods from early times. They are Quakers, Unitarians, misers, spendthrifts, & (here & there to save the ship) commercial geniuses. The only conventional one appears to be George's great-uncle Harold Lees who was a rather commonplace country squire but even he increased his fortune by a speculation in the days of early railroads! When one has a son it is interesting to know what he springs from, especially on the mother's side perhaps?

She blithely suggested that—in spite of his son's condition—he extend his lecture tour to Scotland and go up to Oban, 'an occasion to see some fine scenery'.[169] No wonder George occasionally became irritated with her self-centred mother. More sensitively, Lady Gregory, who had anxiously awaited Willy's reports, wrote, 'I trust this may be the last of Michaels troubles for a long time to come. He will not remember anything about it—that is a comfort.'[170] However the Erskine connection was pleasing, especially as Willy had learned of 'a spirited ancestor for Michael' on the Middleton side also while he was in Glasgow.[171] They still hoped to discover more about the relationship between 'Black Eagle' and Anne Hyde.

Michael remained in the nursing home until 16 November, when Nurse Marsh once again returned to Oxford with him, staying until Christmas. Michael ('William' by now dropped) was christened in Oxford on 20 December in the presence of his other godfather, Lennox Robinson. Evidently George and Willy thought Lennox—who presented a silver cup and provided champagne—a more sympathetic mentor than Ezra, who in 1919 had been invited to perform the role if their first child was a boy. Ottoline Morrell seems to have stood as the only godmother; they were all invited by the new Duchess of Marlborough (the former Gladys Deacon) to lunch at Blenheim Castle near Woodstock. 'You will find the duchess an amusing talker, thoroughly read in literature, especially french literature & a great friend of Anatole France,' Willy assured Lennox.[172] Robinson enjoyed the experience, informing his friend Tom MacGreevy, 'Yesterday we went out to lunch at Blenheim, rather amusing, really a very perfect place in its absurd palatial style and the American-French duchess very nice and most intelligent. Lady Ottoline there in a wonderful wig like an old hair rug—hating the Duchess and everything.' What seems to have charmed him as much as his new godson was the Duchess of Marlborough's gift of a Persian kitten (she had earlier given one to Ottoline).[173] As soon as Lennox left, the household—except for George and the housemaid—succumbed to various ailments, the cook with flu, Nurse with a violent cold, and, most worrying, Michael with a touch of bronchitis. George, 'day nurse and night nurse and charwoman all in one', packed Willy, suffering from a cold, off to a hotel, but he too developed influenza. To make matters worse, unlike the placid Anne, Michael was a fretful baby, sleeping by day but keeping his mother awake by night.[174] The pattern would be repeated many times in the next dozen years.

'Sleeps' had begun again in early September while they were still at Thame, but after a number of sessions Dionertes claimed that the 'force was not good . . . it would not be good for about a week as he had to get used to things'—presumably another child distracted the Interpreter too much. The spirit Frazzlepat then joined them—from the thirteenth cone, he was associated both with George and the Black Eagle, and, by using salt water as his link with George, would be less fatiguing. As in the New York sleeps the previous year, emphasis was on George's vision of a lake. Again she was reminded of her experience with Dorothy Shakespear in 1912, as described to her husband: 'At her school there was a place in the garden, where she remembers water and swans. She often—according to her memory—went there for rest and quiet. Yet on returning to the school years afterwards discovered that water and swans were imaginary.'[175] But Frustrators were still about; Willy was advised that sword and incense would help maintain the link between the four of them. 'The strongest protection was however continued communication, I should see the two children fairly often.'[176] George would certainly agree.

Although more and more absorbed in their own researches, they were still being drawn into quarrels in the Order of the Golden Dawn despite the continued suspension of its regular activities. During the past year Miss Stoddart, still searching for the truth about the origin of the Golden Dawn, had been repeatedly urged by both friends and foes to resign; by March 1921 she had been removed as a Ruling Chief of the Stella Matutina, her fiefdom restricted to the Amoun Temple. Still she stubbornly refused to withdraw or give up the Temple properties, though even those in sympathy felt the cause was hopeless and that she 'had no supporters except Mr Yeats & possibly Mrs Yeats'. A Tarot reading she sent to 'Nemo' suggested that within a few months the entire Order would be broken up. 'If this is true,' she wrote George, 'then it is what you told me two years ago—"That this trouble was permitted so that the Order might be purified & only the earnest students left to carry on." ' Nemo replied that it would not be possible under the present circumstances to 'split members & properties & so form a new Order'. Both she and Demon advised passive resistance, and to await developments.[177] By April Felkin's daughter issued a ballot supporting her father's authority against the rebel chiefs. But in May word came from Rudolf Steiner in Switzerland denying any formal connection with the Felkins: 'self-deception is possible and forces may enter which are beyond the power or understanding of those physically present . . . The Order is decorative and useful to those who need it and are able to distinguish between mere ornament and reality.'[178]

On a trip to London Willy interviewed both Miss Stoddart and her sympathetic co-Chief Dr Hammond, but came away with nothing new. 'I think if we want to get rid of our followers—about four in all—in the order we can put them into Steiners care and they will do their ceremonies, with his motherly care in the background,' he reported to George. He recommended a meeting of the interested parties, but nothing seems to have come of his suggestion until November, when Dr Felkin officially suspended Miss Stoddart. Willy then became active again, advising Dr Hammond on the wording of a short statement that separated the two camps. The loyal members included George's cousin by marriage, Mrs Erskine.[179] But by then Miss Stoddart herself was succumbing to grand-scale delusions; when George and Willy again intervened, it was to try and rescue the Order properties. They do not seem however to have resigned for another year or so.[180]

However, contact with Order members was not confined to 'Il faut chercher' and her companions. In late November they collaborated on a devious reply to a fellow Adept which benefited considerably from Georgie's knowledge of astrology and her early studies in the British Museum:

Our information about Lunar Symbolism is derived from such vague & general sources that I hardly know how to direct you. The most authoritative source I can think of is in the books of astrology. All our astrology is derived from a book attributed to Ptolemy but I have not my copy of his book nearby me at the moment. . . . Your [brother] might take a typical modern book 'Pearce's text book of Astrology' (2 vols). Another authoritative book is that by Morin de Villefranche (Micinus?). There is a french translation in the British Museum. There may be something in Frazer, but allusions to the moon are rare & scattered in folk literature, & I cannot think of any one book that deals with the subject. Perhaps the most important source of symbolism is Greco-Latin philosophy and mythology. There is a very important dialogue by Plutarch describing the passage of souls from the lunar to the solar influence. And I know from the letters of a friend who died in Ceylon that the Singalese have precisely similar symbolism. The symbolism of sun and moon are part of the language of my mind but I have forgotten the sources of that language. . . . My own poem 'The Phases of the Moon' in 'The Wild Swans at Coole' (Macmillan) might interest him, though hardly traditional enough to help him much.[181]

George might still be reluctant to broadcast their researches widely, but clearly she was unable to stop Willy from speaking freely and excitedly about the philosophy they were receiving.

Once again events in Ireland made them shift course. On 6 December the Anglo-Irish Treaty was signed in London; the terms gave the Irish Free State Dominion status similar to Canada's and the six northern counties the power to secede. George immediately cast a horary, so excited that she did not include the question. A week later the Dáil met in Dublin, eventually accepting the Treaty by 64 to 57. Ominous though that narrow margin was, the decision was made to move not to Cork but to Dublin. Despite her husband's unease, George seems to have cast the deciding vote. 'I am in a deep gloom about Ireland,' Willy confided to Olivia,

for though I expect ratification of the treaty from a plebiscite I see no hope of escape from bitterness, and the extreme party may carry the country. When men are very bitter, death and ruin draw them on as a rabbit is supposed to be drawn on by the dancing of the fox. In the last week I have been planning to live in Dublin—George very urgent for this—but I feel now that all may be blood and misery. If that comes we may abandon Ballylee to the owls and the rats, and England too . . . and live in some far land. Should England and Ireland be divided beyond a hope of remedy, what else could one do for the children's sake, or one's own work? I could not bring them to Ireland where they would inherit bitterness, nor leave them in England where, being Irish by tradition, and my family and fame, they would be in an unnatural condition of mind and grow, as so many Irishmen who live here do, sour and argumentative.[182]

But George was determined; even before the Treaty was ratified, Lennox had been instructed to look out for a house in Dublin.[183] And despite many European adventures in the years to come, George and her children would remain firmly committed to Ireland.

Part III

Directions 1922–1928

Life's been rather too hectic . . . all Willy's irons having to be kept hot . . .
and letters, telegrams, telephones have all been buzzing
(George to Tom)[1]

All the pseudo-mystico-intellecto-nationalistico stuff of the last fifteen years
isnt worth a trouser-button, or rather as a trouser-button is a most necessary
article one might say a pillowcase button! As long as there was any gesture in
it, as long as there was a war on and so on and so on, it was worth it.
(George to Tom)[2]

Nationality throws out personality and there's nothing in his verse worth
preserving but the personal.
(George to Tom)[3]

The saint is responsible to God alone—man of genius to himself as well
(the control Thomas)[4]

12

BALLYLEE

At least Dublin was in the same country as Ballylee, although sometimes it would not seem so. Lennox sent a list to Oxford of houses for sale, but still George and Willy delayed. George was exhausted from nursing a house full of invalids; in addition, Michael was a demanding baby. His second operation had been expensive, and once again she had to dip into her capital. Relieved to receive a cheque from Lolly for Cuala sales, Willy wrote gloomily, 'I have given it to George & it will make her annual account ballance [*sic*] (apart from what she had to sell out for Michaels second operation). It has been a year of great expense with nurses & doctors apart even from the operation. I live in alarm at the thought of JBY's next account.'[5]

The situation in Ireland was still unsettled; the Treaty, which was approved on 7 January, was repudiated by 'the Irreconcilables', led by de Valera, over the wording of the oath of allegiance. Two days later Arthur Griffith succeeded de Valera as President and the next week Dublin Castle transferred power to Michael Collins as Chairman of the Provisional Government. Almost immediately a split occurred in the Volunteers (or Irish Republican Army) between the intransigent 'Irregulars' and those incorporated into the Free State army, led by Richard Mulcahy; threat of a civil war hung over the country. Meanwhile, as much to give George a change as from any enthusiasm to enter Irish politics, Willy accepted an invitation to attend the international Irish Race Conference in Paris, where they arrived on 18 January. The Conference, presided over by de Valera despite—perhaps because of—the situation at home, included among its delegates Maud Gonne and Jack Yeats; both brothers spoke on 23 January, Willy during the afternoon on the theatre, Jack that evening on art. It is doubtful whether the Yeats men saw much of each other, for while Willy was prepared to support the Treaty, Jack was vehemently opposed. However, George enjoyed this opportunity to see the Pounds, although Ezra's impatience with his former mentor was by now obvious: Yeats, he had decided, was 'at the walnuts and wine stage', his contribution to the meeting 'affable, but no impact', though forgiven because he was still 'a damn good lyric poet'.[6]

George and Willy were in Paris until 26 January. The experience—where the question of Ireland's fate hung over the meetings despite the international composition of the delegates—does not seem to have dulled their desire to move; immediately on their return to Oxford Willy wrote asking Lady Gregory to put George up while she inspected Ballylee. Still worried about his wife's exhausted state he promised, 'If she goes to you she will be no burden for the sooner you send her to bed the better,' adding almost as an afterthought, 'On her way through Dublin she may perhaps look at a Dublin house with a view to our going there next autumn when it gets too cold at Ballylee.'[7] A series of astrological maps were drawn on 30 January, the major question being Willy's 'Life in Ireland if I return'. Then Rafferty wired that building was commencing on Ballylee—what kind of flooring did they want in the castle? Things were moving ahead at last. Not content with Lennox's list, they also consulted Gogarty about their move to Ireland:

We shall be settled there in an almost completed tower the first week in April. Do you know of a house that would suit us? Nothing modern, no modern improvements if possible to run the servants into extravagance, ancient names cut on the glass of the windowpanes, if possible. Mountjoy Square, Rutland Square, Stephens Green, Ely Place, that street where Dillon lives—all sound pleasantly. My wife goes to Ballylee for a couple of days in March to see that all is ready for our April flitting and will look at Dublin houses if there are any for her to see. Surely the Castle rats must be leaving their comfortable holes.[8]

While George and Willy were turning their thoughts towards Dublin, Jeanne Foster wrote concerning JBY's failing health. But almost as her letter reached them, at 6.55 a.m. on 3 February, the old artist died. As Willy had feared, the winter had been too much for him, but it was also discovered that he had been suffering from tuberculosis. A flurry of telegrams between Quinn, Jeanne Foster, Gurteen Dhas, and Oxford determined that his body would remain in the United States next to the Foster family plot in the Adirondack mountains.[9] Mrs Foster made all the arrangements for the funeral and burial, while John Quinn as always attended to the financial matters; together they cleared and packed the old artist's few belongings. The unfinished, long-promised self-portrait, which JBY had made his final excuse for remaining in New York, would return without him.[10] Willy dictated a letter to Lily assuring her that all was for the best, 'for he has had no growing infirmities, no long illness'. 'If he had come home he would have lived longer but he might have gone infirm, grown to feel himself a useless old man. He has died as the antarctic explorers died, in the midst of his work and the middle of his thought, convinced that he was about to paint as never before. . . . I think we did all for him that could be done and that there is nothing to regret.' To Lolly he spoke of the pleasure their father had received from her 'vivid letters'.[11] But the news deeply affected George. Almost immediately they began to plan for Cuala a further selection of his letters—to be made by her—and portions of his autobiography—to be arranged by Willy. JBY's *Early Memories* was published the following year, but the larger volume of letters, which had been mooted even before his death, was not edited until 1946, and then not by George.[12] 'I wish he could have lived to see us in Dublin,' Willy wrote to Olivia. 'He was fond of George.'[13] Eventually three boxes reached Gurteen Dhas; one containing his few personal belongings, the others books. Quinn sold as many of JBY's paintings and drawings as he could, and sent the remaining sketchbooks and drawings home with the long-awaited self-portrait. John Butler Yeats died as he had lived, poor in all but what he most believed in—the creativity of the artist and the ferment of the intellect.

That unsuccessful pressure to call the old patriarch home somehow made their decision to move to Ireland now even more imperative. George was determined to move her family to Dublin, and soon. On 11 February at 1.15 p.m. she consulted the stars, 'Am I right to go to look at houses in Dublin at once? Moon going to sextile Jupiter which promises no unexpected obstacles. Comfortable journeys. Significator of houses is conjoined with Venus sun in the neighbourhood of mid heaven trine Jupiter square Mars. This promises that a satisfactory house will be obtained but . . . it will either not be the house expected or it will be acquired in some unexpected way.' Two weeks later she annotated the horary reading: 'Correct. Got different house & circumstances generally unexpected. G. Yeats Feb 26 1922.'

George left Oxford on 12 February, stopping off in London on the way—probably to consult her solicitor. She was in Dublin by the next day and immediately began to look at houses, but remained uncertain of her choice, which seems to have been between two properties. Finally, in the lawyer's office, she decided on the south side of the river, a large eighteenth-century house in Merrion Square. Working hard to complete more of his memoirs, Willy wrote, 'I hope you do not think my not going over leaves you too much responsibility.' 'If you do a wire tomorrow will bring me over on Friday—even a wire on Friday will. I have not gone because as I trusted your judgement I thought it would be an extravagance to go. Between lost days and money spent I might go near spending the difference between our Oxford and our Dublin rent and taxes. Your letters have been more undecided and despondent than your telegram led me to expect, and so perhaps you really want me over.' The children and he were all well, he assured her; and if they could rent a portion of the new house at £50 a year and also let the stable, they 'would have a very cheap house'.[14] As it turned out, she was able to let the top floor for six months 'to two young men of our acquaintance' (names still unknown), thereby providing some security while they were in Galway. Informing Olivia that Merrion Square was to Dublin 'what Berkeley Square is to

London', Yeats confessed that he felt 'very grand especially as I remember a street ballad about the Duke of Wellington'. The rooms were so large and stately that 'our carpets will look like postage stamps', but there were fine mantelpieces and a view of the Dublin mountains. By now he had decided that the situation in Ireland 'will come right in three or four months'. 'We shall have a pleasant energetic life,' he predicted, 'if the Treaty is accepted at the general election, and turmoil if it is rejected. . . . It is right for us to go, though I left all for George to decide.' But Augusta Gregory warned them, 'It is an anxious time—disorder here & there—& this likely to increase until this government is well in the saddle.'[15]

Although Willy's Saturn had 'suggested delay', George's Mars 'carried the day' most successfully. It was an auspicious time financially as well as astrologically. 'By a most strange stroke of luck she bought for a very small sum . . . and within three days could have re-sold at a profit of £600.'[16] The lease, purchased from Dr Richard Atkinson Hayes, cost £1,650; the annual rate was £100. George, who signed the offer to purchase, was able to arrange a bank mortgage; with the £500 expected from Willy's memoirs, there was no need to deplete their capital further. If need be, he could do another American tour to help pay the mortgage off, 'so the house will be so much extra estate for Ann or Michael to inherit'.[17] His father's death had provided a timely release.

Built about 1789 (not 1740 as Willy claimed), number 82 on the south side of Merrion Square could not have been more conveniently placed for a triumphant return to Dublin.[18] The top-floor office of the *Irish Statesman*, where AE and Susan Mitchell worked and held Friday afternoon tea sessions, was two doors away at number 84;[19] the National Gallery and Leinster House (purchased that year to house the Dáil and Séanad) marked the west side of the square; while from the other end of the street one came upon a breathtaking view of the Dublin mountains. Although now the square was chiefly occupied by the medical and legal professions, former residents had included Sir William Wilde, Daniel O'Connell, and Sheridan LeFanu—as well as many distinguished members of the old Parliament, including the Right Honourable William Gregory of Coole Park. Charlotte Payne-Townshend, now Mrs Bernard Shaw, had once lived on the south side. Although the houses on the south and east of the square are inferior in design to the grand mansions opposite, number 82 had a drawing room with three great windows, marble mantelpieces after Adam, fine ceilings, and a handsome staircase. There was a long garden at the back (the lot was 137 feet deep and 75 feet wide to the stable lane); little Anne thought that the far end, dark and overgrown with bushes, 'was where the Snow Queen lived'. As they grew older the children would be sent in with their dog to play amongst the dusty bushes of the locked square.[20] In 1927 Senator Yeats spoke in favour of having the square opened to the public 'for the health of the Dublin children and the delight of all the citizens'.[21]

From the lawyer's office George went on to inspect Ballylee, where Rafferty assured her that at least two rooms of the castle would be ready for them by April. When she returned to Oxford on the 20th she was accompanied by Lily, who had all winter been suffering from shingles and neuritis; she was still not recovered from the news of her father's death. 'I am very glad as she is really not well enough to travel alone, and George doesn't mind responsibility,' Lolly felt, echoing a family confidence in and dependence on her sister-in-law that would be put to the test many times over the next thirty years. 'The doctor says she *must* have change—. I think Anne & Michael will be a great pleasure to her.'[22] Meanwhile, Willy's uncle Isaac and the old aunts 'all went all together & looked at the outside of 82 Merrion Square & approved'.[23]

George and Willy immediately cast another horary, deciding that the 'decision to buy 82 Merrion Sq. given in Lawyer's office' was on the whole 'very favourable'. They were promised 'a romantic enterprising life, somewhat disturbed by quarrels, public & private', but satisfactory especially for the theatre, and— most important—'also excellent for children'. There would undoubtedly be 'an element of conflict',[24] but George's script suggested that conflict would 'draw attention to the philosophy . . . Both subjective & objective necessary for you.'[25] There was no turning back now. To his English friends Willy explained that he could no longer stay in England; he must return to serve his country. He had 'much to fight for—an Irish Academy being founded and perhaps a government theatre'.[26] An invitation to accept an honorary degree from Trinity College, Dublin, further sweetened their plans; this would allow him to change from Stephen's Green Club to the University Club, 'where there is perhaps more conversation & less bridge'.[27]

Once again George found suitable tenants for the Oxford house, willing to pay £5 a week for four months starting in April; the final break-up of the house could thus be postponed until late summer. After Lily left they invited Olivia to visit them in Oxford, and they themselves spent a day or so in London. One of the purposes of the journey was to visit (on Dionertes' advice) the College of Psychic Studies; there a trumpet or 'direct voice' medium called up a happy JBY who offered advice to Lily on her continuing ill health and 'proof' related to a little dog in Dublin. Perhaps George, 'who had a desire to go as she thought my father might come',[28] needed this reassurance more than Willy did; it was after her own father's death that she first began to frequent the séance room.

They also went out to Garsington for one last time. George would miss that contact most:

My dear Ottoline, We will come with delight on Thursday. Can you not lunch on Monday (1) do if you can & we will expect you if we see you. I say 'lunch' because when it is tea you go too soon.

I think Joyce lingers too much over all the indignities of the flesh; if he were a french writer he would linger with gaiety as in satire, but being an Irish Catholic he lingers with mingled fascination & disgust. The Irish Catholic is the very devil & Joyce having exploded out of it like a rocket cant forget the delighted surprise of freedom. Willy continues in admiration. I think a great deal *is* very fine but I want a large hot bath after each reading & that's a bore![29]

In spite of her strong reaction, she continued to read Joyce, even smuggling a copy of *Ulysses* back to Ireland.[30]

Willy was sent ahead while George continued the long job of sorting and filing his papers; the large tin box containing the script and notes on the system would go with her by train (again this would be repeated for many years to come). The decision to move to Ireland and the prospect of Ballylee seem to have given her more self-confidence in other ways, too. 'Katherine Scott came last night at 8.15 p.m. and stayed till 12.30 talking about her very American love affairs—I felt so old. Have I already arrived at the age when young women come for advice about their love-affairs?!'[31]

In London Willy meanwhile was visiting old friends, all of whom advised him on furnishings for their new house; Dulac presented them with two large Chinese pictures which would eventually grace the walls of Willy's study, and was 'most vehement' on the subject of Persian carpets. But Michael's birth and his father's death had also made them more conscious of the Woodmass and Erskine connections. Willy enclosed an important note from George's grandmother which had been written to Beatrice Erskine.

'Mrs Erskine had this phrase "it is just as well that all the money should not be left away from the family" which suggests a public spirited animosity one had not thought of I think, and the National Gallery for the pictures. The significance of the phrase only occurred to me next day so I did not question her. It was said in comment on a sentence of mine which was merely "I think a grandmother has every right to see her grandchild & even if the grandmother were in jail for forgery".' His perseverance would result in a meeting the following year with Edith Alice Woodmass herself. But now his father's affairs were foremost, and arriving in Dublin ahead of his family, he took the opportunity to consult his sisters and Jack about JBY's burial. At the Club he was pleased to find 'general optimism except about the trouble with Ulster'; but he missed and longed for George.[32]

Rafferty had received a deposit of £50, but was having difficulty finding wood. However, 'floors or no floors', George was determined to be in Ballylee with the children before the end of March; Willy was to stay at Coole until she had 'all arranged'. There was a strike in England; all the linens and other necessities had to be brought from Oxford by passenger train; they also shifted many canaries, a collie puppy, and the cat Harry, who would soon be joined by Pangur. On

28 March Willy wired from Coole, 'Ballylee all right', following up with an even more satisfactory letter: 'Ground floor room and the rooms on first and second floors will be ready for you. . . . Lady Gregory can keep us as long as you like.'[33] Despite the many rumours that had so distressed George, Ballylee seems to have escaped relatively unscathed during their two-year absence—there had been one forced entry, the locks broken and some windows (which the intruder appears to have mended before leaving). Nothing had been stolen but George's garden syringe. The Molloy sisters too were happy; notwithstanding the unrest at home, news in the papers of English murders had made them more uneasy at night in Oxford.[34]

By early April they were well settled in to Ballylee, and George declared that 'the children have at once increased in weight', whereas Willy was 'glad to be out of Dublin where men talk themselves bitter'. To add to George's happiness, for the first time she and Willy were able to sleep in the tower itself, in the large bedroom above the ground floor. He was delighted to discover how silent stone stairs were. The great elmwood bed designed by Scott had been finished by Rafferty's carpenter, but although they had planned the brilliant Order colours— blue, red, black, and gold—for the fine wooden ceiling, this must wait until Willy was out of the way. Now he wrote at the desk by the window, where he could watch the stares flying in and out of their nest in the hole just above; jackdaws nested in the chimney when not smoked out by the turf fire. The view from the window was of 'river banks fringed now with elm, now with whitethorn, and beyond that rocks and whitethorn everywhere'. Since the canaries objected to sheep's wool and green moss, Olivia sent nesting material, and soon a huge cage with two nests hung there also, promising an embarrassment of progeny. Revelling in his wife's keen eye for natural beauty, he told Quinn, 'It is a great pleasure to live in a place where George makes at every moment a fourteenth-century picture. And out of doors, with the hawthorn all in blossom all along the river banks, everything is so beautiful that to go elsewhere is to leave beauty behind.'[35]

Although Willy usually left the decoration to his wife's discretion, they did not always agree. After Rafferty had finished painting the castle window frames a brilliant red, Lady Gregory was invited to admire them; after her visit she wrote in her journal, 'I say I don't much like them but think they will be better when they fade. He is troubled and gives me all the reasons why they are the only colour that is right with the old stones and I agree politely but not convincingly and at last I say "When one's friends marry one should make up one's mind to have done with telling the truth," and he laughs and says "Quite right", but that the bright red was his idea, G. wanted bright blue.'[36] He spent the summer writing his own poem on Ballylee, rooting it in the turbulent history of the period but again celebrating his good fortune:

The Primum Mobile that fashioned us
Has made the very owls in circles move;
And I, that count myself most prosperous,
Seeing that love and friendship are enough,
For an old neighbour's friendship chose the house
And decked and altered it for a girl's love,
And know whatever flourish and decline
These stones remain their monument and mine.[37]

That summer, when not overseeing the workmen, George busied herself planting flowers and vegetables along the roadside outside the cottage and inside the walled garden; there were roses along the river bank. When the canaries were born, there was some disappointment, for 'George's energetic mind has conceived a project of selling canaries through the newspapers,' and one canary looked 'half sparrow'. 'Who will want half castes?'[38] Despite the worrying news from Dublin and Galway, here all for the moment was peace and contentment, the only disturbance to their night's rest when the puppy barked at a cuckoo. It was now that they decided on a new name for their paradise—Thoor Ballylee. 'Thoor is Irish for tower and it will keep people from suspecting us of modern gothic and a deer park . . . the harsh sound of "Thoor" amends the softness of the rest.'[39]

George was always welcome in the district. Willy took pleasure in the comment of one of Lady Gregory's neighbours, 'Mrs Yeats is so busy and so joyous.'[40] Then too, she paid her servants well, organized transport to bring them to mass in Peterswell, and ordered fish from Dublin for their Friday dinners. When young John Kelly of Dromore, Peterswell (about one mile from Ballylee)—who each year worked with George in her garden—emigrated to America, he carried with him not only a letter of reference but £20. Once she brought down a young girl from Dublin for a holiday, putting her up with Mrs Molloy; thinking there were only two rivers in Ireland, the city-dweller asked whether the Ballylee river was the Liffey or the Shannon.[41] Within a few years 'Chrissie' replaced Mary Anne Molloy and stayed with them until the 1930s; then Mary Martin joined them. Mary Kate, another member of the Kelly family, who came each summer as cook for £1 a week, remembered that chickens and milk were bought from the neighbouring farmers; old Mrs Cusack always presented a goose for St Michael's Day, 29 September, in honour of the young heir. George also patronized local shops: several times a week supplies were purchased in Gort from Gerard Keane, Bartley Finnegan, Paddy Lally (now Sullivan's Hotel), and John Spellman of the Square (now the Archway Tavern). Anne remembers that after some time buying tea out of the barrel marked 'superior', George one morning observed that the same bag filled both barrels, and after that bought from the cheaper label. Once petrol was again available, a car could be hired from Matt O'Connor's Garage in Gort. However, because of their frequent absences, the rate collector Thomas

Coen had to chase them down for annual payments. Little Delia Hynes from the farm below used to pass as George tended her flowers by the roadside—'a fine plain woman', she remembered, always ready with a friendly greeting.[42]

The children too were happy at Ballylee, and both would look back on their summers there with unmitigated pleasure. 'Nana' Reade saw to it that they did not wander unaccompanied into the flower garden or down the banks to the deep part of the river; they spent time across the bridge by the duck shed and across the road where the water was shallow. Anne was delighted when Willy finally persuaded his wife that two Aylesbury ducks should join the menagerie;[43] until they were whooshed into the duck shed, she did not have to go to bed. This was an exciting chore because the first in would escape before there was time to close the door on the second. But at least they could not fly away; one evening, watching George and her daughter struggle, an old farmer remarked, 'Isn't it a good thing them's aren't turkeys?' When talkative Mrs Cusack came by to threaten their quiet she and her mother would hide in the old swing by the river, drawing their feet up so that the wooden sides would conceal their presence. The canaries too were a constant source of fascination. As the young learned to fly, they were sometimes set loose in one of the empty upper rooms; once someone opened the window and they escaped, though all eventually returned but one, which pecked at the window during the night. Once little Anne stole into the forbidden territory of the tower staircase, climbing up to the stranger's room on the top floor, empty but for dust and silence. Peering in, she was frightened by a perfectly preserved brightly coloured dead butterfly caught in a spider's web on the window ledge, and fled down the winding staircase to safety. As Michael grew older, they were allowed to roam further on their bicycles, accompanied by the watchful Nana. The miller who lived down the river—and to Michael's delight always had a rowing boat ready for the floods—once made a crossbow for Anne, but this was decreed too dangerous for a young child.[44]

However, life at Ballylee, no matter how peaceful, could not have been physically easy at any time. George did her share of bicycling to Gort for supplies, especially during these years of civil war. There was no electricity, and the only drinking water at least half a mile away. To fill the great copper boiler on the kitchen range, a large galvanized iron water carrier on wheels was sent twice daily down to the river bank. Young Michael used to watch with fascination a horse 'going round and round attached to a pole that actuated the pumping system that sent the water up to the top of the house' for his bath.[45] It would be another year before the garage was built, housing a boiler to heat the bath water (but never the promised Ford car). One of the young Molloy boys went regularly during the winter months to keep turf fires going against the damp, for the limestone walls wept in wet weather. (Once the wood panelling in the study/bedroom caught fire and consumed some of the ceiling timbers.) There was only one indoor water closet, in the back cottage, reached from the garden door and through the children's bedrooms. Then too, the third room in the tower was urgently needed, for several times a year when the river rose dramatically—sometimes as high as thirteen feet—the ground floor was flooded, and linens, silver, books, and papers had to be moved up the narrow stairs to safety.[46] Once there was three feet of water on the ground floor, but usually the waters receded after twelve to eighteen inches. The new room would not be ready for occupancy for another two years, when it in turn became the bedroom, leaving the present one for Willy's study. Meanwhile it had been turned into a carpenter's shop, where gates and doors were being fashioned. And so Rafferty continued to be a fixture at Ballylee—that is, when he was not home digging potatoes or doing small jobs at Coole and elsewhere—but during these years he had difficulty getting workmen as well as building supplies.

On 14 April 1922 news reached them from Dublin that the Irregulars had occupied the Four Courts, the Fowler Hall, the Kildare Street Club, and the Masonic Hall; young Seán MacBride was once more in the thick of the fighting. Reluctant to become directly involved, yet feeling pressed to do something, they discussed whether Willy should write privately to de Valera. George cast a horary on the afternoon of 16 April asking, 'What will result of letter to Eamonn de Valera be?' Her analysis reveals more than her hopes for the public arena: 'I do not think this letter will cause de Valera to change his plan of campaign but I do think that it will cause him to modify it, changing from militarist tactics to political strategy. I do not think WB will enter into public relations in the matter at all, but will probably be in communication privately and in personal relations with De V. and his party.' The horoscope 'seems' to indicate that 'it would be inadvisable for WB to take public part', for 'such action would greatly interfere with his creative force'. However there was also an indication that 'he would have personal success if he did take a public part.' Willy wrote out his judgement the following day: the effect of a letter would be indirect, with 'no present practical effect'. The stars were inconclusive. But by now the Irregulars were raiding shops, post offices, banks, smashing up printing presses, and derailing trains.[47] George and Willy walked over to Coole to consult about the advisability of his receiving an honorary degree in July from Queen's University, Belfast; as they feared, acceptance from 'the Protestant enemy' infuriated friends like Maud who had shifted to the anti-Treaty side.[48] Even Gregory, like those of her fellow Protestant landowners who had not fled, was receiving threats. Willy spent some nights at Coole until George was assured that there were men patrolling every night round the demesne, for 'Lady Gregory is the first person in the county that would get protection.'[49]

Again George turned to the stars: 'What will happen to Ireland in the near future.' This time they predicted 'successful negociation [sic] . . . suggesting settlement by overwhelming public opinion'. The election on 16 June proved the heavens partly right—the Treaty was ratified 58 to 35. On 28 June Michael Collins attacked the Four Courts; the fighting in Dublin lasted for eight days and spread further. For seventeen days there were no trains, post, or telegrams, and the main roads were blocked by trees and rocks. The sound of shots and the occasional explosion could be heard from Gort, although nothing came nearer the castle. Unable to get to Dublin, George and Willy now found themselves held hostage by events; the Trinity College honorary degree ceremony had to be postponed until December. By July there was no bread to be had in Gort; the captain of the garrison sent a motor to Loughrea for yeast, but the first messenger was shot. Flour arrived in Galway by boat the next day; then the supply of sugar ran out.[50] When post was finally delivered, the fish George regularly ordered from Dublin was too—Lady Gregory was not amused by the spectacle of more than two weeks of malodorous mail spread out airing on the lawn.

Much more serious, little Anne became ill and required treatment in Dublin. By 20 July news reached them that a train might be running from Galway; it was possible to get there by car, but roundabout. George cast another horary: 'Sudden decision to make journey to Dublin. Is it a wise decision and what will be general results.' Without bothering to write out her judgement, hearing that Dr Walsh, the priest who had been at Tillyra, was planning to motor to Ballinasloe, she made plans to take her daughter the next day.[51] George never forgot that journey. Because many of the roads were still blocked, the car frequently had to detour through the fields, which meant making an opening in the dry stone walls, then filling it up again with the heavy stones once they had gone through. The driver and George—who was suffering from a particularly severe attack of rheumatism—did all the opening and closing, while the priest never stirred from his seat. Twenty years later, she was still angry. The story, told frequently by George, became confused in her children's minds with baby Michael's journey from Oxford to be operated on in Dublin the previous year.[52]

While she was away with Anne, Willy and Michael spent the week at Coole. Once medical attention was received, George left her daughter at Gurteen Dhas while she took the opportunity to cross to England. There were arrangements to be made about the Oxford house and, the post still uncertain, Willy's proofs to be collected. She had been reading Cellini's memoirs aloud to her husband during the evenings, and he wanted some books on the artist's work from the London Library. Pleasantly, Dorothy was by now in England with Olivia, which meant an opportunity to catch up on news of the Pounds' activities. Dorothy was actively painting; her illustrations would appear in one of the books Ezra edited during the Paris years.[53] Her style was evolving, influenced by many visits to Italy, and they were now considering a permanent move there. George and Willy still talked of a journey to Italy themselves.[54] But once back in Dublin, she found herself in the centre of public affairs. One evening at the Gogartys she met not only several members of the Dáil, but Michael Collins himself, resplendent in his uniform as Commander in Chief; despite threats to his life, he had walked openly through the streets.[55] It was the last time George would see him. In Dundrum there was much talk of both children. Lily thought Anne 'in colouring George over again', but Stephen Gwynn recognized a likeness to her grandfather. 'I hope so,' the fond aunt wrote to Quinn. 'Her colouring so unlike us made me not look for the Yeats in her.' His godson was 'splendid, a giant, who demands talk & play & kisses and gets them all—he is dark and lively'.[56]

George and Anne returned to fresh danger. So far Ballylee had been left relatively unscathed by the war around them, but now there was talk of their bridge being blown up. A horary assured them that the bridge was safe; but this time the stars were wrong. At midnight on 19 August there was a knock at the door and a stranger politely warned them that in an hour and a half there would be two or three explosions. When George consulted him as to the safest place to bring the children and maids, he recommended 'half way up the tower'. The Irregulars 'behaved very well', she later wrote to Ottoline,

& when the fuses were lit & all the men ran off as hard as they could pelt, one man stayed behind to say 'In a few minutes now. There will be two explosions. *Good night Thank you*'(!) As though he was thanking us for the bridge!

After two minutes, two roars came & then a hail of falling masonry & gravel & then the same man shouted up 'All right now' & cleared off. We had gone round opening all windows to save the glass & nothing was damaged. Not a hole in any roof, though some stones went right over the tower (130 feet & more up) & fell on the cottages on the other side.

It was all over about 1.15 am. Then we went out & put up barricades & lamps burning in the great window on the ground floor. At the time, *after* a feeling of panic when we heard the irregulars knocking at the door & had to go out to speak to them, one felt nothing but a curiosity to see how it was done & to try & save windows etc. But since then we have both felt rather ill & our hearts both hopping & stopping.

Surprised by the noise, Anne was heard to remark, 'Glynn (the carpenter) is making a great noise up in the workshop.' The explosion was heard as far away as Loughrea, but George and Willy thought the noise much less than the air raids in London. The next morning the miller, surveying the damage, remarked, 'It's a pity, it's a pity, it took a long time to make all that worked stone. They won't find many to help them in their work.'[57] It would be a long time also before the bridge was repaired; but enough of the stones remained to walk across single file. Long tree trunks were placed by the stones, allowing room for one horse and cart to make their way gingerly across. Anne used to hide hoping a cart would tip over into the stream. The experience found its way into Willy's poetry.

On 12 August Arthur Griffith had died, succeeded as President by William Cosgrave. Now, two days after their bridge was blown up, Michael Collins was assassinated. George cast another horary: 'Decision to give up smoking until there is peace in Ireland. *When* will there be peace?' She was also missing Ottoline. Willy had written twice and she once, without any response.

Are you angry with us? Not a word from you—almost for months . . . *Do* write—unless one or other of us has mortally sinned, & W., at any rate, says he can think of no crime of *his* committing, he fears some bore to whom he has been rude at Oxford may have maligned him to you! We feel very abandoned & remote.
   All our neighbours have fled the country with the exception of Lady Gregory & Edward Martyn. . . . *Here* we find all parcels & many letters come opened. But I believe that is the postman who has an insatiable curiosity. We have complained both of letters not arriving & not being received by others. But 'tis no use. I think if they tear an envelope too badly they just quietly dispose of the corpse & say nothing.[58]

When Ottoline did write, it was to tell of her own personal tragedy. That summer Lionel Gomme ('Tiger'), her young lover, had died in her arms of an aneurism. Inconsolable, she asked for advice about attending séances; to whom should she go?[59] George's immediate response was to offer to make her a talisman, first consulting the stars as to its advisability. Instructions were included in Dr Felkin's 1914 syllabus for 6=5, but both she and Willy had long been practising the art, and it was often recommended by their Instructors. Long ago Sturm had advised Willy, '*To make a talisman for an aspect arrange it so that the threatened planet is symbolically the stronger.*'[60] She wrote a long letter the next day which revealed much:

My dearest Ottoline. I have been too low in spirits to write to you, but now your letter comes. I was thinking over it last night & the thought suddenly came to me—shall I suggest making her a Talisman? A talisman for health. We have both made many, & often they have some curious power to heal. Maybe it is only that the possession of one puts the possessor en rapport with the makers & through that support comes a suggestion—If the idea amuses or interests you let me know soon as they take a long time to make—we *both* have to do it & the ritual is a long one, & we are soon moving up to Dublin. However, I did an astrological figure for the moment of my decision to ask you, & it seemed to me from the figure that there was a complete change coming, or perhaps came, to you, especially a change for the better in health. If you *want* a talisman it is rendered inoperative if you think of it or show it to another person—suggestion again—because you thereby weaken the link with the makers.

Despite their contented life at Ballylee, Willy was feeling his age that summer; so however was she. But as she told Ottoline, she had her own thoughts about the political situation, reflecting a sense of history and personality that differed from her husband's:

I dreamed very vividly of you a few nights ago, so vividly that I woke with that intimate sense of personality one has after meeting a person from whom one has been long separated.

I was saying (in my dream) to you that I was nearly thirty & I was only now beginning to long for all the things I ought to have wanted at twenty, & a voice kept shouting at me 'No, tell her "Conrad and the terrace" ' and kept on repeating these words. Do you know Conrad?

Collins death is a great loss, greater than Griffith. He was a far better educated man—read Homer in Greek & had that passion for the Homeric heroes that O'Connor has for Trotsky! Griffith was too old and too fixed & bitter a mind to make a statesman. After their civil war was ended I think other men would have soon outrun him. But just now he was invaluable & his death will prolong all this war. Kevin O'Higgins & Duggan are both thought the coming men. Cosgrave of course takes Griffiths place for he is an old hand. Dick Mulcahy *extremely* able but a reserved silent man who is not of the type which gets loved & that is half the battle here.

Any advice she could offer about mediums was, she admitted, out of date. Mrs Handcock in London was 'exceedingly good' and Willy would ask a fellow member of the SPR to send an introduction;[61] Mrs Leonard '*used* to be remarkable' and '*was* excellent', but might now have been spoiled by all the publicity over Oliver Lodge's *Raymond*—if writing, she instructed, say 'Miss Hyde' recommended her. But she admitted that she herself had given up mediums.[62]

Perhaps George was no longer as credulous as Willy, for she does not mention the visit they had made in March to the College of Psychic Studies. Her long letter went off just before the post office workers went on strike; Willy visited Garsington in November when he went to Oxford to retrieve his Kelmscott Chaucer and papers from storage; while there, he and Ottoline talked philosophy. 'We must keep her in our thoughts,' he wrote to George. 'I used to think her interested but as not understanding but I see that I was mistaken.'[63]

After the explosion, the servants were nervous and even Anne somewhat anxious. Furthermore, blowing up the bridge had dammed their little Ballylee River. By 19 September heavy rains led to a flood and they waded through two feet of water to pack and lift all their belongings to safety. Although George had already made arrangements to send the children to Coole for a week while readying Merrion Square, the departure from their castle was ignominious.[64] But despite the hardships, the memory of the pleasures of that summer lived on, carrying them through successive summer retreats for the next six years. Only a few months after they had settled into their new house in Dublin, George and Willy were planning a return journey to superintend the completion of the tower's third room, made even more necessary now that they had experienced flooding. 'However we are not going as somebody has shot our builder and he is in hospital.'[65]

Like the longed-for peace, Ballylee continued to remain a promise unfulfilled. But no matter the delays and other commitments—and there would be many— this blessed place of retreat was where George and Willy were happiest together. The following summer while waiting for Willy during a dramatic storm she finally finished painting the great ceiling in their bedroom:

Damn Blast Hell. No: one cannot write surrounded by all the beastly amplitudes of nature. Millions of unnecessary blades of grass trees, stones, a most damnable quantity of water through & in the ground, and a vast deal more being hurled upon one out of the Heavens, borne down in a 120 mile an hour gale. A jackdaws nest in every chimney & *no* young moorhens. I often like the monotonous profligacy of nature but at this moment no. We are still—at 7 oclock new time—$1^1/_2$ feet out of the flood. . . .

The gale tears down the winding staircase of the Tower so that when I go out of my room my hair is rushed inside out like one's umbrella in a storm!

However I have painted the entire wood ceiling red & blue & now I want some gold paint.[66]

Rafferty's presence was always a deterrent to intruders, but when the castle was unattended there was always that danger, despite the watchfulness of neighbours. They might return to discover doors burst open (although the housebreaker was careful not to damage the wood), or telltale signs of a bed slept in. During the first winter all the mirrors disappeared, one, large and heavy, left in a ditch to be collected later. There was word that a farmer walking home late in an alcoholic daze mistook his own reflection for an avenging spirit and turned teetotal overnight.[67] When Willy wrote in protest to the local authorities about the break-ins, from their neatness suspecting an 'inside job', an ironic message was scrawled on the cottage wall, 'Tom Kiernan, civic guard Gort, take proper care of this property'— clearly the intruders were local. Lady Gregory assumed that many of them were men 'on the run', merely looking for a quiet and dry place to sleep. But George lamented the theft of her rose bushes; Willy suggested planting birch trees instead.[68]

George was well aware that, without the support at Coole, Ballylee would not have been possible. The two neighbouring houses were open and co-operative, especially during the civil war when supplies were difficult and even the post slipped through with difficulty, if at all. When they were away, Lady Gregory kept a sharp eye on Ballylee, and when the floods overtook them, Coole offered harbour. Even when there were no natural or political disasters to contend with, there was regular traffic to and fro: George, being the younger, was the most frequent messenger, regularly dropping by with newspapers and telegrams for Coole, taking with her post and other messages on her visits to Dublin. Lady Gregory could always count on one or both to assist her in entertaining unexpected or difficult visitors; fruit was sent over to Ballylee for the children's tea; Gregory was included in family celebrations (Michael was delighted with a silver fruit knife presented to him on his sixth birthday); they shared workmen, local gossip, and local responsibilities.

Coole was not merely a stopping-off point while George prepared Ballylee for the summers. Augusta Gregory was fond of Willy's son and daughter, and the feelings were reciprocated. Michael and Anne were always invited to spend a few days at Coole during their holidays, when big John Diviney (known locally as 'Blocker') would bring them over in the pony and trap; the two children took turns getting down to open the gates.[69] Once they arrived, endless hours were spent raking the large gravel area outside the house with the little rake and hoe kept especially for them in the porch.

Gregory took her quasi-guardianship seriously. When Anne had nightmares, she would appear at the bedroom door with milk and ginger biscuits; little Michael was patiently nursed through teething sessions. She told them stories and read to them, and when they left packed each a special bag of treats for the journey. Michael pleased her enormously when, 'Reading some fairy story about "The Three Wishes" ', she asked 'what he would wish for if such an offer came. He said "Coole—the house". I said that would be too big for him, wouldn't a part of it do, but he said "No, the house, just as it is".'[70] Anne and Catherine Gregory, eight and ten years older, were too big to be playmates; once when invited to tea at Ballylee with their mother and grandmother, they teased little Michael because he looked like the elf in *Puck of Pook's Hill*, and were never invited back.[71] Anne Yeats recalls that on one occasion Lady Gregory accompanied their family to Rosses Point in Sligo, sitting on a sand dune 'like a black pyramid fully dressed in her usual black clothes'.[72] And when both their parents were away, Gregory visited Anne and Michael regularly at Ballylee or Merrion Square.

Sometimes George made a surprise visit to the tower with Anne, and Lady Gregory would turn from her gardening to find her merry visitors. Anne was already showing promise as an artist. 'Our children are robust,' Willy wrote to Ezra, 'and Anne has made a painting of two cats which would fill me with pride if I were the author.'[73] But despite George's pleasure in watching the children wading in the river, feeding the ducks and geese, playing boisterously in the yard, the visits she made to Ballylee alone or with Willy were most precious. With only a dog for company, she would go in the spring for 'three glorious days of solitude & cabbage planting', or in the late autumn to plant her rose bushes; she watched anxiously for the return of the grey heron and moorhens; she painted and repainted, making Ballylee her own. Willy felt the same longing for the castle, and, were it not for the winter damp, would have lived in that 'perfect tranquility' all year long.[74] As Rafferty completed each room, they followed him with excitement: 'Are you in the old bedroom or have you moved up a floor?' Willy wrote from London, telling her of the stained-glass window by Burne-Jones given to them by Ricketts and Shannon. 'I think it might go in the top room or top landing of castle, as I think we have no window in Dublin suitable. It commemorates St Cecilia and is rather charming.'[75] The window was decreed by realistic George too valuable to be left at Ballylee, but when they were together even the flood could be an adventure. 'The flood is upon them at Ballylee,' Gregory recorded in her journal, 'two feet of water in the ground floor rooms—they had to send the maids away, their rooms being flooded. And George is ill, got a chill wading out to rescue a gosling, and W. says he has to do the cooking—"there are sausages and I longed to cook them in memory of Woburn Building days, but didn't like to as George couldn't eat them".'[76] Years later, George recalled sweeping out the 'worms and maggots, and very hard to clean, but great fun'.[77]

As life in Dublin became more demanding, they would escape to Ballylee with 'no children, no telephone, no callers' to disturb them.[78] She confided to one friend, 'It is so impossible to read when any moment some one may dash in to ask a question, or the children yell and quarrel, or are ill and have to have their hands held and hot bottles put to their feet, and continual surprises thought out for them, for like their male parent a "surprise" makes them quite well—or happy— for at least . . . three hours.'[79] On such visits, while George read, Willy worked contentedly at his philosophy. He was also beginning to pursue his wife's earlier studies. 'I write verse and read Hegel and the more I read I am but the more convinced that those invisible persons knew all.'[80] Away from George in London during the summer of 1924, he envied her retreat to Ballylee: 'one good thing in your letter is that you are getting rest & if I were with you as well I fear it would not be as complete a rest. Do not persuade yourself out of that rest—you will always need long periods of it. Once I have this book finished I think I would be [a] quiet companion for you but till that is through I cannot be myself at rest. All blessings be upon you my beloved.'[81] Now when he was at Coole without her, he missed that companionship.

I am working well and keeping well, and the woods in their autumn colours at evening when I take my walk are magnificent. My only distress is absence from you and I miss you always, and when I see a lovely sight—evening light on the beaches and light—long for you that I may talk of it. Is not love being idle together and happy in it. Working together and being happy in it is friendship. I wish you would write to me, but I know you are always busy.[82]

Throughout 1922 and later, the creation of the new philosophy was in fact closely linked with the tower. In May and June there were sixteen 'philosophical sleeps' (dealing primarily with the state of the soul after death) which were 'talked out' during the day and typed by George. Frequently they were alerted to the significance of an idea by the smell of incense or jasmine; and their dreams were on the whole now good omens. Then George began talking in her sleep. 'She seemed a different self with more knowledge & confidence' and 'spoke of the different spirits by name'. The next day her actions followed the ghostly instructions, whereby she 'thought out questions for Dionertes'. It was this July that they decided 'to give up "sleap" "automatic writing" & all such means & to discourage mediumship, & to get our further thought by "positive means" '. If help was needed, they could always call and it would be given.[83] Unable to get to Dublin, where they had hoped to consult a medium, that was the only assistance there was that summer.[84] Dionertes would not return until the following July, when, over a series of sleeps ending in November 1923, he helped clarify further the moments of crisis and historical phases and cones; then there was silence until March 1924. As the Instructors had suggested, work at the system must continue through discussion alone. Dionertes had insisted that the system should enter into all the details of their life, not just Willy's work.

Although George was still opposed to publication, by September 1922 she had become reconciled to Willy's record of their system 'to show to a few people'. The 'philosophical sleeps' apparently over, and his long poem 'Meditations in Time of Civil War' finished, Willy turned to the task with renewed energy. 'Now I am busy writing out the system—getting a "Book A" written that can be typed and shown to interested persons and talked over.'[85] That he considered this but the first draft was significant—after all, as early as 4 March 1918 the guides had acknowledged that the philosophy 'may be in the book'. George soon accepted the inevitable; by the end of 1922 Yeats had promised his publisher 'the first hundred pages' of a book 'entirely unlike any other work of mine'.[86] Throughout 1923 he worked on the book, scrupulously noting (when he could) what came from George's Instructors and what was his own; the distinction would become more and more important although difficult to maintain when he and George moved from revelation to discussion. The civil war delayed work further, and it would not be until April 1925 that he was prepared to surrender his manuscript. But long before that, the process of writing that would lead to *A Vision: An Explanation of Life . . .* had begun.

Not that there had not been plenty of warning. Despite renewed cautions, Willy had talked freely if not entirely openly of their work on the system. 'An Image from a Past Life', 'The Phases of the Moon', 'The Double Vision of Michael Robartes', 'The Fool by the Roadside', and 'All Souls' Night' had all been published by 1922. In notes to these and other poems he had resurrected the characters John Aherne and Michael Robartes, who 'take their place in a phantasmagoria in which I endeavour to explain my philosophy of life and death'. The first intimation was in fact as early as 1919, when his coy preface to *Michael Robartes and the Dancer* announced his intention of publishing Robartes's mass of 'letters and table talk' and exposition of the *Speculum Angelorum et Hominum* of Giraldus.[87] He first planned a series of dialogues involving these two quarrellers and the persona Yeats, eventually abbreviated in *A Vision* to Owen Aherne's sly 'Introduction' and ornate discussion of 'Desert Geometry—or The Gift of Harun Al-Raschid'.[88] This lengthy poem, most revealing of all, was first published in June 1924 in the *Dial* alongside the temporarily suppressed 'The Lover Speaks' and 'The Heart Replies'; then all three were included in the Cuala volume *The Cat and the Moon and Certain Poems* (1924). If George's spirits had truly come to give Willy images for his poetry, then she must have known from the beginning that the system would eventually be less than private knowledge. What she did not wish was to have her co-authorship formally made public. Yet 'The Gift of Harun Al-Raschid' could only be interpreted as Aherne does: 'I am inclined to see in the story of its origin a later embodiment of a story that it was the first diagram drawn upon the sand by the wife of Kusta ben Luka, and that its connection with the lunar phases, the movements and the nature of the *Four Faculties* and their general application to the facts of human life, were fully explained before its geometrical composition was touched upon.'[89] Even Dulac's 'Portrait of Giraldus from the Speculum Angelorum et Homenorum [*sic*]' is an only partially disguised portrait of W. B. Yeats.

His wife could not escape, though the poetry would be more widely and profitably read than *A Vision* or his other notes. The Arabic colouring to the Solomon and Sheba poems was carried forward in 'The Gift of Harun Al-Raschid', completed in 1923. Willy obviously enjoyed writing the notes for his sister's press:

According to one tradition of the desert, [Harun's new bride] had, to the great surprise of her friends, fallen in love with the elderly philosopher, but according to another Harun bought her from a passing merchant. Kusta, a Christian like the Caliph's own physician, had planned, one version of the story says, to end his days in a monastery at Nisbis, while another story has it that he was deep in a violent love-affair that he had arranged for himself. The only thing upon which there is general agreement is that he was warned by a dream to accept the gift of the Caliph, and that his wife, a few days after the marriage, began to talk in her sleep, and that she told him all those things which he had searched for vainly all his life in the great library of the Caliph, and in the conversation of wise men.

Kusta ben Luka as the philosopher of Chance and Choice had been introduced in 1921 in a note to *Calvary*, published in *Four Plays for Dancers*. Both he and Harun Al-Raschid were historical figures of roughly the same period as the golden age of Byzantium (his learned friend Sturm would set him right on the Caliph's actual dates), although the desert tribe of Judwali Arabs ('Fanatical in matters of doctrine . . . tolerant of human frailty') appears to have been Yeats's own invention.[90] But Orientalism was in the air: George and Willy had known *The Arabian Nights* since childhood and were reintroduced by the evocative versions produced by Edmund Dulac and Laurence Housman; George had read much on the magic and astrology of Syrian religion; more recently Sturm had lectured to the London Theosophical Society on the philosophy of the Arabian alchemists; W. S. Blunt entertained his guests dressed in flowing Arab robes, and his wife Lady Ann had published *The Bedouin Tribes of the Euphrates*; James Elroy Flecker's *Hassan* was one of the theatrical successes of 1922. Even 'Il faut chercher' may well have contributed to the comic framework Willy was weaving about the system, for Miss Stoddart's derisory description of the new ceremonies Felkin received from his mystical adept Ara Ben Shemesh smacked of legendary Arabia. 'The Turban & carpet slippers would finish you both I am quite sure . . . F. R. likes such things & what they represent & evil powers find them useful.'[91] Dr Felkin had always been intrigued by geomancy; in 1908 Yeats recorded that 'Felkin told me that he had seen a dervish dance a horoscope. He went round and round on the sand . . . circle to centre. . . . He then danced the connecting lunar . . . planets and fell in a trance. This is what I saw in dream or vision years ago.'[92]

Willy's tribute to his own bride was reflected in Ben Luka's promises: 'when I choose a bride I choose for ever'; 'I would have found the best that life can give, | Companionship in those mysterious things.' And she herself, 'youth's very fountain, | Being all brimmed with life', 'all those gyres and cubes and midnight things | Are but a new expression of her body | Drunk with the bitter sweetness of her youth'.

But the poem carries alongside this gratitude a fear of its very origins:

> It seems I must buy knowledge with my peace.
> What if she lose her ignorance and so
> Dream that I love her only for the voice,
> That every gift and every word of praise
> Is but a payment for that midnight voice
> That is to age what milk is to a child?
> Were she to lose her love, because she had lost
> Her confidence in mine, or even lost
> Its first simplicity, love, voice and all,
> All my fine feathers would be plucked away
> And I left shivering. The voice has drawn
> A quality of wisdom from her love's
> Particular quality.

Time would prove, as always, at least a partial truth.

But in the autumn of 1922 the Yeats family once again enjoyed a new beginning. On 20 September Anne and Michael went off with their luggage on John Diviney's trap to be sheltered at Coole for a week. After two days at the Hibernian Hotel while they oversaw the final details of the move, George and Willy settled into 82 Merrion Square, just in time for the autumn equinox. By the time the children arrived on the 26th, not only had a new kitten been installed but George had made all sufficiently presentable that the first 'Monday at home' was announced that week. 'The children arrived in good spirits, and all well and Anne I think very pleased with her new house,' Willy reported. Within a month Anna had discovered a new word, 'She has just said "I am importantly happy." ' Having discovered that 'Nana' was teaching Anne Roman Catholic prayers, her mother insisted that hence-forth they be restricted to the Lord's Prayer and what the children called the 'God

Bless Prayers'.[93] Even those, to her parents' amusement, were liable to continuing modification. 'The children are well, and your godson has eight teeth,' Willy reported to John Quinn, 'And nothing ails Anne but her theology. When she says the Lord's prayer she makes such interjections as "Father not in heaven—father in the study," or "Dada gone to Coole". Then again, finding Kingdom difficult to pronounce, she has been accustomed to say "Thine is the Kitten, the Power, and the Glory." But owing to the growth of her intelligence has lately noticed that my cat Pangur is not a kitten, so the last form has been, "Thine is the Cat, the Power, and the Glory." '[94] Although Catholic prayers were forbidden, Anne remembered occasional visits with Nana or her sister to the convent in Leeson Street and 'the smell of polished linoleum'; walks might also lead them to Nurse Reade's mother in Dublin who, charmed by the little girl, 'used to give me wet kisses which I hated', and doubtless prayers on departure.[95] Nothing could prevent Anne's quick ear from picking up kitchen colloquialisms; one day George overheard her yelling, 'Sacred Heart, the cat is eating a canary.' Anne was full of moral indignation, for she said the 'cat had his tea'.[96] But George fretted over Michael; although he was growing, he was still not as sturdy as she wished. It would be many years before she could give up her watchfulness over the son she had longed for and come so close to losing.

Although their new drawing room was now beautiful, 'the rest of the house needs much more paint than we can afford at present, being in Victorian dum-duckety'.[97] George would soon relieve that drabness by sewing bright cushions and curtains and painting Willy's high-ceilinged study which was at the back of the house, overlooking a narrow strip of town garden and stable at the far end, 'joined by an open double doorway to the front room overlooking Merrion Square'.[98] Once again the Blake engravings lined the stairs, and on a visit to London, rationalizing that he could recover the £10 by writing an essay, Willy bought a set of Blake's 105 etchings of Dante.[99] His father's drawings also covered the drawing room walls, while Sato's Japanese ceremonial sword hung near the fine marble fireplace. Eventually JBY's self-portrait would find its rightful place in the dining room.[100] Merrion Square was to serve as a contrast to Ballylee, but also under George's influence Willy's tastes were changing. On a visit to London, Lady Gregory told May Morris with amusement 'how Yeats when he first came to Coole so much under her father's influence used to abuse our old mahogany—"a copy of marble"—and was all for plain or painted wood. But now he is in Merrion Square he is himself putting in mahogany.'[101]

A visitor two years later described her first impressions as she was received 'in a very large hall',

the olive-tinted walls of which were hung with clever rough color sketches in narrow gilt frames. . . . the deep orange curtains at the foot of the stairs parted, and the maid returned to take me up to the drawing room. . . . Tall pale green bookcases filled with inviting looking books caught my eye first, and then a series of beautiful portraits in oils which hung on the walls. A log fire crackled in the large open fireplace. Deep easy chairs were everywhere—one beside the fireplace had a tiny stool before it on which stood a small portable typewriter with paper in it—one leaf had fluttered to the floor. A large carved table laden with books, flowers in a stand in the middle of the floor, tall candles everywhere![102]

During the first few weeks in Dublin they were awakened at night by only the occasional shot, 'perhaps fired out of high spirits or by accident', Willy told Olivia. 'Life is interesting here & I think George enjoys it & one gets used, or at least half used to the sound of shots or bombs.' But 'everywhere one notices a drift towards Conservatism, perhaps towards Autocracy. . . . We are entering on the final and most dreadful stage. Perhaps there is nothing so dangerous to a modern state, when politics take the place of theology, as a bunch of martyrs. A bunch of martyrs (1916) were the bomb and we are living in the explosion.'[103] The violence would come closer still. One night 'a terrific explosion' on the other side of the square cracked their kitchen windows. Then on Christmas Eve two bullets entered the house itself:

One into the nursery, where it broke up against the wall—a fragment hitting George on the shoulder without injuring her—it did not break the skin. She had Anne on her knee. We had both gone up to sooth the children who were scared at the noise—Republicans firing from the roof. The second bullet came through a drawing room window & pierced our folding doors into the bedroom where it struck the wall. Mary Ann is ill & scared & will go home for a time, but George & I are quite cheerful & I dont think the children mind.[104]

Anne's first memories of the civil war were of noise, but George noticed that baby Michael 'smiled whenever a particularly loud explosion came'.[105] From then on each night the children were carried through to their parents' bedroom at the back of the house. George's beautiful drawing room curtains were lined with black, to be used again during the Second World War.[106] Accustomed to the sound of gunshots and threat of explosions, Gregory lunched and dined with George and Willy in their new house, and thought them 'very well content'.[107] However, soon life in Merrion Square would become more interesting still.

13

MERRION SQUARE

During a philosophical sleep early in January 1922 their Instructor had announced, 'I am to say that in near future you will receive a suggestion & an offer which they say you must think deeply before refusing.'[1] A week later Lady Gregory, delighted to hear that Willy was moving to Dublin, suggested that 'It wd be splendid if you were Minister of Fine Art! It was merged in another Ministry at the reconstruction, & I thought then they probably didnt mean to refill it—but I daresay they might to get you in. You shd be a great strength to them if they want the support of intellectuals.'[2] A few months later when he arrived in Dublin Willy rejected his old friend's suggestion that he speak publicly on the political situation; 'I could do no good in this whirlpool of hatred; & doing no good would be doing harm. I at least can refuse to hate & stay at home & write.'[3] Yeats was never to become a member of the Dáil, but by the end of the year it seemed highly likely that Dionertes' prediction would come true and he would indeed be speaking out in a public forum. On 2 December, while he was lecturing in England, Gogarty arrived at Merrion Square and wrote 'Senator Yeats' in the fog on the doorplate. Several hours later that evening a more formal invitation was issued through George:

10.30 p.m. Such an excitement! I heard knocking—Maids not in. All alone in the house. I looked out of the window & saw the maids looking scared and 3 men talking to them, with two more standing by a large & very dirty car. I proceeded down the stairs in dressing gown to demand what it all meant, but before I got down, Delia opened the door with her key & brought in 2 of the men & said 'Two gentlemen from the Provisional Govt to see you'. I skedaddled upstairs & dressed & hurried down. Two young men immaculately dressed asked if I thought you would accept nomination to the Senate. So I said as far as *I* knew you would but I couldnt commit you. So I am to wire to you tomorrow early & get a reply which I am to send to Cosgrave. The young men said the maids looked very suspicious of them—I had looked at them out of the window in my dressing gown & one of them 'secretary' to Cosgrave said he was glad they had passed the test.[4]

Of the thirty Senators appointed for six years by Cosgrave as President of the Executive Council, Yeats was to be one of the representatives of the 'Cultural Panel'. One of his proposers was Desmond FitzGerald, poet and friend of

Pound, who had been in the Post Office with Pearse and was now a member of the Dáil for Dublin and Minister for External Affairs.[5] Gogarty, who took some credit for the appointment, implied that Yeats had earned a senatorship through his former (but relatively brief) membership in the Irish Republican Brotherhood; when George challenged him—'You kept that dark'—Willy responded, 'Never say again that I can't keep a secret.'[6] Although the appointment had been expected for some time, even discussed in the newspapers, it was not without danger: in November Liam Lynch, influential commander of one of the division of Irregulars, included Senators in his category of those to be shot on sight; the government then granted special powers to the army. The Irregulars responded by issuing an order for shooting 'at sight' all members of the Provisional Government who had voted for the emergency powers; residences of all Senators were among those to be burned. On 7 December, after two Dáil Deputies had been fired upon, one of them fatally, Richard Mulcahy permitted as deterrent the execution of four jailed Republicans (leaders from the four provinces and his former comrades).[7] Two days later Senate convened, and on 11 December Yeats was sworn in. As was their custom, George and Willy noted the time astrologically: 'Probably took oath at 12:30.' 'I am on the Irish senate,' he wrote Dulac with some pride, 'and a probable income as senator, of which I knew nothing when I accepted, will compensate me somewhat for the chance of being shot or my house burned or bombed. We are a fairly distinguished body much more so than the lower house, and should get much government into our hands.' Since the Senate met only in the afternoons, he was able to continue work on the philosophy each morning, and the additional £360 a year was more than welcome.[8] It would mean no more long lecture tours; while away in England he had been homesick, missing George 'constantly & am always wondering if I am as much missed'. She also had looked forward to his return: 'The house seems very empty and lonely.' And he worried about her going out alone at night amidst the constant gunfire.[9]

Although work in the Senate meant even less time for poetry, George encouraged Willy to accept the appointment. She was indignant when she heard that George Russell was wavering: 'I heard yesterday evening that AE had refused to give an answer either way (formally) about the Senate but said he must consult his wife. They think he is going to back out. So dont repeat what I said. He hasnt the moral courage of a flea!' From then on her attitude towards Russell—whom Lily and Lolly referred to as 'The Strayed Angel'[10]—would be ambivalent; she was convinced that one of the reasons he refused was not his wife's decision but his colleague Susan Mitchell's strong Republican stance.[11] But even before the swearing-in ceremony, George was fully engaged in the political debate, serving as Willy's eyes and ears in the situation around her while he was absent, and entering in all his activities when he was there. Her daily letters vividly describe not only their home life but comment on public events. When for instance

Erskine Childers was arrested, she sent Willy a telegram and then followed it up with a letter explaining why he should join in the protest:

I hope you weren't angry with me for wiring you about Childers? It is not so much a question of Childers, as of the other men. If they don't shoot Childers there is a better chance for the others, and any way it is a good thing for the ministry to see that people *do* care. . . . They will probably have to shoot men, but if they do it in this way and before the Constitution is passed in England the country will turn as it did after the Maxwell executions. . . . there is great feeling about these unauthorised shootings.

Yeats immediately replied with a telegram to be forwarded to Ernest Blythe (one of Cosgrave's Ministers), but Erskine Childers, already court-martialled and found guilty, was executed the next day. In Leeds, Willy awoke to 'a volley or rather . . . two volleys one close on the other as if two squads of men had been told to fire but had not fired exactly together. I said "Childers is dead".'[12] Four days later while at a dinner party, George provided more details of the executions and the government leaders who ordered them—doubtless most of the information received from Gogarty, although she was also a regular visitor to the Arts Club.[13]

Concerned that his being publicly associated with the Senate 'will bring Maud and her ilk down upon you with prayers for intercession', she was soon actively defending Willy's reputation amongst the Republicans:

Maud Gonne is publishing wide and broadcast your statement that you wouldnt do anything for Miss Macswiney. Also that you want the English government back—that you are not even a free stater. I was told this twice, both times by republican women who wanted to know was it true. I think the way they make hay, or try to make hay—of your reputation for the sake of propaganda is too disgusting. I have set in motion amongst the de Valera feminine branch a contradiction of the second statement, although I find on roundabout investigation that it is not believed outside the Despard group. I am not at all sure from the evidence that the second statement has its origin in M. G. It sounds to me more like Helena Maloney. It is a very poisonous thing to start just at the moment. Number one woman who came to me on the matter gave herself away most beautifully. She was saying that only three letters of protest about Childers were received by the Gov. So I said I knew of four for a fact that were sent to Blythe. And she said 'O but they wouldnt come under the heading of government letters if they were personally addressed to him.' So I said 'You mean he would have opened them himself instead of their being opened by the officials who open government letters?' And she said 'yes' So I said 'And therefore the republicans wouldnt get told about it'. She got very red and said nothing more.[14]

Willy's response to Maud's 'vindictive slander' once again indicated his relief at having selected otherwise: 'She had to choose (perhaps all women must) between broomstick and distaff and she has chosen the broomstick—I mean the witches' hats.'[15]

However, they continued to keep a watchful eye on Maud, Iseult, and Seán. When Maud was jailed in 1923, the stars were consulted on her behalf: 'M. G. in gaol will she be released in time to save life.' When Iseult was arrested a few weeks later, George delivered by hand a letter to Maud at Roebuck House reporting what Willy had learned and pledging assistance.[16] Later still Maud sought his help when Seán was arrested.[17] Soon Willy too was threatened, they believed by Maud's more aggressive supporters.[18] Whether this was true or not, Maud became more and more scornful of Yeats's activities; when the new designs for coins were selected by the committee chaired by Willy, she vented her anger in a letter to the press: 'designed by an Englishman, minted in England, representative of English values, paid for by the Irish people.'[19] George preserved the newspaper clipping.

During the height of the civil war George herself seems to have been determined to carry on in the calm manner that Dorothy had always admired and Quinn and JBY had observed.[20] One evening she and a companion left the cinema to find themselves in the middle of a particularly aggressive shelling; they had to bolt through blasts of machine-gun fire near Merrion Square, finally taking refuge in the Arts Club on Upper Fitzwilliam Street for several hours until there was a lull. She returned home to find Anne awake and the servants 'weeping and praying' in the dark. 'My advent brought a more pagan spirit, and they all cheered up and ate caramels.' Her only comment about the dangers —'A stirring life.'[21] After this incident, however, she seems to have decided that more discretion was necessary. When Augusta Gregory was visiting, she arranged to take her to the Abbey Theatre in a taxi instead of walking.[22] This may have been the occasion Anne remembered: 'One night it was particularly noisy with a great number of shots going round the place, and Mother thought it would be best to take the tram and get home quicker. Lady Gregory refused . . . she wasn't going to be intimidated . . . and Mother told me, "I felt like saying, 'It's all very well for you, but it isn't *my* (bloody) country!'" '[23] On 17 March 1923, the Pillar Picture House around the corner from the theatre was blown up; but despite threats from Republicans, the Abbey stayed open.[24]

For all her bravado in letters to Willy, George was aware of the risks. A horary asks simply, 'Query will this house be raided or burned? Jan. 6 1923 8.45 p.m.' It was no idle question; during January and February that year the houses of thirty-seven Senators were burnt, including Kilteragh, Senator Horace Plunkett's home in Foxrock on whose grounds Lennox Robinson lived. Gogarty, who had already been captured by gunmen and made a daring escape by diving into the Liffey (after which he carried a revolver and had an armed guard), moved his practice to London for a year until things quietened down, returning each week for Senate meetings.[25] Willy, back again in London on business, urged George to join him in Holyhead, leaving Lily in charge at Merrion Square: 'I am writing letters & little system but alas my head is full of poetry which I long to write. Ah if only you & I had a chance of a couple of weeks anywhere out of reach of bombs and business.' But George was firm: 'I don't think I had better go away just now. Last night there was a great burning of houses, & I don't want Lily to come here & get a bad shock.' Instead she asked their armed guard to come in earlier each evening; soon they were coming as early as 4 p.m. (occasionally while having tea in the hall they gave Anne lumps of sugar). As news reached him of the conflagrations in Dublin, and doubtless influenced by Gogarty's retreat, Willy became even more alarmed for his family: 'I was awakened at 6.30 this morning, by what seemed a shot. I have been anxious about you all since.' They had already stored all the paintings and manuscripts—including the script and their work on the system—in the bank. Now he urged her to consider taking a house in Wales or Chester until the worst was over, 'for you are in great need of rest. It is very possible that you may have to move them to Wales having insured house & its contents against war risks for (say) three months. Gogarty has impressed upon me that nervous shock may be very bad for Anne's kidneys. The boat from Holyhead to Dublin is I think 11/6 so I could do all I had to do without much expense.'[26] George's reply moved him deeply:

I *do* feel that things now are at the Climax—and therefore that one should if it is in anyway possible, stick it out. If it is, in any way, any use being here at all—that is to say if it is to be of any use in the future—this is the decisive moment. . . . It is *just* possible that Dev. may at last have the courage to dissociate himself from the extreme element. Do not think that I for one moment do not realise the upset to you that all this is, or that I neglect the possibilities of danger to you.

I am not suggesting that you should come back—except for the Senate—but I do think that a general removal might be a bitter mistake. Anne has slept through *every*thing. That she is a little deaf may be a godsend to her! She is sleeping as she has never slept before & curiously enough seems to have lost all sense of fear at strange noises.

It seems strange to me that I have no feeling of fear over the future, but this very lack of anxiety increases my belief that there is no need for fear, for if I do not fear for you when you are my whole world surely my instinct is right?

He stopped trying to persuade her; not only was her courage impressive (and strikingly similar to Lady Gregory's), but 'I realized how rarely you express emotion from the great pleasure that last sentence of your letter gave me. Years have past since you have written me, if indeed you ever did write me such a sentence. It has filled my heart full.'[27] Like Willy, her daughter recalled how undemonstrative George was, conveying affection instead through her large expressive eyes and, most of all, her actions.[28]

A few weeks after her refusal to leave Dublin, George called round to Ely Place to discover Mrs Gogarty in tears, having just read in the paper that Renvyle had been burned down.[29] However, unlike George, Willy did not think de Valera would ever change: 'He is a theologian turned politician & could take for his motto a saying of I think Newmans, "better that the human race should perish than that one sin be committed." '[30] At 9.15 p.m. on 4 April George cast another horary: 'House being watched? If so, what reason.' The answer was depressing: 'I should say the house *is* being watched.' Even the armed guards were becoming restive. 'We are rather weary of being tied to the house,' Willy confessed. 'We think if we went away the government might not keep their guard here and so we talk over plans of Italy but know they are not to come true this year.'[31] Italy may have been out of the question, but his wife was determined not to lose out on all entertainment: one day Lily visited them to find that George had bobbed her hair and was planning to attend a fancy dress party dressed as a Mexican Indian, 'the cut off tresses in her belt as a scalp'.[32]

She did manage a quick trip to join Willy in London mid-February, leaving Lennox Robinson, his sister, and mother to sleep at 82 Merrion Square. Yeats was delighted to have his wife to himself for a few days ('I hate all absence from you'), and they celebrated by visiting old haunts—dining at the Mont Blanc Restaurant on Gerrard Street, visiting a few mediums at the College of Psychic Sciences, among them the famous Mrs Blanche Cooper, and making friends with Dulac's 'new love' Helen Beauclerk, whose 'very strange' horoscope they had both judged.[33] It would have been almost normal except that, at the Laverys, when a servant 'let a glass fall with a crash, every Irish person of the party had jumped'.[34]

But Willy had another surprise for her: he had been to see her grandmother, and for the first time George was invited to visit 7 Southwell Gardens. She remembered that experience vividly, for as they passed a portrait in the hall, she asked Mrs Woodmass, 'Is that my grandfather?' Not immediately recalling that Nelly had been a legitimate offspring, the old lady replied, 'That was my husband'.[35] Willy continued to visit his wife's grandmother and eventually his charm paid off; just months before her mother's death in 1927 Nelly had been brought back into favour also. Indomitable to the end, Edith Alice even died 'very gracefully'. During her last days Nelly observed: 'Half paralysed, she speaks & swallows with difficulty but every day she is carried into the dining-room dressed up in silks and laces and a wonderful head-dress and is as beautiful as ever. She has iron pluck and no one knows what she thinks or feels. Her brain is as cute as it ever was.'[36] Although George never received the oil paintings of her ancestors, she and Harold were provided with voluntary settlements; and almost at the last moment a second codicil granted Nelly a life annuity of £500.[37] Michael and Anne recalled a few memories of Nelly, but they do not seem ever to have visited the dreaded old lady of Southwell Gardens. Nor were they aware that a maternal great-great-aunt, Agnes Steeds, had lived in County Dublin until her death in 1925.

By 2 May 1923 seventy-seven Republican prisoners had been executed; on 27 April de Valera ordered the Republican campaign suspended, and arms were dumped in May. George had been right. Meanwhile Senate affairs engrossed them both more than they had bargained for. 'Here one works at the slow exciting work of creating the institutions of a new nation,' Yeats wrote to Olivia.[38] He depended upon George to read to him (and discuss) the 'blue book' reports and to do some of the research for his committee work. Frequently now the visits to Ballylee included long evenings of reading for the Senate. George enjoyed some of these tasks more than others. 'Willy is taking himself seriously at the moment— as a legislator,' she wrote to an absent friend:

—and Spengler's 'Decline of the West' is being read (by me to him) and when not read, talked about; or your new Irish Coins—God Help You—or your Maynooth which has 'approached' the 'President' to declaim against the resolution recently passed by the school teachers that a local rate be struck for the maintenance of the schools and that the management of the schools be under local committees . . . its all tried on the dog first . . . or your local farmer 300 yards from Ballylee who recently knocked down a girl of eleven and kicked her when down because she called names at him, and got fined 5/- and costs (7/0) for doing so.[39]

During his two terms Yeats was to head committees on Irish manuscripts, new Coinage, and the 'Federation of the Arts' in Ireland; became exercised over the threat to author's copyright; and with the support of the Chief Justice almost succeeded in rerobing the judges.[40] George listened to and typed out his speeches; many years later she described the preparation, which they both enjoyed: 'Yeats would stride, tall and silver-haired, up and down the length of his study, shaping and rehearsing a passage, dictating it to her when it satisfied his ear, now and then breaking into laughter over some witty phrase, or mischievous illustration of a point.'[41] During the debate on divorce he sent one memorable speech, which was never given, to AE; publication in the *Irish Statesman* guaranteed greater publicity than if buried in the cloth-bound proceedings of the 1925 session.[42]

The speech he did make, 'unique in the history of the Senate' according to the Clerk of that body, was deliberately crafted beforehand; George told Joseph Hone that 'He had been extremely nervous while rehearsing his oration at home; he was deathly white when he rose, and when he had finished the sweat was pouring from his brow.' In this case at least the results of such effort were satisfying: 'By all accounts it was terrific—at least WB was, everyone was frantically excited while he was speaking.'[43] George too was pleased with its impact:

The Divorce Speech has at any rate made people sit up—and whether they do so on a hard backed chair with their mouths in a horizontal line, or in arm-chairs with their mouths open, dont seem to much matter. But the Magical Sleep of hypocrisy & custom has had an abrupt waking! They are shocked at the mention of their immaculate

O'Connell—but last night a good Catholic told W. the follow[ing] story—a man went to O'Connells house & found many pretty servant-girls waiting upon O'Connell. The man said 'What a lot of pretty maids you have. Where are they to be had?' And O'Connell's reply 'Upon the fur rug in the dining-room'.[44]

Yeats always took his duties as Senator seriously, missing sittings only through illness or commitments elsewhere; the Senate sat a total of 245 days during the two terms he was in office, but there were many other hours devoted to committee work and 'intrigue'.[45] When he was in London George was even busier, 'all Willy's irons having to be kept hot'. She also seems to have marshalled a wide circle of informants: 'G. Yeats came in saying she had been told there was a split in the Cabinet and that we might be without a Government by 4 o' c,' Lady Gregory recorded during one visit to Merrion Square.[46] Her involvement seems to have been generally acknowledged and accepted: 'I know pretty well what he wanted in reference to the matter,' she wrote confidently to Desmond FitzGerald on one occasion; 'shall I come over at 4-30, or will you wait till he is back?'[47] Sometimes she preserved notes on the swift passage of events:

March 11th 1924 dined at the Glenavys. . . . O'Higgins who was full of the army mutiny. Said he was very glad it had come at last, . . . praised O'Connell . . . March 12. Heard that Executive Council sat from 10 to 6.16 next morning . . . 13th Rehearsal of 6 p.m. of Hawks Well . . . went to Hippodrome in evening with L.R. Wednesday March 19. Executive Council have requested the resignation of General Seán McMahon. Chief of Staff General O'Sullivan Adjutant General General S. O'Muirthile Quartermaster General & head of I. R. B. General Mulcahy resigned . . . It is difficult to foresee what will come.

The notes end, typically, with a horary figure—'what will be result of Executive action in demanding resignations of army council? 9.30 p.m. (10 GMT) March 19. 1924.' The judgement concludes, 'In what other country would an army council order a raid on a suspected meeting in a public house without the warrant of either government or chief of army?'[48]

Despite the internal strife between army and government leaders, in August 1924 Ireland celebrated the end of the civil war with the Tailleann Games, to which many international figures were invited. Asked by Gogarty to take charge of the distinguished guests (or 'eminent sons' of their respective countries), Yeats and consequently George were kept away from Ballylee while they attended —and hosted—numerous social events. 'George brings back much news of Dorothy and a little of Ezra and under her incitement I have asked Joyce to come and stay for a few days. If he comes I shall have to use the utmost ingenuity to hide the fact that I have never finished Ulysses.'[49] Pound was also invited:

You will be nominally the guest of the Nation and I enclose you a very magnificent invitation card. This means that you will see the Games which will probably be a great bore and the Horse Show which is about the only thing we do really well and be present when I crown in the name of the Irish academy certain books—the best Irish products in that line of manufacture for the last three years, produced by citizens of the Free State living in Ireland. I shall have a small Committee acting with me, selected by myself and you will hear Joyce sufficiently commended I hope, though certainly not crowned, for he is excluded by the terms of reference. You will also probably be invited to certain country houses, and will be generally be made much of, and meet everybody who is to be met, and have admirable opportunities for your usual violence and brutality.

He concluded less flippantly with 'I need hardly say that we shall be delighted to see you and if you can bring Dorothy too, so much the better. George is in England at present but this invitation is of course from us both. In fact, we have refused to have anybody else in order that your temperament may have full sway and exercise.'[50] Although the invitations were backed officially, neither Joyce nor Pound came.[51] Intrigued, Ezra would come only if he did not have to pass through an English port and could have the facilities of the Abbey Theatre and the Catholic pro-Cathedral choir for a production of his Villon opera. That far Yeats and his theatre were not prepared to go.

On 1 August George and Willy entertained the 'Brazilian ladies from the Papal Court' in the afternoon and that evening a theatre party for the Swedish Minister, Erik Palmstierna, who would become a good friend. The next week they gave a dinner party for eighteen guests, including G. K. Chesterton and Compton Mackenzie. The weeks leading up to the games themselves were packed with garden parties, official banquets, and other cultural events, some of which George enjoyed more than Willy. 'A wonderful concert and a wonderful house,' Mackenzie observed while attending John McCormack's concert at the Theatre Royal. ' "Wonderful, wonderful", Yeats replied in the voice of one who has just been initiated at Eleusis. "But oh, the clarity of the words," he almost moaned. "The damnable clarity of the words!" '[52] In Gogarty's version of the story, the song was Yeats's 'Down by the Salley Gardens'.

That week Yeats also hosted a reception at the Royal Irish Academy to honour the prizes awarded for literature (invitees were asked to respond to 'The Secretary 82 Merrion Square', that is, George). One of the four awards went to Iseult's husband Francis Stuart, whose first book of poetry had been published while he was in jail. Maud and Iseult attended the ceremony of crowning with wreaths of bay, but Maud left immediately afterwards, having instructed her son-in-law *not* to address Willy as 'Senator'. The rest of the party—including Chesterton who accepted on behalf of Stephen Mackenna—then went across the road to the Bonne Bouche for tea; Stuart always remembered that the three men of distinction, en route to a garden party in the viceregal lodge, were dressed in top hat and morning coats.[53] One can only surmise what Ezra and Dorothy would have thought of it all. The following week Yeats was once more off to London on official business.[54]

To Ezra Willy dismissed his labours offhandedly, 'This week we meet every day so I cannot get to Ballylee but in normal times meet about one afternoon a week. It is old age's substitute for golf.'[55] But they both worked hard, for George also accompanied Senator Yeats on official journeys around Ireland. The tour of the Shannon electricity scheme was more enjoyable than most: 'we motored from Ballylee to Limerick . . . lunched . . . saw all and understood devilish little . . . motored back via Killaloe and the mountains. On the whole a very perfect day.'[56] Some, though by no means all, of their adventures were reflected in his poetry, such as the famous visit to St Otteran's School in Waterford. George's gay description (liberally scattering dots and dashes throughout for emphasis) provides a vivid and refreshingly colourful context to Willy's reconstruction of the experience in 'Among School Children':

Willy has been in the thick of—I *wont* use an epithet—Education Bills. We were at Waterford last weekend to see the Sisters of Mercy's schools. . . . We lunched with Mother De Sales on Sunday . . . . . terrible O terrible . . . pale greenwashed walls and sacred pictures of the late eighteenth century, a dreadful plaster—very whitened plaster—Christ in the centre of a mantelpiece draped in red p[l]ush with tassels flanked on either side by two oriental and purely mundane figures, one of each sex, very markedly so and these in their turn flanked by two of the worst vases I have ever seen. . . . pale biscuit coloured 'mat' ground fluted tops so narrow as to be useless for any purpose, wide bulgey stomachs covered with lilies and roses intertwined, spreading at the base into claws . . . . The small central table decked in dark blue felt cloth embroidered in brown and grey . . . . . Then we were conducted into another room for lunch. . . . The Reverend Mother did not eat with us Perhaps one does not eat in the presence of a man? Alone I have several times lunched with all the nuns and so on and enjoyed it prodigiously. But O Tom—the lunch . . . . soup, half sherry . . . chicken with brandy sauce . . already my head reeled, but though I refused port the brazen William drank two large glasses after refusing whiskey and brandy that were urged upon him.. an adorable pudding with brandy sauce. Then we went down to the schools, very empty and freezing of a Sunday afternoon . . . spent near two hours over curriculums, Montessori apparatus, P. N. E. U. (otherwise known as Parents National Educational Union . . . it invaded Ireland about the time we chucked you over!) Willy asking blushing nuns how often the floors were washed . . . . asides to me from Sister Mary Ellen 'O DEAR! I wouldnt mind saying ANYTHING to you . . . but a man . . O/DEAR . . .' 'Do the children come clean?' Or do the Sisters have to wash them? More blushes Then at last back to the Convent where the Reverend Mother awaited us with hot milk. I started off boldly and joyfully being half frozen . . stopped . . . realised . . . twas hot brandy with a dash of milk. But I had to drink more than half for the Reverend Mother with a most baffling and unequalled courtesy kept handing me the glass. I was in dread I wouldnt be able to walk straight down the drive, remembering the black and white-framed faces that watched our arrival from all the windows. On Monday I refused to go again . . I couldnt face it twice. They make one feel ashamed, ashamed of life and drinking and smoking and caring for nothing not even husband and children or relations (who really does?) or anything but a line written in a book and a particular person that is but a part of one's own supreme egotism. As I typed that I thought it was rather Catholically phrased . . one instead of I . . . Its curious how the pious avoid the 'I'. 'We', like royalty but with so great a difference and distinction. Arrogance and humility.[57]

Lighthearted and somewhat ironical though her tone is (reflecting her relationship with her correspondent), the remarks also reveal George's aesthetic decorum, acute observation, and sympathy; it is impossible not to assume that husband and wife reviewed the experience that evening in the privacy of their Waterford hotel room. In addition to Plato, Plotinus, Gentile, Burke, Kabir, Alfred North Whitehead, and the Irish school inspectors, the philosophical fabric of 'Among School Children'—in particular the penultimate stanza ('Both nuns and mothers worship images . . .')—gained something from the acute and very human observations of George Yeats.

Throughout the years he was on the Senate, Willy was also deeply committed to assisting Lady Gregory in honouring the codicil that should have given Hugh Lane's collection of Impressionist paintings to Dublin rather than England's Tate Gallery. This meant many hasty journeys to London, and again George was involved, not only in his packing and hotel arrangements—she worried that he might not be comfortable or warm enough—but in dealing with the voluminous correspondence that always followed his many various publications. She handled most of the requirements from publishers, sorted out those enquiries she knew Willy would wish to deal with himself, and became adept at writing what she called 'jelly' letters, tactfully deflecting other requests. Because of her linguistic abilities, she determined who got translation privileges, and soon she took over from Eva Ducat as musical adviser as well, approving or rejecting the settings to his poetry. Then there were always copyright matters, which she and Willy discussed before she wrote the formal letters. 'I generally write to these people as "George Hyde" Secretary . . . It does away with the "Personal Influence" nuisance!', thereby with one stroke providing some distance for herself and keeping her father's name alive.[58]

It was more difficult to retain anonymity with those who knew her (or realized that Yeats had no secretary). On behalf of one translator Ezra knew enough to tackle her directly: 'Dear Jarge . . . for gawd sake clear the traks & let the man get on with his job.' Friendship did on this occasion—indeed on most requests from Ezra—open the gates. But in matters of Willy's fame and finances, she was firm. Concerning one request for a smaller royalty on the setting for a poem, her answer was simply scrawled below the agent's letter, 'must pay 2d—or not publish'.[59] Even the preservation of proofs was within her domain. And the storage of manuscripts, which sometimes yielded surprising results, as when she discovered Yeats's early drafts of *Oedipus*; Willy immediately began work on the choruses. Of one file she explained to Yeats's bibliographer, 'There is the accumulation of over forty years in it and I have bursts of energy about twice a year and sort and tabulate and find lost documents.' Well might he say to his sister, 'George looks after such things.'[60] Good-hearted Lolly sometimes tried to circumvent the process; to one disappointed supplicant she wrote, 'Don't say I said this—but Mrs Yeats opens & does his letters for him —& anxious to save him work—might not have produced yours at a good moment. *Don't repeat* this—she just casually mentioned it when we were going upstairs after lunch—& said "You never write introductions do you? Will I answer that?" "Yes" said W. B. . . . . George—who is as good as gold—only wants to save W. B. work.'[61] Like many seekers over the years, Lolly and her protégés never succeeded in getting past George. Even the more favoured Lily had finally to confess, 'Never tell folk I can get them to see W. B. because I can't. He was never very approachable, now he is very unapproachable. The senate gives him much work, committee and other work. Then he has his writing and letters and the Abbey. He has to rest in the afternoon, and so must protect himself from callers. He could get no peace.'[62]

George was as committed as Willy to perfection of the work. As an artist she cared about its appearance and Willy described her reaction on receiving the first two volumes of the Macmillan collected edition, designed by Charles Ricketts: 'Yesterday my wife brought the books up to my study, and not being able to restrain her excitement I heard her cry out before she reached the door "You have perfect books at last".'[63] Nor was she averse to criticizing the poetry itself. While he was rewriting 'The Death of Cuchulain', she pointed out the physical impossibility of 'his head upon his breast'. 'It was an oversight of course,' he replied rather huffily, but revised the line to 'with head bowed on his knees Cuchulain stayed'.[64] Her matter-of-factness was a necessary complement; once at the Club when asked 'how it felt to live with a genius—she replied, "Oh alright, I never notice" '.[65]

When Yeats's time in the Senate was coming to an end George, loyal though she was to their nationalist aims, was indignant at Gregory's argument that Yeats should stay on. Not only were she and Willy both beginning to feel that the new Republic was not fulfilling its promise, but she feared that he would lose sight of his main responsibility. Had not the script years ago cautioned that the man of genius was responsible to himself as well as to God?[66] Country must come third—well after poetry. 'He is always full of verse that never gets time to be written,' she fretted to her good friend Tom MacGreevy.

There is really nothing more he can do, and he hasnt been well again for some time. . . . He talked to Lady G. about it and she said she thought he ought to remain in 'to keep a worse man out'. That's how your enlightened country looks on poets. . . . He becomes more and more wrapped up in matters that are purely Irish and therefore insular, and provincial. I have been reading nothing but poetry just lately *not* his!! and it has made me realise how damnably national he is becoming. Nationality throws out personality and there's nothing in his verse worth preserving but the personal.[67]

She was chastized in turn by MacGreevy, 'God forgive you for saying that I am more disruptive than you are—you treating Ireland like a boy in the street kicking a rusty tin can.'[68] But there was always the danger that political enmities, boiling so close to the surface, might again erupt. In November 1926 Yeats apologized to Lady Gregory for not going down to see her; 'am told the country is not very safe for Senators just now. Gogarty was going to see a patient in or near Loughrea and was advised not to. He came round last night to tell me this.'[69]

George had known all along what she was getting into, and the multiple roles she would be expected to play as the poet's wife. An incident early in their marriage was a salutary lesson: Willy returned home in excitement over something he saw in a Bond Street window; expecting a hat or something equally attractive, George rushed off to discover the new portable American 'Noiseless' typewriter. When her mother told her this story, Anne was conscious of the disappointment in her voice, still there many years later.[70] But Willy was also aware of how much he expected from their partnership, and the heavy demands he made: 'Your mother writes that the book has just come & her letter is one of those gracious kind letters she writes so well. I seem to have given you "a great & splendid life"— ah if I only had.'[71]

In addition to being 'the perfect wife', George was determined to be the perfect mother. 'Nothing has been happening here except work and work and work and the children alternately in bed! Michael is in bed now with something and a slight temperature but we dont quite know what . . . He just says he doesnt feel well, I hope he isnt sickening for something.'[72] Michael's health was a concern until well into his teens: he was shy, gentle, and self-absorbed, interested in details, and always a perfectionist. Whereas Anne had gabbled from an early age, Michael for a long time would not say more than yes or no, then greeted his parents on their return home with his first complete sentence, 'Yesterday I had a stomach ache.' Their approach was the same when learning other languages, Anne chattering ungrammatically in French or German while Michael refused to speak until he had completely mastered them. But Anne, though sturdy, boisterous, and good-tempered, was in fact more nervous than Michael, as Lily noted. 'George took them both to the pantomime to a box, and Anne cried at the acrobats, while Michael looked on with deep interest and no fear, and witches and giants have to be left out of stories for Anne. She is so gay and quick that unless you know her you would think her fearless.'[73]

Anne was also quick to pick up not only the usual childhood diseases, but further complications, and seems to have spent nearly every Christmas in bed. In 1922 it was tonsilitis, followed almost immediately by scarlet fever; a reception George had planned for the marriage of one of the Pollexfen cousins had to be cancelled.[74] 'We are certainly a house of sickness,' Willy acknowledged with resignation.[75] Although day and night nurses were frequently required, George always took the main responsibility for nursing the children herself, despite how 'wearing and rather exasperating' she found it 'looking after a sick child whose conversation is unlimited and vocabulary small'.[76] At the time Michael was still a baby, but Anne clearly remembered the aftermath of her scarlet fever. The room had to be fumigated and everything possible burned. When her favourite doll was cast into the flames, 'Father without consulting mother went off to Lawrence's Toy Shop in Grafton St, and bought me an identical doll. Mother said that he was very hurt when I would have nothing to do with it, I knew perfectly well as mother said that it wasnt MY doll, mother said she could have told father I would know the difference at once.'[77]

Over yet another Christmas Anne came down with pneumonia compounded by severe dysentery. Again both a day and night nurse were required; perhaps because one of the nurses was named Miss Graves, Anne refused to let her mother out of her sight. Anne was seriously ill for over a month, and although directly involved in the preparations celebrating the Abbey's twenty-fifth anniversary, George was unable to attend all the special events.[78] 'George never goes out for more than half an hour, as Anne won't complain to the nurses, or doctor, but only to Nanna or her mother. Nanna is with her while the nurse is at her lunch and dinner,' wrote a worried Lily.[79] Though she rarely complained, on this occasion George did admit that she was 'so bored these days seeing no one I want to see and more or less "on duty" all day, and W. out every evening (because I am "on duty" just as he is in the middle of being read to or typed for, and then he is left for an hour or so & doesnt like it) and Lennox buzzing in at five (when I am "off" for an hour or so) and staying for a short time and then going to rehearsals.'[80]

They continued to be 'a house of sickness'. A year later first Willy, then Anne, came down with the measles. Immediately after one of their visits to London, Willy went to bed with a cold and one of the servants had all her teeth out. More serious, at the same time Michael required a delicate operation on an ear duct, a malformation which he inherited from George who had it in both ears; during his two nights in the nursing home, George and Nana Reade shared the night watch.[81] Pursuing all of Willy's interests while tending to her children's needs was beginning to wear George down. Whenever either Michael or Anne was ill she found it hard to concentrate on anything else; her apology to a correspondent would be echoed many times, even after both children had reached maturity: 'I said I would send this some months ago and would have done so but for a serious illness of my eldest child . . . which made me too anxious to think of anything.'[82]

Lolly was later to write to John Quinn, 'Anne & Michael are delightful children, Anne like a sprite, & Michael a giant—full of good humour—it is so pleasant to see Willie with them.'[83] Lily's more detailed record was perceptive:

Michael is a great character, and will I think be a somebody, in what direction impossible to see yet. He appears to reason in quite a grown-up way. Anne is getting rather shy now, she is charming, not pretty, but will be. Her figure is very good, tall and light, and she says pleasant things to you, and gives warm kisses, and she and Michael kiss each other every night as she has her own room now. . . . Michael gets the best of most things from Anne and Mama. He is the 'man' and also the Baby.

The family looked eagerly for resemblances to Willy in Michael, but thought Anne more like her mother in size and colouring. Lily noted that Anne was like her mother also in other ways: 'she and Anne always seem to give out light. Michael is more grave. I love to see Anne carrying anything. She comes along bearing it aloft as if it was a precious gift, and perhaps only an old dress from Cuala to stitch.'[84] Michael was indeed like his father; the caricaturist Isa MacNie remembered his entering a room after Willy, hands behind his back and keeping pace 'in the most sedate manner possible . . . just a miniature image of him'.[85] Once while visiting Merrion Square when their parents were away, Lady Gregory was amused at the 4-year-old's grave demeanour: 'found Michael alone in the nursery, glad to see me, pulled out a chair and said "will you sit down".'[86]

Michael and Anne were good friends, not yet at the age when differences are expressed physically. Once when they were 6 and 4, their mother overheard them after they had been put to bed: 'they were acting the scene of being caught. Anne was being the angry George and Michael was the caught children.' Shortly after this incident, Anne was given a bedroom to herself.[87] To prevent her from sleepwalking or, when she was supposed to be in bed, 'climbing upon the window seat of the top floor front window to look out at the women and children sitting on the coping stones of Merrion Square', George used to tie a string to the doorknob of Anne's room. If the string was broken next morning, Anne had been up. Her mother once used this device in a strange hotel: the string was then passed from Anne's big toe through the window to George's foot; unfortunately, that time someone cut the string outside. George was scrupulous in treating the two fairly; when one had a birthday, the other had a 'half-birthday', and although she was not herself demonstrative, there was never any doubt that the children were loved. When visiting Anne after her illness even Lily was a little shocked to find her 'dressed in cowboy trousers & having her tea—with lovely sugar cake—the kind we only get on birthdays—but children now get every day'.[88]

Writing from Ballylee while Willy was in London, George kept him aware of their development. 'The children are well, and I made the surprising discovery that Michael can count up to six though he cant say the numbers! I asked him to give me three sticks and to my amazement he carefully chose out three, then four when I asked for them and so on. He has learnt it all by himself. He is becoming very engaging, and much more active.'[89] He also, Gregory noted, had learned his alphabet on his own.[90] On another occasion George urged Willy to bring back 'a mechanical toy—he has got to the age for them and spent all yesterday (his birth-day) with a tin motor with a key that Mrs Reade (the charwoman) sent him'. Willy dutifully went to Harrod's for toys, selecting for Michael 'a mechanical duck with wings that wag, some sort of a cart that chimes when pulled', and 'a top for Anne which changes its notes when banged on the head while spinning'. Then, not wishing to leave George out, he offered to bring back an Italian address book for her.[91] When home he often played boisterous games with his children, and was tolerantly amused by their actions. Once when Anne was too young to read but old enough to draw, she took a piece of paper from the desk in her father's study; 'there was uproar next day when father couldn't find the poem he was working on, mother came at once to me and reclaimed it, when asked why I had taken it I replied tearfully . . . "There were only scribbles on it".'[92] On one momentous occasion their father was sent in to deal with a noisier eruption. He remained silent for a few minutes, then solemnly chanted the eighteenth-century lines

> Let dogs delight to bark and bite,
> For God hath made them so:
> Let bears and lions growl and fight,
> For 'tis their nature too.
>
> But, children, you should never let
> Such angry passions rise;
> Your little hands were never made
> To tear each other's eyes.

He then majestically departed. The children were awed into good behaviour and neither ever forgot the occasion.[93]

But George's memories of these happy times were overshadowed by one particular incident that she frequently recalled: 'When Michael was about three or even four, WBY had taken Anne to the postbox to post letters. Michael had not been taken and was very jealous; one or two mornings later, when I was bringing him downstairs, he saw WB going to the bath, he just looked over his shoulder and said, "who is that man?" '[94] As with her other 'set pieces', this one was reported with variations by others, probably representing her own different moods. David Clark recalled that George 'told the story with great delight, and obviously much admiration and sympathy for her son'; Ellmann added that Yeats 'was inclined to be partial to Anne over Michael'; when she told the story to Brigit Patmore George's version had Michael stating, 'I don't like the man (meaning Willie), the man I pass on the stairs!' James Stephens's recollection is coloured by his own love of a good story:

Yeats was seeing me out. We were walking down the stairs, when up the stairs came a maid carrying in her arms Yeats' son, then aged about three years. The huge-headed infant gazed very sternly at his father, and Yeats, thinking he ought to say something to his own baby, murmured a couple of lines from John Donne . . . The infant looked at him with no reference, and roared in a titanic voice: 'Go away, Man!' Yeats and I went abashed away.[95]

Although concerned to provide the atmosphere he needed, George was always aware that Willy's absorption in his writing deprived the children of a full-time father. 'He had to be absolutely alone, so completely alone that even when an infant was in the room and silent, he had still to be alone, because no personality must be there at all.'[96] George could not even sew if she was with him; and her gramophone was for many years at the far end of the house. The household was after all, dependent upon his writing, and the phrase 'Father's working' was not simply a casual warning. Tom MacGreevy's version of George's recollections (although he mistakes Michael's age by two years) is polished by these mixed emotions:

I didnt see W. B. He was escaping pneumonia but only barely—was delirious all Wednesday night. Anne inquired dutifully for her father each morning but Michael (aged 4) said nothing so his mother asked why. 'Did father' he replied solemnly 'ask for me when I was sick?' And there was no answer because his father hadn't. Half the time the father doesn't realise they are there and one time Michael going upstairs on a message turned back and when asked why said 'There's a man on the stairs' pretending he didnt know who it was.[97]

Constantly urging her to take more rest, Willy realized that George herself was not as robust as she looked. She suffered from rheumatism which would eventually become painfully incapacitating arthritis; a tendency to bronchitis and pneumonia regularly threatened; the ulcer that perforated later in life may have been incipient for some time; and she pushed herself to the limit. The afternoon nap or 'two and four' she had been accustomed to was not always possible once their Dublin life and the demands of children gained momentum. She also was susceptible to many of the children's diseases. In March 1923 she came down with scarlet fever just as the children were almost recovered; once again the house became a nursing home and Willy was sent to stay at the club.[98] Later that year she encountered Bethel Solomons who immediately ordered her to bed—she had jaundice.[99] She had to endure many painful visits to the dentist, and her rheumatism sometimes was so bad she could not hold a pen. But she rarely gave in. On one occasion, when she was suffering from an especially painful bout of pleurisy, Willy was at Coole. 'My dear: I have just heard of your illness—Lennox has written—& I am wiring Delia for news. It is great ill-luck for you my poor child. You have been working too hard & taking no care of yourself. I would like to return (but stay at Club) to be near you but cannot yet decide. I don't want you to be thinking "he is uncomfortable" or something of the kind.' She persuaded him not to return, and he cheered her by relating Galway gossip and, even more important, his delight at Rafferty's progress at Ballylee. 'You will have the whole castle ready to inhabit very soon,' he wrote her. 'The room above—the top room—is the great surprise. It is magnificent—very high . . . It will make a wonderful sitting room or study Five or six pounds will make it habitable. So you will have a spare room for a friend. There has been no flood since the day we left & the house looks perfectly dry & habitable. The little enclosed garden seems all right. It looked a pleasant friendly house.'[100]

With Dr Cahill's collusion and a professional nurse in attendance, that time George was spared both an imminent visit from Lady Gregory and Lolly's interference. But she suffered another serious bout the following year; the stress was taking its toll:

The last few weeks—on looking back—seem an endless turmoil. A good deal of Senate & business, a good deal of Lady Gregory & a hell of a lot of pain. I have & have had a 'dry pleurisy' which is infernally painful. I am almost ashamed of always having something the matter & feel obliged to say 'very well thank you' when I long to say 'like Hell' & to be sympathised with & coped with & for, & patted & tucked up! I am up & about again but rather gingerly & the arrears & futures of letters & so on fill me with despair.[101]

Like their father before them, both Yeats sisters worried about what George really thought of them. As Lily pointed out, this was in part because she was not, like the rest of them, a compulsive letter-writer, but waited until she had something to say. 'George Yeats writes to no one she is the worst correspondent I know, when I see her writing I tear upon the letter in fear—are the children ill or are they selling all and going to live in Tibet for the next few years, this is how one feels when people only write when they must make some announcement—far better to write even postcards about nothing at all.' But she added a postscript to her comments: 'A long letter from George this morning I withdraw.'[102] The sisters would soon have further earnest of George's care. Not only was business suffering from the civil war, but Cuala's landlord had given them notice. As the end of their lease approached, they still had not found any place to house the Industries. Willy sent reassuring words delivered by JBY in the séance room: 'the message was simply "The time must come—to hold on—to persevere—not to give in—business will be better." We were to tell you this.'[103] Willy and George considered purchasing 'a large old Dublin house', which they would rent at a reasonable rate to Cuala.[104] Then once again plans had to be changed as they faced yet another financial crisis.

On holiday in England in July 1923 Lily, who had been in poor health for some time, collapsed and was sent to a nursing home. The first diagnosis was tuberculosis, but soon the doctor in attendance discovered that the major difficulty was in her breathing. Willy, who had gone over to see her, was at first hopeful that five or six weeks of treatment might suffice; but complicating matters was the latent animosity between the two sisters, exacerbated by their widely different temperaments and the economic circumstances that dictated their confined living space. Each thought the other lazy and selfish. From her hospital bed in London Lily insisted to her brother that 'She will never go back to Lolly.' Nor would she see her, though in typical Yeats fashion she wanted Lolly to write her a daily postcard.[105] Within a few weeks however the diagnosis was much more serious, and a series of specialists were consulted. When George heard the bad news, she burst into tears. Even Jack, who normally did his best to keep a distance from family affairs, was drawn into the discussions, 'I do not think Lolly ought to go over at present,' he advised George. 'Could you come here tomorrow and see me. Anytime that suits yourself.'[106]

It would not be until 1929 that Lily's problem was discovered to be a retrosternal goitre,[107] which accounted for the noisy, tortuous breathing and slow movements that so exasperated Lolly. In the meantime, however, Lolly took matters into her own hands, insisting that Lily's problem was 'simply neurasthenia, a bad attack'.[108] She first consulted Dr Frank Purser, a family friend, who bypassed the doctor in attendance and conveyed his opinion to one of the London specialists; then, after getting their cousin Lucy Middleton to do a psychometric reading, she went to London herself. Lolly could be charming and convincing: despite the resident doctor's disagreement, the consultant was persuaded to change his diagnosis. Having originally assured Lily that 'there was nothing of the nature of hysteria associated with her condition', he now claimed that there was 'no organic disease of the throat'. On his next visit he told Lily that she should 'get out and walk about, and forget everything about the noise, in fact that she should be up and about some useful work before she reached the stage of being an old lady, and that it might be well worth her while to adopt a baby as a means of occupying her time'.[109] To Willy he reported that her 'disorder' was 'purely functional', the 'higher regions of the brain' needed 'something better to do'. Perhaps the most deadly blow was his comment that 'the patient appears to me to be thoroughly enjoying' her illness.[110] One can almost hear Lolly's injured tones in his words. But Lolly felt vindicated: 'W. B. has been most generous & paid these two doctors & also gave me a cheque to go to London on,' she informed John Quinn, 'but he never speaks to me of Lily—neither does George. They *seem* vexed I interfered, but I *had to*.'[111]

Surprisingly, considering their affection for Lily and frequent annoyance with Lolly, Willy and George were also persuaded. Although George seems to have remained silent beyond the inevitable preliminary horary ('Question of Lily 11:30 a.m.'), when Willy received the last of the many medical reports he agreed with the consultant. 'I have very little doubt that you have found the true solution. . . . You mention a neurologist in your letter and I would be very much obliged if you would recommend me one in case we find it necessary to call one in. I would prefer to have my sister moved to Dublin and have her treated there where the family physician can give the necessary information about her past.' To the doctor who had attended his sister for the previous nine months and indignantly rejected these opinions (and Lolly), he was placatory:

It is right for me to say from my general knowledge of my sisters' temperaments that I do not think his diagnosis improbable considered as a diagnosis of present conditions. The whole family are exceedingly nervous and suggestible. I remember once being crippled with rheumatism and my instant cure by an unexpected half hour's animated conversation. We are not a normal family. . . . It is impossible for us to prevent my sister Elizabeth going to see the patient unless the patient will write . . . and say that she does not want to see her. It is obviously exceedingly important for the future of both women that we shall keep ourselves out of their personal conflict.[112]

They paid for more than Lolly's journey to London. Although they doubtless shared the ongoing charges, George took responsibility for the accounts for all the costs of Lily's year of treatment, hospitalization, and convalescence in France; the total expenditure was over £400, two and a half times an average annual salary.[113] Although this was a heavy toll on their finances George tried to reassure Lily, who was properly appreciative:

What you said about the expensive [sic] of my illness is balm to me. You and Willy are so good and generous, and it does worry me often and of course most when I am less well, as then I see no immediate end to it.

I don't like to write and thank you over and over, but I want you to know I am not just opening my mouth and swallowing all my gifts without a thought of the givers. I know that my kind of illness would be far worse and harder to endure in an ordinary house.[114]

The additional expenses did, however, require a certain amount of financial juggling—a situation all too familiar. 'Neither I or George have forgotten that we must owe you much money,' Willy wrote to Quinn concerning the outstanding debts over his father, 'but we must ask you to leave it for a little till this illness of my sister has been paid for. Cuala, which was nearly killed by war & civil war, has begun to do well & to pay its debts, & we shall pay ours.'[115]

Lolly did eventually find a house in Ranelagh which could accommodate the Cuala Industries and the two sisters, but the rent was too high; it would appear that despite Willy's urging, at the last minute Lily could not face the emotional upheaval of telling Lolly what she really thought, though she confided not only to Ruth in her weekly letters but also to George. And so, after a year's absence from Ireland, Lily returned to Gurteen Dhas. Despite her determination to live apart and gain 'the freedom that I have all my life longed for', circumstances would force the two incompatible sisters to coexist until the end of their lives.[116]

'George does not write to you about Lolly's plans,' Willy wrote on the eve of her return, 'because neither she nor I think we should influence you in any way, or give any opinion.'[117] George always treated them fairly, inviting them on separate visits and scrupulously making certain that each received full attention. But like Willy she was fonder of Lily. 'George said the other day that my placidity and silence was just as maddening to Lolly as she was to me,' Lily wrote. 'I wonder? I am not very silent, but I can't talk to her, as she dislikes most people and I like people more than anything else. I don't mean crowds always walking in and out of one's house. I hate that. But I love to watch people and think over their characters.'[118] Although George and Willy tried to stay out of the sisters' quarrels, they could not avoid other responsibilities. As soon as he heard of Lily's collapse her brother had written in resignation to Lady Gregory, 'I imagine that whatever happens George & I will now become responsible for Cuala.'[119] That commitment would continue until all—Willy, Lolly, Lily, and George—were gone.

On first hearing the devastating news of Lily's breakdown, George had posed a question to the stars: 'Am I going in for a wild-goose chase in proposing to undertake charge of embroidery section of Cuala?' There were always concerns over Cuala's financial situation, now exacerbated by the need to find new quarters. Lolly and Willy had quarrelled many times over the running of the press, and George was frequently drawn in as peacemaker: 'George has put off her Ballylee visit to next week that she may help me with Lollys accounts tomorrow. Lolly & the auditor both come. The help is partly to take the form of drawing off Lolly that I may be alone with the auditor.'[120] George's horoscope confirmed the auditor's report: 'We think the only thing to be done is give up our ground floor to the Cuala Industries George to take entire charge of the embroidery & to take Lilly's place on board of both. . . . We are moving our dining room to the basement.'[121] Explaining to Ezra why they could not contribute to one of his worthy causes, Willy elaborated on the situation: 'we are taking the derelict Cuala industries into this house & hardly yet know what our responsibilities are. Our ground floor is to be given up to embroidery and a printing press. Both my sisters have been worsening in health of late, & the industry has not benefited. For a few months at least we shall not know what our income is.'[122]

George took up the embroidery department with her typical enthusiasm and energy. She designed bedspreads and other articles, and did some of the sewing and embroidery herself; at least some of this work could be done at Ballylee.[123] By September Willy reported to Coole that 'George is very busy with Cuala—full of projects plans for embroidered blouses and the like.'[124] He was proud of this additional proof of his wife's artistic skills: 'Since my sister's illness my wife has taken charge of the Cuala embroideries and is making a success. They needed a new and younger eye'; 'My wife is full of energy of mind and body and will I think greatly improve the work. She knows what people wear and has seen modern art. My sister's work had become too sere, a ghost of long past colours and forms.'[125] The business arrangements were also refined; although Lily and Lolly continued

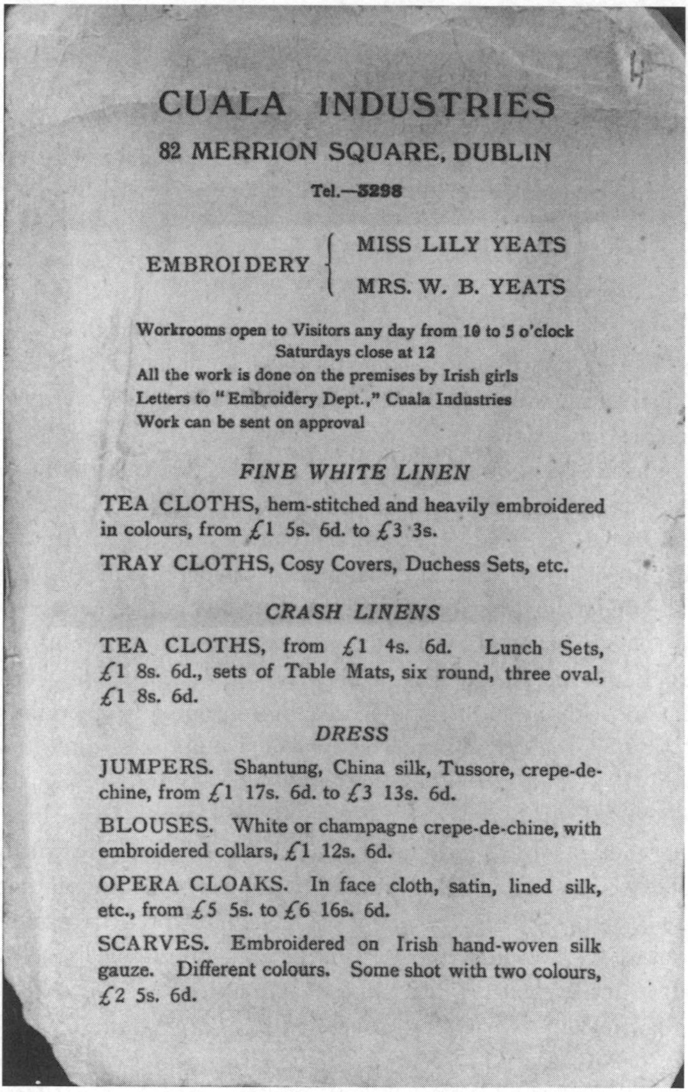

CUALA INDUSTRIES

82 MERRION SQUARE, DUBLIN

Tel.—5298

EMBROIDERY { MISS LILY YEATS
MRS. W. B. YEATS

Workrooms open to Visitors any day from 10 to 5 o'clock
Saturdays close at 12
All the work is done on the premises by Irish girls
Letters to "Embroidery Dept.," Cuala Industries
Work can be sent on approval

FINE WHITE LINEN

TEA CLOTHS, hem-stitched and heavily embroidered
in colours, from £1 5s. 6d. to £3 3s.

TRAY CLOTHS, Cosy Covers, Duchess Sets, etc.

CRASH LINENS

TEA CLOTHS, from £1 4s. 6d.   Lunch Sets,
£1 8s. 6d., sets of Table Mats, six round, three oval,
£1 8s. 6d.

DRESS

JUMPERS.   Shantung, China silk, Tussore, crepe-de-
chine, from £1 17s. 6d. to £3 13s. 6d.

BLOUSES.   White or champagne crepe-de-chine, with
embroidered collars, £1 12s. 6d.

OPERA CLOAKS.   In face cloth, satin, lined silk,
etc., from £5 5s. to £6 16s. 6d.

SCARVES.   Embroidered on Irish hand-woven silk
gauze.   Different colours.   Some shot with two colours,
£2 5s. 6d.

Fig. 4. Cuala Industries advertisement announcing George's involvement in the Embroidery Section.

to be partners, Cuala ceased to be a society and—most important—there were separate accounts for press and embroidery.[126] George was also busy designing the bookcases and cupboards for Willy's new study, for Cuala's move into 82 Merrion Square on 23 August (at 11.05 a.m. according to Willy's horoscope) necessitated considerable reorganization.[127]

Lolly was delighted to be in the centre of Dublin and the thick of things:

We have the fine lofty diningroom for the Printing Press—walls white & yellowish ivory paint—no curtain so the sun . . . shines in—we have blue curtain to shelves & our Cuala prints & poems on the walls—the floor dark oak—it looks very well. The study in front is the Embroidery Room with some of our embroidered banners on the walls & a great press full of beautiful coloured embroideries—& six pretty girls working round a scrubbed white table—a dark oak floor—then in 'the return' I have this room for myself—with my own Kerry & Donegal & Sligo sketches on the white walls—a dresser with pale yellow china—I have tea up here for lunch in our Dublin way—*the quiet is wonderful.* I hear nothing—but the canaries singing on the landing outside my door—& sometimes Anne's piping voice when she & Michael go out for a walk. It is far quieter than Dundrum.[128]

Like his sister Lolly, Willy looked forward to 'living in a house where there is so much going on'.[129]

Meanwhile George took charge of sales, including journeys to Birmingham—where she stayed with the Yeats family friends, the Cadburys. Mrs Emmeline Cadbury was a long-term supporter of the Cuala Industries, but there may have been other connections, for George had been to school with some Cadbury daughters. She later told Lily how much she had enjoyed the visit to the Quaker household, 'beautiful and full of peace'.[130] She also attended the annual Arts and Craft sales in London, where Cuala traditionally had a stall. Once, to avoid the silk tax, she took with her a silk shawl, cloak, and rest gown ordered from Cuala, which she posted to Willy's cousin Hilda who in turn posted them on to Belfast.[131] 'I do hope you are not tired of Cuala & me & the whole bother of us?' Lily fretted. From her hospital bed she sent advice to George, not all of it welcome, for George was not as happy as her sister-in-law with the social side of Cuala. 'How would the Lynds do for a sale? Sylvia is very friendly. All they would have to do is ask all their friends and give them tea. You would do the entertaining, only you have to go to it yourself. The personal touch is very necessary.'[132] Ruth, who was over from Australia for the year and familiar with Lily's methods, was also called upon: 'How is the embroidery doing? George ought to get people in every day if she can.'[133]

Lily had returned to Dundrum by August 1924, but even then she was only strong enough to go in for three days a week. 'I had a rather depressed letter from Lily,' George wrote to Willy from Ballylee. 'I suppose I shall see her on Monday but not alone unless a miracle supervenes. She says "Lolly I find just the same, cross and full of venom. I have not yet found any topic we can talk on." . . . She says she will go in every second day, going in a little later than Lolly and coming out a little earlier, so as to get a calm journey.'[134] Early in 1925 space was found for the Cuala showrooms on the second floor of a red-brick eighteenth century house at 133 Lower Baggot St (Roberts' builders and decorators below, a private flat above). The official opening was on 25 February, followed by a series of 'At

Homes' which once again involved George. Lily was again not well. Fortunately the senior 'girls', Sara Hyland and May Courtney, were dependable.

'May comes out by the 5 train and sees me every day, and George goes in and out, and the girls are so good and responsible. Isn't it well I brought them up to know the whole business. People are beginning to drop in to the new place, which is just right. . . . The stairs are very well kept, and the whole place in shining condition.' But despite Lily's belief that all was operating smoothly, George continued to shoulder much of the responsibility for the embroidery department. Lily was not well enough to start work in the new quarters until the beginning of April 1925:

I went into the new Cuala yesterday for the first time. I took a cab to the tram. The rooms are very nice, but the noise is horrible. I suppose I'll get used to it. The old Cuala I liked best of all, with the Adam [fireplace] and the meadow and the hills. Willy came out to see me the other day and we had a good talk. Lolly he told me wrote to George after the move and said she was so glad to be at last in a place of her own that she felt like a champagne supper. Tactful! to the woman who had put us up rent free for a year and a half.

She was also sensitive enough to realize that George, who 'naturally is only half warm over it. She has so much to do and so many interesting activities', continued to be 'nice as possible, be[ing] obviously very glad to fling up Cuala and get back to her own life'.[135]

But George could not shed Cuala as easily as Lily inferred. She continued to look after the sales in London; at least it provided an opportunity for a few days of holiday afterwards, and sometimes Willy was there too. Then in March 1925 the sisters' overdraft was so extensive that the bank refused to honour any further withdrawals. In May Willy wrote firmly to Lolly. 'I should like to see the Craig & Gardner audit before definitely selling out stock to pay off Cuala overdraft. In the meantime I have sent down to Mr Jackson a sufficient amount of securities to guarantee your present further overdraft, I asked him if he can see his way with the additional securities to allow it to continue for another month. Could you arrange with Craig & Gardner to finish audit by June 7.'[136] By July Lily was reporting that 'Cuala and all business in a very bad state.' Finally, in October 1925 Willy paid off the overdraft and a mortgage of £1,976 was arranged with his sisters. 'I have now paid off your overdraft—including Lilly's bill of £245—& the total sum paid off is £2010.11.1. I have also guaranteed a future overdraft for each of your two departments of £100 each . . . I am making such arrangements as will guarantee to you both the income on the investments which I have bought back from the bank.' He calculated that over the past twenty years, even with occasional gifts from the Cadburys and Lily's friend 'Phillida' Boston, there had been an average annual deficit of £135.[137] The Pollexfen and Steamer shares Lolly and Lily had deposited with the bank as security would turn out to be worthless; and despite the auditor's frequent warnings that they were selling at a loss, Cuala would continue to go well over the annual deficit. Alarmed at the despondent tone of Lily's letters, Ruth wrote from Australia inviting her to come to them for a year. But Lily did not feel up to the long journey, 'So that rather settles it for the moment,' George replied. Besides neither she nor Willy could provide the fare.

I am not sure that in any case Willy or I, and certainly not I, would feel very inclined to take part in a decision that ought to be Lily's and Lily's only. It is too great a responsibility. And apart from that I don't think we could do much financially. Lily may have told you that Willy is paying off the Cuala overdraft . . . and I think that is as much as we could do for some time anyway. However thank you for your letter. I really think Lily is better, certainly her breathing is better, and I don't think life is the strain it was.[138]

Ruth continued to do her best for Lily. Trained by Cuala and JBY, she became an interior designer in Australia, and was so successful that in 1926 she was put in charge of the decoration and furnishing of the Prime Minister's residence and the new Government House in Canberra. Embroidered firescreens were commissioned from Cuala and, most important, the design and manufacture of two bedspreads for the Duke and Duchess of York's visit to open Parliament. Designed by Jack and Cottie, and embroidered by Lily and Sara Hyland, they were displayed for five days in Freke's window in Dublin before being shipped to Australia. But the temporary success was not enough to save Cuala embroidery, and both departments would continue to limp along with infusions from Willy and George. To make matters worse Jack, who had been providing Lolly with illustrations for cards and broadsheets, seemed to be sinking into another depression. 'I know you are doing a great deal for Lilly and Lolly and it is very good of you,' he wrote to Willy. 'But I can do no more. The last two or three drawings for prints I have given against my will. These reproductions are a drag and a loss to me in my reputation.'[139] Jack's last drawings for Cuala were done in February 1926, and Sturge Moore was encouraged to design further ornaments for the press. In 1927 Willy started giving Lily an allowance of £100 which George continued after his death; she also gave her the occasional holiday. 'George gave me a present to go away for a week on. She says I am much too white. I think of going to Glengariff or some warm spot in Kerry, in comfort, to an hotel. She is good and generous.'[140] Again and again their own plans for Italy had to be shelved.[141] Then when Lily had another breakdown in 1931 the embroidery department was finally closed down. 'George is extraordinarily good, so comforting, and you can trust her,' a grateful Lily wrote to Ruth. 'She is so big in her ways and mind, and Willy the same. They fill me with hope and comfort.'[142]

When Cuala finally moved out in 1925 George and Willy were delighted to take back all of 82 Merrion Square. He immediately wrote to Lady Gregory, 'I want you to come and stay with us. George has changed her rooms so there is a room empty and of no use unless you occupy it.'[143] When he was next in London, George instructed him to buy 'a jug and basin etc, & while you are at it get a *slop pail to match*, and you might if you feel like it get a couple of bedroom chairs (for your own room.) as we are short of them. You know you are going to move into the large room at once, & my room will be a guest room for Lady G. when necessary (& I go into dressing room when she comes).'[144] Despite the demands of Cuala, George made certain her own house was always properly staffed and hospitable. 'George does it in a lavish way,' Lily noticed. 'The day of our sale she had 5 in the house, her own three, then Mrs Reade and a boy to help. Nurse I have not counted in the five. She has Nurse's young sister as a tweeney now . . . She says no Maids now will stand being fussed after . . . , and 82 is not an easy house, so many stairs and basement kitchen.'[145] Sometimes George hired a chef to cater to larger dinner parties.[146] And when one of the servants was married, the wedding breakfast was held at Merrion Square. Little Anne, observing the dining table arranged the evening before, crept down from the nursery with all her dolls and stuffed animals, gravely placing one at each chair.[147] But impoverished as they were, Lily and Lolly always had two servants at Gurteen Dhas.

During one of the many crises over Cuala, a worried Willy wrote to George, 'We may have to sell this house and give up Ballylee. It has been a shock though not unexpected.'[148] Once again, however, when their finances were at a low ebb, good fortune smiled. On 7 November 1923 Willy wrote to Quinn that there was a chance he might receive the Nobel prize for literature; a week later the official telegram arrived from the Swedish Minister in Britain.[149] There is more than a ring of truth in the story that when the editor of *The Irish Times* phoned to congratulate him, his first words were 'How much, Smyllie, how much is it?'[150] George and Willy stayed up 'until 1 am answering the telephone & being interviewed, then at 1 ock went down to the kitchen & fried sausages, next morning marched out and bought new stair carpets'.[151] When the official letter arrived, he was told the amount would be 114,935 Swedish crowns and 20 ore—roughly £6,800.[152]

Although the Swedish Academy insisted that personal attendance was not mandatory, almost immediately Willy received requests to speak; in any case he and George were determined to be present for the ceremony on 10 December. Willy went ahead to London on 1 December, and George, after leaving Willy's trusted cousin Violet Gordon in charge of all correspondence, followed a few days later, sooner than she had planned but telegraphed for by Willy. She would have to deal with a Cuala sale on her way through, but was excited at being in London as well as Sweden: 'tomorrow evening I shall be "totting" it down the Tottenham Court Road!'[153] On 6 December they left by way of Harwich, Esbjerg, Copenhagen, and Malmö; George later remembered that Willy had 'long talks with a Danish merchant' on shipboard.[154] When they arrived in Stockholm on the 8th, they were met at the Central Station by author and permanent secretary of the Swedish Academy Erik Hal Karlfeldt, who was to guide them through the next eight days.[155] As soon as they arrived at the Grand Hotel, George sent a message to a friend in Dublin, 'You might call on the family & report? (12.30–1 or 2–3 or 5–6 or 9 a.m.–11 a.m.!!).' She added, since other responsibilities had followed them to London, '[Francis] Stuart to be released—J. Campbell inquired into. Tell Miss Townshend.'[156] The week was crowded, with Willy's presentation followed by a banquet on the 10th and his lecture on the 13th.

George was also in the spotlight; the day after they arrived 'An interview with Mrs Yeats' appeared in the daily newspaper:

Youthful and charming with her bright blue eyes, kind of symbolizing Yeats's ideal of beauty. She said she hoped women would draw advantage from what they had already achieved so far. Irish women had been fighting for Irish freedom and not had much time for political and social issues up to now. She had done her social duty as a nurse for $2^1/_2$ years during the war; women should pay attention to political and social problems, particularly the latter, since there were so many social issues to be dealt with in Ireland they might leave politics to men for the time being—with a twinkle in her eye.[157]

At the Nobel banquet in the newly opened City Hall she was escorted by the Prime Minister, Ernst Trygger. During the next days they watched the return of the Crown Prince and Princess after their honeymoon, visited art galleries and the National Museum, returned to the City Hall to admire its glowing mosaics, and dined at the English Ambassador's. The day after his lecture Willy was ill, and tea with a group of prominent Swedenborgians had to be postponed until the day of their departure. On the 15th, they attended a performance at the Dramatic Theatre when *Cathleen ni Houlihan* was a curtain-raiser to Goldsmith's *She Stoops to Conquer*.[158] George also had time to do some shopping and took back with her a stool upholstered with Swedish 'hemslöjd' material and some Danish knives; she treasured both purchases until her death.[159]

Maurice Bowra recalls how much Yeats enjoyed describing the presence of the 1921 laureate Anatole France, who was there 'with three mistresses and four parrots'.[160] Then on the morning of 15 December, when George was packing, they received a lesser literary luminary. Robert McAlmon, the American poet and friend of Ezra Pound (his expatriate Contact Publishing Company would later publish Pound's work in Paris), was staying in the same hotel. When he telephoned their room he was immediately invited up for coffee, but when Willy started to talk about 'truth and beauty and art', McAlmon 'pleaded another engagement and bolted'. 'Mr Yeats was entirely likeable, amiable, and sympathetic. If he had been nearer my own age I would have stopped his sermon on beauty. As it was, I knew it was hopeless. He was hardened into the poetizing mould.'[161]

After leaving Stockholm on the 16th, George and Willy spent a few days in Copenhagen, Amsterdam, and Antwerp before returning to London. She immediately went on to Dublin in time for Christmas, while Willy stayed on to visit Olivia, whose husband had recently died, and his sister Lily, who was enchanted by his tales:

He came on Xmas Eve and was delightful, told me about the splendours of Stockholm. He said it was like the Prisoner of Zenda, a fine spectacle. There was the giving of prizes. He had to walk backwards up five steps coming from the King. There was a banquet. He sat by a Princess, George by a Prince, who talked with her in French the whole time and told W. B. that she spoke without accent . . . He was told by the Swedish Minister here that on no account was he to go without a fur coat, so George looked out one he had in America some years ago, and at the cost of £10 got it recovered. He wore it, and when they reached London he was covered with hairs so went to a furrier who said the only cure was a new lining at £25. When they got to Sweden it was too muggy, snow melting, warmer than usual and coat far too warm. . . . The prize has made a boom in his books, and he is seeing MacMillan and his agent so as to get the most out of it.[162]

Anne never forgot that Christmas either:

I had an enormous Christmas stocking at the foot of my bed, there were so many presents that they overflowed the capacity of the stocking, an arm chair was brought in from the landing to hold the extras, and there was a postcard from Santa Claus saying he was sorry to have to use the chair as well as the stocking, what made the whole thing so convincing, and unforgettable was the postcard, it was a pink card with snow falling, signed by Santa Claus. The card was Swedish, I suppose I thought that Sweden was where Santa came from.[163]

Lily had another visitor that season. John Quinn, having received mixed reports, sent Jeanne Foster over to London to check up on her. He himself had been in France, Germany, and Italy with Mrs Foster throughout most of September and October, but had avoided crossing the channel. London was no place for anyone tubercular, he wrote urgently to Willy; but he also had advice about the Nobel prize, which he feared would be wasted on Ballylee. 'I have always felt that it is a pity to take an old house and make it over when there are so many good houses that are more comfortable.'[164] It was the last letter Yeats was to receive from his American friend, for John Quinn died on 29 July 1924. Quinn had been pleased at the dedication to him of *The Trembling of the Veil*, though typically he had suggested the honour should go to Lady Gregory instead. It is to be hoped that he was also gratified by Willy's last letter to him:

You needn't fear that we shall spend any of that money on Ballylee, I put aside the proceeds of my last 'lecturing tour' for that purpose, and I have still a substantial sum left, which is intended in part for the concrete roof, for we still live, when there, protected not very perfectly by stone floors alone. We are not in a mood to spend much on it at present, for with Cuala and the Senate, neither of us can be long away from Dublin. Its chief use for some time to come will be to house the children, my Wife and I going down for but a few days at a time.

As for the Nobel funds, £6,000 was invested on the advice of a stockbroker (yielding 5 per cent, not the 8 per cent Quinn assumed) and £500 went on paying off their mortgage. The remainder was spent on Lily's medical expenses and house furnishings, including bookcases, stair carpets, plates, dishes, knives and forks, and 'something I have always longed for, a sufficient reference library'.[165] Other plans included help from his friend Dulac: there was a space between the new bookcases which he would like to fill with a Chinese picture.[166] On Willy's return to Dublin, a secretary was engaged to assist with the many letters of acknowledgement; and the Arts Club gave a dinner in his honour. Then life went back to normal—or as normal as it would ever be.

The pressures of their life in Dublin were making both of them restless, especially when Willy could not join George at Ballylee or on one of her Cuala trips to England. He continued to miss her, especially 'when the shadows lengthen'. 'Gogarty drove me up towards the mountains last night & that renewed the desire I feel so constantly to go with you somewhere into the mountains for a few days away from all our complications & preoccupations.'[167] In May 1924 George spent two weeks in England, visiting friends, buying clothes (a green coat 'which looks so old fashioned and is yet upon the very top of the fashion'), going to theatres, and 'a frivolous flippant visit to the Academy mostly enlivened by a badly behaved companion & an immense feather in my hat which tickled the nose of every fat dowager!!' Still recovering from a bout of pneumonia, she spent several days in hospitable Ipsden House, surrounded by Herbert Reade's books and comfort. She was not excited by Liam O'Flaherty's *The Black Soil*; 'perhaps I am not interested in the setting, having my mind filled with a different form at the moment—but I do feel it is good & real achievement.' But she too longed to travel: Tom MacGreevy and Lennox Robinson were in Spain, Beatrice Erskine in Palestine, her brother Harold in Florence, and the Pounds in Assisi. Once again she remembered days in Italy: 'No, one cant write letters sitting under a lime tree full of bees,' she replied to one of Tom's effusions, '—it reminds me of "die Schone Tage Von Aranjuez sub Nun Zu Ende".' Later at his request she glossed her quotation as being 'from a play of Schiller's but I cant remember which. In fact, though I was compelled to read them at school, it is the only thing I remember from them. It isnt Philip V pining for home, at least as far as I remember, it is a pining for something, a dream, that is past. I dont know that Milan is essentially the thing that I remember but the Garden and the Cathedral are a part of it.' When longing for Italy, she tended to lapse into 'Georgie'.[168]

Adding to their longings was the knowledge that Dorothy and Ezra had decided to move permanently to Rapallo. 'George and I have had dreams of getting to Italy, but when the moment comes something always prevents it,' Willy wrote to Pound in May. A few months later he visited Dorothy and Olivia who with Ezra were planning a tour of Italy. 'I wish we could too but that will be too soon probably,' he told George, adding, 'No I think I would sooner be alone somewhere with you at least for a time than even with Ezra and Dorothy.'[169] Italy would beckon sooner than they thought, however, for by October Willy's blood pressure was so high that he was advised to give up all lectures and 'go to another country and climate'. 'I am trying to get a secretary in order to finish this book and calculate that in three months I shall be in Italy,' he told another friend. 'My life has been too exciting it seems and I must now pay for it.'[170] On his next visit to London the subject was again broached: 'Olivia told me that Dorothy wrote to you urging the charms of Sicily in January. Have you weighed them?' Within a few days the decision was made—they would join the Pounds in Sicily if it did not upset George's many plans.[171] George was in London for the usual Cuala sale, and Willy was once again away over Christmas, this time staying with the Tuckers in Sidmouth.[172] Although he was away from the children, he was able to escape the Cuala 'At Home' at number 82, and, given his blood pressure problems, possible confrontations with Lolly. Then on 5 January George joined him and they left, at last, for Sicily.

Syracuse did not live up to expectations. The Pounds had been in nearby Taormína since late December, but Ezra was 'crabby'. 'Taormína was nothing but a British suburb, while Siracusa was a wasteland with Greek ruins,' he complained. George and Willy seem to have moved on to Palermo fairly quickly, to be joined there later by Dorothy and Ezra.[173] From Palermo they made day trips to Monreale and Cefalù and brought back many professional photographs of all the architectural sites on the island; because they visited the twelfth-century Cappella Palatina in Palermo—'a gem of medieval art' according to George's Baedeker—on a dark day, the mosaics of the cathedral at Monreale were far more exciting.[174] But Sicily was on the whole a disappointment, and the long-awaited extended holiday with the Pounds did not last much more than a fortnight. In retrospect Willy would remember chiefly the brilliant sunshine and Ezra and the hotel bus driver going about in 'smoked glasses'. By 23 January he and George were in Naples, visiting Pompeii on the way, where George thought the frescos disappointing.[175] Revelling in 'perfect weather—warm sun and brilliant sky, sea. One sits in the open air, or walks without a coat,' they were amused by the Neapolitans' reaction to a brief rain shower: 'Every cab horse was covered by a mackintosh, the horses' heads put under a mackintosh and every cab man unrolled a green umbrella.'[176] After a week in Naples they moved on to Capri for ten more days; the Cave of Mithras would enter the text of *A Vision*. Their last stop was Rome, where they arrived on 16 February and immediately embarked on a week of intensive sightseeing.[177] By then both were well and rested, and Willy was able to dash up two flights of stairs in the Borghese Palace without breathlessness. Again their photographic collection was primarily of mosaics, examples from all the major churches, museums, and especially the Vatican.[178] George was delighted to be back in Rome; perhaps it was on this journey that she started collecting spoons from various hotels as souvenirs.[179]

She was home in time for Anne's sixth birthday (and the opening of Cuala's new showrooms). Although both Gregory and Robinson had reported regularly on the children's welfare, and Nana Reade was entirely dependable, she was as always relieved to be back to them. But Willy stayed on in London; the manuscript of *A Vision*—which had accompanied them everywhere they went for so many years—was to be handed over to the publisher, although 'Perhaps even at the last moment I will shrink from parting with it.'[180] Werner Laurie would have to wait for two more months, but since he had been holding the first hundred pages or so for almost two years, one more deferment was not unexpected. 'I have been delayed in part by the inherent difficulty of work of this kind but partly by all kinds of distractions arising out of the condition of this country,' WBY had written in March 1923 when first negotiating publication. 'Please do not count on my being able to finish the whole work by any specific date until we have had further correspondence. . . . If we had peace here I could finish easily enough and may be able to do so in any case. I have hundreds of pages of notes which I have to keep stored in the bank out of reach of the incendiaries. I hope that another fortnight or three weeks may enable me to get the hundred pages typed and finished.' Six months later he had sent the 'first big bundle'. 'Such wisdom of life, results of much toil & concentration, as has been granted me, that part of me that is a creative mystic, that made out of the shadow of Swedenborg is in this book.'[181] But still he had delayed. While he was struggling with 'the most crucial part of the book', Dionertes once more came to his assistance, and in a philosophical sleep in March 1924 George reported on 'the office of spirits at 15 and 1 in communications with the living'.[182] 'It is not easy to break through into the other world,' Yeats explained a month later. 'I have but one overwhelming longing and that is to finish it, for it [is] my old man of the sea, and all I can say is that I see no reason why I should not, illness apart, do so in about six weeks. Do not however count on this.'[183] It is to be hoped the publisher did not.

George was also beginning to weary of the albatross; that summer she wrote from Ballylee, 'You ought to finish the book on October 24—then it will be exactly seven years since we started it. I feel that if you dont finish then you will go on for another 7 years at the one book!'[184] She was more prescient than she realized. Dissatisfied with what he had written, Willy started afresh; 'the difficulty has been to combine the part that should be literature with the part which can be nothing but technical exposition of geometrical symbolism.' 'You have in this book', he wrote his publishers, 'a side of me of which my readers know nothing—the symbolism that is at the back of my work—thoughts that have persecuted me for years.'[185] In order to understand better Vico's philosophy of recurrence, George had given him Croce's *The Philosophy of Giambattista Vico*.[186] When they were in Rome she and Joseph Hone combed the bookshops for works on the antecedents of Fascism, and discovered Gentile's *La Reforma dell'educazione*, which George translated and summarized for Willy.[187] The flourish of dates at the end of each book promised completion at last: 'Syracuse, January 1925' for book IV, dedication and book III 'Capri, February 1925'.

By mid-April 1925 it was George who promised delivery to Werner Laurie: ' "A Vision" is finished but there is about a week's work to be done on the typescript. I hope to be able to send it to you, through Mr Watt, in ten days time.' As if to confirm the official significance of the occasion, she signed her letter 'Georgie Yeats'.[188] And then on 23 April 1925, Willy wrote triumphantly to both Dulac and Lady Gregory, 'Yesterday I finished my book.' All that remained was for George to check the corrected typescript and make the diagrams. He was delighted with Dulac's designs for the frontispiece and 'The Wheel', which 'would take in the whole British Museum'.[189] It was appropriate that George should put the finishing touches to the manuscript; book IV records, through Owen Aherne's asides, the experiences she went through during the philosophical sleeps, and records those sessions almost verbatim. The final words of book III, the last to be completed while they were alone on Capri, echoes the excitement of their honeymoon over seven years before: 'Sun in Moon, Moon in Sun'.[190]

14

DUBLIN

A Vision was finally published on 15 January 1926. Described in Yeats's introduction as 'The Way of the Soul between the Sun and the Moon', not only in substance but in dating the book recorded the passage of their lives together. The concluding poem, 'All Souls' Night', had been written in Oxford and Dulac's 'Portrait of Giraldus' discussed there; book I was 'Finished at Thoor Ballylee, 1922, in a time of Civil War'. Of the poems interleaved between the various chapters, 'The Wheel', 'The Phases of the Moon', and 'The Fool by the Roadside' depended upon George's early script; 'Leda' was an example of how to read the historical cones provided during George's philosophical sleeps; and 'Desert Geometry or the Gift of Harun Al-Raschid' was a barely concealed description of her methods. Eight and a half years of collaboration were echoed, sometimes in George's own words, throughout this fragmented report of their encounter with another universe. But when the book appeared it was dedicated not to George (who steadfastly refused the honour), but to 'Vestigia', one of the few remaining who 'met nearly forty years ago in London and in Paris to discuss mystical philosophy'. Had Horton been alive, he would have been the first choice; he would, however, have disapproved of *A Vision*, and even more if Yeats had dealt with the Beatific Vision and sexual love.[1] Perhaps in response to what she read either here or in *The Trembling of the Veil*, 'Vestigia Nulla Retrorsum'—Moina MacGregor Mathers's motto in the Order of the Golden Dawn—that year issued a new edition of her husband's great work, *The Kabbalah Unveiled*.

Although admitting the 'quixotic' aspect of MacGregor Mathers's character, 'Vestigia' strongly objected to her husband's portrait in Yeats's memoirs, and this had led to a renewal of their acquaintance; Yeats, in attempting to appease her, would visit her periodically in London until her death in 1928.[2] However, although she offered some clarification of the Order's murky history ('though a certain portion must remain private to yourself, for the present'), by 1923 George and Willy's own involvement in the Golden Dawn seems to have ceased. There had been one flurry of renewed interest when on a visit to London Willy reported a conversation with Stoddart, who told him 'that if Hammond consents we can have all the orders properties. She seemed to me much better than usual and gave me a long description of a tower vision she had in 1914. . . . A ruined tower and the Phoenix born from the fire on the top. She seems to think it must be a real place. It got very ruinous as you got up.' Excited more by the offer than the vision (which in any case was similar to her own bookplate), George replied immediately, 'You must try and get the Order properties!!!!!! *We shall have to pay for them, but it will be well worth it*.'[3] Whether her interest was purely historical or to assist with the philosophical sleeps we will never know; presumably the properties would have been stored in the upper room of the tower. But evidently Willy's appeal to Dr Hammond was unsuccessful, and with 'Il faut chercher's' release of the Temple properties their interest waned. In any case, although the Stella Matutina had served them well, they had in every sense moved on. In July 1923, when adding a note to a further autobiographical fragment, Yeats emphasized, 'to prevent needless correspondence, that I am not now a member of a Cabbalistic society'. Three years later when his bibliographer asked for confirmation of the authorship of two early Golden Dawn pamphlets, George replied, 'He says you may attribute them to him, but asks you not to quote or give a synopsis as the Order still exists though it is now in different hands and he is not an active member.'[4]

This did not mean, however, that their interest in séances had ceased. Whenever he was in London Willy visited the College of Psychic Sciences and sought out mediums, reporting back to George of instances of levitation, spirit photography, and direct voice communications. Later he would even postpone his return from an American tour in order to consult the celebrated 'Margery' Crandon.[5] At one recorded session of a sitting with Eileen Garrett, the spirit of MacGregor Mathers himself appeared; at another, 'somebody, who seems to be my father, came and said "You have a son who is slow to learn but he is slow and sure. When older he will be brilliant." '[6] Willy's play *The Words upon the Window-Pane* initiated a lively discussion with George about survival after death, drawing on the experiences of both. So sensitive did she remain that Willy hesitated to involve her while writing the final version of the system. 'If I dictate to George it would almost certainly put her nerves all wrong. I don't want any more mediumship.'[7] Instances of George's trances would continue in spite of his caution.

The Nobel prize brought renewed acquaintance with a friend who, they soon discovered, shared their interest in parapsychology. In 1924 they had given a party for Erik Palmstierna, the Swedish Minister in London, with whom from then on George held intimate conversations about occult matters. He remembered sitting 'in Yeats's kitchen, the dining-room being used for the Cuala Hand Press, discussing Swedenborg and Tagore, the incipient materialism in Ireland after the liberation, the history of the Abbey Theatre, the value of words and their power to convey musical impressions'.[8] Later Palmstierna would describe George as 'a remarkable instrument of the soul' who spoke in a low voice on 'the spiritualistic way of thinking'.[9] He himself had read and studied widely in psychology and was convinced of the reality of extra-sensory experience. But also appealing to George was Palmstierna's friendship with the d'Aranyi sisters. Over a number of years he and Adila experimented with a form of planchette, using letters of the alphabet and simple words with a glass as a pointer; the messages they received were eventually published in 1937 and 1940. Even Jelly, who claimed no occult gifts, was drawn into the 'glass game'. This led in 1933 first to advice on the tempo of Bach's Sonata in E minor, and then the whereabouts of Robert Schumann's long-lost Violin Concerto in D minor.[10] After a series of psychic and mundane adventures, Jelly d'Aranyi eventually gave the first performance in England with the BBC Symphony Orchestra on 16 February 1938.[11] Although George was away in France on that special occasion, Jelly performed in Dublin frequently from the 1920s until she moved to Florence thirty years later, and always the two friends would meet. George treasured a 1927 recording of Schubert's Trio in B flat with Jelly (violin), Felix Salmond (cello), and Myra Hess (piano); but she did not always care for Jelly's concert selections. Once when César Franck's Symphony in D minor was being played, she sat outside in the lobby until it was over.[12] Palmstierna meanwhile was an important link between the two.

Walter Rummel, another musician with occult interests, also visited the Yeatses in Dublin, providing news of Olivia and the Pounds. So enamoured did he become of Ireland that he returned as frequently as possible, not always at the most convenient time. 'Rummel rummels on Saturday and stays at the Yeats—arriving on *Thursday* to George's disgust,' Lennox reported in February 1926.[13] But on this occasion he proved invaluable, for his visit coincided with the riot in the theatre over O'Casey's *Plough and the Stars*. On the second night there was an attempt to kidnap Barry Fitzgerald, who was playing 'Fluther'; Gregory described the scene with much relish: 'It was thought safer for the Players to stay in the theatre between matinee and evening performance. So there was a meal made ready for them. And G. Yeats brought Rummel who had been giving a concert and he played for the actors in the auditorium, Chopin—several pieces. During Beethoven's Moonlight Sonata, Yeats fell asleep and awakening said he had dreamed there was a storm going on. . . . The players were delighted.'[14]

For some years Rummel had been Isadora Duncan's beloved 'Archangel', until he took up with one of her former pupils. Not surprisingly and much to George's delight, on this same visit his reputation as a lover became the subject of considerable speculation:

Rummel was here for three days and was really rather pet and good, Mrs Walter Starkie (they dined here to meet him) said to Mrs Bethel Solomons some days later 'I was so afraid of him . . . he is SO ALARMING . . . He is SUCH a CHASER of women!' I wonder did she think he would assault her in our drawing-room? *He* said of her 'She is quite pretty but very hard I wonder how her husband ever managed to make love to her? But perhaps he didnt.' So that's that . . . Anyway at the moment he is very happily married and no one has ever existed before etc etc.[15]

On his next visit Rummel was once again in love, with both the country and yet another lady; and again George played hostess:

Walter wrote that he and his Patricia would like to come and stay here from January 17 to 30th. I simply cant . . . Its reduced now to five days from the 17th and five days before the 30th . . . ludicrous isnt it? They will go to his sister-in-law for the interregnum. He is giving a concert on the 30th . . . It isnt a bit of use, Dublin will never click . . . and he loves it. So feminine. Why DO the Irish always love the unattainable . . . HE isnt Irish but begins to regard it as his adopted country. Its a beastly nuisance. One can cope with Walter, I've know him long enough to tell him to run away and play. But Patricia????? Anyway I suppose they'll play with each other. . . . Lennox will be an angel and ask them—or him—out to Dalkey, but when he comes here he just sits and wont get away into a corner and have a little passionate conversation with them. He really is hopeless in the mass. And Walter has never, even now, learnt to talk to more than one person at a time.[16]

Rummel seems always to have been in search of the unattainable; by the time he had ceased performing in Dublin he was with his third wife.

Although repeatedly invited, Olivia never came to Dublin; Willy's gossip may have put her off: 'Our ministers and their wives would interest you—the two or three we sometimes see. They are able & courageous but as yet—I admit— without play of mind. Honest modern-minded men swimming still in seas of conspiracy of others' making when no one's letters are safe and no one's telephone wires.'[17] But other friends from George's former London years passed through: Dorothy's school friend Hilda Strutt, whom they had visited in Bath; the Australian poet Fred Manning, who had been in love with Dorothy and thought Senator Yeats 'chastened and subdued' in Dublin.[18] Erskine Childers's sister Sybil, their colleague from the Golden Dawn, was offered hospitality more than once. 'She is nice & I always liked her but with a sick child it makes guests difficult,' George moaned. 'She came back from India 6 months ago & says people have been beastly—on account of Erskine. What swine!'[19] Judith Masefield, who was interested in an acting career, paid a visit; Ragnor Ostberg, the designer of Oslo's new City Hall, was entertained at a lavish dinner and reception; Kazumi Yano, Japanese poet and translator of Yeats and Gregory, stayed with them in Ballylee and Dublin, and sent special powder for cleaning the ceremonial sword.[20]

Then there were the Stuarts, by now living in some hardship in Glencree, County Wicklow, to whom Willy gave up his own bedroom; George had to put a large sign on the door so that he would not absent-mindedly wander in.[21] Although George had always accepted Willy's quasi-guardianship of both Maud's children, she would see comparatively little of them in Dublin except when there

were domestic or political problems. Much to their disapproval, Seán had disappeared into the Irish Republican Army; when Seán was arrested on the occasion
of Kevin O'Higgins's murder, Yeats found it 'something of a nightmare':

He was and probably is a friendly simple lad but has been subject to a stream of terrible
suggestion and may not have been able to resist. Any one ordinary would think him
devoted to making peace & quite harmless but there are others who have a different story
and it is impossible to sift out the truth. In England you have never met the hatred that is
commonplace here. It lays hold upon our class, I think, more easily than upon the mass
of the people—it finds a more complicated and determined conscience to prey upon.[22]

By 1935 Seán was Chief of Staff of the IRA, eventually becoming a barrister, party
leader, and statesman. No one could have predicted that as a campaigner for
human rights he would be awarded both the Nobel and Lenin peace prizes. After
a lapse of many years, Seán MacBride would enter George's life significantly
again in 1948.

Iseult's marriage was always a concern, although both George and Willy did
their best to make Francis Stuart welcome. While imprisoned for fifteen months
for his Republican activities, at Iseult's suggestion he sent Yeats a copy of his first
volume of poetry, *We Have Kept the Faith*; it earned him one of the Academy
awards during the Taillteann celebrations. After his release, for which George
and Willy had both campaigned, he went around to meet them for the first
time, only to have the door opened by one of the Senator's uniformed guards.
'Luckily', he recalled, 'George Yeats leaned over the stairs and saw me and said,
"Oh, let him in".' She was, he decided, 'a nice woman', but he did not think she
took her husband too seriously. 'I remember, especially at the dinner table, I
would get involved in serious discussions, which he loved. . . . I would get quite
carried away until I would see George's face watching us as much to say, "Well,
now how are you going to extricate yourself?"'[23]

Later, Willy would become enthusiastic about Stuart's novels, although often
in despair over his treatment of Iseult and their children; she had indeed chosen
'a young man . . . and all for his wild sake'. When Iseult was ill in May 1925, Willy
visited her daily; when she was pregnant with her son Ion, George learned that
Francis had 'bought a horse and is having it trained at the Curragh for racing, and
all their money or rather his money is going on it'.[24] Stuart was absent at the birth
of their children. Willy's worry led to another poem, 'The Death of the Hare':

> Then suddenly my heart is wrung
> By her distracted air
> And I remember wildness lost
> And after, swept from there,
> Am set down standing in the wood
> At the death of the hare.

However, even before the crowning with wreaths, his involvement with the aspiring revolutionary became closer still. In June 1924 Yeats was actively soliciting subscriptions for a monthly literary magazine founded by the Stuarts, the writers Liam O'Flaherty and F. R. Higgins (who had edited Stuart's volume of verse), and the painter Cecil Salkeld. Hoping for 'an admirable row' and the upset of Dublin complacency now that the war was over, Yeats wrote but did not sign *Tomorrow*'s first editorial, urging artists everywhere to 'call back the soul to its ancient sovereignty . . . We proclaim that we can forgive the sinner, but abhor the atheist, and that we count among atheists bad writers and Bishops of all denominations.' Lady Gregory disapproved of his involvement, fearing trouble —she would also recognize in his call to 'the soul' their frequently stated ambition in the early years of the theatre movement to recall to Ireland 'its ancient sovereignty'.[25] Willy's enthusiasms had extended further than she could follow. For the second issue he gave them 'Leda and the Swan', which AE had already refused to publish in the *Irish Statesman*. George was not too happy about his contributions either, though as she explained to Gregory she appreciated her husband's constant demand for intellectual stimulus:

GY here overnight getting Ballylee ready for the children. . . . She, though she didn't support me when I told him so—is sorry Willie is writing for them, says everyone will recognise the manifesto as his though he doesn't believe they will, and that he has given them his Leda poem and a fine thing among his other poems in the Cuala book, but is, now it is known it goes into *Tomorrow*, being spoken of as something horribly indecent. However she says he was feeling dull in Dublin and it has given him a great deal of amusement.[26]

The first issue of *Tomorrow*, as Yeats had hoped, was indeed suppressed for blasphemy, not because of his poem but because of a short story by Lennox Robinson, 'The Madonna of Slieve', about the rape of a simple girl who imagines her child is the Christ. The second issue that August was its last. The result was more serious for Robinson, who was forced to resign his position with the Carnegie Trust. This time George's astrology was more optimistic than accurate —a horary cast when the Trustees were meeting suggested that 'The querent shall not be removed.' Gregory, a Trustee herself, fought for Lennox even as she had fought for Synge's *Playboy*, which she had not liked either. Fortunately, at George's urging, Robinson's salary as producer had just been increased; unrepentantly irrepressible, Willy advised the Stuarts to appeal to the Pope.[27] Perhaps George and Willy remembered Ezra's involvement in Wyndham Lewis's iconoclastic *Blast*; the next book of poems for his sister's press, which included 'Sailing to Byzantium', would be entitled *October Blast*.[28]

By far the most frequent visitor to Merrion Square was Augusta Gregory. Willy was at last able to repay his long-time benefactor the hospitality he had enjoyed for so many years at Coole. 'This will make a great difference to me, both here & in Dublin,' she wrote on hearing the news of George's house purchase, '—& all possible help is needed on the side of sanity in Ireland now—for we cannot but feel very anxious.'[29] Very soon number 82 became her Dublin refuge, where she could count on a warm and comfortable welcome far beyond that she was accustomed to at the Russell and Standard Hotels—although she was punctilious in stating that if her arrival would be inconvenient, she could 'always stay the Russell'. Gradually the rubric altered slightly and she felt comfortable enough to invite herself: 'If you & George are kind enough to ask me I will go to you— but otherwise to the Russell'; 'I know George will be kind enough to invite me, if convenient, but if not I can quite well go to the Russell.' But Willy was always welcoming: 'When you come on Wednesday you will of course stay with us. Dont go till you have to do so.'[30] Sometimes, if her journey to Dublin was unexpected, Yeats met her at the Broadstone station and insisted that she go to them. George always had a room ready for her (it was in fact her own that she gave up), and when an operation for cancer was necessary, both of them sat at Lady Gregory's hospital bedside, then took her to Merrion Square for recuperation: 'such a good night in quiet and fine linen!'[31] Her journals are full of appreciative comments about George's kindness, Willy's thoughtful attendance, and the sense of holiday she had when with them. Letters of thanks were not mere empty formalities: 'that week with you was a wonderfully happy rest'; 'thanks to George's kindness & your improvement & the childrens liveliness I enjoyed my visit'; 'I am much the better for my luxurious visit to 82.' Gradually the visits became longer, extending at times to three or four weeks: 'Here I am safely. . . . I feel quite a new being after my happy weeks with you and George & the children—all so kind—& I am full of courage—tho' prospects are not very bright. . . . I look forward to seeing George next Monday—for as long as she will stay.'[32] Sometimes, however, George was nursing both Willy and Lady Gregory at the same time while coping with other business:

My dear Ezra Non poss: In other words since William was ill and convalesced we have had Lady G staying here . . . for a month . . . and all has been held up in consequence. There IS a mass of verse bad and goodish . . . But it has to be sorted . . . And until there is once more solitude in the house it seems impossible to get this done. In two weeks I hope it will be done! By then I will see that a batch is sent you. I dont know whether you will want to use it or not.[33]

It was not all theatre business for their guest in Dublin. After attending one of Willy's 'Mondays', Gregory commented in her journal, 'It is supposed to be for men only, and might be better so,' but even so, 'it was an interesting evening'; possibly Gogarty's witticisms became a little too indecorous.[34] After their move to Dublin George, unlike Mrs Gogarty who presided throughout the evening, always discreetly withdrew, reappearing only to serve refreshments (tea for AE, whiskey and white wine for other guests).[35] George ran messages and operated the telephone for Gregory. Both avid movie-goers, she and Willy took Gregory to see her first colour film (Zane Grey's *Wanderer of the Wasteland*, filmed in the Arizona desert), although she disapproved of their occasional preference for the movie house over the Abbey. (Once when turned away by a full house, they were seen crossing over to the Metropole to see *Anna Christie*.[36]) Willy was not always there: 'Dublin seemed lonely without you, but George was very kind, & taxied me one evening to the Abbey.' Sometimes George was not there either, but Augusta Gregory was always encouraged to use 82 as her base, and when the children were also absent she even appreciated being affably greeted by the big dog Thor. Occasionally Anne and Catherine Gregory also stopped off with their grandmother on the way between the Liverpool boat and the train to Gort.[37]

Satisfying though they were to Willy, such visits were not always sweet and easy for George, no matter how much she appreciated Lady Gregory's generosity and long friendship with her husband. Sometimes her guest's resolution became too much for her. 'Lady G. was here for one whole month . . . . . only left yesterday, and I have been sitting in the smallest possible nutshell in order to preserve a moderate outward sanity.'[38] As Lily once remarked, 'Lady Gregory is here and staying at W. B.'s. George finds her I think rather overpowering. Who doesn't?'[39] 'As she grows older she grows very strong and obstinate,' Willy observed with affectionate amusement.[40] But though she enjoyed telling a good story herself, his old friend could be both prudish and unamused. Anne once purchased a squeaky cushion from a Grafton Street toyshop and put it on Lady Gregory's chosen chair. When it squeaked, 'Lady Gregory just stood up, removed the cushion and sat down again. Mother was so cross on my behalf.'[41] As she grew older (and suffered from rheumatism and recurring cancer), she also became more forgetful. George gave vent to her exasperation rarely, and only to close friends like Lennox and Dorothy.

But they were both true gentlewomen; George remained generous and hospitable to her husband's benefactor, just as Lady Gregory in turn had accommodated Willy's marriage. Other times they acted in collusion, and the Lane pictures were always a ready excuse: 'I am not quite certain that George has not conspired with Lady Gregory—she was at Coole on Friday—to send me on this wild-goose chase for the good of my health,' he wrote to Olivia of a planned trip to London. 'I have been doing too much philosophy and writing too much verse.'[42] When the Gregory medallion was struck by the Irish Academy of Letters, George bought one as a gift for her; designed by Spencer Simson, Willy thought it after the Mancini painting her best portrait. Her reaction was typically selfless and as always inclusive: 'Very kind of you & George giving me the medallion— something for the children to inherit.'[43] Despite the occasional and inevitable irritation, the relationship between the two women would remain cordial and co-operative until Lady Gregory's death.

'I think you will find Dublin a very different place with the new life in it & find yourself contented there,' Gregory had written just before their move.[44] Dublin society in turn approved of Mrs Yeats, if Lady Dunsany's reaction was any indication. 'Mr and Mrs Yeats staying. . . . I had not met Mrs Yeats before, but they seem a happy well-assorted couple; she is practical, appreciative, not a shadow, and has a sense of humour (being English it has not been lost in the late mess) and we thought him improved in little ways.'[45] When the French Society was established, George became a regular attender; meetings there and social encounters with consul-generals to the new nation were a good way to keep up her languages. She seems to have avoided the Society for Psychical Research, although Willy was a member of the Irish Astrological Society. Inevitably many of their dinner invitations had to do with Willy's connections in the Senate, for Dublin was too small to draw a hard and fast distinction between politics and the arts. There were frequent invitations to the viceregal lodge (nicknamed 'Uncle Tim's Cabin' by Gogarty), where Timothy Healy, the first Governor-General, sometimes took them aside to discuss the progress of the campaign to regain Hugh Lane's pictures.[46] On the occasion of his first visit to the Abbey Theatre George knowledgeably made certain that whiskey was available for the three ADCs. [47] As time wore on, George became less sympathetic to Willy's involvement in the Senate—it was immersing him in a milieu that she felt was beneath him, taking too much time from his work as a poet: 'to spend hours listening to rubbish in and out of the Senate and going to committees and being visited by fishermen's associations, and Freddie Ryans' and nincompoops and miaows and bow-wows of all sorts mostly mongrels is a bit too much.'[48]

Perhaps, other than the Gogartys, the couple they saw most frequently were Mary and Joseph O'Neill, Irish scholar and Permanent Secretary to the Department of Education. Willy regularly attended the O'Neills' 'At Homes' in 2 Kenilworth Square on Thursday and the Gogartys' in Ely Place on Friday. George was friendly with both wives, though privately she referred to poet Mary Devenport O'Neill as 'the White Heron' (or 'herring'), a possible reference to the long dialogue Mrs O'Neill held each week with Yeats over *A Vision*.[49] George and Willy both admired Kevin O'Higgins, Minister for Justice and External Affairs and vice-president of the Executive Council, though she found dinner parties there 'just pleasant and a little dull'.[50]

George hated 'small talk' and longed for the bite and intelligent discussion she had been accustomed to in London, in her mother's and Olivia's circle and at her clubs. Since November 1921 she had been an out-of-town member of Dublin's United Arts Club; on 2 November 1922 the Club held a dinner to welcome them to Ireland; within months of their move to Merrion Square she was appointed honorary secretary. Soon Willy's needs became too demanding for her to deal with the innumerable complaints and suggestions that accompanied the monthly committee meetings, and by the end of 1923 she had resigned her office. However, she remained on the general committee, along with her brother-in-law Jack.[51] The Club was a place to have dinner when Willy was away or at a meeting, a cup of afternoon tea, or simply an evening of conversation. 'I sat on at the Club last night till nearly eleven talking to the Manchester Guardian correspondent. A simple, rather pleasant young man who was interested in mystical things, mainly in the direction of "orders" and rituals.'[52] Not that the conversation was always sedate: 'My wife says that members of the Arts Club have become incredibly [candid] about their love affairs.'[53]

In true Dublin form even—or especially—the gossip had wit and the spice of malice. And the two friends she spent most of her time with were Club regulars. Lennox Robinson, 'Lynx' or 'Tinche' to his friends, had been around for as long as she could remember—she met him first at gatherings for the Irish Players in London, and her marriage had brought them into close partnership, for Yeats was Lennox's hero, ideal, and colleague. He was the natural choice as one of Michael's godfathers. George probably first met Thomas MacGreevy at the Club, most likely through Lennox, for the two men had at one time shared lodgings and continued to confide in each other. Tom and Lennox's was a delicate though necessary friendship, for MacGreevy was unduly sensitive, ready to take umbrage and always scenting disloyalty; behind his back they all called him 'Tamsie' or 'Painsy' (after the hymn 'We may not know, we cannot tell | What pains He had to bear'[54]). Both men encouraged George in her support of Willy; she could count on their help for innumerable errands ranging from having the telephone mended and measuring filing cabinets when she was at Ballylee to checking on the children's welfare or keeping Willy occupied while she was further away. Both were probably homosexual by nature, although Tom's deep Roman Catholicism locked him into celibacy and abstinence. But Lennox once reported in good humour, 'I've bought a pair of Oxfords—crudest strawberry colour and a jumper up to my neck—apricot—together they justify Dublins worst suspicions about me!!'[55] Since most of Dublin did suspect this, neither was a threat to the good name of Mrs W. B. Yeats; she could invite them without compunction to join her for dinner at the Club or an evening at the movies. They were all fond of film; her earliest surviving letter to Tom is an invitation on Arts Club stationery to join her at the Corinthian cinema to see Chaplin in *Pay Day*: 'It's my last chance as my nurse goes on a week's holiday tomorrow & I shant.'[56] They had dined and gone to the 'Pictures' just a few days earlier.[57] In the company of either she could relax, say what she thought, and joke, confident that she would be understood. She sometimes signed her letters to both 'Georgie', an indication of this camaraderie and freedom; with Tom and Lennox, she need not always project the strong 'George' image that Willy required. And all three corresponded regularly with each other.

'I thank you for your delightful letter,' Willy once wrote to George. 'You are much the best letter writer I know, or have known—your letters have so much unstrained animation, so much natural joyousness.'[58] There was an art to letter-writing, and just as she had mastered the skill of automatic writing, George learned to excel in it. No longer was she the reluctant correspondent who had maintained a silence during Willy's epistolary courtship or an equally stubborn refusal to enter into JBY's demand for immediate response. Apart from her daily reports to Willy (by November 1922 often signed 'Dobbs'), the friends she honed her skills on were Lennox and Tom. They wrote to each other when she was at Ballylee or one of them was abroad, even when they were all based in Dublin. All three loved to tell and hear a good story. Just as important, all had a refreshing attitude towards Yeats. The Monday 'At Homes' were privately referred to as 'Church' because of the regular attendance of AE ('the Prophet'), whom Tom did his best to avoid. On one occasion George reprimanded him, 'You really might have come to Church this evening; coming to the door and then going away when you heard Russell was here!'[59] Lennox and Tom were also friends with Hester Travers Smith (daughter of the critic Edward Dowden), whose artist daughter Dolly had the confidence of both. As early as 1923 Tom seems to have written to Dolly about Lennox's drinking, which would eventually thrust him into permanent alcoholism; 'I am so sorry Lennox is being difficult. Dublin is worse than most places in those ways.'[60] In later years that rapport would at times be threatened.

Lennox had boarded with Hester when he first moved to Dublin from Cork and was soon drawn into the circle she had formed to experiment with the ouija board and, occasionally, automatic writing. He turned out to be an apt pupil; as they sat blindfolded at the table 'the replies to questions came with extraordinary rapidity and clearness'; in London they displayed their skills before members of the Society for Psychical Research. Lennox was present on the occasion when the spirit claiming to be Hugh Lane came to one of Hester's sittings, 'seizing my arm so violently that the "traveller" was frequently knocked from the table to the floor'.[61] When the divorce from her philandering doctor husband was final, Hester moved to London, took back the name of Dowden by deed-poll, worked first as a journalist, and then became a full-time professional automatist and psychic counsellor.[62] By the time George had arrived on the scene, Hester Dowden was in London and Lennox was manager of the Abbey; having moved outside the centre of Dublin, he ceased to be involved with such experiments. He remained, however, an interested and sympathetic observer of all psychic matters; a firm believer in George's astrology, he regularly had her cast progressions for him, and through her consulted the stars before he made significant decisions.

Only six years older than she, Lennox quickly became George's devoted pal. Together they gambled on the sweeps, went to the races (both horse and dog), the opera, the cinema, and the theatre; they shared their experiences in gardening and breeding canaries. She sympathized with his lingering affection for Iseult, and he in turn listened to her trials as general nurse, secretary, wife, and mother. Lennox took his duties as godfather seriously, and when she was travelling sent regular reports on the children:

I'm sending you a wire today to say that all here is well—I dashed into 82 for a minute yesterday evening to retrieve my fountain pen which I had left there and put my head in at the nursery door and said 'Hallo'. Ann of course responded and rushed across the room, but Michael *shrieked* 'Hallo' out to me across the room with his arms out, roaring laughing and so demonstrative that I am sure he regretted it as soon as I was gone and he will probably cut me next time to put me in my place.

The children were awfully well when I saw them (Monday last) I think you'll find Michael strangely developed and effusive when you come back. Ann seems very pleased with her school.[63]

Even if she was only in Ballylee, he included in his surveillance the garden and the canaries. 'I called to see the children on Tuesday but they were all fast asleep (2.30 p.m.) so I invited myself to dinner there yesterday and we had a most lively meal. They are to come to Sorrento for the day on Saturday (or if not Sunday) and have ordered their dinner (jelly-with-cream-on-top). They looked very well, Michael with a bit of a cough—the garden looked blooming—the greenhouse a little on the wet side but that is better I suppose than the other extreme.'[64] One of the characteristics of gentle, generous Lynx that George would come to appreciate most was his discretion, about her own feelings as well as the state of Willy's health. With his ear and sympathy, she did not feel quite so alone. 'I seem to be inflicting a hell of a lot of letters on you & I hope I'll stop soon—but its your fault for being such a perfect oyster!' she wrote on one occasion. 'I feel I can pour out all the vapourings & they wont go further or be supposed to be "complaints".'[65]

But apart from holding up the Poet (as they frequently referred to him in their letters) their strongest bond was the theatre—Abbey productions, his and others' playwriting, and, perhaps most of all, the Dublin Drama League. In 1918, based on a suggestion from Lennox, a meeting had been called by Yeats, Robinson, James Stephens, and Ernest Boyd to establish a theatre group independent of the Abbey Theatre. Subscription-based, the League's aim was to give play-wrights, actors, and audience an opportunity to experience the contemporary 'unpopular' European plays restricted by the Abbey's charter and unlikely to be seen elsewhere in Dublin.[66] The League's first productions in 1919—at the Abbey on its 'dark' nights—were translations of Srgjan Tucic's *The Liberators* and Leonid Andreyev's *The Pretty Sabine Women*, both produced by Robinson; Maud Gonne played Hecuba in Euripides' *The Trojan Women* (again produced by Lennox) in 1920. Back in Oxford or on the American tour, George did not see these early productions, although she had been privy to the discussions from the beginning. However, knowledgeable and up to date about European literature, once she arrived in Dublin she thrust herself with enthusiasm into the League's activities. Gradually she took over from Willy as one of the prime movers, and by 1923 (perhaps earlier) was honorary general secretary. Ostensibly Willy was president until 1928, but Lennox as vice-president did most of the work; George remained active through its first incarnation and again from 1941 until the League disestablished itself (for the second time) a year later.

Labyrinthine as the League's structure was, with subcommittees dedicated to play selection, production, and playgoers, eventually it was Lennox and George's partnership (including a great deal of pressure behind the scenes) that tended to hold the project together. For its first ten years the League, as critics later admitted, 'was primarily responsible for revitalizing Irish drama after the civil war, paving the way for the Gate Theatre established by Hilton Edwards and Micheál MacLiammóir in 1928, and inspiring the experiments of O'Casey, Beckett, Johnston, and Robinson himself'.[67] Its members were encouraged to participate as actors, translators, producer/directors, and designers. So successful were they that by 1925 a Players' Section—which soon became known as 'the Dramick' after a delivery boy's distortion—was formed to give less experienced members an opportunity to perform in the League's 'At Homes'; within two years 'the Dramick' became a separate organization and as the New Players opened the Abbey's new experimental Peacock Theatre.[68] However, George disapproved of Lennox's one-time professional appearance, as Lewis Dodd in a production of Margaret Kennedy's *The Constant Nymph*, directed by Shelah Richards of the New Players. 'Did you see it in London. I did & thought it too idiotic for words & Noel Coward as L. Dodd too beastly for anything. Its a low play.'[69]

As vice-president (later president) and general secretary, Lennox and George were finally responsible for the finances (the subscription was 18s. 6d., later £1 1s.), the production—including hiring designers—and choice of plays—including commissioning new translations. Lennox, who had never performed before, acted in thirteen of the League's seventy-three productions (borrowing his stage name, 'Paul Ruttledge', from the hero of Yeats's *Where There is Nothing*) and produced fifteen. Even Tom MacGreevy was drafted to act (in two plays), produce (twice), and translate (Lenormand's *Time is a Dream*).

In order to keep interest high and increase the subscription numbers, the League also held 'At Homes', which Lennox later recalled as 'Horrors, some amateur or semi-amateur performance in a drawing-room with tea and sandwiches but they brought in snobbish members'.[70] He excepted from this description two open-air performances in his back garden, with the sea as backdrop.[71] He should also have remembered the first performance in Ireland of Yeats's 'drawing room' plays: *At the Hawk's Well* (in the drawing room of 82 Merrion

Square, 30 March 1924) and *The Only Jealousy of Emer* and *The Cat and the Moon* (for the first time on the Abbey stage, 9 May 1926). Produced under George's watchful eye and with Lennox as both director and Second Musician, these were profoundly successful contributions to the League's activities.[72] Just four weeks after his performance as Chorus Leader in *At the Hawk's Well*, Lennox appeared again in the leading role of Pirandello's *Henry IV*, claimed by those who saw it as 'one of the finest pieces of acting seen on the Dublin stage'.[73] 'Dear Henry the Fourth', wrote George, 'In case you are arranging at once about the Musicians . . . When I spoke of the Musician who speaks, to WBY, he at once said, off his own bat so to speak, "O Lennox can do that, and he can play the drum, it will be much better to have an intelligent person to play the drum" . . . (NB. A musician is not an intelligent person) So you can cope with that problem too . . . A nice busy month you'll have varyfying [*sic*] your personality, so to speak.'[74] Despite her pleas, Lennox refused to play the eponymous hero in Flecker's *Don Juan*, although he did direct the production.[75] However, although she admired his acting, she later thought him 'quite dreadful in verse on the wireless', and could not 'endure his theories, and execution, of poetry reading'.[76] Like Willy, with whom she did not always agree either, she held her own strong views on such matters.

Despite the avowed aim to remain separate from the Abbey Theatre's offerings, ten of the League's productions became part of the Abbey repertoire, including Susan Glaspell's *Trifles* and Eugene O'Neill's *The Emperor Jones*. In responding to George's request for permission, a delighted O'Neill expressed the hope of seeing their production, and also that the League would do more 'now that you know that any one of them you care to try is available'.[77] Although invited several times over the years, O'Neill never visited Ireland, although his plays continued to be produced by the League, the Abbey, and later the Gate Theatre. *The Emperor Jones* was by far the most successful, with actor-playwright Rutherford Mayne powerful in the title role and a striking stage design by Dolly Travers Smith, who was especially invited to Dublin for the purpose—with far-reaching consequences as we shall see. Lolly, a member of the League, thought she had never seen 'a play so well produced at the Abbey. The Forest was really terrifying.'[78] Even Lady Gregory was impressed and hoped that Dolly lived in Dublin.[79]

Other invitations led to further surprising results. Denis Johnston was first drawn in to the League to play Ulysses in Lennox's 'At Homes', later performing in Strindberg and Pirandello, finally directing Toller's *Hoppla!* for the League before moving on to direct other expressionist plays for the New Players. After his own *The Old Lady Says No!*, rejected by the Abbey, was so successful at the Gate Theatre, George and Lennox were determined to get his next play. According to Johnston's diary, during the summer of 1930, 'Lennox and George Yeats must have been told by Shelah [Richards] that I had written one act of a new play, because they came in one night and demanded that I read it to them. They shouted with laughter at places and wanted to know what happens next. Trouble is I don't know what happens next.'[80] By the time Johnston had figured out what the next act would be, the League had retired, but the following April the Abbey produced his 'very queer interesting play', *The Moon in the Yellow River*.[81] Johnston would later credit the League with 'introducing to Dublin all the *avant garde* plays of the time'. Lennox, he claimed, neither understood or liked expressionism, but he 'and the older generation that he represented, taught us and showed us Strindberg, Pirandello, Benavente, Schnitzler, people whose plays we would never have seen—and maybe not even have read'.[82] Before moving to London Sean O'Casey was also elected a member of the play subcommittee; but although the League tried to persuade him to allow a production of *The Silver Tassie* after its rejection by the Abbey, O'Casey adamantly refused as long as Lennox or anyone by the name of Yeats was connected with it.[83]

But the League's productions frequently drew upon Abbey resources, a practice much disapproved of by Lady Gregory:

Perrin told me of the Drama League using our costumes, properties and stage for rehearsals without any payment. And as there was a meeting of the League at 82 I told Yeats and Robinson of this, and also that it is not fair taking all our best actors for the D. L. plays, not leaving them time to get up fresh, or old work of our own, so that we fall back on used up plays, such as have been arranged for this autumn. I said that Yeats for domestic reasons couldn't stand up against the League, but I left it to L. R. to do so.[84]

A few months later matters came to a crisis. The second night's performance of Benavente's *The Passion Flower*, on 10 November, had to be cancelled because of the illness of one of the Abbey actors who was playing a leading role. According to M. J. Dolan, who had replaced Lennox as theatre manager, 'although the Drama League knew this at 4 o'c the people who arrived were kept waiting outside the Theatre till 8, and then sent away in very bad humour.' Although Dolan was himself a member of the cast, he complained to Gregory that the public 'don't distinguish between Drama League performances and ours, and lay the blame on us'; furthermore, in an obvious effort to separate himself further from the offenders, he objected to having to clear away 'all the mess' of the League performances. Attempting to appease both sides, George said 'they would give up having the Abbey players in future they give too much trouble, so a separation would probably be best'.[85]

For the next few years cast lists ceased to depend upon the permanent Abbey ensemble except as producers, but the problems still rankled. Gregory once again took her complaints to Lennox, later confiding to her journal, 'I am rather in disgrace with G–Y for saying I would like the new [Abbey] Director not to be connected with the DDL . . . the Drama League performances have been making crisis (not in themselves but around about) that 5 days were lost in that last *Passion Flower* in one way or the other and before that there had been grumbling at the using of our wardrobe and properties etc.' A proposal that no actors should be used without consent of the Directors (principally Gregory and Yeats, though Lennox had recently been appointed a Director) would hardly have eased Willy's domestic conundrum.[86] But after this temporary lull, Abbey players again found their way onto the programmes. The disagreement did not interfere with traffic between Coole and number 82.

It may well have been with the League in mind that George turned to playwriting herself:

I drank four gins and its about two weeks ago and in the exhilaration produced thereby read Willy a play and he thought there was a play in it—in the first two scenes of it and damned the third fully comprehensively and thoroughly. I had a nervous breakdown for a week because when I had read one scene I realised what I was up to—he didnt know I ever did anything—but such small encouragement as I got has rather given me something to do, or to look forward to, not to production because I'm too critical to believe I'll ever do anything good enough, but at any rate to going on and not just getting through each day as it comes.[87]

Although George finished the play, 'and it finished me', she rejected it as too 'impersonal' and 'really too punk for words'. However, 'rather proud of having done it, one got a sort of freedom', she moved on to a second play, 'more "ambitious" (I seem to hear that phrase as a commonplace of reviewers) with a theme more like to myself and what intrigues me'.[88] Unfortunately, neither manuscript seems to have been preserved, nor is her playwriting mentioned again. We will never know what intrigued her, but clearly she needed a further outlet for her own creativity now that the days of automatic writing were over. She later moved on to a novel.

Dublin however suspected that she was a closet writer. When in 1926 the Abbey produced *Mr Murphy's Ireland*, a play about the Black and Tans by 'Elizabeth Harte', speculation was rife that either George or Lennox had written it. 'I'm glad Lennox told you *I* didn't write "Mr Murphy's Ireland" ', George wrote to Tom. 'Everyone in Dublin thinks I did! Beastly. I wouldnt write a better play but I wouldnt write one bad just in the way *it* is bad.' O'Casey suspected Lennox, who emphatically denied authorship, 'for there's a great deal of the novelette about it'. It was many years before Ernest Blythe let it be known that the author was Elizabeth Healy, daughter of the Governor-General. George was especially annoyed because she had tried to persuade Lennox not to produce the play.[89]

If anyone other than Willy read George's work, it would have been Lennox, who had a healthy respect for her critical astuteness. Before submitting a translation to the New Players, he asked, 'Could you throw an eye over this before you go down and tell me if you think it will do—will it shock the holy? It shouldnt but they're so queer . . . Make a little mark in the margin at anything that seems badly translated and I'll try and get it better.'[90] The following year he gave her the script of *The Big House*, his play about the dying embers of the Ascendancy tradition, set in the period 1918 to 1923, which Christopher Murray aptly describes as the charting of 'both the inevitability of the destruction of the house and the sense of outrage . . . at the action which seeks to drive out a people as if they had no right to be there.'[91] George 'found some dull spots, especially in the opening scenes', but preferred it to O'Casey's *The Plough and the Stars*, and was overwhelmed by the defiant character of Kate Alcock, Anglo-Irish daughter who refuses to give in.

Not once, nor twice, nor three times, but at least six times (and then not for moments, but for minutes) she touches the heights of modern tragedy. I read the Plough three times over and it left me stone cold, save for the touches of humour, but this play of yours gripped at my vitals. Great tragic drama in the theatre used to give me cramp in the muscles of my stomach, and I fancy the right actress in the part of Kate could produce that effect. It is certain to make a big splash in the Abbey, and probably elsewhere, though in order to get the full effect one must know the psychology of the two Irelands.

Probably aware that Kate was modelled on Mary Spring-Rice, daughter of Lord Monteagle, George had herself watched the beginning of the flight of Protestant landed families from Clare and Galway.[92] In urging Lennox to make Kate even more distinguished, George reveals much of her own response to the civil war and its aftermath, all she had observed in both town and countryside: 'She can be herself, and ready to serve Ireland, without talking down to the natives, just as she can be a Protestant without the assistance of John Bull. If this class, now on equal footing in this country for the first time in history, has anything really great to offer, we want to know about it. Personally I think they have all the brains, but then they had all the opportunities for developing them.'[93] On this point she agreed with Willy, who the previous year had thundered out his own declaration, 'We are one of the great stocks of Europe. . . . We have created the most of the modern literature of this country. . . . the best of its political intelligence.'[94] But her visceral reaction to the play was also more personal: like Kate, she would always be an outsider, 'something outside, different'.[95]

When *The Big House* was first presented at the Abbey, it had 'a terrific' but mixed reception, again sharply observed by George:

a dear old thing of some sixty Unionist winters got up at the matinee when the Black & Tan began drinking out of the decanter and said 'This is a revolting play'—The poor darling had an impediment in her v's which sounded luscious but ineffective. And after the first act Countess Con Gore Booth Markievicz said 'what a wonderful creation the English Bounder ("Capt Despard") is'. And Dermod O'Brien said (this I did *not* repeat [to Lennox]) 'Anybody who didnt know the Lynx would think he had been born in the Slums'.[96]

Lennox's play also gave rise to a revealing exchange between George and Tom, who as a confirmed nationalist disliked *The Big House* as much as she approved of it. Railing against the play as 'sadly indifferent', 'soothing . . . with Anglo-Ireland as the stainless heroine in the snow', Tom thought the only solution to Robinson's 'fearful Englishness' was to become an exile in London, as he himself was.[97] In defending the Anglo-Irish, George found consolation in her own foreignness while at the same time being impressively clear-sighted about England:

Chewing the cud over your expostulations on Anglo-Ireland the other day it occurred to me that truth was only to be discovered in an uncivilised country by the highly civilised and slightly mad foreigner. By foreigner I mean the object of your animosity, the Anglo-Irishman; probably the 'native' can achieve the high civilisation and slight madness necessary by a prolonged visit to some other country provided that he does not return to the motherland out of patriotism.

Patriotism would destroy any country, its going to destroy England very soon. Up to about the middle of the war we wernt patriotic, everyone else was doing everything much better than we were, everyone elses goods were much better than ours. Then in spite of winning we began to come rather badly out of it, our unemployment is worse than anyone else's, we are very well hated by every other nation, we have a royalty who knits and collects postage stamps, breeds first rate bulls and fifth rate race horses, and so we have had to become patriotic to explain all these things to ourselves and hide them from the world. For heavens sake dont become a wild goose Tom. I dont really like fat undulating Arnoldian country but your writing of it made me hate this arid stony ghost ridden country.[98]

She was becoming more and more separated from her native land; Willy had roots here, she had only Willy's. Yet her children were and would always be Irish. Her own attitude would remain, like so much of her intellectual and occult pursuits, ambivalent. 'I find it curious that I can divide my mind into two and believe myself loyal to my own country and at the same time no less loyal to my adopted country (adopted in the marriage sense)', she was to comment many years later after spending more than half that married life in Ireland.[99] Meanwhile, as she watched Willy become more and more embroiled in Irish politics, she worried about their future. As she had complained to MacGreevy a few months earlier, 'there's nothing in his verse worth preserving but the personal.'[100]

George in turn was annoyed with Lady Gregory's role in the *Silver Tassie* controversy, for it was she who bundled off Yeats's comments to O'Casey without consultation. The row that this precipitated fell mostly on Yeats, whom George was once again nursing back from a serious illness. This time she showed her exasperation with Gregory to her sister-in-law, complaining that 'She, obstinate old woman, will never even say she is sorry.'[101] But at other times George's reports on the quality of Abbey productions were useful to both Directors, and Willy frequently took her advice about casting his own plays.

George had always been a keen theatregoer, and ever since her first visit to Dublin, she had taken an active interest in the Abbey Theatre. As secretary of the Drama League, she became even more familiar with its internal workings. And as wife of one of the founding Directors, she did her best to promote it. There were dinner parties before those performances which needed either social or political acceptance, such as the first night of O'Casey's *The Plough and the Stars*. 'The Yeats had a great dinner at Jurys before the play—the Jamesons, Gogartys, O'Higgins, Blythe, Starkie, Coopers, self,' Robinson informed the absent MacGreevy. George then went on to a dinner party for Walter Rummel, but 'became so nervous suddenly about Willy that she left her coffee and made for the Abbey to find the most unexpected row on'.[102] When the play was revived three months later there were rumours that 'the anti-Casey republicans' were threatening to blow up the theatre. However, the only weapon hurled from the gallery was a stink-bomb, which Willy grabbed before it went off. He and George left the auditorium and emptied its contents down the drain. George later claimed that she kept the case as a souvenir.[103]

But George also realized, now that Lady Gregory and Yeats were no longer contributing as many works themselves, that the Abbey required more than Lennox's plays and the newly discovered O'Casey if it were to survive. 'I wish to goodness you'd write a play,' she wrote to Tom.

The plays coming in to the Abbey now are really too unspeakable. There's a solemn play of Brinsley's just in. I like the first act but havent read the rest yet. Lennox says he knew exactly what was going to happen after the middle of the first act, but I am not sure there isnt something to be said for that method. Anyway I feel the Abbey ought to do it if only to encourage Brinsley [Macnamara] to stop writing vulgar comedies It would really be rather dreadful if the Abbey collapsed, having got the audience, from lack of playwrights. A so much worse death than financial failure through lack of audience.[104]

However, at the same time she seems to have been primarily responsible for dissuading Willy from risking exposure of his Noh plays to an Abbey production. 'Willy has given up the ghost about the Noh plays & is going to ask Arthur Shields to produce one. . . . I rebelled at first but once he makes up his mind its quite useless saying or doing anything.'[105] She seems to have won that battle, but not her lobby for the acceptance of a play by Seán O'Faoláin:

about the civil war 1922–23 which is devilishly near being a very fine play (he was a republican). Its got an emotional and intellectual intensity which is startling. The Abbey wont accept it, I forget why, but it may be they think the second act loose and dont understand the third. Nor do I for that matter. Willy, with his usual formula for a first play, says 're-write it'. Lennox, with his usual formula, says 'write another' and I would say only obviously I dont say it, 'write another but use more than half of this material again with re-writing'. But the creature may be going to America on some sort of scholarship and of course he'll be completely ruined.[106]

O'Faoláin did go to Harvard, and while working for his third master's degree compiled his first book, a selection of *Lyrics and Satires from Tom Moore* which was published by Cuala. But the Abbey did not see a play of his until 1937, when it was booed.[107]

George's interests went beyond the plays themselves. She was a keen judge of acting and design, to such an extent that Willy again tried to lure her into practice. On visiting Cambridge to see Terence Gray's production of *The Player Queen* in 1927, he wrote excitedly, 'I think you must go to this theatre & study it. It is apparently the one centre of scenic & lighting experiment now in England.'[108] Although her designing seems to have been restricted to assisting with the occasional production—she recalled wearing roller skates to help Dolly Travers Smith paint the backdrop for *Fighting the Waves*—she always took special note of costuming and decor for both the League and the Abbey. And, although usually shy at social events, for the League she was prepared to be more visible. A painful attack of dry pleurisy prevented her from being a member of the chorus in Euripides' *Iphigenia in Tauris* for one of Lennox's 'At Homes', but she rose to the occasion on the next:

The opening At Home was on Thursday in the Engineers Hall and very successful I think, the 'piece' was a reading of *Over-ruled* by Mr Tulloch, Redding, tall Johnston and George Yeats! Redding started being shocked at the first rehearsal and got more shocked. George Tulloch started cutting things at the last moment, everyone else in the cast got great fun out of it and the audience (with one shocked exception) loved it. The females of the Government were there in force Mesdames Cosgrave, Blythe, O'Higgins, Kennedy.[109]

On occasion she was also prepared to disagree strongly with her husband on production matters. When the League produced Shaw's *Heartbreak House* with a largely Abbey cast and Mary Grey (Mrs Bernard Fagan) reprising her role as the original Hesione Hushabye, her analysis was far more complete than Willy's:

Mary Grey is charming . . . Delightful . . . As a person. But as an actress!! o GOD . . . Have you ever seen her act? I didnt too much dislike her as 'Mrs Ushabye' (Heartbreak House) but she was stagey in the English sense to the nth degree; she waved, moaned, schwärmerei'd, gushed and 'drew herself up' threw back her head and yearned, and convinced you that all the time she was really in love with and had never been in love with any one but, her husband. Quite excellent—I'm sure that's what Shaw wanted, but somehow it was undistinguished and a little provincial . . . though I bit Willy's head off when he said it was. Chiefly because he was exalting Abbey acting against 'the English Stage Cliche' and I'd been very cock-a-hoop on Saturday night that Ireland hadnt won the triple crown (football—in case you dont know the allusion—Ireland has won against England, Scotland, but they 'couldnt beat little old Wales'—and W. was surprisingly annoyed about it . . . when I arrived on Saturday night from Gort he said . . . before anything else 'Well I suppose you know that Wales beat Ireland and so we havent got the triple crown') Anyhow he was most abusive and as he was being really very cross and unpleasant coming home from the Abbey and going on like a thorough paced Irish-anti-Englishman and Mrs Liz (or is it Leah?) Clarke just in front, and she'll probably write and tell you all about it . . . AND he gets so loud when he is excited! Eileen Crowe certainly was what one never thought she could be . . . distinguished . . . almost aristocratic (in the intellectual sense) . . . Will Shields amazing as Captain Shotover, a really beautiful performance, Stevenson . . . rather inadequate but odd . . . I must say the Abbey 'got there' and I dont know that Mary Grey did.[110]

Aware of the excessive responsibilities she carried, Lennox appreciated George's need to get away, and when he was travelling encouraged her to go out to his house, either with the children or alone: 'so good for discipline if you do.'[111] When they first met, he was still living in the gatehouse of Kilteragh, Sir Horace Plunkett's hospitable, Swedish-designed house in Foxrock situated 'between the Dublin mountains and the sea'.[112] George's horary of 7 October 1924 for 'LR House bought at Dalkey' dates his move to Sorrento Cottage eight miles south of Dublin, 'on the rocks facing Killiney Bay with the Wicklow Mountains, Bray Head, and the Sugar-loaves making an almost over-painted, too theatrical a backcloth'. Lennox loved his 'small but well-planned and comfortable' house with its four acres of garden sloping steeply to the sea; 'It had been neglected and it was fun getting it gradually into order.'[113] Most of all, he loved entertaining, and Sorrento rapidly became a substitute for the parties he had enjoyed at Kilteragh. Michael loved the rocks, sitting for hours 'fishing' with an old stick and piece of string; later, when Lennox purchased a player-piano, his godson would immediately demand music and, dragging a chair across the drawing room, sit 'with his nose against the pianola'.[114] George revelled in the sea air, the view, and, most of all, the privacy.

The children adored being at Dalkey & so did I & it would have been lovely to stay longer but with you & Tom away Willy seems to have no one to hold his hand in the long evenings & he is a little 'off' Gogarty at present. Lately there have been swarms of hard-faced Americans there & none of them talk anything but sex & politics without even the saving grace of Quinn's lady who said after a lengthy conversation 'but I *do* like music *too*!' All nerveless & unwillable & rotten with age no matter how young they are.

It was on this occasion that she recorded 'A conversation on a windy day in March': 'George Yeats. Why do you like Norman? He is a vile little boy. Anne Yeats. But he has lovely hair & eyes as cold as any March wind——or one might call it "Any woman's reply on being asked why she loves a scoundrel——" '[115]

George's story of Anne Yeats and young FitzGerald would enter Yeats's crucible and become the poem 'Father and Child':

> She hears me strike the board and say
> That she is under ban
> Of all good men and women,
> Being mentioned with a man
> That has the worst of all bad names;
> And thereupon replies
> That his hair is beautiful,
> Cold as the March wind his eyes.[116]

But grateful as she was for the Dalkey retreat, George preferred it when Lennox was nearby. 'One misses you terribly when your away. So glad you arent going to India though one oughtnt to say if you wanted to go.'[117] In turn, Lennox sometimes joined them at Ballylee: 'Got back all right last night—everything rather wild and wet it blew a storm here, all rather depressing and I thought of you two so snug in your tower . . . It was lovely at Ballylee, I thought I was only there $2^1/_2$ days but I find it was $5^1/_2$.'[118]

Whereas Lennox was a trusted pal, Tom MacGreevy, born only a year later than she, was more like a younger brother who could be confided in, asked to run messages, complained to, and frequently contradicted. He too felt himself to be an outsider in Dublin, having arrived only shortly before she did. Born in Kerry, MacGreevy had been a junior member of the civil service until the First World War; as second lieutenant in the Royal Field Artillery he fought at Ypres and the Somme, and was twice wounded. When he was demobilized he entered Trinity College as a mature student, taking an honours degree in political science and history. By June 1919 he had met both Lennox Robinson and Hester Travers Smith, and found a congenial base at the United Arts Club; Dolly remembered meeting him while he was still in uniform.[119] Having 'walked on' in an Abbey production of *Androcles and the Lion*, it was not long before he too became a dedicated committee member of the Dublin Drama League. After graduation from Trinity, he was appointed assistant secretary to the Irish advisory committee of the Carnegie Trust, where Lennox was employed as an organizing librarian. But like Lennox his ambition lay in the arts. Unlike Lennox, however, while Tom was working at one thing, he was always restless to begin the next: literature, music, the ballet, and most of all painting consumed him. Later, when contrasting himself with Samuel Beckett, with whom he taught in Paris, he confessed that he had 'always been as much interested in living as in writing about living'.[120] He wrote few poems, anguishing over each draft; yet Yeats, doubtless encouraged by George, spoke of him as 'the most promising of all our younger men. . . . I know from his criticism, his talk, how rich he is in imagination and in knowledge, and with proper encouragement he should be able to do again many times what he has done once.'[121]

It was Tom's talk and ideas that most charmed George, and by 1923 they were friendly enough for her to summon him to dinner at the Club ('I shall be dining here at 7.15 tonight. Dine with me if you arent doing anything else'), a film ('Will you come to Charlie tonight? Probably you cant. Anyway, if you arent at 82 by 8.10 *I wont expect you*'), or tea and an adventure: 'Dear Mr Mcgreevy Please excuse typing but I have already written thirtysix letters today and should burst if I had to push a pen. I cant even type corectly now! My only free time before next Monday is tomorrow after 4 and before 7–30. If you can come in to tea and strvague somewhere afterwards. Yours Mrs Yeats!'[122] Such meetings were important to both of them, for despite how busy she was during the day George was, as Lily frequently noted, easily bored. 'Tuesday 82 M. Sq. D——m. I want to be amused. Are you as busy as Lennox this week? And if *not* will you dine at the Club on Friday & gossip with me afterwards (W. has McManus coming in the evening) as I shall be at a loose end. Yours George Yeats.'[123]

Formal and correct to cover his insecurities, MacGreevy had difficulty unbending at first, but George was always good at breaking through the barriers of shyness: 'I wish I could think of an alternative to "Mister MacGreevy" but I cant, & "Tom" has the unpleasantest association in my remote youth.'[124] From then on 'Dearest George' received all his woes, fears, and—most important—his writing. She had no compunction about telling him when she did not like his poetry, but was equally encouraging. 'You never yet did anything as good or better than "Aodh Ruadh O Domhnaill". I've read it again and again and there isnt a word to spare or a misplaced word and I take my hat off to you. Willy has been away yesterday and today so he hasnt seen it but I'll be very surprised if he doesnt get it at least as much as I've got it. I'll show it to him tomorrow and write to you again!'[125] The poem was frequently anthologized, becoming, as he once crossly put it, his 'Innisfree'. And although George like Willy clearly believed it his best, she continued to respond to each new offering, writing of one frequently revised poem, 'I do think its improved, if my recollections of its father and grandfather are correct, but I still feel that each variation is its own theme and the main theme is built up out of all the variations instead of vice versa. WB. of course thought it too modern, too difficult, too Ezratic, and was intolerant of it because it hadnt the tightness of Red Hugh.'[126]

Tom enjoyed practising elaborate diplomacy, one of the reasons he liked to gossip. But George was also tactful, as when she deflected him from hopes of his translation of Valéry being published by Cuala. Responding to two more poems he sent, she wrote, 'Yes, I like them both; Willy thinks them obscure—I dont think I do. I like the plains of Ireland best. I'm afraid as far as the Cuala Press is concerned there's no hope of Valery, but I am certain W. would gladly give you the introduction to Macmillan.'[127] And when a quarrel threatened to erupt between Tom and Lennox because he took offence over a professional matter, she tried to make him see reason by using her own experience with WBY's work:

Dont be too cross with Tinche because he asked to see one scene of the french translation of Whiteheaded Boy. Every writer has to do that. Personally I have never given permission to any translator, no matter who he was, without seeing a 'specimen'. It is the usual custom. In two cases I refused permission (one French and one German) to men whose own work I admire quite a lot! They simply couldnt translate. Its a totally different art, and I'm not at all sure that any good writer can translate, or any good translator write! Its the same sort of difference as music and opera. I should certainly, had you suggested doing a translation of W. B. have made the same demand.[128]

But Tom was quick to see a slight, and sympathetic as George was, she sometimes became the stern elder sister, reminding him on one occasion that 'other people are nearly, or quite, as sensitive as you are yourself. However as I said its no business of mine but I wanted to modify a general statement into what I really meant. See you tonight.'[129]

When MacGreevy moved to London in 1925, George missed his regular presence in her life. 'I wish you were back here,' she wrote. 'Willy said last night very solemnly "Now McGreevy is not here we have to do our own gossiping" and there's nobody here now who has more than one idea in six months.'[130] The friendship continued, however, in lengthy letters and occasional meetings in London or Paris: 'Write a line to say how London feels—I am homesick for it.'[131] Nor was he allowed to forget the children. 'The enclosed may amuse you. It isnt much like Anne but rather good of Michael,' she remarked on sending him the well-known photograph of Willy and children in the castle garden.[132] Tom carefully preserved Anne's first printed letter from Ballylee, which informed him, 'I HAVE LOST TWO TEETH . . . AND THERE IS A DEADSHEEP [sic] DOWN ON THE RIVER'; it was annotated 'Composition and writing Anne's unaided work. Spelling by George Yeats.'[133] And when Willy was in London, she made certain that Tom knew his address.

While in London MacGreevy boarded with Hester Dowden at 15 Cheyne Gardens, and he sent more chat about that circle than she cared for. When George did finally meet Hester, who frequently visited Lennox, she had taken an instant 'violent dislike': 'She's the unbending hard essence of everything I loathe mentally emotionally and temperamentally. She makes me think of lumpy beds Russian fleas, and ipechacuana [sic] wine. (If you never had the latter ask the chemist to give you a sip.)'[134] Another equally strong response had unexpected repercussions:

Dear Thomas-Grumble-Grumble. Do your worst but for God's sake type it! I hate cross-word puzzles—jigsaws—missing words & you *are* so economical with your paper composed with handiwork & ink. What the devil am I to write about anyway? I've nothing to tell, or confess, or compel, or gossip. I've read nothing for weeks & I havent your magnificent certainty that one need not be even superficially reasonable. How you have the nerve to expect me to believe that you dont like living in 'the Nunnery'—I see you being drawn into corners all day, by all, & confidences being murmured into your ready ear—I always said you were a missed-priest & living in a magnificent vortex of vicarious enjoyments! All this is a little drunk but its late & Im clearing off letters—yes that's rather rude—but you deserve it—I go to Ballylee Thursday morning for three glorious days of solitude & cabbage planting & on my return will write you a sober & sane & reasonable letter, though what the devil I shall put in it I dont see—Undying hate to Hester, greetings to yourself Yours affly George Yeats[135]

This particular letter strayed further than George had intended, for by mistake she sent it to Lennox. It was not the first time she had erred with her chums.

I grovel . . . Really to do it twice is too much! When I got up from Ballylee on Saturday night I found a letter enclosing one to Lennox that I had sent in mistake . . . I rang up Lennox to find that I had sent yours to him, and I suppose you got one beginning 'DearestE.' But you havent sent it back! I wrote to you about two oclock in the morning of Tuesday last and evidently put all three in the wrong envelopes. I only hope Lennox didnt read yours before observing that it wasnt for him, for the last remark 'undying hate to Hester' . . . Write me a line soon to tell me that you're not too irritated with my stupidity in twice sending you the wrong letter . . .

Lynx had of course read it, but tactfully sent it directly to Tom. 'George was sending me a package today and sent me the enclosed—obviously for you. I havent told her of her mistake as it would annoy her.'[136] There may have been some jealousy, or more likely distrust of Hester's methods, in George's violence, for the professional automatist—the same age as Nelly Tucker—seems to have held both Tom and Lennox in emotional thrall or blackmail; even Willy occasionally attended Hester's Sunday evening 'At Homes' at 15 Cheyne Gardens.

However, Tom was not always as sensitive as Lennox to George's attitudes. Just as he kept pressing George to visit Hester, he concocted the extraordinary idea of having Yeats made Ireland's High Commissioner to London. 'Now don't say no quick about the High Commissionership. It would be a splendid chance for Ireland to do itself credit. And we'd all have a very intriguing and interesting time. How should it be done I wonder. I'll tell Lennox.' By now accustomed to Tom's more lunatic ideas, George did not even reply, but Lennox was prompt with his disapproval: 'Have a heart—or rather a head! Can you imagine WB coping with an office, entertaining the dull people that must be entertained— or George—even less.'[137]

Their letters, with talk of books, music, and art, provided George with the release she needed. Tom sent her Valéry's *Eupalinos*, which she reserved for Ballylee. 'I want to keep those phrases so beautifully measured and that thought so whittled into precision, until I am a little measured and whittled! Not that I am ever really either.' The gift made up for 'two rotten books' given to her by AE for review, 'A Savonarola by "Mrs Charlotte Eliot" with a clumsy introduction by T. S. Eliot . . . . . . perhaps the author is his mother or his sister . . . Its New England tract with a substratum of history . . . very little . . . and is written in incredibly bad rhymed verse that smacks of blank verse too.' No review seems to have appeared under her name in the *Irish Statesman*, perhaps because the author was indeed Eliot's mother.[138] In November 1925 MacGreevy was appointed assistant editor of the arts magazine the *Connoisseur*; he was somewhat embarrassed by the editor's conservative tastes, such as the preference for Wheatley's *Cries of London* 'over a design by Picasso, Matisse or Braque'. George's response, although typically even-handed in her appreciation of social and literary history, reflects her interest in decoration:

As for the Connoisseur, I grew up surrounded by it, and to me it is a part of history. Stagnant history, vieux jeu and anything else you like, but if you orientate it in your consciousness as far from both sun and moon as possible it has qualities, very English, Ruskin pottery pale green walls and a chaste bowl of flowers (all of one sort please) standing on a table runner of liberty silk with a fringe 'to contrast' upon a table from Maple's antique department. Always very well-bred, but not quite of the best public school, and of the cheaper house at the University. In about two generations Dublin will have reached that stage and please God I'll be dead then. All these Lytton Stracheys and Sitwells ('Discursions') make fun of it and the Albert Memorial and the Albert Hall, and Ruskin pottery and pale green walls because they grew up in families that were brilliantly clever in a public and spectacular way whereas they are clever in a personal negative and journalistic way and they amuse one because they have selected a form of gossip that panders to one's feeling of superiority to a previous generation. Wheatley's cries of London *in their day* were quite as enthralling as any illustrative artist of today and not a whit less good of their kind. This is not to say that I don't fully sympathize with you for preferring Picasso or Brancusi. But I am less disruptive than you.

Typically, she concluded by saying she did not like the last poem he had sent her, and recommending Osbert Sitwell's recently published *Discursions on Travel Art and Life* for its 'prose poem' on 'Cats' and a section on the King of Sicily's interest in lavatories.[139] Despite his qualms, MacGreevy held the position at the magazine until February 1927; it paid his debts and allowed him some time to write.

Tom worried that George would miss the music she had so loved while in London. Hester Dowden was a fine pianist and had a large collection of recordings which he much appreciated. 'I hear you have a gramophone. Do say whether you play it for yourself and whether you'd be interested to hear of records we've found successful and what new ones you have found.'[140] George replied immediately:

Oh yes, I play it myself . . . have a secret collection of records, the 24 preludes a la Chopin d'apres Cortot . . . O shades of Rummel . . . The Unfinished, Vesti la giubba Pagliacci-Caruso . . . In questa tomba escura lascia miripesar . . . grand, but it ought to be sung by a soprano or at least a mezz.sopr . . . You do need that antithesis to give you the same shock that the sudden solo rising out of the base and worldly choir at Westminster Cathedral gives you. Caruso really isnt the goods for it. And a lot of Westminster and Chapel Royal (Windsor) choir carols . . . really good . . . And the children have Come back to Erin, Laughing policeman, Toy Drum Major, and so on. They dont cotton to anything else, though Anne for some queer reason likes 'No, Pagliacci non son' and Michael always did like the 24 preludes.[141]

Tom at once sent her a recording of the Brahms Trio, 'a great joy'. But when Willy was 'working', no sound must be heard; George's record collection remained secret until she presented it to Anne in her mid-teens. Frank O'Connor later recalled that she listened to the gramophone in the kitchen, but neither of her children recalled its being played.[142]

While in London MacGreevy occasionally lectured at the National Gallery, and his greatest desire was to become the director of the Gallery in Ireland. Although his first application for the post was premature, George encouraged him and Willy, a member of the board, wrote in his support. She kept him informed of the deliberations:

The present situation as regards the N. G. seems to be this . . . that if the Board decides they want a whole time man Bodkin will not be elected and your name will go up. But this is terribly private. There seems to be an inclination to have a whole time man, and most of the Board seem to dislike B. personally but on the other hand they seem—some of them—to think he might be a good man. Several have seen W. but W. unfortunately has been suffering from nerves, probably his high blood pressure, and I gather he has been rather cross . . . . He would I need hardly say prefer you but I cant sound him as to what he is really doing as he gets very irritable when asked anything . . . I suppose the next Board Meeting will produce something tangible in the way of news about things.[143]

Yeats felt that an application from Tom would be helpful, for it would give him 'a sort of claim to special consideration when next there is a vacancy'.[144] Of the seventeen candidates who applied, MacGreevy came in second to Thomas Bodkin; his turn would not come until 1950.

In August 1925 they all met in Italy. Willy and Lennox had been asked to lecture at Mürren by Henry Lunn, who ran a tourist bureau, and George leapt at the opportunity of a week in Switzerland. However, Willy did not enjoy his role; Hugh Kingsmill remembers him sitting gloomily outside the Palace Hotel in Maloja, next to a lively, friendly Robinson. When called upon to lecture, 'Yeats recited "Innisfree" with an air of suppressed loathing. . . . An aristocrat had been superimposed on the poet, and his small black eyes, hard as marbles, looked out upon the world with a mixture of contempt and mistrust.'[145] The rest of the journey was not much better. MacGreevy, who had been 'Lunning' in Lucerne, joined them in Milan on 28 August and they spent a few days touring the city. That is, Lennox, George, and Tom enjoyed themselves while Willy, who dismissed the cathedral as 'Nottingham lace architecture', sat in the Hotel Manin reading *The Times.* 'We'll go to Verona, we will go to Lugarno, *or we'll go home.*'[146] They went home. George bought a cuckoo clock for the children, who had been staying at Coole. But she still longed for the Italy of her dreams. When Tom sent her a postcard of Milan the following year, she 'nearly wept',

and it wasnt until your letter this morning that I realised that you wernt there!!! If I hadnt been an ass I would have noticed Teddiedwards head on the stamp, but I didnt, and the scrawl indicating your address was romantic in its squirls but uninforming . . . Anyway I felt hideously jealous and homesick. I am never really homesick for England but Italy . . . everything nice has always been in Italy. So I felt vile and like selling all I have just to get to Italy which would be a folly, and middleaged people with children cant be too foolish.[147]

At least once a year George visited her mother in England. The Tuckers had moved to Sidmouth in 1923, first to Kenyon Cottage next door to the Woodlands Hotel, then to Alkerton Cottage. Olivia and Dorothy, who spent most of the summer months in England with her mother while Ezra went to his mistress in Venice, were often there when George went down to Sidmouth; with the four of them together it must have been like old times. Later Dorothy's son, at school in England and in the care of his grandmother, would also be there; Omar Pound remembers the Tuckers' small house being 'crammed with Victorian clutter'.[148] George's visits to London were often rushed, especially when she was in charge of a Cuala sale, but she and Tom always managed to meet for at least dinner at Gennaro's and a film. In November 1925 her aunt Ghita, now widowed, as well as her mother needed consolation, for her young cousin Billy Spurway had been killed in a flying accident. Then Eva Ducat came up to London to have dinner with her. Aware of MacGreevy's love of secrecy, she made it clear that 'I dont mind anyone knowing I am in London—I shant have time to see anyone——& I do *not* want to see Hester!'[149] Sometimes Nelly joined her daughter and son-in-law in London, bringing with her a whirlpool of energy and complaints. 'We are going to stay at Orchards Hotel, Portman St, George & Nelly & I,' Willy wrote to Olivia, 'pray that there may be no rats in the rafters.'[150] Such visits were hardly relaxing; George's script had after all placed Nelly in phase 19, where 'the natural characteristic' is to 'dramatize'. 'George and I were perpetually on the watch that she might not think when we made some arrangement for ourselves that we were avoiding her,' Willy described one such occasion. 'She is overflowing with kindness (wanted to come to London again and look after me in November) but she is always on the watch for the wolf with "privy paw". George and I have been alternately wolf.'[151]

George introduced MacGreevy to many of her London friends, including the Dulacs and Olivia Shakespear. Olivia found him 'rather a little dear and amuses me'. George reassured Tom that 'By "amuses" she means interests and entertains. Its a word the old gang used a lot.'[152] Olivia in turn introduced him to Herbert and Georgina Reade.[153] Gregarious Tom was soon invited to Ipsden and meeting 'dear little 'Erb' every other week in London, and with Olivia attending private soirées at the Fowlers ('Two Brahms sextets and Mrs Shakespear in the most magnificent dress and shoes'). There were public concerts and the ballet: 'I go to hear Gerhardt—the first time Mrs Shakespear came with me and wished and wished you were with her when Gerhardt sang Brahms.' And he met Harry Tucker: 'An encounter with your step-father at Mrs Shakespears. I think he must have thought me rather awful, but I liked him—so gentle and friendly and dignified and unlike me.'[154] But he was not introduced to Nelly Tucker until October 1926. George was hesitant, 'You'll probably like her but I dont know. Lennox said the other day that his mother & mine were rather alike——They *are* and are NOT!'[155]

Her reluctance was natural, for although since her marriage and Nelly's move to Sidmouth the situation between them had been easier, her mother was finding it difficult to adjust to the ageing role of Yeats's mother-in-law. 'I am tending sweet peas & rearing chrysanthemums, contemplating the flight of sea-gulls, following the sun. When I was a young woman Yeats used to call me the "Gad Fly": but what does the gad-fly do when it has lost its sting?' She was more blunt with her niece Grace, claiming that every woman upon reaching 50 (her age when Georgie married) should be 'pole-axed'.[156] But when George finally arranged the intro-duction, Nelly was immediately charmed by this courtly young man whose 'extreme correctness' reminded her of 'a très bien young Frenchman'. She took it upon herself to take Tom around, though 'George says you dont want "ordinary dinner parties" & she rather doubts my knowing people you'll like!' 'I believe in being all things to all men. I like human intercourse & the insides of people's pretty, warm houses reconcile me to their empty minds.'[157] Any time Nelly was in London, Tom squired her to the Prom and art galleries, took her to tea and to par-ties. She rather enjoyed managing this would-be cosmopolitan from the country: 'Hearing about another party at Mr Fowler's reminds me to jog your elbow, forgive if futile but did you paste-board Mrs Stackable after that party Jelly played at we took you to? Mrs Stackable is Mr Fowler's sister-in-law and lives with him & does hostess. If you leave cards she'll ask you to more parties . . . she's always out but very friendly if in, but rather the "kitchen sink" order.'[158] Mother and daughter were more alike than George would care to admit.

Much to George's annoyance ('I dont *at all* approve of your clandestine correspondence with my mother!'), Nelly soon began writing flirtatiously to her 'dear gazelle':

You make me wish I were your own age, we could play a good game. The Englishman takes the game of flirtation as seriously as all other games, and all other races (except the Irish) can't learn the game. Luckily I spent some of my youth in Ireland so got my fling at my favorite pastime. . . . I'm as busy as ever. All the roses are being propped up on 10 foot stakes & bulbs put in & potting sheds cleaned and creepers trained & grass seed sown. I have dyed all my cushions a fine Chinese blue. (Do you like Japanese prints? I do. We have a good many) On Thursday Fanny Davies played here and played her best, her Schumann *is* the best, but she's the schoolmarm always. Jelly is neither schoolmarm nor school girl, dont forget her recital on Dec 17 & send me another card to tell me about it.[159]

By encouraging his ambition to be a true artist, Nelly saw herself as one also. 'I am careful not to go on living in the same way,' she insisted. 'Love must be kept firmly in the present, it is a thing without past or future . . . The fact remains that, fundamentally and however painfully, we *are* artists and artists we shall remain, and we both know that art is the only thing that matters and the one thing that makes the world tolerable . . . We've had Jelly d'Aranyi here, more so than ever in every way, and in beauty. She has so flattered me that I am a mass of pomp.'[160] Years later when her own world had dwindled through Harry's illness, she took comfort in her friendship with Tom: 'I have always known that you, and Jelly d'Aranyi, and I myself, are the Trinity who know that nothing matters, nothing really counts, for us, except the Arts, in the Arts alone can we find our salvation, whatever it may lie.'[161]

George at first tried to discourage the developing intimacy, telling her mother not to ask Tom down for Christmas, 'as nothing for you to do here, & you have friends near London, and would be very bored here'.[162] But MacGreevy was delighted to have someone else to pour out his soul to, sending books and writing long reports of his activities, hopes, and plans. Like George, Nelly had strong opinions about writers and writing and did not hesitate to disagree with him; when for example he sent her his monograph on Richard Aldington, she was equally outspoken:

I dislike Aldington's work; it bristles with personal grievances. Of course you like it because it misjudges England—but then—you are our natural enemy, who may become a friend any day, while R. Aldington is an ill-conditioned relation. . . . I have Harry as a safety valve; but he knows me too well, & agrees too much with my opinions, so I run no risk of contempt—one *must* take risks! If you are in London on Saturday you might hear Jelly d'Aranyi play Beethoven Sonatas with Myra Hess at Wigmore Hall. . . . You might also call on Olivia Shakespear who is also rather a unique event. Dont forget to tell me what you think of Yeats by John, if you can trust yourself inside our Academy just for that.[163]

But Nelly was gentler than her daughter when he became self-pitying. 'No—there is *not* "one wholly sympathetic being in all the world". We are lucky if we can ever find one even very partly sympathetic with a small part of our being. . . . the only way is to do the sympathizing, it cultivates the imagination, like no other form of activity! . . . Art is an amusing hobby, game, trade or mistress, the best man ever made for himself.'[164]

She refused, however, to satisfy his curiosity by introducing him to her own family; 'my son came up and renewed my satisfaction in seeing him where and what he wishes to be, which is all a mother ought to ask. My sister & my brother brought me the usual dissatisfaction born of love where is no liking.'[165] But inevitably Tom went too far, by including George in their exchanges:

Please please PLEASE, dont mention my name to my mother when you are writing to her more than is consistent with the usual necessities. I got from her on Xmas day a long letter most of which was devoted to something or other that I am supposed to have said and which I gather came to her via you (during the last two months) I imagine it was some joke you made about your correspondence (hers and yours) and which she has not sufficiently carefully read to get the correct context. I just answered that I didnt know what she meant as it was the first I had heard of it. It doesnt matter but it is irritating. Did you say I was shocked at the tone of her letters or something of that kind? Dont tell her I didnt whatever it was or we shall arrive at a point that quite illogically makes me think of Mme du Deffand's story of the old lady's dog who bit a large piece out of a guest's leg, whereupon the old lady cried out 'WILL it make him sick'? My mother loves to make a whirlpool and especially if she can suck me in to it, and she has probably worked herself up into an annoyance with me in order to amuse herself over the Xmas holidays. That was why I said gaily to you in London 'you are not to discuss me with my mother'.[166]

Contrite, Tom promised never to mention her to Nelly again; 'I suppose nothing will ever put an end to this parents business.' 'WHY WHY WHY is it that we all have to deceive our parents?' George wrote in response. 'Is it because they began our lives by deceiving us.'[167] And there the matter ended. A few years later, George was amused to find that her mother—who claimed not to be sentimental—had kept a packet of Tom's letters.[168]

Soon, however, another event conspired to create a rift in the three-way friendship; this time it came from Cheyne Gardens. Lennox like Tom was a frequenter of Hester Dowden's salon in London, and ever since he had boarded with them in Dublin had been a wise and helpful counsellor to her daughter Dolly, fifteen years his junior. Like her mother, Dolly was psychically inclined; there are stories of her prevision and sighting of ghosts and Hester was impressed by Dolly's great skill with the ouija board and automatic writing.[169] The relationship between mother and daughter was always incendiary, more so once Dolly determined to pursue her art studies and seek studio space outside the controlled and controlling circle. George observed the friendship between Dolly (or 'Dolche') and Lynx with a hopeful eye, and as early as 1925 suspected that something more committed might come of it. However, after seeing both in London, Willy reported, 'Dolly (not engaged to Lennox I think).'[170] But even though she was aware of his homosexual tendencies, George thought marriage a possibility for her lonely friend. Years ago he had, after all, conceived a passion for Iseult. 'I think, though I'd throttle you if you ever let on to him or to anyone else that I said this,' she wrote to Tom,

I think that he is very soon going to take steps that will most effectively put an end to the rumours and gossip of the Oscar Wildish sort. He hasnt in so many words told me so, but he has gone as near it as anyone could. I havent the vaguest idea who it is for one never sees him with any one here and he hasnt been in London for ages. But I am perfectly certain that I am right. It may be secret, but I know from something he said a few weeks ago that one will hear fairly soon. I havent the vaguest idea what he is thinking about it, but he *has* said very often that he is lonely. I wouldnt tell you this but your letter really seems needlessly worried. And I havent told anyone else, though I did tell Willy tonight, for Iseult was here, and there is to be a baby in September . . . I think, or know, that L. has lost interest *there* but if he is told that sort of thing and thinks Harry is behaving badly, it will all start up again. And I do really believe that if he got married he'd have a decent chance of being happy. In any case its no use harrowing him over something that he is powerless to control, or help. Do you agree? But perhaps he has told you? And is that why Hester is not going to Dalkey!!!! I am rather puzzled, he doesnt seem very cheerful but that may partly be worry about money. . . . I do very much feel that if its going to come off it will probably be a great success and even if it isnt a success he wont be much worse off than he is now. And he's an affectionate sort of person who's likely to get accustomed to anyone quite soon if he gets his dream even for five minutes. If he doesnt he'll make her life 'a little hell' as Bella says in the White Blackbird.[171]

Tom's offhand—perhaps deliberately casual—suggestion that 'Only Hester is really able for him. Domestically they are both impossible' provoked a scornful response from George:

Of course I dont agree with one single word you say. But then I hardly ever do. But this time from the very beginning to the very end I utterly disagree . . . I'm sure Hester is more than equal for Lennox, he'd not have a chance once she was certain of him. Of course I must say I've never met the Lennox you always tell me of and only once got a faint glimpse that you *might* be right when he bit Hester hard last year at Dalkey. But she'd just been so hideously rude to him that a saint would have bitten back. . . . I gather you are rather liking Hester at present!!![172]

In 1926 Dolly was planning an exhibition of her paintings in Dublin. When Lennox consulted George about the propriety of Dolly's staying at Sorrento Cottage without her mother as chaperone, she offered 'a spare room' at Merrion Square. Lennox would 'hate to know that he was discussed like this', she explained to Tom, 'but you know how all Dublin would have talked about his "new irregularities" . . . Put it to her that she'd be very welcome and the maids will look after her with assiduous and rather inefficient attention, and beds will await her with warm welcome if she will sleep in them.'[173] Having heard so much from Lennox and Tom, George and Dolly were surprised to like each other immediately. 'I love Dolly,' George enthused. 'Dont generally much like females but she adds one to the small collection I do like—Dorothy, Eva and Jelly.'[174] The friendship would be a lasting one and when Dolly returned to London George was as bereft as Lennox; together they issued the invitation to design *The Emperor Jones* for the League. To Tom George again broached the subject of a more permanent arrangement: 'Any chance do you think of her staying over permanently? Willy snorts at the idea, but I'm not so sure.' Again Tom refused to rise to the bait: 'Dolly has been in high spirits, you all gave her a grand time and London has been duller for her in consequence.'[175]

When Dolly departed, George missed her 'horribly'; 'I wish she did live here.'[176] She and Lennox immediately found further commissions so that Dolly spent more and more time in Dublin, designing for the Abbey as well as the League, and in between working in Harry Clarke's stained-glass works. Always, she was welcome at Merrion Square, where she thought Michael 'a pet' and Anne 'dreadfully knowing and coy'.[177] Even Willy liked 'Chinatown', as he dubbed her because of her slightly Oriental appearance, and always made a point of including her in his invitations to Lennox. He also appreciated her skill as a theatre artist. 'You ask me what I think of the work you have done for us in Dublin. We are greatly indebted to you, you have transformed the whole look of our stage. . . . You have one very great advantage which is that you combine aesthetic sensitiveness and novelty with a grasp of the necessities of the stage, you have never brought us an impracticable design.'[178]

And he recognized the company she offered George. Now there was a trio of chums who went to the races, films, and theatre together. George assisted her in painting sets and accompanied her to parties; Dolly played small roles in several productions. Eventually, although returning to London for other design commissions, she took a permanent studio/room in Dublin, dubbed 'the Grimery', but frequently came to Merrion Square, yet another person to check on the children when George was away.[179] When Lennox went to America to lecture, he missed their company: 'I learned to play craps on board ship—the dice game the niggers play— and a very good gamble it is and when you and Dolly and I get together next I'll win all your pennies.' 'On the whole I'm getting along fairly happily only get an *awful* Europe-ache every now and then—don't want Ireland (except Dalkey garden) but want a cafe in Spain or France or Italy and you and Dolly.'[180] As she had with Tom, George played a protective older sister role with Dolly, even taking her to Ballylee, a most certain sign of their friendship. The two women had a great deal in common: they were both psychic and trained artists; they chose as mates men considerably older than themselves; their birthdays were both in October, just ten days apart; and perhaps most of all, both experienced difficult, uneasy relationships with their mothers. As time went by they would also share the same weaknesses.

Tom did not return to Dublin for a visit until October 1927, after he had taken a teaching position in Paris. Plunged into a new artistic circle that included Joyce, Beckett, and Aldington, he was already distancing himself from his old friends. 'You havent written for such an age that I wonder if I have been putting all my feet into it somewhere?' George wrote, inviting him to stay at Merrion Square. 'L. R. tells me that you are to be in Florence for a week—lucky devil— and so I write to the address he provides. Dolly, as you know, is over, so it is all rather a lark. There is great excitement in the family that "Mister McGreevy" is really coming back. They always think that you are very foolish to live anywhere but here.'[181] The visit was not an unqualified success. 'Tom MacGreevy arrived yesterday & some obscure quarrel between him, Dolly Dowden—otherwise Chinatown—& Lennox Robinson is disturbing life,' Willy reported to Olivia. 'I think the trouble is that Tom came here when he should have gone to Lennox and as Dolly's cap is set at Lennox she too feels aggrieved. I am hoping that peace and night may come together for all, with George added, are now turning Lennox's greenhouse into a cage for canaries. We had a noisy & cantankerous dinner at a restaurant last night.'[182] But unsuspecting Tom still hoped that Dolly might 'nerve herself to risk Paris on her £2 a week for a year or so'.[183] Nor did he realize quite how much he was out of sympathy. 'George has had another missive from Tom,' Lennox wrote Dolly, 'and I believe we are going to escape this August, he's just going to stay on and on in Paris and be a starving poet, he said to G "I dont think there is any lonelier person in the world than me." Isnt it just so pathetic!'[184]

When Dolly and Lennox finally married in 1931, Tom would become lonelier still. Once again he felt betrayed, and for some years his relationship with George also cooled. Apart from occasional flying visits, it would not be until MacGreevy returned to Ireland in 1941 that they would pick up their old ties in the same close way. He and Hester seem to have been the only people who did not realize that marriage between Tinche and Dolche was inevitable. But Hester at least recognized that Tom's feelings for Dolly were not sexual; she suspected the same of Lennox and became even more 'gloomy and difficult'.[185] George on the other hand hoped for at least a happy companionship, and had made her feelings clear to Dolly long before the formal engagement. 'I suppose I ought to write you a formal congratulatory letter,' she wrote Dolly on hearing the news, 'but I cant do that because my congratulations are so entirely to Lennox for doing something that will make him terribly happy for the first time in his life, for I never changed my early opinion which I propounded over a wheelbarrow of weeds in the garden at 82 . . . I wonder if you remember your reply? I do. I do think you'll do all that and I dont think anyone else could have done it. So that's that.'[186] As she had for the Pounds so many years before, sometime this summer she cast the Robinsons' horoscopes, identifying the 'Joint aspects LR & Dolly'.

Yeats's congratulatory letter to Lennox was also predictable: 'You will get a charming able wife. You will work better, be far more content.'[187] Aware of his own satisfactory marriage, Willy continued to pay court to his wife. No matter how engrossing his activities and writing while he was away, his heart, he frequently assured George, 'is with you always'. 'I am too busy to have any thoughts except that I want greatly to be back home with you drinking a bottle of Muskatel [sic] and telling you all the news.'[188] He sought advice of their London women friends in searching out gifts to bring back to Dublin: Olivia advised on 'some very pretty black & gold evening shoes . . . They have funny tops' which he thought 'very pretty'. 'If by any chance you have gold brocade shoes let me know & I [will] find you something in a Liverpool curiosity shop perhaps.' George replied with affectionate tact: 'I am delighted at the idea of the shoes. They are just what I want. Indeed I had tried a couple of months ago to get some here but with no success.' However, Willy was not always as successful in identifying headgear as he was shoes. Like the other Yeats women, George loved hats, the fancier the better. Once at a garden party he could not find her, and when she was pointed out to him replied, 'I know my wife, and that is not she.' He did not recognize her in a new hat.[189] He was more triumphant with jewellery: 'I warn you however that you will feel moved to welcome me for I shall bring you a large and striking Hungarian brooch which will make a sensation in the Arts Club. I think the broach [sic] you lost was Hungarian. . . . The stones are green, red & white. I got it at a place Mrs Hamilton Fox recommends.'[190] When George was returning from London he once mistook the date and made a dinner commitment; George received an apologetic note, 'I have been upset all day to think you must return to an empty house.'[191]

They were happiest together at Ballylee, the Siberian sledge dog Thor their only companion. 'I shall have a whole month without the children and Willy will be content and happy and well at Ballylee and so I shall have all the day to frolic in.' Willy appreciated their retreat as much as she did. 'We have been here for some days,' he wrote Olivia on another occasion, '—in perfect tranquility—no children, no telephone, no callers. No companion but a large white dog which has a face like the Prince Consort—or a mid-Victorian statue—capable of error but not of sin.'[192] Sometimes George went alone, or took Anne and Thor, leaving Michael with his beloved Nana to go every day to the sea or have other treats to make up.[193] As much of the summer as possible was spent at Ballylee, Willy returning to Dublin for meetings and then as briefly as possible. Neither was pleased when town invaded their peace:

We had a fearful influx of visitors here The entire Gogarty family complete with Kevin O'Sheil and Mercedes Car; Willy's uncle Isaac his cousin Hilda, his cousin Guy complete with wife, in a Canadian car, and Lady G. All unexpected. Could God have sent a more difficult plague to the Egyptians? Willy *has* got such a lot of relations, and the maids always say 'at home' to them and to clergy who call, and one cant tell them that relations and the 'cloth' (is that a purely English term for clergy?) are not always longed for. Since Anne was ill they call far more . . . to see the dear children . . . which unfortunately includes 'Willy's dear little wife' as Aunt Fanny called me once in public. She's at least three inches shorter than I and about 75 and the wife of a doctor . . . therefore she thinks my children very badly brought up because they eat unwholesome food. Dont you hate people who make you feel 'guilty' without knowing why? Only one's own sex can do it, and they *do* do it sometimes.[194]

But at times not even the tower was far enough away, and George's letters to Tom increasingly included a litany of complaints: 'There is a fearful lot to be done and I am so tired, and so cross.' 'Nothing has been happening here except work and work and work and the children alternately in bed!'[195] Detachment was not always possible when, in addition to frequent illnesses, there were money worries. When an unexpected large bill came from Heal's for furniture which Willy could not pay, he asked George if she could meet it 'and charge to me either the whole ultimately or the part that went to pay for the things in my room. Or would you prefer that I sold out something? I am most anxious that you sell out nothing more—you must keep a rampart round the children.'[196] Once again, travel plans had to be shelved: 'I'm afraid there's not a ghost of a chance of our all going to Italy in September,' Lennox informed Tom; 'the Yeats will be at Ballylee till the middle of August and I gather are very hard up and no talk of going abroad.'[197]

Money did occasionally turn up when most needed. When Ellen Chapman, Mayor of Worthing and her father's step-aunt, finally died in 1925, George was at last able to look forward to receiving the rest of her inheritance:

we shall probably come to London for ten days to celebrate the death of my Great-aunt-law-devil. Through whose decease I hope to get my father's money, at least the share of it that he left me. My brother who is already very rich gets two thirds but my share ought to be £250 a year and *might* be £300. As I have been trying to get Willy to leave the Senate after the education Bill is through—he is always full of verse that never gets time to be written—it may help to induce him to.

Probate on Mrs Chapman's will was granted the following February, and the fortunate Harold also received a collection of watercolour drawings.[198] But George and Willy did not go to London in April after all. 'I do want to go abroad next September and in spite of my devil-great-aunt's death I shant, we shant, be able to do both. The present plan is to go to Ballylee about May 15 till August 1 and then . . . to Spain? . . . in September. If it isnt Spain it will be Italy. And if it isnt Italy it will be France. And it may be neither and none.'[199]

When, in July 1927, grandmother Woodmass finally died the Tuckers, but not the Yeatses, attended the funeral. 'The whole affair was horrible,' Nelly wrote Tom, disagreeing with both her daughter and *The Times* on the actual date of death, 'but she departed in peace—she just slept away. Relations are worse than the seven worst devils. She was very rich.'[200] Most of the estate went to Nelly's brother George, who then remarried (and later left this wife too).[201] But Harold and George again received some money, which eased the Yeatses' financial strain for the time being and once again turned their minds to the sun.

Dear E. P. Yours of some ancient date?? Anyway, herewith certain pomes. If you want any, or both, or either, send word quick quick quick, for WB doesnt know the bloody moon is gone to you and is imagining that I am serialising it with Dial, or trying to do that . . . And dont fuss about cash, tisnt necessary as Autobiographies have done well this year for us—ONLY, for God's sake, dont separate the bloody moon series or he will undoubtedly burst.

We have an invite to a villa at Alassio unless a female of my acquaint: is more flighty than I think likely and so we shall arrive in Genoa circa January ('I know you will not want to leave the children for Christmas') and it seems the moment to stay for two or three days at Hotel Mignon Rapallo IF IT and D. and YOU are still in occupation at that date . . . . . ?[202]

The unspecified woman was probably Lady Gregory's friend Mrs Lucy Phillimore, whose novel *Paul: The Jew* had recently been serialized in the *Nation*; George and Willy had been taken by Gregory to Kilmacurragh, her country house in Kilbride, earlier that month.[203] A wealthy, restless widow with strong socialist tendencies, although brought up in England Lucy (or 'Lion') Phillimore had embraced the Irish cause with enthusiasm. She was also mystically inclined; efforts to consult her late husband through the offices of Mrs Leonard (now so popular she charged thirty-five shillings a session and had to be booked well in advance), may have been suggested by the Yeatses.[204] But, although they would frequently encounter Lucy Phillimore in the south of France as well as in England and Ireland, more important to George was the possibility of renewed friendship with Dorothy and Ezra.

Perhaps far more than Willy, George needed a break away from Ireland. She was getting tired of Dublin society and indeed of Irish politics and attitudes. 'Everything here is rather vile at the moment; at least there has been and is rather a wave of mental and moral dishonesty which sickens one,' she had complained to Tom the previous year. 'People like Professor Magennis starting new parties and calling themselves little Irelanders as an excuse for the worst philistinism. Vile vile vile. I begin to wonder if you are not right to leave English speaking countries!'[205] For three months in the spring of 1927 Willy was involved in the controversy over the Copyright Act. But the most devastating blow to their hopes of a new Ireland was the assassination in July 1927 of Kevin O'Higgins, Minister for Justice and External Affairs and a good friend. George and Willy had come up from the quiet of Ballylee for a few days, and heard the news on their way to dine at the Gresham Hotel. Turning away from the door they walked the streets for hours, trying to come to terms with the loss of a friend, and 'the one strong intellect in Irish public life'. At O'Higgins's funeral, they recognized the choral music as part of a prevision they had both experienced before the murder. 'The night before George had suddenly called the dog out of the way of what she thought was a motor car,' Willy wrote to Olivia, '—there was no car—and a moment after when inside our own door we both heard two bursts of music, voices singing together. . . . You will remember the part the motor car had in the murder. Had we seen more he might have been saved, for recent evidence seems to show that those things are fate unless foreseen by clairvoyance and so brought within the range of free-will.'[206]

Although there seems to have been general knowledge of the real assassins, they were never charged; but many others were arrested, including Seán MacBride (even though Senator Bryan Cooper had seen him on a ferry from England at the time of the murder). Willy thought that Maud and Iseult did not seem anxious, thinking it 'a mistake or an electioneering move'—but he himself was.[207] Seán was arrested under the new Public Safety Act, which Yeats had voted for, providing broad measures for search and detention; this, as well as Willy's efforts to permit her son to visit his dying old nurse, initiated yet another controversial exchange of ideas between the two old friends. 'Not to vote was the easy, popular thing but I would have despised myself,' he wrote in defence. But he also dictated a statement 'of what I believe to be the ancient doctrine . . . of the effects of hate & love. The whole of mystical philosophy seems to me a deduction from this single thought.' It was yet one more attempt to deal with the concept of 'victimage' as discussed in George's script and 'sleeps': 'A Victim is a person so placed in life that he would be excited into the most violent hatred or into some other bad passion, if he did not dissolve that passion into the totality of mind, or to use the common language into God. Until that act of Victimage takes place, an act not of simple renunciation, but of sanctification, the passion remains passing from mind to mind from being to being among the living and the dead.'[208] The challenges raised by their 'system' continued to haunt him, and Maud continued to accuse him of insincerity ('For your poetry you will be forgiven, but sin no more'[209]).

The summer in 1927 at Ballylee was more by necessity than choice, for whatever money George received from her grandmother's will contributed to paying, once again, the Cuala overdraft. And again financial help came just in time to assist with the next crisis. In the autumn Willy received an offer from William Edwin Rudge, who wished to have the rights for six months of sixteen or more pages of poetry and would pay a substantial sum for the privilege of publication in his private Fountain Press in New York. Writing against time, Willy came down with influenza in October. 'He is *not at all* seriously ill,' George assured Lady Gregory, 'but is rather weak and has to be kept very quiet.'[210] But his collapse was worrying all the same, for congestion of the left lung followed. It had been a year of sickness, starting in January with severe rheumatism chased out by flu; privately George thought that he had not been 'what I, being of a fussy mind, consider "well", ever since'.[211] This recurrence was serious enough to have caused delirium and his doctor recommended a journey out of the Dublin winter into the sun.

Advised by Lennox, whose most recent journey to Spain had been earlier that year with Hester and Dolly, George made arrangements for their longed-for holiday. The proofs for *Oedipus* were handed over to Lady Gregory to finish 'especially as to stops', a copy of their wedding certificate ordered for the issuance of new passports, hotels booked through Cook's travel bureau, sisters-in-law entertained at the new Jammet's restaurant, and, most important of all, assurance elicited that the children would be regularly checked on. Although they were leaving sooner than originally planned, 'George is very happy over it,' Lily reported, 'and, wonderful woman, speaks and reads Spanish, although she has never been there.'[212] Her last public gesture before leaving was to invite Sean O'Casey and his bride Eileen Carey, in Dublin on their honeymoon, to join them for dinner at the Moira Hotel.[213]

However, the journey to Spain would not be the restful holiday George anticipated.

PART IV

TRANSITS 1929–1939

All that matters is to lead or be led—to renew or be renewed—the form or object is no great importance—stagnation is the evil

(the control Thomas)[1]

A philosophy created from experience, burns & destroys; one which is created from search, leads. ('Definitions')[2]

The nervous system of a psychic is terribly subject to certain kinds of strain.

(Willy to Augusta Gregory)[3]

such small encouragement as I got has rather given me something to do, or to look forward to, not to production because I'm too critical to believe I'll ever do anything good enough, but at any rate to going on and not just getting through each day as it comes. (George to Tom)[4]

Had I known that all this might happen I should certainly never have had a family. (George to Tom)[5]

Some day of course he will have to die but I do hope it will be in Dublin or at least London. . . . More than ever I believe that no one should be dependent on anyone. (George to Lennox)[6]

15

RAPALLO

They left Ireland on 3 November 1927; Willy once again had a temperature and all was left up to the thermometer. But the next day George and Willy embarked from Tilbury on the SS *Morea*, a P. & O. Royal Mail liner bound for Gibraltar and Marseilles under Captain E. J. Thornton.[7] Naturally they travelled first class (£15 each). They planned to spend most of the time in Seville and be back in Dublin in time for Christmas.[8] The children proudly flourished a telegram from London.

As usual, it was a rough passage across the Bay of Biscay. Back in Dublin a worried Lennox read that liners were twelve hours late because of the gales. He wrote advising a return home by way of Madrid; at least that way George would see the Prado.[9] Reaching Gibraltar on 9 November, George and Willy went immediately to the Hotel Reina Cristina down the coast in Algeciras, where Lynx had once stayed with Horace Plunkett.[10] The hotel, under English management and designed primarily for English and American guests, was described when it was built in 1901 as 'a handsome two storey building standing in its own grounds', occupying 'a commanding position on the sea front facing Gibraltar, the Straits, and the African Coast beyond, as well as, inland, the Sierra de la Palma and the mountain ranges which rise behind it as far as the eye can reach'.[11] Set in two acres of gardens, the Reina Cristina was up to date and luxurious, with electric lighting and—a must for Willy—fireplaces in all rooms. Doors led out from the dining room, library, smoking room, and great hall to a fine patio or inner courtyard with marble columns, floor, and fountain; their fellow traveller John Hall persuaded his wife, George, and Willy to perform there for his motion picture camera. Hall later sent the Yeatses some stills, but the film itself, complete with scenes of their arrival at Gibraltar, HM ships *Tourmaline* and *Splendid* rigged for Armistice Day, and birds flying over from Tangier, would remain hidden for sixty years.[12] George was especially delighted to meet the tall elegant Jean Hall, just three years older than herself. A Canadian by birth, Jean Nesbitt had been studying piano in Vienna when she met John Hall, a prominent and wealthy British industrialist nineteen years her senior. She too had a young family, was fluent in languages, well read, and happiest in the company of men. The two women became fast friends, and in the following years the Yeatses visited the Halls both in Charnes Hall, Staffordshire, and their London flat at St James's Place.[13]

As it turned out, Lennox's recommendations as tour guide would soon be abandoned. Although the sky on most days was clear, the temperature ranged only between 57 and 67 degrees Fahrenheit in the shade; this was not the sun Willy longed for, and so George made arrangements for them to move on to Seville sooner than planned. But while at the Reina Cristina, they delighted in the magnificently lush gardens and the colourful wildlife. 'Today there has been rain but yesterday and the day before bright sun,' Willy wrote to Lady Gregory; 'and today, now that the rain has stopped, the butterflies are lighting on the roses in the hotel garden . . . at sunrise some hundred or so white herons will come flying from beyond Gibraltar and go to sleep in some dark trees. Tomorrow we go . . . by motor to Seville—some six hours journey—to far greater heat . . . P. S.—The first two or three herons have just arrived.' He was charmed by the idea that the birds 'fish in the Mediterranean on the other side of Gibraltar which is some ten miles off, & then fly home to the gardens here for a night's sleep'.[14] A year later, more correctly identified, they would appear in 'At Algeciras—A Meditation upon Death':

> The heron-billed pale cattle-birds
> That feed on some foul parasite
> Of the Moroccan flocks and herds
> Cross the narrow Straits to light
> In the rich midnight of the garden trees
> Till the dawn break upon those mingled seas.

The Yeatses left the Reina Cristina on 14 November, and just in time. Three days later the authorities announced a case of smallpox in Algeciras; everyone leaving was required to be vaccinated. (The following year a fire almost completely destroyed the hotel itself.) The trip by private car was 'a beastly long uncomfort[able] journey' over some bad roads, and when they arrived in Seville George discovered that the 'very nice' inexpensive pension she had booked (only fifteen pesetas, approximately ten shillings, a day) had no heating. They went instead to the Grand Hotel Seville, 'a poem & *not* cheap'; but it was warm and comfortable, even luxurious—hot and cold running water in all 100 rooms and, most important, a lift, for even writing a letter seemed to exhaust Willy. Worse, his lung began to bleed, which alarmed Willy more than it did George: 'I think the tide has turned & that Spain isnt going to be the absolute wash-out it seemed at first!' she reported to Lennox. 'When WB began calling Seville "Siena" I felt all was up. The Alcazar gardens have "registered" & in time he may take notice elsewhere—His main preoccupation is "my lung" which still registers blood. He will probably have to have inoculations or some'at when he gets home. . . . I career round all morning while W. is still in Hutchykutch & see & see & see.'

But even before Lennox could reply, he received another letter. George had spoken too soon. After ten days they were to move again, this time to Cannes where, at any rate, there would be doctors she could consult. 'Here they speak pidgeon English & pidgeon French & there are no facilities of any kind.' Although his cough and symptoms were much worse, she still did not think there was anything seriously wrong. Willy had no temperature and was actually gaining weight; probably, she decided, he has 'a "bug" in his lung'. However, he was hating it in Spain and for the first time afraid he might die.

'WB of course is making his last wills & testaments at all hours of day & night —Hurrying to finish a poem—but has not been able to begin yet. "Of course I shall never be able to go on with the autobio: now—" etc. etc. All poppycock— However in the same breath he talks of writing a poem on the Herons at Algeciras in "a few years time"——Do for Gods sake write news. What a pillaloo!' Although George would have preferred to go directly home, Willy was desperate for the sun. She thought of returning to friendly Algeciras, but Jean Hall wrote that it had turned very cold there.[15] Despite her mornings of sightseeing, 'I couldnt enjoy it with so vast an acreage of depression all around,' she told Lennox. 'I never saw W loathe anything so much!' They left Seville by train on 23 November.

The journey to Cannes was a nightmare: George arranged for a sleeper as far as Madrid where Willy went to bed in the hotel after a mere half-hour in the Prado, then another to Barcelona where he again spent the day in bed and she left him only long enough to go to Cook's travel office. 'I simply darent leave him all alone in the hotel. He was really so very done up & collapsed I thought he might start a really bad haemorrhage any moment. At B[arcelona] I was in a blue funk but decided to get him through & it worked out all right.' Finally, after yet another sleeper, they reached the small Hotel Château St Georges on the route de Frejus, in a quiet residential area west of the old town; about a mile from the centre of Cannes, it was just ten minutes away by tram or twenty minutes' walk along the seafront. She still hoped to be home in three or four weeks. 'I dont believe you two ought to be allowed out alone together any more,' Lennox wrote in sympathy. 'I'm sure you must always have a butty of either sex or both—I dont mean a hermaphrodite I mean possibly 2 butties.' He still hoped she had managed to enjoy herself a little in Spain, and if only for a moment forget the 'round table'—a reference to his play in which the round table in the heroine's bedroom represents 'All the silly things that we do again and again, this stupid going round and round the mulberry bush, this dance that leads to nowhere'.[16]

Despite the fact that Cannes was a success ('William purrs all day—on the hotel verandah; he hasnt moved elsewhere!'), it was still all 'round table' for George. Willy, who thought the beach like Rosses Point in Sligo, wanted to stay for six weeks; she relented and made plans to 'fetch out the infants' for Christmas. Nurse Reade would take them as far as London, where George planned to meet them and accompany children and Nurse across France. She herself was close to collapse, though fighting valiantly to maintain her customary calm:

Of course the 'grandparc' is a small garden & though it is—almost—'jusq'au plage' there is a road & the railway in between! However there's grand view of sea & roses on terrace etc. & a mile away is Cannes. He ought to have been brought straight here, but how could one foresee etc etc, or know how deep was the Spain complex! *And* he can be kept in touch with detective stories here—It looks grand at night—all stars & little lights round the bay—& the first night when I was feeling mad & was in my room looking out on 'nature' (villainous word) some one here began playing the moonlight [Sonata] & it just got me.[17]

Within a week however Willy, who had been feeling well enough to attempt a walk and write some verse, had another relapse; as he was reluctant to see a doctor in France, George wrote to Dublin for a new prescription. But finally it was necessary to call in medical help. At first they expected to return by mid-January; now they would be in Cannes at least a month longer. By this time, despite George and Lennox's caution, rumours were circulating in Dublin about Willy's health. George wrote to Gogarty, counting on his irrepressibility to counter them, but also probably hoping for medical advice:

I hear—that in spite of all our efforts—it has got round Dublin that Willy has some 'disease of the lung' & so I hasten to write to you as the best centre of contradiction. The haemorrhage in the lung was due to very high blood pressure (it was *260*) & since the B. P. has come down to 230 the haemorrhage has practically ceased. There *is* a small spot on the lung—since the congestion last October I imagine—& the man here thinks it quite unimportant. The blood pressure is what he concentrates on. W. is allowed no reading (but detective stories) no work & no exercise at present. No food after 4.30 p.m. at all. No wine, nothing but toast for tea & breakfast. The diet suits him admirably.[18]

Gogarty had assured Lennox that 'it can't be really serious lung trouble, not at his age and with sound lungs all his life'. However, alarmed by George's letters, Lennox volunteered to take Anne and Michael at least as far as Paris.[19] Then George discovered that the children could not be separated from her passport. To make matters worse, the British Consul was very rude when he saw that her passport was Irish.[20] But she needed Lennox's support more than ever, and after a series of confusing telegrams it was agreed that he would join them in Cannes after Christmas and, if she could arrange it, take the children back with him to Dublin. Lennox wrote frequently and cheerily: 'Once upon a time a—comparatively—young-looking man boarded a train at Cannes with two young children. His hair was dark, his step light. Twentysix hours later an elderly grey-haired man who tottered as he walked was helped by two porters out of the continental express at Victoria. He was followed by two young children.'[21]

But not even dear Tinche could raise her spirits. While George sank more deeply into a depression, Willy rose from his to a gaiety 'outside ones control, a something given by nature'. On 29 November, both wrote letters reflecting completely opposing moods. To Olivia Willy confessed that, 'staggered' by his 'first serious illness', he had 'hardly expected to recover but now I do expect to. George is planning already winters abroad & various contraptions, which will make it possible for me to give up everything I really don't like & keep everything that I like.' As always in his letters to Olivia, he paid tribute to his wife: 'I need not say that George is all goodness & kindness.' George on the other hand, after informing Lennox that 'William is re-planning his future! Resigning from everything he can resign from,' alarmingly continued, 'No Ballylee—that anyway will be a relief—a house near sea—perhaps Killiney—winter months here. I have given up the future & so apart from getting rid of 82 I cant be bothered. All I want is to get back & really get that done. . . . No, I felt for years that life was quite unnecessary & if only a landslide would remove me they could have jointly a nurse a governess a secretary & a housekeeper & all get on so much better.'[22]

Black as her depression was—'no Ballylee'—the fragmented situation would get still worse for George. While in Dublin, Augusta Gregory daily went to Merrion Square to see the children, 'romping and reading and telling stories'; but by late November Michael was in bed with a sore throat, and the doctor at first feared scarlatina.[23] Lennox, busy with a production in Cork, depended upon Dolly's occasional reports. By the time George met nurse and children in London on 15 December, Michael was seriously ill and had to be taken immediately to a nursing home. Horrified by how thin and pale her son was, she seethed, 'Dr Crichton was a bloody fool to let Michael travel over. He ought never to have allowed it.' The Dublin doctor did send a long letter with Nurse Reade, recommending a specialist who in turn insisted that Michael, 'having every kind of complication glands, throat, a wheeze & gastritis', travel no further. He might just be well enough to travel in a week's time if in a sleeper. Afraid to leave Willy alone any longer, she thought first of taking Anne ahead ('she is very fit & can quite well sit up'), leaving Michael to follow with his beloved Nana. 'It really all turns my brain to water,' she confessed. 'When Paterson sent Michael out of the room this morning & began telling me all that was the matter with him—I just disgraced myself for life by bursting into tears. . . . its all desperate.' She found herself unable to leave her little son, and so she and Anne stayed on in the nursing home with him. While there Dr Patterson discovered that Michael was allergic to eggs and milk, a condition he fortunately outgrew. George also had to persuade him that it was all right to eat the boiled sweets prescribed; always dutiful, Michael had been trained not to eat before meals. Worried that Willy would be 'fussed' at her not returning as early as expected, she wired to Cannes for a medical report; the doctor replied that Willy was reading too much. But by the time she returned with Anne to her husband on Christmas Eve, George was relieved to find him much better and cheerful.

Michael and the faithful Nana Reade arrived the next day, and from then on the children spent most of their time paddling on the beach with buckets and spades. Anne was intrigued that foodstuffs had to be kept in a basin surrounded by water as protection from ants. Michael was overjoyed when he saw a fisherman draw in his net, wash a fish in the sea, and eat it raw.[24] Even Willy came down to the beach in his shirt sleeves. Gradually the children turned brown from the friendly sun, and Michael, delighted to shed his bandage, began to put on some weight. But the experience had been a portent—for the next ten years George would find herself torn apart by conflicting duties, and desperate when either child was ill.

Clearly, the children would not be ready to return with Robinson in early January; but even so, Lennox must come out at their expense. 'Willy is looking forward so much to seeing you & wants to ease his mind on you,' she pleaded. '—he gets restless wondering what the Abbey does etc—And one feels when in expensive London nursing homes that being a little more bankrupt—a year hence—wont matter at all. So please dont fuss at the cost of your journey. And please dont have any nonsense about travelling second.'[25] She could not however, take gossipy Tom at the same time, sympathetic as he was. She told MacGreevy only that Michael had been unexpectedly delayed in London by a cold, and although it would be nice to see him, 'apart from conversation with William there are no attractions. Its the usual Riviera resort, though it doesn't afflict us much as we are a little way out from the town.' What is more, she was suffering from 'hellish neuritis all up my left arm from finger tips to shoulder & some days can hardly use it at all'.[26] It would be several months before Tom was informed of their future plans, and much longer before George recovered her own health and equanimity.

What she did not dare tell Tom was that in London it had been discovered that Michael suffered from a tubercular gland. Both she and Willy were aware of the power of the dreaded word, especially in Ireland. 'One does not want to spread the suggestion that he has tuberculosis,' Willy wrote to Lady Gregory. 'A tubercular gland is the slightest possible form of that infection.' But he broke the news that their return would be even further delayed; instead of taking Michael home, they were on the advice of the helpful London specialist sending him to 'a home-school in Switzerland', l'Alpe Fleurie in Villars-sur-Bex, 4,000 feet above sea level. 'In a month's time we go to Rapallo and George will leave me there, more or less in charge of the Pounds, and take Michael to Switzerland. When we go to Rapallo nurse takes Anne back to Dublin, Anne is in the most vigorous health. George will fetch me from Rapallo at the end of March, and I shall spend a few days in London before going to Dublin.' Furthermore, Lennox had been asked to arrange for the sale of 82 Merrion Square and look for some place on high ground near the sea.

They doubted whether they would be able to afford summers at Ballylee as in the past, although the neighbourhood must not think they were abandoning it. 'When we get home George will go there to see what repairs may be necessary after possible damage done by the floods this year.'[27] Gregory's reply was as always both encouraging and cautious: 'It will be sad seeing Ballylee shut up—but you will have to come & stay here, not to forget us. And a new house may inspire new poems there must be "Mrs Frenchs" or the like everywhere in Ireland.'[28]

Lennox had arrived on the last day of the year, bringing with him the works of Teresa of Avila (requested by Willy) and welcome news of Dublin. He paddled in the sea with the children, escorted George to shops and the casino, and with Willy discussed the Abbey repertoire and new ballet school, plans to 'simplify' *The Only Jealousy of Emer* as a ballet for Ninette de Valois, and a new project, the Academy of Letters. 'Probably it sent up his blood pressure but better that than lethargy,' he informed Gregory on his return. 'Yeats is certainly better than he has been but very far from well, he is very weak and lazy, I feel that he should be stirred up but probably I'm wrong. . . . He wants a little society, the hotel people are impossibly dull.'[29] One day they motored over to St Raphael to lunch with Lucy Phillimore, but the excitement exhausted Willy. Another day they went into Cannes to watch the carnival 'Battle of the Flowers'. After he left, Lennox sent George his remaining francs to gamble away in the casino: 'you are so damned moral when you are alone and haven't someone crude and low like me to tempt you.' But privately he informed Dolly, 'The situation in Cannes is pretty bad, I think the poet just ready to lie in bed all day.'[30]

Two years earlier when Willy had suffered from a fever, George had predicted, 'I foresee a moment not very distant when he will take to his bed permanently! However if he likes it why not.'[31] But to be in a foreign country, without friends, and so uncertain of the prognosis, was a different matter. However, Lennox's visit had given her strength too. She adapted to a new regime of keeping her husband active and, by whatever means possible, the poetry alive:

That ass-doctor came earlier than expected and filled W. with despair by telling him he need not expect ever to get back his original health etc. etc. So W. proceeded to have a complete breakdown, and 'of course he had never realised before how completely his interest in life had been in his work and if he isnt going to be able work and etc and etc' and 'You must tell Lennox. I know he has always thought I did not take my fair share of the burden of the Abbey . . . etc. etc.' So I made him dictate the beginning of a scenario for ballet, many letters and walked him into town today and he ate an enormous meal at the Majestic grill room and then wandered about looking at a seaplane which was taking people for short flights and landing near the Majestic on the sea, and only at 2–30 did he remember that he must be getting tired! I shall be thankful to get him to Rapallo and watch Ezra ginger him up! . . . You left a horrible vacuum behind you which is only just beginning to be lived down.[32]

But Willy once again collapsed with flu, and this time George turned to MacGreevy for help. 'Next time you have a leisure moment *do* write to Willy,' she urged, 'and dont say I asked you to! He really needs rousing badly, and has got it rooted in his head that he mustnt do anything, think anything, read anything!'

I have been working him on to an idea of a series of philosophical questions to be asked of various butties—Haldane—Lewis—Bertie Russell and so on, and until he remembers he mustnt think he prances about in bed full of joy, then suddenly flops down 'I must stop. My blood pressure will go up' . . . . But if something isnt done he'll sink into awful depths of depression and despair. . . . I hope to get him to Rapallo, in fact well or ill I am going to get him there on or near Feb 17. Except for this continual fatigue he is ever so much better, I had really thought he would be well in no time. . . . Either philosophy or ballet schemes please![33]

A fracas in the hotel also helped revive the listless poet: 'We have had the revolutionary temperament here,' he informed Olivia. A couple from the Russian Embassy in Paris accused Willy of having consumption and tried to persuade various guests to leave. George and Willy offered to depart for the sake of the hotel. However, the plot backfired, and the manager asked the trouble-makers to leave. Since then, 'our allowance of clean sheets and of baths has been increased; and the communists are doubtless trying somewhere else to create the revolutionary situation'.[34] George's knowledge of French and Spanish was proving invaluable. Meanwhile they had decided that, if the school was a success, Anne would join Michael in Switzerland; she had suffered far too many winter illnesses in Dublin. 'Michael has got back his colour and his plumpness and is in great spirits at the thought of Switzerland,' Willy wrote to Coole, 'he has just said to Anne "When you come out to Switzerland next October I will introduce you to my friends and say 'This is my sister'." ' 'It was like "God caring for the ravens"—one of my family mottoes—the way that American private press enabled me to make an utterly unforeseen £400 as if in preparation for all this expense.'[35]

On 13 February 1928 Anne and Nurse Reade left Cannes for Dublin, and the following day George took Michael and Willy to Rapallo. They stopped en route at Menton so that Willy could consult a specialist recommended by the London doctor, who had suggested 'that the ancient cure of bleeding at regular intervals' might ease his blood pressure, which increased during his coughing spells.[36] When they arrived in Rapallo on the 17th, Dorothy and Ezra were there, and George felt more secure at last. But nobody realized that they would be at the Albergo Rapallo, a small hotel on the seafront next door to where the Pounds had established themselves, until 1 April.

George had appealed to the Pounds for help in January, after it was clear that Willy would not be well enough to return to Ireland. Both replied immediately. Ezra offered detailed descriptions of the available hotels, even offering to spend a night in the Rapallo, taking a thermometer with him to make certain the proprietor was not bluffing in his promise of warmth; he advised on appropriate terraces (including their own but five flights up) and where best to eat out of the wind. Dorothy, delighted to have the prospect of 'Coz' nearby, volunteered to take Willy for walks—short or long—while George was with Michael in Switzerland.[37] Relieved by the promise of support and clearly delighted at the prospect of being with her old friends again, George had reported to Dorothy from Cannes, 'William is much better. Dont think he is likely to "give trouble" while I'm Swissing. Anyway a wire could fetch me back in 12 hours. We arrive D. V. at Rapallo 6.55 p.m. on Feb 17. If one can dine, say at 7–45 (Here one has to do it at 7 sharp or give notice!) will you and E dine with me and come up play with W after?? Both males will go to bed on arrival, Michael because he is made to, and Willy because he always wants to!' She was reluctant to be far away from them. 'We both agree that [Portofino] VETTA would be hell of a way away, and I think W will probably find Rapallo sufficiently "country" without moving from "Albergo Rapallo". I hope he will begin soon to be able to walk. For months he has only gone 1,000 yards at the outside—if 1,000 yards is what I can walk in 15 mins. My space sense is not good.' She was also anxious to borrow books and hoped for a lending library that could provide the four detective novels Willy consumed each week. (They once bought 'a crime fiction' advertised as 'Murder at Keyes', but on opening it found 'a ghastly sentimental novel within the cover "The Eternal Love".'[38]) Reading the works of the ascetic contemplative St Teresa to him was not providing her with much pleasure. But Willy looked forward to talking over matters of punctuation in his poetry with Ezra.[39]

So delighted were they with their new environment that within days the Yeatses had decided to establish a permanent base in Rapallo, and even before she left for Switzerland with Michael on 22 February George had regained sufficient energy and optimism to seek out a possible flat. News from Dublin of Anne—she heard every second day—was promising: 'always in rude health, positively vulgar health'.[40] But Michael was losing weight again. While she was settling their son into his new school, Willy walked by the seafront in the morning, dozed each afternoon in the sun on the roof garden which opened out from the Pounds' rooms, and—resolutely obeying doctor's orders not to work—wrote the occasional letter. To Olivia he outlined their plans: their first thought was to keep 82, letting out all but one floor; furniture would be shipped to Italy where they might live from August to April so that the children, both in school in Switzerland, could spend their holidays there. Seemingly unaware of the depth of his wife's depression, he added 'George is longing for the freedom of flats & a daily help & all heavy meals out. . . . We shall live much more cheaply & this change of place & climate at my time of life is a great adventure one longed for many a time.' However, all this was still secret from Nelly. Nor did he mention Ballylee. He concluded by providing an up-to-date report on her own daughter: 'Ezra and Dorothy seem happy & content, pleased with their way of life. Dorothy & George compare their experiences of infancy & its strange behaviour. George instructing Dorothy out of her greater store. If we carry out our plans, & settle here they will renew all their old friendship & to George at any rate that will be a great happiness.'[41]

George did indeed look forward to spending time with her 'dearest Coz', though their lives had ceased to follow parallel lines. Dorothy and Ezra had arrived at a convenient *modus vivendi* of dignified silence—summers in England for Dorothy with her mother and son Omar, while Ezra went to Venice with his mistress Olga Rudge. Olga and Ezra's daughter Mary, living in Italy with a foster mother, was never spoken of. Dorothy remained as private as ever, withdrawing to her studio to paint or sitting room to read. George had chosen another path, concentrating on keeping husband and children on the same lifeline. But that choice was beginning to take its toll.

Meanwhile, leaving Willy in the care of the Pounds, she was at the Pension Henriette in Villars-sur-Bex (now the ski resort Villars-sur-Ollon, in the canton of Vaud, near Montreux). L'Alpe Fleurie itself was a large verandahed wooden chalet on a slope overlooking the Rhone valley and facing the 10,000-foot high 'Dent du Midi'. Grandfather Woodmass may have climbed it during his mountaineering days. Michael loved the funicular cog-wheel train that chugged up from Bex, and the tea and cream cakes at the Palace Hotel across from the school. There was also an excellent luge or toboggan run below at Villars. George wrote to Willy that Michael was delighted with the snow 'and the St Bernard dogs dragging sledges'.[42] From Rapallo Willy assured her all was well; 'Ezra explains his Cantos & reads me Cavalcanti & we argue about it quite amicably.' He told Lily that he looked forward to their seeing 'the sights together for the first time since we left home'.[43]

Finally satisfied that the school and Michael were right for each other, George returned to Willy on 2 March. She would have to become accustomed to a life of geographical uncertainty. Dutifully she sent a long report to Coole describing Willy's improved health, the new flat, and her son's school. Gregory was delighted with the photographs of Michael, replying to Willy: 'How well he looks, & happy & robust . . . Michael is quite himself tho he looks more like you than before. . . . that question of giving up 82 had been so long in your minds it is as well to have it settled definitely.' However, she still assumed they would eventually return to Ballylee.[44] To Tom George announced, 'We have revolutionised existence.' It was too early to say how long they would have to remain in Italy, and even though the Pounds were nearby, she hoped it would not be year-round. Ezra probably hoped so also, although he seems to have enjoyed the stimulus of having Willy 'next door'.[45] But until she returned to Villars with Willy at Easter George would not know whether Michael was happy enough to remain until June. If Michael is content, 'I shall come over to fetch him June 15 or so and bring him to Ireland until Sept: when he would return to Villars. If not then we would have to bring him home with us April 10—and come to Rapallo, say in July. In that case Anne would go [to] a school at San Remo instead of Switz: and for the present Michael would stay with us in Rapallo.' As for Willy, 'If only I had known W. might crock up—and his "crocking" is, I think personally, really more close to nervous breakdown than anything.' The lung was perhaps only slightly affected, but unless there was some tubercular infection, which she doubted, this could not explain his continued physical exhaustion. 'Its rather distracting,' she admitted, for although the mountain air suited Michael, it would not at all suit Willy. 'I really havent the slightest idea how W. will develop. He has always, constitutionally, been so strong that I should never be surprised if he didnt perk up all of a sudden to what he was before.' But all the doctors agreed that he must winter in a good climate. Willy meanwhile was 'very happy at the idea of getting out of all responsibilities, no more committees, no more Senate, no more anything but his own work'. As for George herself, 'We shant have a servant sleeping in, so that, except in holidays, we shall be very free and can lock the front door at any moment and buzz off where we like! And I shall at least have the benefit of "no responsibilities".' But at the moment, 'I cant see outside an infinitesimal area—W & M.'[46]

'I think the only desire George has ever expressed to me has been this desire to go to Italy, where she was very happy as a child,' Willy had told Lady Gregory years ago.[47] These were not the ideal circumstances George had longed for, but she would have to make the best of it. She was only 35, and already the future promised little but anxiety and exhaustion. To MacGreevy she confessed, 'had I known that all this might happen I should certainly never have had a family!' On looking over her long unrestrained letter she then wrote at the top, 'Private "burn this when read" '.[48]

In 1928 Rapallo, on the eastern side of the Ligurian Riviera and sheltered in the Gulf of Tigullio about eighteen miles below Genoa, was still comparatively unspoiled by tourists, despite every guidebook's boast of nine times more sunshine than in England. Palm trees flourished and Pitosforos evergreens with their orange blossom flowers scented the air in the piazzas and along the seafront; private villas dotted the wooded hills behind. Whereas the winter inhabitants had at the turn of the century been primarily English, now there was a strong German community, the most prominent member being the Nobel laureate Gerhart Hauptmann, who took his lunch at the Caffé Aurum on the other side of the hedge from Ezra and Dorothy. George was relieved to discover an English circulating library on the via delle Americhe; nearby—should he ever be required—an English chaplain was in residence at the Church of St George, which they considered attending in an effort to seek out 'material here for a social circle'.[49] Lily would have enjoyed a visit with her sister-in-law to the exhibition rooms of Zennaro, manufacturer of 'artistic laces and embroideries', also on the via Americhe. And it was in this pleasant residential district—within a week of their arrival—that George found the ideal flat, 'with balconies & the most lovely view imaginable'.

Number 12 via Americhe (now number 34 Corso Cristoforo Colombo) was newly built; as the first tenants in number 8 on the fourth floor they were able to choose the colours and—to the builder's regret—'keep out ugly tiles and plaster ornaments of all sorts', and eliminate glass in the doors. There were balconies on three sides from which they could enjoy the morning sun and views of both sea and mountains, with French windows off the dining and sitting rooms; the ceilings were high and the floors in the hallways marble. Altogether there were nine rooms: for Willy, a study with two French windows and balconies with doors both into the entrance hall and his bedroom 'so that he can paddle in and out without being seen'; a small study for George; schoolroom and night nursery for the children, though Michael would sleep in George's bedroom (overlooking the sea) at Willy's end of the hall; a large boxroom ('linen room and glory ole!'); bathroom and two lavatories; and even in the children's holidays a spare room for guests. The kitchen, coal, and coke room provided steam heating, and there was both gas and electricity for light and heating.

For Yeats Rapallo was the fulfilment of a dream: 'This is an indescribably lovely place, some little Greek town one imagines—there is a passage in Keats describing just such a town.'[50] The views over Rapallo and the bay were spectacular; there was a lift from outside their door down to the narrow entrance hall. (On his arrival Michael duly counted the eighty-two steps up to their flat.) George signed a five-year lease on 17 March 1928, and during the next month measured floors, marked where the electric outlets should be, and identified what furnishing would be required. Willy described the furniture in the Genoa shops as 'twists and waves and twirls. . . . English lodging house furniture somehow exalted into an incredible energy; Michael Angelo dreaming of Tottenham Court.' When they insisted theirs be as plain as possible, the craftsman was in despair at their 'brutto' taste.[51] The rent was 9,000 lire (approximately £98) per annum; food was comparatively cheap, and they dined out regularly, often with Dorothy and Ezra, with whom they lunched every day.[52] It was but a short, pleasant walk up the via Americhe, across the via Gramsci bridge, then through the piazza IV Novembre to the Pounds' flat on the via Marsala or, if the wind was not too cold, along the seafront where the Ristorante Rapallo welcomed them each day. By the end of February Willy was strong enough to walk about the harbour 'for an hour without fatigue', but, convinced by the statement of his doctor in Cannes that he suffered 'from the overwork of years', he was still self-consciously nursing himself. 'I am directed to walk slowly and even turn my head slowly that the speed of thought may slacken, and to avoid prolonged excitement even in conversation, and to keep away from winter cold and out of all crowded places as far as possible.'[53]

Already 'much in love with Rapallo', he longed to be settled in their new flat, 'for the one centre of all my hopes is to [be] back in my study and not in Dublin where there is so much besides my study', he wrote to Lady Gregory on St Patrick's Day, warmly inviting her to come herself and occupy their guest room. He was now well enough to work on alternate days, 'some paragraphs for *The Vision* or for a little book I am writing for Lolly, an account of this place, and Ezra and his work and things that arise out of that'. He was not yet his old self, but 'wonderfully better' than when he arrived. As for the children, he and George had clearly made up their minds even before their trip to l'Alpe Fleurie for Easter.

I am well satisfied to think that Anne and Michael will get their schooling in Switzerland instead of Dublin. They will know Ireland from Ballylee and Coole. . . . (and they very naturally much prefer Coole to Ballylee). Then too they will grow up with perfect French and Italian and then they will come here for Xmas and as they grow older will see Rome and Florence and the few people they meet will be intellectual persons. I would not have liked London for them, or anywhere that would bring them into contact with people much richer than themselves, and I dreaded Dublin because people much poorer are even worse.[54]

Their hopes for Anne and Michael as competent Europeans would eventually come true, but over the next five years they themselves would spend less than twelve months in the new Rapallo flat.

Back in Dublin Lily and Lolly chafed at not receiving regular letters from George. Having been instructed not to raise any alarms, Lennox kept assuring them that all was well in Rapallo. But all was not well with the sisters-in-law, for in her haste to see to the needs of Willy and Michael, George had botched the plans for Anne's birthday party. Cottie had not been included in the guest list she had sent to Willy's cousin Violet Gordon, who was a trusted friend of George's age. Letters of complaint followed her to Villars, from where she wrote to Cottie:

Private! I have just had a letter, rather agitated, from poor Violet! Lily and Lollie are blaming her because when she sent out the invitations for Anne's birthday party she didn't send you one. As a matter of fact this was what happened. I wrote to Violet from Cannes four weeks and a few days ago and enclosed a *very full list* of everyone to ask. After two weeks, hearing nothing from her, I concluded that [as] she is a very prompt correspondent, she hadn't got the letter. (She *hadn't*.) I wrote in gt haste the day Willy Michael & I left Cannes another letter asking her to send out 'invites' *at once* & enclosing in my haste a list of children only, except for Lily & Lollie who I started with, as I am in mortal fear of their susceptibilities! At the end of the list I said 'and anyone else I have forgotten'. But she, very naturally, as she only got this *2nd* letter on Monday evening Feb. 20, sent out the invitations to my list & didnt go any further. So for God's sake if anyone is to be blamed, blame me! And I'd hate you to think I did it out of anything except sheer haste. I cant imagine that you would think I really did it on purpose & this letter is only in case 133 Lr Baggot Street makes mischief—Lily said to Violet 'will you make it all right with Cottie'—make allowances, as you always do—for temperament & add a piece to mine as to tell the truth my only interest or thought for the past month has been to get Willy settled with the Pounds at Rapallo so that *I* could bring Michael here & see him happily settled in. . . . I have just now remembered that there are others! I never put down Lennox, Aunt Fanny, the Starkie child (Anne has been to *two* parties there—) Oh, I mussed it all up—

The three sisters-in-law, accustomed to their 'rock' George, would never be able to grasp how genuine her threat was: 'I feel its my turn & if anyone gets temperamental except me I shall howl them down quite easily!'[55] But Lily and Lolly were easily mollified by the photographs she sent of the children playing on the beach.

On the way through London Anne had been introduced to Olivia, who reported to Dorothy that Anne had 'the most charming manners'.[56] More important, she once again encountered her grandmother, who was in London for a sociable five weeks. 'Darling Anne Yeats made herself quite the most lovely thing in my life,' Nelly wrote. 'As the manageress of the Hotel said "She is a great little girl, so *sensible*".'[57] Anne was especially proud because she was already taller than her diminutive Granny. She remembered being taken 'to a real restaurant with white cloths on the tables and a swing door into the restaurant to have an ice cream and of our being put out because granny wasn't wearing a hat (I thought for years that we were put out because she WAS wearing a hat).' It is hard to imagine either Nelly or George without a hat, but whatever the reason for the confusion —the restaurant may not yet have been open for afternoon tea and ices—the reunion was a resounding success. From then on Nelly wrote her granddaughter letters at the end of which there was usually a riddle, such as 'why did the fly fly' (because the spider spied-er), 'why did the bull rush' (because he saw the cowslip), 'why did the house fly?' (because it saw the kitchen sink), 'why did the lobster blush?' (because it saw the salad dressing).[58] Michael's turn would not come until later, but Nelly was obviously happy with young children. This may have been the same period in which young Brigid Younghughes visited her much older sister Gwynne and husband Harold. Nelly rented an ice cream machine so the youngster could make ices with lots of strawberries and cream, made a point of instructing her ungenerous son *not* to count the number of cakes she ate at tea, and sent her out on a tour of London with car and driver.[59]

Lily was delighted to have her little niece nearby once again:

Anne came into Cuala with all lights lit, which is always the effect her entry has on me. She is going to be good-looking and does not wear the big glasses now. . . . The girls asked her what she had liked best and she said, 'The boat I came home on.' . . . Her grandmother went to London to see her and was very pleased, Nurse says, and thinks her very Yeats. She told Nurse she was glad the children have their father's figure. George makes a good effort, but her legs are so curious, ankles very thick. She is very conscious of it and wishes for long skirts to become fashionable.[60]

Nurse Reade was obviously a bit of a chatterbox herself. George had good reason not to want to be discussed by her mother. Anne went to Gurteen Dhas over Easter (without Nana), where each day ended with a noisy card game of 'Old Maid'.

George and Willy left Rapallo on 30 March in time to spend Easter with Michael. Although the guidebooks promised adequate medical attention for the English visitor, before they left George—who throughout her life suffered from poor teeth—had 'two hellish' operations on her jaw. Either on this occasion or later, her Rapallo dentist when drawing out a back tooth broke away two or three pieces of the jaw; back in Dublin she would undergo two more operations to remove the fragments.[61] But she was greatly relieved to find that her son seemed 'very happy—is evidently enjoying life—& is obviously much better—his legs better—they were v. crooked—& getting much less tired—I shall be able to leave him here knowing that he will be happy & well looked after.'[62] Satisfied with his progress, they made their way back to Dublin by way of Paris, where they lunched with MacGreevy, who confessed that he was 'very frightened' of being jobless in Paris. Although she sympathized, George may not have cared for her mother's solution: 'If the worst comes to the worst and you are on the pavement in July, come to us & overhaul Harry's collection. You can have all expenses & every comfort and a pound a week & as much time to yourself as you like.'[63] They then went by boat from Cherbourg to Queenstown, thus avoiding the fatigue of changes from Calais to London, Holyhead, and Kingstown. Willy was still not strong and already looking forward to the return to Rapallo where he could 'put off the bitterness of Irish quarrels and write my most amiable verse'. 'They are already though I do not write, crowding my head,' he told Gregory. When he received his copy of *The Tower*, he had been astonished 'by its bitterness'.[64]

George had been away from her daughter for two months and, although receiving thrice-weekly reports from Nurse Reade, missed the rapid changes in her energetic 9-year-old. Lennox was also relieved to have them back in Dublin. Plans had changed so frequently and rapidly that, apart from putting the house on the market for them, he was still uncertain as to their arrangements. There were no houses that were worth looking at, he reported, all 'too big and too dear'; and the first offer on number 82 had come from a neighbour—Dr Cahill—and was far too low (only £1,200). But he had oiled and powdered the ceremonial Japanese sword as soon as he returned, the canaries were flourishing, the Dublin Drama League and the Abbey were both busy, and now in mid-February the first daffodils were up.[65] George and Willy were also undecided. When they told Lennox of their thought of keeping number 82 and renting out the lower floors, he pointed out that the necessary renovations, if possible at all, would be prohibitively expensive. However, he did have potential tenants who would take great care of their books and other possessions. But George had already determined that 'What furniture we dont bring here will either be sold or stored; stored because we may find it better to have two rooms in Dublin rather than stay in Digs.' In any case, with Willy's future health uncertain and possibly 'working less', and Michael having to be in Switzerland or the south, 'we shall have to live as comfortably and as cheaply as we can'.[66]

Willy was still confessing to 'gusts of exhaustion', and as soon as they arrived in Dublin George arranged for a thorough overhaul. The doctors' report was not unexpected. 'They say he is much better but must do very little work yet, for a year anyway,' Lily was told. 'He looks very fine and is quite slim. He is to have vaccine treatment for his chest. He sounds rather bronchial. Their plans are not quite settled yet. It will be winter abroad, I fear, for some years.'[67] Always fashion conscious, the sisters were intrigued by the boots George had brought back from Switzerland, creating 'much interest by walking round town in them, worn with very pale stockings. . . . black rubber with black fur, worn over ordinary shoes'.[68] Lady Gregory came for a three-week visit, and there were others to entertain while they still possessed 82 Merrion Square. Then came the controversy over *The Silver Tassie*; O'Casey had sent the entire correspondence to AE for publication in the *Irish Statesman*. Again there were fears for Willy's blood pressure.

George was sounding somewhat frantic when she wrote to MacGreevy apologizing for not yet having read his translation of Valéry on Leonardo:

Give me one more week! I am on the verge of becoming completely potty and dotty, have had Lady G. here for two weeks, shall have her for another week at least, am negociating [*sic*] the sale of this house which rather breaks my heart, have to arrange for removal of furniture to Rapallo, removal of furniture to a flat here (all by August 1) fetch Michael on June 20 for summer holidays and decide where to go . . . probably a furnished cottage at Sutton for I have refused to open Ballylee this year. . . . Honest to God, I cant read it decently and reasonably for six days, and William is in such a state of k-nerves too! But one way or another all will be comparatively settled in a week. . . .

The truth is that I dont want to sit in judgment on the Leonardo all alone, I want to read at least bits of it to Willy, and in the state of k-nerves he's in, to say nothing of Lady G. being here, and me 'that occupied' I cant do it until after Sunday next.

However, number 82 was at last in the process of being sold: 'I have told all, the lawyer, the house agent, the buyer, that if they dont agree by Friday next I give up the ghost, moisten the lips and start again; and this afternoon they all respectively telephoned that they couldnt b[e]ar to worry me and they would surely agree in two days time and "Mr Butler" (the buyer) and "Mr Brindley" (the Agent) and "Mr Walsh" the lawyer, have all telephoned to the one tune "Whatever you want, we'll do!" It is all a mixture of Tchekov and Laytone and Johnstone.'[69] Evoking the contrasting moods of Chekhov's *The Cherry Orchard* and a popular close-harmony duo suggest that at least she had regained her sense of humour.[70] But not surprisingly, she soon went to bed with a severe headache.

The sale ('rather horrid, but inevitable') of 82 Merrion Square for £1,500 to the architect Professor R. M. Butler (who would use it for offices) was definite by the end of May; George had two months in which to sort and pack what went to storage for Rapallo, what stayed for their new home. It was only at the last moment that they finally found a suitable flat, around the corner on Fitzwilliam Square. Number 42 West belonged to the gynaecologist Bethel Solomons, recently appointed master of the Rotunda Hospital. Although he and his family moved to the Master's Lodge, he wished to retain at least part of the house for his private practice. The Yeatses were trusted friends and in any case planned to be away for six months of the year; the rent for the two upper floors was only £100 a year. But although not much more than the cost of their Rapallo flat, in Italy they had twice the number of rooms.[71]

'Life has been pretty hectic,' George admitted to Tom. 'But Willy is now recovering from the O'Casey behaviourisms—he was really knocked up for two days, and had to stay in bed. And before that there seemed no end to the amount there was to do—a long German thesis to be translated to him (a Bonn student writing for a "doctorat") then just as that was finished, all the O'Casey stunt.'[72] In time she would be more sympathetic towards O'Casey, who received Lady Gregory's rejection of *The Silver Tassie* just when his son was born and finances were tight.[73] But now, pragmatic as she was, while packing up the house she had been so proud of it was just too much; for many women, the loss of a loved home comes next only to a death in the family. Then, too, Lennox, Gregory, and Willy's sisters were all distressed by the move, and George found herself having to console them at the same time. 'I loved the house, and I hate change,' Lily told Ruth. 'George says it has served its purpose and I suppose I ought to feel that way also. I feel it is the end of the Yeatses as Irish. Anne and Michael will be cosmopolitan and have no abiding place.'[74] Augusta Gregory mourned the loss of her Dublin base and the sense of family she had there. 'Dublin . . . seems terribly empty without you. I dread going there,' she wrote after the move had taken place. She would be a guest in Fitzwilliam Square, but less frequently.

George returned to Switzerland in mid-June to collect Michael. It was not an uneventful journey, for just as she was packing for herself and Willy—who planned to spend the week in London—she mislaid her passport. Gregory, still in residence, begged her to 'sit quite still and pray to St Antony of Padua'. Willy had to go without her; then her house guest continued, 'About 11 o'c when I was in bed she came up, having in a quiet moment remembered she had locked it in the cupboard of my room!' But there was no respite: George's extra day was spent typing letters for Gregory.[75] George and Michael returned by way of Paris where they lunched with Tom. Scrupulously fair as always with her children, this time it was Michael's turn to visit his grandmother. They spent two days in Devon with the Tuckers, and then went on to Cornwall where Harold, until 1927 a curate at Falmouth, was now vicar. Michael remembers going out in a boat at Looe.

There had been considerable dithering over Ballylee; first Willy told Lady Gregory that George and the children definitely would be there for the summer, then George decided Willy would not be strong enough for the walk to Coole and feared the damp of Ballylee; finally she definitely announced that she would not open the castle that year.[76] She took Anne and Michael instead to Brooklawn, a furnished house in Howth; while Nana looked after the children and the maids took care of the housekeeping, she went daily into Dublin to prepare 42 Fitwilliam Square and to keep Willy comfortable at Merrion Square.[77] 'Do not trouble to send Chrissie,' Willy reassured her. 'After all I made my breakfast every day for years. . . . I am in high spirits but miss you much when the shadows lengthen.' Besides, the Senate was meeting almost daily. George sent the servant anyway.

George returned not only to packing and storage, but to Drama League business and Willy's last session as Senator. There were also the children's entertainments to see to—Anne was riding in the children's division of the Horse Show; George was a life member of the Royal Dublin Society and also the zoo, where they went regularly to feed the monkeys. Willy reported that 'yesterday the proprietor of a menagerie said to a friend of Georges "There will be rain, the lions are roaring & the serpents oily." '[78] And again, she was decorating their new home herself. 'George has made our flat at 42 Fitzwilliam Square charming,' Willy wrote to Coole from Howth. 'My study is about as big as the old & looks out over the square—blue walls & ceiling & gold coloured curtains. Her dining room I have not yet seen, but Lennox saw it & was loud in its praise—he spent a night here to keep me in talk while George was in Dublin.' The rooms were large, but not quite so 'lofty' as those in Merrion Square.[79] According to their landlord, she also painted the sitting room black, which he assumed was 'as an aid to inspiration'.[80] By the middle of August Willy was packed off to Coole for a fortnight to avoid the pressures of Taillteann week while George moved the last of their furnishings into number 42. But now Anne was ill, and so from Coole Willy went on to Kilmacurragh, the country home of Lucy Phillimore, with whose 'syllogistic mind' he proceeded to enjoy 'a blazing row'.[81] The quarrel does not seem to have prevented them from exchanging later visits in Italy, and while Willy was staying in the dark eighteenth-century Wicklow house, George took the children to school in Switzerland.[82] 'Left this morning and returns next Wednesday—once upon a time you and I had a like energy,' Willy proudly told Olivia.[83]

He was anxious to return to Rapallo in September, but George held out for October or even November, admitting to Lolly that there was little for her to do there. Her sister-in-law was pleased; perhaps George would begin to like Dublin after all.[84] With Willy's resignation from the Senate, George too was busily divesting herself of responsibilities, finally resigning as honorary secretary to the Drama League, which in any case would soon suspend productions as a result of the opening of the rival Gate Theatre. They had already given up other 'At

Homes' 'because only the bores came'; once they moved into Fitzwilliam Square, formal entertainments would be restricted to Willy's 'Mondays'.[85] One of the pleasures of the summer was lunching with Dolly and attending the theatre and the races with Lennox or both.

On 28 September Yeats formally resigned from the Senate; but he was not removed from controversy. 'At the moment . . . I am preoccupied with politics,' he wrote Ezra. 'I started the thing off some six weeks ago by an interview with "The Manchester Guardian" & it has gone on hotly.' The issue was a censorship bill, over which for the first time in years he and Maud agreed.[86] But the mood of the new Free State was against him. The day after his resignation he published an article denouncing the Act in the *Irish Statesman*. George was amused at his look of utter incomprehension when a woman standing in the receiving line of a reception at the viceregal lodge commented, 'My, Mr Yeats, you *are* a brave man.'[87] Finally, a few days later, George and Willy went to Ballylee. Just before they left they had Lily over to lunch and she was delighted to see them in such good form. 'It was so invigorating and good. They were playing with each other like hares in the moonlight. They were really putting book-plates into books and darting at each other to see if it was really his or her book. "Darling, that book is mine," George would say. "It's mine now", W. B. said, dabbing in his plate. They were playing like children.'[88] Her description is a salutary warning to scholars attempting to prove facts by the state of the Yeats library alone.

'I'm so glad to think you will come here—the summer has already felt long without you—any of you,' Gregory had written. She was still distressed by their move from Merrion Square and plans for Italy. 'I feel Dublin will be a lonely place without you—and—82. My visits there have been such a happiness and help. I am glad to have seen you in your new surroundings—the rooms look so pleasant & comfortable. But I'll always have a feeling of affection for 82 M. S. where I received so much kindness & help on my (often troublesome!) visits.'[89] For her too the old order was changing; in 1927, no longer able to maintain the estate, she had accepted Margaret's decision to sell Coole to the government, with the proviso that Lady Gregory could keep the house during her lifetime. The Yeatses' visits there would be more pleasant, however, for the widowed Margaret had recently married Guy Gough of nearby Lough Cutra. ' "Aunt Augusta" they say is fifteen years younger since she gave away her daughter-in-law,' Lily in turn informed Ruth. 'Captain Gough is rich and what is known as "a very decent fellow", which I think means dull but knows how to behave.'[90] Both George and Willy always found their neighbour Guy cordial, and now that Margaret had her own home apart from Coole she too was more enthusiastic about Willy's attendance on her mother-in-law.

It was the last time they would be together in Ballylee. Willy was once again at work on his revisions to *A Vision*, but George's active role in the partnership was almost over—though not quite. 'Doubtless I must someday complete what I have begun,' he had written in the first edition, and, not knowing whether he was 'a goose that has hatched a swan or a swan that has hatched a goose', had awaited the reviews with some trepidation.[91] But there were few responses, apart from the expected lengthy essay by AE and, surprisingly, Seán O'Faoláin's cogent and on the whole positive description of the 'system'.[92] 'A Vision reminds me of the stones I used to drop as a child into a certain very deep well. The splash is very off and very faint.' He advised Olivia to read 'The Gates of Pluto' section; 'it is overloaded with detail and not as bold in thought as it should have been but does I think reconcile spiritual fact with credible philosophy.'[93] But Olivia thought the book 'rather terrible—all so unending & no rest or peace till one attains an unattainable goal'. She was thankful 'not to find anything about Love in it. (I don't mean sexual love) I believe men are so made that they naturally hate one another & all their talk about Love is Bunkum.' Besides, of contemporary poetry she now only read his '& occasionally Ezra's'.[94]

Although George was relieved that the poetic flow might now be unhindered, neither she nor Willy had really been satisfied with this first attempt to codify their system. Despite Dionertes' insistence that the philosophy should enter their entire lives, not only the 'Beatific Vision' but much of the script was never used. It was probably therefore not surprising that while they were in Cannes Dionertes had made himself known again through an already-overwrought George. The incident was distressing: Willy returned from a walk to find his wife—in a trance —locking the door. Nurse Reade, returning with Anne, then tried to enter; shocked into alertness, George fell. The next day Dionertes returned, saying angrily, 'It cannot happen again'—that hour was his.[95]

George's philosophical sleeps that followed the publication of *A Vision* in 1926 appeared to take a slightly different form from those earlier. Although 'as usual' Dionertes was unaware of his immediate surroundings (Willy 'had to assure him several times that voices out in the street were not in the room'), he was reluctant to reply to direct questioning, seemed more hesitant to make definitive pronouncements. Instead, the exploration continued along Socratic lines, Dionertes responding with questions himself and Willy providing answers which were then discussed. The process was in fact similar to the dialogues George and Willy had held while analysing the script, with Yeats then selecting what he thought important or what was obviously a correction of his previous thought. Now when Dionertes or another came the visit was usually to confirm what Willy had already written: 'The spirit last night after giving sign confirmed statement that spirits come in to our sleep as the Dramatis Personae of our dream.'

Sometimes however the visit was less pleasant, though no less important. In May 1929 Dionertes' presence was particularly disturbing to both of them:

He was petulant & distressed—everything so difficult. He should not have come. Threatened never to come again. When it was over I had to take aspirin & George found she had been crying from exhaustion. He had said 'she is wet'. I had looked to see if water was dropping from ceiling & finding that it was not had said 'she must have spilt water on her neck at dinner' He objected first to my use of word marriage to describe relation between Husk & P. B. [Passionate Body] P. B. was too ephemeral for such a word . . .[96]

Willy was so upset by the interview that he confided in Lady Gregory. 'Yeats himself had come in, some time before lunch, a good deal upset by words, occult, connected with his work, correcting some mistake in it—spoken by George in her sleep—she unconscious of it.'[97] Willy began to dread these nocturnal visits, insisting to Olivia that he did not want 'any more mediumship'.[98] But George's trances continued, although now rarely, until the second version of *A Vision* was published in 1937.[99]

Was it now or earlier that they had what George later described to Ellmann as their 'first and only serious quarrel'? Although finally agreeing to the publication of *A Vision*, she had never wanted her contribution to be made public any more than she had wanted Willy to employ the fictional framework of Giraldus and his colleagues.[100] As late as September 1924 he had written to his publisher, 'If I could write the story of their coming to me—but that I certainly cannot do— it would have a much larger sale than "The Trembling of the Veil". Some day I shall continue "The Trembling of the Veil" but it will not contain this story. (This is not for publication).'[101] But now that Yeats was continuing his development of the system in a new edition, beginning with his essay addressed to Ezra, she was powerless to stop him.

From WBY's point of view, publicly recording his wife's involvement was both an acknowledgement of their partnership and documentation of the *reality* of his sources. He wanted to be able to claim with pride, 'Where got I that truth? | Out of a medium's mouth . . . , | Out of dark night where lay | The crowns of Nineveh.'[102] In 1947 George was somewhat equivocal in her discussions with Richard Ellmann: 'Sometimes he believed in *A Vision*, sometimes not. He generally thought of the anti-self as a spirit, but not always. . . . He wasn't sure how much control Daimon had. He didn't doubt until he began to put it all on paper after several years.'[103] But there was no doubt that Yeats took the concept and the general philosophy George had provided very seriously indeed. 'I want it to be taken as a part of my work as a whole, not as an eccentricity. I have put many years of work into it,' he told Harold Macmillan when submitting the second version.[104] And George never denied the material herself.

So why was she so against admitting her commanding and pervasive share of the work? As I have already suggested, there were good reasons both social and personal. As the Victorian product of a Victorian mother, she was too proud and dignified to want to be looked upon as one more of the freaks that had come out of cabinets in the late nineteenth century.[105] Furthermore, despite her apparently relaxed and controlled appearance in public, except when in the role of Mrs W. B. Yeats she was naturally shy and reserved; formality always balanced the sympathy with which she approached strangers. But there was a much more intimate aspect to her denial. The 'incredible experience', begun in desperation and misery, had altered—indeed made possible—their lives together, including the fulfilling mystery of the marriage bed. From the beginning it was a partnership founded on extraordinary trust and commitment. But as the guides kept insisting, it was *her* power they drew upon. Secrecy kept that power—wherever it came from—pure. By broadcasting to the world a dry factual account of their great and exciting experiment, Willy exorcized both George's virtue and her presence. Although publicizing her mediumship, he eliminated her in other ways, especially her scholarship; in *A Packet for Ezra Pound*, for example, he sidesteps any responsibility for Pico, 'my wife had burnt her translation when she married me, "to reduce her luggage" '.[106]

The symbolic power of Ballylee was also at stake. It was not only illness that marked Yeats's last visit in 1928. February had seen the publication of *The Tower*. So anxious had he been that his symbolism be rooted in earth, in preparation for the cover design Sturge Moore had been sent photographs of the 'gaunt desolate old Irish Tower beside a bridge blown up in the Civil war'.[107] Now, with that magnificent volume and *A Vision* both published, from now on, while still 'this blessed place', the tower had become emblazoned on his heraldic shield for all to recognize, assess, and debate. Proud as she might be of the poetry she had done so much to make possible, the penalty was an inevitable dissipation of the original magic; by remaking the imagery, Yeats had once again taken possession of the tower itself. On 15 October 1928 when she left Ballylee, George sent a brief note to Lady Gregory striking in its departure from the customary 'roofer': 'I was sad at leaving Coole & the woods today. Your long-suffering kindness to me these eleven years has made many things easy that might—otherwise—have been most difficult. Till we meet again Yours affly George Yeats.' Touched by this rare display of emotion, Gregory pasted the message in her journal adding, 'But the kindness has been from her rather than from me.'[108]

Although George would occasionally return with the children for brief visits to Ballylee, and as late as 1931 Willy would speak optimistically (but unrealistically) of staying there, the tower years had effectively ended. Nothing could have marked the ruthlessness of separation more strongly than George's willingness to rent out the property to strangers. In 1930 Gogarty had enquired on behalf of potential tenants, Pamela Travers and Madge Burnand. Having been there with Dolly some time that summer, George wrote a pragmatic reply:

As I told you on the phone, Ballylee will be available from *July 15*. The main disadvant-
ages are:
*a. no indoor 'accomodation' [*sic*] except one earth closet*
B. all water for bath or washing up has to be taken from the river by bucket. There is a
large galvanised iron water carrier on wheels which we get filled twice a day.
c. Drinking water has to be fetched either half a mile or a mile according to flood or
drought.
d. The nearest shops are 4 1/2 miles away; this would not matter if the tenants had a car.
E. The garden will not produce much in the way of vegetables, unless there is a man to
cope with sowing and weeding one or two days a week.
There are four bedrooms (six beds) two sittingrooms, one kitchen, one garage (with
boiler to produce hot bath water). The kitchen has a small range with copper boiler for
hot water: the range works well.
When floods arise they generally subside within 24 hours. When there is a flood there is
one sittingroom and one bedroom, 2 beds in the tower into which one may retreat. The
two cottages and the dining room (tower) and garage flood roughly 12–18 inches.
*indoor 'accomodation' is in the far room of the back cottage and is reached either from
the garden door or through the two back bedrooms.
In wet weather the limestone 'weeps' so that you have to keep turf fires or oil stoves (there
are two) going, otherwise there is an awful dampness. In July, August Sept: everything is
as a rule dry.
    Against all the above I will add that there has not been a flood for twentythree months
in spite of last winter and summer's rains. I just want to make sure you know the worst.[109]

    However, George remained emotionally involved in the tower, once chastising
Lennox for what she mistakenly thought were 'low-handed hits at Ballylee'.[110]
But to Lady Gregory's delight, once again Coole became Yeats's western home.
For the last three summers of her life not only Willy, but George and the children
came to stay. When Willy spent the longer winter of 1931–2 attending to the
weakening chatelaine, he dutifully reported on regular inspections of the rapidly
deteriorating cottage and castle. Anne and her cousin passed by in 1934, but were
not given a key. When she grew older Anne tentatively asked whether she might
go there to paint, but George's monosyllabic refusal was so abrupt that she gave
up the idea of ever returning.[111] Eventually a few pieces of furniture and memories
were all that remained.
    With Yeats's determination to continue his work on the system, other dreams
were also systematically excised by George. Although he encouraged Lily, the
family historian, to include the story of the Butler connection in her great 'Family
Book' ('It unites us with so much that is greatest in Irish history'), once Michael
was at school in Switzerland George had a different opinion. 'George thinks that
you should not put the Duke of Ormonde story in the family book (which goes to
the National Library) as we have no real evidence,' Willy wrote to his sister. 'She
is afraid it might come out when Michael was at Oxford let us say [and] give his

fellows a chance to ridicule him. She thinks you should write what you remember of it, and let us have it for the chest of family treasures—my Japanese sword, my Nobel medal, the old Bible, the family book and so on.'[112] More and more, her attention would be concentrated on the children. She and Willy were relieved about Michael who was now talking more and, having learned to box and play croquet, getting stronger.[113] They were also delighted at Anne's development. 'Do you notice how pretty your daughter is getting?' George remarked to her husband in Lily's (but not Anne's) hearing one day at lunch. Anne in turn was becoming more aware of her parents, one day asking Lily, 'Do you know that Father is the greatest living poet of the age?'[114] As they grew up, both children had reason to regret the poems their father wrote about them. But Anne was by nature a very happy child. 'Yesterday and tomorrow never trouble her,' Lily noted approvingly. When asked if she was sad about being away from Michael, she replied, 'I miss him but am not sad. I never have been sad and I never will be sad.'[115]

Whereas Michael was interested in how things worked, Anne early displayed talents as an artist. By the time she was 4 she was taking painting lessons twice a week, half an hour at a time, from Aunt Lolly.[116] When she was 6 she won first prize (£1) in the Royal Dublin Society National Competition for children in the 5-to 8-year-old class for a painting of the shop across from Cuala (including a policeman at the corner). 'Her eye for proportion is remarkable,' Lily observed. 'You say to her, "Where does the man's head come on that shop" "There" says Anne, not a moment's hesitation. Willy is so proud of her work. To explain to her in school they have to draw for her. Another of those darned Yeats at work. If we only had the money-making art as well.'[117] The following year Lolly again submitted one of her prize pupil's paintings, and again Anne won first prize. 'She is a *wonderful observer—sees everything at a glance—& can put it down*—like someone with *inherited knowledge* of drawing,' Lolly enthused. '—not a bit like any child of 7 I ever taught before—she has not to catch her interest by pretty colour etc. it is apparently the *form itself* that thrills her.'[118] However, in 1927 Anne's work was the cause of yet one more quarrel between Willy and his younger sister. 'Lolly has gone to bed in tears and rage,' Lily reported.

Willy it appears had told her Anne's paintings were not to be sent in to the R. D. S., as he thinks she ought not to be getting prizes for work done under direction while she just scribbles as badly as any other child when working alone. I did not know he had made this request. Anyway Lolly did, and sent off three paintings, and Anne got a special prize, and Willy has written with fires to Lolly, who is banging round on me and everyone, and says she acted as she always does, from the highest motives etc. and is always blamed etc. etc. and George and Lady Gregory and many others are behind it. . . . I think Willy is right. Anne does wonderful work while Lolly is here to put her down and make her see and concentrate. Now she ought to get no more prizes or praise till she works alone. I am sure people think the work is not her own at all, because of the silly scribbles she does alone.[119]

One can hardly blame Lolly for being disappointed, for she was a brilliant and stimulating teacher, able to draw out the best from her students. Years later Anne described her aunt's method as 'a new way of teaching painting using a large watercolour brush, direct, no drawing and filling in, and because she made one use the largest watercolour brush available and petals on leaves or stalks had to be bold and courageous, there could be no rubbing out, what was put down was there for all time, but at least it looked clean and fresh as all good watercolours should'.[120] Lolly was also the first to understand and teach the Irish hand and its great curved strokes with the knowledge of the correct pen angle, using the broad-edge pen; her pupils were taught to write the names of plants and flowers in Irish on their canvases. As well as instructing other teachers in her method, she had among her own young students many who would later become well-known artists: Mainie Jellett, Melanie and Louis LeBrocquy, and of course Anne Yeats.

George was determined that her children, unlike their father, be independent. Once when Lolly, who was very proud of her elegantly small feet, commented on the size of Anne's, George sharply retorted, 'she has to be able to stand on them'. Training began in small ways—when first allowed to go out alone, the children could walk to one crossing, then later as far as two, etc.; they enjoyed finding roundabout routes so that they could walk further before getting to the permitted crossing. Michael spent 'his first night by himself all on his own' with his godfather at Sorrento Cottage, 'and felt very important'.[121] By the time they were 11 and 13, George sent them together on an 'independence trip' to Cork and Blarney (ascertaining that the Hones, who were staying in St Anne's Hydro, would keep a wary eye). When Anne was 14 and enamoured of Shakespeare, she went to Stratford-on-Avon on her own for a week. Later each would travel across Europe alone, on routes carefully prepared ahead of time by their mother.

In an effort to instil a sense of household economy a penny penalty was instituted for careless breakages; Father broke the first dish, Mother the second. The children said nothing, but were inordinately pleased.[122] From Willy they learned an elaborate sense of courtesy. But George also imbued them with her own strong sense of justice and fair play, and, although herself prepared to bend the truth somewhat when the social situation required it, was vehement in her insistence on honesty. Anne remembered once being sent to her room to write out the Beatitudes ten times for telling a 'black' lie. When Anne was 5 George started taking her to the children's service at the 'Peppercanister Church' every other Sunday, until one day after the vicar's sermon she was heard to ask in an uncompromisingly clear voice, 'what's "an unfortunate marriage"?' But George's own frankness was transparent when, while she was being taught the catechism on the alternate Sundays, her daughter suddenly realized Mother did not believe a word of it.[123] George's articles of faith would remain much broader than the Church of Ireland's, no matter how much she and Willy felt Anne and Michael should have a solid, socially and spiritually acceptable, foundation. And she herself, like Willy, would be buried with full Anglican rites.

The requisite social niceties were instilled very early. There were the usual treats such as ice cream in Fuller's every Saturday morning, but from an early age both children dined out at the fashionable Dublin restaurants, albeit at an early hour; the grill room at Jammet's was especially favoured. Lily described the preparations for Anne's ninth birthday while her parents were in Rapallo: 'she came at 6 o'ck with Nurse to Cuala, and then Nurse went off and Anne took us out to lunch at the Hibernian, paying herself and taking the change home to Nurse in a piece of paper, tipping the waiter out of other money. She did not understand doing it out of the lunch money.'[124] George's children were not going to be caught unprepared and self-conscious, if she could help it.

The same anxious attention was given to their formal education. Lily recorded with approval her brother's ambition to see his children educated 'so that they would appreciate good literature, know modern languages, and be disciplined. The rest they must leave to themselves.'[125] Before Anne was 6, a bookplate was ordered for her; 'my wife wants to have it ready for the first sign of interest in books,' Willy explained to the designer, his old friend Sturge Moore. Three years later he was worrying because she *was* interested: 'We are struggling with Anne's desire to debauch her intellect with various forms of infantile literature presented by servants etc.'[126] Although Willy disapproved of the comic papers, George felt such reading better early rather than later, because they would always regret having been deprived; Mother won, and they were each allowed to collect two comics a week from the local newsagent. As Anne grew older she was given free rein— anything but modern novels which, her mother felt, 'might make her unhappy' —an interesting comment given young Georgie's reading habits. (Needless to say, *A Vision* and all things occult were also on the prohibited list; George never discussed such activities with either child.) George was much more concerned about Michael, and because she was likely to chastise him for reading 'rubbish' instead of 'good books', he always did his best to conceal his reading material from her. Not knowing of his mother's passion for music, he always explained that he himself turned to music because it was not emphasized in the household.[127]

That famous visit to the Montessori school in Waterford was of more than public interest to George and Willy, for the subject of their children's schooling was a matter of great concern and much discussion. Anne remembers going along the canal to St Margaret's Hall, Dublin High School for Girls and Kindergarten, on Mespil Road; then both children went to Nightingale Hall off Morehampton Road, which Anne attended from January 1925 until the spring of 1928.[128] Anne took school with her usual frank carelessness; it was something—especially learning sums—to be endured. On the other hand Michael, who joined her a year later, worried about the strange new world where he would be separated from his beloved Nana Reade. 'Michael has gone to school, *hating* the idea, afraid "he wouldnt do it properly"', his godfather observed, 'but after one day of it he adores it and woke at 4 in the morning yesterday asking wasnt it time to go.'[129] Always shy and reserved, her son's precision was cherished by George in one incident when the children returned home unexpectedly. When asked why, 5-year-old Michael replied gravely, 'Miss Wilson has departed this life.'[130] While the children were in Cannes, George hired a governess to teach them French; although Anne returned to the surviving Miss Wilson for another term, their European education had begun in earnest.

The children spent more than two years in their Swiss school. Since l'Alpe Fleurie was part clinic, there was considerable emphasis on outdoor sports, which both children enjoyed. Photographs of the two of them skating were sent to Coole, provoking a response similar to Lily's: 'both look radiant—as if they mean to carry joy with them through the world.'[131] But despite the improvement in his health and languages, Michael's timidity was harder to overcome; perhaps because of the violent thunderstorms, to which he was unaccustomed, he started to walk in his sleep, hiding behind doors and jumping out at passing teachers. Once Anne had joined him in September 1928, he too seems to have adjusted to the new regime, although the difference in age meant the two children did not share many activities. Anne went skiing with the older children, while Michael had to be content with skating on the rink attached to the hotel across the road.[132] 'Nurse called in and told us about the children,' Lily reported the following January, 'Anne is so tall they hope she will stop growing for a while. She talks quantities of French and some Italian, but Michael has the best accent. . . . There is an Irish teacher at the School who makes great pets of them.'[133] Anne was as usual plagued by arithmetic: 'They allowed you to do your sums in English until you had enough French, and then to work in French until you had enough German! So when I came back, I couldn't even look a sum in the face.'[134] Soon Willy was able to report with gratification, 'They are both well, Michael working hard but Anne refusing to work at anything but French. Michael has perfect French and never will speak a sentence unless he is quite sure it is correct, but Anne talks helter-skelter as it comes, which is all very pleasing as it is in their horoscopes, and confirms our science.'[135] On their return to Rapallo for the holiday her father, coached by George, gave Anne a stern lecture: 'He said her grandfather had worked very hard, he worked hard, Uncle Jack and Aunts Lily and Lolly worked hard, Michael worked, and she was the one idle one in the whole family. She was much impressed and asked if she worked hard even at arithmetic in French would he be pleased. Michael was jealous and had to get a little lecture also.'[136] Michael became so interested in Germany that he expressed a wish to go to school there. The Italian doubtless came from their linguistically proficient mother while holidaying in Rapallo (an indication of their stages of health, their first word in French was 'encore'—more, in Italian 'basta'—enough). George also invented a language of their own, which they occasionally spoke for the rest of their mother's life. But her punctiliously correct son was distressed when he realized that their private form of 'Double Dutch' gibberish was not a real language. When they returned to Ireland in 1931, George hired a French governess, and later Michael accompanied her to the French Society meetings.

Willy never did learn any Italian, remaining dependent on George's linguistic skills, but he was anxious to get to the sun and away from Dublin. 'When I get to Rapallo I am a honey bee—here I am a wasp,' he wrote to Maud.[137] And to Ezra from Coole,

I am longing for Rapallo to get away from damp and political agitation. The Government has just introduced an Evil Literature Bill which will enable the pietists, if they have the nerve, to make it illegal to import into the country any book on the Roman Index. The Government hate the Bill as much as I do, but for the moment the zealots are all powerful, in the struggle between Free State and Republic each party promises them whatever they want. I have been interviewed and may probably write but I can speak no more, it makes me too ill and in any case I shall be in Rapallo before the fight comes.[138]

Tom MacGreevy passed through Dublin in September 1928, causing yet another rift with 'Tinche' by staying at Fitzwilliam Square rather than Sorrento Cottage.[139] While Lennox was busy with preparations for an American lecture tour, George wrote on his mother's behalf to Jephson O'Connell:

May I introduce you to Mrs A. C. Robinson. You may remember that about a year ago you were good enough to give Mr Lennox Robinson (her son) some information as to how he might retrieve a sword which was appropriated by the British Military during the Black & Tan period. The sword belonged to Mrs Robinson's great grandfather & it would be very kind of you if you would give her some assistance in retrieving it. She will write to you. Yours most sincerely George Yeats[140]

Colonel O'Connell arranged for the sword and dagger to be returned to the Robinson family, and promised George he would visit them in Rapallo. While Willy went on ahead to London, George stayed at Fitzwilliam Square to make final arrangements for the move to Italy. In addition to Willy's books and papers —which would travel with her—there were the children's prized possessions, essential if they were to be happy on their visits. These included Anne's dolls and a large white playhouse which had been their mother's Christmas gift. (Although big enough to hold both children and an adult, with a door they could walk through and windows to look out of, fortunately it folded like a screen for storage.) Besides, she wanted to report on the opening of Lennox's new play, *The Far-Off Hills*. By now she too was ready for a rest and anxious to begin their new life. Willy arranged to meet her in Staffordshire, where they were to spend a few days visiting the friends they had known at Algeciras, Jean and John Hall.

But even at departure life did not go smoothly for George. Later she described to a sympathetic Curtis Bradford an experience at Holyhead which must have taken place at this time:

The English customs official at Holyhead that winter morning decided that the box of manuscripts was the perfect hiding-place for a bomb, so he started through it. The papers began to blow. The official, George Yeats, other passengers all tried to retrieve them. Suddenly it all seemed hopeless to Mrs Yeats; she quit trying to save them, and sat down to wait. As she told me this story, I had a powerful impression of the fatigue and misery she had felt as a young woman burdened with too many responsibilities.[141]

George and Willy finally left for Rapallo at the end of October 1928, spending several days in Villars on the way to visit the children. While there, Willy was asked to give a reading; a small audience of less than twenty assembled in the vast ballroom of the 'placid' Hotel Victoria. John Collis, who happened to be passing through, recalled how by his reading and demeanour 'the great magician simply changed the room from an unholy of holies to a place of harmony and inspiration'.[142] It may, however, have been now that the altitude made him sufficiently upset to cause a hurried retreat.[143]

Once in Italy, Willy settled down contentedly to work, 'writing daily and satisfied with what I write, I am confident of a rather fruitful winter', he wrote to Gregory.

In the evening I have Ezra who is in the most amiable of moods. I feel as one used to feel in a ship at sea before they discovered wireless, for Eason, who was to have sent us the Irish papers has forgotten all about us. I don't know what has happened to the *Irish Statesman* and its libel action, or what is being said about the censorship. . . . I keep well, the climate suits me, and the fact that the two very damp days brought the old symptoms shows that Dublin in winter never will do again, and I get through my days without fatigue and manage to keep warm. If I can write verse I shall have all I should ask of life, and more than I ever hoped for, aided by this incomparable scenery.[144]

In this relative isolation Pound's friendliness was essential, 'for I see that in the winter he must take Russell's place on Monday evenings'. Ezra would continue to fascinate and infuriate. 'He has most of Maud Gonne's opinions (political and economic) about the world in general, being what Lewis calls "the revolutionary simpleton". The chief difference is that he hates Palgrave's *Golden Treasury* as she does the Free State Government, and thinks even worse of its editor than she does of President Cosgrave. He even has her passion for cats, and large numbers await him every night at a certain street corner knowing that his pocket is full of meat bones or chicken bones. They belong to the oppressed races.'[145] Sometime now he decided to dedicate the first essay of his revised system to Ezra, 'hater of abstraction', who had pronounced that 'no one should be allowed to read [A]*Vision* till he was 40'.[146]

George, meanwhile, in their cramped temporary quarters in the Albergo Mignon around the corner from Dorothy, waited impatiently for furniture to arrive. Lennox had written from New York thanking her for the report of his play, adding wistfully, 'I'll be hoping to hear from you of Rapallo and the flat. I can just see you sailing about it now scumbling here and scumbling there, talking fluent Italian and draining gin and its.'[147] But still the marvellous flat with its electrical gadgets remained empty. She made arrangements to hire a live-in cook and a daily servant for the holidays, ordered stationery in anticipation, and wrote on it to Tom. Although hungering for news, she was 'fearfully busy—not so much at the flat for the furniture has not yet arrived—but W. has been so well—really better than for the past 3 years—& has been writing a lot & so there has been a lot to type & correct & his writing is worse than I have *ever* known it'.[148] Finally, after a month on the road, their belongings arrived on 23 November, and after George had hung pictures, arranged the furniture, and hung up the mosquito nets, she and Willy moved in. The empty rooms had looked small in comparison with Fitzwilliam Square, but now, he wrote to Lily, 'after our small hotel bedrooms, they look immense. It will be a pleasant place clean and luminous with amazing views from all the windows and great balconies to sleep on in the sun'. To Gregory he exulted in anticipation, 'Electricity is so cheap here that we shall be able to warm ourselves by touching a button.'[149] In celebration—since Dorothy refused to join them for champagne—he dated the introduction to his revised *Vision* 'November 23rd 1928 and later'.

Tom invited himself for Christmas, and stayed until 1 January; Governor-General and Mrs MacNeill were visiting nearby and regularly lunched with them and the Pounds. Nana Reade also came from Dublin in time to be with the children. This would be her last holiday with them, as she prepared with George's encouragement and help to train as a maternity nurse in Dublin's Rotunda Hospital. George was determined to send Nurse off in grand style, and with MacGreevy's connections was able to arrange a papal audience while they were in Rome for a week in early January. Anne was intrigued by the thought of the Pope's blessing—did the blessing include Nana's clothes and the paper and string round the holy medals; would it wash off? Michael grieved at the loss of his beloved nurse, and secretly felt guilty because he loved her more than his parents. George took them to all her favourite haunts—the zoo, the Colosseum, the Villa Medici, the Villa d'Este gardens (where Michael fell into a fountain). The children then returned to Switzerland and Florence Reade, relieved of her duties after almost ten years, to Dublin and her new life.

'May you be well and flourishing and gay always,' a grateful MacGreevy wrote George from icy Paris; he assured her he had been most discreet in describing his visit to her mother (who thought his news 'very graphic').[150] But illness continued to dog them both. Willy was in bed for a few days in Rome; three days after their return to Rapallo George succumbed to 'flu-bronchitis-old right lung' and spent 'ten days solid in bed and crawled thereafter around feeling beastly'. 'I feel I was very vague the whole time you were here,' she wrote Tom in February, 'but I had the devil of a pain in my back the whole time which was apparently a form of pleurisy or so the doc said when I had flu and it still continued it is now coped with and departed.'[151] Within days of her recovery they learned that Lady Gregory had been operated on for cancer. 'I wish we had known before,' Willy wrote, blithely dismissing from memory his wife's recent illness. 'George would have gone back to look after you. . . . when you can travel accept George's invitation—she is writing this post—& come to us here & stay till we all go back to Ireland together. Here you will have comfort, quiet, & if you want it a little fairly pleasant society & books.'[152] Touched by their invitation, Gregory gently refused: 'It sounds wonderful, & I like to dream of it—though I know it must be but a dream! I am not fit for journeys.' Then George's bronchitis returned, and Willy himself had rheumatism. 'When one wasnt in bed the other was.'[153]

Once recovered, both Yeatses renewed their activities with customary energy. 'William is exceedingly well, has been writing verse hard, and says he is full of themes,' George informed Tom:

—yesterday came dashing along from his cot to announce that he was going to write twelve songs and I had got to purchase 'a musical instrument' at once and set them to music . . . All said songs being of a most frivolous nature! I have been painting all the old green study furniture chinese red—rather in fragments because I couldnt do much at a go—and it looks rather good I think—so far the bookcases and desk are completed, the rest in a state of chassis and wetness. I think it stirred William up! He says he has shed off one old personality with the Ninetyish greens![154]

That winter Lily went to London for a further set of X-rays, finally receiving confirmation that her illness was not psychosomatic, but that 'an abnormally large and irregularly shaped thyroid gland pressed down on an assortment of nerves, muscles, and ligaments in her chest and throat'.[155] Writing with an offer to 'stump up' part of the costs for her treatment, George admitted she was bored:

Its been vile here—cold, east and north wind and now two days sirocco so that not a single window in the flat has been able to be even a chink open (they are all the french window type) all that time. A real hurricane full of sand which has even crept through the minute cracks of the windows and fallen on the floors—all gritty! Lordy, give me winters in Dublin! At least there's something to do there . . . There's so little to write about—no doings to relate, and of course no theatres or cinemas except at Night (cinemas) and the three people we know have all been ill—so its a gloomy letter. I count the days to Dublin.[156]

News from Lolly was also problematic. Disturbed by the account of the automatic writing in *A Packet for Ezra Pound*, she took the manuscript around to AE, begging him to ask WBY to at least 'take the smells out' of his description of the spirit world. 'AE has written advising this,' Gregory wrote in her diary, 'and so should I if my opinion were asked.'[157]

Lennox arrived for a week on his way back from the United States, cheering up both George and Willy. He was distressed however 'that W is still so wedded to hutchy-cutch, he's like his own man in The Player Queen . . . *Its too snug he was in the bed* and I believe you keep Willie too snug. Stop brushing out the crumbs. Four days accumulation of toast and biscuit crumbs would drive even Willie out of bed.'[158] Willy continued to see Ezra daily, and, he informed Coole, 'We see almost as much as you do of travelling Americans and there are stray celebrities occasionally.'[159] The 'celebrities' included Richard Aldington and Brigit Patmore, Basil Bunting ('one of Ezras more savage disciples'), the young musician George Antheil, who had recently written the incidental music for a Berlin production of *Oedipus Rex*, and the poet and playwright Gerhart Hauptmann 'who does not know a word of English but is fine to look at—after the fashion of William Morris'. The Pounds then arranged a formal meeting with the other Nobel laureate, who was just two and a half years older than Yeats—'the first dinner coated meal since I got here', Willy informed Olivia.[160] George described the occasion for Lennox:

William enjoyed himself prodigiously, talked without a pause to Mrs. Haupy for 2 hours —'He is looking very mischievous tonight' said Haupy. Haupy also talked incessantly. He is quite adorable! He monologued—with the occasional sentence from self in atrocious German & It[alian] (mixed) & was only interested in the fact that William looked so young! He didnt care a bit that they were both Balzacians & Plutarchians, & Dostoeiveskians. . . . He asked what I was going to do with Michael & I said M. wanted— at present—to go to school in Germany & I was thinking of Max von Baden's school—*His* grandson is there! So there was great love & enthusiasm on both Hauptys' parts & when I said I thought M. should go for a year first to a 'family' that he might learn German before plunging to school & they said 'we will find that family'.[161]

The dinner was evidently a success, for the following month the German poet invited them to his place. The experience was good copy for George, who again regaled Lennox with an account of the evening:

Really it is most distressing that the strain on the nerves caused by making sufficient guttural ejaculation to suggest a comprehension of conversation completely misunder- stood interferes so devastatingly with what should be delightful appreciation of lashings and lashings and *lashings* of excellent cold champagne! ('I must have my—yes, literally MY—champagne straight off the ice! Why do you not remember that' says Haupy crossly to his German Butler). Talking German through champagne is like playing chess to prevent sea-sickness. . . . And food and food and more and more food from 8 to 10.30, and all a failure with William because the ice 'Sarah Bernhardt' is served en bombe without a knife and the fork and spoon dont get a sufficient purchase to provide a decent helping. One got the elidings. AND such a good ice too![162]

Ezra had been an early champion in Paris of the young iconoclastic composer-pianist George Antheil, known to both Tom and Lennox. George thought him 'terribly pet', and proceeded to help his young wife Böski find an inexpensive place to stay ('I shall adore bargaining when its not for myself'), and loaned them furnishings and blankets.[163] Much to their delight (Lennox had made the suggestion the previous year when they met in Paris[164]), Antheil promised to write music for Yeats's new ballet *Fighting the Waves*. Willy, Ezra, and Hauptmann in turn helped Antheil write his 'glandular detective story' *Death in the Dark* (published in 1930 under a *nom de plume* by Faber and Faber).[165] Certain tricks of speech suggest that George also had a hand in the writing. As for Richard Aldington, George found him unchanged 'except that he looks very neat and respectable, has the same giggle and the same slightly vague perception about everything'.[166] She and Willy (wearing heavy woollen socks over his gloves) braved the wind and snow to dine with Aldington and Patmore at their hotel on the bay. George laughed and caught at the Italian children playing round their table; she spoke of her own, confiding that Michael's attitude to his father had improved now that he was at school. Brigit was horrified by Mrs Yeats's courage when, in response to one of Willy's more nonsensical flights of oratory, 'with her eyes fixed on some ice pudding, . . . said in a low voice, "Willie talking poppycock?"'[167]

George managed to avoid various friends of Lily and Lolly by pleading doctor's orders not to attempt the east wind. But in mid-March they stayed with Lucy Phillimore in Monte Carlo, 'a wondrous land of the rich with no side-walks upon the roads which are intended only for murderous motorcars'.[168] And then she went to Switzerland to be with the children for five days over Easter. On the way back there was a mild railway accident. She was thrown down in the corridor and lost her purse; when she recovered it some £4 worth of francs had been stolen.[169] George was anxious to be home, her mood swinging up and down, she confessed to Lennox. She thought Antheil's music for *Fighting the Waves* 'stupendous. Terriffic', and the composer himself 'adorable, quite crazy, and probably a genius, so one forgives him being exceedingly tiresome and hysterical!' 'But he plays magnificently—If he weren't short, stout, flabby, broken nosed, dubiously shaved, & black of finger nail, he'd have half Europe at his feet. Probably a mercy for him he hasn't—At present he is growing a moustache & partial beard—and they have a flat with no hot water so washing is difficult & he *looks* unspeakable—But oh he is a terrible pet.'[170] Ezra had been in Venice with his mistress for some weeks; the British fleet was in and there were too many visitors about Rapallo; George experienced her first earthquake and was 'devastatingly sick'. Willy was 'writing with diabolical rapidity' and healthier than he had been for four years; he would have liked to stay on a month longer. Finally, on 27 April, they left for London, breaking the journey overnight at the Hotel Terminus in Paris where they had tea with Betty Duncan (who had left the Arts Club and was living in Paris) and George spent the evening with Tom. To circumvent her mother's threat to join them in London, even 'if it is only for one night', George went straight on to Dublin. 'If I don't,' she explained to Lennox, 'I'd have to stay some days with her which would blow a lot of cash—and I'll be seeing her anyhow in August or Sept. And again on the way out here in Nov[ember].'[171] Besides, she was not too keen to meet her mother with Willy's revelations in *A Packet for Ezra Pound* already in the press. On her part, Nelly regretted that the Yeatses were 'always beyond some barrier of water. I hate the sea when it is a high road & I am afraid to fly.'[172] Willy stayed on in London for two weeks to visit friends and a couple of mediums. At his last séance (with Mrs Garrett) he received the assurance that his son, now 'slow and sure', would 'be brilliant'. Thus encouraged, he went to the Round Pond to look for a model yacht for Michael.[173]

George meanwhile was unpacking and arranging 42 Fitzwilliam Square, entertaining Lily and Lolly to lunch with stories of the children, attending the last Drama League production until 1936 (Lennox's *Give a Dog* . . .), and generally enjoying being back in Dublin. Once Willy returned the social round began in earnest. George sold ices at a fête to raise funds for the Rotunda at Clontarf Castle; she insisted that Willy, a hospital governor, make an appearance; 'She says Dr. Solomons never charged her any fees, so she must help the hospital.'[174] One evening Lily, who by good fortune was dining with Miss Beatrice Marsh in the flat below George and Willy, saw them off to dinner at the viceregal lodge. 'George ran into the hall and was showing me her dress, of blue-green and black with a long side tail. She looked like a mermaid and had a handsome cloak of black with a big collar. I had only half seen her when a call for help came from above. She rushed off saying, "It must be his stud." Why do men only have one stud? If I owned a man I would buy him a gross of studs and be happy ever after. They had a motor like Cinderella's coach waiting for them.' Beatrice Marsh returned from the Abbey Theatre to find the Yeatses pacing up and down waiting for someone to come home and let them in. They seem to have been in the habit of forgetting their keys.[175] Willy made his mark at Fitzwilliam Square in other ways, according to Dr Solomons: 'I still retained rooms there. I then had a temporary secretary, who, poor girl, was very ugly. She came into my study one day, remarking: "I met a queer gentleman on a landing upstairs, as we passed he stopped and, looking at me, said 'Horrible, horrible' and walked on." '[176]

In June Lennox drove George and Willy down to Glendalough, where they celebrated Willy's birthday at the Royal Hotel. Ostensibly the trip to the country was because Willy was not sleeping well, but George was also aware that he was suffering from writer's block. The journey was a success—Willy began writing before they reached the hotel. It was also an opportunity to drop in on the Stuarts, where Francis was successfully running a poultry farm. Willy impressed Iseult and her husband with his endless questions about the hens.[177] By now he was feeling so well he casually remarked one day that he could 'easily winter in Dublin'. George was afraid to hope.[178] In July, 'to escape charming Americans with introductory letters', he went to Coole for three weeks;[179] George enjoyed the solitude at number 42, and outings with Lennox, then went to Switzerland to fetch the children, now tall and sunburnt. It was not only friends and family who recognized Michael's striking resemblance to his father. After George had returned to the carriage, having put the children to bed, a stranger in the compartment asked, 'Do you mind telling me if that boy is a Yeats because 41 years ago I was in Sligo and two boys used to be there who were Yeatses.' They were, he said, 'some years older than I was, but your boy looks to me just like them.'[180] This year's treat on their way back through England was a five-shilling flight over the countryside from Croydon. Anne was delighted at seeing a cricket match from the air, but George later admitted being terrified all the time her children were in flight. On her return to Dublin Willy met her with the news that he had been invited to lecture in Japan, and was tempted. But, as he had predicted to Olivia, George made up his mind for him 'in five minutes being in her decisive youth'. He lamented the loss of this 'adventure for old age—probably some new impulse to put in verse'. But George was 'quite firm—Michael's health would not stand it and of course she is right. I am relieved and disappointed.'[181] Frequently the children's health was used as her excuse to avoid causing him alarm about his own.

George returned in time to host a dinner at Jammet's for the opening night of *Fighting the Waves*. As usual her sister-in-law took note of her appearance: 'George looked most handsome in a big cloak with a high black velvet collar. She had that look she often has, as of a light shining out from her. Anne has the same look. It is most attractive.'[182] Antheil had, with much urging from Lennox throughout the summer, produced his music on time. The ballet, danced and choreographed by Ninette de Valois, with masks by Hildo von Krop (who was present for the première) was, Willy proudly informed Olivia, 'my greatest success on the stage since *Kathleen-ni-Houlihan*'. In the same letter he sent her *A Packet for Ezra Pound*, adding, 'heaven knows what will happen when it reaches Mrs Tucker'.[183] Word has not come down of Nelly's reaction to this Cuala publication, which would form an introduction to *A Vision B*, but Ezra was considerably aggrieved by Yeats's description of his *Cantos*, grumbling 'CONFOUND uncle Bill YEATS' paragraph on fuge [*sic*] | blighter never knew WHAT a fugue was anyhow. More wasted ink due his "explanation", than you cd. mop up with a moose hide.'[184]

Although Willy kept insisting that he was 'almost finished' with the philosophy, work on revisions to *A Vision* would continue for another four years and result in a quite different book. 'Four or five years' reading has given me some knowledge of metaphysics and time to clear up endless errors in my understanding of the script,' he explained. But his 'conviction of the truth of it all has grown also'.

Making Michael Robartes his mouthpiece, and having proved 'the immortality of the soul', the deductions would be discussed 'with an energy and a dogmatism and a cruelty I am not capable of in my own person'.[185] George's contribution had not entirely ceased and, now that her role was made public, there was no sense denying her active participation in the construction of the system. But apart from occasional messages, she seems to have given up controlling the direction of *A Vision B*. Whether at her request or not, he was also anxious to distance her from his revisions as much as he could, explaining that 'I am trying to dictate some of the final version of the system. It has been all in manuscript for some months but it is very hard to get a possible typist. If I dictate to George it would almost certainly put her nerves all wrong. I don't want any more mediumship.'[186] When she did precipitate a visit from Dionertes, the message was to urge him in another direction, dealing with the problem of hatred, not love.[187]

Determined to give the children as much of a holiday as possible away from their cramped quarters in Dublin, George (delayed once again by the dentist) took them to Coole for a week on her own; Jack and Cottie were also guests and she was impressed by how well read her brother-in-law was, and pleased at how well he got on with Michael and Anne.[188] Then joined by Willy they spent some happy days in Sligo, staying at a hotel on Rosses Point where the children could swim. It was also an opportunity for Willy to show off his children to the Pollexfen relatives; Michael—who loved his own solitude—was especially intrigued by a cousin 'who hates the world and never sees anyone but the postman'.[189] When the children went back to Dublin in preparation for their return to school, their father once again departed for Coole. Lily observed with approval that Willy's children were 'very strictly brought up, and very obedient'—and also apparently unaware that their father was unlike other men. But she would miss George's comforting and 'radiant presence'.[190] Then George began packing up for their return to Italy; she had persuaded Willy to go later 'so as to get the benefit of the Italian May'.[191] The journey through London would be a sad one, for her old friend 'Erb Reade had died during the summer; there would be no more journeys down to Ipsden.

As usual, Willy went ahead to London, leaving George to collect and sort what was to be taken to Rapallo, and to indulge in theatre, film, and the races with Lennox, who won £4 at Racedale, but 'little Georgie Yeats put her shirt with 10 on him and made £8!!'[192] Willy meanwhile was hitting another kind of jackpot. While visiting Dr Carnegie Dickson, a long-time member of the Stella Matutina who with a colleague revived the Amoun Temple after its closure by Miss Stoddart, he had discovered 'the most curious things about the Order', and was promised sight of some of the early papers belonging to Coroner Westcott, founder of the Golden Dawn.[193] He was told that the philosopher C. D. Broad was a member (a 5=6), and to learn more, he was planning to visit the Hermes Temple in Bristol.

True to their oath of secrecy, he closed with 'This all very private of course. Better destroy this.'[194] Apparently, although they had ceased to be active members of the Stella Matutina, its history continued to intrigue them both, especially as it entwined with the details of their own philosophy: at Bristol he learned of a 'frater' who had while attempting to accomplish a Tattwa also received a vision of an arrow being shot at a deer.[195] Willy had also ordered tickets for *The Silver Tassie* (one for Jean Hall), and wanted her to keep Sunday free for a film society showing of *Potemkin* with Dulac. What he did not at first admit was that he had caught a cold while attending a performance of Shaw's *The Apple Cart* (which he hated), and by early November had been consulting Dr Dickson in his professional capacity; he was coughing 'a good deal of blood' and was going to see a specialist. Although he assured her it was merely 'a slight setback', George arrived in London the next day and moved him from the Savile Club to the Knightsbridge Hotel where she could insist he remain in bed.[196]

Their departure for Rapallo was delayed for almost three weeks while Dr Young (the same specialist who had seen Lily) took a series of X-rays and assessed his condition; George assured Lily and Lolly that 'it is nothing at all to worry about. He has again had haemorrhage from the left lung. He had it about a year and a half ago, and then the doctors said it was not serious. . . . he is now in very good spirits but just has to stay quiet for a short time.'[197] As a precaution George also sent a copy of Dr Dickson's prescription to Gogarty; she and Willy were both interested that one element was mistletoe. Willy hoped that 'Probably it is in reality the equable temperament of the Druids that descends to us through this visible symbol. Why not?'[198] When George complained to Lennox that Dr Dickson had referred to her as Yeats's 'better-half', Tinche replied, 'It's almost too good to be true.' But he confided to Tom, 'It may sound awful to say but I wish now he would die quickly. I cant bear this petering out. He was in splendid form in Dublin before he left and I saw him for half an hour at his club in London, he looked like the Sargent drawing and was full of fun and life— then three days later—this. But anything better than this crawling round in heavy overcoat to a café in the middle of the day, a slow walk, then bed.'[199] However, the X-rays indicated that Willy's lungs were clear; in celebration the Yeatses moved to the Grosvenor Hotel and entertained the Dulacs and other friends to dinner. Despite the fact that he coughed up blood again the next day and had developed a cold, George and Willy left London for Italy on 21 November 1929.

16

FITZWILLIAM SQUARE

This time George had included a portable wireless set in her luggage. The Italian customs officers waved aside it and the usual cartons of books and papers after the first revealed a collection on Italian art. But they did insist on George removing the rug from a large parcel up above the compartment seats—whereupon a nest of canaries began to sing.[1] Otherwise the journey to Rapallo was uneventful, if overheated. 'William arrived intact,' George reported, but 'the train was so steam-heaten (God it was HOT) and he slept in | one fur muff reaching from foot to waist. | 1 large pussy rug. | 4 Blankets | Endless underwear (pure wool) | and he was just so COLD & nothing would stop him sneezing.'

Rapallo was not only damp, but empty. The only visitors so far were Basil Bunting and 'Momma & Poppa' Pound, all 'parked for the winter in flats', and 'Haupty' had written her 'a charming letter full of idiomatic German all about I dont know what but I gather *they* arrive in January or so. Really German is an intolerably difficult language when handled by one who is inordinately polite!'[2] She was delighted to meet Siegfried Sassoon again, 'the same as ever, as nice as always, full of very incoherent conversation & nerves'. However George could not help but compare his wealthy travelling companion to Lennox, burdened back in Dublin by family and financial worries:

Damn all the rich young men prancing round the world beautifully existing remote from a gross world by money & money & money. We'd a long afternoon of Stephen Tennant yesterday—so very tall, incredibly slim, with that pale delicate Ninetyish complection, large sad hazel eyes surrounded by the long dark up-turned eyelashes that so admirably match 'blond cendrée' hair with a deep wave in it from brow to nape of neck—long small boned hands ending in marvellously pollished [*sic*] pointed nails issue from 3 inches of beige silk cuffs (no turn-back; one large, individual, button) which in their turn emerge from brown suiting. But I didnt care for his taste in scent. He had just spent a week in Paris and had I am afraid been missled [*sic*] by one of these new Parisian Perfumes which disdain association with any flower—'La Songe' 'Rêve d'amour' 'Pour troubler' and how it troubled the flat! Traits of Parisian artistry hung & clung & clutched invisibly—and a windless night too——He'll spend the winters carrying his scent like a flag through all the most expensive hotels of Southern Italy—rich—rich

Even his sentence structure compared unfavourably with Lennox's. 'He hadn't much conversation "Fancy!" "Really" "How lovely!" and it *was* such a pity to *just* miss Gertrude Stein in Paris—Yes, an inversion, but would "just to miss" mean the same.'[3]

George's letters continued to report on life in Rapallo; it had been raining steadily since they arrived, and although Willy finally was relieved of his cold he had developed 'a new trick', night-time fevers. George arranged to have a wood stove put in to supplement the electric heat. Ezra paid the occasional visit, seeking fresh reading material and cheering Willy 'by looking intelligent'. Of the new books the Yeatses had brought from London, 'He read a little here and a little there in as much silence as I would permit, and grumbled at intervals that they were "a dull lot". When the *Times Supplement* begins to arrive he will read that, devouring it in monosyllables.'[4] Alone and worried, George was feeling less sympathetic towards her old friends, who were determinedly inhospitable to the English visitors. 'Ezra has refused to come & meet them, which alternately infuriates & amuses me. He says he cant be bothered with people who are not serious students or "Pilgrims" & Dorothy *may* come in for coffee afterwards "but I find it so difficult to talk to people now"—My statement that Sassoon was a terribly nice person was not well-received—One *does* want a good brain as well you know! Or rather a brain good in a parallel line to the Ezratic brain. They make one sick!' Willy obviously agreed; a diary entry later that year commented, 'Pound's conception of excellence, like that of all revolutionary schools, is of something so international that it is abstract and outside life.'[5]

More worrying was the way Willy's temperature kept zooming up every night, accompanied by a rapid heartbeat. He was suffering from such exhaustion that to dictate a letter was a strain, and by mid-December his condition had become so alarming that George called in a doctor, who suspected typhoid. On 21 December Willy himself was sufficiently concerned to dictate a brief will, bequeathing everything to George 'knowing that she will employ it according to my known wishes, for the benefit of my children'; his signature was witnessed by Basil Bunting and Dorothy, and then, for good measure, Ezra. Finally he agreed to stay in bed. Somewhat delirious, on the 26th he dictated a 'chaotic' letter to Lennox resigning from the Abbey; George wisely burnt it and resignation was never again mentioned. She kept a record of the blood, stool, and urine tests, and faithfully recorded his wildly fluctuating temperature and pulse. When Willy kept getting out of bed to read his charts, George presented him with an edited version. Finally, when reports from the three blood specialists were inconsistent, in early January she wired to Carnegie Dickson for the names of specialists in intestinal and tropical diseases—only to discover that the first one he recommended had just died.[6]

Exhausted, she was finally able to find an English nurse in Florence who took over night duty, but not without a struggle. 'Lord—the fuss there was about the nurse!' she wrote to Lennox.

He was too ill to realise I couldnt literally do night and day, to say nothing of the fact one wanted a trained person . . . He told the doctor he wouldnt have one, so doc. said I was getting over tired. So he said 'ask her if she wants me to have one'. So when I told him he must large tears rolled down his face . . . but after three nights he accepted her without difficulties and likes her now. I broke it to him gently today that when he was well enough to just ring at night when he wanted anything she would come on at day, he remarked 'I dont see what there is for her to do in the daytime she'll insist on soaping me all over at night as well as in the morning'. The first morning he told her 'my wife washes me' nurse remarked 'Mrs Yeats is asleep' 'I will wait until she is awake'.

Dorothy had come in two or three times and done some essential shopping for George but Ezra, fearing infection, stayed well away. Fortunately Basil Bunting was willing and helpful, and Willy now liked him. There was only Lennox in whom to confide her deepest fears and misery.

I hope in a week the nurse will be able to go on day, and the first day that happens I shall go down to the Aurum and drink three Luigi's one on top of the other! (A luigi is orange juice, gin, 5 drops of curocoa[*sic*] . . .) Except balconies I havent been out I really forget for how long. Eight days anyway. Nor read anything, nor written any letters . . . . . . I dont know a single soul who is at the moment having a gay and joyous life so there is no one for one's mind to contemplate as an oasis. What's happened to the world? That you should be having hell with the Theatre apart from other hells at home so to speak with brother is hideous. That sort of thing is so much worse than illness, illness is only work and boredom bar two or three days of panic that William might die *here*. Some day of course he will have to die but I do hope it will be in Dublin or at least London. Here one is absolutely helpless. More than ever I believe that no one should be dependent on anyone.[7]

Still the doctors were baffled. Summoned by George, Dr Niccola Pende, a consultant from Genoa, visited Willy on 22 January and eventually diagnosed brucellosis or Malta fever and 'Bacillus of Bang' (the cause of abortions in cattle). George began reading up in medical journals, and—wishing to contradict any theory that Willy had congestion of the lungs—sent copies of her husband's charts to Gogarty, who also suspected Malta fever. Willy may have contracted brucellosis from contaminated milk in Galway, or, as the specialist suspected, in London. It has since been suggested that the culprit may have instead been an 'occult pulmonary lesion' caused by his coughing blood in London.[8] But whatever the cause, Dr Pende's treatment—serum injections from an institute in Milan combined with arsenic and a 'most stimulating' diet—seemed to work. Willy rapidly gained strength on the diet—three or four eggs a day; scraped beef,

1. 'Mrs W. B. Yeats' by Edmund Dulac, exhibited at the Leicester Galleries, London in June 1920.

2. The Montagu Woodmass family (Nelly, Jack, Ghita, Harry, George).

4. William Gilbert Hyde Lees at Eton.

3. Portrait of Edith Alice Woodmass by Laura Hope, June 1905, from a photograph by Alice Hughes, 1897.

5. Edith Ellen Hyde Lees in 1908.

6. The Grove, Fleet,
Georgie Hyde Lees'
birthplace.

7. The young Georgie.

8. Georgie in 1910.

9. Georgie in her early twenties.

10. W. B. Yeats in 1914.

11. Dorothy and Ezra Pound, about 1912.

12. Harold Hyde-Lees at thirty.

13. Ashdown Forest Hotel, where the automatic writing began.

14. Stone Cottage, where the Yeatses spent their honeymoon.

16a and b. W. B. Yeats's ring with the astrological symbols for Venus and Saturn.

15. George at Gurteen Dhas, 1918.

17. Portrait of George by John Butler Yeats, May 1920.

18. W. B. Yeats with his daughter Anne, April 1919.

20. Thomas MacGreevy *c.*1921.

19. The Yeatses in San Antonio, Texas, 14 April 1920.

21. Sketch of George by John Butler Yeats on the back of the menu for the Poetry Society of America dinner, Hotel Astor, New York, 29 January 1920.

22. George in February 1920, photographed by Underwood and Underwood in New York.

23. Baby Anne Yeats with her aunts and uncle (Cottie, Lolly, and Jack Yeats) in the garden of 61 Marlborough Road, Donnybrook, 1920.

24. Anne and Michael
Yeats with Florence
('Nana') Reade,
Ballylee, *c.*1926.

25. Thoor Ballylee
tower and cottage in
the 1920s.

28. Nelly Tucker in middle age.

26. Dolly Travers Smith (later Mrs
Lennox Robinson), Ballylee, *c.*1930.

27. George and Michael Yeats with
Lennox Robinson *c.*1929.

29. George at Ballylee, 1930.

30. Anne, George, WBY and Michael Yeats in the garden at Ballylee, 1929.

31. 'Riversdale', watercolour by Anne Yeats c.1933.

32. 'Chrissie' with Ahi I, George, and Anne with Pangur, Riversdale, c.1934.

33. 'Clouds and Fir-cones, Rapallo', watercolour by Dorothy Pound, 1942.

34. Hotel Idéal Séjour, Menton, where W. [Yeats died.

35. Jack, Michael, George, and Anne Yeats at W. B. Yeats's reinterment in Drumcliffe, 17 September 1948.

36. Michael Yeats with his daughter Caitríona, 1951.

37. George and Ezra Pound, February 1965.

38. Drumcliffe churchyard.

chicken, port, egg-flips with brandy (doubtless George's great-aunt's recipe), and 'very dry French champagne in the evening "even if the temp. rises to 105"'; a concerned Hauptmann provided the champagne. When William Rothenstein passed through, visiting his old friends the Hauptmanns, George saw him only briefly and Willy not at all.[9] She had no time to write the lengthy frequent reports expected in Gurteen Dhas; but Augusta Gregory was grateful for George's weekly bulletins—usually telegrams, and occasionally, when there was a nurse to relieve her, a more detailed letter. By 9 February George was able to report that Willy's temperature had been normal for seventy-two hours and he had spent half an hour in a wheelchair in his study; but it would be some time before he could even walk or stand alone.[10]

Christmas had been a disaster. Bunting agreed to travel to Switzerland to fetch Anne and Michael in easy stages, stopping overnight in Milan on 19 December; George warned them *not* to sing 'Bye Baby Bunting', which until then had not occurred to either child. But when her son and daughter arrived at the flat, she was unable to spend any time with them; again Basil came to the rescue, taking them out on expeditions. All this in addition to medical expenses and six weeks of professional nursing was proving very costly. This time it was Lennox who came to the rescue; Gogarty, he reported, knew of someone who was prepared to buy a manuscript. At the same time she received money from no less than three publishers, and a proposal from Macmillan for a complete 'edition de luxe' which would surely bring in more cash. 'You inaugurated such luck!' George wrote gratefully to Lennox:

Youre a grand thrower of bridges over torrents. And you'll snort at my credulity but at my fussiest (cash fuss) moment which was Friday 1—7.30 p.m. I suddenly heard your loudest voice say 'thats allright George'—& I ceased entirely to fuss. I suppose you saw Gog. on his Friday evening so I was several hours too early, & 'sub-conscious' [though] it hadnt occurred to me you'd be doing anything. In fact I feel rather compunctious at having 'mentioned' the subject at all & worried you, but lordy you inaugurated great luck! . . . 'Cross' with you for 'nosing in like this'—Its perfect that anyone exists who doesnt say 'Can I do anything' 'What shall I do'—And it will set in motion the selling of an MSS which will have to be done—for expenses arent by any means going to stop yet! At the best we'll have to have the nurse another 2 weeks for Willy can do nothing for himself—is very weak. More likely a month at the present rate of progress! God, she is a bore![11]

George's intuition had been on target: Lennox replied that he had gone to Gogarty at four in the afternoon, not in the evening, but the sale of any manuscripts could wait until she returned. He continued to do his best from a distance, sending her books and providing suitably sanitized versions of Willy's condition to Lily and Lolly. Meanwhile, according to Basil Bunting a different rendering of Willy's recovery went round Rapallo: 'he began to think he had been bewitched, so that the doctors were helpless: what he needed was a powerful and well-disposed wizard. . . . he did at last convince himself . . . into believing that his illness was caused by a certain ring he wore, and the next time he was strong enough to venture out, he and Mrs Yeats made their way to the end of the mole and cast the ring into the sea, with the appropriate formula; and it seemed to work, for that time he did not relapse.'[12]

By the end of February Willy was strong enough to go out for a drive. He was anaemic, had lost more than twenty pounds ('is very thin, his legs spindly looking, too thin to carry his big shoulders'[13]), and grown 'a beautiful silky beard, grey like my hair but a very black moustache'.[14] George thought the 'Imperial' quite becoming, but when a photograph was sent to Ireland Gregory's reaction was 'Quite dreadful! Banish it! It takes every spark of intellect from your face,' and Gogarty wisely advised him to shave it off or he would not be able to forget his illness. Lennox sent a copy to *The Irish Times*, but agreed that 'individuality dies behind all that hair. He is like John Dillon, J. B. Yeats, Christ, anyone who has ever had a lot of hair on his face.' Willy was determined to keep it long enough to show Ezra and the children.[15] Pound was still avoiding him. 'I am afraid that if he delays much longer William will get a bit frivolous when he *does* come—phrases have been rehearsed,' George reported. However, tales of Ezra's mother (whether relayed by Dorothy or Bunting) offered some light relief:

Its just dawned on me that in three or four weeks you'll be crossing the little old Pond as Mrs Homer Pound lightly and so originally calls it. That woman has all the lecture-hounds beat to a frazzled cock-hat . . . but she just has so much more general knowledge than I have for she knew that Masoch and Masaryk were pronounced so nearly alike that you could get 'em mixed up. Son informing Mama that what was the matter with her was that she was masochistic . . . 'What's that?' says Mamma (turn up your voice on 'that' please) and son explaining all about Masoch till he gets tired and goes off for a little walk, leaving Mamma really completely in possession for she says 'Well, *I* always heard Masaryk did so MUCH for his country!'

In any case, Ezra and others would soon be departing for the summer, and she rather dreaded the ensuing boredom; however, it might make Willy realize how quiet life would be there year-round. 'I do feel one might as well have colds in the winter in Ireland as be ill of Malta and Abortus fever for four–six months in Rapallo!' She would have agreed with Gogarty's dismissal of Rapallo as 'the Bray of Genoa'.[16]

A letter from London contained further surprises. Writing to enquire about Willy's health, Carnegie Dickson told the astonishing story of the recovery of some of the Golden Dawn's original properties. Invited to assist at the consecration of a Meditation Room in an Anglican vicarage in the north of London, he and his wife were amazed to find the original Pastos, painted by 'Vestigia' (Moina MacGregor Mathers), in use as an altar. It had been bequeathed to the vicar by Helen Rand ('Vigilate'), one of the early members of the Order, and was now returned 'after many adventures & vicissitudes to the faithful remnant of the old group! Without our seeking it!' The good doctor hoped it would be 'a symbol of renewed life & activity & *harmony* in the old Order'. He had also borrowed *A Vision* from the accommodating clergyman; 'I am much interested therein— including the dedication! It's a funny world.'[17]

Lennox, meanwhile, was on his way to the United States to earn some much-needed cash. Lonely and distressed at leaving his ageing mother and by the terminal illnesses of two friends, he wrote to George, 'I know you are hard about dying and about caring whether people do or don't. I can't get used to it, it always seems to me a kind of insult, a victory, something that shouldn't be.'[18] He may have been more sanguine than George about her attitude towards death, but what he did not tell her was the reason for his year-long depression: 'I think the failure of W. B. is at the back of it all,' he confided to Dolly. 'He has been the biggest thing in my real life and with that prop gone (and it seems to be) I feel helpless.'[19] However, George's next letter included news of 'a most interesting event' that cheered them all. One afternoon when Willy's fellow Senator, Samuel Brown, called,

I ambled in after (leaving them alone for tea) with William's medicine just in time to hear W. saying 'We shall probably be trying an experimental winter in Dublin'. You men of genius really have a genius for casualness! At the moment I naturally faded away, reserving a large sized pin, a hatpin, to be used later on a probably unwilling moth. But I do think when you go and throw your hat over the fence like that you must expect a large-sized bull to spear it? No, terribly mixed metaphors; 'horn' it should have been the word.[20]

By the end of the month Yeats had definitely decided to spend the next winter in Ireland, a comfort also to Lady Gregory, who was finding Dublin 'terribly empty'.[21]

Ezra had finally come out of hiding, having pleaded illness; 'no not ill but fussy. If he gets a gnat sting he fusses,' George complained to Gregory. 'Today I met Ezra for the first time—you know his dread of infections,' Willy wrote to Olivia; 'seeing me in the open air and the sea air, he sat beside me in front of the café and admired my beard, and declared I should be sent by the Free State as Minister to Austria. . . . Certainly I need a new career for I cannot recognise myself in the mirror.' He was beginning to feel more himself and able to join the other winter visitors at the Caffè Aurum about 11.30 on sunny mornings: 'I go out every day or two for an hour but have discovered that I must spend the rest of each day in bed and there read nothing but story-books. Having exhausted the detective literature of the world I have just started upon the Wild West and shall probably, if my illness last long enough, descend to Buffalo Bill.'[22] But he was still not over the nervousness that had accompanied ill health. In early April he and George spent two weeks in Portofino Vetta, 'on a mountain top about five miles from Rapallo in a hotel with large woody grounds about it and views over miles of mountain and sea'. They were intrigued to learn that Nietzsche had lived for some months in a small house (now a restaurant and hotel) nearby.[23] 'Here I can step in and out as I please, free from the stage fright I had in Rapallo whenever George brought me to the little café by the sea,' he confessed to his diary, and felt 'almost well again . . . Here no mountains shut us in; I think three weeks should make me well as ever.'[24] He was also reading Swift's diaries, and, encouraged by George, once again contemplating a play about the Dean.[25] On their return to the flat they were visited by Masefield and his daughter Judith, who were in Monte Carlo for the ballet season. With the recent death of Robert Bridges, George correctly predicted that Masefield would be made the next Poet Laureate; although there was considerable speculation in the newspapers, neither of them expected Yeats to receive the appointment. However, this may have been part of the reason for Willy's visits to a few clairvoyants, where nothing new or exciting turned up.[26]

But meanwhile George herself was getting bored, a condition not alleviated by reading aloud, for 'some three hours a day for some weeks', William Morris's *The Well at the World's End*:

These over fertile writers ought, for the sake of younger generations, to undergo a Marie Stopes treatment. So treated Morris might have felt Chaucerian language incompatible with that vast efflorescence which covers everything he writes about, one cant read a description of a field and a tree without shivering to think how many leaves make the tree and how many blades of grass have gone to the greenness of the field. Horrid. Even when he describes bare places their lonely vastness is all pebbled, or still worse, sand. No. I do NOT like it. Then the clothes are encrusted with Embroideries . . . Cuala . . .[27]

A chance encounter with an Anglican nun from the Oxford Mission to Calcutta, who was spending three weeks of her six months' leave in Rapallo, provided welcome company:

apart from being an admirer and a Nun she is a very charming person with whom I have been for three weeks hobnobbing a very great deal. We were sitting this morning on the top of a mountain after $1\frac{1}{2}$ hours drip and pant walk (its very hot here now!) and she suddenly remarked 'Did you ever meet in Ireland a playwriter called Lennox Robinson?' So I said feebly 'yes, I have met him', and she said 'I met him at Oxford when I was a student there' (that must have been between 1910–1913) and you just made such an impression that she has read all your published plays! . . . Today we breakfasted, walked, ate lunch in a chestnut grove, walked home, parted at about 3.30, will probably never meet again, yet if we do we'll probably just start again where we left off: she's really one of the most intelligent people—no, I ought to say women—I ever met. Gosh, when I gradually found out all the stuff she'd read during six years in India, Calcutta, Darjeeling, and all round-a-bout, and I thought of what I'd read the last six years, and still more what I could remember of what I'd read, I just felt nothing so much as slug.[28]

Then on 8 May 1930 the children returned, quite pleased at the prospect of spending a month in Italy—a relief to George, for they could not afford holidays in Ireland this year.[29] Like Lily and Lolly, Lady Gregory regretted their absence: 'The children will have grown out of all knowledge when I see them again. Give them my love—& tell them I have got a new boat—not so heavy as the old one. And that Mr. Ross had caught 12 pike one day.'[30] By June Willy's beard was gone, swept up with hair clippings from the entire family into the canaries' nest. 'I hope at least you made a bracelet or the fillings of a brooch from it,' chided Lennox.[31] The weather was now warm enough for paddling in the bay. George taught Anne and Michael to float, then at their request demonstrated herself, only admitting later that she could neither swim nor float; their father, however 'swam like a fish, dived under them and tickled them in the water'.[32] Willy read them 'The Rime of the Ancient Mariner' and 'The Lay of the Last Minstrel' (Anne liked the sound of his voice), and he and George again discussed their children's education. 'Like most parents, I suppose,' he wrote to Coole, 'I want them to have none of their father's defects. I would like Michael to start Greek when he is twelve or less, & do not care if he never learns a word of Latin. He has some French & German & will soon know both well. Anne has good French & will never I think forget it. She works to please others, Michael to please himself.'[33] While in Rapallo both children also sang in the church choir,[34] and Willy taught them the moves for chess, taking Michael to a café each week to play. Anne felt discriminated against, for her father only took her out for ice cream, perhaps prompting 'her first act of independence':

At lunch she was not to be found and Michael said, with a voice full of disgust, 'Anne has run away'. Meanwhile a friend of George's and mine had met her on a country road 'talking to herself and trying to walk like a queen in a faery tale' and asked her to lunch. Anne accepted but insisted on eating her own food and unpacked a knapsack. She brought out (wrapped in separate pieces of newspaper) biscuits, a bottle of lemonade, a looking-glass, a comb, a brush, and a piece of soap. She said she would go home 'after dark' but was persuaded to do so at the end of lunch by the suggestion that George and Michael were probably making ices.[35]

On another occasion George was amused by Anne's pulling Michael out of the road with the caution, 'Do be careful, Michael. Don't forget you are the only young Yeats.'[36] Some time this summer they went down the coast of Levanto.[37]

A further diversion was the arrival of the 'suicidal cat', inevitably dubbed Pangur. There are various versions of how the cat came to spend its days on Willy's bed, and how it earned its notoriety. Michael believed Pangur was 'suicidal' because it used to lie on the track in front of his electric train, leaping to safety at the last minute. Bunting's version was more theatrical: it had belonged to the current mistress of the Italian playwright Sem Benelli, and when his company went on tour a home was required. Benelli's secretary deposited the cat at Bunting's door, but when ignored, the animal leapt three storeys from the window sill to the garden, dislocating a shoulder. Ezra then suggested that Willy, still convalescing, would have plenty of time to caress the beautiful Persian. But eventually he too was preoccupied with work; shut out on the balcony, Pangur again 'cut an attitude, proclaimed its intention of suicide, and jumped down, four stories this time', breaking a leg. Predictably, Willy's version to Gogarty (dictated to George) elaborated on Benelli's complicated amours, but he was delighted with the presence of the 'very white cat with a very fluffy tail and very blue eyes', which 'sleeps off enormous meals upon my bed'.[38]

George took the children back to school on 15 June, leaving Willy in the English-speaking environment of Portofino. To her consternation, for it left little time to pack and make all the necessary travel arrangements, on her return he insisted that they depart two weeks earlier than planned. In addition to all their books and papers, there were now five canaries: two dark 'like mamma; three, orange yellow, like papa', she exulted to Lennox. 'Even William who is somewhat unobservant in memory remarks that they "are very large for their age, arent they?" Didnt I tell you that the little dark feathered bird was a bird of great value?'[39] Willy also insisted, to her disgust, that they return with Wyndham Lewis's *The Apes of God*, measuring 'something near 14 × 8 × 6, filled with 625 odd thick-papered pages covered with the ugliest print imaginable' and 'so heavy that it cannot be read in the hand but must be parked on the middle when read in bed, so heavy that it causes a dent in the middle so that if pages are turned without a backward heave of the book at each turning (that in itself prevents rapid reading) the page crinkels [sic] or tears. He argues that any realistic novel must necessarily be disgusting. I maintain that the book is a realistic novel: William maintains that it is a satirical pamphlet; we quarrelled about it, about that terminology, until 11.30 last night.' George had sublet the flat to Ezra's parents, who were delighted to be 'in' for American Independence Day on 4 July.[40] Pangur the Persian cat remained behind and, receiving plenty of attention from Homer Pound, reformed. George also left Ezra's parents one of the young, surprisingly large, canaries. There is no word of the outcome of that conjunction.[41]

The Yeatses sailed on 3 July 1930, arriving in Southampton on the 9th. After dinner with Dolly in London, George went on to Dublin while Willy stayed on for another week. Olivia had been suffering from bronchitis, and George, her memories fresh from many experiences with doctors, advised Dorothy to bypass a general practitioner:

Personally if I were bronking in London I should go to R. A. Young, 57 Harley St. and get overhauled and if he decided inocculations [sic] wld do good I should ask him to pass me on to Carnegie Dickson (7a Upper Harley St—difficult to find as it's the far end of H. St, across Marylebone Rd, almost next the Park) to find the bug and make the serum. Whether C. D. wld want to give the injections himself in order to watch the results

I don't know. I suggest him because he not only takes endless trouble but is exceedingly intelligent and will modify the strengths of doses to suit the general make up of patient (I don't know if he would want to give the injections himself or if OS's doc: would. . . . (When I was done I got too much at first and had a madly itching rash for weeks!) I believe inocculations don't by any means always cure people, but if Young and C. D. think it would do good, and they're both very honest people, it might be well worth trying. If you decide to take her to Young it might help if you had a chart of her temperature, pulse, *breathing*, over a week or two or more. And most certainly mention what you say in your letter about the illness affecting her eyes. Couldnt you get her to Young before she goes away? The inocculation is a lengthy business, takes three months . . . once a week, and if youre wise you spend the 24 hours after each go doing nothing, preferably in bed.[42]

Almost as soon as he returned to Dublin Willy travelled to Renvyle to have his portrait painted by Augustus John, an arrangement made by the industrious Gogarty. Mrs Gogarty had rebuilt their western retreat but now it was, as it had been with the previous owner, a hotel, which had been opened 'with appropriate pomp and ceremony' on 26 April 1930.[43] George lost no time reclaiming Fitzwilliam Square: 'The flat resounds with hammers and files on copper tubing,' she wrote Willy, 'and your new gas fire in the study looks grand, and your new bedroom almost has its gas fire and electric fire; you'll find a salamander heat in your two rooms when you return.' There was no other news apart from the caretaker's annoyance over the theft of their dustbin, but the next day she was going with Lily and Lolly to a viceregal garden party. 'Perhaps I really want an excuse for wearing a brand new large hat even though it must top an old, old, dress. I shewed you the new stuff for your new bedroom curtains and quite forgot to shew you the lovely—or so I think—length of brocade in many colours that I got in London for my new evening dress . . . Yours forever George.'[44] Her 'old dress' did not come up to Gurteen Dhas standards; Lily noted that her sister-in-law 'looks very well and gay', but thought 'her clothes pitched on her'.[45]

The Longfords had agreed to drive Willy to Renvyle, and George wrote to Pakenham Hall with her daily report.[46] 'Please don't go and get colds or nuisances of that sort and do control your dislike of giving trouble by remembering that milk and biscuits for the night and hot water bottles for the day give very little trouble.'[47] Still fearing a relapse, she advised him to hire a car to go from Galway to Coole after the artist had finished; of the painting itself, showing him sitting in a chair covered with rugs, Yeats later described it as 'Portrait of the Poet in his Last Long Illness'.[48] Augusta Gregory was delighted to have him back, 'so full of life, of discovery, of creative work. And he talks more brilliantly than ever.'[49] But she herself was beginning to fail noticeably, and the cancer had returned. 'Every time I meet her I think she's a bit less on the spot than the time before,' Lennox had warned George, unkindly adding, 'She can only keep two subjects in her mind now, long ago she used to be able to keep three.'[50]

Encouraged by George, Willy would spend most of the summer at Coole, work-ing peacefully on his 'Swift play'. He later admitted that his wife not only urged him to write *The Words upon the Window-Pane* but 'added the detail about the medium refusing money and then looking to see what each gave'.[51] George contributed more, for the play itself provoked a further exploration of their own experiences with the spirit world. 'I have just finished a beautiful & exciting second part to my commentary on the Swift play,' he wrote. 'It is an interpretation of the seance in the light of Plotinus Ennead V.7—& is a thought that has been exciting me for weeks.'[52] The passage in his essay quoted Plotinus' statement that we should not 'baulk at this limitlessness of the intellectual; it is an infinitude having nothing to do with number or part'; he was quoting from George's copy of MacKenna's translation, and prefaced it by one of her own experiences: 'Once a friend of mine was digging in a long neglected garden and suddenly out of the air came a voice thanking her, an old owner of the garden she was told. She said, "Have you not been reborn?" "Yes," was the answer, "but I am still in the garden." '[53] Willy's essay initiated a debate about mediums and memory, in which George objected to his assertion that there was always an element of dramatization in the medium's performance:

I think that the reason I did not very much like Part II Windowpane is that your argument—the dramatisation of the secondary and tertiary personalities of the medium, seem so close to the old psychical research theory of the 'subconscious' or at least that I cannot personally understand what you mean except in those terms. If I had to interpret that 'commentary' I could not say that any 'spirit' were present at any seance, that spirits were present at a seance only as impersonations created by a medium out of material in a world record just as wireless photography or television are created; that all communic-ating spirits are mere dramatisations of that record; that all spirits in fact are not, so far as psychic communications are concerned, spirits at all, are only memory. I say 'memory' deliberately, because 'memory' is so large a part of all psychic phenomena. I dont remember any case in which a spirit (communicating through a medium) had during the latter part of his life or during any part of his life been cut off from that every day faculty of memory. Those people who were wounded in the head during war—they dont come—the insane dont come???—the spirits who tell us about their houses, their horse racing, their whiskeys and sodas, their children, their aunts and God knows whatnots, their suicides, were all mainly preoccupied during their lives with those things. Have we any record of a spirit communicating who had been at any period of his life been so physically or mentally incapacitated that memory, even 'subconscious' memory, had been obliterated?

Evidently Willy had struck a sensitive chord with his suggestion that 'even honest mediums cheat at times either deliberately or because some part of the body has freed itself from the control of the waking will, and almost always truth and lies are mixed together'. She apologised 'for this diatribe—it all comes out of an idea I had lately that small nations have long memories, big nations have short memories, small nations make Empires'.[54]

'I like your comment on my note,' he replied by the next post. 'My difficulty has been that we have been told that the dead recover memory from us, that they have seperated [*sic*] themselves from the "acquired faculties". They can see in the *Passionate Body* but all names, all logic, &·all that we call memory is from us.' He enclosed 'a page of comment', adding, 'I half think of giving your letter (without your name) as a footnote with the comment I sent or something like it.'

Note on GY's letter I do not consider the fully separate spirit a passive mirror of timeless images but as a timeless act. This act appears to us through the antimony [*sic*] of past & future & loss of memory in the living man would be present in the act also. It may make communication difficult. If I think of John Smith who lost his memory from a blow on his head, I not only transfer that loss to the dramatization, in so far as that dramatization is from my suggestion, but think of him in just that part of his life, which is absent from his present state. If my 'subconscious' could think of him as he was when most alive, most completely himself, and do so with as great intensity as it now thinks of his tragedy he would enter & direct the dramatization. It is because whatever is in time, is also in the timeless moment, that one is compelled in the pursuit of moral coherence to believe in rebirth. I admit the difficulty of timeless moments, but in some sense their selves [are] but parts of time; but what can we do with antinomies but symbolise their solution by some kind of Platonic myth.

Still excited by her remarks, he then sent 'a different comment' to 'GY's letter':

Remember how many of what seems the laws of spirit life are but the pre-possessions of the living. A number of communicators have warned us against cremation on the ground that it is a shock to the departed spirit yet to think so would be to think that eastern races that have studied these things for centuries are more ignorant that we who have hardly studied at all. If I think of a man as having lost his memory from a blow on the head, my 'un-conscious' rejects him as possible testimony. I am more moved by my correspondents statement that I have turned a seance into a kind of wireless apparatus & denied that the spirits are there at all. If I drop that word 'unconscious' adopted out of mere politeness I may be better understood: the Daimon of a living man is a dramatist— what am I but my daimons most persistent drama—it dramatizes its fancies, characters out of fiction have written through the planchette—it dramatizes its knowledge, & when that is knowledge of other daimons it is as though it has lent them its dramatic power. The Spirit is thus present in a representation which is the child of the living & the dead. The separate daimon is not a passive timeless mirror but a timeless act which with your help enters time once more[55]

The exchange is perhaps the closest we can come to the daily discussions that took place about and around George's automatic writing and later 'sleeps'. They were clearly moving towards a final position on the automatic script, but Willy would tussle with the question of impersonations by mediums for years to come. He later revised part II of his introduction, clarifying his argument and deleting a long section about the daimon, including the remark, 'Dramatisation or medium passes from daimon to daimon at the suggestion of some spoken word, or some association in the unconscious mind of some sitter.' But now, too busy with observing rehearsals of *The Dreaming of the Bones* and attending to Michael's needs (making up parcels of fudge for a school sale), George had no 'time to digest the two commentaries' before he returned to Dublin. The debate obviously continued, for the following winter, after attending séances in New York, he again took up the discussion both with George and in correspondence with his old friend Everard Feilding, proposing that a medium might adopt or dramatize 'a suggestion apparently coming from an external supernormal source'. But *The Words upon the Window-Pane* was admired by at least one well-known practising medium for 'its instructive realism and its acute cynical observation of some typical people who attend seances'.[56]

Despite her declaration to Lennox that it would be 'a relief' not to spend any further summers in Ballylee, she was still deeply attached to the tower. When Robinson wrote her from Massachusetts of 'a Norman Castle . . . covered with cow-dung', she immediately took umbrage at what she mistakenly considered 'low-handed hits at Ballylee'. Lennox hastily had some explaining to do.[57] That August she joined Willy in Coole for a few days to inspect Ballylee, then returned to Dublin for an operation, probably another attempt to repair the damage done by the Rapallo dentist to her jaw. But, as she complained to Dorothy, she was not to recover in peace:

Had an operation when I got back here and imagined W. safely disposed of for three weeks! But no, Lady G had to have an op: and the two of them buzzed up to Dublin the day after I had my stitches out, and since then—thats 11 days ago—life has been a perpetual fro and to and to and fro, but thank God I've had such a bad cold these last four days I couldnt risk giving it to her!! Christ how she repeats herself now . . . she'll tell you the same saga quite literally three times in less than an hour, and repeat it again the next day, and the day after that too. Burn when read . . . . . . She has recovered in her usual miraculous manner, may be going home tomorrow or Monday. She wants W to go down to Coole for most of September, and I hope he will—he doesnt seem to mind the reiterations. Personally they send me nearer lunacy than anything I ever met.

Her long letter continued with messages for Ezra, who had been left in charge of the business and tax arrangements for the Rapallo flat, and finished with a story for both:

Dudley Digges told me a nice tale of Goldman (or is it Goldwynn?) the movie Director who had a button-hole factory before he went into the movies. He sent for John Barrymore and said to him 'I must have you for my new picture . . . I shall spend five hundred thousand dollars . . . perhaps seven hundred thousand dollars . . . you will have such a romantic part . . . the most pewtifull clothes . . .' (he runs his hands round Barrymore's coat collar to demonstrate) 'such lovely fur' (suddenly grabs the buttonhole on the coat collar) 'Cheesus! What a lousy buttonhole!' Yours frivolously George.[58]

Although towards the end of his life even Ezra would acknowledge 'that stupid, suburban prejudice'[59] and she herself would make a Jew one of her closest confidants, George's 'nice tale' betrays the usual anti-Semitism of her class and period.

George seems to have gone briefly to England in August, for she was not present when the Abbey Theatre revived Yeats's much-revised morality play, *The Hour-Glass*. As usual, Lily and her sister were present on opening night: 'Willy just in front of me and as keen as if he saw it for the first time, people craning their necks to see him and he quite oblivious of them. Maud Gonne came, late of course. She looks a ruin and quite 90. She looks desperately old and ill.'[60] Although George kept two servants, the flat on Fitzwilliam Square was never meant to be more than a pied-à-terre, and Willy was staying at the Stephen's Green Club while she was away. 'I will call about 11.30 that you may have some sleep after your journey but if you want me before that telephone me here,' he wrote on her return, adding, 'Hourglass successful at Abbey. Masks wonderful.'[61] They rarely invited guests to Fitzwilliam Square for more than tea, and George's diary lists numerous luncheon and dinner engagements at the Shelbourne Hotel or the Kildare Street and United Arts Clubs. 'The old conservative haven of the rich, the Kildare St. Club, now admits women as guests to lunch and dine with members,' Lily reported, 'but we go in by a side door labelled "Servants". George says I did not see the label but it recalls the entrance to a bathroom, we will say. Willy told the committee that the lights are so unbecoming no woman would come a second time.'[62] Much to George's relief Lennox was now back from his American tour; still worried about their finances, she needed his advice about a likely purchaser for Willy's manuscripts. Then Willy returned to Coole. 'WBY has arrived, safe & well,' his hostess wrote, 'He came in sunshine & alas, awoke to rain—but I've established him in the "Playroom"—with a fire—he has the bedroom next it. I hope you will come whenever it suits you to inspect Ballylee ... I like hearing Willies news of Michael & Anne ... P. S. Willie is to stay as long as he can stand me! Come down now & again to inspect him!'[63]

To Ezra George was relieved to report that William was 'exceedingly well, producing a large amount of activity, some of it I think rather good value'.[64] In addition to his new play about Swift he was busy composing the second framework or preface to *A Vision B*, sending drafts back to Dublin for George to type. However, fearing further mediumship, he avoided dictating the major part of the system to George.[65] She in turn kept him informed of activities in Dublin. The previous November Jack and Cottie had moved around the corner to 18 Fitzwilliam Place, and although the two brothers saw little of each other outside of family gatherings, George and Willy were amused to discover through a postman's confusion that Punch's caricaturist 'W. Bird' was none other than Jack Yeats.[66] Of the Abbey productions, George disliked and was bored by Brian

Cooper's detective drama *Let the Credit Go* ('but then—when one has read all the first class detection of the world!'). However, she enjoyed the audience it attracted, 'The pettest old things have errupted [*sic*] into the Abbey . . . ancient whitehaired, fearfully eighteenth century old things, with diamond stars in their hair.' 'I only hope that they will be so large that when added to the past weeks of profit there may be during the next six months—as result of these accumulated hundreds— some play I DO want to see!'[67] She again went down to Coole for two or three nights, taking Willy the freshly typed manuscripts and books he needed. It may have been now that Lennox went with her and Dolly to see 'our beloved Ballylee', before he set out for a Swiss sanatorium with the dying artist Harry Clarke.[68]

There was constant worry over finances; Cuala expenses were also a threat and Willy spent considerable time negotiating new designs for Lily.[69] To his agent he dictated an urgent request to consult with his publishers, especially over the projected 'edition de luxe':

I find that my average income from Macmillan (London) calculated over some five years is £211. I havent the papers to calculate with equal accuracy what I receive from the American firm but the average is certainly somewhat higher. The present year, that ending June 30 1931, will certainly fall very much below the average in both countries. It will probably fall to the level of 1929 £131 from London and a proportionate amount from America a year when there was no new book or recent new book.[70]

Anne and Michael also had to be provided for; they were now ready to leave l'Alpe Fleurie 'where there is more play than lessons, and a great deal of resting in hammock chairs out of doors'.[71] The children 'dominate our plans, and for their sake we shall try and settle in Ireland again', Willy had earlier written to Masefield.[72] The Rapallo experiment had not been entirely successful despite the advantages of climate but, Willy informed Lady Gregory, George decided that he was 'not fit for town life, and when I get back from England (where I go on Friday) I shall probably find that we have shifted to a furnished house at some place like Dalkey'.[73] He claimed that her decision was determined by his irritation at Denis Johnston's production of *King Lear*; but George was also thinking of the children. The flat in Fitzwilliam Square was not suitable for full-time habitation; besides, she disliked some of the strange admirers who too easily tracked down Willy when he was in Dublin. And so when Vera and Joseph Hone announced their plan to spend some time in Switzerland, she arranged to rent their house in Killiney for four months. Cottie wrote mischievously to Gregory, 'the garden is in terraces if Willie goes *all* the way down & *all* the way *up* three times a day he will become quite a slimkin, am I really suggesting he is a *little* fat? No, no, *portly*.'[74] Again there was talk of spending the summer at Ballylee, but George had also intimated to Gogarty that she was prepared to rent out the tower from the middle of July 1931.[75]

While in England Willy went to Oxford, visiting the Morrells at Garsington and the Masefields at Boars Hill. 'I like to think that you are staying with Masefield,' George wrote, 'you must have met him for the first time just about the time you first stayed with Lady G. . . . If you get the opportunity look up Force Stead at Worcester College, and if you go there, look up Sheagan Dorman, Lennox's nephew and take him to Fullers to feed on ices and cream buns! You wont get any value out of him, but you like ices, and he adores cream buns!' Stead was mourning his hopeless love for 'a Nymph' considerably younger than himself; did they recognize the parallel with Willy's passion for Iseult? As for Sean Dorman, George was fond of Lennox's nephew; knowing that he liked meringues, she always offered them when he was invited to tea. To commemorate this thirtieth anniversary of their first meeting, Masefield sent a copy of the limited edition of *The Wanderer of Liverpool* (1930), which he embellished with original drawings and additional poems. George treasured it enough to stipulate in her will that it be left to Anne. He also built a model ship, the *George and Willy*, which always occupied a prominent place in the drawing room.

In Oxford Yeats planned also to visit May Morris, whose correspondence with John Quinn survived among the letters Lennox had been asked to edit and shown to George.[76] Again George stressed her belief that the art was more important than the artist. 'If you go over there do remember to talk to her about those two lovely poems in the Quinn letters,' she urged.

She wrote beautiful letters damnable perhaps that he did not burn them, although had I been able to write letters like that my personal vanity would have been pleased that they survived seeing that they contained so much that was impersonal, so little that was personal, so much praise of a man who gave her birth and of his house and of his friends—even his and her criticism of his friends, in those letters, had such nobility and justice that it was impersonal. Her own criticism of your gestures, lecturing, was justified, although she cut it, because she did not know you well enough to know that you do it unconsciously in private life. Anyway, if she isnt going to give that poem, those two poems, to the Quinn book, put the fear of God into her and make her publish them.[77]

Willy returned in time for the Abbey production of *Words upon the Window-Pane*, and four days later, on 21 November, George herself left for London and Switzerland. This time, instead of passing through London, she brought the children back by way of Paris, Cherbourg, and Cork. 'Michael shed some tears leaving Villars but "Anne, little wretch, did not".[78] Willy proudly informed Olivia that 'Anne has I am told perfect French. She is growing very pretty and remains very much of a flirt. On Saturday night she was roused up to see Lennox and put her arms round his neck. Next morning she revealed that owing to her sleepiness she had not known who it was. "But", said George, "you put your arm round his neck". Upon which Anne said without the slightest sense of shame "Oh I could see it was a man".[79] George immediately engaged a French governess for three hours each morning—who was shocked that Anne knew far more about the pagan gods than she did the scriptures. Wanting both children to be 'good classical scholars', Willy would have liked to send Michael 'to a school at Cambridge where Greek and Latin are learned in the same way and spoken, but we must keep him under our eyes for a couple of years yet'.[80] They decided on Baymount School for Boys in Dollymount as preparation for the College of St Columba in Rathfarnham and then university. Anne, on the other hand, spent eighteen months as a boarder at Hillcourt (now Rathdown) School for Girls in Glenageary, run by the three Palmer sisters, and then, when she opted for art school, her formal academic life was over.

Apart from some time at the Abbey helping Dolly paint the backdrop for Lennox's adaptation of Sheridan's *The Critic*, George devoted the Christmas season to the children's entertainment. Once again their plans were delayed by illness; Vera Hone suffered a bout of bronchitis and could not yet leave the Killiney house. Then Michael succumbed to the measles, and while Willy was out of harm's way in Coole Anne went down with a high fever. George nursed her daughter in Fitzwilliam Square while her son was sent on to South Hill with one of the maids, who took along her nephew, 'aged 15, 6 feet tall, and adored by Michael'.[81] George's rheumatism had also flared up again. 'They are the crockiest family,' observed Lennox with considerable justification.[82]

Still at Coole, Willy inspected Ballylee; but he longed for news from Dublin. 'I thought that it was I who have the grievance about letters. You in the midst of the great world every moment writing with news and I with nothing to tell.' To which George, tied to one sick child in Dublin and overseeing another not quite recovered in Killiney, replied, 'When you return I will tell you all about that fantastic "Great World" in which you imagine I am living.' However, when Willy arrived on 6 February 1931, he was met at the Broadstone with news that Anne was still not well enough to be moved, so he spent five days at the Standard Hotel waiting to be summoned to South Hill. Finally on 19 February he wrote to Augusta Gregory from that 'beautifully situated house, in the near distance the sea through intervening eucalyptus boughs'. George was expected that night. 'She has been kept in Dublin by Anne who is still sufficiently ill to make the carrying of her downstairs today a matter of much discussion. Michael is here and seems as well as possible.' Arrangements had been made through Tom MacGreevy for Alan Duncan, son of the Arts Club founder Ellen Duncan, to come from Paris as Willy's secretary for a month; it seemed that *A Vision B* might be finished at last.[83] He was dictating the 'final' version and looking forward to working on 'other things', including an essay on Swift and another new play *Resurrection*, both by-products of the system. Alan Duncan would stay until 15 March,[84] by which time the children were at last well enough for George to attend a new Abbey production (*Money* by Hugh P. Quinn) and spend the night in Fitzwilliam

Square. She saw little of Lennox, whose mother and sister were both seriously ill, but Tom passed through on his way to visit *his* mother in Tarbert.

Anne (now referred to as 'the interruption' by her brother) finally started school on 1 May. 'Anne has been home today after her first week at school, very happy and pleased with everything and apparently doing well with her lessons,' Willy wrote to Gregory, who was in Dublin on theatre business. 'Are you returning home on Tuesday? I ask you because Michael has been promised a sight of you and will be upset if George cant arrange to bring him in.'[85] George finally decided that Michael would be better off going to school than with a governess; for ten months from 8 June he went each day by electric tram to Mount Temple preparatory school for girls and boys at 3 Palmerston Park, Rathmines, where his aunt Lolly taught painting classes. Four other little boys who were to go to Baymount at the same time as Michael were also attending the school, which was run by Miss Ellen Sweeny ('very protestant, she's the daughter, sister, aunt, of vast hordes of protestant clergy!'). 'He seems pleased and excited, and I think he needs companionship of people of his own age,' George explained to her husband. 'He is much better without Anne, but she is 2^1/$_2$ years older and very "bossy" in spite of all that he is very lonely without her.'[86] A secret advantage was that, by walking to the next fare stage, Michael saved twopence each day, 'just enough . . . to buy a favourite chocolate bar'.[87] Despite being at Hillcourt for only one term, Anne returned for the summer bearing two honours certificates for drawing, and 98 per cent in her French. But her parents most appreciated a remark in one of her school essays: 'I admire Desdemona because of her singular love for a black man; most people have a peculiar dislike and distrust of black men.' 'I was delighted with your letter and Anne's admiration for Desdemona,' Willy wrote from Coole. 'I hope however that she herself has not idealised Othello's complexion. It might be an embarrassment in five years' time.'[88] Michael's school reports were—and would continue to be—consistently favourable.

Yet once more, a holiday in Ballylee was simply not financially viable. Lily was again ill. On inviting her out to Killiney for several weeks' rest, Willy discovered that the bank had refused any further overdraft; she could not pay the embroidery staff their salaries. After a visit to the bank he undertook to pay Lily half her salary, £92 a year, and guarantee 'a small overdraft'. His sister, still at war with Lolly, was grateful for how 'interested and fine and generous' her brother and sister-in-law were.[89] Fortunately Lolly's printing division was paying its way, but the future of the entire embroidery section was in doubt. 'What however is quite certain,' Willy informed Gregory from Fitzwilliam Square,

is that George and I will be very hard up for the next twelve months, or until the edition de luxe brings in some money, as I have published nothing for a long time, and as we are going to be hard up we shall in all probability have to stay on in this flat instead of getting a house outside Dublin, and there will be no visit for George and Anne and Michael to

Ballylee. The children will be able to get down to the sea on fine days, Howth, or Blackrock where there are sea swimming baths, Anne is learning to swim at the Blackrock baths which is near her school which is at Glenageary.

He was taking six of the seven volumes of the projected 'edition de luxe' to Macmillan in London, now more necessary than ever.[90]

On 26 May Willy was to receive an honorary degree from Oxford, but from London had to wire to George, 'Where do I lunch on Tuesday?'[91] As usual, they wrote to each other almost daily while he was away. At Wadham College (where an unidentified 'Miss Lee' asked to be remembered to his wife) he was asked 'what had of recent years so deepened my poetry'. He also saw Force Stead; George had been right in that he wanted help over his frustrated love affair. In London, Olivia told him that Mrs Homer Pound had been robbed of jewellery (kept in an unlocked drawer), but he was able to assure George that no damage had been done to their Rapallo flat.[92] George's letters were also cheerful and full of news. However, his new book for Cuala, *Stories of Michael Robartes and his Friends*, even with prints and poems, would come to less than thirty pages. 'I've racked my brains to think of any enlargements but the book seems to me so complete in itself that I cannot imagine how any more pages can be grafted in'; it would eventually be published at 46 pages. The Abbey was doing well, AE had cleared 'just under £3,000' on his lecture tour in America, and—to her sorrow— the horse she had fancied for the big Derby Day race had 'collapsed'.

Then, there was a rather nightmarish lunch yesterday with that Miss Daking . . . She interests me tremendously as a human being but lord god in heaven William no one who talks so much can think, and that woman talked incessantly from one to five thirty . . . honestly I dont think I said more than 150 words, perhaps less, during the sitting. I got down to my most English sub-soil and said 'quite' that I might alternate the 'yes, yes.' or 'no, no' which were necessary as punctuations. Had I not been compelled to meet Michael the interview would have been even longer and I am sure I would have begun punctuating with 'how true'.

What distressed her most about this visitor was her hands: 'Queer curtailed fingers, short in the third joint with the very short nails that mean obsession, or the half-developed. No, perhaps that is too personal a judgment; I've known three people with those short, abnormally short, nails who were obsessed.'[93] Years later she would object to Seán O'Sullivan's portrait of Yeats, insisting that Willy's fingers were 'tapered to very thin, square edge—with round nails—not pointed nails on round fingers' as in the painting.[94]

On his return from England Willy and George entertained the Swedish State company of actors who had come to see the Abbey in performance.[95] Then Willy went almost immediately back to Coole, briefly overlapping with Jack and Cottie.[96] The meeting was cordial; on his return, Jack told George 'he has *never*' seen his brother 'in such good health'.[97] The experience led to further signs of congeniality. 'Jack and Cottie are keeping themselves to themselves at the moment,' George reported. 'Although on Saturday when Anne and Michael and I were returning home we saw him in the distance and the children said with one voice "he is crossing the road to speak to us!" '[98]

But Lady Gregory was much weaker; despite her operation the cancer would recur and rheumatism had made her lame. Margaret and Guy Gough urged Willy to spend as much of the winter at Coole as possible, and George encouraged the plan. Now the tables were turned: although Gregory still insisted on reading to him—for one thing it took her mind off the pain—Willy tended to her medication, fended off tiring visitors, and tolerated others, patiently answered her questions over and over, and did his best to offer distraction from her weakening condition. In Dublin, George served as eyes and ears for them both, once again keeping them informed of the political and cultural action there, forwarding doctors' advice and prescriptions, discreetly deflecting unnecessary Abbey worries. July had been 'bleak and drenching',[99] but there was glorious weather for the Horse Show at the beginning of August, where Cuala as usual had a stall; Lolly returned home 'disgruntled', convinced she had been snubbed by both sisters-in-law.[100] George and the children were then invited to Coole, but the visit was delayed while Anne went into Elpis Nursing Home for a few days to have a septic ingrowing toenail removed. 'George was to come to pictures but Anne is in Elpis having toe off or something and G. being perfect mother cant leave her,' Lennox complained to Dolly. However he and George had been 'to the dogs' the previous week, where both lost money but enjoyed themselves. On 24 August George finally brought the children to Coole, but only for four days. 'They are cheery little visitors,' Gregory wrote in her journal, pleased that she could provide something new to delight them; driving on the 'side-car' was 'not allowed in Dublin'.[101] The Italian critic and philosopher Mario Rossi was another welcome guest at Coole; when his family left Willy changed his plans and stayed on to assist the ailing chatelaine. Although spending sleepless nights because of the pain, she still refused to take any drugs. It may have been the last time she saw Anne and Michael. 'She was very fond of the children,' Lily later recalled, 'and Michael felt very affectionate towards her. Last time he was there he went back and gave her another hug, and on the train was seen eating seed cake, at which Anne exclaimed, "Thought you hated seed cake!" "But", said Michael, "Lady Gregory gave us this." '[102]

MacGreevy was in Paris, pleased by the praise Yeats had written for his small book on Eliot; but he continued to have difficulty separating critical response to his writing from personal relations, and was feeling more and more isolated. Dolly, having spent most of the winter in Dublin either working at Harry Clarke's glassworks or the Abbey, was back in London fighting with her mother. George played the stern elder sister, writing 'a frigid letter because I dont think she has a chance in a competition of throwing fits with Hester—Hester has far more experience'.[103] Hester Dowden's battle with her daughter may have been part jealousy, certainly possessiveness, for on the evening of 20 July Lennox had called round to Fitzwilliam Square to 'spill both beans' to George. He and Dolly had decided to get married. When the news got out, the results were to be expected. Taken completely by surprise, Tom felt hurt, angry, and deserted; and complained to Hester. Hester offered him little comfort: 'I know that you loved and admired Dolche but I didnt think like that. . . . Dolche might have given you more pain if you had asked her.' But she herself had doubts: 'If Lennox was in love with Dolche why did he spend his holiday in Paris with you?'[104] Most of Dublin was equally surprised, for those who knew of Lennox's passion for Iseult realized that it had never completely subsided; 'whenever I see her my heart stops, and when we meet I can say nothing but banalities,' he had confessed to Tom only six months before.[105] Those who suspected his homosexual tendencies were even more astonished; Lady Gregory sent best wishes but privately thought a long engagement might have been more advisable.

George was happy for both of them. Lennox was lonely; only last year he had written from Ann Arbor that all he wanted was 'a café in Spain or France or Italy and you and Dolly'.[106] She had long recognized that for many years Dolly had been in love with Lennox, and had even challenged her soon after they had met, 'over a wheelbarrow of weeds in the garden at 82'. Remembering the details of her own wedding with regret, she urged them both to be married in church. 'She's awfully pleased,' Lennox told Dolly, 'but insists on Chelsea Old Church . . . G says she still wants to be re-married in a church . . . I'm all for 8 a.m. in the morning at that nice old church, G. says W. B. Y will come over to "give you away"!!!! Anyhow it seems simple and decent and registry seems neither.' To Dolly George was even more insistent, perhaps projecting Dolly's fears that Hester might make a scene:

I have a terrible prejudice against registry offices—nasty frowzy places. . . . Sorry, I'd mislaid my theme for the moment, which was Chelsea Old Church or any old church in remote Dublin (having the Grimery you can easily establish 'residence') and the Poet as Best Man. But then you see, I have a hopelessly romantic—or sentimental, mind—he really would do it quite nicely & I would see that he had the doings. Also, in Church one's relations may weep quietly in or in front pews which is quite OKE in the best 1830 tradition, whereas in registry offices the formality may lead to outbursts. . . . speaking Dolly with full experience of registry offices, and a very great prejudice in favour of the church, I have, as you see, very strong feelings on the subject!

In lieu of the customary honeymoon Dolly and Lennox were accompanying the Abbey company on an American tour (where Dolly would spend more time with the actors than with Lennox), and George enclosed a cheque to be spent on clothes for the journey. On their return 'We might then prance around and get cups and saucers and dinner plates and whatnots' as a 'formal and official wedding present'. As a parting shot she advised them 'dont *for God's sake get* photographed on the doorstep (of church or registry) as Sheelah & Denis did —your proportionate heights are about the same'.[107] She was probably remembering Gregory's comment that the wedding photo of Denis Johnston, so much taller than Shelah Richards, made them look like an 'If'.

But George's full-hearted approval created a rift with Tom that would take many years to heal. 'I'm feeling annoyed with you,' she chastised him.

Why didnt you write to Dolly? *This is private.* I said to her that it was because she had not written to you herself. I think you might write to her. . . . If you really cared for Dolly you would have written to her because she has loved LR for a long time, and so you might be glad that she is happy about it all, instead of being rather a pig. I can say that to you very frankly because of some things you told me many years ago. I want Dolly to be completely happy, but that means that her friends will be happy and friendly too. Burn when read—!

To soften her message and in recognition of his own loneliness, George closed her letter with, 'I hope you will really decide on that cottage near Dublin so that we see more of you. There are damn few intelligent people in Dublin, and they get fewer and fewer.' Tom was not to be mollified, however, replying indignantly,

I sent a word to the Lennoxes for Xmas, thinking over what you said. . . . it brought back the kind of upset that the whole business has been. I had of course sent my good wishes etc for both of them to Lennox who told me in about a dozen words. Dolly made no sign which was nice of her. I also sent my second Dolphin [his poems] to them jointly but got no acknowledgement. . . . God knows my feeling that I don't ever want to see Dolly again hasn't modified. . . . It was as if she had annihilated me and I don't feel that I exist . . . It has paralyzed me somewhere. . . . She was my faith in not letting oneself be run away with by one's instincts, in sticking to what was sensible and good, in refusing to become a flamboyant figure of the kind who has so often stirred W. B. to his own kind of great poetry.[108]

Lennox, he continued, is 'not a human being in the full sense—though he is a dear phenomenon enough', but 'Dolche is a human being and responsible for what she does'. 'And I'm terrified to think of her in that beastly country of speakeasies and general disgustingness.' Once again beset by family illnesses, it was two months before George was able to respond to his outburst. Then, aware of how hard up he was in Paris, she arranged for the *Irish Press* to be sent to him.

It is a disappointing paper I think; its literary articles are bosh; the political leaders are Pooh; and in fact the only thing I can find to say about it is that I take it every day instead of the Independent.

I dont agree with you about all sorts of things. But I wont write to you about them! Dolly has written a good many letters to me and I think she is happy, and I do not think that that land of speak-easies and blah blah can change her from herself. In fact what I really think is that you should know that she has a quality that cannot be qualified, or interchanged, or dis-integrated, and if you dont know that——Yours affly George Yeats[109]

It is doubtful whether Tom's stiff letter of congratulation to Lennox was ever posted; and throughout the winter Dolly never did hear from her 'Tamsie'. Eventually he would come round, and call on the Robinsons on his next visit to Dublin; but it was a long time before he could forgive George for not siding with him.

Willy was hardly surprised by Lennox's engagement. To 'Chinatown', his nick-name for Dolly, he wrote, 'I approve of you. You will be a great ornament to our neighbourhood. You have both done very well for yourselves. Congratulations, good luck.' His note to Lennox reflected his own satisfaction in the married state: 'You will work better, be far more content.'[110] Lennox was 44, Dolly fifteen years younger. Despite Hester's 'devilish' attitude over the matter and George's pleas, the marriage took place in the Chelsea Register Office on 8 September 1931 with the bride's mother and the groom's brother as witnesses. Very soon the story went round Dublin 'that Lennox Robinson when asked by a certain woman, who has been spreading the tale, "whether he was very much in love", replied—he had been married a week—"How could I love a plum pudding?"' [111] But despite his gradual decline into alcoholism they remained together, and in the early years especially George enjoyed having her two friends in Dublin.

Meanwhile George desperately needed space of her own, and Dolly's 'enormous room'—part living quarters, part studio—would be an ideal retreat. Always referred to as 'the Grimery', this was probably the upper flat of one of the buildings on North Frederick Street, where the Clarke glassworks were situated; Norah McGuinness, Shelah Richards, and the actress Meriel Moore had been occupants at various times during Dolly's absences.[112] 'I do want a room to work in and have peace in during the endless summer holidays to say nothing of the fact that if you'd lease it to me during the winter (at what you pay) t'would be a godsend,' George wrote.

After that yous might want to keep it for the evenings you're at parties and dont want to pay 16/- for taxis to Dalkey; but if you *dont* want to keep it I'd like the 'first refusal'. Its £16 a year isnt it? We'll probably be staying on here for a year or two and I might be very glad to take it on. . . . I think I gave you a kitchen table and a bed and if you dont want them I'll reclaim them IF YOUS DONT WANT THE ROOM. If yous want the room the table and the beds are yours for all time. Anyway we can settle that up when you come back from those united states, but while you ARE in that bloody country you might well let me pay the six months rent for if you dont I'll have to find something else which wont be half as cheap.

Dolly agreed, but as late as November George was still having difficulty getting the extra keys from Shelah and Meriel.[113]

From Coole Willy wrote to Olivia, 'I shall be here for some time. Lady Gregory is really very ill, constantly without sleep through pain and dreads my going.'[114] And to Sturge Moore, 'I shall be here for months, going to Dublin for a week now and again, or my wife coming here.'[115] To George he admitted, 'Her judgment is vigorous, but her memory comes and goes.'[116] It would be a long winter, punctuated by hasty journeys to Dublin to attend to theatre and other business. Apart from a brief time away in September 1931, probably to see her mother (and Dorothy who was in Sidmouth with Olivia and Omar), George remained in Fitzwilliam Square, relaying news of the children and various friends, sending the requisite books, supplies, and advice, dealing with publishers, sometimes even casting and costuming his plays (with the main company on tour in the United States, she had seen more of the remaining actors than he), and generally serving as secretary and research assistant.

She was also becoming practised at deflecting seekers and well-wishers alike. 'I'm glad you heard W. B. in Donegal—yours is the only letter from Ireland,' she wrote to Monk Gibbon of Willy's first BBC broadcast from Belfast.

Personally I like that poem 'In Memory of Con Marckiewicz' and Eva Gore Booth as well as anything he has written for some years. The other poem you speak of I don't like so much because I like so very much the tightly packed later poems, but so many people like the Anne Gregory poem that I am sure I am wrong-headed even if I insist on sticking to my wrong-headedness! . . . Willy comes back to Dublin (from Galway) tomorrow, and I'll hand over your letter to him. Whether he will have time to write interestingly on all the things he thinks about Gerald [sic] Hopkins I don't know—that phrase sounds rather snubby, but it isnt; what I really mean is that he will only be in Dublin for three days and will then probably be returning to Coole with his old friend who is very unwell, so, his leisure being curtailed, he may not have time to write at length on a theme which interests him tremendously.[117]

The situation was frustrating for both of them, for George could not make her own private arrangements until she knew Willy's, and with Gregory's health deteriorating, he was more and more tied to Coole. 'If you cannot make "plans", I think you must say so in order that I may know what to do about a number of problems that I find difficult . . . Please do not think that I am "feeling neglected" —your own phrase!'[118] She made certain he was not indifferent to the children either. In December after spending a week in Coole catching up on typing—he was still making corrections and additions to *A Vision B*—she wrote,

It was really very pet and nice of you to be up when I was going yesterday, thank you. I found Michael very well, bursting to tell all his doings during the week—the plot of the play at the French Society—the lion cubs at the zoo and the charms of Rupert . . . (your cousin) the conversation he had with someone at the French Society 'I didnt know him,

he was French, and I dont think he knew me, I like talking to people I dont know' . . . . .
. . . A thrilling cinema (gunmen) and a star for composition! Two mice caught in his
cupboard, his crocusses all much bigger, thank goodness painting classes were over
for the term, how many hours until Anne returned from school on Friday, what was a
moon's nebula (that stumped me,) kippers for breakfast twice, no chicken since I went
away, and so on ad infinitum.[119]

But Anne was 'in profound disgrace at school for not working'. 'She wrote to me
"Miss Palmer blew me up and made me go to late prep. every day last week.
I think the results were good for I got 8 out of 10 for arithmetic, 14 out of 15 for
Geometry, 10 out of 10 for French, 12 out of 15 for Algebra, but don't think I shall
be much higher in the class because I didnt work at the other subjects".'[120] Willy
wrote that he missed George 'greatly', but was delighted by Anne's remarks. 'She
could not have written like that if she was afraid of you, or if she did not want to
please. There was nobody I could have written to like that. I would have been
afraid to tell of my short comings, & I would not have thought of them as Anne
does without moral fuss.'[121] But once again Anne was in bed over Christmas,
with 'a terrific temp: and throat'; the doctor feared diphtheria. 'Please write to
her about her "linotype" and don't forget to read the inscription on the back of
the calendar!' George wrote, explaining that 'a lino-type is *cut* in linoleum'.[122]
She bought gifts for the children on his behalf and Willy dutifully wrote to both
children; he had Anne's calendar by his bed, and—cautious as always in his
judgement—would have praised her linotype more, 'but I don't feel I know
how it was done . . . If it is her own design, & if the treatment of wall & ground
is her invention it is very remarkable.' He assured Michael that the salted
almonds he had sent his father were 'excellent . . . no cook in the world could
have made better'.[123] When Anne was well enough to be left in charge of one of the
trusted housemaids, George took Michael to the pantomime and also to the Gate
Theatre, where she disliked Colum's *Mogu of the Desert*; criticizing in detail
the staging, music, and performance. She was reading Walter Pater's *Marius the
Epicurean* in bed 'for tranquility of mind'; Willy especially enjoyed her 'most
amusing letter' on the Drennan letters which, she reported, 'are both "amusing
and instructive" as I was told on being given Mrs Gatty's "Parables from Nature"
as a school prize'. In the same letter George elaborated at some length on a court
case concerning a medium and a sweepstake ticket.[124] 'You are much the best
letter writer I know, or have known,' he wrote her; 'your letters have so much
unstrained animation, so much natural joyousness.'[125]

Sometimes in spite of herself irritation erupted. Worried about his fading
eyesight, she sent him a new lamp; his question 'What oil do I put in it' produced
the expostulation: 'The lamp of course consumes lamp oil, paraffin. What in
Heaven's name else could it consume?! Its very form shouts paraffin oil; you
could surely not have imagined that it demanded Sanctuary oil, or olive oil?' But

she went on to joke about arranging rehearsals for *The Dreaming of the Bones*, 'if it is to be done it must be got going—anyway, have you thought out who is going to shake dem bones when you is gone back to Coole? ("bones" is a name negroes give to dice—shaking the "bones" . . . very low).'[126] She had very little gossip to relay, though 'Maud has been terrifically busy! She got in a meeting that had been banned twentyfour hours earlier than the banned one.'[127] Occasionally she had to chastise him for passing on some of the information she did provide: 'Dossie Wright has a new daughter; Mr and Mrs Dermod O'Brien went to the Arts Ball as "*Fig Leaves*"!; Denis Johnston went down to the Abbey to ask permission to stay there for Hallow'een night to lay the ghost. Now for God's sake keep this last piece of news to yourself and don't impart it to Lady G.' As usual, she had to warn him to be discreet. 'If you repeat this I shall never again write you a letter to Coole containing anything frivolous or serious.'[128] But their relationship was subtly changing, and more and more frequently she was signing herself 'Dobbs'.

Cuala too was in transition. By September it had become clear that neither Lily nor the embroidery division would ever recover, and so it was decided that Lily was to 'fade out slowly, probably by Xmas. A sudden end would damage the Press and also it all takes time.' 'George is extraordinarily good, so comforting, and you can trust her,' Lily wrote to Ruth. 'She is so big in her ways and mind, and Willy the same. They fill me with hope and comfort.'[129] On 3 December 1931, Lily attended Cuala's final embroidery sale, and by the beginning of January George had wound up all the division's affairs and paid off the overdraft. George 'does it so graciously, no fastening of a hook in your jaw over it', Lily wrote about the arrangements. 'I never should have taken up the work after my illness. The eight years have been a very great strain, and each year a small loss, adding up.' Taking a thousand preference shares in the company as recompense, Willy had to withdraw £1,000 from his Nobel account to square Lily's account, and a further £800 was found for Lolly's. In addition, he and George committed £7 a month to Lily on the understanding that she would through her own efforts try to match it. Impressed by her sale of embroidered pictures of the Abbey Theatre and the Customs House, Willy suggested she undertake a series of 'famous houses'— Vanessa's at Celbridge, Coole, etc.—and also seek drawings or paintings from AE that might be adapted. Cuala's last completed order was for the Stations of the Cross designed by Brigit O'Brien, and by then only three of Lily's 'girls' were left. One of them married, and the remaining two, Sara Hyland and May Courtney, decided to carry on as a 'Mendery and dressmaking establishment', paying rent to Lolly for room and telephone expenses and acting as Lily's agents.[130] George admired their courage and supported them in every way possible, taking in the first bundle of mending. 'It is easy to do propaganda when propaganda is altruistic!' she explained.[131] Until the last month of his life Willy continued to seek out new subjects for Lily to embroider (urging her to design some herself, even suggesting colour of thread and appropriate frames), and George watched over her favourite sister-in-law until her death.[132]

Still concerned about Anne's health, she took the children to Killarney for a week while Willy went to Dublin to see his dentist. 'We had an excellent journey,' she reported,

—arrived in gales, storms and floods! No front rooms overlooking the lake could be used because the wind so terrific. The next morning dead calm, some sun, floods vanishing. Today a summer's day, and the lake dead smooth and transparent and the children have gone off with an old boatman for a 'grand tour' which is to take 3–4 hours! We had a long drive yesterday (outside car) all round the Muckross estate up to Torca Mountain etc. Anne has done a quite excellent sketch from the covered in verandah, and proposes to start another tomorrow so as to get two done! She is getting back her colour and energy.

They had the entire hotel to themselves and, deprived of animals while living in the flat, George especially enjoyed the various dogs and 'a regally colossal black cat' who were allowed in the house outside 'the season'. 'Such is German discipline— the manager is a German—that the animals, or so I was told, understand that from Whitsun until September 15 they must cease to be house dogs and cats. I doubt very much that the cat would permit this code to be imposed upon him, he did not seem at all obedient. He was a very determined cat.' Michael delighted especially in their return journey from Clifden to Galway by bus and train, count-ing the lakes as they passed. Meanwhile Willy wrote of his excitement over Francis Stuart's new novel *Pigeon Irish*; in turn George had enjoyed reading *The Most Unfortunate Day of my Life*, a recently published fragment by Maria Edgeworth illustrated by Norah McGuinness. 'Printed in fine type on handsome paper it seems an incomparable piece of style—of its own kind—the grandfather and grand-mother of all the Virginia Woolf's and Stella Bensons and all of those modern novelists who seem to write with the astonished eyes of an imaginary child.' She reported unfavourably on the current Abbey productions, especially disagreeing with the casting and direction ('NO, NO!'), and warned of the government-appointed director Walter Starkie's need to be consulted both about the Abbey and Willy's new plan for an Irish Academy of Letters. Most important, however, was the appointment she had made for them both to visit W. L. Scott, the headmaster at Baymount School, before Michael started there in May.[133]

Anne was much better for the holiday, but now she had an ingrown toenail on the other foot, which would eventually require another operation. Spurred by George's tale of the animals and perhaps remembering that his daughter had become a member of the SPCA 'Band of Mercy', Willy wrote to Anne:

I hear you are almost well again. I have no news except that the head forester here a little while ago counted sixty two wild swans on the lake, that is seven or eight more than I ever saw. A little before that he saw a flight of twenty five herons rising from the bank & I never saw more than two or three. He says that wild swans & herons are increasing all through the west of Ireland & explains it by the greater gentleness towards beasts & birds of the people especially the children. I have been writing a poem which contains a description of a wild swan suddenly flying up from the side of the lake. Your affectionate father WB Yeats[134]

But then he overlooked Anne's birthday. Noting that he even misdated his apology, George was tactful: 'I sent on your letter to Anne, crossing out the "almost" and commenting in a letter of my own on the fact that you had dated your letter March 8. . . . I told her that you had asked me to read it to "see if it was legible", and that I hoped she would be as amused as I was to see that you lived always a week or two behind time or in advance of time. (She wont mind the date because she will remember that you came to Dublin a week too early once!)' Then Michael's headmistress had written, 'I never knew so nice a little boy, he is so solemn and yet merry, so innocent, but he's clever'; at which George wryly commented, 'Its like an epitaph on an eighteenth century tomb.'[135]

Willy made a brief visit to Dublin to vote in the general election on 16 February. George usually cancelled his vote for Fine Gael by casting hers for Fianna Fáil, and this time de Valera and Fianna Fáil formed the new government. When she had time to consider the implications of de Valera's win, especially concerning the proposed Academy and the relationship between the Gate Theatre and the Abbey, she wrote to Coole,

I do very much wish that I could see you to talk over a few of these things now that the political situation is clearer. If you think that you cannot come to Dublin again before you go to London, I wonder if you could come to Galway for a night—I would make an excuse to go there . . . a friend . . . because I dont think Lady G. ought to have the burden of a visitor. I really do believe that this is the moment to start things off, and the few people I have seen since you went away all say the same thing—we are tired of politics, we want an intellectual movement politics are the death of passion and passion is the food of the intellect. Please do agree that either you come up, or we have an assignation in Galway![136]

Replying that he agreed 'about everything', Willy came to Dublin early in March, arriving in time to have lunch at Fitzwilliam Square with Ruth Draper; George also seems to have been in charge of the arrangements for the actress's one-woman show at the Abbey.[137] Unaware that Miss Draper's Italian lover, the poet and anti-Fascist Lauro de Bosis, had recently been killed, George later described the party to Lily: 'They had Mrs. Walter Starkey to meet her. She is Italian. Miss D. attacked Mussolini, Mrs. S. defended him. In the end Mrs. Starkey was in tears and talking a mixture of Italian and English. George felt Miss Draper was noticing it all to produce later.'[138] Lennox was still not back from the American tour, but to George's pleasure Dolly had returned. Willy then spent most of April in London, during which time he set in motion many of the activities which would engross his last decade: with Shaw he discussed plans for the Academy of Letters; he met Shri Purohit Swami, whose autobiography had so entranced him that winter; delivered Lady Gregory's autobiography to her publisher; attended a meeting of the Ghost Club; saw Ottoline; and to various English officials put his case for the Irish government's objections to the oath of allegiance. All this was reported, almost daily, in detail to George. Especially gratifying was the news that Macmillan had begun to set his 'edition de luxe'. On 10 April he gave his second BBC broadcast, 'Poems about Women', which George, who had listened to it with Dolly, thought 'too slow, so very much slower than you lecture or read'. Then he invented 'urgent business' in Dublin to escape a final dinner party, and was home on the 21st.[139] There were family matters to attend to, house-hunting and other rites of passage: 'Michael goes to school, his first real school, early in May and George is getting him his first long trousers (white cricket trousers) tomorrow morning.'[140] A week later he returned to Coole.[141] He continued to consult George about the rules for the Academy and who should be elected: 'I want your ideas on the subject—I am afraid of my own impulsiveness.'[142] The lump in Lady Gregory's breast was larger; she sat outside the hall door for an hour, the first time she had been out for months. The next day she signed the contract—arranged by Yeats—for her autobiography.[143] 'Old age, as I see it in her, suggests somebody passing into trance,' Willy had written; but it was worse when his old friend struggled to remember and she fought back tears.[144] George sent regular parcels of mail, books, and personal belongings he required. Once she included a hairbrush; 'It has made me realize that all my life I have wanted to scratch my head and never have been able to do so hitherto,' he wrote in thanks.[145] Willy stayed at Coole as long as he could, but by mid-May the theatre, Academy, and other business—including a visit to Michael's school —called him to Dublin. George and Willy were dining out when urgent word came summoning him back to Coole. Although he caught the earliest train next morning, Yeats was not, after all, present when his old friend died at midnight on 22 May 1932.

When death finally came to Augusta Gregory, Willy was devastated by the loss. 'The blow has been heavy,' he wrote to Sturge Moore. 'I feel that never again dare I see that neighbourhood which is so full of memories.'[146] It marked the end for him not only of Coole, but of Ballylee. But the loss was not only his: for George, too, the old order had passed away with Lady Gregory.

17

RIVERSDALE

The flat in Fitzwilliam Square would soon no longer be available, and George began serious house-hunting in April 1932. 'We must move next winter and want an old detached house with a garden,' Willy had written to Olivia on his return from London.[1] By mid-May they had found a little house in Willbrook, Rathfarnham, 'old enough for dignity'; originally called 'Sallymount', it was now named 'Riversdale'.[2] George paid £700 for the lease, held by the General Presbyterian Fund and due to run out in March 1945; the annual rates were a reasonable £39. The house itself was 'rather squat and square', only two storeys high, and the rooms small with the exception of one opening out into the conservatory and walled garden, which would become Willy's study. They disliked the plate-glass windows in the house, but the splendour of the creeper-covered seventeenth-century farmhouse (which 'might be in a Calvert woodcut') lay in the gardens—flower, fruit, vegetable, rock—and tennis, bowls, and croquet lawns. 'We shall outdo Celbridge for years to come,' Willy exulted.[3] 'I never expected to own anything as beautiful as this little house,' he had written on the very day of Lady Gregory's death.[4] To George he said if he could not have this, he would never take another.[5] The property, slightly more than four acres, and surrounded by fields, had once been part of an old orchard; George let the field beyond the expanse of lawns for grazing.[6] The house, flanked by gates off Ballyboden Road, was approached by a curved driveway past a gatehouse on the right with a walled fruit garden (plums and apples) beyond. The windows were low and 'everywhere look out upon some garden'. A river, crossed almost at the gate by an old moss-covered arched bridge, ran parallel to the road. When Lennox heard of their plans, he was concerned that the waste water from the local laundry across the fields would be a threat to the children; George however pointed out that the stream flowed towards the Bloomfield Laundry and away from their property.[7] Behind the house across the cobblestoned yard were stables which would become the children's playrooms and—when he was old enough—Michael's bedroom, 'a most ingenious and amusing place for hens', and various sheds.[8] A summerhouse abutted the croquet lawn. Hedges separated the various gardens and, beyond that, trees sheltered them from neighbours at the rear and sides.

There was no electricity (except in the gatehouse); heating and light were by gas. Until Yeats appealed for assistance to the Ministry of Posts and Telegraphs the nearest telephone was half a mile away in the village public house; the Minister (P. S. O'Hegarty, bibliographer and collector of Yeatsiana and destined to become Michael's father-in-law) immediately dispatched workmen to Riversdale, so that by summer's end they could once again protect their privacy.[9] Although they were surrounded by country, the Whitechurch bus (number 47, still a single-decker) passed the gate; but 'just too far from Dublin to go there without good reason and too far', Willy hoped, 'for most interviewers and the less determined travelling bores'.[10] When news of the sale reached the neighbourhood, the local rector's young son was heard to say in excitement, 'Do you know the Fiddler of Dooney has bought Riversdale?'[11] Soon the artist Seán Keating also moved into the neighbourhood.[12]

George and Willy were enchanted by the gardens. 'I shall have a big old fruit garden all to myself—the study opens into it and it is shut off from the flower garden and the croquet and tennis lawns and from the bowling-green,' he told Olivia. He would be able to go through the glass-door 'to share the gooseberries with the bullfinches'; through the window to his left he could see pergolas covered with roses and to the right, borders of phlox amongst the old apple trees. Ricketts's gift of the Burne-Jones window hung in the window into the greenhouse, its proper home at last.[13] To George's delight the gardener, John Free (himself just 21), agreed to stay on for three days a week and with his help she soon had the grounds exactly as she wished. 'I made John arrange so that we could leave open the gates into the lawn when we have a party without fear of the hens escaping,' she informed Willy before the move. 'This has been done most skilfully!' A long narrow bed blossomed in the spring with a mass of pink tulips and forget-me-nots. However, although she hated arum lilies, she did agree to keep a large bed when the young gardener explained that it supplied 'all the funerals in Rathfarnham'. Fortunately they were unobtrusive, on the far side of the croquet lawn. In the autumn there was myrtle in blossom on one side of the hall door and verbena on the other, and the walls glowed with the berries of the barberry shrub.[14]

George gained possession on 27 June 1932, in time to be settled in for the children's holidays. The entire house required cleaning and distempering; 'the last people did up the rooms without taking the pictures off the walls or moving the cupboards,' she complained.[15] As always, she tackled Willy's rooms first, herself painting the walls and ceiling of the long room which would be his study a rich lemon yellow, with green and black doors. On the right of the entrance hall, this was originally two rooms divided by a folding door in the Georgian tradition; the front half held Willy's long worktable and low bookcases all round protected by black sindon, while the other end was the sitting room, with yet more bookcases and easy chairs ranged on either side of the turf-burning fireplace. Prominently displayed was the Japanese sword, surrounded by paintings. A smaller study, 'the gold room' (again with a fireplace), opened out of his upstairs bedroom; outside the window she hung a meat bone to attract the tomtits.[16] 'At first I was unhappy,' he confessed to Olivia, 'for everything made me remember the great rooms and the great trees of Coole . . . but now that the pictures are up I feel more content. . . . George's fine taste has made the inside almost as beautiful as the garden which has some fame among gardeners.'[17] Both knew it would be the last environment she would create for him.

On 6 July Willy wrote to his daughter, 'Your mother is tired out putting things into bundles and boxes to take them to Rathfarnham. As I am greatly in the way she is sending me to Glendalough tomorrow where I shall stay for more than a week getting more & more impatient for my new study. The study walls are to be all yellow like a buttercup.'[18] The Stuarts' poultry farm at Laragh was within easy drive of the Royal Hotel, but he complained to George that he found Francis Stuart 'rather flat' without Iseult, who was in Dublin visiting her mother; however, she returned in time for the weekend, when he escaped noisy children in the hotel by joining her at Laragh.[19] Lonely and excited by the prospect of their new house, he returned from Wicklow two days too early, and was sent to his club until 20 July. George meanwhile was ensuring there would be enough warmth at Riversdale. On Sunday night she made a special trip into Dublin to collect the 'gas fires' from the flat; 'the gas fitters declared that their work would be "delayed" if they did not get them today. . . . and as all work has been so much delayed.' But she admitted for the first time that all the hard work was taking its toll: 'I feel that I am getting too old for this kind of thing: my pace is got slow, I dont get through things with the rapidity that I managed even five years ago! Of course when we moved five years ago it was Dublin to Dublin which made a difference.'[20] She would soon turn 40.

Two years earlier while still in Rapallo, Yeats had confessed, 'I shall hope like the tramp Davies in one of his poems, for a small house and a large garden. I have always wanted to live always in one place and have never managed it yet.'[21] It looked as if he would finally realize that dream. 'He is as happy as a boy home for the holidays,' Lily observed. 'He reads and writes and wanders in and out of the gardens and has scuffled the paths.' The long study was especially ideal for his method of dictating to George, when he would 'tiger up and down' as he spoke. One evening when Gogarty was visiting, he too started walking up and down the room, each time getting nearer to Yeats's worktable, where he picked up a pen and a piece of paper, then suddenly threw them down again saying, 'no Willy I'm damned if I will!' According to George, the poet had been mischievously willing him to draw a donkey and put his name under it.[22] Outdoors, Willy played croquet 'with great enthusiasm', becoming so proficient that regular guests such as AE rearranged their visiting hours to avoid a game. Even Lolly was forced to play; one unfortunate woman (probably Cottie) deliberately let him win and was never invited to play again. Even the children were pleased with their new home, rising at 7 a.m. to garden.[23]

Willy tore himself reluctantly away for a lecture tour to the United States, where he hoped to earn enough not only for renovations to Riversdale but to establish the Irish Academy of Letters. Alan Duncan was accompanying him as secretary and general assistant, but George spent the week with him in London before he sailed, 'to give last instructions to Alan. She feels no clothes will ever be sent to the wash.'[24] She arrived at the Orchard Hotel in Portman Street, where Willy joined her from his club, in time to celebrate her birthday. It was also an opportunity for them to visit friends, Ottoline in particular, tour the bookshops, and there were always letters to write; George never seems to have travelled without her typewriter. Then Willy and Alan sailed from Southampton on the SS *Europa* on 21 October, and George went to Sidmouth to see the Tuckers. '19' (Nelly)

was being sane and sensible bar the fact that she insisted on motoring me to Exeter that I might catch a train which left twenty minutes later than the one I had intended to take from Sidmouth on the grounds that it would bring me to London at nine p.m. instead of at 10 p.m. Actually the train stopped at every station and arrived in London at ten minutes to 11. I examined my conscience severely and finally decided not to tell her; if she does it to anyone else its their own fault for not looking up the train themselves!! She and Harry came to the station (Exeter) and it seemed heartless to write and say 'your train dont arrive at 9 p.m.'.

There was news of young Omar Pound, who was now at school in England. 'Harry is taking his uncle-hood to Omar seriously.'

He solemnly asked me, when we were alone 'At what age did Michael read?' and I said 'about five' upon which Harry sighed heavily, and looked worried and finally said 'Omar cant read anything, he was six in October'. I said 'He has probably decided he prefers being read to' upon which Harry cheered up a little and then got depressed again and said 'he ought to be coerced. He is spoilt.' From what I hear Omar is the most spoilt of all only children, but I am inclined to think also from what I hear that in about a year, or maybe two, Dorothy, who apparently Omar obeys where he obeys no one else, will import him to 'school abroad'.[25]

Despite Harry's concerns, Omar remained in England, and distinguished himself as a teacher and poet; but within months 'Uncle Bunk' himself would be seriously ill.

When George returned to Riversdale and the family on 24 October she once again travelled with animals, this time two kittens. From London Yeats had written to the secretary to the High Commissioner,

My wife, to whom I am dictating, wants to import two kittens into Ireland; one which is for me is a grey persian. She would be greatly obliged if you would send her a postcard to the Orchard Hotel saying if a permit is necessary for such importation. She once tried to smuggle a pug puppy through in her pocket; she had known nothing of the regulation until she reached Holyhead. She was found out, but as it was so small that it had to be spoon-fed the customs at Dun Laoghaire decided that it was 'no dog.'

George was assured that no permit was now required for cats or dogs.[26] Parents and children alike had missed the pleasure of animals when they moved from Merrion Square into the flat. When the little pug (which Anne thought she had smothered in her doll carriage) died of distemper in 1926, he had been immediately replaced by Thor, the large white friendly Samoyed, which Willy had described as having 'a face like the Prince Consort—or a mid-Victorian statue—capable of error but not of sin'.[27] Anne was still small enough to hide under the nursery table when first introduced to him; but by the time they moved from Merrion Square Thor was blind and would never have survived the stairs and new surroundings of Fitzwilliam Square. Now at Riversdale George switched to keeshounds, Dutch barge dogs, all named Ahi—the tradition continues in the family to this day. But the Riversdale bestiary also included smaller animals: Michael was again allowed to keep rabbits (always named Peter and Pamela), whose progeny eventually numbered twenty-three. And Anne once reduced Aunt Lolly to hysteria by allowing her pet mouse to run down her sleeve when they shook hands.

While he was in America George kept Willy informed of the progress of house and family. Both children had been home for their half-term holidays: Anne had grown taller, Michael looked well but was still prone to septic outbreaks. Both sisters-in-law had been invited for overnight visits (separately), and Lolly 'managed to keep off all controversial subjects the entire time, which was remarkable'. As an extra measure of protection, George was arranging for a telephone to be installed at Gurteen Dhas. In turn she and Anne attended a party hosted by Lily and Lolly; then Dolly had stayed a night while Lennox was away. As for Willy's cat, 'he is very affectionate, perfectly square, and since I beat him for trying to pounce on a wren he turns his face away from all sitting birds, this may not last but future smacks await him.' Several weeks later 'The cat continues to be angelic!' but a little too bold:

Last night he could not be found and as it was fearfully wet and a wind that cut one in half was blowing I left him out and left open my half door in the pantry and locked the inner door. This morning again he was nowhere, we all hunted and called, no reply until at last John went into the shed where the chicken food is kept in large bins with very heavy tops. John called, 'miaow, miaow' from a bin! He had somehow managed to get inside the corn bin, although how he had pushed up the heavy cover with his head I cant imagine and the lid had fallen and he was trapped in the corn: A good thing, as John remarked that he hadnt tried the bran bin for it was very full and he would have suffocated very quickly without air. In future that door will have to be kept shut!!

Willy thirsted for all the news. 'I picture to myself the little house in the yard put in perfect order, a playroom there.'[28] George arranged to restore the three lattice-windowed rooms over the stable as soon as possible, much to the children's delight: 'They have their books and toys there and keep the rooms clean themselves, polish the floors and all.'[29] Absorbing as the two kittens were, there were other adventures to relate. To her relief the tenants they had inherited left the gate lodge ('Really God is very good at times') and she and Chrissie gave it a thorough cleaning. Again, ensuring that he was not left out, she sent Willy all the details:

I got Roberts to send out a man to report on the roof etc (for damp) and to estimate for a door to what he called 'the privvy'. The present 'privvy' hath no door and hath been used for a rubbish heap of bycycles [sic] (all broken) disused clocks, jam jars, empty bottles, and portions of bedsteads and mattresses. Question how did the Rileys (our last tenants) manage?! The roof does not need much, chiefly a little pointing, but the gutter system has to be inaugurated for at present the rain has no trap and so gently and persuasively runs into the walls—hence damp.

She was delighted when the young gardener asked if he might move in and deduct the rent from his wages.

I gave him carte blanche to do what he liked with the ground round it, the result was that he spent his last Saturday half holiday with his two immense brothers clearing out all the half cut down holly trees, and the general mess in front. Today he is going to clear some more. Then he plans to 'continue the lawn' down from the cypress trees so that 'the lodge will set off the house'. I think we shall have a model lodge! He is making most of his own furniture—has made a very good kitchen table and a washstand in our tool shed working there after he finishes with us at six p.m. When I first asked him if he had any furniture for the lodge he said 'well, I've got a lot of pictures'.[30]

John soon had it 'like a doll's house with pink curtains and frills and roses and green tubs full of plants.'[31]

Despite her work on Riversdale—'You wont know the house when you come back!'—as always she kept him abreast of Dublin affairs. Each Abbey production was faithfully criticized, and the acting commented on; he was escaping bus and railway strikes. (During the 1930s Dubliners suffered considerably from strikes ranging from rail and bus to laundry and printing, frequently in combination.) The new Governor-General insisted on conducting both private and formal duties in Irish, prompting her to wonder, 'will there be an official Interpreter for the occasions when foreign Ministers visit this country to sign treaties?' She had lunched with the Childerses, where Molly's mother Mrs Osgood announced continually 'that at her age one renounces the world . . . Gosh, what she needs as a preparation for Eternity is a Trappist Nunnery.' And Sean Dorman had grown a moustache, which seems to have become fashionable—'DON'T YOU DARE TRY IT.'

Christmas festivities began with a party at 'the Lennoxes', where George was invited to stay the night. 'I gather that we all stay in bed until at least 11 a.m. on the following day,' she wrote, 'as Sean Dorman will be sleeping in the bathroom and no power can awake him before eleven. I think the guest room, unlike the other bedrooms, *has* a basin and jug in it and if I find it hasnt I shall brush my teeth and wash my face into the kitchen sink! OR yank Sean out of bed. OR bribe Sean to exchange beds. I really don't like to leap into an astonished world as late as all that . . . on Xmas eve . . . when one remembers all the things one has forgotten to buy.' She had not seen Michael for a month, but both children were soon home for their holidays, Anne 'as usual with a sore throat, cold, cough'. By January all three had succumbed to the flu, and George's flow of news was reduced to reports from the newspapers and discussions with 90-year-old Dr Croly from the nearby dispensary.[32] The only consolation was that Nana Reade was free to nurse them.

She signed her letters 'Dobbs', sometimes 'George Dobbs'. Willy in turn dutifully sent postcards to the children, and Alan Duncan regular reports of his employer's health to George. But they were both counting the days until his return. 'I look forward to being home with great excitement,' Willy wrote. 'Perhaps I shall ask you to meet me somewhere, where we can be together for a little without distracting business. I shall deserve that reward if I bring you five or six hundred [pounds].' George replied, 'When you arrive back to Southampton I shall meet you and we can do a little jaunt somewhere—I suggest not London —then you might return here for a few weeks and do your London Academy lectures in April or May. I do think London is much nicer then, also you would be less cold and foggy.' On 9 December she wrote, 'Six days more and you'll be through—unless you give those extra eight lectures. PLEASE dont forget that you must cable the name of the boat that you are sailing on. I would so like to come and meet you.' But Willy stayed on to deliver yet more lectures, and to attend several séances with the famous medium Mrs Crandon. Besides, although, as he admitted, 'I am longing for you & constantly picture our meeting,' he realized that if he returned on 1 January as originally planned 'you will not, perhaps, be able to get away from the children in time'.[33] He knew his wife well.

By early 1933 he was still hoping they could go for 'a few days in some country place. I too count the days, then London for a few days. You must want to buy clothes.' But despite his delayed departure, when Willy arrived in England on 27 January, George was just recovering from an operation 'for acute antrums', caused by the severity of her flu.[34] She met Willy instead at Kingstown. He had brought back 'about £700' for George and £600, 'all the money it wants', for the new Academy.[35] Three days after his return he too contracted the flu, and was bedridden until the middle of February. By early March, however, he had regained his energy: 'I play croquet constantly and can still keep up my dignity by beating the children.'[36] Anne was disappointed to discover that he could also regularly hit the bull's-eye with her air rifle; it had not occurred to her that you only need one eye to shoot.[37] The lease on the Rapallo flat was due, but Ezra arranged for his parents to take it for another year; neither George nor Willy was keen to go to Italy in May to dismantle it.[38]

Willy resumed his 'Mondays' and George reserved Saturday afternoons for her own 'At Homes', which were attended primarily by women who lived nearby. Dolly and Lennox lived close enough to drop in regularly, and Gogarty motored out from Dublin with his usual panache. Despite the distance from the city centre, visitors soon found their way to Rathfarnham: Signe Toksvig —who was surprised to find she liked both Yeatses and Dolly Robinson; the young poet Robin Wilson, George's 'slow-minded' friend; and E. R. Dodds, who brought along Louis MacNeice. Though struck by Willy's elegance, with his 'smooth light suit and a just sufficiently crooked bow tie', MacNeice was disappointed that the older poet talked about the moon and spiritualism, not poetry.[39] Nancy Maude, Dorothy's old school friend who had by now left Joseph Campbell and their bare Wicklow life, lived close by in 'a little red brick villa of the worst style', pleased to be able simply 'to turn a tap'.[40] Iseult was cordially invited to stay the night ('George says she can put you up "at a moment's notice"'); Francis Stuart remembers the 'hothouse degree of warmth' and the 'enormous fur-lined slippers he wore in his study'.[41] George invited Sybil Childers, their colleague from the Golden Dawn, to stay as she did not get along with her sister-in-law Molly.[42] Not all the guests were familiar or distinguished. One August, probably in 1934, she invited a young Waterford schoolboy with writing ambitions to have tea with her husband. 'George Yeats, in a lawn-green dress and bright pinny, opened the glass-panelled door smilingly . . . "You're in beautiful time for tea" . . . reappeared with a tray that was laden with a variety of hillocks: thinly sliced bread; pats of butter; homemade jam; scones with a powdering of flour; iced pastries; and a pot of tea under a cosy'. Willy accompanied the boy to the bus and—doubtless prompted by his wife—gave him a two-shilling piece for tram fare.[43]

Another frequent visitor was Captain Dermott MacManus, formerly an officer in the English army in India, but now determinedly anti-British. Somewhat to George's dismay, although he claimed such activities renewed his verse 'by giving it foundations',[44] Yeats once again plunged into politics, 'trying in association with ex-cabinet minister, an eminent lawyer, and a philosopher, to work out a social theory which can be used against Communism in Ireland—what looks like emerging is Fascism modified by religion'.[45] Yeats's dalliance with Fascism remained largely theoretical, but throughout the summer of 1933 he watched with excitement the growth, under the leadership of General O'Duffy, of the Army Comrades Association, better known as the 'blue-shirts' and later the National Guard. 'I find myself constantly urging the despotic rule of the educated classes as the only end to our troubles,' Willy wrote to Olivia. 'Our chosen colour is blue, and blue shirts are marching about all over the country. . . . The chance of being shot is raising everybody's spirits enormously.'[46] Soon the National Guards started saluting with the straight-armed Fascist salute; shortly afterwards they were banned by de Valera; eventually they formed a coalition with various other discontented fringe parties and in time evolved into Fine Gael. George noticed that when MacManus brought O'Duffy for 'secret talks' with Yeats, 'they spoke on different lines and neither listened to the other'.[47] 'Whether it succeeds or not in abolishing parliamentary government as we know it today, it will certainly bring into discussion all the things I care for,' Yeats declared.[48] It was the discussion Willy thrived on, and Dermott MacManus became a lifelong friend; 'I know no man who in the service of his convictions has lived a life of such danger,' Yeats would later claim.[49] That September all four Yeatses spent a week as paying guests at Woodville Grange, the MacManus family home in County Longford, where George taught Anne and Michael to row on the lake to the rhythm of 'Rabin-dra-nath Ta-gore'. For the rest of his life, when Willy was in Dublin MacManus was a weekly visitor; soon they both became disillusioned with the National Guard, as their interests turned more towards the East.

According to Willy, George always 'hated blue-shirts' but soon became embroiled herself in a neighbourhood quarrel with political overtones. As told by her amused husband, when she caught her next door neighbour's collie in her henhouse and missed a white hen—her best layer—she wrote to complain. 'If they do nothing I will go to the police.' John the gardener returned with word that Mrs Weldon had drowned the collie, and three other dogs for good measure. Horrified by what she had instigated, George was plunged into further gloom when the white hen returned. Willy restrained her from confessing, for 'you feel a multi-murderess and if you write, Mrs Weldon will feel she is'. He insisted that she put the hen into the pot.[50] And the incident took its place in his revisions to 'Three Songs to the Same Tune'—' "*Drown all the dogs*", *said the fierce young woman*'. Whether for this reason or others, George, who 'hated' O'Duffy for whom the three 'marching songs' were written, thought them 'terrible'.[51] But it would not be the last we hear of the Weldons.

In the summer of 1934 Tom MacGreevy passed through with his good friend witty Monsignor Browne; he called on the Robinsons 'who were very amiable', but was told 'the WB's . . . felt resentful about my not calling or ringing up. Can't be helped.' Once he had taken umbrage, Tom found it hard to back down, but 'Father Paddy . . . wanted to see the W B Yeatses so I had to ring them up and we dined there last night and had great wars with W. B. but all in friendliness and urgent requests that we should come again at the end, and appeals to me to stop in Dublin etc.'[52] It would not be George's fault that their relationship remained rocky for some time:

My dear Tom, No you weren't wrong in your memory of the 'laughter-loving side' of my character, where I was at fault was in not dotting the 'I' of the first part of my letter which was an almost exact transcription of a letter I had received that morning from a female to whose house I had refused to go to 'listen-in' to the royal wedding—*And* in leaving you to understand that 'postcard—when there are so many interesting things to be written about' referred to *letters* to George Yeats. I had thought that your postcard was a fore-runner of a possibly renewed correspondence. I dont change much, & in one respect I dont change at all. I dont change towards my friends. Yours affly George[53]

When news reached her that Monsignor Browne was ill, she again initiated a correspondence. 'Yesterday I was talking with Dr Paddy Brown's sister and she told me that Dr Moore thought he would completely recover. I write this to you because I think you may care to hear the latest of him. She told me, what I had not known, that his illness was inflamation of the muscles of the heart. I dont know what news you have had of him, but as I do know that you and he are great friends and that he may have been too ill to write to you, I send this.'[54] Like her husband, George never confused friendship with loyalty, especially in a town where the form of malice was often appreciated more than its accuracy. Once, when defending Gogarty, who could never resist the opportunity to turn a tale for its wit, she was challenged: 'But don't you know . . . that the man is sitting somewhere at this minute saying the most scandalous things about you?' To which she replied, 'And don't *you* know . . . that a man may do that and still be the most loyal friend you ever had?'[55]

More and more frequently, however, Willy had occasion to travel to England, not only to consult with Bernard Shaw about the Academy of Letters, but to further his own theatre plans; he and George both felt that the subsidized Abbey, now so closely watched over by a Board which included government representat-ives, was no longer sufficiently independent or even capable of satisfying his requirements. George also recognized his grief over the loss of Coole, and his need to seek out the intellectual stimulation he had once depended upon there, which Dublin had never been able to provide. But always he was encouraged to follow all the happenings at home. 'Am on the track of a brass-knocker,' he wrote from London in April 1933; she replied by describing how 'terrific' the garden was looking, 'the late tulips have shot up and thickened their buds so that they will be fine when you come back. . . . Next year I shall have about two thousand under the fruit trees which will people that bare space and die down before the trees grow thick in green.'[56] Although George took advantage of Willy's absences to have further work done on the house—repainting the bathroom and 'Aunt Jane' (the water closet); cleaning the outside water tank, etc.—major decisions had to wait for his participation: 'When you come home we will seriously go into the question of the lofts: and when we go into that question we shall also have to see about the heating of the "Vinery". It might be possible to do it quite cheaply.'

While Yeats visited all his pals in London, George enjoyed herself with hers in Dublin. 'Tomorrow, I regret to tell you, I go to Punchestown with Dolly and Lennox . . . . that is because on Thursday last Lennox got a cheque for £400 from Alber Wickes . . . I have insisted that I pay my own expenses; hope to recover them by mug punting of the "blind prick" sort! Added of course to slight following of form and instinct guided by seeing the annimules prancing round the paddock before each race.' Ever practical, she was 'taking a limited amount of cash with fivepence earmarked for my bus fare from Dublin to Willbrook'.[57] Although she usually used the Bible for the 'blind prick' exercise, this time she seems to have opened a book on Indian philosophy, which is underlined at 'The shifting nature of the world conceals the stable reality' and annotated, 'Marked by my wife who had opened the book at random to find what horse would win at Punchestown. W. B. Y.'[58]

George and Dolly frequently went to the movies, with or without Lennox, and all three attended the Abbey and the Gate productions, George forwarding her criticisms on to Willy. They also went as a threesome to parties and even private dances when the occasion demanded, and Lennox and Dolly frequently asked George to join them for dinner when she was alone.[59] But Lennox was now drinking so heavily that it was an increasing worry not only to his friends but to the Abbey; what was worse, Dolly was beginning to accompany him into that slow decline. Both were depressed, and George watched with anxiety the marriage she had had such hopes for. 'I think L. R. is really being very sober,' George reported in December 1934,

I stayed a night there and for the first time for some months it was very pleasant—the two of them were not being on each other's nerves. I didnt naturally mention the theatre to Dolly seeing that L. R. had so recently made the gesture of resigning. I saw her a few days later and she began on it herself and I gathered that they were now discussing together all these things, an excellent sign dont you think? They are having a party (of a large kind) next Saturday. It is to start at 5 p.m. and I am bidden to stay the night which I am doing. I think the less I say about anything the better, so I shall avoid talking about it. You say in your letter 'I have written Lennox a vehement letter which he can talk about if necessary'. Not, I think, to George!

Others also made certain she was entertained, so that even she had to flee Dublin occasionally. 'Last Saturday I went to Howth for the night to Mrs Gasking —when you are away people think I am lonely and entertain me. I told you Sorrento Cottage always asked me when you were away. When we were in Dublin the Dermod O'Brien's used to do it and a couple of times the Marquis

McSwineys.'[60] Ironically, the guest house in Baily was named 'Innisfree', but George and Willy's correspondence ceases to refer to Ballylee. Willy's absence also provided a good time to take care of her own medical problems while he was away: December 1933 marked an unspecified operation which kept her 'delightfully comfortably luxuriatingly in cot' for at least five days.[61] As usual, when Willy returned he in turn came down with a lingering cold and went to bed for six weeks, although this year Anne seems to have escaped her usual Christmas illnesses.

By now Anne had left Hillcourt (where the fees were £120) and was studying art at the Royal Hibernian Academy of Painting, Sculpture and Architecture on St Stephen's Green (where admission was free for students whose work qualified). Unlike her brother, who was an earnest student, although a keen reader Anne had not enjoyed the formal learning process; her passions were drawing and theatre. George was relieved when, given the choice of a year at Alexandra College for the Higher Education of Ladies (which she considered 'genteel and over English') or art school, her sensible tomboyish daughter immediately opted for the latter. And so from January 1933 until March 1936 Anne attended the Academy, spending three hours painting from the live nude model every morning, and another two hours drawing from the live nude model in the afternoons. Only 13, she was younger than the other students by 'at least fifteen years', but was proud that she never missed a day, and received an honourable mention from Beatrice Glenavy, who judged the end-of-term competition.[62]

But while Anne was at art school, George made certain her study of languages and literature continued at home under parental supervision. 'Her sole education is languages, the Academy Art school and my conversation,' wrote Willy (with some justifiable exaggeration) to an old friend.[63] Originally this meant regular conversation and written essays for her father; as for reading, everything but modern novels was allowed, although since Anne found nothing more contemporary than Hardy (from her mother's collection) and Balzac (from her father's) this injunction seemed to her somewhat unnecessary. However each week there were 'fewer and fewer corrections' in the essays she submitted to her father, and soon 'the idea was quietly dropped'. Sometimes she played three-handed whist with her parents, but such recreations were rare.[64] She later described the experiment in learning from Father's conversation:

When I was about fourteen mother decided that father was overworking . . . I was to go in to the study after supper each night and engage him in conversation, a truly frightening prospect!!!! I did try, night after night, but it was to put it mildly unsuccessful, until I hit on the idea of as it were dropping a pebble in the pool, and waiting for the ripples, this was a great success, father talked vividly at length and enjoyed himself. This of course defeated the object of the exercise which was to rest his mind, but it didnt seem to do him any harm.[65]

While he was away, Anne was encouraged to send him criticisms of the plays she attended, especially the Abbey's; Anne's own collection of programmes is marked by her judgement of performers and decor. Yeats was proud of his daughter; 'She & I are close friends.'[66] As always, however, he was cautious about expecting too much of his own children: 'at six or seven she was an artistic prodigy but is now just an ordinary talented art student. I shall know nothing of her for another three years.'[67] Anne would always remember those days at Riversdale where 'all were a unit', for it was now that she got to know her father. It would be another five years before Michael and Willy held similar conversations; for most of his life Willy was to his son 'a formidable, towering figure . . . like living with a national monument'. But as a young boy he sat listening to his father's entertaining conversation at the dinner table, 'wondering whether, when I grew up, I would be able to tell stories as well as he did'.[68] The only occasions Michael recalls of the family out together were the regular visits to the Abbey and 'going home in a horse-cab . . . listening to my parents tearing the night's performance to shreds. The acting, the direction, the play itself, were all condemned.'[69]

Anne was also being trained in other ways: she lunched (baked beans on toast, buttered bread, and tea for 1s. 3d.) at the 'DBC' in Merrion Row every day except Monday. On that day she went for lunch to great-aunt Fanny Gordon at 26 Morehampton Road, taking the precaution of eating her usual lunch beforehand; her elderly cousins were unfamiliar with a young teenager's appetite.[70] In the autumn of 1933 Charles (Charlotte) Lane-Poole, cousin Ruth's eldest daughter, came from Australia to spend a year with aunt Lily. The 20-year-old Charles immediately became a regular at Riversdale, young enough for a close friendship with Anne, yet old enough for George to ask her assistance in tending to children, and even, when necessary, Willy. From now on Lily's weekly report to Ruth showed her brother's family through the lens of the beloved Charles: 'she spent the whole of yesterday at Willy's, deputed by George to give Willy his lunch and see him to the bus and to look after Anne, who had a painful little operation on her nose the other day.'[71] George too was delighted with this 'remarkable' young woman, and suggested that Charles join Anne for lessons in French and German; one arrangement with a tutor from Trinity College abruptly ceased when Charles informed her that he received his young charges in his pyjamas.[72] At other times Charles was invited to adult gatherings with Lily, George, and Willy. (One advantage to all her older relatives was that Charles had her own car.) Soon Anne had 'given up all her other friends for Charles'. In July 1934 they went to the west of Ireland, visiting Ballylee on the way to Galway and the Aran Islands; George did not give them a key, and they were unable to get in.[73] The following summer they went riding in Wexford.[74] George was pleased to see Anne with someone older and sensible, but even so once had to chastise them both for sitting through the film of *The Scarlet Pimpernel* a second time without paying.[75]

Much in love with Shakespeare and a regular theatregoer, Anne had created a model theatre of her own, serving as director, designer, actor, and dramaturge of 'The Pegasus'; not only Charles but her brother, mother, and friends were drawn into the company. 'Anne has roped Michael into theatre work,' George informed Willy.

He suggested she should stage a scene from the Merchant of Venice and has in consequence found himself set down to learn five parts and use a different voice for each! He also re-set all her electric lights with proper bulb holders so that the bulbs can be changed for coloured light if necessary. The present programme is Merchant of Venice and Dark Lady of the Sonnets . . . We have arranged the old tent poles so that it is possible in two minutes to put them together and have the whole end of the nursery curtained off with an opening for the theatre itself. I dyed old sheets black for curtains.[76]

When Charles returned the following year to embark on a landscaping course at the Glasnevin Gardens, Anne postponed her birthday celebration so that she could be present for a new production.[77] Clearly George agreed with Dr Montessori's method of 'self-motivated education', or as Willy had put it in 'Among School Children', 'the best modern way'. Despite her training in independence, George kept a wary eye on her daughter, who was still young enough to ease out of homework; when both parents were away she was not allowed to stay out at Riversdale with the servants, but sent to Gurteen Dhas. 'Anne is very merry and quick and much more affectionate since Charles came,' Lily noticed. 'She is very intelligent and deals with Aunt Lolly with a firmness that is very amusing.' 'Lolly used to begin in the evening her usual exhausting restlessness and complaining. Anne, very irritated, used to run at her, take her shoes off, tickle the soles of her feet and also rumple her head. Lolly is very ticklish and was helpless.'[78]

Their daughter was also, however, to receive all traditional rites including confirmation, apparently more at Willy's wish than George's. 'George is quite aloof from it all,' her sister-in-law noted. 'It is Willy that insists . . . and he is quite right.'[79] When godmother Lily searched out her own confirmation veil for Anne's acceptance into the Church of Ireland, George was dismayed at what was expected, 'Good Lord, must she have a white dress and veil?' She was frank about her attitude towards organized religion; of a successful Abbey production (*A Saint in a Hurry*) she complained, 'I DO not like the play. Production good, scenes good; but unadulterated religion and self-righteousness all through for nearly three hours, with my joy in religion and the only sinner not enjoying his sin, is unbearable.'[80] However, her daughter unwittingly delayed the ceremony until Easter of 1935:

There was a circular Summer House beside the lily bed where I used to read, once when I was reading Balzac's Peau de Chagrin (The Wild Ass Skin) I forgot to go to the vicarage for my weekly confirmation class, when I remembered, I cycled down to apologise to the Rector Canon Sullivan, who said 'Thats all right Anne', but a day or so later he told mother that he didnt think that I was 'Quite ready' for confirmation and that we would leave it until next year, so I had all the lessons to do all over again. I suspect that he had never heard of 'The Wild Ass Skin' made enquiries and decided that it was thoroughly immoral.[81]

Somewhat to her parents' surprise, Anne requested permission to become a Girl Guide. As a member of the Robin Patrol of the Rathfarnham Church, she eagerly attended the weekly meetings, proudly wearing her uniform, which soon had many badges. (Lily thought Anne, usually careless of dress, looked much better in uniform.[82]) Knots were a special love, and she could soon tie fifteen knots blindfolded; but when Anne asked if George would serve as patient while she practised bandages for her first aid badge, George, still pained by memories of her wartime nursing, refused. Even the Guides could however become a political landmine. Anne was hurt by Gogarty's outspoken disgust on seeing her dressed for a meeting, but she herself recognized a greater problem when Lady Shaw of Bushy Park offered to present the local troop with a Union Jack. Anne wisely consulted her mother; Willy wrote in protest, and the flag was neatly stored on a church cupboard shelf. Its location was eventually discovered many years later by none other than Gráinne Yeats.[83] By the time Anne was 16, art and theatre had become one. In August 1936 she was hired by the Abbey as assistant to Tanya Moiseiwitsch, the theatre's first full-time professional stage designer, and in addition joined Ria Mooney's school of acting in the Peacock Theatre.

Michael meanwhile was living with some thirty other young boys in the nineteenth-century castellated country house of Baymount in Clontarf. Surrounded by fields and gardens, the school like l'Alpe Fleurie emphasized fresh air and exercise, but it was also academically respectable; Michael soon became a member of the spelling team, which routinely gained first place in competitions with British schools. Like his mother he enjoyed films, and gained great popularity as a narrator of the plots he picked up during summer outings with George. By the time he left Baymount in July 1935 he had also became interested in politics; as 'a committed de Valera republican' among boys destined for English public schools and the British army, he was a distinct minority.[84] Since he had little conversation with his father at this age, apparently neither recognized how opposing their views were. However, noting this new interest, from about 1933 on George used her influence to get the highly coveted tickets for attendance at the annual Budget Speech in the Dáil. She was also pleased to see that unlike his sister he was making friends at school, 'though that may be because the boys at Michael's school are on the whole a more intelligent lot than Anne's girls were'.[85] He became proficient at chess, urging his mother to play with him; one of the few occasions he recalls when George was visibly angry with him was when—seeing his future advantage—he attempted to dictate her next move.[86] But to his great regret he was never allowed to study music—perhaps because Anne's violin lessons ceased when her teacher found she could not tune her instrument. His sister later claimed her only successes were curing Michael of an irritating habit of drawling by imitating him on her fiddle, and frightening the junior children at school by imitating ghostly sounds on the E string.[87]

'My son aged 12½ toils through the ordinary curriculum and will go to St Columba's in a year or so and then to College,' Yeats had written of their agenda for Michael.[88] It would not have occurred to his parents that there was any alternative to boarding school. Attendance at private schools was not only customary for the middle and upper classes, for their son it was a guarantee of the kind of training which was expected of a gentleman and a scholar. Such was the division in Ireland, the schools had to be Protestant, which inevitably meant pro-British; even Trinity College now admitted many Roman Catholic students, and at this stage neither George nor Willy was keen on the possibility of mixed marriages.[89] Then too George recognized that Michael had not inherited his father's self-sustaining poetic nature and was convinced that he needed formal education. She may also have felt that her beloved son required the masculine environment provided by his teachers; certainly his absent-minded (and increasingly absent) father could not serve as a role model. But such was the habit of privacy in the Yeats family, neither Anne nor Michael would have spoken of any unhappiness at boarding school. His mother would have been devastated to learn that Michael in particular resented school regulations that forbade him cycling the short distance to Riversdale from Columba's on any but the few allowed holidays. He vowed that none of his own children would be sent away from home.

And so in September 1935 Michael was once again a college boarder, albeit much closer (about three miles) to home; he stayed there until entering Trinity in the autumn of 1939. St Columba's College, again a Church of Ireland school, was perched 500 feet up on the side of Two Rock Mountain; adhering strictly to the public school tradition, although classrooms were heated, the dormitories were not. Growing fast and still susceptible to colds and septic outbreaks, Michael would spend considerable time in the dispensary, where he had plenty of company. Despite, perhaps because of, their diverging political views, his best friend throughout his college years was Brian Faulkner, who would eventually become Prime Minister of Northern Ireland. Insisting that Willy visit the school, George took him to meet the warden, Revd C. W. Sowby, 'who was remarkably impressed by the practical tenor of his enquiries on sanitation, ventilation, heat and so on, until Mrs Yeats, who was walking behind . . . called out, 'Don't mind him, he is only showing off.' '[90] It is probably just as well that George had not heard the recollections of an earlier boarder, Sean Dorman, Lennox's nephew, especially the game in which the boys cycled down the long steep hill to the college without using brakes.[91] Although he does report having attended a cricket game to watch his son play, that was probably the only official visit Willy made, for he did not care for Warden Sowby. He and George both preferred to consult Michael's room teacher, George White, who was once invited to Riversdale to discuss their son's future. But it was with George that the master normally discussed Michael's performance, and Mr White 'came to have a great admiration as well as affection for her'.[92]

Meanwhile life at Riversdale continued to bring pleasure. Both children were accustomed to the mixture in their father of practicality and absent-mindedness, delighting in one story in particular which has now gone into the annals of Yeatsiana. 'Apart from his regular periods of work, my father might begin the process of composition at any time,' Michael recalls.

All the family knew the signs, we were careful to do nothing that might interrupt the flow of thought. Without warning he would begin to make a low, tuneless humming sound, and his right hand would wave vaguely as if beating time. This could happen at the dinner table, while playing croquet, or sitting in a bus, and he would become totally oblivious to what was going on around him. One afternoon my sister, Anne, got on a bus on her way home to find the poet already sitting in a front seat, obviously deep in the throes of composition. So she left him alone and took a seat near the back. In due course they both got off the bus at the family gate and, as they went in, he looked at her vaguely and asked, 'Who is it you are looking for'?[93]

At other times he could be disconcertingly observant. Anne remembered once being in his study, her clothes in a considerable state of disrepair, her fingernails —as George would put it—'in mourning' from the day's play or gardening. 'Father looked at me thoughtfully and said that perhaps brightly coloured patches would look good on my clothes, and another time he suggested that I should paint my finger nails with gold paint (this at a time when to paint your nails with even pink varnish was to be considered "fast").'[94]

Inevitably he and George related their children's preoccupations to the astrological and Dionertian predictions: 'George said it is very strange,' he wrote to Olivia when Michael was 13 and Anne 15,

that whereas Michael is always thinking about life Anne always thinks of death. Then I remembered that the children were the two dispensations. Anne collects skeletons. She buries little birds and beasts and then digs them up when worms and insects have eaten their flesh. She has a shelf of very white little skeletons. She has asked leave to go to the geological museum to draw skeletons. Then she loves tragedies, has read all Shakespeare's, and a couple of weeks ago was searching the reference books to learn all about the poison that killed Hamlet's father.

He then added a postscript: 'When George spoke of Michael's preoccupation with life and Anne's with death she may have subconsciously remembered that her spirits once spoke of the centric movement of phase 1 as the kiss of Life and the centric movement of Phase 15 (full moon) as the kiss of Death.'[95]

When the children were home there was much croquet at which Father was frequent victor, and in between both kept active. George was 'always very busy with her flowers'; on a visit to Oxford Willy sent her 'a new flower in the College garden . . . a blue poppy which has just arrived from China'.[96] Lennox recalled Willy's childlike delight in the fruits of his own garden. 'Eating roast beef I remember him leaning across the table to his wife and gravely enquiring, "*Our* horse-radish, George?*" to which she would as gravely reply, "*Our* horse-radish, Willie".[97] When away he contemplated the changes he would find: 'Have you had the Aviary made? That is one [of] the events I look forward to.'[98] George dutifully provided all the 'newses': 'a vast quantity' of sand and slates had arrived in preparation for work on the courtyard; Seán O'Faoláin was back in Ireland; a biography of Constance Markievicz was being written—did Willy have any memories?[99] When home, his wife's efforts at farming sometimes evoked a mixture of pride and wry amusement. 'George is facing a dire domestic perplexity,' he informed the always receptive Olivia. 'In her energy, which never abates, she has increased the number of our hens & now there is an overwhelming deluge of eggs. It is no use selling them for owing to the English tariff you can buy them for eight pence a dozen, and there is no use preserving any more, all possible bowls and tubs are full.'[100]

Willy was again writing verse, his first since Lady Gregory's death; this pleased George, who was even prepared to put up with his dalliance with Fascism if it resulted in new poems. Fascism in turn was interpreted through his continuing work on the system. 'I send you a typed copy of the suggestions for discussion which I have made out,' Willy wrote to the 'ex-cabinet minister' (Desmond FitzGerald) in his small discussion group. 'I have purposely left undeveloped section IV. We would probably develop it differently and I don't want to press my own conclusion. What I think most important is to preserve the dynamic element of Fascism, the clear picture of something to be worked for. We have to take everything we legitimately can from our opponents, to ask ourselves for instance how much even of the materialistic theory of history we can re-state & absorb.'

Although he did not speak of his wife's involvement, section IV of his document, entitled 'a new philosophy', bore familiar overtones of George's script and reading: 'Though the conflict of positives is true it is not, any more than the dialectic of Hegel, a solution of the antinomies which are insoluble by the human intellect, though they are solved in the heroic life, in the saintly life, in the work of art. Practical result. The Fascist philosophy is accepted but there is something in man, which lying deeper than intellect, is not affected by the flux of history.'[101] A letter to Olivia that summer echoes George's response to his *Window-Pane* commentary: 'History is very simple—the rule of the many, then the rule of the few, day and night, night and day for ever, while in small disturbed nations day and night race.'[102] His experiences in New York seem to have once again confirmed his belief in the supernatural. 'When I saw at Mrs Crandon's objects moved and words spoken from some aerial centre, where there was nothing human, I rejected England and France and accepted Europe.'[103]

After Willy's return from London and just two days after Michael had gone back to school, George once again produced a page of automatic writing, which included the instruction 'Read again . . . think it out' and, on a second sheet, 'I have no message I want to go home.'[104] Six months later, after years of silence, Dionertes returned. 'George three nights ago lit incense,' Willy wrote on 17 October 1933.

I did not ask why nor perhaps did not know. Presently she went into trance and Dionertes came, giving sign. He insisted on being questioned. I asked about fifteenth multiple influx. He said 'Hate God'. We must hate all ideas concerning God that we possess, that, if we did not, absorption in God would be impossible . . . Later on George went two or three times into momentary trance and always to repeat 'hatred, hatred' or 'hatred of God'. I was, the voice once said, 'to think about hatred'. What seems to me the growing hatred among men has long been a problem with me.[105]

This may have been the encouragement Yeats needed to complete *A Vision B*, for by the following January he had 'faced at last and finished the prophecy of the next hundred years'. 'Now George's work begins,' he wrote to Olivia, 'to draw the diagrams—and the book is done.'[106] But as usual he was overly optimistic. Two months passed before he alerted his publisher that he could expect 'in a week or two' the typescript, suggesting that it accompany his *Collected Plays*. 'It is a book which will be very much wanted by a few people—I get letters already asking for it—but will puzzle the bulk of my readers. I want it to be taken as a part of my work as a whole, not as an eccentricity.' Harold Macmillan replied immediately, suggesting *A Vision B* be published in the spring of 1935, but after reading the manuscript he admitted to Yeats's agent that 'the subject matter of the book is one that makes a very limited appeal. To most ordinary minds it appears to be quite mad, and I cannot believe that the sale will be anything but a very small one.'[107] (Evidently his publisher had never read the first version.) The 'arbitrary, harsh, difficult symbolism' of his revised philosophy still did not satisfy him, but at last it was over, and he could return to poetry—or so George hoped.[108] Again she rejected the dedication he had drafted as early as 1931: 'To my Wife who created this system which bores her, who made possible these pages which she will never read & who has accepted this on the condition that I write nothing but verse for a year.'[109] He was also distancing himself in terminology from their notebooks: 'I have constructed a myth,' he pronounced of this revised version, 'but then one can believe in a myth—one only assents to philosophy.' And he was reconciling himself to the fact that 'I shall have a few very devoted readers . . . Perhaps if I recover my health and am not too poor I may travel to meet such men.'[110] Instead, promise of such an encounter arrived in the post.

Yeats first heard of Shri Purohit Swami from Sturge Moore, who was aware of the Indian's lectures in April 1931; on his next visit to London Moore introduced the two men and Willy, after casting his horoscope, immediately encouraged him to write his autobiography.[111] Shri Purohit, who cautiously consulted an astrologer as to how long his friendship with Yeats might last,[112] started on the task at once and so eager was he to consult Yeats that George had to send him a telegram (signed 'Secretary') to prevent his arrival at Fitzwilliam Square.[113] The manuscript arrived while Willy was still at Coole; he found the first instalment 'beautiful', while the second 'overwhelmed' him so much that he gave it to Augusta Gregory to read. 'I am perhaps particularly susceptible to the kind of emotion it arouses & need her confirmation of my belief for as I said "it seems to me one of the great books of the world".' As he had advised Synge many years before, he added, 'he should not be afraid to describe any supernatural events *which he has himself seen*. You said he left some out.'[114] The relationship between Sturge Moore and the Swami would become a thorny one, and on his next visit to London in April 1932 Yeats found himself playing the mediator: Moore had taken umbrage at a well-meant but—to western eyes—insulting gesture of dividing a fee as thanks for his editing. 'You cannot imagine how much silly boasting I have cut out,' he complained to his old friend; but Willy was determined to accept the Swami as unique, possibly in his own way a saint.[115] Perhaps he had at last found a mortal being with the wisdom of Dionertes. 'When I spoke of certain events in the poem as symbolic,' he explained to Shri Purohit, 'I did not mean that they were not also real. I know several cases where an event was brought about by spiritual powers to symbolise certain doctrines.'[116] And he enthusiastically enlarged to his learned doctor friend of the Swami's qualities: 'He is a true Indian saint and monk, having upon his forehead the Indian stigmata (the little mound that is probably on the forehead of your Buddha).' To which Sturm scathingly replied, 'the lump on your Swami's forehead appeared to me to be a small wen or cyst and not a stigma. There is a chakra between the eyebrows, but it is deep in the head and is not physical.'[117]

Olivia was not too sure about the Swami's genius either, although she found him 'a Pet—& so engagingly simple—outwardly, not at all the professional saint'. But on the excuse of reporting to Willy, she attended many of his lectures, even taking along friends such as Eva Ducat. 'I feel I may be sailing under false colours with all these people, because I am *not* a convert, tho' very much interested.' 'They don't seem to realize that I am a sheer Agnostic & don't believe in anything —though of course I think anything is possible. I listen to everybody, & wonder how you can all believe the things you do! And all different things.'[118] She herself was 'getting tired of Yogis & unbelievable miracles', but although she disapproved of 'the pack of silly women' who attended his lectures, she found his philosophy 'hard & relentless & logical' and would remain a concerned friend to the Swami until he left England.[119] The fly in the ointment was the Swami's close companion, Gwyneth Foden, who insisted on serving as his hostess and jealously guarded her charge. Olivia was blunt in her dislike: 'She is what I call "twittery" & an egoist; & talks too much about herself.' As the Yeatses and others would eventually discover, many of her tales were false, such as the addition to her name of an appropriated title, the published claim to be 'the only European woman ever permitted by the Hindu priests to dance in their temples', her life-threatening mysterious illnesses, her own threats of suicide, perhaps even the child she claimed (to a select few) to have had by the Swami.[120] George became increasingly dismayed at the energy her enthusiastic husband devoted to correcting the Swami's prose and writing lengthy introductions to his books. But despite Olivia's distrust and George's displeasure, Willy continued to find the Swami's talk 'very luminous', visiting him as often as possible on his trips to London, and—although once incautiously describing her as a 'Cleopatra of the suburbs'—was inclined to excuse his companion: 'She is good hearted & her vanity is on the surface so one forgives her.'[121] That tune eventually changed, but certainly Gwyneth Foden was generous to a fault (providing she had her own way), and over the next few years George and Willy would both have reason to appreciate her practical assistance.

The Swami's autobiography, *An Indian Monk: His Life and Adventures*, was published by Macmillan in November 1932 with Yeats's introduction. 'Very interesting, but rather unbelievable,' Sturm commented. 'Yeats goes in off the deep end. He will believe anything, provided it is strange enough.' Sturge Moore was still nursing a grudge, and on receiving his copy wrote to Shri Purohit, 'Had I not cut out huge portions of your M. S. your book would have given you away, and would not even have deceived Yeats who had set his heart on it, and on the picture which it draws of Indian life, as he confesses. He always attributed any remonstrance I made to my resentment.'[122] Undeterred, on his return from America Yeats read the Swami's translation of the adventures of his master, Bhagwan Shri Hamsa, and devoted many months to condensing the narrative and writing yet another introduction. George was distressed, for his introduction had taken seven weeks, and this may have been one of the reasons that he could not ask her 'to be my typist in the case of this essay because it would induce somnambulism'. But the essay, he told Olivia, 'has grown to have great importance in my scheme of things'.[123] He was especially intrigued by one particular concept which reminded him of George's 'sleeps': 'I think we both mean the same thing about "dreamless sleep",' he explained to the Swami. 'The sleeper has no wisdom but he is lost in the abyss of wisdom.'[124] After he had tactfully deflected the Swami and Mrs Foden from their choice of title ('Love's Pilgrimage' 'would suggest to the public a sentimental novel'), *The Holy Mountain* (his own suggestion) was published by Faber and Faber in September 1934, with a considerably longer introduction by Yeats.[125] 'I do not find anything the matter [with] the Swami's book, it is his master's book that is incredible,' he protested at Olivia's criticisms. 'I have so many wonders that I have gone completely to the miracle workers.'[126] As thanks the Swami sent him a copy of his translation of the Gita and, not to be outdone, Mrs Foden made a gift of a green sari for George.[127] Recognizing the inevitable, George had decided she should meet the Swami herself on her next visit to England. 'George, by the by, wants you to arrange for her to meet the Swami & I had better not be there,' Willy appealed to Olivia.[128] But the meeting was delayed, ostensibly because George had to see to some new boots for Michael, mainly because Willy's blood pressure was once again dangerously high. It would appear that George and the Swami (and Mrs Foden) did not meet for at least another year, by which time he and Willy had begun to discuss working together on a translation of *The Ten Principal Upanishads*. George would always begrudge the time her husband spent rewriting the Swami's English, time that would have been better spent at his own creations, especially given the precarious state of his own health.[129]

She may have had even deeper fears of the Swami's influence: in his being encouraged to devote the remaining years to the study of another's words, did she not recall Willy's early eager response to the automatic script, offering to spend the rest of his life piecing together the system? That previous commitment had already taken him sixteen years and the end was still not in sight. But at least the 'mythology' he then constructed had led to deeper poetry; and it had a ground bass of their shared wisdom. The Swami on the other hand was leading him away from her. And in her opinion he was no substitute for Tagore. Soon Yeats introduced MacManus to the Swami, explaining that 'He is interested in Indian thought, more perhaps in Hatha yogi than Raja yogi but is learned and sympathetic'; together under the Swami's tutelage they studied the Yoga-sutras and Tantra or the 'Higher Hinduism'.[130] George made her feelings known in other ways: 'It is a remarkable thing,' Willy once told his typist, 'but whenever I read the Swami to my wife she falls asleep.'[131] Obviously the threat of somnambulism could cover a range of needs. By the time she did meet the Swami, other factors had made her situation even more complicated.[132]

In 1934 they were seeing WBY's *Collected Poems* through the press. Willy was also writing the next instalment of his memoirs, the first chapters of which were 'sensational and exciting and will bring George much household money when she sends them out to English and American magazines'. So busy was he with the Swami and other projects, however, that *Dramatis Personae* would not be published by Macmillan until May 1936. The thrifty George farmed out sections to the *London Mercury* and the *New Republic* even before Lolly produced her Cuala volume in December 1935.[133] But Shri Purohit still pressed for attention. Neither Willy nor George had been able to suggest an acceptable biographer or editor for Lady Gregory's papers. 'You need not be afraid,' Willy reassured the

Swami. 'I shall not begin my life of Lady Gregory until I have written my essay for you. I hope to begin the essay, or my preliminary study for it in a couple of days.'[134] In any event, the projected life was reduced to a section of his own memoirs. His nine-page introduction to the Swami's two-page translation of the 'Mandukya Upanishad' duly appeared the summer of 1935—a harbinger of greater things to come.[135]

Other 'mysteries' followed George and Willy through these years. In March 1933 Erik Palmstierna and Adila Fachiri, neither of whom had 'ever attended spiritualistic séances or experiments of any kind', started experimenting with 'the glass game'. Adila's sister Jelly d'Aranyi was then summoned by the unknown messenger who eventually identified himself as Robert Schumann; he was determined to have his missing 'D minor Concerto', which Joseph Joachim, Clara, and Brahms had suppressed as unworthy, played by Jelly. By July great-uncle Joachim had suggested through the glass that the missing manuscript might be found in Berlin, and a month later Baron Palmstierna 'discovered' it in the Prussian State Library. Although the story would not be made public until 1937 when permission was finally given to copy the manuscript, Palmstierna had been a guest at Willy's birthday luncheon party in London in June 1933. It is highly unlikely that the experience was not related to a sympathetic audience which included other believers such as Sturge Moore and Dulac, or that Jelly's dear friend Nelly would not have been told.[136] Later Palmstierna published further accounts of the work he and Adila continued to pursue.

Also in 1933 Willy started to see apparitions, which returned at least ten times. The first was 'the passage of a coat hanger slowly across room—it was extraordinarily terrifying'. By November the apparition had come a seventh time—'a child's hand and arm and head—faintly self-luminous—holding above . . . a five of diamonds or hearts.' Did it promise five months or five years? 'Five years would be about long enough to finish my autobiography and bring out *A Vision*.' By the time it made its tenth and last appearance he saw 'in broad daylight, an arm waving goodby at the edge of a screen beside my door'.[137] Such reminders were cause for further frustrations, for somehow in the past four years, ever since Spain and Rapallo, one of the greatest mysteries—joint sexual satisfaction—had been lost. In August 1933, while correcting the proofs of his new book, *The Winding Stair*, Willy had confessed to Olivia that he found the 'Crazy Jane' and other love poems 'exciting and strange. Sexual abstinence fed their fire—I was ill yet full of desire. They sometimes came out of the greatest mental excitement I am capable of.'[138] That desire had never left him, and ever since facing certain mortality in this first serious illness, Willy had become more sexually demanding. But as his demands increased, George—amidst the worry and exhaustion of her husband's recurring illnesses, the children's needs, even the restoration of Riversdale—found herself less and less able (or willing) to meet them. Was she simply too tired? Or had the temptation to seek solace in alcohol, the threat hanging over her all her life—the dependency inherited from father, grandfather, and even great-grandfather—already begun to take hold? Apparently she was betraying a lack of sympathy in more public ways, or at least it seemed so to Willy. By 1935 Willy confessed to Iseult that 'everything was terrible. He and his wife had gradually been alienated—he said she was a mother rather than a wife—that she had humiliated him in public.' In relating this incident to Ellmann years later, Iseult generously added, 'But George must have put up with a lot.' And when Willy remarked, 'If only you and I had married,' she burst out with, 'Why we wouldnt have stayed together a year.' Iseult did not tell Ellmann whether Willy had confided in her about George's drinking.[139]

Letting go—when did it begin? As early perhaps as 1933, when George was simply too tired for sex. Perhaps even earlier, for little by little, once the great shared work was done, her role had dwindled to copyist, editor, housekeeper, and nurse. While still in Cannes she had told Lennox, in a rare burst of self-pity, that 'they could have jointly a nurse a governess a secretary & a housekeeper & all get on so much better'.[140] Although her native cheerfulness and energy had gradually reasserted itself once Willy recovered, the stresses remained. For the Rapallo experiment proved to be a transition period in more ways than one. Willy's series of illnesses and the shock of her little son's condition had not only exhausted George physically, but drained her emotionally. Her marriage from the start had pulled more out of her than even she thought possible. Now, while Willy bounced back with the famous Yeats vitality, she had not the same store of energies to draw upon. Survival became a day-to-day process, as she channelled her strength into doing what had to be done. The fun of 'keeping all Willy's irons hot' had dissipated; all that was left was watching over his health and business affairs, and caring for Michael and Anne. More and more the children had to be considered. In addition, her own health was draining her; the arthritis that would later cripple her had already taken hold. And much as her husband remained the focus and *raison d'être* of her life, she could no longer meet all his physical needs. Many years later Charles Lane-Poole would recollect that although she had always considered the Yeatses' marriage a happy one, there was no sign of 'touching' or warmth.[141] When her father-in-law had first heard of her family's tendency to alcoholism, he had reassured himself that George 'has lots of self control'; he could not foresee the stresses her marriage would generate.[142] Whereas a 'gin and it', or their favourite wine, or even Hauptmann's champagne, had previously served as a mild stimulus to after-dinner conversation with Willy and banter with Lynx, now alcohol served to dull the senses, damping down the very awareness and memories she had cultivated for their philosophical forays. Increasingly that physical dependence on the rush of energy had to be fed by 'pink ladies', 'brandy Alexanders' (especially once her ulcer started bothering her), even whiskey in her tea.

Willy himself was suffering from impotence both sexual and creative; ever since Lady Gregory's death and the loss of Coole he had been alarmed by how little poetry he was writing. 'For a year now I have written little but prose, trying for new foundations.'[143] He was also becoming more emotional—almost at times sentimental. 'I have a longing for remote beauty,' he admitted. 'I have been reading Morris' Sigurd to Anne and last night when I came to the description of the birth of Sigurd and the wonderful first nursing of the child, I could hardly read for my tears. Then when Anne had gone to bed I tried to read it to George and it was just the same.'[144] When it finally came, the burst of energy produced a new harshness and impersonality that startled his friends and even himself. Generous and understanding though he was, Dulac refused to write the music for the new dance play *A Full Moon in March*, finding the 'love and blood' theme unpleasant: 'the Queen is not remote enough and the swineherd too vehement, they seem to have been forced into a kind of realism that is out of tune with the otherwise symbolical spirit of the play . . . the power behind the point is let loose without restraint . . . one has the feeling that the emotional impulse has run away with the hand that should direct its course.'[145] And his old friend AE on receiving a copy of *The Winding Stair* asked, 'Why do you growl about your age when you never were so vital in youth? . . . actually you seem more packed with psychic vitality than you were forty years ago.'[146]

This time, however, the vitality was surgically induced, and would prove only partially successful. Concerned about his impotence, Yeats had been told of a surgeon in London who was a specialist in the Steinach 'rejuvenation' operation. There had been considerable publicity over previous experiments with pig testes and goat or monkey glands, but this procedure was far less invasive, consisting of vasoligature and vasectomy in the belief that this would stimulate production of male sex hormones, hence 'reactivation' or 'rejuvenation'.[147] Developed by the Austrian physiologist Eugen Steinach, the practice had become so popular in the 1920s that even Freud had undergone the operation. It has been suggested that Sturge Moore, who was operated on by Geoffrey Keynes, first introduced the subject to Yeats, but it seems more likely that he heard of the procedure in June 1933, and discussed it with his good friend Dulac.[148] Back in Dublin Willy and George proceeded to carry out their own research, based primarily on a book (*The Conquest of Old Age*) which described the procedure and included photographic evidence of the positive effects on a number of patients. They also looked up in *Who's Who* the London surgeon known to have performed the operations, Dr Norman Haire, and probably read his own study, *Rejuvenation*, published in 1924.[149] A sexologist, gynaecologist, and obstetrician, Haire originally came from Australia, and after settling in England in 1919 became active in the birth control movement. Within two years he was writing about the work of Steinach and from there moved to numerous lectures and publications on marriage, sexual knowledge, and sex ethics. His own philosophical position is summed up in *Hymen, or the Future of Marriage* (1927): 'Just as a piano needs tuning so that it may give the sweetest music, so I believe, our sexual morality needs readjustment—a little loosening here, and a little tightening there—if individual and communal life is to be as harmonious as possible.' He was also in favour of legalizing polygamy.[150] Haire's conclusions about the vasoligature suggested that there were no ill effects, and although not universally successful, when it was, 'may lower high blood-pressure; increase muscular energy; stimulate appetite for food; relieve insomnia and indigestion; cause improved nutrition of skin and renewed growth of hair; improve power of concentration, memory, temper, capacity for mental work; and possibly increase sexual desire, potency, and pleasure'.[151] What more could a 69-year-old poet ask for? Especially one who was convinced that poetry and potency were directly related: Ezra promulgated and even George's discarnate Instructors had emphasized the essential link between 'creative genius' and 'sex intercourse', and one of the characteristics of the unhappy Hunchback (phase 26) was that he suffered mental distortions due to repression or distortion of sex.[152]

Yeats was back in London again in December 1933, and may have consulted the Australian miracle-worker then. Finally, after another postponement due to illness, he and George travelled to London in April 1934, when the operation was performed in the Beaumont House Hospital. George, who had left the children in the charge of Charles and the servants, stayed with him for almost ten days before feeling confident that all was well. But having returned to Dublin in stormy weather, she fretted about his weakened state:

I wired to you today 'all news good' adding that the Abbey made a profit of £83 . . . If you are able to see Macmillan on Tuesday or Wednesday I imagine you will travel Thursday night staying at Queens Hotel Chester the night. Dont forget to wire for room. WHY DONT YOU GET A SLEEPER FROM LONDON TO CHESTER? Dont think of the fifteen shillings! It would be well worth it for the sake of being able to lie down. You ought to arrange at once for your reservations. Send me a wire saying if you start Wednesday, Thursday or when. Hope you are feeling better on your legs today. I had a fearful crossing—had to hold on to prevent falling out of my bunk, but was not seasick at all. This wind will have blown itself out by the time you start.[153]

Willy returned to Dublin on 20 April, and was soon back to his usual routine, playing croquet, correcting proofs for the de luxe edition, and optimistic. 'I am out in the garden at a little green-baize-covered table the gardener has carried out for me. It is too soon to know whether I have benefited by the operation but I feel as if my blood pressure was down—I am not irritable and that is a new event.'[154] A few days later he told his publisher, 'That operation has almost made me a young man. I do not yet know how it has affected my blood-pressure, but it has given me back my energy. I no longer feel myself at the end of life putting things in order or putting them away. They say that I shall lose this first stream of vitality in a few weeks and then recover it in greater measure.'[155] But much to George's relief, he refused to accept the presidency of the Swami's newly established London Institute of Indian Mysticism.

Only Olivia, Harold Macmillan, Lennox, and the poet Fred Higgins (who was involved both in Abbey management and the Academy) had been officially informed. 'I will tell nobody,' Olivia had promised. 'The Swami is coming to tea tomorrow & is sure to make enquiries about you, but I'll lie to him!'[156] However, as George once said to Tom, 'Dublin has a million tongues and I am sure some of them will blab.'[157] Word soon got round town of the 'gland old man', doubtless spread by both Higgins and Gogarty, who was miffed that he had not been consulted. Yeats 'has undergone Steinach's operation, and is now trapped and enmeshed in sex', he wrote to an American friend. 'When I parodied his poem into, "I heard the old, old men say Everything's phallic"', little did I think he would become so obsessed before the end. He cannot explode it by pornography (as Joyce) or jocularity as I try to do.'[158] Certainly either Haire or the operation itself had loosened Yeats's tongue and increased his interest in sexual matters; probably a combination of both, for with the frank, outspoken Australian he had discussed not only his inability to have an erection—a condition which apparently the operation did not correct—but his distress over George's lack of interest in their sexual relationship.[159]

Another phase of their lives together was also ending. On 5 June, once George was convinced that Willy was fully recovered, they left by Cork and Cherbourg for Rapallo to hand over the flat to the senior Pounds and pack up their furniture. It would be the last time George, Willy, Dorothy, and Ezra would be together. As was to be expected, the meeting between the two poets was a mixed blessing: Ezra's response to Willy's new work (*The King of the Great Clock Tower*) was summed up in one word, 'Putrid!'; it was written, he expanded, in 'nobody language'. Already fearing that he 'had grown too old for poetry', Willy was at first deflated, then rose to the bait. When the play was successfully staged at the Abbey later that year he made certain Pound received the newspaper accounts,[160] and when Cuala published the text in October, his preface included Pound's judgement. George was no doubt more concerned by the Pounds' enthusiasm for Mussolini and the economic theories of Social Credit. And, suffering from chronic rheumatism, she hurt her back while packing up the flat. They returned by way of London, where Willy visited his friends while George went directly to Sidmouth to see her mother.

Olivia, Dorothy, and Omar soon joined her there, but a more welcome and unexpected visitor was Grace Jaffe (née Spurway), who had come from the United States to spend the summer with her mother, now widowed and also living in

Sidmouth. Grace remembers a long private conversation with her beloved older cousin over tea, during which George told her that she had given up her occult activities because it was 'bad for the children'. To her cousin's disapproval, she persisted, however, in her belief in astrology.[161] There was more need than ever for George's regular visits to Nelly, for the previous year Harry Tucker had shown the first symptoms of 'softening of the brain' and arteriosclerosis, probably the condition now diagnosed as Alzheimer's disease. He recovered sufficiently from his first attack, which had been shocking because of its accompanying violence. But 'the old days are gone, never to return, when we were "happy as the days are long"', Nelly wrote to Tom. 'He has received great care & his memory is uncertain, though his mind is still active & he is himself a marvel of goodness & patience in spite of much distress about his memory & head noises.' Even though she found her husband's brain 'still vastly superior to most of the brains I'm in contact with', she admitted she was 'a soul in hell'. Although like her daughter she took comfort in her garden, as 'valet, nurse, & constantly on duty' she could not leave Harry for long, even to enjoy her 'one abstraction', contract bridge. Fortunately Jelly d'Aranyi stopped by in Sidmouth fairly often on her tours, and these concerts were supplemented by an excellent wireless.[162] Trying to convince herself that her brother's condition was 'all lack of proper circulation—& not his brain', Olivia frequently stayed in a nearby hotel; though sorry for her sister-in-law, she found her 'tiresome'. 'I am worried about Nelly, who is always on the verge of a breakdown—according to her own account,' she had written to Willy in May, but 'one doesn't know what is play-acting or what is true'.[163]

It had been a decade of loss for Nelly: two of her aunts (Nelly Munn of the travelling bathtub and Agnes Steeds of the egg-flips) had died in 1924 and 1925, followed by her mother after a late reconciliation in 1927; her brother George remarried in Canada shortly after, and Nelly was concerned about his first wife and their children, one of whom was permanently in a mental institution. Her nephew Billy Spurway had died in a flying accident, and the history of her niece Annie Spurway, Grace's sister, was somewhat bizarre: in 1924 she had married her own great-uncle, who died in strange circumstances seven years later, and Annie herself was mentally unstable.[164] George and Ireland seemed 'farther off than ever!' Nelly complained to Tom. A copy of his poems which she had just received produced the outburst, 'I have no use for "God" in the Person Singular . . . Art made the Gods. . . . in the Arts alone can we find our salvation, whatever it may lie.'[165] By February 1935 Nelly was told by her doctor to go away alone for a fortnight.[166] Although she was herself unwell, the advice may also have been protective, for Harry was beginning to lapse occasionally into the violent condition that would eventually require permanent hospitalization. But for the next few years George would find 'Bunk' on the whole pleasant, if erratic both physically and emotionally.

Grace remembers that George spoke of her own concern over Willy's health. His blood pressure was high once more, and his London doctor had advised injections—which she was to give.[167] Evidently the Steinach procedure was not as efficacious as they had hoped. The summer was spent quietly at Riversdale, their major excitement the arrival of furniture from Rapallo. 'We put that wardrobe you made a design for the embroidered doors of a few years ago into my son's room,' Willy told Sturge Moore. 'I was in the room yesterday and found it more beautiful than my memory of it. It has now got the exactly right surroundings.'[168] There was the annual summer party at Gurteen Dhas, at which both brothers made an appearance; the success at the Abbey of *The Resurrection* and *The King of the Great Clock Tower* with striking costumes designed by Dolly (but Joseph Holloway noticed that Yeats was walking lame[169]); the Horse Show, to which George treated Lolly; a printers' strike that cut off all newspapers; and laundry and train strikes threatened, although still there were the usual summer visitors. George lovingly tended her garden, but Willy was restless; his letters to Olivia included more and more outrageous tales of others' sexual adventures. Of his new poem 'Ribh Prefers an Older Theology' he wrote to her, 'The point of the poem is that we beget and bear because of the incompleteness of our love.' He then added, 'Strange that I should write these things in my old age, when if I were to offer myself for new love I could only expect to be accepted by the very young wearied by the passive embraces of the bolster. That is why when I saw you last I named myself an uncle.'[170] He returned to the theme two months later when speaking of his introduction to *The Holy Mountain*: 'There are moments when I long to escape from this practical life—Academy, theatre etc—that I might go to see the one or two people who understand such things and begin again my old spiritual adventures.'[171] Instead, still seeking the 'Beatific Vision', he embarked on a search for the spirit through the flesh.

The journey to Rapallo had retrieved fragments of their past; the next led to a new pattern for their future life together. Early in October 1934 George and Willy were once again on their way to Italy, this time to Rome where he had been invited to speak at the Fourth Congress of the Alessandro Volta Foundation. Most of their expenses were paid by the Italian government, and George left Anne at Gurteen Dhas. Yeats's own lecture was on Ireland's national theatre, but he created more stir when as chairman he cut off Marinetti, founder of Futurism, unaware (or having forgotten) who he was or what he was saying; George in the audience was helpless to rescue him. When the conference ended, George stayed on in Rome and then went on to enjoy the mosaics in Ravenna; she did not return to Ireland until 20 October. Even that visit was not long enough; years later she would write to Tom, 'It does seem very hard for you to get five days in Rome instead of Lallapaloozing there for weeks—That is what one needs there. To be blindfolded for three days for every day one looks.'[172] Willy meanwhile went eagerly back to London for the first of many romantic assignations.

Yeats had met the poet and actress Margot Ruddock on 4 October; she had written to him several times proposing a project dear to his heart, a poet's theatre. In arranging that interview, he had written, 'Do not think that I await our meeting with indifference. Shall I disappoint you or shall I add to the number of my friends?' He could not have been more ripe for a romantic adventure; the day after they met she was 'My dear Margot' and he had arranged to have a copy of *An Indian Monk* sent to her. From Rome he wrote again to arrange a meeting, explaining that 'my wife stays on and then goes straight to Ireland'; he was already rewriting *The King of the Great Clock Tower* 'giving the Queen a speaking part, that you may act it', but he also saw her as a replacement for Florence Farr Emery as speaker of his verse.[173] It was not long before they were lovers. Margot was 27, fifteen years younger than his wife; he was nearing 70.

Yeats stayed on in London until the end of October, excited about the possibility of a 'poetical theatre', his committee Ashley Dukes of the Mercury Theatre, Rupert Doone of the Group Theatre, Dulac, and, although he had not yet named her to George, Margot. 'Organizing is like a bumble-bee in a bottle,' he wrote to Riversdale to explain the delay in returning. 'One tries all directions until one finds the neck.'[174] He had however introduced Margot to the Dulacs—who cast her horoscope—and the Swami—who borrowed money from her. He was also staying in 'a little self-contained flat' at 44 Seymour Street, managed by a Miss O'Dea and recommended by Margot; the cost was 'little more than half' what he paid at the Savile Club, and it had the added attraction of privacy.[175] 'I hope you are progressing with your theatrical schemes,' wrote Olivia, 'your renewed activities are most interesting—I should not perhaps say "renewed" but "accelerated"—Don't you feel rather as though you had been wound up again?'[176] Once back in Dublin, he flung himself into Academy matters, writing his new play for Margot, advising on her own poetry. His letters and poems were revealing; clearly he would never take to heart John Quinn's motto, 'Never fornicate through an ink bottle.'[177] Still excited by the clandestine nature of his affair, he was receiving Margot's letters at the Kildare Street Club, but that was an inconvenience. 'Write an occasional letter to me at Riversdale. . . . My wife knows that we work on the theatre project. It is more natural if you write there.'[178] Worried that 'this nervous inhibition'—his impotence—would return and make him an unsatisfactory lover, he was plunged into 'utter black gloom'; but by now George was far more aware of the situation than he guessed, and called in Gogarty as entertainment for him. Willy on his own consulted Dermott MacManus, who claimed to have 'cured himself' of impotence by Oriental meditations. Willy was sufficiently careless in other ways, telling Margot, 'you are of course at liberty to tell any intimate friend you can trust'.[179] Perhaps aware of the dangers of his situation, especially Margot's high-strung impetuousness, he wrote a new will— his last—again appointing George the sole executor. By 6 December he was back in London and with Margot. Dulac, with whom they dined, wrote to him, 'Let me say again how happy we are at your happiness.'[180]

Left to tend to affairs in Dublin and ensure a happy Christmas for their children, George faithfully reported on the Abbey—the houses were small but the acting, costumes, and with one exception the setting of Lady Gregory's comedy *The Canavans* delighted her and Dolly both: 'the house rocked with laughter. I didnt much like the setting for the Mill room. It was all painted like brand-new pitch pine though not so yellow, which somehow looked wrong when they speak of the "thatch" overhead.' But a week later she was 'disgusted' by a new play, *At Mrs Beam's*, 'to the roots of my soul both by the play, by the acting . . . and the scene'. In Riversdale there was also a new production of Anne's 'Pegasus Players'. The sisters-in-law were duly entertained to lunch on Boxing Day: 'Charles may have a "hunt" but for my own sake I hope not for if she comes I can more easily separate off the controversialists.' And the turf fire side of his study had been 're-yellow-washed' by John. She was also practising her Italian by attending society meetings. Most important, Michael had done 'very well' in his exams.[181] But she was now writing to Willy only once a week.

'Are you back?' Willy wrote to Olivia in late December, 'Wonderful things have happened. This is Bagdad. This is not London.'[182] Once again he harked back to *The Arabian Nights* for romantic parallel. Baghdad was entered through Harley Street, where Yeats was receiving daily injections from Dr Haire in an effort to 'get [his] body back to the normal'.[183] If the consulting room, with its 'silver ceiling and walls hung with exquisite Chinese embroideries on silk', was exotic, Haire's dining room was even more so, 'with highly coloured dragons writhing like vorticism-gone-mad all over the ceiling. More silken tapestries here, too, and in the drawing-room, where an almond tree blossoms in paint on the ceiling.' Willy was invited to a formal dinner, where another guest was the writer Ethel Mannin, as free a soul in her own way as her host. Her good friend Haire, she wrote approvingly, was not only 'the most infallibly amusing person' she had ever met, but 'believes in the right to be happy, not merely as a theory, but as a practical working philosophy of life'.[184] A *bon vivant* in every other way, the doctor was a teetotaller, and so at the end of the evening Willy and Mannin had adjourned to her flat for burgundy. She remembered his vivacity and excitement at this first encounter: 'Open another bottle, child!'; she was only eight years younger than his wife. Whether engineered by the sexologist, or initiated by Mannin, the relationship deepened into a sexual one, and within days Willy was writing in gratitude to his new friend: 'My Dear Your serious & kind letter has come. We probably wrote at the same time but you will not get mine till tomorrow for I delayed the posting of it. You are right, the knowledge that I am not unfit for love has brought me sanity & peace.' Later she would admit that 'the operation didn't give him the new lease of vitality he had hoped from it', although she 'did [her] best for him'.[185] But for the time being, Willy felt he had been blessed; one letter ends with the words, 'Mother Goddess I put your hand to my lips.'[186] They met for his 'beatitudes' at Seymour Street until he returned to Dublin. A dinner arranged for her to meet the Dulacs, however, was not a success; Willy fell asleep in the host's chair. Ethel did not care for the Swami either, and although 'the temple & the mystic ceremony' seem to have occurred infrequently, they remained good friends for the rest of his life—if occasional argumentative ones, for he consistently resisted her attempts to draw him into political debate.[187] Despite his excitement over these encounters, he was, he told George, 'sorry to be delayed in London for I am getting homesick'. By 7 January 1935 he was 'homesick, idle & tired, longing for garden, canaries, country roads, Higgins' stories, etc.', but Norman Haire had done him 'much good', and he was happy.[188]

Whatever the London adventures, his longing to be at Riversdale seems to have been genuine, for he was also exhausted, and once again within days of his return was ill in bed with a fever, coughing up blood. Aware of his distress over not being able to communicate with Margot, George wrote privately to Dulac, 'Willy returned with a chill—very cold journey from London and is now recovering from a congestion of the left lung—you might pass on this information (*as from yourself*) as letters are being looked for and have not arrived. From which you can gather that he has discoursed largely on the subject. He is getting well, but it may be rather slow, by that I mean that he won't be out of his room for another week. Love to both from both.' Edmund replied immediately, thanking her less for the medical report than the tacit recognition and generous understanding of his support in Willy's amorous adventures. It was just as well that the projected season of plays in London had to be postponed.[189] George also recognized her husband's delight in intrigue, and doubtless watched with some amusement Willy's efforts to conceal from her his amorous correspondence with both women ('I go to a dentist tomorrow and so can post under no eye but my own'; 'Write here and as you will, there will be no accidental opening'; 'I thought it unwise to leave on the hall-table letters, which might become a theme of domestic meditation').[190] To Mannin he described his situation: 'Cough—cold—eggflip—sleep—exhaustion —temperature—doctor What more is to be said.'[191] By the end of January his condition was so serious that the new young doctor at Rathfarnham grew alarmed and called in reinforcements, thereby plunging Yeats into further gloom. In order to use a portable X-ray, 100 yards of wire had to be run from the gardener's lodge to Willy's bedroom; John Free, Lily reported, 'was immensely pleased and very proud'.[192] That accomplished, George turned once again to Gogarty:

I cannot telephone to you because every word I say can be heard by WB. in his bedroom. He had a 'relapse' on Sunday night. Yesterday, Monday, Dr Shaw (51 Rathfarnham Rd.) brought out Dr Stewart with his portable X Ray apparatus. Today at 2.45 p.m. Shaw told me that the print showed not much of a serious nature in the left lung but showed a considerable enlargement of the heart. What I want you to do, if you will consent, *is to allow me to ask Shaw to consult with you* as 'you are Willy's oldest friend in Ireland & know him physically & *temperamentally* better than anyone else.' . . . Dr Shaw asked me to get from Carnegie Dickson the X Ray that was done in London Oct–Nov. 1929. I expect to get this print tomorrow. If you will allow me to make the suggestion to Shaw, I would like to ask you to see Shaw when this No I X Ray comes Will you phone to me?[193]

Years before, when they were both members of the Golden Dawn, Dickson had thought Yeats tubercular; he told George that the 1929 X-rays had disclosed 'a great many healed spots which made him think his original conjecture very probable'.[194] Congestion of the lungs could well mean permanent weakness and a loss of the much-prized new-found vitality.

George had other equally pressing reasons for seeking Gogarty's co-operation, and fearing not only Willy but the telephone operators listening in (as they sometimes did),[195] she was compelled to put them in writing. In the heart of her letter (marked 'Private') she outlined with extraordinary pitiless honesty her blueprint not only for Willy's remaining years but her own: 'I do not want Willy to be made an invalid ["&" struck out] or a fool. I think too that *if* any of these things are serious, I would rather he died in happiness than in invalidism. He may not have told you of all his past 18th months activities. One of them is that he has been very much in love with a woman in London. I tell you this that you may understand why I am most anxious that he should not be tied to an unnecessary invalidism.'[196]

George sometimes charged her husband with ruthlessness;[197] now she applied the same harsh pragmatism towards her own situation. Certain that Gogarty had broadcast the 'humbug' Steinach operation, she could be equally sure that he would turn his witty rhyming spotlight on Willy's folly. And so, just as she had appealed to Gogarty's quickness to deny the rumours circulating when Willy was ill in Rapallo, she now enlisted his sympathy and understanding of the role she herself had chosen to play. 'After your death,' she would later say to her husband, 'people will write of your love affairs, but I shall say nothing, because I will remember how proud you were.'[198] But what would history say of her part? Would she appear the foolish bystander, a deserted helpless Griselda, or worse still, his unfortunate 'procuress'?[199] George was a proud woman; the struggle for due recognition would bother her for years to come. But she would have to deal with that problem later. Now she had to concentrate on keeping not only the poet's dream but the poet himself alive. The admission to Gogarty was also a plea for Dublin's understanding; there was more poetry to come from that well. She was well aware that in making herself vulnerable, she put her identity as Mrs W. B. Yeats in jeopardy. Although Gogarty was never the most discreet person in whom to confide, she had no other choice.

But George was too astute not to recognize her own responsibility for the path they were now on. Had she not rescued their marriage and ensured the continuation of his poetry by encouraging this belief in the relationship between creativity and sexual satisfaction? Again, when the stream was dammed after Augusta Gregory's death, she had once again built a congenial ambience within which he could write, but Riversdale had not been enough to release the flow. She had supported the Steinach operation not so much for its sexual promise as for the intellectual excitement it might produce—and eventually did. She no longer felt capable of providing the physical relationship he so desired; now she must face the full consequences of that release. For fifteen years she had been able to provide all he needed—far more than 'a small old house, wife, daughter, son, | Grounds where plum and cabbage grew' which he had described in a late poem.[200] Had she allowed herself to age too quickly? Willy's new loves were both younger than she, Mannin by not that much. Ironical that Lennox had written jokingly of his recovery in Rapallo, 'Its a mercy anyway that Willie is being a little human again and eating and drinking—but you needn't hope he'll really take to either drink or women, he's terribly Protestantly virtuous.'[201] No one would have guessed that first serious illness would lead to his impotence, George's exhaustion, and the current situation.

But in condoning Willy's infidelity was she not also simply accepting the temper of the times? The conservative attitude had been that Edward should not have renounced the throne for Mrs Wallis; mistresses were an acceptable part of life's pattern—look at the history of royalty, even of her own grandparents. Even so-called 'idea' plays on the London stage—Shaw's *The Apple Cart*, Maugham's *The Constant Wife*—accepted the social hypocrisy. But George had little sympathy with anything that involved the break-up of families. Upon learning that Betty Duncan had eloped for a second time, leaving children behind, she had replied acidly, 'I dont feel any enthusiasm over that sort of thing. And it wont last I imagine any more than the previous efforts. One hopes she wont have a third family! Who is going to pay for the Goldrings? Or do they just go on the rates?'[202] Her own mother had resolutely stayed within marriage for—among other reasons —the sake of her children, and so would she.

After all, there had always been other women in Willy's life, celebrated in the personal poetry she so valued. Maud was easily put in her place—an icon kept alive by the very poetry she had engendered. By her own actions Iseult had removed herself from the centrality of Willy's life; though still firmly in his affections, she was no longer a serious threat to their own partnership. The complexity of his relationship with Olivia was a different matter: George had known of that close friendship since she was a child; it had sustained him through numerous love affairs and strengthened their marriage. With that other pillar of stability gone, Lady Gregory of Coole, Olivia's ironic self-imposed detachment was even more necessary to Willy. And she herself could count upon Olivia's support and encouragement. Ethel Mannin she would never meet, nor apparently did she want to; she could be dismissed as a necessary accomplice of Norman Haire. But Margot—that was a different matter. How far would her headstrong poet go?

'I don't expect he will be able to get to London much before the middle of March,' she wrote to Edmund at the beginning of February. But the same day he suffered another collapse brought on by a lengthy visit from Margaret Gough's solicitor; Margaret refused to recognize the codicil in which Gregory had left publication of manuscripts to Yeats's discretion. There were other projects being planned. 'Several Dublin societies are preparing for my next birthday,' he wrote to Mannin. 'The alarmed secretary of one has called upon my wife: "O Mrs Yeats don't let him slip away before June." '[203] The Swami meanwhile was trying to keep excitable Margot calm. 'I have requested Margot to control herself when she sits on the committee, listen to all what they say by one ear, and leave it out by the other, till you come here. She confessed that it is very difficult, but I told her that hence it was worth doing.'[204] As always, Olivia thought of George's situation: 'What an anxiety for George—I hope she isn't worn out. I suppose you had a nurse.'[205] But as always, the burden of care had fallen on her; there is no reference to any other nurse. By early March he was correcting proofs, playing croquet, sending poems to Margot, and reading Balzac and *The Arabian Nights* daily. Economically he sent the same quotation from Scheherazade to both Margot and Ethel, recommending it as a motto for 'a very advanced book upon the education of children': 'it is not shameful to talk of the things that lie beneath our belts.'[206] But he admitted that the collapse had strained his heart. After a few hours of work, he told Olivia, 'George comes and says "That's enough serious literature" and puts "a wild-west" into my hands. "Wild-west" is the only form of popular literature I can endure. Like the old writers its writers live with the visible and so help rather than injure my own literary sense.'[207] George would later advise a hostess, 'I find the only way to make him rest is to plant him in a room by himself with a detective story and leave him sternly alone.'[208]

Willy was not well enough to leave for London until 24 March, this time taking rooms in Seymour Street opposite Miss O'Dea's. The rent including breakfast was only £2 a week, but there was no gas fire and he quickly caught a chill; he held off seeing a doctor for three days, determined to arrange the London production of his plays and see Margot. Ethel Mannin was in Monte Carlo with 'a friend'. 'My visit here was necessary—there were things I only could decide,' he wrote defensively to George on the 30th, and five days later insisted that he was well enough to dine with the Dulacs and 'get that star-map for Anne'. Although George had parcelled up the items he had forgotten to pack, she was not writing as regularly as he wished. He continued to address her so, but she had stopped signing herself 'yours ever, Dobbs', reverting once more to 'George'.

When she did write it was to caution him against travel over the Easter bank holiday weekend. 'I think you are right. Certainly today I feel very unfit for the journey,' he replied, then added, 'Why don't you come over & have a week or fortnight of London & put me into better spirits.' Mrs Foden was going to Russia and had offered him her flat at 19 Lancaster Gate for three weeks. 'I could not put you up but we could ask friends there—there is a great handsome room.' By 10 April, acknowledging her letter about the proofs of *A Vision*, he was more urgent: 'I hope I shall hear that you are coming over.'[209] None of George's letters in this exchange survive but, with Anne and Michael home for the Easter holiday, she would doubtless have been reluctant to leave them. Uneasy about his condition, however, she sent a prepaid telegram to which he replied, 'Nearly well again. Yeats.' 'The "Yeats" made her shout with joy,' Lily reported. 'There she had her man. No other man would so end a telegram to his anxious wife—and then all the 8 paid for words wasted.'[210] By mid-April he felt well enough to write an essay and pursue the theatre project: 'This is a good day. I have climbed the stairs without getting out of breath. All last week I was crawling about & panting.' He assured George that he was 'reasonably happy' and still 'without my wild desire to return to Dublin at all costs—probably the prospect of that big room next the Park. I am well enough to look up my friends.' He did not admit that the doctor was still visiting him daily to administer injections. However, within days of moving into Mrs Foden's flat, 'a great room with Chinese tapestries', he was again coughing up blood and Dulac was sufficiently alarmed to telegraph for George. Once again George had to set everything aside, and before the end of April was in London.[211] This time she seems to have felt confident enough to leave Anne and Michael at Riversdale with only the servants to watch over them—Mary Martin, 'a steady, reliable woman', and John Free the gardener. The family rallied round, Lily and Charles motoring over regularly for tea; Lily thought that in time Anne would become a better hostess than her mother, who 'gets shy'. Then, as their mother's absence continued, Willy's cousin Violet Gordon took over, looking after Michael's clothes when he returned to Baymount for his last term, then taking Anne back with her to Morehampton Road.[212]

Although the laboratory report found no traces of tubercular bacilli, Willy would not be well enough to return to Dublin with George until 9 June.[213] When Gwyneth Foden returned—she was expected back on 12 May—they moved a few doors away to 17 Lancaster Gate Terrace. By mid-May he was well enough to receive visitors though still not going out, and he immediately wrote to Sean O'Casey, who had extended the olive branch of sympathy earlier that year. As usual he had his own private agenda—a production of *The Silver Tassie*—but charmed O'Casey by asking his advice on other literary and theatre matters. The Abbey had been closed since December, and with Lennox more and more often incapacitated, Yeats was determined to revive it by inviting fresh blood onto the

Board and gently ousting Robinson by hiring a producer (preferably Irish) from England. The new Directors, who included Fred Higgins, Brinsley Macnamara, and Ernest Blythe (all chosen by Yeats), were determined not to be taken in by his 'craftiness, . . . the complexity of his mind, . . . his capacity for using people for his own ends'—the ruthlessness of which George accused him.[214] As usual, however, Yeats had his way: the young Englishman Hugh Hunt (recommended by Masefield) was appointed managing director, by the end of the year bringing over as designer the even younger Tanya Moiseiwitsch, and O'Casey was charmed into giving the Abbey his play. Four months later, while on a brief visit to Dublin, O'Casey lunched at Rathfarnham and played the inevitable game of croquet with Yeats. He would conflate the discussions of these two visits in his autobiography:

At Lancaster Gate, Mrs G. Yeats was there watching over her famous husband. Pushing death away from him with all the might in her little hands. Anxious that he should not do too much. When dinner was on the table, she left the two men alone to eat it, and Sean felt the lack of her quiet charm and her good looks . . . The room seemed to be thronged with poem-books from all persons; while on the mantelpiece lay a pile of Western Tales of cowboy and Indian chief, sliced here and there by a detective story, which were there, he told Sean, to ease a mind tired and teased with a long concentration of thought on the imagination of others.

The younger playwright watched with alarm as talk brought on a coughing spell. 'The cough shook the fine frame of the poet again; the breast ebbed and flowed spasmodically; and the fine hand grasped the arm of the chair with tenseness . . . —It hampers me, this, he said, in little gasps; comes on so often, so often.'[215] *The Silver Tassie* was produced at the Abbey Theatre on 12 August, leading to a controversy which gave Willy much joy and George more worry.

Meanwhile there was a backlog of work and correspondence to deal with; as usual the typewriter seems to have travelled with her. Friends such as Ottoline Morrell and the Dulacs came to Lancaster Gate, and this is probably when George finally met the Swami. George enjoyed a flutter on the racecourse with Helen and Edmund Dulac ('Robin Goodfellow' yielded 'wicked but nevertheless fortunate winnings'); but when Ethel Mannin came to dinner she disappeared.[216] Willy's excitement over Margot appeared to be ebbing, doubtless due in part to his debilitated state and Mannin's return to England. But now a new project engrossed him, reviving the sense of partnership with his wife. Oxford University Press had commissioned him to prepare a new anthology of modern verse, and both he and George plunged into an orgy of reading, 'finding wonderful things'. Poetry, he decided, 'has become philosophical and profound in the last ten years'.[217] He was also discovering new poets, one of whom especially intrigued him. They discovered that Ottoline knew Lady Dorothy Wellesley sufficiently well to take him down to her country house in Sussex.[218] From Lancaster Gate Willy wrote to

Ottoline, 'The idea came into George's head—she was out shopping—& into my head—I was here—that I must have this book which contains Lady Dorothy's latest work. Ten minutes ago George arrived with her copy, five minutes ago Bumpus messenger with my copy. Did the thought first come to me or first to George? Which transferred to which?'[219]

Anne remembers that such coincidences occurred frequently in Dublin; her parents would not have considered them mere accidents. Nor would Yeats consider his meeting with Dorothy Wellesley anything but preordained. 'I wish I knew some benevolent hostess or cheap lodging, for I long for conversation on something else but politics,' he had lamented after Gregory's death. Thanks to *The Oxford Book of Modern Verse*, that wish would finally be granted.[220] That his hostess was the Duchess of Wellington was an added boon; perhaps the atmosphere of Coole might again be created. On 3 June he and Ottoline went down to Penns in the Rocks, Dorothy Wellesley's home in Sussex. As usual, George made the arrangements. 'In haste!' she wrote to 'Dear Ottoline'. 'I hope you will be able to stay at Withyham on Monday—*NOT* because Willy needs a "nana" but because he needs your genius for finding the stimulating thought in conversation. Yours ever George Yeats. Your parlour maid has just telephoned to say that you *can* go on Monday. I am so glad. I wire to Lady Dorothy Wellesley; so do tell me on the phone when you call for Willy on Monday.'[221]

George may have taken this opportunity to visit Nelly in Sidmouth. But despite her concern over the children in Dublin, she also enjoyed being back in London. As always she went to the cinema:

George made us all laugh the other evening with her account of a cinema she saw in London. They have places where you pay 7d and just see a newsreel. She got the Jubilee procession and doings, and somehow it was shown before the Royal Censor had seen it. She saw the King putting down his coat at the back with both hands as he got out of the coach at St. Paul's while the queen gave him a vicious look. Then on the balcony at Buckingham Palace Princess Mary's boy scratched his head. The Duke of Kent blew out a great sigh of weariness, and the queen poked Princess Margaret Rose into good behaviour. She saw the same film some days later, all these homely human touches gone. The audience, she said, laughed hard.[222]

Buoyed by the success of Willy's overnight visit to Penns, they returned to Dublin on 9 June, in time to prepare for the celebrations around Yeats's seventieth birthday. George invited Lily and Lolly to dinner on the 13th, and Michael had permission to be home for the day; Jack, Cottie, Charles, and Violet Gordon came in the evening. Never one to miss a detail, Lily described the occasion: 'He got 42 cables and telegrams, £10 to buy a present from an American, some brandy bottled before Waterloo from an English admirer, an original Blake drawing from English writers and artists, all their names in a vellum book. . . . We had duck and green peas, meringue and cream, coffee, and champagne to drink Willy's health. Jack was in good talk and so was Willy, full of plans and hope and life, and looking handsome, which is an achievement at 70.' A public dinner given by the PEN Club with 250 in attendance took place in the Hibernian Hotel on 27 June; George bought enough tickets for all Willy's relatives. 'It was a proud evening for the Yeats,' wrote Lily. 'Aunt Fanny was quite overcome, and I thought that stoic George was also.' Anne, given her first 'perm' for the occasion, was less happy seated next to the Swedish Consul. She kept her annotated copy of the menu: 'Peas' instead of the French beans; speeches by Hackett, WBY, Masefield, and O'Faoláin 'interesting', Desmond McCarthy 'dull'.[223] The unflattering newspaper photographs of the dinner indicate that George had little time to attend to her own appearance: John Masefield, who was representing the English authors, brought his wife with him; not only at Willy's insistence did George have to rise early to meet them early that morning (and see them off the next), but she gave up her own room and slept over the stable.[224]

Willy was still far from well; 'congestion of the lungs has left me an enlarged heart,' he told Mannin. What was worse, his young doctor had enjoined 'for the present' complete celibacy. He would obey until he could see Norman Haire, but he was convinced that he had been worse before the operation.[225] With George's approval he refused an offer to receive an honorary degree from Harvard and lecture there for a term; 'forbidden all bodily & mental activity' and 'denied all exercise except croquet, the first command from a doctor that has given me unmixed pleasure', his plans to return to London and Sussex that summer were also abandoned.[226] Then there was another blow with the death of AE, his oldest friend; Yeats's encouraging telegram arrived the evening before Russell's death in Bournemouth, 'and it pleased him very much'.[227] A massive funeral took place in Dublin on 20 July; along with other members of the Academy of Letters, Yeats met the steamer at 6.30 a.m., then joined the mile-long procession to Plunkett House in Merrion Square and on to the service and the graveside, where Frank O'Connor spoke on behalf of the Academy. Afterwards he swore to George that he would never have 'the sort of funeral AE had': Gogarty's aviator friend Lady Heath organized a flight of three civil aeroplanes who dipped in salute over the Royal Mail boat; when there was talk of the Irish tricolour being spread on the coffin, Yeats declared, 'if this was done he would snatch it away with his own hands'.[228] Willy was depressed for weeks, refusing to attend the annual summer party at Gurteen Dhas, fearing that his old friend would be talked of. 'I am suffering at present from AE's funeral,' he admitted to Dorothy Wellesley. Recognizing the depth of his loss, George pierced the gloom by recalling his own poem 'The Choice', declaring that 'AE was the nearest to a saint you or I will ever meet. You are a better poet but no saint. I suppose one has to choose.' There would be no 'heavenly mansion' for Willy, but he could strive still for 'perfection of the work'.[229]

He and George continued work on 'our' anthology; George selected the poems from his own work, a list Willy approved of with the exception of 'Three Things', which he insisted be included.[230] Even Anne was sent down to the summerhouse to read through three volumes of Alfred Noyes—who did not make the cut; there would be further trouble over that particular poet.[231] Willy was amused by George's dismissal of Edna St Vincent Millay whose poetry, she claimed, was 'all hot lobster and mountain tops'; he thought that her description 'perfectly expressed what Eliot, Doone, perhaps Dulac, think of romantic acting and poetry. . . . the Elizabethans were full of "hot lobster" ', but he also admitted that his own *Shadowy Waters* probably deserved the phrase.[232] 'Have you forgiven me for my long silence?' he wrote to Margot in mid-July. 'I could hardly help it, illness reducing my working hours, and then that great mass of letters, at first those that had come while I was ill in London.' He was considering whether she should be included in the anthology: 'I would like to take the opinion of one or two friends. I like you too much to be a good judge.'[233] Whether George was consulted we do not know, but he and 'Lady Gerald' were now corresponding regularly, about both her own poetry and the anthology. George, he wrote, had tears in her eyes when he read out Wellesley's poem 'Fire'.[234] A warm invitation to Penns now included George and Anne: 'My daughter (sixteen) longs to know your daughter (sixteen). Could she come too?' George could (or would) not come, 'she will be engaged with my son's birthday and other matters'.[235] 'Other matters' included a journey to England with Michael to make up for Anne's travels with her father;[236] few people recognized George's innate shyness.

Willy and Anne left Dublin on 13 August; they stayed at Penns for ten days. It was Anne's first visit to a 'great house' and she found it 'very intimidating'. She was also embarrassed by her clothes, which had been made by a dressmaker under Violet Gordon's supervision earlier that summer, 'clothes the wrong length the wrong shape and made apparently of checked chintz like chair covers'. Although much to her disgust relegated to the nursery (where 'they played awful music all day and talked of things quite unknown to me'), the other girls seemed in her eyes to be sophisticated and worldly. But her misery evaporated when costumes were rooted out: Anne chose 'a pair of black slacks, a white shirt, a man's top hat and a tall walking stick . . . I looked very smart, I felt terrific and very happy.' Willy disapproved of the trousers, but was pleased that his daughter 'beat Victoria's greatgranddaughter at croquet'. The other highlight for Anne was seeing Rex Whistler driving away in an open motor car 'covered all over with splashes of paint like a palette'.[237] On her return to Dublin Lily noted approvingly that her niece, 'looking a handsome girl, her hair well arranged', seemed finally to have 'begun to treat her appearance with respect'.[238]

From 'this delightful place, where there is fine talk & beautiful gardens', Willy wrote reassuringly if somewhat naively to George, 'Anne is very happy—there are two girls of her own age. Last night however she played crocket [*sic*] with Lady

Dorothy myself & two grown up guests. In the first game she was worst. Then Lady Dorothy took her as partner (she had seen that Anne was nervous) & began to encourage her & praise her. Anne soon had that joyous animated look she gets & beat everybody including Lady Dorothy.'[239] Penns in the Rocks was living up to all his expectations—in addition to the anthology, they discussed a new selection of Wellesley's poetry and Willy began to contemplate a new series of *Broadsides*, 'another attempt to unite literature and music'.[240] Anne then joined Michael —after his own travels with his mother—for a week of playgoing at Stratford-on-Avon; this was probably the occasion when, after being bitten while boating, she came up in a rash all over her body and, mortified, had to consult a doctor.

After a few days in the British Museum reading '45 books' and getting 'about a dozen or so extra poets', Willy returned to Dublin on 30 August ahead of his children, summoned by George to attend to yet another theatre crisis.[241] Haire had given a good report of his heart, but meetings with Margot were probably somewhat restrained. He had deflected her offer to meet him at the boat (after all, his daughter would be with him), and ardour seemed to be cooling:

I understand what you feel about the word 'love'. I too hate that word and have I think avoided it. It is a name for the ephemeral charm of desire—desire for its own sake I do not think that it is because I have grown old, that I value something more like friendship because founded on common interest, and think sexual pleasure an accessory, a needful one where it is possible . . . I am still ill—if I can avoid any effort that puts me out of breath, or any chill for a few months, I should be as vigorous as ever. . . . I want to be as much alone as possible that I may write poetry again.[242]

If, as later rumour insisted, there had been plans to run away together, those letters of his which survive suggest it was a very brief fancy. The London theatre project had again collapsed, but Nancy Price, founder of the People's National Theatre Company, was anxious to produce a Yeats festival; Yeats appointed Margot his representative, 'Do what plays of mine *you* like or you *and she* like.'[243] Still hoping Margot might perform in *A Full Moon in March*, he sent her a revised version of the play for Nancy Price, asking her to return the early manuscript for 'my wife's careful mind covets it'.[244] Eventually Price settled on *The Pot of Broth*, *The Hour-Glass*, and *The Player Queen*, but for three matinées only. Margot would play a small part in another of the company's productions the same season at the Duke of York's Theatre; however she was not cast as the Player Queen, as she and Yeats had hoped, but played the 'real Queen', Decima.

The trouble at the Abbey was over the production of O'Casey's *The Silver Tassie* which opened the day before Willy and Anne had left Dublin. Brinsley Macnamara had sided with the Irish nationalists and clergy who considered the play blasphemous, and now with his usual skill Yeats managed to oust him from the Board of Directors. 'He has really given us a great advertisement. The Abbey has not been so prosperous for years—every seat sold. I have been very polite, no man was ever stabbed more courteously—poor devil.' He thought again of George's charge that he was ruthless.[245] As usual there were complications: 'We are accepting into our friendship (but not our theatre) the man we put out. Higgins said to my wife "I cannot quarrel with the man. I like the way he looks at a glass of porter. He gives it a long look, a delicate look, as though he noticed its colour and the light on it." '[246] But he was pleased with Hugh Hunt's work as the new broom.

In between Willy's theatre business and settling Michael into his new school, George was deep in correspondence over the publication in the *London Mercury* of *Dramatis Personae 1896–1902*, arranging for photographs and insisting that the dates be included in the title 'whether you are able to use the whole material or only two thirds of it'.[247] 'I must apologise for the household,' Yeats wrote to Wellesley on discovering that George had forgotten to post a manuscript to her. 'My wife has been greatly overworked, typing large parts of my Autobiography etc.'[248] They were both also working hard on the anthology, George typing out most of the poems as well as his constantly changing introduction.[249] They consulted Raphael's ephemeris for Dorothy Wellesley's horoscope, which 'greatly surprise[d]' him, for 'your profile gives a false impression, it suggests cumulative energy, masculinity. You are not sensual, but emotional, greatly wishing to please and to be pleased; fundamental common sense but too impatient for good judgment until deliberation call up this common sense; deeply imaginative but the star that gives this makes drugs attractive.'[250] It would be some time before he learned of and met the love of her life, the BBC producer Hilda Matheson, whose death led Wellesley towards the drug of alcohol.

Meanwhile the two corresponded about their work 'as one poet to another'; she would figure prominently in the introduction to the anthology. 'You have brought a new pleasure and interest into my life and I thank you.'[251] He told her of his plans to extend the scope of the *Broadsides*, and he was anxious for her to meet the author and music critic W. J. Turner, whose assistance was also enlisted.[252] He went to Penns again when *The Player Queen* was produced, spending more time there than in London, thanking his hostess in Carlyle's words: 'Penns in the Rocks is the perfect country house, lettered peace and one's first steps out of doors in a scene umbrageous, beautiful.'[253] Sussex would figure more and more largely in his future plans. Wellesley attended the opening matinée on 28 October at the Little Theatre in Hammersmith and hosted a dinner party afterwards; Yeats joined them, but probably did not bring Margot. He was still trying to keep the different strands of his life as separate as possible.

Willy's journey to England lasted for only two weeks, and almost did not take place at all. Just days before the date of his departure he noticed 'a small spot' on his tongue; his doctor advised an operation and all depended upon the laboratory report. 'I have had a good many small swellings in various parts of my body, certainly harmless, and this is probably of the same nature though in an unusual place,' he assured the Swami. Although dictating the letter to George, he added, 'Please say nothing to Margot, all her future may depend on her concentrating on her part.' After the medical report arrived he wrote again, enclosing his previous letter. 'An infection of which I knew nothing, and received in early youth is producing this curious result. Though the spots have so far been harmless, a spot might come let us say in my brain, I must therefore have treatment. . . . Next Wednesday I receive the first of the series of injections which must last for a month, then I can go away for three months with no treatment except a medicine to drink after my meals; then I must return for another month's injections.'[254]

Once more George appealed to Gogarty to help deflect publicity:

I could not explain on the telephone the real reason why WB could not lunch on Friday because we suspect the telephone operators of supplying information to the newspapers. He had a growth removed from his tongue by Pringle on Wednesday. It was examined microscopically and we heard last night that it was not malignant, but he is to have some treatment. With the exception of Tuesday afternoon when he taxies into Pringle he will be 'in' all the week, so if you happen to be passing do drop in to see him. By Monday he will probably be talking easily; does so now with a little thickness of speech.[255]

The operation delayed a much more significant departure. Ever since June he and the Swami had been planning to go away together that Yeats might 'put into good English' Purohit's translation of the *Upanishads*. 'That will serve the double purpose of saving my life & bringing my Muse back to life. . . . I plan while away to write many poems.'[256] Originally they spoke of India—which had long been a dream for both George and Willy—but, doubtless at George's urging, for Lennox and Dolly had spent the month of June there, settled on Majorca instead. All the travel arrangements were in the hands of Gwyneth Foden, who was accompanying them, after which she and the Swami planned to return to India together. 'It will be an odd trio!' Olivia remarked with amusement.[257] From the beginning Willy had to quell Foden's enthusiasm, rejecting her 'most generous offer to pay expenses all through the winter', insisting on a single cabin on the steamer and (probably George's caveat) that their hotel be 'on flat ground & close to long flat beach'.[258] By November, after the journey had been postponed several times, she was 'My dear Gwyneth'. For Yeats, the expedition was becoming more and more urgent, and he pressed himself to settle theatre and Cuala business and complete the anthology. 'The very fact that I am going with a man whose mind I touch on only one point, means peace.' Finally on 28 November he wrote to Penns:

I await Friday with longing, on that day a curtain blots out all my public life, theatre, Academy, Cuala. My work on the anthology is finished—the rest, the business arrangements, are my wife's task. . . . I am planning a new life, four months in every year in some distant spot and nothing to do but poetry—the rest of the year mainly in Dublin and work for my family. . . . My public life I will pare down to almost nothing. My imagination is on fire again.[259]

Such plans by now had a familiar ring. So did his dissatisfaction with *A Full Moon in March*; he was already thinking of a new play, 'a three act tragi-comedy in short lines, rhyming now and again, more or less "sprung verse"' which when completed as *The Herne's Egg* he judged 'the strangest, wildest thing I have ever written'.[260] He finally sailed on 30 November, a 'wet, blowy and unpleasant' day.

George accompanied him to Liverpool, using as her excuse that she wanted to see the cathedral and the art gallery; but after presenting Mrs Foden with roses, she immediately returned to Ireland. 'I'm sure Mrs Foden thought it most odd of me not to wait to see the boat steam out of the docks,' she later wrote. 'I felt too like the dog who sees his masters going for a walk and leaving him at home.'[261] As it happened the boat did not leave until the next morning, but Yeats's journey through the Bay of Biscay was unusually rough, and George returned in a gale, 'one of the worst crossings I have ever known, accompanied by sheet lightning all the way'. Anne and Mary Martin had hot water bottle and bed ready for her when she arrived at Riversdale next morning, while Gwyneth Foden protected her two charges (and her roses, which she discovered gracing the captain's table) 'with insatiable energy'.[262] By mid-December Yeats and his companions had settled in a warm and 'very new white hotel' and met the British Consul, Commander Alan Hillgarth. Willy faithfully sent 'Dobbs' regular reports of his health and daily schedule; 'My heart has never quite recovered from the strain of those four days of storm otherwise I am very well & am doing beautiful work. . . . I do not think my head was ever so full of imaginative inspiration.' The hotel manager was typing the *Upanishads* for no payment and he estimated they were spending 'when all extras are counted, less than £3.5.0 a week'. Mrs Foden continued to envelop them in 'benevolent storm'; George was amused by his description of the Swami, 'very wide & unpassable in his pink robes', walking in front of him on the stairs to ensure that he did not walk too fast. But he was anxious for news, the gain or loss in each new play at the Abbey, suggesting that Anne give him that news 'as her department'.[263]

George in turn wrote frequent accounts of life at Riversdale and in Dublin. The two large chestnut trees by the bridge were dangerous and would have to be removed. Michael was doing well at Columba's, coming first on the total of marks for all exams, but had returned with no seats in any of his trousers. 'His voice has broken; I havent got accustomed to it yet and keep on thinking there is a strange man in the house. Nothing is happening here but preparations for Christmas—as usual I shall be glad when it is over.' The Christmas party was, however, a success 'if one is to judge by noise—Michael as a widow with a baby in her arms was admirable but the play (in which everyone had to improvise their parts from a scenario) ended in a free fight on the floor; no casualties'. After Christmas Michael went off to Bangor to visit his new school friend Brian Faulkner—the first of many adventures they would share—Brian 'in his bath singing "God Save the King", Michael outside the door shouting the "Soldier's Song".[264] She went alone to see the film of *The Informer*, pronouncing it 'very clever sensitive acting and production. The first time brutality on the films hasnt left me with a bad taste in my mouth.' Puzzled by the use of the word 'shebeen', for the first time in her life she sat through a show for a second time and then realized O'Flaherty was employing this as a discreet name for a brothel. When attending a film, she would become so engrossed that on leaving the cinema she would not at first know where she was.[265]

She and Lennox, along with her good friend Olive Craig and Lord Longford, had been responsible for the revival of the Drama League which opened in January in the Torch Theatre with Benavente's *His Widow's Husband*, produced by Ria Mooney, and Cocteau's *Orpheus*, produced by Robinson and Shelah Richards. George approved of the first, but criticized Lennox's casting in the second. There was the usual concern over attracting audiences again, for both the League and the Abbey were suffering from the popularity of the Gate Theatre, which had been established by Hilton Edwards and Micheál MacLiammóir. When Dolly bought a notice at Woolworth's to put on the gate at Sorrento Cottage, painted in black on white 'SHUT THE GATE', 'Lennox came home and saw it "O if only we could write Hilton Edwards name on the back and send it through the post." '

There was also another confession on the domestic front:

I am inaugurating a third war against our neighbours, the Weldons. This one is going to be strictly silent. Their maid has for the past three weeks been climbing into our premises and taking wood from our river walk and upper field (some cut up by us) she does this quite regularly on Wednesday, Saturday and Sunday. I am having John barb-wire the gaps in the fence between us and them. John is afraid to speak to her about it because he says 'she'd say I hit her'. The Weldons have far more timber than we have, and in any case I don't see why *we* should keep them in fuel for their fires!! I think I told you we had a cattle feud; their hungry cattle breaking in to us for 'eats', incidentally through the same hole that the maid has now re-opened for her raids! Mary, in a vigorous denouncement of the maid's behaviour ended up 'no wonder their cattle break in' (i.e. bad example given by human being)[266]

As always fiscally prudent, she asked him to take note of how long an airmail letter (which cost twopence halfpenny extra) took compared with the ordinary post: 'The post office *says* it takes two and a half days instead of five.'[267] She sent him newspapers, more detective novels, and fresh material for the anthology: 'Do let me have back this stuff as soon as you can. We shant be safe until the material is at the OUP!! I also badly need that excuse for the people who are constantly sending manuscript poems for your "consideration"!!'[268] Clearly they were back on their former companionable terms.

Yeats had left instructions that his wife conduct all business affairs in his absence, and she was busy not only with the anthology and his publishers but with permissions and other requests. All letters and fees were to be sent to 'Georgie Yeats' until further notice.[269] Proofs of his autobiography were going forward with publishers both in England and America. Turner had refused the offer to be English editor of a new expanded series of *Broadsides*, which left Dorothy Wellesley as a possibility. 'I want you & Higgins to decide,' Willy wrote from Majorca; George would act as business secretary to that project too.[270] In a burst of energy she spent thirteen and a quarter hours finishing the index for the anthology. 'Really the whole thing could go off any day now if that kitty-bitch Margaret Gough would reply.' She was also typing Russell's letters to him as the next project for Lolly's press. 'So many of them are "a yard wide and all *wool*" but I think I have selected a bunch which are interesting as a whole book. I am putting in very little of the cloudy supernatural, they are so very badly written.'[271] She suspected the 'supernatural' element was responsible for an unnerving experience:

I havent any news to write about, in fact writing at all is part of an act of defiance and challenge to a poltergeist who has three times since four o'clock today thrown a brass ash-tray from my typewriting table to the floor with a loud clang. The last occasion occurred about 11.15 p.m. when I had carefully placed said ashtray in the middle of the table so that I might be sure that the vibrations caused by the machine were not the agent or propeller of its action! I have now lit one of Swamiji's incense sticks, put on a kettle for a hot water bottle, a mug of bovril, with which I shall retire to bed, plus a further incense stick—its a little like the story of Father Benson who went to investigate a haunted room armed with a piece of the True Cross and a revolver—as soon as I feel I have not succumbed to fright. Needless to say the darned thing only jumped off the table when my mind was completely absorbed in my work. I have been working since ten this morning on the AE letters— I began to wonder if the passages I was typing when it jumped had anything to do with the matter. It didnt do it while Anne was in the room (7.30 to after 10).

After that, there was no more poltergeistery. Cuala published *Passages from the Letters of AE to W. B. Yeats* in June 1936; although page proofs were corrected by George, her name does not appear as editor or compiler.[272]

Enclosing 'the usual' monthly instalment for Lily, she added the latest news from Majorca: 'He calls "Palma" "Palermo" throughout his letters . . . very muddling to future biographers. He dates his last letter "probably Thursday" and the post mark is undecipherable, so I dont know how long letters take.'[273] Awareness of the significance of such details had been reinforced by the arrival of a professor from Hull University, who had been commissioned to write a biography.[274] Dr Oliver Edwards embarked on his assignment with enthusiasm, and he and George were to become firm friends. Not only did she enjoy his company, she was soon energetically involved, searching out dates and letters, urging Lily to write her memories of their childhood, and even enlisting Willy's cousin

Violet Gordon in the hunt for early records. 'I think I only realized, when Edwards was going into records for his book, how little I had of a kindly nature from the older generation,' she wrote Vi. 'I have gone through so many bitter letters from relations of his own generation, through two little account books kept daily over a period of two years of his entire expenditure at the age of 28 and 29; accounts which show such items as "borrowed sixpence from Symons" that I would like to have your "record" to put into the file.'[275] After Edwards's first visit on New Year's Day, 1935, she had written excitedly to Willy who was in London, 'lordy I do know so much more than I ever knew about your life! In the last 48 hours I have done more research for "data" than I ever did since I took on with you. I think I did it with great discretion. . . . This is all long-winded and dull to you, but it hasnt been dull to me because all these investigations have quickened my memory of the strange, chaotic, varied and completely unified personality that you are.'[276] Her husband would continue to amaze and intrigue her, and Oliver Edwards plodded on with his book until the end of his life; it was never published.

Another more private and personal project does not appear to have survived either. 'I wish she wouldnt call you my "belovedest" or "your beloved"', she wrote crossly to Willy of a recent letter from Mrs Foden. 'And I wish you hadnt told her I was writing a novel.'

You are so indiscreet that I fear you may even mention I dont like you referred to as my 'belovedst', so you had better put this letter in the fire at once, or, failing a fire, down the half-way. How the devil am I to 'write a novel' if people ask how it progresses and I get involved therefore with biographical matter? I am doing it to amuse myself, and if I attempt to publish it shall do so under a pseudonym. Probably it will be burnt, but it is meant as an interest to myself, is not Irish or English, has no autobiographical or biographical associations. So leave me to stew in my solitary juice.[277]

Sadly for *this* biographer, like her artist's portfolio, the plays she had written earlier, and other literary projects later, the novel was indeed most likely consigned to the flames.

18
MAJORCA

Only after George saw Willy off at Liverpool did she remember that she had forgotten to pack his medicine glass; however, he and Mrs Foden could get one in Palma. She was also worried about the stormy passage he suffered; he did admit, 'My heart was a little upset by the rolling of the steamer I had to hold on to things so hard & so often but that will soon mend.' However, he was able to send her a revised introduction to the anthology, done on the voyage. Besides, a week after they arrived in Majorca they had settled comfortably in to the Hotel Terramar in San Agustin, recently built and boasting central heating, its own sea beach on the C'as Catalá coast, and 'all comforts'. Within days Foden had arranged for him to have a room on the ground floor to avoid the stairs, but despite that warning signal, he was enjoying the scenery: 'My window is wide open and the sun streams and lights up the white walls.' Most important, he was spending each morning at his play, 'a strange faery tale', and had also written 'rather a fine lyric'; the afternoons were devoted to letters and an hour's work with the Swami. George suggested that 'As soon as you get one act of your play done you really ought to make a clean copy or you will forget your own writing!' but she wondered what they did in the evenings.[1]

She soon found out, for Willy's frequent letters were graphic in their detail. Gwyneth Foden had been somewhat of an embarrassment on the liner—she quarrelled with the purser as soon as they got on board; the bad weather did not sufficiently subdue her activities, but she won over all the Hindu stewards by appearing at the ship's concert in the dress of a sacred temple dancer. In the hotel she soon became a liability, bored when the others were working well, sulking when Yeats dismissed her book on Russia, and angrily threatening concerning the only other guest, an Englishman, who had refused to use the same bathroom as the Swami. Early in January 1936 Willy became ill, and food poisoning was diagnosed by the Spanish doctor Consul Hillgarth had recommended; in this emergency Foden was once again 'devotion itself'. But the transformation did not last, and soon Willy told the Swami that 'if she did not return to normal in a few days' he must insist on her return to London; after many lengthy interviews Shri Purohit announced that she would once again be 'normal'. 'When she is good she is very very good—if it would only last,' Willy reported to George.

But George was worried. 'Six nights ago I suddenly woke up and heard you saying "O,O,O,O," continuously like a groan, forgetting that you were away I ran into your bedroom to find Michael fast asleep. I hope you haven't had a return of your congestion of the lung? . . . I didnt write all this before because I hate to seem fussy.' Replying to her 'curious, &, at the time, accurate vision', Willy confessed, 'When you had your vision I was not actually groaning (that was dream dramatization) but I was ill & in pain. Every breath was painful the doctor here discovered that what I thought muscular rheumatism was food poisoning. He cured me in a couple of days but not of the difficulty of breathing. I am quite well except that a slight phisical [*sic*] exertion makes me pant.' The doctor insisted he stop all writing except for the work on the *Upanishads*, so he sat daily on the terrace of the hotel manager's villa; he enclosed a violet plucked from the villa garden. Within days of this letter his breathing became much more difficult and he was confined to bed. Always careful in business matters, he and the Swami signed a formal agreement sharing the royalties of the work they had done together. The same day his letter to George, dictated to the Swami, describes his situation: 'to go to England or Ireland at present would kill me. I must wait for the warm weather.' Would she care to come out and nurse him, thereby saving the twelve shillings a day charged by a professional nurse? He realized it was difficult to find some place for Anne to stay in Dublin, and Michael's holidays must be considered.[2]

Even before this resigned letter reached her, George had left Dublin in response to a wire from the Swami; despite her suspicion of aeroplanes as 'dangerous and inconsequent objects', she must have flown from London to Barcelona, for she reached Majorca at 8 a.m. Sunday morning, 2 February.[3] That evening she typed a reassuring letter to Lily and Lolly:

I found Willy with a nice nurse, propped upright in bed with every available pillow, rather weak and slow in speech but not looking as bad as I had expected. I saw the doctor this morning after he had seen Willy at 9.30 and he gave me the history of the illness. He had wanted to send for me two weeks ago but Willy refused as he said he would be better in a week or two. . . . Willy has had some kidney trouble and his heart has not been behaving very well. The doc. thought him better today; he was very bad on Wednesday and Thursday but they wired 'slightly better today' to London to relieve my journey.

The British Consul and his wife arrived with thoughtful and unsolicited offerings of 'pillows, a wonderful padded bed-rest with side pieces (he has to be propped upright) a wicker-bed table, fifteen detective and wild west stories, three magazines, and a bed pan!' But she warned Willy's sisters that his recovery would be slow, 'as he gets "set back" '.[4]

The next day she wired Lennox and Dolly, for word had reached the newspapers that Yeats was 'gravely ill' and 'suffering from a heart attack'. George saw 'a garbled version of it in a Spanish paper' on her way through Barcelona, but only later discovered that Foden on her own initiative had given an interview to the Reuters newspaper reporter. 'Now no information is given except through the doctor whom I asked to be cautious,' she wrote to Dorothy Wellesley, who had telegraphed to Dublin for news.[5] 'I fear we shall see the end of the Arch-Poet soon,' Gogarty wrote to an American friend, 'kidneys working a dilated heart too hard.'[6] The Swami wrote to Margot that 'the inevitable is coming'; having already had a vision of Willy ill, she offered to fly out immediately, but fortunately was dissuaded by the news that George was on her way.[7] By the middle of February Gwyneth Foden, having quarrelled with the Swami and been frozen out by George, had returned to England ('Gott sei dank!'[8]). 'She's never had to deal with a rock before,' commented Willy; later he told Wellesley he himself had turned her out at the beginning of his illness.[9] It would not, however, be the last they heard of 'the Foden'.

George was right, Willy's recovery would be 'a long business'. Warned by Oliveres Jiminez, the local doctor, that the specialist in Barcelona was unsatisfact-ory (in his hands the patient 'would die in two weeks'), she wrote for advice to their old friend Carnegie Dickson in London. Having learned from the Rapallo experience, she began taking daily notes from the moment she arrived, observing every change in Willy's physical condition and recording the doctor's unsuccess-ful attempts to find a suitable medication. They conclude with a summary as of 22 February:

General condition, exceedingly nervous, this I believe to be to some extent the result of having had no proper attendance at night before Feb.2. Spanish nurse with no English slept in a room near him but did not attend unless bell rang, he only rang once—spent three or four nights with very little sleep breathing very bad, no one within call except Spanish waiter 'who was instructed to call Mrs Foden in case of need'. Nurse was only brought in on January 29th. Previous to that he was nursed by Mrs Foden.

When breathing easy is very cheerful, planning new work etc and likes Wild West read to him by the hour![10]

These observations, along with a letter from Dr Jiminez himself, she also sent to Dickson, who replied immediately to both, suggesting as consultant a chest specialist in Barcelona and alternative medication for Yeats's heart. When Gogarty received a letter from the doctor describing his condition—'we have here an antique cardio-renal sclerotic of advanced years'—he exclaimed, 'Why! It sounds like a Lord of Upper Egypt.'[11] Slowly, Yeats began to improve, but it may have been now that he told George that 'it was harder to live than to die'. A few months later he would write to Wellesley, 'I need a new stimulus now that my life is a daily struggle with fatigue. I thought my problem was to face death with gaiety, now I have learnt that it is to face life.'[12]

By March life at the hotel 'had become impossible', George wrote to Gurteen Dhas:

it is full now and very noisy, and as his room (and mine) are on the ground floor it is unceasing—it is beginning to get on his nerves. I consulted with the doctor and he agrees to having Willy moved to a small villa which I can get a few yards down the road. It has all modern conveniences including steam heating (very necessary) and in a week's time we can get it. It will cost about half what it costs to live here for the three of us (W, self and nurse) . . . and that is an important consideration as goodness knows when it will be possible to move Willy home. . . . As far as I can see it will be three months before we can trek home at the present rate of progress. He will have to come home by sea as the train journey would be impossible. Hours to wait in Barcelona between the arrival of boat from Palma and departure of train for the border, then at border a long wait standing about with passports and so on.[13]

Once again other responsibilities had to be shelved. George wired to Macmillan asking that Tom Mark pass the final proofs of *Dramatis Personae*; it was the beginning of a close collaboration that would last for many years. Michael fortunately was still at St Columba's, but hurried arrangements had to be made for Anne. She stayed first with Olive Craig, George's friend and fellow committee member on the Drama League, then went to the Robinsons in Sorrento Cottage for a week, then back to the Craigs. Seeing her at the Abbey with Olive and her architect husband Frank, Lily was told that Anne was 'no trouble' and very good with their two children. 'Poor George does have a strenuous life,' Lily admitted. 'This is the second time Willy has been seriously ill far from specialists and nurses and home, and she has had to leave the children and her house and garden.'[14] However, sympathy did not stop her from complaining that reports from Majorca were too brief and far between. Anne's seventeenth birthday passed without celebration. But when the aunts suggested their niece stay in the room next to Lolly's at Gurteen Dhas, George politely rejected the offer, as not being good for either Anne or Lolly. However 'she cant go on indefinitely staying with friends', and by the end of February it was arranged that Anne sail out to join her parents.[15]

About 23 March George took Willy to the villa Casa Pastor, which she thought 'an ugly little modern mushroom but fine large sitting room all windows on the sea, and terrace, and steam heating which is essential'. Later when he was feeling better Willy would describe it as 'a charming but melodramatic house—tall marble pillars, white walls ornamented with stucco panels, a wide balcony going all the way round, the summer villa of a Palma stockbroker suggesting a film'.[16] Willy sat on the balcony, looking out over miles of woods and sea. His rooms, George informed Wellesley, 'are on road level so that he will be able to go out for walks in his pram—lovely country within five mins: walk'.[17] The 'pram' was a wheeled chair which the Dulacs at her request arranged to be sent out from London; it would be Anne's job to push her father about and—with some effort—up and down the steep road off the villa.

There, work began again on the *Upanishads*. George privately thought the Swami worked Willy too hard, but she would later 'with little wheezes and hoots of pleasure' regale Donald Pearce with a description of the poetic process:

It was all very businesslike. . . . Most days the Swami and he would sit on the verandah of our cottage, where it was fairly cool and shady. First, the Swami would translate a bit of text into his very limited English, then W. B. would set to work improving on it. They would mumble and talk over it, line by line, till they got a version that satisfied them both. Sometimes it was very amusing, though. For they were so serious and solemn about everything. But the Swami, you see, always ate large quantities of rice. So you would hear them saying something like 'the ineffable wisdom of the blessed sushupti,' and next moment you'd hear, saving your presence, you'd hear a loud rrrrppf! from the Swami. Or W. B. would be saying, 'the deep and dazzling darkness of the Eternal Mind,' followed by rrreeeeppp! again from the Swami![18]

Once work on the *Upanishads* was completed (except for Yeats's finishing touches), they immediately embarked on a translation of the aphorisms of Patanjali; the Swami was determined to stay as long as the Yeatses did before returning to India. Yeats was secretly relieved that Purohit was not going back to London 'now that his work is complete'; 'He says there are only three people he regrets not seeing again—Mrs Shakespear, Omar, and Margot Collis [Ruddock].'[19] The Swami would have part of his wish granted unexpectedly just before he sailed on 13 May.

Feeling 'like a child of five left in charge of a Tiger in a wire cage, and . . . tired of being sent for when the Tiger escapes',[20] George alarmed Willy by telling him that he must never go away again without herself or Anne. 'That will suit me not at all,' he complained; 'as age increases my chains, my need for freedom grows. . . . I repent of nothing but sickness.'[21] By now he was convalescent, 'all unpleasant symptoms gone and all organs sound—but still weak'. To Mannin Willy wrote, 'Yesterday for the first time for months I put on my ordinary clothes. Only twice for months, some days ago and then last night, have I known that I was a man full of desire.'[22] The same day to Wellesley he described the 'long list of things I must not eat'. 'I imagine myself unrolling at a restaurant something like a ballad singer's sheet at a fair. There was a consultation, and one doctor was a monarchist, the other a socialist, and it needed the energy of the British consul to make them meet (my wife had selected the socialist on expert London advice), and they disagreed as to the cause of my illness, and both theories are allowed for in the list of forbidden foods.'[23]

George relaxed enough to send a pattern to May Courtney, one of Lily's 'Cuala girls', to have 'a pretty silk dress' made.[24] As for sightseeing, perhaps she had time to trace the path of Raymon Llull, who had been born in Palma and whose name she had studiously recorded in her copy of Hermes Trismegistos so many years ago. Or to visit the cathedral, 'filled with a pale light', but (according to Clifford Bax) like the dark cathedral at Barcelona 'disfigured by a glass of indescribably sour colour'.[25] Some outings may have been possible once the children were with her; George made careful preparations for their respective journeys. Anne arrived first, having crossed on 20 March to Liverpool, where her cousin Rupert Gordon met her and put her on a boat in Birkenhead which called at Palma on the way to the Suez Canal. By far the youngest on board (she counted 'at least eleven different kinds of hearing aids'), Anne later complained that she had 'eight mothers' looking after her—not counting cousin Charles, who had helped with the packing. Having waited until the end of term and his confirmation, Michael did not arrive until 5 April. Accompanied as far as London by one of the masters of St Columba's, to his sister's envy he was to travel overland; he was delighted at the thought of sleeping on the train. Lennox arranged that in London he was then met by Tom MacGreevy, who put the 14-year-old on the boat for Paris. But although armed with his mother's careful instructions—four typewritten pages—once Michael arrived in Barcelona he could not find the special bakery she had suggested, and still recalls with chagrin that the taxi driver took advantage of his youth by driving him back the short route to the station by a roundabout way. Despite the misadventures, George was determined that her children, unlike their father, would learn to look after themselves, although she drew the line at bullfights.

Michael returned to school at the beginning of May, but Anne was to wait and go back with her parents; it would be the end of her days as an art student. In addition to wheeling her father about in his 'pram' (terrified that she would lose control as they went downhill), she remembers that a monkey broke loose and ate both the laundry in the shed and her father's heart pills. Of the Swami she recalls little but her mother's barely concealed disapproval and his appetite for bananas. One day while at work Yeats was startled by the sudden appearance of St John Ervine, whose ship called at the island.[26] Then the calm was once again broken by another less welcome visitor.

About 10 May—the very day of the highly combative presidential election in Spain—Margot Ruddock appeared outside the villa, luggage in hand. George, looking out of the window at 6 a.m., saw her walking around the long verandah, directed her in, and gave her breakfast. As Yeats later recorded the incident for publication, she told him she had 'come to find out if her verse was any good'; he told him he 'was amazed by the tragic magnificence of some fragments' but that her technique was worsening. Margot then left 'in pouring rain, thought, as she said afterwards, that if she killed herself her verse would live instead of her. Went to the shore to jump in, then thought that she loved life and began to dance.' Whether this version coincided with George's recollections, she never said. But it is likely it was George who sent her to sleep at the nearby pension where the Swami was staying; he gave her dry clothes and slippers and some money. The rest of the story has conflicting details depending upon whether Yeats, Margot herself, or others relate it. By now clearly unbalanced, Margot departed for Barcelona where her daughter had been born two years previously; adventures with her friend's dog led to her being confined to a bedroom, from which she escaped through the window, falling through a barber's roof and breaking a kneecap. After being X-rayed she once again escaped, to be discovered hiding in a ship's hold, singing her own poems and insisting that she must return the Swami's slippers. At this stage the British Consul (probably 'the courageous but splenetically anti-Red' Norman King[27]) became involved and contacted the Yeatses. After arranging for Anne to stay up the road with the American sculptor Mary Klauder Jones (who had just completed busts of both the Swami and Yeats), George and Willy travelled to Barcelona, and found her in the Enfermia Evangelica calmly writing an account of her four days' madness. They arranged for her to go to England in the company of a nurse, guaranteeing all expenses including the clinic's and a claim by the Peruvian Consul (one of six involved) that in her fall Margot had injured 'a valuable dog'. George later told Ellmann the dog was a prize Pekinese and that she 'had to take care of the owner's wrath and compensation—Margot apparently being completely uninjured while the dog was splattered about the pavement!'[28] This may have meant a further trip to Barcelona, for Anne recalls her mother describing how she arrived alone in the midst of general political and social chaos, and could find no place to eat or sleep until a baker, nervously defying the anarchy surrounding him, took her in. No wonder George grew exasperated whenever Margot's name was brought up.[29]

'A madness has always a kind of spiritual ecstasy,' Yeats wrote to the Swami; within days the newspapers had got hold of the 'horrible phantastic melodrama'.[30] Various items were published by the busy but doubtless delighted Reuters correspondent: 'Poetess Falls from Window', 'Condition said to be "Grave"', 'Visit to W. B. Yeats'.[31] Margot's actor husband Raymond Lovell congratulated her on the 'magnificent publicity', and provided more newspaper fodder.[32] When Gogarty learned of the escapade, he mischievously suggested that 'Frustration applied by Mrs Yeats may have been at the bottom of this affair.'[33] On his return to England Yeats arranged for the publication of some of Margot's poems in the *Mercury* with a preface by him; he would eventually publish the story, in still another revised form, alongside her own version, as an introduction to her volume of poetry.[34] By July 1936 she was asking him to send money for the Swami's return to England that she might work with him; 'The Shri Purohit Swami is my God and his good name and the good name of India are my responsibilities.'[35]

The Swami, however, had left within days of Margot's arrival, bearing with him a public letter 'to young Indian poets' in which Yeats urged them to 'write in your mother tongue . . . for you cannot have style and vigour in English'.[36] Despite his continuing affection for the Swami, clearly he like George felt the task of rendering Purohit's translation into elegant English too difficult and time-consuming. Safely on board ship, the Hindu sage sent his thanks to both of them, adding, 'It seems that I went to Europe for you, and am going back when you think I should do so. I will be always with you in Spirit though not in person.'[37] George would have been less pleased if she saw a letter he wrote some months later, urging Yeats to spend the next 'two or three years' writing his own memoirs: 'You asked me in Palma whether it is advisable for you to write original things or write your reminiscences. I am in favor with the latter. You asked me to write my tale, I wrote it, now it is my turn to ask you to complete your autobiography.'[38]

The publicity over Margot's escapade spurred Gwyneth Foden to action once more. She sent flowers to Margot, and a letter to George:

Your illustrious husband cannot claim that his visit to Palma was a flaming success can he? The tragedy in Barcelona—is one which by super-human effort on my part I did not do likewise & moreover they both knew it—that prince of evil darkness & yr husband conduct [sic] did not redound to their credit—If I opened up my mind to you It would cause you infinite pain I'd never hurt another woman—so keep silent The ghastly episode in San Agustin caused wounds that can never heal—your husband is an old man—& if he is preparing to meet his maker—he should go down on his knees & ask God's forgiveness & make every retribution in his power before he leaves this world—The dual personality of ['Willie' struck out] your husband will stand out in my memory—one the poet of charm—the other I dare not think of. If he has any chivalry left he will give it to you & your children.[39]

The original cause of Foden's grievance appears to have been Purohit's refusal to accompany her back to England; she insisted that 'Yeats is dying; Yeats is dead—you have got to look after me.' 'It has all been a witches cauldron,' Willy wrote to Olivia. 'Better not speak of it, but do not be surprised if you too get one [of] her mad, sometimes threatening letters.'[40] Foden complained of her treatment to the British Consul, who told her she could 'do nothing'.[41] But she continued to cause trouble: she claimed the Criminal Investigation Department were investigating the Swami; Dulac promptly made enquiries and found the charge groundless. She went to Faber and Faber, who were publishing the translations, saying he knew no Sanskrit, and wrote to T. S. Eliot, one of Faber's editors, with accusations of the Swami's immorality and homosexuality; Eliot ignored her letters. She found a willing accomplice in Margot's estranged husband, who took money from her and at the same time accused the Swami of using 'undue influence' to extract considerably more from Margot; through her solicitors Margot temporarily silenced her. She also made some effort to discountenance Yeats in Ireland, writing to Seán O'Faoláin that she had reliable information from Purohit's own family about 'things of a nature that dispelled that saintship for ever'.[42]

She continued to harass Commander Hillgarth, now in England, and sent further charges to Lady Elizabeth Pelham who had studied with the Swami (and paid some of his expenses), spent time at his master's ashram in India, and would continue her yogi studies intermittently with Yeats. And she sent registered letters to George: 'If Mrs Foden is indebted to Mrs W. B. Yeats for returning the silver cup & saucer she lent Mr Shankar Purohit she thanks her.' George and Willy both received anonymous messages, enclosing letters from others she had enlisted in her vendetta against the Swami. She went so far as to send telegrams in Yeats's name giving the wrong date for his return.[43] Then she turned her attention to India, endorsing the grievances of the Swami's estranged daughter, and writing to the press and police in Bombay. The result was simply to forge a close alliance among those suffering from her hysterical missives and who were prepared to take legal action if necessary. But Foden persisted in claiming that the Swami had mistreated her. 'God knows what the truth of the whole situation is and how far it is important that we should know it. It seems to me quite beyond the unravelling of any human being,' wrote an exasperated Elizabeth Pelham, who relayed summaries of these activities to the Swami's master in India.[44]

In December 1936 Foden again wrote to George, forwarding 'a pair of sandals S. P. gave W. B. in October 1935 to take back with him as a gift for you— . . . W. B. went without them.'

This reminds me—do you remember my asking you in front of S. P. at the Terramar Hotel—if you had received certain gifts I had sent through W. B. from time to time You admitted none—save the Green & Gold saree—S. P. admitted to you that he was present when these were given W. B. I'm thankful for this incident—it is one upon which you will not think I'm a liar—a painful accusation that has been laid against me—W. B. a great talker is none so careful what he says about people—and should know that London & Dublin are perfect whispering galleries of Gossip. I wont go into painful details—I would spare you all the pain I can—for there is no-one for whom I feel sorrier for. But in time perhaps not in W. B.'s time—but in your childrens time—they will come to realise that their father owes me a deep debt of gratitude.[45]

George returned the sandals with the cool response, 'Mrs Yeats cannot receive presents from or through Mrs Foden.'[46]

After a year of such bombardments Foden tried a new tack: a letter to Mrs Sturge Moore describes a mysterious illness and explains that she had offered 'material . . . of historical value' to Mrs Yeats, who, although engaged in 'writing her husband's biography', did not 'appear interested when I approached her with the fact. . . . I did not press the matter—she was openly friendly to me—but I felt an inward chilliness that was not conducive for me to be more informative.' Claiming that she had 'nursed Mr Yeats in Palma singlehanded—he would not allow me to send for Mrs Y', she now offered these valuable papers to Sturge Moore, who promptly insisted on 'an entirely free hand' with the manuscript.[47] Marie Sturge

Moore wisely appealed to George, sending her all the relevant correspondence and explaining that 'Tom thought he ought not to neglect this chance of suppressing probably undesirable documents.'[48] Doubtless happy to get a few things off her chest, George immediately replied at length and in detail:

I am typing this because I want to deal clearly with the question of Mrs Foden. She is not truthful and personally I doubt that she is going to have an operation. She wrote to me on March 2 1936, in the course of a long letter 'Why I tell you this is because a nursing home is out of the question so a bed is to be found for me in one of the WOMEN'S HOSPITALS where I can go as a paying patient according to my means'. She wrote a similar letter to Lady Elizabeth Pelham who went to see her and found her looking quite well and extremely active; a few days later she called on the Dulacs without warning and as she saw Edmund looking out of the window he could not refuse to see her! My impression is that she wants to have an excuse for going to see you to talk of all her grievances and incidentally slander Purohit Swami and WBY. I think personally that it would be very unwise to see her or write to her. She is a very hysterical and unpleasant person.
I will now deal with her letter to you.
    1st. I am not writing my 'husband's biography'.
    2nd. She has not offered me any of her 'journals' reports conversations etc. She has informed me in several letters that she had kept a journal. This was intended to be, I thought, a form of threat; in a letter dated 11/12/36 she says '. . . but in time perhaps not in W. B.'s time—but in your childrens time—they will come to realise that their father owes me a deep debt of gratitude.'
I have kept all her letters, anonymous and signed, and I hope you will keep this letter written by her to you. I have replied to no letter from her since she left Palma on Feb. 21 of last year. She behaved abominably from the moment I arrived at Palma as the result of a telegram from Swami saying that Yeats was ill.
    Sorry to write at such length. I should be very sorry if you and yr husband got mixed up in this untidy mess. I don't believe she has the slightest intention of handing over her documents to yr husband, and I do think she wants an excuse for making your acquaintance![49]

A few weeks later Willy received a postcard addressed to the Swami with the request 'Mrs Foden does not know Mr Purohit address herself forward please'. He did not send it on, explaining to Purohit that

I will not assist her plans & because it was meant for my eyes not yours. It is headed like a letter she sent me 'in hospital'. As she does not name the hospital I think it most unlikely she is there at all. There is a statement about a child (I have known that story for months, & true or false it does not affect my friendship for you in any way). I have put the post card among other Foden documents (I cannot send it back to her as she gives no address). It says by the by that though she has just been successfully operated upon for cancer she does not expect to live long. I think this all drama.[50]

And that seems to have been their final word on Gwyneth Foden.

It was not, however, quite the end of the Margot story. 'When I am in London,' Willy wrote to Olivia from Majorca, 'I shall probably hide because the husband may send me journalists and because I want to keep at a distance from a tragedy where I can be no further help. . . . I shall be at the Savile but help me to remain there in obscurity.'[51] The next chapter of his adventures with Margot would once again involve a controversy over the Swami, and lead to a serious quarrel with his old friend Dulac.

George, Willy, and Anne left Majorca on 26 May, with three hundredweight of luggage. Before the ship stopped at Gibraltar Willy called Anne to his cabin, advising her if she had any problems to go immediately to the British Consul for assistance. Amused, neither she nor her mother told him that Anne had already thoroughly explored Gibraltar on her own on the way out. But this time, although the journey across the Bay of Biscay was so rough everybody else took to their berths, her father was strong enough to remain upright—until he too was sent below by the captain.[52] After seeing Willy off from Charing Cross to Dorothy Wellesley in Sussex, and holding a business meeting with Watt, George and her daughter went on to Dublin. Michael's prize-giving ceremony (he won for mathematics and 'general knowledge') had been set for 9 June, but she arrived to discover that Michael along with several other boys was in quarantine for scarlet fever and the ceremony put off. 'Now she will only see her son through glass like a fish at an aquarium,' wrote Lily. But the case was a mild one and the invalids seemed—seen through a window—to be enjoying themselves. 'Just as well he got it at school. George has had enough of illness. It would have meant sending him to hospital or having two nurses.'[53]

As always, George was glad to be home, especially considering the political crises engulfing Spain; by July Majorca would be in the hands of the nationalists attacking Barcelona and the Revolution was well under way. 'Garden looking good,' George reported to Willy immediately after her arrival, 'animals all well and so on and thank heaven no more rabbits—a disappointment for Michael but no one else! . . . The cat has been ratting again and looks more disreputable than ever.' Her first day was spent answering calls from all of Willy's relations and deflecting questions about the Barcelona escapade. But, having interviewed Willy's agent in London, she was already busy correcting proofs and making out the list of acknowledgements for the anthology.[54] She was quite happy to hand over her husband's care for a time to Lady Dorothy, who on her own initiative consulted Dr Dickson about Yeats's medication. 'W. B is not coming back at the moment to G's relief,' Lennox wrote to Dolly, 'though Olive says she wants him back as soon as possible (*she knows*). I think I know that G. at any rate wants to play roulette on Sat—and not have Willy.'[55] While he was still away George also took the opportunity to have her husband's room repainted a deep cream colour.

Dublin meanwhile buzzed with its own excitement, all of which was reported to Willy; she and Anne attended a garden party arranged by the Drama League in a house looking 'as though it has just been delivered from the shop—no traces anywhere of the residents—and and and the ornaments!!' As always, she refused to be photographed, giving as her excuse that newspaper photographs as 'advance publicity' were of no use and she personally loathed them. Anne however was photographed by herself, 'examining a bird-bath or sun-dial kind of object'.[56] George also met Gogarty there, though doubtless he did not confide in her his diagnosis of her husband's condition: 'The poet it seems has swollen ankles from kidney trouble and a weak heart. This looks as if we will be staging a popular funeral . . . "Popular" is put for well-attended.' The Dublin wit would continue to predict Willy's imminent demise, 'But what does one expect as the result of Steinach's operation at 70 years of age?'[57]

George was relieved when Wellesley wired of Willy's safe arrival, and his own letter followed saying that he was now less tired. 'I had immoral ideas of sending the list of acknowledgements to the OUP without letting you see them,' she confessed, 'but decided that you might want to alter the opening phrase (!) and perhaps add a word or two at the end about help from friends.'[58] On his return from Sussex Willy spent a week in London, entertaining Mannin and Ruddock both, and showing to Sturge Moore the latest messages from Foden; though his infatuation by now seems to have been over, he felt some responsibility for Margot, and was determined to further her career if at all possible. George then went over to Holyhead on 29 June to see him through customs, taking care on their return that she was not in the newspaper photograph showing the delegation—Gogarty, Higgins, Hayes, Starkie—who met him at Kingstown pier. Even though she arranged for a cabin on the return journey, it was a long day: an 8.25 train in order to catch the mail boat at Kingstown (now Dun Laoghaire), landing at Holyhead at 11.45, and departing again at 2.30 for arrival in Ireland at 5.25 p.m. This would become a regular routine.

Once home Willy was disappointed at how weak he was—Anne could beat him at croquet (the mallet seemed heavy), and for most of the summer George or his daughter wheeled him about in his 'pram'. Rather fancifully, he decided that Anne was 'in love with an entomologist'—her elderly cousin Rupert Gordon had interested her in insects—thus explaining her search for a slater or woodlouse so she might count its legs through a prized large magnifying glass.[59] Lily's report of her niece's new interest was more accurate:

We had Anne here on Sunday. The School girl had come uppermost again, and she wore a very antique thick skirt, showing all the scars of its hard life, a grey blouse, no stockings, brown socks and plenty of great bites. But she is a dear, not so wise with Aunt Lolly as Michael is, very little and Anne would show her irritation. She is now keen on insects and is collecting them. She got a dog flea, a hen flea, but had great difficulty in getting the flea that fattens on man. She has never seen one. One doesn't now, but Mary managed to get her one. She is reading books on insects and knows something on the subject. Rupert started her and gave her a collecting case etc.[60]

The aunts' attitude towards Anne altered with every appearance, each one perceived as yet another 'miracle'. 'Today she is a slim peaceful seventeen, her hair waved and combed back and caught in a bunch of little curls at the nape of her neck. Her long brown arms are charming, and so are her ways . . . Her colour is much paler. I thought she was going to have George's too strong colouring, but no, and her figure is like Willy's when a youth.'[61]

Michael was still in quarantine, but although well into recovery had to undergo yet another operation, this time to have his adenoids removed. As usual, when Lily visited Riversdale there was much discussion about the young heir. 'George says he is not like her people. He is at first glance like Willy, who is in appearance more Pollexfen than Yeats. Then when you know him better he is not line for line his father at all, and yet very like. He has lots of character and has humour. He has small, deep blue eyes, hair almost black, his skin fair, silent and definite, knows his own mind, is adored by his friends, and by his mother. He burns a deep brown in the sun.'[62] His mother was especially pleased at how easily he had made friends at school; the doctor had told her Michael was 'a card' who kept all the others in the infirmary amused. Brian Faulkner—who was not among the chosen few to be quarantined—was apparently desolate; they had been close friends from the first day, when the young northerner discovered that Michael's collars were made by his family's linen company.[63] Michael was finally released and back in class until the end of term in late July.

When Willy was home, the day revolved around his schedule: up about 4, working at proof sheets until about 5.30, then back to bed, breakfast at 7.30, 'and then write poetry, with interruption for rest, till 12'.[64] 'When the air is clear I have good health,' he told Mannin, 'When it is cloudy & damp I lie awake at night (writing much) and sleep during the day. It is a curious experience to have an infirm body and an intellect more alive than it has ever been.'[65] He did not keep his sleeplessness to himself: George was frequently roused by a call from the next room, 'Are you awake?' Once she was, she would stumble down to the kitchen to make Ovaltine, often to find on her return up the stairs that, satisfied with the attention, he was already asleep.[66] Afternoons in the household were devoted to croquet and the occasional visitor, although illness, he was to write, 'has enabled me to get rid of bores, business and exercise'.[67] He was not straying far from the garden, unless George pushed him down some of the country roads in his wheelchair. 'Mondays' continued to be sacrosanct, but now Higgins and Gogarty dropped by to visit the poet whenever they felt like it; Lennox and O'Connor came in to report further theatre business; and at least once a week MacManus joined him for long private discussions about Hindu philosophy and Spanish politics. George welcomed them all in, provided tea or something stronger, and escaped to her gardening or to listen to music at the far end of the house.

On 10 August Willy accompanied his wife to the Abbey for the first time since his illness; the audience broke into applause when he entered. The occasion was a production of his *Deirdre*, with Jean Forbes Robertson in the starring role; that weekend George held a reception in her honour at Riversdale.[68] Both George and Willy loathed the production, as she described in an illustrated letter to Anne who with a friend was visiting Olive Craig and her family in the country:

'Deirdre' was bloody (I am assuming that neither you nor Olive will give voice to my true opinion on that play—) the production was bloody, the 'famous actress' was, as your father wrote in his own pen-work to MacLiammoir, 'a Camberwell canary, a Blackpool sparrow' (and I forget the other epithets.) The costumes were HELL:: Deirdre wore large golden hair plaited for about two feet below her ears and ending, as far as I can remember in about six inches of wound gold coils and about nine inches of curls below; her dress was of the purest white (in my young days you would call the material nun's veiling) embroidered with tre-foils (disguised shamrocks) in scarlet and gold. You may remember that she and Naisi arrived on horseback. We had the horses hoofs most realistically portrayed off-stage by Barney. For some reason unknown to me her incredible nun's-veiling-scarlet-and-gold costume had a bright green tongue-leaved edge. This may have been because the costume maker had created the costume two inches too short . . . Anyway Deirdre had ridden a-horseback for many miles—side-saddle of course as the dress was very narrow—and her gold crown and so on and so forth were speckless.

Naisi was killed (off scene) with a scimitar (probably a scimitar used in 'HASSAN') and the very curious thing was that in the final death scene Naisi's throat had not been cut. Now this was curious because we had a marvellous exhibition of blood on scimitar (see diagram enclosed A) which suggested head being cut off. The death exhibit was most beautiful. Naisi lay dead complete with Deirdre in a lighted square (see diagram B) flood-light from right. Torches came from right also. Poor lambs, poor torches! Madame Tussauds chamber of horrors, (black curtains framed their background) The public has adored it.[69]

Clearly George already considered Anne a designer in training, but she was not yet impressed by the Hunt–Moiseiwitsch contribution to the Abbey.

In late June 1936 Ottoline and Philip Morrell spent two weeks in Ireland visiting Francis Hackett and his wife Signe Toksvig in Wicklow; Ottoline came to tea at Riversdale. Ottoline 'was a hen who had layed [*sic*] a very big white egg & wanted all the yard to know', Willy told Wellesley. 'The egg was our friendship, which was not only "important" to me & you but to my wife (this when she got George to herself for a moment) for I would be safe in your hands "You were no minx".'[70] By now all of his London friends clearly knew of his relationship with Margot; but Ottoline would also have been aware of Dorothy's own relationship with Hilda Matheson, and this was most likely the gist of her quiet aside to George. George on her part seems already to have accepted Wellesley, just three years older than she, as an integral part of her husband's circle; her own letters from Majorca had been warm, and later, when the two women finally met, they established their own friendship. George would not have been slow to realize that, just as the script liberated Willy from his obsession with Maud Gonne, it had prepared him for the open acceptance of (and undisguised interest in) Wellesley's sexuality. Most of all, she appreciated the shared responsibility for Willy's health and enthusiasm, a luxury she had not enjoyed since Lady Gregory's final illness. He had hoped in Riversdale to 're-create to some measure the routine that was my life at Coole, the only place where I have ever had unbroken health'.[71] But she was quick to recognize that Riversdale could never provide the intellectual stimulation of those early years at Coole. Yeats's first visit to Penns had offered that opportunity, and their correspondence while he was recovering in Majorca had sealed the working relationship between the two poets. Significantly, he quoted Gregory's favourite maxim while stressing what he hoped was their common aim: 'ours is the main road, the road of naturalness and swiftness, and we have thirty centuries upon our side. We alone can "think like a wise man, yet express our selves like the common people." '[72] By midsummer they were collaborating on ballads. Sussex would from now on become his Galway; Lady Dorothy his new confidante. Very soon they were 'My dear Dorothy' and 'My dear W. B.', signing 'with love and affection'. His return to Penns that autumn sealed the compact: she spoke of Hilda Matheson, he of his adventures with Margot. Theirs would not be an ordinary romantic liaison but a special 'intimate understanding'; from Riversdale he sent his love to her '& a somewhat lesser love to Hilda your Providence (is not every poet a drunken sailor?)'.[73] The Sinbad motif had altered somewhat with age. If George did not know the truth before, she would surely have learned it now.

Illness continued to dog the household that summer of 1936. George still could not leave Willy alone; when Mary Martin was on holiday she brought in a 'temporary' who found Riversdale too lonely; so that she could go to see Lennox's new play at the Gate Anne was summoned home from holiday. 'So you've damn well got to come back on 25th and stay in the following night (preferably two nights) . . . I cant leave yr father alone unless either you or Mary are here. So that's that.'[74] Willy had another relapse, recovering just in time for his journey to London to deliver the BBC 'National Lecture' on modern poetry. Before he accepted the invitation, George had cautiously insisted he 'read aloud with suitable expression for three quarters of an hour'.[75] Delighted with the £100 fee 'which put my finances right', it also meant another visit to Penns. George was confident enough of the relationship to send a long letter explaining her husband's needs:

Dear Lady Gerald WB is quite well again; he is much better now than when he was staying with you last June. He *was* ill—in fact when I got yr letter (about Broadsides) in which you asked for news of his health, he was rather ill. So I didn't write. At that time I was very doubtful if he would be able to get over to England.

He is now sleeping very well, has no breathlessness, & his heart is excellent. The result—the doctor & *I* say of digitalis—*he* says diet! I enclose a typed slip with diet. About 'rests'—very difficult to say. At present he lives in a routine: comes down at 3 p.m., goes for a drive or walk in his 'pram' or wanders about garden. Sees people & always rests after a couple of hours of talk. That is to say he is firmly left alone.—But when he is away I don't believe he'll stay in bed until 3. So he probably ought to lie down or sit by himself for at least 2 hours between tea & dinner & one hour at least between lunch & tea! However, as Edmund Dulac said to me, 'He is the most obstinate man I have ever known'. I find the only way to make him rest is to plant him in a room by himself with a detective story and leave him sternly alone.

   I am glad he can go to England now, because I doubt very much if he will be able to go over again, at any rate unaccompanied.* In any case he will have to 'stay put' from abt October 20 to mid-April. Yours George Yeats
*This is of course private.

Willy wrote rather wryly, 'I understand that my wife has sent you a list of ideal rules for my conduct—Well'—but did not object.[76] As it turned out, he stayed till the beginning of November and with George's blessing was back at Penns by early March; as usual, she took the boat to England both coming and going, to see him through customs.

Yeats's departure gave George time to concentrate on other matters. Michael had come home from St Columba's in August still unwell; by the end of September the ' "bugs" in his throat' delayed his return. He finally went back to school in mid-October, having once more missed the prize-giving ceremony. Anne was in bed with a bad cold, and George herself was again back in the care of the dentist. But she was looking forward to the party for Lennox's fiftieth birthday; as usual she would stay the night at Sorrento Cottage, and she was having a new dress and coat made for the occasion. However, Willy was always on her mind. In answer to a telegram she wrote,

I am so sorry that I sent you off with so incomplete papers etc. I let myself get distracted with that Broadcast and all its alterations, and then, too, with Anne in bed, I hadnt an assistant. I hope you are looking after yourself and that you will remember that if you get a cold I would rather come over at once and not wait until you are very ill! I have a suitcase ready packed and English money, so you will probably NOT get a cold. On previous occasions I was unprepared, and to be unprepared is tempting misfortune You were so well I dont expect a 'wire', but you must not be cross with me if I telephone to Dulac (cheap rates at night after nine) to ask how you are. You can always explain it by saying 'my wife is very fussy'.[77]

She was doubtless relieved by the reports he faithfully sent back to 'Dobbs': 'All goes well . . . I could not get a good green for a shirt—we shall have to get that in Dublin under your eye but I have ordered two red shirts. I have bought the needful socks etc.' He shared the ham sandwich she had supplied for the train journey with 'Gypsey Nina' whom he was thereby able to 'draw out—you remember my habit in that matter which used to shock Lady Gregory'. His travelling companion so charmed him he arranged for a copy of his selected poems to be sent to her.[78] Life was almost normal again, but on 3 October George phoned Edmund Dulac just to make sure. Edmund reported that Willy was 'exceedingly well, very much better than . . . last June'.[79]

Willy too was now easier in mind about George. Even before his departure for Majorca her drinking had become more obvious. The previous Christmas dinner had been spoiled, as Lily delicately put it, 'by George being in one of her boisterous moods and carrying on a kind of rough horseplay with Anne and Michael who, being half Yeats, don't like it or respond. Michael is now two inches taller than his mother . . . George boasted that she could wrestle with Charles and floor her. "Charles was just being polite," said Michael.'[80] It was not until much later that innocent Charles, recollecting George's slow careful walk and manner at such times, realized that she was often under the influence of alcohol; Anne, having observed her staggering, seemed more aware.[81] But back in Riversdale in the summer of 1936, all seemed once more to be under control. Willy had been sufficiently concerned to confide his fears to Wellesley in June; by August he was able to write more happily,

I think you were right about my wife. She has not been overworked for a long time now—unless she may be just at the moment with the proofs of the anthology which go off in a couple of days. She has made a list of first lines etc. There have been [no] more of the old symptoms, and the household is happy—my anxiety [which] was acute for many months was I think needless. We have all something within ourselves to batter down and get our power from the fighting. I have never 'produced' a play in verse without showing the actors that the passion of the verse comes from the fact that the speakers are holding down violence or madness—down Hysterico passio. All depends on the completeness of the holding down, on the stirring of the beast underneath . . . Without this conflict we have no passion only sentiment and thought.[82]

But he realized that he 'must be in Dublin before wintry weather sets in or make [my] wife miserable'.[83]

How much George's recovery was due to Yeats's apparent disaffection with Margot is difficult to say. When he arrived in London he had taken Margot out to dinner, worried that she might not have 'enough either of coals or of food'. The strain that meeting provoked created such havoc that he fell asleep at the table the next evening when entertaining Mannin and the Dulacs. 'Next time I ask you to dinner I will choose the other guest or guests for the sake of their talk & yours,' he promised Ethel.[84] From Penns he wrote to George that Lady Dorothy was sending her 'some rare plant or bush. It must root and grow.'[85] This would be the first of a number of gifts from one gardener to another. George listened to his broadcast with approval, and was excited when he wrote that he was buying her a wireless through the BBC. 'Thank you so very much. I hope you told the BBC that we have not got electric light so cannot have an instrument which "plugs into" a main.' He would later forget this important fact and send the barber crawling about looking for an outlet,[86] but accepted her advice to have the machine sent direct from London so that they would not be delayed by customs on his return; the Bush wooden radio finally arrived on 7 January, and as the only 'short wave' in the area, was often in demand. The wireless became a source of amusement for the children also; one of George's set pieces was a description of Willy cupping his ear and saying, 'I beg your pardon?' when he could not hear distinctly; Anne and Michael rushed out of the room to giggle.[87] In return George sent the latest Dublin gossip and a press cutting 'from a New York paper called "Time" which may amuse you . . . they give photographs of the king with Mrs Simpson on his recent holiday!!'[88] Back in London Yeats was confined to his room at the Savile with a cold, but revived sufficiently to attend a 'quite beautiful' rehearsal of his project for a series of broadcasts combining singing and speaking verse; directed by Hilda Matheson, Margot was one of the performers, but although satisfactory in her role obviously was not otherwise. 'Blot out what I told you about Margot,' he wrote to Wellesley on 29 October. 'I cannot endure that moral torture chamber where hysteria manufactures thumbscrews daily of some "new" pattern. All I can do for her is get her poems published and find her work if possible.'[89] An indication of where his thoughts were tending was his application for membership in the Eugenics Society just before he returned to Dublin. George met him at Holyhead as usual.

It was probably now that he brought home with him a large reproduction on canvas of Paul Gauguin's *Ta Matate* which they hung in the dining room over the fireplace. Anne, who sat opposite at the table, at first hated it; it was the first modern painting she had seen and was certainly the most modern in Riversdale.[90] Meanwhile George and Willy were both immersed in work—preparations for the new series of *Broadside*s, discussions with Watt concerning the Macmillan and Scribner de luxe editions, dealing with the mass of correspondence provoked by his broadcast on modern poetry, 'a bust up in the Academy of Letters', and (George's job) final work on the accounts for *The Oxford Book of Modern Verse*.[91] Her work on the anthology also led to higher earnings; spurred by the demand Ezra made for printing his own poems, George began negotiating an increased fee for Willy's. She and Anne attended a formal reception on behalf of the Municipal Gallery on 12 November, as did Lily, Lolly, Jack, and Cottie; Willy stayed home, pleading exhaustion, for he was collaborating with Wellesley on 'much curious love poetry'.[92]

Then on 19 November 1936 Oxford published their anthology, and an avalanche of criticism descended on Riversdale. Sending MacGreevy a cheque for his contribution, George quoted Jack Yeats's comment, 'I see that a catch harvest can be made quickly by reviewers, who have never written a verse, now, immediately; just by raising their pure disinterested voices up into the clear air on behalf of the poets who are out of your anthology.'[93] Although—always punctilious herself—she was annoyed by the critics' errors, George was not distressed; though upset by some of the attacks, Willy was delighted by the hornet's nest stirred up by his introduction and selection. So was the press, who sent him an additional £250 in recognition of the sales—15,000 copies were sold in the first three months and an immediate reprinting was required. Rousing him from depression while keeping down his blood pressure was always a challenge for George. To make light of his moods, she would often quote to the children her own adaptation of Rabelais:

> The devil when well, the divil a saint was he
> The devil when ill, the divil a saint would be[94]

Willy then read a book persuading him that the diaries which revealed Roger Casement's homosexual tendencies were forged;[95] in a burst of ferocious energy he sent off to the *Irish Press* (de Valera's paper) a ballad denouncing Alfred Noyes by name. Wellesley and Mannin both wrote to him in urgent protest. Fearing that they would believe he 'hate[d] the people of England' and humbled by Noyes's 'noble' letter to the newspapers explaining his own role and calling for a government investigation, he withdrew his attack. 'It would be a great relief to me if they were so submitted & proved genuine. If Casement were a homosexual what matter!', he wrote defensively. 'Forgive all this my dear but I have told you that my poetry all comes from rage or lust.'[96] A more painful fallout from the anthology, especially for George, was the alienation of Ottoline Morrell; resentful that he had praised Turner's *The Aesthetes*, which mocked her and her husband, she rejected his clumsy efforts at conciliation. He also feared that she might have felt neglected for Dorothy Wellesley (George always recalled that Ottoline dismissed Wellesley's friendship, claiming that Yeats simply preferred her cook's prowess). Although he sent George copies of their correspondence, she wisely stayed out of the quarrel. Neither she nor Willy ever saw her again, and a year later Ottoline was dead.[97]

George had told Tom, 'The family is well—WB very much better than he was last summer and much less absorbed in his physical condition which is very good.'[98] But whether from the excitement over the Casement incident, the rejection by the Abbey of *The Herne's Egg*, or the attacks on his anthology—probably a combination—he once more fell ill, succumbing to influenza. Unable to get a nurse during the epidemic, George was again busy nursing her husband.[99] She could do little, however, for the depression that continued to engulf him. 'You say I seem far away,' he wrote Wellesley,

—I am far away from everybody & everything. Something happened to me in the darkness some weeks ago. . . . Everything seems exaggerated—I had not a symptom of illness yet I had to take to my bed. . . . I felt I was in an utter solitude. Perhaps I lost you then, for part of my sense of solitude was that I felt I would never know that supreme experience of life—that I think possible to the young—to share profound thought & then to touch. I have come out of that darkness a man you have never known—more man of genius, more gay, more miserable.[100]

George later described his mood to Peter Allt: 'Once when continually ill in 1937, he rang his bell for me in the night to ask me to stay with him for a while and said, "When I am ill I feel I am becoming a Christian and I hate that." ' He repeated this to Wellesley: 'when I am ill I am a Christian & that is abominable.'[101] Once again he was reminded of his own mortality. Anne, whose room was near her father's, and who had been given George's record player, remembers playing the Gregorian chant over and over until finally her mother told her to stop; her father thought he must be dying.

By February 1937 Willy was well enough to be left while George went into Dublin; she was surprised by the deference of shopkeepers, until she learned that Willy's Casement ballad had been published in the papers that morning.[102] Although she sometimes wished he would write something else and blamed Higgins for the emphasis on ballads, George appreciated the traditionalism Yeats was attempting, and would later reject any other way of singing them. It was she who suggested that the poem 'He and She' (his 'centric myth') was ideal for singing; and Willy paid attention to her criticism. When she objected to the repetition of 'himself' in the first verse of 'The O'Rahilly', he offered a revision; but George 'on the whole' preferred the original, and so it remained.[103] But partly because of the failure of his experimental broadcast by Radio Eireann from the Abbey stage on 1 February ('every human sound turned into the roar, grunt or bellow of a wild beast. I recognise that I am a fool'[104]), all his future programmes would be carried out in London. Once again he suffered a relapse.

The one bright ray was news conveyed by Gogarty that a group of American admirers had formed a 'Testimonial Committee' to present him with a cheque for £1,000, with promise of further payments of £500 a year for four years; 'it will give my old age what it needs of rest and change,' he wrote to the chief organizer, Dr Patrick McCartan. 'I am at present full of creative power, and if that power stays with me I may owe it to you and your friends.' He insisted on the gift being made public, for 'if it were kept private it might seem that I was ashamed of taking the money whereas I am proud that I should have been thought worthy of it'.[105] According to Gogarty, when learning of the generous gesture George asked him 'to arrange that it be given with enough flourish not to make it look like an alms'.[106] The gift also relieved him from dependency on George's careful accounting; now, he informed his chums in the Academy with glee, he would not have to turn to his wife for funding.[107] The money would be sufficient, he told Lily, 'to allow me to go abroad for the three months of the year when I am always ill—Jan, Feb, March & have enough taxis. I am always stern with myself (or I hope so) and I will take nothing that will not increase my working capacity. If I can reduce fatigue and illness I shall increase that capacity.' In 1935 he and George had paid off an old embroidery department debt of £350.[108] Now his sister was having difficulty meeting household expenses for Gurteen Dhas, and had borrowed several times from George to pay her bills. While continuing to seek out contemporary designs for her (which she often thought 'queer' or 'too fussy'), now he could afford to offer £5 advance for each piece of embroidery she completed.[109] Whenever his sister finished a panel, George packed it in his luggage when he travelled to London, thereby avoiding tax: 'when he takes it George says to the Customs, "A piece of embroidery by his sister", and the man, "Yes, ladies like doing fancy work", and no more about it.'[110] The day after the cheque was formally presented, he sent Lily and Lolly £25 each, which allowed Lily to pay her taxes and rent. Lily was grateful, but relieved also for her brother: 'With his bad sight and his mind far off it is very unsafe and exhausting for him to have to stand waiting for buses.'[111] By this time he was blind in one eye, one of the reasons, George claimed, he frequently did not recognize people on the street.[112]

Also, Cuala was in difficulty again, and continuing to lose money. In 1934 another cash infusion for the press had been necessary, at which time Yeats insisted on taking part in the management, but this had meant even more rows with Lolly.[113] He had taken to meeting her for tea at the Shelbourne, 'because there he could not shout at her'.[114] In exasperation he had once (rather unfairly) said to Sturge Moore, 'I have two sisters, one of them is an angel, the other one a demon.'[115] Once after a depressed night and another battle with Lolly, he begged George to take over the press; she wisely replied that Cuala needed the cachet of his name to survive at all.[116] But George was in fact relieving him of a great deal of the day-to-day responsibility, handling proofs, suggesting new books, and dealing directly with the press. After hearing of one particular 'Lollipop' tempest, she had shouted with laughter, 'Lolly's life is a series of short dramatic one-act plays.'[117] Not all Lolly's antics could, however, be laughed away. Privately George thought the typesetting 'the worst in the world', and resented the time taken by Lolly's 'little chats', which tended to go on non-stop for hours.[118] Meanwhile Mr Scroopes of the Bank of Ireland was alarmed at the increase in Lolly's over-draft, and once more threatened to cut off his supply. After going carefully over the accounts and previous audits, Willy and George determined that the Cuala income would have to increase by £150 a year if solvency were to be recovered. Lolly, who suffered from high blood pressure at the best of times, became ill with worry, aggrieved that she as the person running the business was not consulted: 'If I dont know what the Bank says to him—or he to the Bank I am all at sea—

and I am not a child after all,' she complained to George.[119] Willy temporarily assuaged Scroopes by promising a complete overhaul, comparing the situation at Cuala with the Abbey Theatre, which was finally under Fred Higgins's management making a steady profit. Both institutions, he pointed out, depended upon 'vigorous literary production in Ireland'.[120]

It was time to deal with 'the great problem of my life, put off from year to year, and now to be put off no more', Willy wrote Wellesley; 'and that is to put the Cuala Press into such shape that it can go on after my death, or incapacity through old age, without being a charge on my wife'.[121] In September 1937 he dictated a Memorandum on the 'Future of the Press':

I hope presently to propose a re-organisation based on the following considerations. I am old and in bad health and if the Press is to go on and earn salaries for the workers I must arrange for others to take my place. My sister Elizabeth is old and in bad health, she will no doubt survive me, but there must be such control of the press as will secure the future of the others engaged in it. Furthermore I see no chance of success unless the Press remains as it has always been closely associated with the Irish intellectual movement. I think however before re-organisation it is most desirable to prove that the Press is paying and can pay better. A few years ago I calculated more than two books but not as many as three books a year (assuming that the other activities of the business continued to earn what they earned at that moment) would make the Cuala firm solvent. Then my illness came and I could not deal vigorously with the situation. I did not consider that it was possible to get between two and three books a year of sufficient merit and for that reason I started the *Broadsides*. It is not however possible to publish a continuous series of *Broadsides*. We must leave a gap between the volumes.

His solution was to introduce a new bi-annual 'written mainly by myself in the line of my old *Beltaines* and *Samhains*'.[122] This would become *On the Boiler*, what he described as his own *Fors Clavigera*; he seems to have conveniently forgotten his denunciation of Carlyle in their early work on the 'system'. Whether the promised reorganization would ease George's responsibilities was another matter; and when *On the Boiler*, despite Yeats's hopes that it would create 'a rumpus' to 'advertise Cuala', was finally published, it was not after all by the press.[123] Reminding Lolly that he had already spent 'more than £2,000' on rescuing Cuala, Willy would bulldoze his plans through the following summer.

Willy was in England from 5 March to 24 April 1937, staying for most of the time at the Athenaeum, to which he had recently been elected under a special rule waiving the entrance fee. George as usual accompanied him across the Irish Sea, then went on to spend a 'rather hectic' but 'very pleasant week end' with the Tuckers in Sidmouth. She was back in Dublin by 11 March, snowed in so that 'nothing can be done in the garden damn it', and 'doing teeth and not very much else'. Her mouth was too sore even to write the local gossip, but she was sufficiently exercised to seek confirmation on one point: 'I am told that "The Mothers' Unions" of England have sent a letter to the King's Proctor asking that Mrs Simpson's divorce should not be made absolute! Is this true? What frightful hypocrites people are.'[124] Almost daily letters between 'My dear Dobbs' and 'dear Willy' follow their activities—he was 'keeping wonderfully well', had ordered a new suit, asked her to send him his red shirt that he might test it against a new 'dull red pull-over', and ordered his Jaeger 'sleeping suit trousers' as instructed. Comfortably in his new club, he was dining out most evenings and preparing for the first of his series of broadcasts. He had seen Margot more than once: having thrown up her part in a provincial repertory company, she would now have to be included in his second programme; this meant rehearsals and staying longer in London than he had intended. Also, he wanted to visit Penns, for Wellesley was just back from a holiday. Even better news was that his agent had now negotiated a fee of seven guineas per poem. George in turn dealt with Cuala affairs and her children's needs, all his correspondence, attended the Abbey productions, and relayed local news. Heavy snowfall had turned to equally heavy wind and rain and she encouraged him to stay on in England; 'it would be much better to return to somewhat warmer weather.' He confessed to Wellesley that he had been 'in a very excitable state, the result I suppose of illness, strangely miserable, and this has given my poems a new poignancy'.[125] The same message was sent to Ethel Mannin with a request for advice, but the meeting may not have materialized; their relationship, he later wrote, should be preserved 'as an occasional joy, not among the necessities, but among the ornaments and luxuries'.[126]

That Willy hired a locker in the club in order to leave his dress clothes in London indicated the direction his thoughts were tending; Dublin was not providing the release—emotional and sexual as well as intellectual—that he required. A week after he arrived in London he had written to Shri Hamsa, the Swami's master, 'I have thought of going to India with my own book of spiritual philosophy in my hand and hiding myself there for some time. But there is a practical difficulty of a personal kind which seems under present circumstances to make that impossible.' A few days later he was blunter to the Swami,

Lady Betty [Elizabeth Pelham] of whom I have seen a good deal has suggested my going to India next October—if your master could have me, and has offered to come too . . . please tell him of the operation I went through in London and say that though it revived my creative power it revived also sexual desire, and that in all likelihood will last me until I die. I believe that if I repressed this for any great period I would break down under the strain as did the great Ruskin. I am sorry to be kept from what might have brought me wisdom.[127]

Judging from the protracted correspondence between Yeats and Lady Elizabeth, at least one incident had occurred between them which made her determined that never again would either 'be led away by imagination from the right and the true path'. But although she finally decided not to return to the ashram at Lawasha (which she had visited in 1935), she clearly valued his friendship: 'If you ever feel the necessity to talk over some point with a fellow student, that is really inhibiting free thought or action, please use me as a waste paper basket or as an element in the proposition. I am absolutely at your service there.' They would continue to meet to discuss the Swami's problems with both Foden and Margot, his manuscripts, and their own spiritual experiences.[128] Yeats, however, wanted more. 'In my own life I never felt so acutely the presence of a spiritual virtue, and that is accompanied by intensified desire,' he wrote Wellesley, adding in a postscript, 'No—no—I shall not make love to Hilda. She would not have me, and besides she is sacred—and I dont want to.'[129]

George and Michael, home for the holidays, listened to 'In the Poet's Pub' on 2 April. She wired her approval immediately, and followed with a letter the same day:

The Broadcast was entirely delightful. I dont like most of the pomes, as you know, but the result of the performance seemed to me most exciting. You spoke in your natural unrestrained voice, a voice very unlike the artificial one of the 'Modern Poetry', and whatever listeners thought of any other portion of the twenty minutes a whole lot of people will have been glad to hear the real Yeats evidently enjoying himself. The whole production during its twenty minutes sounded as if you and the speaker and the drums were really enjoying yourselves and that you had locked the door on the solemn portentous BBC and had no intention of unlocking the door until you had your final laugh—which we heard *very* distinctly! . . . From certain intonations I believe you were the 'chorus'??

The 'pomes' she did not like were by Newbolt and Chesterton; but she was pleased by Michael's reaction: ' "I prefer poetry done that way" which is the nearest he ever got to any statement about "poetry". (He knew all the pomes so I think he must have been secretly reading your anthology.)'

Despite Willy's disclaimer that he was growing 'impatient to get home', she encouraged him to stay on for the second programme, to be broadcast on 22 April. Since the BBC would reduce his fifteen guinea fee by £5 if he did not, he agreed; 'I am also most anxious to make these broadcasts as good as possible as they about pay for my legitimate London expenses—I mean by legitimate not purchase of clothes etc.'[130] There were other reasons for delaying his return: he had been introduced by Helen and Edmund Dulac to their good friend Edith Shackleton Heald, to whom he was immediately attracted. But even so after his second broadcast, 'In the Poet's Garden', he was anxious to be home. 'For three weeks now I have been longing for Dublin,' he wrote his wife. 'O how I long for home the cat & the dog, you & Anne Higgins & the local gossip.' He also had advice from Wellesley about the garden: 'We were all wrong about the "lily pond"—Dorothy says John should put back all the mud, baskets should be sunk in mud, & left "to rot away" but that the right time for planting is May.' He would return in time to see the roses sent from Penns flourishing around the front door, the arum lilies tall and white, and small sprouts on the water lilies.[131] Doubtless at Holyhead, when met by George, he coincided with Michael, who was off on a weekend bicycle tour of Wales by himself; his mother had arranged the hostels in advance.[132] And from his daughter he would hear the latest news of the Abbey.

Ever since September 1936 Anne had been working as assistant to Tanya Moiseiwitsch, the promising young stage designer Hugh Hunt had brought over from England; as part of his contract Hunt had insisted on improved stage lighting and, for the first time, a full-time designer and scene painter. The agreement was that she would train her own successor, and Anne landed the job. 'Having tried various art students and rejected them,' the proud father wrote, 'she has asked for my daughter, having seen her work. If all goes well my daughter will earn in her nineteenth year some £5 a week, which will enable her to quarrel with her family and take a flat of her own if she wants to. She is timid but draws with a bold sensitive line and is completely stagestruck.'[133] Observing Anne's enthusiasm with the 'Pegasus Players', Yeats had some years previously written to Lolly, 'I am going to ask Anne to design some stencils (private) to use on certain stage costumes I shall want her to do this unaided except that I shall give the symbols. I do however want her to be taught pattern. The stencils are for a play I have finished.'[134] When she returned from Majorca Anne brought with her 'a jolly book on costume through the ages, good drawings well arranged, periods and dates clearly shown'; the Abbey position may already have been in her parents' minds. On 21 August 1936 George had written to Anne,

Unless you refuse, & I don't think you will!!, you go from Monday September 7th every day from 11–1.30 to work on scene painting, designing, etc. at Abbey Theatre. Miss Moisewitsch is to teach you all she knows, with a view to your being employed at Abbey in her place when she leaves. This will not be for a year probably. . . . After 3 months, *unless you are thrown out*, you will be paid a pound a week; *if* you are taken on when she leaves, you will probably get £4 a week. When you get £1 a week it will be your dress allowance. *When* you get £4 you will contribute part to me for living expenses unless you decide to have a flat of your own. You will go to art school every afternoon for the present.

I didnt tell you anything about it before because I hadnt made final arrangements with Hunt. About 2 weeks ago the question of an art student to work under Moiseiwitsch arose (2 previous ones sent by Atkinson Metropolitan S. of Art left Abbey because they really wanted to be portrait painters) & so I ramsacked all your drawers etc to find any theatre work to submit!! I hope you will like this idea as much as I think you will!! You will sometimes have to work in the evenings at Abbey & in any case will *always* have to be at Abbey for dress rehearsals. *You will have an opportunity of really learning *all* the theatre work etc. & if you will work & use your head, it will be the beginning of a career.* I felt I must put a parental exordium into this letter.*!!!! Please let me know what you think of this scheme.[135]

'It will be good to pin Anne down,' Lily felt, recalling her own experiences as a 16-year-old student when she was 'expected to spend a month making a careful drawing of the Apollo or the Dancing Faun'. 'Art schools are no good for a girl of her sort. She wants someone working with her all the time till she gets some sort of real interest.'[136] However, concerned that Anne would 'dilute her energy with green room gossip', George insisted to Willy that as far as possible her formal training continue:

As it seems impossible for Anne to go with any regularity to the '2 to 4' life classes at the Hibernian Academy, I have told her that she must go three evenings a week to the night schools at the School of Art. On the days that she has to work in the afternoons at the Abbey she will have, if she is going to School of Art class in the evening, to have a dinner in Dublin. I am *absolutely determined* that she must continue her drawing at one art school or another, and I know you will back me up in this. The difficulty about irregular attendance at the Hibernian Academy etc is that she will take up the place of a regular student, and as she may be irregular it does not seem to me to be fair.[137]

Moiseiwitsch remembers the appointment somewhat differently; having been 'given' Anne as an assistant, she found it quite daunting to have 'a Yeats' working with her.[138] However, she was pleased to have someone younger than herself, and the two soon became fast friends. Very soon, although ostensibly 'on trial' for the first three months (when she received no salary), Anne was working such long hours at the theatre, and reading everything she could, that her parents feared for her health. After her apprenticeship her salary was ten shillings a week, increased the following year to thirty shillings. But she was happy; recalling her first job, which was to paint the archway to 'Heaven' in Dunsany's play *The Glittering Gate*, she thought it could not have been more appropriate.[139] Now that Charles had returned to Australia, Tanya ('Tottie') soon became Anne's ('Moop') closest companion, in and outside the theatre. George sometimes joined them for a film at the Corinthian, taking them afterwards to the Broadway Soda Fountain on O'Connell Street; George ordered a 'pink lady' (a blend of gin, crème de cacao, grenadine, and cream), while the two girls had sodas. Tanya remembers George slurping through the straw to put the young woman at ease—and that engraved in marble on the counter was the café name mispelled 'Brodway'. The young designer spent Christmas 1936 at Riversdale; 'Ahi and Pangur on all the best chairs, and George, Anne and Michael on the floor, is such a beautiful picture.'[140] Yeats gave her a copy of the anthology, and invited her to put her feet up beside his on the hassock in the sitting room. Anne was shocked when he took down the great Japanese sword for Tanya to inspect; 'he never did that for me!' But Willy was not well, and his presence at the dinner table oppressive; after finishing his special diet, he departed with the words, 'I will now remove the chill my presence is causing.' After he left the atmosphere did indeed lighten and the floodtide of conversation broke out.[141] George enjoyed the company of both young girls; Lily observed that at the awards reception given by the Academy of Letters in the Peacock Theatre, 'George was in high spirits and gave Anne a cigarette.'[142] Like her parents and most of her colleagues in the theatre, Anne would become a smoker.

While continuing to assist Tanya (she worked on *The Dear Queen*, *Casadh an tSúgáin*, and the *Playboy*), Anne joined Ria Mooney's school of acting in the Peacock Theatre, where she designed and painted sets, designed costumes, performed in productions of the newly established 'Experimentalists', a young company performing on a limited budget in the Peacock Theatre, and learned a great deal about stage management. George as always encouraged and assisted, even drawing some measured diagrams for one of Anne's design proposals, but allowed her daughter to make her own way.[143] In June 1937, Anne spent her holiday in London, staying in a boarding house in Sussex Gardens (£2 10s. a week including breakfast) where, feeling very grown up, she delighted in the magical disappearance of the bed into the wall and the unfamiliar woven curtains and upholstery. She saw her father a few times when he was in London, and Helen and Edmund Dulac kept a friendly eye on her, introducing her to a number of young stage designers; after she had left Dulac sent a warm invitation for her to call them whenever she returned, 'We have both taken a great fancy to her.'[144] However, most of her time was spent at the theatre, in London and as far as Oxford and Canterbury (three times to see *Murder in the Cathedral*). George had instilled independence in her daughter, but not a dress code; consequently, unfamiliar with London customs, she was embarrassed by not knowing when to dress formally. Her father was more protective, advising her not to look into the windows of the 'rubber shops' in Charing Cross Road; but the window displays were discreet, and Anne too innocent to recognize contraceptives, so she returned to Dublin and her mother none the wiser.[145] She also returned with many books, and, according to George, 'in a state of high combustion and longing to fling paint around . . . she had seen & learnt a vast amount'.[146]

The following winter Frank O'Connor, managing director at the Abbey in Higgins's absence, recommended that Anne study theatre design in Paris; as 'an exercise in independence' George insisted that Anne discuss these plans with O'Connor and Tanya herself. She was in favour of the plan, but Willy was not, preferring that she study in London. George and O'Connor, however, won, and Anne spent four months in Paris, boarding with Léa Rixens, 18 rue du Molin de Beurre, XIV, widow of the artist Émile Rixens and a close friend of the Dulacs.[147] With £2 10s. provided by the Directors for living expenses, supplemented by 'pocket money' from George, and armed with introductions to various designers in Paris, in mid-November Anne set off on her own. She returned to Dublin with an umbrella, forty-nine books, much more self-confidence, and a surer sense of her own work.[148] Now given greater responsibility, in April 1938 she designed the sets and costumes for a revival of her father's *On Baile's Strand*. Striking out with her own vision of the play, she used the bronze doors adapted from one of Robert Gregory's designs to great effect, and changed the traditional costumes. The conservative players complained at this break with tradition, but George and her aunts approved. Willy was absent for his daughter's first solo flight on the Abbey stage, but pleased with what he heard from George and his sisters. He was however present four months later for her production of *Purgatory*, and shortly after her father's death, she would design the first play of her uncle Jack's to receive professional production. George and O'Connor had been right.

Michael's education was also of some concern. His parents had decided that he would spend one more year at St Columba's, and take the entrance examinations for Trinity College. Since he could not enter college until he was 18, the intervening year would be spent in Germany (Michael's own preference) or elsewhere so that he could retrieve his languages. 'He is now greatly interested in world politics and reads quite deep books on the subject,' Lily observed. 'I am glad he is to go to Trinity, Papa and his father and grandfather were there, the grandfather in the 18th century. George adores him, but with Willy he is shy, while Anne and he have always been companions.' Recalling her vision of 1911, she wondered whether her nephew would become a diplomat. His aunt's vision of the 'tall young man . . . in and out of the Embassies' would prove correct in all details,[149] but George had more immediate things on her mind. When she next accompanied Willy to England in September, Michael journeyed with them, then she and her son went off on their own for a week's walking tour of Wales; Michael was delighted that their arrival coincided with the release of the three Welsh Nationalists who had been sent to Wormwood Scrubs for bombing a Royal Air Force camp, and who were to arrive that afternoon for a reception at the Eisbeddfil Pavilion. As usual George described their adventure to Willy,

After we left you at Holyhead we proceeded to Caernarvon, together with some twelve thousand Welsh Nationalists, all going to the Home Rule meeting at Caernarvon to welcome the three men who had been imprisoned etc. Michael insisted on attending the meeting, but as it was all in Welsh consented to leave after about $^1/_2$ an hour. We then walked around and got caught up in a huge crowd awaiting the exit of the three heroes. About six police and three ambulance men dealt with the thousands; very unlike Dublin. From 8 p.m. until after 10.30 we only heard two words in English, from the police at intervals, 'keep back', also very unlike Dublin! The police mainly talked Welsh, flirted with the girls, one chewed gum unceasingly, in fact 'a good time was had by all'. When Lewis emerged from the hall he had to be pushed through the crowd with the assistance of three police and two ambulance men. . . . The Caernarvon meeting of Welsh nationalists was held in a colossal building called THE PAVILION. It is the size and shape of the Mormon Temple at Salt Lake City, but made of galvanised tin, painted black, with small windows painted white. Sound, or rather acoustics, almost as good as the Mormon Temple.[150]

Having her son to herself had revealed some facts about his education that disturbed her: 'I am not at all inclined to keep him on at St Columba's after the end of this next year (end of summer term 1938 when he will be nearly seventeen) and the Sorbonne might be a better place for him for a year than Germany,' she wrote. 'I was infuriated to find that he has now been started on "the Second Book of Virgil" "which we have to do for School Certificate and Intermediate" with no sense of the construction of The Aeneid. They just have to "do" the Second book; "it is five hundred lines". Damn school. I'm not exalting Virgil but damning a system which gives you "500 lines" and no circumference.' 'I am certain you are right about Michael,' Willy replied immediately. 'He is being taught Virgil as I was taught it at the High School & I was damnably ill taught. There too the intermediate was the excuse & the real reason was I imagine second rate teachers. I think he should do well at the Sorbonne, as he knows French and would find himself among hard workers. I will ask Dulac about it.'[151] But despite his parents' concerns, Michael returned to St Columba's, where he suffered yet more illnesses and gained more prizes. George ensured however that he had time with his father, taking him to London when she accompanied Willy, but as always giving her son his own space and time. They were all noticing a greater resemblance to Jack. 'George is so bored by the dull country between Euston and Holyhead so travels by night,' Lily wrote, 'but Michael said, "no," he wished to look out of the window, so he stayed at the hotel for the night and came by the early mail in the morning, and had a comfortable journey and looked out of the window, while George, it being Sunday, and Sunday being the night the commercial travellers come to Ireland, had a very uncomfortable journey, surrounded by the travellers talking shop. She was delighted with Michael, because she thinks it is just the sort of thing Jack would do.' While at Euston Michael had a linguistic adventure, apologizing to a cockney porter for not understanding a word he said. On discovering he came from Dublin, the porter offered his hand to the tall young boy: 'Shake, I was there once for a week,' after which the two got along famously.[152] Their plans for Michael would change yet again. The following summer he took the Oxford and Cambridge Schools examinations, gaining credits in English, French, Irish, Elementary Mathematics, and Additional Mathematics, giving him entrance to Trinity. Perhaps because of the threatening situation in Europe, they cancelled plans for his study abroad, and in the autumn of 1938 he returned again to St Columba's, to concentrate on history and mathematics. 'George says he is at the stage of knowing what he dislikes but not knowing what he likes,' Lily reported. 'They think he is rather young for Switzerland yet and can do that later. Also George finds having Willy around for the winter enough without Michael.' His father still considered him '100 per cent schoolboy' and admitted that he did not yet understand him.[153] However, encouraged by George, who arranged for him to attend special meetings of the Dáil, Michael's interest in politics continued, and would eventually provide the only genuine point of contact with his father.

Willy had returned to Ireland in July 1937 once more embroiled in a mare's nest created by Margot and the Swami. Until now he had ignored Gwyneth Foden's accusations that Shri Purohit had borrowed £100 from Margot to pay his expenses in Palma; but Margot, 'under some sort of emotional excitement', probably due to the broadcast, now admitted this was true. Although her loyalty to the Swami was 'unshaken & unshakable', because of her extreme poverty and his own belief that the loan had made their work on the *Upanishads* possible, he wrote to the Swami insisting that 'your debt to Margot [be] a first charge upon the *Upanishads* and that you may be in a position to do so I shall forgo for the present my claim for the repayment of the £50 I gave you to pay your ticket to India'. Assuring him that 'in all your dealings with me you have been a man of scrupulous honesty', he insisted that Margot be paid in full within the year in such a manner that 'nobody must be in a position to say that I paid Margot'. To ensure this further, 'After (say) five years time, for I know that you are a poor man—I will expect the £50 to be paid out of the royalties to my heirs or to me.' Before sending the letter, he showed a draft to Elizabeth Pelham for her approval.[154] Swami replied agreeing to the terms, saying that he owed Margot a total of £120, but had already sent fifty and given her the equivalent of ten in Palma. Later Margot would say the total was £125, and again Yeats asked as a point of honour that the full amount be paid. Once Willy reached Riversdale and consulted George, his demands grew simpler and he forgave Swami the £50 he and George had paid towards his passage home. By the spring of 1938 the Swami had paid his debt in full to Margot, but despite assurances of affection, the relationship between the two adepts became increasingly more formal. Yeats agreed to write an introduction to the *Aphorisms* of Patanjali, to be published by Faber, but handed over to Elizabeth Pelham the Swami's translation to the *Awadhoota geeta*. 'It is not work for me. I am not in great sympathy with anything but the *Upanishads* and the *Aphorisms*.' Explaining that he had 'no longer the strength', he also rejected the shaken Swami's offer to arrange a lecture tour. 'All my life now is arranged that I may do my creative work with what energy remains. I work for a couple of hours before I get up and then I am tired for the day.'[155] When Margot announced her intention of going to India, the Swami asked nervously, 'Is it going to be another edition of Palma?' Willy advised him that 'you should make up your mind if you want her or not & if you do not tell her not to come. She is wild & unballanced [*sic*]. I tried to get Elizabeth Pelham to see her but she has I think rightly refused. She feels that she can take no fresh responsibility.'

Shortly after performing in Yeats's fourth broadcast in October 1937, Margot once again collapsed and was committed to a mental institution. A registered letter sent by Yeats in the summer of 1938 provoked no reply. 'I must conclude either that she grew wilder than usual and was shut up, or that she had made up her mind in some fit of excitement to cut us both out of her life,' he wrote to the Swami. 'If she has simply cut us both out of her life we have nothing to complain of. She may even be quite right. We put her out of relation with her habitual surroundings.' Just weeks before his own death, Willy wrote to Shri Purohit that he knew nothing of her whereabouts. 'She seems to have had you much in her mind—thinking one night that you were dead. I have no way of learning anything. I never knew any of her friends or relatives. She was a tragic beautiful creature.'[156] Margot never recovered and died, aged 44, in 1951.

19
MENTON

On 26 May 1937 at an Academy of Letters dinner, Yeats made an announcement that would have further repercussions for his life with George. Declaring his retirement from public life, henceforth he 'would live like a butterfly & write poetry'. The Abbey Theatre and the Academy were at last both prosperous enough to get on better without him; 'A new generation must feel that it is in complete control. I have set myself free to go where I please.'[1] It would not be so easy for him to let go the reins on either institution, but other interests beckoned. While at Riversdale Willy had finally written to the Swami that he 'must give up India for the present. I was ready to risk going so far from my doctor but I now find that if I did so it would cause my wife great anxiety. She has not tried to prevent me in any way, but I have found out in various ways how great her anxiety would be. I most sincerely hope to go later.' However, there was always next year. *A Vision* would soon be out, 'and only in India can I find any body who can throw light upon certain of its problems'.[2] Although not untruthful—George did indeed disapprove of such an unrealistic plan—he was as always presenting that portion of the facts which suited the occasion. For by now he was in regular correspondence with Edith Shackleton Heald, who seemed to be more complaisant than Lady Elizabeth Pelham. Within days of his letter to the Swami he was writing to her, 'I am sorry to wait so long before I again ask you for a friendship from which I hope so much. You seem to me to have that kind of understanding, or sympathy, which is peace'; and to Dulac, 'My correspondence with the lady is all that I could wish and I am grateful to you.'[3] A successful journalist, Edith lived in the Chantry House, an eighteenth-century Georgian country house in Steyning which she and her sister Nora Shackleton Heald, editor of the *Lady*, had recently redecorated for their retirement. Older than George by seven years, she would be his last lover. 'Were you younger,' he wrote before their affair began, 'a true intimacy would be impossible . . . I think the finest bond is possible when we have outlived our first rough silver—& that it may be very sweet to the old & the half old.'[4] 'If all is as I would have it, I may consult her about my domestic arrangements,' he wrote to Dulac.[5] Ever eager to be of assistance, his friend arranged for a service flat at 52 Holland Park that Yeats might save on expenses and have more privacy than at the club. Waxing and waning as he did in appearance and weight, he was not so attractive to some observers. Signe Toksvig saw the Yeatses at the Abbey Theatre that May and fled without speaking: 'He has got enormously fat and bulges in his untidy clothes, and his hair is wild and streels every which way, not romantic, but like an old uncombed woman's.'[6]

George, who very likely already recognized that he had a new romantic interest, was not concerned about his spending more time in England, in fact seemed to encourage it. In June 1937 Willy returned to London, waiting however to attend a garden party George was giving for Anne on the 6th. Then, leaving his wife to complete the final details for the new collected editions and deal with the ongoing *Broadsides*, he set off to rehearse for his third BBC programme. The day after he arrived, Edith dined with him at the Athenaeum and all went as Willy hoped. 'Your birthday today', George wrote on the 13th, 'I hope you were enjoying it with the Dulacs and Miss Shackleton.' Edith had driven him and the Dulacs down to Steyning; from Penns, Willy somewhat ingenuously described the Chantry to George: 'They have a charming old house with an immense garden in the middle of an old country town—house, furniture, pictures, garden all perfectly appropriate. They are two elderly women. Yesterday the younger of them motored me here.' The same day he wrote to Edith in words reminiscent of his earlier speeches to Margot, 'I am happy & at peace—my only dread that I may not please you.'[7] But he dutifully reported to Riversdale that he was entertaining Edith to lunch and including her in his London circle; Olivia however never seems to have been introduced. Again George's awareness of Dulac's complicity does not seem to have affected her own relationship with Edmund and Helen. From now on, as Willy divided his English country visits between Penns on the Rocks and Steyning, she welcomed the additional support in keeping her husband physically well and intellectually stimulated. Sometimes she was uncertain as to his whereabouts—mail would be forwarded to Penns on the Rocks when he was at the Athenaeum; only after his most recent letter would she know he had by then decamped to Steyning. The inevitable delays were not always accepted by his agent or publishers with her equanimity. It would appear, however, that Dorothy Wellesley observed Edith's encroachment on the poets' territory— especially in the same county—with a resentment equalled only by Edith's of her. Ladylike on the surface, both showed their true feelings in other ways. 'He is tired after a week of tempestuous grand ladies but seems happy here,' Edith wrote to Dulac after retrieving Willy from Penns. Hilda Matheson wrote on behalf of Wellesley after Yeats's death, 'I suppose we must be prepared, from various rumours I have heard, for a whole crop of unworthy or silly or tiresome books about WB. No doubt Edith Shackleton will be one of them.'[8] By July he was planning a winter journey to the south with Edith and her sister; 'Ah if we were already there on some warm southern beach, lined with palm trees & the moon the only other inhabitant.'⁹ Although he invited George to join him, it was understood this would be after Edith had left.

But he also needed the quiet of the flatlet in London. After his first visit to Steyning, he admitted that although he had 'a pleasant time', 'there have been too many people staying or calling & I have talked too much & am tired. I long for Holland Park where I shall not speak to a soul until 3.30 when I set out for the club if I do set out.' He enclosed a photograph of Edith, Helen, Edmund, and himself in the Chantry House drawing room.¹⁰ Obviously nothing was being kept from his wife, despite the occasional ingenious evasions his nature enjoyed; but he apologized for seeing so little of his daughter who was by now in London, though he did ring her up 'from time to time'.¹¹ However, Anne was thoroughly enjoying herself at the theatre, responsible to no one. From now on, as he spent less time in Ireland, he and George would conduct more business by post than together at Riversdale. Patrick McCartan was in Ireland bearing good will and a cheque from the Testimonial Committee, and on Willy's behalf George gave a luncheon party for him at the Kildare Street Club; there was a flurry of letters over whether Yeats needed to return earlier than planned, and what the precise terms were for the proposed gift from the American committee. In addition she was trying to rouse Higgins over the monthly *Broadsides*—he was not answering her appeals for help over musical settings—and searching out 'lost' manuscripts Willy urgently requested. She was also preparing the various volumes of the two de luxe editions for Watt to send to Macmillan and Scribner (who were 'screaming hotly about "copy" '). Always conscious of what his work would look like to future generations, she was especially anxious that all details be included in these editions: 'Perhaps you will not think it necessary to give each play its own date, but students of your work may be glad of it.'¹² Yeats accepted most of her suggestions about the ordering of material and the accounting arrangements she made with Watt and his publishers; he in turn faithfully reported all business arrangements he was making with Macmillan about the new volumes they were bringing out in the regular series.¹³ Whether or not he realized that this was preparation for George's eventual responsibilities as literary executor, he also recognized that he was asking a great deal of her. 'My wife gives valiant aid, but her children and her house weigh her down, and there is so much to do between theatre and Cuala,' he admitted to Wellesley.¹⁴ As usual his absence was an opportunity to have the study repainted.

But now Yeats was embroiled in a quarrel with Dulac, who had been put in charge of the music and composed some of the settings for his broadcast 'My Own Poetry'. After hoping that Margot would renege when learning that she was singing only one piece (she did not), Willy insisted on rehearsing her for 'The Curse of Cromwell'; but Edmund demanded his own professional musician and speaker for the poems for which he was responsible. As usual, there are various versions of the row, according to George 'WBY's the most exotic':[15]

Dulac had lost his temper with the BBC people who had left his name out & had denounced them over the phone. He was within his right. When my rehearsal began I told him his musical rehearsal would follow as he could keep silent. He came up into the little room like a musicians gallery where I was with George Barnes of the BBC & interrupted & when I refused to listen said 'You are not in your Abbey Theatre now' & presently I said 'Take that man away'. He went declaring he would take his music with him. I finished my rehearsal in peace, & Helen pacified Dulac. I doubt if the BBC ever saw anybody in such a fury as I was . . . I never found out what Dulac wanted except that he wanted to interrupt me. I beleive [sic] that I rejected for bad speaking a speaker he wanted rejected for not following his music. When his musical rehearsal came he asked for & was granted a professional singer. God help that professional singer next rehearsal if she or he attempts to pour humanity out of a bottle.

Other 'stormy rehearsals' followed; Yeats objected first to the professional singer engaged by the BBC and insisted that the announcer say she was produced by Dulac and not by him, then to the unfortunate harpist whom Dulac brought in to play chords behind the words of the songs, thus in Yeats's ears 'making the music too important'.[16] George unwittingly added fuel by writing to say 'how very enchanting "Cromwell" was—the last stanza perhaps not so good, but all the rest quite lovely. A vast improvement on her [Margot's] last broadcast. The singer of course impossible, though the music delightful.' Astonished by his wife's praise of Margot, Willy sent her letter on to Dulac, saying 'on the subject, music, we have never been in agreement. She has, I think, generally disliked "folk" settings. I had indeed awaited her letter with alarm. Of one thing you may be quite certain—she means exactly what she says.' Apologizing for his own violence, he innocently asked if he could send George a copy of Edmund's setting of 'He and She'. Dulac, who had already complained that Willy's behaviour had been 'unfair and very disturbing' and Margot's performance 'incredibly bad . . . "plummy" and theatrical', grew even more indignant:

George is very kind and generous. Her 'of course' about the singer is a bit of a give-away though. I don't know what you mean by wanting George to go over the music with somebody. . . . I am not likely to set any more of your poems and don't see the point of submitting to God knows what kind of criticism what will never be used again. If, however, George wants the music for herself I can get a copy made from the original . . . I also know now that, on certain grounds, one can never be sure of where one stands with you.[17]

Having received a blow-by-blow description of the saga, George merely asked, 'You dont say if you and Dulac are friends again. I think you probably are, because you have a genius for remaining the friend of people to whom you say the most abominable things! (I am thinking of your letter in which you tell me you said in the midst of the BBC row "Take that man away"). Are you broadcasting with him later?'[18]

George's forecast was as always accurate. After a further exchange of charges, denials, explanations, and expression of grievances independently to Turner and anyone else who would listen, the two friends were reconciled. Signing himself '*always* affectionately', Dulac seems to have had the last word: 'I am glad we have all simmered down. Some obscure grievance in you must have wanted an outlet. [If] found in these discords let us rejoice it is over.'[19] Edith reported that 'the Poet' was pleased by Dulac's letter, adding, 'He is in perfect agreement with your thesis and rather wondering what he has been fighting about!' But just to be sure, Edmund sent his own conclusions to George. 'WB seems calmer about this silly affair of poetry singing. . . . as matters stand there is nothing to be done about it unless one were to start at once an institution for the training of performers, musicians, and . . . publics. Meanwhile I shall not waver from one point: he, or any other poet, should not allow "inspired amateurs" to play about with his work. In all this quarrel it is the only point I have endeavoured to make. He does not seem to have understood it.'[20] Having almost exhausted the subject, Dulac and Yeats agreed to cancel their planned BBC debate on poetry and music.

Equally disturbing for Willy on this trip to England was the 'very painful' situation at Penns. Dorothy Wellesley, overtired from escorting her daughter through 'the season' and coronation events, had suffered an emotional collapse and was apparently hallucinating. 'Talking to her is sometimes a strain because she forgets what she has said or what I have said,' he wrote to George. 'The whole thing comes from an attempt to go back, in the interests of her daughter, into a world she cast off.' He urged her son and daughter to arrange for medical attention and a professional nurse. Telling nobody there what he was doing, he 'used our old Order methods of cure . . . & apparently with success for the moment', but after a week's recuperation at Steyning he was 'only just recovering from the strain'.[21] He asked George to send him more sleeping tablets; he was ready to go home. However, when he returned the following spring, he was delighted to discover that his spell had been permanently beneficial. 'When I was at Penns last Autumn & alarmed about Dorothy I meditated by myself & got the impression first of a garden & then of green trees & I told Hilda & said that I thought green trees were the best surrounding for Dorothy . . . At dinner the other night she began talking of her dreams & described a constant dream of a garden followed by green trees.'[22]

Yeats returned to Riversdale before the end of July 1937. 'If you are to be here all August and September you could probably instruct Mary to keep off all the Americans who are now beginning to inflict us,' George had warned. 'There have been eleven in the past six days wanting to shake your hand . . . The horrid creatures have their cheap trips in the summer months.'[23] The Americans he was committed to were Patrick McCartan and his colleague on the Testimonial Committee, who were in Dublin for Horse Show week; arrangements were being made for the Academy to honour them at a dinner at which he planned to make his own statement. Thanks to their generosity, there was much discussion between Willy and Edith, and George and Willy, over winter plans. When Heald suggested the Riviera, he was doubtful. 'My London doctor—Young in Harley Street—warned me against the French Riviera years ago because of the cold wind at sunset. I will make what enquiries I can & let you know. I need exemption from damp and chill but most of all I need quiet for when I lose that my ankles swell & then comes the devil.' But after consultation with George, 'My wife thinks that I should not reject the French Riviera because of what my doctor said some years ago, when I had a lung attack. What I need is a good lodging, much milk (not goats milk) & a piece of level ground, warmth & a clear sky.' He was amused that this time it was George who urged him to return to his diet of milk and fruit and salad from their own garden; it was, he pronounced with satisfaction, the 'fate of all successful revolutions . . . to become the next orthodoxy'.[24] He was already making arrangements for his return to England. Hilda wrote that Dorothy was better, but when he described his winter plans to Wellesley, 'to be back in Ireland during November and December (where I have to keep an eye on the Abbey), and then get to a warm climate with friends and dig myself in to some inexpensive spot until spring', tactfully he did not mention who those 'friends' were.[25]

George escorted Willy back to London on 11 September, and until the end of October he shifted between the Athenaeum, Penns, and Steyning. By now he was dictating business letters (including those to his wife and daughter) to Edith, who was also typing drafts of his poems and final plays. If George felt that she was being obliterated from his creative life, she did not show it. On 22 September he sent her a cutting from that morning's *News Chronicle*: the BBC had announced that Jelly d'Aranyi would be performing Schumann's long-lost Concerto for the first time on 20 October in the Queen's Hall, with the BBC Symphony Orchestra; full details were given of the role of the spirit messages.[26] 'My uneventful life leaves me with nothing to record,' he replied when acknowledging her long and 'most amusing letter' about the departure of the Abbey company to the United States. Unfortunately, Fred Higgins was accompanying them, which left the organization of the *Broadsides* entirely in George's busy hands. Willy had however seen Dr Young; although there was an increase of albumin, he was pronounced 'much better than at any of [his] previous visits'.[27]

Keen to observe Anne's progress, and knowing that Willy would be concerned about performances at the Abbey while the major actors were away, George made a point of attending the theatre regularly. *The Man in the Cloak*, a new play by Louis d'Alton, came in for harsh judgement. 'If Clarence Mangan was the cringing, self-pitying, horror, that D'Alton has made of him I dont think he is worth making a play about. If such a play had been presented at any other theatre I would have walked out after the first act. The newspapers today praise it. "In Siberian wastes" . . ."Pain as in a dream" and so on, "You'll think of me through Daylight hours, My virgin flower, my flower of flowers, My dark Rosaleen!"' She then added tellingly, 'Perhaps I hate the play because you have taught me to hate the weak.'

In his absence, she was doing 'a mass of dull work, clearing out old typescripts and so on', and asked, 'Can I now burn all the old typescripts of "A VISION"? I will not do so unless you tell me that I may.'[28] The long-planned revision was finally coming out on 7 October, he told her; to the dismay of many future scholars, 'all old proofs etc' could therefore be destroyed. When his six copies of *A Vision* arrived, he sent three to her 'as you are part author'.[29] He also sent a copy to the Swami, though 'My wife did not want me to send you this book as she thought it was so out of your tradition it could only bewilder you.' Although he still believed in the discarnate Instructors, work on the *Upanishads* and *Aphorisms* had broadened his view:

It is meant for Europe. The stories at the opening and ending at page 60 are about the kind of people who in Europe are interested in spiritual things. The section called 'Dove and Swan' may interest you, but leave the complicated geometry alone, unless you have a genius for such things. The creators of geometry said they did not themselves make use of it but that it was the only way they had of getting their thought through or rather this was implied. They said they had 'assembled it' for my benefit.[30]

Yeats did not mention George's participation; if the Swami was not yet aware of her spiritual capacities, the introduction would fill him in. The American edition appeared the following February. Most reviewers were bemused by the whole thing, but he appreciated the generosity of Charles Williams (who had not been included in the anthology): 'He is the only reviewer who has seen what he calls "the greatness and terror of the diagram".'[31]

By mid-October 1937 Yeats's plans for the spring were 'getting clear'. 'I think of Cap-Martin at Monte Carlo where life just now is cheap, a hotel advertises food & lodging for 8/- a day,' he wrote George. The Heald sisters could come for any one month; could she come before or after? 'It should be pleasant & sunny & Anne will be fairly near.' He sent her some new poems and had in mind 'a long Noh play on the death of Cuchulain'. He also tried to persuade Olivia to join them—doubtless after Edith had left. George replied that she would love to join him at Cap Martin, though January would be difficult because of Michael's holidays. She had meanwhile created a small sitting room for herself upstairs at Riversdale; as her husband's business manager she needed an office.[32]

To George's relief, both Edith and Dorothy kept a watchful eye on Willy's health and followed her instructions concerning his medication; but she kept an emergency bag packed just the same. However, she was the next casualty, felled by 'an overwhelming cold' that turned her brain to 'cotton wool' and made it difficult to arrange for Anne's study trip to Paris. Within a week she was in bed with a bad case of influenza. In Higgins's absence work on the *Broadsides* was also delayed, though she struggled in to Dublin to prod the printer and designer. Willy in his turn grew alarmed, urging her to ignore his business letters until she was better, and wiring Anne for news of George's condition. On 20 October he wrote unromantically from Steyning, 'If a certain date is given correctly in *A Vision* this must be the anniversary of the marriage. Last night I had a nightmare. I was in a crowded house of horrible people, who all said you were dead (I have been anxious about your cold). Then I found you in the form of a large cold cooked chicken. I took you up & then bit by bit you came to life. I woke up very content.'[33] What George thought of this unflattering image of herself as mother hen is not recorded; she was already feeling 'revolting' and had an ulcerated throat, which would at least save her from telephones for some days.

She was still planning to meet him in England at the end of the month for a planned visit to Jean Hall, who, at vast expense, had recently restored and moved into the twenty-three-bedroom Broughton Hall. Anne was to accompany them before going to Paris—and there were her clothes to see to also. George was 'certain she will buy none in Paris—all her money will go in books as it did in London. She bought one summer frock because I threatened her with stoppage of allowance if she didnt!' Now or a little later she presented her daughter with the expensive plum-coloured hat that would cause her as much embarrassment as pleasure—when she passed by Trinity College on her way to the Abbey, the students would circle her to read the embroidery on the wide bottle-green ribbon around the headband—'Je' on one side, 't'aime' on the other.[34] However George then had another relapse and went back to bed. Then Pangur died, 'a slight blow to me—Mary and the gardener think me heartless because I said "I must get a kitten for myself at once".'[35] But as she reminded him, she had learned to be strong. 'My Own Poetry Again' was broadcast on 29 October. Although he insisted she should not meet him ('I shall manage all right. I am much stronger now'), George as usual went to Holyhead when Willy returned to Ireland on 1 November.[36]

The spur that led to Cuala's reorganization had been a poorly published *Broadside*. Unfortunately the wrong version of Dorothy Wellesley's ballad had been printed with the wrong music, and furthermore, Wellesley complained, the illustration was 'vulgar and unsuitable'. To make matters worse she was just recovering from the death of her beloved great Dane, Brutus; Lady Dorothy did not have George's resiliency. 'It is only one of the things that have gone wrong,'

Willy apologized. 'Higgins and I were away. My wife has had flu and was, I think, much worse than she will admit. I knew she had lost grip of things and would have returned at once but for my broadcast. . . . I was never sent a proof. If only there were an Irish Hilda Matheson.' He was about to reorganize Cuala and make Higgins managing director. 'If he had been here there would have been no errors in your poem and a wrong artist would not have been chosen.' Two weeks later he was still excusing George; 'When my wife is ill and Higgins away I have no help here—hence the errors. My wife struggled on fearing that I might come home and catch her influenza.'[37] There was no acknowledgement that he may have agreed to George's choice of artist (Harry Kernoff, who 'has a harsh side'), but he was beginning to realize that his wife had been left with too much to handle. He himself was mainly confined to the house; 'Willy is not in very good health ever since his illness two years ago, kidney trouble,' Lily worried. 'I don't suppose he will ever be very well again, but will have to be slow and careful. His mind is as vigorous as ever.' By mid-December he was admitting, 'I do my editing under difficulties.' He did not seem to realize that Wellesley herself had suffered a serious accident and was in hospital for more than two months.[38]

Despite the determination to let his Dublin institutions take care of themselves, the Abbey was continuing to dominate their thoughts. Lennox, depressed and alcoholic, was threatening suicide; they hoped he would submit to psychoanalysis. Frank O'Connor, newly appointed managing director, believed Robinson was 'drinking deliberately, as a substitute for suicide. Ten or twelve years ago he made up his mind that he could not attain the intensity needed for great art.' Yeats recalled Lennox speaking to him in despair 'at being so inferior to Synge'. In an effort to encourage him to give up drinking, O'Connor had appointed Robinson head of the school of acting, but his public criticism (during a debate at the rival Gate Theatre) of O'Connor and Hunt's play *The Invincibles* led to a demand by the Board for his dismissal.[39] Yet he was the theatre's longest-serving Director aside from Willy, and one of the Abbey's most prolific playwrights. Fearing that any disturbance would damage their negotiations with the government over financing necessary repairs and rebuilding, Yeats took the chair '& had to strain what influence I have to get it withdrawn. . . . He has stopped drink & thereby soured his temper without recovering his intelligence.'[40] Although the idea of a two-week 'Abbey Theatre Festival' in August 1938 seems to have originated with Lennox, he could no longer be trusted; Higgins (seen by some as responsible for a 'web of intrigue') had replaced Robinson as the 'heir apparent'.[41] When Lennox elected to produce and cast *The Player Queen* for the 1938 Festival without Yeats's permission, the reaction was swift and lethal. 'My letters to Lennox Robinson were personal mainly concerned with the Academy of Letters,' WBY wrote to the secretary of the Board. 'I made him no statement, & gave him no message intended for the Board of the Abbey Theatre. Should I decide to ask the board to give a part in my play to an English actress—& I have decided nothing of the kind—I will bring the matter before the Board myself. . . . I could not live a peaceful life if Lennox started casting my play behind my back.'[42] Dolly and Lennox continued to make efforts to 'reform in the temperance direction', but such attempts seemed to be short-lived. Dolly however continued painting (she held an exhibition at the Gallery, 7 St Stephen's Green, in October 1938), and during these years Lennox wrote some of his finest plays.[43] George suggested Cuala might publish Lennox's memories of his early years as a complement to a volume or two of Willy's letters to Lady Gregory, but Willy was 'not quite sure if his work is of the type that sells well through a private press'. Neither project came to fruition.[44] As the years passed, George saw less and less of her two friends. She was fighting her own private battles, but for her alcohol was not yet the crutch of consolation it would later become. Meanwhile life for her would continue to be a jumble of children's needs, Willy's interests, and the increasing dissatisfaction of both of them with the political and cultural life of Ireland. She would later write to Edith, 'nobody can feel more passionately than I feel for him that he has to return to this desolate place!'[45]

Ever since he had arrived home from London Willy had been struggling daily with fatigue. Thinking this might be the fault of the climate (and perhaps stress over the Cuala reorganization), George suggested taking him to France ahead of Edith and her sister, but he needed his library while writing the introduction to Patanjali's *Aphorisms*, and would not budge.[46] Seán O'Faoláin brought Elizabeth Bowen to tea, and remembered how George kept imploring him not to leave, 'He likes her! He likes her!'[47] Depressed by recurrent illness and the grey weather, Yeats dreamed of getting away to the sun: 'As I look out on the snow covered fields (snow has just turned to rain and soon all will be slush) I think with joy of our getting out of the train into warm bright air, or almost bright and warm air, certainly into the encouraging presence of palm trees.' He instructed Edith to fix their departure for the south of France 'as soon after Jan 3 as you like, but let me have a few days rest with you before we start if that is possible'. For the first time someone other than George was responsible for his travel arrangements. Yet still he desired his wife's approval, writing to Edith: 'Your paragraph about all the people who might or might not come with us to Monte Carlo was valuable, though I hope neither the lady from Belfast nor anybody else will come. I want you to myself. I read the paragraph to my wife and she laughed at the idea of our not going alone. That means her blessing. With her the start is all important. Other peoples minds are always mysterious and I wanted that blessing.'[48] Years later Edith would tell Ellmann that Willy was 'puzzled and hurt when George ceased to have an interest in sex';[49] how much this was evasion of the actual situation on his part is debatable, but there appears to have been some truth in the statement.

Christmas 1937 was the last they would spend at Riversdale. Michael went without his parents to aunt Fanny Gordon's family gathering on 25 December. 'Jack and Cottie and Michael came in after dinner,' wrote Lily. 'We all chattered like starlings, nothing of the least importance said. Jack was very funny, showing us how he had seen a man playing a mechanical piano with feeling and emotion. Michael must be now 6 ft. He was silent but not an oppressive silence as he heard and saw and was interested.'[50] Anne remained in Paris, by now working regularly in the studio of theatre designer and teacher Paul Colin, and visiting as many theatres and galleries as she could fit in. Lennox, who visited over the holiday, had sent her a letter of introduction to Granville-Barker and her father sent one to Gordon Craig. Both men entertained the young woman courteously, and Craig continued to correspond after she returned to Ireland. When Anne reported that Craig seemed vastly amused at her having 'no notion of art school drawing', George asked, 'Was this because he thought your drawing vile, or because he thought your designs lively & active & unfinished? I cant see that "art school drawing" is a vital necessity, though I *do* regret that your drawing isnt a little better than it used to [be].'[51] Lennox also introduced her to other friends, most of whom thought she was his daughter; Anne reported that her French was infinitely better than his. George kept her fully informed of all the theatre activities and gossip of Dublin, providing detailed criticism of design and direction. She did not care for the ballet: 'I do *not* like poems spoken to dancing! Especially badly spoken to poses. We did all that sort of thing fifty years ago, only then we did it with one mouth, two arms and two legs. Now it is done with one or more mouth, and other peoples arms and legs. Both have comic value.' Tanya was away ill and her assistant (always referred to as 'ninetofive' because of her determined attempt to keep to a schedule) was not too dependable. Everyone at the theatre—Cyril Cusack especially—missed her. 'So far Lolly has shown no alarm at Cyril Cusack's lamentation at your absence from the Abbey. I have no doubt I will hear reverberations of auntish anxieties over niece's association and acquaintance with nice but undesireable young men. My ears are cocked. A most unsuitable motherly letter so burn when read. Mothers really ought to guide footsteps . . . Independence is unknown to Lollipops.' She happened to mention to Lily, confidentially, that it was time for Michael to have evening clothes. 'Broadcast throughout Ireland proceeded from one telephone remark. Good publicity agents, your aunts!!!!!' But Michael had sensibly decided he was still growing too fast. There was a new white Persian kitten at Riversdale, 'most excellent kitten, well-mannered, but somewhat too active'; she assured Anne it would still be very much 'energetically and abundantly "kitten"' by the time she returned.

George was sending 'suitable extracts' from her daughter's long letters home to the Abbey. Frank O'Connor, who had brought Evelyn Bowen around to meet the Yeatses, suggested that Anne stay on in Paris despite Tanya's absence, since 'there is nothing of any interest coming on at the Abbey'. Willy had suffered another bad spell, and was 'very much afraid of the journey' to the south of France, although George thought that it might be managed if he went by the new train ferry. 'He and his friends would get into their sleepers at Victoria and get out of them in Paris. Sounds easy.' However, not having heard from Anne for some time, he once again wanted her safely on this side of the channel: 'father got very worked up, decided you were wasting your time, wrote to the O'C about it, saw him twice, wanted you re-called to Dublin, wrote to Ninette de Valois (Sadler Wells) to know if you could be taken on there, got answers suggesting you went for three months from January 1st; the O'C obviously wanting you to stay in Paris. I was called in and agree with the O'C. Your father was rather disgruntled because I had not backed him up.'[52] She explained later to her husband why: 'I did not like disagreeing with you about her going to Sadler-Wells-Old-Vic but I thought that if she were re-called to a new position she might lose her independence and so lose also the conviction that she is making her own career. I think I told you when we were both in London circa January 6th–8th, that Ninette de Valois had said to me that Anne could go there at any time.' Once in France himself Willy finally conceded defeat, writing to his daughter that 'all you tell us is good so you need have no fear of my "sidetracking you" '. But he could not resist adding, 'you can always go to the "Old Vic" any time if you want to & work under a lot of different producers. But tell your french instructors or any others that their ladders & stairs & platforms will soon be as dead as crinolines or glass cases full of wax flowers. Hamlet must act not pose.'[53]

On 5 January 1938 George and Michael accompanied Willy to London; did she meet Edith then? George took the night boat back to Ireland on the 9th, leaving Michael to return on his own the next day. She got home in time to receive Willy's wire telling her of his safe arrival in Monte Carlo. His windows at the Hotel Terminus looked on to 'blue sea & bright sunlight & the shore and mountainside you remember. Much such a view as we had at Rapallo.' 'Fearing she may have heard I passed through Paris and think I should have seen her,' he sent a letter to be forwarded to Anne, asking George first to 'put spelling right & make it legible'. He wrote Anne again, thanking her for her Christmas letter. 'Extraordinary', Anne wrote to Tanya, 'I have had two letters from Father in a fortnight, I cant get over it.'[54] She was reading his essays with pleasure, but when she tackled *A Vision* could make 'neither head nor tail of it'.[55] She dined with Sylvia Beach, who played her recordings of Eliot and Joyce; Anne preferred Father to either of them.[56] She was doing so well with her theatre studies O'Connor suggested she stay an extra month.

But again Willy fell ill, this time a 'violent digestive upset' from 'some sort of foliage, red-cabbage or the like'. By the time he wrote to George he had recovered. He and Edith (they were alone) were still in the expensive hotel, but Edith must join her sister in Paris by 5 February. He suggested that, unless George was tired of housekeeping, they might take a flat for two months. 'It would be cheaper than a hotel. If you would like this Edith Shackleton & I could probably find one. We could take it for two months.' George advised him to avoid both cabbage and endive, but on the whole preferred not to cope with a flat and servant for two months. 'We might find a flat that we could take *next year* for three months. So often one finds that there are not enough bedclothes pillows and things to eat off etc!' There was only so much she could leave up to Edith's discretion. She also warned him that the Dermod O'Briens would be staying nearby at Cap d'Ail; 'neither of us would like a great deal of Mrs O'Brien's company I think.' Tactfully she asked, 'Shall I arrive on the 5th, or do you want me to over-lap?' With strong memories of his previous collapses she concluded, 'Do look after yourself,' adding in a postscript, 'Of course if it were *necessary* I could now come out *any time*, as Michael has gone back to school.'[57] That emergency bag was still packed and ready. But before she left there were various business matters to attend to. Willy had left her with the final corrections of his poetry for serialization and publication by Cuala; she sent a 'bunch of poems 2 copies of each' to the editor of the *London Mercury* so that he might make a selection, asking him also to arrange for American publication; what he did not want she would send elsewhere. She was concerned about copyright, but Watt could arrange an interim one of six months. Not since her hasty flight to Majorca had she trusted an editor to correct the proofs himself, but she would send the proofs Yeats corrected for Cuala once he returned them to her; time was short, for Cuala was publishing *New Poems* in May. She was still corresponding about proofs and typing out corrections the night before she left for Menton.[58] Wellesley wrote to Willy that George had replied to a wire from her, assuring her 'with the tact I expected' that the 'news is very good'.[59] Having had enough experience with postal failures—the Rathfarnham post office seemed to make its own rules—she now kept a 'postbook' recording all the letters she forwarded.

Willy meanwhile was working well, and 'content with life'; he was still correcting proofs for *New Poems*, which 'for the moment please me better than anything I have done. I have got the town out of my verse. It is all nonchalant verse.' Optimistically, he declared he was finishing 'my belated pamphlet and will watch with amusement the emergence of the philosophy of my own poetry, the unconscious becoming conscious. It seems to increase the force of my poetry.'[60] Whether George approved the sentiments of *On the Boiler*, she could at least appreciate the spur to his verse. On 22 January, even before his wife's rejection of a service flat reached him, he and Edith had moved. 'This [is] a charming hotel with the sea in front & my window wide open, & cheap (12/- including food),' he wrote from the Hotel Carlton in Menton. 'Come as much earlier as you like but not later than Feb 4 as Edith Shackleton must go on Feb 5. I look forward greatly to your coming & to your being here with me in this beautiful weather.' He was feeling so well that he was planning the future and negotiating his next BBC broadcasts; 'I think with pleasure of spending what will be left of spring & then summer and autumn in Dublin working with Higgins & then returning here to this bright dream.'[61] On her way through Paris George had dinner with her daughter at the Hotel Palais Lyon; 'we gossiped and ate the whole time—it was *grand*,' Anne later wrote to Tanya.[62] She left Paris that night, arriving in Menton the morning of 4 February with the usual luggage—typewriter, publications, 'and the first eight years of your letters to Lady G. which I can type while on holiday . . . To say nothing of various other things.' 'You will find me working in bed as usual,' Willy had written. 'Your room will be ready & the weather all probability clear and sunny.' Edith met her train.[63]

George too had been looking forward to sharing that 'bright dream', and getting away from the cares and responsibilities that oppressed her in Ireland. 'I am giving everyone the address "C/O Thomas Cook and Sons Mentone, France"', she explained to Willy, 'because after a month more in Mentone we might like to wander somewhere else. In any case it will prevent Lolly discovering ancient butties and planting them on us. She is very anxious to do this; "Violet has friends in Mentone if you feel lonely". NO, NO, NO!! If we find a flat or villa we like I think we must still keep ourselves free of an address except to friends outside Dublin!'[64] Even Lolly had written hoping that her overworked sister-in-law would 'have a good time—& see & do something you *want* to do & not be always doing things for other people *all the time*—Have some relief.'[65] George was familiar with the town—on that anxious first journey to Rapallo, they had stopped to consult a specialist, and they had often passed through on their way to visit friends in Monte Carlo. Her knowledge of the area began even earlier, for Harold Hyde-Lees had been assistant chaplain of the parish of St John during the winter of 1923. Nestled between the sea and encircling hill and stretching along a wide, crescent-shaped bay, the small town claimed to be the warmest on the coast, protected from cold winds and heavy rainfall; lemon trees grew in the hills above, their scent pervading the plazas and streets. Almost at the Italian border, it was only six miles north-east of Monte Carlo by road, and within easy driving distance of the airport at Nice.

Life soon became a pleasant restful routine for both of them. Thanking Anne for the crystallized fruit she had sent with her mother, Willy described his days:

I like the box. Now that the fruit are eaten it serves as a tray for small oranges which I eat in considerable numbers. I like your letters to your mother & myself—so full of animation. At your age I think I was melancholy, weighed down by the troubles of the world, but you are gay & that is much better. But then you have not my difficulty in spelling, or if you have do not care, & that is a great help in letter writing. You would like this bright, serene, artificial place where the sun & the sea always shine. Your mother has hired a wheelchair & pushes me along by the sea. In the morning I write poetry & after lunch she pushes, then I sleep & write letters & read [Jack's] new book 'A charmed Life' which is as delightful & inconsequent as the Bible. You can begin it any where as you can the Bible & it is almost as improving. Now I am going to lie down & go to sleep, as your mother has very properly told me to do. Your affectionate Father W. B. Yeats (getting on in years but amiable).[66]

He was writing poetry, which he had begun to think he never would again, and he soon finished his 'big essay' (as least the first draft). He admitted to Edith that he was 'often bored' and would like to talk to 'those people about me, who have interesting heads', but, unlike George, he did not know their languages. However, he was keeping 'marvellously well' and 'the life is good for my mind and body'. George did her best to keep him interested. One day they noticed an exhibition of paintings by the daughter of Richard Le Gallienne, whom he had known many years before in London; 'it was the first day show just opened —pictures charming, & humorous exaggerations of Victorian life—much that was delightful & Miss LeGallienne herself fat & plain with one of those quite natural faces which in a moment you seem to have known all your life—no mask, a kind of cousinly good will. LeGallienne was an over sexed sentimental goose, with no taste, yet what children he has had? I go to see him on Friday. He has a villa here.'[67] He was relieved that George was prepared to show 'good will' towards Edith, whose 'powers of observation' she had noted; George even sought (though without success) some wallpaper Edith had admired.[68]

However, they soon began looking for cheaper lodgings; their expenses, including Willy's extra milk and mineral water, came to about £11 a week plus 15 per cent service tax; he wondered whether Ethel Mannin might know of something suitable. More and more convinced that he would return, he again contemplated the possibility of taking a villa, telling Ethel that he did not like 'the nightly crowd of unknown faces' in the big hotel on the Promenade.[69] In her letters to Anne George was more blunt about their fellow residents.

We are having incredible weather. This is a rather fearful place—full of retired English army people and the like; they talk of nothing but politics in loud and piercing voices. Your father only penetrates to that part of the world between one and three, and at dinner in the evening. He sang all through lunch yesterday to the frank astonishment of a few foreigners and disguised horror of the British!! The British look like people who had to learn some poetry by heart at school some forty or fifty years ago, but who have never thought of it as emanating from an individual; I am sure they think 'it' grows like a cabbage or a fish by some peculiar dispensation of providence.[70]

Still not anxious to accept a villa, George looked elsewhere. On 1 March they moved to the Hotel Idéal Séjour, avenue Virginie Herriot in Roquebrune, a few miles closer to Monte Carlo on the other side of Cap Martin. A true country hotel, its sign proclaimed 'Maison repos arrangement pour famille'. 'It is a very charm-ing spot, not on the sea-shore, but in among the trees and it has a large garden and mountains visible through the trees,' Yeats wrote enthusiastically to Edith. 'This seems the perfect hotel, very clean, good taste, a garden, shady trees, fine mountain scenery, cooking excellent (all done by proprietor). £3.10 a week including taxes & tips, a largish room with a balcony. You would love this place.'[71] So small that it probably did not have more than six guest rooms, the hotel had a separate restaurant reached from a side entrance; they had their tea in the garden. There was no further word of the Lady Gregory letters George was to have typed, but by now Willy had written at least seven new poems in addition to his '30 or 40 page pamphlet', all of which required clean copies made by his wife.[72] Although it seemed a pity to be leaving when the cold weather was gone and 'all is blue & warm', he was already looking forward to London, his BBC programmes, and Edith. 'It will not be possible to go by Newhaven—George finds difficulties connected with time & luggage. She says "Tell her I will put you into the train at Victoria & send you to Steyning at once"!' he wrote on 2 March.[73]

Even before they left the Hotel Carlton George's calm was shattered once again by worrying news from home. On 19 February she had received two wires from St Columba's informing her that Michael's leg had been injured while he was playing hockey and he had blood poisoning; he was rushed into a Dublin nursing home and examined by specialists. After speaking to Dr Collis and the headmaster on the telephone, she was less frightened than at first. 'I had plans all laid to deposit yr father in the English nursing home next door, while I rushed to Dublin,' she wrote to Anne, 'but I don't think now I will have to. Septic legs are the devil & of course I visualized Michael laid out on an operating table & so on.' She had avoided telling 'Lollipops' about the nursing home. 'In fact there was a general conspiracy on all sides to prevent her knowing anything about it until he was returned to the San!! She would have driven Mrs Sowby mad—to say nothing of Dr Collis—by telephoning every ¹/₂ hour.'[74] She was relieved for other reasons too when Anne had returned home from Paris. On 13 March Hitler annexed Austria; the trains were crowded with anxious people hurrying home for fear of war.

George and Willy arrived in London on 23 March 1938, staying overnight at the Grosvenor Hotel. He made George's apologies to Dorothy Wellesley, who had once more extended a warm invitation: 'I wish George would accept your invitation but she asks me to explain that she is hurrying back to Dublin to our son Michael who is home from school with a septic leg.' Yeats then went to Penns on his own the next day, explaining to Edith that he could not refuse. 'She would have thought it very unkind as on the 30th she goes away for months.'[75] Once again he did not stop in London long enough to see Olivia. By the time George got to Riversdale on the 24th Michael had been sent home because of an outbreak of chickenpox at the school. Within days he was felled by that as well.

George's report seemed designed to keep Willy safely in England:

Had hoped for a note to say you were well or some remark of the sort. If you arent, ask Edith to say so! Michael very much better today. He had three days of temperature between 100 and 104 and I was alarmed, but on the fourth day he dropped to 95.6 and has remained there, and the leg now seems very comfortable. It is to be 'unwrapped' on Friday Michael of course *looks* horrible. I dont suppose you remember Anne aetat $1^3/_4$ weeping when she first saw her face in a mirror after chicken pox! Hers was nothing compared with Michael's, but Michael has had constant applications of a lotion which poor Anne's doc didnt give her.

Meanwhile Michael's leg was better, but 'He has gone "septic" everywhere he can, assisted or perhaps instigated by chickenpox, and my entire time is taken in putting on and taking off dressings. As soon as one section clears another one breaks out.' Tending to Michael would keep her busy through most of the summer. Late in April she was finally able to take him away for a week's holiday, but only as far as the Claremont Hotel in Sutton. 'He needs a change very badly,' she told Willy. 'He cant go far from Dublin owing to his infernal leg. He looks allright when you see him on profile from the left side, but the right side of his face is horribly scarred. Some of this will tone down with time! Anyway he is no longer infectious. He has not been able to wear spectacles very much so I have had to keep him amused as he cant read much without them. In fact I am rather tired!'

George was however keeping a wary eye on the Abbey. Having heard, doubtless through Anne, that *The Player Queen* was being proposed for the Theatre Festival in August, she at once sent Hunt and Lennox messages that Yeats must be asked for permission. 'I think I suggested a year or more ago to you that you ought to write a note to the Abbey Board that no play of yours was to be put on unless your permission was given before rehearsals were started.' She had returned to Anne's excitement at being assigned the design for *On Baile's Strand*, and encouraged her daughter to discard the cloak by Charles Ricketts traditionally worn by Cuchulain. 'She felt timid about the cloak of Cuchulain because he says "Nine Queens out of the Country under Wave have woven it with the fleeces under sea and they were *long embroidering at it* . . ." My own feeling is that those few words would not make the audience wait for a heavily worked coat. She made a design which seemed to me to fit so much better with all her other things that I regret the importation of Ricketts.' When George finally saw the production, she thought it 'rather better done . . . than any play for a long time'. Unable to leave Michael for long, she had gone to the gallery (from where she hoped to slip away unnoticed), and 'heard every word of Cuchullain's without the slightest strain, and that at the Abbey is pretty good!!' Having seen nobody but doctors, she was dependent upon the telephone for the latest gossip. 'Frank O'Connor's departure with Mrs Speaight seems to have put ideas into the heads of quite a number of people, who are either upping and doing likewise, or contemplating the divorce of spouse or spouses after years of—shall we call it toleration?' This does not sound like a deserted wife. But she was tired from being once again 'the perfect mother'. As for Riversdale itself, the family hedgehog 'drowned itself' in the lily pond; and the two roses sent by Dorothy Wellesley that had not flowered last year ('Austrian Copper' and 'Austrian Yellow') were now in full bud.[76]

Meanwhile Willy was delighted with his week at Penns, 'which seems at last to have become the centre of intellect I have longed for'. The conversation 'better than on any previous visit' with the right guests, including 'selfless & able' Hilda Matheson, Turner, and Clinton Baddeley, who had been one of his verse-speakers, all 'connected with our conspiracy "Modernity" in literature'. The house was becoming 'a centre of activity at last'. He was pleased by a recent article on his work that praised his language for being 'public' while regretting that it was not applied to the subject of politics. George would not have been so surprised by MacLeish's insight; she of all people recognized the distinction between the rhetoric of the 'public' Yeats and the equivocality of the private 'Willy'. The poet's response to the article and recent discussions at Penns resulted in the first version of 'Politics', which would become the last poem in his next Cuala Press volume.[77] While at Steyning he had written 'a fine lyric' and was writing a new play 'which will be something for Anne to do a setting for'. 'It is in verse & will be strange & powerful but very short. It will make part of my next book of verse.' He was concerned that there be enough new poems for another Macmillan volume 'or your income would fall too much'.[78] He did not realize that in New York, although Scribner's were holding in their safe the complete revised copy of his works and the prefaces and introductions, with Yeats's list of the order in which all should be printed, nothing was yet set in type. Although George would spend considerable energy searching out the illustrations (even arranging for a new photograph of the bust of Maud Gonne in the Municipal Gallery), captions for which WBY was to approve in proof, an internal memo suggests that 'There is no great rush about the Yeats. . . . I suppose we ought to go through the motion of sending proofs to Mr Yeats for Titling. Then, if he doesn't respond, we'll have to fix up the titles ourselves.'[79] The Macmillan de luxe edition was also on hold in London. The only new volume due to come out was the expanded *Autobiography*, to be published in August by Macmillan of New York. There would be many lean years to come.

Cuala was as always a topic of debate. 'I hope you are not giving too much thought to Lolly's complaints!!' George wrote reassuringly. 'You know what she is. If she does not like her new hat she immediately thinks up every grievance she ever had and pours it all out. I have been watching her weekly accounts very carefully and I do not think she has anything to complain of.' Besides, now that de

Valera had settled his economic differences with Britain, 'The new pact removes duties from all the things she sends to England (also on Lily's embroideries!) and this *must* within a year make a very considerable difference in both their sales.' However, she took issue with one of his suggestions for Cuala:

I have three letters from you regarding the new Cuala Book. I dont know *a*. What Lolly wrote to you. *b*. What you have written to Lolly. I do not agree at all with your idea of scrapping 100 copies of 'New Poems' published by Cuala. Your last book of poems published by them was in an edition of 450 followed by a book of Frank O'Connor's poems 250 copies, and that year was the best they have ever had. I have no belief in the 'Collectors'' desire for small edition only, because your poems have always sold from Cuala in the larger editions and as far as I know no complaint has ever been made by any 'collector' about the number of volumes issued. Nor do I think that the printing etc of the Cuala books is so good as to induce any 'collector' to buy them for any reason except desire to read the contents in a 'first edition', which desire would be as completely satisfied by a first edition published by Macmillan and co.

You may remember that you and I went very thoroughly into the question of the number to be published by Cuala, with especial reference to that good year when your last volume of poems was published by them, and that we were in complete agreement about numbers. I am sorry if I seem to oppose you; I only do so because I think Lolly has probably been Lollyish. It is *nonsense* for her to say that she has 'a lot of unsold books at the end of the year'. What she is at is that you are away and she thinks she can work you up when you are alone.

But they agreed that *On the Boiler* should be printed by a commercial press and sold by Cuala on a profit-sharing basis.[80] That was a decision George would come to regret.

She was becoming concerned about Willy's new burst of energy:

Dear Miss Shackelton [*sic*] A letter of WBY's dated May 5th suggests that his next week is going to be very full. Do, please, extract from him his prescription for the digitalis mixture and make him take it twice a day while he is still with you! *You* know his habit of packing in to the last week all the people he wants to see, and *I* know his habit of arriving home very exhausted. If he seems tired, *three* times a day. That journey from London to Dublin is most fatiguing. Yours affly George Y

Edith's reply, now missing, was clearly reassuring, for George wrote less formally a week later, to 'Dear Edith'. 'Thank you so much for your letter. I should have known that you would see about the "digitalis" & you must forgive me for fussing. He needs so much intellectual stimulus that you & others can give, but he unfortunately also needs that very mild heart stimulus.' She signed herself 'Yours affly George Y.'[81] Evidently they had arrived at a certain unspoken *modus operandi*; George acknowledged Edith's role in keeping Willy happy, and she was relieved to have him taken care of, but despite the warm salutation, they could never be friends.

Willy returned on 13 May. It was a bad crossing, but George as usual met him at Holyhead. And again as always, he immediately succumbed to the 'wet air & cloudy skies'. His last week had indeed been an exhausting one, but George was pleased to hear that Hilda Matheson had arranged for him to lunch with Arnold Toynbee; he had long wanted to meet the historian whose thought he believed similar to his own scheme, but had been shy of making a direct approach.[82] Apologizing to Olivia for not stopping in London to see her, he reported on how he found his world: 'the Mentone doctor said I may have several years . . . Michael is back at school after various ailments incident to his age but Anne is & has been in robust health. She thinks of nothing but her theatre work, & neglects her appearance & everything else.'[83] Unusually in his letters to Olivia, there was no reference to George. He was more expansive to Edith: 'On Sunday my son was here, tall & elegant having just won a mathematics prize with a score of either 98 or 100 percent my wife not sure which. My daughter has returned from Paris with greatly increased confidence in her own opinion.'[84] George faithfully attended Michael's prize-giving ceremonies, but alone. Mary Lane-Poole, Ruth's younger daughter who was now visiting Gurteen Dhas, noted with admiration how well dressed she was for such occasions, looking 'very fine—black with some green in your hat'. But fond as George was of hats, she was beginning to take less care of her appearance.[85]

Willy meanwhile was already making plans for next winter's escape: he proposed that George go out with him in mid-November and then back to Ireland for Michael's Christmas holidays while Edith joined him; his wife would then return when Edith left. Later it was decided that instead of George coming home, Michael would go out to spend Christmas with them; Edith would step in when his wife and son returned to Dublin.[86]

Summer at Riversdale was the usual combination of fuss over Cuala and —despite Yeats's hopes—more trouble at the theatre. Frank O'Connor had resigned, in part because he was now living with the actress Evelyn Bowen (Mrs Robert Speaight), a distress to the conservatively Catholic government. Hugh Hunt had turned out to be less satisfactory than they hoped, and had finally blotted his copybook with his production of two of Synge's plays, which roused Seán O'Faoláin to public protest. Yeats summoned a special meeting of the Board at which it was decided to remove the plays from Hunt's jurisdiction; 'We are trying to arrange that he goes amicably but go he must. It has been a slow business getting rid of him.' 'It looks to me as if I shall have to re-organize not only Cuala but the Abbey,' he wrote cheerfully. 'Though we are prospering financially we have discovered an astonishing muddle in our accounts. I hope to know tonight what has happened. I alone have sufficient authority to control events.'[87] As George was well aware, her stubborn husband would never give up that control easily. George's dissatisfaction with the English producer had doubtless confirmed his own fears. After seeing Hunt's production of *The Shewing-up of Blanco Posnet* she wrote,

I liked Tanya's settings, hated her costumes, and returned home on the last bus trying to remember Stephens poem 'the noise of silence' and failing to remember it, cursing and swearing all the way about noisy productions, noisy to the eye and to the ear, screaming yelling howling shouting gesturing—booo. But I suppose the only alternative is contained in that horrible word 'restrained'. Certainly when the stage yells and shouts the audience takes its cue. Now do please not repeat my violent remarks to 'your Board'.[88]

Hunt stayed on long enough to steer the theatre through the Abbey Festival in August. Tanya remained only five months longer, and in February 1939 Anne, only 20, was left with full responsibility as head of design.

When Willy was away there were various guests at Riversdale. Some of Anne's friends in the company might spend the night. Tanya was always welcome for a weekend and was generously entertained when her young stepsister came on a visit (and slept in the absent poet's bed). Her mother, now married to John Drinkwater, lunched with George—a much pleasanter experience than George remembered with the poet's first wife in New York.[89] Once Willy returned, although George did her best to protect him from an excess of visitors, some were more welcome than others. Gogarty brought in Montgomery Hyde (private secretary to Lord Londonderry) and Baron Franckenstein, ex-minister of the Austrian Legation in London, 'We were given a warm welcome,' Hyde recalled. 'Gogarty always cheered him up, he told us, while his wife wound him up.'[90] Towards the end of June, on one of their periodic visits from America, Mary and Padraic Colum came to tea. Struck by the familiar swift entry and eager voice, they were shocked to see him wearing a black patch over one eye (later this was replaced by plain glass). For the first time, Mary wrote, 'I saw him in the role of a parent concerned with the future of his children: his daughter was present, and he talked about her work as a stage decorator with a father's interest.' They never saw him again.[91] Vernon Watkins, son of the founder of the occult bookshop in London they had both frequented so regularly, stopped by and was encouraged by George to visit Ballylee; he later sent her a photograph, and later still, expressing sympathy at her husband's death, recalled his visit to Rathfarnham. 'How beautiful it was—that afternoon when we talked together. In a moment I saw how wonderfully your devotion and tender love sustained him I believe his poetry was greatly sustained by it, too, and in that case the world owes you an incalculable debt!'[92] Another guest was Shotaro Oshima, who had come from Japan to attend the Abbey Festival. George had given careful thought to the decor, and Oshima was pleased to observe a series of Japanese prints of kabuki performances lining the hallway and, laid out in the sitting room, Sato's sword and Yano's gift of two festival dolls (dairibina) on the mantel-piece. He remembered her warm friendly greeting 'as if I had been her intimate friend for many years', but was chastised for insisting on photographing his hero: 'Why didn't you say so before he went upstairs. He has been very ill of late and has not seen even his brother and sister. It was with a great effort that he saw you. He is very tired.'[93] 'Mrs Yeats does protect my brother from many callers,' Lolly had told an American benefactor. 'Sometimes we think she overdoes her watchdog duties, but probably *she knows* best.' Lolly herself once officiously warned Patrick McCartan that Mrs Yeats might not let him in. George tried to conserve Willy's failing energy in other ways, objecting to Lolly's frequent requests for autographs and 'short messages' in Cuala publications.[94] In June 1938 some of Yeats's visitors got a shock. Having had success with blue pomade to brighten his white hair, Willy next tried a stronger dye; Anne returned home to find her father's head 'a beautiful brilliant blue' which she thought lovely. But when one of the actors arrived at Riversdale to discuss Abbey affairs, George took him aside and warned him not to mention the strikingly original hair; Shields could not take his eyes off it. The blue effect lasted some considerable time.[95]

On 8 July George accompanied Willy to England, staying the weekend, pre-sumably to visit the Tuckers. Her return was delayed by a sudden impulse:

I only arrived home this morning having decided to prance round and about Liverpool, my decision being partly influenced because I could not get a berth on Liverpool-Dublin boat Monday night, and the Tuesday boat was an old boat. I had forgotten that Tuesday was July 12th. I got involved in a colossal crowd about 9 p.m. on emerging from a cinema, in Lime Street. About fifteen thousand 'Liverpool Irish' were waiting for the Orange procession. As I had never seen an Orange procession I decided to wait. The crowd got thicker and thicker; it started more or less with elderly 'shawlies' and their men, and then 'shawlies' with infants of all ages, and finally youth and youth entirely intoxicated male and female. The females all wore little orange paper caps like the caps the American navy wear, but instead of patriotic emblems on the caps they had such remarks printed on them as 'Squeeze me' 'I'm no angel', 'Atta Boy'. I thought of getting out of it, but the crowd was too thick, and I finally managed to get against a wall with a stout American sightseer in front of me. Two nuns idiotically appeared in the middle of Lime St. and a man jumped out at them and they were surrounded by men booing. Police on horseback rushed the crowd; foot police finally surrounded the two nuns and got them into a car and a little later a black Maria arrived and departed with a few men. My stout American just went on saying 'Oh My! Oh MY!! OOHH MMYY! OH MY!' in crescendo, until the procession itself arrived about 10.15 p.m. and the crowd unlocked itself and I got away from him. The procession most orderly; banners, uniforms, females in white with sashes etc, and drums and drums and drums. The nastiest crowd I've ever been in, and I've been in a lot! . . . Liverpool crowds smell horrible!'

When she arrived back at Riversdale, Mary Martin provided a coda to her tale for Willy:

When I told Mary, she said 'Liverpool Irish are funny People. I was in Liverpool once when a new piece of land was to be blessed for the building of a new chapel. The streets were lined with Catholics from all the Sodalities and there was a lovely procession with all the representatives of the Sodalities in uniform carrying candles and they all went to the place where the Bishop was blessing the land and the candles were all lit and the moment the land was blessed they all came away and they went wild and murdered everybody and Dora said "that's nothing" & took me down some side streets which were beautifully decorated with banners and streamers across the street and figures of the Blessed Virgin in every window and everybody was drinking pots and jugs of beer and dancing in the streets and you wouldnt think they were Catholics at all.'[96]

Willy, who was excited by the surfacing of 'a new crazy Jane poem' ('I had almost forgotten that poor lady'), enjoyed George's 'most vivid & vital letter'. He had news to tell her in turn, 'the strange tale of Ottolines death', which he had heard from Wellesley. Ottoline had gone to a nursing home to see her husband who was being treated for heart problems. When told that Philip had only a year to live, 'the shock was so great that she had to be given a bed & died almost immediately. Her temperature, when she heard the news, went up to 105.' 'Phillip is of course alive & in fair vigour so far as one knows.'[97] George's reaction to this story is not known; it was one more break with the early years of her marriage. The Liverpool adventure, however, would not be her last that summer. When Michael had finished his exams the two of them sailed to Glasgow, where after visiting the Arts and Crafts Exhibition (Cuala items were on display in the Irish pavilion) they travelled around Loch Lomond, planning to stop 'when we see places we like'. Leaving Michael to pursue his travels, she then met Willy at Chester on 8 August. As always she stage-managed their return, sending a postcard (of Robert Burns's cottage in Ayrshire) to Anne: 'I meet yr father on Monday & we shall be home in time for dinner. Do wear yr new frock *if* you can get home in time!!'[98] The two-week Theatre Festival had already begun, and Anne, as the only member of the family in Dublin, had attended the opening reception in 'a most striking evening dress', in which she duly paraded before her father. Michael too had pleased his father: 'I have received my sons school report—as good as possible. There is one boy he cannot beat at examinations, his friend Falconer [*sic*], but he has been testing him by "intelligence tests" & finds him lacking. Clearly my family is growing up.' However, alarmed at the sight of his swollen ankles, once they reached Riversdale George ordered her husband to bed for three days.[99]

Anne's most successful achievement was the design of *Purgatory*, during which she had to fight off Hugh Hunt's desire for more than the simple bare tree and backcloth stipulated by the playwright. George had reported the controversy to Willy in England. 'Hunt is threatening to have a MOON in the backcloth of "Purgatory". Anne is refusing. If she does not win, she is going to say that she does not wish to have her name on the programme as designer of the setting. He talks of having a round hole (stage left) covered with gauze and lit from the back. I told Anne to say that you did not want a moon, only moonlight.' This may have been when Hunt was heard to mutter as he, Tanya, and Anne worked on the set, 'Father says . . . Father says.' But although none of them could be certain it was Yeats's last play for the Abbey, Hunt was as aware as Anne that the production was historically as well as aesthetically significant. He continued to call up George with various questions:

He asks if, as 'Purgatory' comes between three other plays, it should be introduced by music, or 'percussion' or drums. I said that as far as I knew you did not want any of these things; that you wanted a bald production, no noises off, the whole to be concentrated on the two characters OLD MAN and BOY, and the appearance of the woman at the lit window of the burnt out house.

   I told him that Anne had told me that he had an idea of a moon in the backcloth, lit; and that I thought you wanted an indication of moonlight but NO MOON. He asked if he could cut the line about 'I will cut a stick out of that tree' and if you would give him a line instead, as the OLD MAN would probably have a stick in his hand. I agreed, but gave him your address at Steyning so that he could write about this Please reply to him by return!!!'[100]

Anne persevered, and opening night on 11 August was a triumph for both her father and herself.

   The next night Willy and George returned to the Abbey for *On Baile's Strand*, revived with Anne's designs and 'a magnificent Cuchulain'. 'I have not seen it for years,' Yeats wrote to Edith, '& it seemed to me entirely right—ornate elaborate like a Crivelli painting. My daughters designs for it & Purgatory—especially for this—were greatly admired. Purgatory perfectly acted. House crowded.'[101] *Purgatory* had raised considerable debate, apparently instigated by an American Jesuit priest who took exception not only to the play's theme but to Yeats's curtain speech. To both Heald and Wellesley Yeats took pains to correct the newspaper report: 'My speech is misreported. I said: "I have put nothing into the play because it seemed picturesque; I have put there my own conviction about this world and the next".'[102] But in general he was dissatisfied with the Abbey.

The new players, who join us through our school, have such misshapen bodies that one of the old players, a man who incarnates our traditions, threatens to go to America because he cant stand rehearsing them. Ireland is getting a proletariat which in Dublin is pushing aside the old peasant basis of the nation. We talk of getting players from the country but dont know how to do it. . . . The Festival drew great crowds but our performances were not as good as they should have been—Hunts fault & the new players and the aging & stiffening of some old players. I am talking by hearsay for I went only twice. Some of the acting in my two plays—the two I saw—was magnificent.[103]

'Hearsay' was doubtless from George as well as O'Faoláin. The theatre however continued to challenge him, and provide new stuff for poetry. Having seen his Cuchulain so beautifully acted, he returned once more to that play cycle, this time a play about Cuchulain's death: 'It is necessary to wind up my plays on that theme.' At the same time, annoyed by a book of essays about Rilke, he hastily wrote the lines 'Draw rein; draw breath. | Cast a cold eye | On life, on death. | Horseman pass by.'[104] George denied that he wrote these in the margin as he told Wellesley, but the old player's criticism and Rilke's ideas on death would be drawn together in his next magisterial poem, 'His Convictions', later retitled 'Under Ben Bulben'. In what would prove an even more significant gesture for his wife, he then decided the lines provided the inscription for his own tombstone. It was but a short step to his next crucial decision, that he be buried in Drumcliffe churchyard, at the foot of Mount Bulben in Sligo. When he told Lily about these instructions she objected, 'You have broken with tradition. There has not been a tomb-stone in the family since the eighteenth century & went on to prove it. I asked why that was & she said "O I suppose because it has always been a gay family".'[105] His sister informed him that Yeats and Sligo had recently been in the news for other reasons. 'I hear that the Land Commission have bought the Hazelwood property including Innisfree—the woods and house are I think to be used by the forestry dept—but Innisfree? Will they put up notices "This way to the 'Bee Glade' " "—beware of the bee, anyone interfering with the bee will be severely dealt with" "The beans must not be eaten they are the property of the Land Commission" etc etc.'[106]

George discreetly absented herself when two more friends met with him in August; it would be his last encounter with both. When Ethel Mannin and her future husband passed through Dublin Yeats entertained them to dinner at the Shelbourne, taking along Higgins to make up the foursome. Ethel recalled it as 'a joyous lively occasion'.[107] And, finally, Maud Gonne, looking 'like a ruined cathedral' (the elderly Sarah Purser's words), came to tea. 'A motor will call for you at 4 or a little after,' Willy wrote in his invitation. 'I have wanted to see you for a long time but—'. It was a nostalgic meeting during which he startled her by saying, 'Maud, we should have gone on with our Castle of the Heroes.'[108] But two months later reading her autobiography *A Servant of the Queen* upset him so much he had a bad night. 'Very much herself always—remarkable intellect at the service of the will, no will at the service of the intellect,' was how he described the book—and his ancient love—to George.[109]

He was having trouble with his breathing and was anxious to be away. First Cuala business had to be settled, but Lolly was ill and had gone off for a rest. Convinced that his sister was 'neurasthenic', Willy dismissed many of the symptoms which clearly spelled angina. Conspiring with Lily, George persuaded Lolly to see a doctor and to give up her painting lessons—she was 70 years old and still offering two classes in schools and one private class at home. 'Willy is to make up the money of the lessons to Lolly. George had not told him so yet but would break it to him soon. George is a strong rock.'[110] But Lolly too was sturdily independent; she was still seeing some pupils at Cuala after her brother's death.[111] Then on 26 September Willy's aunt Jenny died, leaving only Fanny Gordon of his father's generation. Her will left the miniatures, family portraits, and a sixteenth-century marriage cup with the Butler crest to Willy, and a silver tea set that had been presented to his grandfather Yeats to George. She was 82.

The greatest blow was, however, the news that Olivia Shakespear had died on 3 October. Willy had lost one of his oldest friends; for George it was not only a further break with her own childhood, but also with her 'dearest Coz'; it was unlikely that there would be any more happy encounters in Sidmouth as when Dorothy, Olivia, and Omar visited the Tuckers. Although retaining a tenuous contact with Omar, she would not see Dorothy again. Olivia's passing was a further anxiety to Nelly, for 'Harry's grief is tragic to see. I can do and say nothing—'[112] Dorothy was too ill to return to London, and so Ezra was deputed to clear out his mother-in-law's flat. He wrote to George on 9 October,

Coz is down with fever so various details devolve on me. I want to get as much of the letter writing done while I am here with typewriter. 1. D/ has recollection that William once stated that he wanted a certain embroidered portier of Olivia's. All of which may have or have had basis in fact (or fancy, or some esoteric reason, association or what not) and he may long since have forgotten said object, but IF he remembers and wants it I am deputed to see that he gets it. 2. I remember that a quarter of a century ago some bloke stole a lot of his first editions. If there are any that HE hasn't got and that exist in Olivia's set the same might be restored to him. I am open to further suggestions. Any chance of your being in London about Nov. 1st?[113]

He asked that she reply to Dorothy, but Dorothy was still too ill to deal with such matters. 'I wrote to Dorothy about Portiere etc,' a worried George reported to her husband, 'but I heard a couple of days ago from her that she is not coming to London & has sent my letter to Ezra. He suggests sending your letters in a sealed packet "to Lennox or whoever will ultimately be editing 'em". I have written *not* to do this!! Asked him to send them to Athenaeum addressed to you. You can bring them back on your return from S. of France.' All too aware of what they might contain, she added, 'If posted to Dublin they will be opened (& I am sure greatly enjoyed) by the customs!' Mindful of his own mortality, Willy apparently destroyed some of his letters to Olivia before they departed for France.[114] Nelly was also doubtful of Ezra's good sense in disposing of Olivia's belongings. She wrote to him suggesting that her sister-in-law Kitty Woodmass, George Montagu's first wife, was 'competent & will take away anything Dorothy likes to give her. She's a good scavenger (as she says).'[115] She told Dorothy that 'Georgie' had written that Willy was once more ill, 'dropsy now, all sorts of complications!'[116] Willy had been in bed with lumbago at the time, but this may also have been an excuse to forestall any suggestion that George herself could travel to Sidmouth when she next crossed over with her husband.

On 6 October 1938, Cuala Industries finally became a limited company with George and F. R. Higgins as directors alongside WBY and—of course—his sister. 'It is not perhaps *quite* what I wanted, but I think it *will* serve,' Lolly wrote to an American supporter, 'and I will not be in further under such a strain as I will share the responsibility [of] Cuala with 3 other Directors.' On 12 October Willy controlled the reconstructed board's first meeting at which shares were distributed, one ordinary share to each director and £1,000 in preferred shares to him. A new auditor, F. R. O'Connor, was also appointed; at first Lolly approved of him, but as his demands for precision became more apparent, she later remembered the matter differently. 'They appointed him Auditor of the new company *at our first meeting*. I felt it was useless to protest. The man was sitting there. I did open my mouth to protest, and Mrs. W. B. put her hand on mine to keep silent. W. B. was of course in an irritable mood—*not at all well*—so she may have felt it best to let things go through, and I *subsided*.'[117]

At the next meeting George was in the chair, where she would effectively remain for the rest of her life. The remaining ordinary shares were distributed: 250 to Higgins, 100 each to WBY, George, and Lolly, and five each to Eileen Colum, Esther Ryan, Maire Gill, and Kathleen Banfield 'as members of the staff in recognition of their services'. Essie Ryan had worked at the press for thirty-seven years, Maire Gill for thirty-two. In order to save George and curb Lolly's correspondence, Kathleen Banfield was to learn to type. George reported in detail on the first meetings she chaired in Willy's absence:

The Cuala meeting went off amicably except that Lolly's Minutes were rather a joke. The arrangement now is that Higgins keeps rough minutes and Lolly is to copy them into the book. There was a slight contretemps over the Minutes as Lolly had written them out like an essay—no paragraphing—and all out of sequence. As Chairman I pointed out that the various matters which came under finance were not kept together, upon which she declared that the agenda from which she had written up the minutes had no 'finance' written on it. She had lost the agenda and an undercurrent of argument was kept up all the meeting (suppressed by me frequently) and at the last moment she remembered the agenda was in the printing room!! She fetched it in triumph and said 'I was right, the word finance was *not* on the agenda'. The word was 'accounts'. Fred and I nearly got the giggles, but he apologised nobly for having written accounts instead of finance. As she seemed ruffled I took her firmly out and gave her a pale sherry and sandwiches at the Shelbourne and she became most amiable. I have suggested to her that she should have the cup of tea at four which she is accustomed to. She says she gets too exhausted to think if she misses it.[118]

The agreement with the bank stipulated that Lolly send weekly reports to George and Willy; it was not long however before she became distressed by her lack of control and George would spend considerable time placating her. Lolly was pleased when a group of American admirers, tireless James Healy among them, formed 'The Cuala Associates' 'to foster a broader appreciation in this country of Cuala achievements'. Not only her brother's work was appreciated.[119]

Willy meanwhile had finally escaped to England. The political news grew more threatening as Hitler's claims advanced, but he was still determined to get to 'some warm place', even if it turned out to be Cornwall. However, despite his own poetic predictions, Yeats found it hard to believe in war.[120] When Chamberlain made his famous promise of 'peace with honour' after the Munich agreement of 30 September, he wrote to Wellesley, 'I share the general relief; war would have meant to me spending what remains of life here, where the winter climate makes me ill, or among unhappy & probably impoverished friends. You would have outlived even a long war (& it would have been very long) but I would never have got out of the dark tunnel.'[121] To Heald he admitted that he was 'just emerging from the fatigue that follows over work, partly caused by difficulty in constructing my little play The Death of Cuchulain. I want the quiet of your personality & your talk.'[122] He would continue to work on the play for the next two months. Yeats left Ireland on 25 October, delayed a few days by a hurried trip to the dentist to repair his broken dentures. He arrived, he told George, to find war fever high at both Steyning and Penns in the Rocks, for Sussex was considered a safe area to billet refugee children. At Steyning there was 'great indignation over the mismanagement of the billeting'. At Penns he witnessed 'an indignant dispute between Dorothy & Hilda' over the government orders to provide trenches for any house with a certain number of staff. In Hilda's absence Dorothy had filled up the trench; 'Under no circumstance will I sit in a dug-out with my employees listening to the gramophone.'[123] He thought it wise to avoid Dulac until On the Boiler was published.

George returned from Holyhead to yet another family illness. Michael had another fever and was in the college sanatorium; the problem seemed primarily 'growing pains'. Young Mary Lane-Poole, who fortunately had a car, drove her immediately to St Columba's, but discovered 'Nothing much wrong—High temperature for 2 days for no apparent reason. He looked rather pale yesterday but will be allowed up today. He slept for almost 48 hours & Collis thinks he was just overtired. He has been working very hard & is of course growing fast.'[124] No sooner was Michael up than Anne sprained her foot at work and was confined for a week to her father's chair and footrest. 'Lordy what a household we are,' she wrote with some exasperation to Willy at Steyning. There was also a tram and bus strike in Dublin, which was a 'damn nuisance'. However, by the end of November they would be starting for France; 'I am making arrangements for departure then. I shall want cheques to buy tickets and Cooks cheques about

ten days in advance.' Wellesley and Matheson were planning to join them and
had issued an invitation to stay in their villa, but this was postponed until after
Christmas and Michael's departure as Dorothy was once again in the doctor's
care. This time Willy was able to pay for George's (and Michael's) expenses and
new clothes for the journey; he sent her a cheque for £150. 'I doubt if you have left
your self anything for clothes,' he later wrote, enjoying his new-found largesse,
'Would you like £50.' He was also pleased with Ezra's response to his recent
poems: ' "rather good" which for him is rapturous approval.' Now that the weather
had turned damp, he was anxious to leave even earlier, but George was committed to the Cuala Christmas sale, for Lolly had printed her name as co-host on
the invitations. 'I shall be glad to get away for a time, freedom from the telephone
will be a rest.' She was 'rather dreading the two long afternoons at Cuala; Lolly
seems to expect me to stay from 3. to 6.30 each day . . . bloody. I shall have
to make appropriate remarks to all the people I have known and avoided for the
last twenty years.'[125] However she was anxious to placate Lolly 'as far as possible';
one evening they had a special outing to the cinema.[126] As soon as the second
day of the sale was over, George left on the night boat for London via Liverpool,
bringing with her a large number of books and, of course, her typewriter. At
the last moment Willy had added two more volumes to their list, Gregory's
Cuchulain of Muirthemne, which he wanted 'for place names in my play', and
Milton.[127] She had also taken the precaution of getting 'cartes de Tourisme' from
the French Legation, 'which will save the nuisance of getting Cartes d'identité in
France (compulsory for a stay of more than two months.)'.[128]

They were to leave Victoria station on the ferry train the evening of 26 November; Lily was impressed by her sister-in-law's 'preventative for seasickness, a meal
of kippers and apples, no tea. Tea is fatal.'[129] Like Willy, George longed to return
to the sun and olive trees of their hotel. However, Dorothy Wellesley was anxious
to meet her, and had even travelled to London 'to buy clothes that she may be
able to entertain Mrs Yeats properly'.[130] Shy of such an encounter, and explaining
that she already had a luncheon engagement for Saturday, George was resigned
to the inevitable: 'I will come to lunch at the club (Carlton Gdns) at 1.30 on
Friday unless I find a letter at the Grosvenor Hotel saying I am not to. I dont at
all want to dine on Friday as I said in a previous letter!! But if you have made
the arrangement I suppose I must . . . What a very obstinate person you are!'[131]
Her luncheon engagement included attending the theatre, where as usual she
described the setting of Shaw's *Geneva* in detail for Anne, along with instructions
for the menus at Riversdale once Michael returned home from St Columba's
('chicken for lunch and sardines for supper').[132]

The original plan had been to go first to Beaulieu-sur-Mer, to a hotel with a
beautiful garden recommended by a friend. But on arrival they found it impossible.
'All the trains ran just behind it and to make things worse there were children

in the Garden and a wireless in the dining room,' George wrote to Anne. 'The children were permanencies, being the progeny of the proprietors, nice children, but of the age when you *must* bycicle and trycicle [*sic*] and scream!!' Making the trains the excuse, they returned to the Idéal Séjour, 'perfect as ever'; they were the only guests, and the weather was warm.[133] Although Willy could walk in the gardens adjoining the hotel, George again hired a bath chair from Nice so that she could wheel him along the promenade. Ireland seemed far away; Lily complained that, after the first telegram to Anne announcing their safe arrival, there had been no word.[134] By mid-December Wellesley had settled with Hilda Matheson in La Bastide, a villa in the hills above Beaulieu where she had spent several winters as a child. Every few days George and Willy would be motored by Hilda to La Bastide; W. J. Turner and his wife were staying and there were a series of dinner guests, including the Austrian musician Artur Schnabel and his wife.[135] On her arrival Dorothy was astonished at how healthy Willy looked, and he read with excitement his new play, *The Death of Cuchulain*; both she and Hilda thought George 'very nice'.[136] They frequently called in at the hotel, and George was able to leave Willy long enough to go on some excursions with them, such as lunch in the ancient hill-town La Turbie. On 22 December Willy outlined to Edith their current arrangements and future plans:

My son is expected. He should have been here by 2 p.m. but then it was to be 4. Now is to be 12 p.m. at the earliest. The hotel proprietor, who is always in bed by 10 is keeping himself awake in the hall. It is 10-30. The mischief is all caused by the weather. Here it has been cold but I was able to sit out after lunch as usual. . . . My wife says you may fix any date in January you like to arrive on. She has merely to arrange with my sister about Cuala. When & if we go to Dorothy I do not know—Dorothy seems overwhelmed by the cold of her villa & the warmth of our hotel. . . . All friendly here except the cats, which look at one as if they expected to be eaten—perhaps they do. The Rapallo cats did not seem to mind—not in the same personal way.[137]

Michael finally arrived at midnight. They all dined Christmas Day with Wellesley and her guests; Willy was 'full of charming stories', primarily for his son's benefit. The two male Yeatses had at last found common ground in their interest in politics; it was now that Michael corrected his father's interpretation of the Czechoslovakian takeover, his explanation 'dumbfounding' Willy. 'I have become very fond of Michael,' he told his wife.[138] He also was showing more concern for George's wishes. Back in Ireland Anne, busy at the theatre, had gone to the Gordons for the usual Christmas dinner. After a trip to Corsica by himself, Michael left for Ireland on 15 January; George made arrangements to return after Edith arrived on 27 January; Wellesley and Matheson planned to leave in early February. Offering to pay for the hire of a car ('I have plenty of money'), he wrote to Edith about her later arrival, 'I am sad over the delay, but I must weigh this against the fact that it has pleased my wife who hates going back to housekeeping now that she is not anxious about our son.' However, he was also aware of the responsibilities she faced in Dublin, adding, 'On the other hand the end of January is about as long as she should stay here. She has a lot to do in Dublin Broadsides, etc. Our not going to Dorothy's villa was her work—she found Dorothy worried about lack of heating, etc, and thought I should be safer and Dorothy less worried if we stayed on here where we are very comfortable.' He was clearly enjoying his current domestic arrangements: 'Dorothy and Hilda are kind people. I dine there every second or third day and am fetched and sent home. We are arranging a new set of Broadsides.'[139]

On Christmas Eve Yeats had told the recalcitrant Higgins, 'I have almost finished my "Death of Cuchulain". It will enlarge my next book of verse. It is a play with a dance in it, but not for the multitude.'[140] However, that along with the Christmas gaiety of exciting talk and games of chess with Michael had tired him. One evening, having still heard nothing from Higgins, they (Willy, George, Dorothy, and Hilda) 'fired' him as editor of the *Broadsides*; another night he awoke from a dream and at 3 a.m. dictated to George the prose draft of 'Cuchulain Comforted'. By the 13th the poem, a new experiment in *terza rima*, was finished.[141] From Anne they heard that the Abbey was 'in chaos'; Tanya was leaving, having had great difficulty working with their new producer Frank Dermody, 'who passes from one fit of hysteria to another'. Anne was now 'sole designer of costume and scenery and a week ago in the general despair was asked to produce as well but had no time'. Willy wrote to his daughter, 'I am glad you are our designer now. It sets my imagination off—damn dark scenes.'[142]

With his wife's help, Willy was setting his affairs in order. His doctor, who had also attended him the previous year, told George that though Willy's body was failing rapidly he might live for another six months or even a year. Although they both knew that he had not long, he thought he had still time to complete the essays for a second *On the Boiler*, and dictated a synopsis to George.[143] Still anxious to further Lily's embroidery, he asked if Michael Rothenstein would be interested in making a few designs based on some of his poems (after his death one eventually arrived which Lily thought 'very good, queer of course and modern').[144] The next day he wrote to Elizabeth Pelham, whom he had not seen for some time:

I know for certain my time will not be long. I have put away everything that can be put away that I may speak what I have to speak & I find my expression is a part of 'study' In two or three weeks—I am now idle that I may rest after writing much verse—I will begin to write my most fundamental thoughts & the arrangement of thought which I am convinced will complete my studies. I am happy and I think full of energy of an energy I had despaired of. It seems to me that I have found what I wanted. When I try to put all into a phrase I say 'Man can embody the truth but he cannot find it.' I must embody it in the completion of my life. The abstract is not life and everywhere draws out its contradictions. You can refute Hegel but not the saint or the song of sixpence.[145]

Lady Elizabeth would later send this passage to George, who recognized its importance to future biographers. He wrote a further poem, 'The Black Tower', and read it to the assembled group; pleased with a song Dorothy had written for the *Broadsides*, he sent Hilda out to make a tune for it.[146] On 22 January he dictated corrections to *The Death of Cuchulain*, and a long memorandum to Augusta Gregory's executor, T. J. Kiernan, concerning what he thought important in her unpublished diaries: 'It is some years since I have seen them, and I admit that the latter part which moved me deeply might not affect someone who knew Lady Gregory less in the same way; to me those fragmentary sentences called up very clearly that simple and profound woman. There are certain passages however of obvious importance.' He expected to be in the south of France until some time in March.[147]

The Dermod O'Briens, who were staying once again at Cap d'Ail, called at the hotel on 22 January; George was out but Yeats gaily entertained them to tea in his bedroom. George was still planning to leave on Saturday the 28th ('if Miss Shackelton's car does not break down while driving across France(!!)'). She was going to travel straight through, hoping to catch the Liverpool boat, and would want 'all ALL ALL the Abbey news at Breakfast' in Anne's room, especially about Higgins who has never written. She was looking forward to being home: 'Longing to see what you look like, I have almost forgotten.'[148] But on the 24th Willy was too tired to join the Turners, who were due to leave the next day, for dinner at the villa; by then George and the doctor realized the end was much nearer than they had expected, and he was receiving morphia injections to ease the pain. On the morning of the 26th he rallied enough to dictate three small corrections to his last poems.[149] Wellesley came for a few minutes in the morning; George asked her to come back in the afternoon 'and light the flame', and on her return she sat on the floor by his bed, holding his hand, while Willy 'struggled to speak'. On Friday the 27th, he was worse, with considerable pain in his heart; he then lapsed into a coma. Dorothy saw him for a few minutes; Edith arrived from Paris in time to sit by his bedside that evening. At 2 a.m. on 28 January the doctor still hoped he might rally, but by 5 a.m., watched over by George, the pain and breathlessness were acute; at 2.30 p.m. he died. Alone with her husband for the last time, George slipped off the signet ring from the fourth finger of his left hand; she then cut off a lock of hair from just above the forehead. For about two hours he was beautiful; 'then the features began to change, and after three hours seemed to sink away.'[150] George asked Edith not to give the news of his death to anybody, not even her sister Nora in Paris, until the children could be told. She wired to Anne, then sent a brief letter. 'Until last night there was a faint hope, but about 3 this morning the doctor told me it would be a matter of a day or perhaps of hours. I have wired Lennox asking if you could stay there for a few days. I will wire you there. I am so glad he had the news that you were to be designer at the Abbey while he was still able to be very pleased about that.'[151] It was the last time she would turn to Lennox for assistance.

Mindful of Willy's wishes, George also needed to make certain arrangements before Ireland heard of his death. She phoned Dermod O'Brien, who that evening brought over from Monte Carlo the Anglican chaplain, Canon Tupper-Carey.[152] After prayers were said over the poet's body, George calmly discussed the funeral arrangements. An early service was necessary for spiritual as well as political reasons: Dionertes had said eighteen years ago, 'I need a ritual of burial'; the Communicators had frequently warned them against cremation which was a shock to the departed spirit.[153] She permitted no photographs to be taken, and dissuaded O'Brien even from making a sketch; 'I will never forget the noble beauty of him as he lay there (in death) with the suspicion of a smile as if he had just had some humorous thought,' he later wrote to George.[154] At the time of Yeats's death, the Moon was in conjunction with Saturn, 'that major planetary timekeeper' so symbolic of his life with George.[155] She kept the hawk and butterfly ring she had given him twenty years before, their signs—Venus and Saturn—incised in the circle within.

It was only on Sunday that the rest of the family in Dublin were informed. Through Dorothy and Hilda, a telegram was sent to Vita Sackville-West at Sissinghurst Castle, who was entrusted to telephone the family in Dublin.[156] In this way it was hoped to avoid word leaking out beforehand. Jack seems to have received the message; barrister and trusted friend of the family Con Curran and his wife Helen drove Jack out to Gurteen Dhas late on Sunday afternoon, discreetly waiting in the car while he broke the news.[157] At George's request, Mabel O'Brien wrote an account of Willy's last days for Lily and Lolly, Jack, and aunt Fanny Gordon.[158] That night George suggested Edith share the vigil, leaving her to watch over WBY until 4 a.m. When she returned to the quiet room, George gave Edith his small Oxford dictionary, his big-barrelled fountain pen, and the manuscript of 'Are You Content?'[159] On the back of the manuscript were ten lines of 'The Spirit Medium'; the juxtaposition of the two poems might be interpreted as a mute acknowledgement of the role the two women had played in the poet's last years.[160] On Sunday at 7.15 p.m. his body was taken up the steep narrow path to the cemetery chapel of rock-bound Roquebrune, high above the bay. That night, George stayed at the villa in Beaulieu with Dorothy and Hilda; Edith remained below at the Idéal Séjour.

Dermod O'Brien accompanied George to the undertakers at la Maison Roblot, where they paid for a ten-year concession on a selected grave site on the second terrace, overlooking the sea.[161] It was as well to be cautious, though both assumed the grave would be necessary for only six months. Later O'Brien settled accounts with the undertakers and clergyman on George's behalf; it was their understanding that the regulations specified at least a year should pass before disinterment, but the representative assured him that an earlier removal could be arranged if required.[162] At 3 p.m. on Monday, 30 January, Canon Tupper-Carey read the Anglican burial service over the freshly dug grave; beside him were George, Dorothy and Hilda, Edith, and Mabel and Dermod O'Brien. Some distance away stood an unidentified man. According to O'Brien, who sent a letter to Lennox the next day, also present were two elderly Irishwomen, Annie and Molly O'Brien, daughters of the anti-Parnellite MP J. F. X. O'Brien. George left the next day, carrying with her postcard photographs of the steep narrow alleyways of Roquebrune and its ancient chateau. On 11 February the undertakers, according to her instructions, placed the plain flat marble marker with the inscription 'W. B. YEATS, 1865–1939' on the grave, but the clerk's entry in the municipal death register read 'Butler, Yeats William'.[163]

MRS W.B.

PART V

MAPPING 1939–1968

'Have I met my wife of that life again'
'Yes . . . She whom you had to defend from tendency to drink.'
(Willy and the control Ameritus)[1]

all these investigations have quickened my memory of the strange, chaotic,
varied and completely unified personality that you are
(George to Willy)[2]

I dont change much, & in one respect I dont change at all. I dont change
towards my friends.   (George to Tom)[3]

I do not wish either you or Michael to live with your aunts at Gurteen Dhas,
Churchtown, Dundrum, because I have brought you up, as I believe, with a
sense of freedom . . . and I do not want either you or Michael to lose the
sense of truth because external circumstances, however difficult, make it.
It is really one of the few things that matter.   (George to Anne)[4]

The link must never be broken. . . . the only importance is *not to break the
link* unless *you are true as far as you can* you break the link
(the Instructors)[5]

20

PALMERSTON ROAD

When George arrived in London on Wednesday, 1 February 1939, she phoned Lily to say she wished a family council to be held before any further public announcements were made. Knowledge of Willy's death had not reached the family until Sunday, 29 January, the same day word spread to the newspaper offices and over the wireless.[6] After Jack heard the news he rang his sisters to say that Willy was 'seriously ill'; later that day when he arrived at Gurteen Dhas, his silent open-armed gesture told it all. As requested by George, Lennox took Anne out to Sorrento Cottage, and asked Tanya to stay with her. Michael, back at school, told the master he wished to remain at St Columba's. After a day in London, during which she made preliminary enquiries about transporting the body from France to Ireland, George crossed over the next morning. Meanwhile Lennox, encouraged by the Abbey Board of Directors in a final effort to have the remains brought back to Ireland, had left on Monday evening for France, flying from Croydon to Paris and taking Michael with him. The two reached Roquebrune late at night, and when Dorothy and Hilda realized next morning that it was the young Yeats who had accompanied Robinson, there was only time to drive them to Roquebrune, tell Michael 'all he might like to hear', and take them back to the train. They arrived back in Ireland just after George; she could hardly contain her fury.[7] Never again would Lennox be trusted. Both children were in shock for days. Michael remembers nothing about the mad expedition with Lennox; Anne could not get warm.

The entire nation reacted without, it seems, much thought of the widow's wishes. Despite the statement in the *Irish Press* on 30 January that, according to Reuter, the funeral would 'probably' take place that day, and the poet be buried at Roquebrune, everyone wanted the body brought back to Ireland immediately. Maud Gonne wrote to de Valera, President Hyde, and Higgins, urging that Yeats be buried in Ireland. On behalf of the Abbey Board Higgins replied, 'We are making every endeavour to have the remains brought home to Ireland . . . I know personally that he had a passionate desire to rest in Sligo. He told me so frequently, and I do think that eventually that will be his resting place. We are using whatever pressure we can marshall to have his wishes carried out.'[8] The Abbey message to George had been aggressive in its urgency: 'Ireland insists that Yeats be buried here Dean of St Patrick's offers grave in Cathedral'; de Valera's wire was only slightly more circumspect, 'We hope that his body will be laid to rest in his native soil.'[9] A flurry of cables crossed the Atlantic: Patrick McCartan offered £100 towards the cost of removal; P. S. O'Hegarty replied, 'uncertain if question money', and Lennox, 'making every effort to bury Yeats in Ireland'.[10] Geraldine Cummins obligingly produced an automatic script dated 1 February purporting to come from WBY, expressing his concern about the quarrel over his being buried away from Ireland and 'the sea'.[11] Apparently nobody was as aware as Willy had been of George's strength of character.

On the evening of Tuesday, 2 February, she and Anne joined Lily, Lolly, and Jack at Gurteen Dhas. Her argument as to his temporary interment in France was clear—Willy had wanted to be buried on the mountain of Roquebrune, 'and then in a year's time *when the newspapers have forgotten me*, dig me up & plant me in Sligo'.[12] The family agreed; they had, after all, for months known of his wishes for his final resting place; the Drumcliffe churchyard where his great-grandfather had served would eventually be fitting closure. To satisfy the obvious need for a public ritual and to placate the Dean, a memorial service would be held at St Patrick's Cathedral. George then phoned Con Curran for assistance in dealing with the press; when he arrived, she told him what she had quoted to the family to emphasize the poet's wishes, and gave him a copy of 'Under Ben Bulben' with its clearly stated final stanza:

> Under bare Ben Bulben's head
> In Drumcliffe churchyard Yeats is laid,
> An ancestor was rector there
> Long years ago; a church stands near,
> By the road an ancient cross,
> No marble, no conventional phrase
> On limestone quarried near the spot
> By his command these words are cut:
>   CAST A COLD EYE
>   ON LIFE, ON DEATH
>   HORSEMAN, PASS BY![13]

Curran distributed the poem and her quotation to all the major newspapers that evening; it was also read in a televised broadcast in London by Gogarty.[14] George did not repeat Yeats's remark, which was later passed on to Ellmann, 'I must be buried in Italy, because in Dublin there would be a procession, with Lennox Robinson as chief mourner.'[15] His poem 'will bind my heirs thank God', he had written to Wellesley five months before. 'I write my poems for the Irish people but I am damned if I will have them at my funeral. A Dublin funeral is something between a public demonstration & a private picnic.'[16] To the treasurer of the American Testimonial Committee, who sent a draft for £200 'to assist in this difficult time', George later elaborated, 'He wanted to have a funeral to which all his friends would go, not as representatives of some public body or other, but as individuals. He did not want to "lie in state" or to have a "public" burial.'[17] Willy never forgot the lesson of AE's funeral, and George, who sympathized fully, was committed to honouring his wishes. It would not be the last time she would have to orchestrate public events.

Letters and wires kept flooding in to Riversdale; George distributed to the press on 6 February, the day of the memorial service, a long alphabetical list of telegrams and messages of sympathy. She did not include those which were most personal—touching notes from former servants (Peggy, Bridgie, Mary, Florence Reade) who remembered her kindness and the happy atmosphere of Merrion Square and Ballylee; the Gordon family; Helen Lawless who had known her as a small child; Dr Dickson of the Order; Jean Hall, who offered to send the film taken at Algeciras; Eva Ducat, who invited her to London.[18] All spoke feelingly of her own contribution to the poet's life and happiness. The memorial service in the cathedral was conducted by Dean Wilson, who twenty years earlier had baptized Anne in Donnybrook.[19] The entire family were present at the service, but not some of their closest friends, for Roman Catholics were forbidden to enter the Anglican cathedral. Lily noted that 'George is fine and brave as she always is. Michael looks poorly and Anne very white and too calm.'[20]

Coincidentally, the Dean's brother, James Wilson, was the rector of Drumcliffe, and had been alerted before Yeats's death of his wish to be buried in the west of Ireland. The day after the memorial service he wrote to George, assuring her that two grave sites had been selected for her to choose from; he also asked permission for the proposed new parish hall to be called 'The W. B. Yeats Memorial Hall'. George replied the next day, 'very pleased to have the Parish Hall called after WB' and that she would call on him shortly concerning the site.[21] On 8 February she and her children, accompanied by Jack, arrived at the Great Southern Hotel in Sligo, and the next morning visited Drumcliffe. Jack later told Lily how interested the children had been in the rectory: Anne and her uncle admired the building itself, especially the staircase; Michael the beautifully kept church records. When they left the rectory Michael said, 'That house has the same smell as Coole'; according to his mother his last visit to Lady Gregory had been when he was only 6.[22] George liked the old sexton, 'a real character'.[23]

Jack stayed in the west only long enough to help select the grave site and walk around Sligo, returning on the mail train the next day after lunching with Oliver Edwards, who was still pursuing his research on WBY.[24] But before leaving, Jack discussed with George the logistics of Willy's return:

it is hoped to be able to bring him by sea to Sligo. He would travel from Liverpool by the line originally founded by the Pollexfens and then called 'The Sligo Steam Navigation Company'. He used to travel as a boy from London to Sligo on these boats, as he tells in his autobiographies. This line was bought by the Burns and Laird Co. a few years ago, but the boats are still those originally belonging to the old line—the only new one was 'christened' by Jack Yeats only, I think, four or five years ago, before the B. & L. bought the line.

Since there were 'still some very old people in Sligo who might like to meet him at the Quay', they chose September as the latest month possible before the weather turned, even though this was earlier than Willy had wished.[25] George, Anne, and Michael stayed on in Sligo for another day or two. There was the matter of the headstone to be ordered; she remembered Willy's admiration of a simple design at Glendalough in 1918.[26] On 22 February George wrote thanking Con Curran for his 'very great kindness during the last three weeks'. She had heard that day from the Sligo Steam Navigation Company who assured her that 'it will be quite easy to bring WBY by sea from Liverpool to Sligo'. However, 'There may be some "customs" difficulty, but I think this could be easily overcome. These are the things which, I confess, rather horrify me. I may again ask your help.'[27] The company representative in Sligo also reminded her that a transport permit would have to be issued by the prefect of the department of place of death; Rupert Gordon then made enquiries in Liverpool of the Anchor Line which had a fortnightly service from Marseilles—in 1939 boats were scheduled to leave on 9, 18 August and 23 September.[28] By May the 'homecoming' was planned for the first week of October, the Drumcliffe parishioners had painted the church gate and railings, the grass margin around the plot had been widened, and the National Library was planning an exhibition of manuscripts and other memorabilia. In anticipation, and possibly as a promise of more to come, in April George presented the library with the manuscript of 'The Wanderings of Oisin'.[29] According to one source, at some time during the negotiations, apparently 'the French government offered the services of a destroyer'.[30]

George's return to Dublin meant facing numerous acknowledgements of the messages of condolence and the onerous task of executorship. She arranged to have a secretary for two afternoons a week, and a card printed: 'Mrs W. B. Yeats thanks you for your kind message of sympathy February 1939'. But even then a personal note was usually added from 'George'. Others—Tom MacGreevy, for instance—required individual letters relating the events of Willy's last days. To some she also sent photographs, usually informal snapshots such as one of him reading, oblivious to the camera.[31] Maud wrote, of course. So did Iseult, who sympathized with the 'sad and wearing time' George must have experienced alone in Menton and the emptiness she must feel now; but she confessed it was a relief to know that Willy would no longer have to suffer his 'obsessing misery' with old age.[32] Many expressed their own desolation: 'I have lost my dearest and most intimate friend, from whom I had no secrets—absolutely none,' wrote Dermott MacManus; George's reply recognized his need for comfort: 'You were one of the few men for whom WBY had a real affection. I think you knew that. If you are ever in this neighbourhood and felt inclined to drop in—please do.'[33] On the whole, however, George dreaded meeting people, most of whom greeted her with the plea to 'bring him back'. She even avoided the Abbey, choosing to attend dress rehearsals to observe her daughter's work.[34] She never did care for the 'first night' society, also avoiding opening days at the Academy whenever possible.[35] Her letter of thanks to Desmond FitzGerald was a plea for understanding: 'I do not care whether Dublin, as I am continually told, regrets that he is not to be buried at St Patrick's When he returns to Sligo I hope you may find it possible to be among the people (*not* "representing the Seanad") who will come to his "planting" in Drumcliffe. . . . I am convinced that his wishes were conveyed in that poem "Under Ben Bulben" which I sent to the newspapers on February 3rd. You may not agree, but I rather wish you would!'[36]

An exchange with Elizabeth Pelham, whom she had never met, was especially revealing; from Lady Elizabeth's reply it is possible to comprehend George's own attitude towards death: 'I too felt about your husband as you describe in yr first letter & in a far lesser degree I expect than you because you were much closer to him naturally than me. I was such a fool I did not say it when I first wrote, not being sure of yr. reaction—I mean the "feeling of no sorrow" & the feeling of the new beginning of death. Sometimes it shocks people if one says so.'[37] This was yet another reason George wished 'Under Ben Bulben' to serve as Yeats's final statement:

> Many times man lives and dies
> Between his two eternities,
> That of race and that of soul,
> And ancient Ireland knew it all,
> Whether man die in his bed
> Or the rifle knocks him dead,
> A brief parting from those dear
> Is the worst man has to fear.
> Though grave-diggers' toil is long,
> Sharp their spades, their muscles strong,
> They but thrust their buried men
> Back in the human mind again.

There were immediate accounts to be settled. Photographs of WBY had to be ordered and inscribed for the fifty members of the American Testimonial Committee; a special note of gratitude went to Patrick McCartan describing how much the funds had meant to her husband: 'That he was happy during those last two months in France could I think not be doubted and several Irish and English friends who were staying fairly near and who came to see him often can all tell you how magnificently his vitality lasted until five or six days before his death.' Later that year she presented McCartan with an early typescript version with many manuscript corrections of 'Cromwell's Curse'.[38] On 24 February Hilda Matheson (charged with, among other details, returning the bath chair to Nice) wrote, acknowledging George's cheque, 'Your sums tally with my notes, except that the extra shilling seems redundant. Thank you very much. I cant think how you coped with accounts as well as everything else.'[39] There were also delicate matters to do with WBY's will: he had instructed that the ceremonial sword be sent to Junzo Sato's 'eldest surviving or only son'; but, conscious of its significance to the poetry (and also their early philosophical experiments), George wrote to Sato asking if Michael could inherit it. Sato replied, 'I did not present the sword with the intention of having it sent back to Japan. I shall be very happy to give it to your son.'[40] Letters were gathered together and sent back to their authors, again with a formal note; fortunately for future scholarship many escaped the net. And publishers were pressing for information and confirmation.

The most urgent message came from R. A. Scott-James, who was alarmed to learn that one of the poems he had been given for publication in the *London Mercury* had already been published in *The Irish Times*. Had others also appeared there? Also, he had been told by Edith Heald that there were a few more recent poems; could he have them for the March number, which would also include 'appreciative articles'? George's reply, marked 'Personal', is a clear expression of how she saw herself as caretaker of WBY's works and wishes:

I found your letter on my return from Sligo last Saturday Feb 11th, and I wired to you at your private address to go ahead with the poems you had as I could not send you copies of the two last poems in time for the March 'MERCURY'.

I published the poem originally called 'His Convictions' and re-named by him on the Thursday morning before he died 'Under Ben Bulben' (in his own writing on the typescript which you had returned to him a little time before) because there had been some activity in Dublin to have a burial at St Patrick's Cathedral; I decided to use that poem to ensure that this activity should not continue. After that publication in the 3 daily newspapers no one in Ireland could decently press what was against his own written wishes.

The reason that I could not send you the two last poems written at Cap-Martin in time for the March number was that I had not been able to make the final copies as the corrections in these were, also, in his own writing, and some in my own hand which had been dictated. These two poems are called CUCHULLAIN [*sic*] COMFORTED and THE BLACK TOWER. If you should care to put them in the Mercury in April, I will send them to you. They will come out, I hope early in May, in a book of the Cuala Press, together with a play finished on January 23rd (one act, verse) called CUCHULLAIN DEAD [*sic*], and other poems. The poem called CUCHULLAIN COMFORTED is in 'terza rima'. He had thought of trying this as a new metre form, which he might use in the future.[41]

George was only 46, with two teenaged children and a legacy. She would miss the mind's bite, the give and take of ideas, the warmth of the laughter and gossip. But with his death she reclaimed that greater part of him, his work. For the next thirty years she would steer the 'Yeats industry' on its extended voyage. Lily early recognized that George, despite her wit and intelligence, had been 'always shy about herself and keeps back'. During Willy's lifetime, she had been able to hide behind the role of anonymous 'Secretary', even claiming that 'Mrs Yeats never gives interviews.'[42] But now that simple escape was no longer possible. There were times when she used the device of ostensibly turning to the men in the family: Jack was deferred to as the new 'head', although Anne noticed that George usually got her own way. Even Michael was startled to learn that he was sometimes used to deflect an unfortunate request or situation. But it did not take long before everyone realized that 'Mrs W. B.' was indeed the 'sole Executrix'; the very wording of Yeats's will made that clear—again and again the directive surfaces—'to my wife who knows my wishes. . . . I give her the fullest power . . . as she may think best'.[43]

The question of an 'official' biography arose immediately. Harold Macmillan wrote that Joseph Hone had already 'been approached from other quarters'; naturally he would like to be the publisher, in both England and America. It would be a great help if she would give her own views as to the right person to attempt the task. 'I understand that Mr Hone had originally in mind a short book, and I think that he would undertake the fuller work if he were asked to do so.' Would she provide, in the strictest confidence, her own opinion—or whether someone else might be 'better equipped for such an undertaking'? He would also like to bring out a 'complete and definitive edition' of WBY's works early in the autumn. George sent her reply within a week:

I hope that Macmillan's will be 'associated with him as his publishers' as long as his family owns the copyright of his work. He would most certainly wish this. Regarding an 'official' biography I think that Joe Hone would be quite the best person to undertake it. Yeats thought his 'George Moore' a good, thorough if unimaginative book, and I do not know of anyone who could do better this kind of book. It would have, I think, to be written by an Irishman, and it would also have to be written by a man with whom I could personally work because there is a vast amount of material for biography which, I think, should in recent years be used with some discrimination. I am not destroying any of this material, it will be at the free use of his biographer, I merely do not wish it to be used as sensational literature. I have spoken to Joe Hone about his doing an 'official' biography, and he says he would like to do it but 'I am very slow'.

However she could not resist a slight dig at the publisher for the long-delayed 'edition de luxe', 'which Yeats always said you would only bring out after his death'. 'There will of course be the last two small books of poems published by the Cuala Press, one called "NEW POEMS" and one which will be called "LAST

POEMS" which will be published in April of this year, to be added. I think that the two Cuala Books, "New Poems" and the forthcoming one which will be called "Last Poems" should be published by Macmillan's in London and America in May or June of this year.'[44] Harold Macmillan hastily replied that they hoped to publish the long-delayed special edition in September. He had heard of an unpublished heroic play which WBY had read to some friends (evidently Dorothy and Edith had not been silent since their return from France); that would be included of course. He would also appreciate her suggestions of 'some appropriate name' for the 'edition de luxe'. George had thought of that point too: although she must have been aware that Willy had considered the name for Scribner's American subscription series and then rejected it as having 'a thin sound', she selected 'The Coole Edition', for 'He owed so much to Lady Gregory that this title would commemorate.'[45]

Scribner's edition too was awaiting her attention. Despite an exchange between the American and English agents suggesting that 'The death of Yeats relieves us, I suppose, of the necessity of doing anything more about the captions for the illustrations,' George soon had the American special subscription series in hand also. By mid-February she had passed the proofs of captions, and was requesting proofs of the volumes that she might make a few corrections from the typescripts. Scribner's were now promising the first volume for October; there was little more for George to do on the projected eleven-volume 'Dublin Edition'.[46] As it turned out this was just as well, for after many postponements (including an offer as early as May 1939 to sell a set of electrotypes to Macmillan), in 1953 the project was definitely shelved; besides, Macmillan's would keep her sufficiently busy for years to come.[47] By April she had changed the titles of volumes X and XI in the Coole Edition, and was suggesting a possible further volume be made up of 'some autobiographical material in MSS, and also some uncollected essays'. She hoped with this volume, *Essays and Autobiographical Fragments*, 'to give to the subscribers to the English and American EDITIONS DE LUXE an opportunity of adding it to their "complete" edition'.[48] In an effort to reassure Scribner's, she wrote through her agent that Macmillan of New York would not be issuing the English de luxe edition in the United States.[49] Later that month, when Tom Mark sent a few questions about the accuracy of quotations and asked 'if you would rather let questions like this be decided here', her response was immediate and decisive, if tactful:

When you have made your own list of corrections to the completed volumes of POEMS would you send me the complete proofs? You see I am left 'literary executor'. WBY wrote to you in September (or October) 1932 about punctuation and generally asking your help, without which he knew he could never get his work into the final form he wished. There are, however a few metrical 'tricks' as he called them, and tricks of repetition of words and phrases, deliberately used, which we should, I think, carefully preserve.[50]

However, although she insisted on retaining Sturge Moore's cover design, she was prepared to accept Harold Macmillan's suggestion of the title for the next trade volume to be published, *Last Poems and Plays*. More significantly, she felt she had the authority to alter the order of the poems. Although she was prepared to accept responsibility, she would not be around for the academic skirmishes that would later arise from those and similar decisions.[51]

George's instructions to Watt, the literary agent, were equally clear and forceful: 'To begin with, please continue to give permissions for Anthologies as before. Subject to your approval I suggest that permission to quote poems in Magazines should be charged the rate of two guineas.' She was alert to all the nuances: 'Mr Allan may quote one verse from Dialogue of Self & Soul *if it is inset in his text*.' In another case, the quotations were not accurate or came from a very early version. And she would like to know from the Society of Authors (which she soon joined as literary executor to the estate) the exact number of lines of allowable quotation as set out in the Copyright Act.[52] Finally, there was the problem of Higgins and *On the Boiler*. The proofs had finally arrived from the Longford printing firm and she needed to consult him about the cover (for which Jack had made a design), the title page, and other points.[53]

George had evidently made it clear to Hone that the suggestion he be the official biographer had been Macmillan's, not hers. Aided by her memory, advice, and co-operation (except for the 'purely personal letters' between herself and WBY, and anything to do with the automatic script), he expected to take two years, during which he was meticulous in consulting all the family. 'J. M. Hone has started on the life and has been over to see me several times,' Lily wrote; '— he sighs and makes notes and sighs again—but is I think quite happy and enjoying the work.' In addition George urged Lily to write down her early memories of the family; it kept her not only occupied, but happy.[54] Apparently without George's express encouragement, Lennox Robinson was also embarking on a small book to be published as soon as possible by Constable. Lennox's book would never be completed, and what he managed to salvage appeared a year later as a brief essay in one of the many books of tributes.[55] Meanwhile, Oliver Edwards was in town for four days and wished to consult her concerning *his* book on WBY. This is probably the occasion when Edwards also asked to see the automatic script. She showed some to him, but her obvious reluctance made him hesitate to do any more than take a quick glance.[56] That project too was never completed; but soon she was approached by others, including a proposal from a young assistant tutor at Cambridge for an annotated 'Selected Poems'; T. R. Henn was firmly turned down, but would later become a trusted friend.[57] To nobody's surprise, by early March she had to spend several days in bed. Besides, Michael was home from school for a day.[58]

There was yet one further public display to endure. John Masefield had been busy organizing a memorial service in London, to be held at the Church of

St Martin-in-the-Fields on 16 March. Having been alerted by Lily, George wired him to point out that date was the hundredth anniversary of JBY's birthday; this information was duly included on the programme. Before she could leave the country, however, it was necessary to write a new will and appoint guardians for Anne and Michael. Work on WBY's estate was making its slow way through the solicitors' office: the American copyright in his works went to Anne, the English and European copyrights to Michael, his shares in the National Theatre Society Limited and all other property to George. When probate was granted on 31 August 1939, his taxable estate in Eire was £3,830, his personal estate in England and Eire together (including the valuation of his copyright fees and royalties) £8,329 9s. 11d.[59] With her new will, dated 15 March, George filed a letter to Anne regarding her own property:

In the event of my death before I return to Ireland on Tuesday March 21st 1939 I wish to make it quite clear that I have signed today at Whitney Moore & Keller's my last Will. This will divides between you and Michael absolutely all the property and monies belonging to me at the time of my death, whether left to me in trust for you and Michael under your father's will dated 1934 (Whitney Moore and Keller's, 45 Kildare St Dublin) or in my personal possession at the date of my death.

After describing the disposition of her effects, she continues with the most important directions:

In my Will I appoint as executors and Guardians my brother H. M. Hyde Lees and Rupert Gordon, the latter to act as Guardian only until you are twentyone years of age. I do not wish either you or Michael to live with your aunts at Gurteen Dhas, Churchtown, Dundrum, because I have brought you up, as I believe, with a sense of freedom which I do not think they would understand; and I do not want either you or Michael to lose the sense of truth because external circumstances, however difficult, make it. It is really one of the few things that matter. I suggest that if such necessity arises before you, Anne Butler Yeats, are twentyone years of age, you should temporarily arrange to stay with Violet Gordon who understands my feelings in this matter. Yours affly George Yeats[60]

This and the will were both witnessed by her long-time Riversdale staff, Mary Martin and John Free, but Anne would not see the letter for almost thirty years. The next day George left for England.

The memorial service in London was held at 3 p.m. on 16 March. Typical of his own overblown style of address, the Poet Laureate had at first planned something elaborate ('W. B. would, I feel sure, like to have read at the service something of Blake, something of William Morris, and some Plotinus and perhaps something by some Buddhist writer').[61] In the end the service was quite simple; whether Masefield was influenced by George or others is not known. There were no readings from other writers; V. C. Clinton Baddeley, with whom Willy had worked on the BBC broadcasts, read 'The Withering of the Boughs' and 'A

Dialogue of Self and Soul' before the lesson from Isaiah, chapter 55, and 'Under Ben Bulben' between two hymns, 'Praise to the Holiest in the Height' and 'The Day Thou Gavest, Lord, is Ended'. There was no address, and the service ended with the Dead March from Saul. Una Ellis-Fermor, who had become friendly with Lily the previous summer during the Abbey Theatre Festival, wrote that 'It was a good service, all triumph and thanksgiving, as it should be.'[62] George had told Masefield she would attend, but asked that her presence not be announced, and her request for privacy was honoured. No one recognized her, or at least publicly acknowledged her presence. She stayed with Dorothy Wellesley in her London flat.[63]

The next day it was back to business. George met with Harold Macmillan and Thomas Mark to discuss outstanding and future publications, including the projected two-volume edition of the *Collected Poems*; no doubt she also took the opportunity once again to make clear her own authority as literary executor.[64] With Dorothy and Hilda she discussed two projects that had already been initiated by WBY: a new series of *Broadsides*, to be edited by Wellesley and Higgins under George's direction at the Cuala Press, and a performance of Yeats's work at Edy Craig's Sussex theatre, The Barn. George spoke of a particular actor she preferred, but apparently the choice of plays was not yet settled. There would be much correspondence to follow, adding heavily to her load as Dorothy and Hilda urged her to arrange for Abbey players to participate in the festival. While there, however, she probably consulted Dorothy in preparing the final text for the Macmillan 'edition de luxe'. When sending Macmillan WBY's two final Cuala volumes she commented, 'You will see that he re-wrote (for about the ninth time) the Three Marching Songs which were published in "A Full Moon in March". I have discussed with various poets the question as to whether the *final* versions *only* should be published, and there seems to be unanimous agreement that *both* versions should be printed as they are, on the whole so different.'[65]

Before leaving for Ireland George also had lunch with the Dulacs; there is no word that Edith Heald was included in the party. However, George was distressed by Dulac's account—circulated by the typist Miss Jacobs—that Wellesley was planning to publish her own book on WBY; as a close friend of Edith, Dulac was vehemently against the idea.[66] She was back in Dublin in time to chair a Cuala board meeting on 21 March, and then wrote to Hilda repeating what she had heard, at the same time reporting her discussion with Higgins over the projected new *Broadsides*. Hilda was as always protective of her lover, advising George that Miss Jacobs, who had previously done some work for Dorothy and was one of the few who could read Yeats's writing, had at his suggestion been given some of the letters of 1936 and 1937 to type. The thought of publishing these extracts on poetry had not, Hilda assured her, occurred to Dorothy until after his death. She would now like to do so, and Hilda herself thought it should be done quickly.

Before proceeding any further, Dorothy would submit to George the extracts and her short introduction. Even Turner, she said, had been approached to write his reminiscences. The two camps were drawing up their battlelines. As for the *Broadsides*, 'You will I hope tell me quite frankly any points of difficulty from your end—for instance financial.' Although Dorothy was already approaching authors in England for contributions, the planned new series of illustrated ballads eventually had to be shelved. Dorothy meanwhile wrote separately that discussions were proceeding with Turner and Clinton Baddeley over the proposed programme at the Barn Theatre. They were thinking of *Words upon the Window-Pane* and *Resurrection*, but would love to present *The Death of Cuchulain* as having 'far greater significance'.[67]

George, who realized that WBY had always expected that his letters to Wellesley would be published, found it difficult not to give permission for the project, although she had misgivings. She also recognized that to many of Willy's friends, the Dulacs in particular who were strong socialists, acquiescence meant signalling her support of Wellesley rather than Heald. At any rate, by mid-April Dorothy had approached Harold Macmillan suggesting the letters might come out about the same time as the poems they refer to, and providing a sample of the correspondence.[68] Macmillan was placed in 'rather a quandary', he wrote to George. 'I understand from her that you would like these letters to be published, but after reading through them myself, I rather wonder if you have seen them lately and are fully acquainted with what they contain. . . . If they were published in their present form some of them would certainly involve you, as the owner of the copyright, in a number of libel actions, while others would not convey to an ordinary reader what they were meant to express to an understanding friend.' George replied the next day:

Of course no letters containing personal matter of the sort you outline must be published. I have already had to deal with this in two other cases. I have insisted that no letters or portions of letters can be printed until I have seen the copy. As Lady Gerald is a personal friend I would prefer her not to know that you have written to me. Could you write to her that many of the letters contain references to people who are still alive of a kind which it would not be possible to publish, and that as 'Mrs Yeats' is the copyright owner she would be responsible in the event of any libel action taken by any of these people. You might ask her if I have seen the letters!

WBY *did* say to her that some of the letters might form part of a book; but, as in the case of the letters to Lady Gregory from which he had planned one or more books for Cuala Press, he knew that they would need drastic expurgation. In regard to the Lady Gregory letters he told me several times that if they were not edited either by him or by myself I was to go through the entire collection and remove all letters dealing with certain personal and public affairs *before* handing them over to any editor. I hope this makes my opinion quite clear?

Acting upon her cue, Macmillan gently rejected the proposal.[69] Wellesley became even more determined; 'since I was the only writer present during his last days I feel that I owe a certain duty to posterity.' Macmillan then sent a copy of their exchange to Watt, who was also intent upon protecting the widow and the copyright. George's brief annotation on his letter was as always to the point: 'I can deal with DW myself.'[70]

Wellesley and Matheson then approached Oxford University Press. Hilda reported that Sir Humphrey Milford was 'delighted' with the letters she had sent him. She then injudiciously added, 'They are, at Dorothy's request, making suggestions of desirable deletions mainly frank remarks about other writers. But they—he & D—are anxious to send them to you as soon as they are tidied up so that you may take out anything that you think wise.' Alarmed at what seemed to be a pre-emption of her authority and control, George wrote back. The letter is not extant, but Hilda's attempt to backtrack makes clear that George was having serious second thoughts about the entire project; she was having trouble enough preventing publication of an 'undignified series of little books'. Dorothy's intention, Hilda tried to assure her, would be to present WBY's letters with as little commentary as possible, simply sufficient annotation to supplement the conversation and letters, the briefest possible introduction, 'concluding with a very short & simple account of the last days'. All would be 'admirably restrained' and, doubtless with Edith in mind, she finished up by urging that 'this duty should be done by a friend who was present rather than "written up" by some journalist who was not'. Dorothy meanwhile sent her own emotional plea: 'I just want to tell you that I quite understand that you really don't want anything published about him at all. To be the wife of a genius must be hard, to be the widow of a genius perhaps impossible.' She did not know how she could get through the Barn performance and felt sure George would turn down the letters, 'even in spite of the long continued row about the Ballad of the Serving Maid'. Of course Dorothy did attend the Yeats festival at the Barn Theatre on 2 July, along with Elizabeth Pelham, the Turners, and William Rothenstein. And Oxford published *Letters on Poetry from W. B. Yeats to Dorothy Wellesley* in June 1940; the press was instructed that all royalties be sent to the widow.[71] George had obviously let off steam about the problems of correcting the Coole Edition too; by mid-July the two friends were so distressed by her obvious overwork that Hilda sent a wire offering 'to go as your representative & knock him [Harold Macmillan] on the head'.[72]

George also had to deal with the Abbey Theatre, especially awkward now that her daughter was chief designer. 'I return The Death of Cuchulain,' she wrote to Lennox. 'I am rather sorry the Abbey has decided to produce it as I think it a bad play and one that should only have been printed and never performed. However, as I dont want to have a row or anything approaching an argument with the Board I suppose it will have to be done.'[73] Lennox took the hint, and the play was not performed on the Abbey stage until 1949, when Anne designed it for the Lyric Theatre (her own last theatre work). In the midst of all this turmoil, Sturge Moore wrote that his daughter Riette, about Anne's age and also interested in a career in the arts, was planning a visit to Dublin; George felt compelled to invite her to Riversdale and arrange for introductions. On 13 June, Willy's birthday, she insisted on being left alone for the day; it had always been a festival of celebration. Then Michael came down with the measles, fortunately a mild attack. (While at Trinity he would succumb to the mumps two years in a row and, later still, whooping cough.) To make matters worse, with the delay in probate she was running out of cash, and had to apply for an advance on royalties; Watt arranged that Macmillan send an advance of £200. George was, as Hilda recognized, 'pretty near the end of [her] tether'.[74]

Her first thought had been to spend the summer in Ballylee. She had in fact spoken longingly of this to Dorothy and Hilda while in London, and even sent them photographs. 'I am more pleased than I can tell you to hear of your plan of going back to the Tower,' Dorothy had written. 'I am sure it will be a very great solution for you in every way. From the photographs it seems to me a place entirely after my own heart; especially I liked the photograph of W. B. with the children.'[75] But instead of a nostalgic flight to Ballylee, she moved to Rathmines, where she would live for the next thirty years. George never returned to the tower, and rejected Anne's request to go there to paint with such abruptness that she did not dare visit it until after her mother's death. 'After a time', Hone wrote in 1942, 'no further effort was made to keep up the place. There is scarcely a sign to-day of Mrs Yeats' once pretty garden, and the rats and the winds have claimed the thatch of the cottages. The tower defies the gales, as it has done for centuries, and as it is well roofed the rains do not penetrate into the poet's chamber, which still contains the heavy oak furniture made on the spot for it, impossible to remove down the narrow winding stair.'[76]

Leaving Riversdale was also a wrench, so painful that George could not talk about it. But her income was now too reduced to justify the expense of the upkeep of the gardens, especially with the ongoing commitment of £84 a year to Lily and the expenses of Cuala. Besides, she argued, the lease would run out in six years and the fields would inevitably be sold as building lots. Then there were the children to consider: Michael planned to enter Trinity in the autumn, and Anne worked long late hours at the theatre; somewhere closer to Dublin with better bus service was essential.[77] She alerted Joe Hone that the manuscripts would be stored for safe keeping in the bank during the move, but she was waiting until the beauty of the gardens would ensure a higher sale price. Finally in mid-May the house went on North's real estate books. Meanwhile, Joe Hone started to work in the Riversdale library while she occupied her little sitting room upstairs. She gave him a list of Yeats's letters he could take home—to Lady Gregory ('a few references to Maude [*sic*] in these which WBY particularly asked me to see were not pub-lished'), Olivia Shakespear ('he had been through these himself'), all the Abbey Theatre correspondence. Of that between herself and Willy, 'purely personal letters not included. There are a few references in the letters to people and events which are private, but they are not things which you would be interested in probably.' It was a pattern she would repeat for the rest of her life—no authors received access to everything, only to what she had decided they would require for the stated pro-ject. Although she assured him that 'of course no books will be sold or anything else that belonged to Yeats', some books, chiefly bound sets of the classics, did find their way to Greene's Book Shop on Clare Street during the move.[78]

George had been actively looking for a house since March. To Anne, who was in Paris during the Abbey's holiday period, she wrote that she liked a 'nice friendly sort of house, in good repair' on Wellington Road; Michael got special permission from St Columba's to see it, but someone else bought it before she was ready to make up her mind.[79] Eventually she settled on a Victorian two-storey terraced house at 46 Palmerston Road. The original rental was for five years at an annual rent of £90 and taxes; George told Lily that 'When she gave her name the landlord took £20 off the rent in one blow as a tribute to Willy. It pleased her very much.' (By 1961 the rent had crept up to £135.) Palmerston (originally Carlisle) Road was a well-established thoroughfare by the late nineteenth century; Rathmines had been a township since 1847 and until the 1930s had been predominantly middle-class Protestant. Now with the increase in population and improved trans-portation system—the area was served by one of the new double-decker buses—the population was changing, with civil servants, students, and workers moving in. It was, however, still sufficiently conservative to frown on Sunday gardening—but even that would change, perhaps influenced by the activities at number 46. George and her family knew the area well—Lolly had taught at Miss Sweeny's (later Mount Temple) school at 3 Palmerston Park; the Donagh MacDonaghs lived down the road at 14, Monk Gibbon's mother at 44 (she then moved across the road to 30), later Seán Lemass would occupy 53 and Mayor Alfie Byrne 42.[80]

George moved in on 26 July, the same day she signed the purchase of the remainder of the lease (from Daniel O'Sullivan, army captain). This time she saw no reason to do the redecorating herself, arranging only for the walls to be dis-tempered and the mantelpieces painted to match the woodwork.[81] The bus stop was nearby, but the front hall door was reached by many steep steps. There were two large reception rooms off the high-ceilinged wide hall. Overlooking the back garden was the dining room or 'Red Room', graced by three Jack Yeats paintings, the Mancini portrait of Yeats, a tablecloth embroidered by Lily, a cupboard of Cuala books, first editions, and fine bindings behind glass on either side of the gas-fitted fireplace. Above the sideboard hung Sato's sword. As if to signal her deliberate withdrawal from the public eye, this soon became her sitting room; the family took their meals on a lower level in the black and white tiled kitchen on what had once been the children's nursery table. Double doors—opened only for Anne's twenty-first birthday party—separated the sitting room from the study where the 'working library' of occult, poetry, art, and reference books competed for wall space with yet more pictures (Shannon, Rossetti, Blake). Here the lapis lazuli, enshrined in Yeats's poem, had pride of place on the mantel, and beneath a window looking out over the front garden stood the 'gilded Moorish wedding chest' with Lady Gregory's letters; steel filing cases and cupboards held WBY's manuscripts; on the floor against the wall, two padlocked green footlockers held the automatic script; the tables were stacked with papers, letters, uncashed cheques, more books, George's typewriter, and overflowing ashtrays. The gas fire whistled eerily when lit. Curtis Bradford's impression was that she was 'camping, as it were, among the huge accumulation of WBY's manuscripts, books, and memorabilia'.

But it was her life too that was being recollected. Like a palimpsest, the furniture in these two large rooms recorded their twenty-two years together, ranging in time from the large leather armchair Lady Gregory had donated to Woburn Buildings, now betraying the clawmarks of generations of cats, through the more elegant furniture of Oxford and Merrion Square, the red enamelled furniture she had painted in Rapallo, to the comfortable armchairs and divans of Riversdale. The long hall was also memorably furnished—four tall brass candlesticks from the Coole dining room (and which Yeats always said had once stood by a bier); a long chest piled high with bundles of press clippings, parcels to go out, and books and articles that had come in about Yeats; on the walls many paintings by John Butler Yeats and one of Lily's embroidered pictures. Upstairs there were sufficient bedrooms for the three Yeatses and Mary Martin, the maid, who came with them from Riversdale; until Michael and Anne left home, guests could only be accommodated when someone was away. At the end of the main hall, three or four steps down the stairs to the kitchen level, the telephone was installed in the 'return'; as her arthritis and hearing worsened, George arranged to be nearby each morning precisely at 10 o'clock. Descending the next thirteen steps, one passed an innocuous-looking cupboard with the 'magic box' on top.[82] Unlike the warm glowing colours of Fitzwilliam Square and Riversdale, this house was cold, grey, and neutral; in later years George refused even to have the windows recaulked ('that was the landlord's job'), or after the war years to remove the blackout curtains (the hall was 'too shabby'). That was one more responsibility she could relinquish; no longer need she create an environment for the poet. Controlling the presentation of his work would be another matter. Lily finally visited Palmerston Road later that summer, and found it 'a good very roomy house. The pictures and books look well, but it has no charm like Riversdale, and no feeling of Willy's presence, which I miss.'[83]

For George the greatest joy was, as it had been at Riversdale, her garden. When she moved in the grounds were a shambles with slugs nesting in bits of broken crockery; the owner went so far as to sue the former tenants for lack of care. George set to work, rescuing the small front garden from a sea of slaters (woodlice) by creating a rock garden, planting rosemary and lavender near the gate. Later, when Kathleen Raine visited her in the spring, she was struck as she entered the gate by the beauty of the anemone pulsatilla (beloved also by Blake) 'and many rather rare species of daffodils and other spring bulbs'.[84] The deep back garden, bordered by high walls, was surrounded by long herbaceous beds bright with lily of the valley and iceberg poppies; her beloved roses were everywhere, and there were apple trees in the lawn, behind that the vegetable garden. Anne, who gardened with her on Sundays, was trained to water the flower beds (if they were not still wet on Monday morning she had not given them enough), and stake all the plants. St Patrick's Day was considered a lucky day for pruning the roses and planting potatoes. Before she left Riversdale George had carefully taken cuttings from the myrtle tree by Willy's garden door.[85]

Her world was changing around her in other ways, too. Michael was in his last term at St Columba's; during holidays he tended to spend more time in the north or travelling around the country with his good friend Brian Faulkner.[86] George was not always certain where he was. 'Please write a note to say how you are, & when you are returning,' she wrote to him at Clifden on 15 August 1939. 'The house is beginning to look human, & John is now cleaning up the garden.' He was still away on his eighteenth birthday, and had still not sent a note in the stamped addressed envelope she had provided. But there was more news of the household: 'Pangur departed for 3 days & nights, but returned this morning at 6 a.m. & proclaimed the fact in howls all over the house!' His school report had come, 'good as usual, though the Warden makes an adverse criticism of your religious knowledge & interests! Based on the Oxford Group versus Oxford Movement I expect!'[87] That autumn Michael entered Trinity College to study not mathematics, as was supposed, but history; he joined the debating team, won a cup at chess, and became more and more dedicated to politics. Absorbed in his studies and what would become his future career, her son was growing up and away.

Anne too was distancing herself. Working hard at the Abbey, she usually returned late and, discouraged from disturbing the household by turning on the hall light, learned to carry the supper tray her mother left ready in the hall up to her room in the dark. Her twenty-first birthday party in February 1940 was a disaster—the theatre circle and the Yeatses simply no longer mixed. Grief also separated the two women; both turned inward, unable to talk about Willy's death. Anne rebelled passively by becoming increasingly private; more and more George found solace in alcohol. Ironically, about this time Jack Yeats began to take a much closer interest in his niece. In June she designed and painted the set for his *Harlequin's Positions*, directed by Ria Mooney for the Experimental Theatre at the Peacock Theatre; it was the first of his plays to receive a professional production. Always courteous and formal, he relished the experience, and delighted in Anne's designs. Invited by letter, she would visit him in his studio in the afternoon; he offered her a glass of madeira, perhaps a cigarette, and would then 'talk of the old days of circuses and fairs, variety shows, and he sometimes sang an old music-hall song with his very rusty voice'. But unlike his brother, he never spoke of his own work. Once he took her to an old-fashioned tented circus. Later he started to send her the occasional cheque, 'at varying intervals and for varying amounts, so that they were always pleasant surprises rather than an allowance'.[88] Was kind, childless Jack consciously assuming a paternal role along with the titular headship of the family? It is possible, for Cottie had for some time been alarmed by George's drinking and the subsequent tension in the household.[89] But he was also very fond and proud of his 'bonny' niece.[90] Later, when she began to exhibit her own work, he bought her paintings, and when Cottie became ill, he asked Anne to write 'a little letter' that might cheer her up. When 'Mrs Jack' died on 28 April 1947 he came close to breaking; luncheons and afternoon meetings with Anne became even more important to him. From then on he regularly spent the winter months in Portobello House, the nursing home in which Cottie had spent her last days. Tom MacGreevy was his executor; Anne was the main beneficiary of his estate.[91] However, he steadfastly refused to take any responsibility for the Cuala Press, even though George asked him to replace WBY on the board.

That spring in 1939, while their mother packed up Riversdale, Anne planned a theatre trip to Paris, and Michael expected to spend a few weeks in Germany before his father's 'replanting'. Then on 3 September Britain declared war on Germany. Once again their plans were turned inside out; not only was Michael's journey to the Continent cancelled, but Yeats would remain in foreign soil longer than his prescribed year. Within a year any 'unwarlike travel' between the islands was banned by the British. Anne and Michael lightened their mother's spirits by celebrating her birthday in October; 'Michael had been the man of the family and told her she must not go out, it was too wet,' she told Lily, pleased. Her sisters-in-law presented her with a drawing by their father of Willy at one year, asleep on the floor with the cat beside him. But within days George suffered further disappointment as Harold Macmillan postponed publication of *Last Poems and Plays*. The two 'editions de luxe' were again delayed; the Coole Edition, Mark informed her, 'has to wait for better times'.[92] 'This is a blow to George, who wants cash,' Lily reported to Ruth, as she herself resignedly went out of her black mourning clothes.[93]

Although remaining neutral throughout the war, Ireland was sufficiently tied to the economy of England to feel the direct effects of what was always referred to as 'the Emergency'. Soon the use of gas for cooking was rationed; households might at any time be visited by the 'glimmer men' looking for illegal use of the stove. The Electricity Board appealed for all to economize as much as possible, and stalwart George did so conscientiously. Unfortunately the neighbours did not; much to the Yeatses' indignation when rationing was introduced, the basis of the allowance was the amount of electricity the household had consumed during the previous billing period. This meant, Anne recalled, 'that we had 40 watt bulbs for the rest of the War and our neighbours could have the lights blazing when ever they fancied. We used to save electricity by listening to the news on our neighbour's radio (the walls between the houses were so thin this was possible).' Fortunately they still had the battery-operated wireless WBY had purchased through the BBC; when Michael was not listening to the opera, he enjoyed annoying his sister by switching stations, thereby producing piercing whistles.[94] George listened secretly to Pound's broadcasts from Italy to America which began in January 1941; no matter what he said, the sound of Ezra's voice brought a lost world somewhat closer.

Lily and Lolly were in need of more attention. 'I have never minded loneliness,' Lily had written to George, 'but now it is ghastly and gets worse. Willy & I were always close friends and our childhood together is never out of mind now. I cannot speak of it to Lolly who is so uncompanionable.' She worried that her sister-in-law found her dull and uninteresting. However, that next winter when she suffered a series of visits to the dentist to have all her teeth out, 'kind George, without telling me, appeared the first time at the dentist's also the second time . . . and she and Maria hustled me into bed'.[95] Lolly also required considerable attention; her chest pains were becoming more frequent and severe, and there was, as always, the press to deal with, which meant reining in the impulsive publisher. 'Lolly is sometimes a raging furnace & sometimes all serenity after the meetings,' Lily observed.[96] The minutes of each meeting contain hints of the other directors' attempts to repress Lolly: copies of all letters must be made before any are sent out; no privately printed book orders are to be taken except with approval of the directors; a general meeting of the staff is to be held 'for a complete free discussion on the working of the business and to put forward any ideas they could'; detailed weekly statements of all lodgments must go to the bank, and a detailed account of each day's work from 9 to 5 be kept; 'no Director or official must write on or verbally discuss the financial affairs of the company with any person or firm without the full consent of the Board.'[97] This last was probably the final straw for Lolly, who enjoyed writing to clients and friends alike of her struggles to keep the press afloat; in fact her letters extracted another injection of £100 from loyal Emmeline Cadbury and a gift of £300 from Charlotte and Bernard Shaw ('so now Higgins and Mrs Yeats can let themselves rip').[98] But when Higgins asked Pat McCartan for assistance in raising another £300 in ordinary shares for Cuala Limited, Lolly felt compelled to inform him that neither she nor George had anything to do with the request. 'When Mrs Yeats and Mr Higgins had as it were taken things in hand—as I say—it is all a little difficult for me—but that cannot be helped & things are improving—but they act without discussing the matter with me first & have to come to me in the end of course as I have run Cuala since 1903.'⁹⁹ No matter how unreasonable she often seemed to her fellow directors, Lolly had some justification for her complaints. Even Lily recognized that George, too, could be unpredictable. 'I don't think George is easy, but then Lolly is impossible . . . George is sometimes all amiability and then again all against one. But then I am sure she is now unhappy and lonely and worried.'¹⁰⁰ George did her best to make Lolly feel appreciated. 'I spent last week-end with Mrs Yeats—I thought it would make me feel sadder—but in some queer way—I got serenity and even slept well—Yet it was my brother's room that I slept in—and I was happy—I liked to think of him in that room.'¹⁰¹

There was still the commitment of *On the Boiler*. Having decided to farm out the printing, they had suffered nothing but delays from the small country press Higgins had recommended. When the proofs finally arrived, the board refused to accept delivery of the entire edition, writing sternly to the Longford Press, 'We regret to say that we are unable to offer for sale any of the copies of "On the Boiler" as printed by you. Your printing is so deplorable in type and inking— apart from the many typographical errors in the text—we feel it would seriously damage the reputation of the Cuala Press if the work went out over our name.'¹⁰² It was agreed that, except for four copies, the entire printing would be destroyed; it was eventually carted away by a Dublin waste paper firm. George then took the text to Alex Thom & Company in Dublin, who produced a second printing in September. By November Lolly was in bed with a bad cold and George, their 'strong rock', was working almost full time at Cuala. Reluctantly she went in each day for the Christmas sale, which despite their fears turned out to be better than the last.

But all was not so well with Lolly, and by mid-December the doctor had decided that she needed professional care. George took her in to St Patrick Dunne's Hospital on 14 December; indomitable as ever, Lolly insisted on dressing 'just as if going to town', and walked to the car. Lily kept Ruth in Australia fully informed. 'When they got her in and to bed things were so bad that they did not expect her to live through the night. George stayed the whole night and Jack was there for a while. Lolly did not know him. They gave morphia. . . . It is kidney. She is not in pain but in much discomfort and a good deal swollen. George is splendid, goes twice a day, and if not at the hospital is at home and ready to come at once.' True to form, Lolly was not an easy patient; one day George, who seemed to be the only one who could control her, was so shocked by Lolly's rudeness to the doctor that she wrote a letter of apology. Things then calmed down for a while, Lolly claiming 'it was a good thing she made that row as now she is being properly looked after'. But two days before Christmas George slipped on the ice and broke a bone in her wrist; unfortunately, it was her left hand. Suffering from pain and a cold, she too had to go to bed. Anne and Michael visited Lolly on the 25th, taking flowers and gifts; Lolly was especially pleased with George's thoughtfulness in sending a blue pile bedjacket.

By 13 January 1940 it was obvious that Lolly was dying. Helping her into the ambulance to take her to a nursing home, George slipped on the ice and broke her arm again. In spite of this she was at her sister-in-law's bedside all the next day. At 6 p.m. on 16 January 1940, just twelve days before the anniversary of her brother's death, Lolly died peacefully and with little pain.[103] She was 71, and almost to the last the vivid, sometimes outrageous, always interesting, 'purple Miss Yeats'. The funeral, strictly private, was held the next day; during the service the coffin, awkwardly placed, tipped off the trestles. Anne whispered, 'There's Lolly having the *last word*'; George was amused, but Jack was not.[104] In her will Lolly left all her Irish first editions and set of Cuala books to Trinity Hall, the women's residence whose warden, Margery Cunningham, was a lifelong friend; George saw that a copy of all future publications went to 'The Elizabeth Yeats Library'. When probated, her estate was valued at £639 1s. 10d.[105] Appropriately, the last two volumes Lolly saw through the press were poems by her brother and his good friend Gogarty, while a third, by the younger Irish poet Louis MacNeice, was on its way.[106] Cuala closed its doors for the week, but by mid-February Esther Ryan and Maire Gill had set and printed a memorial tribute written by Lily (and severely edited by George to save space).[107] Jack paid for the funeral, and arranged for a headstone; from then on he sent Lily a bottle of brandy every month.

Lily was also unwell, had not been out of the house for two months, and was becoming depressed, afraid she was only a nuisance. There were domestic problems at Gurteen Dhas as well: Maria, who had been with them for so many years, had long been a secret drinker; finally it was necessary to find institutional help for her and arrange for a younger maid. Once again it was her sister-in-law who came to the rescue; Mary Cronin and Bridget O'Reilly tended to the ailing Lily. George frequently brought over freshly cooked meals, and one day pleased Lily very much by saying over the telephone, 'Do you know I am very fond of you?' Later she would occasionally go out to stay at Gurteen Dhas; 'She can bolt to the sitting-room if anyone comes in who bores her.'[108] Meanwhile Cuala went on. The next board meeting tidied up matters: the competent Eileen Colum, Padraic's sister, was given more responsibilities and elected a director; Lily was officially appointed 'paid designer' at a salary of £2 15s. a week which, with what George already gave, increased her annual income to a more comfortable £300. George replaced Lolly as secretary to the Industries; at her suggestion the royalties due her (£161 18s. 6d.) were cancelled.[109] She herself was now, as Willy had wished, not only a director of the press, but publisher and editor.

However, her wrist simply would not heal. She had always typed, once admitting to Tom MacGreevy, 'my writing is too vile & I can scarcely think except upon a typewriter for I have written on one for so long'. By late February, even though the plaster was finally removed, she still could not type. On 6 April her arm was once again reset.[110] Such operations were always a danger because of the constant risk of pneumonia; she had never completely recovered from the 1918 influenza. There were other unidentified health problems also and she was back in hospital in June. Sympathetic to her loneliness and difficulties (her own husband was in the United States), Martha ('Neenie') Gogarty invited her to visit Renvyle. George's reply provides some further details of what she had been going through:

Dear Mrs Gogarty I have been in hospital for a slight op & only found your letter on my return yesterday. I would have *loved* to come to Renvyle but cannot go away for another month alas. If you are at Renvyle in the autumn, & the hotel is not full, I would love to be asked again. It is so very delightful of you to ask me.

I hope my arm will be allowed out of plaster at the end of this month, but the combination of arm & a few internal stitches has rather incapacitated me for the moment. Yours affly George Yeats[111]

It would not be Ballylee, but it *was* the west of Ireland, where Anne was at that moment, on a cycling tour of Kerry with friends. Finally in late June her arm was pronounced 'two-thirds right', but she could never again turn her left wrist. The typewriter was permanently set aside; as the rheumatism got worse, writing became even more difficult. She was, after all, left-handed.

Although still helpless with her functional arm in plaster and sling, George needed to keep the press going; she and Higgins both wrote letters to America offering to sell shares in the limited company; in July she followed up with a cable asking 'if impossible could loan be arranged guaranteed by deposit of Yeats manuscripts with MacCartan pending arrangements'. The meticulous and practical James Healy responded to her letter and, later, a cable with a series of questions about the organization of Cuala. He advised that good business practice would seem to be to borrow to pay off existing debts, rather than to try to operate under wartime conditions; with the likelihood of the United States entering the war, nothing could be done about subscriptions for stock in Cuala at this time.[112] Although George 'entirely agreed' with him, there were purely sentimental reasons—though very real and serious—for keeping Cuala open: not only was it the only source of income for Lily, but 'three of the four workers have been at Cuala for over 30 years and to throw them out of employment would cause them great hardship'. Of the two printers, trained in a very specialized occupation, Essie Ryan had been there since 1903 and Maire Gill since 1908; Eileen Colum started in 1904.[113] However, George admitted it was impossible to foresee what sales there might be; there had been very few reviews of *On the Boiler*, for the English papers seemed to be reviewing 'nothing but war books

& fiction'. Masefield had contributed *Some Memories of W. B. Yeats*, and she herself had provided two essays by WBY (*If I were Four-and-Twenty*) which he had intended for Cuala before being published by Macmillan but were by now deleted from the Coole Edition. Orders for these and other books came in daily, but slowly. If only they could collect their English and American accounts; she was sending out polite requests for payment without much success.

Her correspondence with Healy was delicate: he had been a member of the Testimonial Committee and, an avid book collector himself, was always keen to purchase books, especially if inscribed by authors and George herself. He was also invaluable in making contacts with officials in America, especially since not even the Department of Foreign Affairs could elicit payments for her. When no reply came she arranged for an overdraft with the bank by transferring some personal securities.[114] Later that summer Healy cabled that he was granting the loan personally, but further embarrassment ensued—the money never arrived. George turned to Patrick McCartan for help, and the following January a cheque for £100, which had apparently been sent through a third party, finally reached her. This was not, unfortunately, the end of the story. Five years later George received a letter from James Healy referring to his loan account of twice that sum; worried, she wrote immediately to clarify the situation, but had no reply. Panicking, she wrote again three months later, 'Surely you cannot think that *I personally* pocketted the additional £100?' Any slur on the Yeats name could never be tolerated, and her own pride was at stake: 'This mis-understanding harms not only the Cuala Press but myself personally.'[115] The matter was finally cleared up by a soothing letter from Healy, who realized that the second cheque had never reached her. Because of currency restrictions, it was not until 1951, ten years later, that the sum ($400) was finally repaid, when George arranged for it to be deducted from her American royalties.[116]

George's visit with Michael to Renvyle House finally took place in late August 1940, after each Cuala 'girl' in turn had taken her holidays. 'It is so difficult in these days to keep the Press going that one is afraid to neglect any chance of business in England by not being "on the spot".'[117] Meanwhile that same August, thanks to Lily, Bernard Shaw once more came to the rescue:

I remembered that when we started the Industry G. B. S. had said in a p. card that some day he would give us a book and correct the proofs with a view entirely to the look of the page. I told George this on the telephone. She said to write and remind him and I did. I got no answer for a month, then had a letter saying he had thought of a book for us. Letters written by him and Willy to Florence Farr over thirty years ago were in existence, and he thought F. Farr's executor could be got to consent to the publication of them. His he said he would like to look over as they were probably too intimate, and Willy's? George would have to read as they were probably libellous. Now G. B. S. says print his all of them. He and F. F. had a love affair, but at 85 I think people no longer care, and hand it all out. George is very pleased. It ought to be a very good seller and interesting book.

Shaw was his usual generous help, but wartime conditions delayed the proofs, and the volume, edited by Clifford Bax with a brief introduction by George, did not appear until November 1941; a trade edition engineered by Shaw, who was adamant that royalties go to the widow rather than to the press, was then published five years later.[118] Quoting from Willy's correspondence and her own memories, George provided a few pages of background in her foreword to WBY's letters; this is one of the few occasions on which she allowed her name as author.[119] Not all of her exchanges with Bax are extant, but apparently (although it rankled to the end of her days) she did not challenge him concerning his well-publicized claim that WBY had not compiled the Oxford anthology himself. However, she had known his name ever since her early years of study: he too had attended Heatherley School of Art, was a theosophist, had been the first to translate Rudolf Steiner's work into English, and for five years (1909–14) was editor of *Orpheus: A Quarterly Magazine of Mystical (of Imaginative) Art*.[120]

Even before WBY's death plans were in train for the publication of *A Lament for Art O'Leary*, a translation from the Irish by Frank O'Connor, with illustrations by Jack. This was resurrected and finally published in June 1940; three years later, on the fortieth anniversary of the press, Jack Yeats's play *La La Noo* appeared. On the whole, however, Jack kept his distance from the workings of Cuala as he always had from Willy and his family: 'I . . . am not on a footing which, in any way, would give me the right of any knowledge of the working of the Cuala Press, financial, domestic, or otherwise. At no time even during the life of my sister Elizabeth [had I knowledge] of how any wheels turned.'[121] Just as he concealed his work in progress from others, he protected himself. Lily on the other hand was keenly interested in anything to do with the family. She admired her sister-in-law's courage, energy, and care with the printing, noting with approval the improvement in inking and setting: 'George is pretty strict and won't let even one damaged type in.'[122] George had always been an excellent proof-reader; she was also a good business woman, and finally under her aegis authors received contracts for the first time. But she badly needed more assistance on the board. Higgins, who had publishing experience, was helpful on financial matters, accompanying her in discussions with the bank and the auditor; however his responsibilities as managing director of the Abbey made it difficult to keep him sufficiently involved concerning editorial matters. Besides, with Anne at the Abbey, circumstances with Fred could sometimes be strained.

Then, on 8 January 1941, Fred Higgins died suddenly of heart failure. George now had to find not only more board members for Cuala, but a co-editor for herself. She immediately thought of Seán O'Faoláin as a director, and Frank O'Connor as co-editor. Some years previously she had established her own relationship with O'Connor (or 'Michael/Frank', as she referred to him, combining his real name, Michael O'Donovan, with his pen name) and his wife the Welsh actress Evelyn Bowen, both of whom she liked and admired. O'Connor, who had been dismissed by the Abbey Board and was expecting to be involved in a libel suit which he thought might endanger Anne's position, urged her to visit them in Wicklow incognito. 'I would love to come & see you & Mrs O'Donovan,' George replied, 'but must I come "incognito"? I am a very bad diplomatist & might forget that I had not seen you. I will write to ask what day I may come when I am out of plaster.' Having published his *Lament for Art O'Leary* (considered by many the finest of Cuala's books), she had been keen to follow up with another. 'Do you really think your translation of "The Midnight Court" is too vigorous for the virgin eyes of the Cuala Press—workers & subscribers? I wish I could see it??' *The Midnight Court* did not go to Cuala, but O'Connor did. Effectively banned from work in Ireland under de Valera's government because of his civil marriage to a divorced woman, he replied at once, accepting her invitation. George was relieved:

Thank you very much. With you as 'Editor' my burden, timidity, sense of responsibility (literary) will be vastly lightened. I have asked, before I had your letter, S. O'F. to become a director. Havent had a decision in writing from him yet. Higgins never told me that he had discussed 'Court' with S. O'F. nor did he discuss the possibility of subscribers only. In fact with all my contacts with Higgins on matters concerning Cuala he never committed himself to anything bar that one vehement statement. Apart from that one instance he made objections to almost everything but left me to say 'no'. That is why I want two people who can both say 'yes' or 'no' with the kind of direct speech which I knew from 1917–1939.

She was sincere in her wish to hear once again that 'direct speech'; after listening to one of his radio broadcasts she wrote, 'I hope you will not think I am doing an Anglo-American Gush if I say that every word I have heard you say—wireless in Ireland & England—conversation—has given me a delighted excitement that I had thought died when WB died.'[123]

Both new directors began energetically, O'Faoláin making a number of excellent suggestions concerning the printing activities of the press. Both men also introduced new authors: at O'Faoláin's urging Elizabeth Bowen gave Cuala her autobiographical *Seven Winters*, and O'Connor brought in both the artist Elizabeth Rivers and the poet Patrick Kavanagh. But O'Faoláin resigned from the board later that year on the grounds of ill health. Collaboration with O'Connor, though sometimes stormy, continued. Occasionally George had to force him to disagree openly with her: 'Isn't "*NO*" what you really want to say? I wish you didn't find it so difficult to just say "NO" or "YES" or "I MUST" or "I WANT! I always feel when you talk to me that there is something positive you want to say and that some clumsiness of my own has stopped you saying it. I think you will have to forget that I am WBY's widow.'[124] Other times, 'Michael/Frank' spoke equally frankly to her. At his suggestion she considered taking up the abandoned project of the Lady Gregory letters:

I am really dubious about selling value of a selection of the letters to Lady G. There may be a very few which have individual interest but the great mass has only historical value. Students of Yeats or of the period in which he lived might buy the book, but . . . ? I cannot help feeling that a book of some sixty pages, selected from a correspondence 1896–1932, would have to be sixty admirable pages; & I dont see the material! I must show you some, you will judge. Vast numbers remain to be typed; I find that the typists so mis-read the writing that it takes me almost as much time to correct as it would to type. Such errors as this . . . 'I lunched with Lady Lyttleton yesterday, I was my dearest & all went well' . . . On investigation 'I was *very discreet*.!'

   Letters to his father or letters to Olivia Shakespear might be better? Serious suggestion I will try & type so that you can see a general outline.[125]

She did however start making summaries of some of Yeats's letters to Gregory in a duplicate book which had originally been Anne's 'allowance account'. Her notes started in 1909 and concluded with Willy's meeting with Edith Heald. Perhaps some memories were simply too painful to record.

   O'Connor also encouraged her to consider writing 'a little book on W. B.' 'It may be too soon for you to begin, but it just occurs to me that if you have been helping Hone your mind may well be full of impressions which would be more easily fixed now than later on.' But again she was dubious and even more reluctant. 'I composed the "enclosed" & kept it over for further consideration. I didnt want to send you a purely instinctive reply,' she finally responded. 'You suggested to me some years ago that I should write some comments, and now the mechanical typing of the Lady G. letters has got me going at white heat because there are so many things lost; did you not say when you & Evelyn were having tea before Betty [Elizabeth Rivers] went away "to write a life of Yeats should be like pursuing a ghost".'[126] Suggestions that she write her own account of WBY's last years had come from others, including their Oxford friend W. F. Stead, who had taken a different tack: 'You must have played a very large part in all his writing for these last twenty years or so; I remember how often you seemed to hold the key to many mysteries when "A Vision" was taking shape in 1920–1922. Is it too much to hope that you may write an account of his later years, and what happened at the end, for which he had long been prepared.'[127] But, shrinking from revealing herself publicly, especially after two years of self-imposed solitude, she was too timid to pursue the project. The day the first reviews of Hone's biography came out, all with slighting references to herself as medium and to WBY's 'silly side . . . the trivialities of occultism', she arrived at a production meeting with O'Connor and Elizabeth Rivers considerably the worse for drink. She immediately wrote to her co-editor,

Sorry. The combination of two molars yanked out on Friday morning and New Statesman review knocked me out. I couldnt even say why to you and Elizabeth. One oughtnt to allow such things to take control, but the fact that unfortunately *I* do should give you complete confirmation of why I cant do that 'little book about Yeats for Cuala'. You saw my capacity for emotional display and black out. I am terrified with no reason for terror about this Life, afraid now that it is on the market that I will meet people in Dublin who will ask me what I think of the book, so I will slink as I did after Yeats death round back streets to avoid the people who said 'You *will* bring him back, won't you' to avoid the avid mouths that ask me 'what do you think of Hone's . . . . . .'

Her apology to O'Connor crossed with an angry letter from him; he had been only dissuaded by his wife from resigning immediately; he had seen Robinson destroy himself through alcohol, and could not bear to see it happen to George, whose relationship with Yeats he had always considered ideal. The letter touched her deeply; her reply was unusually revealing:

Thank you—I never knew that you had written 'after his death of Yeats marriage'. I had avoided reading anything that was printed about him. A lack of courage. When this is all over I would like to know what you wrote, & if you would tell me where you wrote it I will find the paper.
   I am grateful to you for writing to me that 'this is the last big job you will do for him'. That phrase will be in my mind for ever. It is the first time anyone has written such a sentence to me. Yours George.[128]

The challenge lingered—as late as 1950 she told one scholar that she was going to publish 'a chronological book on Yeats'.[129]
   The partnership with O'Connor also continued. Knowing how hard strapped he and Evelyn were for funds and, echoing a statement she had once made to Willy that 'Frank O'Connor is a writer who must go on writing,' she once sent him a cheque as a gift. He brought her Sobranie cigarettes from England ('Such beautiful smokes. They spoil one for all other cigarrettes [*sic*]'.) She admired Evelyn's 'finished' acting, and would like to have seen her in *The Player Queen*. They joined each other for tea and suppers, and Evelyn remembered her once saying wistfully that nobody came to see her any more.[130] Although his support was strong, including two more of his own books, O'Connor eventually resigned from the Cuala Press in 1944 on some unidentified matter of principle. By then his marriage to Evelyn was beginning to disintegrate and he was spending most of his time in England. However, he and George remained friends for the next twenty-five years.
   On 14 January 1942, in order to save over £100 a year in rent, George moved Cuala from 133 Lower Baggot Street into Palmerston Road, where at the low annual rent of £20 the Press took over two rooms on the lower level, next to the kitchen. Even so, often she would have to forgo the rent in order to balance the

Industries' books. George cast her net wide in an effort to find new outlets for the cards, even, as Lolly used to, asking regular subscribers from Canada and the United States for advice and help. New projects were initiated, such as a series of Christmas booklets, the first of which was *The Wren Boys*, complete with the traditional St Stephen's Day rhyme, music, and a hand-coloured frontispiece by Jack Yeats. But every year the auditor (another F. R. O'Connor) warned her that 'some effort must be made to put the business on a profit-earning basis'; each year the Industries failed to do so.[131] Although tentative efforts were made to find new directors—Geoffrey Taylor, Elizabeth Rivers—George continued to run the Press herself with the help of the staff. Later, when Molly Gill was seriously ill, she personally bore all the medical costs; when she herself was incapacitated, Eileen Colum came in each day to deal with correspondence. But the war and customs tariffs took their toll: typing paper was scarce and expensive and she took to doing preliminary work on the back of old duplicate typescripts; her clothing coupons went towards the purchase of linen for the spines of books; the binders could only work with gas for an hour and a half each day.

In October 1943 George herself became a Cuala customer, arranging for the private publication of fifty copies of *Mosada*, Willy's first published volume, with his corrections; these were distributed to his oldest friends and a few private collectors as her own mark of gratitude for their loyalty.[132] By December 1943 there was only enough paper left for three more books, one of which was Yeats's *Pages from a Diary Written in Nineteen Hundred and Thirty*, anonymously edited by George. 'The Yeats Diary will, I think, be interesting,' she explained. 'A good deal of the thought in it will be familiar to anyone who knows Yeats' work after 1930, a good deal of it has been far better written in fragments, but 1930 was a good germinative year.' From April 1944 no cards or prints could be exported. By this ruling Cuala lost all their English and American customers; however, since nothing could be imported, the sale in Ireland of Christmas cards increased. George complained to Lily that she was 'so busy colouring cards that she hates the sight of them and says that she will get her own in Woolworth's'. Finally at the end of 1945 Cuala was permitted to export 2,000 cards to the United States.[133] George continued to make plans for new books, but she admitted, 'I suppose anyone less of a damn-blast-hell fool than I would let the press die.'[134] In 1946 Cuala announced the publication of *Landor and Ireland* by Maurice James Craig, but although the author received an advance of £10 from the press, the book did not appear. An illustrated book on Georgian Dublin by John Betjeman (at the time press attaché to the English representative in Ireland) was mooted but came to nothing. Neither did a volume of letters between WBY and Sturge Moore, which had been suggested by the Moores and tentatively agreed to by George, to come out after Hone's biography.[135] The last book to appear with the Cuala imprint was *Stranger in Aran*, written and illustrated by Betty Rivers, now a close friend, which was published on 31 July 1946. With prints and cards she kept the press going—and the remaining 'Cuala girls' in work—for the rest of her life.

Even after she ceased publishing, George's feeling of responsibility towards young Irish poets—the original aim of the press—continued to weigh heavily. Worried that Patrick Kavanagh's *The Great Hunger* might be censored, she managed to send the hundred unsubscribed copies to J. G. Wilson of Bumpus in London for preservation and sale; fifty were returned after the war. Unable to accept Kavanagh's next volume, *A Satirical Pilgrimage*, she recommended it to Faber, at the same time sending Eliot a copy of Cuala's *Dafydd ap Gwilym* by Nigel Heseltine, in the hope that Eliot might consider further translations by him. One of her final proposals had been an anthology of the last decade of Irish poetry; she was keen to include a poem or two by 'a very young airman who was killed in 1942 . . . who might have achieved something'.[136] Even in the 1950s and 1960s she kept a close eye on who was writing, or should be but was not.

In the summer of 1944, George had a visitor who was preparing an article on Cuala and the woman who ran it. Lily continued to prod her to put her name on the circulars and bills, and also in the colophon of the books now that she was doing both Willy's and Lolly's work. But George did her best to remain at some distance.[137] However, that day she was more than usually forthcoming, even exhibiting family treasures including the door knocker from Riversdale (never used again). After her death R. M. Fox published his memories of the visit:

a most unassuming woman with a magnificent leonine head, a grey-black mane of hair, a firm jaw and deepset eyes. Of medium height, she was sturdily built. She was a rock of quiet commonsense . . . She was a familiar figure at displays of Irish industrial goods with her stand of Cuala Press cards and broadsheets . . . I went to the premises of the Cuala Press to see it in operation. I rang the bell at the side and she opened the door and led the way to her flat above. . . . Three women ran the press and a large part of their work consisted in swinging the heavy handle round and printing the broadsheets which— with hand-printed Christmas cards—kept the press busy in its latter days . . . After the broadsheets had been printed, the pictures were handcoloured and hung up over lines of cord to dry, which gave the basement the appearance of a busy washing day.[138]

Usually, however, George remained as much in the background as she could. Anniversaries of WBY's birthday and death were always traumatic; Edith Heald for example sent flowers on 28 January. In June 1940 T. S. Eliot delivered a memorial lecture at the Abbey; George, Anne, and Michael hid themselves in the gallery, but when Hone reneged on the vote of thanks Monk Gibbon at the last minute was asked to take his place. He spoke from his seat, immediately behind the Yeatses, who were thus thrust into the spotlight. Aware of Gibbon's resentment at being left out of their anthology and the Cuala list, George thanked him for his 'magnaminity'.[139]

But, as she had revealed to O'Connor and Rivers, the greatest strain was when Hone's biography appeared. That first review by Raymond Mortimer in the *New Statesman* set the tone for many that followed: the book was informative but dull; thorough in places and uncritical in others; and because it was authorized, highly selective. Even Gogarty acknowledged that there were 'inevitably some reticences' and 'little attempt to assess the work'.[140] One review however was so appreciated by George for its sensitivity and insight that she wrote to the author, whose critical articles in the *New English Review* on Yeats and Cuala she had followed for some years. Speaking of Yeats, Herman Peschmann had written that George herself 'became for him amid storms private and public an anchorage; yet something far more than an anchorage—a springboard for that extraordinary burst of fertility, in poetry of stark simplicity and strength, in his last years: a full study of that part of his life cannot yet be written and, wisely, no attempt is here made.' But he regretted that WBY's 'attitude to spiritism, astrology, cabalism and "black magic"' had not been probed more completely, and wished for an 'adequate account of his poetic development, or a co-ordination of it with his life'.[141] George's response revealed not only a fair assessment of Hone's biography, but her own attitude towards Willy:

You gave me an undeserved tribute which pleased me tremendously! I liked the book (Joe Hone's 'Life') because, to me, it did not spoil my own image of the man. When the book was started I arranged with Joe that I should see no script or part, because if I were to ask for that the writer would have no freedom. When I read the book I was sure that I was right in making that decision. It was a most difficult task—to write of a man at a time when so many of his friends and relations were still alive. The lack of co-ordination of Yeats' poetic development with his life was almost inevitable in a book of this sort. To begin with, the 'Collected Poems' (Macmillan) arranged by Yeats himself, are far from being in a chronological order—as *un*-chronological as many of the poems published in magazines etc. Then, unless a biographer's mind is naturally so concerned and saturated with poetry that he is compelled against his own will to write from that bias, what can he do but tell a story that will make a picture? Someone else will write another 'Life' from the only 'point of view' that I myself care for at all—poetry.

She spoke of her own work, 'collecting dates of the writing of poems, re-writings—, so that material shall be available both for a dated "collection" and for a different life'. Then, tantalizingly, she added, 'That problem "Nobody ever felt certain about Yeats' faith in the occult. Did he really believe or was it just a play-ing with fantastic images, etc". I myself find it difficult to know. Of this side in his life I am writing.' Although this last reference gives us a hint of the 'little book for Cuala' she was contemplating at O'Connor's suggestion, no notes concerning occult studies survive. When the second edition of the biography appeared after Hone's death, the corrections and appendix were provided by George from her own carefully annotated copy.[142] But although she spoke openly of Yeats and his beliefs to a chosen few (and was prepared to joke about Joe Hone's 'allergy to dates'), never again, apparently, did she commit herself on paper.

For many months George went to town as little as possible, and did not even answer the telephone, leaving the maid to say she was 'not well'.[143] When it came to theatre, however, George was more prepared to go public. In May 1941 the Dublin Drama League was again reorganized; Lennox was elected president, and George the general secretary. Other members of the committee included Jack Yeats, Micheál MacLiammóir and Hilton Edwards of the Gate Theatre, George's friend Sybil LeBrocquy and her artist son Louis, Frank O'Connor, and playwright Denis Johnston. Johnston chaired the inaugural meeting and effectively served as chief administrator; three committees dealing with playgoers, writers, and production, each with its own secretary, were also appointed.[144] However, with each disagreement (and inevitably there were many), George found herself in the eye of the storm. The first squall was over the production of Frank O'Connor's *The Statue's Daughter*, to be produced at the Gate Theatre in December 1941; Joseph Holloway noted in his diary that George as secretary sat prominently at a table in the vestibule.[145] There had been some concern that the play would be rejected by the 'playgoers' committee', but it was the 'production committee' that eventually almost caused the League to founder. Evidently before the third performance two members of the cast refused to go on unless they were paid in advance. Ria Mooney promised the dissidents their money, and the show went on. The same performers appeared the following week in the League's second production, Eliot's *The Family Reunion*, apparently without the same guarantee. A third offering that same month, a double bill of Buchner's *Wozzeck* and Blanaid Salkeld's *Scarecrow over the Corn*, would mark the final farewell to the Dublin Drama League. By the middle of January 1942 Sybil LeBrocquy, secretary to the playgoers' section, found herself embroiled in a legal quarrel. The matter was not settled until May, when George sent a personal cheque for nine guineas to the actors involved before their claim went to court. The League once again capsized.[146] Later that year, however, George rejoined the United Arts Club, perhaps because Tom MacGreevy was once again living in Dublin.

A more significant theatre crisis struck much closer to home, for with her father's death in January 1939 Anne became one of the casualties of a struggle for power among the Abbey directorate. In August 1939 the Abbey Board, having changed its constitution in order to do so, dismissed O'Connor as Director, thereby removing Anne's mentor and protector. Directives began to come down demanding that old materials, stock sets, and curtainings be used, avoiding whenever possible all sets with wallpaper decoration. In part this was due to wartime economy; it was even more a reversion to old habits and Anne, trained in Paris at O'Connor's insistence, became suspect. Anxious to learn more about production, she attended rehearsals at the Gate Theatre, where Micheál

MacLiammóir was only too willing to offer advice. She recalled, 'The usual set at the Abbey was three white flats, I put in two flats. And the word came down: "Quit going to the Gate rehearsals. Your work is getting arty." '[147] In spite of the fact that Fred Higgins was the Abbey's managing director, by the end of 1940 her designs were being rejected; she was demoted to assistant, her salary reduced accordingly. In April the following year she underwent an operation for a hernia caused by the heavy work at the theatre; while she was still recovering, the Board informed George that her daughter's contract was terminated. While George was tending to her daughter in hospital, Michael was visiting the Faulkners in the north when Belfast suffered its first big air raid. Telephones were out of order, and George could get no news of her son. To her relief he arrived home safely, but tired, in the middle of the night. No wonder George had difficulty keeping her mind on Cuala; 'when anything happens to my family my bones lose their marrow and my head dithers,' she apologized to O'Connor.[148] The following month Germany dropped bombs on Dublin in the Strand Road area, killing over thirty and injuring another eighty.[149] By December, with the bombing of Pearl Harbor, the United States had entered the war. Michael went back to Trinity; for the next four or five years Anne freelanced, working with other young designers such as Louis LeBrocquy, designing or stagemanaging for the Peacock Theatre, the Cork Opera House, the Olympia and Gaiety theatres, and Austin Clarke's Lyric Theatre, where once again she designed some of her father's plays.

For some time George had also been worried about Nelly Tucker. Many of her mother's letters, doubtless indiscreet as usual, never arrived, but occasionally she could be reached by telephone. There was reason for concern apart from enemy attacks on the coast: since 1939 Harry Tucker's dementia had become so severe that he was permanently confined to a nursing home in Torquay. Forbidden to visit for fear of increasing his violence and hallucinations, Nelly sold Alkerton Cottage and moved in to a hotel, devoting each day to preparing little gifts to be sent to her husband 'in hopes of a lucid moment'. Then in March 1940 Nelly's sister Gertrude Spurway, who had been living in Sidmouth, died. Although they had never been close, the relationship had been amiable, and it was one more door closed for Nelly; less than a year later her last remaining uncle, Cecil Woodmass, also died. At first too busy and ill to visit her mother, George was by then unable to cross the channel; as Archdeacon of Portsmouth her brother Harold was determined to stick to his post, refusing to retreat to his house in the country. Writing to Dorothy, Nelly reported that 'Harold has had a bad slump, & Georgie has too many poor relations in Ireland. So I am left with a very small income, as I pay all extras & comforts for Harry.' Her two children had always been her 'chief source of supplies'.[150] Then in mid-January 1942 George received word that her mother was seriously ill. With great difficulty she managed to get a permit to enter England; returning home furious after an entire day fighting through red tape at the British office, she sputtered, 'Now I know what it's like to be black.' One of the problems was that, having married just a year too late to qualify for the new state law granting her the nationality of her husband, she was not legally entitled to an Irish passport. Although finally given one out of consideration of her situation, George never bothered returning to fill out the official forms when the new law came into force. (Anne always felt it was because she resented the £25 this would have cost; she kept on voting anyway, and was never challenged.) After a horrendous two-day journey, George arrived in time to spend two weeks by her mother's bedside in Torquay. Nelly died on 2 February 1942 at the age of 74. Jelly d'Aranyi, performing in Scotland, was devastated by the news; she loved Nelly very deeply, as she wrote to 'dear Dobbs'; Nelly had been 'a most perfect friend and company', and she had been worried at not receiving the customary immediate reply to her letters.[151] An obituary did not appear in *The Times* until 12 February; described as the eldest daughter of the late Montagu Woodmass of Chester, there was no reference to her first husband William Gilbert Hyde Lees or to her late mother Edith Alice of Southwell Gardens, London. 'Poor George has had so many of these rushed and anxious journeys, and January been a distressing month, Willy January '39, Lolly January '40,' wrote Lily. 'I don't think this is a great sorrow, just a sadness. The mother was very temperamental and difficult, but it is a distressing experience if not a deeply felt one.'[152]

Typically, George revealed nothing of her own feelings. She stayed on to pack up her mother's papers and belongings, and make arrangements for Harry Tucker, who would at last have to be 'certified', a move until now avoided. Nelly, who had held power of attorney only, had always feared this would happen if she died first. After seeing the solicitors in Sidmouth, George then went on to her brother in Portsmouth; since the Pounds were in Italy, Harold was made Harry's temporary guardian.[153] The visit was not an entire success: Harold had been irritated by the police surveillance accorded him because of his Irish brother-in-law. He was also angered by George's drinking; probably aware of his own potential genetic weakness and branded by the memory of his father's deathbed he was, according to his sister-in-law, 'terrified of alcohol and very mean about it', and 'horrid, not at all sympathetic' to George.[154] She spent a night in London on her way back; she visited the bookshops, distributed Cuala leaflets, saw the exhibition of works by Jack B. Yeats and Ben Nicholson—'admirably hung & lit'—at the National Gallery, and made a special point of visiting Omar Pound at Charterhouse school in Surrey.[155] Foraging about in a secondhand bookshop on Charing Cross Road, she discovered (and bought for 2s. 6d.) a copy of *The Wanderings of Oisin* with the inscription 'W. B. Yeats This copy is not to be lent as I have made corrections in it that I do not want to lose.'[156] All the books she ordered for herself arrived except Joseph Harsch's *Pattern of Conquest*, a reporter's account of Germany during the first years of the war.[157] Then, her permit almost up, she returned to Dublin. Thanking Edith for the flowers that had arrived in her absence, she apologized for not telephoning: 'You are so often in my thoughts. I am so thankful Willy did not live to see this war, & I am sure you feel the same about it.'[158] Her own feelings about Ireland's neutrality were mixed, as she admitted to Oliver Edwards: 'I find it curious that I can divide my mind into two and believe myself loyal to my own country and at the same time no less loyal to my adopted country (adopted in the marriage sense).'[159] But her children were Irish, and in Ireland she would remain.

The very day George returned to Ireland, Harold's wife Gwynne died of heart failure, according to the doctor a direct result of the strain of the frequent raids. From this time on her brother spent all his free time with Gwynne's mother and sister Eleanor; most of his money would go to their comfort.[160] When George received 'about four hundred pounds' from her mother's legacy, it went towards the costs of publishing at Cuala.[161] She conscientiously took over her mother's responsibilities with young Omar Pound, at Christmas sending some promised stamps. She also arranged a gift of £5 three times a year until he was 21, 'In memory of my mother and your grandmother (who often gave me tips when I was young)':

I am a hopeless correspondent as you already know. Partly because it is difficult to write letters to people one cannot meet fairly often. I do like *getting* letters, and, if I may say so, yours have a vital vivid turn of phrase which fills me with curiosity about what you are planning to do when you get out of school. I wish we could meet, though I know that if we did we should talk of everything else because people only talk of what they want to do to people of their own generation. When the war is over, perhaps you would make this house a headquarters for an Irish holiday; if you have a bycycle [*sic*] we could plan an amusing fortnight—my son is not so very much older than you are! (By the way, are you 15 or 16?)

I wish you would tell me your home address. Your affectionate 5 times removed cousin George Yeats[162]

Dorothy, stranded in Italy, could not now keep a watch over her son; unlike her 'step-pest' who insisted on such ceremonies for her children, she was very annoyed when she heard Omar had been baptized.[163] In 1944, when Omar was bombed out in London, George offered to take him in, but he could not get across to Ireland.[164] He would not visit Dublin until 1951.

Not surprisingly, for a time George was not well, feeling 'seedy' and suffering dizzy spells.[165] Other family illnesses followed. On 3 September 1943 Lily suffered a stroke which left her paralysed and bedridden. George punctiliously reported to Healy that 'the £200 cabled to me immediately after WBY's death by the Testimonial Committee has been used entirely for Miss Yeats'

I was at the time obliged to use a part of the money for my own and our children's expenses, but the money was in a separate account and was replaced in that account as soon as I was able. The Testimonial Committee may be glad to know that they have helped WBY's sister as well as himself. The money has been used for payment of nurses etc in order that she might remain in her own home instead of having to go to a hospital. I have kept full accounts showing the exact way in which this money was spent. I hope you will regard this as 'confidential' as we should not like to see reports in newspapers about what is really a personal family matter. Miss Yeats has not been able to read or write—her sight is very bad and her right hand is paralysed—but someone might read her a paper or a letter containing matter which would undoubtedly distress her very much She is 78 years old and is bearing her helplessness most gallantly.[166]

The following year aunt Fanny Gordon, JBY's remaining sister, died. Again, Lily provided Ruth with details:

George went to Violet's assistance at once and found her quite stunned, so she took a taxi and went to see Jack, who characteristically refused all responsibility, so George went on to Mount Jerome, where a very light-hearted young man turned over a large book, and seeing our Aunts Grace Jane and Jane Grace, and our Grandmother Jane Grace, remarked, 'there seems to be a dearth of originality of names in your family.' Then George said that she couldn't give the exact date of the funeral as they had to wait to hear from Rupert, so he took down another book, flicked over the leaves, and said, 'The booking is light just now', as if it were a theatre.

Anne was in Portmarnock, and Michael and George attended the funeral at Mount Jerome. 'There were wasps—attracted by the wreaths no doubt—and one circled incessantly round Michael and myself; M. behaved in most exemplary manner, stood stiff as a toy soldier!'[167] A few months later Violet Gordon had an operation and naturally sent for 'our strong rock' George, who stayed with her until her brother Rupert Gordon arrived from Liverpool.[168] With Violet's death in early January 1945, George had lost another trusted friend. Eileen, Violet's younger sister, moved into Palmerston Road for more than a month.

'The Emergency' would continue to cause financial hardship. When Harry Tucker died in 1943, there were difficulties in separating Nelly's property from his as both had been stored together. With restrictions on travel even more inflexible, George appealed for assistance to Desmond FitzGerald, now a Senator: 'They are unfortunately things which only I can do as I know what belonged to my mother and what to my step-father . . . My trouble is that until these things are settled a. I don't get any money which I need badly. b. My brother doesnt get furniture—he would like it as he has been in Portsmouth for six years. c. Only I know about the prints and pictures. The great collection belonged entirely to my stepfather.'[169] This time she was unable to get a permit to leave the country. Although presumably Harold brought some small items to Ireland when he visited his sister, the Tuckers' belongings would still be something of a mélange nine years later when he finally consulted Dorothy Pound about distribution of the library.[170] Money was a continuing concern, for by now all of Yeats's books were out of print. George told Lily that she only got £10 on the English editions in 1944, and was uncertain about American royalties.[171] However, she withheld cashing a cheque from the BBC for broadcasting rights until she had been assured that Marie Sturge Moore, whose husband had recently died, was paid for her share of the royalties.[172] Shortly afterwards, George herself had an accident: as she and Anne were about to board a stationary tram in Dawson Street, she was knocked down by a motorbike. Anne took her to Mercers hospital, and although nothing was broken, the shock kept her in bed while she recovered from 'external bumps & bruises & cuts'. Although her coat was torn and two policemen took all the particulars, typically as 'Mrs W. B.' she refused to make any charges against the young driver.[173]

By now a fluent Irish speaker, Michael graduated from Trinity in December 1943 with a first-class degree in history and political science and received the gold medal for oratory.[174] He then proceeded to study economics and statistics at University College, Dublin, and, finally, law. He had also enlisted in the 43rd Battalion of the Local Defence Force, quartered in Rathmines, and drilled every Thursday evening; he achieved a bull's-eye the first time he took his ancient Lee-Enfield rifle to the firing range, but, unlike his father with Anne's airgun, never succeeded in duplicating the feat. During the election campaign in 1943, Michael joined the Fianna Fáil party; when in 1944 he gave the inaugural address as auditor of the Trinity College Historical Society, he chose as distinguished guest speakers Jan Masaryk, Minister for Foreign Affairs in the Czechoslovak government in exile, and the Taoiseach, Eamon de Valera. In 1948 he stood alongside Seán MacEntee as one of the three candidates for the Dáil from Dublin South-East; he did not get in, but the baptism of fire would prove invaluable.[175] Having joined not Fine Gael, his father's allegiance, nor Clann na Poblachta, the party recently established by Seán MacBride, Michael became even more distanced from his parents' old friends. 'So my Godson is going F. F and not with Sean MacBride!', Lennox wrote with some astonishment. 'I am sure Willie would have liked the latter for old sake's sake. Michael doesn't simply exist for me, I dont know him at all.' But he was also aware of how this divided George's loyalty: 'I'd really be afraid to meet George, she would hedge all the time and be completely hostile.'[176] George regularly voted for her son's chosen party. When Michael was called to the bar, much to Lily's delight he wore his grandfather's eighty-two-year-old gown and wig.[177] One of his guests was uncle Jack, who had recently received an honorary degree, thereby, Lily proudly noted, becoming the sixth member of the Yeats family to hold a Trinity degree.[178]

More and more all three Yeatses were going their own way. 'I think that this secretiveness is part of the modern girl,' Lily wrote of Ruth's concern over her own daughter:

I don't believe Anne tells her mother where she is going to. When Anne comes to see me she talks to me about her work and answers anything I ask her, and then says, 'I must go now, as I have an appointment.' Not a word about who it is or what it is. It makes me feel as if I were an acquaintance and not a near relative. Michael I think is better this way and tells his mother most of his doings, though I think he and Anne know little of each other. I know George told me a story of how she was out one evening, leaving Anne and Michael, and the next morning she said something to Michael about Anne. He said that he hadn't seen her, and so George said, 'Why, she had dinner with you last night'. 'Oh, I forgot', said Michael.[179]

But George had always encouraged her children to make their own way. Lonely as she was, she accepted and encouraged their independence. However, her own reliance on alcohol grew during these years. Like many who seek consolation or forgetfulness in alcohol, she was usually able to hide it sufficiently to carry on; but then there would be relapses when everything was just too much to bear. The tenuous balancing act between two responsibilities—care of Willy and care of her children—had collapsed. Nor can we ignore the toll of those long years of soul-straining, when she summoned the dark secrets of the unconscious while drawing on all her practical energies to create the sunlit atmosphere of serenity required for Willy's poetry.

Although Anne would always enjoy the theatre, increasingly she came to realize that what she really wanted was to be a painter. She started attending night classes at the National College of Art, beginning with watercolour and wax, and would experiment with many different media throughout her long career. She also approached her uncle, asking him to teach her. But Jack, who had never had a pupil, replied that it 'would be quite impossible . . . All my energy has to go into painting my pictures.'[180] He did, however, buy two paintings from her successful first exhibition in 1946, and, except for a few productions with the Lyric Theatre, Anne then left stage design behind. One of her last designs, in December 1949, could not have been more appropriate—her father's last play, *The Death of Cuchulain*, for the Lyric Theatre on the Abbey stage. In 1946 she moved to the top flat of 16 Exchequer Street over offices and a hardware shop. Nicknamed 'Checkers' not in emulation of the English Prime Minister's residence but because it was full of draughts, it was reached by fifty-six steps, and she shared a lavatory one flight down. But for ten shillings a week it was her own, with lots of studio space, and she was happy. George provided an old two-ring gas cooker from Cuala, a French clay casserole, and a suggested household weekly budget of £2.45 which thoughtfully included half a cake. Anne painted the large room herself, sensibly removing her clothes to save on spills.[181] She would be there for eleven years, and from then on stayed at Palmerston Road for no more than ten days at a time, over Christmas or when her mother was ill. The arrangement was better for both of them; Anne was distressed by her mother's drinking, and she and George found it difficult to admit their true feelings. Things gradually improved, especially once she joined her mother for a drink (which they jokingly called 'a knird') over dinner. After George quit smoking, she surrounded Anne with so many ashtrays at the kitchen table that Anne stopped, at least in her mother's presence. There were happy times too; sometimes they danced round the kitchen table, each on her own side. She still spent Sundays helping with the garden, and later they always had lunch together at least once during the week. Every few weeks they met for an early dinner at the Hibernian; George enjoyed her food, but had a very small appetite. Together they went to the zoo, where George was a life member, taking seeded lettuces for the giant tortoise and windfall apples to the monkeys—George observed that Anne's aim always improved when she had been painting. Anne remembers her commenting that in a mural she painted for the Church of Ireland, the Christians had little heads, while all the pagans had proportionately larger bodies. Proud of her daughter's abilities, George tried not to interfere, though she worried when, like her father before her, Anne suffered from a creative block; on those occasions George might suggest a journey to a new country, 'to tell her what it was like'. Once when Anne was in Dubrovnik George sent a postcard saying with evident relief, 'Grand letter! Glad paint is in your mind—had been afraid—'[182] When the wartime restrictions lifted, Anne travelled as much as she could—to France (where she stayed above Sylvia Beach's bookshop and again visited Gordon Craig), Italy, Yugoslavia, Sicily.

In 1956 George and her daughter went to Holland to see the Rembrandt exhibition, then went on to Italy. They stopped in London on the way, visiting the art galleries. George, who regularly read *Elle* and *Oggi* to keep up her languages, put together two sets of Scrabble so that they could practise their Italian beforehand. Anne remembers how proud her mother was when in Verona she was mistaken for a native speaker from near the Austrian border. One evening they went for a walk; behind the firmly closed shutters of one shop there were chinks of light, 'and the air was full of the sound of singing birds'. Also on this journey Anne learned from George how to sit still and become 'invisible', aware of everything passing around her. Those 'marvellous 18 days in Italy' were George's last journey outside Ireland. From then on she enjoyed vicariously Anne's travels and frequent invitations to exhibit abroad, demanding not postcards of works of art, but views of the countryside. Italy would always remain a source of happy memories. Sometimes she wrote notes in Italian to keep Anne on her toes, and when Anne travelled through southern Italy and Sicily in 1965, she had George's recollections of the journey she and Willy had made forty years before.[183]

The two Yeats women were more attuned than they realized: just as George and Willy had frequently made the same purchase, Anne would arrive with something from one of the food shops on Chatham Street only to find that her mother had bought it herself the day before. It became a game between them, and 'nine times

out of ten' when Anne paused before a shop, George had already been there.[184] They
also shared a love of and tales about animals. Anne always remembered the occasion
when George discovered that a mouse was eating the chocolate she habitually left
by her bedside; she set a trap using a fig, but the next day, although the fig was gone,
the pips were neatly ordered beside the unsprung trap. When Ahi, the old dog who
came with George from Riversdale, died in 1944 she would suddenly waken to the
silence. He had slept in her bedroom for so many years she was used to his snoring.
Ahi was followed for a short time by a shorthaired dachshund called Patrick (or
Dachle); after he died there remained only the succession of cats. She and Anne
used to take one to Howth on the bus and walk it on a lead; two ('the yellow peril'
named Pluto and a beautiful grey) regularly took themselves off to a neighbour every
Sunday.[185] Another cat was called 'Lugh', but none was again named Pangur. In
1947 Anne joined the committee of the Irish Exhibition of Living Art as honorary
treasurer; Norah McGuinness, who had illustrated one of her father's books so
many years before, was then president and despite the age difference they became
fast friends. In addition to her painting she illustrated books, painted murals, taught
art privately in Checkers and, like her aunt Lolly before her, at several schools—
the Hall School (now Rathdown) in Monkstown, St Stephen's School for boys in
Harcourt Street, and Park House School. George proudly told Lily that 'One
school was so anxious to get her that they changed the hours of all the classes to
fit her convenience, so she must be good. She is very strict.'[186] On Saturdays after
her class she often joined Dolly Robinson for lunch and backgammon. 'She is full
of beans & most delightful company but never speaks of George,' Dolly noted.

George herself began to see a little more of Lennox and Dolly after WBY's
death; when accepting one invitation she confessed, 'Oct 31st sounds grand—
something to look forward to.'[187] But a visitor noticed that, now that her children
had their own careers, she was much alone.[188] She had few guests during the war
years. In the summer of 1942 Oliver Edwards introduced her to a young student
assistant; at the end of August George invited her to stay while Anne was away.
Impressed by her hostess's generosity, young Daphne Bush was struck by her
'lively, humorous, rather brisk and matter-of-fact personality' and 'quick, bright
glance of appraisal'. But she was shocked when after dinner as they sat by the fire
George suggested 'in a humorous, half-conspiratorial sort of way "Let's listen to
Ezra" and she tuned in to one of Ezra Pound's political broadcasts from Italy'.
Daphne was unable to accept George's invitation to spend part of her Christmas
vacation working on the Cuala Press, and they never met again.[189] Ebullient Jelly
d'Aranyi performed in Dublin three or four times. Although she does not seem to
have stayed at Palmerston Road, Jelly appreciated the clothing coupons George
gave her. On one tour Jelly, shopping for clothes with the coveted coupons,
received an invitation from Prime Minister de Valera, 'An Taoiseach', which she
understood as 'the teashop at four o'clock'.[190]

There was yet one more public responsibility due WBY, however. Now that Ireland was returning to normal after 'the Emergency' years, it was time to consider the return of Yeats's body. The arrangement she and Dermod O'Brien had made with the cemetery at Roquebrune was for ten years and time was passing. George sent Jack, Anne, and Michael to tell Lily that 'There is a movement on foot to bring Willie's body back, but it won't be till June.'[191] Rumour had it that the Sligo Corporation was keen to make arrangements of their own to bring the remains back to Ireland, a usurpation George could hardly allow. It had been her last promise to Willy. She then wrote a polite letter to the Mayor of Sligo, informing him that 'the family were making arrangements to have the remains brought back from France this summer'. The Mayor immediately wrote that Corporation 'in deference to the family's decision are taking no action', adding however that some members 'thought the Government should have undertaken and completed the task before now'. Corporation's deliberations on 5 January 1948 were picked up by *The Times* the next day.[192] When word reached London it caused consternation in several quarters, causing Edmund Dulac to break a long silence and reveal a carefully kept secret. He had, he said, been on the point of writing to her of the events of the past seven months. In June 1947 Edith Heald had visited Roquebrune, but WBY's grave was nowhere to be found. The local curé informed her that the concession must have been for one year, for another body had rested in that plot since 1946; Yeats's bones would then have been taken to the ossuary and would be impossible to identify. To avoid scandal, he and Edith had therefore concocted a plan: they had already purchased a 'concession à perpétuité' and he had designed a monumental stone to be placed there in honour of Yeats's memory. As far as any visitor was concerned, it would appear that the tomb and the stone had been there always, thereby preventing any awkward questions. Under the circumstances, he suggested that she turn down the idea of the reburial, telling the Sligo Corporation that owing to the war the cemetery had been disturbed and Yeats's remains dispersed. He offered to send his monument to Ireland instead, if she wished. A few days later, urged by Edith to be more precise and emphatic, he wrote again to tell her that the abbé had written to say that W.B. had been buried in the 'fosse commune' which he interpreted as the 'Pauper's grave', and that no concession had been purchased at all. George's reply crossed with Dulac's second bulletin: 'Dear Edmund, The grave was taken for *Ten* Years—not one—M. Roblot told Dermod O'Brien & myself that this was the sale at Roquebrune. I have the receipts. When I got your letter I consulted the French Minister here—I gave him your letter. He has written personally to the Abbé This of course strictly private—When he gets an answer to his letter—I will write to you. Yours George Yeats.' She twice underlined the word 'Ten'. Then, after receiving his second message, she took to the telephone. The French Minister had assured her that 'it would be quite easy to get the remains and bring them back'.[193] Among her carefully filed records was not only the original accounting from Dermod O'Brien, but a receipt from Maison Roblot for 2,225 francs.[194]

The private exchanges between Dulac and l'Abbé J. B. Biancheri, Heald, and her lesbian lover the painter Gluck were far less sympathetic to Mrs Yeats, whom they immediately blamed for mismanagement if not downright carelessness; nor does it seem to have occurred to them that it was none of their business. It was also clear that his antipathy to Wellesley, referred to slightingly as 'the Duchess', had surfaced in the impulsive Dulac; rumour had doubtless reached them that both Dorothy and George were drinking heavily. Edith was naturally devastated by her experience the previous June, and the kindly curé, whom they had contacted in search of assistance, had been most sympathetic. It was Biancheri who had helpfully telephoned the current director of la Maison Roblot, who could find no record of the purchase of a concession for 'la poëte Yeats'. At first it was assumed a concession must have been taken for one year only; then with still no evidence it was decided that Yeats must have been buried in the 'fosse commune', which carried a time limit of only five years. All, including Biancheri, convinced themselves that the mistake was entirely the widow's. As the harried officials in la Maison Roblot were asked again and again for further details, their answers like the abbé's became more and more definite. But still they could find no records, though it was admitted that towards the end of the war years there had been considerable activity enlarging the cemetery. No one seems to have explained the technical terms being used by the French authorities: 'fosse commune' does not mean a 'pauper's grave' as Edith and Dulac charged, but that part of the cemetery owned by the municipality or commune. Moreover, a 'concession temporaire', as applied to individuals, simply meant not 'perpétuelle'; such 'temporary' leases were purchased for five, ten, even twenty-five years, and it appears that ten was customary for the cemetery at Roquebrune. In any case that is the term George was convinced she had been granted.[195]

There is no record of George's private conversations with the French Ambassador in Ireland, the genial and flamboyant Count Stanislaus Ostrorog, or of his correspondence with Biancheri, but within months the transfer from France to Ireland had become a formal intergovernmental affair. This was doubtless encouraged by the Minister for External Affairs in Ireland's new government, none other than Seán MacBride, with whom George then had several private discussions. The abbé, who, Dulac noted, 'seems to take a real interest in the matter', had sworn both himself and the funeral director to secrecy; he reported that an 'inspecteur de police' (which they translated as 'a detective') would arrive at Roquebrune in March to participate in the formal exhumation and identification procedures. This encouraged Biancheri to return once again to the records, but unfortunately in his haste he only muddled the story further by stating that the register indicated that 'Butler William Yeats' had been buried on 28 January, two days before the ceremony had actually taken place. Doubtless aware of the mounting significance of the situation, he now suggested to his English correspondents that there may have been a copyist's error—or confusion between a five- and ten-year concession. However, he himself very much doubted whether it would be possible to identify the bones in such a short time; in any case absolute certainty was impossible. He did not mention that, according to strict governmental regulations, the family should have been informed when the coffin had been moved; if removal was necessary from the 'private' area where concessions were leased for individuals or families, it would be to the 'fosse commune' or area owned by the municipality itself.

Dulac again wrote to George, repeating the abbé's assurances. Since she appeared determined to face what would surely be a painful task, he could only hope it would not be too distressing. As for the stone, he sent a photograph in case she would like it for Drumcliffe. In that case he and Edith would put a simple tablet on the wall over the 'concession à perpétuité' they had already, with the obliging curé as go-between, purchased in Roquebrune. He would be grateful if, now that she had 'taken charge', she would keep him informed of progress. George does not seem to have replied. Nor did she reply to the next letter from London on the subject. Now Gluck, distressed by Edith's anguish and frustrated by their lack of success in persuading George to abandon her plans, took it upon herself to write to George, for the first time disclosing her part in the Roquebrune visit. Identifying herself not only as Edith's interpreter but someone who had 'so far . . . preserved the utmost secrecy', her letter forcefully repeated all Dulac's information, adding (with its insulting implications) that her enquiries had been the first in eight years. She herself could not 'view this re-burial with equanimity' and, although with 'no desire to make things worse than they are', urged Mrs Yeats to 'reconsider any scheme for re-burial'. It is not hard to imagine George's reaction to this abrupt demand from a complete stranger; once again she telephoned Edmund. Dulac was furious at Gluck's interference and 'impertinence', especially since George assumed Edith was using Gluck to intimidate if not threaten her; besides, now he and Edith would both be cut off. The good abbé meanwhile had on their behalf secured the concession for their memorial.[196]

Gluck and Dulac were not accurate in stating that no previous enquiries had been made. In 1941 George had received a reassuring note from Yeats's old friend Allan Wade; he and his wife had visited the cemetery before their enforced return to England in June 1940. The grave, he reported, 'looked tidy and well kept'; unfortunately the censor would not allow him to send photographs he had taken of the grave and stone marker.[197] Then Michael Yeats received a letter from another English stranger. Albert Emery had read the notice about the proposed reinterment and wondered about the fate of the grave next to Yeats, in which his brother-in-law Alfred Hollis had been buried in early February 1939; that grave had also been leased for ten years. When Emery, his wife, and daughters had visited Roquebrune in February 1947 (four months before Edith and Gluck), they too had discovered that all the graves in that part of the cemetery had disappeared. Local officials explained that 'there had been fighting around Roquebrune and that in the confusion all burial records had been lost'. Perhaps there was now more information available? Michael's reply was courteously sympathetic but not encouraging, admitting that 'The position with regard to the cemetery at Roquebrune would appear to be more than a little confused.' He himself had been told that the remains were 'removed to an unmarked corner of the cemetery'.

In the case of my father certainly, and probably also in the case of your brother-in-law, the concession given was a ten year one, and should not therefore have expired until early next year. But it would seem that during the war changes occurred in the administration of Roquebrune cemetery, and conditions were for a time much disturbed—you will remember that fighting took place in and around Roquebrune. The new administrators of the cemetery may not have been able to gain access to the prewar records of burials; in any event, they have clearly made a mistake as regards the time for which certain of the concessions were granted. As far as the remains of my father are concerned, they have been traced and are now lying in a vault ready to be taken home as soon as transport can be arranged. But you will understand that the circumstances in this case were exceptional.[198]

All that Michael could suggest was that Mr Hollis's coffin 'would be found near where his father's remains had been discovered', that is, in the municipality's corner of the cemetery, 'unmarked' because not privately subscribed.

Meanwhile, government wheels kept churning through diplomatic red tape. About 17 March 1948 Abbé Biancheri had been invited to assist at the exhumation; called to the bedside of an ailing parishioner some distance away, he was unable (and doubtless unwilling) to accept. He reported on 31 March that the research and exhumation had taken place, as the law required, in the presence of the police, the Mayor, the official coroner, the inspector from Paris, and the cemetery caretaker. The bones were placed in a new coffin which now rested in the chapel, but Biancheri had no information as to the date of departure. Municipal records confirm that in March 1948 Yeats's body had indeed been exhumed and, again according to the regulations, immediately placed in a new coffin; presumably the tarnished nameplate from the original coffin (noted by the press) was transferred at the same time. To assist in the enquiry, the family had offered further details: not only was Yeats a very tall man with 'a particularly massive bone structure', he had been buried in the truss he had worn due to 'a long-term hernia problem'.[199] But still there was delay. In June Dulac sent Edith a newspaper item suggesting that there was confusion at Roquebrune because 'the local authorities had lost their lease on the land. The cemetery was moved; graves switched around.' 'No wonder', the columnist added, 'Yeats' grave could not be located when the exhumation was ordered early this year.' No sources for this information were offered, but Michael Yeats is again quoted: 'I'm afraid things were messed up locally. We are assured all has been straightened out now and that the coffin will come to Ireland in a few weeks as soon as suitable transport is found.'[200] The newspaper article seen by Dulac was probably several months out of date, for by early summer negotiations were well along. By mid-June George was able to tell Lily that 'all the formalities in France are over, but they have yet to be completed on this side before she knows the final date of Willy's reburial'.[201] In August George wrote to Seán MacBride, 'You will have seen that the papers have got wind of the Corvette. Do let me have a date as soon as you can. I gather that Sligo is going to have a general holiday on the day of WBY's arrival. Another tale is that the County Council "has tons of sand ready to put on the roads". This piece of information puzzles me. Why sand? WBY would have loved to know.'[202]

Finally on 25 August the corvette LE *Macha* departed Dun Laoghaire on its way to Nice. It was the first time the Irish navy had been outside territorial waters; calling in at Gibraltar on the way, Commander MacKenna had to explain to the Admiral's office that a courtesy call could not be made 'with swords', as they hadn't any. When the Irish Ambassador Seán Murphy and his attaché flew in to Nice, the plane crashed on landing; no one was hurt but there was a slight delay in the round of official visits. On 16 September Yeats's coffin, which had been resting for five months in the cemetery chapel, was carried down to the town square, preceded in state by Abbé Biancheri with his young cross-bearer. After a brief speech by the deputy Mayor and an oration by a local poet, the Irish flag was draped over the coffin and, accompanied by a French guard of honour and a military band (with additional side drummers and trumpeters), the hearse then proceeded through Nice. Now fully aware of the situation, the government of France was determined to accord as much honour as possible to the distinguished poet before his remains finally left their territory. As the ship left the port, a young priest was seen to rush out and make the sign of the cross. Both George and the Protestant Irish poet would have appreciated the French Catholic blessings. The journey home took eleven days; because the port at Sligo was too shallow for the draught and equipment of the *Macha*, disembarkation took place at Galway, where the Yeats family was welcomed aboard. The procession then travelled by road to Sligo, where at the borough boundary it was met by the Mayor, members and officials of Sligo Corporation, and government officials from all quarters. An army bugler sounded the General Salute, then a military guard of honour watched over the remains for several hours in front of the Town Hall before the cortège wound its way to Drumcliffe and the final ceremony.

It was inevitable that even now controversy followed George and her family. Indignation had been publicly expressed that the greatest Irish poet was not being accorded a full state funeral; government press releases apologized that there would be no state ceremonial except for the military guard of honour; they had bowed to the wishes of the family. Seán MacBride represented the government; Eamon de Valera, leader of the opposition, accepted George's letter of invitation. Just as the Yeats family had rejected burial in St Patrick's Cathedral, now they insisted that the ceremony be as private as possible under the circumstances.[203] Nobody however could control the crowds at Drumcliffe; this was a holiday with well-known figures to gawk at and appeal to for autographs. When Jack, George, Anne, and Michael arrived, a pathway for them had to be forced through to the grave site. George was jostled as she cast her handful of soil on the coffin at the service of committal. There was no oration; the Mayor concluded the ceremony with the final lines from 'Under Ben Bulben'. Even then the rumour was being circulated (by Louis MacNeice among others) that the casket held the remains, not of the Irish poet, but an unknown Frenchman. More public still was the doubt cast by John Ormond Thomas, author of the *Picture Post* article published a few weeks later. He and his photographer had been in Roquebrune and were now in Sligo; much to George's dismay, they were still there the next day.[204]

That was not the only battle George had to fight. Two weeks earlier she had written to Frank O'Connor:

My dear Michael Jack dropped a bombshell on me yesterday. He called me away from the Cuala stall at 1 p.m. & said he wanted to talk to me. He put his foot down on having any address or oration at Drumcliffe. Michael went to see him in the evening. But, as Michael said, if he was a younger man we could have combated his decision. As it is, Anne, Michael and I want to tell you that *we* were united in asking you to make the oration, but we feel that we have to obey Jack's wishes. Michael Anne & I hope that you will come to Sligo for Friday Sept. 17th. Your room at the Great Southern Hotel was booked before this catastrophe occurred. Perhaps I should say that I had discussed with Jack on Saturday Aug 21, and that he had agreed fully.

You can imagine how difficult it is for me to write to the only man in Ireland who would give a noble and imaginative address, to say that Yeats' brother has decided that there is to be no address. We (A. M. & I) know that there is a political basis about it. We feel that, as I have said, we must agree with Jack's decision.

I hope that you will forgive us all and if you can come to Sligo that you will stay with us.[205]

Knowing how difficult the entire ceremony must be for Jack so soon after his wife's death (Cottie had died 28 April 1947), George could hardly demur. O'Connor, who had already gathered from External Affairs that Jack was being 'generally obstructive', was relieved to be freed of the obligation; but he was sorry for George, 'who has strain enough on her without becoming involved in political dogfights'.[206]

There is no mention of his being present at the ceremony. However, 'Michael/ Frank' published his address, with its tribute to George, in advance: 'Yeats was probably the most fortunate of all great poets; fortunate in his father, in his friends, in his marriage, and in his children.'[207] Another figure missing at the graveside was Oliver Gogarty, still in the United States; George invited his son Noll to stand beside the family during the service.[208]

During August she had also been fending off worried telephone calls from the Mayor of Sligo, who was annoyed at not being kept officially informed of all the arrangements. He had been told by Seán O'Faoláin that the corvette would be putting in at Galway rather than Sligo; this had distressed the local citizens— could she not do anything about it? George turned to Tom MacGreevy, asking his assistance in keeping any more details out of the press for as long as possible. Evidently kind Tom, now that he was back in Dublin, had become her confidant once more, to the extent that Seán MacBride had suggested he serve as George's liaison with the Ministry. Earlier that year MacGreevy himself had been in Paris, to be made Chevalier de l'ordre de la Légion d'honneur by the French government for his services to the Arts; did he also serve as George's intermediary there while in France? It would be the kind of task 'diplomatic Tamsie' would have greatly enjoyed—and kept secret.[209] Tom described the occasion as 'one of the beautiful days of my whole life'; although 'Intrusive bad manners showed themselves momentarily, once in the morning at Galway and once at the grave- side, photographers of course, but neither of them was Irish and neither of them represented an Irish paper, so let them be.'[210] Four years later he sent George his published account of their journey from Galway to Sligo, ostensibly describ- ing a bus tour of Connemara and the Burren. Thanking him for his 'beautiful description', she recalled, 'You will remember you told me that you were not sure how you could do it (after the Sept 1948 journey) and now you have put that journey into its right setting & thank you so much. Your description is the only one which will live.'[211] Anne's memory of the day is kinder; having no dark coat, she had had to borrow one from a friend. 'It was very strange to be attending your father's funeral nine years after his death. It was pouring with rain. As we drove through Sligo about 10 o'clock in the morning I was wondering why so many people were sleeping so late with their curtains drawn. And then I realised it was a mark of respect for my father.'[212]

MacGreevy returned to Dublin with Jack Yeats and Michael immediately after the re-interment. However, one guest remained in the background, refusing to be recorded by the press or photographers, or to join the six clergymen for the final service. Not even Anne and Michael remember his being there, but a letter from George to MacGreevy the day after the burial makes it clear that Harold Hyde-Lees, of the Anglican dioceses of Bath and Wells and Sarum, had come to support his sister at the ceremony and remained with her in Sligo:

I cannot use that inadequate word 'thank you'. It is impossible to express such gratitude as is in my heart. I only hope that some day it may be possible for me to do something for you & that if the day ever comes you will tell me. How few people would have had the sensitivity to know that I should like to hear that your 'charges' had been deposited safely in Dublin. For that telegram I also owe a deep debt of gratitude.

I took flowers (from Lisadell) yesterday. As I had expected, every leaf & petal had been taken as 'momentoes' on Friday evening! Nothing was left but wires & moss. That horrible Picture Post couple are still here, but Harold & Anne are buttresses. I believe after Monday all will have gone. Blessings on you.

When she returned to Dublin, George took Tom and Harold to lunch at the Gresham Hotel. Harold did not stay long, but always remembered finding 'all those steps at 46, Palmerston Road . . . even in 1948 . . . wearisome'.[213]

George had been determined to remain in control as much as government courtesy would allow. The invitations had gone out from Palmerston Road, and she paid the bills once the coffin arrived on Irish soil: £46 10s. for the motors from Galway Docks to Drumcliffe; £8 for grave expenses and ringing of bell; £140 for the monument and kerbing. Her diary has the careful note that 'Mrs Margaret Diamond (Monumental Sculptors) has given the curb & little plaque to mark site of grave also limestone chips—O'Connell Street Sligo'. As a mark of gratitude, she sent Seán MacBride one of WBY's manuscripts, making it quite clear this was for him personally, 'for keeps'; his letter of thanks describes the gift as 'three mss books', but unfortunately does not say which ones.[214] One further family council meeting was still required. On 26 September Jack wrote thanking George for sending him copies of the Sligo newspapers, adding that he would be delighted to see her about the 'portrait question'. On 28 October there was a small ceremony aboard the LE *Macha*, when Michael presented a portrait of Yeats to Lieutenant General D. McKenna, chief of staff, and the officers of the ship; present were George, Jack, Anne, Seán MacBride in his official capacity, and Tom MacGreevy. It was not until 1952 that the keeper of the Roquebrune cemetery found the simple marble tablet that George had arranged for Yeats's temporary grave; in 1953 Dulac's handsome stylized design of 'Pegasus ascending to the stars' was affixed to the cemetery wall where it remains still.[215] It would not be the last the world would hear about Yeats's bones, but given the documentation George kept and the many false assumptions made by Edith, Dulac, Gluck, and Biancheri, evidence suggests that it probably *is* Yeats who lies at the foot of Ben Bulben. As the inquisitive curé had warned, the necessary research would be very difficult, but not impossible.[216]

In April 1948 Willy's cousin Eileen Gordon (known in the family as 'the blonde butterfly') had married. 'George came and told me all about Eileen's reception about two days before her wedding. . . . Eileen is a good hostess, but none of the guests (George said) were younger than Aunt Fanny. She said that if there was a long ring at the door before the guests had arrived she expected a stretcher to come in. Michael looked a mere baby.'[217] On 16 October Lily had even more exciting news to relay to Australia, for Michael was officially engaged. He had met Gráinne Ní Éigeartaigh, daughter of P. S. O'Hegarty, at Trinity College, where she was enrolled in modern history and political science while at the same time studying singing, piano, and harp at the Royal Irish Academy of Music.

She is rather small, with a kind of demure prettiness. She does not 'make up' or smoke. She wears her hair long, brushed straight back. She dresses plainly, but Michael is very happy, and I think they will suit each other very well. It seems impossible for us to get away from the name Grace. Our grandmother was Grace and her mother was Grace, and then Aunt Gracie. They hope to be married in Spring. She is the youngest of four. Her two sisters and brother are all married. Her father is a very clever man. He was Post Master General here for some time. Her mother belongs to a clever family. She is a niece of Sir Samuel Dill. The family are all Irish speakers. They used to go to Donegal every summer and grew up Irish speakers.

George, who had scrupulously avoided appearing at any restaurants where Michael might be entertaining his current girlfriend, had known of her son's interest for some years. When Michael finally brought her to the house, Gráinne remembers being greeted on the stairs with the comment that it was 'about time' they met.[218]

   Gráinne and Michael were married on 14 May 1949 at 12.30 p.m. in St Philip's Church; a reception followed at the O'Hegartys' home, Highfield House in Rathgar, which had once been Edward Dowden's home. (The Robinsons' wedding gift provided a nice touch—it was a dinner set which Dolly had recently inherited from her mother, Dowden's daughter.[219]) By this time, with the re-interment over, Anne had managed to get George out of black clothes and into brown, but Lennox, who attended his godson's nuptials, did not think much of her appearance:

We married Michael Yeats yesterday with such pomp and ceremony. Red carpet into the church, ushers with white rosettes asking were you for the bridegroom or the bride. I said bridegroom and put in the backest pew but seeing Jack in the second moved up and sat beside him. George joined us. She had a small shiny new black hat, a big dull brown coat which came down to her heels and, perhaps, a blue dress underneath—but she looked so drab, I do think she might have bought herself a dress for her beloved Michael's wedding. Michael was in immaculate bridegroom clothes, bride very charming in white with lovely lace lent by the Currans who lend this lace for every nice wedding. There was lovely music and then we went round the corner to your grandfather's house where the Hegartys threw a very splash party. I had been in the house a few times with Hester, on a Sunday night when there was always a cold chicken but I didn't know there was such a lovely spacious garden behind it. . . . Thinking over Michael's wedding I am glad we didn't do it like that; I think birth, marriage, and death are very private affairs and should be done privately.[220]

George never said what *she* thought, but whatever Michael wished was all right with her. Besides, still remembering her own registry office wedding, she would have liked the ceremony, although being somewhat dismayed that her son should have chosen something as conventional as the Lake District for his honeymoon. During the first twelve years of their married life her son and daughter-in-law lived on Oakdown Road in Churchtown, not far from Gurteen Dhas. As far as Gráinne was concerned George was the 'perfect mother-in-law', who never interfered. George in turn, although preferring the piano to the harp, admired Gráinne's voice and musicianship. She also appreciated her daughter-in-law's forthright manner.

George was not quite so keen on Gráinne and Michael's insistence that their children begin life by speaking Irish, but was delighted at the thought of a family. 'I am immensely pleased about my grandchild. Michael & Grainne now definitely call it "*he*"—I hope they won't be disappointed if it is a "she" —As "it" has to be brought up as an Irish speaker they have made a vow never to speak to each other except in Irish. Grainne says "when he is three years old he will probably be able to talk in English too." Anne & I think we shall be able to do a little "infiltration" before then.'[221] Caitríona Dill Yeats was born in 1951, followed by Siobhán Máire in 1953, Síle Áine in 1955, and Pádraig Butler in 1959. George managed to overcome the language barrier by her tone of voice and gestures, but her good friend Olive Craig, a strong Unionist, was very worried when George took Caitríona for the night while her parents were away. George however coped, occasionally babysitting both at Churchtown and Palmerston Road. When Michael came down with whooping cough just before Siobhán was born, he returned to be nursed by his mother.[222] George was godmother to Síle, who remembers the frenzied excitement when, a rare occasion, 'Gramma' came out to Sunday lunch at Dalkey, where the family had moved in 1961. But what Gráinne and Michael recall vividly was George's appearance at the hospital on the birth of her only grandson; it may have been the only occasion when she was obviously drunk in public. Willy would hardly have objected either.[223]

Lily did not see her nephew married or live to enjoy the new generation of babies. She died on 5 January 1949, having been paralysed for five and a half years and holding on until her brother was brought back to Ireland. As they had shared a home, Lolly and she rested in a common grave. Now only Jack was left, who wrote of his sister, 'Her memory and interest in everyone and their lives remained with her always. I treated her as my book of reference.'[224] George was one of three executors of the tiny estate, in which capacity she had considerable correspondence with Lennox who, regretting the loss of Sorrento Cottage, wanted to take over Gurteen Dhas. After much scurrying back and forth, arrangements finally fell through and the Robinsons remained in their flat in Monkstown. Now called Hillbrow, the Yeats sisters' house still stands, but no longer looks out on fields as it had during Lily and Lolly's day.[225] Apologizing for not answering personal letters, George admitted, 'for some time my existence had been rather complicated. You know me well enough to know how all these things knock me out. I have always been quite good in emergencies but not during long years of strain.'[226] Her life would remain complicated for the next twenty years.

21

SEEKERS AND FRIENDS

In the spring of 1950 Stephen Spender was invited to dinner at the University Club to meet George: 'Mrs Yeats is an elderly, robust, somewhat stocky lady, wearing glasses with thick lenses—the sort of person who is described as a "body". She struck me as extremely intelligent, alive and friendly, with a very independent existence of her own, no nonsense about her, and definite irony.'[1] In Dublin she is remembered as 'a warm friendly personality—forthright and easy in manner. What we now call "her own woman".' Everyone knew her as 'Mrs W. B.'[2] These descriptions would be echoed by generations of scholars who were fortunate enough to find their way to 46 Palmerston Road. Years of rheumatism and bronchitis had shrunk George's strong frame by at least four inches; her hair, still abundant, was turning grey; encouraged by her drinking, that high colouring was now even more noticeable, and her teeth, always a problem, were worn down and stained by nicotine. Age and ill health had made her careless of her appearance now that she need not perform alongside the public poet; besides, loose-fitting clothes and comfortable shoes made movement—increasingly more painful with serious back problems—easier. She walked slowly but confidently, no shakiness there; when she smoked, she held the cigarette carefully between forefinger and thumb. Gradually her arthritis made getting up so difficult that she could not bear having anyone help her out of a chair or a car. Especially after she developed stomach ulcers in the mid-1950s, she looked far older than her years. Illness never however weakened that strong, musical, 'magnetic' voice; one visitor recalls her reciting 'Meditations in Time of Civil War' so beautifully it caused shivers.[3] Nor was it possible to forget the bright, penetrating, darting eyes that seemed to look deep inside or at the very least read one's thoughts.

Although she was welcoming and sympathetic, something in her manner invited decorum, for some even awe; in the presence of that 'fine and delicately poised mind' automatic writing and the occult seemed more believable. But there was also a ready twinkle or a sharp whistle which suddenly dissipated any awkward shyness. Like a Beckettian character she had three laughs—silent open-mouthed acknowledgement; an abrupt aware 'Ha!' with the head tilted back; and the full rich laughter of pure, almost malicious enjoyment. As Lily had always said, she disliked the boring and dull in both people and writing. Intolerant of any pretension, dishonesty, or the second-rate, she often startled too-worshipful visitors with a deliberately matter-of-fact statement about WBY's (or another scholar's) human weaknesses. Apparently simple questions on art, literature, music, or even sport could have a 'wicked spin' on them, and one soon realized that without any pressure this extraordinarily learned woman was subtly conducting the most rigorous intellectual examination imaginable. If the scholar passed this test, manuscripts appeared and—especially in the earlier days—workspace in the 'Yeats study', sometimes even lunch or strong coffee and sweet cake, was provided. The first shock of her appearance soon dissipated; nobody ever doubted being in the presence of a remarkably fine, quick-witted intelligence. As more and more 'seekers' (her word) climbed the steps requesting admission and her health deteriorated, her manner could sometimes become abrupt; manuscripts would then be temporarily deposited with kindly Alf MacLochláinn at the National Library. If she had been drinking, the afternoon sessions might be either more gossipy or occasionally challenging; something said weeks before might be recalled and roundly denounced. Rarely was there any obvious sign of her alcoholic habits, although those who claimed to know her well suggested a gift of John Jameson Green Stripe would not go amiss, and at least one visitor observed her fondness for strong candies to disguise the facts.[4]

As her daughter observed, George 'only worked one to one . . . You never asked mother anything directly; you had to wait for it to come out.' Those fortunate enough to become friends would be invited to join her in a drink at the Hibernian, or lunch at the Unicorn Restaurant or Shelbourne Hotel (where the maître d' made certain she had her favourite table); then the atmosphere lightened as she indulged her penchant for good story-telling. But she never gave up control of the situation—or of the manuscripts, kept 'in usable disarray'[5] and doled out to whom and as she saw fit. She freely admitted that each seeker, no matter what explanation was proffered, was categorized. The process was much the same as when she and Willy years before had placed friends and strangers in their appropriate phases of the 'system', only now the divisions were simpler—poetry, drama, prose: 'It's not what *you* think you are, it's what *I* think you are!'[6] Later she would claim that WBY had instructed her to hand out materials piecemeal—poetry to one, prose to another, etc. I suspect that this was her usual stratagem to find a male authority for what she wanted to do herself, and it may well have been a wise decision. Anne would later recall that 'Mother worked on the principle that if people asked her for something she'd say if she had it, or she hadn't. She never volunteered anything.'[7] Although she obviously grew to trust some scholars more than others and more and more material was gradually revealed, she continued to hold the key. As always, she made no secret that the poetry interested her most, and had little patience with scholars who she felt had not read it carefully enough. Nor could she forgive a turgid style. 'They all come bringing books and I can't read them they are so badly written.' She kept the growing pile of critical studies on a table in the hall, and invited visitors to take whatever they wished; 'I don't know in the least what most of them are talking about, and WBY would not have known either.' Much of the scholarship she considered too narrow and myopic, busily grinding down the poetry into footnotes. 'A question I am often asked is "Who was 'Some old Cardinal' "——Personally I dont think it matters in the least. But all the Mincing-Machines do.'[8] She frequently dismissed those who refused to accept the significance of the occult or 'magic' in Yeats's work: 'They all come here and they don't have a sense of what they are looking for.'[9] Even Richard Ellmann, with whom perhaps she spoke most unguardedly about her own life, was reprimanded: ' "Do you not believe in ghosts at all?" she asked me. "Only in those inside me," I replied. "That's the trouble with you," she said with unexpected severity.'[10]

Although she downplayed her own role, comparing herself to 'a hen picking up scraps' and describing (somewhat unrealistically) how she donned an apron with a large pocket for hidden treasures rescued from wastepaper baskets, George obviously was responsible for preserving the bulk of Yeats's early drafts. Some discarded pages literally had to be pieced together, others uncrumpled and smoothed out. Perhaps Willy had not always been as aware as she claimed of how an event would look to posterity, but certainly she was.[11] On WBY's death Charles Lane-Poole had written to Lily saying that George was, next to her own, the best mother she knew. Lily passed the compliment on to George, 'who was very pleased. She gets very few bouquets and deserves many. I fear that after all the business and letters are done, that she will find her life bare, after all the years of devotion to Willy.'[12] Lily need not have feared; requests flowed in to publish, edit, or consult the manuscripts George had so carefully preserved.

Some of these early seekers became lifelong friends to whom she herself could turn for assistance. Oliver Edwards tirelessly pursued his research on WBY, although by now George must have realized that he would never be able to let the book go. But she enjoyed his quiet wit and his company; when he and his wife Barbara spent a winter in Enniskerry, they were often invited to join her at the theatre and stay the night. Oliver assisted her with Welsh and German translations planned for Cuala, and in turn she could vent her impatience with the narrow-minded reverence of others. For example, when the broadcasting station would not permit the line 'Throw likely couples into bed' in 'Three Songs to the One Burden', she provided an earlier version, 'Marry off the better sort' and immediately received a barrage of complaints. 'Various comments here have been of the "how *could* you" . . . "I cant *bear* to hear the ballads sung like that" . . . "rather as if they were being sung in a public house" (exactly what I wanted, those ballads should be thought of as if they could be sung anywhere and in the

traditional manner, not in the Rathmines-educated-in-Cheltenham manner.) . . .
"*all* the poetry left out . . ." etc. etc'. With Edwards she could also argue precise
points of pronunciation:

No I *dont* agree with you about the pronunciation of 'Pollex*fenn*'. Firstly because Yeats
invariably read that rhyme as Pollexfen (Pōllŭxfĕn) and men, but also because his work
abounds in these half rhymes . . . now would you pronounce 'demesne' as demean in
order that it may rhyme with green? (lst stanza of Henry Middleton) or perhaps you
thought like Clinton Baddeley that the word is pronounced demean? It is 'demayne'. Or,
that a ballad singer in Ireland who would probably pronounce 'poor' as 'pore' would be
more correct because the word would then rhyme with 'more'? (Come gather round me
Parnellites). Then again if you pronounce it 'fenn' the rhythm of the word is altered it is
almost impossible to get the 'oll' sound of Poll if you have to stress *enn*. I think Lennox
Robinson quite dreadful in verse on the wireless, and I cannot endure his theories,
and execution, of poetry reading. I am glad you like the old stone cross sung . . . many
people here were horrified at its being sung. . . . Glad 'Barbara' like[d] the bass better
than the tenor; she will have noticed that the tunes were not all from the broadside tunes.

And whereas with most seekers she was circumspect, with Oliver she felt free to
float some of her own interpretations. 'Have you ever studied the Cuchulain of
the plays up to Hawk's well and the Cuchulain of Hawk's well to the last play? I
decided recently that at some moment before the writing of Hawks well the poet,
probably unconsciously, had begun to identify himself with Cuchulain. (Do you
see in a short poem called The Witch the seed of the Well? The same theme in a
different dimension. (Maud of course "one long sought with desire").' However,
the conclusion to this long letter should give all critics pause:

Yeats did NOT write those lines on the margin of Rilke. He *did* write Under Ben Bulben as
a direct result of reading that essay 'Rilke and the conception of death' by William Rose
(who sent him the book—'R. M. Rilke. Aspects of his mind and poetry') The finished
poem had grown into something quite different from the notes written after reading
the essay, but then that always happens. But I do think that students of that particular
poem need to have read the essay *after* having studied the poem . . . I should have liked
to hear your lecture at Cardiff. Thank you for leaving me out. I am quite sure that 'wives'
are a part of literary gossip, just as I hate reading a poet's work for the first time if I know
anything about him (or her), or about the circumstance from which a poem arose.[13]

Not all her correspondence with Oliver Edwards was serious; she was relieved
to discover that his precise mind sometimes was in error. 'What a comfort to *me*
to feel I was right for once. How rude I am being. But I have for years thought of
you as a metronome, and now I see you in a totally different way.' He was also one
of the few outside her family with whom she could indulge her love of parodic
doggerel. On one occasion he left behind some race cards, which she returned
with an outburst occasioned by the latest wartime regulation:

> Was it for this—these cards that spread
> ruin on every race-course side
> for this that Sean Lemass has said
> all paper must at home abide
> for Cuala cards and prints alone
> and all the paper that will save
> makes betting easier for our own
> Mug-punting Irish fool or knave.

I think Lemass, minister for supplies, is the only racy gent in the Cabinet, MacEntee punts a bit perhaps. Lemass hath said thou art not to export cards or prints or pamphlets. Books I am lying very low about as the Order mentions books in bulk. I am tapping another source. . . . I have been exhausting my useless fury with 'Supplies' by re-painting the bathroom; the only paint available is a foul-smelling flake white, so the department looks like a cabin on a fifthrate mediterranean liner, and when you lie in the bath and waggle your legs to make a faint chou chou chou the illusion is complete. You and Barbara must try it next time you come. The bathroom looks loathsome, but so clean you almost have to wash before you go into it at all. I'll have guest beds all next week.[14]

As she would be with most of these early scholars, no matter the state of their scholarship, George remained loyal to Edwards. During the war he asked permission to quote 'Reprisals', Yeats's poem about the death of Robert Gregory that his mother had rejected.

I am sorry for asking you not to use that fourth Robert Gregory poem (never published). I have privately pulled what string I have, which is extremely slight, to get Michael over for this meeting at St Andrews. I may say that the British authorities here have tightened up permits for delegates from Trinity in the last year, and it is rather touch and go if Michael will get his Permit. I enclose copy of letter from St Andrews. He, Michael, is almost certain of his permit (subject to *one* delegate only instead of the two mentioned in the letter I enclose) and he sees Collinson today to confirm that permit. I am afraid that if you use that fourth Robert Gregory poem in the North you might destroy Michael's chance of going to St Andrews. These things get out even when there is no Press Reporters, & permits are sometimes cancelled—as I know.

She was also sensitive to the fact that Robert Gregory's son was fighting in another war. But she made sure that Oliver was granted the first right to publish the poem in 1948.[15]

One of the few scholars able to visit her during 'the Emergency' was a young tutor at St Columba's, Peter Allt. In 1941 he published an article claiming that although Yeats could not be considered a Christian poet, his work was 'notable because it faces and admits the most terrible truths about the human soul; and honesty of this kind is achieved by only the very greatest poets.' Whether this article became the catalyst for their lengthy discussions, within two years they were deep in correspondence over both substantive and technical details, leading to Allt's efforts to collate all the early versions of Yeats's poetry, searching for textual variants. By 1944 he was contemplating, with her encouragement, a variorum edition of the poetry.[16] Significantly, for a further article he received permission to quote the following passages from her own letters to him, in support of his decision not to deal with 'such points as punctuation, staggering, etc':

Yeats 'always said "I know nothing about punctuation." He once said to me, "I never know when I should use a semicolon or a colon. I don't like colons." He also disliked a dash, and detested brackets. He did use brackets a good deal in *later* work (himself in MSS.) But punctuation, apart from a comma and a full stop, were, I think, mainly outside influence'.

'I wrote the following note into my copy of C. P. in November, 1933 (the date W. B. Y. gave it to me): "When W. B. Y. was correcting the proofs of this book he said, *I have spent my life saying the same things in different ways. I denounced old age before I was twenty, and the swordsman throughout repudiates the saint—though with vacillation"* '

'I feel quite certain that Symons made the decision not to stagger [lines] because he *saw* his poems on the page, whereas I don't think Yeats ever did; he sang his proofs and often forgot to consider whether song and printed word corresponded.'[17]

Despite this apparent dismissal by George, the question of Yeats's punctuation would vex scholars for years to come. Lolly once wrote to John Quinn, 'We have a time of it putting in punctuation for W. B. He has a lordly way of disregarding it altogether, so we put it in as we go along and then let him have it in proof.' He himself admitted to his publisher about certain points, 'I am a babe in such things', and George was fond of telling how, after about half an hour's dictation, he suddenly said, 'Comma'. Oliver Edwards also favoured less punctuation, 'Excess of punctuation is a symptom of illiteracy.'[18]

With George's encouragement, Allt approached Macmillan suggesting a variorum edition of the *Collected Poems* based on the volumes corrected by Yeats for the Coole Edition; she recommended however that should the volume be reset with the variants added, the poems 'should be chronological and not in date of publication'.[19] Allt's proposal was rejected and, the war finally over, he eventually left for Cambridge. However, a few years later when Russell Alspach proposed his own variorum edition to Macmillan of New York, George delayed replying as long as possible in order to give Peter Allt an opportunity to complete his thesis.[20] By 1947 Alspach and Allt were discussing collaboration; in 1953 Peter completed his doctorate, and a year later was dead. The long-anticipated variorum edition of the poems was published under both names in 1957. Clearly George had a special relationship with the young scholar, whose ceremonious formality in manner and correspondence was reminiscent of the young Tom MacGreevy. In 1948, after a visit to Ballylee, Allt described meeting several local men sitting on the bridge who recalled 'the Senator'; he predicted to them that Michael himself would soon be in the Senate. Then, with a sensitivity sadly missing from her correspondence with Dulac earlier that year, he spoke with feeling of how the years in that 'wonderful place' must have been the happiest in the poet's life. Offering to arrange for Yeats's famous lines to be carved on a stone at last, he added, 'But it ought to be done by your orders, I think.'[21] Unfortunately, if George replied to this gentle offer, her letter does not survive. It would be another twelve years before the poem was erected on what finally became a designated National Monument.

Peter Allt, a graduate of Trinity College, had known George's son as a student at St Columba's and later when Michael taught history there for a time. The next young man to be allowed access to the manuscripts was another of Michael's colleagues, for A. Norman Jeffares had graduated from Trinity the same year as George's son, also with first-class honours (albeit in different disciplines). In 1946 'Derry' Jeffares was at Oxford, writing a thesis on Yeats and aided by access to many of the early autobiographical materials. Not only was George helpful in answering his questions and deciphering the manuscripts, when the thesis was completed a year later she read his typescript and, although insisting that some passages be revised or deleted (' "Diana Vernon" ' must *not* be identified with Olivia Shakespear'), provided new illustrations to enhance his book *W. B. Yeats: Man and Poet*. In turn, she could count on him to run errands if her son was not available. The relationship would be a long and fruitful one, with George continuing in her role as active participant. When Jeffares was granted permission to edit selections from Yeats's works in a series of volumes, she carefully read through the proofs, correcting certain factual errors and insisting on the rephrasing of certain passages that referred to her automatic writing.[22] Although the hapless editor was not responsible, she also objected to the cover designed by Macmillan: 'I don't like it, neither would W. B. . . . Isn't it time these people learned that there is more to Ireland than shillelaghs and shamrocks.' Chastened, one of the firm's directors travelled to Dublin to assure her that the offending shamrocks would be removed.[23]

While Derry Jeffares was eagerly transcribing many of the early diaries, George received a letter from an American sailor who had been a doctoral student at Harvard, his interrupted dissertation a study of Yeats's mystical system. Might he, when he had leave, come from London to speak with her? George replied immediately, carefully explaining that although she would be in charge of the Cuala stall during a book fair at the Mansion House for one of the weeks he expected to be in Ireland, he was to phone and leave his number with the maid. Neither was disappointed at the meeting in September 1945: Richard Ellmann, who had feared that the poet's widow would not want to talk about her mystical experiences, found her sympathetic and remarkably intelligent; George thought him the first visitor who had really understood WBY's poetry. Not only did she show him the manuscripts and diaries, she gave him a number of rare pamphlets relating to the Golden Dawn, and promised him ready access to other materials when he returned the following year. She also suggested other people he should meet both in Ireland and England. Here at last was someone intent on the 'system' and aware of the central place it took in the poetry. Soon she was asking 'Dicky' to call her George.

From America that winter of 1945 several parcels arrived from Ellmann's grateful mother with highly coveted delicacies (tea, coffee, fruit cake, condensed soups, chocolates). The tea was especially prized, for it had been rationed to half an ounce a week per head for most of the war; George shared it with family and Cuala workers, but she kept the gift of stockings for herself.[24] In turn, she asked Ellmann to find out what had happened to Ezra Pound, who, after being locked in a cage and then a prison camp in Italy, had been flown to the United States. At first she was relieved that Ezra was in the United States, thinking he would presumably receive better treatment than in Italy 'where he would have been in the custody of un-intelligent military officials who think poets are punk'; but the news grew worse, for Ezra was charged with treason and confined in St Elizabeth's Hospital for the Insane in Washington, DC.[25] Ellmann sent her all the newspaper reports he could, assuring her that the case would probably never come to trial. At her request he also sought out information about Dorothy, who had left Italy to be with Ezra. And he made enquiries at Yale on behalf of Michael, should her son care to pursue his studies in the United States. Those two weeks in September had been important for both George and the American seeker. When Ellmann returned to Ireland in June 1946 their discussions continued; George was frank in her responses to his interpretations and surprisingly forthcoming about her own life. She thought he was too sceptical about *A Vision*, but, although she obviously reread the automatic script in order to answer some of his questions, refused to let him study the notebooks himself, with her customary dismissive phrase, 'That's too personal.'[26] They went to the Abbey Theatre and frequently dined out together; she wrote introductions for him to Edith Sitwell (who was shocked by some of his questions), the Dulacs, and other friends. To Eliot she wrote, 'Unlike many of the young men who are now writing about WBY Dicky Ellman [*sic*] seems to me to have a purpose which is neither gossipy paragraphs or the easy way to get a Ph. D.'[27] Ellmann introduced her to the American scholar John Kelleher, who liked her very much but was startled by her appearance ('not at all what I expected the wife of a famous poet to be . . . big and hearty and had a fine forthright laugh'); they were both embarrassed when George paid for dinner at the Unicorn Restaurant, which Anne was busily decorating with unicorns, giraffes, lions, and peacocks, but Kelleher declined to have her cast his horoscope. As she and Dicky came to know each other better, she released more and more manuscripts to him, even lending him an old valise so that he might take them to his room at the Arts Club, and allowing him to microfilm manuscripts. After he explained that the rituals had been published in America, she also released some of the proscribed Golden Dawn materials and alerted him privately to members still alive in London. Observant concerning the difficulties of Palmerston Road, his requests home became more specific—would his mother send fifty or a hundred large strong envelopes and some sellotape for Mrs Yeats? Through him she also had—for the first time—contact with Ethel Mannin, who had entrusted him with some of Yeats's letters; there is no word of what transpired between the two women, or whether they even met, for Mannin told Hone that Yeats had always said—probably with delight in the thought of intrigue—that George was 'suspicious' of her.[28] That first Christmas George presented Ellmann with Yeats's copy of *The Poetical Works of John Milton* which had a draft of 'News for the Delphic Oracle' in pencil on the rear endpaper. When he required an extension on his Rockefeller grant, she promised to write a supporting letter. But apart from their friendship the greatest gift was arranged after he had returned to America: in November 1947, while George was once again in bed with bronchitis, a ton of coal was delivered to Palmerston Road, ensuring for the first time in six years a warm winter.[29]

Lily met many of these seekers; in fact that year Una Ellis-Fermor, while she was writing her book on the Irish dramatic movement, became a paying guest at Gurteen Dhas. As Hone and Edwards had discovered, Lily's big 'family book' was especially useful for biographical information, and Ellmann soon followed. 'I had a young American writer to see me last Sunday. He is working at Trinity doing a thesis on Willy. He looked so young and full of health. He had the usual beautiful teeth.' She was also visited by Derry Jeffares; the two scholars had by now met, both hot on the same trail. Both were destined to be pioneers.[30]

Although Ellmann's *Yeats: The Man and the Masks* first appeared the year before Jeffares's *W. B. Yeats: Man and Poet*, the two books were frequently reviewed together, often with a nationalist bias. Mary Colum, for instance, wrote slightingly of the 'young naval man' who had had tea with the poet's widow, claiming that 'few people in Dublin took the spirits, the frustrators, communicators and so on with any seriousness'. In the first of a number of articles implying that all George brought to the marriage was a large dowry, Colum asserts that 'The strength, originality and depth of his later poems came undoubtedly from the fact that he had acquired leisure and some financial security.' Later she would boast—perhaps on her sister-in-law Eileen's evidence—that one of her reviews had made George cry. This was probably caused by the gratuitous remarks made in her favourable review of Jeffares's 'very fine book . . . without straining the credulity of the reader':

The accounts of Yeats's attempts to find himself a wife would be hilarious if it were really possible to laugh successfully at anything he did. . . . Mrs Yeats was a good helpmeet but her part in 'A Vision' can be overestimated and has been fantastically so by the author of a recent book. She was a young Englishwoman about twenty-five years his junior whom the poet married in his fifty-third year, and until her marriage she had never been in Ireland. He became infatuated with domesticity and with being a pater familias. His marriage, it should be realized, did not add to his economic burdens—quite the contrary —and his creature comforts were well looked after.[31]

Evidently many critics were not yet comfortable enough to accept the mystical in Yeats's poetry. Typically generous, George wrote to console Ellmann when the first reviews came out: 'I think I told you when I saw it in typescript how fine a thing you had done. You must not be bothered by criticisms of Edmund Wilson who does not know his stuff, or Horace Gregory, or [Horace] Reynolds etc. You must accept the fact that these critics have never read Yeats, and have never read any poetry at all unless they were compelled to, out of a necessity which made them love poetry which they could not create, and must therefore criticize.'[32] When Derry's book appeared in April 1949 she read it carefully again, annotating her copy for future reference. Ten years later, when Ellmann's book on James Joyce appeared, it was dedicated to George Yeats; gratified that her faith had been justified, she praised its 'particular quality of understanding which makes the book exciting to read'. 'At last Dicky has learned to write' was her comment when the tribute was mentioned.[33] Dicky and Derry would remain coupled in her mind:

I was fascinated to hear that Dick was appearing in a Chicago court to declare that Tropic of Cancer—or was it Capricorn was not obscene!! I don't know if either is 'obscene' but personally I think both are disgusting. But then I am very old—About 2 years ago a friend of mine . . . brought them over to me & asked me to send them back by some voyager to London. After long waiting to find a suitable missionary—difficult—I got Derry Jeffares to take them.[34]

Ellmann and Jeffares had opened the floodgates. Others came and went after the war and on through the 1950s and 1960s: from India, France, Germany, Sweden, the United States, Canada, Britain. When she was familiar with the research and the letters requested were *to* rather than *by* Yeats, she would arrange to send papers to England through the Irish Embassy, or with apparent casualness simply hand them over. However, she always remembered what she had loaned and to whom; at any time a peremptory request for return might arrive.[35] Most scholars were greeted courteously, but she instructed them to phone at 10 a.m. precisely; not only was she becoming deaf in her left ear, the more arthritic she became the longer it took to climb up or down the stairs to the telephone on the landing above the kitchen. When Anne was home she made the dash for her, sometimes causing confusion since her voice, especially on the telephone, was similar to her mother's. During the summer of 1946 Birgit Bramsbäck came from Sweden to study the Cuchulain legend in Yeats's work; when she returned three years later George welcomed her back warmly, 'for I have such a pleasant memory of you'.[36] For Bramsbäck she recalled the hospitality she and Willy had received during the Nobel prize journey. While Ellis-Fermor was in Dublin George asked her to consider editing the play *Diarmuid and Grania*, that strange hybrid created by Yeats and George Moore, in part so that unsuitable applicants could be told that it was already undertaken; too busy, the English scholar eventually gave way to an approved younger American.[37] In 1948 T. R. Henn, whose family had Sligo connections, wrote from Cambridge asking if he might discuss Yeats's interest in pictures. Not only did George lend him slides, she carefully read and annotated his manuscript *The Lonely Tower*, sending him seven pages of notes that corrected his dates and quotations, and adding valuable information about attributions and sources.[38] This was what she enjoyed most, working with those seekers who were intent on searching out WBY's creativity, in a sense reliving his work. Those were the few who were invited to sit around the kitchen table with her, magnifying glass in hand, poring over Yeats's more illegible lines. Some, like Tom Parkinson with the poetry and David Clark with the plays, worked closely with George assembling, sorting, ordering and dating the manuscripts. Parkinson spent two summers going through 'six thousand pages of drafts, fair copies, and final versions'.[39] For Clark's use, she deposited the manuscripts of the plays in the National Library of Ireland, but invited him to work on the books in the house. Once he asked her something about the *Vision* manuscripts, and was 'most startled when she snapped back, "Oh, I don't give two pins for all that". Then, realizing what she had said, "I mean, it's the poetry that's important".'[40]

George showed most concern for the poets who came to her wishing to study Yeats when she felt they should be writing themselves. Her parting words to Jon Stallworthy, whom she had assisted in his study of the early drafts, were 'Don't spend all your life on Yeats'; her greeting to Kathleen Raine was 'A poet has no right not to write.' She then added to Raine, who had not published for some time, 'you need a rabbit-bolter', explaining that this was the terrier sent down the rabbit-hole to make the rabbits come out. 'I was WBY's rabbit-bolter.'[41] She enjoyed talking about William Blake and was so impressed by Raine, who was then writing *Blake and Tradition*, that she presented her with one of the books she had come to see; later Denis Saurat's *Blake and Modern Thought* was returned to the library, still bearing its inscription 'For Kathleen Raine Christmas 1958 George Yeats.'[42]

She was delighted when John Montague moved back to Ireland in 1958 and took to calling by when he was in the neighbourhood. Here was someone with whom she could let go, who did not want anything from her but good talk. She had already read his poetry when, at tea in the Shelbourne Hotel, Tom Parkinson introduced them, but Montague was not prepared for her 'entrancing . . . extraordinary sense of humour'. They discussed writing, poetry, and poets; she lamented how many of the books about WBY were badly written and—always her severest judgement—dull, and confessed that she found one scholar-poet's verses 'intolerable'. Over a glass of sherry they would mischievously devise a scheme to get Austin Clarke on the booze (to relieve his gloom) and Patrick Kavanagh off it (so he ceased to waste his energies). 'The only thing that earned her unreserved scorn was not working.' And she repeated what she would say again to Kathleen Raine, 'A poet has no right not to write.' Once she showed John the 'magical stuff', emphasizing the significance of astrology, but was almost relieved when he did not pursue the subject. Oddly, for Montague was interested in George Steiner, they never discussed anthroposophy. John got the impression that for her much of the excitement went when Yeats died; she did not enjoy being 'the keeper of the museum', especially when scholars were either too obsequious or wanted to pry into her own feelings about Maud Gonne. She liked Montague's French wife Madeleine; they remembered her sharing a drink from a bottle hidden under the Cuala stall at the Book Fair. Once he brought Theodore Roethke to visit her; on the way the two poets bought a large bouquet of roses, concealing a bottle of sherry within. As Montague described it, the introduction was catastrophic: 'The door . . . opened slowly, all the more because the carpet had got curled into it. "Hello, John," said George Yeats, bending to smooth the rug with her left hand. The wait was too much for the tense Roethke, who now shot out his right hand in greeting. "Mrs Yeats, I brought you some flowers!" he bellowed, whereupon she straightened her back, scattering most of them across the floor.' Almost crippled by rheumatism at the time (with which Roethke sympathized), George soon soothed the nervous visiting American. When they said their farewells to her, she was almost asleep on the sofa, and 'Ted tucked the rug around her with great tenderness.'[43]

Next to poets, philosophers were appreciated. When Virginia Moore (a poet as well) told George she wished to understand better Yeats's religious and world view, the response was 'I don't want to be a curmudgeon so yes, you will be very welcome'; she also recommended a furnished flat nearby. Theirs seems to have been an immediate rapport: unlike most, who underwent rigorous interviews, on that first day Moore was given one of the early 'magic' notebooks and invited to stay for lunch. Daily from 9 to 4 through the autumn of 1952 Moore would work on the manuscripts, one book at a time; then the two would talk, continuing downstairs in the kitchen over supper. Their daily discussions ranged over religion (Moore had been a student of contemporary theologians Paul Tillich and Reinhold Niebuhr), philosophy and early arcana, poetry. Like so many others, Moore considered George 'the most intelligent woman she had ever met . . . could talk with her about anything. . . . She spoke from the centre—true.' 'If she never had any connection with Yeats, I would have been very impressed with her.' The admiration was mutual; George once startled her by leaning forward and saying intently, 'Don't underestimate yourself.' And she read the manuscript of

The Unicorn: W. B.Yeats's Search for Reality with approval. Seven years later she remarked of the *Vision* notebooks, 'Perhaps those are for Dr Moore.' George replied to her letters, but they never met again.[44]

George began to call the summers her 'American season'. Now that first generation of scholars sent their students and colleagues; most would be assured of an appointment. Perhaps because of this, she was especially aware of the need to assist local scholars; she read Arland Ussher's manuscript and loaned him materials on the Tarot and Blavatsky; she was generous with advice and help when Liam and Jo Miller were setting up the Dolmen Press and later for Liam's history of Cuala. But she was distressed when Ulick O'Connor, who refused to believe she had no letters by Gogarty, quarrelled with her. After O'Connor's biography of Gogarty was published George admitted having enjoyed it and, delighted to have the author pointed out to her one afternoon in the Hibernian Hotel, discreetly peered at him from behind a pillar.[45] Predictably, she did not care for 'Monkey' Gibbon's less than flattering book on her husband; when it was published she phoned him concerning the attribution of the photograph of Yeats on the book jacket and frontispiece, but refused to discuss the work itself.[46] As time passed she ceased to accept book-length manuscripts—though she seems to have read nearly everything that was published. She continued however to offer words of advice, for example pointing out to one scholar the Dante references he had missed in 'Cuchulain Comforted'. But she would not grant permission to quote from the unpublished poems or play scenarios. She was still adamant that what Yeats had not wished to see in print, she did not.[47]

One seeker, however innocently, crossed the boundary between permission to transcribe and right to publish. When Curtis Bradford arrived in Dublin in 1954 to teach American literature at Trinity College for the winter, he was introduced to George by Professor H. O. White, an old friend of Lily. After a pleasant dinner during which she surprised him with her extensive knowledge of Henry James and Emerson, George invited Bradford to Palmerston Road, and throughout the winter allowed him to see and transcribe many of Yeats's unpublished manuscripts. George apparently gave him permission to discuss with Scribner's his wish to publish in journals the three 'Prefaces' Yeats had written especially for the defunct special American 'Dublin Edition', but Macmillan of New York, who by now owned the copy, refused, claiming they wished to publish themselves (although no date was offered).[48] A few years later, without further consultation with her, he submitted over 800 pages of Yeats's unpublished prose to Rupert Hart-Davis. Startled by the size of the typescript, Hart-Davis wrote to George asking whether indeed Bradford had her permission to publish; he presumed not. George exploded, replying angrily that she had given no such permission, but that Bradford 'seems to have decided that he has a right to publish'. On her behalf the publisher wrote to the offending scholar, quoting the phrase. Puzzled and hurt by George's refusal—for he could not understand why she had allowed him to make such extensive transcriptions if he was *not* to publish—Bradford made things worse by his own letter to her, arguing that sufficient time had passed that nobody still living would be upset by the publication of the autobiographical Journals and Memoirs, and that these, the 'Leo Africanus' papers, and the unfinished novel *The Speckled Bird* were of major interest to scholars; furthermore, he claimed, only he and she could read Yeats's crabbed hand. It may have been the final claim that steeled George in her decision. At some stage in the argument she told him that Michael Yeats did not wish publication; probably this was simply her usual stratagem, but after George's death he upheld his mother's decision. At his own death Bradford left the papers to Grinnell College where he had taught for many years; the bulk of Bradford's monumental scholarship remains unpublished.[49] Fortunately the story has a happier sequel. In 1958 George signed an agreement giving Bradford permission to publish *Yeats at Work*; two years later he arrived in Dublin and was allowed to read the manuscripts of those poems, plays, and prose selections included in the volume, which was finally published in 1965. However, this time Bradford worked not at Palmerston Road, but in Trinity College, where George temporarily deposited the necessary manuscripts. It must have been on this visit that she read and required alterations to his article on 'Yeats and Maud Gonne'; although she did not always agree with his conclusions, she would no longer forbid. He then embarked on *The Writing of 'The Player Queen'*, but there is no record of any further meetings with George Yeats; that impressive volume did not appear until both he and George were dead. In 1970, when Michael and Anne revived the Cuala Press, the first volume issued was Bradford's edition of *Reflections*, transcribed so many years before from the prohibited journals. His own essay on George, written in 1955 and revealing as much about the author as it does about his subject, was not published until after her death.[50]

Occasionally, as in my case, she initiated the meeting. From her old friend Sybil LeBrocquy she heard of my work on the theatre for my doctoral thesis and invited me to tea. After the traditional 'interview', she sent me off on the bus with a bag full of papers, and occasionally I worked at Palmerston Road. But since WBY was only one of the cast of characters who interested me, our talk ranged widely over lunches at the Unicorn or tea and the occasional drink (brandy Alexanders) at the Hibernian. I never saw her incapacitated, although once she had clearly resorted to alcohol when searching through old letters for an answer to a question. Once too, picking up on a casual remark of mine, she suddenly quizzed me on the distinction between 'Spiritus Mundi' and 'Anima Mundi'; my stumbling explanation must have been satisfactory, for she offered me the 'magic' books. But I was not ready for that and she did not pursue the subject. Despite my reluctance to embark on Virginia Moore's territory, from 1959 we met regularly each summer, usually at the Hibernian Hotel—although during Horse Show week George liked to frequent the Shelbourne where she could eavesdrop on the wealthy tourists. She was once highly amused by an earnest discussion between two women over the ethics of accepting a souvenir Eiffel Tower when she herself had 'missed' Paris. Eventually George decided the two Ann(e)s should know each other, and even suggested her daughter seek out unpublished drawings by Jack Yeats for my edition of Synge's plays. I was not the only young scholar who was actively encouraged; she was delighted when Oxford University Press and Macmillan appointed poetry editors (Jon Stallworthy and Kevin Crossley-Holland respectively) under the age of 30.[51]

Sometimes if the research on Yeats (especially the prose) did not particularly interest her, the seekers did. She would then let down her guard in other ways, indulging her liking for witty stories. Bradford remembers her saying mischievously about the fire at the Abbey Theatre in 1951, 'I've always thought it was WB. Lennox Robinson was about to revive *The Player Queen* and planned to take the role of Septimus. Of course WB would never permit that.' She then quoted from 'In Memory of Eva Gore-Booth and Con Markiewicz' the line 'Bid me strike a match and blow', striking an imaginary match and puffing an imaginary flame.[52] Donald Pearce recalls her 'brimming sense of fun' and open laughter; but he once made a careless remark—intended as a compliment—that clearly hurt her. She brooded on it for some days, then burst out, 'You people come in here as often as you like, with your questions and your literary troubles, and you think I have nothing else to do but look after them. Well, that's not all I have to do with my time.' Her powdered face was flushed purple. 'And *you* even tell me that what I ought to have been is a businesswoman!' Pearce did not return to Palmerston Road for several weeks, and the incident was never mentioned again. Perhaps because she had revealed so much, she was prepared to offer more. Once he was deliberately left alone with the chests in which the automatic script was stored; another time she showed him the lock of hair cut on Yeats's deathbed, and even slipped the treasured signet ring onto his finger. He was one of the few to copy down the scurrilous 'Poem of Lancelot Switchback' with which, she told him, Yeats hoped to shock Dorothy Wellesley.[53] Pearce introduced other Americans: Hugh Kenner remembers being shocked when she said of WBY in what he thought a derogatory manner, 'He never could spell,' but was pleased that she spoke highly of his article on the deliberate construction of each volume of the poems.[54] Pearce's last memory is happily frivolous, when she taught him as he went down the steps towards the bus stop, 'the correct response to "Tootle-oo!" is always "Pip! Pip!"' It may have been with him that she picked up the habit of using the Americanism 'So long'.[55] When his edition of Yeats's Senate speeches was published, George especially liked a quotation from Ezra Pound's *Cantos*:

> If a man don't occasionally sit in a senate
> How can he pierce the darrk mind of a
> Senator?)[56]

Ezra's incarceration continued to distress her. Often she would lash out at Americans for their treatment of a poet—any poet, but especially her friend Pound.[57] To David Clark she raged, 'It's like caging a tiger,' protesting that somebody 'so completely alive, so bursting with splendid energy', should be locked up. Some—Paul de Man, Virginia Moore—were asked to visit Pound and report back.[58] In 1947 she was especially relieved to hear from Ezra himself, who asked her in his inimitable way for 'Poisonl gnuz of people' as 'max. relief I can get here'. She wrote immediately to Eliot for information, quoting Ezra's letter to her. 'The first I had from him since 1939. Have you heard from him and have you written to him? . . . Can you suggest to me any books that EP would like to have? I would so gladly buy them to send to him. It is horrible to me to think of him incarcerated in a State Lunatic Asylum.' Eliot replied that he had seen Ezra that July and found Pound sane if more extreme in his ideas; he hoped that more salubrious surroundings might be found for him after the congressional elections. Unfortunately Eliot had missed seeing Dorothy, who had not yet arrived from Italy, but had since learned from her that she was now in Washington and once more in funds. He himself had sent books, but recommended avoiding political or economic subjects; however, Faber was planning to publish the next batch of Cantos. Although George wrote to congratulate him when Eliot received the Nobel prize, there is no record of books she herself may have then posted to Washington.[59]

However, in 1954 after another request from Ezra she sent him Willy's copy of *The Holy Guide* by John Heydon (1662). That book was never returned to the Yeats library, but over the next ten years 'My dear Jarge' would receive unsolicited bulletins complaining that she did not write ('Wot the HELL Do yu do with yr mind?'), wanting to know about Irish political commentators, requesting information about Yeats's knowledge of Greek (the pronunciation of 'Sailing to Byzantium'), or—and this she did answer—permission to quote in an anthology he was compiling for young readers.[60]

Dear E. P. NO charge for any Yeats poems you want to put into Anthology—I gather—YOUR form of communication is a little difficult for ancient persons like me—that you 'plug for early short poems'—as far as I am concerned your selection is right—don't quite know what you mean by '*post-Elephant*'—I wld certainly agree that Mat Arnold in TOTO should not be included—*But* I don't know *who* is the '*Dover Bitch*'? Personally, I would like a bit of Golding? Also, I think 1890ish stuff not very exciting or useful for our young generation—if you are thinking of persons aged 10–18? I find that persons of that sort of age do not really want to read 1890—like to read Cummins E. P. Skelton—the inevitable Blake—Love to both George Yeats

Ezra replied with 'Benedictions', explaining that 'Elephant' referred to Eliot, 'Dover Bitch' to Arnold's poem 'Dover Beach'; he had been quoting their old text on magic by Ennemoser to Eliot, and recommended she read Niebuhr.[61] But although Pound continued to send the occasional communiqué her way, George would not be drawn into further discussion.

Rarely was there anything from Dorothy, and then only a one-word 'Greetings' in the margin. To one of Ezra's visitors in Washington she admitted she had 'led a hell of a life these last sixteen years, first the bloody war, and these nine years here'; now her one purpose was to keep her husband 'happy and reasonably well' that he might complete the *Cantos*.[62] The parallel with George's life during the late 1930s is striking, when she too was trying to keep her husband's poetry alive. Finally in 1958 Ezra, officially certified 'insane' and therefore not liable for trial, was released in the care of his 'committee', Dorothy, who remained in charge of his funds until his death. That summer both, in the company of a young woman called his 'secretary', went to stay with Ezra's daughter Mary at Brunnenberg. From there Ezra wrote to George, 'Mountain air a pleasant change from D. C. Yrx deeV-oted E. P.' But he could not breathe for long in the Tyrol, and less than a year later was writing from the Grande Hotel in Rapallo: 'We got an attic, and an elEvator that works, at least for the present, as that at v Marsala has NOT for the past 49 years.' But Ezra once more returned to the Tyrol. By 1962 Olga Rudge, mother of his daughter, had taken charge and Dorothy was alone.[63] Although 'Uncle Billyum' was still on a higher plane than Eliot, Ezra remained unrepentantly audacious, as his parody of 'Under Ben Bulben' makes abundantly clear:

> Neath Ben Bulben's buttocks lies
> Bill Yeats, a poet twoice the soize
> Of William Shakespear, as they say
> Down Ballykillywuchlin way.
>
> Let saxon roiders break their bones
> Huntin' the fox
> Thru dese gravestones.[64]

Ill health continued to plague George. 'Nothing to be done about it except acknowledge old age,' she wrote to Ellmann when she was only 59.[65] Winters were spent fighting recurring bouts of bronchitis, and labour unrest with the inevitable accompanying strikes by railway and lorry drivers made the ordinary affairs of housekeeping even more difficult; when even the banks were on strike, the local grocer in Ranelagh cashed cheques for her. By the early 1950s the devoted Mary Martin had left; she had not been well for some time and the kitchen at Palmerston Road was getting her down. Eventually she found a new position working for a blind man; having been trained never to disturb WBY's papers, she was well suited. From then on George had only part-time help—Teresa arrived for a few hours in the morning a couple of times a week; the gardener occasionally when he felt it necessary. Eileen Colum came in each day to deal with Cuala, but by 1954, having no assets or liabilities, the Industries were no longer registered as a limited company. In 1961 Esther ('Essie') Ryan, who had joined Cuala in 1903, died; eventually only Molly Gill was working in the printing room off the kitchen.[66] With no live-in domestic help, George prepared all the meals herself; thanks to her early Red Cross training, she was an excellent cook: Anne remembered her delicious ossobucco, Virginia Moore a lamb dish done with herbs and strips of onion. She enjoyed Elizabeth David's recipes, and was intrigued when I once sent her a copy of Alexandre Dumas's cookbook. When it was time for a talk with visitors, she brought in with her a Cona coffee-machine and sweet cake. Visiting her in April 1957, Kathleen Raine noticed that she also carried a hot water bottle for her back.

With the founding of the Yeats International Summer School in Sligo in August 1960—always referred to by George as 'the Yeats Racket'—more visitors came calling. Conscious of her role as guardian of Yeats's name, George continued to invite them to tea. She enjoyed stories of the events at Sligo, and added to her own repertoire the one about the rowing boat that sank on its way to Innisfree, sending earnest students and their lecturers wading through waist-high water back to shore. Despite the claims of the tourist industry she insisted that not even WBY could identify the fabled island, and related with delight the story of his rowing round the islands of Lough Gill in unsuccessful search. When O'Connor lectured at the School, she saved *The Irish Times* report.[67] Aware always of public impressions, she was distressed when a photograph suggested that Yeats's headstone was cracked. Bookseller John Keohane, whom she knew well, was asked to investigate and, if necessary, arrange repairs; 'Whatever will students think of me for being so neglectful?' The 'crack' turned out to be only a shadow picked up by the camera, but Keohane assured her that he would look at the grave at intervals to make sure nothing was amiss. George responded immediately with customary generosity:

I am deeply grateful for your kindness in going out to Drumcliffe and reporting on the condition of the tombstone. You can imagine what a relief it was to me. I do not know how to thank you—I wonder if you have in your private collection a copy of 'A Lament for Art O'Leary' Illustrated by Jack Yeats? If you have not, I should so much like to send you one of my three copies. 75 only were printed by the Cuala Press. Greetings to your wife & to yourself.[68]

She had reason to be concerned about what people might think. On one occasion she and Anne went up to Belfast to shop and watch the newsreel of the royal wedding; they missed their train and were taken by the taxi driver to a bed and breakfast in the nationalist Falls Road area (where the first thing they saw was a

Cuala print of 'Innisfree' in the hall). Anne remembered that on their return to Dublin George received several abusive anonymous letters and phone calls for having gone into the north.[69]

As early as 1944 George had decided that the manuscripts must be presented to the nation, and discussed how to avoid death duties with Richard Hayes, director of the National Library of Ireland. At first she had considered presenting some of the papers to Trinity College as well, but within five years of WBY's death her plans were quite clear. To the ever-interested Healy she explained, 'while tabulating and sorting MSS [I] found that there [are] in some cases duplicates, and these I have set aside. By DUPLICATES I mean *identical* MSS. My plan in the arrangement of MSS is that variants, corrected typescripts etc should all go to the National Library. Also books in which Yeats had written corrections, so that there shall be a complete collection, in as far as *I* am able to make it complete, for students of the future.' By 1955 she told MacGreevy she was 'gradually sorting out all the MSS which is going to the Nat. Library (All the Abbey stuff & letters from Irishmen etc) so that I can send it off soon. Much less trouble for A. & M.' By late September the following year, in an effort to reduce the number of visitors to the house while recovering from her first serious ulcer attack, she had sent off all the plays to the National Library. 'I have been very unwell for more than a year, & unfortunately, since August 4 to Sept 12 I had 3 professors here studying MSS (verse). I am very over-tired & must have 3 weeks rest which has to include some hospital treatment.' By the early 1960s, as scholars needed them, she deposited various notebooks and letters to Yeats in the library manuscript room; many remained there. But she was not yet ready to give up the poetry.[70]

If there had been any second thoughts about a gift to Trinity College, they were abandoned in August 1959 when Jon Stallworthy arrived to work on the poetry manuscripts, armed with letters of introduction to Bethel Solomons (who telephoned George on his behalf) and the librarian of Trinity. George applied her usual test, presenting him with three notebooks which he was to read in the College manuscript room. However, when he was abruptly turned away by the librarian without even being given a chance to explain his presence, George promptly took him and the notebooks in a taxi to MacLochlainn and made it very clear that *all* the papers would go to the National Library. After many days of struggling with Yeats's handwriting, Jon realized that she had deliberately given him papers that bore no relation to the poems he had come to see; but he had successfully passed the test (and learned to decipher Yeats's hand); from then on he worked happily either at the library or, when enough problems had been accumulated, over the kitchen table with George at Palmerston Road.[71] When she donated a further batch of papers to the library in 1963, the directors were moved to call it 'one of the most munificent gifts since the founding of the state'.[72] Characteristically, however, she wrote to Michael, 'will think about my own letters to WBY, but do not think I shall change my mind. His to me will be handed over to you in a sealed package "do not open until after my death"(!)'[73]

WBY's letters to others were another matter. Shortly after his death Macmillan heard from Allan Wade, Yeats's first bibliographer, hoping that the Coole Edition would include various items on the theatre that had so far escaped publication. George herself replied, and immediately after the war both Allan and Margot Wade were her guests at Palmerston Road. Wade's visit was purposeful; he was dedicated to the task of preparing a complete bibliography, and once that had been embarked upon, an edition of Yeats's letters; he returned to England with permission for both. With George's help, the bibliography was published in November 1951. Work on the letters was even more collaborative:

Did Roger Lhombreaud Merton College Oxford write to you about 3 letters to Rhoda Symons? They are dated 1909. He is doing a book on Symons. In haste G.Y. I opened this to thank you for letting me know Norman Haire had died. I know he had some letters but did not know you had not seen them. Shall I write to the executors and ask them to send you either the letters or copies? About the Joyce letters. Would it be any use my offering the Joyce letters *I* have to Yale if they will send copies of WBY to Joyce? If you think it *would*, let me know.

When Wade's edition of the letters appeared in 1954, she thanked him for the 'magnificent book . . . The best memorial Yeats could have.' A year later Allan Wade was dead. Concerned that his estate might not be adequate, George wrote to Rupert Hart-Davis offering to add some spare copies of Cuala editions to the library he was selling for Margot Wade; a few years later she quietly arranged that £50 from royalties also go to her old friend's widow.[74]

Her relationship with Macmillan was not always as smooth as it was with Hart-Davis. Always on the lookout for misprints, she was determined that when the new collected edition appeared, it would be a suitable commemoration of the poet and his work. Within months of Yeats's death, while she was correcting proofs of the two volumes of poems—considered by her the definitive edition since Yeats had passed the proofs himself—she was corresponding with various scholars over details of punctuation and interpretation, suggesting that rhythm 'which was achieved after much difficulty' should remain sacrosanct, and that although even ballad forms were used by WBY 'in a most personal way', the meaning was deliberately 'impersonal'.[75] Her most serious long-reaching discussions were with Thomas Mark, that 'admirable scholar' who had been working as Yeats's in-house editor since 1932 and who had often been given by the poet himself *carte blanche* concerning punctuation.[76] Sometimes Yeats had consulted him on other matters: 'My wife and I arranged the contents of the American edition, & she was very urgent about the placing of the introductions to the *Wheels and Butterflies* plays. I am not quite certain what we did, or if we did right. I would like your opinion.'[77] But now as literary executor George had the final authority. Moreover, as she often reminded Mark, she remained the link between the creative and editorial processes:

Thanks to Macmillan allowing 'Essays' to go out of print I have no copy, but in the American Macmillan edition, p.104, line 10 'by Moeris and the Mareotid lakes' it should be 'M*ae*ris' *as dipthong*. The reason I particularly mention this is that your eagle eye will notice in the second line of 'Under Ben Bulben' (one of the new poems I shall be sending you,) 'Round the Mareotic lake'. That 'c', instead of 'd', was a subject of much discussion between WB and myself, he wanted it for sound, and I finally discovered a respectable authority for it!

Occasionally she challenged the punctuation Mark was fond of adding, deleting where she felt his comma altered the sense. She made trips to the National Library to check spellings of the Gaelic words. At other times she provided the context for changes Yeats had made in the text:

'A Nativity' Yeats altered *gnat* to *moth* deliberately. He thought gnat created a wrong image. He said to me 'No! One *swats* gnats and mosquitoes';
'Lapis Lazuli' deliberate punctuation by WBY who read the two lines

> Their eyes mid many wrinkles, their eyes
> Their ancient, glittĕrĭng eyes, are gay
> (glittering eyes and gay read on a higher note);

'Colonel Martin' reference as in 'Last Poems' and Macmillan ed. is the *original* version. The longer one was really created by F. R. Higgins for purpose of singing. I persuaded WBY to replace the original;
'The Song of Wandering Aengus' I several times heard him end line 3 as 'by the door', but on one occasion (at a lecture) he stopped & said 'No: I must start again', & then said the line 'on the floor'. So I think perhaps leave it as printed?[78]

Other major decisions made by the two dealt with the choice of poems for the final volume, and in what order those last poems should be printed. 'Certainly put "Under Ben Bulben" at the end of the volume. Its present position was WBY's, but I think now it should undoubtedly be at the end as you suggest. I should be inclined to omit that Huddon and Duddon poem from *A Vision*; the Antigone poem makes a fine end to *The Winding Stair* section, and the Huddon and Duddon is not a good poem.'[79] It would be many years (and then to the dismay of many of his readers) before 'Politics' would conclude the final volume, as Yeats seems to have intended.[80] But the argument about authorial versus editorial intention will never, it seems, be over, and George always admitted responsibility for the decision to end the Macmillan edition of the collected poems with 'Under Ben Bulben'.[81]

By February 1940 Macmillan had published *Last Poems and Plays* and it was clear to George that the Coole Edition would be postponed indefinitely. Although the fine paper had already been purchased, '*de luxe* publishing at such a time was considered unseemly'. Tom Mark soldiered on with his proof-reading, adding new material to the volumes already approved by Yeats before his death; he was becoming even more pedantic and fussy in his later years.[82] George no longer felt inclined to answer his questions as promptly; besides, her arm was in a cast for three months and there were family matters to attend to. She was also dismayed by the fact that Macmillan had allowed so many volumes to go out of print; even Eliot had written to her in 1946 about the difficulty of getting copies of Yeats's work, adding that it was more than time for a new collected edition of the poems.[83] Three years later the American scholar Marion Witt complained that only the 1933 *Collected Poems* was available, and that most of the other volumes had been out of print for many years. It was perhaps not surprising that Harold Macmillan had had difficulty getting a reply from her—why should she bother if they did not? Finally, when it appeared that a new edition would indeed appear, George was once again in regular communication with Thomas Mark;[84] in November 1949 a limited two-volume edition of the poems was published, and in July 1950 a new trade edition in one volume. A new edition of the plays, adding the last five Yeats had finished, appeared in 1952, and an updated volume of *Autobiographies* in 1955.

But it was outside pressure that appears to have finally urged Macmillan to further projects. In 1955 Witt proposed that Oxford University Press publish an edition of Yeats's uncollected prose which she had prepared.[85] The request, which was denied, did however lead to four new publications: *A Vision* (1956) 'reissued with the author's final revisions'; *Mythologies* (1959); *Essays and Introductions* (1961); and *Explorations* (1962). Only the last volume publicly announced that the passages were 'selected by Mrs W. B. Yeats', but she was involved with the preparation of all four. Most of the revisions to *A Vision* were provided by George.[86] She firmly insisted upon the chronological ordering in *Essays and Introductions* when the three essays especially written for Scribner's Dublin Edition finally appeared; the publishers had hoped to put them at the head of the volume but reluctantly agreed to her ordering, for 'you have been so obliging, kind and helpful that we ought to meet your wishes and we will move them accordingly'.[87] To MacGreevy she admitted that she did not care for the title *Mythologies*, chosen by Yeats in 1938; she liked even less his change from 'Discoveries' to 'Explorations'.[88] Communication with the publishers had improved when 'Rache' Dickson, now a director of Macmillan, began to make periodic trips across to Dublin. After they met in January 1959, she said if his name was on the envelope she would open it. 'That didn't mean that she would deal with the matter contained, but at least she was aware of it, and a long-distance call to Dublin would produce the answer.'[89]

Perhaps because later that year Dickson made the mistake of offering to buy out George's rights for a fee her agent considered highly unsatisfactory, even this arrangement did not ease the passage of *Explorations*, which seems to have been discussed at their first meeting.[90] 'I shall look forward with great interest to seeing your list of material,' Dickson had written in August 1960. He wrote again the following April:

I hear indirectly that you are distressed about the cuts suggested in the marked copy sent to you of ON THE BOILER. I don't know whether this is the reason why I haven't heard from you in reply to my letters of last August and January of this year, but if it is I wish that I had known that. We are perfectly ready to print ON THE BOILER without any alterations at all. The suggested cuts were indeed only suggestions, and they can be ignored altogether. Do let us get on with EXPLORATIONS. The other books have done very well, and it is a pity not to add this valuable material to W. B. Y's published work.[91]

Since in December 1960 George told another correspondent that she was writing to Macmillan about various misprints in the *Collected Poems* and *Collected Plays*, it is possible that the silence Dickson speaks of had only to do with the projected new volume.[92]

That word 'indirectly' hints at how George had her own ways of making her dissatisfaction known; she had effectively bid farewell to Thomas Mark in 1949 when work on the two-volume 'definitive edition', *The Poems of W. B. Yeats*, was finished. 'When I was in London in 1942 I found in a bookshop in Charing Cross Road a copy of WANDERINGS OF OISIN inscribed "W. B. Yeats This copy is not to be lent as I have made corrections in it that I do not want to lose." I should like you to have it as a token of gratitude for your many years of sensitive care in seeing WBY's work through the press.'[93] After that generous gesture, correspondence between George and Mark seems to have ceased, although he was privy to her discussions with Dickson. When *Explorations* appeared, the order followed an undated list in George's hand.[94] By August 1961 Dickson was discussing with George the revisions to Hone's biography; she provided corrections to the text and 'a one-page Epilogue which described the burial in Drumcliffe churchyard'.[95] By then Derry Jeffares's four volumes of selected works were in preparation; in 1964 Lovat Dickson retired and returned to Canada, and George's active contribution to the publication of Yeats's works ended. In 1967 however she honoured another commitment when she sent Roger McHugh the letters from Margot Ruddock to Yeats 'together with many of her poems and other material referred to in this edition', insisting that 'the letters should not be censored or cut in any way'. A professor at University College, Dublin, McHugh had already edited the letters of Yeats to Katharine Tynan, and had asked for permission to edit the Ruddock correspondence as early as 1964, but George did not feel it should be published during the centenary year.[96] Her sense of ceremony, like Willy's, was great.

Not that she ever tolerated unauthorized liberties. A regular listener to the BBC, she once wrote a strong letter pointing out the omission of a line from a reading of 'The Cat and the Moon'. Hasty letters of apology arrived from both the producer and the secretariat.[97] One of her last public objections occurred in June 1965 when a correspondent to *The Irish Times* quoted an early unauthorized poem; she was delighted when Arland Ussher responded asking for information, 'which gave me the opportunity of replying with some history . . . As the damn thing is not copyright any one can use it as a re-print!' Her own firm letter appeared a few days later:

In his letter of June 16th Mr. Arland Ussher asks for an explanation regarding a poem called: 'Mourn—and then Onward.' Writing to his sister, Lily Yeats, on Sunday, October 11th, 1891, Yeats says: 'I send you a copy of *United Ireland* with a poem of mine on Parnell, written the day he died to be in time for the press that evening'—the poem was printed in *United Ireland* on October 10th, 1891. It was reprinted by the *Irish Weekly Independent* on May 20th, 1893; also on one or two other occasions by other papers.
    No revisions or corrections were ever made by Yeats, and it has never been included nor ever will be in book form.[98]

She could not always avoid public appearances. When W. R. Rodgers planned to broadcast a programme making use of interviews with people who knew Yeats, he enlisted Frank O'Connor's help. But even 'Michael/Frank' had difficulty persuading a reluctant George to participate; in bed suffering from a bad bout of bronchitis, she wrote apologetically, 'apart from not knowing when I may have a voice again, I have got cold feet about the idea. So better call it off alltogether. Sorry to seem so changeable.' Eventually, however, she agreed to be interviewed, and the recording includes some of her best 'set pieces' on WBY.[99] A few years later, she had to suffer in a very public box during the Abbey's golden jubilee celebrations. In telling the story afterwards George quoted Henry James's remark at a dull speech, 'we are not here to enjoy ourselves'.[100] Finally, as her back became ever more painful, she refused to go out at all in the evenings except for very early suppers with Anne in the grill room of the Hibernian. Declining an invitation from H. O. White to attend a production at the College, she explained:

I find it a bit difficult to sit up late, & should not like to go to the Trinity Players production & leave early—as one can at an ordinary theatre—and this is a lovely programme. The two plays I have most heard praised are 'Dreaming [of the Bones]' & 'Purgatory'— both unfortunately for *me* at the end of the programme. But best arranged for sequence. I don't know what you feel, but I never care very much for '[The Land of] Heart's Desire' or 'Pot [of Broth]'. Perhaps I am predjudiced [*sic*] by WBY's opinions on his own early work![101]

Nor was all of the publicity attractive. In 1961 the opera *Elegy for Young Lovers* by Hans Werner Henze was produced at Glyndebourne. As described by W. H. Auden, who with Chester Kallman provided the libretto, its main character was 'a cross between W. B. Yeats and Stefan Georg and is very libellous. (Setting, an Austrian mountain resort; time, c.1910). Like W. B. Y., he gets ideas from a lady who has visions.' Two characters seem to be modelled on George—the mad visionary widow who comes out of her madness on learning that the body of her bridegroom has been found after forty years and gets drunk, and the devoted 'secretary' who supports him from her own inheritance. Although she never mentioned the opera, with her lifelong interest in music George was bound to have read at least some of the reviews.[102]

Ever since Yeats's death fewer friends were calling at Palmerston Road. In August 1950 Dorothy Wellesley visited Ireland, during which time her fur coat was stolen. She gave George a copy of her privately published book *Beyond the Grave: Letters on Poetry to W. B. Yeats*, which included five photographs of the tower sent her by George in 1939. The book was as much a tribute to Hilda Matheson, who had died in 1941, as it was to Yeats: 'genius actually demands a competent friend, without which it cannot live. It is love and affection; it is somebody who is able to deal with practical life.' George took the opportunity of Wellesley's visit to request the return of the manuscript of *The Death of Cuchulain*.[103] The following year Omar Pound, accompanying the blind Wyndham Lewis to Ireland, came up from Cork to see her.[104] George must have been pleased to learn that he too was a poet.

For many years one of George's closest friends was Olive Craig, who had taken Anne in when her parents were in Majorca, and who frequently joined her on theatre outings. A Trinity Scholar, she enjoyed probing for meaning, sometimes provoking George to flights of fantasy:

Olive & I went to 'Iceman Cometh' Gaiety Sunday Night. Even Olive thought it could have been cut by one hour. But it was an exceedingly good production and two quite outstanding performances. There were two Priests in front of us who had evidently been given their cues—they rose and left exactly one minute before the three ladies of pleasure made their entrance! . . . Olive was re-searching for the inner meaning all through the first act, I wildly suggested 'What's wrong with the twelve disciples and the three Maries at the foot of the Cross'. Pure frivolity which she took seriously. Not sure however that one couldnt work it out that way very neatly! I must try to get a copy of the play.[105]

George regularly visited Olive's cottage at Malahide; one fine Christmas they sat on the sea wall to pluck the turkey, but the wind changed before they could escape a cloud of feathers. Olive, who for all her learning was somewhat impractical, could always be counted on to provide an amusing story. 'Neenie' Gogarty did not forget her either; to one invitation George replied, 'Many thanks for your letter. I am being lent a cottage at Malahide for end July to mid-August so could not come to Galway for races although it sounds a delightful idea. I want to be in reach of Dublin for Horse Show week—Cuala always has a stall. Do let me know when you are in Dublin again.'[106] Another staunch friend was Sybil LeBrocquy, who continued to be a powerful, witty force behind most literary and artistic projects in Dublin and was herself a Swift scholar. Although George sometimes found Sybil's energy a bit overpowering, she appreciated her generosity and loyalty.

Still the seekers kept coming. She was beginning to need a 'closed season' herself, and in June 1954 Anne flew with her to England. In London they saw new plays and the latest French films, visited art exhibitions and the Battersea fun fair, travelled to Greenwich and Richmond by boat (twice) and to Putney Common on the bus, dined in small restaurants—George delighted the Italian waiters by ordering a 'Strega' after dinner—lunched in Soho with Rupert Hart-Davis, and met with the Wades. Obviously George was determined to revisit *her* London. Then they took the train to Somerset where Harold had retired to a curacy in Watchet in a tiny church that 'smelt of prayer'. Harold, a big man with a barrel-shaped, asthmatic chest, drove them around the country in his small Morris car, visiting yet more art galleries; Anne remembers having to sit in the middle of the back seat, on the ridge, to provide balance, and although they went to the top of hills to see the view, they were never allowed to get out of the car. Either now or on a previous visit to Ireland (Gráinne remembers taking her baby daughter around to Palmerston Road in a carrycot to see him), Anne shocked her uncle by talking of her love affairs; later Harold spoke disapprovingly of her conduct to his cousin Grace Jaffe.[107] Harold's intolerance was well known: on one of his rare visits to Ireland George had hired a car and driver to take her brother around the countryside; he assumed by the neat appearance of some of the farms on the outskirts of Dublin that they must have crossed over the border into Northern Ireland. However, the journey to Watchet was important to George; from then on she and Harold corresponded, regularly sending each other birthday gifts. When George was in hospital her brother—otherwise overly thrifty—sent Anne money to buy her such delicacies as strawberries, grapes, nectarines, and figs. In 1961 'Dobbs' sent 'Hokel' photographs of 'the Grandwees':

Very many happy returns to you. I cannot send you a birthday present—customs nuisances—& so I send a cheque in the hopes that you will buy yourself some thing you would like to have & would not buy yourself. Herewith various snapshots of all my grandchildren—I do not often see them now that the family has moved out to Dalkey, but they look like the snaps!! So much better than 'studio' photographs with which you & I suffered from. How are you? I know I never write, but I think a great deal about you.[108]

Another unexpected visitor was Grace Jaffe, who arrived in Dublin in 1954, as instructed by her cousin, only after Horse Show week was over. Although Grace had made arrangements to stay elsewhere, George insisted that she move to Palmerston Road, where she slept in Anne's bedroom. Meals, Grace recalled, were somewhat haphazard, and the dark house was 'a mausoleum rather than a home', 'a bit like living on a tomb-stone'. George hired a car and driver to show her cousin around Dublin and the neighbouring countryside; Grace did not meet either Anne or Michael, although she did see one of Anne's paintings hanging in an exhibition of modern art (she would eventually meet Michael and Gráinne in Illinois in 1967). But the most memorable part of the visit occurred during their last evening together, while Grace, who was teaching sociology, waited to be collected for an appointment to tour a home for unwed mothers. As when she was a little girl, Grace confided in her adored older cousin about her extramarital affairs, her recent divorce, and her conversion to Roman Catholicism—finally bursting into tears. Once again George comforted her, 'You know Grace, that all human love is a reflection of Divine Love.' She in turn spoke of her own unhappiness in the last years of her marriage when Willy had turned to other women, and admitted that she had once tried to write her memoirs of WBY, but later burned them. As time passed, they forgot about food, making do with large tumblers of whiskey. When Grace returned to the house there was a tray of sandwiches by her bed, but her cousin was nowhere to be seen. She left the next morning, worried because she had been unable to rouse George; although Grace was unaware of the situation, evidently the stress of the evening's discussion had sent her cousin once again to seek forgetfulness in alcohol. Sometimes memories were simply too much to bear.[109]

Grace was back in England three years later, but this time she spent time with her cousin Harold. Again the visit was traumatic, for Harold would suddenly launch into an irrational tirade reminding her of the tantrums he had experienced as a child. A man of harsh judgement and many prejudices, he left at his death in 1963 an estate valued at close to £130,000, most of it including the prized family possessions and portraits going to distant cousins in England. George received one-fifth of the residue from his estate and some etchings and drawings by Muirhead Bone; Michael was left Augustus John's *Woman Seated*; but to her mother's sorrow, Anne was not even mentioned in her godfather's will. The regret was more emotional than financial, for by now George's own situation was much more satisfactory: in addition to her inheritance from her father, she was receiving well over £1,000 a year from royalties; occasionally she sold extra copies of rare books and pamphlets.[110] Just in case Harold had not remembered his domestic help either, George sent £50 to his servant Annie Dunn who had been with him for eleven years; however his will instructed that each of his servants receive £100. Michael attended his uncle's funeral and for the first time met some of Gwynne's sisters, for whom Harold had made handsome provision.[111] Shortly afterward, when Anne took a very nice photograph of her mother, George refused a copy saying she no longer had anyone to send it to.

By then most of the figures featured in her story were either distanced or had died: Maud Gonne and Walter Rummel in 1953, Iseult Stuart in 1954, Lennox Robinson in 1958. Fortunately Tom MacGreevy was back in Dublin; after years of precarious existence in England he was now living with his widowed sister and her family. For a time he served as art critic for *The Irish Times*, then published his study of Jack Yeats's paintings.[112] Finally in 1950 he achieved the longed-for position of director of the National Gallery of Art, which he held until 1963. As she had years before, George read and commented on his manuscripts:

My dear Tom A great many thanks for a very illuminating article on Dante. I wish I had had it when Henn was here. I do really think it preposterous that postman should not allow one to have such things! . . . You have a new (to me) & exciting connection between the Commedia & ? 'The Dream of the Bones' ('Hawk's Well' you say but you describe the 'Bones'.) Now *dont* please regard that as anything critical. Your text is what matters, & matters very much) I wish you would send that article to some intelligent magazine in U.S.A. Would you?? *Please.* My underlinings are almost equal to Lolly's. If you agree with me will you ring up? Yours affly George Thank you also for saying 'you have reason to be very proud of Anne's Exhibition'. I know you would not say that if you did not think it.

'Dante and Modern Ireland', in which MacGreevy recommends the Temple classics George studied as a young woman, speaks of being in Italy with the Yeatses in 1925 and 1928; she would have appreciated both references. At times, however, she could not resist criticizing his writing style. 'When we meet, I hope I shall not anger you with some insistence that you should, often, write "I" instead of "one". That you should be more positive in some passages. That you should *never* say "of course". That you should quite often eliminate an "and". Please forgive these suggestions which are the sort of thing that arose between WBY & GY in the course of work.'[113]

The friendship was important to both of them, although she seems to have continued to treat him as a younger brother, even sending him a hot water bottle for his aching shoulder. They met regularly for tea at the Shelbourne; Anne recalls joining them once when Tom pontificated for so long that George, aware of her daughter's impatience, said, 'Oh come off it Tom,' at which he subsided. Once, too, he expressed great surprise that Michael knew more about Wagner than he did. But just as Tom gave George support in the negotiations over the return of Yeats's body, he served as a much needed confidant on other matters. She must also have reminisced with him of happier days, for she occasionally signed her letters to him 'George "Hyde" '. When his book on Poussin was published by Dolmen Press in 1960, she sent a copy to Harold for his 70th birthday. An exchange shortly after Harold died and after Tom had retired for reasons of ill health reveals much about their relationship:

My dear Tom How very nice of you to write—I think you misunderstood a phrase—a very stupid phrase—of mine when we were talking about the 'archdeacon'. I was remembering a lunch we had in the basement at the Gresham with Harold, in 1948. You liked him I think and it was a very happy memory for me. That is why I wanted you [to] dine with me last Friday! He died in his sleep and is buried at Mirfield with his wife. Michael went over—I was not able to go. Very much to my surprise he had arranged with his executor to be cremated. Before the cremation (at Bristol) the funeral service was at his own church. Then he was taken to Bristol & then to Mirfield where his wife is buried. I find myself rather lonely. Thank you for your kind thought about the mass for him. He would have liked that. Yours affly George Yeats

My dear George. Did I misunderstand something? Actually I felt happy about our party, afterwards as well as during, and the memory of our luncheon with Harold, and the feeling that we were happy at it, remained with me. He had been easy, modest with the modesty of a distinguished man, kindly and gracious probably wondering about a fellow who referred to his mother as 'Nellie', but letting himself see the fun of it. Thinking of all three of you I do realise that I have been a privileged man. But I mustn't be too serious. I think of your mother writing, 'God Almighty, how I am bored by the people around me'. And I think of yourself, when I came home from Spain with a beret, saying, 'Tom, are you going to go round Dublin in that obscene little hat?' The things that for some unknown reason, one likes to remember! You had laughed as you said it.

I can understand your feeling lonely. . . . I expect you and the Archdeacon had lots of childhood reminiscences to laugh over when you could get together. Now you feel the gettings-together are over. But it has happened [to me] to feel that those who are gone do still laugh affectionately with me (and even *at* me, which, so long as it is affectionately, is fine too). . . . Dear George, I don't want to intrude at all, but you know that if at any time you'd like to meet and talk for a while, I have a great deal of leisure now. God bless, Tom[114]

MacGreevy was also a support for her brother-in-law, whom he visited every evening. Jack Yeats was now spending the harshest winter months in the Portobello Nursing Home. In November 1956 it was clear that the old painter was failing. George consulted Tom: 'When I rang up Portobello today the nurse said that Jack had been "walking up and down the corridor". I told her not to say I had rung up. That is what I think he wants, isn't it? You know him so much better than anyone else.'[115] Anne and MacGreevy were by his deathbed on 28 March 1957; she held her uncle's hand, and ten minutes before he died his last words were 'Goodbye Anne'. Tom was chief executor of Jack's will, and Anne his major beneficiary. Later that year, after recovering from an operation herself, she moved from Checkers to a second-floor studio-apartment at 39 Upper Mount Street, where her uncle's brilliant paintings covered the walls and birds sang 'in sunlit cages'.[116]

With Jack's death 'our rock George' was freed at last from attendance on Willy's generation. That year, when Jeanne Robert Foster received no reply to her letters, she left the care of John Butler Yeats's grave site to biographer William

Murphy, having unrealistically decided that George 'never had very much liking for the father of her husband she has no interest in looking after the grave plot and monument'.[117] Foster would not know how ill George was herself; in 1963 she too landed in Portobello. One Sunday afternoon in late March when Anne was fortunately with her the ulcer perforated; an ambulance took her to Adelaide Hospital where her doctor, Maurice O'Connell, managed to rescue her. 'She is at last starting to make progress after a horrid time,' Anne wrote to O'Connor who had sent flowers,

not only did her ulcer perforate but she somehow acquired in the hospital a very badly poisoned right arm and congestion of her right lung, she had also nine pints of blood (I think she is rather glad they left her one pint of her own blood!!) These last two days or so she is much more herself though not up to receiving visitors yet (at least they wont let visitors except Michael & I, go in to her). She is now back in Portobello nursing home and much prefers it, the five other occupants of the Adelaide ward were either deaf or dotty or both, and one of them chattered all night with sketches from Revelations and other thrilling Scriptural books!!! and as she couldnt see any of them since they were behind curtains, they probably became rather nightmarish disembodied voices in the half dark!

It was another week before George herself could scribble a note to Tom, thanking him for his flowers and assuring him that 'number 2 lung is much better today'. She signed the card 'Georgie'.[118]

For the final stage of recuperation Anne took her mother to the Country Club in Portmarnock for a week or two, where to George's delight they were put in a small cottage separate from the main hotel, just a few yards from the beach. George was well enough to listen to the Grand National at Easter, which she claimed an outsider horse always won. (She always bet half a crown each way in the three big Irish races, selecting her horse by opening the Bible at random. Once the pin landed on the Song of Solomon, and something similar to 'Royal Sovereign' won; another time it landed on the phrase 'they shall stumble and fall', and a horse did.[119]) Shortly afterwards, Norah McGuinness loaned them her cottage in Bray, where they went for several weeks with George's cat Pluto, 'the yellow peril'. Norah was horrified when she learned that, after lunch in town, they used to deposit their parcels at the hotel while they played the slot machines on the pier. On her return to Palmerston Road George wrote a brief note to Anne, 'It occurred to me you might be short of money so I send £3. Arrived home safely—lolling in bed——Hope you & Pluto are on speaking terms. I am in *no* hurry to have him back—!!! . . . A great many thanks for all your kindness—Bloody to be so crippled.'[120]

In 1965 George had two unexpected visitors. One was her cousin Kim Ridley, daughter of George Woodmass, with whom she had tea in the Hibernian in April. Beyond a reference to this 'surprising cousin', nothing else was recorded. The other was much more memorable. On 4 February a memorial service for Eliot was held at Westminster Abbey, and to everyone's surprise Ezra Pound travelled from Italy to be present. With 'Old Possum's' departure, Ezra felt even more bereft – 'Who is there now for me to share a joke with?'[121] He answered the question himself by abruptly announcing to Olga Rudge that he wished to fly to Dublin before going home. Once they arrived at the Hibernian, Olga phoned George; although the call came at 3 p.m., for some reason George answered the telephone and, after alerting Anne, took a taxi to the hotel. The two old friends were sitting there when Anne arrived; neither said a word, but she could feel the affection between them. When George asked him if he would like to meet some of the younger Irish poets, Ezra uttered the one word 'No'. George excused herself briefly and, after a few fruitless attempts at conversation, Anne too fell silent. Then her mother returned and 'the curious meeting continued'. Finally photographers emerged, and then Olga Rudge entered to take Pound away. He left Ireland the next morning; they never communicated again.[122] Ezra lived on until 1972, only a few ripples disturbing his pool of silence; just a little over a year later, Dorothy, who had been living near Omar and his family in England, followed him.

POSTLUDE: ODYSSEYS

For close to thirty years Thoor Ballylee remained deserted except for occasional visiting cattle and the nesting crows George had once desired. Seekers would return to Palmerston Road and tactlessly describe the state of disrepair; usually George concealed her distress, commenting only, 'That's the way we found it. It's come full cycle.'[1] Michael and Gráinne on their annual journeys to the west would stop by and lament that they would never be able to rescue it; once they were amazed to find 'a very large horse carriage' ingeniously stored on the ground floor.[2] As the years went by, doors and windows were open to the elements, furniture disappeared, and even stones from the parapet had been thrown into the river. Then in August 1960 George received a letter from the secretary of the Galway Council; could they have her permission to recommend the castle be restored as a National Monument? The campaign which had been initiated by Mary Hanley of Limerick and the local Kiltartan Society resulted in a complete restoration, costing the Irish Tourist Board £10,000. At the same time the Department of External Affairs turned its attention to cleaning up Coole Park, now bereft of house and gardens. During the lengthy reconstruction process, Michael brought over to his mother lists of questions from the architects enquiring about the original Ballylee furniture, colour of paint, floor coverings; George answered them all, but, true to her oath to the Order, never revealed the reasoning behind the remarkable ceiling in the upper room. One of the visitors to the restored tower was Edith Shackleton Heald; she and her companion were allowed to take their picnic tea 'in WB's favourite room overlooking the river'. There is no record of her visiting Palmerston Road on her way to the west.[3]

George attended the opening of the new Abbey Theatre in September 1963, and on the same day Anne's third one-woman show at the Dawson Gallery (her first since 1948). Conscious that Anne and Michael were busy with their own careers, as long as she could she had protected them from the demands of 'the Yeats industry'; she never for example even spoke of her own work with the publishers. By now Anne was travelling more both as an exhibitor and with sketchbook in hand; as early as 1951 Michael had entered the Senate where he served until 1954, returning there in 1961. Increasingly, however, seekers were turning to Michael when George would not answer their letters, and as she became more reclusive he was dealing with many of her financial affairs. (To be fair, she was becoming more and more subject to audacious requests, like the one from an insistent American entrepreneur who wanted to buy 46 Palmerston Road, dismantle it, and transport it to the United States; George acidly remarked that not only had WBY never lived there, the house was only rented.) With the centenary celebrations of Yeats's birth spawning an increasing number of critical studies and seekers and with their mother's increasing ill health, Michael took on even more responsibilities, including attendance at such events as the annual Summer School. Anne, who was travelling in Italy, wrote in April 1965, 'I'm sorry you're plagued by centenarians and am very glad Michael has the formula by now, I'm afraid he has to lunch on it with me in Sicily and you "unwell" but I expect he takes it in his stride, that's where the public training should be a help to him.'[4] That May Michael formally presented Yeats's Nobel medal 'on indefinite loan' to the Sligo Museum.[5] However Anne was back in time to join Michael and Gráinne at a special service in Drumcliffe on WBY's actual birthday, 13 June.

Of the various centenary celebrations George wrote, 'About the only thing that really pleases me is that Radio Eireann is going to broadcast the service at Drumcliffe next Sunday. That, I think, would *really* please WBY.'[6] What else would have pleased her, although she never spoke of it, was the oration at the graveside. George, who had never forgotten Jack's prohibition at the time of Yeats's reburial, insisted that this be given by Frank O'Connor, who drew on his own experience for his remarks:

Another thing he would have wished me to do—and which I must do since none of the eminent people who have written of him in his centenary year has done so—is to say how much he owed to the young Englishwoman he married, and who made possible the enormous development of his genius from 1916 onward. This should be said by someone who was closer to them both than I was, but it was obvious even to a casual acquaintance. It is not too much to say that if Yeats had not married, or indeed, if he had married someone else, that the story of his later work would probably have been very different. In many ways he was a most fortunate man; fortunate in his parentage, because it is not every poet who has a genius for father, and most fortunate in his marriage . . . For a long time before Yeats' marriage he withdrew gradually from Ireland and the Irish theatre to their great loss, but even that hurt he learned to ignore if not to forget. In this again, I think, we in Ireland may owe a debt to Mrs Yeats.[7]

Nine months later 'Michael/Frank' too was dead; they had renewed their friendship on his return to Ireland with his new wife and baby (which, George observed, 'had the head of a curate'). Her encouragement and wise counsel supported him at a time when he desperately needed it.[8]

Now no longer able to travel herself, George gained much pleasure from the long newsy letters Anne sent back to Ireland; interestingly, she wanted picture postcards of people and places, rather than the works of art she had herself collected. 'I've had a sort of feeling that Yugoslavia was not being as good value —possibly because no people to chat with. . . . Don't forget to send me some picture postcards of Dubrovnik within the city walls!'[9] In turn, she kept Anne aware of what was happening at home, news of the elections, strikes, her own activities. Dublin continued to struggle with the effects of local politics:

Very many thanks for two boxes chocs. which arrived this morning!! Beautifully packed & no customs trouble . . . As usual we have strikes. Once again the dustbins remain uncollected. The strike is un-official in Corporation Sewage department—But dustmen do not cross pickets . . . The gardener, who is here today because last Tuesday was wet—wanted to bring in the bins. Told him firmly that bins are in my private garden & no one is entitled to object! As usual the Corporation asks people to bury or/and burn contents. What do they suppose people living in flats are to do? The ESB also again un-official threaten strike but this has been postponed until Saturday.

Nothing much happening here—the gardener does not think much of our incinerating plan. He 'had a drum' which he would give us. This morning at 8.15 I heard a noise in the garden & on looking out I saw immense drum painted dark green being put through the garden gate—left on its side. No gardener. Later I saw this [drawing of cat tail going in] later again [drawing of cat tail emerging].[10]

As she had been with Willy, she was still the practical organizer:

Wonderful letter from ERICE!! . . . It sounds wonderful, anyway something you will never forget. And you must have learnt a lot of Sicilio-Italiano. I imagine you were the first Irish person ever to go to Erice—so perhaps you are a memory forever to them also! How dull you will find it when you [get] back to Dublin. According to my diary you leave Palermo on May 10 & arrive in London on Wednesday May 12. Did you remember to take Irish cheque or chequebook with you so that you can cash with Watt??!! If you did NOT PLEASE LET ME KNOW at once and I will send Watt a cheque which he will cash for you or give you an open cheque which you can cash at his Bank—In other words you could then blow off some steam in London and come back to Dublin less FLAT. Dublin is packed with 450 members of Interparliamentary groups.—coloured & magnificently dressed. At the same moment the Dail elected Lemass as Taoiseach—Dillon resigned as leader of Fine Gael Party on he says age—he is 62 but is actually rather ill I think. Liam Cosgrave now leader of Fine Gael. As you see everything is as usual & Pluto & I are very well thank you.[11]

Always an avid reader, George delighted in the human adventure. 'Spent all last night reading Con Curran's "Joyce Remembered"—Result, very sleepy this morning and annoyed I have to look after the gardener until 2 p.m. when I can read again,' she wrote while Anne was in Yugoslavia.[12] And during the same period, 'Did I tell you I have got Françoise Gillot's "Picasso"—Most of it will be easier for you to understand than it is for me—technical details about lithograph working etc—v. interesting to me but you will know all about it & possibly not find it so interesting.' A fortnight later the autobiography of this artist's wife—so different from herself—continued to intrigue her:

Postcard today from Agrigento—Wed. 21st—One of the best. Most Sicilian postcards are very hideous—Did you get a 'cutting' from me about the 30 French authors & artists who want Gillot book banned? Personally I feel that the end of her book when she describes returning to Vallaures & finds all her things have been removed one of the most unpleasant revelations of her own character—However, when you return & read the book you can tell me what you think about it. Most annoying you were away when I got it & I could not blow off. I do feel there is a great deal of exciting material. I believe Picasso himself has been trying to get book banned. This may or may not be true. Anyway I long for you to get home & read book & tell me what you think about it. As you see, I have no contact with any person who can argue about it with me.[13]

When Anne was home, she regularly brought back from the library novels and detective stories for her mother, but perhaps what appealed to George most in the last years were stories of exploration—in Tibet, or in the tracks of Odysseus. As early as 1949 Ellmann had sent her Henri Michaux's evocative *A Barbarian in Asia*, which had been translated by her old acquaintance Sylvia Beach.[14] It was a perceptive gift, for George had much in common with the Belgian poet and painter, especially his dislocating and allegorical methods and strikingly independent, original vision; even his alter ego 'Monsieur Plume' had a pathos like that of the Chaplin movies she used to enjoy.[15] But the odyssey which caused greatest excitement was Yuri Gagarin's flight into space in 1961, the account of which she avidly listened to on Willy's old radio. Later she bought a book about that too.[16]

Sometime during the first decade of her widowhood George had embarked on a new spiritual odyssey herself. In 1951 a book on clairvoyance, telepathy, and precognition was issued in London; she was sufficiently intrigued to preserve the publisher's announcement.[17] But from the early 1940s she was also exploring new directions. When Grace Jaffe visited in 1954, George admitted that she had seriously considered becoming a Roman Catholic like her cousin. She could, she jokingly told Grace, 'even accept the idea that the Blessed Virgin Mary "went up to Heaven with all her clothes on" ', but she could not tolerate 'the run-of-the-mill Irish priests who went "scuttling over" the Irish landscape in their black clothes'.[18] The memory was too vivid even after forty years—Father Walsh sitting stolidly in his seat while George and the driver opened stone walls in an effort to make their way across the fields with her sick child. Grace had already heard of George's flirtation with Roman Catholicism from Harold, himself often addicted with what he called 'Roman fever'; one of Gwynne's sisters was a cloistered Anglican nun, another a Roman Catholic nun. George may have confided in her brother on her visit to Watchet earlier that year, or when Harold visited Dublin in 1951; Harold was in fact under the impression that she had indeed converted. Certainly she came very close to doing so.

Perhaps Tom MacGreevy, a devout Catholic, was responsible. But more likely another influence was Elizabeth ('Betty') Rivers, who had become a close friend while they worked together with O'Connor over her publications with Cuala.[19] Rivers, who had lived on Inis Mór for a number of years before the war, moved in 1946 from London to Dublin, where she worked with stained-glass artist Evie Hone until the latter's death in 1955. Both women were fervent converts to Roman Catholicism, and evidently both were sufficiently close to George to discuss spiritual matters. As early as 1943 Evie wrote from her sister's country house in Galway,

My dear George When I said I wanted to give you a book I had in mind one which is apparently out of print. I thought you might like things in it and if you didn't you could change it, now my little plan is frustrated so the next best thing I can do is to send you this delapidated copy of mine. I hope you won't mind its bedraggled cover, you cannot change it but you need not read it unless you find it attracted you. I know you will like the reproduction any way, one of my favourite windows in Chartres. . . . With love Yrs Evie

George preserved the letter in *Ancient Devotions for Holy Communion from Eastern & Western Liturgical Services*. Other books in her library that were probably influenced by Evie are *The Roman Missal in Latin and English for Every Day in the Year*, *The Catechism Simply Explained*, and *Progress through Mental Prayer*.[20] Whether Evie, a loyal friend (and cousin of Joseph Hone), ever managed to persuade George to accompany her to mass or a conference with her priest we will never know. However, after Evie's death in 1955 conversion seems no longer to have been a serious consideration. 'Lunched with Betty yesterday,' George wrote to Anne in 1963. 'Nice, but too long. No stimulus to my imagination, nor do I think I probably was to hers.'[21] Within a year Elizabeth Rivers was also dead. But through her last years a brightly coloured gouache by Evie Hone, 'Our Lady Queen of Peace', remained propped up on the mantelpiece in George's bedroom. The parallel between this search shortly after Willy's death and the turn to spiritualism after her father's is suggestive. Four years later, in March 1967, she lost one more link with the past when Tom MacGreevy died.

By the time the new Peacock Theatre was opened in July of that year, George was not well enough to attend and sent her invitation to me so that I might accompany Anne.[22] But nothing would prevent her from being present two months later, although in a wheelchair, at the unveiling of the Yeats Memorial in St Stephen's Green of Henry Moore's massive sculpture *Knife Edge*. The ceremony included readings from Yeats's poetry by Austin Clarke and two young poets, Eavan Boland and Brendan Kennelly; did she also overhear the Dubliner who muttered as the Taoiseach pulled back the drapery, 'Doesn't look a bit like him'?[23] Later at a dinner in honour of the sculptor, Anne watched as George talked to Moore, who was charmed by the detailed description she gave of an exhibition she had

seen of his work. A few days later she wrote to Sybil LeBrocquy, one of the moving forces behind the committee, 'I cannot remember how many years it is since I
was sent a "Hallowe'en" present. How very charming & kind of you! So *many*
thanks. All Souls Night was one of the very few dates WBY used to remember and
this year I was thinking about that, & his poem, mainly because the date of the
unveiling of Henry Moore's evocative, beautiful, statuary. I am deeply grateful
to the Memorial Committee and to yourself that Stephens Green has this knife
edge for ever.'[24] Moore's great statue still stands overlooking the Green; another
of Sybil's projects was not so fortunate. Less than a year later a bust of Yeats by
Albert Power was unveiled at Sandymount Green, near the poet's birthplace; this
time George was unable to attend, but the family was represented by Anne and
Michael, and Yeats's poetry was read by Oliver Edwards. Less than three weeks
later the heavy bust was found by a local resident in the roadway in Sandymount,
having been mysteriously removed from its seven-foot-high plinth.[25]

George gradually closed off all the upstairs rooms at Palmerston Road except
for Anne's, and slept in the sitting room. Ever since her ulcer had perforated,
Michael and Anne had been trying to persuade her to move into a flat, where Anne
was prepared to join her. 'It is splendid to think that Dobbs . . . will not for
much longer have to climb up, and down, all those steps at 46, Palmerston Road,'
Harold wrote when hearing of the plan. 'Personally, even in 1948, I found them
wearisome. When you move get a flat with a lift.'[26] But neither a burglary nor
even dry rot and its messy treatment (twice, in 1963 and 1968) would persuade
George. She kept saying, 'I'll let you know on my birthday.' On the morning of her
birthday she told Anne to look out of the window, where the vegetable garden had
been put into grass; her daughter realized then that George would never move.

On 16 October 1967 Anne joined her for lunch at the Hibernian Hotel and
stayed at Palmerston Road for the night to celebrate her mother's 75th birthday. George had outlived almost all her close friends and her physical world
had narrowed to a few visitors. Now that Michael had moved to Dalkey, she did
not see as much of the grandchildren; besides, her increasing deafness made it
difficult for her to follow the multiple noisy, excited discussions (mainly in Irish)
around the Yeatses' table. 'You know what it would be like to lunch voiceless
in that house!!!!' she once wrote to Anne when a cold prevented her from going
there for Easter lunch.[27] Instead, Michael and Gráinne took her out for quieter
meals. 'Michael & Grainne lunched with me last Friday. I overate, tempted by
G. wanting salmon—neither of them wanted steak—result of USA I suppose.
I took down your typed itinerary which M enjoyed.'[28]

Increasingly Michael was looking after George's financial affairs and the
'Yeats industry'; the literary agent tended to send questions to him so as to give his
mother 'the least trouble'.[29] Besides, a reply, although indirect, was then more
likely.

I had nothing whatsoever to do with the choice of poets or poems included in the 'Oxford Book of Modern Verse'—My only connection was that I typed letters dictated to me by WBY, and collected dates of authors' birth. (signed) George Yeats Put the above into clear language! Please use my phrase 'poets or poems'.
Clifford Bax (Arnold Bax's brother) was the first person to say all over London that WBY had not made the selection himself—(He was *not* included!)
I return the damn correspondance [*sic*].[30]

George never did like answering letters; after her death Michael found almost 200 unopened, many with uncashed cheques. But he too was travelling more. 'Michael popped in on Friday—not for anything—just a visit. He & Grainne go to U.S.A. in October and expect to be back for Christmas. He asked me about travelling a HARP in U.S.A. How could I know—I ask you!! My own feeling if I were travelling a Harp on trains would be to play it to the Negro conductors (and in my day all the conductors were negroes) and they would all do everything— especially if song accompanied the Harp.'[31]

By 1967 Caitríona was also away, studying music in Holland. She dutifully sent letters to her grandmother, who always made a point of inviting her to lunch alone on her visits home. The family now spent summers at their cottage in Carraroe, from where Síle sent news to her godmother. 'Many thanks for your letter,' George replied.

I imagine you are safely back at Cliff House with all the 'Junk'—! Did Michael come down to help move all the livestock (including Grannie, Padraig & yourself . . . !) Or did he stay safely at Cliff House? Your grandfather always hid when I was moving to Ballylee with the 'Junk' prams, bicycles, dog, cat, canaries, sheets, curtains, books (WBY's) 2 children, groceries, house & garden tools—
    Did you learn to bicycle easily or did you fall off a lot as A & M did at first.
    I have been taking cuttings of the Busy Lizzie Grainne gave me last year—one is doing v. well & have hopes of 6 others. Love to all Gramma[32]

Now the whole family gathered at Palmerston Road for Christmas, where there would be a great heap of brightly coloured gifts on the sideboard; the children played with their gifts while the adults sat around George's daybed. Síle always had a long tube of smarties which she invariably opened at the wrong end and spilled over the floor. But despite her increasing physical suffering, George never lost her sense of humour; after one festivity Anne received the following doggerel:

> Of Turkey young
>   and turkey old,
> Turkey hot
>   and turkey cold,
> Of turkey tender
>   turkey tough,
> I thank thee Lord
>   I've had enough[33]

Anne's six-week journey to Yugoslavia, Albania, and Greece in the spring of 1968 was suggested by George 'to tell her what it was like', but really because she thought her daughter depressed and once more facing a creative block. On such occasions she would encourage Anne to go off and enjoy herself, or 'wave a wild tail' (much stronger than 'prancing'). While Anne was away her mother was enjoying Adrian Mitchell's second book of poems. 'This should be sung to the Summer Sligo school,' she wrote:

> My girl Kate's teaching in the States,
> Lecturing from town to town,
> Pays her bills by, gets her thrills by
> Studying the influence of Yeats on Yeats
> (Chorus)
> What's wrong with that?
> What's wrong with that?
> That's what she always wanted to be.
> What's wrong with that?
> If it makes her happy,
> If it keeps her happy,
> That's all that should matter to me.

The influence of Yeats on Yeats—a nice new theme for all the seekers!!!
I read the book after a most melancholy day—Austin Clarke's new book of reminiscent miasma—I look forward to some booming & drum accompaniment from you![34]

It was the last letter Anne ever got from her. On her return to Ireland she realized her mother was very ill, and watched her covertly checking her own pulse rate. Still, that summer George persevered with the daily tasks—writing the order book for Cuala (one to John Keohane on 15 August), discussing with Molly Gill the cards and broadsheets to be hand coloured. She listened to radio broadcasts describing the invasion of Prague by Russia. On the 20th she wrote to the Japanese scholar Oshima, who had visited them so many years before, arranging to meet him for tea at the Hibernian; but this appointment she could not keep. On Wednesday, 21 August, Anne had lunch with her as usual, but left knowing that her mother, seriously unwell, could no longer live alone; at her urging George promised to see the doctor before the end of the month. Depressed at the thought of having to move back to Palmerston Road, Anne fought a migraine for three days as she tried to visualize how she could live and work—move into Michael's old room and use her own down the hall as a studio? She tried to call George on Friday morning at the usual hour of 10, but her mother did not answer. Then suddenly the migraine pain lifted about 3 p.m. That afternoon Molly Gill went upstairs as usual to collect her weekly salary, to find George dead on the sitting room sofa. On 23 August 1968 her heart had at last failed her.[35]

Unsentimental, private, and determinedly independent to the end, George died as she may have wished—alone and true to her Golden Dawn motto, 'Let Nobody Know'. It was almost as if she had waited for the appropriate time—Michael, with the family in Carraroe, had celebrated his forty-seventh birthday on 22 August; Anne was painting again. Below, the weather was cool and cloudy, but dry. Above, the transiting Sun was conjunct her midheaven—always a fortunate event, and her progressed Moon was nearing its cyclical return to her natal conjunction of Pluto and Neptune—signifying a period of profound change, last reached in the year after Willy died.[36] For her, death was not an ending but a portal—it was after all only a change of state, a beginning on the journey towards reincarnation.

But first, there was the journey to Drumcliffe. After a funeral service on Monday, 26 August, in Holy Trinity Church, Rathmines, the procession to Sligo began. With the remaining Yeatses were William and Harriet Murphy, who drove the two cars. Instead of the dinner party they had planned so that Bill, who was at work on his magisterial biography of JBY, could finally meet George, they attended her funeral. Arriving in Sligo about 2 p.m., they were met by the Mayor and other dignitaries who walked with Michael through the town. At Drumcliffe churchyard a coachload of tourists waited, jockeying for position beside her husband's famous tombstone; the children had to force their way through to be by their grandmother's casket as it was lowered into the common grave.[37] For weeks afterwards Anne was cold, as she had been after her father's death, but woke up each morning feeling comforted. Only then did she receive the letter George had written her in March 1939, with its statement of faith: 'I have brought you up, as I believe, with a sense of freedom . . . and I do not want either you or Michael to lose the sense of truth because external circumstances, however difficult, make it. It is really one of the few things that matter.'[38]

In 1969 Anne moved to Dalkey, only yards away from brother Michael, who was by then Cathaoírleach (Chairman) of the Senate. Molly Gill retired, but with the help of Liam Miller and poet Tom Kinsella Anne and Michael revived the Cuala Press to publish further Yeats manuscripts and the work of other poets; only then was a man—a male printer—employed.[39] Six years later Michael was Vice-President of the European Parliament and Anne was enjoying a series of exhibitions around the world.

In 1986 a family of pine martens, the rarest mammal in the British Isles, was discovered nesting in the thatch of Ballylee; today there are baby hawks in the stares' nest. Perhaps none of this would surprise George—not even that, only eleven months after her death, a man walked on the moon.

The link must never be broken. . . . the only importance is <u>not to break the</u> <u>link</u> unless <u>you are true as far as</u> you can you break the link[40]

Appendix

The Death of William Gilbert Hyde Lees

On 18 November 1909 Georgie's father William Gilbert Hyde Lees died at 18 Denbigh Street; his son Harold registered the death on 22 November. The death certificate gave as cause of death 'chronic stenosis of the Larynx' precipitated by 'acute Laryngitis syncope'. But even then there was confusion, for the solicitors' notice to creditors speaks of him as 'late of 145 Merton Road Wimbledon' which is the address of a Dr Bayfield.[1]

Gilbert Hyde Lees's will, dated 23 December 1908, offers a different address still, for apparently at that time he was a patient in a private nursing home for alcoholics run by Mr and Mrs Haydn Dadson:

THIS IS THE LAST WILL AND TESTAMENT of me WILLIAM GILBERT HYDE LEES at present residing at Highshot House East Twickenham in the county of Middlesex gentleman I hereby revoke all former wills made by me and appoint Eric Percy Hill Clerk in the Bank of England sole EXECUTOR and TRUSTEE hereof I bequeath to my son Harold Montagu Hyde Lees all my jewellery family portraits and any of my books that he may choose also my cabinet made out of the boat in which I rowed for Wadham College Oxford and all my private papers which papers I require him to keep in a place of absolute safety

In exercise of the power or powers of appointment amongst my children reserved to or vested in me by will settlement or other document or documents I hereby devise and bequeath all the real and personal estate which shall be subject to the trusts under which the said power of appointment is exercisable as to two equal third parts thereof to my son the said Harold Montagu Hyde Lees and as to the remaining one equal third part thereof to my daughter Bertha George Hyde Lees I give devise and bequeath all the rest residue and remainder of my real and personal estate wheresoever and whatsoever to Arthur Tolfrey Christie now residing at 6 Fawcett Street Fulham Road London absolutely but in the event of the said Arthur Tolfrey Christie predeceasing me than I give devise and bequeath all the said residue of my real and personal estate to my said two children in equal shares but if either of my said two children should die in my lifetime without leaving issue living at my death then I give the share of the child so dying to the other of them or his or her issue living at my death

IN WITNESS whereof I have hereunto set my hand this twenty third day of December one thousand nine hundred and eight W. G. HYDE LEES signed by the above named William Gilbert Hyde Lees as his last will in the presence of us both present at the same time who in his presence at his request and in the presence of each other have hereunto subscribed our names as witnesses

GEORGE P. WALSH clerk to Messrs Head & Hill Solrs 3 Raymond Buildings Grays Inn WC

GEORGE J. TANSLEY clerk to Messrs Head & Hill Solrs 3 Raymond Bldgs Grays Inn WC.

Arthur Tolfrey Christie (1879–1958), by then living in York House, Finborough Road, was granted probate on 18 January 1910; the gross value of the estate was £845 6s. 1d.[2] Little is known of Christie; there is no further suggestion of any close friendship with Hyde Lees and Christie himself soon returned to his native Australia, where he wandered from one rooming house to another, only casually employed throughout a long, unhappy life which ended in a mental hospital. Since there is some evidence of his having a nervous breakdown about 1910, it could be that he too was a patient at Highshot House; or, having served briefly in the Boer War, he and Hyde Lees may have been drinking companions in one of the officers' London clubs.[3] Without any further evidence, William Gilbert Hyde Lees's choice of residuary legatee seems to have been yet another quixotic gesture in an impulsive life.

Abbreviations

The letters and manuscripts of WBY are scattered, sometimes with duplications in different venues; I have identified the places in which I saw the material as quoted, or both places where there is a discrepancy. In the case of multiple references in one note, the order follows the order of quotation in the text. Unless indicated otherwise, when no source is given, the materials were read while in the possession of the Yeats family.

The following abbreviations have been adopted for frequently recurring names of publications, places, and people. Otherwise, for printed sources the usual convention has been adopted of a full citation in the first instance, followed by a recognizable shortened form. Manuscripts are cited by location, and in the case of TCD, NLI, Harvard, ULL, and BL, a call-number is given.

AY	Anne Yeats
Berg	Berg Collections of English and American Literature, The New York Public Library, Astor, Lenox, and Tilden Foundations
BL	British Library Manuscripts Division
Boston College	Yeats Collection, Burns Library, Boston College
Boston University	Special Collections, Boston University
Bryn Mawr	Laurence Housman Collection, Seymor Adelman Collection, Bryn Mawr College Library
Bucknell	Ellen Clarke Bertrand Library, Bucknell University
Delaware	W. B. Yeats Collection, University of Delaware Library, Newark, Delaware
Dorothy	Dorothy Pound, née Shakespear
ECY	Elizabeth Corbet Yeats ('Lolly')
Emory	W. B. Yeats Collection, Special Collections, Robert W. Woodruff Library, Emory University
EPDS	Omar Pound and A. Walton Litz (eds.), *Ezra Pound and Dorothy Shakespear their Letters: 1909–1914* (New York: New Directions, 1984)
Gregory	Augusta, Lady Gregory
GY	George (Bertha Georgie) Yeats, née Hyde Lees
Harvard	Houghton Library, Harvard University
Heald	Edith Shackleton Heald
Hobby	Diana Poteat Hobby, 'William Butler Yeats and Edmund Dulac. A Correspondence: 1916–1938' (Ph.D. dissertation, Rice University, 1981)

HRHRC	Harry Ransom Humanities Research Centre, University of Texas at Austin
Huntington	The Huntington Library, San Marino, California
Indiana	The Lilly Library, Indiana University, Bloomington, Indiana
JackBY	Jack Butler Yeats
JBY	John Butler Yeats
JK	collection John Kelly
Kansas	Kenneth Spencer Research Library, University of Kansas Libraries, Lawrence
Lily	Susan Mary Yeats
LTWBY i and ii	Richard R. Finneran, George Mills Harper, and William M. Murphy (eds.), *Letters to W. B. Yeats*, 2 vols. (London: Macmillan, 1977)
MacGreevy	Thomas MacGreevy, formerly McGreevy
MBY	Michael Butler Yeats
Mills	F. W. Olin Library, Mills College, Oakland, California
MYV i, ii	George Harper, *The Making of Yeats's 'A Vision'*, 2 vols. (Carbondale, Ill.: University of Southern Illinois Press, 1987)
Nelly	Edith Ellen Hyde-Lees, née Woodmass, later Mrs Henry T. Tucker
North Carolina	Wilson Library, University of North Carolina at Chapel Hill
NYPL	John Quinn Memorial Collection, Manuscripts and Archives Division, The New York Public Library
Pound	Ezra Pound
Queen's	Queen's University Archives, Queen's University, Kingston, Ontario
Quinn	John Quinn, New York
R L-P	Ruth Lane-Poole, née Pollexfen, formerly Lily's ward
Robinson	Lennox Robinson, playwright (later married to Dolly Travers Smith)
Shakespear	Olivia Shakespear, née Tucker
Sligo	Sligo County Public Library
Southern Illinois	Lennox Robinson Papers, Special Collections, Morris Library, Southern Illinois University at Carbondale
Stanford	MO273, The James A. Healy Collection in Irish Literature, Department of Special Collections, Stanford University Libraries
Stony Brook	William Butler Yeats Microfilmed Manuscripts Collection, Special Collections Department, Library, State University of New York at Stony Brook
TCD	Trinity College, Dublin
Toronto	Thomas Fisher Rare Books and Manuscript Collection, University of Toronto
Tulsa	Richard Ellmann Papers, The University of Tulsa
UCD	University College Dublin Library

ULL	Thomas Sturge Moore Papers, University of London Library
Wade	*The Letters of W. B. Yeats*, cd. Allan Wade (London: Macmillan, 1954)
Washington	Babette Deutsch Papers, Washington University Libraries, Department of Special Collections
Wellesley	Wellesley College Library, Special Collections
WMM	collection William M. Murphy
YA 1 . . .	*Yeats Annual* (London: Macmillan, 1982–) followed by number and date (nos. 1 and 2 edited by Richard Finneran; from no. 3 (1985) edited by Warwick Gould)
YAACTS II . . .	*Yeats: An Annual of Critical and Textual Studies*, ed. Richard Finneran (1983– , various publishers), cited by number and date
Yale	Beinecke Rare Book and Manuscript Library, Yale University
YL	Yeats Library, books belonging to GY and WBY formerly in possession of the late AY
YVP i, ii, iii	*Yeats's Vision Papers*, ed. George Mills Harper et al., 3 vols. (Iowa City: University of Iowa Press, 1992)

Notes

INTRODUCTION

1. GY to Oliver Edwards, 2 Feb. 1941, NLI MS 27,032.

PRELUDE: BALLYLEE

1. Automatic script, 28 and 31 Oct. 1918, 3 May and 15 Sept. 1919, *YVP* ii. 102, 108, 279, 427.
2. 'To Be Carved on a Stone at Thoor Ballylee' (1918).
3. WBY to Pound, 19 Sept. 1918, Yale.
4. I have drawn on various sources for this description of Ballylee, including WBY's correspondence, Gregory's Journals, memories of AY and MBY, GY's answers to a 1963 questionnaire on furnishings and fittings, the research of Sister de Lourdes Fahy, an unpublished typescript by Oliver Edwards, and ordnance maps of the area.
5. I have no doubt the 'friend of mine' WBY speaks of was GY at Ballylee; possibly the incident is related to a 'drain like excavation' found in June 1919, WBY, introduction discussing 'timeless individuality' in *Words upon the Window-Pane, The Variorum Edition of the Plays of W. B. Yeats*, ed. Russell K. Alspach, assisted by Catherine C. Alspach (London: Macmillan, 1966), 970; *YVP* ii. 317.
6. The Yeatses at various times took colour symbolism from Blake, the Order of the Golden Dawn, and George's automatic script.
7. Passages are adapted from GY's and WBY's own words, with footnotes identifying the source. GY to MacGreevy [?2 Aug.] 1923, TCD MS 8104.
8. WBY to Gregory, 6 Dec. 1919, Berg.
9. GY to MacGreevy, 31 Dec. 1926, TCD MS 8104.
10. 'Black Eagle' was the symbolic name given in the automatic script to the 'fourth daimon', their son Michael.
11. WBY to Pound, July 1919, Yale.
12. GY to MacGreevy, 2 Aug. 1923, TCD MS 8104.
13. WBY to Gregory, 27 Sept. 1920 ('Some New Letters from W. B. Yeats to Lady Gregory', ed. Donald T. Torchiana and Glenn O'Malley, *Review of English Literature*, 6/3 (July 1963), 45–6).
14. GY to MacGreevy, 31 Dec. 1926, TCD MS 8104.

PART I: PROGRESSIONS

CHAPTER 1: ANCESTRY

1. A horoscope cast by GY in the 1920s refers to her grandfather as 'Frederick Montagu'.

2. Her husband, referred to scathingly by the commentator 'Junius' as the parasitical 'cream coloured Bradshaw', was Secretary to the Treasury under the Duke of Grafton and in 1772 appointed one of the Lords of the Admiralty; he was allocated a suite of 'around no fewer than sixty rooms, just off the Haunted Gallery and known as the Haunted Gallery Lodgings' as a summer residence; a family memoir claims that his widow continued to reside in Hampton Court Palace.

3. *The Complete Peerage* (1926), 108.

4. I am grateful to Mrs Hilary Thomas for her assistance in tracking down public documents in order to create family trees.

5. 'Original Records of Early Expeditions in the Zermatt District', *Alpine Journal*, 32 (1918–19), 217.

6. A favourite saying of George ('Juddy') Andrew's; much of this information comes from R. E. Thelwall, *The Andrews and Compstall their Village* (Cheshire County Council and Marple Antiquarian Society, 1972); interviews with Grace Jaffe and AY.

7. Interview with AY; Lily to George, 16 Feb. 1924: 'Keep that receipt for egg flip in the family. It must not be lost. It is life-saving used with discretion, as a diet disastrous.' When she died in Dec. 1925 Agnes Steeds was living at Clonsilla House where she and her late husband had run the Castleknock Stud Farm in the north-west outskirts of Dublin.

8. I am indebted to Dr Grace Jaffe (née Spurway) for memories of her grandmother and cousins during three days of interviews in Oct. 1985; however she admitted that her memory for dates was suspect.

9. Thelwall, *The Andrews and Compstall their Village*, *passim*.

10. Speaking of his son's new wife, on 6 Nov. 1917 JBY reported to John Quinn that 'her father was educated at Eton and Oxford, and that her family own Gainsboroughs and Romneys, which all means money', WMM. In 1928 the portraits were loaned to the Birmingham Gallery by GY's uncle, and returned to him in Sept. 1938; a portrait by Lawrence is in the collection of the Hon. Society of Lincoln's Inn, information courtesy of Brendan Flynn, Curator (Paintings and Sculpture), Birmingham Museums and Art Gallery and the National Portrait Gallery.

11. Nelly to MacGreevy, [?21 Nov. 1926], TCD MS 8129.

12. Grace Jaffe.

13. These in turn were passed on to George Woodmass's daughter Barbara Reyntiens; I am grateful to Anthony Reyntiens for the opportunity to examine them.

14. Nelly to WBY, 29 Oct. 1921.

15. 'Funeral of Mrs Chapman: Striking Manifestation of Affection and Esteem' and 'Mrs Chapman's Noble Life', *Worthing Herald*, 2 Jan. 1926, 1, 11, 20.

16. Courtesy of the Revd Bidwell's grandson, Dr Anthony Bidwell.

17. Information from census records; I am grateful to Pauline and Andrew Rankine for a photograph of the house.

18. Her children always considered 16 Oct. her birthday; a book token from her brother is inscribed 'for 16 October 1955', and her stepfather's gift of a book on Dürer is dated 16 Oct. 1909.

19. Her 1914 astrology workbook includes a number of horoscopes including several for 17 Aug., gradually refining by the use of events and finally determining 16 Aug. at 8.25 a.m., MBY.

20. As given without further comment in the automatic script of 16 Sept. 1919 when the Yeatses were exploring Nelly's psychology; they may have some relation to another question in the script to do with the 'mediums persecution in matter of medical home', *YVP* ii. 430–1.

CHAPTER 2: CHILDHOOD

1. According to the Retail Price Index, figures from before the First World War must be multiplied by 35 to give the equivalent value in 1996.

2. John Montgomery, *1900: The End of an Era* (London: George Allen & Unwin, 1968); Alastair Service, *London 1900* (New York: Rizzoli International Publications, 1979).

3. WBY to Gregory, 29 Oct. 1917, Wade, 634; Helen Lawless to GY, 1 Feb. 1939.

4. Did Gilbert—or Nelly—own this property? The Kensington Directories from 1892 to 1919 consistently name John Joseph Kempster, surgeon dentist, as the chief resident, yet Willy and George Yeats were 'loaned' a flat at this address for a few days in 1918. I am grateful to Graham Buckley for his assistance.

5. Olivia Shakespear's initials appear on the same page, Wayne K. Chapman, 'Notes on the Yeats Library, 1904 and 1989', *YA* 8, 202.

6. Although Georgie's name does not appear in the school records still extant, it is noted that Lady Gregory's granddaughters Anne and Catherine would later attend the other Sister of Mercy school in Clewer, St Stephen's College 'for the children of gentlemen'.

7. Nelly to Dorothy Pound, 8 Nov. 1938, Yale.

8. GY to WBY, 16 Oct. 1931.

9. Eve Knight (comp.), *When You Look Back: A Collection of Letters Written to Children by Illustrious Persons* (London: Cobden-Sanderson, 1933), 62.

10. Richard Garnett in the *Sketch*, quoted in Rodney K. Engen, *Laurence Housman* (Stroud: Catalpa Press, 1983), 116. One critic shrewdly discovered 'Old Religion' in Housman's 'walk through Fairyland'.

11. Preface to *Gammer Gurton's Fairy Tales* (London: Moring, 1905).

12. Cf. the prancing 'golden king and silver lady' of WBY's 'Under the Round Tower' (1918).

13. Laurence Housman, *The Unexpected Years* (London: Jonathan Cape, 1937), 100.

14. 'I wonder sometimes if I have been unfaithful in my friendships; so many have come and gone, not through any active breach or loss of kind feeling, but from the fact that we have each become different people', ibid. 112.

15. Harold entered Eton in 1904 when he was 14, information courtesy P. R. Quarrie of Eton College Library.

16. Grace Jaffe, *Years of Grace* (Sunspot, N. Mex.: Iroquois Press, 1979), 15 and interview. Harold's sister-in-law thought that Georgie was 'very much her mother's favourite. Nelly was a nice woman, but she was not fond of Harold,' interview with Eleanor Younghughes, 1 Aug. 1985.

17. WBY to Gregory, 30 Dec. 1920, Berg; AY recalled her mother speaking nostalgically of a childhood in Florence.

18. A search of the divorce registry 1892–1911 yielded no trace of a decree absolute; there is no record of a separation agreement which in any case would have remained private.

19. Nelly to Laurence Housman, [?winter 1906], Bryn Mawr.

20. A history of the school and reminiscences by various students is included in *I Was There: St James's West Malvern*, arranged by Alice Baird, preface by Nancy (Maude) Campbell (Worcester: Littlebury & Co., 1956).

21. AY in 1974 radio interview with William Furlong (*Audio Arts* (Eo Ipso Ltd.), I, 4).

22. Probably the source of a statement WBY dictated to his wife in Nov. 1921, returning his correspondent's manuscript: 'my life is as busy as the life of a girl at school, there is something to be done in every part of day,' WBY to Miss Boylan, 24 Nov. 1921, Boston University, W. B. Yeats Archive.

23. WBY to F. P. Sturm, 17 June [1921]; Notebook 4, *YVP* iii. 19.

24. AY.

25. I am indebted to Ms Jennifer M. Rampton, registrar of Queens Gate School, and Mrs Irene Johnston for her memories as a student there.

26. Richard Ellmann interview notes with George Yeats, 8 Dec. 1946, Richard Ellmann Papers, The University of Tulsa.

27. Michael G. Reade to me, 30 July and 22 Aug. 1987.

28. J. H. Baker, *The Ipsden Country: The Home of Charles Reade* (Reading: Wm. Smith & Son, 1939).

29. See Appendix.

30. Rachel Grahame, 'The Search for Arthur', M.Litt. thesis (University of Sydney, 1996).

31. See Appendix.

32. Peter L. Petrachis, *Alcoholism: An Inherited Disease* (US Department of Health and Human Services, 1985); David Goldman, 'Genetic Studies on Alcoholism at the NIAAA Intramural Laboratories', *The Search for Inherited Links*, vol. 12/2 (Winter 1987/8) of *Alcohol Health and Research World* (National Institute on Alcohol Abuse and Alcoholism). According to D. W. Goodwin, 'Family Studies in Alcoholism', *Journal of Studies in Alcoholism*, 42/1 (1981), 156–62, there is a three- to fourfold increase in risk among both sons and daughters of alcohol-abusing fathers.

33. JBY to Rosa Butts, 20 Mar. 1920, WMM.

34. Migs Woodside, 'Children of Alcoholic Parents: Inherited and Psycho-Social Influences', *Journal of Psychiatric Treatment and Evaluation*, 5 (1983), 531–7: 'Some children may be overly controlled supercopers who are very successful until midlife when as adults, they may become ill or depressed. Others, in adulthood, may become alcoholic . . .' The 'Caretaker or Family Hero' 'feels inadequate, is unable to cope with failure or mistakes, views himself as responsible for everything and everyone and becomes a workaholic'.

35. Grace Jaffe on a photograph of her cousin; Dorothy Shakespear to Ezra Pound, 14 Sept. 1911, *EPDS*, 58.

36. 'a critical, though kindly older cousin, with a tremendous sense of humour', Jaffe, *Years of Grace*, 164.

37. When a professional astrologer mapped Georgie's progressions shortly after her marriage, a rectification was noted for Nov. 1909 when 'Father died suddenly'. The automatic script gives 'Nov 1909 "Finish" ' as one of Georgie's initiatory moments, second series; another reference in the script to 'Nov 23—glass door' may have something to do with his funeral service, *YVP* ii. 213.

38. Known as 'Oriental aldehyde dehydro genase', Goldman, 'Genetic Studies on Alcoholism'.

39. Nelly to MacGreevy, 5 Feb. 1929, TCD MS 8129.

40. Joseph Joachim (1831–1907); Rummel and other pianists regularly performed in the drawing rooms of friends: Olivia Shakespear could take up to eight or ten with crowding; Eva Fowler had much more room.

41. Nelly to MacGreevy, 21 Apr. 1929, TCD MS 8129.

42. YL, AY. Another book preserved by George was Valentin Scherer, *Dürer des Meisters: Gemälde Kupfer und Holzschnitte* (Stuttgart: 1908), inscribed 'To G H L on her XVIIth Birthday with best wishes from H. T. T' (Harry Tucker).

43. For much of the biographical information about Olivia Shakespear I am indebted to correspondence with John Harwood and his *Olivia Shakespear and W. B. Yeats: After Long Silence* (London: Macmillan 1989); he thinks Olivia and Willy may have met as early as 1898 (140), but I think that unlikely.

44. For example, she dismissed *The Love Letters of an Englishwoman*, published anonymously by Laurence Housman, later to become a friend, with 'The writer is a sentimentalist and a prig.'

45. On the morning of 21 Jan. 1917 there was a memorial service and unveiling of tablets at St Paul's Church, Compstall, to Kenny, John, and Robert, 'The beloved sons of Montagu Woodmass, Esquire and Mrs Woodmass (late of Compstall Hall) and great Grandsons of George Andrew, Esquire, founder of this Church and Village'; I have found no evidence that Montagu (who died on 2 Feb. 1917) or Edith Alice attended; George Woodmass probably represented the family.

46. Nelly to MacGreevy, 11 Mar. 1928, TCD MS 8129.

47. Interview with Grace Jaffe.

48. Probably 'Patience' or ordinary playing cards (Nelly was fond of bridge) rather than the Tarot pack, which at this time had been appropriated by serious occultists (although WBY also consulted Patience cards), Richard Cavendish, *The Tarot* (New York: Crescent Books, 1975) and Stuart R. Kaplan, *The Encyclopedia of Tarot*, vols. i–iii (New York: US Games Systems, 1978–90).

49. 'Psychometry, the reading of objects, or ultra-perception. The faculty of divining by touching a physical object, the character, surroundings and experiences of persons who have touched it', 'memory-divining', Geraldine Cummins, *Unseen Adventures* (London: Rider & Co., 1951), 42, 53.

50. Nelly to Laurence Housman, [?winter 1906], Bryn Mawr.

51. Interview with Grace Jaffe; in 1921 GY cast a horoscope for 9 Aug. 1910 which may have had something to do with these events, Stony Brook.

52. Interview with Grace Jaffe; Grace M. Jaffe, 'Vignettes', *YA* 5, 142–3, and Jaffe, *Years of Grace*, 16–17.
53. WBY to Gregory, 13 July 1921, Stony Brook.
54. Nelly to MacGreevy, 25 Apr. 1928, TCD MS 8129.
55. AY.
56. Erik Palmstierna, *Horizons of Immortality: A Quest for Reality* (London: Constable, 1937), 346–65; he wrote a number of books on occult subjects in the 1930s and 1940s.
57. Nelly to MacGreevy, 24 May 1934, TCD MS 8129.
58. Joseph Macleod, *The Sisters d'Aranyi* (London: Allen & Unwin, 1969), v. 279.
59. Eva Ducat, *Another Way of Music* (London: Chapman & Hall, 1928), 56.
60. WBY respected GY's knowledge of music even if he did not always follow her advice; cf. his notes to *The Great Clock Tower* (1934): 'My wife says "Had you heard Elena Gerhardt or Campbell McInnes or Gervase Elwes you would know that's all nonsense". "But I have heard so and so" I say "and so and so and their words although audible were more bloodless than veal". "O", my wife says, "if you think they can sing".'
61. London Archive Centre Acc.459 D. Misc.190 includes the guest list of the club; George wrote to MacGreevy from the club on Marylebone Road about July 1922.
62. Ducat rejected Peter Warlock's settings to some of WBY's poems.
63. WBY to Gregory, 23 Dec. 1916, Berg; Ducat was one of the witnesses to Helen Lawless's will in May 1934.
64. The ouija board is 'a sheet of cardboard on which the letters of the alphabet are printed. The automatists' fingers rest on a small heart-shaped piece of polished wood called a "traveller" or "pointer". This "traveller" glides lightly over the cardboard pointing to the letters spelling out messages,' Cummins, *Unseen Adventures*, 20. 'Table-tilting' or 'rapping' occurs when a number of people sit around with fingers lightly touching a small-legged table; brief answers to questions are spelled out by the number of times the table shakes or taps.
65. Shakespear to James G. Fairfax, 13 Aug. 1911 (Hugh Witemeyer, 'James Griffyth Fairfax and Ezra Pound in Edwardian London', *English Literary History*, 42/3 (1999), 249). *The Beloved of Hathor* and *The Shrine of the Golden Hawk* were produced by 'the Egyptian Society' in Jan. 1902; according to Mary K. Greer, *Women of the Golden Dawn* (Rochester, Vt.: Park Street Press, 1995), 266, both Farr and Olivia were in the cast. Farr was Chief Adept in Anglia of the Golden Dawn from 1897 to 1900; she resigned in 1902 and went to Ceylon in 1912; GY remembered seeing her twice.
66. As described in the *Harmsworth Magazine* of May 1900.
67. Nelly to MacGreevy, 1 Mar. 1928, TCD MS 8129.
68. To GY, MacGreevy described him as 'gentle and friendly and dignified' (24 Feb. 1926).
69. Nelly to MacGreevy, 8 Dec. 1928, TCD MS 8129.
70. GY to MacGreevy, 28 Dec. 1926, TCD MS 8104.
71. Interview with Sister Brigid Younghughes, to whom I am indebted for the descriptions of Harold.

72. Pound to Dorothy Shakespear, 23 Sept. 1913, *EPDS*, 260.

73. Harold's sisters-in-law often wondered if he himself had Jewish blood, letter to me from Brigid Younghughes, 20 Nov. 1986.

74. Nelly to MacGreevy, TCD MS 8129.

75. Her comment to John Montague is typical of her attitude, 'They all come bringing books and I cant read them they are so badly written' (interview with Montague).

76. She later wrote about Heatherley's in *Kings, Commoners and Me* (London: Blackie & Son, 1934).

77. GY's financial records; in *A Room of one's Own* (1924) Virginia Woolf reckoned £500 to be what a woman needed for an independent artistic life.

78. These were years of considerable unrest throughout Britain: a series of strikes began with the miners in south Wales in Sept. 1910, escalating to include the seamen and dockers in June, followed by a national railway strike in Aug. 1911, Samuel Hynes, *The Edwardian Turn of Mind* (Princeton: Princeton University Press, 1968), 346–7.

79. Interview with Grace Jaffe; Caroline Fox, *Stanhope Forbes and the Newlyn School* (Newton Abbot: David & Charles, 1993), 70–2.

80. C. E. Vulliamy, *Calico Pie: An Autobiography* (London: Michael Joseph, 1940), 160; chapter 5 describes his time at the Newlyn school from 1911 to 1914.

81. She may have contributed a painting to an exhibition at her old school in 1909, *Dorothy Shakespear (1886–1973): An Exhibition of Dreamscapes and Alphabets Organized by David A. Lewis* (Nacogdoches, Tex.: SFA Gallery, 3 Nov.–5 Dec. 1997), 1–2.

82. WBY to Shakespear, 27 Oct. 1926, dated 1927 in Wade, 730.

83. Shakespear to Pound, [Aug.–Sept. 1911], qtd. in *EPDS*, 49.

CHAPTER 3: FRIENDS

1. Dorothy to Pound, 14 Sept. 1911, *EPDS*, 58.

2. See illustration courtesy of Dr Grace Jaffe.

3. Grace Jaffe recalled that Georgie as a child had a mole about the size of a dime or sixpence on her right cheek; her children do not remember one.

4. Lily to JBY, 22 Sept. 1918, NLI MS 31,112.

5. In conversation with me.

6. Iseult's description to Richard Ellmann; the Gonnes, both of whom had pale complexions, also privately disapproved of George's brightly coloured dresses, Richard Ellmann interview notes with Iseult Gonne Stuart, 21 Sept. 1946, Tulsa.

7. ECY to JBY, 13 Mar. 1918, NLI MS 31,113.

8. Lily to R L-P, 21 Feb. 1928, WMM.

9. Grace Jaffe remembers her cousin doing fine heel darning to make the stockings last longer, and sewing buttons more firmly on new blouses and dresses; Dorothy was adamant that she would not cook, although she did needlework and made or decorated some of her own hats.

10. 'W.R. [Rummel] was here playing to Nelly last night & we had the Schumann again: its splendid' (Dorothy to Pound from Brunswick Gardens, 2 Dec. 1910, *EPDS*, 80).

11. Dorothy to Pound, 12 Sept. 1912, *EPDS*, 152.

NOTES TO PAGES 35-7

12. Dorothy to Pound, 15 Sept. 1912, *EPDS*, 157–8; Dorothy's reserve was well known; she did not even tell Georgie details of the wedding plans until a few months before.

13. Dorothy to Pound, 3 Sept. 1912, *EPDS*, 146.

14. In the possession of Omar Shakespear Pound and exhibited in *Dorothy Shakespear (1886–1973)*.

15. Interview with AY. This may have been in 1912, *EPDS*, 159.

16. Dorothy to Pound, 12 May 1912, *EPDS*, 98.

17. Information from Omar Shakespear Pound; Dorothy to Pound, 13 Jan. 1914, *EPDS*, 300. WBY had visited the Grotto with Harry Tucker in 1912, and either he or Georgie preserved postcards showing the underground passages. On the flyleaf of her copy of *Prometheus Unbound* a horoscope is cast in pencil, written above it '[?che] Per domandar il mio futuro 18 Jan 1914 8.10 p.m. GMT.'

18. Dorothy to Pound, 22 May 1912, *EPDS*, 102; Hilda Strutt married Frank Deverell in 1912 and on at least one occasion visited George in Dublin, Omar Pound.

19. Dorothy Shakespear Pound, *Etruscan Gate: A Notebook with Drawings and Watercolours*, ed. Moelwyn Merchant (Exeter: Rougemont Press, 1971), 11.

20. Edie M. Wood and Caroline Bernard.

21. Dorothy to Pound, 5 Apr., 1 May, and 20 Nov. 1913, *EPDS*, 196, 215, and 275. The original owner of the villa was F. A. Searle, author of *Sketches of Tivoli: The Ancient Tibur and its Neighbourhood* (1906).

22. 21 Mar. 1914, *EPDS*, 333.

23. Ermete Trimegisto, *Il pimandro ossia l'intelligenza suprema che si revila e parla ed altri scritti ermetici*, trans into Italian by Dr Giovanni Bonanni (Todi: Atanor, 1913).

24. GY to MacGreevy, 31 Dec. 1926, TCD MS 8104.

25. Dorothy to Pound, 5–29 Apr. 1913, *EPDS*, 196–215. Of her first visit to Italy in 1910 when she and Olivia joined Ezra in Sirmione, Dorothy later said, 'that was the first time I ever saw colour', qtd. in Noel Stock, *The Life of Ezra Pound* (London: Kegan Paul, 1970), 86.

26. 'To Harold from DOBBS', 11 May 1913.

27. There are revealing pencil strokes at p. xv of the preface in her copy of C. Lowes Dickinson's 1898 edition: 'This poem was chiefly written upon the mountainous ruins of the Baths of Caracalla, among the flowery glades, and thickets of odiferous blossoming trees, which are extended in ever winding labyrinths upon its immense platforms and dizzy arches suspended in the air.'

28. Dorothy to Pound, 31 Oct. 1938, Indiana.

29. Dorothy to Pound, 20 Mar. 1914, *EPDS*, 332.

30. 19 Mar. 1912. Richard Aldington, *Life for Life's Sake* (New York: Viking, 1941), 108; Marjorie Perloff, *The Futurist Moment: Avant-Garde, Avant Guerre, and the Language of Rupture* (Chicago: University of Chicago Press, 1986), 172. The public reaction to Marinetti is described in Lawrence Rainey, *Institutions of Modernism: Literary Elites and Public Culture* (New Haven: Yale University Press, 1998), 28–38 and notes.

31. Richard Cork, *Vorticism and Abstract Art in the First Machine Age* (Berkeley and Los Angeles: University of California Press, 1976), i. 99–100.

32. Reed Way Dasenbrock, *The Literary Vorticism of Ezra Pound & Wyndham Lewis: Towards the Condition of Painting* (Baltimore: Johns Hopkins University Press, 1985), 23.

33. Dorothy to Pound, 16 Mar. 1914, *EPDS*, 330.

34. Perloff, *The Futurist Moment*, 175–6.

35. Grace Jaffe told me that after a visit from Nelly there were always treasures left behind in the rectory library.

36. Grace Jaffe, 'Vignettes', 141. 'the best method of learning a foreign language: after mastering a few of the rudiments, take an interesting book written in that language and begin to read it, looking up only a few key words. The rest of the words will come to your mind through the context.' *Years of Grace*, 16.

37. The 1906 Oxford edition by John Sampson with an introduction by Walter Raleigh, who would later support her entry to the Bodleian. Many of these books are in YL.

38. *A Translation of the Latin Works of Dante Alighieri* (*De Vulgari Eloquentia, De Monarchia, Epistolae, Epistles, Eclogues,* and *De Aqua et Terra*), trans A. G. Ferrers Howell and Philip H. Wicksteed, Temple Classics (London: Dent, 1904). Dorothy quotes from the Temple edition of the *Convivio*, second treatise, in her notebook in Apr. 1910, *EPDS*, 17–18.

39. 'Our knowledge of Dante and of Shakespear interacts; intimate acquaintance with either breeds that discrimination which makes us more keenly appreciate the other,' and Dante's 'work is that sort of art which is a key to the deeper understanding of nature and the beauty of the world and of the spirit' (162).

40. His lectures began on 11 Oct. 1909 and lasted until 21 Mar. 1910.

41. *EPDS, passim.*

42. GY to Allan Wade, 24 Nov. 1953, Rupert Hart-Davis.

43. Ezra Pound, *The Spirit of Romance* (New York: New Directions, 1953), 144.

44. Dorothy to Pound, 11 May 1912, *EPDS*, 98.

45. 'Dante and Shakespear are like giants. Lope is like ten brilliant minds inhabiting one body,' *The Spirit of Romance*, 205. In her copy of *Ripostes* (London: Stephen Swift, 1912) 'Effects of Music upon a Company of People' is identified as 'Walter Rummel playing at Eva Fowler's' and 'From a Thing by Schumann' as 'Phantasie F minor'; 'The Return' (which WBY pronounced 'distinguished') is checkmarked. Her library also includes a number of volumes presented by Pound.

46. *Sonnets and Ballate of Guido Cavalcanti*, trans. Ezra Pound (London: Stephen Swift, 1912), inscribed 'Presentation copy' and signed 'Georgie Hyde Lees June 28.1912'. There is an ink stroke all along the left side of 'Sonetto Viii' ('Perche non furo a me gl'occhi miel spenti'); a page is inserted of two poems with translations but not in GHL's hand; Guido Cavalcanti, *Rime*, con introduzione e appendice bibliografica di E[milio] C[ecchi] (Lanciano: R. Carabba, 1910), signed 'Georgie Hyde Lees Rome, May 1913' with annotations p. 23 line 3 'Ad Un Amico', p. 28 line 2 'Per Giovanna' beginning 'Chi e questa che vesa, ch'ogn uomo la mira', p. 55 'Per Giovanna' 'Perche non furo . . .'; bookmark at pp. 72–3 and 136–7.

47. 30 Apr. 1914, *Pound/Lewis: The Letters of Ezra Pound to Wyndham Lewis*, ed. Timothy Materer (New York: New Directions, 1985); *Etruscan Gate*, 11.

48. *Blast*, 1, which appeared on 2 July 1914, concluded with manifestos by poet Pound and sculptor Henri Gaudier-Brzeska trumpeting their personal definitions of Vorticism.

49. Dasenbrock, *The Literary Vorticism of Ezra Pound & Wyndham Lewis*, 14–17; Lewis's definition as given by Douglas Goldring, *South Lodge* (London: Constable, 1943), 65, is quoted by Dasenbrock, 17; Wyndham Lewis, 'Introduction' to *Wyndham Lewis and Vorticism*, catalogue of the 1956 Tate Exhibition circulated by the Arts Council of Great Britain.

50. Cork, *Vorticism and Abstract Art*, i. 286–9; ii. 552; the final image in the 1974 exhibition 'Vorticism and its Allies' at the Hayward Gallery, London, was Dorothy's *Hommages à GB, WL, TSE, EP* (1937 or 1938).

51. *Pound/Lewis*, 17 Aug. 1917: '£8 or £10 for the bronze letter weight ought to satisfy. It would really serve as a letter weight on your desk if it is the thing I think it is. Mrs WBY has the alabaster original.' Pound to John Quinn, 10 Oct. 1918, NYPL. I am grateful to Judith Zilczer of the Smithsonian Museum and Evelyn Silber of Leeds Museums for assisting me in identifying this sculpture, described by the artist only as 'ornement, relief ajouré $7'' \times 2^{1}/_{2}''$, and originally sold to Hulme for £2 (H. S. Ede, *A Life of Gaudier-Brzeska* (London: Heinemann, 1930), 198–9 and 205). Six copies in bronze were cast, but their whereabouts are unknown.

52. Cork, *Vorticism and Abstract Art*, 286.

53. Ellmann interview notes with GY, 8 Dec. 1946, Tulsa.

54. Dorothy to Pound, 5 Dec. 1911, *EPDS*, 80.

55. GY to Oliver Edwards in a comparison with Geoffrey Taylor, 12 Sept. 1944, NLI MS 27,032.

56. Donald Pearce, 'Hours with the Domestic Sibyl: Remembering George Yeats', *Southern Review*, 28/3 (July 1992) (repr. *Yeats-Eliot Review*, 12/3–4 (Winter 1994), 136–43), 493: 'how fond she was of Ezra, saying that she liked him better than any other of W.B.'s literary friends and associates.' I have found no record of a meeting with d'Annunzio; portraits of d'Annunzio depict him as almost bald: George was probably referring to Gerhart Hauptmann, who had a thick head of hair and whom she knew well in Rapallo.

57. Dorothy to Pound, 25 Nov. 1911, *EPDS*, 78.

58. Qtd. by Humphrey Carpenter, *A Serious Character: The Life of Ezra Pound* (London: Faber, 1988), 238. *Ripostes* was a Christmas gift in 1912; *Des Imagistes: An Anthology* is inscribed 'G. H. L. from O. S. [Olivia Shakespear] May 1914'.

59. Unattributable; WBY also gently mocked Ezra's supposed conquests in his poem 'The People' (later retitled 'His Phoenix'), first published in 1916. I am inclined, however, to agree with recent biographers that Ezra remained a virgin until his late twenties.

60. Oliver Edwards thought Pound became 'a very important Synge substitute', 'Ezra Pound Symposium', *Paideuma*, 3/2 (Fall 1974), 167.

61. WBY to William Rothenstein, 14 Nov. 1912, JK.

62. WBY to Gregory, 3 Jan. 1913, NLI MS 30,179; Pound to Dorothy, 2 Jan. 1913: 'The Eagle [WBY] said my criticism was much more valuable than Sturge Moore's: I should *hope* so!' *EPDS*, 175. The elder Yeats also appreciated Pound's 'magnificently belligerent prose', JBY to GY, 19 Mar. 1921, NLI MS 31,109.

63. 'Will you come at 7 and dine with me, that we may have some talk before the others come. You can ask Aldington & anybody else you can think of for Monday evening,' WBY to Pound, 'Sunday' [9 May], Yale.

64. WBY to Gregory, 19 Feb. 1913, Emory.

65. They joined Pound in Sirmione, Italy, late Apr. 1910, went to Venice 6 May, and all three seem to have gone back to Sirmione until later in May.

66. Others certainly did; cf. Dorothy to Pound, 13 June 1910, 'I take it that during your "exile" you have been forbidden to write to me? . . . if anything happens write a word to my Cousin—I know he is to be trusted. I am having tea with him tomorrow afternoon,' *EPDS*, 23.

67. A liaison with 'no intellectual companionship' as described by GY, Ellmann interview notes with GY, 17 June 1946, Tulsa; for a short time in 1908 WBY and Maud Gonne were also lovers.

68. On the basis of an inscription 30 June 1910 to Olivia Shakespear of *Poems: Second Series* (pub. Mar. 1910) with astrological symbols implying 'the transit of the Moon through Sagittarius, by which it entered the relations symbolised here (trine of Sun, sextile of Jupiter, opposition to Mars), [which] occurred on 31 Mar. 1910', Warwick Gould thinks this is a time when they may have had a further affair (*YA* 9, 301, 307); this seems to be confirmed by two horaries drawn by WBY: 'S on her return from Italy June 9 1910' and '1.P M S comes to W June 14 1910'.

69. GY to Allan Wade, 20 Nov. 1953, Rupert Hart-Davis; Card File, automatic script for 28 Mar. 1919; Birgit Bramsbäck informed me that GY told her twice that they met in 1911; Curtis Bradford, 'George Yeats: Poet's Wife' (1955), *Sewanee Review*, 77/3 (Summer 1969), 392; Ellmann interview notes with GY, 8 Dec. 1946, Tulsa; GY's notes to T. R. Henn, Aug. 1948, 'Meeting with Miss Hyde Lees 1911 (not 1912)'; R. F. Foster thinks they met as late as 8 Dec. 1911, *W. B. Yeats: A Life*, i: *The Apprentice Mage* (Oxford: Oxford University Press, 1997), 437. Oliver Edwards in his Sligo lecture says she told him they met in May, but he mentions 1910; Joseph Hone, *W. B. Yeats* (2nd edn. London: Macmillan, 1962), 259 erroneously states that they first met while WBY was visiting the Tuckers in Lynton during the winter of 1911–12.

70. Virginia Moore, *The Unicorn: William Butler Yeats's Search for Reality* (New York: Macmillan, 1954), 229 (but places it in 1910); Georgie attended Heatherley's from Feb. to May 1911, and again Oct. 1911 to Jan. 1912 and may have joined Dorothy in drawing classes for a week in May 1913.

71. Dorothy to Pound, 2 Dec. 1911, '☐ comes to Dante on Thursday [7 Dec.] after all', *EPDS*, 80.

72. 'I have come to feel the worlds last great poetical period is over. . . . The young do not feel like that—George does not nor Ezra,' WBY to Shakespear, 2 Mar. 1929, Wade, 759.

73. WBY to Gregory, 21 Feb. 1912, Berg.

74. At the Quest Society, see Chapter 4.

75. Dorothy to Pound, 21 Sept 1912, *EPDS*, 159.

76. Interview with Birgit Bramsbäck; a copy of G. Trobridge, *Life of Swedenborg with a Popular Exposition of his Teachings* (1913), is in YL.

77. Thanking Dunsany for his letter of sympathy in Feb. 1939, she recalls her 'great delight in your plays which I have known since I was 15'; the Abbey brought Dunsany's first play, *The Glittering Gate*, to London in June 1909 when she was 16.

78. The automatic script offers the tantalizing comment 'End of Apr. 1909 "First Sight"'' as the first of Georgie's 'initiatory moments', second series; elsewhere the date is 'end May early June'. The script for 6 Apr. 1919 asks, 'Why had she emotion like Night mare on seeing me first time,' the answer 'Certain things had to come first— therefore terror.'

79. Dorothy to Pound, 24 June 1912, *EPDS*, 123.

80. The parallel movements are described in George Dangerfield, *The Strange Death of Liberal England 1910–1914* (London: Capricorn, 1961 [1935]).

CHAPTER 4: STUDIES

1. Her father's birthday is mentioned in the automatic script 21 Dec. 1919, *YVP* ii. 519.

2. Trans. William Sloane Kennedy (London: T. Fisher Unwin, 1909); 'When she was 17 she read Lombroso . . . and got interested in spiritualism,' Ellmann interview notes with GY, 8 Dec. 1946, Tulsa. This may be the cause of her Dec. 1909 'initiatory moment' identified in WBY's notes on the automatic script, Card File A34, *YVP* iii. 240–1. There is a copy in YL with WBY's signature and dated 27 Jan. 1911.

3. Richard Maurice Bucke first published *Cosmic Consciousness* (Philadelphia: Innes & Sons, 1901) shortly before his death. Among his examples are Socrates, Jesus, Paul, Plotinus, Dante, Behmen, Pascal, Spinoza, Swedenborg, Blake, Balzac, and Bucke's personal hero Whitman.

4. James's Gifford Lectures at Edinburgh University in 1901 and 1902 were published as *The Varieties of Religious Experience: A Study in Human Nature* (London: Longmans, Green, 1902). In his conclusion he defines 'truth' 'to mean something additional to bare value for life, although the natural propensity of man is to believe that whatever has great value for life is thereby certified as true' (401 n.). All quotations from James are taken from the Harvard University Press edition of *The Works of William James*.

5. She was however sufficiently interested in Henry James to purchase Rebecca West's *Henry James* when it was published in 1916, now missing from YL but included in a list made in the 1920s (probably by GY), and identified as hers. She might have agreed with Pound: 'We lose a great deal if we leave our sense of irony behind us when we enter the dolorous ports of Dante's *Hell*. For sheer dreariness one reads Henry James, not the *Inferno*,' *Spirit of Romance*, 136.

6. Now missing but in the 1920s list.

7. In *A Packet for Ezra Pound* (Dundrum: Cuala, 1929) WBY says his wife had read several volumes of Wundt; the three-volume sixth edition was published in 1908–11, but there is no copy in YL. Wundt was briefly embroiled along with Gustav Fechner in a debate over the American medium Henry Slade, Marilyn E. Marshall and Russell A. Wendt, 'Wilhelm Wundt, Spiritism, and the Assumptions of Science', in R. W. Rieber et al. (eds.), *Wilhelm Wundt and the Making of a Scientific Psychology* (New York: Plenum Press, 1980), 158–75.

8. Letters to his father and mother in July 1911, Carpenter, *A Serious Character*, 156.

9. George Robert Stow Mead (1863–1933) was educated at St John's College, Cambridge, and joined the Theosophical Society in 1884. He helped edit Blavatsky's monthly magazine *Lucifer*, which he renamed the *Theosophical Review* on becoming editor, and 1890–8 was general secretary of the Theosophical Society. Founding the Quest Society in Mar. 1909, he edited the quarterly *Quest* 1909–30, and was the author of more than two dozen books on Gnosticism and related matters. In 1924 after the death of his wife, Laura Mary Cooper, whom he had married in 1899, he became more involved in psychic research, sitting with several mediums.

10. 'I wanted criticism & so gave it. They are accustomed to an average audience of a little over a hundred. They had hundreds last night. The room was quite full,' WBY to Gregory, 2 Feb. 1912, Berg. On 31 Jan. he explained his discovery (which in *A Packet for Ezra Pound* he would cite as from John Philoponus) 'The spirit-body is formless in itself, but takes many forms or even keeps the form of the phisical [*sic*] body "as ice keeps the shape of the bowl after the bowl is broken" (that is the metaphor though not quite the phrase),' WBY to Gregory, Berg.

11. 'As far as I know Yeats was never a member of the Quest Society, but he was a frequent visitor to the weekly meetings in Kensington Town Hall and later in a large studio in Clareville Grove, South Kensington' (Geoffrey M. Watkins, 'Yeats and Mr Watkins' Bookshop', in George Mills Harper (ed.), *Yeats and the Occult* (Toronto: Macmillan, 1975), 308); however, Geoffrey Watkins did not join his father's business until 1919. Dorothy to Pound, 21 Feb. 1912, *EPDS*, 68.

12. 'I have been intensely excited over another of Mead's—"The World Mystery". It is full of interesting things, and I have "correlated" several to vaguenesses of my own! Also a footnote fit for Walter [Rummel], about a "dodecagonal pyramid" with a door of many colours—the pyramid "in a sphere of the colour of night". I have been needing Il Paradiso to refer to,' Dorothy to Pound, 22 May 1912, *EPDS*, 102; in Feb. 1913 she was reading a translation of Philostratus' life of Apollonius of Tyana, about whom Mead published a critical study in 1901.

13. Alan Scott in *Origen and the Life of the Stars* (Oxford: Clarendon, 1991), 90 describes 'gnostic groups' as those 'whose language and imagery has been strongly influenced by Jewish or Christian cosmologies, who even more than Plato . . . are drawn to mythology as a mode of expression, and for whom the belief that esoteric knowledge delivers the individual from evil powers in heaven is of special importance'.

14. A lucid description of the various viewpoints expressed in the *Quest* can be found in Patricia Rae, *The Poetical Muse: Pragmatist Poets in Hulme, Pound and Stevens* (Lewisburg, Pa.: Bucknell University Press, 1997), 81–5.

15. Dorothy to Pound, 16 June 1912, *EPDS*, 114.

16. Foster, *W. B. Yeats*, i. 102; Moore, *The Unicorn*, 455 n. 11. Among volumes once in the Yeatses' library were two editions of *Fragments of a Faith Forgotten* (1900 and 1906), the entire 'Echoes from the Gnosis series' (1906–8), *Quests Old and New* (1913), and *Orpheus* (1896, with its cross-references to Giraldus, Cornelius Agrippa, and Ficino).
17. Early Aug. 1920.
18. Interview with Kathleen Raine. The Neoplatonic 3 Hypostases—the One (beyond being), the *Nous* or Intellect (true being), and the Soul which creates time and space—influenced much medieval thought. GY acquired Taylor's original 1817 edition of Plotinus in 1914; her copy of Iamblichus is included in the 1920s library list; cf. Dorothy to Pound, 20 Nov. 1913: 'I try to read Plato—but find him much too "correlated"! I like Mead's version of him very much. It is full of pictures.' *EPDS*, 275.
19. Published in *A Lume Spolento* (1908); in it Pound first uses the term 'vortex' which he would identify as 'The "cone". . . the "Vritta", whirl-pool, vortex-ring of the Yogi's cosmogony' (qtd. by Perloff, *The Futurist Moment*, 266–7).
20. Carl du Prel, *The Philosophy of Mysticism*, trans. C. C. Massey, 2 vols. (1889), now missing from library but identified as GY's in the 1920s list.
21. 'And it shall come to pass afterward, that I will pour out my spirit upon all flesh; and your sons and your daughters shall prophesy, your old men shall dream dreams, your young men shall see visions: And also upon the servants and upon the handmaids in those days will I pour out my spirit. And I will shew wonders in the heavens and in the earth, blood, and fire, and pillars of smoke. The sun shall be turned into darkness, and the moon into blood, before the great and terrible day of the Lord come,' Joel 2: 28–31.
22. Dorothy to Pound, 9 Oct. and Pound to Dorothy, 11 Oct. 1913, *EPDS*, 269–70.
23. About 11 June 1913, see Dorothy's letter chastising Ezra for interfering with the guest list, *EPDS*, 232.
24. As defined by Sir Oliver Lodge in *Raymond or Life and Death with Examples of the Evidence for Survival of Memory and Affection after Death* (London: Methuen, 1916), 355.
25. 'her initiatory moment of May 1913 produced your critical of Mar. [1917] & your initiatory of May 1913 produced her critical [Sept 1917]', automatic script for 27 Mar. 1919 concerning 18 or 25 May, *YVP* ii. 217.
26. 19 May, 'The Relation of the Individual & the Universe', 26 May, 'Soul Consciousness', 2 June, 'The Problem of Evil', 9 June, 'The Problem of Self', 16 June, 'Realisation in Love'. Tagore's lectures, first delivered at Harvard, of which these were the first five of eight, were published as *Sadhana: The Realisation of Life* (New York: Macmillan, 1913, 1915).
27. Naresh Guha, *W. B. Yeats: An Indian Approach* (Calcutta: Jadavpur University, 1968), 91–2.
28. The book was published in July 1914; on 12 Sept. 1914 WBY wrote Tagore that he had planned to go to India that winter but the war made his journey impossible, JK; 'sleeps' of 14 and 15 Aug. 1920, Notebook 6, *YVP* iii. 46. The automatic script suggests that the Yeatses seriously contemplated a passage to India.

29. A series of three lectures 3, 10, and 17 June at 3 p.m. advertised in *The Times* of 26 May, P. S. O'Hegarty collection, Kansas. I am indebted to Wayne Chapman for this information.

30. 'Do read James Stephens—"Here are Ladies"—It's excellent,' Dorothy to Pound, 20 Nov. 1913, *EPDS*, 275. The prize-giving ceremony of the Academic Committee of the Royal Society of Literature, chaired by Sir Walter Raleigh, took place on 29 Nov 1913.

31. 'Two lectures on the Irish Theatre by W. B. Yeats', ed. Robert O'Driscoll, in Robert O'Driscoll (ed.), *Theatre and Nationalism in Twentieth-Century Ireland* (Toronto: University of Toronto Press, 1971), 66–88; WBY's *Plays for an Irish Theatre* was first published by Maunsel of Dublin in 1911, with a second impression in 1913; Georgie's copy is dated 1914 and signed by her.

32. The Tuckers may well have discovered 'The Prelude' through Mrs Adeney's son William Bernard Adeney (1878–1966), who had studied at the Royal Academy Schools and the Slade in London and at Julian's in Paris; since 1903 a teacher at the Central School of Arts and Crafts and a founder member of the London Group in 1913 (later its president), his work was represented in the 1912 Post-Impressionist Exhibition. Patricia Greacen to GY, 11 Sept. 1956, describes Mrs Adeney as wife of a congregational minister, but the 1916 deeds identify him as 'Medical Practitioner'; the house was later renamed 'End House'. I am indebted to the present owners, Victor and Judith Benjamin, for information about the deeds to the house and a tour of it and the grounds.

33. First pointed out in his book *Early British Trackways* (1922) by the photographer and antiquarian Alfred Watkins, who believed that the network of straight lines linking ancient landmarks had been made by prehistoric man as sighting points, later thought to indicate a change in the earth's magnetic field which can be detected by dowsing or with a pendulum.

34. As told to AY.

35. WBY to Gregory, 17 Aug. 1913, JK.

36. WBY to Pound, 24 Aug. 1913, James Longenbach, *Stone Cottage* (New York: Oxford University Press, 1988), 4–6 and 30; on 7 July WBY had written to Gregory, 'I want to arrange for Ezra Pound to act as my secretary this winter. I propose that we take rooms for himself & me about an hour out of London & I go straight there after Coole,' Berg; Barbara Willard, *The Forest: Ashdown in East Sussex* (Poundgate: Sweethaws Press, 1989).

37. MBY.

38. WBY to Gregory, 22 June 1911, Berg.

39. Described by Alice Welfare (qtd. in Longenbach, *Stone Cottage*, 7).

40. Dorothy to Pound, 4 Sept. 1913, *EPDS*, 250.

41. Noted in GY's copy of *A Vision*; the text was probably *De Principiis*; Dorothy to Pound, 9 Sept. 1913, *EPDS*, 254.

42. Edward Marsh to Rupert Brooke, recording a luncheon conversation with WBY in July 1913, Christopher Hassall, *A Biography of Edward Marsh* (London: Longmans Green, 1954), 237.

43. The editors accept the date of 'the spring of 1912' in WBY, 'Preliminary Examination of the Script of E R', ed. George Mills Harper and John S. Kelly, in Harper (ed.), *Yeats and the Occult*, 130–71; however, Elizabeth Heine dates a horoscope done by WBY for 'Miss Radcliffe Anglesea' in 1911; L. A. G. Strong, *Green Memory* (London: Methuen, 1961), 253–4.

44. Eva Fowler implies this in a note to WBY enclosing script written 'nine or ten years ago', given her by the mother of Elizabeth ('Bessie') Radcliffe.

45. At his death in 1933 Alfred Fowler left £500 to Radcliffe, 'the closest friend of my late wife', will of Alfred Fowler.

46. Eva Fowler to WBY, 22–3 May 1914, *LTWBY* i. 290.

47. 18 May 1913, Stony Brook.

48. WBY to Gregory, 20 May 1913, Emory.

49. Her father Alexander Radcliffe had property at Bag Park, Devon; she married Ronald, later 3rd Baron Gorell, in 1922 and had three children, see his memoirs, *One Man . . . Many Parts* (London: Odhams Press, 1956); WBY's engagements in London in Nov. 1929 include 'tea with Lady Gorell', Stony Brook.

50. About June 1915 Bessie invited WBY to tea to meet her sister, for whom she had requested a 'protective talisman' against the frightening experiences accompanying her own automatic writing, Stony Brook.

51. L. E. Jones, *I Forgot to Tell You* (London: Hart-Davis, 1959), 37–45, describes an earlier clairvoyant experience with Bessie. This may be the 'Mr Jones' WBY refers to as having been present during some of Bessie's automatic writing sessions.

52. When news of Eva Fowler's death in 1921 at the age of 50 reached him, WBY wrote to Gregory, 9 Aug. 'Mrs Fowler has died suddenly—a loss to George and to myself as she was the centre of a little world where we had many acquaintances and I could always stay there at an emergency. It has broken one of my links with London—I have known her for a great many years. She was an egotistical talker but an unselfish and simple woman.' I am grateful to G. M. Harper for this reference.

53. Elizabeth Radcliffe to WBY, 19 Dec. 1913, *LTWBY* i. 277.

54. Dorothy to Pound, 1 Aug. 1913, *EPDS*, 236. There is a postcard of the Tower Arch of St Helen, Ranworth, among the Yeats papers (AY).

55. During an automatic writing session on 26 Nov. 1919 the Yeatses ask the question, 'Words heard before WBY came to Norwich "The two hands & the two wings must be joined together but must not destroy each other" '. 'Ameritus' explains this as the joining of the lunar and solar vision, leading to the experiencing of 'when chance & choice are one', or the Beatific Vision. *YVP* ii. 492.

56. Nelly refers to her 'old friend Richard Pryce' in a letter to MacGreevy, 9 Oct. 1926, TCD MS 8129.

57. Georgie's reading ticket was no. 12677, her number in the register B4334; she was the first new reader to sign the register on that day, British Museum Central Archives. Pound reported to Dorothy on 30 Nov. that 'the Prelude' was 'quite empty', *EPDS*, 283.

58. MBY; I am indebted to Johannes Maczewski for identifying Adolf Heinrich Friedrich Schlichtegroll (1765–1822), a philologist and editor of the annual

Nekrolog der Deutschen; messages had previously come from, among others: George Moberly, Bishop of Salisbury, father of the co-author of *An Adventure*, describing a visionary experience at Versailles, Thomas Creech, Fellow of All Souls College, and a wrongly discharged policeman named Thomas Emerson.

59. In 1948 George told Birgit Bramsbäck, 'I used to go to the British Museum for him looking things up.' letter to me, 3 June 1987; 'from time to time after her first meeting with Yeats she helped him to check the authenticity of information given him by mediums', Richard Ellmann, *The Man and the Masks* (2nd edn. Oxford: Oxford University Press, 1979), 222. A further report on the relationship between Karsch and Goethe in an unidentified hand begins, 'The works of Anna Luisa Kirsch [*sic*] are not in the British Museum Library,' Stony Brook.

60. 'Wer immer strebend sich bemuht | Den konnen wir erlosen' 'page 277 of Philip Reclam press edition, Vol. 6–7'; Mrs Fowler and Elizabeth Radcliffe were travelling during the month of Oct., *LTWBY* i. 273–4; Stony Brook.

61. WBY to JBY, 5 Aug. 1913.

62. *Proceedings of the Society for Psychical Research*, 27 (Jan. 1914), 157–75; the handwriting has been identified as Nelly's by D. G. Gamble, forensic handwriting analyst.

63. 'Mind can influence mind independently of the recognized organs of sense,' Frederic W. H. Myers, 'Automatic Writing, or the Rationale of Planchette', *Contemporary Review*, 42 (1885), 248. WBY took issue with Myers a number of times, as in a lecture on symbols to the Golden Dawn, see Chapter 5.

64. *Human Personality and its Survival of Bodily Death* (1903), *Encyclopedia of Occultism and Parapsychology*, 2nd edn.

65. Ellmann interview notes with GY, 26 Dec. 1946, Tulsa.

66. Pound was also familiar with the French Rosicrucian Joséphin Péladan, whose theories were disapproved by the Order of the Golden Dawn.

67. Birgit Bramsbäck says GY told her this twice (letter to me).

68. Pound to WBY, [?30 Apr. 1914 or later], 'Ezra Pound Letters to William Butler Yeats', ed. C. F. Terrell, *Antaeus*, 21–2 (Spring–Summer 1976), 34.

69. Logie Barrow convincingly argues that spiritualism, secularism, and mesmerism—as well as many other 'isms'—flourished interdependently in the north of England, *Independent Spirits: Spiritualism and English Plebeians 1850–1910* (London: Routledge & Kegan Paul, 1986).

70. See Arnold Goldman, 'Yeats, Spiritualism, and Psychical Research', in Harper (ed.), *Yeats and the Occult*, 108–29 and Moore, *The Unicorn*, especially chapter VIII, 218–55.

71. I have been unable to trace the source of this familiar remark.

72. For detailed discussions see Alex Owen, *The Darkened Room: Women, Power and Spiritualism in Late Victorian England* (London: Virago Press, 1989) and Peter Washington, *Madame Blavatsky's Baboon: A History of the Mystics, Mediums, and Misfits who Brought Spiritualism to America* (New York: Schocken Books, 1993).

73. I am grateful to William H. Gaddes for many hours of discussion on this and related matters; see also Susan A. Greenfield, *The Human Brain: A Guided Tour* (New York:

Basic Books, 1997); Colin Blakemore and Susan Greenfield (eds.), *Mindwaves: Thoughts on Intelligence, Identity and Consciousness* (Oxford: Blackwell, 1987); Jesse E. Gordon (ed.), *Handbook of Clinical and Experimental Hypnosis* (New York: Macmillan, 1967).

74. Everard Feilding, who married the medium Stanislawa Tomczyk, wrote to WBY, 1 Apr. 1933, that his wife 'like yr. wife . . . hates spiritualism & won't talk about it', *LTWBY* ii. 553. Moore speaks of 'The spiritism-hating Dorothy Pound' and says 'the Pounds were annoyed with Yeats' spiritism, which was at its strongest just when they were seeing the most of him (1911–1916)', *The Unicorn*, 258, 356–7.

75. '1912–1916 were the years when W.B. was always frequenting séances. He bored people to death by talking of séances,' GY to Birgit Bramsbäck, quoted in a letter to me 3 June 1987 recording her notes of 1948; 'About 1914 Yeats' talk of spirits became so constant as to alienate his friends,' Ellmann interview notes with GY, 26 Dec. 1946, Tulsa.

76. Ellmann, *The Man and the Masks*, 222; 'Presently Georgie started accompanying him to séances, and helping him check up on data,' Moore, *The Unicorn*, 229.

77. Susy Smith, *The Mediumship of Mrs Leonard* (New York: University Books, 1964), 238.

78. For example, *The Blue Island Experiences of a New Arrival beyond the Veil*, communicated by W. T. Stead, recorded by Pardoe Woodman and Estelle Stead (London: Rider, 1922).

79. 'I have just had a certificate of caution from a well-known American medium who has turned me out of her séances,' WBY to JBY, 5 Aug. 1913, Wade, 583–4; this must have been at a private sitting or small circle at Wimbledon given after the medium's return from Scotland.

80. Birgit Bramsbäck quoting her notes of 1948 in a letter to me, 3 June 1987.

81. Steve L. Adams and George Mills Harper, 'The Manuscript of "Leo Africanus"', *YA* 1, ed. Richard J. Finneran (London: Gill & Macmillan, 1982), 3–46.

82. WBY, 'Report of Séance held at Cambridge House, Wimbledon at 6.30 on May 9th, 1912', MBY.

83. Stony Brook; Foster, *W. B. Yeats*, i. 465 and plate 31 (photograph of Etta Wriedt).

84. WBY to Gregory, 19 July 1915, Berg.

85. Qtd. by Bradford, 'George Yeats: Poet's Wife', 399. 'Julia's Bureau' was closed shortly after Stead's death, but reopened as 'The W. T. Stead Borderland Library and Bureau' in the autumn of 1914 when funding was found, preface to *Lessons from the Beyond by 'Julia'* (London: Rider, 1931), 13–14.

86. WBY to Edmund Dulac, 11 Oct. 1916, Hobby, 81.

87. Sir Oliver Lodge, physicist and 1901–3 president of the Society for Psychical Research, became convinced of 'demonstrated survival' after the death of his son in the war in Sept. 1915; *Raymond or Life and Death with Examples of the Evidence for Survival of Memory and Affection after Death*, based on his sessions with Gladys Leonard, went through many editions, including a revision with an additional chapter in 1922. In addition to sittings with Leonard on 27 and 28 Sept., 12 and 22 Oct. 1915, 28 Jan., 3 and 24 Mar. 1916, Lodge describes sittings with Etta Wriedt

and A. Vout Peters (another of WBY's favourite mediums); *The Encyclopedia of Occultism and Parapsychology* (2nd edn. Detroit: Shepard, 1984) states that Lodge held sittings with Leonard 'every week for several years'.

88. Smith, *Mediumship of Mrs Leonard*, 19–22.

89. GY to Ottoline Morrell, 1 Sept. 1922, HRHRC.

90. From 1919 to 1955, investigators published their results and commentaries on Gladys Leonard's mediumship in the Society's *Proceedings* and *Journal*.

91. Lodge, *Raymond*, 365; Smith, *Mediumship of Mrs Leonard*, 95–154. 'Proxy sitters' are third parties attending on behalf of someone else and know nothing about the persons they represent nor about the wished-for communicators; in a 'book test', claimed to be devised by Leonard's communicators, the control instructs the sitter to look for a book somewhere else, and by checking a certain page and line to seek a message, thereby excluding previous knowledge or telepathy and, when successful, presuming clairvoyance.

92. GY to Ottoline Morrell, 1 Sept. 1922, HRHRC; in mid-July Lady Ottoline's young lover 'Tiger' (Lionel Gomme) had died in her arms of a massive brain haemorrhage and she was seeking advice concerning mediums, Miranda Seymour, *Ottoline Morrell: Life on the Grand Scale* (London: Sceptre, 1994), 439–40.

93. Gladys Osborne Leonard, *My Life in Two Worlds*, with a foreword by Sir Oliver Lodge (London: Cassell, 1931); Una, Lady Troubridge, 'The Modus Operandi of So-Called Mediumistic Trance Mediumship', *Proceedings of the Society for Psychical Research*, 32 (Jan. 1922), 344 ff.

94. Adams and Harper, 'The Manuscript of "Leo Africanus"', 15–17.

95. AY.

96. Letter from Kathleen Raine to me, 25 Aug. 1985.

97. GY to WBY, 21 Dec. 1932.

98. Ellmann interview notes with GY, 17 Jan. 1947, Tulsa.

99. H. Heywood-Smith, 'Early Stages of the Anthroposophical Movement in England', *Anthroposophical Quarterly*, 15 (Winter 1970), 74–6. I am grateful to Margaret Jonas, librarian of the Anthroposophical Society in Great Britain, for these details and other archival material.

100. Moore, *The Unicorn*, 172–8; Geoffrey Ahern, *Sun at Midnight: The Rudolf Steiner Movement and the Western Esoteric Tradition* (Wellingborough: Aquarian Press, 1984).

101. Included in the 1920s library list, but now missing.

102. 'Long before' her own automatic writing began in 1917, as quoted by H. R. Bachchan, *W. B. Yeats and Occultism* (London: Books from India, 1976; 1st edn. Delhi, 1965), 256.

103. Ellmann, *The Man and the Masks*, 222; Moore, *The Unicorn*, 239 and 276.

104. Walter Kelly Hood, '"Read Fechner", the Spirit Said: W. B. Yeats and Gustav Theodor Fechner', *Yeats: ACTS*, 7 (1989), 91–8. Fechner was a colleague of Wilhelm Wundt, with whose writings George was familiar.

105. A. E. Waite, who mistakenly places Steiner's visit a year earlier, is quoted by R. A. Gilbert in *The Golden Dawn Companion* (Wellingborough: Aquarian Press,

1986), 20–2: 'I had a long conversation with him, brought about by one of his women admirers and followers, who was also a Member of the Golden Dawn. She acted as intermediary also, for he could speak no English. . . . It is on record that Rudolf Steiner attended at least one Stella Matutina Meeting on the occasion of his visit to London.'

106. I am indebted to the librarian Mrs W. Poynton for searching the records of the Society for Psychical Research; she found no record of Georgie, Harold, Nelly, or Eva Fowler, but WBY was a member from Feb. 1913 until 1928.

107. *Il pimandro ossia l'intelligena supreme che si rivela e parla ed altri scritti ermetici*. 'I have been trying to read, in Italian, some of the wisdom of Hermes Trismagistus. I believe it to be *very* much diluted for the use of the R. Catholics. It feels like the shell with nothing inside: not even a rattle,' Dorothy to Pound, 24 Mar. 1914, *EPDS*, 335. See also Timothy Materer, *Modernist Alchemy* (Ithaca, NY: Cornell University Press, 1995), 89.

108. See Chapter 5 below.

109. Johannes Aventinus, *Des Hochgelerten weit berühmbten beyerischen geschichtschreibers Chronik* (Frankfurt am Main: Ben Georg Raben, 1566); *Atlas of Ancient and Classical Geography* (London: Dent, 1910); Franz Cumont, *Astrology and Religion among the Greeks and Romans* (New York: Putnam, 1912); John Locke Estens, *The Paraclete and Mahdi; or the Exact Testimony of Science to Revelation and Exposition of the Most Ancient Mysteries and Cults* (Sydney: John Sands, 1912). At some time she consulted works by the Arabian astrologer Aben-Ragel and Athanasius Kircher, appendix C of *MYV* ii. 81–2 and 419.

110. *The Odysseys of Homer*, trans George Chapman, 2 vols. (London: Dent, 1906); *Le sette sposizioni del S. Giovanni Pico de la Mirandola intitolate Heptaplo, soprai sei giorni del genesi*, tradotte in lingua Toscana da M. Antonio Buonagrazia Canonisco di Pescia (Lorenzo Torrentino, 1555); Pico, *Opera Omnia*, 2 vols. (1572, 1573). A black quarto loose-leaf book signed 'Georgie Hyde Lees 16 Montpelier Square' lists Pico's '47 Cabbalistic Conclusions'; her copy of *The Kabbalah Unveiled* is heavily annotated with references to Pico.

111. Ellmann to me in conversation; WBY was very impressed by Pound's 'The Return', first published in June 1912 and set to music by Rummel the following year; he quotes it in full in *A Packet for Ezra Pound*.

112. (London: Watkins, 1911).

113. Heinrich Cornelius Agrippa von Nettesheim, *Opera*, in duos tomos concinne digesta . . . (Lyons: Per Beringos Fratres, n.d.): one volume only into which is pasted carefully studied diagrams of 'The Thirty Two Parts of the Sepher Yetzivah', 'The Tree of Life. The outward and visible Sign of an inward and Spiritual grace', and a list of the twenty-two Tarot trumps. 'I took down from my wife a list of what she had read, two or three volumes of Wundt, part of Hegel's *Logic*, all Thomas Taylor's *Plotinus*, a Latin work of Pico della Mirandola, and a great deal of mediaeval mysticism,' WBY, *A Packet for Ezra Pound*. In the margin of *A Vision* GY wrote, 'GY had read Hegel's philosophy of history,' and later repeated this to Ellmann, Tulsa; Moore also understood that Georgie gained her knowledge of Hegel when

she was in her early twenties, interview Sept. 1987. GY was familiar with Croce before her marriage, Ellmann interview notes with GY, 8 Dec. 1946, Tulsa; she told H. R. Bachchan that she gave her husband Croce's book *The Philosophy of Giambattista Vico* (1913) in Aug. 1924, *W. B. Yeats and Occultism*, 149 n. 4.

114. Jaffe, 'Vignettes', 143–4; Grace attended Miss Sparkes's school from autumn 1912 to spring 1914; Nelly to MacGreevy, 24 May 1934, TCD MS 8129.

115. Dorothy to Pound, 13 Feb. 1914, *EPDS*, 306.

116. Dorothy to Pound, 1 Mar. 1914, *EPDS*, 312; the editors mistakenly identify 'Erb as Herbert Leaf, a Shakespear connection. According to Carpenter, *A Serious Character*, 236, Olivia paid the rent.

117. WBY to Pound, 8 Mar. 1914, Indiana; on 30 Mar. he repeated the compliment, to Homer Pound: Ezra has 'found for himself a very clever, a very charming and a very beautiful wife. I shall be back in time for the marriage,' qtd. in Carpenter, *A Serious Character*, 233.

118. J. J. Wilhelm, *Ezra Pound in London and Paris 1908–1925* (University Park, Pa.: Penn State University Press, 1990), 154.

119. Yeats to Gregory, 21 Apr. 1914, Berg.

120. *Light*, 2 and 9 May 1914, 211–14 and 223–4, Peter Kuch, ' "Laying the Ghosts"? —W. B. Yeats's Lecture on Ghosts and Dreams', *YA* 5, 114–35. Séances with Mrs Wriedt were also described by E. R. Johnson, a painter whose reports of seven sessions in 1912 and twelve in 1913 are quoted in W. Usborne Moore, *The Voices* (London: Watts, 1913), 50–4, and 282–92; Johnson also gave a paper to the Ghost Club on 'Spirit Guides' in July 1913, BL MS 52,271.

121. Carpenter, *A Serious Character*, 228–9, 238.

122. 30 Apr. from Stone Cottage, *Pound/Lewis*, 6–7. In *Blast*, 2 (July 1915) Wyndham Lewis included works by Dorothy Pound, essays by Lewis, Pound, Ford, and Gaudier, and a photo of Gaudier's head of Pound.

123. 'one is a most sensitive materializing medium,' WBY to Gregory, 4 May 1914, Berg.

124. To Birgit Bramsbäck in 1948 GY described Crowley as 'very wicked'. Mathers may also have been responsible for introducing Crowley to Agrippa's magical formulae; see Alex Owen, 'The Sorcerer and his Apprentice: Aleister Crowley and the Magical Exploration of Edwardian Subjectivity', *Journal of British Studies*, 36 (Jan. 1997), 99–133.

125. Moore, *The Unicorn*, 238–9; Nelly to Gregory, 30 Sept. 1917, a letter written in some distress which may explain why she writes 'Mulberry' (which I have not been able to trace) for the more probable 'Marlborough'.

CHAPTER 5: THE GOLDEN DAWN

1. Even the 16th-century Danish observational astronomer Tycho Brahe, who devoted his life to correcting Ptolemy, began his study of astrology by casting horoscopes of famous men, Victor E. Thoren, *The Lord of Uraniborg: A Biography of Tycho Brahe* (Cambridge: Cambridge University Press, 1990), 17.

2. Dorothy to Pound, 21 Mar. 1914, *EPDS*, 333; she was probably reading GY's copy of Pico. Elizabeth Heine has pointed out to me that for her study of mundane astrology

Georgie followed Alfred John Pearce, *The Text-Book of Astrology*, which is in YL. Her personal library contained works by 'Charubel' (C. G. M. Adam); 'William Joseph Simmonite' (Robert Cross Smith, friend of William Blake); the essential *Raphael's Horary Astrology*; innumerable Astrological Manuals by theosophist 'Alan Leo' (William Frederick Allen), and works by 'Sepharial' (Walter Gorn Old), who also published *A Manual of Occultism* (1911).

3. Perhaps this has some connection with one of Georgie's 'initiatory moments' later attributed to Oct. 1910 in the automatic script of 22 July 1919, *YVP* ii. 331.

4. From the thirteen-point table traditionally ascribed to the 'Tabula Smaragdina' or Emerald Tablet of Hermes Trismegistos, quoted in Christopher McIntosh, *The Astrologers and their Creed* (London: Random House, 1969), 118.

5. WBY to Miss Little, 24 Nov. 1921, probably Edith Little, an early member of the Golden Dawn, NLI MS 30,563; *The Tetrabiblos; or Quadripartite of Ptolemy, being Four Books Relative to the Starry Influences*, trans. from the copy of Leo Allatius by James Wilson (London: William Hughes, 1828) is in YL.

6. H. P. Blavatsky, *Isis Unveiled* (Pasadena, Calif.: Theosophical University Press, 1966), i. 259.

7. I am grateful to Elizabeth Heine for her patient and generous explanation of astrological matters and, in particular, the numerous charts among the Yeatses' papers; definitions of most astrological terms are taken from Alan Leo's series of manuals.

8. Thoren, *The Lord of Uraniborg*, 82–3; Brahe later began to distrust astrology because of the lack of dependable tables, but, like Newton after him, believed there must be some relation between the harmony of the universe and prediction, ibid. 218.

9. 'Primary Directions may be regarded as indicating unescapable karma, the effect of repeated thoughts and desires, and perhaps actions too, in past lives'; 'Secondary directions, on the other hand, may be considered as representing the changing mental phases through which we all pass, more or less affecting us according to our readiness to take advantage of opportunities,' Alan Leo, *Casting the Horoscope* (London: Fowler, 1969), 170.

10. A sky map with the arcs related to the earth's daily rotation.

11. GY may have used this incident as proof of the uses of astrology, for the story appears in Birgit Bjersby, *The Interpretation of the Cuchulain Legend in the Works of W. B. Yeats* (Uppsala: A.-B. Lundesquitska Bokhandeln for Uppsala University Irish Institute, 1950), 131 n. 2. That it was of significance to both Yeatses is indicated by their annotations: 'Wed. Nov 17 10 am [1920] letter found in dustbin WBY'; 'Note found when Mercury by retrogression came to exact sextile of Mars ie.21.334 GMT I looked in dustbin on Nov 16 but I did not remove whole contents for examination & consequently missed seeing the paper which was further down than I looked. On Wednesday morning I turned out the whole bin mass of refuse on to the garden path' (GY).

12. 'Kymry' (Hamilton Minchin), who reports the visit in a letter to Yeats in Aug., Stony Brook.

13. Of special significance are (1) book of horoscopes alphabetized signed 'Georgie Hyde Lees 1914'; (2) duplicate book labelled 'Astrology 1850–1916' with an index in GY's hand, which seems to have been used by her from about 1914 as a workbook and then intermittently by both Yeatses through to 1935; (3) light blue MS book entitled 'Horary Figures. Horoscopes. 1914—' which has figures by WBY and inserts by Georgie; (4) 'Book of Blank Maps with Instructions' which WB seems to have used in 1910–11, then picked up by GY from early 1921 through 1923, with occasional annotations by WBY; and (5) a few horoscopes, mainly to do with natural and political events leading to war, in Georgie's Golden Dawn study book, MBY.

14. John Kelleher politely declined, letter to me, 4 June 1985.

15. A single page of horoscopes and notes, NLI 30,764. After the automatic writing began, the Yeatses were obsessed with identifying special 'moments of crisis' in their lives; these were closely related to refinements in their astrological calculations which served as background to the system of *A Vision*, see below.

16. All these dates are identified in the automatic script as 'initiatory moments'— unanalysed predestined moments, 'changes of mind & heart & will' implying 'shock to belief whether mental emotional or spiritual' leading up to a 'critical moment' which 'produces events', *MYV* ii. 231–2. The automatic script of 27 Mar. 1919 states that 'her initiatory moment of May 1913 produced your critical of Mar. [1917] & your initiatory of May 1913 produced her critical [Sept 1917]', *YVP* ii. 217.

17. For some years WBY had been anxious to learn more about Steiner's knowledge of astrology; on 15 Sept. 1912 Felkin wrote to him after returning from Germany, 'I was too much engaged in getting grades & things that I could not go into the Astrology for you this time I will do so when I go over again', *LTWBY* i. 252.

18. Ellmann writes, 'In 1914 she joined a group of Rudolf Steiner Theosophists, and that same year Yeats suggested that she become a member of the Golden Dawn. He sponsored her and saw her through her initiation', *The Man and the Masks*, 222. However, since the Steiner group had broken away from the Theosophical Society in Jan. 1913, she probably joined the new Anthroposophical Society earlier than 1914.

19. Erskine Childers was executed in Dublin in 1922; Sybil stayed with George in Dublin in 1926 after returning from India, and again later.

20. I am indebted to R. A. Gilbert for information concerning Georgie's admission and the various stages of her progress in the Order; his *The Golden Dawn: Twilight of the Magicians* (Wellingborough: Aquarian Press, 1983) and *The Golden Dawn Companion* provide the clearest guides to the relevant documents. Where Amoun Temple directives are unavailable, I am following the pattern described for the Isis-Urania Temple which, although separate from the Amoun Temple under the control of A. E. Waite (who preferred mysticism over magic) continued until 1914 and appears to have shared much the same structure and rituals.

21. Jeremiah 36: 4, 19: when the princes of Judah discover the roll in which Baruch 'wrote from the mouth of Jeremiah all the words of the Lord, which he had spoken unto him', they advise Baruch, 'Go hide thee, thou and Jeremiah; and let no man know where ye be.' See also 1 Samuel 21: 2: 'And David said unto Ahimelech the

priest, The king hath commanded me a business, and hath said unto me, Let no man know any thing of the business whereabout I send thee, and what I have commanded thee.' I am grateful to Peter L. Smith and Margaret Mills Harper for discussing probable sources.

22. Many of these references are listed in Frank Kermode's editorial notes to *The Tempest* (London: Methuen, 1958), 168; in 'The Glass Graduate' Cervantes plays upon the word, citing quotations from the New Testament, Cato, and Horace (*Exemplary Stories*, trans. C. A. Jones (Harmondsworth: Penguin, 1972), 1140–1). I am grateful to Stephen Rupp for these examples.

23. Gilbert, *The Golden Dawn Companion*, 81, 96–7; 'This symbolic sentence in its many-sided forms is certainly most dangerous and iconoclastic in the face of all the dualistic later religions—or rather—theologies—especially so in the light of Christianity,' Blavatsky; A. E. Waite, *The Doctrine and Literature of the Kabalah* (London: Theosophical Publishing Society, 1902), 338 n.; Bachchan, *W. B. Yeats and Occultism*, 256.

24. Ellic Howe, *The Magicians of the Golden Dawn* (London: Routledge & Kegan Paul, 1972), 273 ff.; to add to the confusion about the later history of the Order, by Dec. 1919 Miss Stoddart had moved with the Temple to 56 Redcliffe Gardens, West Kensington. She may have been related to MacGregor Mathers, who had a cousin named Walter MacGregor Stoddart, a schoolmaster. Howe, *The Magicians of the Golden Dawn*, 40.

25. Howe, *The Magicians of the Golden Dawn*, 59–88.

26. W. B. Yeats, *Autobiographies* (London: Macmillan, 1955), 576. Later they would both be embroiled in arguments over the origin of the Order and the 'Cypher manuscripts'.

27. Yeats, *Autobiographies*, 375; Gilbert, *Twilight of the Magicians*, 67. I have drawn much of this description from Z'ev ben Shimon Halevi, *Tree of Life: An Introduction to the Kabbalah* (London: Rider, 1972) and Will Parfitt, *The Elements of the Qabalah* (New York: Barnes & Noble, 1991).

28. Israel Regardie, *The Original Account of the Teachings, Rites and Ceremonies of the Hermetic Order of the Golden Dawn* (5th edn. St Paul, Minn.: Llewellyn Publications, 1986), 18; originally published in four volumes, this was the first publication of the secrets of the Order: rituals, ceremonies, knowledge lectures, diagrams, signs, and symbols. On p. 21 Regardie provides a convenient table indicating the relationship of the names of the sephiroth to the grades of the Order.

29. 'Ritual Z Part Three', Stony Brook.

30. Directions in a manual prepared by Mathers and Westcott, quoted in George Mills Harper, 'From Zelator to Theoricus: Yeats' "Link with the Invisible Degrees" ', in Robert O'Driscoll and Lorna Reynolds (eds.), *Yeats Studies 1* (1971), 80–6.

31. Three notebooks containing her handwritten notes exist, as well as an expanding file containing papers on the Golden Dawn relating to both GY and WBY, MBY.

32. Howe, *The Magicians of the Golden Dawn*, 23.

33. With calculations on the same page tracking the progressed moon through the months from Oct. 1914 to Dec. 1915.

34. Moore, *The Unicorn*, 134.
35. Designed in 1918 by Sturge Moore and incorporating also symbols from 'the System'.
36. Her horoscopes for 2 Dec., 4.40 p.m. and 18 Dec., 10.30 p.m. bracket Yeats's visit of 6 to 10 Dec.; later 'Nov. 1914' was identified as an initiatory moment.
37. *YVP* i. 204; Dorothy to Pound, 30 June 1912, *EPDS*, 127. Subtitled 'an Investigation of the Meanings of the Letters of the Hebrew Alphabet considered as a Remnant of Chaldean Wisdom', *The Way of Wisdom* was published by J. M. Watkins in 1900; Emery died of breast cancer on 29 Apr. 1917.
38. There is also a horary for 9 Apr. 1915 3.45 p.m., MBY.
39. MBY; copy courtesy G. M. Harper.
40. Typed notes in a brown folder, marked 'Passed Quis Separabat [Rowland D W Childers] Oct/15'; 'Lecture 6 4=6 of Philosophus', Stony Brook.
41. 'the highest Degree known to us', 'D.E.D.I.', 'Is the Order of R. R. & A. C. to Remain a Magical Order?' (1901), 8.
42. 'The Condition needed for Entry into the Second Order' by S.A. (W. Wynn Westcott), Gilbert, *Twilight of the Magicians*, 126–9.
43. As recalled in the automatic script of 6 Apr. 1919: 'Why was interpreter upset when taking 5=6 obligation?' 'To accentuate & intensify the pb & pf—to produce clairvoyance—to increase link of CB & PB & weaken spirit.'
44. So described by Evelyn Underhill in *Mysticism: A Study in the Nature and Development of Man's Spiritual Consciousness* (New York: Noonday Press, 1955 [1911]).
45. Gilbert, *Twilight of the Magicians*, 67.
46. Howe, *The Magicians of the Golden Dawn*, 89–90.
47. Regardie, *The Original Account*, 429–32; Moore, *The Unicorn*, 146.
48. Regardie, *The Original Account*, 40.
49. A vivid description of the workings of the Order's early years and some of the major figures involved, related to the astrological significance of the rituals, can be found in Greer, *Women of the Golden Dawn*.
50. 'Impression of 6=5 Ceremony Postulant Frater D.E.D.I. Oct. 16/14', George Mills Harper, *Yeats's Golden Dawn* (London: Macmillan, 1974), 306–7.
51. Regardie, *The Original Account*, 24.
52. 'D.E.D.I.', 'Is the Order of R. R. & A. C. to Remain a Magical Order?'; 4 Mar. 1918, *YVP* i. 371.
53. Quoted by Nelly to Gregory, 30 Sept. 1917, Berg.
54. Gilbert, *The Golden Dawn Companion*, 66–9; Howe, *The Magicians of the Golden Dawn*, 273; Harper, *Yeats's Golden Dawn*, 126 and 306–7; Harper, 'From Zelator to Theoricus', 80–6. According to Howe, *The Magicians of the Golden Dawn*, 276, by 11 Nov. 1914 there were 83 Outer Order members (43 men, 40 women) and 40 in the Second Order; but Gilbert, *The Golden Dawn Companion*, 41 and 166–8, states that by 1914 only 20 Second Order members remained in a total membership of Amoun of 45.
55. If the original 1894 procedures were still followed, Howe, *The Magicians of the Golden Dawn*, 77, 288–9; Gilbert, *The Golden Dawn Companion*, 119. Ellmann

states that GY 'got up to 6=5 (first grade of the Inner—when candidates lie down in Pastos of Rosencreuz)', interview notes with GY, 8 Dec. 1946, Tulsa.

56. Gilbert, *The Golden Dawn Companion*, 106–11.

57. Christina Stoddart to GY, 1 Dec. 1919: 'I find it won't after all be possible to get up Mrs Erskine's 5=6 this week so I won't bother you for any more grades until you come up in Jan,' MBY; 'She was in charge of teaching new people use of Tattwa symbols etc., when they were married,' Ellmann interview notes with GY, 8 Dec. 1946, Tulsa; Regardie, *The Original Account*, 41, 91, 457, and 515 ff. WBY and probably Georgie made use of Ráma Prasád, *The Science of Breath and the Philosophy of the Tatwas* (1890; 2nd edn. with preface by Mead, 1894), 'Clairvoyance: A Lecture by V. H. Soror Deo Date', ed. Warwick Gould, *YA* 14, 265–83.

58. Graham Hough, *The Mystery Religion of W. B. Yeats* (Hassocks: Harvester Press, 1984) offers a readable summary of Golden Dawn practices and its place in the occult tradition.

59. 'D.E.D.I.', 'A Postscript to Essay Called "Is the Order of R. R. & A. C. to Remain a Magical Order?"', in Harper, *Yeats's Golden Dawn*, 269.

60. In the Yeats papers there is a clipping from the *New York Times*, 2 Mar. 1913, 10, 'Dreams of the Insane Help Greatly in their Cure': 'Theories of Dr Freud are put in practical use at Ward's Island and in other institutions in the city that care for the mentally disturbed.' The addresses of Freud and Jung are written in the vellum notebook in use by Yeats in 1913 with information concerning their projected translation into English, MBY. However, the names of Freud and Jung were clearly unfamiliar to the anonymous stenographer recording his lecture, who misspells both, Delaware.

61. Information courtesy R. A. Gilbert.

62. 'Chaos was destitute of the life-swirl or vortex. The vortex is the finger of fire, as it were, or light-spark, shot forth by the light-aeons, in their positive phases,' Mead, *Fragments of a Faith Forgotten* (New York: University Books, 1960), 329.

63. Eight of Olivia's uncles and 'at least eighteen first cousins' were in the army, Harwood, *Olivia Shakespear and W. B. Yeats*, 7; on 8 Oct. 1914 Yeats wrote to Gregory, 'I have no particular news except that an old General, a friend of the Tuckers has said that there will be no keeping the British soldiers from reprisals when they get to Germany,' Berg.

64. GY to Mrs Pound, 7 Apr. 1920, 'I have pleasant memories of your visit to Aldeburgh in 1914,' Yale.

65. Ministering to the Christian slum-dwellers only, not the Jews, *Years of Grace*, 50.

66. May Morris to John Quinn, 7 Oct. 1914, Janis Londraville, *On Poetry, Painting, and Politics: The Letters of May Morris and John Quinn* (Selinsgrove, Pa.: Susquehanna University Press, 1997), 154.

67. Introduction to Lady Cynthia Asquith, *Diaries 1915–1918* (London: Hutchinson, 1968), p. xviii.

68. WBY to Gregory, 14 Jan. 1915, Berg.

69. WBY to Mabel Beardsley, 15 Jan. 1915, JK.

70. Moore, *The Unicorn*, 239.

71. From at least the time of her marriage Georgie was also a member of the Lyceum Club at 128 Piccadilly across from Green Park; in the 1920s Olivia Shakespear belonged to the Albemarle Club nearby at 37 Dover Street, the building later taken over by Oxford University Press.

72. Mar. 1915 is later identified as an initiatory moment; the words 'There will be four' first appeared in the scripts in July 1913 and again on 10 Feb. 1915; Eva Fowler's letters are with MBY, and the Radcliffe papers are in Stony Brook.

73. Wilbur Cross, *Zeppelins of World War I* (New York: Barnes & Noble, 1993), 24–5.

74. Vera Brittain, *Testament of Youth* (London: Gollancz, 1978), 138.

75. In a letter to John Quinn, 21 Mar. 1913, Iseult writes of Maud as 'my cousin', Janis and Richard Londraville (eds.), *Too Long a Sacrifice: The Letters of Maud Gonne and John Quinn* (Selinsgrove, Pa.: Susquehanna University Press, 1999), 106–7.

76. Asquith, *Diaries 1915–1918*, 17; Anna MacBride White and A. Norman Jeffares (eds.), *The Gonne–Yeats Letters 1893–1938* (London: Hutchinson, 1992), 357. From Sept. to Dec. 1914 Iseult was, with Maud Gonne, given the rank of lieutenant to work as a Red Cross nurse in a hospital at Argèles in the Pyrenees, White and Jeffares (eds.), *Gonne–Yeats Letters*, 349 ff.; during summer 1915 she was working with Maud in two French military hospitals in Paris Plage for six months; then from Oct. 1915 she was secretary to an Aviation Society; then back nursing by the end of the year.

77. Cross, *Zeppelins of World War I*, 53.

78. May Morris to John Quinn, 31 Dec. 1915, Londraville, *On Poetry, Painting and Politics*, 167–8.

79. WBY to Gregory, 17–18 Oct. [1915], Berg.

80. Asquith, *Diaries 1915–1918*, 77, 87; Cross, *Zeppelins of World War I*, 27–8, 41.

81. Brittain, *Testament of Youth*, 200.

82. 24 June (qtd. in B. L. Reid, *The Man from New York: John Quinn and his Friends* (New York: Oxford University Press, 1968), 16); elsewhere he described the war as 'bloody frivolity', C. M. Bowra, *Memories 1898–1939* (London: Weidenfeld & Nicolson, 1966), 239.

83. Gregory to JBY, 23 May 1917, NLI MS 30,976; WBY to Lily, 15 June 1915, Boston College; 'Clairvoyant Search for a Will', Augusta Gregory, *Sir Hugh Lane: His Life and Legacy* (Gerrards Cross: Colin Smythe, 1973), 213–15.

84. Radcliffe to WBY, 11 May [?1916].

85. WBY to Gregory, 29 Jan. 1915, Berg.

86. Meuccio's compilation is mistakenly catalogued in YL as *Prophetia et Alia*; I am grateful to Warwick Gould for identifying it. 'Sepharial' was the author of *Directional Astrology* (London: William Rider, 1915) and *Eclipses* (London: W. Foulsham, 1915); GY later purchased his *Primary Directions Made Easy* (London: Foulsham, 1917) and *The Science of Foreknowledge* (London: Foulsham, 1918); also WBY to Miss Little, 24 Nov. 1921, NLI MS 30,563. Leo, *Casting the Horoscope*, 111, dismisses the methods proposed by Morinus as 'practically abandoned'.

87. Stony Brook; three pages exist of Georgie's calculations of 'Primaries W. B. Yeats with RAMC' from July 1884 to June 1915, Stony Brook.

88. Arthur Marwick, *Women at War 1914–1918*, qtd. by Deborah Gorham, *Vera Brittain: A Feminist Life* (Toronto: University of Toronto Press, 1996), 101.

89. Brittain, *Testament of Youth*, 180; *A Great Work in which we all Share* [Toronto Red Cross, 1916]; Washington, *Madame Blavatsky's Baboon*, 167–8. The Endsleigh Hospital seems normally to have operated independently of the Red Cross, although assisted by volunteers; the only reference in the official reports for 1914 to 1920 refers to an invitation 'to supply the household staff' when 'a domestic crisis' arose (*The British Red Cross Society County of London Branch* (London: Harrison & Sons, [n.d.])), 75). I am grateful to the British Red Cross Society Archives for details of Georgie's service, and to William Benzie for identifying the building, which now houses University College London Union.

90. The Kensington Training Centre was organized by the Hon. Gorell Barnes, father of the man who was later to marry Elizabeth Radcliffe; Red Cross Report, 16–17.

91. Asquith, *Diaries 1915–1918*, 248, 285; 'We were there to be useful and not to be taught things,' Brittain, *Testament of Youth*, 309.

92. Constance Babington Smith, *John Masefield: A Life* (London: Oxford University Press, 1978), 135.

93. Howe, *The Magicians of the Golden Dawn*, 275; it is tempting to see this as a precursor to Yeats's 'The Second Coming' (1919).

94. The script and notebooks all identify these dates as an initiatory moment for Georgie.

95. Nelly to Gregory, 30 Sept. 1917, Berg; WBY to Gregory, 22 Sept. 1917, Berg.

96. WBY to Lily Yeats, 15 June 1915, Boston College.

97. Jaffe, 'Vignettes', 143–4; I am grateful to the Principal's Office for details of Grace's attendance at Cheltenham Ladies College, 1914–17.

98. Brittain, *Testament of Youth*, 130; 'One thing is that now at least people will no longer bury their dead as they used. Now they are so many one *must* talk of them naturally and humanly, not banish them by only alluding to them as if it were almost indelicate,' Asquith, *Diaries 1915–1918*, 97.

99. Copy courtesy Omar Shakespear Pound, who discovered it among his mother's papers.

100. Asquith, *Diaries 1915–1918*, 248; Brittain, *Testament of Youth*, 251.

101. Asquith, *Diaries 1915–1918*, 449–51.

102. Red Cross Report, 22; Brittain, *Testament of Youth*, 166, 211, 339.

103. Both of her children in turn sleepwalked, AY.

104. 'Three lectures on certain phases of art and religion in the Roman empire' (London: Constable, 1915), signed and dated 1916.

105. WBY to Gregory, 10 Apr. 1916, JK.

106. Asquith, *Diaries 1915–1918*, 152.

107. WBY to Gregory, 25 May 1916, Berg.

108. Gilbert, *The Golden Dawn Companion*, 41, 66 ff.

109. 'Ritual 5=6', Stony Brook.

110. Harper, 'From Zelator to Theoricus', 80–6.

111. Vellum notebook, Stony Brook; Hobby, 87 ff.

112. *Occult Review*, 24/1, 51–2.
113. Including C. G. M. Adam, *Fresh Sidelights on Astrology* (London: Modern Astrology Office, 1916), which is mistakenly described in Edward O'Shea, *A Descriptive Catalog of W. B. Yeats's Library* (New York: Garland, 1985), 4 as having WBY's bookplate, not hers.
114. Conrad Balliet, 'The Lives—and Lies—of Maud Gonne', *Eire-Ireland*, 14/3 (Fall 1979), 43; WBY to Gregory, 18 and 21 June, 3 and 16 July 1916, Berg; Curtis Bradford claims WBY proposed to Maud in Sept., but all the evidence points to the beginning of July, 'Yeats and Maud Gonne', *Texas Studies in Literature and Language*, 3/4 (Winter 1962), 470.
115. Brittain, *Testament of Youth*, 274, 279–80.
116. Eva Fowler to WBY, 13 Oct. 1916 (misdated 1917 in *LTWBY* ii. 336–7); WBY to Gregory, 19 and 14 Aug. 1916, Berg.
117. Cross, *Zeppelins of World War I*, 93; Charles Ricketts, *Self-Portrait*, comp. T. Sturge Moore, ed. Cecil Lewis (London: Peter Davies, 1939), 265–7.
118. WBY to Gregory, 8 Sept. 1916, Berg.
119. 'The Gogartys came to dinner and Yeats came to tea—he was said to be going to marry Maud Gonne's eighteen year old daughter,' Mark Amory, *Biography of Lord Dunsany* (London: Collins, 1972), 132–3; Lily to R L-P, 12 Nov. 1916, WMM.
120. NLI 30,764; the *Vision* Card File A34 lists this date as Georgie's fifth 'initiatory moment', *YVP* iii. 240–1; the automatic script for 22 Dec. 1919 links it with a 'Madam V', *YVP* ii. 520, probably Madame Vandervelde, wife of the Belgian Ambassador in Dublin in WW1 whom Ellmann met at Buswell's in the 1940s and who boasted she had had affairs with WBY and H. G. Wells. GY was very interested, and wished she had met her, Ellmann interview with me, 31 July 1985.
121. WBY to Horton, 22 Jan. 1917, George Mills Harper (ed.), *W. B. Yeats and W. T. Horton: The Record of an Occult Friendship* (London: Macmillan, 1980), 131.
122. 'Perhaps I had not said definitely enough that I cannot have Iseult on a visit—it is impracticable . . . So please put away this idea from any plans you may make for her. I am sorry you told her you had asked me to have her, for it will make it awkward for me to see her should I be in Dublin again,' Gregory to WBY, [July 1916], Stony Brook.
123. WBY to Gregory, 9 Mar. 1917, Stony Brook.
124. WBY to Emery, 5 Mar. 1917, JK.
125. Recorded by WBY on 26 Aug. 1920, Notebook 6 and Card File D4, *YVP* iii. 39, 278.
126. Nelly to Gregory, 30 Sept. 1917; a horoscope in Yeats's hand for Sunday, 18 Mar., at 9 p.m. is labelled 'I Trevor Square', which is just around the corner from the Tuckers' home at 16 Montpelier Square; another for 9.15 a.m. two days later (coinciding with the equinox festival) is described as 'I. M. of GBY' and Yeats's Vision Notebook identifies this as one of his 'critical moments' leading to 'Nativity of First Child'; the automatic script and Card File C45 discuss this 'evocative moment', the 'unconscious communicator' identified as 'Mrs T', Georgie's mother, *YVP* ii. 202–3. George told Jeffares that she and Yeats discussed marriage in Mar. 1917, letter to me and White and Jeffares (ed.), *Gonne–Yeats Letters*, 40.

127. On 23 Mar. 1917 he consulted a mechanical medium in St Leonards, vellum note-book, Stony Brook; WBY to Gregory, TS copy annotated by GY; MBY.

128. The session took place at Woburn Buildings on 17 May 1917, MBY; Rabshekeh's story is in 2 Kings 18.

129. WBY to Shakespear, 15 May 1917, Wade, 625–6.

130. Asquith, *Diaries 1915–1918*, 398–9.

131. Brittain, *Testament of Youth*, 365.

132. Lily to JBY, 18 June 1917, NLI MS 31,112.

133. Asquith, *Diaries 1915–1918*, 314.

134. Cross, *Zeppelins of World War I*, 137; Sinéad McCoole, *Hazel: A Life of Lady Lavery 1880–1935* (Dublin: Lilliput, 1996), 61; Ricketts, *Self-Portrait*, 279–80.

135. WBY to Shakespear, 10 July 1917, Wade, 627.

136. Gregory to JBY, fragment, [?Nov./Dec. 1917], Stony Brook.

137. *Pound/Lewis*, 94; the drawing has since disappeared.

138. WBY to Georgie, 5 Oct. 1917: 'I kiss the tops of your fingers where they are marked by the acid.'

139. Brittain, *Testament of Youth*, 208.

140. GY told Ellmann that she stopped nursing in Aug., Ellmann interview notes with GY, 17 Jan. 1947, Tulsa; the Red Cross archives give as date of termination Sept. 1917.

141. Nelly to Gregory, 30 Sept. 1917, Berg.

142. WBY to Gregory, 12 Aug. 1917, Berg.

143. Iseult to Thora Pilcher, [? Aug. 1916], qtd. by Balliet, 'The Lives—and Lies—of Maud Gonne', 43; Richard Ellmann, preface to *Yeats: The Man and the Masks* (Oxford: Oxford University Press, rev. edn. 1979), p. xv.

144. WBY to Gregory, 8 Sept. 1917, Wade, 631.

145. A. N. Jeffares, *W. B. Yeats: Man and Poet* (2nd edn. London: Routledge & Kegan Paul, 1949), 190.

146. WBY to Gregory, 18 Sept. 1917, Wade, 632.

147. Ellmann, *The Man and the Masks*, 1979 preface, p. xv; WBY to Gregory, 18 Sept. 1917, Wade, 632.

148. WBY to Gregory, 19 Sept. 1917; the sentences about Maud's conviction omitted in Wade, 632–3; Wade to GY, 27 Feb. 1952, Rupert Hart-Davis.

149. Radcliffe to WBY, 17 Sept. 1917, MBY.

150. Horton to WBY, 23 Oct. 1916, Harper (ed.), *W. B. Yeats and W. T. Horton*, 130.

151. 'Florence Farr: Letters to Yeats, 1912–1917', ed. Josephine Johnson, *YA* 9, 238–9.

152. WBY to Gregory, 22 Sept. 1917, Stony Brook.

153. Hesketh Pearson, *Conan Doyle: His Life and Art* (London: Methuen, 1943), 166 ff. I am grateful to Malcolm Payne of Crowborough for identifying and providing a photograph of 'Rosewood'.

154. Ellmann, *The Man and the Masks*, 1979 preface, p. xvi.

155. WBY to Macmillan, 17 Sept. 1917, BL Add. MS 55,003/49.

156. WBY to John Quinn, 16 May [1917], NYPL; the essay was originally entitled *The Alphabet*.

157. Berg; this and Nelly's next letter are quoted by Harwood, *Olivia Shakespear and W. B. Yeats*, 157–8, where the analysis differs somewhat from mine.
158. Moore, *The Unicorn*, 252–3.
159. Asquith, *Diaries 1915–1918*, 349.
160. Interview with Grace Jaffe, 18 Oct. 1985.
161. MG to WBY, 8 May 1913, 26 or 27 July 1913; White and Jeffares (eds.), *Gonne-Yeats Letters*, 320, 322–3.
162. MG to WBY, ?3 Oct. 1917, ibid. 392.
163. Arthur Symons to Quinn, 22 Nov. 1917, NYPL.
164. Ellmann interview notes with Iseult Gonne Stuart, 21 Sept. 1946, Tulsa.
165. WBY to Gregory, 13 Oct. 1917, Berg.
166. Nelly to Gregory, 9 Oct. 1917, Berg; Gregory to Georgie, 5 Oct. 1917.
167. JBY to Mrs Caughey, 20 Nov. 1917, WMM.
168. The letters between WBY and George are with MBY.
169. Ellmann interview notes with GY, 8 Dec. 1946, Tulsa; Jeffares says Iseult offered to marry WBY in 1910, but was rejected 'because there was too much Mars in her horoscope', *W. B. Yeats: Man and Poet*, 190; WBY used to address his letters to Mabel Dickinson, 'Dear Neptune'.
170. I am grateful to Elizabeth Heine for help in unravelling these references; see her 'W. B. Yeats: Poet and Astrologer', *Culture and Cosmos*, 1/2 (Winter/Autumn 1997), 60–75 for a detailed discussion of the Yeatses' natal horoscopes.
171. WBY to George Russell (AE), ?1 Nov. 1891, *The Collected Letters of W. B. Yeats*, i: *1865–1895*, ed. John Kelly and Eric Domville (Oxford: Clarendon Press, 1986), 266.
172. WBY to Gregory, 10 Oct. 1917, Berg; GY to Gregory, 10 Oct. 1917, MBY; Heine, 'W. B. Yeats: Poet and Astrologer', 69–70; Moore, *The Unicorn*, 216.
173. WBY to Gregory, 13 Oct. 1917, Berg.
174. WBY to JBY, 15 Oct. 1917, WMM; Mary Colum's review of Wade's letters stated baldly: 'On his wedding day in his fifties he was possessed of only ten pounds. But the lady he married, fortunately, had an income,' *New York Times Book Review*, 20 Feb. 1955.
175. AY.
176. WBY to Georgie, 16 Oct. 1917.
177. WBY to Ricketts, 23 Dec. 1917, JK; the automatic script for 17 Apr. 1919 gives the date of conception of the third daimon (which required 'sexual union') as 19 Oct. 1917, *YVP* ii. 255.
178. Two copies of the certificate, entry no. 58 in the Book of Marriages no. 72, exist among the Yeats papers, one issued 19 July 1921, the second 27 Oct. 1927; a horoscope by Willy gives the precise time, MBY.
179. Arthur S. May, *Marriage in Church Chapel and Register Office* (London: Longmans, 1920), 66; the Woolfs were married on 10 Aug. 1912, Leonard Woolf, *Beginning Again* (Hassocks: Harvester, 1963), 69.
180. GY to Dolly Travers Smith, 22 July 1931, Sotheby's sale catalogue 21–2 July 1983, no. 584, copy courtesy Colin Smythe.

181. Pound to Quinn, 3 Nov. 1917, NYPL.
182. Lily to JBY, 2 Nov. 1917, NLI MS 31,112.
183. 22 Oct. 1917, *Pound/Lewis*, 111.
184. Ellmann interview notes with GY, 8 Dec. 1946, Tulsa.
185. Lily to Quinn, 25 Oct. 1917, NYPL.
186. WBY's congratulatory phrase to Pound on his engagement, 8 Mar. 1914, Indiana.
187. WBY to Gregory, 24 Oct. 1917, fragment or unsigned, Berg.
188. WBY to Edmund Dulac, 22 Oct. 1917, Hobby, 102.
189. I am grateful to Allan Pratt for his assistance in identifying the room and showing me around the hotel and grounds.
190. Earlier that year Cynthia Asquith stayed with her husband at an inn in Ashdown Forest near the camp, *Diaries 1915–1918*, 269–71.
191. I am grateful to Christina Bridgwater for this paraphrase of Iseult's undated letter.
192. Interview with Virginia Moore.
193. WBY's horary is on p. 210 of Waite's compendium; GY's is in her blue MS book. GY's errors were as follows: although also consulting an ephemeris, she put Jupiter in Taurus rather than in Gemini, and Venus in Scorpio rather than Sagittarius; WBY put 28 Taurus at the ascendant while GY put 20 Taurus on the ascendant, so her horary is 8 degrees earlier than his. Because of these errors hers is set for a time twenty minutes earlier but in reality was drawn after his, Elizabeth Heine.
194. 'interpreters C. M.' (later corrected to O. M.) 'When you told of the letter', *YVP* ii. 224; 'Oct. 24th–5 1917 4 to 5', automatic script for 22 Dec. 1919, *YVP* ii. 520.
195. Dated by WBY 'Oct 25–26', but GY first dates it 24 Oct., the day he began writing the poem. This appears to be the earliest extant draft, although because of the neatness of transcription it was probably not the first; it is written in a brown leather manuscript book given him by Maud Gonne for Christmas 1912 which also contains accounts of Radcliffe's automatic script, Maud's notes of May 1914 on the bleeding oleograph, and, among other drafts, 'Subject for Poem. I give first praise to woman . . .', NLI 30,358. The copy he sent to Lady Gregory, without numbered stanzas and a few minor alterations in spelling and punctuation, is entitled 'He complains of his heart', and is dated 'Oct 25 & 30', copy courtesy the late Richard Gregory.
196. Moore, *The Unicorn*, 253; GY made this admission to Moore but, misinterpreting Moore's endnote 462 n. 60, which refers to WBY's letter to Olivia Shakespear concerning a later incident, recent critics have assumed that it was GY herself who wrote to Olivia on 9 July 1928. 'Her idea was to fake a sentence or two that would allay his anxieties over Iseult and herself, and after the session to own up to what she had done,' Ellmann, *The Man and the Masks*, 1979 preface, pp. xv–xvii.
197. WBY to Gregory, 29 Oct. 1917, Wade, 633–4.
198. See for example 'Two Songs of a Fool', written, according to George, about 20 Sept. 1918: 'A speckled cat and a tame hare | Eat at my hearthstone | And sleep there; | And both look up to me alone | For learning and defence | As I look up to Providence.'

199. 'She was confident that he would decipher the cat as her watchful and timid self, and the hare as Iseult—a fleet runner,' Ellmann, *The Man and the Masks*, 1979 preface, p. xvi.

200. WBY to Gregory, 29 Oct. 1917, Wade, 634.

201. Moore, *The Unicorn*, 253; 'Had it not been for the emotional involvement, she thinks nothing would have come of it—but as it was she felt her hand grasped and driven irresistibly,' Ellmann interview notes with GY, 8 Dec. 1946, Tulsa, and 'The pencil began to write sentences she had never intended or thought which seemed to come as from another world,' Ellmann, *The Man and the Masks*, 1979 preface, pp. xv–xvii. 'In telepathic experiments I find that there is greater success in results when emotion gives driving force to a thought transferred to another mind,' Cummins, *Unseen Adventures*, 31.

202. According to Wade, 633–4, this letter is postmarked 29 Oct. 1917, but sufficient evidence suggests it was written by the 26th or 27th and simply not posted for several days; I therefore disagree with Harper's contention, based on the date assigned by Wade, that the automatic script did not begin until the 27th, *MYV* i. 3–4.

203. Ellmann interview notes with GY, 9 July 1947, Tulsa.

204. GY to 'Derry' [Jeffares], late Aug. or Sept. 1961; Ellmann, *The Man and the Masks*, 222.

205. WBY, introduction to *A Vision* (2nd edn. London: Macmillan, 1937).

206. Qtd. by Harper, *MYV* ii. 416.

207. Paraphrase by Christina Bridgwater; see also White and Jeffares (eds.), *Gonne–Yeats Letters*, 392.

208. Guha, *W. B. Yeats: An Indian Approach*, 80, points out the similarities to Tagore's poem *The Gardener*, where section VI begins with the lines 'The tame bird was in a cage, the free bird was in the forest, | They met when the time came, it was a decree of fate | The free bird cries, "O my love, let us fly to the wood." | The cage bird whispers, "Come hither, let us both live in the cage" ', *Collected Poems and Plays of Rabindranath Tagore* (London: Macmillan, 1958), 93–4.

209. This section entitled 'His heart replies' is dated 30 Oct. by WBY, Richard Gregory, but WBY's letter to Lady Gregory when he speaks of the poems as 'among the best I have done' is postmarked 29 Oct., Wade, 634; GY annotates 'His Heart Replies' 'Oct 30 in MSS book but Oct 27'. First printed in the *Dial*, June 1924, with the titles 'The Lover Speaks' and 'His Heart Replies'; a cleaner manuscript in NLI 13,589, which is annotated by George 'dates of writing Oct 24 & 27 1917', is entitled 'Owen Aherne and his Dancers', as in *The Tower* (1928).

210. Elizabeth Heine, 'W. B. Yeats: Poet and Astrologer', 70–1.

CHAPTER 6: FOREST ROW

1. T. Werner Laurie published the first edition, referred to here as *A Vision A*, in 1937; Macmillan published a second much revised edition, referred to here as *A Vision B*.

2. This date seems to have been agreed upon during an hour's interval in the session of 22 Dec. 1919, *YVP* ii. 520, Card File O6, *YVP* iii. 349.

3. *MYV* i. 3–4; *YVP* i. 10; but see previous chapter.

4. From a rejected passage attributed to Owen Aherne, quoted in editorial introduction to *A Critical Edition of Yeats's 'A Vision' (1925)*, ed. George Mills Harper and Walter Kelly Hood (London: Macmillan, 1978), p. xii.

5. Jeanne Foster, Quinn's mistress, recalled George's statement to her, qtd. in letter to me from Richard Londraville, 24 Aug. 1989.

6. Dorothy to Pound, 4 Sept. 1913, *EPDS*, 249.

7. WBY to Dulac, 25 Oct. 1917, Hobby, 102.

8. Introduction to *A Vision B*.

9. Allan Wade's TS copy sent to GY, Stony Brook, and NLI 30,560.

10. WBY to Radcliffe, 28 Oct. 1917, qtd. by Harper, *MYV* i. 7; on 9 Nov. Yeats used almost the exact phrasing in a letter to Margaret Gregory's friend Alick Schepeler, with whom he apparently had had a brief liaison, thanking her for her good wishes: 'My wife & I are fellow students in all my interests so I think we should prosper,' Huntington.

11. WBY to Radcliffe, 11 Nov. 1917, *YVP* i. 11.

12. Radcliffe to WBY, 13 Nov. 1917, *LTWBY* ii. 339, where the date is given as 9 not 4 Oct.

13. WBY to Gregory, 29 Oct., Wade, 34 and 3 Nov. 1917, Emory; a typed copy of his second letter bears the following annotation: 'GY: (1) "A Strange thing surely" etc Oct 25/26 (2) "The Heart behind its ribs laughed out" etc. Oct 30 in MSS book but Oct 27.' George was in the habit of providing the dates of completion, MBY.

14. 'He was indefatigable about it, making her do it for 2 or 3 hours an afternoon—3 to 6,' Ellmann interview notes with GY, 8 Dec. 1946, Tulsa.

15. *YVP* ii. 180; *YVP* iii. 256.

16. Geraldine Cummins describes 'the easy and natural way in which Mr Yeats conducted the sitting and thereby drew out the character and personality of the communicator', 'W. B. Yeats and Psychical Research', *Occult Review*, 66 (Apr. 1939), 135; 'I find that in these experiments the particular sitter naturally makes an immense difference. If Mr. Y. is present at a sitting and he concentrates on a card, number, or letter, or even a word, the proportion of successful results is very large compared to those achieved through other sitters. Mr. Y. is not a sitter himself, but he has a very remarkable influence on a séance, and undoubtedly he has great power of conveying thought to controls,' Hester Travers Smith, *Voices from the Void: Six Years' Experience in Automatic Communications* (New York: Dutton, 1919), 83.

17. *YVP* i. 83.

18. WBY to Gregory, 16 Dec. 1917, Wade, 634.

19. Ellmann interview notes with GY, 8 Dec. 1946, Tulsa; T. S. Eliot spent an evening in early Mar. 1917 at the Omega Club 'discussing psychical research with William Butler Yeats (the only thing he ever talks about, except Dublin gossip)', T. S. Eliot to Eleanor Hinkley, 23 Mar. 1917, *The Letters of T. S. Eliot*, i: *1898–1922*, ed. Valerie Eliot (London: Faber, 1988), 169.

20. *YVP* i. 63, also script of Jan. 1919, *YVP* ii. 158 ff.; Yeats to Dulac, June 1920, Hobby, 134.

21. Monk Gibbon, *The Masterpiece and the Man: Yeats as I Knew Him* (London: Rupert Hart-Davis, 1959), 79.

22. Travers Smith, *Voices from the Void*, 7–8. Daughter of Trinity College Professor Edward Dowden, she was well known as a medium both in Dublin and London; familiar to both Yeats and Lennox Robinson, she published messages from Hugh Lane and Oscar Wilde among others; she describes how Hugh Lane's communication violently seized Robinson's hand and arm, pushing them around the board so there was difficulty holding on to the 'traveller', 112.

23. WBY to Gregory, 25 Nov. 1917, WMM; 'The spiritism-hating Dorothy Pound, among other witnesses, has testified to the physical exhaustion induced by Mrs Yeats's mediumship,' Moore, *The Unicorn*, 258.

24. GY to Dulac from Ballylee, 16 Aug. 1922: 'Just at present I am emerging from a bad attack of rheumatism all over, and I can't do much. That is why I am typing this letter; it is easier than grasping a pen,' Hobby, 154–5.

25. Bette London, *Writing Double: Women's Literary Partnerships* (Ithaca, NY: Cornell University Press, 1999), 152 n.; the script for 20 Mar. 1919 begins, 'No longer the medium Thomas—different name Interpreter', *YVP* ii. 200. Cummins also disliked the word medium.

26. Dorothy to Pound, 28 May 1913, *EPDS*, 230–1; Mrs Barker's volumes were *Letters from a Living Dead Man* (1914), *War Letters from the Living Dead Man* (1915), *Last Letters from the Living Dead Man* (1919); R. A. Gilbert, 'Seeking that which was Lost: More Light on the Origins and Development of the Golden Dawn', *YA* 14, 49 n. 24.

27. 'The Manuscript of "Leo Africanus" ', ed. Steve L. Adams and George Mills Harper, *YA*1, 3–48.

28. 10 Jan. 1918, *YVP* i. 237; 'subliminal' was the word used by Myers for 'beneath the threshold of consciousness'.

29. See Chapter 4 for her research on texts mentioned by MacGregor Mathers, including Raymon Llull (or Raymond Lully).

30. Myers, 'Automatic Writing, or The Rationale of Planchette', 243.

31. 7 Nov. 1917, *YVP* i. 64; WBY to Gregory, 25 Nov. 1917, WMM.

32. My own sitting with the highly respected Mrs Ivy Northage of the College of Psychic Studies began with her asking whether we (Colin Smythe and I) wanted her or her control 'Chan', who, she insisted, was far more interested in philosophical teaching than answering personal questions. We chose 'Chan'.

33. 5 Nov. 1917, *YVP* i. 55; 11 Nov. *YVP* i. 78.

34. London, *Writing Double*, 163 n.

35. Cummins, who was first initiated at Travers Smith's ouija board, rejected the term 'automatic writing' altogether; the classicist E. R. Dodds, later president of the SPR, was another sitter with Travers Smith, Cummins, *Unseen Adventures*, 133, 151, 168.

36. *YVP* i. 201.

37. Suggested by Deirdre Toomey, 'The Unwilling Persephone', *YA* 10 (1993), 273. Ochorowicz's medium was Tomczyk who had married Everard Feilding, SPR researcher and friend of both Olivia and Yeats.

38. Script in London, 21 May 1919, *YVP* ii. 285.
39. Also 'Alastor', 'Elder', 'Honoras', 'Marcus', 'the Pylons' or 'Pulons', 'Thalassa'. My suggestions of sources could be elaborated in many directions.
40. *Autobiographies*, 217; Notebook 7 and Vision Notebook 2, *YVP* iii. 75 and 185.
41. 23 May 1920, George's recapitulation of four 'sleeps', Notebook 4, *YVP* iii. 18; see also WBY's essay 'Swedenborg, Mediums and the Desolate Places X': 'Plutarch, in his essay on the daimon, describes how the souls of enlightened men return to the schoolmasters of the living, whom they influence unseen.' *The Collected Works of W. B. Yeats*, v: *Later Essays*, ed. William H. O'Donnell (New York: Charles Scribner's, 1994), 65.
42. Dated Feb. 1924; defined in *A Vision B*, 83 as the 'ultimate self of man'.
43. 'Sleep' of 14 and 15 Aug. 1920, written up by GY in Notebook 6, *YVP* iii. 33.
44. Graham Hough compares the daimon, 'a spirit . . . attached by some affinity-in-opposition to a living man', to the Jungian Anima, 'a contra-sexual image, the interpreter and representative of the unconscious as a whole, always opposite to the Will or consciousness of man; a main agent in what Jung calls the integration of the personality, and Yeats calls Unity of Being'. *The Mystery Religion of W. B. Yeats* (Hassocks: Harvester Press, 1984), 112–13.
45. 23 Mar. 1919, *YVP* ii. 211.
46. 1 July 1920, Notebook 6, *YVP* iii. 28.
47. MBY; NLI; WBY to Shakespear, 9 July 1928, Wade, 744.
48. James's statement is frequently quoted: 'If you wish to upset the law that all crows are black . . . it is enough if you prove that one crow is white. My white crow is Mrs Piper.'
49. Nandor Fodor, *The Haunted Mind: A Psychoanalyst Looks at the Supernatural* (New York: Helix Press, 1959), 58.
50. WBY to Gregory, 15 Dec. 1913, Berg; he recorded later sessions with Mrs Herbine in 1915.
51. 'Anima Mundi, II'; 'There is nothing supernatural about it . . . In magic the "will to know" is the centre round which the personality is rearranged. As in mysticism, unconscious factors are dragged from the hiddenness to form part of that personality. The uprushes of thought, the abrupt intuitions which reach us from the subliminal region, are developed, ordered, and controlled by rhythms and symbols which have become tradition because the experience of centuries has proved, though it cannot explain, their efficacy: and powers of apprehension which normally lie below the threshold may thus be liberated and enabled to report their discoveries,' Underhill, *Mysticism*, 157.
52. Mrs Piper was later a party to the cross-correspondences involving Oliver Lodge's son Raymond (*Encyclopedia of Occultism and Parapsychology*, 2nd edn., 1037–40).
53. WBY to Ethel Mannin, 9 Oct. 1938, Wade, 916–17.
54. Qtd. in the editorial introduction to *A Critical Edition of Yeats's 'A Vision' (1925)*, p. xxxix.
55. WBY, introduction to *A Vision B*, 8–9; Peter Allt, 'Yeats, Religion and History', *Sewanee Review* (Oct.–Dec. 1952), 643–8.

56. 'Hodos Chameliontos II', *The Trembling of the Veil* (1922), W. B. Yeats, *Auto-biographies*, ed. William H. O'Donnell and Douglas N. Archibald (New York: Scribner, 1999), 210.

57. *YVP* iii. 399–400; *A Critical Edition of Yeats's 'A Vision' (1925)*, pp. xii–xvii.

58. Perhaps more if some script was not preserved. Dates and places are usefully tabulated in the editorial introduction to *A Critical Edition of Yeats's 'A Vision' (1925)*, pp. xix–xxi. *YVP* i. 56–7, 58.

59. Janet Oppenheim, *That Other World: Spiritualism and Psychical Research in England 1850–1914* (Cambridge: Cambridge University Press, 1985), 165.

60. Ellmann interview notes with GY, 8 Dec. 1946, Tulsa; Harper, *Yeats's Golden Dawn*, 125–6, 282; *YVP* i. 49 n. 2. Blavatsky claimed direct knowledge from the Mahatmas; MacGregor Mathers consulted his wife's automatic writing; Dr Felkin consulted the Secret Chiefs and the Sun Masters by writing a report and then receiving their comments via his wife's or his own mediumship, Howe, *The Magicians of the Golden Dawn*, 258–9; the transcriptions from Stainton's script of 1873 and 1875 included messages concerning John Dee.

61. Foster, *W. B. Yeats* i. 201–3, 387–8.

62. Qtd. by Bachchan, *W. B. Yeats and Occultism*, 238–9.

63. See Chapter 5 above.

64. Interview with John Montague; Myers describes the planchette as 'no occult instrument, but simply a thin piece of board supported on two castors, and on a third leg consisting of a pencil which just touches the paper . . . two advantages over the ordinary pencil . . . a slighter impulse will start it, and . . . it is easier to write (or rather scrawl) without seeing or feeling what you are writing,' 'Automatic Writing, or The Rationale of Planchette', 237.

65. 17 Oct. 1919, *YVP* ii. 451–3.

66. On 29 Nov. 1917 Marcus chided George for not wearing her sun talisman. *YVP* i. 124. Guha, *W. B. Yeats: An Indian Approach*, 70–2; preparation for the 4=7 grade of Philosophus included the Tattwa lecture on 'the Science of Breath'; all members of the order were instructed in the delicate manufacture of talismans.

67. In this case Thomas was also introducing the new method of 'talking', *YVP* ii. 182.

68. The sword was presented to them in Portland on 20 Mar. by Junzo Sato; Notebook 8, 7 Oct. 1921, records Dionertes' advice 'to draw the Sword & lay a flower upon it for symbol of 3rd Daimon', *YVP* iii. 99.

69. 14 Apr. 1919; see also 17 Apr. 1919, 'do invocation together close', *YVP* ii. 247, 254.

70. 8 June 1919; 19 Jan. 1919, 12.10 p.m. 'Thomas and Rose Now put out candle—you should light it *before* you call me & I want a *permanent* flame if I am to come in the mornings'; 24 May 1919, 'What have you forgotten—two things—prayer & ceremony,' *YVP* ii. 298–9; 180–2; 286.

71. Introduction to *A Vision B*.

72. When Hazard Adams was studying in Yeats's library in 1951 he recalled occasionally hearing whistles from another room as he worked, and in GY's presence 'the emission of sharp whistles when she attempted to bring something in particular to mind', adding, 'It is certainly possible to believe that if anyone is a medium she might have been', letter and interview 1987.

73. Deirdre Toomey suggests a connection with Maud Gonne, 'The Unwilling Persephone', 272, but this seems unlikely under the circumstances, and use of violet scents was common; according to her daughter, GY favoured Roget et Gallet toiletries.
74. *Mediumship of Mrs Leonard*, 215.
75. 'Clairvoyant Search for a Will [1915]', 209–15; 'a spirit may under a curious psychological necessity described by Swedenborg, have built up round itself a fictitious personality,' WBY to Lily, Feb. 1916, Boston College.
76. 12 Nov. 1917, *YVP* i. 81; 20 Nov., *YVP* i. 86.
77. *YVP* ii. 42.
78. Ellmann interview notes with GY, 17 Jan. 1947, Tulsa.
79. Hazard Adams's evocation of the Renaissance term 'mathesis' is relevant here, *The Book of Yeats's Vision: Romantic Modernism and Antithetical Tradition* (Ann Arbor: University of Michigan Press, 1995), 235.
80. '[Yeats's] double gyre extends to a vision in which human life from birth to death is supplemented by an after-life which is purgatorial and runs from death to birth again, taking the form of a "dreaming back", a kind of total psychoanalysis. . . . We notice that the purgatorial theme in Dante also includes the image of moving from death back to birth again, as Dante is traveling towards the place of his original birth as a child of an unfallen Adam,' Northrop Frye, *Words with Power* (New York: Viking, 1990), 161.
81. 25 and 30 Nov. 1917, *YVP* i. 122–3, 126.
82. WBY to Gregory, 3 Nov. 1917, Emory.
83. 21 Dec. 1917, 7 Jan. 1918, *YVP* i. 177, 219; *MYV* i. 147–51, also Gregory N. Eaves, 'The Anti-Theatre and its Double', *YA* 13 (1998), 34–61.
84. Historical cycles were first discussed on 21 Nov. 1917, the twenty-eight phases a few days later, and the mask before Christmas, *YVP* i. 94, 119.
85. 23 Dec. 1917 and 1 Jan. 1918, *YVP* i. 175 and 185.
86. George told Ellmann that WBY 'would not have conceived of "The Second Coming" as the annihilation of intellect without the system', Ellmann interview notes with GY, 17 Jan. 1947, Tulsa. In addition to the poems written to GY, all of which intimate a knowledge of her mediumship, others bearing a more direct relationship to the philosophical system include 'Solomon to Sheba', 'Solomon and the Witch', 'Two Songs of a Fool', 'Another Song of a Fool', 'Shepherd and Goatherd', 'Towards Break of Day', 'An Image from a Past Life', 'The Phases of the Moon', 'Under the Round Tower', 'The Four Ages of Man', 'The Second Coming', 'The Saint and the Hunchback', 'Gratitude to the Unknown Instructors', 'The Gift of Harun Al-Rashid', 'The Spirit Medium', 'The Double Vision of Michael Robartes', 'The Gyres', 'Fragments', and the play *Calvary*.
87. *YVP* i. 199. Dorothy Pound told Virginia Moore she thought the intimacy with Olivia continued even after marriage, but there is no evidence of this, and given Olivia's principles and fondness for GY, it is unlikely (interview with Moore). See script of 6 Sept. 1919: 'Who was my wife jealous of in 1700 incarnation,' 'The woman who is now [upside down writing] Olivia Shakespere.' 'Did that jealousy create a knot,' 'Yes . . . necessitated expiation in life.' 'That expiation now complete,'

'nearly 4 years ago.' Of the four people representing 'four periods of great influences' in his life, Olivia was surely the one GY knew well, *YVP* i. 122.

88. WBY to Iseult Gonne, 18 Aug. 1918, JK.

89. 4 Jan. 1918, *YVP* i. 200.

90. Note to 'An Image from a Past Life', *Michael Robartes and the Dancer* (Dundrum: Cuala Press, 1921).

91. 3 Sept. 1918 and 25 May 1919, *YVP* ii. 41 and 289.

92. JBY to Oliver Elton, 9 Apr. 1911, collection Leonard Elton, courtesy WMM.

93. *YVP* ii. 291–2.

94. *YVP* ii. 405. '*Mandookya Upanishad* with an Introduction by William Butler Yeats', section VII, *Criterion* (July 1935), *Essays and Introductions*, 484; Guha points out that the Yeatses would have first encountered 'Yantra', the geometrical figure of a double triangle used for meditation, in Blavatsky's *The Secret Doctrine*, *W. B. Yeats: An Indian Approach*, 125; it also appears in the Order lectures.

95. MBY.

96. 13 Apr. 1919, 21 Dec. 1919, 25 Dec. 1918, *YVP* ii. 244, 519, 152.

97. 9 Apr. 1919, *YVP* ii. 240.

98. Åsa Boholm, 'How to Make a Stone Give Birth to Itself: Reproduction and Autoreproduction in Medieval and Renaissance Alchemy', in Goran Aimher (ed.), *Coming into Existence: Birth and Metaphors of Birth* (Göteborg: IASSA, 1992), 137; I am grateful to Cynthea Masson for this reference.

99. Heine, 'Yeats and Maud Gonne: Marriage and the Astrological Record, 1908–09', *YA* 13 (1998), 16, 11.

100. WBY to Pound, 15 July 1918, when sending him 'The Phases of the Moon', adding 'After all ones art is not the chief end of life but an accident in ones search for reality or rather perhaps ones method of search,' Yale.

101. 'Vorticism', *Blast*, 1 (June 1914).

102. Although we are not primarily concerned here with Yeats's writing of *A Vision*, I agree with Colin McDowell who has consistently claimed that understanding the geometry is essential; see his ' "Heraldic Supporters": Minor Symbolism and the Integrity of *A Vision*', *YA* 10 (1993), 207–17, 'Yeats's "Vision" Papers: First Impressions', *YA* 11 (1995), 160–3, and 'The "Opening of the *Tinctures*" in Yeats's *A Vision*', *Eire-Ireland*, 20/3 (Fall 1985), 71–92.

103. WBY to Dulac, 25 Oct. 1917, Hobby, 102; WBY to Gregory, 25 Nov. 1917, WMM.

104. 'Kymry' dated his work on the horoscopes from 11 to 17 Nov. 1917.

105. WBY to Dulac, 7 Feb. 1918, Hobby, 108.

106. *A Vision A*, 215.

107. 16 Oct. 1919, *YVP* ii. 451; Ellmann interview notes with GY, 8 Dec. 1946, Tulsa.

108. 20 Nov. 1917, *YVP* i. 87.

109. Mead, *Fragments of a Faith Forgotten*, 329.

110. For example, Ron Heisler, 'Yeats and the Thirteenth Aeon', *YA* 13 (1998), 246–50.

111. 'D.E.D.I.', 1901; 'A system of functions in a circuit through which flows a divine current. Each function creates not only phenomena, but transforms all

the adjacent sub-circuits,' Halevi. *Tree of Life*, 32; also T. Jeremiah Healey III ' "That Which is Unique in Man": The Lightning Flash in Yeats's Later Thought', *YA* 13 (1998), 257–60.

112. Howe, *The Magicians of the Golden Dawn*, 59.

113. 5 Jan. 1918, *YVP* i. 204–7.

114. Parfitt, *Elements of the Qabalah*, 32, 40, 102–3.

115. Notes 'From the Section of the Book "Minutum Mundum" . . . which hath the title of "Liber Hodos Chameleonis" ', Stony Brook.

116. 'Ritual Z Part One', the Opening of 0=0, Stony Brook.

117. Parfitt, *Elements of the Qabalah*, 33–4, 41, 103; also 'the beauty created when everything is synthesized into a complete whole, the harmony that results from living life from a clearly defined centre . . . attributed to both the sun (at the centre of our solar system) and the heart (at the "centre" of our human system)', ibid. 116.

118. 'Impression of 6–5 Ceremony Postulant Frater D.E.D.I. Oct. 16/14', Stony Brook.

119. Margaret Mills Harper, 'The Medium as Creator: George Yeats's Role in the Automatic Script', *YAACTS* 6 (1998), 49–71 and 'The Message is the Medium: Identity in the Automatic Script', *YAACTS* 9 (1991), 35–54; Janis Tedesco Haswell, *Pressed against Divinity* (Dekalb: Northern Illinois University Press, 1997), London, *Writing Double*, 179–209.

120. Martin T. Orne, 'The Nature of Hypnosis: Artifact and Essence', *Journal of Abnormal Social Psychology*, 58 (1959), 277–99.

121. John S. Brownfain, 'Hypnodiagnosis', in Gordon (ed.), *Handbook of Clinical and Experimental Hypnosis*, 220; also in the same volume David Rosenhan on dissociation, 488, and Gordon on hypnotic skills in general, 625–35, and Merton M. Gill and Margaret Brenman, *Hypnosis and Related States: Psychoanalytic Studies in Regression* (New York: International Universities Press, 1959).

122. Most critics have hedged, few going as far as Northrop Frye: 'Not having any explanation of my own to offer of this account, I propose to accept his at its face value', 'The Rising of the Moon: A Study of "A Vision" ', in Denis Donoghue and J. R. Mulryne (eds.), *An Honoured Guest: New Essays on W. B. Yeats* (London: Edward Arnold, 1965), 13.

123. The mind–body controversy that raged during the 19th century is still very much alive. Psychology appears once again to be making room for dualism—not the simple Cartesian belief, but an alternative to the monism that had for so long the upper hand, Greenfield, *The Human Brain*.

124. Ibid. 129–33.

125. Wilder Penfield and Lamar Roberts, *Speech and Brain-Mechanisms* (Princeton: Princeton University Press, 1959), 33–5, 39–55, 229; 'writing . . . takes on an automatic character like speaking and automobile driving' by 'summoning to mind the concept of which the word is a counterpart . . . [or] a series of concepts and the words are produced automatically' (248). More recently, studies have been carried out to explore the brain changes during hypnosis using two types of the current brain scans, BEAM and PET.

126. Geraldine Cummins, *Swan on a Black Sea: A Study in Automatic Writing. The Cummins-Willett Scripts*, ed. Signe Toksvig (London: Book Club Association, 1965), 163.

127. Gordon Claridge, 'Schizophrenia and Human Individuality', in Blakemore and Greenfield (eds.), *Mindwaves: Thoughts on Intelligence, Identity and Consciousness*, 29–41.

128. *Diagnostic and Statistical Manual of Mental Disorders* (4th edn. [DSM-IV] Washington: American Psychiatric Association, 1995), 484–7; James L. Spira (ed.), *Treating Dissociative Identity Disorder* (San Francisco: Jossey-Bass, 1996).

129. Introduction to *A Vision B*.

130. Journal July 1913, *Reflections by W. B. Yeats Transcribed and Edited by Curtis Bradford from the Journals* (Dublin: Cuala, 1970), 51–2.

131. Qtd. by Jeffares, *W. B. Yeats: Man and Poet*, 210; to Herbert Palmer WBY wrote on 9 Aug. 1922 that an automatic script 'is often affected by "telepathic influence" as I could prove to you if necessary', Delaware.

132. Especially the work of Eleanor Sidgwick, Oppenheim, *That Other World*, 120–1.

133. Qtd. by William James, 'Conclusions', in *Varieties of Religious Experience, The Works of William James* (Cambridge, Mass.: Harvard University Press, 1985), 402–3; Underhill describes the voices heard by mystics as 'an extreme form of that dissociation which we all experience in a slight degree when we "argue with ourselves". But in this case one of the speakers is become the instrument of a power other than itself, and communicates to the mind new wisdom and new life. . . . poetry . . . in so far as it is genuine and spontaneous—is largely the result of subliminal activity,' *Mysticism*, 278.

134. Myers, 'Automatic Writing, or The Rationale of Planchette', 235, 241; Oppenheim, *That Other World*, 256.

135. James, 'Conclusions', in *Varieties of Religious Experience*, 408.

136. Stony Brook.

137. Preface to *Psychic Messages from Oscar Wilde*, ed. Hester Travers Smith (London: Psychic Book Club, [n.d.]), p. ix.

138. GY to WBY, 24 Nov. 1931.

139. 'The images from automatic are of the present life in its relation to the *unity of self & the physical unity*,' script of 15 Jan. 1919, *YVP* ii. 175–6.

140. WBY's entry in Notebook 6 on 11 Jan. 1921, *YVP* iii. 65.

141. 'Sleeps' of 19 Oct. and 4 Sept. 1921, Notebook 8, *YVP* iii. 102 and 96.

142. WBY to Quinn, 30 Oct. 1920, concerning his tonsilitis, Wade, 663.

143. 'A Packet for Ezra Pound XII'.

144. 1 Nov. 1924, Lady Gregory, *The Journals*, ed. Daniel J. Murphy (Gerrards Cross: Colin Smythe, 1978), i. 600.

145. *A Packet for Ezra Pound*, 32–3; Cummins recalled his saying to a group of fellow occultists that 'We all . . . differed from ordinary students through our belief that truth cannot be discovered but may be revealed, and that if a man does not lose faith, and if he goes through certain preparations, revelation will find him at the fitting moment,' 'W. B. Yeats and Psychical Research', 132.

146. Moore, *The Unicorn*, 256.

147. Interview Sept. 1987; Peter Allt, Richard Ellmann, Norman Jeffares, Curtis Bradford, David Clark, Arland Ussher, Hazard Adams, Thomas Parkinson, David Pearce, Jon Stallworthy, and myself, to name only a few.

148. GY told Ellmann that Giraldus had been invented as early as Jan. 1918, Ellmann interview notes with GY, 17 Jan. 1947, Tulsa.

149. MacGreevy to GY, 10 July 1929, probably describing the writing of *Les Enfants terribles* (Paris, 1929), TCD MS 8104; 'ecstasy, physically considered, may occur in any person in whom (1) the threshold of consciousness is exceptionally mobile and (2) there is a tendency to dwell upon one governing idea or intuition. Its worth depends entirely on the objective value of that idea or intuition,' Underhill, *Mysticism*, 360.

150. Private conversation with me, 26 May 1998; much later when GY talked to Alf MacLochlainn, then curator of manuscripts at the National Library, he recalled her always being 'very relaxed about it perhaps in a way slightly amused or bemused. It just happened and it just stopped. As one might say, I was playing tennis well that summer, with no hang-ups about any "decline in the powers",' letter to me.

151. Frye, *Words with Power*, 82–3.

152. 6 Nov. 1917 and 18 Oct. 1919, *YVP* i. 61 and *YVP* ii. 454.

153. 12 Nov. 1917, *YVP* i. 84.

154. 10 and 11 Nov. 1917, *YVP* i. 72 and 74.

155. 20 Dec. 1917, *MYV* i. 75.

156. Qtd. by Moore, *The Unicorn*, 277–8, 364.

157. Thomas Parkinson, 'Fifty Years of Yeats Criticism (in Homage to Richard Ellmann)', *YAACTS* 9 (1991), 110.

158. James, postscript to *The Varieties of Religious Experience*.

159. Parkinson, 'Some Recent Work on Yeats', *Southern Review* (Summer 1979), 745–6; Moore, *The Unicorn*, 278.

160. Allt, 'Yeats, Religion and History', 643–8.

161. Note to 'The Second Coming', in *Michael Robartes and the Dancer*, qtd. by Guha with reference to Tantric rituals associated with Yantra, *W. B. Yeats: An Indian Approach*, 125–6. Northrop Frye on the other hand, dismayed by the 'irresponsible fatalism' of *A Vision*, considers the Instructors 'obviously devils. That is, all they knew was the vision of life as hell, and hence, like other devils, they lacked a certain comprehensiveness of perspective,' preface to *Spiritus Mundi: Essays on Literature, Myth and Society* (Bloomington: Indiana University Press, 1976), p. xii.

162. GY told Ellmann that she insisted several times on breaking off the writing because she feared it might 'swallow up poetry', Ellmann interview notes with GY, 17 Jan. 1947, Tulsa.

163. Ibid.

164. 4 Jan. 1918 [postmarked 7 Jan.], Wade, 643–4.

165. For example, Colin Wilson, *Beyond the Occult* (London: Corgi Books, 1989), Betty Shine, *The Infinite Mind* (Glasgow: Harper/Collins, 1999).

166. Perceptive discussions of George's automatic writing are offered by Denis Donoghue, 'The Magic of W. B. Yeats', *New York Review of Books*, 41, 849–55 and Phillip L. Marcus, 'The Authors were in Eternity—or Oxford: George Yeats, George Harper, and the Making of *A Vision*', *YAACTS* 6 (1988), 233–44, later incorporated in Phillip L. Marcus, *Yeats and Artistic Power* (Syracuse, NY: Syracuse University Press, 2001), 128–32; 'What she did with *A Vision* was the greatest of all matrimonial tricks . . . she convinced him she was giving him back his own unconscious which he could then accept through her authority,' interview with John Montague.
167. 'Fragments II' (1933).

CHAPTER 7: LONDON, OXFORD, AND DUBLIN

1. WBY to Lily, 30 Oct. 1917.
2. JBY to ECY, 5 Nov. 1917, WMM.
3. JBY to John Quinn, 6 Nov. 1917, WMM.
4. JBY to ECY, 5 Nov. 1917; JBY to Lily, 6 Nov. 1917, WMM.
5. JBY to WBY, 5 Nov. 1917, *LTWBY* ii. 337–8.
6. JBY to ECY, 29 Nov. 1917, WMM.
7. WBY to JBY, 30 Nov. 1917, WMM.
8. JBY to Rosa Butt, 5 Jan. 1918, WMM.
9. WBY to Quinn, 29 Nov. 1917, NYPL.
10. Pound to Quinn, 3 Nov. 1917, NYPL.
11. *Seventy Years: Being the Autobiography of Lady Gregory*, ed. Colin Smythe (Gerrards Cross: Colin Smythe, 1974), 551; she wrote in similar vein to his sisters and father.
12. Gregory to JBY, fragment, [?Nov./Dec. 1917], Stony Brook.
13. Lily to Quinn, 11 Mar. 1918, NYPL.
14. Lily to JBY, 31 Jan. 1918, NLI MS 31,112.
15. Ellmann interview notes with Iseult Gonne Stuart, 21 Sept. 1946, Tulsa.
16. WBY to Gregory, 3 Nov. 1917, Wade, 633–4.
17. Lily to Quinn, 27 Nov. 1917, NYPL.
18. *A Book of Images Drawn by W. T. Horton and Introduced by W. B. Yeats* (London: Unicorn Press, 1898); Harper (ed.), *W. B. Yeats and W. T. Horton*, 120–39. On 11 Dec. he again invited Horton 'any hour between 8 and 11 & meet my wife', JK.
19. Harper (ed.), *W. B. Yeats and W. T. Horton*, 137.
20. 24 May 1919, *YVP* ii. 288. Since the message came to them at Woburn Buildings, the chair probably refers to WBY's Monday 'At Homes', which Horton frequently attended.
21. 8 and 12 Nov. 1917, *YVP* i. 67 and 81.
22. Richard Aldington, *A. E. Housman and W. B. Yeats: Two Lectures* (1938; Hurst: The Peacocks Press, 1955). The Pounds had lived in the same house as the Aldingtons when first married; at this time H. D. was renting a room at 44 Mecklenburgh Square near other writers such as D. H. and Frieda Lawrence.
23. WBY to Dulac, 10 Nov. 1917, Hobby, 103.
24. Introduction to 'Certain Noble Plays of Japan' (Apr. 1916), in *Essays and Introductions* (London: Macmillan, 1961), 221.

25. In Mar. 1917 Yeats, the Persian scholar Denison Ross, and Dulac produced a report on David Wilson's machine which he claimed could not only speak but produce a 'chemical medium' allowing for photographs of auras etc., Hobby, 87–97.
26. *Stories from the Arabian Nights*, retold by Laurence Housman with drawings by Edmund Dulac (London: Hodder & Stoughton, 1907). George's portrait is number 105 of ' "Somebodies": Cartoons and Watercolours by Edmund Dulac', Leicester Galleries June–July 1920, BL 7859.a.15; inscribed 'To Mr and Mrs W B Yeats from their friend Edmund Dulac', the original painting is now in the possession of Michael and Gráinne Yeats.
27. Dulac to Joseph Hone, 16 Apr. 1940, NLI MS 5919.
28. Colin White, *Edmund Dulac* (London: Studio Vista, 1976); Ann Conolly Hughey, *Edmund Dulac: His Book Illustrations* (bibliography) (Potomac, Md.: Buttonwood Press, 1995).
29. White, *Edmund Dulac*, 76; the cartoon is reproduced in colour on the book jacket of Frank Tuohy, *Yeats* (London: Macmillan, 1976).
30. WBY to Dulac, 27 Nov. 1917, Hobby, 104.
31. WBY to Dulac, 14 Dec. 1917, Hobby, 106–7; GY to Dulac, 2 Dec. 1917, Hobby, 104–5.
32. Dulac to WBY, 15 Feb. 1918, *LTWBY* ii. 344; Hobby, 104 –5.
33. Card File S44, *YVP* iii. 400; 22 Nov. 1917, *YVP* i. 104; 7 June 1918, *YVP* i. 484; 16 Oct. 1919, *YVP* ii. 451.
34. *YVP* i. 251.
35. WBY to Dulac, 27 Feb. 1918, Hobby, 109; Yeats to William Force Stead, 26 Sept. 1934, MBY. 'a vision, whether we wake or sleep, prolongs its power by rhythm and pattern, the wheel where the world is butterfly. We need no protection, but it does,' *Per Amica Silentia Lunae*; 'This great purple butterfly, | In the prison of my hands, | Has a learning in his eye | Not a poor fool understands,' WBY, 'Another Song of a Fool', dated by GY 'Dec.' 18 or Jan 1919' and containing the images found in an automatic drawing of 7 Jan. 1919, *YVP* ii. 163.
36. 'one night when I had given George her ring before sleap he [Dionertes] felt for it on my hand & missed it,' WBY, 12 Sept. 1921, Sleep and Dream Notebook 8, *YVP* iii. 95.
37. Maud Gonne to WBY, 21 Mar. 1916, White and Jeffares (eds.), *Gonne–Yeats Letters*, 370.
38. The script for 25 May 1919 describes fate in George's horoscope as 'spiritual' 'because it is that which drives & inspires the soul'; 'things of the spirit' not 'spiritual' or 'mind' but 'the greek Nous' which implies 'the unique', *YVP* ii. 288–9.
39. WBY to Dulac, 24 Nov. 1917, Hobby, 103.
40. 20 Nov. 1917, *YVP* i. 91.
41. WBY to Gregory, 25 Nov. 1917, WMM.
42. Sturge Moore to Gordon Bottomley, *c.*12 Dec. 1917, copy courtesy R. L. Green.
43. Sturge Moore to Hugh Fisher, 'Dec. 7 or 8 1917', ULL MS 978/24/135.
44. Sylvia Legge, *Affectionate Cousins: T. Sturge Moore and Marie Appia* (London: Oxford University Press, 1980); Ursula Bridge (ed.), *W. B. Yeats and T. Sturge Moore: Their Correspondence 1901–1937* (London: Routledge & Kegan Paul, 1953).

45. WBY to ECY dated 1920 by GY; WBY to Sturge Moore, 26 May 1926, Bridge (ed.), *W. B. Yeats and T. Sturge Moore*, 91.

46. 15 Jan. 1918, *YVP* i. 256–7.

47. *YVP* i. 123; Harper (ed.), *W. B. Yeats and T. W. Horton*, 37.

48. Bridge (ed.), *W. B. Yeats and T. Sturge Moore*, 49, 54, 91.

49. WBY to Gregory, 25 Nov. 1917, WMM; WBY to JBY, 30 Nov. 1917, WMM.

50. ECY to Major Butterworth, also claiming that Carlyle had once lived there, Stanford; WBY to JBY, 12 Feb. 1917, Stony Brook.

51. Bradford, 'George Yeats: Poet's Wife', 395.

52. WBY to Gregory, 16 Dec. 1917, Wade, 634–5.

53. *Autobiographies*, 140.

54. Although later to please Willy she would paint the sitting room walls black in their Dublin flat.

55. AY.

56. Foster, *W. B. Yeats*, i. 160. There had been bedbugs the summer of 1902 when Sturge Moore's sister Nellie had stayed there with a friend when WBY was at Coole, Legge, *Affectionate Cousins*, 204.

57. WBY to Dulac, 24 Nov. and 14 Dec. 1917, Hobby, 103 and 106–7.

58. WBY to Gregory, 16 Dec. 1917, Wade, 634–5.

59. 25 Nov. 1917, *YVP* i. 122–3.

60. 7 Dec. 1917, *YVP* i. 159.

61. Robinson to Dolly Travers Smith, 17 Dec. 1917, TCD 9686.

62. Asquith, *Diaries 1915–1918*, 360–1, 377.

63. WBY to Lily, 20 Dec. 1917, WMM.

64. WBY to William Barrett, 20 Dec. 1917, *MYV* i. 75.

65. 25 Nov. 1917, *YVP* i. 122.

66. 29 Dec. 1917, *YVP* i. 179.

67. 7 Jan. 1918, *YVP* i. 223.

68. 9 Jan. 1918, *YVP* i. 227–8.

69. 'I cannot tell you this and I do not think you will get it by this method with this medium | They dream backwards remember,' 11 Nov. 1917, *YVP* i. 75.

70. I am grateful to Rosemary Hammond, present owner of Stone Cottage, for helping me track down Ashdown Cottage and to the owner Dr D. K. Rycroft, of the School of Oriental and Asian Studies, University of London, and his son for graciously allowing me to photograph the house and gardens.

71. Ricketts to WBY, 17 Nov. 1917, Stony Brook; WBY to Ricketts, 23 Dec. 1917, JK; WBY to Horton, 23 Dec. 1917, Harper (ed.), *W. B. Yeats and W. T. Horton*, 140.

72. Beverley Nichols, repr. in E. H. Mikhail (ed.), *W. B. Yeats: Interviews and Recollections* (London: Macmillan, 1977), i. 135.

73. Ibid.

74. Hal Cheetham, *Portrait of Oxford* (London: Robert Hale, 1971), 79, 197 ff.

75. Gregory to Quinn, 4 Jan. 1918, NYPL.

76. Gregory to WBY, 18 Dec. 1917, 8 Jan. and 4 Mar. 1918, Stony Brook.

77. Asquith, *Diaries 1915–1918*, 398–9.

78. Lily to Quinn, 10 Dec. 1917, NYPL; WBY to Gregory, 4 Jan. 1918, dated 7 Jan. 1918 by Wade, 643.

79. Quinn to WBY, 3 Feb. 1918, *The Letters of John Quinn to William Butler Yeats*, ed. Alan Himber (Ann Arbor: UMI Research Press, 1983), 179; WBY to Quinn, 8 Feb. 1918, Wade, 645.

80. 'The unfinished draft of this play consists of two dialogues, one between an old man and a young girl, the other between an old woman and her son, a young man who is in love with the young girl and wants to marry her. The girl lives in an old tower upon a hill "in charge of all the ghosts of the hill." She comes to see the old man who has a letter for her from her lover, and she tells him that the young man's mother does not want her son to marry: "She says that I am evil and yet has never set her eyes upon me." The old man explains to her that the old woman is jealous of her youth . . . In the second dialogue the mother and her son argue about the girl: the son says that she needs protection, as she has neither friends nor relatives, the mother calls her a beggar-child, and finally curses her son expressing a wish that he might get drowned in the rising river: "May you be drowned with that girl looking on . . .",' Bjersby, *Cuchulain Legend*, 35 n. 3.

81. 18 Jan. 1918, *YVP* i. 273.

82. 11 and 21 Nov. 1917, 5 Jan. 1918, *YVP* i. 74, 99, 202; see especially 'The Choice': 'The intellect of man is forced to choose | Perfection of the life, or of the work . . .'

83. WBY to Gregory, 4 Jan. 1918, postmarked 7 Jan. by Wade, 644.

84. *YVP* i. 250; 21 Jan. 1919, *YVP* ii. 183.

85. WBY to Dulac, 10 Jan. 1918, Hobby, 107.

86. Dulac to WBY, 15 Feb. 1918, *LTWBY* ii. 344.

87. Dulac to WBY, 10 Nov. 1918, *LTWBY* ii. 353.

88. Brittain, *Testament of Youth*, 145; the Yeatses are not mentioned in Brittain's memories of Oxford in 1919 and 1920.

89. Now Littlewoods in the Clarendon Centre.

90. WBY to Gregory, 12 and 14 Jan. 1918, Berg; *The Letters of Sir Walter Raleigh (1879–1922)*, ed. Lady Raleigh (London: Methuen, 1926), i. 169.

91. WBY to Gregory, 21 Jan. 1918, Berg; GY must have renewed the lease on Woburn Buildings—due in March—for another year and then extended it for a further three months, since they did not vacate until 25 June 1919.

92. GY to Lily, 7 Feb. 1918, Boston College.

93. Gregory saw Maud at the end of Jan. 1918 at a Mansion House public meeting concerning the Lane pictures, Gregory to WBY, 'Wednesday' [?30 Jan. 1918], Stony Brook.

94. WBY to Iseult, 9 Feb. 1918, NLI MS 30,563.

95. Script for late Jan., early Feb. 1918, *YVP* i. 306 ff. It is unlikely that this was Hester Travers Smith, as Harper suggests.

96. WBY to Iseult, 9 Feb. 1918, NLI MS 30,563.

97. 23 Jan. 1918, individual cycles are related to the sephira, *YVP* i. 280; both GY and WBY would have been familiar with Chaucer's 'The Franklin's Tale', and Harper suggests GY examined the works of Athanasius Kircher, mentioned on a list of the '28 Mansions of the Moon', in the British Museum, *YVP* ii. 561 n. 81; *MYV* ii. 419.

98. ?18 June 1919, *YVP* ii. 300.

99. This last characteristic, omitted in *A Vision*, is described in the script of 7 Aug. 1919, *YVP* ii. 364.

100. *A Vision A*, 51.

101. 21 Aug. 1920, 'Some New Letters from W. B. Yeats to Lady Gregory', 45. In *A Vision*, individuals are given as examples only between phases 6 and 27; Carlyle was placed at 7, 'assertion of individuality'.

102. Ellmann interview notes with GY, 17 Jan. 1947, Tulsa; Moore, *The Unicorn*, 268.

103. Gregory to Quinn, 12 Jan. 1919, quoted by James Pethica, 'Patronage and Creative Exchange', *YA* 9 (1992), 72–3.

104. I am grateful to Stanley Gillam and Steven Tomlinson of the Bodleian Library, John Kelly, and Selina Guinness for assistance in seeking the Yeatses' records for 1918 to 1920.

105. Moore, *The Unicorn*, 63, quoting GY.

106. 23 Dec. 1917, *YVP* i. 174–5.

107. These were discovered at Stony Brook and are preserved as pages 370–2 of *YVP* i.

108. WBY's summary, 8 Oct. 1921, Notebook 7, *YVP* iii. 78; Bodleian Library records.

109. 4 Mar. 1918, *YVP* i. 369.

110. 4 and 5 Mar. 1918, *YVP* i. 370–2, 374–6; summarized in Notebook 7, 8 Oct. 1921, *YVP* iii. 77–83.

111. 5 Mar. 1918, *YVP* i. 374, 378.

112. I have been unable to trace the ownership of this flat, although in 1902 it is mentioned as an address for Edith Ellen Hyde Lees.

113. WBY tells Horton on 4 Mar. that they plan to leave Oxford on the 8th and go to Dublin on the 12th, 1918 (Harper (ed.), *W. B. Yeats and W. T. Horton*, 140); on 5 Mar. 1918 he tells Dulac they are leaving for Ireland on the 11th, Hobby, 110.

114. A. Norman Jeffares, 'Introduction', *Images of Invention: Essays on Irish Writing* (Gerrards Cross: Colin Smythe, 1996), p. ix.

115. P. L. Dickinson, *The Dublin of Yesterday* (London: Methuen, 1929), 169.

116. Tuohy, *Yeats*, 166; AE to Quinn, 11 Feb. 1918, Reid, *The Man from New York*, 354.

117. ECY to JBY, 13 Mar. 1918, NLI MS 31,113. Roseann Hodgins and Maria O'Brien were long-time servants of the Yeats family.

118. Lily to JBY, 8 Apr. 1918, NLI MS 31,112.

119. JBY to Gregory, 19 Apr. 1918, WMM.

120. Gregory to WBY, 8 Jan. 1918, Stony Brook.

121. ECY to JBY, 13 Mar. 1918, NLI MS 31,113; Lily to JBY, 8 Apr. 1918 , NLI MS 31,112.

122. ECY to JBY, 2 Sept. 1917, NLI MS 31,113.

123. Sara Hyland, *I Call to the Eye of the Mind: A Memoir*, ed. Maureen Murphy (Dublin: Attic Press, 1995), 59.

124. JBY to Rosa Butt, 4 Dec. 1907 and 3 Jan. 1908, qtd. by Foster, *W. B. Yeats*, i. 375 and 600 n. 86.

125. 'George regrets that Cottie does not go on with her portrait painting,' JBY to ?Lily, 24 May 1920, WMM. I am grateful for William Murphy's help in deciphering this letter.

126. GY to MacGreevy, 10 July 1926, TCD MS 8104.
127. William M. Murphy, *Family Secrets: William Butler Yeats and his Relatives* (Syracuse, NY: Syracuse University Press, 1995), 394 n. 17.
128. 11 Mar. 1918, *YVP* i. 379.
129. 18 July 1918, *YVP* ii. 12–15; 8 Oct. 1921, Notebook 7, *YVP* iii. 82.
130. 30 Mar. 1918, *YVP* i. 404–5.
131. WBY to Dulac, 19 [Apr.] 1918, Hobby, 111–12.
132. ECY wrote to her father on 4 June 1918 that GY 'went back to Galway on the 7.30 a.m. train on Sunday taking the Cuala kitten with her', NLI MS 31,113.
133. Lydia R. M. Thomas to GY, 7 Feb. 1939.
134. Gregory to WBY, 13 Mar., 17 and 18 Mar. 1918, Stony Brook; WBY to Gregory, 10 Mar., Stony Brook, 18 Mar., NLI MS 30,593, 19 Mar. 1918, Berg.
135. Most likely GY had read this in Robin Flowers's popular translation.
136. Lily to JBY, 8 Apr. 1918, NLI MS 31,112; WBY to Ellen Douglas Duncan, 16 May 1918, qtd. in 'A Fair Chance of a Disturbed Ireland: W. B. Yeats to Mrs J. Duncan', ed. John Unterecker, in Robin Skelton and David R. Clark (eds.), *Irish Renaissance* (Dublin: Dolmen, 1965), 105.
137. Katharine Tynan Hinkson to JBY, 11 Aug. 1918, WMM.
138. Frank O'Connor, 'Reminiscences of Yeats', in *Leinster, Munster and Connaught* (London: Robert Hale, 1950), qtd. in *Interviews and Recollections*, ii. 333; Ellmann, *The Man and the Masks*, 1979 preface, p. xxiii.

PART II: CONJUNCTIONS

1. GY to WBY, 1 Feb. 1923.
2. WBY to GY, 6 Aug. 1920.
3. 10 Nov. 1918, *YVP* ii. 119.
4. 4 Mar. 1918, mirror writing, *YVP* i. 371; Notebook 7, *YVP* iii. 78.

CHAPTER 8: COOLE

5. WBY to GY, 4 Oct. 1917.
6. First published in the revised edition of *The Celtic Twilight* (1902); Georgie had purchased the 1912 reprinting in Oct. 1913.
7. WBY to Quinn, 4 Sept. 1918, NYPL; Mary Hanley and Liam Miller, *Thoor Ballylee: Home of William Butler Yeats* (2nd edn. revised, Dublin: Dolmen, 1977), 10–12.
8. Oct. 1914, Stony Brook; on 16 Mar. 1916 Maud wrote, 'I hope you will get your castle. It seems to suit you so well. It is a dream which should be realised—It would help you with your work I think,' White and Jeffares (ed.), *Gonne–Yeats Letters*, 369.
9. WBY to Gregory, 16 June 1917, TS copy annotated by GY, Stony Brook; Maud Gonne to WBY, 25 Apr. 1917, 'How charming your Western castle looks in the photo you sent Iseult. We are longing to see it. Can it really be possible you got it for £35?' White and Jeffares (ed.), *Gonne–Yeats Letters*, 390.

10. Correspondence between Sir Henry Doran, the Board Inspector Mr Edmonds, W. F. Bailey and the Estates Commissioners' Office, Lady Gregory, and WBY, Nov. 1916 to Apr. 1917.
11. WBY to Gregory, 29 Jan. 1915, Berg.
12. WBY to Shakespear, 15 May 1916, Stony Brook; Wade, 625–6.
13. Gregory to JBY, 23 May 1917, Stony Brook.
14. Gregory to JBY, fragment, [?Nov./Dec. 1917], Stony Brook.
15. WBY to Gregory, 29 Oct. 1917, TS copy with GY's annotations, Stony Brook, differing slightly from Wade, 633–4, and 25 Nov. 1917, WMM.
16. WBY to Gregory, 4 Jan. and 22 Feb. 1918, Wade, 643 and 647.
17. Most of the following description of work on Ballylee draws on Rafferty's correspondence and detailed accounts, including George's cancelled cheques, NLI MS 30,663.
18. WBY to GY, 28 May 1918.
19. Gregory to WBY, 28 Nov. 1917, Stony Brook.
20. WBY to Lily, 4 Feb. 1918, WMM.
21. Gregory to WBY, 4 Mar. 1918, Stony Brook.
22. GY to Lily, 7 Feb. 1918, NLI MS 31,112.
23. JBY to Mrs Caughey, 20 Nov. 1917, WMM.
24. Gregory to WBY, 'Monday' [Jan. 1918], Stony Brook.
25. Elizabeth Longford, 'Lady Gregory and Wilfried Scawen Blunt', and Lady Gregory and James Pethica, 'A Woman's Sonnets', in Ann Saddlemyer and Colin Smythe (eds.), *Lady Gregory: Fifty Years After* (Gerrards Cross: Colin Smythe, 1987), 85–122.
26. Gregory to WBY, 15 Nov. 1920, Stony Brook.
27. WBY to Georgie, 4 Oct. 1917.
28. JBY to Mrs Caughey, 20 Nov. 1917, WMM.
29. WBY to Georgie, 4 and 6 Oct. 1917.
30. WBY to Quinn, 23 July 1918, Wade, 651; WBY to Dulac, 1 July 1918, Hobby, 114–15.
31. WBY to JBY, 13 Feb. 1917.
32. Jeanne Sheehy and George Mott, *The Rediscovery of Ireland's Past: The Celtic Revival 1820–1930* (London: Thames & Hudson, 1980), 134.
33. Gregory to WBY, 16 Aug. 1917, Stony Brook.
34. Letters from Scott to WBY in 1918 discussed details of the building and furniture.
35. WBY to Dulac, 1 July 1918, Hobby, 114–15.
36. Lily to Quinn, 11 Mar. 1918, NYPL.
37. WBY to Maud Gonne, 13 May 1918, White and Jeffares (eds.), *Gonne–Yeats Letters*, 393–4.
38. WBY to Miss Norah Annie Bretherton, 27 June 1918, JK.
39. WBY to Quinn, 5 June 1922, NYPL.
40. WBY to Quinn, 23 July 1918, NYPL.
41. A correspondence took place in 1918 with Miss M. Redington of Athenry.
42. Lily to Quinn, 18 Sept 1920; GY to Birgit Bramsbäck in 1948, qtd. in a letter to me 2 Sept. 1988.

43. WBY to Gregory, 13 Nov. 1916, Stony Brook; Gough to Burke, 30 Oct. 1917, either Myles J. Burke, Clerk of the Gort Rural District Council and of the Union, or the Major F. C. Burke, Resident Magistrate at Gort, Stony Brook.

44. Lily to JBY, 4 June 1918, NLI MS 31,112; WBY to Gregory, 28 Feb. 1920, Berg.

45. WBY to GY, [?18 Aug.] 1918.

46. Ricketts to WBY, 3 Sept. 1918; WBY to Heald, 28 Nov. 1937, Wade, 901.

47. WBY to GY, 18 Aug. 1924. The window was sold after George's death.

48. *Autobiographies*, 140; WBY to Pound, 19 Sept. 1918, Yale.

49. 'A Prayer on Going into my House' (Apr. 1918).

50. Recalled by AY in her speech opening the Yeats Flower Show, Drumcliffe Church, 27 June 1991; for a description of the house and grounds see Lady Gregory, *Coole*, ed. Colin Smythe with a foreword by Edward Malins (Dublin: Dolmen, 1971).

51. Masefield to Cottie Yeats, 1 May 1905, qtd. in Smith, *John Masefield: A Life*, 91.

52. Lily to JBY, 26 Apr. 1918, NLI MS 31,112. Lady Gregory did, however, daily feed the three outdoor cats in the flower garden, but apparently Pangur preferred pork to rats, Anne Gregory, *Me & Nu: Childhood at Coole* (Gerrards Cross: Colin Smythe, 1970), 94–5.

53. WBY, Sleep and Dream Notebook 7, *YVP* iii. 81–2.

54. Sleep and Dream Notebook 7 and Card File D37x, *YVP* iii. 81, 83, and 291; script for 16 and 17 Apr. 1919, *YVP* ii. 250–4.

55. Gregory to WBY, 'Monday 18th' [Feb. 1918], Stony Brook.

56. WBY to Gregory, 22 Feb. 1918, Berg; Wade, 637.

57. WBY to Dulac, [probably 19 Apr. 1918], Hobby, 111–12.

58. WBY to Clement Shorter, 17 May 1918, Wade, 649.

59. WBY to Dulac, 20 Apr. 1919, Hobby, 131.

60. WBY to Gregory, 29 Apr. 1918, Berg.

61. WBY to Dulac, 9 Apr. and late Apr. or early May 1918, Hobby, 111–13.

62. '12 p.m. new time—11 p.m. Thursday Apr. 25th', *YVP* i. 437, inaccurately identified as from Ballinamantan.

63. 12 May 1918, *YVP* i. 443.

64. A single handmade volume containing work by 140 poets, 120 painters, and 9 composers, inscribed on vellum pages and published in 1991.

65. Recorded by W. R. Rodgers, 16 Feb. 1949, BBC Sound Archives.

66. WBY to Lily, [?June] 1918, Boston College.

67. JBY to WBY, 13 Apr. 1918, WMM. His sketch of a man and a woman seated in a rowing boat, both holding fishing poles, is reproduced in Hone, *W. B. Yeats*, 246.

68. WBY to Katharine Tynan Hinkson from 'Ballylee Castle', 23 Sept. 1918, MS Eng. 884.22, Harvard.

69. Probably a Corona typewriter, which folded for portability; later she had a Remington portable typewriter.

70. WBY to Dulac, 1 July 1918, Hobby, 115; WBY to GY, 18 Aug. 1918.

71. WBY to Shakespear, Wade, 681.

72. Anne and Michael Yeats; letter to me from John Keohane, 31 Oct. 1994. Gregory was frequently accused by the local people of maligning them in her plays about the mythical village of Cloon, Elizabeth Coxhead, *Lady Gregory: A Literary Portrait* (2nd edn. London: Secker & Warburg, 1966), 78.

73. As recalled by Donald Pearce in 'Hours with the Domestic Sibyl', 496–7. To Shakespear, 22 Nov. 1931, WBY described this 'local satirist and a really terrible one' as 'an old woman who lives in a little cottage near Gort', Wade, 785–6.

74. Lily to JBY, 24 May 1918, NLI MS 31,112.

75. ECY to JBY, Easter Sunday 1918, NLI MS 31,113; *Journal of Irish Literature*, ed. Robert Hogan, special Joseph O'Neill number 12/2 (May 1983).

76. Austin Clarke in Francis MacManus (ed.), *The Yeats We Knew* (Cork: Mercier, 1963), 93–4 and 'Some Memories of W. B. Yeats', *Guardian*, 12 June 1965, 7.

77. 27 June 1918, *YVP* ii. 2.

78. 25 May 1918, *YVP* i. 456.

79. WBY to Pound, 15 July 1918, Yale.

80. WBY to Pound, 6 June 1918, Indiana.

81. Pound to Quinn, 13 Dec. 1919, NYPL.

82. Ulick O'Connor, *Oliver St John Gogarty* (London: Jonathan Cape, 1964), 148, Oliver St John Gogarty, *As I Was Going down Sackville Street* (London: Sphere Books, 1968), 197–206, and Oliver D. Gogarty, 'My Brother Willie was your Father's Friend', *Bibliotheca Bucnellensis*, NS 7 (1969), 3–4, repr. in Jim McGarry (comp.), *The Dream I Knew* (Collooney, Sligo: Jim McGarry, 1990), 72. I am grateful to Oliver Gogarty and John Keohane for information.

83. Oliver St John Gogarty, *Mourning becomes Mrs Spendlove* (New York: Creative Age Press, 1948), 216.

84. AY.

85. Pound to 'Cher Maitre' [WBY], 10 Mar. 1918, 'Ezra Pound Letters to William Butler Yeats', ed. Terrell, 35–6.

86. 'The Shadow of Noon' in Apr. and 'Landscape' in June, repr. in Londraville and Londraville (eds.), *Too Long a Sacrifice*, appendix 2, 242–3.

87. Yeats to Pound, 6 Sept. 1918, Yale.

88. 14 May 1918, *YVP* i. 445.

89. WBY to GY, 28 May 1918; Lily to JBY, 23 May 1918, NLI MS 31,112.

90. GY to Pound, 24 May 1918, Indiana; Ann Saddlemyer (ed.), 'George, Ezra, Dorothy and Friends: Twenty-Six Letters 1918–59', *YA* 7 (1990), 7–8; the notes to this article have been superseded by this book.

91. Margaret Ward, *Maud Gonne: Ireland's Joan of Arc* (London: Pandora, 1990), 85.

92. Clement Shorter, husband of the poet Dora Sigerson Shorter, was the editor of the *Sketch* and *Illustrated London News*; he would privately publish Yeats's *Nine Poems* in Oct. 1918 as he had 'Easter, 1916' in Sept. 1916.

93. GY to Pound, 28 May 1918, Yale.

94. WBY to GY, 28 and 30 May 1918.

95. Both Lily's and Lolly's letters to JBY dated 4 June 1918, NLI MS 31,112 and 31,113.

96. Lily to JBY, 13 June 1918, NLI MS 31,112.

97. WBY to Dulac, 10 June 1918, Hobby, 114.

98. 16 June 1918, *YVP* i. 508–9.

99. WBY to GY, 15 July 1919.

100. WBY to Lily, 17 July 1918, Stony Brook.

101. Ivor Montagu, 'Students of Film through the World have Lost their Most Respected Pioneer', *Sight and Sound* (Spring 1970), 107; Missy Daniel, 'Iris Barry ?1895–1969', in Barbara Sicherman and Carol Hurd Green (eds.), *Notable American Women: The Modern Period. A Biographical Dictionary* (Cambridge, Mass.: Harvard University Press, 1980), 57.

102. WBY to Gregory, 14 Aug. 1918, Berg.

103. WBY to Maud Gonne, 18 Aug. 1918, White and Jeffares (eds.), *Gonne–Yeats Letters*, 395.

104. WBY to Gregory, 6 Dec. 1919, Berg.

105. 'He is being sent to France to count marmalade pots or peel potatoes, something of that sort.' Lily quoting GY to JBY, 8 Apr. 1918, NLI MS 31,112.

106. WBY to GY, 18 Aug. 1918 (two letters).

107. WBY to Iseult, 18 Aug. 1918, NLI MS 30,563.

108. Iseult to Yeats, [? Aug. 1918], qtd. in Geoffrey Elborn, *Francis Stuart: A Life* (Dublin: Raven Arts, 1990), 77.

109. Wilhelm, *Ezra Pound in London and Paris 1908–1925*, 196–7 citing Francis Stuart's *Black List/Section H*; Elborn, *Francis Stuart*, 30.

110. 2 Sept. 1918, *YVP* ii. 37.

111. WBY to Gogarty, 7 Sept. 1918, Princeton.

112. Gregory to WBY, 25 Oct. [1918], Berg.

113. GY in conversation with me, 1959; Pearce, 'Hours with the Domestic Sibyl', 496.

114. WBY to Quinn, 4 Sept. 1918, NYPL; WBY to Clement Shorter, Wade, 652.

115. ECY to Quinn, 12 Sept. 1918, NYPL.

116. WBY to Pound, 19 Sept. 1918, Yale.

117. NLI 13,587.

118. A copy in YL has a slip inserted with Hebrew characters and English equivalents in pencil, probably in GY's hand. 'Strongly influenced by cabalistic and astrological magic, the *Key* sets out the . . . choosing of a suitable time and place, the weapons, robes and "pentacles" or diagrams which the magician will need, the drawing of the magic circle, the incantations for summoning spirits and for compelling their obedience,' Richard Cavendish (ed.), *Man, Myth and Magic* (Radstock: BPC Publishing Ltd., [1969]), 1181.

119. 'Estrangement', *Autobiographies*, 464.

120. NLI 30,358, reproduced in *The Wild Swans at Coole*, ed. Stephen Parrish (Ithaca, NY: Cornell University Press, 1994), 133.

121. Berg, reproduced in *The Wild Swans at Coole*, ed. Parrish, 73.

122. 28 Jan. 1919, *YVP* ii. 192.

123. George Russell to WBY, 2 June 1896 (*Letters from AE*, selected and edited by Alan Denson (London: Abelard-Schuman, 1961), 17–18).

124. 24 Sept. 1918 from Dublin: 'The child the father the grandfather the great grand & the great great . . . all have looked upon the mountain & have seen more than the reality & all with different eyes,' *YVP* ii. 67.

125. First published by Bradford, who places it several years later, 'George Yeats: Poet's Wife', 396. The draft of yet another Solomon and Sheba poem has been published by Stephen Parrish (*YA* 6 (1988), 211–13 and *The Wild Swans at Coole*, 413); undated, it seems to serve as bridge between the two 1918 poems.

126. A lengthy correspondence ensued until Yeats finally managed to get Iseult to find and return the book, one of a set of Fenimore Cooper's novels, Stony Brook.

127. WBY to Gregory, [early Feb. 1909]; Gregory to WBY, [Dec. 1906], Stony Brook.

128. AY, quoted by William M. Murphy, *Prodigal Father: The Life of John Butler Yeats (1839–1922)* (Ithaca, NY: Cornell University Press, 1978), 643 n. 22; M. B. Yeats, *Cast a Cold Eye* (Dublin: Blackwater Press, 1999), 5–6.

129. JBY to Isaac Yeats, 26 Oct. 1920; JBY to ECY, 7 July 1920, qtd. in Murphy, *Prodigal Father*, 509.

130. James Pethica, ' "Our Kathleen": Yeats's Collaboration with Lady Gregory in the Writing of *Cathleen ni Houlihan*', *YA* 6 (1988), 3–31.

131. Gregory, *Me & Nu*, 33; Gregory to WBY, 8 Dec. 1922, Stony Brook.

132. Lily to JBY, 4 June 1918, NLI MS 31,112; WBY to Pound, 6 June 1918, Indiana.

133. WBY to Maud Gonne, 18 Aug. 1918, White and Jeffares (eds.), *Gonne–Yeats Letters*, 395.

134. Lily to JBY, 28 Sept. 1918, NLI MS 31,112.

135. WBY to Sturge Moore, 17 Nov. 1918, Bridge (ed.), *W. B. Yeats and T. Sturge Moore*, 31, 33–4; WBY to Dulac, 13 Dec. 1918, Hobby, 117–18.

136. WBY to Maud Gonne, White and Jeffares (eds.), *Gonne–Yeats Letters*, 396–7; I have found no evidence for Hone's statement that Maud wrote and offered them the house, *W. B. Yeats*, 320–1.

137. WBY to GY, 3 Oct. 1918.

138. Mark Bence-Jones, *Twilight of the Ascendancy* (London: Constable, 1987), 52, 181.

139. Gregory to WBY, 28 Nov. 1918, Stony Brook; I am grateful to Sister Mary de Lourdes Fahy of Gort for sorting out the two Dooley families for me.

140. Lily to JBY, 9 Oct. 1918, NLI MS 31,112; Francis Stuart, Thomas Davis Lecture, in McManus (ed.), *The Yeats We Knew*, 39; Rafferty to GY, 9 Nov. 1918, NLI MS 30,663.

141. 8 to 28 Oct. 1918, *YVP* ii. 71–101.

142. Recalled to Ellmann by H. O. White, who attended with the increasingly disapproving playwright Daniel Kelleher, a devout Roman Catholic, Ellmann interview notes with H. O. White, 19 June 1946, Tulsa.

143. 2 and 8–11 Nov. 1918, *YVP* ii. 108 and 114–20, 144.

144. WBY to Gregory, 16 Oct. 1918, Hone, *W. B. Yeats*, 314.

145. Rafferty to GY and WBY, Oct. and Nov. 1918, NLI MS 30,663.

146. *Encyclopedia Britannica*; Gina Kolata, *Flu: The Story of the Great Influenza Pandemic of 1918 and the Search for the Virus that Caused it* (New York: Farrar, Straus & Giroux, 1999). It is suspected that the flu was also unique in that it left in the survivors a predisposition to Parkinson's disease.

147. In a letter to Ellen [Mrs James] Duncan he writes, 'I have had 24 hours of fever and cold. I am better but am too weak to go to lecture tonight.' 'A Fair Chance of a Disturbed Ireland', 101.

148. WBY to Lily, 18 Nov. 1918, Boston College.

149. Probably Francis C. Purser; although in his letter to Gregory Yeats refers to Frank Parsons, there is only an A. R. Parsons listed in the medical directory whereas the Pursers were family friends.

150. Lily to Quinn, 7 Jan. 1919, NYPL; WBY to Gregory, 26 Nov. 1918, Berg, and 29 Nov. 1918, TS copy annotated by GY, Stony Brook.

151. Gregory to WBY, 'Wednesday' [27 Nov. 1918], Stony Brook.

152. Maud Gonne to WBY, 1 Nov. 1918, White and Jeffares (eds.), *Gonne-Yeats Letters*, 198-9.

153. Pound to Quinn, 15 Nov. 1919, NYPL; copy annotated by Pound for Lennox Robinson in 1930, Emory.

154. Qtd. in White and Jeffares (eds.), *Gonne-Yeats Letters*, 400.

155. Karl Beckson, 'Arthur Symons's "Iseult Gonne": A Previously Unpublished Memoir', *YA* 7 (1990), 203.

156. Lily to JBY, 31 Jan. 1918, NLI MS 31,112; Lily to Quinn, 28 Nov. 1918, qtd. in Murphy, *Prodigal Father*, 485.

157. Nancy Cardozo, *Maud Gonne: Lucky Eyes and a High Heart* (New York: New Amsterdam Press, 1978), 330; WBY to Gregory, 14 Dec. 1918, TS copy with annotations by GY, Stony Brook; Pound to Quinn, 2 Dec. 1918, NYPL; Francis Stuart, in McManus (ed.), *The Yeats We Knew*, 39.

158. Lily to Quinn, 29 Nov. 1918, NYPL.

159. ECY to Quinn, 11 Dec. 1918, NYPL; Gogarty, 'My Brother Willie was your Father's Friend', 6.

160. Quinn to WBY, 20 Dec. 1918, *LTWBY* ii. 357-8; *Letters of John Quinn to William Butler Yeats*, 203.

161. Lily to Quinn, 7 Jan. 1919, NYPL.

162. R. F. Foster, *Modern Ireland 1600-1972* (London: Allen Lane, 1998), 488 ff.

163. 11 Dec. 1918, *YVP* ii. 132.

164. 16 to 21 Dec. 1918, *YVP* ii. 133-49.

165. 25 Dec. 1918, *YVP* ii. 152.

166. 7 Jan. 1919, *YVP* ii. 162-3; 26 Nov. 1920, Notebook 6, *YVP* iii. 57. The evolution of the poems is traced in George Mills Harper and Sandra L. Sprayberry, 'Complementary Creation: Notes on "Another Song of a Fool" and "Towards Break of Day" ', *YAACTS* 4 (1986), 69-81.

167. WBY to Gregory, 5 Jan. 1919, Berg.

168. 9 Jan. 1919, *YVP* ii. 167-8; WBY to Gregory, 29 Jan. 1919, Berg.

169. WBY to Gregory, 20 Jan. 1919, Hone, *W. B. Yeats*, 315-16.

170. WBY to Ellen Duncan, 10 Jan. 1919, misdated in 'A Fair Chance of a Disturbed Ireland', 99–100; 'Psychical Phenomena: Advice to the Church and the Press', *Irish Times*, 27 Jan. 1919.

171. Gregory, 3 Feb. 1919, *Journals*, i. 35–6; Cummins described it as 'the most moving and eloquent lecture on Psychical Research I have ever heard', 'W. B. Yeats and Psychical Research', 137.

172. JBY to Quinn, 15 Jan. 1919, *J. B. Yeats Letters to his Son, W. B. Yeats, and Others*, ed. Joseph Hone (London: Faber, 1944), 258–9.

173. *YVP* ii. 194–5.

174. WBY to Pound, 16 Jan. 1919, Yale.

175. WBY to Betty Goldring, quoted in Sotheby's sale catalogue of James Gilvarry's collection, no. 560; Douglas Goldring, *Odd Man Out* (London: Chapman & Hall, 1935), 172 and 232.

176. Gregory, 3 Feb. 1919, *Journals*, i. 34–5.

177. Gary James Phillips, 'The Dublin Drama League: 1918–1942', Ph.D. dissertation (Southern Illinois University, 1980), 11. I am grateful to Dr Phillips for sending me a copy of his dissertation.

178. 24 Jan. and 9 Feb. 1919, *YVP* ii. 189 and 197–8.

179. Amory, *Biography of Lord Dunsany*, 200.

180. Lily to JBY, 11 Feb. 1919, NLI MS 31,112.

181. WBY to GY, 'Wednesday' [?19 Feb. 1919].

182. On the back of a draft of 'The Second Coming' WBY has written: 'Pangur c/o H. D. 63 Beecham Avenue, Ranelagh', NLI MS 13,588; Thom's *Dublin Directory* lists no Beecham Avenue, but includes a George Downes at 63 Lr. Beechwood Avenue, Ranelagh.

183. Lily to JBY, 25 Feb. 1919, NLI MS 31,112.

CHAPTER 9: ANNE

1. Bethel Solomons, *One Doctor in his Time* (2nd edn. London: Christopher Johnson, 1959).

2. Lily to GY, 6 Feb. 1924; Lily, writing from a London nursing home, mistakenly attributes this incident to the birth of Michael, which took place in England.

3. WBY to Gregory, 26 Feb. 1919, Berg.

4. Brigit Patmore recalling a visit with WBY to Dulac's studio in the early 1920s, *My Friends When Young*, ed. Derek Patmore (London: Heinemann, 1968), 93.

5. WBY to Shakespear, 25 Aug. 1934, Wade, 828 and Elizabeth Heine, 'Yeats and Astrology: "Supernatural Songs"', in Bruce Stewart (ed.), *That Other World: The Supernatural and the Fantastic in Irish Literature and its Contexts*, ii (Gerrards Cross: Colin Smythe, 1998), 285–8; WBY, 'Conjunctions' (Aug. 1934). The subjective was represented by their son Michael's birth time at the conjunction of Jupiter and Saturn, reflected in the accompanying couplet.

6. 20 Sept. 1919, *YVP* ii. 435; the phase of the Fool, 'the Child of God', was 28.

7. 'I am at work on my poem about Anne,' 1 Apr. 1919, later selected by George in her summary 'WBY to Gregory Letters', MBY.

8. 31 Mar. 1918, *YVP* i. 406; Ann Saddlemyer, 'Reading Yeats's "A Prayer for my Daughter"—yet again', in Toshi Furomoto et al. (eds.), *International Aspects of Irish Literature* (Gerrards Cross: Colin Smythe, 1996), 69–81.

9. WBY to Elkin Matthews, 6 Apr. 1919, JK.

10. WBY to Lily, 9 Mar. 1928; Whitney, Moore & Keller, 'Result of Search in Irish Land Commission on behalf of Mr W. B. Yeats', 8 Jan. 1930, Stony Brook. For the Yeats family trees, see Foster, *W. B. Yeats*, i. pp. xx–xxiii.

11. 5 Mar. 1918, *YVP* i. 374.

12. Script for 24 Sept. 1918, *YVP* ii. 67–70; WBY, 8 Oct. 1921, Notebook 7, *YVP* iii. 83; *YVP* ii. 200–1.

13. Quinn to WBY, 4 Apr. 1919, *Letters of John Quinn to William Butler Yeats*, 213.

14. 20 Mar. 1919, *YVP* ii. 200–2.

15. See Chapter 5; in his card file WBY identifies the person who unconsciously set the process going as 'Mrs T', who the editors erroneously assume is Hester Travers Smith, *YVP* iii. 264.

16. 21 Mar. 1919, *YVP* ii. 202–6.

17. 20 Mar. 1919, *YVP* ii. 200.

18. WBY to Gregory, 3 Mar. 1919, Berg.

19. ECY to Alfred de Lury, 5 Mar. 1919, Stony Brook.

20. Lily to JBY, 7 Mar. 1919, NLI MS 31,112.

21. Jack BY to Elkin Mathews, 26 Mar. 1919, WMM.

22. JBY to Julia Ford, 1 May 1919, 'Letters to an American Patron', ed. Michael Stanford, *YAACTS* 11 (1993), 184.

23. *Freeman's Journal* (Dublin), Saturday, 1 Mar. 1919, 3; Lolly conjectured that the author, identified only as 'K', was probably Daniel Lawrence Kelleher ('D. L. Kay'), who had published *The Glamour of Dublin*. ECY to Alfred de Lury, 5 Mar. 1919, Stony Brook. I am grateful to Paul Murray for searching out the poem.

24. JBY to Julia Ford, 1 May 1919, 'Letters to an American Patron', 184; Thom's *Dublin Directory*, 1919 and 1920, lists the proprietor as Miss Moeran.

25. 20 and 21 Mar. 1919, *YVP* ii. 200 and 202.

26. Robinson summarized their dialogue in *Curtain Up: An Autobiography* (London: Michael Joseph, 1942), 118–21.

27. 29 Mar. 1919, *YVP* ii. 223–4.

28. 15 Apr. 1919, *YVP* ii. 250–1 and 562 n. 94.

29. Louis Esson to Padraic Colum, 2 May 1920, Berg.

30. 28 May 1919, *YVP* ii. 290; 25 July 1919, *YVP* ii. 338.

31. 5 Apr. 1919, *YVP* ii. 232.

32. 25 Aug. 1919, *YVP* ii. 388.

33. 28 Mar. 1919, *YVP* ii. 221.

34. 29 Mar. 1919, *YVP* ii. 224–5; Card File V 1–13, *YVP* iii. 421–4.

35. Lily to JBY, 5 June 1919, NLI MS 31,112.

36. JBY to Julia Ford, [?summer 1919], 'Letters to an American Patron', 185.

37. ECY to Quinn, 15 Apr. 1919, NYPL.

38. Susan Mitchell to JBY, 29 Mar. 1919, MBY; Hilary Pyle, *Red-Headed Rebel: Susan L. Mitchell Poet and Mystic of the Irish Cultural Renaissance* (Dublin:Woodfield Press, 1998), 64–71.

39. ECY to JBY, 'Whit Monday' 1920, NLI MS 31,113.

40. Lily to JBY, 20 Apr. 1919, NLI MS 31,112.

41. WBY to Pound, 9 Mar. 1919, Yale.

42. WBY to Quinn, 14 June 1919, NYPL.

43. ECY to JBY, 18 May 1919, NLI MS 31,113.

44. 12 Nov. 1917, *YVP* i. 83.

45. GY in BBC broadcast June 1949, qtd. in 'W. B. Yeats', in W. R. Rodgers (ed.), *Irish Literary Portraits* (New York: Taplinger, 1973), 15.

46. WBY's notes, 1 May 1921, Notebook 7, *YVP* iii. 75; 30 May 1920, Notebook 6, *YVP* iii. 21; GY's notes, Vision Notebook 1, 89, *YVP* iii. 176.

47. *The Works of William Blake*, ed. Edwin Ellis and W. B. Yeats, 3 vols. (London: Bernard Quaritch, 1893), i. 310 and table, 314.

48. Lily to JBY, 20 Apr. 1919, NLI MS 31,112; ECY to JBY, 18 May 1919, NLI MS 31,113. Their cousin Revd Gibbon may also have been present although not officiating: 'I am also under the impression that my father baptised one, if not both, of Yeats's children, though I seem to remember his saying that the christening took place in Donnybrook church,' Gibbon, *Masterpiece and the Man*, 37.

49. WBY to ECY, 29 Aug. 1919, envelope, Boston College.

50. WBY to GY, 7 May 1919; John Mitchell's furrier shop was on Wicklow Street.

51. WBY to GY, 8 May 1919; the Dublin Bread Company, familiarly known as 'the DBC', had restaurants in Dame Street and on Stephen's Green North.

52. ECY to JBY, 18 May 1919, NLI MS 31,113; WBY to Gregory, 23 Apr. 1919, Berg.

53. Lily to R L-P, 7 May 1929, WMM; the book was either *Feeding and Care of Baby* (London: Macmillan, 1913), which was reprinted fourteen times and in a revised edition still available in 1937, or *Natural Feeding of Infants* (Dunedin: The Royal NZ Society for the Health of Women and Children, 1917), both by Sir F. Truby King.

54. JBY to Julia Ford, [?summer 1919], 'Letters to an American Patron', 185.

55. ECY to JBY, 18 May 1919, NLI MS 31,113.

56. Gregory to WBY, 13 May 1919, Stony Brook.

57. Gregory to WBY, [July 1916], Stony Brook; WBY to Gregory, 11 May 1919, Berg; WBY to Gregory, 2 May 1919, Berg; NLI 30,179; the passage was marked by GY for inclusion in her (unpublished) selection of the Yeats–Gregory letters.

58. WBY to GY, 13 May 1919.

59. Death certificate of Charles Herbert Hyde.

60. Lily to JBY, 5 June 1919, NLI MS 31,112.

61. 28 May 1919, *YVP* ii. 291–2.

62. WBY to GY, 8 May 1921; Stoddart to 'Nemo', 1 Dec. 1919; Howe, *The Magicians of the Golden Dawn*, 260–83; Harper, *Yeats's Golden Dawn*, 125–45; Gilbert, *Twilight of the Magicians*, 73–6. The most up-to-date history of the Order's early years is provided by R. A. Gilbert, 'Seeking that which was Lost', 33–49.

63. Howe, *The Magicians of the Golden Dawn*, 278.

64. 4 and 7 June 1919, *YVP* ii. 295–7.
65. 8 June 1919, *YVP* ii. 298–9.
66. 21 July 1919, *YVP* ii. 329–30.
67. 22 July 1919, *YVP* ii. 331.
68. 12 Jan. 1919, *LTWBY* ii. 360–1.
69. WBY to Dulac, 20 Apr. 1919, Hobby, 131.
70. WBY to GY, 13 May 1919.
71. 6 May 1922, Notebook 8, *YVP* iii. 105.
72. Qtd. by Quinn to WBY, 14 June 1919 (*Letters of John Quinn to William Butler Yeats*, 218–19); Quinn's accounting was probably included in his letter to WBY of 4 Apr. 1919.
73. WBY to Lily, 10 Jan. 1918, Boston College; WBY to Clement Shorter, 29 Jan. 1918, JK; WBY to JBY, 1 Sept. 1919, WMM.
74. Gregory to GY, 8 Nov. [1918].
75. 25 and 21 May 1919, *YVP* ii. 288 and 284.
76. [?16] June 1919, *YVP* ii. 299.
77. On 16 Feb. 1919 GY records both questions and answers, *YVP* ii. 557 nn. 134–5; *MYV* i. p. xiii.
78. 21 May 1919, *YVP* ii. 284.
79. [?19] June 1919, *YVP* ii. 304.
80. WBY to Gregory, 20 June 1919, Berg.
81. 20 June 1919, *YVP* ii. 304.
82. WBY to Gregory, 29 Oct. 1917, Wade, 633–4.
83. To Ellmann GY later confirmed that the first stanza referred to Iseult, Ellmann interview notes with GY, 17 Jan. 1947, Tulsa.
84. 14 Jan. 1918, *YVP* i. 251, 254.
85. Horton to WBY, 22 Dec. 1918, *LTWBY* ii. 359.
86. Eva Fowler to WBY, 13 Nov. 1913; 'Elizabeth Morison' and 'Frances Lamont', *An Adventure* (London: Macmillan, 1911); 7 further impressions, 2nd edn. with additional material 1913 (Macmillan, 2 impressions), 3rd edn. with new appendices but previous material left out (Chapman, 1924). The 4th edn. with preface by Edith Olivier (Faber, 1931) is in YL; the first two editions, now missing, are on the 1920s library list.
87. Lucille Iremonger, *The Ghosts of Versailles* (London: Faber & Faber, 1957), 43–6, qtd. in Michael H. Coleman, *The Ghosts of the Trianon* (Irthlingborough: Aquarian Press, 1988), 100–1; *Occult Review*, Jan. 1912, 9–10. I am indebted to Colin Smythe for making available to me copies of the letters from Ralph Shirley (editor of the *Occult Review*) to Margaret Gregory, 10 Dec. 1911, and WBY, 3 Jan. 1912, and E. Morison to Margaret Gregory, 9 Jan. 1912.
88. C. Anne E. Moberly to WBY, 20 Mar. 1918, *LTWBY* ii. 346; the book referred to may have been the revised edition of *An Adventure* with further appendices which finally appeared in 1924.
89. Possibly the anonymous *The Story of Meadow Farm: A Psychic Adventure* (London: Arthur H. Stockwell, [n.d.]), date stamped by the British Library 16 Apr. 1919, which, although concerning a pension near Interlaken, describes an experience in a style similar to Lady Gorell's later publications.

90. Elizabeth Radcliffe to WBY, [?May 1918], Stony Brook.

91. 22 June 1919, *YVP* ii. 313.

92. 10 Sept. 1919, *YVP* ii. 414.

93. 6 Apr. 1919, *YVP* ii. 235.

94. 20 Mar. 1919, *YVP* ii. 201.

95. 10 Apr. and 4 May 1919, *YVP* ii. 243, 250.

96. 19–21 June 1919, *YVP* ii. 303–4, 313.

97. 16 May 1918, *YVP* i. 449–52.

98. 23 July 1919, *YVP* ii. 332–3.

99. 26 June 1919, *YVP* ii. 317.

100. Lily to JBY, 27 June 1919, NLI MS 31,112.

101. 30 June 1919, *YVP* ii. 323.

102. 2 and 3 July 1919, *YVP* ii. 324–5.

103. WBY to Gregory, 5 July 1919, Berg.

104. 27 and 30 June 1919, *YVP* ii. 320 and 323.

105. WBY to GY, [?9] and 10 July 1919.

106. WBY to GY, 10 and [?11] July 1919.

107. WBY to Quinn, 11 July 1919, Wade, 658–9.

108. WBY to Pound, 16 July 1919, fragment, Yale; NYPL.

109. WBY to JBY, 16 July 1919, Stony Brook.

110. JBY to WBY, 26 Aug. 1919, NLI MS 31,109.

111. WBY to Quinn, 9 Aug. 1919, NYPL.

112. Lily to Quinn, 30 July 1919, NYPL.

113. WBY to Gregory, 25 July 1919, Berg.

114. 31 July 1919, *YVP* ii. 348.

115. GY interviewed by W. R. Rodgers, 16 Feb. 1949, BBC Sound Archives. I am grateful to Richard N. White for explaining the properties of the mayfly to me—they surface in May, live for a brief time, and as a delicacy for hungry trout are much prized by fly fishermen.

116. 1 and 2 Aug. 1919, *YVP* ii. 351–3.

117. 5 Aug. 1919, *YVP* ii. 359.

118. 8–15 Aug. 1919, *YVP* ii. 366–79.

119. Oliver St John Gogarty, *It isn't this Time of Year at All!* (London: MacGibbon & Kee, 1954), 145–7.

120. Gogarty, *As I Was Going down Sackville Street*, 199, 204–5.

121. 22 Aug. 1919; the editors erroneously identify Robert Blake as William Blake's younger brother, *YVP* ii. 381–3; 572 n. 171. Tradition claims that the ghost was Ethelred Henry Blake (1824–38), not his brother Ethelstane, Guy St John Williams, *A Sea-Grey House: The History of Renvyle House* (Renvyle House Hotel, 1995), 79–81.

122. WBY to Miss Jacobs, 30 July 1919, in response to her letter of 25 July, Stony Brook.

123. Sir Kenelm Digby, Knight, *The Closet of Sir Kenelm Digby, Knight, Opened*, ed. Anne Macdonald (1910), now missing but identified as belonging to GY in the 1920s library list.

124. 24 and 25 Aug. 1919, *YVP* ii. 386 and 388.

125. 26 Aug. 1919, *YVP* ii. 390–1.
126. 13 and 14 Sept 1919, *YVP* ii. 422–6; Card File V13, *YVP* iii. 424.
127. 15 Sept. 1919, *YVP* ii. 427–8.
128. 6 Sept. 1919, *YVP* ii. 408–9.
129. 24 Aug. 1919, *YVP* ii. 387.
130. 10 Sept. 1919, *YVP* ii. 414.
131. 18 Sept. 1919, *YVP* ii. 434.
132. In her interview with Rodgers GY emphasized that Anne was not in the room with Yeats while he was writing the 'Anne poem'; while his daughter was sleeping outside at Ballylee in her cradle by the river, he could look at her from the window on the stairs inside or walk down in the garden to her, BBC Sound Archives.
133. Gregory, 2 Sept. 1919, *Journals*, i. 88.
134. Lily to Quinn, 9 Sept. 1919, NYPL.
135. WBY to Laurence Binyon, 11 Sept. 1919, JK.
136. Lily to Quinn, 9 and 29 Sept. 1919, NYPL.
137. Lily to Quinn, 29 Sept. 1919, NYPL.
138. 24 Oct. 1919, *YVP* ii. 463.
139. 15 Sept. 1919, *YVP* ii. 427.

CHAPTER 10: OXFORD AND NEW YORK

1. WBY to GY, 7 Oct. 1919.
2. Lily to JBY, 4 June 1918, NLI MS 31,112.
3. Lily to JBY, 18 Nov. 1919, repeating a story told to Gregory by GY, NLI MS 31,112.
4. Lily to JBY, 2 Aug. 1920, NLI MS 31,112.
5. ECY to JBY, 8 Jan. 1921, NLI MS 31,113.
6. This description is drawn from Lily's and ECY's letters to JBY and the memories of L. A. G. Strong, Joseph Hone papers, NLI MS 5919. After a period as 'The Shamrock Tea Rooms', boasting a 'Yeats Room' decorated with WBY's poems and Cuala prints, the ground floor later housed 'Wendy News', the upper floor part of Critchley Ward & Pigott, chartered accountants.
7. Lily to JBY, 2 Aug. 1920. Inserted in GY's copy of Frederick Litchfield, *Illustrated History of Furniture* (1899) are five photographs of chests, carved panels, and tapestries, one with an identification by GY, 'old iron round chest in Town Hall Slaidburn West Riding Yorks', and a newspaper clipping 'Old English Furniture' giving prices of a sale at Christie's, including a Chinese lacquer cabinet carved with mountain landscapes similar to the one they owned.
8. Bowra, *Memories*, 232; T. MacGreevy, 'W. B. Yeats—a Generation Later', *University Review*, 3/8, 8.
9. The d'Aranyi sisters also frequently performed at Ottoline Morrell's 'Thursdays', Seymour, *Ottoline Morrell*, 281–2.
10. David Cecil, introduction to *Lady Ottoline's Album*, ed. Carolyn G. Heilbrun (New York: Knopf, 1976), 3–14; Strong, *Green Memory*, 236–7; John Cowell, *No Profit but the Name: The Longfords and the Gate Theatre* (Dublin: O'Brien Press, 1988), 19–20.

11. Bowra, *Memories*, 232.

12. GY to Ottoline Morrell, 15 Dec. 1919, HRHRC.

13. Sandra Jobson Darroch, *Ottoline: The Life of Lady Ottoline Morrell* (London: Chatto & Windus, 1976); Seymour, *Ottoline Morrell*, especially chapter 14. Evelyn O'Donovan Garbary (the former Mrs Robert Speaight) described to me how Ottoline turned up to the Speaights' London flat one winter day dressed entirely in white, instead of in the customary dark winter garb.

14. WBY to Gregory, 21 Aug. 1920, 'Some New Letters from W. B. Yeats to Lady Gregory', 45.

15. Bryan V. O'Connor to 'W. B. Yeates Esq', 26 Nov. 1919; Strong to WBY, 15 Oct. 1920, Stony Brook.

16. L. A. G. Strong, 'Yeats at his Ease', *London Magazine*, 2/3 (May 1955), repr. in Mikhail (ed.), *Interviews and Recollections*, i. 147.

17. L. A. G. Strong, 'W. B. Yeats', in Stephen Gwynn (ed.), *Scattering Branches: Tributes to the Memory of W. B. Yeats* (London: Macmillan, 1940), 215; Birgit Bramsbäck, quoting GY in a letter to me, 3 June 1987.

18. 13 Oct. 1919, *YVP* ii. 445.

19. E. F. Jourdain to GY, 19 Dec. 1919, Stony Brook.

20. Brigid Younghughes, Gwynne's youngest sister, to me, 25 Sept. 1985.

21. I am indebted to Sister Brigid Younghughes and the late Eleanor Younghughes for their memories of Gwynne and Harold.

22. WBY to A. H. Bullen, 15 Nov. 1919, Wade, 659.

23. 'there are certain scripts to be finished & if all goes well brilliantly finished', 22 Nov. 1919, *YVP* ii. 491.

24. 23 Sept. 1919, *YVP* ii. 441.

25. 12 and 13 Oct. 1919, *YVP* ii. 442-5.

26. The script for 21 Dec. 1919, Gilbert Hyde Lees's birthday, notes 'Her father is born again today . . . born but only in the womb—not yet born into life . . . ,' *YVP* ii. 519.

27. 16-21 Oct. 1919, *YVP* ii. 451-8.

28. 23 Oct. 1919, *YVP* ii. 460-3.

29. 4 Nov. 1919, *YVP* ii. 470.

30. WBY to Dulac, 24 Oct. 1919, Hobby, 132. This was most likely the Lyceum Club at 128 Piccadilly; the Three Arts Club, where George sometimes stayed, was further off at 19A Marylebone Road.

31. Lily to JBY, 5 Nov. 1919, NLI MS 31,112.

32. WBY to Gregory, 7 Nov. 1919, Berg.

33. 6 Nov. 1919, *YVP* ii. 475.

34. 8 Nov. 1919, *YVP* ii. 476.

35. WBY to Gregory, 6 Dec. 1919, Berg.

36. 9 Dec. 1919, *YVP* ii. 506.

37. *c.*22 Dec. 1917, *YVP* i. 177.

38. WBY to Iseult, 17 Nov. 1919, Elborn, *Francis Stuart*, 35; Lily to JBY, 10 Nov. 1919, NLI MS 31,112.

39. 20 Nov. 1919, *YVP* ii. 486-8.

40. 30 Nov. and 6 Dec. 1919, *YVP* ii. 498 and 501–2.

41. 'A People's Theatre: A Letter to Lady Gregory', *Irish Statesman*, 29 Nov. and 6 Dec. 1919, repr. in *Dial*, Apr. 1920.

42. Stoddart to 'Nemo', 1 Dec. 1919, Harper, *Yeats's Golden Dawn*, 130; R. A. Gilbert informs me that Caroline Beatrice (Mrs Steuart) Erskine is entered on the roll of the Second (Inner) Order as no. 267 on 16 Dec. 1919. I am grateful to Professor Wallace McLeod for information on the Freemasons.

43. WBY to Gregory, 29 Dec. 1919, Berg. The 'Sir John (or James) Plasten who is connected with one of the colleges' named in WBY's letter to Gregory, 27 Dec. 1919, is not listed in the Oxford Directory for 1919–20; their tenant was probably Sir Thomas Henry Penson, lecturer in modern history at Pembroke College.

44. GY to Ottoline Morrell, 15 Dec. 1919, HRHRC.

45. 25 and 23 Dec. 1919, *YVP* ii. 522–3.

46. WBY to Quinn, 31 Dec. 1919, *MYV* ii. 386.

47. Notebook 5, *YVP* iii. 20–1.

48. AY.

49. JBY to Lily, 26 Jan. 1920; Quinn to Lily, 25 Jan. 1920, Murphy, *Prodigal Father*, 505 ff. Much of my description of JBY and his surroundings is dependent upon W. M. Murphy's books and articles on the Yeats family and his unpublished transcriptions of JBY's letters to Rosa Butt and his daughters.

50. JBY to JackBY, 28 Apr. and 5 Sept. 1918, 5 June 1919, AY.

51. JBY to Julia Ford, 6 Jan. 1911, 'Letters to an American Patron', 170.

52. Qtd. by Reid, *The Man from New York*, 418.

53. Quinn to WBY, 28 Jan. 1920 and 7 Aug. 1919, *Letters of John Quinn to William Butler Yeats*, 230 and 220.

54. JBY to Gregory, 27 Jan. 1920, Berg; JBY to Lily, 26 Jan. 1920, Murphy, *Prodigal Father*, 505; JBY to Frank Yeats, 15 Feb. 1920, 'Some New Letters of John Butler Yeats', ed. Thomas S. Lewis, in Raymond J. Porter and James D. Brophy (eds.), *Modern Irish Literature* (New York: Twayne, 1972), 341.

55. JBY to Isaac Yeats, 2 Feb. 1920, Murphy, *Prodigal Father*, 505.

56. JBY to Rosa Butt, 23 June 1920, WMM; JBY to Lily, 20 June 1920, Murphy, *Prodigal Father*, 505.

57. Richard Londraville, 'Jeanne Robert Foster', *Eire-Ireland*, 5/1 (Spring 1970), 38–44; Reid, *The Man from New York*, 313.

58. '*Dear Yeats,*' '*Dear Pound*', '*Dear Ford*': *Jeanne Robert Foster and her Circle of Friends*, ed. Richard and Janis Londraville (Selinsgrove, Pa.: Susquehanna University Press, 2001), 89.

59. See Chapter 2 above.

60. Margaret Widdemer, *Golden Friends I Had* (New York: Doubleday, 1964), 61.

61. GY's annotated programme of the dinner, MBY.

62. JBY to Lily, 15 Feb. 1920 and JBY to ECY, 13 Feb. 1920, Murphy, *Prodigal Father*, 507.

63. *Common Conditions*, ed. Tucker Brooke. Elizabethan Club Reprints, no. 1, inscribed 'To Mrs Yeats with the sincere regards of The Elizabethan Club Yale 18 Feb. 1920', YL, uncut.

64. GY to AY, 9 Oct. 1963.

65. AY.

66. Letter to me from Alf MacLochlainn, 14 May 1985.

67. JBY to Rosa Butt, 20 Mar. 1920, WMM.

68. Divorced Australian wife of the musician Benno Moiseiwitsch and mother of Tanya Moiseiwitsch, the Abbey Theatre's first full-time stage designer.

69. JBY to [?Lily], 24 May 1920, Stony Brook; Lily to JBY, 12 June 1920, NLI MS 31,112.

70. JBY to Lily, 15 Feb. 1920, Murphy, *Prodigal Father*, 507.

71. JBY to GY, 21 Aug. 1920, NLI MS 31,109.

72. JBY to GY, 28 Sept. 1921, NLI MS 31,109.

73. JBY to JackBY, 7 May 1920, AY.

74. JBY to [?Lily], 24 May 1920, Stony Brook.

75. GY to Oliver Edwards, qtd. in his lecture to the Sligo Summer School of Aug. 1973, audio tape courtesy the late Georgie Wynne.

76. JBY to [?Lily], 24 May 1920, Stony Brook.

77. Ellmann interview notes with GY, 1 July 1946, Tulsa.

78. WBY to Gregory, 28 Feb. 1920, Berg.

79. JBY to Rosa Butt, 20 Mar. and 23 June 1920, WMM.

80. JBY to JackBY, 28 Feb. 1920, AY.

81. Jeanne Foster's verbatim report, ed. Richard Londraville, 'An Evening in New York with W. B. Yeats', *YA* 6 (1988), 166–85.

82. The Pond agency did in fact fail by the end of the year. I am grateful to the late Karin Strand for sending me details of the tour.

83. WBY to Gregory, 28 Feb. 1920, Berg.

84. 29 Feb. 1920, Notebook 1, *YVP* iii. 8.

85. Qtd. in the *Chicago Tribune*, 1 Mar. 1920, page 1, sec. II. col. 2.

86. AY.

87. Burton Rascoe, 'Meetings with W. B. Yeats', repr. in Mikhail (ed.), *Interviews and Recollections*, i. 119.

88. Notebook 1, *YVP* iii. 8.

89. WBY to Shakespear, 14 Mar. 1920, Wade, 661.

90. WBY to Gregory, 30 Mar. 1920, Berg.

91. Enclosure with letter from Quinn to WBY, 29 Apr. 1920, *Letters of John Quinn to William Butler Yeats*, 233.

92. Junzo Sato to Oliver Edwards, 2 Mar. 1935, NLI MS 27,023; Shotaro Oshima, *W. B. Yeats and Japan* (Tokyo: Hokuseido Press, 1965), 132–3, 121–30.

93. WBY to Dulac, 22 Mar. 1920, Hobby, 132–3.

94. 21 and 24 Mar. 1920, *YVP* ii. 534–6.

95. 1 and 28 Mar. 1920, *YVP* ii. 533 and 537–9.

96. *YVP* ii. 539.

97. 9 Nov. 1918, 9 and 21 Jan. 1919, *YVP* ii. 116, 168, 182–3.

98. 8–13 and 21 Dec. 1919, *YVP* ii. 503–11 and 519.

99. Ellmann notes 1946–7, Tulsa; 6 Apr. 1920, Notebook 8, *YVP* iii. 86.

100. 'We had one of those little sleeping compartments in a train, with two berths, and were somewhere in Southern California. My wife, who had been asleep for some minutes, began to talk in her sleep, and from that on almost all communications came in that way,' *A Vision B*, 9–10.

101. 17 Oct. 1933, Curtis Bradford, *Yeats at Work* (Carbondale: Southern Illinois University Press, 1965), 134–5.

102. *A Vision B*, 10.

103. WBY, 18 Sept. 1922, Notebook 8, *YVP* iii. 109.

104. Notebook 2, *YVP* iii. 9–12; for example, 'Byzantium' and *Purgatory*.

105. 13 Apr. 1920, Notebook 2, *YVP* iii. 13.

106. Robinson to GY, Dec. 1928, MBY.

107. 17 May 1920, Notebook 4, *YVP* iii. 17.

108. JBY to GY, 1 Nov. 1920, NLI MS 31,109.

109. WBY to Gregory, 28 Feb. 1920, Berg.

110. WBY to Gregory, 30 Mar. 1920, Berg.

111. WBY to Gregory, 14 June 1920, Berg.

112. JBY to JackBY, 16 Mar. 1920, AY.

113. GY to Miss Bates, 12 May 1920, Wellesley.

114. AY.

115. The specialist was Henry Craig Fleming, *Letters of John Quinn to William Butler Yeats*, 237–9.

116. JBY to Rosa Butt, 23 June 1920, WMM.

117. Pound to Quinn, 21 Feb. 1920, NYPL.

118. Ezra Pound, *Instigations* (New York: Boni & Liveright, 1920).

119. Pound to Quinn, 1 June 1920, NYPL.

120. GY to Mrs Homer Pound, 7 Apr. 1920, Yale.

121. GY to Allan Wade, 6 Sept. 1953, Rupert Hart-Davis.

122. JBY to Rosa Butt, 23 June 1920, WMM.

123. JBY to [?Lily], 23 May 1920, Stony Brook.

124. Jeffares to GY, 23 Sept. 1947.

125. Pearce, 'Hours with the Domestic Sibyl', 494. The introduction to *A Vision B*, 25, concludes, 'now that the system stands out clearly in my imagination I regard them as stylistic arrangements of experience comparable to the cubes in the drawing of Wyndham Lewis and to the ovoids in the sculpture of Brancusi. They have helped me to hold in a single thought reality and justice.' Quinn had by then an impressive collection of the artist's works, including *Mademoiselle Pogany*, *Bird*, *The Penguins*, *Portrait of Mme P.B.K.*, *Muse*, and *Head*, Reid, *The Man from New York*, *passim*.

126. Reid, *The Man from New York*, 419; Murphy, *Prodigal Father*, 642 n. 17; letter from Richard Londraville to me, 1 June 1989.

127. JBY to Rosa Butt, 25 Jan. 1921, WMM. Either Ellmann misheard or GY deliberately misled him on 5 July 1946: 'Yeats and Quinn had a quarrel lasting about 10 years because Quinn thought Yeats had tried to snaffle a niece of his Yeats said, "If it had been your wife, yes, but a niece—never". JBY tried to settle this for a long time. At

last Quinn "forgave" Yeats—which meant a great show of magnanimity,' Ellmann interview notes with GY, 5 July 1946, Tulsa.

128. JBY to ECY, 18 May 1920, WMM.

129. WBY to Gregory, [?18 May] 1920: 'Today I go to have a record taken of myself for a new kind of moving picture—a picture that talks as well as moves,' Berg.

130. 'For Madame Yvette Guilbert with all my admiration and homage W. B. Yeats May 26 1920, this book which John Quinn has bought that his homage may be linked with mine' 'And John Quinn signs his name with that of his friend Yeats as a measure of his homage . . . ,' James Gilvarry collection, Christie's sale catalogue no. 498, New York, 7 Feb. 1986.

131. An offer repeated by WBY to JBY, 27 Oct. 1920, Murphy, *Prodigal Father*, 510.

132. JBY to Rosa Butt, 20 Mar. 1920, WMM.

133. JBY to Frank Yeats, 15 Feb. 1920, WMM; JBY to Rosa Butt, 20 Mar. 1920, WMM.

134. WBY to Quinn, 30 Sept. 1921, qtd. in Reid, *The Man from New York*, 493-4.

135. Ellmann interview notes with GY, 5 July 1946, Tulsa.

136. Review of J. B. Yeats, *Letters*, ed. Joseph Hone, by Mary M. Colum, 'J. B. Yeats' Limberness and Grace', *Saturday Review of Books*, 29/45 (9 Nov. 1946), 16.

137. JBY to GY, 24 May 1920, NLI MS 31,109; see illustration.

138. Quinn to WBY, 1 May 1920, *Letters of John Quinn to William Butler Yeats*, 232-4.

139. Notebook 4, *YVP* iii. 20.

140. JBY to Lily, 29 May 1920, Murphy, *Prodigal Father*, 508-9; 'I am glad to know that you got through without any annoyance of any kind,' Quinn to WBY, 4 June 1920, *Letters of John Quinn to William Butler Yeats*, 235.

141. 31 May 1920, Notebook 6, *YVP* iii. 22.

142. WBY to Gregory, [?18 May] 1920, Berg.

143. Quinn to WBY, 4 June 1920, *Letters of John Quinn to William Butler Yeats*, 235-6.

144. Lily to JBY, 12 June 1920, Murphy, *Prodigal Father*, 509.

CHAPTER 11: MICHAEL

1. Foster, *Modern Ireland*, 497.

2. WBY to Gregory, 18 May 1920, Berg; Hone, *W. B. Yeats*, 323.

3. Gregory to WBY, 1 June 1920, Stony Brook.

4. Lily to JBY, 12 June 1920, NLI MS 31,112.

5. WBY to GY, *c.*12 June 1920.

6. Lily to Quinn, 20 June 1920, NYPL.

7. WBY to Robinson, 23 July 1920, JK.

8. Lily to JBY, 12 June 1920, quoting from 'A Prayer for my Daughter', NLI MS 31,112.

9. WBY to Fagan, 13 June 1920. I am grateful to James Pethica for providing me with a copy of this letter. James B. Fagan was manager of the Duke of York Theatre and also lessee of the Royal Court Theatre where the Abbey Theatre frequently performed.

10. WBY to Gregory, 25 June 1920, Stony Brook.

11. Gregory to WBY, 16 June 1920.

12. Notebook 6, *YVP* iii. 24.

13. WBY to Dulac, 19 June 1920, Hobby, 134.
14. 28 and 30 June, 1 July 1920, *YVP* iii. 26-8.
15. WBY to Lady Ian Hamilton, 19 June 1920, JK.
16. Felkin to Stoddart, 21 July 1920, Harper, *Yeats's Golden Dawn*, 129-30; Hammond to 'Care Frater' [WBY], 28 Sept. 1920, *LTWBY* ii. 369.
17. Rothenstein to GY, 9 July 1920, Stony Brook; William Rothenstein, *Men and Memories* (London: Faber, 1932), 377-8; Rathindranath Tagore, *On the Edges of Time* (Calcutta: Orient Longmans Private, 1958), 134-5; Rabindranath Tagore to WBY, 19 July 1920, Stony Brook.
18. WBY to Gregory, 25 June 1920, Stony Brook.
19. WBY to Gregory, 14 June 1920, Stony Brook; Gregory to WBY, 8 July 1920, Stony Brook.
20. WBY to Gregory, 15 July 1920, Berg.
21. 21-9 July 1920, *YVP* iii. 29-31.
22. ECY to JBY, 26 July 1920, NLI MS 31,113.
23. Gregory, 10-11 Jan. and 13 Apr. 1920, *Journals*, i. 119, 139.
24. Maud Gonne to WBY, 29 July 1920, White and Jeffares (eds.), *Gonne-Yeats Letters*, 405-7.
25. WBY to Gregory, 29 July 1920, Stony Brook.
26. WBY to Gregory, 3 Aug. 1920, Stony Brook; both Boccaccio and Chaucer had written of the patiently loyal but abused wife Griselda; Yeats's 'Two Songs of a Fool' (1918).
27. Mead, *The Doctrine of the Subtle Body in Western Tradition* (1919); Mead may have been doing research for *The Gnostic John the Baptizer: Selections from the Mandaean John-Book Together with Studies on John and Christian Origins, the Slavonic Josephus' Account of John and Jesus, and John and the Fourth Gospel Proem* (London: John M. Watkins, 1924).
28. GY to WBY, 3, 4, and 6 Aug.; WBY to GY, 4 Aug. 1920.
29. WBY to GY, 6 Aug. 1920.
30. Reported by Daphne Fullwood in a letter to me, 13 Nov. 1985.
31. GY to WBY, 8 Aug. 1920.
32. 12-15 Aug. 1920, *YVP* iii. 31-3.
33. Notebook 6, 29 Sept. 1920, *YVP* iii. 48. The 1861 census for Great Warley, Essex, includes as head of household (with three servants) Sarah Bonham, unmarried, age 53, an officer's daughter born in Dominica. Her father Brigadier General Bonham of the 69th regiment served for sixteen years in the West Indies. I have found no connection between the Bonhams and Gilbert Hyde Lees.
34. WBY to Gregory, 21 Aug. 1920, 'Some New Letters from W. B. Yeats to Lady Gregory', 44; Gregory to WBY, 25 Aug. 1920, Stony Brook.
35. JBY to George, 16 Aug. 1920, NLI MS 31,109.
36. Lily to JBY, 2 Aug. 1920, NLI MS 31,112.
37. Lily to Quinn, 2 Sept. 1920, NYPL.
38. WBY to Gregory, 21 Aug. 1920, 'Some New Letters from W. B. Yeats to Lady Gregory', 45; Lily to JBY, 18 Aug. 1920, NLI MS 31,112.

39. WBY to Gregory, 21 Aug. 1920, 'Some New Letters from W. B. Yeats to Lady Gregory', 44.

40. T. S. Eliot, *The Sacred Wood: Essays on Poetry and Criticism* (London: Methuen, 1920) signed 'George Yeats' but on flyleaf 'OM 1920', YL.

41. GY to 'Lady Ottoline', 26 Aug. 1920, HRHRC; Constance Garnett translated *Letters of Anton Chekhov to his Family and Friends* (London: Chatto & Windus, 1920).

42. Smith, *John Masefield: A Life*, 182.

43. WBY to Quinn, 3 Mar. 1921, *Letters of John Quinn to William Butler Yeats*, 231.

44. Ottoline Morrell to GY, 10 Sept. 1920, recipient misattributed as WBY in *LTWBY* ii. 367.

45. James O'Reilly, quoted by Gogarty, 'My Brother Willie was your Father's Friend', 5.

46. WBY to Quinn, 9 Sept. 1920, NYPL.

47. Notebook 6, 1 Sept. 1920, *YVP* iii. 41.

48. 20 May 1921, Notebook 7, *YVP* iii. 76.

49. 26 Nov. 1920, Notebook 6, *YVP* iii. 57–8.

50. 15 Dec. 1920, Notebook 6, *YVP* iii. 61–2.

51. Notebook 6, 29 Sept.–7 Oct. 1920, *YVP* iii. 48–53.

52. 1 Sept. 1920, qtd. in Elborn, *Francis Stuart*, 45.

53. [?16 Sept.] 1920, qtd. in part ibid. 45–6.

54. WBY to Quinn, 30 Oct. 1920, Wade, 663; 22 Sept. 1920 horary: 'Ought WB to have operation now or not'; on the other side of the page in automatic writing came the answer 'No' 'not now'; 24 Sept. 1920 1 p.m. horary 'should WB have his throat operated on by Gogarty'. I am indebted to Elizabeth Heine for dating these and other horoscopes.

55. Lily to JBY, 30 Sept. 1920, NLI MS 31,112.

56. Lily to Quinn, 11 Oct. 1920, NYPL; Sir Horace Curzon Plunkett's home was Kilteragh, Foxrock.

57. Gogarty to Horace Reynolds, 25 Apr. 1946, bMS Am. 1787, Harvard.

58. Lily to Quinn, 11 and 14 Oct. 1920, NYPL.

59. 'Mrs Yeats once explained to me that he was accustomed to distinguish those pages of manuscript that were to be discarded from those that were to be kept and filed by referring to the latter as "*history*"; early drafts of certain poems, abandoned ideas for a play, alternative versions of some essay—all had their place in an intellectual and personal "history" that was as objective to his scrutiny as if it were not his own but the life of another man.' *The Senate Speeches of W. B. Yeats*, ed. Donald Pearce (London: Faber & Faber, 1961), 22.

60. WBY to Pound, 7 Oct. 1920, Yale.

61. 'All Souls' Night' (1920).

62. He first met GY 'in 1920 and we were soon warm friends, a real friendship which never faltered'. Dermott MacManus to MBY, 26 Aug. 1968.

63. WBY to Gregory, 27 Sept. 1920, 'Some New Letters from W. B. Yeats to Lady Gregory', 45.

64. Maud Gonne to GY, 22 Oct. 1920, White and Jeffares (eds.), *Gonne–Yeats Letters*, 416.

65. WBY to Quinn, 30 Oct. 1920, Wade, 664.

66. WBY to Gregory, 27 Sept. 1920, 'Some New Letters from W. B. Yeats to Lady Gregory', 45.

67. WBY to Quinn, 9 Nov. 1920, NYPL.

68. JBY to GY, 1 Nov. 1920, NLI MS 31,109.

69. 19 Nov. 1920, Notebook 6, *YVP* iii. 55; Pound to Quinn, 9 Oct. 1920, NYPL.

70. WBY to Gregory, 26 Nov. 1920, Berg.

71. Sturge Moore to GY, early Dec. 1920; T. Sturge Moore, 'Yeats', *English: The Magazine of the English Association*, 2/11 (1939), 273–5.

72. GY to Dulac, 15 Dec. 1920; WBY to Dulac, 27 Dec. 1920, Hobby, 153 n., 136–7.

73. WBY to Gregory, 2 Jan. 1921, JK.

74. WBY, *Per Amica Silentia Lunae*, XXII. Later the automatic script was stored and transported in a lowly tin box while the chest held the Lady Gregory papers.

75. Vance Palmer, *Louis Esson and the Australian Theatre* (Melbourne: Georgian House, 1948), 26, 36.

76. 'Now all three are, I think, one, or rather all three are a discrete expression of a single conviction.' 'If I Were Four-and-Twenty', *Irish Statesman*, 23 and 30 Aug. 1920, reprinted in *Living Age*, 4 Oct. 1920.

77. WBY to Gregory, 18 Dec. 1920, Berg.

78. Strong, *Green Memory*, 246.

79. Robert Graves, *The Crowning Privilege*, The Clark Lectures (London: Cassell, 1955), 117.

80. WBY to Gregory, 12 Dec. 1920, Berg.

81. WBY to Gregory, 26 Nov. 1920, Berg.

82. JBY to GY, 1 Nov. 1920, NLI MS 31,109; WBY to JBY, 28 Sept., 27 Oct., 9 Nov. 1920; JBY to WBY 19, 21, 22 Nov. 1920, NLI MS 31,109; Quinn to Pound, 1 May 1921, qtd. in Rainey, *Institutions of Modernism*, 188–9 n. 22.

83. WBY to Gregory, 30 Oct. 1920, 'Some New Letters from W. B. Yeats to Lady Gregory', 46–7.

84. Nora Desmond in *Evening Telegraph*, 30 Oct. 1920.

85. Foster, *Modern Ireland*, 497–500 and 'Chronology'.

86. On the morning of 21 Nov. 1920 the IRA killed eleven unarmed British officers in Dublin; in the afternoon the Black and Tans fired into a football crowd at Croke Park, causing a stampede and twelve deaths.

87. WBY to Gregory, 26 Nov. 1920, Stony Brook; Gregory to WBY, 2 Dec. 1920, Stony Brook; Gregory, 28 Nov. 1920, *Journals*, i. 207.

88. WBY to Gregory, 6 Dec. 1920 , NLI MS 30,593.

89. Given by GY to Oliver Edwards, who published it in *Rann* (Autumn 1948).

90. Gregory to Quinn, 2 Jan. 1921, qtd. in Mary Lou Kohfeldt, *Lady Gregory: The Woman behind the Irish Renaissance* (New York: Athenaeum, 1985), 251.

91. Gregory to WBY, 19 Jan. 1921, Stony Brook.

92. Gregory to WBY, 15 Nov. 1920, Stony Brook.

93. 'Mr Yeats at Oxford: Surprising Vote at the Union on Irish Self-Government. Eloquent Speech', *Westminster Gazette*, 18 Feb. 1921; 'Mr Yeats Breaks Silence:

Passionful Speech at Oxford Union', *Daily Herald*, 18 Feb. 1921. The motion for complete self-government was carried 219 to 129, Strong, *Green Memory*, 247; John Stewart Collis, NLI 5919, qtd. by Anthony J. Jordan, *Willie Yeats and the Gonne-MacBrides* (Dublin: for the author, 1997), 168.

94. WBY to Gregory, 24 Feb. 1921, Berg.

95. Gregory to WBY, 21 Dec. 1920, Stony Brook; WBY to Gregory, 27 Dec. 1920, Berg.

96. WBY to Gregory, *c*.8 Feb. 1921, Stony Brook.

97. Pound to Quinn, 30 Dec. 1920, NYPL.

98. Notebook 8, 18 Sept. 1921, *YVP* iii. 95.

99. WBY to Gregory, *c*.8 Feb. 1921, Stony Brook.

100. WBY to Gregory, 30 Dec. 1920, Berg. Helen T. M. Lawless and Skerrett Edward George Lawless lived at 32 via Romana Florence; her husband died in 1935 at age 75, she in 1947 at age 85; Eva Ducat was witness to her will in 1934.

101. WBY to Gregory, 1 Jan. 1921, JK; Gregory to WBY, 4 Jan. 1921, Stony Brook.

102. Gregory to WBY, 1, 19, and 23 Jan. 1921, Stony Brook.

103. WBY to Gregory, *c*.8 Feb. 1921, Stony Brook.

104. Dulac to WBY, 13 Jan. 1921, *LTWBY* ii. 374–5; WBY to Dulac, 28 Feb. 1921, Hobby, 138.

105. WBY to Gregory, 6 Jan. 1921, Berg.

106. Brigid Younghughes remembers meeting Willy sometime in 1921 on a tour of the Wye Valley with Harold—and, presumably, their wives.

107. Notebook 6, 11 Jan. 1921, *YVP* iii. 65.

108. Notebook 8, 18 Feb. 1921, 6 Apr. and 18 Sept. 1921, *YVP* iii. 84–8, 94. Basil Blackwell and Dorothy Sayers had both been present at one of Bond's sittings with the medium 'John Alleyne' (John Allen Bartlett). *MYV* i. 177–80. 'When I took my hands out of my pocket on our way to Glastonbury they were strongly scented, and when I held them out for my wife to smell she said, "May flower, the Glastonbury thorn perhaps",' WBY, introduction to *A Vision B*.

109. WBY to Sturge Moore, 17 Feb. 1926, Bridge (ed.), *W. B. Yeats and T. Sturge Moore*, 72–3.

110. WBY to F. P. Sturm, 18 Feb. and 23 Oct. 1918, 20 Dec. 1920; F. P. Sturm, *Umbrae Silentes* (London: Theosophical Publishing House, 1918), YL; Notebook 8, 18 Feb. 1921, *YVP* iii. 85; Sturm to WBY, 20 Feb. 1921, Richard Taylor (ed.), *Frank Pearce Sturm* (Urbana: University of Illinois Press, 1969), 75–9.

111. WBY to Sturm, 17 June [?1921], Stony Brook.

112. Sturm to WBY, 26 Aug. 1929; in spite of this, on 9 Oct. 1929 WBY sent him a copy of his 'Six Propositions'. Taylor (ed.), *Frank Pearce Sturm*, 99–101.

113. WBY to Shakespear, 4 Mar. 1926, Wade, 711–12.

114. Gregory, *Journals*, i. 646 n. 8.

115. WBY to Gregory, qtd. in Hone, *W. B. Yeats*, 338.

116. Gibbon, *Masterpiece and the Man*, 42–3.

117. WBY to Wade, 13 Feb. 1922, NLI MS 30,560.

118. WBY to Gregory, 24 Feb. 1921, Berg; Lily to JBY, 13 Feb. 1921, NLI MS 31,112.

119. JBY to GY, *c.* Feb. 1921, NLI MS 31,109.
120. WBY to Quinn, 3 Mar. 1921, *Letters of John Quinn to William Butler Yeats*, 231.
121. WBY to Lily, 21 June 1921, Boston College.
122. WBY to Gregory, 22 Mar. 1921, Berg.
123. Notebook 7, 26 Mar. 1921, *YVP* iii. 74–5; WBY to Gregory, 24 Feb. 1921, Berg.
124. Gregory to WBY, 3 Mar. 1921, Stony Brook.
125. Lily to JBY, 17 Apr. 1921, NLI MS 31,112; WBY to Shakespear, 9 Apr. 1921, Wade, 667–8.
126. WBY to Gregory, 10 Apr. 1921, Berg; this sentence omitted by Wade, 668; WBY to Gregory, 29 Apr. 1921, JK.
127. WBY to Gregory, 5 Apr. 1921, Berg.
128. WBY to GY, 8 and 9 May 1921.
129. WBY to Quinn, 30 May 1921, NYPL; Quinn to WBY, 17 June 1921, *Letters of John Quinn to William Butler Yeats*, 259.
130. 17 May 1921, Notebook 7, *YVP* iii. 76.
131. ECY to JBY, 24 May 1921, misdated 1919 in Gifford Lewis, *The Yeats Sisters and the Cuala* (Dublin: Irish University Press, 1994), 155.
132. WBY to Robinson, [?21 June 1921], Stony Brook; WBY to Dulac, 17 July 1921, Hobby, 141.
133. WBY to Gregory, 1 July 1921, Stony Brook.
134. WBY to Shakespear, 1 Aug. 1921, Wade, 672.
135. WBY to Nugent Monck, 1 Sept. 1921. I am grateful to D. H. Hoeniger for providing me with a copy of this letter.
136. Section VII of 'Hodos Chameliontos', *Autobiographies*, ed. O'Donnell and Archibald, 215–16.
137. WBY to Gregory, 13 July 1921, Stony Brook.
138. Interview with Grace Jaffe.
139. Rafferty to GY, 28 Oct. 1918, NLI MS 30,663.
140. Gregory to WBY, 31 July 1921, Stony Brook.
141. WBY to Gregory, qtd. in Elborn, *Francis Stuart*, 51–2.
142. Lily to JBY, 8 Nov. 1921, NLI MS 31,112.
143. *A Vision B*, 17.
144. WBY to Gregory, 1 Aug. 1921, Stony Brook; Lily to JBY, 6 and 23 Aug. 1921, NLI MS 31,112.
145. 11 Feb. 11.45 a.m. 'what day w [William] or s [Stuarta] born?' By 26 Mar. 1921 the name 'Michael' was proposed 'if a boy', Notebook 7, *YVP* iii. 75.
146. WBY to Gregory, 9 Aug. 1921, Stony Brook.
147. Notebook 8, 18 Sept. 1921, *YVP* iii. 94–5; WBY, 'Conjunctions' (Aug. 1934).
148. Murphy, *Prodigal Father*, 523–4.
149. WBY to ECY, 22 Dec. 1921, Boston College.
150. 'A second child, a daughter like the first, has been born to the wife of Mr W. B. Yeats, the poet, at Cuttlebrook House, Thame. Mr Yeats made a surprise marriage four years ago to Miss George Hyde-Lees, only daughter of the late Mr W. G. Hyde-Lees, of Pickhill Hall, Wrexham,' *Star*, 24 Aug. 1921.

151. Gregory to WBY, 22 Aug. 1921, Stony Brook.

152. Lily to JBY, 16 Sept. 1921, NLI MS 31,112; WBY to Gregory, 9 Sept. 1921, Berg; Notebook 8, 5 Sept. 1921, *YVP* iii. 97; 'A Packet for Ezra Pound', section VII; Notebook 8, 12 Sept. 1921, *YVP* iii. 95.

153. Lily to JBY, 4 Sept. 1921, NLI MS 31,112.

154. 'There was a very questionable moment whether he would live or not, he was a very small infant at the time. WB wrote that poem because he wasn't sure if Michael would live or not.' GY to W. R. Rodgers, BBC Sound Archives.

155. A. N. Jeffares, 'W. B. Yeats and his Methods of Writing Verse', *Nineteenth Century and After* (Mar. 1946), 123.

156. Lily to JBY, 16 Sept. 1921, NLI MS 31,112.

157. Lily to R L-P, WMM; Lily to JBY, 22 Sept. 1918, NLI MS 31,112; WBY to Lily, 1 Sept. 1921, Boston College.

158. Lily to WBY, 22 Jan. 1922, Stony Brook.

159. Gregory, 18 Sept. 1921, *Journals*, i. 292–3.

160. The photograph, dated by Lolly 18 Sept. 1921, is published in Pyle, *Red-Headed Rebel*, 206.

161. Lily to JBY, 16 and 27 Sept. 1921, NLI MS 31,112; ECY to JBY, 19 Sept. 1921, NLI MS 31,113.

162. JBY to GY, 28 Sept. 1921, NLI MS 31,109.

163. WBY to JBY 30 Sept. and 29 Oct. 1921; JBY to GY, 9 and 16 Oct. [?1921], AY.

164. WBY to Quinn, 25 Aug. 1921, Wade, 673; Quinn to WBY, 19 Sept. 1921 and 30 July 1922, *Letters of John Quinn to William Butler Yeats*, 269, 288.

165. WBY to Gregory, 19, 27, and 29 Oct. 1921, JK.

166. Lily to JBY, 8 Nov. 1921, NLI MS 31,112.

167. WBY to GY, 29 Oct. 1921; GY to WBY, 30 Oct. 1921, Stony Brook. I am grateful to Dr A. J. Hutchison for medical explanations.

168. WBY to GY, 6 Nov. 1921.

169. Nelly to WBY, 29 Oct. 1921.

170. Gregory to WBY, 3 Nov. 1921, Stony Brook.

171. WBY to GY, 11 Nov. 1921; he heard of this from a distant cousin, Agnes Raeburn.

172. Robinson to MacGreevy, 15 Dec. 1921, TCD MS 8103; WBY to Robinson, 15 Dec. 1921, Sotheby's sale catalogue no. 580, 21–2 July 1983; Wilhelm, *Ezra Pound in London and Paris*, 226.

173. Robinson to MacGreevy, 19 Dec. 1921, TCD MS 8103; Seymour, *Ottoline Morrell*, 435.

174. WBY to Ottoline Morrell, 6 Jan. 1922, JK; WBY to Gregory, 12 Jan. 1922, Stony Brook.

175. WBY to Sturm, 17 June 1921, Stony Brook; Notebook 4, 23 May 1920, *YVP* iii. 19.

176. Notebook 8, 7 Oct. 1921, *YVP* iii. 99.

177. Stoddart to WBY, 18, 21, and 29 Mar. 1921, *LTWBY* ii. 376–80; Harper, *Yeats's Golden Dawn*, 308–9; Stoddart to GY, 21 Mar. 1921.

178. Stoddart to WBY, 21 Apr. 1921, Harper, *Yeats's Golden Dawn*, 139; Collison to 'Frater', 8 May 1921 (Howe, *The Magicians of the Golden Dawn*, 280); 'Whatever

may eventually happen I mean to hold on & investigate in every possible way giving the Order every chance before finally deciding. Honestly I don't see much hope for it but I am certain we are being helped by some strong good forces.' Stoddart to WBY, 18 Nov. 1921, *LTWBY* ii. 400–1.

179. WBY to GY, 5 and 8 May 1921; Stoddart to WBY, 10 May 1921, *LTWBY* ii. 385–6.

180. Although Moore, *The Unicorn*, 177, says WBY and GY probably both ceased to be members in 1919, they seem to have remained on the fringes until early 1923, when Stoddart also left, Howe, *The Magicians of the Golden Dawn*, 283.

181. WBY to 'Miss Little', 24 Nov. 1921, NLI MS 30,563; identified on the letter as 'Paget's aunt', she is probably Edith Little ('Pherometha'), who was admitted into the Isis-Urania Temple of the Golden Dawn in May 1905; the astrologer 'Zadkiel' (Alfred John Pearce) had also briefly been a member of the Order, Gilbert, *The Golden Dawn Companion*, 162, 145; *The Tetrabiblos; or, Quadripartite of Ptolemy*. The friend who died in Ceylon was Florence Farr Emery.

182. WBY to Shakespear, 22 Dec. 1921, Stony Brook; Wade, 675 has a slightly different transcription.

183. WBY to Gregory, 2 Jan. 1922, Berg.

PART III: DIRECTIONS

1. GY to MacGreevy, 28 Nov. 1926, TCD MS 8104.
2. GY to MacGreevy, 31 Dec. 1925, TCD MS 8104.
3. GY to MacGreevy, 31 Dec. 1925, TCD MS 8104.
4. 10 Nov. 1918, *YVP* ii. 119.

CHAPTER 12: BALLYLEE

5. WBY to ECY, 12 Jan. 1922, Boston College.
6. Pound to Quinn, 21 May 1921 and 21 Feb. 1922, NYPL; other speakers on cultural affairs were Evelyn Gleeson, founder of the Dun Emer Industries, Arthur Darley, composer and violinist, and Douglas Hyde.
7. WBY to Gregory, 27 Jan. 1922, Berg.
8. WBY to Gogarty, 1 Feb. 1922, qtd. in 'My Brother Willie was your Father's Friend', 5.
9. In her will Jeanne Robert Foster left the plot to the care of W. M. Murphy, Jeanne Robert Foster to WMM, 6 June 1957.
10. Foster to WBY, 26 Jan. 1922; Murphy, *Prodigal Father*, 537–9; Jeanne Foster to WBY, 5 Feb. 1922, *LTWBY* ii. 405; Jeanne Foster to GY, 12 Feb. 1922.
11. WBY to Lily, 13 Feb. 1922, Boston College; Wade, 676; WBY to ECY, 3 Feb. 1922.
12. 'Chatto & Windus has accepted my father's letters—the two Cuala books—on condition of their re-arrangement in a shape like "Samuel Butler's Note Books" & George is to make the re-arrangement under my eyes,' WBY to Gregory, 26 Nov. 1920, Berg; *J. B. Yeats Letters to his Son*; J. B. Yeats, *Early Memories* (Dundrum: Cuala, 1923).
13. WBY to Shakespear, 17 Feb. 1922, Wade, 678.
14. WBY to GY [dated 14 Feb. 1922 but probably a day or two later].

15. WBY to Shakespear, 17 Feb. 1922, Wade, 677; Gregory to WBY, 11 Feb. 1922, Stony Brook.

16. WBY to Shakespear, 1 Mar. 1922, Wade, 678; also WBY to H. J. C. Grierson, 7 June 1922, Wade, 687.

17. WBY to Gregory, 23 Feb. 1922, JK; Bradford, 'George Yeats: Poet's Wife', 395. They sold the lease in 1928 for £1,500.

18. I am grateful to Miss Ellen Cooper, managing director of Pembroke Estates Management, 14 Fitzwilliam Place, for finding a copy of the original lease, and to Jim Brennan and Rochford Brady for searching out the Memorials. Thom's *Dublin Directory* for 1923–8 states the city rate was £100; the ground rent was £30.

19. Robinson, *Curtain Up*, 123–4.

20. Memorials; AY.

21. 9 Mar. 1927, *The Senate Speeches of W. B. Yeats*, 133–6.

22. ECY to Quinn, 15 Feb. 1922, NYPL.

23. WBY to Gregory, 9 Mar. 1922, Berg.

24. Astrological chart drawn on 21 Feb. 1922.

25. MBY.

26. Hilda Doolittle to Vera Hone, 23 Feb. 1940, Hone papers, NLI MS 5,919; WBY to Shakespear, 1 Mar. 1922, Wade, 678.

27. WBY to Gregory, 15 Mar. 1922, Berg.

28. Notebook 8, 23 June 1922, *YVP* iii. 108; WBY to Jeanne Robert Foster, 27 Mar. 1922, Richard Londraville.

29. GY to Ottoline Morrell, [11 Mar.] 1922, HRHRC.

30. Even though *Ulysses* was never officially banned, there was a great deal of self-censorship in Ireland. GY told Birgit Bramsbäck that although the customs officers detained her, they did not seize the book (letter to me, 2 Sept. 1988).

31. GY to WBY, 19 Mar. 1922; I have been unable to identify Ms Scott.

32. WBY to GY, 21 Mar. 1922. The Chinese paintings from Dulac were left to AY.

33. WBY to GY, 28 Mar. 1922.

34. WBY to Shakespear, [? Apr. 1922], Wade, 680; Gregory, 20 Feb. 1922, *Journals*, i. 332.

35. WBY to Quinn, 5 June 1922, Wade, 682–3. Details of Ballylee are drawn from WBY's letters to Shakespear, [?Apr.] and May, 7 June 1922, Wade, 680–2, 685–6, and to H. J. C. Grierson, 7 June 1922, Wade, 686–7.

36. Gregory, 8 Sept. 1922, *Journals*, i. 392.

37. From 'Meditations in Time of Civil War'.

38. WBY to Shakespear, 7 June 1922, Wade, 685–6.

39. WBY to Shakespear, [?Apr.] 1922, Wade, 680–1.

40. WBY to GY, [? 4 Nov] 1924, quoting Rita Daly of nearby Castle Daly.

41. GY to MacGreevy, [?2 Aug. 1923], TCD MS 8104.

42. Interview with Mrs Delia McAllel, Gort, 1 Oct. 2000; additional information courtesy Sister de Lourdes Fahy, Sisters of Mercy Convent, Gort, and, through her, Father Martin Coen's interview with Mary Kate Callinan (née Kelly).

43. MBY, *Cast a Cold Eye*, 4.

44. Memories of AY and MBY.
45. MBY, *Cast a Cold Eye*, 6.
46. GY to Gogarty, 6 Jan. 1931, Bucknell; AY, 1974 radio interview; Marilyn Gaddis Rose, 'A Visit with Anne Yeats', *Modern Drama*, 7/3 (Dec. 1964), 300.
47. Terence de Vere White, *Kevin O'Higgins* (1948; Dublin: Anvil Books, 1986), 84–5.
48. Wilhelm, *Ezra Pound in London and Paris*, 314.
49. Gregory, 26 May 1922, *Journals*, i. 359.
50. Gregory, 8, 12, and 20 July 1922, *Journals*, i. 373–4, 378.
51. Gregory, 20–2 July 1920, *Journals*, i. 378–9.
52. AY; MBY, *Cast a Cold Eye*, 5.
53. B. C. Windeler, *Elimus*, with illustrations by Dorothy Shakespear (Paris: Three Mountains Press, 1923).
54. WBY to Shakespear, 27 July 1922, Wade, 687–8; WBY to Pound, 18 May 1924, Indiana.
55. Gregory, 31 July 1922, *Journals*, i. 382.
56. Lily to Quinn, 13 Aug. 1922, NYPL.
57. GY to Ottoline Morrell, 1 Sept. 1922, HRHRC; Gregory, 20 Aug. 1922, *Journals*, i. 387.
58. GY to Ottoline Morrell, 27 June 1922, HRHRC.
59. Seymour, *Ottoline Morrell*, 440.
60. 'decision to ask OM if I shall make her talisman.' Horary 31 Aug. 1922 7.45 p.m.; Gilbert, *The Golden Dawn Companion*, 123; Sturm to WBY, 5 June 1906.
61. 'I have written to Lady Ottoline . . . & have sent her a letter to Mrs Handcock which I think will do the trick. I haven't seen that lady for a long time; the last two occasions . . . were mere goozle compared with my earlier interviews,' Everard Feilding to WBY, 26 Sept. [1922], *LTWBY* ii. 364, misdated 1919.
62. GY to Ottoline Morrell, 1 Sept. 1922, HRHRC.
63. WBY to GY, 27 Nov. 1922.
64. Gregory, 20 Sept. 1922, *Journals*, i. 396; WBY to Quinn, 19 Oct. 1922, NYPL.
65. WBY to Ricketts, 5 Nov. 1922, Wade, 690–1.
66. GY to MacGreevy, [?2 Aug.] 1923, TCD MS 8104; true to her oath of secrecy, years later George told her son that she had merely 'used up the remains of some old paint pots that were lying around', MBY, *Cast a Cold Eye*, 5.
67. MBY, *Cast a Cold Eye*, 6–7.
68. WBY to GY, 11 May 1924; WBY to Shannon, 1 July 1924, JK; Gregory to WBY, 4 Jan. 1923, Stony Brook.
69. MBY, *Cast a Cold Eye*, 6.
70. Gregory, 29 Nov. 1927, *Journals*, ii. 220.
71. Gregory, *Me & Nu*, 117.
72. AY, unpublished memoirs.
73. WBY to Pound, 29 July 1923, Indiana.
74. Robinson to MacGreevy, 28 Oct. 1926, TCD MS 8103.
75. WBY to GY, 18 Aug. 1924.
76. Gregory, 12 June 1926, *Journals*, ii. 107.

77. GY to Bramsbäck, 1948, qtd. in a letter to me, 2 Sept. 1988.

78. WBY to Shakespear, 23 June 1927, Wade, 725.

79. GY to MacGreevy, 15 May 1926, TCD MS 8104 .

80. WBY to Shakespear, 23 June 1927, Wade, 725.

81. WBY to GY, 20 Aug. 1924.

82. WBY to GY, 3 Oct. 1924.

83. Notebook 8, 18 Sept. 1922, *YVP* iii. 106–9 and illustration, and Notebook 9, 16–21 June 1922, *YVP* iii. 116–18.

84. 'Do you know of a good medium in Dublin?' WBY to Robinson, 24 June 1922, Lennox Robinson Papers, Southern Illinois.

85. Notebook 8, 13 Sept. 1922, *YVP* iii. 110; WBY to Shakespear, 9 Oct. 1922, Wade, 690.

86. WBY to T. Werner Laurie, 13 Mar. 1923, Emory.

87. Note to 'The Phases of the Moon' (1922); preface to *Michael Robartes and the Dancer*.

88. *A Vision: An Explanation of Life Founded upon the Writings of Giraldus and upon Certain Doctrines Attributed to Kusta ben Luka* (London: T. Werner Laurie, 1925), pp. xv–xxiii, 9–11; these early drafts are published in *Yeats's Vision Papers*, iv, ed. George Mills Harper and Margaret Mills Harper (London: Palgrave, 2001). I am indebted to George and Bobbie Harper for copies of the transcriptions.

89. 'The Dance of the Four Royal Persons by Owen Aherne', *A Vision A*, 11.

90. Frye, 'The Rising of the Moon', 19; A. Norman Jeffares, *A New Commentary on the Poems of W. B. Yeats* (London: Macmillan, 1984), 445–6; S. B. Bushrui, 'Yeats's Arabic Interests', in A. Norman Jeffares and K. E. W. Cross (eds.), *In Excited Reverie* (London: Macmillan, 1965), 280–314.

91. Stoddart to WBY, 29 Mar. 1921, *LTWBY* ii. 379–80.

92. Qtd. from an unpublished notebook by Moore, *The Unicorn*, 463 n. 3.

93. AY.

94. WBY to Quinn, 5 June 1922, Wade, 684.

95. AY, unpublished memoirs.

96. GY to WBY, 23 Nov. 1922.

97. WBY to Gregory, 30 Sept. 1922, JK.

98. Gibbon, *Masterpiece and the Man*, 44–50.

99. WBY to GY, 2 Dec. 1922.

100. The self-portrait, sent by Quinn, arrived in Sept. 1923, but by then the Cuala Industries had taken temporary possession of the dining room.

101. Gregory, 14 May 1923, *Journals*, i. 452.

102. Nancy Pyper, 'Four O'clock Tea with W. B. Yeats', *Musical Life and Arts* (Winnipeg), 1 Dec. 1924, 161–5, repr. in Mikhail (ed.), *Interviews and Recollections*, i. 158–9.

103. WBY to Shakespear, 9 Oct. 1922, Wade, 690, and 7 Nov. [misdated Dec.] 1922, Stony Brook.

104. WBY to Ricketts, 5 Nov. 1922, Wade, 690–1; WBY to Gregory, 26 Dec. 1922, JK.

105. GY to WBY, 24 Nov. 1922.

106. AY.

107. Gregory, 10 Nov. 1922, *Journals*, i. 408.

CHAPTER 13: MERRION SQUARE

1. Mid-Jan. 1922, *YVP* iii. 104.
2. Gregory to WBY, 31 Jan. [1922], Stony Brook.
3. WBY to GY, [?22 Mar. 1922].
4. GY to WBY, 2 Dec. 1922.
5. Earnán de Blaghd in McManus (ed.), *The Yeats We Knew*, 73.
6. Hone, *W. B. Yeats*, 350; however, Pearce believes his prestige as a poet, urged by Gogarty, was the main deciding factor, *The Senate Speeches of W. B. Yeats*, 14–15.
7. A list of outrages to Senators is provided by Donal Joseph O'Sullivan, *The Irish Free State and its Senate: A Study in Contemporary Politics* (London: Faber, 1940), 100 ff.
8. WBY to Dulac, ?19 Dec. 1922, misdated 1 Dec. in Wade, 693–4, Hobby, 142–3; WBY to Shakespear, 30 July 1928, Wade, 745. In 1924 the average man earned £3 a week, Rainey, *Institutions of Modernism*, 63.
9. WBY to GY, 29 Nov. 1922; GY to WBY, 1 Dec. 1922.
10. Clifford Bax, *Rosemary for Remembrance* (London: Frederick Muller, 1948), 52; GY to MacGreevy, [n.d.], TCD MS 8104.
11. GY to MacGreevy, 24 Apr. 1926, TCD MS 8104.
12. WBY to GY, 23 Nov. 1922.
13. Gregory, 27 Nov. 1922, *Journals*, i. 415.
14. GY to WBY, 23 and 28 Nov. 1922. Charlotte Despard, radical Republican sister of Lord French, the Lord Lieutenant, had recently purchased Roebuck House with Maud Gonne; Helena Moloney, former Abbey actress who had been imprisoned in 1916 and was now president of the Irish Congress of Trade Unions, also at times lived with Maud.
15. WBY to GY, [2 Dec. 1922]; WBY to Shakespear, 5 Jan. 1923, Wade, 696–7.
16. WBY to Maud Gonne, 3 May [?1923], White and Jeffares (eds.), *Gonne–Yeats Letters*, 430.
17. WBY to Shakespear, 7 Sept. 1927, Stony Brook.
18. Gregory, 12 Apr. 1923, *Journals*, i. 445.
19. Maud Gonne MacBride, *An Pobhlach*, Dec. 1928, NLI MS 30,911.
20. 'I found George Yeats exceedingly companionable. She is as Quinn says "calm" always calm,' JBY to Gregory, 8 July 1920, WMM.
21. GY to WBY, 24 Nov. 1922.
22. GY to WBY, 1 Dec. 1922.
23. AY in Saddlemyer and Smythe (eds.), *Lady Gregory: Fifty Years After*, 20; MBY, *Cast a Cold Eye*, 37.
24. Robinson, *Curtain Up*, 131–2.
25. J. B. Lyons, *Oliver St. John Gogarty* (Lewisburg, Pa.: Bucknell University Press, 1976), 34.
26. WBY to GY, 21, 30, and 31 Jan. 1923; WBY to Gregory, 31 Jan. 1923, JK; GY to WBY, 30 Jan. 1923.
27. GY to WBY, 1 Feb. 1923; WBY to GY, 2 Feb. 1923.

28. AY; Charles (Charlotte) Lane-Poole also recalled that neither George nor Willy were 'touching' people, interview Jan. 1997.
29. Gregory, *Journals*, i. 436; this entry is dated 19 Feb. 1923, but Renvyle was destroyed on 29 Feb. O'Connor, *Oliver St John Gogarty*, 199.
30. WBY to GY, 3 Feb. 1923.
31. WBY to Jeanne Foster, 8 Apr. 1923, WMM.
32. Lily to Quinn, 8 Apr. 1923, NYPL.
33. WBY to GY, 30 Nov. 1922, 10 and 13 Feb. 1923; on this or another occasion WBY was impressed by a book test given him by Mrs Cooper, as recounted by Cummins, 'W. B. Yeats and Psychical Research', 133.
34. Gregory, 18 Feb. 1923, *Journals*, i. 436.
35. Ellmann interview notes with GY, 8 Dec. 1946, Tulsa.
36. Nelly to MacGreevy, 1 Feb. 1927, TCD MS 8129.
37. Will of Edith Alice Woodmass.
38. WBY to Shakespear, 28 June 1923, Wade, 698–9.
39. GY to MacGreevy, 1 July 1926, TCD MS 8104.
40. Ronan Keane, ' "Had I the heavens' embroidered cloths": Yeats's Role in Robing the Judiciary', *Irish Times*, 9 June 1990, 2–3.
41. *The Senate Speeches of W. B. Yeats*, 20.
42. Ibid. 156–60; W. B. Stanford, 'Yeats in the Irish Senate', *Review of English Literature* (July 1963), 73, 75–6.
43. O'Sullivan, *The Irish Free State and its Senate*, 167–8; Hone, *W. B. Yeats*, 370; Robinson to MacGreevy, 11 June 1925, TCD MS 8103.
44. GY to MacGreevy, 28 June 1925, TCD MS 8104.
45. O'Sullivan, *The Irish Free State and its Senate*, 629; WBY to Shakespear, 18 Dec. 1922, Wade, 690.
46. Gregory, 12 Mar. 1924, *Journals*, i. 516.
47. GY to Desmond FitzGerald, 17 Jan. 1923, UCD.
48. NLI MS 30,064.
49. WBY to Shakespear, 28 June 1923, Wade, 698–9.
50. WBY to Pound, 17 June 1924. The invitation read: 'We, on behalf of the Distinguished Visitors' Committee of Aonach Taillteann have the honour to invite you, Ezra Pound Esq. M.A. an Eminent Son of your Country, to be the Guest of our Nation, from 1st Aug. to 10th Aug., 1924. Signed WBYeats Chairman Oliver St J. Gogarty Vice-Chairman H. M. Laughlin, T. W. Maddock Hon Secretaries,' Indiana; Pound to WBY, 19 June 1924, 'Ezra Pound Letters to William Butler Yeats', ed. Terrell, 39–40.
51. Desmond FitzGerald to Pound, 11 July 1924, Mary FitzGerald, 'Ezra Pound and Irish Politics: An Unpublished Correspondence', *Paideuma*, 12/2–3 (Fall–Winter 1983), 383.
52. Compton Mackenzie, 'Sidelight', *Spectator*, 193 (1 Oct. 1954), 395.
53. Stewart Donovan, 'Remembering Yeats: An Interview with Francis Stuart', *Antigonish Review*, 71–2 (Autumn–Winter 1988), 59.
54. WBY to Gregory, 6 Aug. 1924, Sotheby's sale catalogue no. 552.

55. WBY to Pound, 29 July 1923, Indiana.
56. GY to MacGreevy, 1 July 1926, TCD MS 8104.
57. GY to MacGreevy, 26 Mar. 1926, TCD MS 8104.
58. GY to Watt, 3 June 1925, Stony Brook. I am grateful to Narayan Hegde for providing a copy.
59. Pound to GY, 14 June 1928, MBY; Saddlemyer (ed.), 'George, Ezra, Dorothy and Friends', 14; Watt to GY, 7 Jan. 1927.
60. 'Georgie Yeats' to A. J. A. Symons, 25 Mar. 1926, HRHRC; WBY to Grierson, 21 Feb. 1926, Wade, 710; WBY to ECY, 8 July 1919, Boston College.
61. ECY to Monk Gibbon, 31 Mar. 1926, Queen's.
62. Lily to R L-P, 1 Oct. 1925.
63. WBY to Ricketts, 5 Nov. 1922, Wade, 691.
64. WBY to GY, 12 Nov. 1924; AY.
65. Ellmann interview notes with Isa MacNie, 17 Aug. 1946, Tulsa.
66. 10 Nov. 1918, *YVP* ii. 119.
67. GY to MacGreevy, 31 Dec. 1925, TCD MS 8104.
68. MacGreevy to GY, 7 Jan. 1926, NLI MS 30,859.
69. Gregory, 19 Nov. 1926, *Journals*, ii.149.
70. The portable model of the 'Noiseless' typewriter was introduced in 1921.
71. WBY to GY, 9 Nov. 1922.
72. GY to MacGreevy, 8 Dec. 1926, TCD MS 8104.
73. Lily to R L-P, 26 Jan. 1926.
74. On 10 Jan. 1923 Hilda Pollexfen married the Revd Charles Lloyd Graham.
75. WBY to Shakespear, 5 Jan. 1923, Wade 696-7.
76. GY to WBY, 23 Nov. 1922.
77. AY, unpublished memoirs.
78. Ibid.
79. Lily to R L-P, 3 Jan. 1926.
80. GY to MacGreevy, [31 Dec. 1925], TCD MS 8104.
81. Robinson to MacGreevy, 25 Oct. 1926, TCD MS 8103; Lily to R L-P, 20 and 28 Oct. 1926.
82. GY to A. J. A. Symons, 25 Mar. 1926, HRHRC.
83. ECY to Quinn, 16 Jan. 1923, NYPL.
84. Lily to R L-P, 6 Apr. 1926 and 8 Sept. 1925.
85. Isa MacNie, BBC interview, 'W. B. Yeats', in Rodgers (ed.), *Irish Literary Portraits*, 14.
86. Gregory, 5 Feb. 1925, *Journals*, i. 625.
87. Lily to R L-P, 16 Apr. 1925.
88. Lily to Monk Gibbon, 23 Jan. 1926, Queen's.
89. GY to WBY, 19 Aug. 1924.
90. Gregory, 11 Aug. 1924, *Journals*, i. 572-3.
91. GY to WBY, 23 Aug. 1924; WBY to GY, 28 Aug. and *c*.2 Sept. 1924.
92. AY, unpublished memoirs.
93. AY; MBY, *Cast a Cold Eye*, 31; the poem is by Isaac Watts.

94. GY to Rodgers, BBC Sound Archives.
95. David Clark, unpublished memoir; Ellmann, *The Man and the Masks*, 1979 preface, pp. xxxiv–xxxv; Brigit Patmore, 'Some Memories of W. B. Yeats', *Texas Quarterly*, 8/4 (Winter 1965), 157; Stephens, *James, Seumas & Jacques*, ed. Lloyd Frankenberg (New York: Macmillan, 1964), repr. in 'W. B. Yeats', in Mikhail (ed.), *Interviews and Recollections*, ii. 297.
96. GY to Rodgers, 'W. B. Yeats', in Rodgers (ed.), *Irish Literary Portraits*, 15.
97. MacGreevy to his mother Margaret McGreevy, 18 Oct. 1927, TCD MS 10,381.
98. WBY to ECY, 4 Mar. 1923, Boston College.
99. 'George has jaundice—I hope however she may be well by next week—which keeps her in bed a good deal at the moment,' WBY to Gregory, 2 Nov. 1923, Berg.
100. WBY to GY, 7, 8, and 10 Apr. 1924.
101. GY to MacGreevy, 28 June 1925, TCD MS 8104.
102. ECY to JBY, 'Whit Monday' 1920, NLI MS 31,113; Lily to JBY, 18 Jan. 1922, NLI MS 31,112.
103. WBY to Lily, [?late Mar. 1922], Boston College.
104. ECY to Quinn, 31 July 1923, NYPL.
105. WBY to GY, 27 July 1923.
106. JackBY to GY, 11 Feb. 1924, Stony Brook.
107. J. B. Lyons, 'A Creative Family', *Consultant* (Nov. 1995), 32–6.
108. ECY to Quinn, 31 July 1923, NYPL.
109. Dr Robert Simpson to WBY, 20 Mar. 1924, Stony Brook, qtd. in Murphy, *Family Secrets*, 225.
110. E. D. Waggett's report sent to WBY on 26 Mar. 1924, qtd. in Murphy, *Family Secrets*, 226.
111. ECY to Quinn, 24 Mar. 1924, NYPL.
112. WBY to Waggett and to Dr Robert Simpson, both 3 Apr. 1924, Stony Brook.
113. Accounts with Roseneath Nursing Home, Winchmore Hill, N21, Stony Brook; Murphy, *Family Secrets*, 224–34, 445–8.
114. Lily to GY, 9 Feb. 1924.
115. WBY to Quinn, 3 Nov. 1923, NYPL.
116. WBY to Lily, 10 June 1924; Lily Yeats, 'My Wishes', *c.* Mar. 1924, *LTWBY* ii. 449–50.
117. WBY to Lily, 18 June 1924, Boston College.
118. Lily to R L-P, 12 Dec. 1932.
119. WBY to Gregory, 17 July 1923, Berg.
120. WBY to Gregory, 26 June 1923, Berg.
121. WBY to Gregory, 19 July 1923, Berg.
122. WBY to Pound, 29 July 1923, Indiana.
123. GY to MacGreevy, 10 Aug. 1923, TCD MS 8104.
124. WBY to Gregory, 10 Sept. 1923, Berg, dated on envelope.
125. WBY to Sturge Moore, 1 Nov. and 18 Aug. 1923, Bridge (ed.), *W. B. Yeats and T. Sturge Moore*, 50 and 49.

126. Lily to R L-P, 27 Sept. 1923.
127. Hyland, *I Call to the Eye of the Mind*, 122.
128. ECY to Clement Shorter, 6 Sept. 1923, Berg.
129. WBY to Sturge Moore, 18 Aug. 1923, Bridge (ed.), *W. B. Yeats and T. Sturge Moore*, 49.
130. Lily to R L-P, 3 Sept. 1926.
131. Lily to R L-P, 28 Oct. 1926.
132. Lily to GY, 9 Feb. and 16 Mar. 1924.
133. Lily to R L-P, 27 Sept. 1923.
134. GY to WBY, 21 Aug. 1924.
135. Lily to R L-P, 17 Mar., 2 and 7 Apr., and 29 July 1925.
136. WBY to ECY, 12 May 1925, Stony Brook.
137. TCD Cuala Archives; WBY to 'my dear Sisters', 29 Oct. 1925; Vincent Kinane, 'Some Aspects of the Cuala Press', *Private Library*, 2/3 (Autumn 1989), 119-29.
138. GY to R L-P, 17 June 1925.
139. JackBY to WBY, 31 Oct. 1925, qtd. by Lewis, *Yeats Sisters and the Cuala*, 170.
140. GY to James Healy, 14 Aug. 1940, Stanford; Lily to R L-P, 13 Sept. 1927.
141. Robinson to MacGreevy, 25 July 1927, TCD MS 8103.
142. Lily to R L-P, 27 Sept. 1931.
143. WBY to Gregory, 23 Apr. 1925, NLI MS 30,593.
144. GY to WBY, *c.*24 Aug. 1925.
145. Lily to R L-P, 17 Dec. 1925.
146. Lily to R L-P, 1 Dec. 1926.
147. AY.
148. WBY to GY, [undated].
149. Erik Palmstierna to WBY, 14 Nov. 1923.
150. Robert Smyllie to Rodgers, 'W. B. Yeats', in Rodgers (ed.), *Irish Literary Portraits*, 10.
151. Lily to Quinn, 22 Nov. 1923, NYPL.
152. E. H. Karlfeldt to WBY, 15 Nov. 1923, Stony Brook; WBY to Quinn, 29 Jan. 1924, NYPL, and to Gregory, 13 Jan. 1924, Wade, 701.
153. WBY to Dulac, 25 Nov. 1923, Hobby, 159-60; V. M. Gordon 'for Mrs W.B. Yeats' to MacGreevy, 5 Dec. 1923, TCD MS 8104; GY to MacGreevy, [n.d.], TCD MS 8104.
154. Jon Stallworthy, *Between the Lines: W. B. Yeats's Poetry in the Making* (London: Oxford University Press, 1963), 96.
155. Birgit Bramsbäck, 'William Butler Yeats och Sverige', *Tvärsnitt*, 1 (1986), 8, translated for me by the author; Birgit Bramsbäck, 'William Butler Yeats and the "Bounty of Sweden"', *Moderna Språk* (1988), 97-106.
156. GY to MacGreevy, [?8 Dec.] 1923, TCD MS 8104.
157. *Dagblad*, 9 Dec. 1923; summary and translation courtesy Birgit Bramsbäck, 5 Oct. 1989.
158. Bramsbäck, 'William Butler Yeats och Sverige', 12.

159. In a letter to me of 3 June 1987 Bramsbäck described seeing them when she visited Palmerston Road in 1948.
160. Bowra, *Memories*, 234.
161. Robert McAlmon, *Being Geniuses Together 1920–1930* (rev. edn. San Francisco: North Point Press, 1984), 227.
162. Lily to R L-P, 26 Dec. 1923.
163. AY, unpublished memoirs.
164. Quinn to WBY, 23 Nov. 1923, *Letters of John Quinn to William Butler Yeats*, 291–3.
165. WBY to Quinn, 29 Jan. 1924, NYPL; WBY to Gregory, 13 Jan. 1924, Wade, 701–2.
166. WBY to Dulac, 28 Jan. 1924, Wade, 703.
167. WBY to GY, [?June] and 27 July 1924.
168. WBY to GY, 11 May 1924; 'Georgie Yeats' to MacGreevy, 15 May 1924, TCD MS 8104; GY to MacGreevy, 31 Dec. 1925, TCD MS 8104.
169. WBY to Pound, 18 May 1924, Indiana; WBY to GY, Sept. 1924.
170. WBY to Sturge Moore, 21 Oct. 1924, Bridge (ed.), *W. B. Yeats and T. Sturge Moore*, 55.
171. WBY to GY, 29 Nov. and 2 Dec. 1924.
172. Robinson to MacGreevy, *c.*18 Dec. 1924, TCD MS 8103; Gregory, 30 Dec. 1924, *Journals*, i. 615.
173. 23 Jan. 1925, Wilhelm, *Ezra Pound in London and Paris*, 344; Robinson to GY, 22 Jan. 1925.
174. Stallworthy, *Between the Lines*, 97; among the many photographs are ones in an envelope marked 'Mosaics (Sicily) G.Y. Capella Palatina'.
175. GY to MacGreevy, postcard 30 Jan. 1925, TCD MS 8104.
176. WBY to Dulac, *c.*12 Feb. 1925, Hobby, 172–3.
177. WBY to Gregory, 14 Feb. 1925, G. M. Harper.
178. GY's collection includes many full-size photographs of works in the Museo Capitolino, Museo della Terme, Palazzo Doria, the Vatican, and all the major churches and basilicas, AY.
179. MBY.
180. WBY to Gregory, 14 Feb. 1925, courtesy G. M. Harper.
181. WBY to T. Werner Laurie, 13 Mar. and 7 Sept. 1923, Emory.
182. Notebook 9, 21 Mar. 1924, *YVP* iii. 119.
183. WBY to Werner Laurie, 20 Apr. 1924, Emory.
184. GY to WBY, *c.*24 Aug. 1924.
185. WBY to Werner Laurie, 12 Aug. and 22 Sept. 1924, Emory.
186. Bachchan, *W. B. Yeats and Occultism*, 149 n. 4.
187. Hone, *W. B. Yeats*, 367–8.
188. GY to Werner Laurie, 14 Apr. 1925, Emory.
189. WBY to Dulac, 23 Apr. 1925, Hobby, 173–4; WBY to Gregory, 23 Apr. 1925, Berg; WBY to Dulac, 5 May 1925, Hobby, 174.
190. *A Vision A*, 215; to Sturm he wrote on 20 Jan. 1926, 'You will get all mixed up if you think of my symbolism as astrological or even astronomical in any literal way . . . The two movements are Lunar and Solar.' JK.

CHAPTER 14: DUBLIN

1. 'Dedication', *A Vision*, pp. x–xii; Moina Mathers (born Mina Bergson) married MacGregor Mathers in 1890; the most complete biography is given by Greer, *Women of the Golden Dawn*.
2. Moina MacGregor Mathers to WBY, 4 Feb. 1924, *LTWBY* ii. 451.
3. WBY to GY, 19 Nov. 1922; GY to WBY, 23 Nov. 1922.
4. WBY, 'A Biographical Fragment, with Some Notes', *Criterion* and *Dial* (July 1923), repr. in *Autobiographies* (1926); 'Georgie Yeats' to A. J. A. Symons, 25 Mar. 1926, HRHRC; 'D.E.D.I.', *Is the Order of R.R. & A.C. to Remain a Magical Order?* and *A Postscript to Essay Called 'Is the Order of R.R. & A.C. to Remain a Magical Order?'*, both written in 1901.
5. WBY to GY, 22 May 1923; WBY to Shakespear, 1 Jan. 1933, Wade, 804.
6. 28 May 1927, James Lovic Allen and M. M. Liberman, 'Transcriptions of Yeats's Unpublished Prose in the Bradford Papers at Grinnell College', *Serif*, 10/1 (Spring 1973), 25; WBY to GY, 9 May 1929.
7. WBY to Shakespear, 23 Oct. 1930, Wade, 777.
8. Bramsbäck, 'William Butler Yeats and the "Bounty of Sweden"', 97–106.
9. Erik Palmstierna, 'W. B. Yeats: Ett silhuettklipp', *Dagens Nyheter*, 6 Feb. 1939, qtd. by Bramsbäck, 'William Butler Yeats och Sverige', 7.
10. Palmstierna, *Horizons of Immortality* and *Widening Horizons* (London: John Lane/Bodley Head, 1940); Palmstierna, *Rifts in the Veil* (London: Andrew Dakers, 1951).
11. Palmstierna, *Horizons of Immortality*, 330–65; Macleod, *The Sisters d'Aranyi*, 186–203.
12. MBY; what remains of George's record collection is now in the possession of Gráinne Yeats.
13. Robinson to MacGreevy, 10 Feb. 1926, TCD MS 8103.
14. Gregory, 13 Feb. 1926, *Journals*, ii. 64.
15. GY to MacGreevy, c.15 Mar. 1926, TCD MS 8104.
16. GY to MacGreevy, 31 Dec. 1926, TCD MS 8104.
17. WBY to Shakespear, 26 May 1924, Wade, 705.
18. Manning to William Rothenstein in 1926, qtd. in Kaiser Haq, 'Forgotten Fred: A Portrait of Frederic Manning', *London Magazine* (Dec. 1983/Jan. 1984), 75.
19. GY to MacGreevy, 13 Apr. 1926, TCD MS 8104.
20. Lily to R L-P, 1 Dec. 1926; Yano to WBY, 15 Aug. 1927, *LTWBY* ii. 477–8; Kazumi Yano, 'At Thoor Ballylee 45 Years Ago', *Yeats Society of Japan Annual Report*, 7 (1972), 26; Robinson to WBY, 19 Jan. 1928.
21. Elborn, *Francis Stuart*, 77.
22. WBY to Shakespear, 7 Sept. 1927, Stony Brook, passage omitted in Wade, 728.
23. Elborn, *Francis Stuart*, 63; Donovan, 'Remembering Yeats', 60.
24. GY to MacGreevy, 1 July 1926, TCD MS 8104.
25. Qtd. by Elborn, *Francis Stuart*, 67.
26. Gregory, 14 July 1924, *Journals*, i. 563.

27. £400 per annum payable quarterly was agreed upon 14 July 1926, GY to MacGreevy, 1 July 1926, TCD MS 8104; Robinson, *Curtain Up*, 135–6; Gregory, 20–3 Oct. 1924, *Journals*, i. 591–3.

28. *October Blast* (Dundrum: Cuala, 1927).

29. Gregory to WBY, 26 Feb. 1922, Stony Brook.

30. Gregory to WBY, 1, 28, 31 Mar. 1924; WBY to Gregory, 28 Jan. 1924 ff., Stony Brook.

31. Gregory, 1 to 14 June 1923, *Journals*, i. 460–7.

32. Gregory to WBY, 28 Feb. 1927, Stony Brook; 'Lady G. was ill all night and I am divided between running errands and sleep-fighting,' GY to MacGreevy, 11 Feb. 1927, TCD MS 8104.

33. GY to Pound, 20 Feb. [1927], Yale; Saddlemyer (ed.), 'George, Ezra, Dorothy and Friends', 9–10.

34. Gregory, 10 Mar. 1924, *Journals*, i. 514–15.

35. Gibbon, *Masterpiece and the Man*, 53–4.

36. Gregory, 23 Sept. 1925, *Journals*, ii. 44–5; Joseph Holloway, 14 Aug. 1924, *Joseph Holloway's Abbey Theatre*, ed. Robert Hogan and Michael J. O'Neill (Carbondale: Southern Illinois University Press, 1967), 235; 'Tomorrow Im taking WB and George to "The Gold Rush",' Robinson to MacGreevy, [21 Jan 1926], TCD MS 8103.

37. Gregory, 2 Apr. 1926, *Journals*, ii. 87.

38. GY to MacGreevy, 27 Feb. 1927, TCD MS 8104.

39. Lily to R L-P, 22 May 1928.

40. WBY to Shakespear, 21 June 1924, Wade, 706.

41. AY in Saddlemyer and Smythe (eds.), *Lady Gregory: Fifty Years After*, 20; the shop may have been the Grafton-Street Bazaar, run by C. and F. Leechman.

42. WBY to Shakespear, 27 Apr. 1925, Wade, 708.

43. WBY to Gregory, 29 Mar. 1923, Berg; Gregory to WBY, 2 Apr. 1923, Stony Brook.

44. Gregory to WBY, 13 Mar. 1922, Stony Brook.

45. Lady Dunsany's diary, 23 Apr. 1924, qtd. in Amory, *Biography of Lord Dunsany*, 196–7.

46. WBY to Gregory, 3 Feb. 1926, Berg; *Journals*, ii. 61.

47. Gregory, 10 Jan. 1926, *Journals*, ii. 59.

48. GY to MacGreevy, 31 Dec. 1925, TCD MS 8104.

49. WBY's notebook of their weekly conversations, NLI MS 13,576; M. Kelly Lynch, 'The Smiling Public Man: Joseph O'Neill and his Works', *Journal of Irish Literature*, 12, 3–72.

50. GY to MacGreevy, 24 Apr. 1926, TCD MS 8104.

51. Letter to me from Patricia Boylan, 10 Aug. 1988 and interview 15 June 1989; see also Patricia Boylan, *All Cultivated People: A History of the United Arts Club, Dublin* (Gerrards Cross: Colin Smythe, 1988).

52. GY to WBY, 4 Feb. 1923.

53. WBY to Ottoline Morrell, 7 Dec. 1925, HRHRC.

54. From the hymn 'There is a green hill far away' by Cecil Frances Alexander.

55. Robinson to GY, [?11 May 1925].
56. GY to MacGreevy, [30 Nov. 1922], TCD MS 8104.
57. GY to WBY, 23 Nov. 1922.
58. WBY to GY, 28 Jan. 1932.
59. GY to MacGreevy, [?1923], TCD MS 8104.
60. Dolly Travers Smith to MacGreevy, 27 Oct. 1923, TCD MS 8103.
61. Robinson, *Curtain Up*, 78–81.
62. Edmund Bentley, *Far Horizon: A Biography of Hester Dowden Medium and Psychic Investigator* (London: Rider & Co., 1951).
63. Robinson to GY, 22 Jan. and 6 Feb. 1925.
64. Robinson to GY, 27 or 28 May 1927.
65. GY to Robinson, 29 Nov. 1927, HM 51873, Huntington.
66. WBY to Robinson, 13 Sept. 1918, Sotheby's sale catalogue no. 579, 21–2 July 1983.
67. Gary Phillips, review of Brenna Katz Clarke and Harold Ferrar, *The Dublin Drama League 1919–1941*, *Eire-Ireland*, 16 (Winter 1981), 133–4; Phillips, 'Lennox Robinson on the Dublin Drama League: A Letter to Gabriel Fallon', *IcarbS*, 4/2 (Spring 1980), 75–82.
68. Their first production was Kaiser's *From Morn to Midnight*, directed by Denis Johnston, 13 Nov. 1927, Phillips, 'The Dublin Drama League: 1918–1942', 123–7.
69. GY to MacGreevy, 19 May 1927, TCD MS 8104; she must have seen Coward in *The Constant Nymph* in Oct. 1926 at the New Theatre, London.
70. Phillips, 'Lennox Robinson on the Dublin Drama League', 78.
71. *Iphegenia in Tauris* (11 July 1925) and *The Cyclops* (31 July 1926), both by Euripides.
72. Dulac's costumes, masks, and music were utilized for *At the Hawk's Well*; Norah McGuinness designed masks and costumes for the 1926 productions and danced 'The Woman of the Sidhe'. Casts are reproduced in Brenna Katz Clarke and Harold Ferrar, *The Dublin Drama League 1919–1941* (Dublin: Dolmen, 1979).
73. Qtd. by Phillips, review, *Eire-Ireland*, 134.
74. GY to Robinson, [?Mar.] 1924, Huntington.
75. 'I like Flecker's Don Juan but we couldnt produce it unless you played Don Juan— no dont snort—you *could* but I doubt if you *will*,' GY to Robinson, [?1 Apr.] 1926, HM 51868, Huntington.
76. GY to Oliver Edwards, 2 Feb. 1941, NLI MS 27,032.
77. Phillips, 'The Dublin Drama League: 1918–1942', 176; Eugene O'Neill to GY, 6 Jan. 1926.
78. ECY to MacGreevy, 21 Jan. 1927, TCD MS 8106.
79. GY to MacGreevy, 29 Jan. 1927, TCD MS 8104.
80. Qtd. in Joseph Ronsley, 'Initial Response to Denis Johnston's *The Moon in the Yellow River*', in Furomoto et al. (eds.), *International Aspects of Irish Literature*, 236. In a letter to me Ronsley suggests that Johnston's original entry, dated Oct., was written first, then elaborated on some years later and dated July—an unlikely date since Robinson was in the United States until mid-Aug.
81. Robinson to MacGreevy, 26 Mar. 1931, TCD MS 8103.

82. Denis Johnston to Michael J. O'Neill, qtd. in M. J. O'Neill, *Lennox Robinson* (New York: Twayne, 1964), 113–14.
83. GY to O'Casey, 3 May 1926, NLI MS 27,027; O'Casey to Gabriel Fallon, 3 and 11 Sept. 1928, *Letters of Sean O'Casey*, i: *1910–1941*, ed. David Krause (London: Macmillan, 1975), 310–11.
84. Gregory, 26 Sept. 1924, *Journals*, i. 586.
85. Gregory, 18 Nov. 1924, *Journals*, i. 604–5.
86. Gregory, 5 Dec. 1924, qtd. in Phillips, 'The Dublin Drama League: 1918–1942', 85.
87. GY to MacGreevy, *c.*15 Mar. 1926, TCD MS 8104.
88. GY to MacGreevy, 24 Apr. 1926, TCD MS 8104.
89. GY to MacGreevy, 19 Sept. 1926, TCD MS 8104; Robinson to MacGreevy, 27 Aug. 1926, TCD MS 8103; *Letters of Sean O'Casey*, i. 204 n.
90. Robinson to GY, 'Wednesday' [?Aug. 1925]; title unknown.
91. Christopher Murray, introduction to *Selected Plays of Lennox Robinson* (Gerrards Cross: Colin Smythe, 1982), 17.
92. Robinson, *Curtain Up*, 98. Seventy families left County Clare alone between 1919 and the early 1930s, Terence Brown, *Ireland: A Social and Cultural History 1922–1985* (London: Fontana, 1985), 116, cited in Christopher Murray, 'Lennox Robinson, *The Big House, Killycreggs in Twilight* and "the Vestigia of Generations"', in Otto Rauchbauer (ed.), *Ancestral Voices: The Big House in Anglo-Irish Literature* (Hildesheim: Georg Olms Verlag, 1992), 109–19.
93. GY to Robinson, 'Wednesday' [19 May or mid-June 1926], HM 51866, Huntington.
94. 11 June 1925, *The Senate Speeches of W. B. Yeats*, 99.
95. *The Big House, Selected Plays of Lennox Robinson*, 169.
96. GY to MacGreevy, 19 Sept. 1926, TCD MS 8104.
97. MacGreevy to GY, 3 July 1926.
98. GY to MacGreevy, 26 July 1926, TCD MS 8104.
99. GY to Oliver Edwards, 20 Apr. 1944, NLI MS 27,032.
100. GY to MacGreevy, 31 Dec. 1925, TCD MS 8104.
101. Lily to R L-P, 5 June 1928.
102. Robinson to MacGreevy, 10 Feb. 1926, TCD MS 8103; Lily to R L-P, 18 Feb. 1926.
103. WBY to Shakespear, 22 Apr. 1926, Wade, 713–14; Bradford, 'George Yeats: Poet's Wife', 399. This particular memento has since disappeared.
104. GY to MacGreevy, 8 Dec. 1926, TCD MS 8104; this play may have been Brinsley Macnamara's *The Master*, finally produced by the Abbey on 6 Mar. 1928.
105. GY to Robinson, 'Thursday' [?8 Apr. 1926], Huntington.
106. GY to MacGreevy, 1 July 1926, TCD MS 8104.
107. Seán O'Faoláin, *She Had to do Something*, 27 Dec. 1937.
108. WBY to GY, 23 May 1927; GY owned a copy of *Max Reinhardt and his Theatre*, ed. Oliver M. Sayler (New York: Brentano's, 1924).
109. Robinson to MacGreevy, 28 June and 24 Oct. 1925, TCD MSS 8103/98 and /104; both performances were directed by Robinson.
110. GY to MacGreevy, [*c.*15 Mar.] 1926, TCD MS 8104; Will Shields's stage name was Barry Fitzgerald.

111. Robinson to GY, 22 Mar. 1926.

112. Bence-Jones, *Twilight of the Ascendancy*, 144.

113. Robinson, *Curtain Up*, 137.

114. Robinson to MacGreevy, 'Thursday' [early Sept. 1925], TCD MS 8103.

115. GY to Robinson, 'Maundy Thursday' [?1 Apr. 1926], HM 51868, Huntington.

116. In her annotated 1933 edition of *Collected Poems* GY wrote 'Anne Yeats & Fergus Fitzgerald' next to the poem, Wayne Chapman, 'George Yeats, *The Countess Cathleen* and O'Hegarty', *YA* 9, ed. Deirdre Toomey (1992), 277; WBY's Mar. 1926 diary entry, where the boy is referred to as 'Norman', also borrows GY's comment 'I should put this into verse for it is the cry of every woman who loves a blacguard,' NLI MS 13,576, qtd. in *The Winding Stair (1929): Manuscript Materials by W. B. Yeats*, ed. David R. Clark (Ithaca, NY: Cornell University Press, 1995), 103.

117. GY to Robinson, 'Thursday' [8 Apr. 1926], Huntington.

118. Robinson to GY, [?10 June 1926].

119. I am indebted to Susan Schreibman for assistance with MacGreevy's biography.

120. MacGreevy, unpublished memoirs, qtd. in introduction to Susan Schreibman, 'Weeping over a Lost Poetry: An Annotated Edition of Collected Poems of Thomas MacGreevy', MA thesis (University College Dublin, 1985), p. xvii; I am grateful to Susan Schreibman and J. C. C. Mays for making this available to me.

121. WBY to Harriet Monroe, 30 Dec. 1928, qtd. in *Collected Poems of Thomas MacGreevy*, ed. Susan Schreibman (Dublin: Anna Livia Press, 1991), p. xxxiii.

122. GY to MacGreevy, [?Sept 1923], [30 Nov. 1922, misdated c.1923], and 26 Sept. 1923, TCD MS 8104.

123. GY to MacGreevy, [n.d.], TCD MS 8104.

124. GY to MacGreevy, [?early Dec. 1923], TCD MS 8104.

125. GY to MacGreevy, 26 Mar. 1926, TCD MS 8104.

126. GY to MacGreevy, 26 July 1926, TCD MS 8104.

127. GY to MacGreevy, 8 Dec. 1926, TCD MS 8104.

128. GY to MacGreevy, 8 June 1928, TCD MS 8104.

129. GY to MacGreevy, fragment [?Sept. or Oct. 1923], TCD MS 8104.

130. GY to MacGreevy, c.15 Mar. 1926, TCD MS 8104.

131. GY to MacGreevy, 28 June 1925, TCD MS 8104.

132. Taken by Tomás Ó hÉidhin (1872/3–1943), son of Bartley and Mary Hynes, who at the same time seems to have photographed the interior of Ballylee.

133. AY to 'Mr McGreevy', [?Aug. 1924], TCD MS 8104.

134. GY to MacGreevy, [29 Oct. 1925] and 10 July 1926, TCD MS 8104.

135. GY to MacGreevy, 9 Mar. 1926, TCD MS 8104.

136. GY to MacGreevy, c.15 Mar. 1926, TCD MS 8104; Robinson to MacGreevy, 'Wed.night' [17 Mar. 1926], TCD MS 8103.

137. MacGreevy to GY, 19 Oct. 1926, NLI MS 30,859; Robinson to MacGreevy, 28 Oct. 1926, TCD MS 8103.

138. GY to MacGreevy, 24 Apr. 1926, TCD MS 8104.

139. MacGreevy to GY, 30 Dec. 1925, NLI MS 30,859; GY to MacGreevy, 31 Dec. 1925, TCD MS 8104.

140. Goldring, *Odd Man Out*, 182; MacGreevy to GY, 30 Dec. 1926, NLI MS 30,859.

141. GY to MacGreevy, 31 Dec. 1926, TCD MS 8104.

142. Ellmann interview notes with Frank O'Connor, 13 Oct. 1946, Tulsa; MBY and AY.

143. GY to MacGreevy, 27 Feb. 1927, TCD MS 8104.

144. Robinson to MacGreevy, 24 May 1927, TCD MS 8103.

145. Hugh Kingsmill, 'Meetings with Yeats', *New Statesman and Nation*, 4 Jan. 1941, 10–11.

146. MacGreevy to GY, 22 Sept. 1962, NLI MS 30,859; Hone, *W. B. Yeats*, 371.

147. GY to MacGreevy, 31 Dec. 1926, TCD MS 8104.

148. Qtd. by John Harwood in a letter to me, 5 Nov. 1985.

149. GY to MacGreevy, 29 Oct. 1925, TCD MS 8104.

150. *YVP* ii. 429–30; WBY to Shakespear, 24 Sept. 1926, Wade, 717–18.

151. WBY to Shakespear, 27 Oct. [1926], misdated 1927 in Wade, 730–2.

152. GY to MacGreevy, 31 Dec. 1925, TCD MS 8104.

153. Shakespear to WBY, 21 June 1925, 'Olivia Shakespear: Letters to W. B. Yeats', ed. John Harwood, *YA* 6 (1988), 63–4.

154. MacGreevy to GY, 30 Dec. 1926 and 24 Feb. 1926, NLI MS 30,859.

155. GY to MacGreevy, 19 Sept. 1926, TCD MS 8104.

156. Ibid.

157. Nelly to MacGreevy, 1 Nov. 1926, TCD MS 8129.

158. Nelly to MacGreevy, 30 Oct. 1926, TCD MS 8129.

159. GY to MacGreevy, 8 Dec. 1926, TCD MS 8104; Nelly to MacGreevy, [? 21 Nov. 1926], TCD MS 8129.

160. Nelly to MacGreevy, 5 Feb. 1929, TCD MS 8129.

161. Nelly to MacGreevy, 24 May 1934, TCD MS 8129.

162. Nelly to MacGreevy, [?early Dec. 1926], TCD MS 8129.

163. Nelly to MacGreevy, 8 June 1931, TCD MS 8129.

164. Nelly to MacGreevy,13 Jan. 1928, TCD MS 8129.

165. Nelly to MacGreevy, 11 Mar. 1928, TCD MS 8129.

166. GY to MacGreevy, 28 Dec. 1926, TCD MS 8104.

167. MacGreevy to GY, 30 Dec. 1926, NLI MS 30,859; GY to MacGreevy, 31 Dec. 1926, TCD MS 8104.

168. Nelly to MacGreevy, 12 July 1928, TCD MS 8129.

169. Cummins, *Unseen Adventures*, 33–4, 100; WBY to Shakespear, 9 July 1928, Wade, 744.

170. WBY to GY, 28 Apr. 1925.

171. GY to MacGreevy, 1 July 1926, TCD MS 8104.

172. MacGreevy to GY, 3 July 1926, NLI MS 30,859; GY to MacGreevy, 10 July 1926, TCD MS 8104.

173. GY to MacGreevy, 28 Sept. 1926, TCD MS 8104.

174. GY to MacGreevy, 9 Nov. 1926, TCD MS 8104.

175. GY to MacGreevy, 31 Dec. 1926, TCD MS 8104; MacGreevy to GY, 11 Jan. 1927, NLI MS 30,859.

176. GY to MacGreevy, 29 Jan. 1927, TCD MS 8104.

177. Dolly Travers Smith to MacGreevy, 17 Jan. 1927, TCD MS 8103.
178. WBY to Dolly Travers Smith, 11 Nov. 1929, TCD MS 10,662.
179. Location unknown, but probably an upper flat in North Frederick Street, near the Clarke glassworks; I am grateful to Nicola Gordon Bowe for advice.
180. Robinson to GY, 19 Oct. 1928 and 30 Apr. 1930.
181. GY to MacGreevy, 8 Sept. 1927, TCD MS 8104.
182. WBY to Shakespear, 2 Oct. 1927, Stony Brook; passage omitted from Wade, 729.
183. MacGreevy to GY, 9 Dec. 1927, NLI MS 30,859.
184. Robinson to Dolly Travers Smith, 16 July 1929, TCD MS 9686.
185. Hester Dowden to MacGreevy, 12 Aug. 1931, TCD MS 8136; Robinson to MacGreevy, 'Wednesday' [22 July 1931], TCD MS 8103.
186. GY to Dolly Travers Smith, 22 July 1931, Sotheby's sale catalogue no. 584 21-2 July 1983, courtesy Colin Smythe.
187. WBY to Robinson, 23 July 1931, JK.
188. WBY to GY, 16 Nov. 1926.
189. AY to William Murphy, 19 May 1988, WMM.
190. WBY to GY, 30 Nov. and 2 Dec. 1922; GY to WBY, 1 Dec. 1922; WBY to GY, 25 May 1923.
191. WBY to GY, 29 Mar. 1925.
192. GY to MacGreevy, 24 Apr. 1926, TCD MS 8104; WBY to Shakespear, 23 June 1927, Wade, 725.
193. Lily to R L-P, 26 Apr. 1927.
194. GY to MacGreevy, 10 July 1926, TCD MS 8104.
195. GY to MacGreevy, 24 Apr. and 8 Dec. 1926, TCD MS 8104.
196. WBY to GY, 3 Nov. 1925, TCD MS 8103.
197. Robinson to MacGreevy, 25 July 1927, TCD MS 8103.
198. GY to MacGreevy, 31 Dec. 1925, TCD MS 8104; probate was granted 5 Feb. 1926.
199. GY to MacGreevy, 15 Mar. 1926, TCD MS 8104.
200. Nelly to MacGreevy, 8 Aug. 1927, TCD MS 8129; Nelly says here that her mother died on 23 July 1927, two days later than stated in the published obituary.
201. George Woodmass married Flora Sharpe in 1928; later he settled on the Channel Islands leaving his wife in Victoria, British Columbia. I am grateful to Mary Petersen and Pam Duncan for finding Flora's grave site.
202. GY to Pound, 8 Sept. 1927, Yale; Saddlemyer (ed.), 'George, Ezra, Dorothy and Friends', 10. 'Sailing to Byzantium' and 'Blood and the Moon' were both published in the third issue of the *Exile* (Spring 1928).
203. Gregory, *Journals*, ii. 194, 205, 265.
204. *Signe Toksvig's Irish Diaries 1926–1937*, ed. Lis Pihl (Dublin: Lilliput Press, 1994), 109; Gregory, *Journals*, i. 77–8. Other novels by Lucy Phillimore were *By an Unknown Disciple* (1918) and *Paul: The Christian* (1930).
205. GY to MacGreevy, 8 Dec. 1926, TCD MS 8104. Wm. Magennis, TD, a Professor of Metaphysics at the National University, in 1925 founded the short-lived Clann Eireann ('The Irish People's Party') after breaking with Cumann na nGaedheal over the Boundary Commission report.

206. WBY to Shakespear, [?July 1927], Wade, 727.

207. WBY to Shakespear, 7 Sept. 1927, Stony Brook.

208. WBY to Maud Gonne, 7 Oct. 1927, White and Jeffares (eds.), *Gonne–Yeats Letters*, 439.

209. See ibid. 432–3 for the entire exchange.

210. Gregory, 12 Oct. 1927, *Journals*, ii. 207.

211. GY to MacGreevy, 15 Mar. 1928, TCD MS 8104.

212. Gregory, 27 to 31 Oct. 1927, *Journals*, ii. 209–10; copy of marriage certificate issued 26 Oct. 1927; Lily to R L-P, 31 Oct. 1927.

213. GY to Sean O'Casey, [? late Oct. 1927], Berg.

PART IV: TRANSITS

1. 14 Jan. 1918, *YVP* i. 252.

2. 'Definitions', Vision Notebook 1, 82, *YVP* iii. 174.

3. WBY to Gregory, [*c*.8 Feb. 1921], Berg.

4. GY to MacGreevy, [*c*.15 Mar. 1926], TCD MS 8104.

5. GY to MacGreevy, 15 Mar. 1928, TCD MS 8104.

6. GY to Robinson, 9 Jan. 1930 [misdated 1929], HM 51886, Huntington.

CHAPTER 15: RAPALLO

7. I am grateful to T. Finlayson, Gibraltar archivist, for making the relevant issues of the *Gibraltar Chronicle* available to me in Dec. 1994.

8. GY to Thomas Bodkin, [early Nov. 1927], TCD MS 7001.

9. Robinson to GY, 17 Nov. 1927.

10. Robinson to MacGreevy, 23 Nov. 1922, TCD MS 8103.

11. *Cook's Excursionist and Tourist Advertiser*, 11 May 1901, 10.

12. I am grateful to Hilary Thomas and Mrs Lees of Stafford for helping track down the original film, which is now with the British Film Institute.

13. I am indebted to Patrick and Elaine Hall for hospitality and information about Jean and John Hall and handing over to me the rights to the Algeciras film.

14. WBY to Gregory, 13 Nov. 1927, qtd. by Gregory, 21 Nov. 1927, *Journals*, ii. 217; WBY to Maud Gonne, [*c*.10 Nov. 1927], White and Jeffares (eds.), *Gonne–Yeats Letters*, 443.

15. GY to Robinson, *c*.15 and 19 Nov. 1927, Huntington. According to the *Gibraltar Chronicle* the foreign exchange rate in Nov. 1927 was 28.67 pesetas to the pound.

16. Robinson, *The Round Table* (1922); Robinson to GY, 25 Nov. 1927.

17. GY to Robinson, 27 and 29 Nov. 1929, HM 51873, Huntington.

18. GY to Gogarty, 12 Dec. 1927, Bucknell.

19. Robinson to GY, 6 and 9 Dec. 1927.

20. Robinson to Dolly Travers Smith, 13 Dec. 1927, TCD MS 9686; WBY to Heald, 21 Feb. 1938, Wade, 905.

21. Robinson to GY, 14 Dec. 1927.

22. WBY to Shakespear, 29 Nov. 1927, Wade, 732–3; GY to Robinson, 29 Nov. 1927, HM 51873, Huntington.

23. Gregory, 26 Nov. 1927, *Journals*, ii. 219–20.
24. GY to Robinson, 19 Dec. 1927, Huntington; AY; Lily to R L-P, 24 Jan. 1928.
25. GY to Robinson, 19 Dec. 1927, Huntington; WBY to Shakespear, 12 Dec. 1927, misdated 21 Dec. by Wade, 733.
26. GY to MacGreevy, 26 Dec. 1927, TCD MS 8104.
27. WBY to Gregory, 18 Jan. 1928, Stony Brook.
28. Gregory to WBY, 1 Feb. 1928, Stony Brook.
29. Robinson to Gregory, 13 Jan. 1928, Berg.
30. Robinson to GY, 31 Jan. 1928; Robinson to Dolly Travers Smith, 16 Jan. 1928, TCD MS 9686.
31. GY to Robinson, 'Thursday' [?8 Apr 1926], Huntington.
32. GY to Robinson, 17 Jan. 1928, HM 51875, Huntington.
33. GY to MacGreevy, 19 Jan. 1928, TCD MS 8104.
34. WBY to Shakespear, 12 Jan. 1928, Wade, 735–6.
35. WBY to Gregory, 7 and 10 Feb. 1928, Berg.
36. WBY to Gregory, 18 Jan. 1928, Stony Brook, and 10 Feb. 1928, Berg.
37. Ezra and Dorothy Pound to GY, 20 Jan. 1928, Saddlemyer (ed.), 'George, Ezra, Dorothy and Friends', 11–12.
38. GY to WBY, 'Thursday' [29 Oct. 1931], '"Yours Affly, Dobbs": George Yeats to her Husband, Winter 1931–32', ed. Ann Saddlemyer, in Susan Dick, Declan Kiberd, Dougald McMillan, and Joseph Ronsley (eds.), *Omnium Gatherum: Essays for Richard Ellmann* (Gerrards Cross: Colin Smythe, 1989), 286; the notes have now been superseded by this book.
39. GY to Dorothy Pound, 2 Feb. 1928, Yale; Saddlemyer (ed.), 'George, Ezra, Dorothy and Friends', 13.
40. GY to MacGreevy, 15 Mar. 1928, TCD MS 8104.
41. WBY to Shakespear, 23 Feb. 1928, Wade, 736–7.
42. I am grateful to Toni O'Brien Johnson and John Martin for assistance in describing the setting.
43. WBY to GY, 27 Feb. 1928; WBY to Lily, 28 Feb. 1928.
44. Gregory to WBY, 18 Mar. 1928, Stony Brook.
45. Pound to Louis Zukofsky, 5 Mar. 1928, Barry Ahearn (ed.), *Pound/Zukofsky: Selected Letters of Ezra Pound and Louis Zukofsky* (New York: New Directions, 1987), 8.
46. GY to MacGreevy, 15 Mar. 1928, TCD MS 8104.
47. WBY to Gregory, 30 Dec. 1920, Berg.
48. GY to MacGreevy, 15 Mar. 1928, TCD MS 8104.
49. Gregory, Nov. 1928, *Journals*, ii. 337.
50. Gregory, 26 Feb. 1928, *Journals*, ii. 235. The reference is to Keats's 'Ode on a Grecian Urn'.
51. Gregory, Nov. 1928, *Journals*, ii. 337; WBY to Shakespear, 23 Nov. 1928, Wade, 748; also Desmond Chute in Mikhail (ed.), *Interviews and Recollections*, i. 140.
52. Copy of lease; WBY to Sturm, 9 Oct. 1929, Stony Brook. I am grateful to Matilde Frisenda for allowing me to explore the flat in Rapallo.

53. Gregory, 26 Feb. 1928, *Journals*, ii. 235.

54. Gregory, 19 Mar. 1928, *Journals*, ii. 243–4.

55. GY to Cottie Yeats, 1 Mar. 1928; I am indebted to Bruce Arnold for alerting me to this letter among the Jack Yeats papers in AY's possession.

56. WBY to GY, 25 Feb. 1928.

57. Nelly to MacGreevy, 1 Mar. 1928, TCD MS 8129.

58. AY to WMM and me.

59. AY and Sister Brigit Younghughes.

60. Lily to R L-P, 21 Feb. 1928.

61. WBY to Gregory, 21 Aug. 1929, JK.

62. GY to MacGreevy, 3 Apr. 1928, TCD MS 8104.

63. MacGreevy to GY, 16 Mar. 1928, NLI MS 30,859; Nelly to MacGreevy, 22 Mar. 1928, TCD MS 8129.

64. Gregory, 26 Feb. 1928, *Journals*, ii. 235.

65. Robinson to GY, 21 Feb. 1928; Robinson to WBY, 19 Jan. 1928.

66. GY to MacGreevy, 15 Mar. 1928, TCD MS 8104.

67. Lily to R L-P, 17 and 24 Apr. 1928.

68. GY to MacGreevy, 15 Mar. 1928, TCD MS 8104.

69. GY to MacGreevy, 14 May 1928, TCD MS 8104.

70. The characters of *The Cherry Orchard* mourn the sale of their property; the black American singers Turner Layton and Clarence 'Tandy' Johnstone were popular in England during the 1920s.

71. WBY to Sturm, 9 Oct. 1929, Stony Brook.

72. GY to MacGreevy, 8 June 1928, TCD MS 8104.

73. Saros Cowasjee, *Sean O'Casey: The Man behind the Plays* (London: Oliver & Boyd, 1963), 112.

74. Lily to R L-P, 28 May 1928.

75. Gregory, 17 June 1928, *Journals*, ii. 278.

76. WBY to Gregory, 24 Feb. 1928; Gregory, 7 Apr. 1928, *Journals*, ii. 248; GY to MacGreevy, 15 Mar. and 14 May 1928, TCD MS 8104.

77. Brooklawn, owned by Mrs Sanderson, Dun-Griffan Road, Howth.

78. WBY to Gregory, 6 Aug. 1928, Berg.

79. WBY to Gregory, 30 July and 6 Aug. 1928, Berg.

80. Bethel Solomons, qtd. in Jon Stallworthy, *Singing School: The Making of a Poet* (London: John Murray, 1998), 217.

81. Gregory, 10 Sept. 1928, *Journals*, ii. 317.

82. Kilmacurragh is described in *Signe Toksvig's Irish Diaries*, 103, 116.

83. WBY to Shakespear, [*c*.12 Sept. 1928], Wade, 746–7.

84. ECY to MacGreevy, 21 Aug. 1928, TCD MS 8106.

85. AY; AY inherited the silver tea set and special trays.

86. WBY to Pound, 23 Sept. 1928, Yale.

87. GY to Curtis Bradford, qtd. in 'George Yeats: Poet's Wife', 399.

88. Lily to R L-P, 3 Oct. 1928.

89. Gregory to WBY, 8 Aug. 1928, Stony Brook.

90. Lily to R L-P, 3 Oct. 1928.

91. WBY to Werner Laurie, 16 Jan. 1926, Emory.

92. Seán O'Faoláin, 'Mr Yeats's Metaphysical Man', *London Mercury*, 37/217 (Nov. 1937), 69–70.

93. WBY to Shakespear, 4 Mar. 1926, Wade 711–12.

94. Shakespear to WBY, 14 Feb. 1926, 'Olivia Shakespear: Letters to W. B. Yeats', 68.

95. WBY describes the incident in his introduction to *A Vision B*; GY also discussed it with Virginia Moore (*The Unicorn*, 332).

96. 'Sleep of Mar. 9th 1928', TS with MS addition 2 Apr. 1928; 'Rapallo Notebook 1928–1930', Stony Brook.

97. Gregory, *c*.30 May 1929, *Journals*, ii. 442.

98. WBY to Shakespear, 23 Oct. 1930, Wade, 777.

99. GY to Henn, T. R. Henn, *The Lonely Tower: Studies in the Poetry of W. B. Yeats* (rev. edn. London: Methuen, 1965), 193 n. 1.

100. Ellmann interview notes with GY, 26 Dec. 1946 and 17 Jan. 1947, Tulsa.

101. WBY to Werner Laurie, 22 Sept. 1924, Emory.

102. 'Fragments II' (1933).

103. Ellmann interview notes with GY, 17 Jan. 1947, Tulsa.

104. BL Add. MSS 55,003/161.

105. An excellent description of this phenomenon can be found in Owen, *The Darkened Room*.

106. *A Vision B*, 20.

107. WBY to Kazumi Yano, 23 June 1927, JK; WBY to Sturge Moore, 2 June 1927, Bridge (ed.), *W. B. Yeats and T. Sturge Moore*, 111.

108. GY to Gregory, 15 Oct. 1928, Berg; Gregory, *Journals*, ii. 327.

109. GY to Gogarty, 6 Jan. 1931, Bucknell; Gogarty to WBY, 17 June 1930, *LTWBY* ii. 512.

110. GY to Robinson, 29 June 1930, Huntington.

111. AY; photographs of AY and Charles Lane-Poole, 20 July 1934.

112. WBY to Lily, 28 Feb. and 9 or 19 Mar. 1928.

113. WBY to Gregory, 30 July 1928, Berg.

114. Lily to R L-P, 17 and 2 Apr. 1928.

115. Lily to R L-P, 10 Apr. and 28 Feb. 1928.

116. ECY to Quinn, 17 Sept. 1923, NYPL.

117. Lily to R L-P, 5 Aug. 1925.

118. ECY to Monk Gibbon, 17 June 1926, Queen's.

119. Lily to R L-P, 5 July 1927.

120. AY's opening speech at the Yeats Flower Show, Drumcliffe Church, 27 June 1991.

121. Robinson to MacGreevy, 'Wednesday', TCD MS 8103.

122. AY to WMM, May 1988.

123. AY.

124. Lily to R L-P, 28 Feb. 1928.

125. WBY to Lily, 2 Sept. 1929.

126. WBY to Sturge Moore, 26 June 1924, Bridge (ed.), *W. B. Yeats and T. Sturge Moore*, 53; WBY to Shakespear, 25 Apr. 1928, Wade, 743.

127. AY and MBY.
128. The principal of St Margaret's, 50 Mespil Road, was Miss Edith Badham, LLD; Nightingale Hall was listed officially as the High School, 47–51 Wellington Place, run by the Misses Florence and Edith Wilson.
129. Robinson to MacGreevy, 'Friday' [8 Jan. 1926], TCD MS 8103.
130. AY.
131. AG to WBY, 17 Apr. 1929, Stony Brook.
132. MBY, *Cast a Cold Eye*, 8; AY and MBY.
133. Lily to R L-P, 27 Jan. 1929.
134. Vinod Sena, 'Interview "Images and Memories": Anne Yeats in Conversation', *Yearly Review*, 3 (Dec. 1989), Dept of English, University of Delhi, ed. Vinod Sena and G. K. Das, 87–8. I am grateful to Dennis Duffy for providing me with a copy.
135. WBY to Gregory, 24 Mar. 1929, Berg.
136. Lily to R L-P, 7 May 1929.
137. WBY to Maud Gonne, 6 Sept. 1928, White and Jeffares (eds.), *Gonne–Yeats Letters*, 447.
138. WBY to Pound, 26 Aug. 1928, Yale.
139. GY to MacGreevy, 'Thursday' [early Oct. 1928], TCD MS 8104.
140. GY to J. O'Connell, 11 Oct. 1928, Emory.
141. Bradford, 'George Yeats: Poet's Wife', 397.
142. John Stewart Collis memorandum, Hone papers, NLI MS 5,919.
143. GY to McCartan, 22 June 1937, John Unterecker, *Yeats and Patrick McCartan: A Fenian Friendship* (Dublin: Dolmen 1965), 403.
144. Gregory, *Journals*, ii. 351–2.
145. Ibid. 248.
146. Ellmann interview notes with GY, 17 Jan. 1947, Tulsa.
147. Robinson to GY, 6 Nov. 1928.
148. GY to MacGreevy, 21 Nov. 1928, TCD MS 8104.
149. WBY to Lily, 27 Nov. 1928, Boston College; Gregory, *Journals*, ii. 351.
150. MacGreevy to GY, 13 Jan. 1929, NLI MS 30,859; Nelly to MacGreevy, 5 Feb. 1929, TCD MS 8129.
151. GY to MacGreevy, 11 Feb. 1929, TCD MS 8104.
152. WBY to Gregory, 7 Feb. 1929, Berg.
153. Gregory to WBY, 11 Feb. 1929, Stony Brook; GY to Lily, 27 Feb. 1929.
154. GY to MacGreevy, 11 Feb. 1929, TCD MS 8104; GY later drew up a list of the 'Sequence of poems written at Rapallo Feb. & Mar. 1929' and dated their composition, NLI MS 30,891.
155. Murphy, *Family Secrets*, 240.
156. GY to Lily, 27 Feb. 1929.
157. Gregory, 14 Feb. 1929, *Journals*, ii. 393.
158. Robinson to GY, 8 Mar. 1929.
159. WBY to Gregory, 21 Jan. 1929, NLI MS 30,593.
160. WBY to Shakespear, 2 Mar. 1929, Wade, 758–9.
161. GY to Robinson, 'Monday' [4 Mar. 1929], Huntington.

162. GY to Robinson, 21 Apr. 1929, Huntington.

163. GY to Robinson, 7 or 8 Mar. 1929, Huntington; Antheil to GY [summer 1929], Stony Brook.

164. 'by some happy chance—if chance there be—meeting George Antheil one night in some Paris cafe I suggested to him, though I only knew his music by reputation and by a pianola version of his *Ballet Mechanique*, that he should compose the music [for *Fighting the Waves*],' Robinson, *Curtain Up*, 69.

165. Eliot also had a hand in the book by 'Stacey Bishop', Linda Whitesitt, *The Life and Music of George Antheil 1900–1959* (Ann Arbor: UMI Research Press, 1981), 45.

166. GY to MacGreevy, 11 Feb. 1929, TCD MS 8104.

167. Patmore, 'Some Memories of W. B. Yeats', 158.

168. WBY to Gregory, 24 Mar. 1929, Stony Brook; *Journals*, ii. 416.

169. Robinson to GY, 7 Apr. 1929; Lily to R L-P, 9 Apr. 1929.

170. GY to Robinson, 'Friday' [19 Apr. 1929], Huntington; GY to MacGreevy, 16 Apr. 1929, TCD MS 8104.

171. GY to Robinson, 'Sunday' [14 Apr. 1929], Huntington.

172. Nelly to MacGreevy, 21 Apr. 1929, TCD MS 8129.

173. WBY to GY, 9 May 1929.

174. Lily to R L-P, 29 June 1929.

175. Lily to R L-P, 27 May 1929.

176. Solomons, *One Doctor in his Time*, 178.

177. Elborn, *Francis Stuart*, 82–3.

178. Robinson to Dolly Travers Smith, 29 June 1929, TCD MS 9686.

179. WBY to Shakespear, 2 July 1929, Wade, 764.

180. Lily to R L-P, 13 Aug. 1929.

181. WBY to Shakespear, 31 July and 8 Aug. 1929, Wade, 765–6.

182. Lily to R L-P, 18 Aug. 1929.

183. WBY to Shakespear, 24 Aug. 1929, Wade, 767.

184. Pound to J. D. Ibbotson, 14 Apr. 1936, *Ezra Pound: Letters to Ibbotson 1935– 1952*, ed. Vittoria I. Mondolfo and Margaret Hurley (Orono: University of Maine, 1979), 35.

185. WBY to Shakespear, 13 Sept. 1929, Wade, 768–9.

186. WBY to Shakespear, 23 Oct. 1930, Wade, 777.

187. Bradford, *Yeats at Work*, 134–5; James Lovic Allen and M. M. Liberman, 'Transcriptions of Yeats's Unpublished Prose in the Bradford Papers at Grinnell College', *Serif*, 10/1 (Spring 1973), 19.

188. Lily to R L-P, 5 Nov. 1929.

189. Lily to R L-P, 16 Sept. 1929.

190. Lily to R L-P, 20 Sept. and 5 Nov. 1929.

191. WBY to Shakespear, 13 Sept. 1929, Wade, 768.

192. Robinson to Dolly Travers Smith, 27 Oct. 1929, TCD MS 9686.

193. Gilbert, *The Golden Dawn Companion*, 41.

194. WBY to GY, 25 Oct. 1929.

195. E. Yarrow Jones to WBY, 25 Jan. 1931, Stony Brook.

196. WBY to GY, [?30 Oct. 1929] and 3 Nov. 1929.

197. Lily to R L-P, 12 Nov. 1929.

198. WBY to Gogarty, 16 Nov. 1929; the prescription reads 'Rx Guipsine (T.M 310351) Pills (Extra—Phara p.894. 19th Ed. Vol. I) Mitte 100 sig.1 t.c.d.', Boston University, W. B. Yeats Archive.

199. Robinson to GY, [?23 Nov. 1929]; Robinson to MacGreevy, 28 Nov. 1929, TCD MS 8103.

CHAPTER 16: FITZWILLIAM SQUARE

1. AY.

2. GY to Robinson, 'Sunday' [24 Nov. 1929], Huntington.

3. GY to Robinson, 30 Nov. 1929, HM 51877, Huntington.

4. Gregory, 9 Dec. 1929, *Journals*, ii. 475.

5. GY to Robinson, 'Monday' [2 Dec. 1929], Huntington; WBY, *Pages from a Diary in 1930, Explorations*, selected by Mrs W. B. Yeats (London: Macmillan, 1962), 294.

6. GY's Letts Diary for 1930, NLI MS 30,759.

7. GY to Robinson, 9 Jan. [1930, misdated 1929], HM 51886, Huntington.

8. Lyons, 'A Creative Family', 36; J. B. Lyons, *Thrust Syphilis down to Hell and Other Rejoyceana: Studies in the Borderlands of Literature and Medicine* (Dublin: Glendale Press, 1988), 291–4.

9. William Rothenstein to WBY, 5 Jan. 1930, Stony Brook.

10. GY to Gregory, 9 Feb. 1930, Berg.

11. GY to Robinson, 13 Feb. 1930, Huntington.

12. Basil Bunting, 'Yeats Recollected', *Agenda*, 12/2 (Summer 1974), 38.

13. Lily to R L-P, 30 Mar. 1930.

14. Gregory, 22 Feb. 1930, *Journals*, ii. 507–8.

15. Gregory to WBY, 26 Mar. 1930, Stony Brook; Robinson to GY, 4 Apr. 1930; Gogarty to WBY, 9 Apr. 1930, NLI MS 30,584.

16. GY to Robinson, 4 Mar. 1930, Huntington; Gogarty to WBY, 9 Apr. 1930, NLI MS 30,584.

17. Carnegie Dickson to WBY and GY, 3 Mar. 1930, Stony Brook.

18. Robinson to GY, 4 Apr. 1930.

19. Robinson to Dolly Travers Smith, 12 June 1930, TCD MS 9686.

20. GY to Robinson, 17 Mar. 1930, HM 51890, Huntington.

21. Gregory to WBY, 26 Mar. 1930, Stony Brook.

22. WBY to Shakespear, 4 Mar. 1930, Wade 772–3; Gregory, 5 Mar. 1930, *Journals*, ii. 510.

23. WBY to Gregory, 7 Apr. 1930, Wade, 773.

24. WBY, *Pages from a Diary in 1930, Explorations*, 289; the extract is dated 7 Apr.

25. 'When I have finished my present task "Stories of Michael Robartes" . . . I shall begin my spiritualistic play about Swift,' WBY to Gregory, 2 Aug. 1929, NLI MS 30,179.

26. Rapallo Notebook 1928–30, Stony Brook.

27. GY to Robinson, 17 Mar. 1930, HM 51890, Huntington.

28. GY to Robinson, 1 May 1930, HM 51892, Huntington. I have been unable to identify the literary nun.

29. GY to Robinson, 4 Mar. 1930, Huntington.

30. Gregory to WBY, 29 May 1930, Stony Brook.

31. Robinson to GY, 12 June 1930.

32. AY.

33. WBY to Gregory, [?14 May 1930], Emory, misdated 25 May.

34. AY.

35. WBY to Shakespear, 1 June 1930, Wade, 775–6.

36. Lily to R L-P, 11 Aug. 1930.

37. A map of Levanto issued by Hotel Stelle d'Italia is inserted inside back cover of the fourth part of the *Tale of Genji* (1928).

38. MBY; Bunting, 'Yeats Recollected', 40–1; WBY to Gogarty, 20 Mar. 1930, Sligo.

39. GY to Robinson, 1 May 1930, HM 51892, Huntington.

40. GY to Robinson, 29 June 1930, Huntington.

41. According to a recent version by AY, the cat eventually ended up with 'a blind sculptor', Charis Chapman, 'Across the Atlantic: Impressions of England, Ireland and Anne Yeats', *South Carolina Review*, 32/1 (Fall 1999), 210 n. 2.

42. GY to Dorothy, 15 July [1930], Omar Pound.

43. Williams, *A Sea-Grey House*, 90.

44. GY to WBY, 'Wednesday' [23 July 1930].

45. Lily to R L-P, 29 July 1930.

46. Cowell, *No Profit but the Name*, 77–8. Lady Longford, who had known the Yeatses when she was a student at Oxford, was presented with a copy of the Séanad report on coinage signed by WBY and dated 22 July 1930.

47. GY to WBY, 'Wednesday' [23 July 1930]; Gregory recommended Walsh's Garage in Gort, 1 Aug. 1930, Stony Brook.

48. Ninette de Valois, *Step by Step: The Formation of an Establishment* (London: W. H. Allen, 1977), 185.

49. Gregory, 10 Aug. 1930, *Journals*, ii. 552–6.

50. Robinson to GY, 9 Mar. 1930.

51. WBY, *Pages from a Diary in 1930*, *Explorations*, 322.

52. WBY to GY, 1 Nov. 1931.

53. Plotinus, 'Seventh Tractate: Is there an Ideal Archetype of Particular Beings?', in *The Divine Mind, Being the Treatises of the Fifth Ennead*, trans. from the Greek by Stephen MacKenna (London: The Medici Society, Limited, 1926), iv. 70; Yeats's '*The Words upon the Window-Pane*: A Commentary', part II dated Nov. 1931, was first published in the *Dublin Magazine*, Oct.–Dec. 1931 and Jan.–Mar. 1932.

54. GY to WBY, 24 Nov. 1931.

55. Stony Brook.

56. Everard Feilding to WBY, 4 Apr. 1933, *LTWBY* ii. 854–5; GY to WBY, 27 Nov. 1931. Cummins recommends the play 'to students of psychical research', *Unseen Adventures*, 88.

57. GY to Robinson, 29 June 1930, Huntington; Robinson to GY, 15 July 1930.
58. GY to Dorothy, 22 Aug. 1930, Yale; Saddlemyer (ed.), 'George, Ezra, Dorothy and Friends', 16–17.
59. Michael Reck, 'A Conversation between Ezra Pound and Allen Ginsburg', *Evergreen Review*, 12/55 (June 1968), 29.
60. Lily to R L-P, 26 Aug. 1930.
61. WBY to GY, 29 Aug. 1930.
62. Lily to R L-P, 8 Sept. 1930.
63. Gregory to GY, 11 Sept. 1930, Stony Brook.
64. GY to Pound, 29 Sept. 1930, Yale; Saddlemyer (ed.), 'George, Ezra, Dorothy and Friends', 17.
65. WBY to Shakespear, 23 Oct. 1930, Wade, 777.
66. AY, 'My Uncle Jack: Some Reminiscences', May 1991, lecture at Princess Grace Irish Library, Monaco.
67. GY to WBY, [?27 Sept. 1930].
68. Robinson to GY, 'Saturday aft.' [3 or 10 Oct. 1930].
69. WBY to Gregory, 10 Mar. 1931, Stony Brook.
70. WBY to Watt, Jan. or Feb. 1931, Stony Brook.
71. Lily to R L-P, 1 Oct. 1930.
72. WBY to Masefield, 7 May 1930, 'W. B. Yeats to John Masefield: Two Letters', ed. Paul Delany, *Massachusetts Review*, 11/1 (Winter 1970), 161.
73. WBY to Gregory, 29 Oct. 1930, Wade, 777–8.
74. Cottie Yeats to Gregory, 31 Dec. 1930, Berg.
75. GY to Gogarty, 6 Jan. 1931, Bucknell.
76. Robinson to GY, 15 July 1930. Robinson's edition was never completed but see Londraville, *On Poetry, Painting and Politics*.
77. GY to WBY, 'Saturday' [1 Nov. 1930]; Sean Dorman, *Limelight over the Liffey* (Cornwall: Raffeen Press, 1983), 9.
78. Lily to R L-P, 1 Dec. 1930.
79. WBY to Shakespear, 2 Dec. 1930, Wade, 780.
80. Lily to Ruth, 22 [? Feb.] 1931; WBY to Shakespear, 27 Dec. 1930, Wade, 786.
81. Lily to R L-P, 11 Feb. 1931.
82. Robinson to Dolly Travers Smith, 24 Jan. 1931, TCD MS 9686.
83. WBY to GY, 4 Feb. 1931; GY to WBY, 5 Feb. 1931; WBY to Shakespear, 9 Feb. 1931, Wade, 781.
84. WBY to Gregory, 19 Feb. 1931, Berg.
85. WBY to Gregory, 9 Mar. 1931, Stony Brook.
86. GY to WBY, [3 June 1931].
87. MBY, *Cast a Cold Eye*, 10.
88. WBY to GY, 8 Aug. 1931.
89. Lily to R L-P, 21 July 1931.
90. WBY to Gregory, 20 May 1931, Stony Brook.
91. Lily to R L-P, 26 May 1931.
92. WBY to GY, 28 May 1931; Bowra, *Memories*, 235–6.

93. GY to WBY, [3 June 1931].

94. Ellmann interview notes with GY, n.d., Tulsa.

95. *Signe Toksvig's Irish Diaries*, 118; Lily to R L-P, 30 June 1931. The company performed an old favourite, *Paul Twyning* by George Sheils.

96. ECY to Monk Gibbon, 22 June 1931, Queen's.

97. GY to WBY, 'Friday' [31 July 1931], ' "Yours Affly, Dobbs" ', 282.

98. GY to WBY, 16 Oct. 1931, ibid. 284.

99. *The Times* (London), 4 Aug. 1931.

100. Lily to R L-P, 6 Aug. 1931.

101. Gregory, 23 Aug. 1931, *Journals*, ii. 623.

102. Lily to R L-P, 24 May 1932.

103. GY to WBY, 5 Aug. 1931.

104. Hester Dowden to MacGreevy, 12 Aug. 1931, TCD MS 8136.

105. Robinson to MacGreevy, 27 Dec. 1930, TCD MS 8103.

106. Robinson to GY, 30 Apr. 1930.

107. Robinson to Dolly Travers Smith, 22 July 1931, TCD MS 9686; GY to Dolly Travers Smith, 22 July 1931, Sotheby's sale catalogue no. 584, 21–2 July 1983.

108. GY to MacGreevy, 5 Nov. 1931, TCD MS 8104; MacGreevy to GY, 11 Dec. 1931, NLI MS 30,859.

109. GY to MacGreevy, 4 Feb. 1932, TCD MS 8104.

110. WBY to Robinson, 23 July 1931; WBY to Dolly Travers Smith, 24 July 1931, Sotheby's sale catalogue no. 584.

111. WBY to Shakespear, 4 Jan. 1932, fragment, Stony Brook.

112. Dolly's various addresses were c/o H. Clarke, 6 N. Frederick Street and 32 N. Frederick Street; 6 and 7 and 33 N. Frederick Street were also Clarke studios.

113. GY to Dolly Travers Smith, 22 July 1931, Sotheby's sale catalogue no. 584; Dolly Robinson to GY, 28 Nov. 1931.

114. WBY to Shakespear, 30 Aug. 1931, Wade, 783.

115. WBY to Sturge Moore, 22 Oct. 1931, Bridge (ed.), *W. B. Yeats and T. Sturge Moore*, 169.

116. WBY to GY [early Aug. 1931].

117. GY to Monk Gibbon, 17 Sept. 1931, Queen's.

118. GY to WBY, 26 Oct. 1931, ' "Yours Affly, Dobbs" ', 285.

119. GY to WBY, 15 or 30 Dec., ibid. 293.

120. GY to WBY, 24 Nov. 1931, ibid. 290.

121. WBY to GY, 'Wednesday' [25 Nov. 1931].

122. GY to WBY, 22 Dec. 1932, ' "Yours Affly, Dobbs" ', 293–4.

123. WBY to GY, 24 Dec. 1931; WBY to MBY, 23 Dec. 1931.

124. WBY to GY, Oct. 1931; GY to WBY, 16 Oct. 1931, ' "Yours Affly, Dobbs" ', 284.

125. WBY to GY, 28 Jan. 1932.

126. WBY to GY, 1 Nov. 1931; GY to WBY, 3 Nov. 1931, ' "Yours Affly, Dobbs" ', 289.

127. GY to WBY, 24 Nov. 1931, ibid. 290.

128. GY to WBY, 'Sunday' [1 Nov. 1931], ibid. 288.

129. Lily to R L-P, 27 Sept. 1931.

130. Lily to R L-P, 20 Oct. 1931 and 4 Jan. 1932; WBY to Lily, 6 Jan. 1932; Murphy, *Family Secrets*, 244–5; Hyland, *I Call to the Eye of the Mind*, 155.

131. GY to WBY, 4 Jan. 1932, ' "Yours Affly, Dobbs" ', 296.

132. WBY to Lily, 6 Jan. and 14 Mar. 1932, Stony Brook.

133. GY to WBY, 21 and 25 Jan., 1 Feb. 1932, ' "Yours Affly, Dobbs" ', 296–9.

134. WBY to AY, 3 Feb. 1932.

135. GY to WBY, 2 Mar. 1932, ' "Yours Affly, Dobbs" ', 301.

136. GY to WBY, 29 Feb. 1932, ibid. 300.

137. WBY to GY, 1 Mar. 1932; 'Georgie Yeats' to Francis Hackett, 1 Mar. 1932, Royal Library Copenhagen, courtesy Lis Pihl; GY to WBY, 2 Mar. 1932, ' "Yours Affly, Dobbs" ', 301.

138. Lily to R L-P, 24 Aug. 1938. De Bosis disappeared while flying over Rome, dropping anti-Fascist leaflets.

139. WBY to GY, Apr. 1932; GY to WBY, 12 Apr. 1932, ' "Yours Affly, Dobbs" ', 303.

140. WBY to Gregory, 22 Apr. 1932, JK.

141. 'I return to Coole Park tomorrow and shall be there until May 12th. I hope that while I am away Starkie, George Russell, and Frank O'Connor will draft a set of rules, the minimum necessary for registration.' WBY to Shaw, 26 Apr. 1932, M. J. Sidnell, 'Hic and Ille', in Robert O'Driscoll (ed.), *Theatre and Nationalism in Twentieth Century Ireland* (Toronto: University of Toronto Press, 1971), 177.

142. WBY to GY, [early May 1932].

143. Gregory to Kiernan, 9 May 1932, T. J. Kiernan, 'Lady Gregory and W. B. Yeats', *Dalhousie Review*, 38/3 (Autumn 1958), 305–6; Colin Smythe, foreword to Gregory, *Seventy Years*, pp. vi–viii.

144. WBY to GY, 8 Feb. and 10 Jan. 1932.

145. WBY to GY, 30 Apr. 1932.

146. WBY to Sturge Moore, 4 June 1932, Bridge (ed.), *W. B. Yeats and T. Sturge Moore*, 173.

CHAPTER 17: RIVERSDALE

1. WBY to Shakespear, 22 Apr. 1932, Stony Brook; Wade, 794, reads 'next month' for 'next winter'.

2. Bradford, 'George Yeats: Poet's Wife', 396.

3. WBY to Shakespear, 2 Oct. 1932, Wade, 802; Lily to R L-P, 8 Aug. 1932; WBY to Shakespear, 25 July 1932, Wade, 799; WBY to Gregory, 15 May 1932, Berg.

4. WBY to Gregory, 22 May 1932, Stony Brook.

5. Ellmann interview notes with GY, 8 Dec. 1946, Tulsa.

6. Memorial; Lily to R L-P, 8 Aug. 1932.

7. AY.

8. WBY to Gregory, 22 May 1932, Stony Brook.

9. WBY to P. S. O'Hegarty, 14 Aug. and 26 Sept. 1932, Kansas.

10. WBY to Shakespear, 8 July 1932, Wade, 799.

11. Lily to R L-P, 3 July 1933; WBY's 'The Fiddler of Dooney' (1892) was frequently reprinted in anthologies.

12. GY to WBY, 9 Dec. 1933.
13. WBY to Shakespear, 8 and 25 July 1932, Wade, 798; WBY to Heald, 28 Nov. 1937. He states that the gardens had been created by 'a Mrs Nugent' who lived there till her recent death, but according to the Memorial, the lease was purchased from the heirs of Mrs Ruth O'Regan Phillips, a widow who had lived there since 1905.
14. GY to WBY, [?11 July 1932]; AY; Lily to R L-P, 5 Oct. 1932; ECY to H. O. White, 31 Jan. 1934, TCD MS 3777.
15. Lily to R L-P, 11 July 1932.
16. Lily to R L-P, 5 Oct. 1932; WBY to Shakespear, 2 Oct. 1932, Wade, 802. I am grateful to the late AY for her detailed description of the house and grounds of Riversdale and the offer of her own painting as illustration.
17. WBY to Shakespear, 25 July 1932, Wade, 799.
18. WBY to AY, 6 July 1932.
19. WBY to GY, July 1932; Francis Stuart, in McManus (ed.), *The Yeats We Knew*, 30.
20. GY to WBY, 'Monday' [?11 July 1932].
21. WBY to Masefield, 7 May 1930, 'W. B. Yeats to John Masefield: Two Letters', 161; the poem he refers to is 'Truly Great' by W. H. Davies.
22. AY.
23. Lily to R L-P, 5 Oct. 1932; AY.
24. Lily to R L-P, 5 Oct. 1932.
25. GY to WBY, 24 Oct. 1932.
26. WBY to T. J. Kiernan, 19 Oct. 1932, Berg; Kiernan to GY, 21 Oct. 1932, Berg. Kiernan, an old friend of Lady Gregory and frequent visitor to Coole, had formerly been inspector of taxes; he eventually became an ambassador.
27. WBY to Shakespear, 23 June 1927, Wade, 725.
28. WBY to GY, 4 Nov. 1932.
29. ECY to H. O. White, 31 Jan. 1934, TCD MS 3777; Lily to R L-P, [?5 Aug. 1933].
30. GY to WBY, 2 and 23 Nov. 1932.
31. Lily to R L-P, 4 Feb. 1935.
32. GY to WBY, letters throughout Dec. and Jan. 1932.
33. WBY to GY, 12 Nov. 1932; GY to WBY, 23 Nov. and 9 Dec. 1932; WBY to GY, 25 Dec. 1932.
34. GY to Pound, 11 Jan. 1933, Yale; Saddlemyer (ed.), 'George, Ezra, Dorothy and Friends', 18.
35. WBY to Shakespear, 29 Jan. 1934, Wade, 804.
36. WBY to Pound, 2 Mar. 1934, Yale.
37. AY, 'Faces of my Father', *Irish Times*, 1 Dec. 1976, 10.
38. GY to Pound, 11 Jan. 1933, Yale; Saddlemyer (ed.), 'George, Ezra, Dorothy and Friends', 18.
39. 7 July 1933, *Signe Toksvig's Irish Diaries*, 250; GY to WBY, 3 June 1933; Louis MacNeice, Sept. 1934, *The Strings are False: An Unfinished Autobiography* (London: Faber, 1965), 147–8.
40. WBY to Shakespear, 27 Jan. 1934, JK; this section omitted from Wade, 819.

41. WBY to Iseult Stuart, 5 July [? 1934], NLI MS 30,564; Francis Stuart, in McManus (ed.), *The Yeats We Knew*, 38.

42. GY to WBY, 24 Apr. 1933.

43. Diarmuid Brennan, 'As Yeats was Going down Grafton Street', *Listener*, 6 Feb. 1964, 236–8.

44. WBY to Dulac, 27 Sept. 1933, Hobby, 181–2.

45. WBY to Shakespear, early Apr. 1934, Wade, 808–9.

46. WBY to Shakespear, 13 July 1933, Wade, 811–12.

47. Ellmann interview notes with GY, 28 Oct. 1946, Tulsa.

48. WBY to Shakespear, 17 Aug. 1933, Wade, 813–14.

49. 'neither of us wanted to see General O'Duffy back in Ireland with enhanced fame helping "the Catholic front",' WBY to Mannin, 11 Feb. 1937, Wade, 881–2.

50. WBY to Shakespear, 27 Feb. 1934, Wade 820–1. A slightly different version of the incident is told by Frank O'Connor in 'Reminiscences of Yeats', 256 ff., repr. in Mikhail (ed.), *Interviews and Recollections*, ii. 335.

51. Ellmann interview notes with GY, 28 Oct. 1946, Tulsa.

52. MacGreevy to Margaret McGreevy, 30 Mar. and 5 Apr. 1934, TCD MS 10,381.

53. GY to MacGreevy, 'Monday', TCD MS 8104; possibly Nov. 1934 at the time of the marriage between the Duke of Kent and Princess Marina of Greece.

54. GY to MacGreevy, 12 Dec. 1934, envelope dated 17 Dec., TCD MS 8104.

55. 'O. St John Gogarty', in Rodgers (ed.), *Irish Literary Portraits*, 179; Terence de Vere White, *A Fretful Midge* (London: Routledge & Kegan Paul, 1957), 181.

56. GY to WBY, 24 Apr. 1933.

57. Ibid.

58. The book was S. Radhakrishnan, *Indian Philosophy* (London: George Allen & Unwin, 1923), i. 452, YL.

59. Dolly Robinson to MacGreevy, 11 Feb. 1934, TCD MS 8103.

60. GY to WBY, 14 Dec. 1934; Thom's *Dublin Directory* lists Mrs Gaskin, 'Innisfree', Carrickbrack Road, Baily.

61. GY to WBY, 9 Dec. 1933.

62. AY, unpublished memoirs, and Sena, 'Interview "Images and Memories"', 87–8.

63. WBY to Ernest Rhys, 3 May 1934, Wade, 821.

64. AY, 'Faces of my Father', 10.

65. AY, unpublished memoirs.

66. WBY to Mannin, 30 Dec. 1934, Sligo.

67. WBY to Dorothy Wellesley, 8 July 1935, *Letters on Poetry from W. B. Yeats to Dorothy Wellesley*, ed. Dorothy Wellesley (London: Oxford University Press, 1964), 8.

68. MBY, *Cast a Cold Eye*, 28–9.

69. Ibid. 36.

70. AY, unpublished memoirs.

71. Lily to R L-P, 28 Nov. 1933.

72. Letter from Charles Burston (née Charlotte Lane-Poole) to me, 18 Sept. 1989.

73. Lily to R L-P, 1 May 1934; AY.

74. Lily to R L-P, 5 Aug. 1935.

75. AY; the film was shown at the Grand Central cinema in Oct. 1935.
76. GY to WBY, 5 Jan. 1935.
77. Lily to R L-P, 25 Feb. 1935.
78. Lily to R L-P, 17 Sept., 8 and 23 Oct. 1934.
79. Lily to R L-P, 15 Apr. 1935.
80. GY to WBY, 4 Dec. 1935.
81. Lily to R L-P, 1 May 1934; AY, unpublished memoirs.
82. Lily to R L-P, 27 May 1935.
83. AY, Gráinne Yeats; MBY, *Cast a Cold Eye*, 31–2; Gibbon, *Masterpiece and the Man*, 86.
84. MBY, *Cast a Cold Eye*, 12–15.
85. GY to WBY, 29 Dec. 1932.
86. MBY.
87. AY, unpublished memoirs.
88. WBY to Ernest Rhys, 3 May 1934, Wade, 821.
89. Lily to R L-P, 27 Oct. 1931.
90. Hone, *W. B. Yeats*, 421.
91. Dorman, *My Uncle Lennox* (Fowey: Raffeen Press, 1986), 48–51. I am grateful to Kildare Dobbs and Richard White for their memories of St Columba's.
92. George White to MBY, 26 Aug. 1968.
93. MBY, *Cast a Cold Eye*, 35.
94. AY, unpublished memoirs.
95. WBY to Shakespear, 25 Aug. 1934, Wade, 827–9; Jeffares, *W. B. Yeats: Man and Poet*, 284–5.
96. WBY to GY, 7 June 1933.
97. Lennox Robinson, 'William Butler Yeats: Personality', in Jeffares and Cross (eds.), *In Excited Reverie*, 21.
98. WBY to GY, 26 Dec. 1934.
99. GY to WBY, 3 June 1933.
100. WBY to Shakespear, 17 Apr. 1933, JK.
101. WBY to Desmond FitzGerald, 30 Mar. 1933, UCD.
102. WBY to Shakespear, 13 July 1933, Wade, 812.
103. WBY to Shakespear, 9 Mar. 1934, Wade, 807.
104. A page on Riversdale stationery dated 10 May 1933, NLI MS 30,011.
105. Bradford, *Yeats at Work*, 134–5; Allen and Liberman, 'Transcriptions of Yeats's Unpublished Prose in the Bradford Papers at Grinnell College', 19. Bradford misreads 'Dionertes' as 'Dionastes'.
106. WBY to Shakespear, 27 Jan. 1934, Wade, 819.
107. WBY to Harold Macmillan, 9 Mar. 1934, BL Add. MS 55,003/161; Harold Macmillan to H. Watt, 31 Dec. 1934, Stony Brook; BL Add. MS 5,576/462, qtd. in Finneran, 'On Editing Yeats', 120–1.
108. *A Vision B*, 23.
109. Unpublished dedication, dated 1931, white vellum notebook, quoted by GY to James Healy, 21 June 1940, Stanford.

110. WBY to Shakespear, 9 Feb. 1931, Wade, 781.

111. Advertisement for a course of eight lectures on 'The Bhagwad Geeta' at the Fellow-
     ship Club, 51/52 Lancaster Gate, on Thursday evenings commencing 30 Apr. 1930,
     BL Add. MS 45,732/4; Swami to Sturge Moore, 9 June 1931, Stony Brook. This
     contradicts Geoffrey M. Watkins's claim that his father John M. Watkins 'was
     responsible for introducing Yeats, through the Hon. Mrs Davey, to Shri Purohit
     Swami', 'Yeats and Mr Watkins' Bookshop', 309. 'You will remember you were
     sent to me by Mr. Fletcher of the Society of Friends and how I wrote you an
     introduction to Masefield and how I arranged for you to meet Yeats here.' Sturge
     Moore to Swami, 8 Nov. 1932, BL Add. MSS 45,732/66.

112. Shankar Mokashi-Punekar, *The Later Phase in the Development of W. B. Yeats*
     (Dharwar: Karnatak University, 1966).

113. 'Secretary' [GY] to Swami, 94 Lancaster Gate, 29 July 1931, telegram, Delaware.

114. WBY to GY, 10 Mar. 1932; WBY to Sturge Moore, 9 Feb. and 10 Mar. 1932, BL
     Add. MSS 45,732/29 and 36.

115. Sturge Moore to WBY, 28 Mar. 1932, BL Add. MS 45,732/50.

116. WBY to Swami, 31 July 1932, Mokashi-Punekar, *The Later Phase in the Develop-
     ment of W. B. Yeats*, 260.

117. WBY to Sturm, 7 Jan. 1935, Stony Brook; Sturm to WBY, 20 Mar. 1935, Stony
     Brook, Taylor (ed.), *Frank Pearce Sturm*, 105–6.

118. Shakespear to WBY, 14 May 1932 and 28 Oct. 1933, 'Olivia Shakespear: Letters to
     W. B. Yeats', 83 and 91.

119. Shakespear to WBY, 3 Mar. 1934 and 17 July 1932, ibid. 95 and 86–7.

120. Shakespear to WBY, 17 July 1932 and 14 June 1935, ibid. 86–7 and 99; clipping from
     the *Daily Sketch* (n.d.) with photographs of the Swami and Foden, MBY; Elizabeth
     Pelham to WBY, 30 July 1936, *LTWBY* ii. 583–5; John Harwood, 'Yeats, Shri
     Purohit Swami, and Mrs Foden', *YA* 6 (1988), 104–7.

121. WBY to GY, 30 June 1934; WBY to Shakespear, 16 June 1935, Stony Brook, omitted
     in Wade, 835.

122. Taylor (ed.), *Frank Pearce Sturm*, 56; Sturge Moore to Swami, 8 Nov. 1932,
     TS carbon, BL Add. MSS 45,732/66.

123. WBY to Shakespear, 24 Oct. 1933, Wade, 815.

124. WBY to Swami, 27 Sept. 1933, Delaware; Mokashi-Punekar, *The Later Phase in the
     Development of W. B. Yeats*, 261–2.

125. WBY to Swami, 16 Feb. 1934, Delaware.

126. WBY to Shakespear, 27 Feb. 1934, Wade, 820.

127. Swami to WBY, 6 Nov. 1934, Stony Brook.

128. WBY to Shakespear, 24 Oct. 1933, Wade, 815.

129. Jeffares, *W. B. Yeats: Man and Poet*, 285.

130. WBY to Swami, 11 July 1935, Delaware; Kathleen Raine to me; Santosh Pall,
     'Yeats and India', in Abhai Maurya (ed.), *India and World Literature* (New Delhi:
     Indian Council for Cultural Relations, 1990), 491.

131. Hone, *W. B. Yeats*, 382 n.

132. The flyleaf of no. 4/750 of *The Geeta: The Gospel of the Lord Shri Krishna*, trans. Shri Purohit Swami (London: Faber & Faber, 1935) bears the inscription 'My dear Mrs. Yeats. Thank you for your kindness and god bless you. Purohit Swami', YL.

133. WBY to Shakespear, 27 Feb. 1934, Wade, 820.

134. WBY to Swami, 26 July 1935, Delaware.

135. 'Mandookya Upanishad with an Introduction by William Butler Yeats', *Criterion*, 14 (July 1935), 547–59; see *Later Essays*, ed. William H. O'Donnell (New York: Scribner's, 1994) for text, notes, and commentary on these publications.

136. Palmstierna, *Horizons of Immortality*, 334–51; Macleod, *The Sisters d'Aranyi*, 186–203.

137. Allen and Liberman, 'Transcriptions of Yeats's Unpublished Prose in the Bradford Papers at Grinnell College', 19; WBY to Shakespear, 11 Nov. 1933 and 27 Jan. 1934, Wade, 817–19.

138. WBY to Shakespear, 17 Aug. 1933, Wade, 814.

139. Elborn, *Francis Stuart*, 77; Ellmann interview notes with Iseult Gonne Stuart, 21 Sept. 1946, Tulsa. The discussion Iseult recalls probably took place about 28 Nov. 1935, just before Yeats departed for Majorca.

140. GY to Robinson, 29 Nov. 1927, HM 51873, Huntington.

141. Conversation with Charles Burston, Jan. 1998.

142. JBY to Rosa Butt, 23 June 1920, WMM.

143. WBY to Sturge Moore, 7 Sept. 1933, Bridge (ed.), *W. B. Yeats and T. Sturge Moore*, 177.

144. WBY to Shakespear, 24 Oct. 1933, Wade, 816.

145. Dulac to WBY, 9 Dec. 1934, *LTWBY* ii. 567–8.

146. AE to WBY, 11 Oct. 1933, *LTWBY* ii. 559–60.

147. David Hamilton, *The Monkey Gland Affair* (London: Chatto & Windus, 1986); Virginia D. Pruitt, 'Yeats and the Steinach Operation', *American Imago*, 34 (Fall 1977), 292; Virginia D. Pruitt and Raymond D. Pruitt, 'Yeats and the Steinach Operation: A Further Analysis', *YAACTS* I (1983), 112.

148. Stephen Lock, ' "O that I were young again": Yeats and the Steinach Operation', *British Medical Journal*, 287 (24–31 Dec. 1983), 1965, quoting Jon Stallworthy; however, on 10 July 1934 WBY wrote to Moore recommending Peter Schmidt, *The Conquest of Old Age: Methods to Effect Rejuvenation and to Increase Functional Activity*, trans. Eden and Cedar Paul (London: Routledge, 1931), adding, 'The surgeon I went to is Norman Haire 127 Harley St. He is expensive & I think Dulac could tell you of some one else probably as good who would charge much less,' ULL, MS 978/2/76.

149. Schmidt, *The Conquest of Old Age*; Norman Haire, *Rejuvenation: The Work of Steinach, Voronoff and Others* (London: Allen & Unwin, 1924).

150. Norman Haire, *Hymen; or the Future of Marriage* (London: Kegan Paul, Trench & Truebner, 1927), 8.

151. Haire, *Rejuvenation*, 209–12, 254–5.

152. 28 May 1919 and 26 Dec. 1919, *YVP* ii. 292 and 526; also 31 July 1919, *YVP* ii. 349.

153. GY to WBY, 15 Apr. 1934.

154. WBY to Shakespear, 10 May 1934, Wade, 822.
155. WBY to Harold Macmillan, 15 May 1934, BL MS Add. 55003/166.
156. Shakespear to WBY, 6 Apr. 1934, 'Olivia Shakespear: Letters to W. B. Yeats', 96.
157. GY to MacGreevy, 15 Mar. 1926, TCD MS 8104.
158. Gogarty to Horace Reynolds, 9 Mar. 1955 and Oct. 1934, bMS Am. 1787, Harvard, qtd. by Lyons, *Thrust Syphilis down to Hell*, 191–2.
159. Haire to Ellmann, qtd. by Ellmann to me; cf. Stephen Lock: 'Most reports mention that immediately after the operation there was an increase in sexual interest, and that this persisted for about a year,' ' "O that I were young again" ', 1965.
160. Richard Ellmann, 'Ez and Old Billyum', in *Eminent Domain* (New York: Oxford University Press, 1967), 81–2; WBY to Shakespear, 7 Aug. 1934, Wade, 826–7.
161. Jaffe, 'Vignettes', 148.
162. Nelly to MacGreevy, 18 Nov. and 25 Dec. 1933, TCD MS 8129.
163. Shakespear to WBY, 8 Oct. 1933, 4 Feb. and 3 Mar. 1934, 'Olivia Shakespear: Letters to W. B. Yeats', 90, 93–5.
164. Interview with Grace Jaffe.
165. Nelly to MacGreevy, 24 May 1934, TCD MS 8129.
166. GY to Shakespear, 13 Feb. 1935, JK.
167. WBY to GY, 30 June 1934.
168. WBY to Sturge Moore, 24 July 1934, Bridge (ed.), *W. B. Yeats and T. Sturge Moore*, 180. The design had been worked by Ethel Pye.
169. Holloway, 30 July 1934, *Joseph Holloway's Irish Theatre*, ii: *1932–1937*, ed. Robert Hogan and Michael J. O'Neill (Dixon, Calif.: Proscenium Press, 1969), 35.
170. WBY to Shakespear, 24 July 1934, Wade, 824–5.
171. WBY to Shakespear, 17 Sept. 1934, Wade, 829.
172. Ellmann interview notes with GY, 24 Sept. 1946; GY to MacGreevy, [?1955], Mrs Elizabeth Ryan; Giuseppe Galassi's *Roma o bisanzio: i mosaici di Ravenna e le origini dell'arte Italiana* (Roma: La Libreria Della Stato, 1930) inscribed 'George Yeats Rome "volta congress" 1934', and a guide to Ravenna in Italian signed by her, YL.
173. WBY to Margot Ruddock, 24 Sept., 5 and 11 Oct. 1934, Roger McHugh (ed.), *Ah, Sweet Dancer: W. B. Yeats–Margot Ruddock. A Correspondence* (London: Macmillan, 1970), 20–3.
174. WBY to GY, [?27] and 30 Oct. 1934.
175. WBY to Ruddock, 5 Oct. 1934, McHugh (ed.) *Ah, Sweet Dancer*, 21.
176. Shakespear to WBY, 25 Nov. 1934, 'Olivia Shakespear: Letters to W. B. Yeats', 97.
177. Reid, *The Man from New York*, 81, attributed to Dion Boucicault.
178. WBY to Ruddock, 3 Nov. 1934, McHugh (ed.), *Ah, Sweet Dancer*, 24.
179. WBY to Ruddock, 27 Nov. 1934, ibid. 32–3.
180. Dulac to WBY, 9 Dec. 1934, *LTWBY* ii. 568.
181. GY to WBY, 11, 18, and 27 Dec. 1934.
182. WBY to Shakespear, dated 27 Dec. 1934 but more likely a few days later, Stony Brook; qtd. by Harwood, *Olivia Shakespear and W. B. Yeats*, 189.
183. WBY to GY, [?30 Dec. 1934].

184. Ethel Mannin, *Confessions and Impressions* (London: Hutchinson, 1936), 189–94.
185. Ethel Mannin papers, Boston University; Gogarty to Horace Reynolds, 9 Mar. 1955, bMS Am. 1787, Harvard, qtd. by Lyons, *Thrust Syphilis down to Hell*, 191–2.
186. WBY to Mannin, 15 Nov. [?1936], Sligo.
187. Ethel Mannin, *Privileged Spectator* (London: Hutchinson, 1939), 81–5; WBY to Mannin, 31 July 1935, Sligo.
188. WBY to GY, 3 and 7 Jan. 1935.
189. GY to Dulac, 22 Jan. 1935, Hobby, 209–10; Dulac to GY, 24 Jan. 1935, Stony Brook.
190. WBY to Mannin, 27 Sept. 1936 and 15 Nov. [?1936], Sligo; WBY to Ruddock, 'Wednesday', dated Jan. 1935 in McHugh (ed.), *Ah, Sweet Dancer*, 35.
191. WBY to Mannin [?29 Jan. 1935], Sligo.
192. Lily to R L-P, 4 Feb. 1935.
193. GY to Gogarty, 29 Jan. 1935. I am grateful to Philip Marcus for a copy of this letter.
194. Ellmann interview notes with GY, 8 Oct. 1946, Tulsa.
195. Lily to R L-P, 4 Feb. 1935.
196. GY to Gogarty, 29 Jan. 1935.
197. WBY to Dorothy Wellesley, 3 Sept. 1935, Wade, 839–40.
198. This must have been told to Ellmann by GY, *The Man and the Masks*, 1979 preface, p. xxix.
199. A story by Seán O'Faoláin seems more wish-fulfilment than fact: 'George was mother and wife to him, and more, almost his procuress; she was understanding about what she sympathetically called his "girls": as when for example she once advised him when they were discussing the logistics of one of his romantic excursions not to ignore his mistress on the railway platform and occupy a distant carriage until the train moved out, as he was proposing to do, but rather to go forward to her and greet her joyfully before the world,' Seán O'Faoláin, *Vive Moi!*, ed. and with an afterword by Julia O'Faoláin (London: Sinclair-Stevenson, 1994), 308.
200. 'What Then?', *Last Poems*.
201. Robinson to GY, [?10 Mar. 1928].
202. GY to MacGreevy, 28 July 1929, TCD MS 8104.
203. GY to Dulac, 1 Feb. 1935, HRHRC; WBY to Shakespear, 5 Feb. 1935, Wade, 830–1; WBY to Mannin, 1 Feb. 1935, Sligo.
204. Swami to WBY, 4 Feb. 1935, Stony Brook.
205. Shakespear to WBY, 7 Feb. 1935, 'Olivia Shakespear: Letters to W. B. Yeats', 98.
206. WBY to Ruddock, 25 Feb. 1935, McHugh (ed.), *Ah, Sweet Dancer*, 36; WBY to Mannin, 4 Mar. 1935, Wade, 832.
207. WBY to Shakespear, [?4 Mar. 1935], Wade, 832–3.
208. GY to Dorothy Wellesley, 19 Sept. 1936, Yeats, *Letters on Poetry*, 97–8.
209. WBY to GY, 30 and 31 Mar., 4, 5, 8, and 10 Apr. 1935.
210. Lily to R L-P, 15 Apr. 1935.
211. WBY to GY, 15 and 22 Apr. 1935; Lily to R L-P, 29 Apr. 1935.
212. Lily to R L-P, 29 Apr. and 7 May 1935.
213. John Oliver for Carnegie Dickson, at the request of Dr R. A. Young, to WBY, 10 May 1935, Stony Brook.

214. Earnán de Blaghd, Thomas Davis Lecture, in McManus (ed.), *The Yeats We Knew*, 61–5.

215. O'Casey to WBY, 19 May 1935, Stony Brook; Sean O'Casey, 'Black Oxen Passing By' and 'The Friggin Frogs', *Rose and Crown* (London: Macmillan, 1952), 136 and 145; 43–4.

216. WBY to Mannin, [?27 May 1935] and 28 May 1935, Sligo; Dulac to GY, 7 June 1935, Hobby, 213.

217. WBY to Ruddock, 17 Sept. 1935, McHugh (ed.), *Ah, Sweet Dancer*, 49.

218. Yeats, *Letters on Poetry*, 1.

219. WBY to Ottoline Morrell, 1 June 1935, JK. The volume by Dorothy Wellesley was *Poems of Ten Years 1924–1934*.

220. WBY to Shakespear, 11 Nov. 1933, Wade, 817.

221. GY to Ottoline Morrell, [30 May 1935], HRHRC.

222. Lily to R L-P, 17 June 1935.

223. AY.

224. Lily to R L-P, 17, 24, and 30 June 1935.

225. WBY to Mannin, 24 June 1935, Sligo; passage omitted from Wade, 835.

226. WBY to Francis Stuart, 1 July [1935], NLI MS 30,564; WBY to Dulac, 6 July 1935, Hobby, 205.

227. Pamela Travers to WBY, 18 July 1935, *LTWBY* ii. 578.

228. GY to MacGreevy, 6 Mar. 1939; *Irish Times*, 22 July 1935; Gibbon, quoting Mrs Constantine Curran, *Masterpiece and the Man*, 186.

229. Lily to R L-P, 30 July 1935; WBY to Wellesley, 26 July 1935, Wade, 838. Yeats's short poem 'The Choice' (1931) opens with the lines 'The intellect of man is forced to choose | Perfection of the life, or of the work, | And if it take the second must refuse | A heavenly mansion, raging in the dark.'

230. Hone, *W. B. Yeats*, 451; but see WBY to Wellesley, 23 Dec. 1936: 'You chose those two Kipling poems, my wife made the selections from my own work. All the rest I did.' Yeats, *Letters on Poetry*, 115; Wade, 875–6 and 'she [GY] has informed this author that she had nothing whatsoever to do with the choice of poets or poems', Taylor (ed.), *Frank Pearce Sturm*, 56.

231. GY to WBY, 9 Jan. 1936; AY.

232. WBY to Ruddock, 25 Feb. and [late Mar.] 1935, McHugh (ed.), *Ah, Sweet Dancer*, 36, 38–9; WBY to Wellesley, 6 July 1935, Wade, 837.

233. WBY to Ruddock, 13 July 1935, McHugh (ed.), *Ah, Sweet Dancer*, 41.

234. WBY to Wellesley, 27 July 1935, Yeats, *Letters on Poetry*, 18.

235. Wellesley to WBY, 21 June 1935, ibid. 7; WBY to Wellesley, 26 July 1935, ibid. 11.

236. This is probably when George and Michael made the tour of the Lake District, AY.

237. AY, unpublished memoirs.

238. Lily to R L-P, 1 Oct. 1935.

239. WBY to GY, 19 Aug. 1935.

240. WBY to Wellesley, 25 Sept. 1935, Yeats, *Letters on Poetry*, 29; Wade, 841.

241. GY to WBY, [?29 Aug. 1935], and WBY to GY, 29 Aug. 1935.

242. WBY to Ruddock, 11 Aug. 1935, McHugh (ed.), *Ah, Sweet Dancer*, 42–3.

243. WBY to Ruddock, 21 Sept. 1935, ibid. 51.

244. WBY to Ruddock, 9 Sept. 1935, ibid. 46.

245. WBY to Ruddock, [1 Sept. 1935], misdated 25 Aug. ibid. 44; WBY to Wellesley, 3 Sept. 1935, Yeats, *Letters on Poetry*, 22.

246. WBY to Wellesley, 25 Sept. 1935, Yeats, *Letters on Poetry*, 29; Wade, 841.

247. GY to R. A. Scott-James, 3, 5, and 18 Oct. 1935, HRHRC.

248. WBY to Wellesley, 14 Oct. 1935, Yeats, *Letters on Poetry*, 35.

249. 'I think you have got a copy of the second book of the Rhymer's Club; if you could lend it to me, my wife can type out of it two poems which I want,' WBY to Gogarty, 24 Oct. 1935, Gogarty, 'My Brother Willie was your Father's Friend', 13.

250. WBY to Wellesley, 15 Nov. 1935, Yeats, *Letters on Poetry*, 37; Wade, 842.

251. Wellesley to WBY, 1 Oct. 1935 and WBY to Wellesley, 18 Nov. 1935, Yeats, *Letters on Poetry*, 31 and 39.

252. WBY to W. J. Turner, 6 Nov. 1935 on Wellesley's behalf inviting him overnight to Penns, H. W. Hausermann, 'W. B. Yeats and W. J. Turner 1935–1937 (with Unpublished Letters)', *English Studies* (Aug. 1960), 242.

253. 18 Nov. 1935, Yeats, *Letters on Poetry*, 38–9. During WBY's visit at the end of Oct. Vita Sackville-West was invited to Penns, after the dinner describing him in her diary as 'handsome man with a fine head but also unfortunately a fine tummy', Victoria Glendinning, *Vita: The Life of V. Sackville-West* (London: Weidenfeld & Nicolson, 1983), 279.

254. WBY to Swami, 15 and 20 Oct. 1935, Delaware.

255. GY to Gogarty, 'Saturday', 19 Oct. 1935, Bucknell. The surgeon was probably Seton Pringle FRCS, of the Royal City of Dublin Hospital, who practised at 7 Fitzwilliam Place; the infection may have been neurofibromytosis.

256. WBY to Mannin, 31 July 1935, Sligo.

257. Shakespear to WBY, 18 July 1935, 'Olivia Shakespear: Letters to W. B. Yeats', 101.

258. WBY to Gwyneth Foden, 5 and 28 July, 11 Aug. 1935, HRHRC. I am indebted to Joan Lawrence for copying this and other letters.

259. WBY to Wellesley, 15 and 28 Nov. 1935, Yeats, *Letters on Poetry*, 37 and 39–40; Wade, 842–3.

260. WBY to Turner, 25 Nov. 1935, Hausermann, 'W. B. Yeats and W. J. Turner', 243; WBY to Mannin, 19 Dec. 1935, Sligo.

261. GY to WBY, 9 Dec. 1935.

262. GY to WBY, 4 Dec. 1935; Lily to R L-P, 2 Dec. 1935; WBY to Mannin, 19 Dec. 1939, Sligo.

263. WBY to GY, 15, 21, 26, and 28 Dec. 1935; GY to Ellmann, interview notes with GY, 17 Jan. 1947, Tulsa; WBY to Mannin, 19 Dec. 1935, Sligo.

264. Lily to R L-P, 23 June 1936.

265. AY.

266. GY to WBY, 18 Jan. 1936.

267. GY to WBY, 9, 18, 20, and 29 Dec. 1935, 6, 20, and 21 Jan. 1936.

268. GY to WBY, [?early Jan. 1936].

269. GY to League of British Dramatists, 6 Dec. 1935, BL Add. MS 56,862/6; GY to Macmillan of New York, 9 Jan. 1936, NYPL.
270. WBY to GY, [?6 Jan. 1936]; WBY and GY to Wellesley, 6 July 1936, HRHRC.
271. GY to WBY, 20 Jan. 1936.
272. GY to WBY, 21 Jan. 1936.
273. GY to Lily, 18 Dec. 1935.
274. Austin Clarke to WBY, 15 May 1934, *LTWBY* ii. 562.
275. GY to Violet Gordon, 7 Jan. 1935.
276. GY to WBY, 1 Jan. 1935.
277. GY to WBY, 29 Dec. 1935.

CHAPTER 18: MAJORCA

1. GY to WBY, 4 Dec. 1935; WBY to GY, 15 Dec. 1935 and [?6 Jan. 1936]; WBY to Mannin, 6 Jan. 1936, Sligo; GY to WBY, 9 Jan. 1936.
2. GY to WBY, 20 Jan. 1936; WBY to GY, [24 and 27 Jan.] 1936.
3. GY to WBY, 24 June 1937.
4. GY to Lily and ECY, 'Sunday' [2 Feb. 1936].
5. Dolly Robinson to MacGreevy, 5 Feb. [1936], TCD MS 8103; GY to Wellesley, 10 Feb. 1936, JK.
6. Gogarty to Reynolds, 21 Feb. 1936, bMS Am. 1787, Harvard.
7. Swami to Ruddock, 29 Jan. and 1 Feb. 1936, McHugh (ed.), *Ah, Sweet Dancer*, 72–3.
8. GY to Wellesley, 12 Mar. 1936, JK; misdated 16th and reference to Foden omitted in Yeats, *Letters on Poetry*, 52.
9. Ellmann interview notes with GY, 17 Jan. 1947, Tulsa; WBY to Wellesley, 26 Apr. 1936, the reference to Foden omitted in Yeats, *Letters on Poetry*, 60–1.
10. Stony Brook.
11. Gogarty to Reynolds, 14 Nov. 1936, bMS Am. 1787, Harvard.
12. Ellmann, *The Man and the Masks*, 1979 preface, p. xxxi; WBY to Wellesley, 20 Nov. 1937, Yeats, *Letters on Poetry*, 149.
13. GY to Lily and ECY, 2 Mar. 1936.
14. Lily to R L-P, 18 and 25 Feb., 2 Mar. 1936.
15. GY to Lily and ECY, 2 Mar. 1936.
16. GY to Wellesley, 12 Mar. 1936, JK; WBY to Mannin, [postmark 8 Apr. 1936], Sligo.
17. GY to Wellesley, 12 Mar. 1936, JK.
18. Pearce, 'Hours with the Domestic Sibyl', 490–1.
19. WBY to Shakespear, 10 and 26 Apr. 1936, Wade, 852, 854.
20. Lily to R L-P, 24 Mar. 1936.
21. WBY to Shakespear, 10 Apr. 1936, Wade, 852.
22. WBY to Mannin, [postmark 8 Apr. 1936], Sligo.
23. WBY to Wellesley, 6 Apr. 1936, Yeats, *Letters on Poetry*, 54–6; Wade, 848–50.
24. May Courtney to R L-P, 16 Apr. 1936.
25. Clifford Bax, *Inland Far* (London: Lovat Dickson, 1933), 227.

26. St John Ervine, 'At the Play', *Observer*, 5 Feb. 1939.

27. Tom Buchanan, *Britain and the Spanish Civil War* (Cambridge: Cambridge University Press, 1991), 41.

28. Ellmann to his parents, 14 Sept. 1946, Tulsa.

29. AY.

30. WBY to Mannin, 14 June 1936, Sligo.

31. Dublin *Evening Herald* front page, 13 May 1936.

32. Various details drawn from Hobby, 214–19; WBY to Shakespear, 22 May 1936, Wade, 856; McHugh (ed.), *Ah, Sweet Dancer*, 93–8; WBY to Swami, 25 May 1936, Delaware; WBY, introduction to Margot Ruddock, *The Lemon Tree* (London: J. M. Dent, 1937), pp. ix–xiv and 2–9; Hone, *W. B. Yeats*, 478.

33. Gogarty to Reynolds, 20 July 1936, bMS Am. 1787, Harvard.

34. Ruddock, *The Lemon Tree*, pp. ix–xiv.

35. Ruddock to WBY, [?July 1936], McHugh (ed.), *Ah, Sweet Dancer*, 113.

36. Dated 12 May 1936, reproduced in 'Yeats and India', *Yearly Review*, 3, 112–13.

37. Swami to WBY, 18 May 1936, MBY.

38. Swami to WBY, 16 July 1936, MBY.

39. Unsigned fragment addressed to GY, dated 18 May 1936, Stony Brook.

40. WBY to Shakespear, 10 Apr. 1936, Stony Brook; sentences omitted in Wade, 852.

41. WBY to Swami, 25 May 1936, Delaware; John Harwood provides a useful summary of many of these activities in 'Appendix: Yeats, Shri Purohit Swami, and Mrs Foden', *YA* (1988), 102–7.

42. Foden to Seán O'Faoláin, 19 Oct. 1936, copy of letter in Ellmann's possession, qtd. in Guha, *W. B. Yeats: An Indian Approach*, 129.

43. WBY to Sturge Moore, 1 July 1936, Stony Brook.

44. Elizabeth Pelham to WBY, 8 and 30 July 1936, *LTWBY* ii. 582–5 and a series of letters throughout July and Aug. 1936, Stony Brook.

45. Foden addressed to 'Mr W. B. Yeats', but clearly meant for GY, 11 Dec. 1936, Stony Brook.

46. WBY to Swami, 21 Dec. 1936, Delaware.

47. Foden to Mrs Sturge Moore, 28 Jan. 1937 and Marie Sturge Moore to Foden, 17 Feb. 1937, ULL, MS 978/31/188, 194.

48. Sturge Moore to GY, 4 Feb. 1937.

49. GY to Marie Sturge Moore, 6 Feb. 1937, TS carbon, MBY.

50. WBY to Swami, 27 Feb. 1937, Delaware.

51. WBY to Shakespear, 22 May 1936, Wade, 856.

52. AY, unpublished memoirs.

53. Lily to R L-P, 8 and 16 June 1936.

54. GY to WBY, [?10 June 1936].

55. Robinson to Dolly Robinson, 19 June 1936, TCD MS 9686.

56. GY to WBY, 15 June 1936.

57. Gogarty to Reynolds, 15 June and 14 Nov. 1936, bMS Am. 1787, Harvard.

58. GY to WBY, 17 June 1936.

59. WBY to Wellesley, 30 June 1936, Yeats, *Letters on Poetry*, 66–7; Wade, 858; WBY to Dulac, 1 July 1936, Hobby, 206.

60. Lily to R L-P, 21 July 1936.

61. Lily to R L-P, 13 July 1936.

62. Lily to R L-P, 5 July 1936.

63. Lily to R L-P, 23 June 1936.

64. WBY to Wellesley, 26 July 1936, Wade, 859.

65. WBY to Mannin, 1 Aug. 1936, Sligo.

66. AY.

67. WBY to Turner [postmark 24 Aug., but dated 29 July], Hausermann, 'W. B. Yeats and W. J. Turner', 245.

68. Holloway, *Joseph Holloway's Irish Theatre*, ii. 57; Lily to R L-P, 17 Aug. 1936.

69. GY to AY, 20 Aug. 1936.

70. *Signe Toksvig's Irish Diaries*, 341–3; WBY to Wellesley, 14 July 1936, Yeats, *Letters on Poetry*, 73.

71. WBY to Shakespear, 8 July 1932, Wade, 799.

72. WBY to Wellesley, [postmark 20 Apr. 1936], Yeats, *Letters on Poetry*, 58.

73. WBY to Wellesley, 29 Oct. and 8 Nov. 1936, ibid. 99–100.

74. GY to AY, 20 Aug. 1936.

75. WBY to Wellesley, 21 July 1936, Yeats, *Letters on Poetry*, 82.

76. GY to Wellesley, 19 Sept. 1936, ibid. 97–8; WBY to Wellesley, 1 Oct. 1936, ibid. 98.

77. GY to WBY, 30 Sept. 1936.

78. WBY to GY, 1 Oct. 1936; WBY to Macmillan, 29 Sept. 1936, BL Add. MS 55,003/202.

79. GY to WBY, 5 Oct. 1936.

80. Lily to R L-P, 31 Dec. 1935.

81. Charles Burston, interview 5 Jan. 1988; AY.

82. WBY to Wellesley, 5 Aug. 1936, partially omitted in Yeats, *Letters on Poetry*, 86. Without the reference to George, this phrase is usually interpreted quite differently.

83. WBY to Mannin, 4 Oct. 1936, Sligo.

84. WBY to Mannin, 4 Oct. 1936, Sligo. In *Privileged Spectator*, 81–2, Mannin seems to have conflated the events of this evening with an earlier dinner; at neither did she feel warmly towards the Dulacs.

85. WBY to GY, [9] Oct. 1936.

86. AY.

87. Daniel Hoffman recalling George's conversation over tea at the Shelbourne, 27 Mar. 1962, Daniel Hoffman, 'Visiting Mrs Yeats', *Boulevard*, 12/1 and 2 (Winter 1997), 134.

88. WBY to GY, 12 Oct. 1936; GY to WBY, 13 Oct. 1936.

89. WBY to Wellesley, 29 Oct. 1936, JK; passage omitted in both Yeats, *Letters on Poetry*, 100 and Wade, 865.

90. AY, unpublished memoirs. Later reconciled to it, for many years the print hung in her kitchen, again opposite where she sat.

91. GY to Watt, 8 Dec. 1936; Watt to GY, 10 Dec. 1936, North Carolina.

92. WBY to Mannin, 30 Nov. 1936, Sligo; Wade, 869.

93. GY to MacGreevy, 13 Dec. 1936, Elizabeth Ryan.

94. AY. Motteux's translation reads, 'The devil was sick, the devil a monk would be; | The devil was well, and the devil a monk he'd be.'

95. W. J. Maloney, *The Forged Casement Diaries* (Dublin: Talbot Press, 1936).

96. WBY to Wellesley, 18 Feb. 1937 and 4, 7, and 9 Dec. 1936, Yeats, *Letters on Poetry*, 109–11 and 127–8.

97. WBY to GY, [?12 Mar.] and 10 Mar. 1937; Sturge Moore, 'Yeats', *English: The Magazine of the English Association*, 2/11 (1939), 276.

98. GY to MacGreevy, 13 Dec. 1936, Elizabeth Ryan.

99. GY to Marie Sturge Moore, 6 Feb. 1937, TS carbon, MBY.

100. WBY to Wellesley, 28 Jan. 1937, Yeats, *Letters on Poetry*, 122–3.

101. Qtd. in Allt, 'Yeats, Religion and History', 648; WBY to Wellesley, 28 Feb. 1937, Yeats, *Letters on Poetry*, 130.

102. WBY to Wellesley, 8 Feb. 1937, Yeats, *Letters on Poetry*, 126; Wade, 880.

103. Ellmann interview notes with GY, 9 July 1947, Tulsa; GY to Oliver Edwards, 2 Feb. 1941, NLI MS 27,032; WBY to GY, [9 June 1937]; GY to WBY, 11 June 1937.

104. WBY to Mannin, 2 Feb. 1937, Sligo.

105. A total of $US6,000 (approximately £1,200) was contributed in all, less than planned but enough under the circumstances. WBY to Patrick McCartan, 22 Jan. and 21 Feb. 1937, and Eugene F. Kinkead to Patrick McCartan, 22 June 1939, Unterecker, *Yeats and Patrick McCartan*, 384–5, 392–3, and 423; WBY to Heald, 26 July 1937, bMS 338.12, Harvard.

106. Gogarty to McCartan, 16 Apr. 1937, Unterecker, *Yeats and Patrick McCartan*, 398–9.

107. Ellmann interview notes with Frank O'Connor, 15 Aug. 1946, Tulsa.

108. WBY to Scroopes, Bank of Ireland, 18 Dec. 1937, TS copy.

109. WBY to Lily, 20 Aug 1937, Boston College.

110. Lily to R L-P, 21 Aug. 1937.

111. Ibid.

112. AY quoting GY.

113. WBY to Shakespear, 25 July 1934, Wade, 825–6; the Purchases and Royalties book for 3 July 1934 lists a loan of £126 to the Cuala Press, TCD Cuala Archive.

114. Lily to R L-P, 3 Sept. and 31 July 1934. George also told this story to Mrs Constantine Curran, Elizabeth Solterer to WMM.

115. Qtd. by Gibbon, *Masterpiece and the Man*, 148.

116. WBY to Wellesley, 2 July 1936, Yeats, *Letters on Poetry*, 69.

117. Lily to R L-P, 5 June 1928.

118. GY to Pound, 19 Aug. 1928, Yale; Saddlemyer (ed.), 'George, Ezra, Dorothy and Friends', 15; GY to WBY, 24 Mar. 1937.

119. GY to ECY, 30 Dec. 1936; ECY to GY, 31 Dec. 1936, TCD Cuala Archive; WBY to Mannin, 17 Dec. 1937, Sligo; Wade, 903.

120. WBY to Scroopes, [3 Jan. 1938], TS copy.

121. WBY to Wellesley, 5 Sept. 1937, Yeats, *Letters on Poetry*, 144; Wade, 897.

122. Enclosed with letter to ECY of 16 Nov. [1937].

123. WBY to GY, 25 Apr. 1938.

124. GY to WBY, 15 Mar. 1937.

125. WBY to Wellesley, 24 Mar. 1937, Yeats, *Letters on Poetry*, 132–3; WBY to Mannin, 24 Mar. 1937, Sligo.

126. Ethel Mannin, lecture to Yeats Summer School, Sligo, Boston University, Ethel Mannin Papers.

127. WBY to Shri Hamsa, 12 Mar. 1937, qtd. in Mokashi-Punekar, *The Later Phase in the Development of W. B. Yeats*, 264; WBY to Swami, 21 Mar. 1937.

128. Pelham to WBY, 11 Mar. 1937, *LTWBY* ii. 587–9; Stony Brook.

129. WBY to Wellesley, 4 May 1937, JK; postscript omitted in Yeats, *Letters on Poetry*, 135 and Wade, 886–7.

130. GY to WBY, 1 Apr. 1937; WBY to GY, 9 Apr. 1937.

131. WBY to GY, 18 Apr. 1937; WBY to Wellesley, 4 May 1937, Wade, 886.

132. Lily to R L-P, 27 Apr. 1937.

133. WBY to Wellesley, 24 Aug. 1936, Yeats, *Letters on Poetry*, 89–90.

134. WBY to ECY, [n.d.], Boston College. The play was probably *A Full Moon in March*.

135. GY to AY, 21 Aug. 1936.

136. Lily to R L-P, 23 June and 28 Aug. 1936.

137. GY to WBY, 30 Sept. 1936.

138. Interview with Tanya Moiseiwitsch.

139. AY, unpublished memoirs.

140. Moiseiwitsch to AY, 24 Jan. 1941.

141. Interview with Moiseiwitsch.

142. Lily to R L-P, 28 May 1937.

143. GY to WBY, 11 Mar. and 3 Apr. 1937.

144. Dulac to WBY, 11 July 1937, Stony Brook.

145. AY, unpublished memoirs.

146. GY to WBY, 7 July 1937.

147. White, *Edmund Dulac*, 182–3. Later well known as a Resistance fighter in the Second World War, her face was used for the Victory stamp for France which Dulac designed.

148. Lily to R L-P, 14 Mar. 1938.

149. Lily to R L-P, 2 Aug. 1937.

150. GY to WBY, 19 Sept. 1937.

151. GY to WBY, 11 Oct. 1937; WBY to GY, 13 Oct. 1937.

152. Lily to R L-P, 16 and 25 Jan. 1938.

153. Lily to R L-P, 17 and 23 July 1938.

154. WBY to Swami, 7 July 1937, MS fragment of 'First Draft', Stony Brook.

155. Swami to WBY, 5 Aug. 1937, *LTWBY* ii. 592–5; WBY to Swami, 23 Aug. and 6 Sept. 1937, Delaware.

156. Swami to WBY, 8 Jan. 1938; WBY to Swami, 2 Mar., 3 Oct., and 22 Dec. 1938, Delaware.

CHAPTER 19: MENTON

1. WBY to Heald, 29 May 1937, bMS 338.12, Harvard.
2. WBY to Swami, 15 May 1937, Delaware.
3. WBY to Heald, 18 May 1937, bMS 338.12, Harvard; passage omitted in Wade, 888; WBY to Dulac, 27 May 1937, Hobby, 224–5; passage omitted in Wade, 890–1.
4. WBY to Heald, 29 May 1937, bMS 338.12, Harvard.
5. WBY to Dulac, 1 June 1937, Hobby, 226.
6. *Signe Toksvig's Irish Diaries*, 437 n. 31.
7. GY to WBY, 13 June 1937; WBY to GY, 16 June 1937; WBY to Heald, 16 June 1937, bMS 338.12, Harvard.
8. Heald to Dulac, 14 July 1937, Hobby, 255; Matheson to GY, 30 Mar. 1939.
9. WBY to Heald, 26 July 1937, bMS 338.12, Harvard.
10. WBY to GY, 28 June 1937.
11. WBY to GY, 24 June 1937. Warwick Gould quotes a guest at Steyning who claimed WBY was introduced as a widower; given the directness of the Heald sisters, the familiarity of the Dulacs with George, and George's own knowledge of the situation, this seems unlikely. However the visitor, noting the relationship between the poet and Edith, might have assumed such was the case, Warwick Gould, review of Diana Souhami, *Gluck 1895–1978*, in *YA* 9 (1992), 344.
12. GY to WBY, 12 June 1937.
13. GY to WBY, 12, 13, 16 June 1937; WBY to GY, 23 June 1937.
14. WBY to Wellesley, 17 Dec. 1937, Yeats, *Letters on Poetry*, 150–1; passage omitted in Wade, 902.
15. GY to Hone, 18 June 1942.
16. WBY to GY, 28 June and 1 July 1937; Michael Yeats, 'Words and Music', *Yeats Society of Japan Annual Report*, 8 (1973), 13–17; Hobby, 229–43, 251–61; WBY to Dulac, [8 July 1937], Wade, 893. Dulac's musicians were his friends Olive Groves, soprano, and Marie Goossens, harpist, White, *Edmund Dulac*, 175.
17. GY to WBY, 5 July 1937; WBY to Dulac, 8 July 1937, and Dulac to WBY, 4 and 7 July, Hobby, 229–34.
18. GY to WBY, 7 July 1937. Ninette de Valois says the quarrel was patched up by 'two devoted wives', but Helen Beauclerk seems to have borne the brunt of the fallout, Ninette de Valois, *Come Dance with Me* (London: H. Hamilton, 1957), 96.
19. WBY to Turner, [?10 July 1937], Hausermann, 'W. B. Yeats and W. J. Turner', 250; Dulac to WBY, 12 July 1937, *LTWBY* ii. 591–2; Hobby, 254–5.
20. Heald to Dulac, 14 July 1937, Hobby, 255; Dulac to GY, 27 July 1937, qtd. by GY to Hone, 18 June 1942.
21. WBY to GY, [?8] and 15 July 1937.
22. WBY to GY, 31 Mar. 1938.
23. GY to WBY, 7 July 1937.
24. WBY to Heald, 6 Aug. 1937, bMS 338.12, Harvard; passage not in Wade, 895; WBY to Heald, 10 Aug. 1937, bMS 338.12, Harvard.
25. WBY to Wellesley, 5 Sept. 1937, Yeats, *Letters on Poetry*, 144; Wade, 897.

26. ' "Spirit Notes" Reveal Lost Concerto', *News Chronicle*, 22 Sept. 1937.

27. WBY to GY, 27 Sept. 1937.

28. GY to WBY, 28 Sept. 1937.

29. WBY to GY, 29 Sept. 1937.

30. WBY to Swami, 4 July 1938, Delaware.

31. WBY to Heald, 10 Dec. 1937, Wade, 901.

32. WBY to GY, 13 Oct. 1937; WBY to Shakespear, 12 Oct. 1937, HRHRC; GY to WBY, 17 Oct. 1937.

33. WBY to GY, 20 Oct. 1937.

34. GY to WBY, [?22] Oct. 1937; AY.

35. GY to WBY, 21 and 25 Oct. 1937.

36. WBY to GY, 28 Oct. 1937; Lily to R L-P, 1 Nov. 1937.

37. Wellesley to WBY, [31 Oct. 1937]; WBY to Wellesley, 2, 11, and 20 Nov. 1937, HRHRC, partially omitted in Yeats, *Letters on Poetry*, 146–9.

38. Lily to R L-P, 18 Nov. 1937; WBY to Wellesley, 17 Dec. 1937, ibid. 150–1.

39. Hugh Hunt, *The Abbey: Ireland's National Theatre 1904–1978* (New York: Columbia University Press, 1979), 159.

40. WBY to Heald, 10 Aug. and 7 Nov. 1937, bMS 338.12, Harvard.

41. Letter to me from Hugh Hunt, 13 Apr. 1987.

42. WBY to Eric Gorman, 9 Apr. 1938, Emory.

43. Robinson to Dolly Robinson, 16 Jan. 1936, TCD MS 9687.

44. WBY to ECY, 16 Nov. 1937.

45. GY to Heald, 12 May 1938, bMS 338.12, Harvard.

46. WBY to Heald, 28 Nov. 1937, bMS 338.12, Harvard.

47. O'Faoláin, *Vive Moi!*, 308.

48. WBY to Heald, 10 and 21 Dec. 1937, bMS 338.12, Harvard.

49. Ellmann to me, 31 July 1985.

50. Lily to R L-P, 27 Dec. 1937.

51. GY to AY, 19 Feb. 1938.

52. GY to AY, Nov. and Dec. 1937, Jan. 1938.

53. GY to WBY, 4, 11, and 27 Oct. 1937 and 22 Jan. 1938; WBY to GY, 7 Oct. 1937; WBY to AY, 14 Jan. 1938.

54. WBY to GY, 11 Jan. 1938; AY to Moiseiwitsch, 26 Jan. 1938.

55. AY to Moiseiwitsch, 14 Jan. 1938.

56. AY to Moiseiwitsch, 26 Jan. 1938.

57. GY to WBY, 20 and 27 Jan. 1938.

58. GY to Scott-James, 17, 27, and 31 Jan. 1938, HRHRC.

59. Wellesley to WBY, 30 Jan. 1938, Yeats, *Letters on Poetry*, 153.

60. WBY to Wellesley, 26 Jan. 1938, ibid.; Wade, 904.

61. WBY to GY, 23, 24, and 26 Jan. 1938.

62. AY to Moiseiwitsch, 6 Feb. 1938.

63. GY to WBY, 27 Jan. 1938; WBY to GY, 29 Jan. 1938.

64. GY to WBY, 30 Jan. 1938. George's spelling fluctuates between the French (Menton) and the Italian (Mentone).

65. ECY to GY, [?11 Feb. 1938], TCD Cuala Archive.
66. WBY to AY, 10 Feb. 1938.
67. WBY to Heald, 21 Feb. 1938, Wade, 905. The painter was probably LeGallienne's stepdaughter Grace, certainly not the actress Eva.
68. WBY to Heald, 5 and 12 Feb. 1938, bMS 338.12, Harvard.
69. WBY to Mannin, 17 Feb. 1938, Wade, 904; WBY to Heald, 12 Feb. 1938, fragment, bMS 338.12, Harvard.
70. GY to AY, 9 Feb. 1938.
71. WBY to Heald, 24 Feb. and 2 Mar. 1938, bMS 338.12, Harvard.
72. WBY to McCartan, 27 Feb. 1938, Unterecker, *Yeats and Patrick McCartan*, 415–16.
73. WBY to Heald, 2 and 5 Mar. 1938, bMS 338.12, Harvard.
74. GY to AY, 19 Feb. and 6 Mar. 1938.
75. WBY to Wellesley, 15 Mar. 1938, Yeats, *Letters on Poetry*, 160; WBY to Heald, [fragment ?mid-Mar. 1938], bMS 338.12, Harvard.
76. GY to Willy, 30 Mar., 8 and 20 Apr. 1938.
77. WBY to Wellesley, 24 May and 10 June 1938, Yeats, *Letters on Poetry*, 163–5; Archibald MacLeish, 'Public Speech and Private Speech in Poetry', *Yale Review*, 27/3 (Mar. 1938), 536–47.
78. WBY to GY, 6, 25, 26, and 27 Apr. 1938.
79. J. H. Wheelock of Scribner's to A. S. Watt, 24 June 1938, Edward Callan, *Yeats on Yeats: The Last Introductions and the 'Dublin' Edition* (Dublin: Dolmen, 1981), 95; Wheelock to Charles Kingsley, 29 Aug. 1938, ibid. 96.
80. GY to WBY, 29 Apr. 1938.
81. GY to Heald, 6 and 12 May 1938, bMS 338.12, Harvard.
82. GY to Rodgers, BBC Sound Archives.
83. WBY to Shakespear, 18 May 1938, Indiana.
84. WBY to Heald, 24 May and 13 June 1938, bMS 338.12, Harvard.
85. ECY to GY, 10 June 1938; Moiseiwitsch.
86. WBY to Heald, 3 June 1938, bMS 338.12, Harvard.
87. WBY to Heald, 3 and 13 June 1938, bMS 338.12, Harvard.
88. GY to WBY, 23 July 1938.
89. Moiseiwitsch.
90. H. Montgomery Hyde, 'Yeats and Gogarty', *YA* 5 (1987), 158–9.
91. Mary Colum, *Saturday Review of Literature*, 19/3–4 (25 Feb. 1939), 14; Mary Colum, *Life and the Dream* (New York: Doubleday, 1947), 423–4.
92. Vernon Watkins to GY, 1 Feb. 1939, Stony Brook.
93. 3 July 1938, Oshima, *W. B. Yeats and Japan*, 101–3 and plate 38.
94. ECY to James Healy, 18 May 1938, Stanford; WMM; ECY to Healy, 30 May 1938, qtd. by Michael Stanford in 'A Lasting Little Memorial', *W. B. Yeats and the Irish Renaissance* (Stanford, Calif.: Stanford University Libraries, 1990), 52.
95. Lily to R L-P, 7 June 1938; memories of AY and Moiseiwitsch; de Vere White, *A Fretful Midge*, 180.
96. WBY to GY, 13 July 1938; GY to WBY, 14 July 1938.

97. WBY to GY, 21 and 22 July 1938.

98. GY to AY, [early Aug. 1938].

99. WBY to Heald, 11 Aug. 1938, bMS 338.12, Harvard.

100. GY to WBY, 26 July 1938 (two letters written the same day).

101. WBY to Heald, 15 Aug. 1938, bMS 338.12, Harvard.

102. WBY to Wellesley, 15 Aug. 1938, Yeats, *Letters on Poetry*, 184; Wade, 913.

103. WBY to Heald, 4 Sept. 1938, bMS 338.12, Harvard.

104. WBY to Wellesley, 15 Aug. 1938, Yeats, *Letters on Poetry*, 184; Wade, 913; WBY to Mannin, 22 Aug. 1938, Wade, 914; GY to Edwards, 2 Feb. 1941. The essay was 'Rilke and the Conception of Death' by William Rose in William Rose and G. Craig Houston (eds.), *Rainer Maria Rilke: Aspects of his Mind and Poetry* (London: Sidgwick & Jackson, 1938), presentation copy in YL dated June 1938.

105. WBY to Wellesley, 2 Oct. 1938, HRHRC.

106. Lily to WBY, 1 Sept. 1938.

107. Notes of Ethel Mannin's lecture to the Yeats Summer School, Sligo, Boston University, Ethel Mannin Papers.

108. Beatrice Elvery to Monk Gibbon, Queen's; WBY to Maud Gonne, 22 Aug. 1938, White and Jeffares (eds.), *Gonne–Yeats Letters*, 452; Hone, *W. B. Yeats*, 470.

109. WBY to GY, 27 Oct. 1938.

110. Lily to R L-P, 30 Sept. 1938.

111. ECY to Patrick McCartan, 15 June 1939, Boston University, Cuala Press Archive.

112. Nelly to Dorothy, 5 Oct. 1938, Yale.

113. Pound to GY, 9 Oct. 1938, 'Ezra Pound Letters to William Butler Yeats', ed. Terrell, 46.

114. GY to WBY, 8 Nov. 1938; John Harwood, introduction to 'Olivia Shakespear: Letters to W. B. Yeats', *YA* 6 (1988), 59.

115. Nelly to Pound, 26 Oct. 1938, Yale.

116. Nelly to Dorothy, 12 Oct. 1938, Yale.

117. ECY to James Healy, 19 Oct. 1938 and 19 Jan.1939, Stanford.

118. GY to WBY, 1 Nov. 1938.

119. Annabel Parker McCann, 'American Women Rejoice with Irish in Continuation of Cuala Industries', with photographs of the Yeats sisters and illustrations of embroidery and the press, *New York Sun*, 4 Jan. 1939.

120. WBY to Heald, [?late Sept. 1938], bMS 338.12, Harvard.

121. WBY to Wellesley, 2 Oct. 1938, HRHRC.

122. WBY to Heald, 24 Oct. 1938, bMS 338.12, Harvard.

123. WBY to GY, 27 Oct. and 17 Nov. 1938.

124. Lily to R L-P, 28 Oct. 1938; GY to WBY, 1 Nov. 1938.

125. GY to WBY, [?6 Nov. 1938], bMS 338.12, Harvard; GY to WBY, 8, 10, and 22 Nov. 1938; WBY to GY, 6, 9, 11, 13, and 18 Nov. 1938.

126. Lily to R L-P, 12 Nov. 1938. They most likely went to the Metropole, which was advertising *In Old Chicago* with Tyrone Power, Alice Fay, and Don Ameche.

127. WBY to GY, 17 Nov. 1938.

128. GY to WBY, 15 Nov. 1938.

129. Lily to R L-P, 26 Nov. 1938.
130. WBY to GY, 13 Nov. 1938.
131. GY to WBY, 22 Nov. 1938.
132. GY to AY, 'Monday' [28 Nov. 1938].
133. GY to AY, 28 Nov. 1938; WBY to DW, 1 Dec. 1938, Yeats, *Letters on Poetry*, 190–1; Wade, 918.
134. Lily to R L-P, 19 Dec. 1938.
135. Dorothy Wellesley, *Far Have I Travelled* (London: James Barrie, 1952), 62–3, 165.
136. Ethel Smyth to Wellesley, 31 Jan. 1939, HRHRC.
137. WBY to Heald, 22 Dec. 1938, bMS 338.12, Harvard.
138. Yeats, *Letters on Poetry*, 192; Ellmann, *The Man and the Masks*, 1979 preface, p. xxv; Moore, *The Unicorn*, 434.
139. WBY to Heald, 1, 9, and [?14 Jan. 1939], bMS 338.12, Harvard.
140. WBY to Higgins, 24 Dec. 1938, Hobby, 264.
141. GY, notes for T. R. Henn, Aug. 1948.
142. WBY to Heald, 1 Jan. 1939, bMS 338.12, Harvard; WBY to AY, 4 Jan. 1939; according to the inscription in a copy of WBY's *Collected Poems* given her by GY, Tanya finally departed on 27 February 1939, Moiseiwitsch.
143. GY to Patrick McCartan, 20 Feb. 1939, Unterecker, *Yeats and Patrick McCartan*, 418.
144. WBY to William Rothenstein, 3 Jan. 1939, Wm. Rothenstein, 'Yeats as a Painter Saw Him', in Gwynn (ed.), *Scattering Branches*, 53; Lily to R L-P, 24 Apr. 1939.
145. WBY to Pelham, 4 Jan. 1938, Wade, 922.
146. A. N. Jeffares, *W. B. Yeats: A New Biography* (London: Hutchinson, 1988), 351. Wellesley in Yeats, *Letters on Poetry*, 194, writes that the tune was for 'The Black Tower', but in *Far Have I Travelled*, 167, she states it was for her poem 'Golden Helen' which is far more probable.
147. TS of *The Death of Cuchulain*, NLI MS 8772; WBY to Kiernan, 22 Jan. 1939, Berg; quoted in Kiernan, 'Lady Gregory and W. B. Yeats', 306.
148. GY to AY, 21 Jan. 1939.
149. GY to MacGreevy, 6 Mar. 1939, TCD MS 8104 with details that differ somewhat from Yeats, *Letters on Poetry*, 195. There is some confusion as to which of these works were corrected as late as 26 Jan. GY to Scott-James, 18 Feb. 1939, implies these were 'Cuchulain Comforted' and 'The Black Tower'; Wellesley definitely names *The Death of Cuchulain* and 'the poem "His Convictions" which he changed to "Under Ben Bulben"'. For exhaustive discussions of the drafts of these works see Jon Stallworthy (ed.), *Yeats: Last Poems* (London: Macmillan, 1969), 194–244, Richard Finneran, *Editing Yeats's Poems: A Reconsideration* (London: Macmillan, 1990), 87–99, *The Death of Cuchulain*, ed. Phillip L. Marcus (London: Cornell University Press, 1982), *passim*, and *Last Poems*, ed. James Pethica, (Ithaca, NY: Cornell University Press, 1997), pp. xxxvi–xli and xliv–xlv; however, none of these has taken into account yet another typewriter, that belonging to Edith Shackleton Heald.
150. Pearce, 'Hours with the Domestic Sibyl', 500–1. Preserved with the hair and the rings is a small package that looks like dried blood.

151. GY to AY, 28 Jan. 1939.
152. *Tupper (Canon A. D. Tupper-Carey): A Memoir of a Very Human Parish Priest*, by his friend Lord Lang of Lambeth sometime Archbishop of Canterbury (London: Constable, 1945); Canon Tupper-Carey left Monte Carlo when the Germans occupied France, and died in England in 1943.
153. May 1920, *YVP* iii. 22; WBY's 'Second comment' on GY's letter concerning his introduction to *The Words upon the Window-Pane*, Nov. 1931.
154. Dermod O'Brien to GY, 1 Feb. 1939.
155. Elizabeth Heine, 'W. B. Yeats' Map in his Own Hand', *biography*, 1/3 (Summer 1978); 'At the time of Yeats's death, Uranus was in conjunction with Pluto opposite his Ascendant, pointing to the radical breaking free of death.' Brian Arkins, 'Towards an Astrological Reading of Yeats', *Yeats-Eliot Review*, 11/3 (Summer 1992), 66.
156. '. . . as no privacy could be secured for telegrams to Dublin. I thought it was rather a roundabout way of doing things, from Beaulieu to Dublin via the Weald of Kent, but did what I was asked,' qtd. by Glendinning, *Vita: The Life of V. Sackville-West*, 299.
157. Lily to R L-P, 4 Feb. 1939.
158. Mabel O'Brien to Lily, 29 Jan. 1939; Lily to R L-P, 4 Feb. 1939.
159. Heald, notes Harvard, bMS 338.12; Heald to Bernard Price, 24 Aug. 1968, I am grateful to R. J. Gluckstein for making available to me the papers in his possession; Gerald Flanagan, 'Yeats' Sussex-haven', *Irish Press*, 13 Nov. 1965, 10.
160. As described in Christie's catalogue for the sale of 5 July 1978, *New Poems*, ed. J. C. C. Mays and Stephen Parrish (Ithaca, NY: Cornell University Press, 2001), 367.
161. GY to Dulac, 9 Jan. 1948, Gluckstein.
162. Municipal record no. 140 dated 7 Feb. indicating 'dépôt au dépositoire de M. Yeats'; Dermod O'Brien to GY, 1 Feb. 1939, providing his accounting; Lily to R L-P, 4 Feb. 1939.
163. Dermod O'Brien to 'Lynx', 31 Jan. 1939, qtd. in Lennox Robinson, *Palette and Plough*, a pen-and-ink drawing of Dermod O'Brien, PRHA (Dublin: Browne & Nolan, 1948), 187–8; Maurice Butat, la Maison Roblot, to GY, 14 Feb. 1939; Municipal Records courtesy the Mayor of Roquebrune.

PART V. MAPPING

1. Automatic script, 26 Aug. 1919, *YVP* ii. 390–1.
2. GY to WBY, 1 Jan. 1935.
3. GY to MacGreevy, [?Dec. 1934], TCD MS 8104.
4. GY to AY, 15 Mar. 1939.
5. Automatic script, 4 Mar. 1918, *YVP* i. 371.

CHAPTER 20: PALMERSTON ROAD

6. R. F. Foster summarizes many of the accounts in ' "When the newspapers have forgotten me": Yeats, Obituarists, and Irishness', *YA* 12 (1996), 163–79; Hilda Matheson and Dorothy Wellesley seem to have had something to do with an account in *The Times*, Hilda Matheson to GY, 24 Feb. 1939.

7. Hilda Matheson to GY, 4 Feb. 1939; Lily to R L-P, 4 Feb. 1939.
8. Higgins to Maud Gonne, [n.d.], qtd. in White and Jeffares (cds.), *Gonne-Yeats Letters*, 453-4.
9. NLI 30,801 and 30,772.
10. Unterecker, *Yeats and Patrick McCartan*, 417.
11. Note written 3 Feb. 1939 by E. Beatrice Gibbes. I am indebted to Revd Dr Charles Fryer for a copy.
12. GY to MacGreevy, 6 Mar. 1939, TCD MS 8104.
13. As printed in the Sligo newspapers; later publications drop the 'e' from 'Drumcliffe'.
14. Lily to Molly and Padraic Colum, 22 Feb. 1939, TS copy NYPL; Gogarty to McCartan, 31 Mar. 1939, Unterecker, *Yeats and Patrick McCartan*, 420. Other poems were read by V. C. Clinton Baddeley, Clinton Baddeley to GY, [early Mar. 1939].
15. Qtd. in Ellmann's 1979 preface, *The Man and the Masks*, p. xxxi.
16. WBY to Wellesley, 7 Sept. 1938, HRHRC.
17. GY to E. F. Kinkead, 21 Feb. 1939, Unterecker, *Yeats and Patrick McCartan*, 419-20.
18. GY never replied to Jean Hall, and the film languished in a bureau drawer for another fifty years, although the Halls sent the Yeatses some stills.
19. David R. Wilson to GY, 18 Feb. 1939.
20. Lily to Mary [Gibbon], 14 Feb. 1939, Queen's.
21. Revd James Wilson to GY, 7 Feb. 1939 with annotations by GY.
22. Lily to R L-P, 1 Mar. 1939.
23. ECY to H. O. White, 26 July 1939, TCD MS 3777.
24. Bruce Arnold, *Jack Yeats* (New Haven: Yale University Press, 1998), 286.
25. GY to E. F. Kinkead, 21 Feb. 1939, Unterecker, *Yeats and Patrick McCartan*, 419-20.
26. I am indebted to John Keohane for his memories of conversations with GY.
27. GY to C. P. Curran, 22 Feb. 1939, UCD.
28. Burns & Laird Steamship Company to GY, 21 Feb. 1939; Rupert Gordon to GY, 28 Mar. 1939.
29. Lily to R L-P, 8 May 1939; 'WBY will be "planted" in Drumcliffe, Sligo, about the first week of October,' GY to W. F. Stead, 14 May 1939, James M. and Mariel-Louise Osborn Collection, Bernecke Rare Book and Manuscript Library, Yale; GY to James Healy, 14 Aug. 1940, Stanford; James McDermott to GY, 6 June 1939.
30. 'Epilogue', Wade, 923; GY to Allan Wade, 20 Nov. 1953 (courtesy Rupert Hart-Davis). GY read and approved Wade's manuscript.
31. Taken by the actor Peter Judge ('F. J. McCormick') during an afternoon tea party at Sorrento Cottage ('Georgie Yeats' to Albert Bender, 19 June 1939; Mills).
32. Iseult Stuart to GY, [n.d.]
33. Dermott MacManus to GY, 7 Feb. 1939, and GY to 'My dear Dermott', 29 Apr. 1939. I am indebted to Colin Smythe for copies of this correspondence.
34. Lily to R L-P, 30 Mar. 1939.
35. GY to Oliver Edwards, 22 Apr. 1944, NLI MS 27,032.

36. GY to Desmond FitzGerald, 10 Apr. 1939, UCD.
37. Elizabeth Pelham to GY, [?mid-Feb. 1939], Stony Brook.
38. GY to Patrick McCartan, 20 Feb. 1939, Unterecker, *Yeats and Patrick McCartan*, 418–20; GY to Patrick McCartan, 11 Aug. 1939, G. M. Harper.
39. Hilda Matheson to GY, 24 Feb. 1939.
40. 'An Interview with Mr Junzo Sato', Oshima, *W. B. Yeats and Japan*, 123.
41. Scott-James to GY, 8 Feb. 1939; GY to Scott-James, 18 Feb. 1939, HRHRC.
42. Lily to R L-P, 21 Aug. 1937.
43. Last will and testament of William Butler Yeats. In a letter to me, 19 Mar. 1987, Hugh Hunt recalls Dolly Robinson saying that George 'exhibited a far more positive side of her character after his death'.
44. Harold Macmillan to GY, 6 and 8 Feb. 1939, NLI MS 30,248; GY to Macmillan, 13 Feb. 1939, TS carbon NLI MS 30,248. The minutes of the Cuala board meeting of 10 Mar. 1939 state that the new book in preparation will be called ' "Last Poems" by W. B. Yeats', TCD Cuala Archive.
45. Harold Macmillan to GY, 28 Feb. 1939, NLI MS 30,248; WBY to Watt, 2 Mar. 1937, qtd. in Finneran, *Editing Yeats's Poems*, 18; GY to Thomas Mark, 15 Apr. 1939, TS carbon NLI MS 30,248.
46. John Hall Wheelock to Charles Kingsley, 1 Feb. 1939, Callan, *Yeats on Yeats*, 98; GY to Charles Kingsley, 15 and 19 Feb. 1939.
47. Macmillan to Wheelock, 19 May 1939, BL Add. MS 55,824/179. See Callan, *Yeats on Yeats*, 87–103 and Finneran, *Editing Yeats's Poems*, 5–23 for blow-by-blow descriptions of the progress (and lack thereof) of Scribner's eleven-volume 'limited, autographed, subscription edition of the complete works of Yeats'.
48. GY to Tom Mark, 13 Apr. 1939, qtd. in Finneran, *Editing Yeats's Poems*, 40; Mark to GY, 21 Apr. 1939, NLI MS 30,248; GY to A. S. Watt, qtd. by Watt to Harold Macmillan, 17 Apr. 1939, BL Add. MS 54,904/171.
49. A. S. Watt to GY, 26 Apr. 1939, NLI MS 30,248; Callan, *Yeats on Yeats*, 100; Wheelock to Macmillan, 12 May 1939, and Macmillan to Wheelock, 19 May 1939, qtd. in Finneran, *Editing Yeats's Poems*, 21.
50. Mark to GY, 14 Apr. 1939 and GY to Mark, 17 Apr. 1939, TS carbon, NLI MS 30,248.
51. Harold Macmillan to GY, 13 June 1939; GY to Macmillan, 14 June 1939; GY to Mark, 14 June 1939, NLI MS 30,248. The first alarm was raised by Curtis Bradford, *Modern Language Notes* (June 1961), repr. as *Yeats's 'Last Poems' Again* (Dublin: Dolmen, 1966).
52. GY to A. S. Watt, 26 Feb. 1939, TS carbon, MBY.
53. GY to F. R. Higgins, 27 Feb. 1939.
54. Lily to Monk Gibbon, 7 May 1939, Queen's; Lily to R L-P, 6 May 1941.
55. Lily to R L-P, 10 Apr. 1939; Gwynn (ed.), *Scattering Branches* included among other contributors Maud Gonne, William Rothenstein, W. G. Fay, Edmund Dulac, F. R. Higgins, and L. A. G. Strong.
56. Joseph Hone to GY, 14 Feb. [1939, misdated 1938]; Oliver Edwards, 1973 Sligo lecture.
57. Harold Macmillan to GY, 9 May 1939, NLI MS 30,248.

58. Lily to R L-P, 5 Mar. 1939; ECY to Gordon Bottomley, 5 Mar. 1939, Berg.

59. *The Times* (London).

60. GY to AY, 15 Mar. 1939.

61. John Masefield to ECY, [after 6 Feb. 1939], Stony Brook.

62. 'Fanny' [Una] Ellis-Fermor to Lily, [n.d.], MBY.

63. GY to Harold Macmillan, 6 May 1939, NLI MS 30,248.

64. Finneran, *Editing Yeats's Poems*, 39–40.

65. GY to Mark, 17 Apr. 1939. I am not as certain as Finneran that she would have consulted Frank O'Connor, whom she did not yet know very well, Finneran, *Editing Yeats's Poems*, 54 n. 1.

66. Ellmann interview notes with GY, 8 Dec. 1946, Tulsa.

67. Matheson to GY, 30 Mar. 1939; Wellesley to GY, 27 Mar. 1939.

68. Matheson to GY, 16 Apr. 1939.

69. Harold Macmillan to GY, 5 May 1939; GY to Macmillan, 6 May 1939, TS carbon MBY; Macmillan to GY, 9 May 1939, NLI MS 30,248.

70. Wellesley to Harold Macmillan, 28 May 1939; Watt to GY with enclosures and GY's marginal note, 2 June 1939.

71. Matheson to GY, 26 and 29 June 1939; Wellesley to GY, 29 June 1939; Matheson to GY, 3 July and 6 Aug. 1939.

72. Matheson to GY, 13 July 1939.

73. GY to Robinson, 18 June 1939, Huntington.

74. Sturge Moore to GY, 26 May 1939; Lily to R L-P, 12 June 1939; Maud Gonne to GY, 21 June 1939; Watt to GY, 23 June 1939; Matheson to GY, 26 June 1939.

75. Wellesley to GY, 27 Mar. 1939, and Matheson to GY, 30 Mar. 1939.

76. Hone, *W. B. Yeats*, 410.

77. Lily to R L-P, 13 May, 17 Apr., and 3 June 1939.

78. GY to J. M. Hone, 4 May 1939, HRHRC. Some, chiefly Greek and Latin texts including Mackail's 1930 edition of the *Aeneid*, went to the Jesuit library in Dublin, John O'Meara, 'On the Fringe of Letters', *Irish University Review*, 27/2 (Autumn/Winter 1997), 310 and John O'Meara to me, 13 Feb. 1998; Maurice Craig saw, but did not buy, the 1905 edition of *Coryat's Crudities*, Maurice Craig, *The Elephant and the Polish Question* (Dublin: Lilliput, 1990), 86–7. Some books were also apparently sold through the Dublin booksellers Hodges & Figgis.

79. GY to AY, 10 June 1939.

80. Deirdre Kelly, *Four Roads to Dublin: The History of Ranelagh, Rathmines and Leeson Street* (Dublin: O'Brien Press 1995), 15.

81. John A. Smyth to GY, 1 July 1939; Lily to R L-P, 27 June 1939; John J. Devlin to GY, 6 July 1939.

82. I am grateful to the late AY for her detailed recollections of the layout of the house; other details are drawn from Bradford, 'George Yeats: Poet's Wife', 387–9, and the personal memories of Birgit Bramsbäck, Kathleen Raine, Virginia Moore, Donald Pearce, and myself.

83. Lily to R L-P, 31 Aug. 1939.

84. Kathleen Raine, letter to me, 25 Aug. 1985.

85. Lily to R L-P, 27 June 1939.
86. MBY, *Cast a Cold Eye*, 24–5.
87. GY to MBY, 15 and 21 Aug. 1939.
88. AY's address at Twelfth International James Joyce Conference in Monaco, 12 June 1990.
89. Mrs Jellett to her sister Bay, 21 Feb. 1939, Bruce Arnold; partially quoted in Bruce Arnold, *Mainie Jellett and the Modern Movement in Ireland* (New Haven: Yale University Press, 1991), 190.
90. Lily to R L-P, 15 Nov. 1943.
91. JackBY to AY, 11 Apr. 1947; MacGreevy to Babette Deutsch, 29 May 1947, Washington.
92. Harold Macmillan to GY, 17 Oct. 1939, BL Add. MS 55,830/281; Mark to GY, 19 Oct. 1939, BL Add. MS 55,830/334.
93. Lily to R L-P, 19 Sept., 18 and 28 Oct. 1939.
94. AY, unpublished memoirs.
95. Lily to GY, 22 Mar. 1939; Lily to R L-P, 17 Nov. 1939. Dentist for all of them was Andrew Ganly, playwright and husband of Bridget, artist daughter of Dermod O'Brien.
96. Lily to GY, 28 Apr. 1939.
97. Minutes of 21 Mar., 4 Apr., 25 Aug., TCD Cuala Archive.
98. Shaw to ECY, 17 July 1939; minutes of board meeting for 21 Mar. 1939, TCD Cuala Archive.
99. F. R. Higgins to Patrick McCartan, 3 Apr. 1939, TCD Cuala Archive; ECY to McCartan, 7 June 1939, Unterecker, *Yeats and Patrick McCartan*, 422.
100. Lily to R L-P, 24 Oct. 1939.
101. ECY to Patrick McCartan, 7 June 1939, Unterecker, *Yeats and Patrick McCartan*, 422.
102. Minutes of the Cuala board meeting for 24 July 1939, TCD Cuala Archive.
103. Lily to R L-P, 18 and 28 Dec. 1939, 15 Jan. 1940; ECY to Lily, 10 Jan. 1940.
104. AY.
105. GY to James Healy, 21 June 1940, Stanford; Lily to R L-P, 22 Apr. 1940.
106. Liam Miller, *The Dun Emer Press, Later the Cuala Press* (Dublin: Dolmen, 1973), 105–19.
107. Lily to R L-P, 10 June 1940.
108. Lily to R L-P, 19 Feb. and 23 May 1940.
109. Minutes of the Cuala board meeting for 23 Feb. 1940, TCD Cuala Archive; Lily to R L-P, 11, 19, and 25 Feb., 9 Apr. and 23 May 1940.
110. GY to MacGreevy, 13 Apr. 1926, TCD MS 8104; GY to James Healy, 20 Feb. 1940, Stanford; Lily to R L-P, 25 Feb. and 21 Mar. 1940.
111. GY to Martha (Mrs Oliver St John) Gogarty, 8 June 1940, TCD MS 10,609.
112. James Healy to GY, 19 July 1940.
113. Lewis, *Yeats Sisters and the Cuala*, 182.
114. GY to Healy, 5 and 27 June, 9 July 1940, Stanford; GY to Masefield, 24 June 1940, HRHRC; GY to A. T. de Lury, 11 July 1940, Toronto; GY to Vernon Watkins,

10 Aug. 1940, VFM 1076, Selected Letters of the Yeats Family to Vernon Watkins, Southern Illinois; board minutes of 15 Aug. 1940, TCD Cuala Archives.

115. GY to Patrick McCartan, 4 Jan. 1941, MBY; Patrick McCartan to GY, 26 Jan. 1941; GY to Healy, 6 May, 22 and 25 July 1946, Stanford; James Healy to GY, 2 Aug. 1946.

116. Harold Latham of Macmillan to GY, 31 Oct. 1951.

117. GY to Martha Gogarty, 23 July 1940, Guy St John Williams (ed.), *The Renvyle Letters* (Monastervan: Daletta Press, 2000), 5.

118. Lily to R L-P, 13 Sept. 1940; G. B. Shaw to Lily, 12 and 17 Aug. 1940; Shaw to GY, 29 Aug. 1940; Clifford Bax to GY, 27 Aug., 4 and 5 Sept. 1940; Shaw to A. D. Peters, [n.d.], NLI MS 30,126.

119. Clifford Bax (ed.), *Bernard Shaw – W. B. Yeats: Letters to Florence Farr* (London: Home & Van Thal Ltd., 1946), 33–5.

120. WBY to Wellesley, 23 Dec. 1936, Yeats, *Letters on Poetry*, 115; GY to MBY, 15 Feb. 1968.

121. JackBY to James Healy, 11 Nov. 1948, Stanford.

122. Lily to R L-P, 23 July 1940.

123. GY to Frank O'Connor, 1 May and 27 June 1940, 11 Feb. and 15 Apr. 1941, Boston University, Frank O'Connor Archive.

124. GY to O'Connor, 'Monday' [6? July 1942], perhaps over *La La Noo*, Boston University, Frank O'Connor Archive.

125. Frank O'Connor to GY, [early May 1941]; 'Friday' [?Aug. 1943], Boston University, Frank O'Connor Archive.

126. GY to O'Connor, 23 Aug. 1943, Boston University, Frank O'Connor Archive.

127. Stead to GY, 28 Apr. 1939, qtd. by George Mills Harper, 'William Force Stead's Friendship with Yeats and Eliot', *Massachusetts Review*, 21/1 (Spring 1980), 24–5.

128. GY to O'Connor, 'Monday' [16 Feb. 1943]; O'Connor to GY [incomplete draft] and GY to O'Connor, 'Monday' [?23 Feb. 1943], Boston University, Frank O'Connor Archive. The review was by Raymond Mortimer, 'Books in General', *New Statesman*, 13 Feb. 1943, 111–12. O'Connor's article may have been 'Two Friends: Yeats and AE', *Yale Review*, 29/1 (Sept. 1939), 60–88, abridged for the *Bell* (Feb. 1941), 7–18.

129. Letter from Birgit Bramsbäck to me 2 Sept. 1988, quoting from notes of a meeting with GY on 2 June 1950.

130. GY to O'Connor, 30 Sept. 1942, 24 Nov. and 30 Dec. 1943, Boston University, Frank O'Connor Archive; interview with Evelyn O'Donovan Garbary.

131. F. R. O'Connor to GY, 18 Mar. 1943.

132. 'I was . . . fortunate enough when I was in London in Feb. 1942 to find a copy of THE WANDERINGS OF OISIN 1st ed. 1889 with manuscript corrections in the margins made to many poems. From that book . . . I had Cuala "print" for me *privately* 50 copies with the "corrections" and a frontispiece of the first page of the MSS written in 1886,' GY to James Healy, 13 May 1944, MBY.

133. GY to Oliver Edwards, 22 Apr. 1944, NLI MS 27,032; GY to Reginald A. Addys-Scott, 4 Dec. 1944; minutes of Cuala Industries AGM for 30 Dec. 1944 and 31 Dec. 1945, TCD Cuala Archives; Lily to R L-P, 20 Nov. 1945.

134. GY to Oliver Edwards, 22 Apr., 12 and 14 Sept. 1944, NLI MS 27,032.

135. GY to O'Connor, 19 or 20 Mar. 1941, Boston University, Frank O'Connor Archive; Marie Sturge Moore to Hone, 6 May 1940; Hone to GY, 8 May 1940; Marie Sturge Moore to Hone, 15 May 1940, ULL 978/2/116.

136. GY to John G. Wilson, 27 Sept. 1952, NLI MS 26,748; GY to T. S. Eliot, 21 Nov. 1944. I am indebted to Valerie Eliot for a copy of this letter.

137. Lily to R L-P, 17 Oct. 1940.

138. R. M. Fox, 'Mrs George Yeats: An Appreciation', *Ireland of the Welcomes*, 14/1 (May–June 1965), 21–2.

139. Letter to me from Monk Gibbon, 27 Aug. 1985.

140. Oliver Gogarty, 'Ireland's Great Poet', *Gazette* (Montreal), 24 Apr. 1943.

141. Herman Peschmann, 'W. B. Yeats (1865–1939)', *New English Review*, 20 May 1943, 41–3.

142. GY to Herman Peschmann, 15 June 1943. I am indebted to Warwick Gould for a copy of this letter.

143. Martha Gogarty to Oliver Gogarty, 12 Mar. 1943, and Brenda Gogarty to Martha Gogarty, 1 Nov. 1943, Williams (ed.), *The Renvyle Letters*, nos. 51 and 60.

144. GY to Denis Johnston, 13 and 29 Nov. 1941, TCD MS 10,066. The organizational meeting was held on 28 May 1941.

145. *Joseph Holloway's Irish Theatre*, iii: *1938–1944*, ed. Robert Hogan and Michael J. O'Neill (Dixon, Calif.: Proscenium Press, 1970), 69.

146. Phillips, 'Lennox Robinson on the Dublin Drama League'.

147. Rose, 'A Visit with Anne Yeats', 300; interview with Evelyn O'Donovan Garbary.

148. Lily to R L-P, 7 and 8 Apr. 1941; GY to Frank O'Connor, 15 Apr. 1941, Boston University, Frank O'Connor Archive.

149. *Irish Times*, 2 June 1941.

150. Nelly to Dorothy Pound, 25 June and 9 July 1939, Yale.

151. AY and MBY; Jelly d'Aranyi to GY, 9 Feb. 1942.

152. Lily to R L-P, 3 Feb. 1942.

153. GY to Frank O'Connor, 18 Feb. 1942, Boston University, Frank O'Connor Archive; Lily to R L-P, 27 Mar. 1942; Nelly to Dorothy Pound, 17 Feb. 1939, Yale.

154. Telephone interview with Eleanor Younghughes, 1 Aug. 1985; interview with Brigid Younghughes, 4 Sept. 1987.

155. GY to Heald, 17 Feb. 1942, bMS 338.12, Harvard.

156. GY to Mark, 8 Apr. 1949, Finneran, *Editing Yeats's Poems*, 127; Jon Stallworthy, *Between the Lines*, 4.

157. GY to Book Order Department, Bumpus, NLI MS 26,748.

158. GY to Heald, 17 Feb. 1942, bMS 338.12, Harvard.

159. GY to Oliver Edwards, 20 Apr. 1944, NLI MS 27,032.

160. Eleanor and Brigid Younghughes.

161. GY to Frank O'Connor, 6 Oct. 1942. The money probably went towards the publishing costs of *A Picture Book* by O'Connor with drawings by Elizabeth Rivers (1943).

162. GY to Omar Pound, 16 Dec. 1942, Omar Pound.

163. Dorothy to Agnes Bedford, 1 May 1940, qtd. in Carpenter, *A Serious Character*, 616.

164. Telephone conversation with Omar Pound, June 1989.
165. GY to Evelyn O'Donovan, 4 June [1942], Boston University, Frank O'Connor Archive.
166. GY to James Healy, 6 Sept. 1944, Stanford.
167. GY to AY, 'Tuesday' [12 Sept. 1944].
168. Lily to R L-P, 25 Sept. and 19 Nov. 1944.
169. GY to Desmond FitzGerald, 16 Feb. 1944, UCD.
170. Harold Hyde-Lees to Dorothy, 2 June and 12 July 1952, Indiana.
171. Lily to R L-P, 15 Jan. 1945.
172. Society of Authors to GY, 22 Jan. 1945 and GY to Society of Authors, 29 Jan. 1945, BL MS Add. 56862/80–81.
173. GY to O'Connor, 'Thursday' [9 Feb 1944?], Boston University, Frank O'Connor Archive; Dolly to Lennox Robinson, 15 Feb. [dated 1948], TCD MS 9689.
174. Lily to R L-P, 15 Nov. 1943.
175. MBY, *Cast a Cold Eye*, 47–8.
176. Lennox to Dolly Robinson, 18 Dec. 1947, TCD MS 9688.
177. Lily to R L-P, 28 June 1948.
178. Lily to R L-P, 18 Feb. 1946. JackBY's LLD was bestowed on 3 July 1946.
179. Lily to R L-P, 29 Oct. 1944.
180. JackBY to AY, 17 Jan. 1946.
181. AY unpublished memoirs; Chapman, 'Across the Atlantic: Impressions of England, Ireland and Anne Yeats', 205.
182. GY to AY, 24 May 1965.
183. AY, unpublished memoirs and letters to GY in May 1965; GY to Alan Denson, 14 June 1956, Indiana; GY to AY, 25 Feb. 1959. They were away from 25 May to 11 June 1956; in the autumn of that year AY was a member of the Irish delegation to China.
184. AY.
185. GY to Oliver Edwards, 22 Feb. 1944, NLI MS 27,032; GY to AY, 19 May 1965.
186. Lily to R L-P, 16 June 1948.
187. Dolly to Lennox Robinson, 5 Oct. 1947, TCD MS 9689; Lennox to Dolly Robinson, 15 Oct 1948, TCD MS 9688.
188. Richard Ellmann to his parents, 14 Sept. 1946, Tulsa.
189. Letter to me from Daphne Fullwood (née Bush), 13 Nov. 1985.
190. Macleod, *The Sisters d'Aranyi*, 165.
191. Lily to R L-P, 9 Jan. 1948.
192. A. J. Dolan to GY, [6 Jan. 1948]; 'Poet's Last Wish to be Fulfilled', *Sligo Champion*, 10 Jan. 1948; *The Times*, 6 Jan. 1948.
193. Dulac to GY, 6 and 9 Jan. 1948; GY to Dulac, 9 Jan. 1948; Gluck's memo of 12 Jan. 1948, Gluckstein.
194. MBY.
195. I am grateful to the offices of the Mayor of Menton and Roquebrune, and especially Mme Cécile Kros, for arranging to send me the regulations concerning concessions and exhumations; also to George Sandelescu, J. G. Gasteaud, and the staff of the Princess Grace Library in Monaco for assisting in my preliminary research; and G. V. Downes for help in unravelling the legal codes.

196. 'Acte de concession de terrain dans le cimetière communal', 17 Feb. 1948; Dulac to GY, 18 Feb. 1948; exchanges between Gluck and Dulac throughout Mar. 1948, R. J. Gluckstein. George must have telephoned Dulac on 3 or 4 Mar. 1948 after she received Gluck's letter.

197. Allan Wade to GY, 28 Oct. 1941, Rupert Hart-Davis.

198. Qtd. in Louise Foxcroft, 'Diary', *London Review of Books*, 22/17 (7 Sept. 2000), 32.

199. This fact too would become an issue for later discussion, since Hollis had worn a leather and steel surgical corset; however, his body was 'bent double' from the tuberculosis that ravaged his slight frame, while WBY remained tall and straight until his death, Madge Cockman, letter to the editor, *Independent*, 8 Oct. 1988; Foxcroft, 'Diary', 32.

200. MBY and AY, letter to *Irish Times*, *Independent*, etc., 4 Oct. 1988; Gluck's typed transcript of 'Epitaph', *News Chronicle*, 22 June 1948 (Gluckstein).

201. Lily to R L-P, 16 June 1948.

202. GY to Seán MacBride, 17 Aug. 1948, typescript copy MBY.

203. I am indebted to Bernadette Chambers, archivist, Department of Foreign Affairs; M. Thierry Terrier of the French Embassy in Dublin, and M. Yvon Roe-d'Albert, Minister of Foreign Affairs and Director of Archives, Paris, for their assistance in uncovering the relevant documents.

204. Maurice Collis, *The Journey up: Reminiscences 1934–1968* (London: Faber, 1970), 82–6; John Ormond Thomas, 'W. B. Yeats Comes Home to Sligo', *Picture Post*, 41/2 (9 Oct. 1948), 10–13; GY to MacGreevy, 19 Sept. 1948, TCD MS 8104. I am grateful to John Keohane and James McGarry for making available to me copies of the local newspaper reports.

205. GY to Frank O'Connor, 29 Aug. 1948, Harriet O'Donovan Sheehy and Boston University, Frank O'Connor Archive. According to James Matthews, 'The Irish government intended to send Minister of External Affairs, Seán McBride . . . but stipulated that Frank O'Connor not be the one to give the oration. Jack Yeats, therefore, decided that no speeches of any kind would be allowed,' James Matthews, *Voices* (New York: Athenaeum, 1983), 326, 421 n. 27.

206. O'Connor to Evelyn O'Donovan, 31 Aug. 1948. I am indebted to Harriet O'Donovan Sheehy for a copy of this letter.

207. *Sunday Independent*, 12 Sept. 1948, 4, John Keohane.

208. Martha Gogarty to Oliver St John Gogarty, 23 Sept. 1948, Williams (ed.), *The Renvyle Letters*, no. 160.

209. GY to MacGreevy, 31 Aug. 1948; MacGreevy to Babette Deutsch, 27 Sept. 1948, Washington.

210. MacGreevy to Babette Deutsch, 27 Sept. 1948, Washington.

211. GY to MacGreevy, 15 Sept. 1952, TCD MS 8104; Thomas MacGreevy, 'Uileachan Dubh O', *Capuchin Annual* (1952), 221–9. I am indebted to Mari McKay for a copy of this article.

212. Qtd. in Michael Moynihan, 'A Poet and his Daughter', *Sunday Times* (London), 14 Aug. 1966, 32.

213. MacGreevy to Wallace Stevens, 28 Sept. 1939, Huntington; GY to MacGreevy, 19 Sept. 1948, TCD MS 8104; Harold Hyde-Lees to AY, 27 May 1963.

214. Seán MacBride to GY, 30 Mar. 1949; I am grateful to Anna MacBride White and Catríona Lawlor for their assistance in trying to find the missing manuscripts, which may have been drafts relating to *At the Hawk's Well*, a performance of which was presented at a diplomatic reception at Iveagh House given by External Affairs and directed by Ria Mooney, GY to Ria Mooney, 26 Mar. 1949, Berg.

215. See plates 2 and 3, *YA* 8 (1991).

216. J. Biancheri to Dulac, 16 Feb. 1948, Gluckstein; Diana Souhami, *Gluck 1895–1978* (London: Pandora, 1988); Rian Evans (daughter of Ormond), 'Whose Body Really Lies Beneath this Headstone?', *Irish Times*, 11 Oct. 2000.

217. Lily to R L-P, 23 Apr. 1948.

218. Lily to R L-P, 16 Oct. 1948; AY; Gráinne Yeats.

219. Lennox to Dolly Robinson, 14 Apr. 1949, TCD MS 9686.

220. Lennox to Dolly Robinson, 15 [misdated 8] May 1949, TCD MS 9686.

221. GY to Ellmann, 1 Jan. 1951, Tulsa.

222. Ellmann to his family, 21 Apr. 1953, Tulsa.

223. Pádraig Yeats now has two sons of his own.

224. JackBY to J. A. Healy, 21 May 1949, Stanford.

225. GY to Robinson, 13 Apr. 1949, Huntington.

226. GY to Ellmann, 18 Jan. 1949, Tulsa.

CHAPTER 21: SEEKERS AND FRIENDS

1. Stephen Spender, 13 Mar. 1950, *Journals 1939–1983*, ed. John Goldsmith (London: Faber & Faber, 1985), 104–5.

2. Letter to me from Elizabeth Curran Solterer, 14 Nov. 1991.

3. Interview with Donald Torchiana, 20 Oct. 1985; letter to me from H. Lovat Dickson, 19 June 1985.

4. This composite description is drawn from published accounts or letters to me by Hazard Adams, Curtis Bradford, John Byars, David Clark, Saros Cowasjee, H. Lovat Dickson, David Greene, Daniel Hoffman, Richard Kain, Hugh Kenner, John Montague, Virginia Moore, Roger Parisious, Thomas Parkinson, Donald Pearce, Kathleen Raine, Ben Reid, Jon Stallworthy, Donald Torchiana, and my own recollections.

5. Parkinson, 'Some Recent Work on Yeats', 745–6.

6. Stallworthy, *Singing School*, 229.

7. Qtd. in Ida Grehan, 'Miss Yeats, and the Problem of Living in a Poet's Shadow', *Daily Telegraph*, 15 Jan. 1971, 15.

8. GY to MacGreevy, 13 Apr. 1948, TCD MS 8104; the line 'and some old cardinal | Pacing with half-closed eyelids' occurs in 'Upon a Dying Lady: VI Her Courage'.

9. Letter to me from Kathleen Raine, 25 Aug. 1985; interview with John Montague.

10. Qtd. in Ellmann, *The Man and the Masks*, 1979 preface, p. xxi.

11. Ellmann interview notes with GY, 9 July 1947, Tulsa; Pearce, 'Hours with the Domestic Sibyl', 491; Parkinson, 'Fifty Years of Yeats Criticism', 110.

12. Lily to R L-P, 10 Apr. 1939.
13. GY to Oliver Edwards, 2 Feb. 1941, NLI MS 27,032.
14. GY to Edwards, 3 May and 19 Aug. 1944, NLI MS 27,032.
15. GY to Edwards, 22 Feb. 1944; *Rann*, 2 (Autumn 1948), 3.
16. J. D. P. Allt, 'W. B. Yeats', *Theology*, 42/248 (Feb. 1941), 81–91; Peter Allt to GY, 26 Dec. 1943 and 10 Jan. 1944.
17. The quotations from GY are in G. D. P. Allt, 'Yeats and the Revision of his Early Verse', *Hermathena*, 63–6 (Nov. 1944), 86, 92, and 101.
18. ECY to Quinn, 3 Aug. 1915, Murphy, *Family Secrets*, 197; WBY to Macmillan [?T. Mark, late June or early July 1932] on title page of proofs of *Mythologies* concerning whether to use a comma or a colon before a quotation, NLI 30,030, courtesy Richard Finneran; Oliver Edwards to GY, 1 Jan. 1943.
19. GY to Peter Allt, [n.d., in response to his letter of 15 July 1945].
20. W. P. Watt to GY, 24 May 1948.
21. Peter Allt to GY, Oct. 1948.
22. GY to A. Norman Jeffares, late Aug. or early Sept. 1961; Jeffares, *W. B. Yeats: Man and Poet*. For Macmillan Jeffares edited *Selected Poetry* (1962), *Selected Plays* (1964), *Selected Prose* (1964), and *Selected Criticism* (1964).
23. Letter to me, 30 Oct. 1991, from John Keohane quoting GY; I am indebted to John Keohane and Michael Gill for recalling the incident.
24. Ellmann to GY, 20 Aug. and 27 Nov. 1945, 11 Mar. 1946 ; GY to Ellmann, 23 Aug. and 19 Nov. 1945, Tulsa; Ellmann to his family, 28 Sept. 1945, Tulsa; GY to Mrs Ellmann, 21 Jan. 1946, Tulsa.
25. GY to Ellmann, 19 Nov. 1945, Tulsa.
26. Ellmann in conversation with me, 31 July 1985; Ellmann to his family, 15 June 1946, Tulsa.
27. Edith Sitwell to John Lehmann, 11 Dec. 1946, Edith Sitwell, *Selected Letters*, ed. John Lehmann and Derek Parker (London: Macmillan, 1970), 143–4; GY to T. S. Eliot, 7 Nov. 1946, Valerie Eliot.
28. GY to Ellmann, 6 Dec. 1946, Tulsa; Ethel Mannin to Joseph Hone, 6 Jan. 1941, HRHRC.
29. Letter to me, 4 June 1985, from John Kelleher; Ellmann to his family, 15 and 18 June, 3 Oct. 1946, Tulsa; GY to Ellmann, 6 Dec. 1946 and 2 Dec. 1947, Tulsa. In May 1947 John Kelleher surprised the O'Faoláins with a gift of two tons of coal, Maurice Harmon, *Seán O'Faoláin: A Life* (London: Constable, 1994), 178.
30. Lily to R L-P, 29 June and 18 Sept. 1946; Ellmann to his family, 30 Aug. 1946, Tulsa.
31. Reported to me by Ellmann, 31 July 1985; Mary M. Colum, *Tomorrow*, 8/6 (Feb. 1949), 58–9; Colum, 'To a Yeatsian Urn' (a review of Jeffares, *W. B. Yeats: Man and Poet* and Donald Stauffer, *The Golden Nightingale* (London: Macmillan, 1949), *Saturday Review*, 28 Jan. 1950, 14–16.
32. GY to Ellmann, 18 Jan. 1949, Tulsa; Edmund Wilson, 'New Light on W. B. Yeats', *New Yorker*, 18 Dec. 1948, 103–7; Horace Gregory, 'Paradoxical Destiny of Yeats as Poet and Man', *New York Herald Tribune*, 14 Nov. 1948; Horace Reynolds, 'Clearing Mist & Haze from a Shy Man', *Saturday Review*, 13 Nov. 1948, 11–12.
33. GY to Ellmann, 17 Nov. 1959; GY to me in conversation, 1959.

NOTES TO PAGES 624–9

34. GY to Richard and Mary Ellmann, [postmark 15 Jan. 1962], Tulsa.

35. GY to Alan Denson, 3 Dec. 1952; letters to me from Alan Denson, 2 July 1985 and 11 Apr. 1995, and from Saros Cowasjee, 30 Mar. 1987.

36. GY to Birgit Bjersby (Bramsbäck), [?Apr./May 1949]; letters to me from Birgit Bramsbäck, 3 June 1987 and 2 Sept. 1988.

37. Una Ellis-Fermor to H. O. White, 24 Apr. 1949 and GY to H. O. White, 29 Apr. 1949, TCD MS 3777; the play was eventually edited by William Becker, and published in the *Dublin Magazine* (Apr.–June 1951).

38. Henn, *The Lonely Tower.*

39. Parkinson, 'Fifty Years of Yeats Criticism', 110.

40. Unpublished memoir by David Clark; I am grateful to him for this, for many conversations, and for the copies of his letters from GY.

41. Stallworthy, *Singing School*, 229; Raine to me, 25 Aug. 1985.

42. Other Blake scholars who were kindly received were Hazard Adams, to whom I am indebted for his memories, and Margaret Rudd (the poet Margaret Newlin).

43. Interviews with John Montague; also John Montague, 'Poetic Widow', *Southern Review*, 32/3 (July 1996), 556–60 and 'Gentle Giant', *Southern Review*, 32/3 (Summer 1996), 566–8.

44. Interview Sept. 1987 with the late Virginia Moore, all of whose papers were burned shortly before her death; GY to me in 1959.

45. GY to Arland Ussher, 22 Sept. 1951, concerning the chapter on Yeats in *Three Great Irishmen: Shaw, Yeats, Joyce* (London: Gollancz, 1952), TCD MS 9041/4194. Unless otherwise indicated, these incidents are my personal memories of GY.

46. Gibbon, *Masterpiece and the Man*; interview with Monk Gibbon, 23 Aug. 1986.

47. F. A. C. Wilson to GY, 8 July, 7 Oct., and 13 Dec. 1957; 24 Sept. 1959.

48. Bradford to GY, 23 Sept. 1955; O'Donnell, 'Textual Introductions', in Yeats, *Later Essays*, 486–7.

49. Rupert Hart-Davis to GY, 19 and 29 July, 24 Oct. 1957; Bradford to GY, 2 and 18 Aug. 1957; Allen and Liberman, 'Transcriptions of Yeats's Unpublished Prose in the Bradford Papers at Grinnell College', 13–27. I am grateful to Mrs Maria Gerson Bradford, David Clark, and M. Liberman for responding to my enquiries.

50. A. P. Watt to GY, 27 Oct. 1958; Curtis Bradford to GY, 12 July 1960. Bradford, 'Yeats and Maud Gonne', 452–74; Bradford, *Yeats at Work*; *Reflections* by W. B. Yeats, transcribed and edited by Curtis Bradford; Bradford, *W. B. Yeats: The Writing of 'The Player Queen'* (DeKalb: Northern Illinois University Press, 1976); Bradford, 'George Yeats: Poet's Wife', 388–404.

51. GY to AY, 19 May 1965.

52. Bradford, 'George Yeats: Poet's Wife', 399–400.

53. According to Jeffares, the poem, recently printed as an appendix to *New Poems*, ed. Mays and Parrish, is by Gogarty, altered somewhat by Yeats, A. Norman Jeffares, 'Know your Gogarty', *YA* 14 (2001), 298–305.

54. Interview with Hugh Kenner, 14 Nov. 1985; Hugh Kenner, 'The Sacred Book of the Arts', *Irish Writing 31*, 24–35.

55. Recalled to me by Stallworthy, 11 May 1987; I am indebted to Jon Stallworthy for many discussions and kindnesses.

56. Pearce, 'Hours with the Domestic Sibyl', 485–501; GY to Donald Pearce, 28 Nov. 1960; *The Senate Speeches of W. B. Yeats*, 25.

57. Letter to me from Hazard Adams, 24 Jan. 1987, and interview with Diana and Hazard Adams, 13 Aug. 1987.

58. Unpublished memoir by David Clark; Patricia Greacen to GY, 11 Sept. 1956; Paul de Man to GY, 11 Feb. 1957; Virginia Moore to GY, 27 July 1953.

59. GY to T. S. Eliot, 7 Nov. 1946, courtesy Valerie Eliot; Terrell mistakenly dates Pound's letter to GY 1956, 'Ezra Pound Letters to William Butler Yeats', 47; Eliot to GY, 15 Nov. 1946 and 20 Jan. 1949, NLI MS 30,102 and 30,179.

60. Pound to GY, 24 June 1951, 8 and 29 July 1954, 14 July 1956, 20 Sept. 1957, MBY; Saddlemyer (ed.), 'George, Ezra, Dorothy and Friends', 21–7; GY to Pound, [mid-July 1954], Yale.

61. GY to Pound, *c*. Nov. 1957, Saddlemyer (ed.), 'George, Ezra, Dorothy and Friends', 27; Pound to GY, 21 Nov. 1957, 'Ezra Pound Letters to William Butler Yeats', ed. Terrell, 48.

62. Dorothy to Douglas Hammond, 27 Jan. 1955, qtd. in Carpenter, *A Serious Character*, 816–17.

63. Pound to GY, 5 Aug. 1958, 'Ezra Pound Letters to William Butler Yeats', ed. Terrell, 49; Pound to GY, 1 Apr. 1959, Saddlemyer (ed.), 'George, Ezra, Dorothy and Friends', 28.

64. Qtd. by Ellmann, 'Ez and Old Billyum', 82.

65. GY to Ellmann, 1 Jan. 1951.

66. GY to the Registrar of Companies, Dublin Castle, Oct. 1954.

67. Letter to me from John Byars, 8 Dec. 1999; Hoffman, 'Visiting Mrs Yeats', 124–38; *Irish Times*, 15 Aug. 1962.

68. Letter to me from John Keohane, 30 Oct. 1991; GY to John Keohane, 24 Feb. 1964. Instead, she sent him a bound set of Cuala *Broadsides* for 1937 with the inscription 'W.P.L. [?Wyndham Lewis] from WBY and G.H.L. Dec. 21 1937' and at bottom of page 'get Harry [?Tucker] to sing them to you', John Keohane.

69. The wedding was probably that of Princess Elizabeth and the Duke of Edinburgh, 20 Nov. 1947.

70. R. J. Hayes to GY, 17 Nov. 1944; GY to James Healy, 14 Aug. 1940 and 13 May 1944, Stanford; GY to MacGreevy, [?Nov. 1955], Elizabeth Ryan; GY to David Clark, 16 July, 16 and 27 Sept. 1956, David Clark; letter from B. L. Reid to me, 24 July 1985; Hoffman, 'Visiting Mrs Yeats', 133.

71. Stallworthy, *Singing School*, 221 and interview 11 May 1987.

72. Qtd. in her obituary, *Time* (6 Sept. 1968), 50.

73. GY to MBY, 'Monday' [?1958].

74. Allan Wade to Macmillan, 4 July 1939; Wade to GY, 19 Nov. 1946; Wade to AY, 26 June 1949; GY to Wade, [winter 1952–3] and 8 Apr. 1954, Rupert Hart-Davis; Rupert Hart-Davis to me, 27 Aug. 1985; Margot Wade to GY, 10 Apr. 1958. In his *Memories of the London Theatre 1900–1914*, ed. Alan Andrews (London: Society for Theatre Research, 1983), Wade describes working with the Abbey Theatre in London.

75. GY to Edwards, 2 Feb. 1941, NLI MS 27,032; Allt, 'Yeats and the Revision of his

Early Verse', 94; GY to John Sparrow, 27 Apr. 1939, courtesy Richard Finneran, and 14 May 1939, JK.

76. WBY to Mark, 8 Sept 1932, Stallworthy, *Between the Lines*, 12.

77. WBY to Mark, 13 Oct. 1937, BL Add. MS 55,003/174.

78. GY to Mark, 15 Apr. 1939, TS carbon NLI MS 30,248; 'GY Notes on "A Note on the Text" ', NLI MS 30,213; GY to Mark, *c.*22 June 1939, BL Add. MS 55,825.

79. GY to Mark, 14 June 1939, TS carbon NLI MS 30,248.

80. Bradford, *Yeats's 'Last Poems' Again*; *The Collected Poems of W. B. Yeats: A New Edition*, ed. Richard J. Finneran (New York: Macmillan, 1983).

81. Interview with Hugh Kenner, 14 Nov. 1985; Richard Finneran, 'The Order of Yeats's Poems', *Irish University Review*, 14/2 (Autumn 1984), 175, quoting from Kenner's letter to him of 2 Aug. 1984.

82. Letter from Lovat Dickson to me, 24 Feb. 1986.

83. T. S. Eliot to GY, 15 Nov. 1946.

84. Marion Witt to A. P. Watt, 15 June 1949, qtd. by Foster, ' "When the newspapers have forgotten me": Yeats, Obituarists, and Irishness', 179 n. 55; Harold Macmillan to A. P. Watt, 12 May 1949, qtd. by Finneran, *Editing Yeats's Poems*, 45.

85. Peter Watt to GY, 11 Oct. 1955.

86. Connie Kelly Hood examined GY's marked copy, given by GY to Russell Alspach and now in the University of Massachusetts Library, *A Search for Authority: Prolegomena to a Definitive Critical Edition of W. B. Yeats's 'A Vision'* (Ann Arbor: UMI Press, 1983), 151 ff.

87. Lovat Dickson to GY, 11 Aug. 1960, NLI MS 30,755.

88. GY to MacGreevy, 17 Aug. 1959 TCD MS 8104; a pencil draft in the Macmillan file when returning the page proofs, originally from the Coole Edition, for *Essays and Introductions*, explained, 'As regards the use of "Explorations" in place of "Discoveries", T.M[ark] remembers that the instruction was given by WBY on material that was presumably returned to him with the first proofs "Explorations" was actually used in these proofs (1932). "Discoveries" was to be the title of the volume containing *A Vision* and its associated essays in the Coole edition. In view of a suggestion Mark has made, we think it would be a good idea to restore "Discoveries" to the *Essays and Introductions* vol. It would only affect twenty page headings and would allow "Explorations" to be used as the title of another possible collection of the remaining prose works.' BL Add. MS 55,896 draft notes with suggested list of works to be included in *Explorations* by Lovat Dickson to GY, 9 Aug. 1959. GY requested that a note indicate 'that Yeats changed the title *Discoveries* for *Explorations*. Mr Mark will remember when,' BL Add. MS 55,896.

89. Letter from Lovat Dickson to me, 19 June 1985.

90. W. P. Watt to GY, 24 Feb. 1959.

91. Lovat Dickson to GY, 19 Apr. 1961, NLI MS 30,755.

92. GY to Vernon Watkins, 11 Dec. 1960, VFM 1076, Selected Letters of the Yeats Family to Vernon Watkins, Southern Illinois.

93. GY to Thomas Mark, 8 Apr. 1949, qtd. in Finneran, *Editing Yeats's Poems*, 127.

94. O'Donnell constructs the order of discussion slightly differently in 'Textual Introductions', in Yeats, *Later Essays*, 464–6.

95. Dickson to GY, 29 Aug. 1961, NLI MS 30,755.

96. 'Introduction', McHugh (ed.), *Ah, Sweet Dancer*, 12; *W. B. Yeats: Letters to Katharine Tynan*, ed. Roger McHugh (Dublin: Clonmore & Reynolds, 1953).

97. Patric [*sic*] Dickinson to GY, 10 Aug. 1948; the offending programme, 'The Poetry of W. B. Yeats', was broadcast on the BBC Third Programme 10.30–11.00 p.m., 31 July 1948.

98. GY to Arland Ussher, 16 June 1965, TCD MS 9041/4196; GY to the editor, *Irish Times*, 18 June 1965.

99. GY to Frank O'Connor, Feb. 1949, Texas. An edited version of the broadcast was published in Rodgers (ed.), *Irish Literary Portraits*, 1–21. I am grateful to the BBC Sound Archives for allowing me to hear the unedited tapes; excerpts from this and a 1974 interview with AY by William Furlong were included in the cassette *Audio Arts*, I, 4 (Eo Ipso Ltd.), 1975.

100. Bradford, 'George Yeats: Poet's Wife', 400–1.

101. GY to H. O. White, 22 Nov. 1955, TCD MS 3777.

102. Auden, 22 Oct. 1959, qtd. in W. H. Auden, *Libretti 1939–1973*, ed. Edward Mendelson (London: Faber, 1993), 663. The opera was produced in England in July 1961 and the libretto was first published in pamphlet form 5 June 1961.

103. Wellesley to GY, 26 Sept. 1950; Dorothy Wellesley, *Beyond the Grave: Letters on Poetry to W. B. Yeats* (Tunbridge Wells, privately published by C. Baldwin, n.d.), 27; GY to Oliver Edwards, 2 Feb. 1941, NLI MS 27,032.

104. Interview with Omar Pound, 16 Feb. 1988.

105. GY to AY, 6 July 1948.

106. GY to Martha Gogarty, 20 June 1952, Bucknell.

107. AY's diary and recollections; letter to me from Rupert Hart-Davis, 27 Aug. 1985; interview with Grace Jaffe.

108. GY to Harold Hyde-Lees, 13 Nov. 1961; Harold Hyde-Lees to AY, 27 May 1963. A book token for 21s. inscribed 'To Dobbs from Harold for 16 Oct. 1955' is tucked into an exhibition catalogue of Portuguese art.

109. Jaffe, 'Vignettes', 150–2; interviews with Grace Jaffe, Oct. 1985.

110. W. P. Watt to GY, 24 Feb. 1959; statement of income from E. A. Woodmass voluntary settlement; Allan Wade to GY, 6 July 1952, NLI MS 30,872.

111. Will of Harold Hyde-Lees; Annie Dunn to GY, 19 Aug. 1963.

112. Thomas MacGreevy, *Jack B. Yeats: An Appreciation and an Interpretation* (Dublin: Victor Waddington, 1945) and *Pictures in the Irish National Gallery* (Dublin: Mercier Press, 1945).

113. GY to MacGreevy, 13 Apr. 1948, TCD MS 8104; TS of 'Dante and Modern Ireland', TCD MS 7994; GY to MacGreevy, 17 Aug. 1959, TCD MS 8104.

114. GY to MacGreevy, 14 July 1964, TCD MS 8104; MacGreevy to GY, 18 July 1964, NLI MS 30,859.

115. GY to MacGreevy, 21 Nov. [1956], TCD MS 8104.

116. AY; Rose, 'A Visit with Anne Yeats', 299.

117. Jeanne Robert Foster to W.M.M., 6 June 1957, qtd. in *'Dear Yeats,' 'Dear Pound', 'Dear Ford': Jeanne Robert Foster and her Circle of Friends*, 243 n. 32.

118. AY to Frank O'Connor, 4 Apr. 1963, courtesy Harriet O'Donovan Sheehy; GY to MacGreevy, 10 Apr. 1963, TCD MS 8401.
119. AY.
120. GY to AY, [n.d.].
121. Ezra Pound, *Selected Prose 1909–1965*, ed. William Cookson (New York: New Directions, 1973), 464.
122. AY, unpublished memoirs; Olga Rudge's account is given in Carpenter, *A Serious Character*, 888. A somewhat different account by Rudge is given in Anne Conover, *Olga Rudge and Ezra Pound* (New Haven: Yale University Press, 2001), 232. See illustration from the *Evening Press*, 9 Feb. 1965, 7. I am grateful to David Clark for a copy of this photograph.

CHAPTER 22: POSTLUDE: ODYSSEYS

1. Moore, *The Unicorn*, 282.
2. MBY, *Cast a Cold Eye*, 7.
3. Heald to Gluck, 22 Nov. 1967, Gluckstein.
4. AY to GY, 7 Apr. 1965.
5. *Sligo Champion*, 28 May 1965.
6. Letter from GY to me, 9 June 1965.
7. *Sligo Champion*, 18 June 1965, John Keohane; O'Connor's oration was published in the *Journal of Irish Literature*, 4/1 (Jan. 1975), 175.
8. Interview with Harriet O'Donovan Sheehy, 15 June 1989; ironically, their son Oliver became a Professor of Moral Theology.
9. GY to AY, 19 May 1965.
10. GY to AY, 28 Apr. and 2 May 1965.
11. GY to AY, 23 Apr. 1965.
12. GY to AY, 2 May 1965; C. P. Curran, *James Joyce Remembered* (London: Oxford University Press, 1968).
13. GY to AY, 14 and 28 Apr. 1965; Françoise Gillot and Carlton Lake, *Life with Picasso* (London: Nelson, 1965).
14. Letter from Kathleen Raine to me, 25 Aug. 1985.
15. Henri Michaux, *A Barbarian in Asia*, trans. Sylvia Beach (New York: New Directions, 1949), inscribed 'To George from Dick 24 June 1949' and as insert a review of the book by Billy Rose. Ellmann translated Michaux's poems *The Space Within* (Henri Michaux, *Selected Writings* (New York: New Directions, 1951)).
16. Several books about space travel appeared during the early 1960s, but probably she read W. G. Burchett and A. C. Purdy, *Cosmonaut Yuri Gagarin, First Man in Space* (London: Anthony Gibbs & Phillips, 1961).
17. W. H. Sabine, *Second Sight in Daily Life* (London: George Allen & Unwin, 1951).
18. Jaffe, 'Vignettes', 151.
19. O'Connor, *A Picture Book*, with fifteen illustrations by Elizabeth Rivers, and *Stranger in Aran*, written and illustrated by Elizabeth Rivers (Dublin: Cuala, 1946).
20. Evie Hone to GY, 6 Sept. [probably 1943]; *Ancient Devotions for Holy Communion from Eastern & Western Liturgical Services*, compiled by S.A.C. (London: Burns

Oates & Washbourne, 1923); *The Roman Missal in Latin and English for Every Day in the Year*, edited by an Irish bishop (Dublin: M. H. Gill, 1938); Canon Henry Taylor Cafferata, *The Catechism Simply Explained* (London: Burns Oates & Washbourne, 1932), with the note in an unidentified hand inside the back cover 'A Map of Life by F. J. Sheed'; Edward Leen of the Holy Ghost Fathers, Blackrock, *Progress through Mental Prayer* (London: Sheed & Ward, 1941). I am grateful to Oliver and Muriel Hone for helping me date Evie's letter.

21. GY to AY, 9 Oct. 1963.
22. Letter from AY to me, 20 July 1967.
23. Told me by Lester Connor, who was present at the ceremony on 26 Oct. 1967.
24. GY to Sybil LeBrocquy, 1 Nov. 1967. I am indebted to Melanie Stewart for copies of the correspondence between GY and her mother.
25. GY to Sybil LeBrocquy, 22 July 1968, Melanie Stewart. The unveiling, by Brian Lenihan, Minister for Education, took place on 1 Aug. 1968; a photograph of the bust is reproduced in Micheál MacLiammóir and Eavan Boland, *W. B. Yeats* (London: Thames & Hudson, 1971), 126.
26. Harold Hyde-Lees to AY, 27 May 1963.
27. GY to AY, 14 Apr. 1965.
28. GY to AY, 28 May 1968.
29. Patricia Butler of Watt Ltd. to MBY, 9 Feb. 1968.
30. GY to MBY, 15 Feb. 1968; George seems to have momentarily confused Sturm with Force Stead, Taylor (ed.), *Frank Pearce Sturm*, 56.
31. GY to AY, 3 May 1965.
32. GY to Síle Yeats, 1 Sept. 1967.
33. GY to AY, Dec. 1967, qtd. by AY to me, 25 June 1993.
34. GY to AY, 28 May 1968; the first stanza and chorus of 'Any Complaints?' published in Adrian Mitchell, *Out Loud* (London: Cape Goliard, 1968). I am grateful to the author for permission to publish these lines.
35. Interview with AY, 1 May 1987.
36. Astrological information courtesy Elizabeth Heine.
37. As described by WMM to me, 5 Sept. 1988.
38. GY to AY, 15 Mar. 1939.
39. Kinane, 'Some Aspects of the Cuala Press', 119–29; John Unterecker, 'Interview with Liam Miller', in Porter and Brophy (eds.), *Modern Irish Literature*, 23–41. In order to have more free time for her own painting, AY finally closed down the press in Sept. 1986 and presented the Albion Press and Cuala archives to Trinity College, Dublin.
40. Automatic script, 4 Mar. 1918, *YVP* i. 371.

THE DEATH OF WILLIAM GILBERT HYDE LEES

1. *London Gazette*, 1 Feb. 1910, 822.
2. Certified office copy of last will and testament of William Gilbert Hyde Lees; statement of probate.
3. I am grateful to Rachel Grahame for her research on Arthur Tolfrey Christie which subsequently became the subject of 'The Search for Arthur', M.Litt. thesis (University of Sydney, 1996).

Index

No entry is included for George Yeats herself, as her relationships and activities are indicated throughout; references to WBY and her children and their interests and activities are restricted to those relating directly to GY. The 'Controls' referred to in the automatic script are included only if discussed in the text. Plates and illustrations in the text are identified in bold type.

Ellmann, Richard (*cont*):
677 n. 75, 679–80 nn. 111, 113, 682 n. 18,
684 n. 55, 685 n. 57, 688 n. 120, 689 n. 140,
692 nn. 199, 201, 697 n. 86, 701 nn. 148, 162,
717 n. 83, 723 n. 127, 769 n. 42, 793 n. 15
Emery, Albert 606–7; *see also* Hollis, Alfred
Emery, Mrs Florence *see* Farr, Florence
'Erontius' 111, 193; *see also* 'Instructors'
Erskine, Lord (fifth Baron Erskine) xxii, 9, 10, 12,
86, 112, 278
Erskine, Dowager Lady Anna 10
Erskine, Mrs Robert Steuart (née Beatrice Caroline
Strong) 25–6, 74, 100, 237–8, 284, 294, 339,
685 n. 57, 721 n. 42
Ervine, St John 244, 503
Esson, Louis 210, 266–7
Estens, John 60
Eton 10, 14, 17, 22, 27, 661 n. 10, 662 n. 15, **Pl. 4**
'Eurectha' 111, 215–16; *see also* 'Instructors'

Fagan, James B. 42, 255, 724 n. 9; *see also* Grey,
Mary
Fahy family 1, 3, 214, 254, 255
Fahy, Sister de Lourdes 660 n. 4, 712 n. 139,
732 n. 42
Fairfax, James Griffyth 25, 29, 36
Farr, Florence (Mrs Edward Emery) 29, 61, 70,
88, 91, 115, 225, 265, 284, 480, 587, 665 n. 65,
731 n. 181
Faulkner, Brian 466, 494–5, 510, 551, 581, 596
Fechner, Gustav 58–9, 672 n. 7, 678 n. 104
Feilding, Everard 62, 434, 677 n. 74, 694 n. 37,
733 n. 61
Felkin, Dr R. W. 66, 70, 72–3, 79–80, 83, 115,
122, 215–16, 238, 256, 283–4, 301, 308, 682 n. 17,
696 n. 60
Finnegan, Bartley 3, 296
Finneran, Richard 777 n. 149, 780 n. 47, 781 n. 65
'Fish' 112, 119, 177; *see also* 'Instructors'
FitzGerald, Desmond 311–12, 318, 468, 569, 599
Fitzwilliam Square 205, 401, 402, 403, 412, 414, 418,
431, 435, 436, 438–9, 442, 445, 449, 451, 453, 455,
470, 580
Fleet, Hampshire 15, 17, **Pl. 6**
Foden, Gwyneth 471–2, 486, 493, 494, 497, 498,
500, 505–7, 509, 521, 527, 762 n. 120
Forbes, Stanhope 31–2
Foster, Jeanne Robert 240, 243–4, 250, 290, 338,
363, 643–4, 693 n. 5, 722 n. 81, 731 n. 9
Fowler, Eva 29, 35, 45, 46, 47, 48–50, 51, 61,
76–7, 83, 86, 107, 182, 277, 664 n. 40, 668 n. 45,
675 nn. 44, 45, 52, 676 n. 60
Fox sisters 52

'Frazzlepat' 111, 283; *see also* 'Instructors'
Free, John 452, 455–6, 459, 481, 482, 486, 521, 536,
574
Freud, Sigmund 46, 54, 73, 118, 245, 475, 685 n. 60
Frye, Northrop 131, 697 n. 80, 699 n. 122,
701 n. 161
futurism 37, 479; *see also* Marinetti, Filippo

Gagarin, Yuri 649, 793 n. 16
Gainsborough, Thomas 12, 661 n. 10
Gaudier-Brzeska, Henri 30, 39, 75, 121, 669 nn. 48,
51, 680 n. 122
Gentile, Giovanni 321, 342
George IV 10
Gerhardt, Elena 29, 371, 665 n. 60
Gibbon, Monk ('Monkey') 445, 579, 593, 627,
716 n. 48
Gilbert, R. A. 678–9 n. 105, 682 n. 20, 684 n. 54,
721 n. 42
Gill, Maire ('Molly') 555, 585, 586, 592, 632, 653,
654
Gillot, Françoise 648–9, 793 n. 13
'Giraldus' or 'Gyraldus' 143, 149, 217, 306, 307, 343,
405, 673 n. 16, 701 n. 148
Gluck 605–7, 611, 786 n. 196
gnosticism 44, 45, 672 nn. 9, 13
Goethe, Johann Wolfgang von 50–1, 112, 152,
676 n. 59
Gogarty, Martha (Mrs Oliver St John, 'Neenie') 157,
178, 197, 226, 299, 315, 349, 351, 361, 377, 431,
586, 639–40, 688 n. 119
Gogarty, Oliver St John 135, 147–8, 157, 167, 178,
186, 203, 226, 264, 265, 290, 299, 311–12, 313,
314–15, 318, 319, 323, 339, 349, 351, 361, 363, 377,
388, 406, 421, 424, 425, 426, 430, 431, 436, 453,
458, 460, 465, 477, 480, 482–3, 489, 493, 500,
504, 509, 510, 517, 549, 566, 585, 586, 594, 610,
627, 688 n. 119, 726 n. 54, 735 n. 6, 754 n. 198,
789 n. 53
Golden Dawn, Hermetic Order of 4–5, 29, 59, 60,
65–74, 75, 76, 79–80, 83, 84, 85, 87, 107, 109, 112,
115, 116, 122–4, 133, 144–5, 185, 188, 215, 225, 234,
237–8, 246, 256, 283–4, 295, 343–4, 346, 420–1,
426–7, 458, 483, 622, 623, 654, 660 n. 6,
665 n. 65, 676 nn. 63, 66, 678–9 n. 105,
681 n. 5, 682 nn. 18, 20, 683 nn. 24, 28, 31,
684 nn. 49, 54, 684–5 n. 55, 685 n. 58, 716 n. 62,
721 n. 42, 731 nn. 180, 181; *see also* Amoun
Temple; Stella Matutina
Goldring, Douglas and Betty (née Duncan) 202,
484, 669 n. 49
Gonne, Iseult ('Maurice', later Mrs Francis Stuart)
77, 83, 84, 85–6, 87, 89–92, 94, 96, 98, 101–4,